Emigrants and Exiles

IRELAND

0 5 10 15 20 25 30 35 40

Londonderry
Londonderry
Antrim

Donegal

U L S T E R

Tyrone

Belfast

Down

Fermanagh
Armagh

Monaghan

Sligo

Sligo

Leitrim
Cavan

Dundalk

Louth

Mayo

C O N N A U G H T

Roscommon
Longford

Drogheda

Meath

Galway

Westmeath

Dublin
Dublin

Galway

King's

L E I N S T E R

Kildare

Wicklow

Queen's

Clare

Carlow

R. Shannon

Kilkenny

Limerick

Tipperary

Kilkenny

Limerick

M U N S T E R

Wexford

Kerry

Waterford

Waterford

Cork

Cork

Emigrants and Exiles

*Ireland and the Irish Exodus
to North America*

KERBY A. MILLER

OXFORD UNIVERSITY PRESS
New York   Oxford

Oxford University Press

Oxford New York Toronto
Delhi Bombay Calcutta Madras Karachi
Petaling Jaya Singapore Hong Kong Tokyo
Nairobi Dar es Salaam Cape Town
Melbourne Auckland

and associated companies in
Beirut Berlin Ibadan Nicosia

First published in 1985 by Oxford University Press, Inc.,
200 Madison Avenue, New York, New York 10016

First issued as an Oxford University Press paperback, 1988

Oxford is a registered trademark of Oxford University Press

Library of Congress Cataloging in Publication Data
Miller, Kerby A.
  Emigrants and exiles.
  Bibliography: p.
  Includes index.
  1. Ireland—Emigration and immigration—History.
2. Ireland—Social conditions.
3. United States—Emigration and immigration—History.
4. Irish—United States—History.
I. Title.
JV7711.Z79U55 1985 325.415 85-4919
ISBN 0-19-503594-1
ISBN 0-19-505187-4 (PPBK)

10 9 8 7 6 5 4

Printed in the United States of America

To Patricia,
Eoghan, and Michael

May my love always prevent them
from feeling like exiles

Acknowledgments

During the last few months of preparing this manuscript for publication, I have often looked at the immense pile of pages before me and wondered in amazement why and how I ever wrote a book of such enormous size and ambitious scope. Perhaps the answers to the question *why* would be best explored with close friends over pints of stout, but surely they are somehow related to the bittersweet and imperishable memories of my first visit to Ireland in 1972 and to my subsequent belief that by attempting to understand and clarify the central motifs of Ireland's tragic history I might also unlock the mystery of my own instinctive affection for that country and its people. It may be that we all—men and women in modern societies—are in some sense exiles from the better, happier lands of our dreams and that Ireland's past emigrants and present inhabitants only more starkly or poignantly reflect a universal dichotomy between aspiration and achievement. However, if we hope ever to close that gap and realize those dreams, we must better understand both those processes which have hitherto controlled us and the inadequacies of those notions with which we have vainly combatted those processes or attempted to obscure their unhappy consequences. In recent years, a few Irish politicians and clerics have once again advocated mass emigration as a "solution" to Ireland's social, spiritual, and political ills. If this book helps prevent those scattered voices from swelling into a chorus, if it serves to dissuade the flight of even one person who might instead join with others to create a truly "new Ireland" from which no one—regardless of class, creed, or sex—needs be an "exile," then this effort will have been successful.

The answer to the question of *how* I ever managed to write this book is more easily given. Its creation was possible only because of the aid, advice, and encouragement of fellow scholars and good friends whose many kindnesses I can never acknowledge adequately. Indeed, I have received selfless assistance from so many people during the decade or more since I began my research that it is difficult to single out only a few for special thanks and praise. Certainly, however, I am most indebted to the following individuals: Kenneth Stampp, who directed my doctoral dissertation with characteristic and unfailing intelligence, firmness, and patience; Bruce Boling, whose brilliant insights into Irish language and culture were absolutely invaluable and whose generously shared research and graceful translations of Irish texts adorn this work; Arnold Schrier, who kindly gave me access to the results of his own pioneering searches for Irish emigrants' letters; Pat

Dowling, who offered me his own hospitality and assistance and also that of the United Irish Cultural Center of San Francisco; Jim Donnelly and David Miller, who graciously took precious time from their own superb research to read my manuscripts and provide sound and much-needed advice; the late Rodney Green, who gave me the opportunity to spend a year at the Institute of Irish Studies in Belfast and who shared his unparalleled good humor and knowledge of Ulster emigration; David Doyle, preeminent scholar of Irish-America, who shared both his encyclopedic knowledge and his indefatigable and much-abused friendship; Líam Kennedy, whose many kindnesses are deeply appreciated and whose brilliant insights into Irish history and the Northern Irish problem were mitigated only by our frequent inability to remember all those insights on the mornings after the pubs closed; and, perhaps most helpful of all, Michael Thorn, whose penetrating criticisms shaped this book in major ways, and whose unfailing counsel and friendship helped both me and my family survive that species of exile known only to untenured assistant professors.

Many other scholars and friends also contributed directly or indirectly to the progress of this book. My interest in history was stimulated by the faculty of Pomona College, particularly by John Gleason, and my understanding of the subject was immeasurably advanced by my professors and fellow graduate students at the University of California–Berkeley, especially by Lawrence Levine, Henry May, Leon Litwack, David Bertelson, Woodrow Borah, and David Brading among the former and by Clarence Walker, Jerry Kellman, Ed Quattlebaum, Mark Johnson, and Steve Maizlish among the latter. When I first began my study of Irish and Irish-American history, I was fortunate to receive good advice from several experts in those fields, including Thomas Brown, Jay Dolan, John Tracy Ellis, Emmet Larkin, and, especially, Perry Curtis, whose rigorous criticism of my first, feeble essays prompted me to greater efforts. During my various trips to Ireland and in later stages of my research, I received valuable assistance and encouragement from, among others, Bill Crawford, Robert Dudley Edwards, David Harkness, David Jones, Joe Lee, Maurice O'Connell, Cormac Ó Gráda, Seán Ó Súilleabháin, Trevor Parkhill, and the brilliant young scholars who were Fellows of the Institute of Irish Studies in 1977–78. I have received so much painstaking assistance from librarians and archivists in Ireland and in North America that it would be impossible to thank them all: however, special acknowledgments are due to Brian Trainor and the staff of the Public Record Office of Northern Ireland, to Alf Mac Lochlainn and the staff of the National Library of Ireland, and to Ann Barry of the Cork Archives Council.

My efforts to locate emigrants' letters and memoirs which remained in private hands were facilitated and encouraged by a large number of people and institutions on both sides of the Atlantic. In this regard, I want to express special gratitude to William Shannon, former U.S. ambassador to Ireland; Tom Jordan of the American Irish Foundation; Jo-Ellen Vinyard and Francis Blouin of the Immigration Sources Project at the University of Michigan; and to my former students Bob Derham and Bridget Lynch. A number of fellow scholars have generously shared with me the results of their own work, often taking time from their own archival research to pester librarians on my behalf: heartfelt thanks to Bill and Erica Gienapp, Bill Rorabaugh, Dan Cornford, Mark Wyman, Vic Walsh, Timothy Meagher, and Dale Light, in addition to many others already named above. Thanks also to my excellent research assistants, Bob Hunt, Sue Mernitz, and Rod and Peggy McHugh, and to my colleagues Tom Alexander and Russ Zguta, for reading and criticizing early drafts of this manuscript.

This work could not have been completed without generous infusions of financial assistance from the University of California, the Ford Foundation, the Mabelle McLeod Lewis Memorial Foundation, the American Irish Foundation, the Queen's University of Belfast, and the UMC Research Council. Special thanks are due to those scholars and friends who acceded to my importunate requests for letters recommending me for the fellowships granted by these institutions.

Nor could this work have been completed without the conscientious secretarial assistance which I have received from Doris Meeks, Carol Jablonsky, Pat Smyth, Phyllis Dussel, and Patty Eggleston during the various stages of this manuscript's production.

Sheldon Meyer, editor of Oxford University Press, his assistant and Irish enthusiast Melissa Spielman, and the copy editor Otto Sonntag have given great encouragement and tireless efforts to improve this work. In addition, I must thank Cambridge University Press for permission to reprint some of the material in Chapter 8, which appeared earlier in P. J. Drudy, ed., *Irish Studies IV: Ireland and America*.

Profound thanks are due to all those generous individuals, listed in the Bibliography, who allowed me access to their families' emigrant letters, diaries, and memoirs, and to the many others who responded to my appeals for such documents. I hope that I have written a book worthy of their kindness and of their ancestors' struggles and sufferings.

In addition, I want to express my deepest appreciation to the many close friends, mostly non-historians, who helped keep me relatively sane and content over the years by indulging my obsession with Ireland, my anemic batting average, and my arrogant tendency to take twenty-five-foot jump shots instead of passing off to the open man. To list all of them would consume far too many pages, but my most heartfelt thanks are to Peggy Meury and her family.

Likewise, I can never forget the many personal kindnesses I received in Ireland from Líam and Judy Kennedy, David and Kathy Doyle, Bert Rima and Barbara Harvey, George and Nora Walsh, Paddy and Teresa Mullen, Irene Mulholland and her wonderful family, and from one other who shall remain nameless but always fondly remembered.

My love for and gratitude to my wife and children are inadequately expressed in my Dedication, as are also my hopes that they have forgiven me my many absences from home while researching and writing this book. Finally, I can never repay my mother, father, and maternal grandmother for their love and support which inspired my initial interest in history and which made it possible for me to pursue that interest to this conclusion.

                                                                              K.M.

Contents

Alas that I ever came to this land
And that I left my beloved Ireland behind;
I'm thinking sadly of that time long ago
When I had cheer, sport, and play.

I got a letter from a relation
Telling me to hasten across the sea,
That gold was to be found in plenty there
And that I'd never have a hard day or a poor one again.

I well remember that fine fresh morning
When I bade farewell to my poor sad mother;
The people of the village kept shedding tears:
"Farewell, James, you'll never come back."

I brought along a bag to put the gold in
And fastened it tight with a cord around the top
Lest I lose all the money;
I was going to buy my mother a horse, and a lamb as well.

Naïvely I went aboard
With my bag on my shoulder, praying to God
To bring me safe to land through storm and wind,
Where I'd be a gentleman for the rest of my days.

Alas, when I landed
I made for the city without delay;
But I never saw gold on the street corners—
Alas, I was a poor aimless person cast adrift.

That's how I spent part of my life,
Going from place to place, with no company at my side;
When night would come, it was cold and wet;
Often I lay stretched out in the woods.

It's far far better to be in Ireland where there's cheer,
Listening to the melodious bird songs,
Than looking for work from a crooked little miser
Who thinks you're only an ass to be beaten with a stick.

Go back to Ireland, my modest young girl;
Listen to me, little lad, and head for home,
Where you'll have a pound and sixpence on fair day
And freedom for a carefree dance together on the dew.

When the day comes and the sky is alight
And the hosts march under the green banner of the Gael,
That day you'll be glorious in the battle
Which will scatter the cursed English across the sea.

Séamas Ó Muircheartaigh

Seán Ó Dubhda, O.S., ed., *Duanaire Duibhneach* (Dublin, 1933), 132–33
(trans. by Dr. Bruce D. Boling, Brown University).

Emigrants and Exiles

Introduction

From the early seventeenth century to the establishment of the Irish Free State in 1921–22, as many as seven million people emigrated from Ireland to North America. This vast flow was of great historical significance: emigration was at once a barometer of the economic and social changes taking place on both sides of the Atlantic and itself a major determinant of the modern shapes of North American and Irish societies. In spite of the diminutive size of their homeland, the Irish played an important role in the commercial and industrial revolutions that transformed the North Atlantic world. However, that role was ambiguous, turbulent, even tragic, for the Irish made no easy accommodation to the changing conditions that buffeted them both at home and in North America.

Historians usually define the "Irish Question" in terms merely of political conflict between English colonialism and Irish and Irish-American nationalism. However, the issue attains more universal import if viewed broadly as the adjustment of Irish society, culture, and identity to the necessities and opportunities of the modern world. Emigration afforded one possible response, Irish nationalism another, and Irish-American nationalism bridged the potential gap between the two. On both general and individual levels, emigration and nationalism epitomized the ofttimes tortuous Irish efforts to resolve the tensions between tradition and modernity.

This book is an essay in transatlantic history. One cannot study modern Ireland without realizing the central importance of massive, sustained emigration; nor should one write about Irish-America without recognizing the crucial significance of the Irish background in shaping the emigrants' reactions to the New World. Accordingly, I have focused on three questions. First, how did the Irish emigrants look on emigration from Ireland? Second, what determined their attitudes? And, third, to what extent did these attitudes shape their actual experiences of emigration and life in North America—coloring, easing, or constraining their objective situations?

Of course, during the centuries of emigration, conditions of Irish and Irish-American life were neither static nor homogeneous: nevertheless, sufficient evidence exists to support the following conclusions. First, both collectively and individually the Irish—particularly Irish Catholics—often regarded emigration as involuntary exile, although they expressed that attitude with varying degrees of consistency, intensity, and sincerity. Second, this outlook reflected a distinctive Irish worldview—the impact of a series of interactions among culture, class, and historical circumstance upon Irish character. Finally, both the exile motif and its underlying causes led Irish emigrants to interpret experience and adapt to American life in ways which were often alienating and sometimes dysfunctional, albeit traditional, expedient, and conducive to the survival of Irish identity and the success of Irish-American nationalism.

Historians often claim that the Irish in North America saw themselves as unhappy exiles, but they usually offer meager proof or explanation: few scholars provide more than cursory treatment of the historical, socioeconomic, and cultural backgrounds of the emigrants, and even fewer utilize evidence showing how the "ordinary" Irish themselves regarded their departures. These deficiencies are linked, for if the Irish in North America *did* see themselves as exiles, that self-image might derive at least as much from their Irish heritage as from their American experience. Furthermore, only evidence of the emigrants' personal opinions would reveal whether the exile motif was merely rhetorical or whether it might provide insights into the very character of Irish emigration and of Irish and Irish-American life. Initially I was skeptical. However, after exploring the metaphor's sources in the Irish background and its personal expression in over 5,000 emigrants' letters and memoirs—in addition to poems, songs, and folklore—I conclude that it is of great importance, both for what it can reveal and for what it sometimes purposely obscures.[1]

Florence Gibson was one of many earlier historians who claimed that the Irish in North America regarded themselves as homesick exiles. "Many Irish-Americans had moved to the United States physically," she wrote, "but spiritually and emotionally they were back home in Ireland." Edith Abbott and Carl Wittke, who possessed extensive knowledge of other emigrant groups, concurred and argued that the Irish "maintained a closer contact with their old homes" and held bitter memories of the " 'wrongs of Ireland,' " which inhibited their adjustment to American life and concentrated much of their attention upon dreams and schemes to free Ireland from English rule. As Thomas N. Brown concluded, the Irish—"the most homesick of all immigrants"—charged their unhappiness "upon the conscience of England."[2]

It would be much easier to dismiss the image of the self-pitying, Anglophobic Irish "exile" as merely a cliché if the Irish emigrants themselves and their spokesmen had not employed it so frequently. Throughout the nineteenth and early twentieth centuries, Irish and Irish-American newspapers and orators characterized those who left Ireland as "exiles," compelled to emigrate—either directly or indirectly—by "English tyranny." Nationalists, politicians, and clerical leaders never tired of "reminding" their audiences that the Irish were being "driven out of Erin" like the "children of Israel." Thus, Irish emigration was "not natural but artificial," claimed Alexander Sullivan of Chicago, "since the poverty of Ireland is produced by English law, and not by the law of nature"; in short, he concluded, Irish emigration was "not a social necessity, but a political oppression." As a British ambassador to the United States lamented, the "great majority" of Irish-Americans "looked upon themselves in their exile as victims of British misgovernment."[3]

In addition, emigrant songs and ballads sung by Irishmen on both sides of the ocean usually expressed a "pervasive note of sadness." Whether commercial or folk compositions, the ballads often sang of inconsolable homesickness. "Oh, Donegal, I long to see your native hills once more," wrote an Ulster emigrant, "[a]s I am now an exile upon a foreign shore." Songs like "Poor Pat Must Emigrate" not only described departures as involuntary but also bitterly blamed the British "yoke that does Ireland enslave" for making them mandatory. "It is not my wish that I part with old Ireland," wrote another composer, and "It's nought but oppression that tears us asunder"; for "The home of my father, his birthright for ages / Was torn from us now by the foreigner's hand." Although some ballads promised that the "exiles" would find happiness in America, more often they prophesied that the Irish would "range the wide world—poor, helpless, forlorn" until Ireland was free.[4]

Even more convincing is the evidence of the emigrants' own letters and memoirs that they often regarded their situation as one of unhappy exile. Again, this feeling was rooted in acute homesickness. In America "I have everything that would tend to make life comfortable," a Catholic from County Limerick admitted, "but still in spite of all I can never forget home. . . . At night when I lay in bed my mind wanders off across the continent and over the Atlantic to the hills of Cratloe." "Even after 67 years" in America, wrote another emigrant, "I still have that longing" for home. In other testaments, homesickness melts into bitter alienation from American life: "i wish i ner came to new york," lamented a woman from County Monaghan; "it is a hell upon erth. . . . i cannot get no rest thinking of home." Indeed, as the author of a popular Irish emigrants' guidebook warned, the burden of homesickness could cripple ambition as well as drain emotion. Thus, Michael MacGowan, an Irish-speaker from Donegal, observed that many of his countrymen in Chicago saw "their lives slipping away . . . while their hearts were away at home"; they "were sad enough," he wrote, and "would have preferred to live [in Ireland] on one meal a day than to have owned the whole of Chicago." Finally, many emigrants specifically blamed their "exile" upon the English government or the English-enforced landlord system—alleged causes of all Irish emigration. "Due to the suppression of the English," related a woman from Limerick, "the Irish were practically driven from their homes"; and as an elderly emigrant in San Francisco declared, "We didn't want to leave Ireland, but we *had* to" because of the effects of centuries of English misrule.[5]

Of course, not all Irish emigrants regarded themselves as exiles, as victims of English oppression, or even as acutely homesick. Certain combinations of cultural, economic, or personal factors could produce emigrants who cared little or nothing about either Ireland or its "sacred cause." Yet large numbers of Irish emigrants certainly did see themselves as involuntary exiles, and their letters and songs suggest why the image offered so pervasive and unifying a sentiment to the politics of Irish-American nationalism.

But what were the causes of this exile motif? The standard, nationalist explanation is simple but misleading. Emotionally, one might wish to accept the rhetoric of such true exiles as John Mitchel, who proclaimed that his people's homesickness and Anglophobia were but natural, since the Irish were in North America "only because of insufferable political tyranny which has made their native land uninhabitable to them." However, the paradox remains of a tremendous gap between the exile image and the objective realities of Irish emigration. For if many Irish in North America indeed regarded themselves as exiles, then they saw themselves as having left Ireland unwillingly—as having been forced to leave. But the vast majority of the Irish who crossed the Atlantic were not involuntary exiles like John Mitchel. Rather, they were voluntary emigrants who went abroad in search of better economic and social opportunities—that is, for the same reasons motivating emigrants from other parts of Europe. Indeed, it is remarkable that so few of these self-supposed Irish exiles ever returned to Ireland, compared with the sizable return migrations of Italians, Swedes, and Greeks—few of whom had ever claimed to be exiles, but who went back to live under regimes at least as repressive in certain respects as England's hegemony over Ireland.[6]

Just which and how many Irish emigrants truly left home *involuntarily*? Political rebels, to be sure. Also, fugitives from the law or from personal disgrace. To be generous, include evicted farmers who subsequently emigrated. Add as well those Famine emigrants of 1845–50 who fled out of sheer panic and fear of death (as opposed to many for whom the Famine was simply the final determinant in their decision). But altogether these compose only a relatively small proportion of the seven million or so Irish emigrants to North America. Despite the prevalence and persistence of the exile image, comparatively few emigrants were compelled by force or famine to leave Ireland, particularly between 1856 and 1921, when most departures occurred. Rather, the Irish emigrated voluntarily in order to better themselves; and at least in theory they could have remained in Ireland, as many of their spokesmen advocated.

Moreover, the exile motif was not merely a consequence of the poverty and prejudice endured by many Irish abroad. Of course, in the middle decades of the nineteenth century, Irish-American destitution was widespread and discrimination severe; even in 1900 many newcomers, especially from the west of Ireland, faced privation. However, throughout the century both prosperous and poor Irish emigrants frequently expressed in their letters the same sentiments of bitter exile. While it might be expected that unemployed and impoverished emigrants often would be pathetically homesick and alienated, the fact that many affluent Irish-Americans employed the same self-imagery indicates the presence of a common cultural tradition which could corroborate but also clash with objective experience. As David N. Doyle has shown, by the last decade of the nineteenth century most of the American Irish had achieved respectably decent levels of socioeconomic status and political influence. It is therefore difficult to explain, on the basis of American conditions alone, why the exile motif persisted, why Irish-American nationalists could continue to evoke it so successfully, and why, as Doyle himself has noted, for all its achievements in 1900 the Irish-American Catholic community was still characterized by a "self-indulgent communal morbidity."[7]

Certainly, the handful of Irish-Americans who *were* political exiles had great personal and symbolic importance in their communities. By dramatizing their own plight as representative of the entire exodus, they strove to delay Irish assimilation and thus command emotional loyalty and financial contributions from potential supporters. By implying that their countrymen were in America by compulsion and not by choice, the nationalists' conceptualization of emigration as exile set the Irish apart from native Americans and helped exacerbate some of the emigrants' most fundamental problems of adjustment and identity. However, even the nationalist leaders' inordinate influence does not explain why the image they propagated was so popular and persuasive that it not only was employed by Irish-American clerics, labor leaders, and machine politicians but also surfaced time and again in the private correspondence of quite ordinary emigrants. What deep, responsive chords did nationalist oratory strike?

The exile image was not just a rhetorical device employed by Irish and Irish-American nationalists. Nor was it merely of American origins—like the St. Patrick's Day parades—simply a product of Irish alienation or self-assertion in the New World. All emigrants in America experienced some degree of estrangement, but the Irish view of themselves as exiles sprang from sources more profound than the poverty and prejudice encountered abroad. In short, there seems no reason inherent in either the actual circumstances of most emigrants' departures or the material conditions of Irish-American life which automatically translated a homesickness perhaps common to all emigrants into a morbid perception of themselves as involuntary exiles, passive victims of English oppression. For, viewed objectively, they had made a rational response both to structural changes in Irish society and to the promptings of their own ambitions for the better material life which recent scholarship indicates they generally achieved.

Although the undeniable difficulties the Irish encountered in North America might prompt and nurture the piteous content of the exile self-image, the concept itself reflected not the concrete realities of most emigrants' experiences but a distinctive Irish Catholic worldview rooted deeply in Irish history and culture. The origins of both worldview and exile image long preceded the English conquest of Ireland and the mass migrations of modern times. Subsequent historical circumstances of rebellion and defeat, despoliation and impoverishment, served to ratify and magnify aspects of preconquest Irish culture which made the exile motif seem more poignant and appropriate. Armed with a worldview so shaped, the Irish experienced the socioeconomic changes associated with the modern commercial and industrial revolutions with certain psychological, as well as political and economic, disadvantages. Usually lacking capital and political power sufficient to shape the emerging market economy to their own profit, the Irish fell back upon cultural traditions which could be adapted to deal with the strains of modernization. The resultant worldview provided an ideological defense against change and misfortune, and the basis for a nationalistic assertion of Irish identity. However, it also reformulated and perpetuated the archaic tradition of emigration as exile in the modern context of conflict with England as origin of both political oppression and economic deprivation.

There were specific social and personal reasons why some Irish emigrants might see themselves as involuntary exiles: reasons which often had only remote, if any, connections with English "tyranny" over Ireland. In addition, many others when departing had neither cause nor desire to proclaim themselves anything but voluntary, even eager emigrants. However, the modernized tradition of emigration as political exile generally both subsumed all specific, individual reasons for grief to a sense of common misfortune and injustice, and suppressed most favorable responses to emigration in the name of self-abnegation and communal solidarity. Also, for most emigrants even the process of emigration—their decisions to leave, their methods of financing the journey, their poignant leave-takings, and the ocean voyage itself—only reinforced a worldview which encouraged the exile self-image and its transportation across the Atlantic.

Thus, millions of Irishmen and -women, whatever their objective reasons for emigration, approached their departures and their experiences in North America with an outlook which characterized emigration as exile. Rooted in ancient culture and tradition, shaped by historical circumstances, and adapted to "explain" the impersonal workings of the market economy, the Irish worldview crossed the ocean to confront the most modern of all societies. From the standpoint of the emigrants' ability to adjust and prosper overseas, the consequent tensions between past and present, ideology and reality, may have had mixed results. However, both the exile motif and the worldview that sustained it ensured the survival of Irish identity and nationalism in the New World.

ONE

The Making of
the Emigrants' Ireland

MOST IRISH EMIGRANTS were children of the soil—sons and daughters of tenant farmers, rural artisans, or agricultural laborers. Today, after two-week tours of the "Emerald Isle," their Irish-American descendants, like the Gaelic poets of long ago, often wax eloquent in descriptions of the loveliness of the Irish countryside—its vivid green fields, the brown and purple shades of its mountains. However, contemporary tourists, like the ancient bards, constitute a caste removed from the average Irishman's centuries-old struggle to wring subsistence or profit from the land and weather. In some respects the Irish climate is favorable, in many areas allowing more than one annual harvest and year-round grazing; the Gulf Stream keeps mean temperatures moderate, varying from 40° to 60° Farenheit between December and July. However, much of the countryside's remarkable beauty derives from the changing clouds and high moisture content of the air, which cause constant variations in the sunlight's strength and quality. In other words, the predominant feature of the climate is rain, falling 180 days per year in the Southeast and over 250 days along the Atlantic coast, often driven by gale-force winds; annual rainfall varies from thirty to fifty inches in the eastern lowlands to sixty to seventy inches in the western mountains. This high humidity produces a dampness which pervades Irish dwellings and which, more important, has helped determine the nature of Irish agriculture, for the climate is more suited to grasslands for livestock and dairy farming than to tillage crops. Thus, although potatoes, oats, and flax have been grown throughout the island, wheat and barley normally have been restricted to well-drained soils in the East; even there, September is frequently so wet that Irish farmers speak in terms of "saving the harvest." Without constant fertilization and drainage, many farmers' fields would become highly acidic or revert to marsh and bog. Despite centuries of reclamation, bogs still cover one-fifth of the country—particularly in the West, where some envelop hundreds of square miles. Since Ireland has no major coal deposits and was nearly denuded of forests by the eighteenth century, the bogs have provided indispensable fuel, peat or "turf," for the farmers' hearths. However, their gloomy presence has severely circumscribed agriculture, especially in the West, where, as population increased, a multitude of tiny holdings crowded onto limited arable soils along the seacoasts and in narrow mountain glens.[1]

Indeed, some contemporary scholars argue that, largely because of geography and climate, Ireland could not have developed into anything other than what it

9

had become by the early twentieth century: a supplier of raw materials, chiefly pastoral products, and of emigrants to more-fortunate countries; a land dominated economically, culturally, and, to a large extent even today, politically by its wealthier and more powerful neighbor, England. Such opinion accords well with the fatalism which is a predominant feature both of traditional Irish character and of many currently fashionable and purportedly realistic economists who serve as apologists for the course and consequences of what is generally known as modernization. However, Ireland—like Holland, Norway, or even Cuba—could have had a different history despite its relative paucity of natural resources. "Geography is not the mistress of the life of nations," wrote one observer on the eve of yet another attempt by Irishmen to alter their country's destiny. "The only final cause in history is the human mind, the thoughts it creates, the ideals which . . . it attains. Geography neither predestined Ireland to be independent, nor foredoomed it to be dependent. It is men, and the wills of men, which make it the one or the other." Vaguely or intensely, many Irish emigrants believed this: for them history was not something finished and unalterable; it lived in songs and stories and traditions which were remarkably archaic and which promised that someday, somehow, the seemingly brief interlude of "Saxon domination" would end and that the mythical glories of the Gaelic past would return. On more than a mere rhetorical level, this dream became the central motif of postconquest Irish Catholic culture, and fear of its realization remained the preeminent obsession of Irish Protestants. In short, however "rational" was the movement of millions of Irishmen and -women overseas in search of a better life, many emigrants rightly or wrongly believed that they were really involuntary exiles from an island which might have nurtured them all had it not been for the malevolence of England.[2]

1

Conquest: Exiles *in* Erin

In modern times a fountain of emigrants bound for North America, Ireland in former centuries was itself analogous to the New World—a prey for foreign settlers and adventurers. By the time transatlantic emigration from Ireland began, English conquest had imposed on the island a system of law and landownership, a religious establishment, and a colonizing population—all alien to Gaelic society and culture. As one Gaelic poet lamented, by the seventeenth and early eighteenth centuries the Catholic Irish had become "strangers at home! . . . exiles in Erin!"[1]

English conquest began somewhat inadvertently in 1166 when the king of Leinster, Ireland's eastern province, invited Norman lords from south Wales to assist him against his rival and nominal chief, Ruaidrí Ó Conchubhair (Rory O'Connor), the *ard rí,* or high king, of Ireland. Within a few years the Normans had seized most of Leinster, and their success compelled King Henry II of England to intervene with an army of his own to enforce the continued allegiance of his adventuresome barons. In 1175 the Norman invaders as well as many native Irish chieftains acknowledged Henry as "lord" or ruler of Ireland; in return he made feudal grants to his barons of the Irish lands they had appropriated, and confirmed submissive native chiefs in their remaining possessions.[2]

Despite its seeming ease, this first Anglo-Norman conquest proved illusory, and the English kings' "lordship" over Ireland long remained more aspiration than achievement. The initial Norman successes had been facilitated by Gaelic Ireland's territorial fragmentation and political disunity. No centripetal forces had compelled effective economic or political cohesion. Urban centers were few, and neither monastic settlements such as Armagh nor Norse coastal enclaves such as Dublin had much influence beyond their immediate hinterlands. Although growing in preeminence since the reign of Brian Bóroimhe (Brian Ború, d. 1014), the high kingship of Ireland was still largely nominal and ceremonial, a focus of dynastic strife rather than of political authority. The diffusion of power among many overlords and petty chieftains prevented a united, national Gaelic resistance to the Norman invasion, but it also inhibited a complete subjugation of the island during the Middle Ages; there were no single, all-important bastions or leaders the Normans could capture or kill to seal their victory. Furthermore, the invaders themselves were divided by self-interest, and English kings were usually preoccupied with more pressing or lucrative concerns than their troubled Irish lordship. Thus, the conquerors' advance became a slow, piecemeal process, and when Norman energies waned in the late Middle Ages, the Gaelic lords reasserted themselves.[3]

Although fragmented politically, preconquest Gaelic Ireland exhibited a remarkable legal, cultural, and linguistic homogeneity. Legally, the island was unified through the so-called *brehon* laws, an elaborate system of rules and customs which, at least ideally, governed socioeconomic and political relationships and which reflected a society organized very differently from Norman England. For example, feudal and traditional Irish concepts of land tenure and succession were quite distinct. In feudal England the king theoretically owned the entire kingdom, granting fiefs of land and titles to his nobles in return for their acknowledgment of his supremacy; they in turn granted parcels of land to a succession of undertenants. By contrast, in Gaelic Ireland territorial divisions were of only secondary importance, and Irish chieftains measured status and wealth primarily by the size of their cattle herds. More important, ownership of land was vested not in the individual but in the free family, or *derbfine,* which included all adult males, legitimate or illegitimate, with a common great-grandfather. In theory, each male coheir was eligible for a lifetime allotment of his family's land; periodically the land was redistributed, sometimes annually but usually on the death of a male co-owner. Theoretically, inherited land was inalienable; no member of the *derbfine,* even its head, had legal authority to sell or otherwise relinquish any of the corporate territory without unanimous approval from the entire *derbfine.* However, land, cattle, and other possessions could be leased through a system of clientship which defined the relative status of greater and lesser free families. The consequent lord-client relationship entailed a grant of protection as well as possessions in return for payments of various goods and services, many of which were quite onerous. Indeed, while seemingly egalitarian in its pattern of landownership and inheritance, Gaelic society was in fact highly stratified into rigid grades of both free and nonfree conditions, each with its own attendant rights and duties. For example, when clients failed to meet their obligations, they could fall into a status of base dependence resembling serfdom, a fate which was becoming increasingly widespread before the Norman invasion.[4]

Gaelic political structure was also based upon a form of clientship, but unlike their counterparts in feudal England those in power had no legal claim to the property of their political subordinates. Under *brehon* law the free families' lands were not even in theory grants from either the *ard rí* or lesser chieftains. The basic political unit was the *túath,* literally "the people"—a group of free and nonfree families which acknowledged the royal supremacy of one *derbfine* among them. In the fifth century there may have been as many as 150 *túatha,* each with its own petty king chosen by election (not by primogeniture, as in feudal England) from among the adult males in the ruling *derbfine.* The kings of lesser *túatha* were clients of more-powerful overkings, paying tribute in the form of goods, services, and hostages; however, this clientship was personal only among the chieftains themselves and did not extend to their subjects. Ideally, the most-powerful overkings would be acknowledged by their peers as provincial kings of Leinster, Munster, Ulster, or Connaught; similarly, in theory the strongest of these would become *ard rí*. Despite the hypothetically peaceful nature of the selection process, succession to both petty and great Irish kingships was in fact usually determined by battle and intrigue; likewise, relationships between kings and overkings were settled primarily by force. Consequently, during the centuries preceding the Norman invasion, Gaelic Ireland increasingly resembled the politically centralized states of feudal Europe. By 1166 the independence of local *túatha* and of weaker overkings had been obliterated by more-powerful families such as the O'Connors and O'Neills, and the position of *ard rí*—legally invisible in earlier centuries—was assuming national importance. However, parochial loyalties still predominated, and the Norman conquest abruptly aborted the Gaelic polity's progress toward unification.[5]

Beneath the surface chaos of constant dynastic warfare, Gaelic society was complex and rigidly ordered. Upward status mobility was possible but uncommon, for the customs of clientship and partible inheritance made social descent more likely. Status was clearly defined: each social rank had its own "honor-price," calculated by property holdings, which defined a family's legal status. Thus, family membership was crucial, and a knowledge of genealogy essential to prove privileged lineage. Honor—*enech*, literally "face"—could be outraged or forfeited in countless ways, especially by the violation of certain *gessa,* or traditional prohibitions. For example, failure to provide hospitality, no matter how burdensome, incurred shame for the offender and his family; a king's loss of honor theoretically brought disaster to his entire *túath*. The guardians of these archaic customs were themselves members of hereditary castes. Lawyer-judges, or *brehons,* expounded a fossilized legal system whose elaborate rules and distinctions bore an ever-decreasing relevance to social reality. More lasting in their cultural influence were various grades of poets, or *filí,* whose duties included the preservation (when necessary, the fabrication) of royal genealogies and historical traditions, and the composition of either praise poems honoring just and generous kings or satires admonishing unworthy successors. Christianity made little impact upon the social fabric, and the bulk of the population was at best imperfectly Christianized. Plural marriage and divorce were common on the highest social levels, and many members of the clergy openly married. Although a church reform movement began in the early twelfth century, Irish Catholicism remained peculiarly distinct from its European counterparts. Its organization mirrored the fragmented nature of secular society and was based on the local monastic settlement rather than on the diocese. Monasteries were closely associated with ruling families; often their abbots were themselves members of local dynasties, passing their offices on to sons or nephews, even going to war with religious rivals. Neither monks nor poets paid much attention to the impoverished masses of Gaelic society–directing prayers and poems to the aristocracy and regarding commoners with ridicule and scorn.[6]

The economy of Gaelic Ireland was predominantly pastoral and subsistence oriented. Since the tenth century both internal and foreign trade had increased under Norse influence; however, stock raising and dairying for local consumption remained preeminent. Farm and settlement patterns were mixed, with noble and free farming families living in dispersed *raths,* or ring forts, while unfree bondsmen inhabited separate house clusters. Small tillage fields were enclosed and exhaustively cultivated in oats and other cereals, but most land remained open pasture or waste for grazing cattle and sheep. Transhumance was common in many areas, and Gaelic society generally seems to have been highly mobile–which inhibited urban development and convinced English observers that the Irish were nomads and barbarians.[7]

Between the late twelfth and early sixteenth centuries, Anglo-Norman influence advanced and then receded in Ireland. The initial success of Henry II's barons inspired other land-hungry men to follow, and, in spite of strife among them, by the end of the thirteenth century the Normans were in control of almost two-thirds of the country. In some respects, their influence was dynamic and permanent, especially in Leinster and east Munster. There they introduced improved husbandry and more-commerialized agriculture; a network of walled towns, castles, and manorial villages; new monasteries, friaries, and parochial organization; and a new territorial framework of manors, baronies, and shires. This attempt to replicate the features of English feudal society, including even a Parliament sporadically held in Dublin and elsewhere, imposed unprecedented degrees of order and economic activity and gave the East and South a commercial and cultural lead over the rest of the island. Perhaps the most novel Norman enterprise was town building, as the invaders not only took over old Viking settlements but also chartered hundreds of others, granting privileges to attract merchants and craftsmen from abroad. However, Anglo-Norman society was predominantly rural, and the primary unit of organization was the manorial village, built around the church and castle of the local lord and surrounded by his demesne, the common lands, and his tenants' scattered strip holdings. Privileged tenants, who held perhaps 250–500 acres in fee and inheritance by primogeniture, were usually English, Welsh, or Flemish. The rest–holders of short leases, tenants at will, bondsmen, and laborers– were predominantly Gaelic, and it seems to have been Norman practice to reduce all native Irish on their estates to the level of *betaghs,* or serfs. *Betaghs* lived in separate parts of the manor, in clusters similar if not identical to those inhabited by the lower orders prior to the conquest, and cultivated their holdings in traditional patterns rather than by the Anglo-Norman three-field system of crop rotation. Although during the Middle Ages Norman farms exhibited an increasing tendency toward consolidation and enclosure, among the subjugated natives scattered open fields–redistributed by partible inheritance–remained customary. Indeed, the legal and social segregation which the Anglo-Normans tried to impose probably ensured the bulk of the Irish a substantial continuity between pre- and postconquest ways of life.[8]

In spite of its initial achievements, the Norman conquest was a failure. Given the distance and disinterest of most English kings, Anglo-Norman Ireland was nearly as politically fragmented as its Gaelic predecessor. Outside the towns almost no English middle class existed, and only small groups of English freeholders lived on the rural estates. Even within eastern districts longest held by the Normans, the majority of the inhabitants were Irish. In more-remote areas the invaders were vastly outnumbered, and in the border marches—even in enclaves within Leinster—many Irish chieftains never submitted. In these circumstances, it was hardly surprising that the conquerors soon assimilated to their subjects, adopting the language, laws, and customs of the natives. Intermarriage was common from the start, but in the fourteenth century England's preoccupation with France, civil strife within Ireland, invasion from Scotland, plague in the towns, and poor harvests in the countryside decimated the Anglo-Norman population and drove many settlers back to England. Taking advantage of Norman weakness, many Gaelic chieftains reconquered their tribal lands. In other areas, Norman lords such as the Burkes of Connaught and the Fitzgeralds of Munster adopted Irish habits wholesale, and Parliament's defensive efforts to proscribe native influences were of little avail against a resurgent Gaelic culture. By 1500 royal control over Ireland was confined to an eastern coastal strip centered in Dublin, known as the English Pale. Beyond that area *brehon* law largely supplanted English common law. Many Norman lords became so Gaelicized that they abandoned primogeniture for native traditions of succession and inheritance, thereby invalidating their feudal titles; even in Kilkenny and east Munster, where primogeniture remained the rule, a synthesis of Gaelic and English customs prevailed. Only the church remained ethnically and culturally segregated, but numerous dioceses and monasteries passed back under Irish control. In the wake of this physical and cultural reconquest, many Norman boroughs and manors disappeared, and farming became more pastoral and subsistence oriented. However, these developments little benefited the mass of Gaelic peasants; instead, the period's incessant martial strife and cultural dissonance encouraged both native and Gaelicized lords to make increasingly oppressive demands for revenue and services from their underlings. The bards still addressed their songs only to the great and powerful, praising either *Gaeil* or *Gaill* (foreigners) as self-interest dictated, and formal religion offered little solace. Indeed, with the exception of mendicant orders such as the Franciscans, the Irish church was so riven with abuses in the late Middle Ages that it made but small impression upon the persistent paganism of the countryside.[9]

Thus, by the beginning of the sixteenth century the English lordship over Ireland was largely nominal. Beyond the Pale, the only area of effective royal jurisdiction, lay the Gaelicized remnants of the Anglo-Norman colony, much of it in a state of "bastard feudalism," bordered by increasing areas, some within sight of Dublin, controlled by the "Irishry." Legally and literally, both "the king's Irish enemies" and the "degenerate" Hiberno-Norman barons were beyond the Pale. However, during the early 1500s two movements for reform and unification emerged. The first originated in the Pale among the lesser gentry, merchants, professionals, and lordship officials of Anglo-Norman or "Old English" background. Relatively cosmopolitan in outlook, eager to expand their jurisdiction and commercial activities, such men opposed both Gaelicization and the arbitrary, uncontrolled power wielded by Hibernicized feudal magnates such as the earls of Kildare. As remedy the Palesmen invited an expansion of royal authority which, they hoped, would quell martial strife, reverse Gaelic encroachments, and encourage commercial expansion. The second and ultimately more important centralizing impulse emanated from the Tudor monarchy itself, especially after the ascension of Henry VIII. Nevertheless, although superficially harmonious, the goals of Palesmen and monarchy inevitably conflicted: while the Old English desired royal support to further their own ambitions, the Tudors aimed to subordinate both Irish *and* Old English to London's control and to govern the island through a new, more trustworthy class of "New English" officials and settlers. Even more ominous was Henry VIII's break with the papacy in 1534, a move which ruinously complicated his Irish policies since most of the Old English, as well as native Irish, remained Roman Catholics.[10]

For a time, however, King Henry's initiatives in Ireland seemed to satisfy both Old English and monarchical ambitions. After subjugating the Kildare earls in the 1530s, Henry's lord deputy, Sir Anthony St. Leger, and his Old English advisers inaugurated a decade of conciliatory reform. St. Leger assumed that the primary issues which divided Ireland and impeded royal jurisdiction were legal and constitutional rather than ethnic or cultural. Because of their nonadoption or abandonment of feudal rules concerning land tenure and inheritance, both Gaelic and Gaelicized lords felt they had no option except resistance to a royal supremacy which legally invalidated their titles and possessions. For St. Leger and the Pale reformers, the only alternative to a costly reconquest was to reconcile these magnates to the crown by legitimizing the status quo through a policy of "surrender and regrant": by persuading native Irish and Old English lords to relinquish their lands to the king on the guarantee that he would regrant them immediately, along with new English titles; in this manner the heads of the powerful Gaelic families of the O'Neills and O'Donnells of Ulster became earls of Tyrone and Tyrconnell, respectively. In return, the grantees promised to conform in the future to English laws and customs, and to oblige their underlords to do likewise. Also, by bestowing lavish grants of former monastic properties, St. Leger initially persuaded both the Irish gentry and the church hierarchy to accept the king's religious "reformation." Consequently, a new era seemed to dawn in June 1541, when an enthusiastic Irish Parliament, attended by Gaels as well as Old English, changed Henry VIII's title from "lord" to "king" of Ireland, an action which symbolized the apparent initial success of St. Leger's conciliatory policies.[11]

However, such hopes were soon dashed, and conciliation was abandoned in favor of new policies of reconquest, recolonization, and ruthless confiscation. Liberal reforms would have been difficult to implement in the best of circumstances, for Gaelic and English legal, social, and cultural traditions were at many points inimical. For example, an Irish chieftain might willingly accept a regrant of his tribal lands and a feudal title and promise to transmit both according to the English rule of primogeniture; however, such arrangements subverted native customs of corporate land tenure, partible inheritance, and succession by election—as well as the interests of innumerable Gaelic nobles who were sure to dispute them. In addition, the new religious issues soon compounded old ethnic antagonisms. Before Henry's reformation, neither the Old English nor the Gaelic community had been disaffected from the papacy, and while both secular and clerical lords initially acquiesced in the Act of Supremacy, actual conversions were few and discontent appeared early among lawyers, lower clergy, and displaced friars. Underlying these tensions was the growing fear of Old English and Gaelic landowners alike that increased royal authority might eventually be employed to undermine their position for the benefit of the New English administrators and soldiers who had begun to flock into the country. St. Leger and the Pale reformers needed time to resolve these problems. That they did not get it was due less to the conservatism of Gaelic society or the machinations of the continental Counter-Reformation than to English rapacity and religious intolerance. Both traits reflected an emergent English nationalism which compounded militant Protestantism, cultural arrogance, and an economic expansionism which found expression in Ireland as well as in North America. The consequent aggressiveness of English policy, accompanied by a savagery justified by the alleged cultural and religious inferiority of the natives, eventually drove Old English and Gaels into the arms of the Counter-Reformation and forced them to define a common identity on the basis of shared characteristics and self-interests.[12]

St. Leger's surrender and regrant policy had barely begun by Henry VIII's death in 1547, and even before then more militant royal officials had undermined conciliation and driven mid-Leinster's Gaelic chiefs into revolt. The English seizure and colonization of that region convinced many Irish lords that crown designs were ultimately confiscatory. Moreover, under Henry's successors, Edward VI and Elizabeth I, England's religious policies became more radically Protestant and repressive, heightened by fears of papal and Spanish intrigue among the Irish. St. Leger's tolerant approach, his hope for Ireland's eventual conversion through education and evangelization, was superseded by harsh demands for immediate conformity enforced by penal legislation. In addition, it soon became obvious to the Old English, even to those who had welcomed royal offensives against Gaelic landowners, that the benefits of such policies would accrue not to themselves but to New English arrivistes, who regarded the Old English not as fellow countrymen but as disloyal "papists," incorrigibly "spotted in manners, habit and conditions with Irish stains," whose properties were equally fair game for confiscation. In the face of these aggressions and prejudices, Gaelic bards as well as Old English lawyers and clerics began to formulate novel, inclusive concepts of Irish nationalism which might transcend ethnic parochialisms and rally Irish opposition to English policies. Thus, while most bards still preached race war between *Gaeil* and *Gaill,* Old English spokesmen—often from refuges in continental seminaries—propagated the reformed Tridentine Catholicism as a common bond for all Irish opponents of New English avarice. Despite their different emphases, Gaelic and Old English revolts against English rule convulsed the late sixteenth century. Shane O'Neill of Ulster rebelled in the 1560s; the earl of Desmond led Munster's Old English and Gaelic chiefs into revolt in the late 1570s and early 1580s; and between 1595 and 1603 the Ulster earls Hugh O'Neill and Hugh O'Donnell led a rising which spread throughout the island and received Spanish aid before it, too, was defeated.[13]

The English victories of the late sixteenth century had momentous consequences, which were challenged but ultimately only ratified by subsequent Irish rebellions. The defeats of Desmond and the Ulster lords rang the death knell for the medieval societies of Gaelic and Gaelicized Ireland. Not all native chieftains were immediately dispossessed, and many aspects of Gaelic and Hiberno-Norman culture survived for centuries. However, the English effectively destroyed the legal and structural foundations of native society which had inhibited Ireland's political and economic integration into the emergent English national system. For example, the crown proscribed the *brehon* laws, abolished traditional Irish titles, and forced the remaining Catholic gentry to observe English rules of inheritance and succession. In addition, the government strove to abolish the networks of traditional obligations which had knit medieval Irish society together, replacing them with purely commercial, contractual relationships: new laws not only required Irish landowners to pay cash rents to retain their properties but also obliged them to demand the same from their tenantry. Perhaps most important, the Elizabethan conquest inaugurated the belated commercialization of a hitherto pastoral and subsistence-oriented Irish rural economy. For the first time land and cattle, the traditional sources of status in medieval Ireland, became marketable commodities, and in response to British and foreign demands for Irish products (foodstuffs, hides, timber, iron, etc.) New English landlords and their emulators among the older gentry established local markets, fairs, and industries and generally began to exploit their estates in recognizably modern ways. To enforce these new patterns, the crown modernized and expanded its administrative machinery, thereby bringing the island under closer control by the Dublin government—itself largely a creature of English policy and New English ambition.[14]

Ideally, these legal and economic innovations should have been accompanied by thorough campaigns for religious and cultural assimilation. Indeed, new laws did proscribe the bardic poets, owing to the "lewd liberty" they purportedly inspired among their native patrons. However, despite penal legislation against the Catholic clergy and despite contemporaries' beliefs that "the inferior and common sort" of Irish could easily be drawn into the Protestant Church of Ireland, neither English nor Irish Protestants made sustained efforts to convert or Anglicize the natives. Nor did crown authorities attempt to exploit the divisions of culture and interest between the Gaelic and Old English gentry, who still held almost 60 percent of the land between them. Most Old English lords and merchants had remained loyal during the late risings, and in religious matters they now sought accommodation, arguing that their Catholicism did not dilute their allegiance to the monarchy. However, in the early seventeenth century Stuart royal revenues and New English avarice alike were best served by the branding of Old English Catholics as "recusants" for their refusal to subscribe to the Acts of Conformity and Uniformity—a stigma which justified both their exclusion from political office and a campaign of legal harassment against their property. Thus, common persecution, increasingly advocated on religious grounds, drove Gaels and Old English closer together into a union cemented by the militant faith of Counter-Reformation Catholicism. In turn, that faith—strengthened as it was by Jesuit missionaries from the Continent—only further convinced Protestants that all the Irish were allies of the papal Antichrist and incorrigible enemies of English rule.[15]

Such beliefs easily justified wholesale confiscations of Irish lands and their resettlement by Protestant landlords and tenants in "plantations" which would satisfy New English land hunger, reimburse royal creditors, reward loyal soldiers, and secure the island against local rebellion or foreign invasion. Plantation schemes abounded during the sixteenth century, often envisaging total extermination of the native Irish, but neither Queen Mary's plantation in mid-Leinster nor Elizabeth's more ambitious plans for Munster seriously reduced the large Catholic majorities in those areas. One energetic grantee planted or restored a half-dozen Protestant seaports and manufacturing towns in County Cork, but most other efforts failed for lack of funds, absenteeism among the new owners, and the reluctance of English tenants to settle in so uncertain an environment. Thus, large-scale plantations did not commence until after 1607 when the Ulster earls O'Neill and O'Donnell fled to the Continent. James I declared forfeit all their lands, six of Ulster's nine counties, and granted them to English and Scottish "undertakers" who promised to settle the area with British Protestants. In addition, the king gave large portions of Counties Antrim and Down, outside the main plantation scheme, to the Hamilton and Montgomery families. By 1630 perhaps 4,000 British families lived in Ulster, primarily in the two eastern counties which offered easy access from the Scottish Lowlands. The settlements suffered a severe setback during the Catholic insurrection of 1641, but received massive reinforcements of Lowland Scots, English,

Welsh, and Huguenots after mid-century—especially between 1690 and 1715, when some 50–80,000 new immigrants arrived.[16]

In several respects the Ulster plantation produced ironic consequences. Its promoters envisaged a loyal, united, town-dwelling Protestant population which would eradicate native Irish influences by sheer weight of numbers or by the superior example of English civilization. However, a large majority of the colonists were Scottish Presbyterians, linguistically distinct from English settlers and hostile to the established Church of Ireland. In addition, while undertakers and landlords established a network of market towns in Ulster, most immigrants preferred to settle in the countryside, inhabiting either dispersed farmsteads or house clusters similar to those of the displaced natives. Although many newcomers were no doubt imbued with modern, entrepreneurial ambitions, a large proportion of the Scottish immigrants were dispossessed smallholders—refugees, in a sense, from the increasing commercialization, consolidation, and enclosure of Lowland agriculture. As a result, in Ulster the Scots often reproduced archaic communal patterns of settlement, inheritance, and farming which were vanishing in the Lowlands and which were again similar to those of the Gaelic Irish. Furthermore, despite the crown's intentions, no wholesale expulsion of the natives occurred. Faced with the difficulties of importing British settlers, most grantees willingly accepted Catholic tenants. Some conversions and intermarriages between natives and newcomers occurred, but the enduring pattern was one of ethnic and religious segregation: by the early eighteenth century Ulster was a mosaic of discrete districts, easily definable as predominantly Scottish, English, or Irish. In most areas outside Antrim and north Down, Catholics remained a majority, usually pushed onto the poorer uplands by the new settlers, but still present and enduringly resentful.[17]

In 1641 the resentment of the Ulster Irish exploded into revolt, and their massacre of several thousand British colonists precipitated a general Catholic rebellion lasting ten years. The rebellion was a complex affair, complicated by the concurrent English civil war. The Catholic gentry united to form the so-called Kilkenny Confederation, which ironically pledged allegiance to Charles I while battling royal armies. The Catholic alliance was tenuous, for the Old English still regarded the monarchy as the guarantor of their titles and estates, while the native Irish, influenced by the papal nuncio, Rinuccini, refused fealty to the Protestant king and demanded the legal reestablishment of Catholicism. Protestant forces were even more divided between royalists and supporters of the rebellious English Parliament. Underlying the religious and political issues was the vital concern of all combatants over the future disposition of Irish land: the Gaels might retake their lost territories; the Old English might protect their still-considerable estates; while the New English and Scottish Protestants might either lose their precarious Irish foothold or securely establish themselves and their posterity in the halls of the defeated Catholics. Ultimately, only the Protestants secured their objectives: in 1649–51, after eight years of shifting alliances and betrayals among rebels, royalists, and parliamentarians, Oliver Cromwell's Puritan army crushed Catholic resistance with such ferocious religious zeal that among the Irish the "curse of Cromwell" became a permanent byword for savagery and defeat.[18]

Ten years of war and accompanying famine and plague had devastated Ireland, temporarily reversing the commercial and demographic progress made since 1600. Perhaps one-third of the Catholics perished, and at the war's end thousands of defeated soldiers and clergymen fled to Europe, while the government transported hundreds of others as slaves to Virginia and the West Indies. For a time Catholic mass was prohibited and priests and bishops were declared outlaws punishable by death. Like their New English predecessors, the victorious Cromwellians preferred confiscations to conversions; by 1658, Catholics were left with barely 20 percent of Irish land, mostly in bleak, infertile Connaught, where some 2,000 Catholic landowners were forcibly resettled to make room for loyal Protestants on their former estates. The government allowed the bulk of the Catholics to remain east of the Shannon, but only to serve as tenants and laborers for the new proprietors. Other edicts sought to expel Catholics from towns and exclude them from commerce.[19]

The Cromwellian conquerors intended these arrangements to ensure permanent Protestant dominion over Ireland, but subsequent events in England gave Irish Catholics a last chance to reverse their fortunes. In 1660 the restoration of the Stuart monarchy provided Catholics some relief: Charles II allowed them to practice their religion openly, much to Irish Protestants' alarm, and indeed during Charles's reign Dissenting Protestants—Presbyterians and Quakers—suffered nearly as much religious persecution as did Catholics. On the other hand, Catholics were still excluded from political office, and the Cromwellian land settlement remained virtually unchanged. However, in 1685 James II, a Catholic, succeeded to the throne and proceeded to appoint Catholics to all Irish civil and military posts in an attempt to secure Irish support in his conflicts with the English Parliament. In 1688 those conflicts escalated into Parliament's "Glorious Revolution" against the king, and Ireland became a battleground between James's Irish and French allies and the Protestant forces led by William of Orange (afterward William III). James proved an inept leader: after futilely besieging Londonderry for fifteen weeks, he suffered total defeat at the Boyne River on July 12, 1690. James fled to France, but the Irish Catholics fought on for over a year until the failure of further French aid forced their commander, Patrick Sarsfield, to surrender at Limerick.[20]

The terms of surrender granted to Sarsfield were relatively lenient, but in fact the Catholic defeat was total, and vindictive Irish Protestants took care it remained so. The Dublin Parliament not only reconfirmed the Cromwellian confiscations but also expropriated nearly 300 additional Catholic estates. By 1700 merely 14 percent of all Irish land remained in Catholic hands, and by 1750 that proportion had fallen to 5 percent as the result of new "Penal Laws" designed to eliminate Catholic landownership. In 1703–4, ostensibly "to prevent the further growth of popery," the Irish Parliament forbade Catholics either to purchase land or to lease it for more than thirty-one years; Catholic profits from leased land could not exceed the annual rent by more than one-third. In addition, a Catholic could not bequeath land at discretion; at his death it had to be divided equally among all heirs, thus fragmenting his estate, unless the eldest son converted to the Anglican church and received the whole for his apostasy. Other laws required that Catholic orphans be raised as Protestants, while Protestant guardians "managed" their estates. As a gratuitous insult to the few remaining Catholic nobles, Parliament forbade them to display coats of arms, carry swords, or possess either a gun or a horse worth more than £5. Catholics could not send their children to Catholic schools, either at home or abroad. Nor could they vote, hold office, serve in the militia, enter the professions, engage in certain kinds of commerce, or live in towns without paying special fees. Additional acts banished Catholic bishops and regular clergy; priests could remain if they registered with the authorities, but in theory could not be replaced when they died. For the discovery of transgressors against these laws, informers could receive rich rewards—even the offenders' estates.[21]

For over one hundred years most Irish Protestants considered the retention and sporadic enforcement of at least some Penal Laws vitally necessary to maintain what became known as the "Protestant Ascendancy" in Ireland. Indeed, the laws reflected the fact that the Ascendancy was divided internally between landlords and tenants, Anglicans and Dissenters, and numerically weak outside eastern Ulster. In 1641, British settlers had numbered little more than 50,000 out of 1.7 million inhabitants, and even after the Cromwellian confiscations the Protestant community still constituted less than one-fifth of the island's people. Cromwell's ex-soldiers were supposed to provide a Protestant Irish yeomanry, but in fact few remained to settle and those who did often chose Catholic wives and assimilated into native culture. Although the last great wave of British settlers in 1690–1715 raised the Protestant proportion of the island's population to about 27 percent, that figure declined thereafter due to Protestant emigrations and conversions. Consequently, outside the Northeast and a few southern towns the Protestant presence remained minimal: throughout most of the countryside a handful of magistrates, ministers, landlords, and privileged tenants represented the Ascendancy to an overwhelming majority of sullen Catholic subtenants and laborers. Eventually, to counter both their insecurity and their internal divisions, Protestant apologists created an ideology as well as a penal code. The latter's severity was justified since the Ascendancy was supposedly more than a mere engine of exploitation: it was also "the just dominion of light over darkness, of truth over error . . . , of liberty and reason over despotism and arbitrary power, . . . of the religion, the arts, the civilization of Protestant Britain over the fanaticism, the ignorance and barbarism of Rome." The bravery of the Protestant apprentice boys during the siege of Londonderry, the victory of the Orange colors at "the Boyne water," and William III "of glorious and immortal memory" became unifying and reassuring symbols for a Protestant people who vacillated between arrogance and fear.[22]

Conquest, confiscations, and persecution had profound and lasting effects upon Ireland's Catholics. However, the Penal Laws themselves were never fully enforced, partly because Irish administrative machinery was inefficient, partly because it soon became obvious that Catholics were powerless to further threaten Protestant hegemony. By the middle of the eighteenth century, affluent Catholics could openly send their sons to Europe for schooling, and the bans on Catholic worship were generally ignored. Few chapels had survived the seventeenth-century wars, but Protestants usually allowed unregistered priests, also educated abroad, to conduct services in private residences or crude "mass houses." A few Catholic gentry retained their estates by feigning conversions, by being unobtrusive, or by cultivating alliances with friendly Protestants. Others managed to secure leases on part of their former holdings, grew wealthy through stock raising, and emerged in the early nineteenth century as an affluent tenantry with social and political aspirations. Many families, denied landownership and professional careers, invested in commerce and flourished in overseas trade with Europe and the West Indies. In short, not all well-to-do Catholics were impoverished by English rule. Moreover, some lower-class Catholics may actually have benefited from the overthrow of their traditional superiors. The conquerors had always claimed that the destruction of the Gaelic and Old English orders would free the common Irish from their lords' oppressive, arbitrary exactions. This was largely exculpatory cant, but many poor Irish do seem to have welcomed the substitution of fixed rents for their former, highly capricious obligations. Also, when obtainable, formal leases brought tenants increased security and, during periods of rising prices, even opportunities for upward mobility. Thus, after the Cromwellian confiscations bardic apologists for the old Gaelic social system complained bitterly of the "insolence" of aspiring peasants: "coarse and brutish . . . , gluttonous and quarrelsome, aping the gentry, trying to dress fashionably, too low to understand the meaning of refinement, but lost in admiration of a man who could talk broken English." Such lines as these from the anonymous satire *Páirlimint Cloinne Tomáis* exposed deep social divisions among Irish Catholics, which conquerors less obsessed with personal profits might have exploited. Even so, during the seventeenth and early eighteenth centuries perhaps more aspiring Catholics converted to Protestantism than is usually acknowledged.[23]

However, that opportunity—if such it was—passed by, and, on the whole, Catholic Ireland under the Penal Laws displayed a remarkable degree of social and ideological cohesion. Certainly many, probably most former Gaelic and Old English landowners and chief tenants were degraded in both status and spirit to the level of those they had once despised. Excluded from either purchasing or renting land for long periods, even affluent Catholics were effectively denied access to the most secure source of profits in a still overwhelmingly agrarian society. Although the Catholic church survived the penal code, official harassment of bishops and priests continued through mid-century, causing standards of clerical discipline and lay observance—never high—to fall to embarrassingly low levels. As for the great majority of Catholics, they remained what they had been before the conquest: impoverished subtenants and laborers. Admittedly, judging by increased exports, the Irish economy was relatively dynamic in the late seventeenth century, although much less so in the depressed early decades of the next century. However, such growth as occurred was relative to a near-zero starting point after the Cromwellian wars and scarcely affected the bulk of the populace, which remained only marginally, if at all, affected by commercialization. Consequently, save for a handful of export merchants, head tenants, and large farmers, during this period most Catholics remained in a fragile subsistence economy, retained primitive farming methods and archaic customs, and so encountered few opportunities which might have encouraged the ambitious to risk communal opprobrium by converting to Protestantism. Moreover, in time the debasement of the dispossessed Catholic gentry resulted in a social and cultural fusion between their descendants and the children of their former inferiors. That fusion can be traced in the compositions of the bardic poets, who suffered the same degradation as their patrons: popular tales and legends began to appear in bardic verse, while the poets' political sentiments passed into peasant folk tradition. Those sentiments were often deeply aristocratic, for the bards still looked down upon the "clownish boors" in whose rough company they now made their livings. However, the eventual result was ideological unification, for the poets diffused a sense of common suffering and resentment, and preached Catholic unity in opposition to "the rabble that rules." Not until the late eighteenth century brought economic expansion and a relaxation of the Penal Laws would social and cultural cleavages threaten the unity of Catholic Ireland.[24]

Finally, the psychological effects of the Penal Laws were perhaps most important of all. Sympathetic observers like Edmund Burke and Arthur Young believed that the system produced among its victims a crippling poverty of ambition and spirit as well as of material goods. Whatever the prevailing official attitude in Dublin or London, the existence of the Penal Laws enabled vindictive and avaricious Protestants to persecute Catholics in the countryside. As late as 1766 the executions of a Tipperary priest and several Catholic landowners on trumped-up charges of treason, and in 1773 the judicial murder of Art O'Leary for refusing to yield his horse to a Protestant claimant, reminded well-to-do "papists" that they existed only on Protestant sufferance. No wonder, then, that thousands of dissatisfied Catholics followed Sarsfield and his defeated troops to Europe and into the armies of France and other Catholic countries. However, while the flight of these "Wild Geese" strengthened England's continental enemies, it left the Irish, as one poet exclaimed, *"Gan triath ach Dia na Glóire"* (Without leader save the God of Glory), and encouraged an attitude of fatalism among those who remained at home. Indeed, although remnants of Gaelic literary culture survived into the nineteenth century, under the impact of the Penal Laws the poets expressed a sense of increasing helplessness. The note of despair had sounded earlier in the 1600s—*"Mo thruaighe mar táid Gaoidhil"* (Pitiful are the Gael), began a lament for the defeated Hugh O'Neill—but in the mid-seventeenth century poets like Phiaras Feiritéir and Dáibhídh Ó Braudair still preached that the conquest could be reversed if only the Irish would repent of the "sins" which allegedly were more responsible for their plight than the armies of Cromwell. "Alas," wrote Feiritéir,

> . . . it is not the strength of those hosts
> Nor the fierceness of the troops from Dover
> Nor the power of enemies that destroyed our hope
> But the vengeance of God on green-sodded Ireland.

The poets attributed many sins to the Irish—gluttony, lust, oppression of the poor—but the faults most frequently enumerated were their disunion at the time of the Kilkenny Confederation and their supposedly "treacherous" treatment of the papal nuncio, Rinuccini, and, through him, of the pope himself. However, despite their bitter indictments of "faithless Ireland," the seventeenth-century bards did not despair; for since the Irish were responsible for their defeats, there existed the possibility they could reform and redeem themselves if they renewed their religious allegiance and united against their foes. In the nineteenth century these themes of self-redemption reemerged in the exhortations of many Irish and Irish-American nationalists. However, Feiritéir died on the gallows at Killarney; after Sarsfield's surrender a chastened Ó Bruadair announced he would compose no more; and in the eighteenth century the remaining poets generally abandoned hope that through their own efforts the Irish could restore Catholicism and drive the "English-speaking rabble" out of Ireland. Their spirits and their patrons crushed by the Penal Laws, the poets created a new genre in Irish literature—the *aisling,* or vision poem. In these new compositions Ireland was represented as a sorrowing maiden, passively awaiting and yearning for the return of her rightful "spouse": either the Stuart pretender, the French king, or any other Catholic leader who might break her shackles. Until such foreign intervention, the poets could only compose self-pitying laments for the vanished glories of the past and express futile prayers for divine salvation: *"An reidhfidh Criost ar gcas go deo?"* asked Eoghan Ruadh Ó Súilleabháin. "Will Christ ever ease our lot for us?" But Christ did not answer; the Wild Geese never returned under the flag of France; and in 1746 the Young Pretender went down to defeat at Culloden Moor. Hope for a savior from abroad lived on in songs and prophecies, and in the nineteenth century a different Ireland, under different leadership, would arise to challenge English hegemony. But as one poet wrote, for his fellow bards and their vanquished lords, "Now it [was] the evening and the end of the day."[25]

2

Change: Ireland before the Great Famine

English conquest alone did not cause the massive Irish emigrations of modern times, although Ireland's political subordination in large measure determined and delimited the Irish economic and social developments which did impel the exodus. Nor was Ireland's widespread poverty by itself sufficient cause for emigration, although between the late seventeenth century and the Great Famine of the late 1840s contemporaries often described Irish society as ubiquitously and hopelessly destitute. Beneath a tiny, opulent, alien aristocracy visitors usually saw what appeared to be a homogeneous mass of impoverished Catholic peasants struggling for mere subsistence. Thus, in 1691 one observer wrote, "A little hut or cabin to live in is all that the poverty of this sort hope or have ambition for," and over 150 years later another traveler declared, "Misery, naked and famishing, . . . covers the entire country. . . ."[1]

Nevertheless, although Irish poverty *was* extensive and intense, and although the contrasts between some landlords' mansions and the squalid "smoking dunghills" inhabited by poor Catholics were stark and appalling, pre-Famine Irish society was much more complex and dynamic than most casual observers realized. Moreover, it was the very dynamism of pre-Famine Ireland which created the economic, social, and cultural preconditions for the massive emigrations of the eighteenth and nineteenth centuries and for the emergence of Irish and Irish-American nationalism. In short, the period from roughly 1750 to 1844, the Great Famine's eve, was formatively crucial for modern Ireland and for the emigrations and nationalist movements which have made its history so distinctive, turbulent, even tragic. During those years the commercialization of Ireland's rural economy and the Anglicization of much of Catholic culture rewove the fabric of Irish society. Economic development brought relative prosperity to some regions and classes, enabling a minority of Irishmen to enjoy unprecedented opportunities for upward mobility and material comforts. However, for a majority of the island's inhabitants, the uneven, halting, even distorted nature of Ireland's commercialization meant emigration overseas or immiseration at home. Indeed, it is arguable that by 1844 most Irishmen were, if not poorer in absolute terms than their ancestors had been in 1691, in some respects more insecure in their deprivation, more dependent for sheer survival upon the impersonal dictates of market forces beyond their control. The consequences of Anglicization were equally profound. By eroding the insularity of Gaelic culture, Anglicization exposed Irish Catholics to the lure of emigration overseas and to the "modern," entrepreneurial values accompanying commercialization, thus threatening Catholic Ireland not only with depopulation but also with cultural subjugation to the Protestantism and materialism of English society. However, Anglicization also provided Catholic spokesmen with new ideological resources which could be combined with traditional concepts to defend the Catholic community against both the old Protestant Ascendancy and the new, disruptive effects of commercialization and mass migration.

In spite of the Cromwellian and Williamite conquests, in the late seventeenth century the bulk of the population of rural Ireland lived much as its ancestors had done. Save in east Leinster, with its strong feudal and commercial traditions, most rural dwellers held all or part of their lands in common, farmed primarily for subsistence, paid rents in kind rather than cash, and were only marginally, if at all, engaged in translocal market activities. Dispersed farmhouses existed, but the most common type of rural settlement remained what historical geographers have called the clachan—a haphazardly arranged cluster of a half-dozen to several hundred farmhouses, usually lacking the shops, markets, manor houses, or public and religious buildings generally associated with village life in England. Clachans were merely communities of families, usually related, which leased and farmed the surrounding land in common. The origins of these clachans are uncertain. Probably most represented survivals of preconquest settlements by the lower ranks of Gaelic agriculturists—hence their predominance in the Irish-speaking West. However, clachans were once numerous in the feudalized areas of south Leinster and Munster, where they may have been old *betagh* settlements or decayed manorial villages, and even existed among Scottish colonists in eastern Ulster. Perhaps clachans and individual farmsteads both represented stages in the evolutionary cycle of a communal, subsistence-oriented agriculture once practiced by nearly all Ireland's inhabitants: the process of subdivision to provide land for offspring would quickly fragment a single holding, and familial ties and cooperative farming methods would necessitate clachan rather than dispersed settlement; in time, when the burden of increased population bore too heavily on the available land, individual households would migrate to other areas and the cycle would recommence. Alternatively, clachans might begin through joint tenancy or partnership leasing of land by related or unrelated farmers—an arrangement attractive both to landlords eager for tenants and to peasants who could pool resources to pay rents and stock their holdings.[2]

Whatever their origins, the farm practices pursued in the clachans were woefully inefficient by contemporary English standards. At least in the Gaelic clachans, a rotation of land use rarely took place. Instead the holding was permanently divided into three portions: the "infield," or tillage land immediately adjacent to the clachan itself; the "outfield" used for winter pasture; and, beyond, the rough grazing land to which livestock and their keepers repaired during the summer—a form of transhumance known as *buailtechas,* or "booleying." Portions of both infield and outfield were usually distributed by a system known as rundale (runrig in Scottish Ulster): by communal agreement every household was allotted small, scattered, and unfenced shares of tillage and pastureland varying in quality. Over time, partible inheritance ensured that each household's share diminished as population increased. Furthermore, whenever the head of a household died, all the land was redistributed; in some clachans reallotments took place every year or so regardless of whether a death occurred. Such practices ensured that all members of the clachans had sufficient land for subsistence, and, though the shares of the various households were not equal, the method of distribution and strong communal pressures guaranteed that no farmer would enlarge, consolidate, or improve his portion at the expense of his neighbors.[3]

However, the English had not conquered Ireland merely to preside over a mass of subsistence cultivators: the island's pacification in the sixteenth and seventeenth centuries was only a preliminary to its commercial exploitation and integration into the expanding world of English merchant capitalism. Confiscations guaranteed not only that Irish landowners would be loyal Protestants but also that they would develop and manage the country's resources with a view to profits and export markets. Accordingly, the conquerors had to eradicate traditional customs of land tenure and inheritance and reduce landlord-tenant relations to a purely commercial basis. Thus, during James I's reign judicial decisions outlawed rundale, and in 1695 the Dublin parliament abolished customary Irish tenure, declaring that those without formal leases were mere tenants at will. Legal developments enabling landlords to fully rationalize estate management were not completed until the mid-nineteenth century, but immediately after the Cromwellian conquest some landlords responded to English demands for livestock by abolishing clachan settlements, evicting their inhabitants, and fencing the land into pastures.[4]

Despite such measures, in the early eighteenth century commercialization was negligible, for the Irish economy grew at a painfully slow rate: prices for Irish farm products were generally stagnant, exports and imports increased just slightly, internal trade and urban growth were limited, and the great majority of Ireland's rural dwellers rarely handled cash or produced more than life's necessities. Spokesmen for the Protestant Ascendancy blamed Ireland's economic ills on discriminatory English legislation, such as the late-seventeenth-century acts which forbade Irish exports of live cattle and woolen cloth and excluded Irish vessels from direct trade with North America. However, other causes were more fundamental. Wars and credit shortages caused overseas demand for Irish goods to fluctuate markedly, thus discouraging investments in Irish land. While some proprietors actively developed their estates, many were only rent receivers or speculators who sold their lands after denuding them of timber. Much of the country remained unproductive wasteland, and poor harvests, famines, and epidemics occurred frequently; in 1753 Ireland's population of about 2.3 million reflected an annual growth rate of a mere 0.5 percent over the preceding sixty-six years. Only beef production was consistently profitable, but cattle fattening and processing occasioned little investment or employment, and, as its critics claimed, the expansion of pasture at the expense of tillage may have increased Ireland's susceptibility to famine.[5]

However, after mid-century the Irish economy grew rapidly. Between 1750 and 1810 the value of annual exports increased from less than £2 million to over £6 million, and the value of yearly imports rose at a comparable rate. Even after 1814, when inflated wartime prices fell drastically, the volume of exports and imports continued to expand. A striking rise in the amount of money in circulation reflected this economic growth: the supply of cash increased more than threefold between 1720 and 1770, and trebled again by 1800; in 1806 an observer remarked upon the "vast effusion of bank paper in Ireland," and by the eve of the Famine there were over 170 branch banks in eighty-nine Irish towns. Seaports such as Dublin, Cork, Waterford, and Belfast flourished in response to increased overseas commerce, and hundreds of inland towns prospered with the expansion of internal trade. Linked by new or improved transportation, an elaborate network of markets and fairs permeated the countryside, facilitating commercial exchanges. Districts without shops or banks had the services of peddlers, pawnbrokers, village usurers—the infamous "gombeen-men" who charged 40 percent interest or more—and traveling agents or factors who advanced loans to country people for a lien on their produce. Although many poor Irish in remote districts still exchanged goods through barter, by the late eighteenth century nearly all regions and social groups were at least indirectly involved in an expanding commercial economy.[6]

The primary cause of Ireland's economic growth was Britain's greater need for foodstuffs and textiles to feed and clothe its increasing urban population and to provision its military forces and overseas possessions. Between 1750 and 1814, Britain's nearly constant embroilment in foreign wars, coupled with its natural population growth, created an expanding demand for Irish grain as well as beef, pork, butter, and livestock. Rising grain prices halted the earlier tendency to convert tillage into pasture, as wheat, flour, oats, and barley now became profitable exports. However, the most significant Irish exports were textiles, principally linen yarn and cloth. Since the early seventeenth century, British officials and merchants had promoted Irish linen manufactures as a complement to English woolens; the chief stimulus was a law of 1696 allowing Irish linens duty-free entry to the English market. Subsequently, linen cloth exports increased from a half-million yards in 1698 to a yearly average of over forty million yards in the 1790s. After mid-century half or more of all Irish exports consisted of linen goods, the vast majority going to England.[7]

Rising domestic demand also stimulated Ireland's economic develop-

ment. Increased production of tillage and textile products for export provided greater employment opportunities, and the influx of cash augmented
investments and purchasing power. Although much capital flowed back to
England in the forms of payments for imports, rents to absentee landlords,
and wartime taxes, before 1814 enough remained to greatly expand the
home market for agricultural and industrial goods. For example, in spite
of English laws prohibiting exports of Irish woolens, during most of the
eighteenth century the industry prospered because of greater domestic
demand; similarly, a large rise in the number of Irish distilleries and
breweries both stimulated local grain production and reflected increased
home consumption. Perhaps most significant, not only did average per
capita income increase prior to 1814, but so also did the size of the consuming population: from perhaps 2.3 million inhabitants in the mid-eighteenth
century to over 6.8 million recorded in the 1821 census. This rapid demographic growth—resulting from high marital fertility and declining mortality rates—was both a direct consequence and a sustaining cause of rural
Ireland's commercialization.[8]

A final factor stimulating economic growth was the promotional activity
of the Protestant Ascendancy. The primary motivation of Irish landlords,
whether residents or absentees, was to increase revenues from their estates.
Many found this impossible, especially if they had granted long-term leases
during the economically depressed early eighteenth century. Others merely
swelled their rent rolls by increasing the size of their tenantry. However,
stimulated by rising prices and by the English enthusiasm for "scientific"
agriculture, after 1750 a growing number of Irish proprietors became "improving" landlords, investing large amounts of time and money to make
their estates more productive and profitable. Landlords such as Baron John
Foster of Louth and Robert French of Galway consolidated common holdings into enclosed farms, introduced new farm implements and livestock
breeds, constructed or rebuilt market towns, erected mills and small factories, and encouraged textile production. Proprietors employed both positive and negative incentives to prod tenants to comply with these modern
"improvements." Sometimes they offered bounties and prizes, temporary
rent reductions and low-interest loans, or gifts of tools, fertilizer, looms,
and spinning wheels. Some landlords even set their wives and daughters
to spinning flax to persuade hesitant tenants to emulate their superiors.
Often little persuasion was necessary; rising prices alone were enough to
lead many "spirited" tenants to abandon clachan life for a compact farm
and an opportunity to earn cash through market production. However,
most landlords had to use coercion to break up rundale settlements, and
"the parent of all improvements" was shorter leases with higher rents
geared to anticipated rises in market prices. By 1800 many leases contained
detailed clauses specifying the improvements which tenants were expected
to undertake and the traditional practices which they were commanded
to abjure if they wished to retain their holdings.[9]

Protestant landlords also used political power to promote economic growth and personal profits. On the local level, landlord-controlled parish vestries and county grand juries used tax revenues to build roads and bridges linking their estates to market towns. On the national level, Protestant proprietors dominated the Irish Parliament, and whether they were allied to the English-appointed Irish executive in Dublin Castle, or members of the Whiggish "Patriot party," all supported commercial expansion. Consequently, before its abolition in 1800 the Dublin Parliament passed legislation to facilitate enclosures, encourage grain production, protect home industries, subsidize transportation and harbor improvements, and prevent "combinations" of either rural or urban workers from impeding "free trade" in land and labor. For sheer physical scale, the most impressive products of government subvention were the Grand and Royal canals, linking Dublin to the Shannon. However, the most ambitious state enterprise was the Irish Linen Board, which promoted linen manufacturing in southern Ireland by offering bounties, conducting training schools, and distributing thousands of spinning wheels and handlooms. These official schemes often failed to achieve their specific goals: jobbery and inefficiency were endemic, and several of the most ambitious state-sponsored enterprises failed spectacularly. However, while often unprofitable to their investors, the projects provided employment and facilitated commercial penetration of the countryside.[10]

Commercialization wrought great changes in the landscape and habits of rural Ireland. Landlords and tenants cleared brushlands and drained bogs and fens to bring more land into cultivation. Clachan settlements, open fields, and medieval common lands rapidly disappeared in regions of relatively rich soil, replaced by dispersed farmsteads with enlarged fields fenced by hedgerows or stone walls. The wealthiest proprietors beautified their estates by constructing mansions surrounded by parks and formal gardens, and affluent tenants built two-story, stone farmhouses to replace the thatched cottages they had formerly inhabited. Indeed, if the most optimistic accounts of late-eighteenth-century Ireland are to be credited, material comforts and an ambitious, entrepreneurial spirit were both becoming widespread. Tenants and subtenants increasingly paid rents in cash, and with growing punctuality; every year, wrote one observer, the "lower classes are becoming more industrious, more wealthy, more independent." By 1800 fashionable, imported clothing was commonplace for many farmers' wives and daughters, and rising consumption of spirits, tea, and tobacco indicated the country people's growing ability to purchase "luxuries." Visitors to the cabins of rural textile workers were delighted to report that "occupiers of mud hovels could enjoy the comforts of a palace provided that manufacturing industry held there its kingly sway." Even in the Rosses of County Donegal, one of Ireland's remotest districts, a traveler in 1784 was astonished to discover that the inhabitants, so "wild and fierce" only thirty years earlier, were now "quite another kind of people, totally altered in their carriage and conduct, their habiliments and habitations, their occupations and manner of living . . . so much improved by their intercourse with others." In short, declared one landlord, in the late eighteenth century "we were in a state of profound tranquility and contentment . . . ; the farmers had . . . tasted the sweets of sober industry; agriculture was increasing most rapidly, and the country wore the face of wealth and comfort and happiness." Even during the depressed decades following the Napoleonic Wars, many observers still believed that "the country is making a visible and steady progress in improvement, and signs of increasing wealth present themselves on all sides," especially among the large farmers and the "rising middle class" in the towns.[11]

However, while not wholly inaccurate, such optimistic claims were grossly superficial. In late-eighteenth-century Ireland conflict was more characteristic than contentment, as open rebellion in 1798 and smaller outbreaks of rural violence amply demonstrated. Furthermore, in 1834 a more acute observer, H. D. Inglis, addressed the issue of whether pre-Famine Ireland was really an "improving country." "The reply ought to depend altogether on the meaning we affix to the word improvement," he wrote. "If by improvement be meant extended tillage, and improved modes of husbandry,—more commercial importance, evinced in larger exports,—better roads,—better modes of communication,—increase of buildings,—then Ireland is a highly improving country." But, he added, "I have found nothing to warrant the belief, that any improvement has taken place in the condition of the people"; rather, "a visible deterioration has taken place in the condition of the labouring classes and of the small farmers" who together composed about three-fourths of the population![12]

The glaring contrast between Inglis's statement and those of other, often earlier writers is not due solely to the fact that during his visit Ireland was suffering from the post-1814 depression, which impoverished many farmers and reduced employment for both agricultural and industrial workers. As early as 1791, another perceptive visitor had exposed the paradox of wretched poverty among the vast majority of the country's people at a time "[w]hen Ireland was supposed to have arrived at its highest degree of prosperity and happiness." Rather, the relative pauperization of the Irish was a direct consequence of the process of commercialization itself, occurring as it did in a colonial appendage to the world's most advanced industrial economy, and under a grossly inequitable system of landownership. Under these conditions, Irish economic development was geared primarily, by 1800 almost exclusively, to the export of raw materials and highly specialized industrial goods for the British market. The result was that Ireland's economy was increasingly subject to overseas price fluctuations and was governed ultimately by the considerations of English merchants, bankers, and manufacturers. Moreover, Ireland's colonial status left its industries vulnerable to competition from cheap English imports, spelling eventual ruin for most Irish manufactories. Indeed, the ironic consequence of late-eighteenth-century Ireland's excellent transportation network was that it facilitated the penetration of English goods rather than stimulated native industries. The weak position of Irish manufactories became most obvious in the immediate pre-Famine decades, after the Act of Union in 1800 abolished the Irish Parliament and its potential to enact protective legislation. However, in the late eighteenth century several Irish trades—especially the woolen industry, which once employed thousands in rural Munster and elsewhere—already suffered severely from English competition. Those industries which did survive—such as brewing, distilling, and linen manufacturing—did so only through the consolidation of firms, mechanization, and concentration near port towns like Belfast, Dublin, and Cork: economically rational responses to market conditions, but ones which reduced rural employment. Thus, Ireland's burgeoning population was eventually left dependent for sustenance and employment upon an agricultural system controlled by a handful of landlords and long-lease holders whose drives for profits and "improvements" not only geared land use for export markets rather than domestic subsistence but also eventually made the great mass of rural dwellers economically superfluous. The "dreadful" consequence, as one foreign visitor exclaimed, was "that the poor Irish have to furnish other countries with such vast quantities of that which they themselves are starving for want of."[13]

Given the extreme concentration of landownership, the commercialization of Irish agriculture was bound eventually to have adverse effects upon most country people. Initially, the inhabitants of an Irish estate might benefit from increased prices and employment opportunities, especially in districts where tillage farming or cottage textile manufacturing, rather than grazing, prevailed. However, as land values, food prices, and population pressure steadily rose, most rural dwellers soon found their economic situation deteriorating as they were forced into an increasing dependence upon market conditions.[14]

Alongside the merchants, it was the landlords and those substantial tenants holding long leases signed before economic expansion who reaped most of the advantages from the rising prices of the late eighteenth and early nineteenth centuries. The great majority of farmers—tenants at will or tenants on short leases negotiated during the price boom—found themselves ground between high rents, tithes, and taxes on the one hand, and frequent recessions and poor harvests on the other. Those with little or no land had to pay higher prices for provisions and grossly inflated rents for small patches of potato ground, while employment opportunities fluctuated according to economic conditions and the effects of weather upon harvests. Meanwhile, there was a great increase in both the absolute numbers and the relative proportion of those with small, uneconomical holdings or no land at all. On poorly managed estates or where textile manufacturing prevailed, landlords allowed or encouraged tenants to subdivide their farms to provide for succeeding generations; consequently, by the 1840s over half of all farms were too small to provide more than a bare subsistence. However, on "improving" estates proprietors reduced the bulk of their dependents to a state of landless poverty by forbidding subdivision and by consolidating smallholdings into larger, commercially profitable farms. Such "improvements" became more common after the postwar depression reduced profit margins both for landlords and for large farmers, forcing them to further rationalize land use and reduce their need for labor. But even before 1814 the rising population made competition for land increasingly intense, as commercial farmers strove to increase acreage and maximize production to sustain living standards, while the rural poor struggled desperately to retain access to the primary means of subsistence. This competition drove rent levels ever upward, intensified social and sectarian conflicts, and obliged those among the "lower Irish" who still had access to scraps of potato ground to engage in a variety of market-oriented activities in order to pay rents and avoid becoming landless "free" laborers, totally dependent upon uncertain wages for their survival. Indeed, it was the stick of necessity, as much as if not more than expectations of material improvement, which led thousands of small farmers and laborers to engage in cottage textile production: for only the constant labor of a poor man's wife and children spinning flax or wool could pay half the rent of a few acres and so enable him to compete for land against the grazier or commercial tillage farmer. However, in the late eighteenth and early nineteenth centuries the rapid decline of rural spinning—first in the woolen, then in the linen industry—severely diminished the incomes of small farmers and laborers and forced them to seek alternative sources of income.[15]

Given the desperate need of these classes for cash and credit, it was no wonder that gombeen-men and pawnbrokers flourished in the pre-Famine countryside—or that fairs and markets were well attended—for declining cottage industry meant that the poor could pay rents only by selling every farm product in excess of the bare minimum necessary for subsistence. "There is nothing too trifling to carry" to market, wrote one observer; "a yard of linen, a fleece of wool, a couple of chickens, will carry an unemployed pair of hands ten miles." Indeed, the growing popularity of tobacco and whiskey among the poor may point to their increasing use as substitutes for the milk, butter, eggs, and pork which small farmers and laborers could no longer afford to consume at home. Other means of earning cash also emerged. Many small farmers distilled grain into *poitín* (whiskey) for local markets—a potentially profitable activity, but both illegal and conducive to "intoxication and intemperate habits." In addition, thousands of petty farmers and laborers became "spalpeens" (*spailpíní*), or migratory workers, leaving their cottages each spring for agricultural or construction labor either within Ireland or abroad, returning to their families in fall with the rent money sewn inside their clothes. Ever since the early eighteenth century, migrants from south Leinster and east Munster traveled to and from the Newfoundland fisheries, and by the eve of the Famine at least 60,000—primarily from north Connaught and western Ulster—made annual voyages to England or Scotland. Others migrated within Ireland in search of potato ground. Landlords would often allow poor families, frequently evicted smallholders, to occupy and cultivate mountain wastes for several years, paying little or no rent. Such tenant reclamation was extensive during the pre-Famine decades, but eventually the proprietor would resume control of the improved land and force the peasant to select "another spot whereon to [re]commence his heartless labor."[16]

In spite of these endeavors, the inexorable processes of commercialization and population growth ultimately gave the majority of Irish only two logical alternatives: permanent emigration abroad or rural pauperization at home. For despite Ireland's economic expansion, the country experienced relatively little urbanization. Between 1700 and 1841 the proportion of people living in towns of 1,500 inhabitants or more merely rose from 7 percent to 14 percent, while the total population approximately quadrupled. In 1841 only 20 percent of the more than 8,175,000 Irish lived in communities containing twenty or more houses. As would be expected in an agrarian, export-based economy, nearly all major towns were seaports; in 1841 Kilkenny, the largest inland town, had only 19,100 people—compared with Dublin's 232,700 and Cork's 80,700. Moreover, if the early-nineteenth-century census reports are accurate, between 1821 and 1841 most large towns experienced demographic stagnation or decline; for example, Limerick fell from 59,000 inhabitants to only 48,400, and once-prosperous manufacturing towns in southern Ireland declined even more precipitously. Even small Irish towns were important trade and service centers for the surrounding countryside, as few farmers would travel more than seven miles to market, and these functions generated a growing middle class of traders, shopkeepers, and publicans. However, most townspeople—artisans and laborers—lived barely above subsistence level in filthy, congested, and disease-ridden slums and "cabin suburbs." In most towns, what population growth did occur was primarily due to influxes of evicted, unemployed paupers from nearby estates. Even Dublin, with its magnificent late-eighteenth-century public buildings and graceful residential squares, exhibited "a degree of filth and stench inconceivable" in its old, working-class quarters. Municipal governments made pathetically inadequate provisions for sanitation and poor relief, and in some slums the infant mortality rate was 50 percent.[17]

Ireland's slow urban development and characteristic urban poverty were both reflections of the uneven process of commercial expansion. An economy based primarily on agricultural exports made subsistence cultivators redundant, but generated little urban employment which could attract excess population from the countryside. Before 1814 most Irish manufacturing took place in rural cottages rather than in towns; afterward, urban industrialization occurred rapidly, but it was centered almost exclusively in eastern Ulster. Indeed, Belfast and neighboring towns such as Lisburn and Ballymena were the only urban centers to experience dramatic growth; between 1800 and 1841 Belfast's population rose from about 20,000 to more than 75,000. Elsewhere after 1814 urban manufacturing quickly declined, and cloth weavers in the Dublin Liberties and in Munster towns like Bandon fell into dire poverty. Thus, outside the Northeast, Irish towns offered little or no employment to would-be migrants from rural areas, and the rapid population turnover in urban centers such as Navan, County Meath, indicates that most of those who did move to towns stayed only a short time before emigrating permanently to Britain or North America.[18]

By the late eighteenth century, economic expansion and transportation improvements had united nearly all regions of Ireland into a complex network of trade. Consequently, aside from potato cultivation, which prevailed throughout the island, a relatively high degree of regional specialization emerged as landlords and large farmers reacted to market demands by concentrating on agricultural activities for which their district possessed some competitive advantage. For example, southeast Leinster, with its relatively rich, well-drained soils, was the center of commercial grain production, while tenants in the mountainous regions of Munster specialized in dairy and pig farming for the Cork provision market. Calves born on these dairy farms were bought by graziers and fattened on the lush grass of the Golden Vale of north Munster or the rich, limestone-based pastures of east Connaught. Cattle raised in Munster were usually purchased and slaughtered for the provision merchants of Cork and other southern seaports; those grazed in Connaught were sold after three or four years at markets such as the great Ballinasloe fair in east Galway, and finished their fattening on bullock farms in County Meath before being butchered in Dublin or shipped to England as live cattle. Sheep raising predominated on poor, mountainous land in western Ireland, while oats, flax, and potatoes were the main crops in eastern Ulster, where most rural dwellers were more actively engaged in textile production than in commercial farming. Indeed, by the late eighteenth century, eastern Ulster was no longer self-sufficient in either oats or flax, with the result that production of those crops became widespread throughout southern and western Ulster and northern Connaught, despite the poor quality of their soils. Ulster's linen weavers also needed more yarn than local spinners could supply, and so domestic spinning became the mainstay of the smallholders' economy in north Leinster and much of Connaught. A similar trade existed in Munster and south Leinster, where the wives and daughters of thousands of petty agriculturists paid their rents by spinning wool for the English market or for local cloth manufacturers in towns like Kilkenny, Clonmel, and Carrick-on-Suir. The degree of regional specialization in pre-Famine Ireland should not be overemphasized: most rural households engaged in mixed farming and some domestic industry. Nonetheless, it is clear that while commercialization was uniting Ireland through internal trade, it was also fragmenting the island into increasingly distinct districts.[19]

Moreover, a highly uneven regional distribution of wealth and population emerged. In general, the most fertile soils—those *capable* of supporting the largest numbers of inhabitants—were devoted instead to capital- rather than labor-intensive commercial activities, and bore the highest rent charges, provided the least employment, and contained the lowest population densities per square mile of arable land. "It may seem a strange remark," wrote a French traveler in the 1790s, "but it is true, that the richer the country in Ireland, the poorer are the people and the lower the labourer's daily wage." Conversely, many regions with poor soils barely capable of affording a subsistence living were grossly overpopulated. For example, in 1841 the rich grazing districts of north Leinster often contained fewer than one hundred persons per square mile, while the barren coasts of County Mayo supported nearly five times that number.[20]

An imaginary line, drawn from Dundalk in County Louth southward to the cities of Limerick and Cork, roughly divided the most intensely commercialized farming districts of eastern Ireland from both the manufacturing counties in the Northeast and the largely subsistence-oriented regions along the Atlantic coast. East of that line, in most of Leinster and east Munster, farms were generally larger and land values higher than in the rest of the island. This was the part of Ireland longest held by the Norman and New English conquerors, and thus it had the oldest traditions of commercial agriculture and impartible inheritance. Consequently, the area had a relatively high proportion of resident proprietors and substantial tenants, and it was here that the trends toward enclosures, abolition of rundale, and other "improvements" made the most rapid and thorough progress. Market towns were numerous and the social structure relatively complex; for example, in 1841 Leinster had a higher proportion of traders, shopkeepers, and publicans than any other province.[21]

This highly commercialized area can be further divided into regions dominated either by grazing and stock raising or by wheat and barley production. The relative proportions of land devoted to cattle or tillage fluctuated in response to changing market conditions, but by 1841 there were two major grazing districts: the north midlands, stretching from the north Leinster coast into the plains of eastern Connaught; and an area of north Munster, centered on the Golden Vale and the Shannon estuary. In the grazing counties proprietors were often absentees, and actual control of the soil was frequently in the hands of speculators and substantial tenants who stocked farms of five hundred acres or more. Grazing generated little employment or tolerance for either tillage or subsistence farming; consequently, aside from prosperous graziers and their herdsmen, most of the inhabitants of these regions were poverty-stricken laborers who clung to the fringes of estates. As an Irish magistrate remarked in 1760, while the pastures of County Limerick contained "the richest land [he] ever saw, . . . the common people are most wretchedly poor." Only cottage textile production allowed these marginal cultivators to compete for land; as that failed, their situation became increasingly desperate.[22]

The fruits of commercialization were more widely distributed in the tillage districts, which ran south along the eastern seacoast from Dundalk to the fertile river valleys of south Leinster and east Munster. Here resident landlords were common, most farmers held between ten and sixty acres—and so were neither destitute nor opulent—and laborers had relatively steady employment. The grain trade stimulated local market towns, and contemporaries frequently remarked that, while agricultural methods were often poor, the small farmers of Wexford and neighboring counties enjoyed better housing and clothing and exhibited a greater degree of industry and "respectability" than their counterparts elsewhere in southern Ireland. Indeed, from at least the late eighteenth century onward, farmers in the Southeast commonly rejected the practices of partible inheritance and subdivision, which were so prevalent in the North and West. However, this meant that population growth in the region produced increasing numbers of landless laborers and that, after 1814, landlords' attempts to consolidate smallholdings and expand pastureland both reduced employment and threatened many farmers with eviction.[23]

Although the landless laborers of eastern Ireland were the island's most wretched inhabitants, the most widespread poverty existed along the Atlantic seacoast, from west Cork to Donegal, and in a belt of poorly drained soil that extended eastward from Sligo Bay across north Leinster and southern Ulster to Carlingford Lough and the Mourne Mountains of south Down. Largely isolated from major trade routes, these regions consisted of mountains, bogs, and land generally unsuited for either stock fattening or commercial tillage farming. Consequently, proprietors allowed, even encouraged dense settlement by subsistence cultivators who would reclaim wastelands and make rent payments through supplementary occupations like spinning, fishing, kelp making, illegal distilling, seasonal migration, or small-scale dairy or pig farming. Joint tenancies, clachan settlements, and rundale survived longer in these desolate regions than elsewhere, and indeed many of their inhabitants were squatters, refugees from the estate improvements carried out in more fertile, commercialized districts. Life was poor and primitive in western Ireland and other areas of poor soil: roads and market towns were few, and most dwellings were mere one-room cabins or huts made of mud, turf, or dry stones. However, though most farms were tiny—the great majority had less than ten acres—there were comparatively few landless laborers, and possession of small patches of potato ground at relatively low rents ensured the inhabitants a greater degree of self-sufficiency than the rural poor of eastern Ireland usually possessed. Nevertheless, increasing population, declining markets for spun yarn and other cottage produce, and the prevalence of partible inheritance conspired to pauperize these districts. By 1841 west Munster exhibited a "most frightful state of overpopulation," and land in Connaught had reached "the nadir of fragmentation"; in County Mayo nearly three-fourths of all farms were under six acres in size. By the eve of the Famine, travelers in the western parts of Donegal, Galway, Cork, and Kerry declared that their malnourished inhabitants were often in "the lowest degree of squalid poverty."[24]

The northern province of Ulster was the anomaly in Ireland's general demographic pattern, for it was at once the most densely populated and the most prosperous region. In 1841 Ulster contained an average of 406 persons per square mile of arable land, and Armagh was the most closely settled county in Ireland. Unlike that of affluent districts in the South, Ulster's landscape was characterized by very small farms: half the holdings in Armagh and Monaghan, and over 40 percent in Down and Tyrone, were under five acres in size. Even in the rich Lagan Valley, where Belfast was situated, over 50 percent of the holdings contained fewer than fifteen acres. Yet, in spite of conditions elsewhere considered synonymous with backwardness and poverty, travelers to Ulster remarked on the province's numerous and busy market towns and on the "neat, pretty, cheerful looking cottages" that dotted the countryside. Of course, conditions within Ulster were far from uniform. Protestant tenants in Islandmagee, County Antrim, were involved in a cash economy from at least the early eighteenth century on, while only a few miles distant the Catholic inhabitants of the Mourne Mountains seemed to a visitor in 1759 "much upon a rank with the American savages." Along the Donegal coast and in the uplands of central and southern Ulster, most rural dwellers fared little better than the peasants of Mayo or Kerry. However, in the Foyle Valley of western Ulster, in the area around Lough Neagh, and especially in Antrim and north Down, living standards were generally higher than in any other part of the island. Indeed, English travelers regarded north Down as "the Yorkshire of Ireland," where "Regular plantations, well-cultivated fields, pleasant little cottage-gardens, and shady lines of trees meet the eye on every side."[25]

Contemporaries gave several explanations for Ulster's relative prosperity. The Protestantism shared by about half the province's inhabitants—especially the Presbyterian faith of the Ulster Scots—purportedly inspired a "spirit of enterprise," thrift, and self-reliance which Catholics in southern Ireland rarely exhibited. Whether Irish Protestants had a more modern, entrepreneurial value system than their Catholic counterparts is problematical, but certainly membership in the Irish Protestant community provided distinct economic advantages. In general, Protestants occupied the most fertile land in the North, and, though Presbyterians and other Dissenters suffered some indignities from the Anglican establishment, they never endured the debilitating economic restrictions which the Penal Laws imposed on Catholics. Furthermore, common religion narrowed the social gulf between Protestant landlords and tenants, and frequent intercourse between Presbyterians in Scotland and Ulster directly exposed the latter to modernizing influences from Glasgow and the Lowlands. Indeed, it was through Ulster via Scotland that several crucial innovations, such as the "Scotch plough" and the threshing machine, first entered rural Ireland.[26]

Other observers believed that the North's comparative affluence was due to the prevalent "Ulster custom" of "tenant-right," which gave northern farmers, both Protestants and Catholics, greater security on their holdings and thus more incentives for investment and improvements than tenants in southern Ireland enjoyed. The definition of tenant-right varied over time, but by the mid-nineteenth century most apologists for the custom argued that it consisted of the "three F's": fair rent, fixity of tenure, and free sale. In other words, a tenant, even a tenant at will, could remain on his holding without danger of eviction as long as he paid a rent commensurate with current market prices. Equally important, upon relinquishing his farm—whether voluntarily or by eviction for arrears—a tenant customarily received compensation from either his landlord or the incoming tenant for "improvements" made on the farm during his tenure. In fact, the ostensible basis of claims for compensation was often a legal fiction, for most tenants turned exhausted lands and ramshackle buildings over to their successors. What outgoing tenants really sold was their permission to occupy, or their goodwill, lacking which few Ulster farmers would have dared assume their predecessors' holdings. As a traditional *notion,* tenant-right was common among farmers throughout Ireland. However, only in Ulster did landlords and lawyers widely observe the custom, because of the North's rather unique historical development: in the seventeenth and early eighteenth centuries, proprietors desperate for tenants had offered unusually attractive leases, and the subsequent prevalence of domestic industry in Ulster convinced landlords that large numbers of petty leaseholds were more remunerative than consolidated farms and extensive agriculture. Consequently, what became the Ulster custom gave northern farmers a certain equity or "interest" in their holdings, and sales of tenant-right generated a considerable flow of capital through the province.[27]

However, the major reason for Ulster's superior economic condition was neither Protestantism nor tenant-right, but rather widespread textile manufacturing. Life in Ulster's many market towns revolved around constant trade in yarn and cloth, and by the late eighteenth century nearly every rural household in the North was involved in weaving or spinning linen. Only a relatively few large tenants were engaged primarily in commercial agriculture; the rest tilled largely for subsistence and paid their rents and shop bills from the proceeds of domestic industry. A skilled weaver could earn 1s. a day, while his wife made 3d. to 4d. spinning yarn; although their labor was hard and monotonous, it enabled them to outbid graziers or commercial tillage farmers for smallholdings. The more successful tenant weavers—those with more than five acres, who could afford to purchase a regular supply of yarn from local merchants—became petty "manufacturers" who employed journeymen and cottiers to weave cloth in return for a few roods of potato ground. These employees constituted the great majority of rural dwellers in Ulster, and were in fact a rural proletariat, exploited by the manufacturers and made increasingly dependent upon fluctuating linen prices as their numbers and rent charges steadily increased and as the size of their holdings progressively shrank through subdivision. Although the northeastern counties remained relatively prosperous, by the early nineteenth century the mechanization of spinning and the constriction of handloom weaving around the Lagan Valley reduced much of the

Ulster countryside to the condition of an overpopulated rural slum, rife with bitter sectarian competition over land.[28]

This brief survey barely indicates the regional complexity of pre-Famine Ireland. Within small areas the quality of soil often varied enormously, and nearly every district had its large, comfortable farms and its tiny, impoverished holdings—its aspiring shopkeepers and publicans living in close proximity to struggling artisans, landless laborers, and crowds of starving beggars. Much depended upon the character and solvency of local landlords, and as a traveler remarked in 1822, "In one district the benevolent mind will find delight in contemplating an intelligent, industrious, and independent peasantry," while "in another, at a distance of only a few miles, the heart will dissolve in pity for the extreme wretchedness of the same class of persons, inhabiting the same soil, and surrounded by the same physical advantages."[29]

Commercial growth in rural Ireland exacerbated sectarian and social as well as regional divisions. In 1834 the first reliable religious census showed a Catholic population of 6,428,000—about 80 percent of the island's total—852,000 members of the established Church of Ireland, 642,000 Presbyterians, and 22,000 "other dissenters," primarily Methodists and Quakers. Anglicans and Presbyterians were concentrated in Ulster, the latter almost exclusively; indeed the Ulster Scots dominated much of the Northeast both commercially and culturally. Outside Ulster, adherents to the Church of Ireland were scattered throughout Leinster and Munster, congregating chiefly in towns and areas of rich soil. Few Protestants of any denomination resided in Connaught.[30]

Poor Protestant artisans, tenant farmers, and laborers were not unusual in pre-Famine Ireland, but outside Ulster and a few large cities—where Anglicans and Dissenters occupied every rung of the social ladder—Protestantism was usually synonymous with upper- and middle-class status. Thanks to the conquest, nearly all landlords were Protestants, usually Anglicans, and the Penal Laws ensured a Protestant preeminence in finance, the professions, and most fields of commerce and industry long after those statutes were repealed. In southern Ireland, rural Protestants were usually privileged head tenants rather than poor smallholders, and along with the gentry they constituted the infrastructure of administrative control over the Catholic majority—serving as estate agents, magistrates, bailiffs, sheriffs, jurors at the local assizes, and, of course, Anglican ministers who derived the bulk of their income from tithes levied on the Catholic population. Their political dominance gave Protestants enormous competitive advantages over Catholic rivals in agriculture or trade, and until 1793 their legal monopoly of firearms assured observers that even in districts where Protestants were badly outnumbered, their "Red Hot . . . zeal" would "always be sufficient to keep the Papists under." Although subsequent events eroded Protestants' political strength, their economic supremacy remained. While most Catholics in the early nine-

teenth century earned less than £5 per year, the average income of Protestants was between three and four times that sum: in the last analysis,
this was the real meaning of the Protestant Ascendancy.[31]

However, during most of the eighteenth century, and even well into the
nineteenth, these differences in political power, social status, and wealth
did not *necessarily* translate into bitter antagonism between Protestants and
Catholics. In spite of the rhetorical hatred for Protestant "upstarts" and
heretics which characterized much Gaelic poetry, and in spite of peasant
memories of defeat and confiscation, postconquest Irish society was initially as hierarchical and deferential as its predecessor. In short, for the
mass of Catholic rural dwellers the names and the religion of their lords
had changed, but the basic social structure and the "rules" that governed
it remained much the same. Indeed, the alien religion and language of the
new proprietors may have caused Catholic tenants and laborers to perceive
them as even more unassailable than their former masters. The conflicts
that did emerge in eighteenth-century Ireland were primarily familial or
social, and they often transcended sectarian divisions; in much of Ulster,
antagonism between Presbyterians and representatives of the Anglican establishment surfaced more frequently than did Protestant-Catholic hostility. Only in areas where large numbers of Protestants and Catholics of
the *same* class competed for land or employment did economic concerns
explode into sectarian violence. These conflicts proved prophetic, for by
the mid-nineteenth century virtually the entire Catholic and Protestant
communities were ranged in hostile opposition. However, this occurred
only after the commercialization of rural society had transformed the
nature of the relationship between the upper and lower ranks, and caused
poor Catholics to perceive the Protestant Ascendancy as based on naked
exploitation rather than on natural superiority.[32]

At the pinnacle of Irish society was a tiny, overwhelmingly Protestant
proprietary class: fewer than 10,000 families literally owned Ireland, and
several hundred of the wealthiest magnates monopolized the bulk of the
land. However, extreme concentration of property and power was not a
novelty in Irish experience, and the new landlords inherited much of the
automatic deference which Catholic peasants had always granted those
who controlled the only means of subsistence. Moreover, the initial pattern
of relations between the new masters and their dependents was established
in the late seventeenth and early eighteenth centuries, when economic and
demographic growth was limited and when proprietors were eager to
secure tenants. Thus, tradition and circumstance combined to produce
gentry-peasant relations which were often almost feudal in nature. This
does not mean that eighteenth-century Irish landlords were not frequently
avaricious and tyrannical. They demanded not only rent from their tenants
but also labor services and endless petty exactions such as "duty fowl"; in
the 1770s Arthur Young testified, "A landlord in Ireland can scarcely
invent an order which a servant, labourer or cottar dares to refuse to
execute. Nothing satisfies him but unlimited submission." In the early

eighteenth century few proprietors invested their incomes assisting tenants
to improve their farms, squandering them instead on such forms of conspicuous waste as horse racing, hunting, gambling, prodigious drinking,
and lavish hospitality. As one critic wrote, "the typical Big House was as
ill-cared for as the [peasant's] cabin"; its "slatternliness . . . was barbaric; there was wealth without refinement and power without responsibility." However, unless they became unusually oppressive, by behaving
in such autocratic and prodigal ways, the new proprietors were fulfilling
their inherited, ascribed roles in a manner which ensured them the respect
of their inferiors. Only if landlords seemed all-powerful patriarchs—maintaining their "honor," for example, by displaying generosity and a readiness to fight duels—could they command the obedience necessary to preserve order on estates rent with endemic squabbles among their tenantry.
Equally important, the reciprocal nature of this relationship guaranteed
tenants that in return for their deference they would receive not only land
and employment but also charity during hard times and protection from
outsiders and from the law. Ideally, the landlords were "real gentlemen"
who were "tender of the poor" and who used their political influence to
secure "jobs" for their dependents as well as profits for themselves. Their
dominance of the judicial system assured that the peasantry would look to
them personally for redress of grievances, rather than to abstract statutes
conceived in Dublin. Consequently, as Maria Edgeworth observed, while
" 'I'll have the law of you, so I will!' is the saying of an Englishman who
expects justice, 'I'll have you before his honour,' is the threat of an Irishman who hopes for partiality."[33]

Thus, during much of the eighteenth century there often existed what
Sir Jonah Barrington called "a happy reciprocity of interests" between
Irish landlords and tenants. His further claim that "good landlords and
attached peasantry were then spread over the entire face of Ireland" was
inaccurate, but the ideal—the generally accepted model—of landlord-tenant
relations embodied paternalistic and deferential values which seem to have
been observed on both sides with remarkable frequency and usually without resort to overt coercion. As long as proprietors played the roles of
indulgent, if authoritarian, patrons, then their clients rewarded them with
what a German visitor called "an obedience as boundless as it is voluntary
and cordial." Indeed, many travelers in pre-Famine Ireland complained
that peasant deference too often descended to depths of shameless dissimulation and obsequious flattery. As late as 1842, William Thackeray
remarked in disgust, "A man can't help 'condescending' to another who
will persist in kissing his shoe strings. They respect rank in England—the
people almost seem to adore it here." However, by this time the behavior
Thackeray criticized was either pathetically anachronistic or grossly hypocritical, for in the preceding decades landlord-tenant relations had changed
dramatically.[34]

Even during the early eighteenth century, landlord-tenant relations were
often strained. Many proprietors, especially among the lesser gentry, could

sustain lavish life-styles only by mercilessly "rack-renting" their dependents. Furthermore, even the wealthiest proprietors could play paternalistic roles only if they were generally resident on their estates; in fact, however, one-third or more were absentee landlords who lived more or less permanently in Britain. Absenteeism had a number of causes. Many of the largest landowners possessed several estates within Ireland or extensive property in Britain. Irish holdings were secondary in importance for landlords such as the marquis of Bath, whose occasional visits to his County Monaghan estate were welcomed like visitations of royalty. Absenteeism also reflected the ambivalent social and cultural status of the Irish gentry. Although they often regarded themselves proudly as distinctively "Irish," most could feel little real affinity with the "native" population, since their superior position was, after all, due to their very separateness. Thus, their own models of proper behavior befitting their status could not be their Catholic predecessors, but rather the English landed aristocrats who made them feel inferior because of their "brogue" and other "Hibernian" traits. Consequently, the Irish gentry often aspired to escape the provincial countryside and to live at least in Dublin, which by 1800 they claimed to have made "one of the most agreeable places of residence in Europe," with an upper-class "society . . . as brilliant and polished as that of Paris." The very wealthiest fled to England, often married English heiresses, and educated their sons there so they would be sure to acquire what came to be known as the Ascendancy accent. Whether they lived in Dublin or London, absenteeism drained revenues from the countryside, heightened the cultural estrangement between landlords and tenants, and weakened the bonds of clientage which formed the mainstay of Protestant control. Recognizing these consequences, many Irish Protestants denounced absentees and argued that without resident, "improving" landlords Ireland would enjoy neither economic growth nor social tranquillity.[35]

Ironically, however, it was the "progress" of the late eighteenth and early nineteenth centuries that transformed landlord-tenant relations in ways that destroyed traditional mechanisms of social control. Responding to rising prices for Irish goods and the British upper-class enthusiasm for scientific agriculture, many proprietors began to take a closer interest in the management of their estates. "[T]he spirit of improvement has gone forth," declared the chief baron of the Irish exchequer in 1764, "and I can perceive by dining with the Grand Juries that a man makes a figure in his community in proportion to the improvements he makes. . . ." In fact, most landlords still put little money back into their estates, preferring merely to increase rents. For example, the rent rolls on the Fitzwilliam estates rose by over 86 percent between 1746 and 1783, and by nearly 90 percent between 1783 and 1815; similarly, the gross rental on the Downshire properties went from £30,000 to £55,000 between 1800 and 1815. Yet both Lord Fitzwilliam and the marquis of Downshire expended 90 percent of their incomes in England, and smaller proprietors were usually even less willing to invest at home. Furthermore, many investments were misapplied to the purchase of seats in the Irish parliament or to the construction of costly Georgian mansions, formal gardens, and Dublin town houses. Consequently, when depression and crop failures afflicted Ireland after the Napoleonic Wars, many proprietors found themselves deeply in debt and forced to rack-rent their faltering tenants to avoid bankruptcy.[36]

What most altered landlord-tenant relations after 1750 was that many proprietors abandoned paternalism for the lure of greater profits. Sir Jonah Barrington was wrong when he claimed that during the early eighteenth century "[n]o gentlemen . . . ever distrained" or "even pressed" tenants for rent, but he was correct in perceiving that a significant change had since occurred. By the early nineteenth century it was common for landlords to raise rents by breaking leases through legal chicanery and by "canting" farms at auction to the highest bidders. In the pre-Famine decades visitors remarked that the Irish gentry's renowned hospitality had become a thing of the past, and the new model landlord was a man like Sir John Benn-Walsh of west Munster, whose "[a]cquisitiveness and improvement were the salient characteristics" of his estate management. Such proprietors strove to create a new pattern of "proper," market-oriented behavior for tenants to follow, and through coercion or persuasion they were often successful. Advocates of "progress" like Edward Wakefield claimed that Irish farmers were fully capable of "improvement" if "encouraged" by resident landlords, especially if they harnessed the peasant selfishness formerly held in check by communal restraints. As a proprietor in Cork declared, "Every good tenant soon found out that a broken tenant being put out [i.e., evicted] might mean a substantial gain to himself, one very dear to his heart; he got the field close to his own house that he had coveted all his life, his own Naboth's vineyard." However, even Wakefield had to admit that many tenants still wanted a "master" or "protector" rather than a "progressive" landlord whose "improvements" included higher rents, shorter leases, consolidation of smallholdings, and prohibitions against subletting. Eventually, and especially after 1814, most farmers realized that the price they paid for deeper involvement in the marketplace was the loss of the security they had formerly known under their old "reckless" landlords.[37]

Of course, habits of paternalism and deference lingered on, especially in the West. The fact that increasing numbers of farmers were becoming mere tenants at will, without formal leases, meant that it was more necessary than ever for them to retain their landlords' favor. Ironically, too, many proprietors continued to demand the same symbols of respect enjoyed by their more indulgent predecessors; in the early 1840s Elizabeth Smith, a landlady in Wicklow who had "determined to get rid of all the little tenants" on her estate, could not understand why they treated her and her husband as "only the receivers of a much grudged rent." However, neither proprietors nor tenants could turn back on what had become an inexorable march toward the brave new world of "free trade" in land and labor. Having eroded their old, informal mechanisms of social control, the landlords could only rely more heavily upon new, bureaucratic forms of coercion. The sentiments expressed by one landowner in 1824—"What the devil do I care how they live, so as they come to work when I want them, and pay me my rent!"—could hardly bind tenants with ties of affection or respect. By signing the Act of Union in 1800, Ireland's Protestant Ascendancy threw itself on the protection of the British government, which responded subsequently by enacting new statutes granting Irish proprietors increased powers to evict tenants in arrears and restrict subdivision and joint tenancies. As a necessary complement to these measures, the Irish legal and administrative systems were reorganized and made more efficient. By the 1830s Irish landlords could call upon some 7,500 members of the new Royal Irish Constabulary and between 15,000 and 25,000 British troops stationed in Ireland to defend the "rights of property" against an alienated peasantry which had turned elsewhere for succor and leadership.[38]

The "middlemen" were just beneath the proprietors in the rural social hierarchy. Middlemen were essentially intermediate landlords. As a class they flourished during the first three-quarters of the eighteenth century, when they secured long leases, sometimes for ninety-nine years or more, from landowners who were more interested in gaining steady, secure incomes than in risking personal investments in their estates. There were several kinds of middlemen: many were graziers who rented whole townlands of 300 to 400 acres; others were mere lease speculators or "land jobbers." Most middlemen were of the "lower and middling" sort of Protestant gentlemen. However, a considerable number were Catholics: some were descendants of the original proprietors, allowed to retain de facto control in areas of poor soil and slow economic growth. Others constituted a class of Catholic nouveaux riches, particularly after 1778, when repeal of the Penal Law forbidding "papists" to take long leases unleashed a small flood of Catholic investment. The primary characteristic of middlemen was their practice of subletting most, if not all, their land to under-tenants, usually on short leases and at high rents. On many estates several layers of middlemen made easy livings by subdividing and subletting to those below them. This became especially true after 1750, when rising tillage and textile prices encouraged middlemen to allow a proliferating subtenantry to replace cattle on their lands.[39]

The rationale for the middleman system was that widespread parsimony and absenteeism among Irish landlords necessitated responsible, resident intermediaries to make investments and improvements. In many areas this mission was fulfilled: in the midlands and the dairying districts of Munster, only the middlemen had sufficient capital to build up large herds of beef or milch cattle; in north Kilkenny middlemen, not proprietors, were primarily responsible for town building and agricultural innovations. However, as rural Ireland grew increasingly commercialized, the middlemen came under heavy attack. In the 1770s spokesmen for "progress" like

Arthur Young correctly charged that many middlemen were neither responsible nor improving, that often they were not even resident on their holdings. To Young and Wakefield, the typical middleman was a "parasite" and a "tyrant" who mercilessly rack-rented his subtenants and burdened them with time-consuming personal services. "They were commonly the small gentry," the Irish Protestant W. E. H. Lecky wrote later: "a harsh and rapacious and dissipated class, living with an extravagance that could only be met by the most grinding exactions." Popularly known as squireens, they were filled with "the pretensions of gentlemen," but displayed only "the education and manners of farmers": they "sublet their lands at rackrents, kept miserable packs of halfstarved hounds, wandered about from fair to fair and from race to race in laced coats, gambling, fighting, drinking, swearing, ravishing, and sporting, parading everywhere their contempt for honest labour, giving a tone of recklessness to every society in which they moved."[40]

No doubt many middlemen exhibited such prodigal traits, as did many landlords. However, the real basis for what became almost a crusade against middlemen was the novel perception that the middleman system, once necessary and useful, now prevented proprietors from reassuming control over their estates and realizing the full value of ownership. In the late eighteenth century, even earlier in Ulster and south Leinster, rising prices showed landlords that short leases granted directly to the actual farmers or weavers would be more profitable than long leases to intermediaries; consequently, when middlemen's leases expired—if they could not be broken beforehand—proprietors often refused to renew them. Conversely, middlemen who did obtain new leases before 1814 made promises to pay high rents, which they often could not keep after the Napoleonic Wars, and so suffered eviction for arrears. In short, during the pre-Famine decades middlemen rapidly disappeared. Their influence lingered on, however, for landlords frequently found that the generosity or rapacity of former middlemen had allowed or encouraged multitudes of impoverished subtenants to settle on their properties. For example, in 1795 Valencia Island, off the Kerry coast, was let on long leases to thirteen middlemen who became absentees and permitted subdivision to such an extent that by 1847 the island's population had risen from 400 to over 3,000. The current proprietor, Lord Fitzgerald, could do little but complain, since in 1847 only three of the original leases had terminated. But other landlords pursued the difficult, often dangerous process of eviction and consolidation on their estates, no doubt cursing their former middlemen as they themselves were cursed by the ejected peasantry.[41]

Certainly, the middleman system had impeded the rationalization of Irish agriculture, and both landlords and those farmers who benefited were pleased at its downfall. However, it is doubtful whether either the Ascendancy's control was strengthened or the peasantry's lot generally improved by the passing of the middlemen. While many had been autocratic and improvident, at least their reign had usually been personal and familiar;

they had encouraged their dependents to proliferate to augment their "honor" or patronage power as well as their rent rolls. By the early nineteenth century they were often grotesque, bankrupt relics of a dying social order, but in their absence tenants increasingly faced only the cold calculations of improving landlords and their salaried agents. As one of the few apologists for the old system lamented, if the middleman had been his tenant's "master, he was also his . . . protector," but now "there is no link between the highest and the lowest."[42]

By the early 1840s the top layer of the actual farming population was made up of about 128,000 "strong farmers." Although they composed only some 15 percent of those who in any sense could be called farmers—those who held more than two acres—they leased the great bulk of Irish soil and so effectively assumed the role of immediate landlords to the much larger, subletting classes of farmers and cottagers beneath them in the rural hierarchy. Strong farmers themselves usually enjoyed the security of fairly long leases, often lasting thirty-one years or for the duration of several "lives" of persons named in the contracts. However, the definition of a strong farmer was flexible, varying from area to area. In closely settled tillage or manufacturing districts, a man with more than thirty acres was regarded as a strong farmer, whereas in the grazing counties substantial tenants commonly held several hundred acres. Outside Ulster most strong farmers were Catholics, although in the richest districts of south Leinster and east Munster a large minority were Protestants. Strong farmers benefited most from the middlemen's demise, for subsequently they became head tenants, holding leases directly from the proprietors. Also, the strong farmers received most of the positive encouragements to improve which landlords bestowed on their tenantry, and their superior resources enabled them to drain fields, erect fences and buildings, enlarge livestock herds, and purchase modern farm implements. Although contemporaries often accused graziers of slovenly farming methods, by the late eighteenth and early nineteenth centuries most strong farmers were actively emulating the ethics and behavior of improving landlords. Their farms were relatively neat; their houses well built—perhaps two storied, with stone walls and roofs which were slated rather than thatched—and well furnished; their clothes were stylish, often imported; and their diet frequently included meat. Strong farmers usually owned at least two horses for farm work and employed modern equipment like iron ploughs and drills for planting potatoes. By definition, strong farmers were commercial farmers: they hired poor men and women to work for them on a regular or seasonal basis, and their output was highly responsive to fluctuating market prices. Especially after 1814 this meant that strong farmers increasingly devoted their holdings to pasture for grazing, since raising beef cattle instead of cereals reduced labor costs and promised maximal economic advantage. However, even strong farmers were driven by the relentless pressures of rents and, after 1814, by falling prices—as well as by desires for profit. Although in the depressed 1820s landlords granted some abatements to head tenants, Irish rents probably still absorbed a higher proportion of farmers' total output than in any other country; in addition, taxes and tithes were a steady drain on incomes. Even strong farmers were not exempt from eviction if they fell into arrears. Livestock diseases or a run of bad harvests could quickly deplete their capital, and the growing tendency of proprietors to grant fewer and shorter leases made them increasingly insecure. In these circumstances, many strong farmers found it impossible to maintain their bourgeois pretensions without exploiting their inferiors even more than they were squeezed by their landlords.[43]

Below the strong farmers were about 253,000 "middling farmers" who held more than ten but fewer than thirty acres. In 1841 they composed some 30 percent of all farmers and were a very heterogeneous group. Except in the northeastern counties, the great majority were Catholics. Sometimes they were head tenants, but more often sublessees of middlemen or strong farmers. Few middling farmers had leases that ran for more than twenty years, and large numbers merely held their lands on a year-to-year basis. Their condition ranged from decent comfort to considerable hardship, for if they were sublessees they often paid several times the per-acre rents charged to middlemen or strong farmers. Like their superiors, middling farmers produced a surplus for the market and paid rents in cash; however, their surplus was relatively small, and their net income precariously low. The more fortunate might own a plough horse or mule, but since most lacked sufficient capital to build up herds of store cattle, they engaged primarily in tillage or dairy farming rather than in grazing; in Ulster many were petty linen manufacturers. Middling farmers often hired laborers or servants, especially at harvest time, but they preferred to depend upon informal networks of kin and neighborhood assistance. Though comfortable, their houses were rarely more than one storied and had mud walls and thatched roofs. Their clothes were similar to those worn by strong farmers, but they had to last longer and consequently were often ragged and patched. Outside the "oatmeal zone" in northern Ireland, potatoes formed a major part of the middling farmers' diet, supplemented, however, with milk, butter, bread, fish, and occasional servings of pork or chicken. Many families in this class strove for profits and respectability, but high rents and, after 1814, falling prices and frequent crop failures left them little capital for investment; outside Ulster their insecurity of tenure discouraged them from making many improvements. Like strong farmers, middling tenants often earned extra income by subletting part of their holdings to poorer men. However, subletting could incur the wrath of improving landlords, and after the Napoleonic Wars many middling farmers already lived under constant anxiety of eviction.[44]

At the bottom of the farming population were some 310,000 small-holders who occupied from two to ten acres of land, and perhaps another 100,000 or more families who in 1845 tilled over 30,000 joint tenancies under rundale or some other form of partnership tenure. Together these petty cultivators accounted for more than half of all farmers. Except in a few Ulster counties, virtually all smallholders were Catholics, usually sub-lessees and mere tenants at will. Given their limited acreage, smallholders tilled the soil primarily for subsistence and paid their inflated rents through supplementary occupations like cottage industry, hired fieldwork for wealthier farmers, the distillation of *poitín,* or the occasional sale of milk, butter, eggs, or young livestock. Because their capital was so small, and their margin of security so thin, most smallholders were highly inefficient and conservative farmers. Critics often charged that "[t]he obstinate super-stition of the common people . . . will not allow them to adopt any improvements in husbandry, or the most trivial changes in their farming utensils": this was especially true where commonage prevailed, but even independent small farmers feared to innovate unless proprietors guaranteed them against potential losses. Smallholders could not afford the luxuries of draining and fallowing fields or of fertilizing them with quicklime; instead, they exhausted the soil by repeated croppings. As landlords often complained, typical smallholdings were covered with "ragwort and thistles, banks without hedges, land saturated with water." The general absence of barns and other outbuildings meant that smallholders collected little manure unless they lodged their few livestock inside their houses at night—a common practice among the rural poor. Few men of this class owned horses or ploughs or could afford to hire labor; consequently, they were dependent upon the aid of relatives and neighbors to till the soil with "loys"—primitive spades adapted for bare feet. Smallholders' living stan-dards ranged from spartan decency to desperate poverty. Most occupied thatched houses with few rooms or windows and with only rude country furniture. In areas where domestic weaving survived, smallholders' families wore coarse homespuns; elsewhere they purchased used garments from itinerant traders: in either case, poverty dictated that the clothes be worn into rags before replaced.[45]

Contemporaries believed that from five to eight acres was the bare minimum of land necessary for a family to maintain an adequate existence, but thousands of smallholders and joint tenants survived on much less. Except in years of bad harvests—which occurred frequently in the early nineteenth century—merely having sufficient food to eat was usually not a problem. An average family might need over four tons of potatoes an-nually to stay alive, but one acre would regularly produce half again that much. The smallholders' tragedy lay in the fact that the commercialization of Irish agriculture made their mere subsistence economically immaterial, unless their needs could profit others more fortunate. Thus, in areas of good soil smallholders had to pay rents perhaps four to five times those paid by strong farmers for the privilege of cultivating land which could have been devoted to pasture or commercial tillage. Many small farmers purposely exaggerated their appearance of poverty in an effort to avoid rent increases, but the intense competition for land drove rent levels for sublessees inexorably upward. By the eve of the Famine, high rents had reduced most small farmers outside the Northeast to an almost exclusive dependence upon a potato diet; all other produce had to go to market. Only dogged resistance, supplementary sources of income, and the fact that many smallholders and joint tenants occupied lands of marginal commercial utility dissuaded landlords from "improving" much of this class out of existence, allowing it to struggle along until the potato blights of 1845–50 destroyed its precarious margin of security.[46]

According to a traveler in 1834, "A little buttermilk added to the potatoes, made the chief difference" between the living standard of the small farmers and that of the laboring poor. But however impoverished many farmers were, the possession of land, a little capital, and a greater degree of self-sufficiency made them superior in status and usually in material condition to the nearly 900,000 families of laborers. Laborers, almost exclusively Catholics, constituted about 56 percent of the pre-Famine rural population; in grazing counties like Cork and Limerick, laborers outnumbered farmers by ratios of three or four to one. Basically, there were two major categories of permanent laborers—cottiers and landless laborers—which evolved in response to changing economic and political conditions. In the late seventeenth and early eighteenth centuries, the prevalence of joint tenancies and rundale provided poor men with land, and so market-oriented landlords and head tenants had to secure labor by demanding fixed amounts of "duty-work" from their lessees. However, the century preceding the Great Famine witnessed a slow transition to a "free" labor market. After about 1750, under the impact of rising prices and the ideology of improvement, proprietors moved to eliminate joint tenancies and to grant individual leases no longer containing the duty-work requirements which tenants increasingly resented and resisted. More than ever landlords and strong farmers needed a reliable supply of cheap labor, since now-profitable tillage farming required large numbers of hands for planting, weeding, and harvesting; however, despite the eradication of many clachans, labor remained relatively scarce. In the late 1770s a landlord in Meath informed Arthur Young that twenty years previously "if he gave notice at the mass-houses, that he wanted labourers, in two days he could have 2 or 300; now it is not so easy to get 20, from the quantity of regular employment being so much increased." It seems that employers and laborers alike preferred security to uncertainty, however, for the late eighteenth century witnessed the emergence of a class of bound laborers generally known as cottiers: workers who received a cabin and from two acres to a few roods of land on which to raise potatoes and graze a cow, in return for a stipulated number of days' service in the fields or, in Ulster, at the looms of their employers. In 1793 the Irish Parliament encouraged the proliferation of cottiers by enfranchising Catholic tenants holding land valued at 40s. or more; subsequently, landlords eager to increase their political influence granted thousands of one-acre holdings to dependent laborers, who thereby became what were known as 40s. freeholders. However, most cottiers had no leases and rarely handled cash; their employers, primarily strong and middling farmers, merely deducted their wages from the amount of rent owed. Although cottiers' wages averaged only a few pence per day, their rents were normally high: perhaps £2 per year for a cabin and potato garden, near towns as much as six guineas. The cottier system gave farmers a controlled labor force, for the yearly agreements between landholders and employees ensured that workers could not change employers or bargain for higher pay during periods of heavy demand. On the other hand, although cottiers were certainly exploited, they did receive land sufficient for subsistence, and they enjoyed greater autonomy than the much smaller class of farm servants who lived under the constant scrutiny of their masters.[47]

On the Famine's eve, cottiers still composed a majority of Ireland's rural laborers. Indeed, their absolute numbers steadily grew because of natural increase and the social descent of many poor farmers and farmers' sons. Landlords and head tenants still found cottiers useful for reclaiming wasteland, and they remained economically important in districts where dairying and textile weaving predominated. However, by the first decade of the nineteenth century, heightened land values, the greater availability of cash, and the growing abundance of rural poor had convinced many employers that granting valuable land in order to secure workers was no longer efficient or necessary. Moreover, after 1814 falling prices forced farmers to increase commercial production at the expense of cottiers' potato gardens, to reemphasize cattle grazing, which required less labor than tillage farming, and to reduce labor costs through mechanization or heavier reliance on unpaid family assistance. In addition, after the war many landlords stood firmly against subletting; in 1829 Parliament's abolition of the 40s.-freehold franchise removed the proprietors' last incentive to allow cottiers to proliferate on their estates. Consequently, many cottiers, as well as evicted smallholders and farmers' sons, were transformed into landless "free" laborers who received cash for their services but were obliged to purchase provisions or rent land for subsistence on the open market. In the immediate pre-Famine decades their numbers grew prodigiously, and by 1841 they and their dependents made up over one-fourth of Ireland's population. Contemporary observers were ambivalent about the emergence of this class: it was economically "rational," but it created grave problems of social control since "independent" laborers were "exposed to all the temptations of an idle, reckless, and needy existence," and often survived only through "a general, habitual, petty pilfering." The most fortunate laborers had steady work with one employer, but the great majority lived and worked very irregularly: squatting on wasteland or beside roads on the margins of estates, traveling from harvests to hiring fairs, often migrating to Britain in search of employment. The superabundance of labor and the decline of rural industry meant low wages, rarely averaging more than 4d. to 8d. per day. Although provisions were usually cheap, most unbound laborers suffered chronic underemployment; few worked more than 200 days annually, and during years of bad harvests demand for their services fell while food prices rose. Many landless laborers acquired land for potatoes through a system called conacre: the seasonal renting from a farmer of a few acres or roods of already-manured soil. The renter provided seed, labor, and an often exorbitant fee; by the 1840s the demand for conacre was so great that rents averaged about £10 per acre. Smallholders, cottiers, and farm servants frequently took land in conacre for commercial uses, but for landless laborers conacre was virtually a speculation in subsistence.[48]

Before the Great Famine, cottiers, landless laborers, and the poorest smallholders—those who can properly be called the peasantry—constituted about three-quarters of the rural population, and their wretched condition gave Ireland its deserved reputation for dire poverty. The very poorest—those three million persons described by a parliamentary commission in 1835 as "subject every year to the chances of absolute destitution"—lived barely at subsistence level, pinched by hunger, stunted by malnutrition, and subject to typhus, dysentery, and other prevailing "fevers." By the early 1840s the rural poor were existing almost entirely on potatoes. In the late eighteenth century Arthur Young had described them as more "chearful," robust, and athletic on their diet of potatoes, butter, and milk than their English counterparts who subsisted largely on bread. However, by the time of the Famine few cottiers or laborers could keep cows or afford milk, and they now relied upon a variety of potato—the "lumper"—which was very prolific but also highly susceptible to bad weather and disease. By 1845 all the potato land set in conacre could provide no more than 75 percent of the nutritional needs for Ireland's laboring population. Consequently, every year between late spring and harvest time, the rural poor suffered extreme privation: eating only one meal per day, or every other day, and consuming their remaining potatoes "with a bone" in them—that is, half raw—to slow their digestion. The poorest cottiers and laborers dressed in cast-off rags, through which naked arms and legs protruded, and lived in one-room, mud-floored cabins without chimneys or windows. In 1841 nearly half a million such hovels dotted the Irish countryside, especially in the South and the West. One traveler described them as "less calculated for any of the comforts or conveniences of life than the huts of the savages I have seen in the back woods of North America": furniture consisted generally of a few broken stools; beds were considered luxuries, and many poor families slept huddled together on straw laid on the bare floor. Ironically, having created or at least allowed such squalid conditions, many upper- and middle-class contemporaries concluded they were due solely to the laziness and indifference of the poor themselves. Certainly, apathy both reinforced and resulted from poverty, malnutrition, and disease, but the really destitute could do little to improve their material condition. The cultivation of their potato patches took less than three months each year, and paid employment was increasingly infrequent. In these circumstances it was understandable that the Irish poor passed much time drinking *poitín,* loitering at fairs, and fighting. Many simply gave up the struggle to hold land or find work and turned to begging on a seasonal or permanent basis. During the summer months, when the preceding year's potatoes had all been consumed, swarms of beggars invaded every town and lined the main roads in the South and the West. No wonder travelers often declared that "decay, rags, beggary, and want, stare one in the face everywhere in Ireland."[49]

Despite class distinctions, most rural dwellers found their primary identity in their families and local communities rather than as members of broader social groups. Among Catholics and Protestants alike, the family was the most important unit. In preconquest Gaelic society an individual's claims to land depended on membership in the *derbfine,* and in spite of English attempts to establish the conjugal family as the landholding unit, the traditions associated with the *derbfine* survived not only in rundale clachans but also in the Irish countryman's proverbial passion for genealogy and his belief that ties with even remote kin were paramount in enabling him to cope with life's trials. Among the Catholic Irish especially, only family members were considered "friends" (*cairde*), while nonrelated neighbors, regardless of intimacy, were merely "acquaintances" (*lucht aitheantais*). Whether an Irishman actually felt affection for particular kin was unimportant; intrafamilial strife was often endemic, but family members strove to present a united front to the outside world. Fierce family loyalties precluded objectivity in business, politics, or law: "To save a relation from punishment, or to punish any one who has injured a relation, an Irish peasant will swear to anything." Similarly, except where sectarian divisions precluded unity, neighbors in a rural townland or parish usually saw themselves as bound together by tradition and self-interest, often regarding outsiders with intense suspicion. Thus, while class differences existed both within and among country families, ideally they were "broken down in a thousand ways" by dense networks of reciprocal obligations.[50]

Family, neighborhood, and class closely coincided in rundale communities, where group subsistence took precedence over individual aspirations which might jeopardize the delicate balance between population and available resources. Although by 1800 most clachans had disappeared, strong kinship and communal ties persisted where now-dispersed farmsteads were held by individual families. For example, despite landlords' opposition, it was common for middling and small farmers to subdivide holdings to provide land for their sons when they married. In 1814–19 Anglican ministers reported the practice among Presbyterian weavers in Ulster, English-speaking Catholic tillage farmers in south Leinster, and Irish-speaking joint tenants in less commercialized western districts. As late as 1845 a priest testified that smallholders in Monaghan "are always anxious to keep their sons at home, and divide with them when they can." Farmers sometimes made similar provisions for daughters, granting them portions of the patrimonial holding if they married landless men. However, farmers usually discouraged such marriages and instead provided for daughters through the "match"—a social institution which not only assured "good marriages" but also cemented alliances between landholding families. The crucial aspect of the match was the bride's dowry or "marriage portion"; small farmers would often save or borrow to give away their daughters with dowries of £50 or more. Matches were frequently the result of the crassest material calculations by parents, and sometimes the betrothed had not even met before being joined at the altar. One observer characterized the system as "little less than licensed prostitution," and many young women connived at their own abductions—runaway love matches—to compromise their marketability and force their fathers to allow them to marry men of their own choosing. However, although a commercial transaction, the match also had traditional functions. It not only reflected patriarchal dominance but also redistributed wealth among local families. In addition, the exchange of dowry money helped farmers provide for their offspring even if they did not subdivide their holdings, for the marriage portions frequently went to noninheriting children rather than to the inheriting son and his bride. Ideally, then, the dowry system helped perpetuate harmony and rough equality both among and within farming families.[51]

Interdependence was the cherished norm between generations in single families and among households in any neighborhood. Within families ties of affection and obligation were underlain by an often explicit economic bargain: in return for a portion of the family holding, a dowry, training in a marketable skill, or at least a share of their brother's marriage portion, children would dutifully assist parents in farm work or in cottage industry, and later fulfill their "sacred duty" to maintain them when they grew too old to support themselves. Similar obligations extended beyond the nuclear family: visitors often remarked that the Irish were "most exemplary in the care which they take of destitute relatives, and in the sacrifices which they willingly make for them"; "[s]hame and fear of degradation prevents their being allowed to beg." Another form of interdependence was the neighborhood *meitheall,* a system of cooperative seasonal farm work involving reciprocal exchanges of labor and farm animals. In some districts the practice was known as cooring, an Anglicization of Irish words signifying both kinship obligations and the cotillage formerly associated with rundale. However, the *meitheall* embraced friends and neighbors as well as relatives. When a farmer announced his intention of cutting hay or digging turf or potatoes, his peers and kinsmen would arrive on the appointed day; instead of money their rewards would be food, drink, music, dancing, and the assurance of assistance in turn. The logical extension of this ethic of interdependence was the proverbial hospitality which rural families gave to neighbors, local beggars, even total strangers. Thus, familial and communal obligations helped to mitigate economic distinctions and to insulate country people from the full rigor of the marketplace.[52]

However, much evidence suggests that the process of commercialization

even eroded traditional kinship and neighborhood ties, fragmenting them
along class and generational lines. The interdependence and assumed
homogeneity characteristic of wide kinship obligations and the *meitheall*
made those systems "highly resistant to change . . . highly inimical to
the development of those individualistic achievement motives, acquisitive
consumption values, or that individualistic competitiveness that seems
necessary for the development of a modern competitive capitalistic farming system." But in the late eighteenth and early nineteenth centuries proprietors and tenants alike responded to the lure of profits or the threat
of impoverishment by taking actions which disrupted those institutions.
The most dramatic index of this change was the crumbling from within
of many rundale communities. Although in remote, western districts landlords usually encountered stiff resistance when they tried to abolish clachan
settlements, in more commercialized areas the inhabitants often abandoned rundale voluntarily. For example, in market-oriented parishes like
Maghera in County Derry and St. Peter's, Athlone, in County Roscommon, contemporaries reported that by 1814–19 rundale farmers had become ambitious for higher living standards. As a result, they were "litigious
about trifles, and [felt] but little compunctions in endeavouring to possess
themselves of their neighbour's property, by whatever means it [could]
be obtained." In such districts joint tenures no longer ensured cooperation, but rather "excite[d] . . . them to over-reach each other in the
divisional lots of the common property . . . , or the number of cattle
each should have on the common pasture, . . . or the quantity of work
done in . . . copartnership." The usual conclusion to such internecine
squabbles was the permanent division of the old common lands, and the
dispersal of individual households onto separate farms. Other clachans
fell apart because population growth, excessive fragmentation of holdings,
and declining incomes from cottage industry reduced them to extreme
poverty. For example, by 1837 the 4,000 inhabitants of the Gweedore
district in west Donegal had among them only one cart, one plough,
twenty shovels, and two feather beds; one poor man held his "farm" in
forty-two different pieces, and twenty-two other families shared a half-acre
field. Starvation haunted such communities whenever the potato crops
failed. In these circumstances, it was perhaps inevitable that "tenants in
common," such as those in Kilmactige parish, County Sligo, would resort
to "the habit of dividing their several proportions, casting lots on the
divisions, and inclosing them; which must tend very much to make them
more comfortable, and better able to support their families." However,
when this happened, the extended kinship group—no longer in a position
to apportion land or regulate its use—lost much of its importance. Social
differentiation also eroded the ideological basis for the *meitheall,* because
it could function smoothly only if its members enjoyed similar status and
farming technology, thus ensuring that exchanges of assistance were more
or less equal. However, when market-oriented tenants enlarged holdings
or adopted new farm implements, reciprocity became impossible. Old

meitheall groups often dissolved in bitter jealousy, and more affluent farmers turned to hired labor rather than exchange horses and horse-drawn machinery with tenants who still depended on spades and sickles.[53]

The concentration of wealth in the comparatively small "improving" sector of the farming population led to the hegemony of a family type which was far better suited than the old *derbfine* to the demands of capitalistic agriculture. In pre-Famine Ireland this type was most characteristic of relatively affluent strong farmers and those of lesser wealth who tried to emulate their success. The primary features of strong-farmer families were impartible inheritance and staunch resistance to subdivision. In short, only one son would be chosen to inherit the farm intact, and, unless the family was quite well off, only one or perhaps two daughters would receive dowries sufficient to enable them to marry men with comparable holdings. Ideally, if family means were adequate, noninheriting sons were apprenticed as clerks to urban merchants, set up in some business or trade, or even educated for the professions; Catholic farmers took special pride if they could make one or more sons into priests. If possible, daughters received genteel educations at convent schools, and at the least they were exempted from fieldwork. Their reputations were closely guarded, but those who failed to receive dowries had few alternatives to spending their adult lives as maiden aunts or, if Catholics, as nuns. There seemed to be no fixed rule of succession to family holdings, and strong farmers often did not designate their heirs until they were ready to retire from active farm management. Since a young man of this class would usually not marry until he was certain he could bring a wife into his father's house and support her, marriages were postponed until relatively late, and the age difference between husbands and wives was often considerable. As a witness declared in 1835, "a comfortable farmer's son is very slow to marry; he not only marries late in life, but he always waits until he gets a girl with a fortune. . . ." Thus, the strong-farmer family carefully calculated and maximized its economic resources, but at the expense of collateral kin and at the risk of fomenting both sibling rivalry and intergenerational strife. The great emphasis such families placed on acquisitiveness and respectability, and the fact they could afford to hire needed assistance, inclined them to draw rigid social lines between themselves and less fortunate relations. Strife among parents and children, especially between fathers and noninheriting sons, was harder to contain, but the age gap between husbands and wives—and the loveless nature of many "matches"—often made the mother-son (especially mother–youngest son) relationship exceptionally close: so much so that jealousy between mothers and their sons' brides was proverbial. Otherwise, potential rebellion by noninheriting children was usually thwarted by a "process of socialization" which instilled "in them a deep sense of inferiority [and] of submissiveness" and an aversion to premarital sexual escapades which might disgrace the family "name" and upset parents' cautious calculations.[54]

These family patterns were most common in Leinster and Munster,

especially in grazing districts, where rapid commercialization and the necessity of large holdings coincided with Norman traditions of impartible
inheritance. Initially, Protestant tenants were more likely than Catholics
to keep farms intact, perhaps a reflection of cultural differences as well
as of the greater commercial advantages most Protestants enjoyed. Whatever their religion, farmers who structured family relationships in these
ways obviously displayed a kinship ideology much different from that of
rundale farmers, and very similar to that of the urban bourgeoisie—
merchants, lawyers, shopkeepers, and traders—with whom they were often
allied by blood and marriage as well as by commerce. Like so many of
their landlords, strong farmers made "improvement" and "progress" their
bywords; their families were designed to further those goals, and their
social and cultural dominance over an increasingly commercialized countryside ensured that their values and life-styles would eventually become
the new models for the rest of rural Ireland to emulate.[55]

However, in the late eighteenth and early nineteenth centuries, the family patterns of the poor majority of the agricultural population seemed
to be developing in the opposite direction—toward a greater propensity for
partible inheritance and early marriage—in response to economic changes.
After 1750, rising grain prices made middling and small farmers more
amenable to subdividing holdings among their sons, and the greater availability of land gave daughters improved chances for marriage. Also, their
greater need for laborers, and their recognition that the periodic planting
of fields in potatoes replenished exhausted soils, made landlords and head
tenants more willing to let acreage to rural dependents. Finally, increased
cottage manufacturing enabled families to subsist on smaller holdings and
increased the economic importance of women and children. Indeed, one
observer believed that petty farmers and laborers treated wives like "beasts
of burden" and regarded children merely as "a valuable acquisition, on
account of the labour which they can perform when they grow up." In
any case, land became more easily accessible to the children of farmers,
cottiers, and laborers, and they responded to this opportunity by marrying earlier and more freely and by producing more offspring. Premarital
sex may also have become more common, as young couples anticipated
the certainty of matrimony. There was a regional as well as a social bias
in these trends. Subdivision and early marriage were most frequent in
remote, mountainous regions where wasteland and cottage industry prevailed and where agricultural output for the market was limited. Thus,
travelers in west Kerry and Mayo claimed that men were usually marrying
in their early twenties and women as young as thirteen or fourteen. However, even in districts of rich soil, subdivision and early marriage were not
uncommon.[56]

Combined with lower infant mortality rates and widespread smallpox
inoculation, these developments caused Ireland's population to soar by
about 75 percent between 1780 and 1821. The social consequences are
more difficult to measure. Farmers' greater willingness to reward dutiful

sons with land may have strengthened parental authority. On the other hand, it is more likely that the increased *general* availability of land and employment reduced farmers' sons' dependence on their fathers' generosity and temporarily weakened the match and dowry system by making marriages for love less economically hazardous. The fragmentation of farms and the greater accessibility of cottage gardens and conacre served to blur social distinctions between smallholders, cottiers, and laborers; however, subdivision and early marriages both reflected and deepened the socioeconomic and cultural gaps between the rural poor and the strong farmers. The two groups had responded to the same economic changes in radically different ways: varying class positions and, perhaps, cultural traditions determined widely opposed kinship ideologies, and strong farmers—like improving landlords—viewed the family practices of their inferiors as "reckless" and "improvident."[57]

The strong farmers' judgments proved prophetic, for partible inheritance under conditions of explosive population growth led inevitably to pauperization. After 1814 rural manufacturing declined, landlords and farmers reduced labor costs, and proprietors marshaled the Subletting Act of 1826 behind their new determination to prevent tenants from subdividing their farms. Despite the depression, among small farmers and cottiers pressures to subdivide remained strong: sons still wanted land, and petty farmers may have felt that several households could pay the rent of a holding more easily than one. Perhaps, too, the rural poor were still induced to marry early "by feeling that their condition cannot be made worse." Certainly, subdivision and early marriage remained the norms in western Ireland and other poor regions. However, throughout much of the country, family patterns among the middling and lower ranks began to shift in the direction of the model displayed by the strong farmers who best survived the postwar crisis. Squeezed by proprietors' threats, falling incomes, and rising rents, tithes, and taxes, most middling farmers and many smallholders now determined to keep their farms intact, will them to a single heir, and force the rest of their sons to seek livings elsewhere.[58]

The effects of these changes, although by no means universal until after the Great Famine, were nonetheless dramatic. In Ireland generally, census figures demonstrate that between 1821 and the Famine both the average ages at marriage and the celibacy rates for men and women rose, while rates of marital fertility and demographic growth consequently declined. The children of commercial farmers married later and more rarely, while at the other end of the social scale landless laborers suffered such economic devastation—evidenced by rising infant mortality rates—that they, too, married less readily and had fewer children. On the broadest level, restricted access to land deeply divided those middling and small farmers who now embraced the individualistic, acquisitive ethos of the strong farmers from those smallholders who continued to subdivide and from the laboring poor. Intermarriage between these two groups became increasingly rare, and socioeconomic relations more strained, as their relative positions steadily diverged. The postwar depression also exacerbated intrafamilial relationships. All but the most affluent farmers had to rely more heavily on the unpaid labor of their sons—which may help explain why many small farmers continued to practice partible inheritance. However, those who chose not to subdivide, and whose straitened circumstances precluded them from providing most of their children with educations, dowries, or alternative careers to farming, had nothing to give their disinherited offspring. As a result, some contemporaries believed that ties between parents and children were deteriorating markedly as "a much more selfish tone" became increasingly "perceptible among the poorer classes of the people." In some areas the incidence of runaway matches may have risen, but, so too, may the numbers of pregnant girls who had to resort to the county assizes to force matrimony upon reluctant farmers' sons. However, the most dramatic change was the growing tendency of mature offspring to refuse assistance to aged parents in spite of communal opprobrium—a trend which made farmers more determined than ever to retain their holdings and keep their sons in suspenseful submission as long as possible. In short, economic developments eroded the most intimate relationships in Irish society, and neither traditional social nor familial bonds remained sufficient to prevent violent eruptions of rural conflict.[59]

Pre-Famine Irish society, both rural and urban, was rife with violence. In the 1820s–1840s Irish authorities recorded, in proportion to population, twice as many offenses against persons and property, and executed three times as many alleged murderers as in contemporary England. From the 1760s through the nineteenth century, the Irish and British parliaments passed a succession of special Coercion Acts and repeatedly reorganized and expanded the Irish magistracy and police forces in a vain effort to quell disturbances.[60]

Some of this strife resulted from individual quarrels, often fueled by whiskey, but much was collective and well organized. The most frequent instances of violence were "faction fights" between groups of men numbering from a few hundred to several thousand, usually armed with heavy sticks and rocks, and often abetted by crowds of women who supplied ammunition and verbal encouragement. Generally, the authorities made few efforts to prevent such conflicts, for faction fighting was largely a reflection of rural parochialism and familism and constituted no threat to the established order. Faction fights usually originated in feuds which grew out of territorial rivalries or disputes between neighboring families. The battles themselves were highly ritualized, and tended to occur by prearrangement at fairs, markets, athletic contests, or religious festivals. Considering the large numbers of combatants, relatively few were killed, although on occasion the carnage was appalling. The original causes of these conflicts were often obscure to those involved. In western Ireland, where faction fighting was most prevalent, an autocratic landlord might settle wagers or personal scores by pitting his tenants against those of a rival proprietor. Generally, the feuds were ancestral, their origins lost to memory, but preserved from a sense of family honor, "a mere love of combat," and a desire to wreak vengeance upon the victors of the last encounter. However, by the early nineteenth century faction fighting in commercial farming districts began to assume explicit socioeconomic dimensions. For example, in north Tipperary conflict arose over competition for land between local families and Catholic newcomers from Ulster; and the greatest faction feud of all—the struggle, lasting from 1806 to 1811, between the "Caravats" and "Shanavests" of Munster—arrayed land-poor smallholders, cottiers, and laborers against strong farmers and graziers. In 1827 alone Ireland witnessed over one thousand faction fights and riots; the urban middle classes loathed these conflicts for the property damage and loss of business they occasioned, but not until the 1830s were priests and police sufficiently numerous or determined to discourage them.[61]

As far as the authorities were concerned, the greatest threats to law and order emanated from the secret agrarian societies—oath-bound combinations of peasants and farmers whose activities convulsed much of rural Ireland from the late eighteenth century to the Famine. The societies operated on a regional basis and assumed a variety of names: during the late eighteenth century Whiteboys and Rightboys were active in Munster and south Leinster, while the Hearts of Oak and the Hearts of Steel terrorized east Ulster; in the early nineteenth century the Whiteboys reappeared, supplemented by the Rockites and the Terry Alts in Munster, the Thrashers and the Carders in east Connaught and north Leinster, the Molly Maguires in south Ulster, and the Whitefeet and the Blackfeet in central and south Leinster. Both Catholics and Protestants formed secret societies, although they rarely combined forces: the Oak- and Steelboys of Ulster were exclusively Protestant, largely Presbyterian, while the southern societies were overwhelmingly Catholic in membership. Despite these differences, the societies' patterns of operation were very similar: through social pressure, intimidation, and violence, they sought to substitute their own rules of proper conduct for those of the state. If transgressors failed to heed written warnings from "Slasher," "Burnstack," or "Captain Moonlight," they were likely to find their homes and hayricks burned and their livestock killed or mutilated; if the societies regarded them as especially obnoxious, they would be beaten, maimed, or murdered.[62]

Many of the specific grievances which the secret societies addressed varied over time and according to local circumstances. For example, in the 1760s the Whiteboys tried to prevent enclosures of common lands in Munster, while the Hearts of Oak were more concerned to abolish compulsory road labor in east Ulster; by the early nineteenth century, however, both complaints had disappeared because there were few common lands left in Munster to protect, and because the Irish Parliament had done away with the corvée. On the other hand, the societies' primary grievances—rents, evictions, wages, tithes, and taxes—were perennial and universal. In general, the secret societies sought to maintain what they regarded as traditional patterns of socioeconomic relations in the face of an expanding free market in land and labor. Like the contemporary English "crowd," they based their notions primarily upon "moral" concepts of customary rights and reciprocal obligations rather than upon considerations of efficiency and individual profit. Usually, the societies did not dispute landlords' ownership of the soil, but they acted on the conviction that all members of the community should have access to sufficient land or food to ensure survival. Ulstermen were "foolish people," declared one estate agent, for they thought "it a great sin to take land while the other tenant is in possession"; similarly, a magistrate in Tipperary reported that "a man who holds the tenement does not care under what circumstances he is put out, whether fairly or unfairly . . . he thinks he ought not to be put out." In retrospect, the secret societies were engaged in "reactive" protests, especially in the late eighteenth century. For example, in the early 1770s the Whiteboys destroyed grain and flour intended for export outside distressed districts, but usually refrained from stealing food. A decade later, the Rightboys strove to secure "the protection of a humane gentry" by petitioning Parliament for redress and by administering what they hoped would be binding oaths to landlords and strong farmers. Their basic conservatism was evident in other ways as well. In general, the societies did not deny their members' duties to pay rents and tithes, but they tried to regulate them below market rates, and they violently opposed the interposition of "parasites," such as rentier middlemen or tithe jobbers, whose profits increased the financial burden of the poor but who rendered no compensatory services. What motivated agrarian "outrages" was not merely distress but rather any detrimental change in a hitherto-accepted arrangement. For example, the Whiteboy movement began when a tithe farmer in south Tipperary demanded new fees from local Catholics; the Steelboys rose in response to sudden rent increases in south Antrim; the followers of Captain Rock combined to fight evictions initiated by a new English land agent on an estate in west Limerick; and so forth. Consequently, secret societies flourished not in the impoverished and economically stagnant far west of Ireland but in rapidly commercializing areas like Tipperary, where the prevalence of cattle grazing put severe pressures upon tillage farmers and laborers alike. "In no part of Ireland," wrote one critic of the societies, "were the people so vicious as in those counties which were supposed to have been most civilized" and "progressive."[63]

Another evidence of the societies' conservatism and pragmatism was that landlords and other authority figures suffered relatively few physical attacks. In 1836 George Cornewall Lewis described the societies as a "vast trades union for the protection of the Irish peasantry," but most of their victims were members of the same social classes as their assailants. In part, this was simply a matter of convenience. It was far easier and more effective to discourage evictions by burning out or assaulting a man who dared supplant an ejected tenant than to confront the landlord who had seized and canted the farm; likewise, it was simpler for local laborers to drive spalpeens out of the neighborhood than to punish the rich farmer who had hired them at less than prevailing wages. However, there was another reason behind this pattern of violence. As an anthropologist wrote of peasant societies generally, the Irish often behaved as if "all of the desired things of life . . . exist in finite quantity," and so "an individual or family can improve a position only at the expense of others." As George Wakefield observed in 1812, "the Irish are illiberally jealous of rising merit among themselves." In short, most rural dwellers regarded competition as something inherently evil, and the most-resented members of the community were often the "upstart" *shoneen* graziers—"jumped up small men who had no [ascriptive] right to claim superior social standing to the rest of the rural population." This reactionary egalitarianism, rooted in proverbial and religious strictures, clashed with newly engendered ambitions for improvement and so created internal divisions both among farmers and among laborers.[64]

The secret agrarian societies claimed to represent the moral sense of a hierarchical but interdependent community. Even British officials occasionally agreed that there was at least an implied "compact between the landlord and the peasantry who have been brought up on his estate, by which the latter have as good a right to protection, as the lord of the soil has to make arbitrary dispositions of his property." However, the maintenance of a "moral economy" in pre-Famine Ireland depended ultimately upon the gentry's adherence to a paternalistic tradition. In the late eighteenth century that tradition still had a tenuous existence: magistrates were often slow to act against secret societies, juries frequently failed to convict, and in the 1780s some Protestant landlords actually encouraged the Rightboys' campaign against tithes. However, outside Ulster, paternalism was always tempered by sectarian divisions between gentry and tenantry, and in the 1790s it began to evaporate entirely. Fear of Jacobinism emanating from the French Revolution, the bloody excesses of the United Irishmen's rising in 1798, the economic depression which followed the Napoleonic Wars, and their wholesale conversion to the ideology of "improvement"—all convinced landlords and government officials that the proper response to agrarian protest was harsh, efficient repression. "Let the legislature befriend us now, and we are theirs forever," the Rightboys had declared in 1786; but the next generations knew, as a Kilkenny schoolmaster put it, that "there is little use in going to law with the devil while the court is held in hell," and that their struggle for land and subsistence in the postwar decades would be a war without quarter. As a result, after 1800 the violence perpetrated by the secret societies increased in frequency and savagery. Open battles with the police became common, and by the early 1840s proprietors in Tipperary and elsewhere had become regular targets for assassins' bullets. *"Ó, a thiarnaí fhearainn ír"*—"O lords of the land of Ireland, who wallow in food, in clothing, in gold and in silver, who have neither mercy nor tenderness for the poor," warned a poet from east Cork. "Don't you know that as you have measured, so it will be measured out to you?"[65]

However, whereas the *ultimate* economic conflict addressed by the secret societies was between proprietors and officialdom on one side and the rest of the community on the other, the most *immediate* source of grievances was the deteriorating relationship between the commercial and subsistence sectors of the agricultural population itself. To some extent, the secret societies' aspirations obscured class divisions. The prevention of evictions was a goal approved by all; small farmers and laborers alike hated "land-grabbers" who monopolized the soil; and when tithes fell heavily on potatoes as well as on grain crops, as they did in Munster and south Leinster, that issue also united poor peasants and substantial tillage farmers. Consequently, a few strong and middling farmers—along with the occasional schoolmaster who penned the threatening notices—often assumed leadership of the secret societies, and during periods of general distress such farmers might participate in large numbers. However, the vast majority of the rank and file were always smallholders, cottiers, laborers, and farmers' sons who faced dismal prospects of obtaining land by inheritance: in short, the land-poor and the landless, whose everyday struggles for subsistence pitted them more often against profit-minded commercial farmers than against either the proprietors or each other. Consequently, the nominal leaders of the secret societies often found it difficult to control their supposed followers, and when farmers discovered that initial protests against head rents and tithes were fast expanding to include demands that they provide more potato ground, lower rents for subtenants and conacre, higher wages, and steadier employment, they were often quick to renege on their oaths of allegiance to Captain Moonlight and even turn informer or organize vigilante groups in defense of property.

Agrarian violence, then, was a two-edged sword, and if a "moral economy" embracing both farmers and lower classes ever existed, it was disintegrating under the impact of commercialization perhaps even more rapidly than the landlords' ethos of paternalism. By the early nineteenth century in many parts of Ireland the relationship between the haughty "jackeens" and the despised "culchees" was characterized by harsh exploitation and seething resentment. "I have been a long time in the commission of the peace, nearly thirty years," declared a Cork magistrate, "and I never sat a court day without witnessing some act of oppression on the part of the farmer on his laborer." As an Irish-speaking emigrant well remembered, laborers were often "cold, naked, without a coat or clothing, working in hardship and anguish under the heel of enemies, with nothing to eat but shriveled potatoes and a rare drop of sour skimmed milk"; even when better food was available, "the cloddish master . . . wouldn't eat it at the same table as the laborer . . . , being churlish and contemptuous of him." Perhaps if the gentry and officialdom of pre-Famine Ireland had been more politically astute, they might have exploited the antagonism between farmers and the lower classes. Threatening notices which demanded that "all farmers . . . return their undertenants to their head landlord at the same rates per acre for which they hold the land themselves," and which expressed the pious hope that "the gentlemen will not allow [the farmers] any longer to tyrannise over the poor," gave evidence that those who numerically dominated the secret societies were still susceptible to the blandishments of paternalism. However, the new political economy dictated that landlords and authorities support the profit-making rather than the subsistence sector of the agricultural population, and so the latter were left to express their discontent through violence. As a result, lower-class attacks on farmers constituted the most numerous category of agrarian outrages, and their brutality often exceeded even the cruel code which usually governed such activities.[66]

Urban life in pre-Famine Ireland exhibited much the same patterns of violence as did life in the countryside. In Dublin, Cork, Limerick, and other large towns, mobs of artisans and laborers often battled with the authorities or each other. Food riots occurred frequently when the poor believed merchants and bakers were hoarding or overcharging, and in eighteenth-century Dublin butchers' apprentices, journeymen weavers, and Trinity College undergraduates engaged in sporadic warfare. The late-eighteenth-century Dublin mob saw itself as the guardian of Ireland's constitutional liberties, and so its members often attacked the houses and carriages of pro-English politicians. However, from the authorities' viewpoint, the most dangerous urban violence was caused by trade unions composed of journeymen artisans such as weavers, carpenters, and wool combers. Like their rural counterparts, the trade unions appealed to precapitalist traditions of "just" wages, prices, and working conditions, which they tried to enforce by a combination of peaceful petitions, violent strikes against master craftsmen/employers, and physical retaliation against nonunion workers. The journeymen made a number of specific demands: that wage levels be adjusted to food prices; that employers hire only union members; that the working day be shortened to twelve hours; and that masters refrain from replacing skilled workmen with either machinery or poorly paid women, children, and unskilled apprentices. Journeymen described their unions as "the moral combination by which we feed our children," but the urban bourgeoisie and both Whig and Radical politicians who dreamed of an industrialized Ireland claimed that unions were conspiratorial monopolies which violated free market principles and prevented Irish manufactured goods from being competitive with English imports. Journeymen vainly countered that the masters' guilds conspired to lower wages and raise prices, but from 1780 onward the Irish and British parliaments passed a succession of Combinations Acts, which made union activity punishable by fines, imprisonment, public whippings, and transportation. Ostensibly, this legislation was designed to "secure to every man the fullest enjoyment of that property he has in his labor . . . and to extend throughout this kingdom the benefits of free trade"; but in 1824 one woolen manufacturer was more forthright: "it is the interest of the masters to employ apprentices," he declared, "and by that means to reduce the wages." However, these acts did not succeed in suppressing trade unions, and the state's abandonment of their welfare, combined with the desperate urban poverty of the postwar decades, only intensified the violence between workers and employers.[67]

Frightened members of the Protestant Ascendancy often claimed that the violence afflicting pre-Famine Ireland had sinister sectarian and political dimensions. In particular, landlords and parsons in the three southern provinces frequently warned that the secret agrarian societies were part of a general "papist" conspiracy to overthrow landlordism and establish an independent, Catholic-dominated state. Generally speaking, such accusations were false. Whether the secret societies were composed of Catholics or Protestants, their goals were basically conservative and pragmatic, and in the vast majority of instances their victims held the same religious beliefs as did their assailants. Protestant Oak- and Steelboys attacked Protestant gentry and farmers, and the members of Catholic societies like the Whiteboys devoted most of their attention to coreligionists, demonstrating no reluctance to boycott Catholic shopkeepers who resorted to the courts to collect debts, or to assault Catholic landlords and strong farmers who disobeyed their orders. Neither priests nor Catholic nationalist politicians were immune from attack, and several of the latter were assassinated for carrying out evictions. The urban trade unions were equally unbiased: after the Penal Laws which restricted Catholic manufacturing were repealed in 1779, workers' combinations united journeymen of both religions in violent strikes against employers of all faiths. Upper- and middle-class Catholics' intemperate denunciations of secret societies and of unions alike provided ample proof that those movements were primarily grounded in class rather than in sectarian antagonism. Lay or clerical, whatever their political views and despite their desires for equality with Protestants, "respectable" Catholic spokesmen almost universally opposed both the activities and the ideology of the societies and unions. If conservatives, they believed in order and deference and, as a Dublin physician put it, that "society is the combination of those who *have* against those who *have not";* or, as a Catholic bishop declared, that "the despotism of gentlemen" was preferable to "the brutal *canaille* of the Trades' Unions and Blackfeet conspiracies." If liberals or radicals, they believed that political freedom and national prosperity were inexorably linked to free-market capitalism. For example, in the 1790s Arthur O'Connor, one of the leaders of the revolutionary United Irishmen, railed against labor unions on the grounds that—as the title of his tract stated—*Monopoly* [*is*] *the Cause of All Evil;* and in the next generation Daniel O'Connell, a constitutional nationalist and disciple of Adam Smith, denounced unions for denying "children their just right" to work in factories and attacked both urban and agrarian violence

as the actions of "societies of traitors" which were "obstacles . . . to the
. . . regeneration of their country."[68]

However, although the Ascendancy's hysterical fears that violence was
the inevitable precursor to revolution were generally groundless, it was
true that the activities of the secret societies and, to a lesser extent, the
trade unions had political and sectarian implications. Catholics could hardly
forget their bitter history, enshrined in poetry and folklore, and both they
and Ulster Presbyterians shared similar prophetic traditions which promised
total deliverance from landlords and Anglican parsons. Such sentiments
might lie dormant under layers of automatic or calculated deference, but
when it became increasingly obvious that neither the gentry nor the government was going to honor its paternalistic duties to the poor, the secret
societies inevitably were forced to question and challenge the basic rules
and structure of an oppressive system. Thus, during their brief existence,
most secret societies slowly moved from mere attempts to regulate rents
and tithes to desperate demands that they be abolished altogether. Similarly, after the Act of Union of 1800 reduced and eventually eliminated
protective tariffs for Irish industries, many trade unions began to see economic salvation in the repeal of that act rather than in merely confronting
employers over wages and working conditions. This progression from specific, local grievances to general, political concerns was accelerated in the
1790s by the ideological impact of the French Revolution, widely disseminated in newspapers, handbills, and ballads distributed by the urban middle-class radicals in the Society of United Irishmen. Although the leaders
of the United Irishmen envisioned a bourgeois republic rising from the
ashes of the Ascendancy, the novel notions expressed in Tom Paine's
Rights of Man often combined effectively, if not always logically, with
millenarian expectations and with the practical complaints of the secret
societies. Consequently, many of the same districts in east Ulster which in
the 1770s had produced the Hearts of Steel were in the 1790s rife with
Presbyterian farmers and weavers who joined the United Irishmen to overthrow rents, tithes, and taxes along with the government which enforced
them. Similarly, from the 1790s onward the oaths of allegiance given in
the South to members of Catholic secret societies often contained at least
vaguely republican sentiments of liberty and equality, which coexisted uneasily with the limited nature of their usual demands and which perhaps
indicated that the latter were becoming merely tactical steps along the road
to more radical ultimate aspirations.[69]

The United Irish leaders preached brotherhood among Irishmen of all
faiths, but in the context of Irish society "political" almost invariably translated into "sectarian." Class-based violence by Catholics was sure to exacerbate Catholic-Protestant relations in most areas where social and religious divisions were largely synonymous. Although the Whiteboys attacked
particular landlords because of their estate management rather than their
religious beliefs, the fact that such landlords were usually Protestant—as
were the magistrates and jurors who prosecuted and condemned their as-

sailants—inevitably gave a sectarian tone to rural violence. As a witness explained to a parliamentary commission in 1824, although agrarian disturbances "broke out in consequence of great distress, . . . once a disturbance breaks out . . . it gets force and continuance from religious distinctions." Furthermore, in those districts where roughly equal numbers of Protestants and Catholics shared the same socioeconomic status, the tensions produced by commercialization were more likely to explode in sectarian struggles for territorial dominance than in class-based agrarian warfare. In the 1780s and 1790s, this was what occurred in mid-Ulster and southeast Leinster, imparting a bloody legacy of religious hatred to all subsequent agrarian agitation.[70]

Superficially, the "moral" claims to land or "tenant-right" made by Protestant and Catholic secret agrarian societies seemed similar, but at bottom they were not only quite different but mutually antagonistic. Protestants' claims were rooted in conquest: they demanded "rights" from their landlords and the government which they believed the British crown had given their ancestors in the seventeenth century in reward for garrisoning Ireland against "papist" rebellion. Thus, in the 1770s the Steelboys argued for just treatment partly on the grounds "[t]hat we are all Protestants," loyal to the Hanoverian succession, and that "not one Roman Catholic is ever suffered to appear amongst us." On the other hand, Catholic claims were founded ultimately in preconquest traditions, and if pressed to their logical conclusion their demands for land inevitably challenged its possession by all Protestants—tenants as well as landlords. Since the premises on which they based their "rights" were so different, rural Protestants and Catholics alike found the capitalist ideal of untrammeled competition for leases and employment between members of the two religious groups even more objectionable than intracommunal competition, although their "improving" landlords and the urban middle classes generally embraced both goals. As an estate agent testified, a Catholic was "considered by a Protestant *of the same class* as inferior to him" and undeserving of equal economic opportunities; since most Catholics adhered to the same perception of an economy of finite resources, they naturally reciprocated such prejudices.[71]

In most parts of Ireland, large-scale competition between Protestant and Catholic tenants or laborers could not occur, because one side or the other had overwhelming numerical superiority. Thus, the United Irishmen could appeal successfully to rural Presbyterians in Antrim and north Down, where Catholics were few. However, conditions were much different in mid-Ulster, particularly in densely populated County Armagh, where cottier weavers of both faiths competed fiercely for potato plots. In the 1780s mid-Ulster Protestants responded to distorted accounts of a Catholic Rightboy "rising" in the South, and to fears that the Ascendancy was about to abandon their interests, by forming a new type of secret society, the purely sectarian Peep of Day Boys, which commenced a "ferocious persecution" of Ulster Catholics, driving several thousands into other parts of the island. In the next decade, fear of the United Irishmen united the region's Protestants: landlords naturally dreaded the very idea of republicanism, while their tenants were alarmed at what they saw as an armed "papist" conspiracy to reclaim the land. Consequently, the northern gentry moved to reestablish symbolically what previously they had been undermining economically in their new roles as "improving," profit-seeking landlords: an organic union among Protestants of all classes, formally embodied in the newly created Orange Order and in the yeomanry corps which in 1797–98 helped suppress the United Irishmen with great savagery.[72]

Sectarian violence not only became a permanent feature of Ulster life but also spread into southern Ireland. After suffering attacks from Peep of Day Boys, beleaguered northern Catholics formed their own sectarian society, the Defenders. In the 1790s the Defenders expanded their organization beyond mid-Ulster and became inspired by French republican ideals as well as by religious tribalism; in 1796 they merged with the United Irishmen in anticipation of a general rebellion assisted by French troops. Meanwhile, conditions in southeast Leinster approximated those in mid-Ulster. Although Catholics had a large overall majority, in many districts there was bitter competition over lease renewals between roughly equal numbers of Catholic and Protestant strong farmers and middlemen. This strife, coupled with economic distress, news of Orange massacres in the North, and agitation by local Defenders and United Irishmen, produced in 1798 a rebellion in south Leinster which soon degenerated into bloody religious warfare. In both northern and southern Ireland the Defenders and their United Irish allies suffered crushing defeats. However, the Defenders went underground and soon became known as Ribbonmen. During the early nineteenth century, Ribbon Societies existed throughout much of the island, functioning as a sort of overarching Catholic secret society. In Ulster, Ribbon activities were almost purely sectarian in nature, engaging Orangemen in frequent battles or "party fights" at fairs and markets. In the three southern provinces, Ribbonmen primarily addressed traditional economic grievances, but their influence imparted more-explicit sectarian overtones to all popular agitation, making southern Protestants more paranoid and the authorities more inclined to harsh repressive measures. Although Ribbon oaths still contained republican sentiments of equality and brotherhood, their savage vow "to wade knee-deep in Orange blood" indicated how much Protestant-Catholic relations had deteriorated since the days of the Rightboys.[73]

Commercialization not only produced social differentiation and strife but also transformed linguistic, cultural, and religious practices in much of the countryside. Perhaps inevitably, the economic dominance of English and English-oriented urban markets produced an Anglicization of both Catholic and Protestant Irish: an increasing conformity to bourgeois standards of speech and manners. Whether the result of voluntary emulation or of calculated coercion, this cultural imperialism reinforced regional and social divisions, undermined traditional identities, and threatened to sunder the bulk of the Irish from their links to the past while bestowing few compensatory rewards other than a growing awareness of a relative deprivation which could no longer be cushioned by cultural insularity.

Before 1750 probably the great majority of the rural Irish, and many urban dwellers as well, spoke little or no English. In all but a few eastern counties—Dublin, Kildare, Wicklow, and Wexford—Catholics were predominantly or almost exclusively Irish-speaking; and even in these counties pockets of Irish-speakers endured. Evidence from the early eighteenth century is scanty, but later travelers usually remarked upon the widespread usage of Irish. In 1775 Richard Twiss reported that the language was "still understood and spoken by most of the common people," and in the same decade Arthur Young found Irish-speakers everywhere but in two Wexford baronies and in Dublin city; as late as 1837 another observer discovered fluent Irish spoken in a glen only ten miles from College Green. In towns farther west, the lower classes as well as merchants and shopkeepers engaged in rural trade spoke Irish: in 1812 Edward Wakefield was astonished that in Cork city "the Irish language is so much spoken among the common people . . . that an Englishman is apt to . . . consider himself in a foreign city"; and in Connaught and west Munster towns, magistrates had to employ translators to administer justice. In late-eighteenth-century Ulster most Catholics clung to Irish in spite of their proximity to large numbers of Protestants. In fact, many Ulster Protestants did not speak an English intelligible to visitors from London. Presbyterians often retained the "broad Scotch," or Lallans, of the Scottish Lowlands, and in isolated areas Anglicans preserved Cromwellian dialects. Throughout much of the island the Protestant gentry spoke a "Hiberno-English" heavily influenced by native speech patterns. Moreover, English-speaking Catholics could not be readily understood by travelers from the metropolis. In south Wexford descendants of Norman settlers still spoke the English of Chaucer, and in general much of the Irish reputation for comic ignorance was due to the pathetic, often ludicrous attempts by Catholics to translate literally their native language's elaborate syntax into the conquerors' idiom. Despite the advance of English, in 1800 probably half the island's population was at least bilingual, and by 1812 there were still some two million people "incapable of understanding a continued discourse in English."[74]

The persistence of Irish, Lallans, and archaic English dialects was due to a number of circumstances: the slow economic growth before 1750; the extreme localism of the countryside, reinforced by inadequate communications; and, especially among Irish-speakers, a fierce pride in their native language. Another contributing factor was widespread illiteracy, which, given the paucity of books in Irish, served primarily to insulate native-speakers from English influences. As late as 1841 the first official statistics on literacy revealed that less than half the population over age five could read or write; only 28 percent could do both. Total illiteracy ranged from 40 to 44 percent in Ulster and Leinster to 61 percent in Munster and 72 percent in Connaught. Even on prosperous, Presbyterian Islandmagee, County Antrim, 50 percent of the people could neither read nor write; and in Galway, Mayo, and Donegal over 85 percent of the Catholics were illiterate. However, among the pre-Famine Irish illiteracy usually lacked its modern connotations of abysmal ignorance and cultural deprivation; and travelers who overcame the initial reticence of the rural poor were often astonished at their mental quickness and natural eloquence. Strictly speaking, Irish country people were not illiterate but preliterate: through the oral medium they transmitted a rich, robust traditional culture.[75]

Irish-speakers, especially, had an intense devotion to the verbal arts. Speech and memory had acquired unusual strength, particularly in the telling and retelling of long, complicated stories—many of which had been in circulation since the eighth century. Indeed, the archaism of Gaelic culture was remarkable, reflecting centuries of relative isolation in a subsistence economy which demanded precedents and repelled threatening innovations. Hereditary storytellers, or *seanchaithe,* strove to replicate tales of ancient gods and warriors exactly as they had received them; and rural genealogists, *sloinnteoiri,* memorized family lineages and so kept alive old claims to land and bitter memories of dispossession. In the uplands of Connaught and south Ulster even the *brehon* tradition survived among families of rural arbitrators. The aristocrats of Gaelic culture were a handful of scholars and poets who preserved ancient manuscripts and still composed highly structured verses utilizing traditional meters and themes. In Munster especially, but also in Connaught and Ulster, "courts of poetry" still met in farmhouses where established bards judged the compositions of younger poets. By nineteenth-century bourgeois standards, many of these poems were far from "respectable," dealing with love and sex in a frank, earthy manner which reflected both the ribaldry of an earlier age and the fact that the Irish language made no distinction between polite and vulgar speech. Other poems found inspiration in recent history. As Daniel Corkery wrote, the verse "is full of the broken altar, the stolen lands, the battered woods, the insulted nation; and the lyric always finishes in hopeful prophecies—the English will yet be begging their bread and wearing clogs." In fact, such poems specifically addressed the interests of the remnants of the Catholic gentry—the rapacious middlemen who sighed for the fall of the Stuarts and despised the potato-eating poor. More egalitarian were their Presbyterian counterparts, the compositions of the "rhyming weavers" of eastern Ulster whose verses in Lallans sang of commoners' struggles against the harsh realities of rural life.[76]

By the early nineteenth century the courts of poetry and the rhyming weavers had almost disappeared. However, many traditional patterns remained. Travelers could still find blind harpists, and a few schoolmasters and farmers still harbored tattered copies of Gaelic manuscripts. Moreover, Irish-speakers' everyday speech continued to demonstrate what one scholar described as "an adventurous, enthusiastic exploitation of vocabulary and idiom; a sense of the rhetorical value of the *unwritable* features of speech,

including the resources of rhythm with all its interlocking components—
tone, stress, time, tempo, pause and silence." Music and dancing also
played a prominent role in rural life, and visitors were often astonished
that a people so poor could exhibit such skill and spontaneous pleasure in
those accomplishments: "We frog-blooded English dance as if the practice
were not congenial to us," one traveler reflected; "but here they moved as
if dancing had been the business of their lives." In retrospect, most traditional customs and beliefs seem mundane, but country dwellers blurred
the modern distinctions between the real and the unreal, and all things
physical—landscape, crops, houses, tools, food—had a mystical significance
and were deemed governed by supernatural forces. For example, livestock
were considered linked to their owners in magical as well as practical ways:
the animals' health and fertility were inseparable from those of the peasants,
who therefore allowed them to share their cabins. The unseen world constantly intruded into everyday life. Catholics and Presbyterians alike believed in the existence of fairies—the "good people" or the "little people"—
who inhabited abandoned farmhouses, ancient ruins, hills, and trees. Their
attitude to the fairies was mixed: in part proprietary, since peasants believed that when the little people of one district vanquished fairy armies
from elsewhere, the human inhabitants of that region would enjoy boundless prosperity. Some fairies performed practical functions: "banshees" signaled approaching death by unearthly wails, and "Red Willy" guarded
illegal stills from detection. However, fairies also were considered potentially malevolent: unless propitiated through gifts or rituals, they would
blight crops, sicken livestock, and steal healthy infants, leaving dead
"changelings" in their place. Many rural Irish also believed in witches
and the evil eye; like the fairies, these also helped to explain the often
cruel, arbitrary nature of the peasants' world. Several of the most distinctive customs revolved around death. Presbyterian wakes tended to be somber, but among rural Catholics "sitting up" with the corpse until burial
was a communal occasion enlivened by heavy drinking and "all kinds of
hilarious sport, such as games, story-telling, practical jokes, and almost
every species of noisy fun . . . until . . . the house of mourning becomes a virtual pandemonium." Some wake games went beyond sport, for
"mock weddings," "couplings," and other sexual rituals which shocked
proper opinion avowed procreation in the face of dissolution and led observers like Maria Edgeworth to believe that "more matches were made at
wakes than at weddings." After the wakes, the corpses were "keened" to
their graves by *mná caoine,* old women who were professional mourners
or relatives of the deceased. Most foreign visitors regarded the keeners'
eerie, discordant songs as mere "howling," but in their pure form these
laments were elaborate recitations of the genealogy and virtues of the dead.
Like the wakes, Irish funerals were often sodden and boisterous, sometimes
punctuated with pitched battles between family factions over final possession of the corpse.[77]

As a contemporary student of Munster Irish-speakers remarked, their keens and their funeral customs both notably lacked conventional Christian sentiments of faith or consolation in an afterlife. Indeed, in the late eighteenth and early nineteenth centuries, most Catholics and many Protestants followed religious customs and beliefs at marked variance from those prescribed in Rome, Glasgow, or Canterbury. In general, popular Irish religion was tribal, traditional, and permeated with magic. For many rural Anglicans the Maypole was as meaningful as the sacraments, and most Ulster Presbyterians regarded the Bible more as a source of apocalyptic prophecies of communal triumph over earthly enemies than as a guide to individual salvation. However, of the three major Irish faiths, popular Catholicism was most distinctively premodern. One scholar estimates that, in contrast to near-unanimous church attendance today, as late as 1834 only 38 percent of Ireland's Catholics heard mass on any given Sunday; while attendance rates approached modern levels in eastern towns such as Drogheda and Kilkenny, in rural parishes they ranged from 72 percent in English-speaking Wexford to a low of 20 percent in Irish-speaking Connaught and west Donegal. Members of the hierarchy complained constantly that rural Catholics were lax in performing religious duties: in 1786 the bishop of Cloyne and Ross lamented that at least one-third of those in his diocese never contributed a penny to their priests; and in 1826 George Plunkitt declared that when he became bishop of Elphin he discovered that "Hundreds of Person's had been married who *had not* made *their first* communion . . . and innumerable couples had lived as man and wife who had never been married and many others in flagrant and notorious adultery." Seventeen years later, another critic sighed, "[T]he ignorance of the people in matters of Religion is frightful, and . . . the doctrine of the Trinity is rarely known or even heard of among them. . . ." In fact, pre-Famine Catholics *were* devout, but their piety was expressed primarily in archaic, communal traditions which had originated in pre-Christian times and had since acquired only a thin veneer of medieval Catholicism. For example, rural Catholics prayed and bathed at holy wells once sacred to ancient Celtic deities; on St. John's Eve—formerly Bealtaine, the pagan New Year—they drove cattle through hilltop bonfires to protect them from disease and misfortune; cults of local saints—often barely Catholicized pre-Christian gods—were celebrated on "patron days" with "patterns," festivals which combined prayer, fasting, and self-mortification with athletic contests, fighting, and what outraged contemporaries viewed as "the most disgusting drunkenness and debauchery." Rural Catholics' attitudes toward priests also reflected pagan and medieval traditions: like their legendary druidic and early Christian predecessors, priests were venerated largely because of purported magical powers to cure sickness, combat witches and fairies, and shield their people from persecution and oppression. All these religious customs had several common characteristics. First, they were "predictive": their adherents sought to assure good health and bountiful harvests by repeating traditional rituals which invited supernatural forces to intervene on their behalf. Second, they were communal: worship was a group experience, designed to perpetuate tribal existence and identity, not to realize personal grace. Finally, these practices and beliefs were obviously antithetical to the spreading "spirit of improvement"—the novel idea that rational, acquisitive individuals could and should manipulate their environment to produce beneficent progress.[78]

Nonetheless, the popular cultures of rural Ireland, secular and religious, performed important social functions for their respective followers. Despite the parochialism of country life, shared language, customs, and beliefs helped to transcend regional boundaries. Irish-speaking poets and scholars ranged widely in their travels, and religious festivals such as those at Gouganebarra in west Cork and Clonmacnoise on the upper Shannon attracted thousands of pilgrims from all over the island. Common cultures also ensured a degree of social unity. Oral literature belonged to entire peoples, to storytellers who could not write and listeners who could not read; despite their elitism, the compositions of bardic poets were applauded by a Catholic lower class which felt linked to its superiors by a culture of common misfortune as well as traditional patron-client ties. Ability to speak Irish could even transcend religious divisions, as Catholic peasants regarded local squires as "sympathetic" if they could converse in the native idiom. Whether Protestant or Catholic, members of the gentry who patronized or at least acquiesced in their tenants' customs had far easier relations with them than did those who expressed disdain. Finally, old habits and beliefs helped cushion their adherents against "improvements" which threatened to upset traditional economic and social arrangements. An ambitious tenant who tried to hire laborers to drain a waterlogged field for pasture could find himself thwarted by his neighbors' conviction that the fairies would take vengeance on the community if their swampy habitation was disturbed; similarly, as a magistrate later reported, it was "a very common trick for people who speak English most fluently when being questioned about matters in which they want to be very guarded in their replies to declare that they 'haven't the English only badly,' so that one cannot elicit inconvenient truths from them." Irishmen such as William Carleton and Caesar Otway, who hoped their lower-class countrymen would acquire an entrepreneurial spirit, lamented the prevalence of what might be called— after the late-eighteenth-century Munster poet and rake—the "Eoghan Ruadh Ó Súilleabháin syndrome": a precapitalist archetype or role model which exalted flamboyant behavior and traditional accomplishments like dancing, hurling, fighting, and drinking over bourgeois ideals of diligence, thrift, sobriety, and respectability. As a result, complained another critic, "one third of the time of the labouring classes . . . is wasted in holy days, funerals, weddings, christenings, fairs, patterns, races, and other recreations."[79]

However, though many old customs and beliefs persisted into the present century, by 1800 the communal cultures of the rural Irish were already undergoing transformation. On the Famine's eve, Lallans and archaic English dialects were virtually extinct, and the extent of Irish was fast diminishing. Belief in fairies continued despite linguistic changes, but many other traditional practices were falling into disuse; in much of the country popular culture was approximating middle-class urban standards. In part these changes were desired and designed by the Protestant Ascendancy. Some landlords, such as Lord Shannon, were careful to bestow favors on "only such as speak English," and many Protestants were eager for the eradication of the Irish language among Catholics since "[i]t makes them consider themselves a distinct people from their countrymen who speak the language of the state; and exposes them to the designing views of those who wish to avail themselves of the prejudices flowing from that distinction." Accordingly, in the government-financed National Schools established after 1831, "[t]he chief lesson to be learned by the school children was ignorance—not to say contempt—of Ireland and everything Irish, and reverence for England and everything English. Even in districts where Irish was the only language spoken, the children were taught that English and not Irish was their native tongue."[80]

However, the process of cultural change was more closely allied to general socioeconomic developments than to official calculations. The advance of trade, communications, and the ideology of rational progress—all emanating ultimately from affluent, urban England—broke down provincial barriers and brought into disrepute customs which seemed merely "barbaric" hindrances to economic advancement. Among both Protestants and Catholics, the promotion of cultural change was undertaken primarily by the "improving" and "assimilating classes" which predominated in eastern Ireland and in towns generally: resident landlords; strong farmers; urban merchants, lawyers, and journalists; and clergymen recruited from the upper and middle levels of Protestant or Catholic society. Among Presbyterians, rational "New Light" ministers and Belfast businessmen discouraged the doctrinal rigidity and anti-Catholic bigotry of their conservative rural brethren. Among Catholics, the church began "the massive task of teaching its adherents to internalise and individualise their religion," while clerics and wealthy parishioners strove to demonstrate their modernity by disavowing both the Irish language and its associated customs. For example, in the early nineteenth century the bishop of Elphin insisted not only that his people be "well catechised and instructed" before receiving the sacraments but also that they make their confessions in English. At St. Patrick's College, Maynooth, candidates for the priesthood received no training in Irish, and after 1820 the hierarchy's hostility to the language only intensified as Protestant missionaries began to proselytize in the native tongue. From Derry, Sligo, and elsewhere came reports that priests were suppressing faction fights, drinking, and wake games, denouncing keens as "only fit for uncivilized society," and striving to replace them with "solemn hymns" in Latin. In many dioceses bishops combined with the local gentry and magistrates to prohibit patterns and other festivals which purportedly disturbed "the tranquility of the country" and encouraged such "intemperance and immorality . . . that religion herself is brought into disrepute."

In Cork and Waterford towns, wealthy and pious Catholics founded teaching orders such as the Christian Brothers to uplift the countryside, and in the 1830s Father Theobald Mathew, son of affluent Kilkenny farmers, joined with Protestant ministers and merchants to preach a nationwide crusade for total abstinence. Although some Catholic nouveaux riches assumed noble Gaelic lineages, the prevalent middle-class attitude toward tradition was best expressed by Daniel O'Connell—lawyer, native-speaker from west Kerry, and political messiah of the rural masses—who declared that "the superior utility of the English tongue, as the medium of all modern communication, is so great that I can witness without a sigh the gradual disuse of Irish." With few exceptions, neither clerical nor secular Catholic leaders protested the National School system on linguistic or cultural grounds.[81]

Given the prejudices of their spokesmen, and what—before 1814—seemed to be the socioeconomic advantages of Anglo-conformity, it is not surprising that many rural dwellers adopted English, forsook old customs, and began "imitating the higher classes in dress and manner as much as possible." Many traditions were abandoned along with the clachans which had nourished them: by 1814–19 Anglican clergymen reported that in eastern Ulster "broad Scotch . . . has been regularly wearing out, as the intercourse created by increasing trade and good roads has facilitated . . . communication with the neighbouring towns"; and in northern Donegal formerly monolingual Irish-speakers "are acquiring a tolerable knowledge of the English . . . since their ideas were whetted by a commercial intercourse in the neighbouring fairs and markets." In southeastern Ireland, marketing necessitated command of English, since few corn or pig dealers spoke Irish, and by 1812 Irish was "scarcely known" and "treated with contempt" east of the Barrow River. Contemporaries frequently remarked that either desires for "improvement" or mounting economic pressures were producing declining observance of holy days and other communal pastimes and that "the disadvantage and embarrassment, to which every man, who is unable to read, is exposed, in transacting business with bank notes, have excited in the wildest districts even a more ardent zeal for educating the children" in English. Indeed, nearly every observer of pre-Famine Ireland reported a rage for education among all classes.[82]

In the eighteenth century educational facilities, especially for Catholics, had been rudimentary. The Penal Laws had proscribed Catholic schoolmasters, and for decades after their repeal the church was too poor to provide education except for a small, affluent minority. Consequently, before the 1830s less than 40 percent of Catholic children received even brief educations. Most of those attended either Protestant schools or private "hedge-schools" taught by Catholic schoolmasters, who ranged in quality from drunken, brutish incompetents to "poor scholars" of genuine learning and accomplishments, often Gaelic poets now bereft of wealthy patrons. Even the best had few instructional tools: "textbooks" often included biographies of "robbers, thieves, and prostitutes, the reveries of knights errant and crusaders, a seditious history of Ireland, tales of apparitions, witches and fairies, and a new system of boxing." Nevertheless, rural Catholics seem always to have had an almost mystical reverence for "the larnin' "— particularly for a classical education—and, next to the landlord and the priest, the schoolmaster was often the most respected man in the parish. Indeed, as displaced Gaelic scholars and poets, many hedge-schoolmasters linked traditional resistance to Anglicization with new French revolutionary ideals, and so served as apostles of a hybrid popular culture which challenged the authority of both landlords and priests. Consequently, Ascendancy figures and Catholic clergy alike sought greater control of Irish education: the former hoped "proper" training would "remedy the infidelity of servants, the drunkenness and negligence of tradesmen, and the continuing dread of nocturnal assault," while the latter believed that instruction under clerical auspices was necessary to "civilize" the populace and blunt the twin threats of proselytism and republican infidelity. In addition, by the early nineteenth century the attitudes toward education held by many rural Catholics, especially the farming classes, seem to have become more utilitarian. Although an ornamental education in Latin, Greek, Gaelic, and what William Carleton called "sesquipedalian and stilted nonsense" remained popular, practical subjects such as English grammar, mathematics, and bookkeeping came into greater demand. In many districts the primary criteria for selecting a schoolmaster had been his political sentiments and "the capability of drinking whiskey and sharing it with the electors," but now farmers sought urban-trained teachers to prepare their sons for material success in a world dominated by English-speakers. As a result, observed a parson in rural Kilkenny, "the English language rapidly advances, for so anxious are the people to speak it in the country, that the mountain farmers who cannot speak English, and who send their children to hedge schools, will scarcely allow them to speak Irish at home."[83]

Travelers in pre-Famine Ireland gave ample testimony to the profound, if ofttimes subtle, consequences of creeping Anglicization: the rationalization and commercialization of popular culture. In the 1770s Arthur Young reported approvingly that cottage weavers in Connaught were demonstrating "increasing civility" by changing their traditional Irish names to the English equivalents. In the 1790s a Frenchman in Cork city was astonished to see Catholics washing clothes in a holy well to which magical powers once had been attributed. In Antrim and Down some Presbyterian farmers were so inspired by the rationalism and egalitarianism of the French Revolution that they tried to make common cause with their hereditary Catholic foes to overthrow the Ascendancy. By 1814–19 parsons were reporting that in Queen's County "[o]ld superstitions are going out of use; even the funeral cry is laid aside"; and that in eastern Roscommon the prizes awarded at country dances, once given to the best female dancers, were now merely purchased by well-heeled young farmers' sons as gifts for their sweethearts. On the eve of the Famine, children in County Longford knew scarcely enough Irish to bless themselves; and in north Tipperary an

American witness to a grave-side funeral saw the mother of the deceased, who had begun to keen, forcibly restrained and admonished by her relatives to "[s]top . . . what nobody does now."[84]

However, all these changes could not add up to the homogenized "west British" culture to which many upper- and middle-class Irishmen aspired. Anglicization was glaringly incomplete: the modernizers were too few, the traditionalists too many, and poverty, parochialism, and self-interest discouraged and prevented most rural dwellers from abandoning all the customs which had cushioned their ancestors against adversity and formed the touchstones of their identities. Few lower-class Presbyterians, and even fewer Catholics, had sufficient economic security to discard religious tribalism for a rational, individualistic worldview which would have stripped them of their pretensions to uniqueness in the face of increasing competition for land and employment. Similarly, peasants who lived far from market centers, or whose destitution gave them little hope of economic betterment, had small motivation to forsake either the predictive celebrations which might still ensure survival or their native language, which—if increasingly associated with backwardness and poverty—still expressed memories, and prophecies, of better days. In short, at least half the Catholic population still clung to Irish and/or to many of the customs once inextricably associated with it. However, the incompleteness of Anglicization culturally fragmented Ireland, reinforcing the regional, social, and generational divisions engendered or exacerbated by commercialization. By the 1840s Irish-speaking and many traditional practices were largely confined to a crescent of poor soil that swept westward from the mountains of Waterford and south Kilkenny, through west Munster and most of Connaught, north to Donegal, and eastward through the Ulster uplands to Louth, north Meath, and the Irish Sea. Cultural differences between regions became so great that Connaughtmen regarded Leinster Catholics as hostile "Saxons," while easterners spoke of their western countrymen with derision and contempt. Culture and class increasingly coincided as well. In late-eighteenth-century Ulster, "New Light" Presbyterians were predominantly middle class, whereas their traditionalist brethren were drawn primarily from the rural poor: a dichotomy which found continued expression in nineteenth-century Belfast politics. In Catholic Ireland, cultural conservatism became synonymous with poverty: in many commercial farming districts strong farmers spoke English, while smallholders, cottiers, laborers, and servants conversed primarily in Irish; in mountainous areas, English-speakers tilled the rich bottomlands, while the wretched cabins of Irish-speakers clung to the hillsides. Finally, in many regions even the generations split along linguistic and cultural lines. Where economic growth was slow, the transition from Irish- to English-speaking might take several generations, with a long intermediate period of bilingualism. However, in some areas the change was so rapid that it produced what Seán de Fréine called "the great silence": a cultural gap between generations so wide that parents and children could scarcely communicate.[85]

If, as one scholar wrote, each language draws "a magic circle" around the people who use it, by the early nineteenth century that circle was rapidly disintegrating in much of the island, exposing those it had formerly enclosed to the demoralization of men who have lost a past without yet gaining a future. The descriptions by Carleton and others of south Ulster, eastern Connaught, north Munster and other rapidly modernizing districts portrayed a rural society which had lost its moorings and displayed only the feverish vitality of cultural chaos: learned *seanchaithe* and poets who seemed comic buffoons when they tried to render traditional wisdom into English; schoolmasters and priests trying desperately, often unsuccessfully to straddle two cultures; farmers at fairs bargaining soberly in English, swearing drunkenly in Irish; arranged marriages between men and women whose native tongues were mutually unintelligible; and Irish-speaking children who entered school possessing everyday vocabularies of over three thousand words but who left a few years later with "their intelligence . . . sapped, their splendid command of their native language lost forever, and a vocabulary of five or six hundred English words, badly pronounced and barbarously employed, substituted for it. . . . Story, lay, poem, aphorism, proverb, all the unique stock in trade of an Irish speaker's mind . . . gone forever, and *replaced by nothing"* save shame for their discarded heritage and resentment that they were still unable to realize the benefits that Anglicization purportedly promised. Perhaps it was cultural demoralization which explains why travelers in pre-Famine Ireland found the English-speaking cottiers and laborers in the midlands so much more pathetic in their poverty than the destitute but still-dignified Irish-speakers of Connemara. Perhaps the same phenomenon, coupled with increasing celibacy rates, helps explain why in the 1820s and 1830s whiskey drinking seemed to transcend its traditional associations and assume almost pathological proportions.[86]

Cultural differentiation along class lines further weakened social bonds already fraying because of economic differentiation, and helped to estrange the culturally conservative lower classes from their traditional leaders. Smallholders, cottiers, and laborers felt fewer compunctions against assaulting proprietors and strong farmers who not only profited at their expense but also no longer shared the same language or patronized the same traditional customs. Such tensions helped inspire rural unrest in Protestant Ulster during the late eighteenth century, but they were particularly acute in the Catholic community, where both the social and the cultural gaps were widest. From the 1760s to the 1820s Catholic Ireland experienced what might be called a leadership crisis. On the one hand, commercialization and Anglicization were making rural Catholics more aware and more resentful of the tremendous and growing material gap between themselves and the Protestant Ascendancy. On the other hand, those to whom the Catholic poor traditionally looked for leadership and protection—the remaining Catholic gentry, the strong farmers, and the urban commercial and professional classes—were in the main not defending their interests, but instead emulating the Ascendancy by exploiting them economically and promoting a cultural offensive against their language and traditions. To the Catholic upper and middle classes, their motives no doubt seemed benign: quelling the "backwardness" and violence of rural society would not only protect property, promote tranquillity, and enable the "spirit of improvement" to bestow its promised blessings but also demonstrate to the authorities that under their leadership the Catholic community was sufficiently loyal and respectable to be trusted with legal equality. Indeed, this conciliatory posture proved effective, since between 1774 and 1793 the Irish government repealed most Penal Laws and granted Catholics the parliamentary franchise on equal terms with Protestants. However, to lower-class Catholics, who reaped little or no benefit from these statutory changes and who desired either protection against a "free" market or a greater degree of equality than a class-ridden political economy would allow, it seemed that their traditional spokesmen were turning their backs on the poor and on the customs which had once linked all Catholics in order to ingratiate themselves with those whom the poor had been taught to consider hereditary enemies. No wonder, then, that in rapidly changing districts the Catholic poor—like their Protestant counterparts—turned to the secret societies for leadership in what *they* considered to be a death struggle over access to land and employment. The fierce denunciations by their traditional leaders—whether "Castle Catholics" or constitutional nationalists like O'Connell—only confirmed their growing sense of cultural as well as socioeconomic estrangement from their betters.[87]

This leadership crisis is best illustrated by the increasingly ambivalent relationship between the Catholic church and its lower-class adherents. By all accounts, in the early eighteenth century that relationship was extremely close: although the church's physical structure lay in ruins and its practical authority was shackled by the Penal Laws, rural Catholics regarded their fugitive bishops and priests as cultural heroes who shared with them the stigmas of poverty and defeat. Until 1766, Irish bishops still received appointments on the approval of the exiled Stuart pretenders, and so at least theoretically were enemies of the Protestant state and the Williamite land settlement. In fact, during this period most bishops and priests represented what remained of the Catholic upper classes, since only affluent families could afford to send sons abroad for training legally proscribed at home. However, deferential rural Catholics unquestioningly accepted their clergy's elite origins, and while Jansenist-trained bishops such as James O'Gallagher of Raphoe might thunder that the sins of their poor parishioners had occasioned God's chastisement in the forms of conquest and confiscations, most clerics were either indisposed or unable to alter their people's semi-Christian religious customs.[88]

However, after about 1760 the Irish church began to move in new, complementary directions. First, although in the 1740s the Irish bishops had persuaded Rome to legitimize the popular cults of several traditional Irish saints, after mid-century the church began its earlier-described crusade to eradicate old religious customs and replace them with conventional forms of Catholic worship such as regular attendance at mass, confession, and devotion to the Blessed Virgin. Second, in order to implement these changes, the church began to reform its own organization and to repair and rebuild its physical plant. That the bishops could now undertake these tasks was due not only to the indifference of a self-confident Ascendancy but also to the economic growth of the late eighteenth century. Thus, bishops began to impose stricter discipline on often insubordinate priests and to build and refurbish cathedrals, chapels, and other religious edifices with the contributions of a more prosperous laity. Neither task was completed until the late nineteenth century, but there was considerable early progress in dioceses such as Clogher, whose bishop reported in 1804, "[w]here not long ago we had the most wretched Cabbins of Chapels not half equal to contain the Congregation; and in others where there was no covering whatever for the People and scarcely a shed to shelter the Priest and Sacrifice; we have lately got many good Chapels erected and covered with the best of slate."[89]

However, these developments had one unforeseen consequence: the financial and organizational necessities of expansion inevitably forged closer ties between the church and the "improving/assimilating" Catholic classes at a time when the social relationship between those classes and the rural poor was deteriorating. For example, it is likely that in the late eighteenth century an increasing proportion of priests were drawn not from the ranks of "gentlemen" but from those of the nouveaux riches strong farmers and urban traders; this was certainly true after 1795, when the establishment of St. Patrick's College at Maynooth, County Kildare, provided for a native-trained clergy. Not only were these new priests more zealous than their predecessors in stamping out old religious customs but they also seem to have been more demanding of dues, fees, and gifts from their parishioners. In part, these demands were necessitated by the church's rebuilding campaign; however, they also reflected priests' desires to win acceptance from Protestant peers by making the "respectable" appearance which many could not maintain out of personal funds: "It is your own interest," one priest told his reluctant flock, ". . . that, in a country where gentlemen of a different religion esteem the Catholic clergy more for their outward appearance and conduct than for their profession, your pastors should appear with decency." In the late eighteenth and early nineteenth centuries, some priests reportedly exacted incomes of £300 or more; many had sliding scales of fees for christenings, weddings, and funerals, and stimulated rival families to exhibit their relative degrees of piety and respectability by competing for the honor of making the largest contributions. Conversely, "rapacious priests" were accused of refusing the sacraments to those who could not meet their demands. In many districts it was common for priests to hold "stations" in private farmhouses to say mass and hear confession—a custom necessitated by the dearth of chapels, but

one which gave rise to accusations that priests were extorting lavish entertainments from wealthy parishioners while neglecting their duties to the
poor. Also, although in the eyes of his flock a priest should ideally have
been "as pure as the Ceder of Lebannan which is Encoruptable wood," as
one rustic put it, many clergymen were in fact accused of drunkenness and
immorality.[90]

All these abuses drew repeated censure from the hierarchy, and in 1786
the bishops of Munster even removed two priests whose avarice and arrogance had made them especially obnoxious to their congregations. However, popular resentment was widespread, manifested in anticlerical sentiments which appeared both in late-eighteenth-century Gaelic poetry and in
the proverbs of the poor: "four priests who are not greedy . . . you will
not find in the country," as Mayo Irish-speakers said. But the most effective
protests were made by the secret agrarian societies, several of which put
clerical avarice high on their lists of grievances to be redressed. In the
1760s–1780s the Whiteboys and Rightboys of Munster and south Leinster,
and in the 1810s–1820s the Thrashers and Carders in the north midlands,
tried to regulate priests' dues and prohibit additional "entertainments." In
the 1780s the Rightboys assaulted priests and farmers who refused to obey
their edicts and in some districts deserted the chapels and marched en
masse to the local Anglican churches. Bishops, priests, and "respectable"
lay Catholics denounced the secret societies for these anticlerical activities,
just as they condemned their violent protests against secular grievances. In
1775 the bishop of Ferns excommunicated "the destestable, lawless and
unmeaning disturbers of the public" who were "drawing on us, and our
holy religion, the odium of our mild government, and the gentlemen in
power"; and in 1833 the bishop of Kildare and Leighlin described the agitators as "thieves, liars, drunkards, fornicators, quarrellers, blasphemers—
men who have abandoned all the duties of religion."[91]

When making such statements, or when joining with landlords in offering rewards to informers on secret societies, churchmen were arguably at
least as deeply concerned about the endangered souls of the "misguided"
poor as about the church's revenues and reputation or the property of their
more affluent parishioners. However, to the Catholic lower classes in these
"disturbed" areas, it seemed that the church was siding against them in
their struggle for economic survival. Indeed, during the late eighteenth and
early nineteenth centuries the church moved in a third direction, which
only served to deepen such suspicions. After 1766, freed at last from the
embarrassing Stuart connection by the Old Pretender's death, churchmen
and prominent lay Catholics began to signify their acceptance of the Hanoverian succession and the postconquest land settlement. These protesta-
tions of loyalty had several causes. Bishops and propertied laymen alike
recognized that further hostility toward the state was hopeless and that accommodation might bring equal citizenship and relief from the Penal Laws.
In addition, most Irish churchmen—like their continental counterparts—
were political and social conservatives by background and training; in re-

turn for their church's freedom to shepherd its flock, they were quite willing to preach obedience to duly constituted authority. The anticlericalism of the secret societies and, later, of the French Revolution only intensified their aversion to social upheaval. Moreover, bishops, priests, and upper- and middle-class parishioners believed they needed government support in order to maintain an increasingly tenuous social and ideological position. Reconciling the ideology of "improvement" with a belief in a natural social hierarchy was difficult: religious equality and free trade were one thing, but the skepticism and "leveling spirit" of the American and French revolutions were quite another. Whether inspired by peasant or by radical notions of equality, the secret societies obviously constituted a threat to upper- and middle-class Catholics' notions of orderly progress and to their hopes of winning acceptance from their Protestant peers. Naturally, those few instances when priests were implicated in, and executed for taking part in, agrarian rebellions—in 1776 and more notably in 1798—were extremely embarrassing. As a result, churchmen not only denounced rural violence, excommunicated United Irishmen, and supported official coercion but from 1795 to 1808 also quietly linked their church to British authority by agreeing to a government veto over episcopal appointments. In 1795 they accepted state funding for St. Patrick's College to dispel the danger of radicalism infecting French-trained priests, and in 1799 they traded support for the Act of Union for a promise of full repeal of the remaining Penal Laws. During the same period, the bishops came close to accepting state payment for all Catholic clergy, which would have freed priests from popular influence and created a dual religious establishment; as late as 1822 Bishop James Doyle of Kildare and Leighlin advocated a "union of the good and the virtuous" among Catholics and Anglicans to suppress agrarian violence.[92]

Such actions stemmed at least partly from clerics' mounting fears that the social discipline and spiritual well-being of their "half-savage" parishioners, as the bishop of Kilkenny called them, could be achieved only by allying the church with a government which could put down rural outrages with one hand, and yet held out the promise of religious freedom and political equality for propertied Catholics with the other. However, in the end these accommodating tactics proved insufficient. Despite William Pitt's pledges in 1799, a full repeal of the Penal Laws was not forthcoming after the Act of Union; and by 1808 disgruntled middle-class Catholics like O'Connell successfully demanded that the bishops renounce the episcopal veto they had granted to the government. More important in the present context is that these accommodations did little or nothing to advance the bishops' goals of modernizing rural religious practices and transforming their people into "good Catholics" or law-abiding citizens. The secret societies continued their nocturnal activities, illegitimacy rates persisted which were embarrassingly high by clerics' and strong farmers' standards, and, as was noted earlier, throughout much of the island mass-attendance rates remained low and predictive customs and magical beliefs

remained common. There were several reasons for this failure. First, despite all its efforts to expand its influence in the countryside, before the
Famine the Irish church simply lacked sufficient personnel. In 1800 there
were about 1,850 priests for a Catholic population of around 3.9 million,
roughly a ratio of 1 to 2,100. By 1840 the situation had worsened; although there were now about 2,150 priests, there were also 6.5 million
Catholics, a ratio of 1 to 3,000. Although between 1800 and 1840 the
number of nuns quintupled, the ratio of nuns to parishioners was only 1 to
6,500. Also, most of the clergy were concentrated in the eastern half of the
country, rather than in the West, where they were most needed. In short,
priests and regular clergy were too few to catechize and instruct a burgeoning population. Second, by temporarily weakening its claims to leadership
in the traditional communal struggle against English/landlord hegemony,
the church may have encouraged an identity crisis among its adherents:
perhaps reinforcing cultural conservatism among the disillusioned rural
poor, while allowing upwardly mobile Catholics to feel fewer compunctions about questioning a faith which increasingly seemed less a standard
of tribal loyalty than a matter of personal utility. Certainly, many country
people either ignored priests' condemnations of their traditional customs or
resumed them after zealous clerics died or departed. In parts of Munster,
Irish-speakers resented priests' efforts to suppress the old language—*"má
thráchtann ar cheart"*—"if it speaks of what is right and true," and even in
eastern Ireland the social distance between the priests and the Catholic
lower classes was often a barrier to effective clerical influence. Yet, in many
instances when the people did embrace modern ways, they found their ambitions thwarted or their material success criticized by clerics who feared
that too much cultural and social change might lead to secularism or apostasy. For example, one priest charged that before 1814 "the easy and plentiful earnings of flourishing manufacture, and of extensive and successful
commerce" caused "religion . . . to weep for the first time . . . over the
faltering fidelity and submission of many a son," and contemporaries cited
numerous occasions of priests forbidding parishioners to send their children to the best available schools because they were taught by Protestants
or because they used Protestant texts as mediums of instruction. Parents
often resented such prohibitions, and occasionally defied them when the
only Catholic schools were "of the lowest and poorest description." As a
result, perhaps zealous Protestants were not entirely fantasizing when they
claimed that some Catholics were becoming so irritated by clerical "tyranny" that they were "quite ripe" for conversion to a more "rational" and
"progressive" religion; it is singular that of the 5,650 names on the Dublin
convert rolls for 1703–99, well over half were entered in the last quarter
of the century—*after* the removal of most penal disabilities. In any case,
what is certain is that Anglicization, like commercialization, was unraveling the fabric of Irish society.[93]

In retrospect, Irish society around 1800 seems analogous to a pattern in a kaleidoscope: turned one way the design forms along sectarian lines, but when turned again the socioeconomic and cultural divisions within each religious community seem most prominent. Ireland was fragmenting at a number of stress points, and in the late eighteenth century it was problematical which divisions would prove most important and which, if any, forces would impart cohesion in the following decades. However, the socioeconomic and cultural developments described in the preceding pages produced their own syntheses in the form of nationwide, mass-based political movements which, because of Ireland's colonial status, were often "nationalistic" in the sense that the issues involved ultimately hinged upon the island's political relationship to Great Britain. These movements emerged under the leadership of middle- and/or upper-class figures who promoted group solidarity across social divisions in order to realize specific and purportedly "national" aspirations. Popular support came from the rural and urban lower classes, whose parochial loyalties were eroding under the impact of commercialization and Anglicization and whose traditional resentments could be broadened and harnessed to achieve the "larger" goals defined by their social superiors. However, given the legacy of British colonialism, it was perhaps inevitable that no collective political movement could fulfill the dream of the United Irishman Wolfe Tone "to unite the whole people of Ireland, to abolish the memory of all past dissensions, and to substitute the common name of Irishman in place of the denominations of Protestant, Catholic and Dissenter." Although national movements obscured class conflicts within each community, they resulted in the emergence of two distinct and largely hostile Irish "nations" or peoples whose separate identities were rooted primarily in religious distinctions and whose political aspirations seemed ultimately irreconcilable. "In the realm of concrete action or reaction we Irish have always been as a house divided against itself," wrote a Clareman later in the nineteenth century. "Over the nakedness of our disunion we have drawn the veils or illusions of politics and religion."[94]

In the late eighteenth century the uneven effects of economic growth strained the political relationship between Ireland and England and divided the Protestant Ascendancy against itself. The greater Irish landlords generally favored the existing political system: an unreformed Irish Parliament which effectively represented only a handful of wealthy families; and an Irish executive composed largely of Englishmen who were responsible only to the king's ministers in London and who employed lavish patronage to ensure that Irish legislation was subservient to English interests. In addition, a body of statutes dating from 1494 declared the Irish Parliament's legal inferiority to the legislature in Westminster; the British Parliament could legislate for Ireland, disallow Irish statutes, and even forbid the Irish Parliament from meeting. Since the late seventeenth century a few Irish Protestants had protested these arrangements, but not until the second half of the eighteenth did a minority of Whiggish "Patriots" in the Dublin Parliament begin to challenge them effectively. The so-called Patriot party was a disparate lot, but generally it represented the aspirations of three groups of Protestants: the lesser gentry who wanted to break the political monopoly of the Tory oligarchy; the Ulster Presbyterians who wanted relief from an oppressive and exclusive Anglican establishment; and the growing commercial and manufacturing classes who desired both freedom from English restrictions on Irish trade and a more broadly representative Irish Parliament which would protect and promote Irish industries. Some reformers also advocated a partial repeal of the Penal Laws, particularly those which restricted Catholics' economic activities and which prevented them from contributing to what the Patriots hoped would be boundless national prosperity; however, few Patriots dared weaken the Ascendancy by granting Catholics political equality, and they naïvely believed that, given equal economic opportunities, propertied Catholics would become Protestants in all but name.[95]

The Patriots' opportunity to bring about reforms came in the late 1770s when economic depression, coupled with high taxes to pay for an unpopular war with the American colonies, gave them widespread support for their goal of legislative independence from England. When the government stripped Ireland of regular army troops for service overseas, the Patriots were able to form militia companies of "Volunteers"; ostensibly designed to combat a threatened French invasion, the Volunteers in fact became a powerful, armed pressure group uniting Protestants of all classes behind Patriot demands. Frightened that the 80,000 Volunteers might emulate the American rebellion, the British government made concessions, repealing all restrictions on Irish trade and renouncing its claims to legislate for Ireland. However, while the Patriot leader Henry Grattan exulted that "Ireland is now a nation," bound to Britain only by self-interest and loyalty to the crown, the "revolution of 1782" was in fact illusory, and in its aftermath Irish Protestants became more deeply divided over the island's political future. Grattan's fragile coalition fell apart: Parliament's improved status satisfied most of the gentry, but the urban middle classes and the Dissenters remained alienated. Although theoretically autonomous, the Irish government remained subordinate to English officials in Dublin Castle as well as grossly unrepresentative of the vast majority of Protestants. Indeed, it was British pressure on the Irish Parliament, rather than Protestant generosity, that was primarily responsible for the passage of the Catholic Relief Acts of 1792–93.[96]

In the early 1790s dissension over the advisability of parliamentary reform and the impact of the French Revolution drove conservative Patriots into the Tory ranks, reduced liberal Whigs such as Grattan to political impotence, and led Radical merchants, manufacturers, professional men, and artisans in Belfast and Dublin to form the Society of United Irishmen. Inspired by revolutionary ideals and driven underground by government persecution, the United Irishmen moved from simply demanding reform to soliciting French aid for an armed rebellion designed to establish an independent Irish republic based on equal citizenship for Protestants and Catholics, universal male suffrage, and protective tariffs which, in Tone's words, would cause Ireland's economy to "spring up like an air balloon, and leave England behind her at an immense distance." However, while the United Irishmen based their hopes for success upon the lower classes, particularly the discontented Presbyterians of rural Ulster, antipathy to Catholics tempered radical inclinations among most rural and working-class urban Protestants who considered the partial repeal of the Penal Laws a greater threat to their security than even rents, tithes, taxes, or low wages. Consequently, in Ulster the abortive United Irish rising of 1798 bitterly divided Protestants into rebels and Orangemen, and outside the North rebellion was almost exclusively Catholic. Moreover, even the victorious Protestant loyalists disagreed over Ireland's political future: the gentry and the Anglican bishops generally favored the Act of Union in 1800 as the best surety for their continued ascendancy, but the predominantly lower-class Orangemen were deeply opposed, fearing on the basis of recent evidence that the British government would be more likely than the Irish Parliament to grant Catholics complete equality.[97]

Thus, despite the very different efforts of Patriots, United Irishmen, and Orangemen, in 1800 there was no Protestant Irish "nation" in the sense of a people united across class, regional, and denominational lines by fundamental agreement on basic political principles; a substantial minority had challenged Protestants' most ancient ideological assumptions, and even the traditionalist majority was divided over Ireland's political status. However, by the middle of the nineteenth century Irish Protestants were virtually unanimous in support of the union with Britain and in opposition to Catholic efforts either to break that union or to weaken upper-class Protestant hegemony. This remarkable unity had several interrelated causes. First, the sectarian violence of 1798, followed by the growth of Ribbonism and increasing Catholic political assertiveness, disabused former Patriots and United Irishmen of their tolerant notions and made all Protestants more dependent on what was, after 1800, *British* authority for the security of their lives and property. Second, the economic consequences of the postwar depression linked the fortunes of the once-radical Protestant merchant and manufacturing community more closely to the British imperial system, while simultaneously increasing the Protestant lower classes' reliance upon their landlords and employers for protection against Catholic competition for leases and wages. Third, in the early nineteenth century the Orange Order expanded throughout Ireland, bringing upper- and lower-class Protestants together in a sectarian alliance. Once the Act of Union was an accomplished fact, Orangemen became fiercely, if pragmatically, loyal to that union as a guarantee of Protestant "rights," thus obviating British fears of future Protestant separatism. By heading the Orange Order, Protestant landlords and magistrates reassumed the social leadership they had partially forfeited during the Oak- and Steelboy agitations, and helped ensure that in spite of the economic distress of the postwar decades such *class*-based violence among Protestants virtually disappeared. For tenants, artisans, and laborers, membership in the Orange lodges preserved the essential element of their "moral economy": at least symbolic recognition of their superior claims to land and employment despite the prevailing ethos of free-market capitalism. Finally, after 1800 the rapid growth of evangelicalism among Protestants personalized and intensified their religious beliefs and united them across denominational and social lines in a millenarian crusade to purge Ireland of sin. To a large extent evangelicalism, with its roots in apocalyptic traditions and its emphasis upon personal salvation, was a natural response of Protestant tenants, weavers, and factory hands to the socioeconomic, political, and cultural discontinuities of the eighteenth and early nineteenth centuries—especially the individualizing effects of commercialization and industrialization. However, the evangelical crusade was not a spontaneous eruption; it was consciously promoted and financed by Tory landlords, Dublin businessmen, and conservative Anglican, Presbyterian, and Methodist clergymen who wanted to purge lower-class Protestants of secularism and radicalism and to unite them against Catholic demands for a liberalization of the political system and disestablishment of the Church of Ireland. By the early 1820s evangelicalism had permeated both the Anglican and the Presbyterian churches and had become a proselytizing campaign to convert seditious and turbulent "papists" into loyal and industrious Protestants. Conversions were few, but that very fact helped solidify Protestant ranks by adding a new ideological dimension to the customary justifications for Protestant privileges: by refusing God's grace, Catholics definitely "proved" their spiritual inferiority, while Protestant tenants and laborers demonstrated their own worthiness through the conversion experience and by their adherence to the supposedly "Protestant" virtues of moral uplift—industry, thrift, and sobriety—enjoined by the middle-class evangelicals. Indeed, it was largely through evangelicalism that the children and grandchildren of Steelboys and United Irishmen at least superficially assimilated to the values and demands of nineteenth-century industrial capitalism. Thus, by the eve of the Famine, Irish Protestants were united in support of the established order, and not even attempts by Ulster landlords and Protestant factory owners to undermine tenant-right and to break trade unions had been sufficient to weaken the loyalty of Protestant farmers and workers to what was, in fact, a class-ridden system.[98]

Despite their common legacy of religious persecution, Irish Catholics were in 1800 perhaps even less united socially and politically than Irish Protestants. While the Whiteboys and the trade unions struggled to restore a "moral economy," the Catholic middle classes embraced the ideology of "improvement" and the ethos of free-market capitalism, which promised them equal economic, social, and political opportunities. While lower-class Catholics clung to their tribal identity, upwardly mobile merchants and professionals claimed that when the Penal Laws were repealed "[t]he Catholic will cease to look on religion as a mark of distinction between him and his neighbour." And while Gaelic poets and itinerant ballad singers prophesied that the Stuarts or the French would deliver them from bondage, propertied Catholics appealed to the principles of Locke and Burke in an attempt to win equality within the British constitution. "If we were freed from the disabilities under which we labour," promised Bishop Doyle later in the century, "we have no mind, and no thought, and no will but that which would lead us to incorporate ourselves most fully and essentially with this great kingdom; for it would be our greatest pride to share in the glories and riches of England." Thus, when in 1797–98 Catholic tenants and laborers died by the thousands in a futile effort to make Ireland an independent republic, their traditional spokesmen, lay and clerical, not only denounced their rebellion but afterward almost unanimously supported the Act of Union, which obliterated the island's fragile claims to nationhood.[99]

During the next four and one-half decades, however, Ireland's Catholics became largely united in a succession of political crusades to achieve full political equality, abolition of tithes, and repeal of the Act of Union. Leadership in these campaigns came primarily from the hitherto politically conservative Catholic middle classes and clergy who realized after 1800 that they could not rely on British benevolence to promote or protect their interests. There were a number of reasons for this increased assertiveness. First, the generally improved economic status of the Catholic rural and urban bourgeoisie contrasted dramatically with its continued exclusion from power and influence. Despite Pitt's pledge that full repeal of the Penal Laws—that is, "Catholic emancipation"—would follow the Act of Union, the High Church Tory prejudices of the crown and House of Lords prevented such reform for nearly thirty years. Consequently, unless Catholics were willing to take an oath denouncing their religion as false and idolatrous, they were barred from Parliament, higher offices in the civil administration, the posts of sheriff and subsheriff, the inner bar and the judicial bench, and military promotion beyond the rank of colonel. Furthermore, in practice they were excluded from the vast majority of positions and honors to which they were legally eligible; in 1828 Catholics held only 134 of the 3,033 minor offices theoretically open to them. In short, the Protestant Ascendancy over Irish political life continued, depriving affluent Catholics not only of the status they felt they deserved but also of protection for their property. For example, in 1812 a prominent Catholic complained that in the Protestant-dominated town corporations "[e]very species of Catholic industry and mechanical skill is checked, taxed, and rendered precarious" by "uncertain and unequal . . . justice" and by "fraud and favoritism daily and openly practiced to their prejudice." Even after 1829, when the passage of emancipation made propertied Catholics eligible for parliamentary seats and other posts, they soon learned, as the British statesman Robert Peel admitted, that their equality was merely "nominal." Before the Famine, Ireland was grossly underrepresented at Westminster, and the Irish electorate was so restricted in size that O'Connell had no consistent success in forming an Irish Catholic "party" to wield influence in Parliament. Although his followers derived some practical benefits from their tenuous alliances with English Whigs and Radicals, by the early 1840s middle-class Catholic hopes for political power centered on a restoration of an autonomous Irish legislature.[100]

Second, although propertied Catholics suffered far less than their inferiors from the postwar depression, economic distress exacerbated sectarian competition at all social levels and intensified Catholics' felt need to acquire power in order to protect their position. The economic condition of middle-class Catholics between 1814 and 1845 is difficult to assess: compared with the lower classes they were prosperous; however, relative to their British and Irish Protestant counterparts, their situation was inferior and somewhat precarious. On the one hand, Catholic traders and graziers steadily invested in land, often assuming the mortgages of bankrupt Protestant squires, until in 1845 Catholics owned more land than in the late seventeenth century. Many others emerged from the prosperous war years as affluent strong farmers. However, in the 1820s–1840s some Protestant landlords in Leinster, in south Ulster, and elsewhere began a concerted effort to expel Catholic head tenants and replace them with Protestants. Such bigoted estate management was not widespread, but there were sufficient incidents both to frighten affluent Catholics and to unite them symbolically with their poorer coreligionists, who suffered evictions far more frequently. In addition, after 1814 declining prices made rents, tithes, and taxes more burdensome for all classes and inspired even propertied Catholics to engage in collective protests. Although head rents may have fallen slightly, between the 1820s and the 1840s county cess rose more than 20 percent, and the new Irish Poor Law of 1838 taxed leaseholders as well as landlords to maintain the island's growing army of indigents. For Catholic graziers and strong farmers, tithes became a special grievance: usually assessed on a per-acre basis, they failed to reflect declining crop values; more important, after reform legislation in 1823–24, grasslands and pastoral products lost the exemption from tithes enjoyed since 1735, thus forcing the wealthiest farmers to contribute. Consequently, in the 1830s affluent Catholic graziers—formerly aloof from anti-tithe agitation—led a widespread and often violent "tithe war" against the Anglican clergy. Finally, while the industrial prosperity of eastern Ulster made middle-class urban Protestants in the North firm supporters of union with Britain, industrial decline and urban stagnation in the three other provinces made their Catholic counterparts eager for the restoration of an Irish parliament which under their dominance would not only abolish Ascendancy privilege but also enact tariffs and other laws to rejuvenate the southern economy.[101]

Third, after 1800 the Catholic hierarchy and clergy began to sense that their church's interests would be best served through aggressive political action, rather than through defensive accommodation. By the early 1820s exhortations by laymen such as O'Connell, combined with growing frustration over emancipation and fear and anger over Protestant proselytization, inspired a new generation of churchmen to unite with propertied Catholics in political crusades which promised to weaken, perhaps destroy the Ascendancy and restore the church to a preeminent position in Irish society. Consequently, the bishops not only renounced the government veto over episcopal appointments but by a large majority supported openly the campaigns for emancipation, abolition of tithes, and repeal of the union. Parish priests were even more unanimous and enthusiastic, partly because they shared the same backgrounds and resentments as the lawyers, traders, and strong farmers. Fourth and finally, upper- and middle-class Catholics, lay and clerical, hoped that their leadership of these "patriotic" national movements would enable them to reassert social authority over the Catholic community and, in the name of religious solidarity, suppress the social and cultural conflicts which had rent Catholic society since the late eighteenth century. Churchmen and propertied laymen alike found themselves in a difficult position. The British government's refusal to dismantle the Ascendancy and grant them and their church equality meant that, despite their basic conservatism, they were obliged to employ democratic arguments to combat Protestant privilege, and forced to rely for mass support on a lower-class populace whose economic and political notions were antithetical to bourgeois ambitions and more often expressed in nocturnal violence against their wealthier coreligionists than in constitutional agitation. However, if lower-class resentments could be channeled into peaceful political movements to secure middle-class goals, then not only might those movements succeed but their very existence might obscure class and cultural divisions, reestablish lower-class deference to clerics and propertied laymen, and enable those ambitious men to create a modern, Irish Catholic "nation" in their own social and ideological image.[102]

In one sense, the success of Catholic nationalism in the early nineteenth century was tied to ongoing structural changes in Irish society: the erosion of parochial barriers to metropolitan influences, growing exposure to market forces centered ultimately in England, improved communications and rising literacy, the decline of Irish, and so forth. Thus, the campaigns for emancipation, abolition of tithes, and repeal were best organized and enjoyed greatest popular participation in Leinster and east Munster—the most commercialized and urbanized parts of southern Ireland, where strong farmers and traders were most numerous and where the church was strongest and most influential. However, in another sense Catholic nationalism long preceded modern developments. Political leaders in pre-Famine Ireland did not operate in a cultural vacuum: they drew upon—and sometimes strove vainly to control—communal traditions rooted deep in the Irish past.[103]

Admittedly, the untutored Irish countryman's notion of patriotism was parochial, but it was also extremely intense. *Dúchas,* the Irish word which conveys the equivalent of "patriotism," means an instinctual identification with those cherished aspects of local life which are familiar and innate, inseparable from one's very existence. Countless proverbs expressed Irish attachment to cottage and kin. *"Is naith an t-ancoire an t-iarta,"* as Irish-speakers said: "the hearth is a good anchor"—not merely in a material sense but as the center of all the local customs and activities, songs and legends, which gave meaning and identity in rural life. Irish-speakers maintained an equally intimate relationship with the natural features of their environment: the shapes and colors of the landscape—the birds, trees, rivers, rocks, and hills of their native surroundings. They lavished names on the land; every field, cleft, and hollow had a distinctive appellation which recalled some ancient owner or legendary occurrence. The same relationship was reflected in Gaelic love poems, in which the singer compared his beloved to the flowers and birds and extolled the beauty of his native countryside to persuade her to marry him. It was also evident in the poets' laments for the once-great forests which the British leveled for timber and to deny sanctuaries to Irish rebels: *"Tá deire na gcoillte ar lár,"* lamented one bard—"The last of the woods is fallen." Even the improved communications of the nineteenth century seem not to have diminished the countryman's close identification with his environment, for the same love of nature continued to appear in the diaries of schoolmasters, the memoirs of laborers, and, later still, in the autobiographies of poor fishing folk from the Blasket Islands and other western districts.[104]

More important, the Irish-speaker's sense of identity was not limited to his immediate neighborhood. Although during his lifetime he might never journey beyond his native parish, he knew that he was a member of a wider community, peculiar in its culture and traditions, and that outsiders assailed him precisely because of that membership. Although the countryman's everyday economic grievances were local and specific, they were inextricably tied to feelings of cultural, religious, and racial exclusiveness. Despite its aristocratic bias, seventeenth- and eighteenth-century Gaelic poetry expressed what one scholar has called "a sense of separateness, a sense of identity and nationality stronger than sectional interests." For personal advancement the postconquest poets often resorted to the grossest flattery of Protestant squires, but when addressing their own people they denounced the churlish "upstarts," wished them "[t]orment and gripping fever in the heat of hellfire," and predicted the day when the British settlers would be "forspent and powerless . . . hanged by a rope or burnt to the bone." The music and traditions of the common people expressed the same sentiments. In the 1820s a student of the Munster keens learned that the Irish language was a cloak for songs which "were rebellious in the highest degree," and travelers in Connaught discovered that the poorest peasants were able and ready to recite stories of "bloody Bess or cursed Cromwell" and to draw analogies between their ancient crimes and more recent incidents of oppression. In short, as a Gaelic schoolmaster wrote, his countrymen "detest[ed]" the English "most cordially." Although their notion of the British government might be vague and remote, there is little doubt that the Catholic poor deeply resented the Protestant Ascendancy and its representatives and that they blamed the English generally for all their own ills and for the downfall of a Gaelic order in which they fancied their ancestors had lived contentedly. Such resentment, usually accompanied by self-pity, rang through the laments of poets and schoolmasters for the "thousand million . . . weaknesses and wants from which we have been suffering since the day . . . the Saxons got a grip on our beloved country . . . , poor tortured Ireland."[105]

Irish national identity and antipathy to the English were mutually reinforcing concepts. In part they were based on a communal interpretation of history which "compress[ed] all the past into one living yesterday" and obscured the significance of all other conflicts save that with the hated "foreigner." The English insistence that preconquest Ireland was barbarous and uncivilized naturally led the Gaelic poets to create a romantic counter-image of a land of saints and scholars, of valiant warriors and contented husbandmen, which had been subjugated through treachery and greed. Although the bards themselves despised the Irish poor, the necessity for communal solidarity and the social upheavals of the sixteenth and seventeenth centuries often obliged them to address all Catholics as if they were "children of kings, sons of Milésius," thus giving the lower classes a spurious share of past glories. The result was a widely diffused sense of dispossession and injustice, and an unusual degree of popular identification with the fallen fortunes of those who had suffered directly from confiscations and Penal Laws. Thus, in districts from west Munster to Donegal, country people continued to honor impoverished descendants of once-exalted families; and in the early nineteenth century a priest in Cork testified that his parishioners fondly recalled the days of Desmond and O'Neill for "the liberty and what they conceive the privileges they formerly enjoyed compared with their present degradation." Similarly, all Catholics who defied Ascendancy laws, however much they exploited their coreligionists, became cultural champions. The peasants celebrated the deeds of common highwaymen and poachers alongside Sarsfield's defense of Limerick; and, as one traveler reported, there existed a widespread "determination to set law at defiance, and . . . a disposition to regard all men as martyrs . . . who have been brought, by crimes however heinous," to the bar of justice.[106]

In 1848 an Irish nationalist fleeing from British troops was pleased to discover that in the remote mountains of west Kerry the people still "cherished in their hearts the . . . imperishable purpose and hope of overturning the dominion of the stranger." The observation was significant, for much of the Irish countryman's resentment against British officials and settlers was based on his perception that, regardless of how long their families had resided in Ireland, they were not truly Irish but *Sasanaigh* (Saxons) or *Gaill* (foreigners): strangers, unwanted intruders in the land of the *Gaeil*. Three major characteristics distinguished those who regarded themselves as "native Irish" from their "alien oppressors": language, religion, and "rightful" title to the soil. Early English attempts to proscribe Irish had made the idiom a badge of national identity. In the seventeenth and eighteenth centuries the Gaelic poets admonished their listeners to scorn English, full of "folly and sound without sense," and cleave to the "sweet

Irish tongue of the beguiling airs; swift, bold, strong as the beating waves."
Despite the language's decline, in the first decades of the nineteenth century Protestant observers still lamented that Irish-speakers "think themselves a sort of aboriginal race" and viewed their speech as a "sacred" possession. While most English travelers in pre-Famine Ireland remarked
upon the courtesy they encountered, the country people's true feelings were
expressed in a language few outsiders could understand. For example, the
novelist Thackeray found his attempts to converse with the Connemara
peasantry "a vain matter . . . the people are suspicious of the stranger
within their wretched gates, and are shy, sly, and silent." As a Maynooth
professor observed, the Irish countryman was not to be known by a "passing glance, or conversation or acquaintance especially if the observer
should happen to be of a more respectable class, of a different country, or
a different creed." However, much was revealed to the rare visitor who
could speak Irish. In 1812 one such fortunate traveler wrote:

> No one can enter into the cabin of an Irishman and converse with him fa-
> miliarly in his own language, without perceiving his strong dislike to the per-
> sons and religion of the Gall. He remembers that his country has been in-
> vaded and conceives that the chiefs of his people have been oppressed and
> extirpated by the English. He still points to the ruins of a castle which was the
> habitation of his own prince of the Milesian race, a prince to whom he
> himself is nearly allied, and with a sigh recounts the years that passed
> since its walls were demolished by the hands of strangers.

In short, behind the veil of the Irish language the Gaels spoke and sang of
wrongs and retribution, and later Irish nationalists believed that this was
the major reason why the government banned it from the National Schools:
its very phraseology contained the seeds of dissatisfaction and rebellion.[107]

The second major distinction between *Gaeil* and *Sasanaigh* was religious. As early as the sixteenth century, Edmund Spenser reported that although the Munster Irish were quite ignorant of Protestantism, "yet they
do hate it, though unknown, even for the very hatred which they have for
the English and their government." Later, as conversions blurred ethnic divisions and as the Irish language began its inexorable decline, the Gaelic
poets placed increasing emphasis on religious rather than linguistic identity. By the early nineteenth century, among Irish-speakers the terms *Gaeil*
and Catholic, *Sasanaigh* and Protestant, had become synonymous, and
popular opinion regarded those who challenged the Ascendancy not only
as secular heroes but as martyrs for the faith. Ironically, although the
United Irishmen aimed to create a radically secularized Ireland, the events
of 1798 and the subsequent Protestant evangelical crusade only strengthened Catholics' religious identification and their animosity toward the
"damned . . . offspring of Calvin and Luther." Although in the eighteenth century Irish countrymen often displayed little resentment toward
Protestant converts, realizing that public behavior had to be contingent on
economic necessity, in the early nineteenth century they assailed "perverts"

and their descendants as detestable "traitors." The Catholic clergy did not originate this religious animosity, but often they helped foster it. The priests "spared no pains," recalled one Irish-speaker, "to plant in my young mind an especial reverence and love for the Virgin Mary, and a corresponding hatred of Protestants" and their "foreign" creed.[108]

Finally, it was the issue of land that kept the cultural and sectarian distinctions burning brightly in Irish hearts. For at the center of Catholics' identity and grievances was their firm conviction that they, not the "usurpers," were the rightful owners of Ireland. Strictly speaking, such beliefs were rarely justified, although some now-impoverished families still clung to ancient deeds and old maps of confiscated estates. However, the passage of time, the social descent of many once-great families, and the still-extant traditions of commonage had blurred the old distinctions between nobles and commoners and had diffused a general sense that all Catholics were somehow the true heirs of dispossessed Gaelic and Hiberno-Norman lords. "I do not know of any change" in the land system "short of a perfect confiscation that would give satisfaction," testified a witness before a parliamentary committee investigating rural discontent; for "[t]here is a great deal of feeling among the lower orders of Roman Catholics that they are the owners . . . of the soil." Thus, while the secret agrarian societies usually demanded only fair rents and security of tenure, ultimately their claims challenged the Ascendancy's very existence. *"But why [should] we pay rent at all?"* exhorted a Ribbonman from County Monaghan in 1851. "That's the question, say I. Isn't the land our own, and wasn't it our ancestors' before us, until these bloody English came and took it all away from us? My curse upon them for it—but we will tear it back out of their heart's blood yet."[109]

Despite the social and cultural changes of the late eighteenth and early nineteenth centuries, these popular, nationalistic sentiments did not diminish; indeed, they may have become more intense even before the organized political movements of the 1820s–1840s. The radical, egalitarian notions spread by the French Revolution and by the United Irishmen offered a modern but a corroboratory justification for the Irish Catholics' belief that they, not the Ascendancy, should own and govern the country. "I believe in a revolution founded on the rights of man," pledged the Wexford rebels in 1798, and "in the natural and imprescriptable right of *all* Irish citizens to the land." Their rising failed, but by doing so it increased the catalog of sufferings and martyrs to be celebrated in new songs of rebellion. Similarly, the long wars between England and France renewed hope of deliverance from abroad; Bonaparte replaced the Stuart pretender as the anticipated savior for the men who assembled at the crossroads to discuss politics. Although the church officially disapproved, from the 1790s the religious component of popular nationalism was strengthened by the mass circulation of supposed prophecies by St. Columcille and "Pastorini" (Charles Walmsley, a late-eighteenth-century English bishop) which respectively foretold the imminence of a Gaelic renaissance and the total extermination of Protestants and their religion. Although the numbers of Gaelic poets steadily dwindled, they were supplanted by hordes of itinerant ballad singers who hawked compositions at fairs and markets throughout the island. Most ballads were in English and wretched in quality, but they were immensely popular and transmitted the old themes of resentment and redemption to generations now incapable of appreciating or even understanding the complexities of Gaelic verse. For the more discriminating, the compositions of Thomas Moore and later of the Young Ireland poets proved equally inspirational. Finally, as popular literacy increased, so did the influence of the press on public opinion; however, again there was ideological continuity, for Irish Protestants complained early on that the newspapers "lowest in principles, or more properly speaking, of bad principles," were the only ones read by rural Catholics. Ballads, songbooks, pamphlets, "seditious" newspapers: as an official in Dublin Castle lamented, all these kept "alive in the heart of the Irish peasant the sense of bondage—the deep, unquenchable hatred of the oppressor."[110]

In short, the middle-class Catholic politicians, lawyers, editors, strong farmers, and clerics who wanted to mount a mass-based political offensive against the Protestant Ascendancy had a wealth of popular bitterness to draw on. As a witness before a parliamentary committee testified in 1825, "upon the whole the Catholic population is a great *mass of discontent ready to be operated upon by any political adventurer.*" However, O'Connell and the bishops faced two major problems. First, although peasant nationalism was genuine and instinctive, it was usually also passive and rhetorical. Both Gaelic poetry and broadside ballads expressed dark dreams of vengeance, but they also reflected the late-eighteenth-century Irishman's lack of faith in his own power to seek retribution from the *Sasanaigh.* Filled with a sense of their own sinfulness and impotence, most countrymen seem to have agreed with Humphrey O'Sullivan that only foreign intervention or the "Omnipotent God will strike off us these Saxon shackles" and "break . . . the tooth of the harrow under which they have been harrying us for hundreds of years." Generally, there was an enormous gap between aspiration and action, between rhetorical defiance and practical deference in the face of Ascendancy domination. Schoolmasters who denounced landlords and magistrates to sympathetic audiences were equally ready to address them for favors in the most sycophantic tones. Whatever their members' real opinions as to the rightful ownership of the land, the secret agrarian societies usually confined themselves to pragmatic goals and appeals for paternalistic indulgence. Fueled by whiskey, old resentments and new grievances often led to rebellious words and gestures, but, as several travelers remarked, "every one knows how easily . . . an Irish mob is reduced to obedience by a very trifling display of firmness and force." Even in the late nineteenth century, many rural Catholics still cringed, hats in hand, before those they regarded as their "earthly lords."[111]

However, would-be Catholic leaders also faced a much different problem. Not only did they have to mobilize and activate peasant nationalism but they also had to control and channel its potential force. O'Connell and the bishops were conservative, constitutional agitators: while they often threatened that violence might erupt if the government did not meet their demands, they sought also to demonstrate that Irish Catholics were respectable and law abiding. However, when rural resentments against the gentry or *Sasanaigh* did break out in concerted action, too often it took the forms of midnight assassinations, pitched battles with the hated "Peelers," or, at worst, the wholesale massacres of Protestants which disgraced the United Irish rising in south Leinster. Furthermore, neither the traditional idiom nor many of the concepts of peasant nationalism were appropriate to the tactics and aspirations of bourgeois politicians. When O'Connell and other leaders delivered their long speeches to stir the Irish masses, they were equally concerned that, through the press, their words made a forceful impression upon British opinion: for such purpose the Irish language was a useless medium for agitation, regardless of the wealth of nationalist sentiments it could express. More important, the popular conviction that Irish soil was the rightful inheritance of *all* Catholics not only challenged Protestant landlords' property rights—which O'Connell did not question—but also threatened the extensive holdings of well-to-do Catholics. Neither the social radicalism of the Defenders nor the prediction of the Gaelic poet Raifteirí that "Land shall be without price" when the *Sasanaigh* lay "troubled and ruined" was compatible with the capitalist ethos of Catholic gentry, graziers, and strong farmers who feared the land hunger of their own, truly dispossessed lower classes. Indeed, it was no accident that neither middle-class Catholic nationalists nor their church took up the popular cry of "the land for the people" until after the Great Famine had decimated the ranks of smallholders, cottiers, and laborers and had eliminated most of them from contention for the spoils.[112]

Thus, in the pre-Famine decades middle-class Catholics had to steer the ship of constitutional nationalism between Scylla and Charybdis: they had to articulate their people's ancient grudges and everyday grievances in such a way that they would be focused exclusively on England and the Ascendancy, not on propertied Catholics; they had to organize a diffuse mass discontent into an effective political movement, but without allowing the consequent agitation to burst into uncontrolled violence or open rebellion. To a large extent, O'Connell, the bishops, and other leaders of the campaigns for emancipation, abolition of tithes, and repeal were remarkably successful. Throughout much of Catholic Ireland the political associations they founded to marshal public support for their goals succeeded in transcending localism and rural-urban divisions, and they constituted almost an alternative government—with its own "magistrates" and arbitration boards—which both enforced social discipline and protected its members against Protestant reprisals. The brilliant tactical device of the "Catholic rent" mobilized the masses behind middle-class leadership by allowing the poorest peasants to join the Catholic and the Repeal associations for dues of only 1d. per month. Ascendancy officials perceptively denounced the

Catholic rent as "the wickedest contrivance of mischief . . . , and the most efficient . . . that has ever been thought of," for "[i]t brings the lowest person in the scale of that persuasion almost into contact with the highest, and . . . forms a stronger bond of union . . . than anything" which had previously occurred. O'Connell's successful enlistment of the Catholic hierarchy and clergy in his crusades restored the church to the "patriotic" status it had enjoyed in the early eighteenth century, and enabled the priests to reemerge as "champions of the people" without forfeiting their social ties to the rural bourgeoisie. In most instances, priests headed the parish branches of the associations, while strong farmers and shopkeepers served as dues collectors: an effective local alliance of secular and spiritual power that virtually compelled lower-class deference to the leaders of "the cause." The clergy also became active in other ways: along with the graziers, they spearheaded the crusade against tithes; they collected money to save tenants from eviction, led boycotts of Protestant shopkeepers, and often forcibly supplanted Ascendancy influence in the fields of education and charity. In their sermons they wisely tempered their formerly strident criticism of lower-class Catholic "improvidence" and instead preached a virtual holy war against Protestants, damning them as alien oppressors and immoral materialists and condemning as "traitors" any parishioners who refused to pay the Catholic rent.[113]

Both secular and clerical nationalists largely succeeded in convincing most Catholics that essentially bourgeois goals such as emancipation and repeal would somehow produce all the glorious consequences which the poets and ballad singers had prophesied. If the peasants "were quiet and would follow their leaders," promised the agitators, "they would lead them to liberty . . . and to the recovery of those lands that were taken . . . formerly by soldiers and marauders." "There is but one thing can save Ireland," declared O'Connell, "and that is repeal! The wellbeing of all of you depends on repeal! With repeal you will be happy and rich, and obtain all you wish and strive for." The nationalists also persuaded the masses that Protestant landlords and Anglican parsons—not Catholic middlemen or traders—were the true "parasites" on Irish society and that ultimately England alone was responsible for all Ireland's woes. The Protestant "aristocracy is the cause of all our miseries," avowed a Connaught priest, for it "has a definite, permanent interest in making the people poverty-stricken." "[The] more wretched the people are," he illogically concluded, "the easier it is to impose hard conditions of rent for farms." "Who . . . is to blame," asked O'Connell, "if we are poor, and cannot clothe and feed ourselves better than we do? . . . Ay, the Saxons are to blame! Whose fault is it that . . . so many human beings . . . die annually of hunger? . . . Ay, the Saxons! Who has destroyed our manufactures and our industry? The Saxons! . . . Yes, the Saxons! the English! despotic England is to blame" for oppressing "our beautiful, much to be pitied Ireland!" Such public utterance of old, half-hidden sentiments helped to erode much of the deference formerly characteristic of Protestant-Catholic relations. As a result, lamented one Protestant in 1838, "[t]imes are greatly changed in every part of Ireland. The gentleman must formerly have given no small provocation before any of the lower classes, even in their liquor, would proceed to incivility, but now, under very careful instruction, much of the former deference is disused, and it is neither safe nor prudent to interfere with them. . . ." "No matter," declared a later American visitor, "if the landlord is an Irishman, and the middleman lays on the exorbitant rents, or the small farmers charge enormously for con-acres. England is at fault for every thing." Finally, through their extravagant promises, and by shrewdly linking their political movements to Father Mathew's contemporary crusade for abstinence from drink, the nationalists were at least temporarily able to restrain the secret agrarian societies and the Catholic trade unions and to maintain order and sobriety among their followers. O'Connell boasted that his agitation diminished rural outrages by giving the peasants a constitutional outlet for their grievances, while the priests served as "a dragchain which restrained the people from violence."[114]

For the leaders of the political campaigns, the results were generally satisfying. In 1828 the priests in County Clare marshaled the Catholic 40s. freeholders to vote O'Connell to Parliament over the Protestant candidate supported by their landlords; in the next year, the Tories capitulated and allowed emancipation to become law. Henceforth, O'Connell and other Irish Catholics sat in Westminster and, by allying with the Whigs, were able to secure Catholic appointments and pass legislation which improved the status of middle-class Catholics and increased the church's influence, particularly in education. Tithes were not abolished, but legislation in 1838 converted them into charges on rents, thus eliminating the hated tithe proctors. Moreover, the position of the Church of Ireland was fatally weakened, and not even a renewed evangelical crusade could prevent its eventual disestablishment in 1869. Only over repeal did O'Connell and his followers suffer total defeat. More important for the future, the political movements of the early nineteenth century helped bind many of the fragments of Catholic society, and they were instrumental in creating the aggressive, ostentatiously Catholic, Irish "nation" which seemed so anomalous in an increasingly secular Europe. However, this success had certain ambiguous consequences. The ties forged between lay nationalists and the Catholic church were mutually constraining as well as beneficial. The church's backing brought political victories, but also forced the nationalists to pursue clerical goals which virtually eliminated any hope that a significant number of middle-class Protestants could be enlisted in their cause; thus, by the early 1840s foreign visitors were describing Irish society as almost totally divided into two bitterly hostile camps. Similarly, on the local level the agitation made Catholicism and popular nationalism so inseparable that in political matters it was difficult to tell, as different critics claimed, whether the priests were absolute "tyrants" over their flocks or "the slaves of the people." Moreover, the somewhat spurious link created between middle-class nationalism and the socioeconomic grievances of the Catholic poor meant that the lower classes were never able to mount an effective challenge to the hegemony of their affluent coreligionists: without middle-class nationalist and clerical support, they were isolated and condemned as "traitors to Ireland"—especially if they sought alliances with working-class Protestants; however, with such support, the social content of their protests was diluted and rendered innocuous.[115]

However, these were problems for the future, as even on the Famine's eve large cracks and flaws remained in the façade of Catholic solidarity. As was noted earlier, widespread participation in the campaigns for emancipation, abolition of tithes, and repeal was largely confined to the commercialized south and east of Ireland; in Connaught and west Munster modern political consciousness remained limited, and in Ulster the Ribbonmen were still the Catholics' primary spokesmen. Throughout much of the country, especially in the West, fear of and deference toward Protestant gentry and magistrates were far from eradicated. "Any man must obey his landlord," said a west Munster tenant in 1853, "when he has got a good landlord." Furthermore, many of O'Connell's enthusiastic followers made only a shallow conversion to the pragmatic gospel of constitutional nationalism. Instead, they viewed him as a new savior and "protector," sent to free them from bondage, and they believed that his limited programs were but preliminary to a last great rising which would destroy the *Sasanaigh,* parcel out their estates, and usher in a pastoral millennium. Consequently, while O'Connell strove to reassure frightened Protestants, sectarian violence wracked the countryside as his deluded adherents anticipated the fulfillment of Pastorini's visions. Yet neither O'Connell nor the bishops had any real answers to the pressing problems of land hunger and poverty, and their failure to achieve repeal peacefully seemed to prove that ultimate national aspirations could not be realized without bloodshed and rebellion. And so the secret agrarian societies continued their midnight activities with only intermittent lulls, and the United Irishmen's legacy of insurrection remained alive in the hearts of the dispossessed and disillusioned. Finally, the political crusades of the early nineteenth century did not really achieve the desired degree of social unity between propertied and propertyless Catholics. As one priest candidly admitted, "Catholics and Protestants oppress the people in about the same way. The moment a Catholic becomes a great landowner he conceives the same egotistical dislike . . . for the interest of the people. Like the others, he eagerly seizes on all means of enriching himself at the expense of the poor." At the other end of the scale, observed a traveler, "[t]he poor men of Ireland . . . seemed . . . to indulge in no transcendental theories of politics. . . . They looked only to their individual wants and wrongs, and sought redress for these in . . . plain practical form[s]. . . ." In short, the Catholic lower classes, particularly the laborers, continued to resist bourgeois and clerical leadership; in the early 1840s they were still forcibly demanding that priests reduce their dues, and still assaulting graziers and strong farmers regardless of their religion or nationalist activities. In desperation, churchmen formed vigilante organizations composed of priests and "respectable" tenants to combat such lawlessness. However, the eventual triumph of those who represented "modern" Ireland awaited the fortuitous catastrophe of the Great Famine and the massive emigrations of those who might have challenged the shape of their creation.[116]

3
Continuity: The Culture
of Exile

In the early nineteenth century, most British statesmen and economists argued that the remedy for Ireland's economic backwardness and social turbulence was the establishment of a capitalistic, extensive agriculture in place of the multitude of miserable potato gardens which still dominated most of the landscape. Such Englishmen were advocating nothing new; Ireland's transformation into an economically subordinate supplier of raw materials for urban, industrial Britain had been under way for over a century. What was novel was their open admission that this transformation could be completed only if accompanied by large-scale Irish emigration. To politicians weaned on the seemingly irrefutable logic of Adam Smith, Parson Malthus, and the Manchester liberals, wholesale depopulation seemed the most rational and humane solution to Irish destitution and disturbance. Not only would the soil be cleared of unprofitable and disgruntled subsistence cultivators and underemployed laborers—thus presaging an anticipated flood of capital investment in more rural improvements—but in theory the fortunate emigrants themselves would inevitably benefit by transferring their labor to overseas markets which needed the strength and stamina so underutilized at home. In short, to Britain's rulers and Ireland's owners, rural-to-urban migration seemed the natural concomitant to the commercialization of Irish agriculture; and since most Irish cities and industries were stagnant or declining, emigration abroad seemed to disciples of laissez-faire the only alternative to poverty and discontent in what they considered an overpopulated countryside.[1]

However, to the consternation of English politicians and Irish landlords, in the eighteenth and early nineteenth centuries most Irishmen and -women did not adopt such a utilitarian attitude toward emigration, preferring to rely on both physical intimidation and a variety of rent-earning strategies to keep a tenuous hold on the land. Particularly exasperating to Irish proprietors and officials was that those they considered most superfluous and dangerous—Catholics, especially smallholders, cottiers, and laborers—also proved the most reluctant to go overseas permanently. From the early 1700s through the pre-Famine decades, puzzled observers wondered at what seemed a general Catholic resistance to emigration. "I am really at a loss to account for it," testified a Galway merchant in 1827, "but, unfortunately . . . they are attached to the place where they are bred, and unwilling to move. . . ." Of course, before the Great Famine many Irish Catholics did emigrate to North America or Great Britain, and during and after that catastrophe they formed a large majority of those who left their native land. However, during the eighteenth century Protestant Irish emigrants outnumbered Catholics by about three to one and continued to dominate the exodus until the late 1830s—a perplexing anomaly, considering that Catholics comprised 70 to 80 percent of Ireland's population, suffered severe socioeconomic and political burdens in their homeland, and before 1820 could have utilized the transatlantic traffic in indentured servants to the same degree as did poor Protestants who could not afford to pay their own way to North America. Equally puzzling is the fact that, although subject to the same general economic and demographic conditions encouraging emigration, far more Catholics than Protestants regarded emigration as tantamount to involuntary exile, compelled by British and landlord oppression. Before the Famine, emigrants' letters, songs, and corroboratory testimony demonstrated this distinction between Catholic and Protestant attitudes, and it became especially marked in the late nineteenth century, when the feeling of forced banishment among Catholics was so strong that it provided bitter nourishment for the flowering of Irish-American nationalism. And yet the vast majority of Irish emigrants, both Catholics and Protestants, left Ireland of their own free will, and most seem to have bettered their fortunes by doing so. Why, then, were Irish Catholics more reluctant to emigrate—more resistant to the lure of American opportunity—than were Irish Protestants? And why, when Catholics did emigrate, did they often regard themselves as involuntary exiles, driven out by political and religious tyranny, rather than as voluntary respondents to the same structural changes in rural society which encouraged Irish Protestants and other Europeans to leave their homes in search of cheaper land and higher wages?[2]

Certainly, Catholic Ireland had a long experience of political exile or banishment as a result of unsuccessful resistance to English rule. The flight of the Ulster earls O'Neill and O'Donnell in 1607, the Cromwellian transportations in the 1650s, and the departure of thousands of Wild Geese after Sarsfield's surrender at Limerick: all provided major themes for Gaelic poets and historic models for future emigrants steeped in the traditional culture. In the bards' laments the exiles were *"Ár gcuraidhe tréana léirscrios uainn tar sáil"* (Our mighty heroes swept from us beyond the sea); Ireland's "chiefs are gone," cried another singer:

> . . . There's none to bear
> Her cross or lift her from despair;
> The grieving lords take ship. With these
> Our very souls pass overseas.

Although some composers admitted, "If Providence has ordained that Ireland should be a new England, . . . to this island 'twere best to bid farewell," most poets—often exiles themselves—declared that their defeated lords went forth "sighing all the weary day and weeping all the night." "Though I journey eastwards across the sea," wrote Uilliam Nuinseann, banished scion of Old English nobility, "my heart has left me as I go: it loves no other realm but Ireland."[3]

Moreover, the exile motif in Gaelic literature embraced the Catholic Irish generally, not just the expatriated chieftains and soldiers. In the seventeenth century those poets who blamed Irish "sinfulness" for their defeats at English hands often drew a striking analogy between Irish Catholics and the Jews of the Old Testament: both had been God's chosen people; both fell from grace, suffered His wrath, and now lay under the "slavery" of their enemies; and both had been banished from their "holy land." *"Cosmhail re Cloinn Israhél,"* recorded one bard in the early 1600s:

> Like the Children of Israel
> under oppression in the east of Egypt
>   the Sons of Míl here about the Boyne
>   are leaving their native land.

"Ye Israelites of Egypt," cried another composer; "ye wretched inhabitants of this foreign land! Is there no relief for you? . . . a second Moses?"[4]

Conceived in the late sixteenth and early seventeenth centuries, these exile themes not only persisted in Gaelic poetry but also found later expression in nationalist literature composed in English. During the late eighteenth and nineteenth centuries, broadside ballads drew parallels between yesterday's banished leaders and contemporary champions such as the exiled United Irishmen and members of secret agrarian societies transported to penal servitude in Australia. Similarly, patriotic orators proudly proclaimed that, like the Jews, the Irish at home and abroad would cleave to their faith, remember their Jerusalem, and redeem their homeland from foreign bondage. However, the image of emigration as exile long antedated the Anglo-Irish struggle. For example, in the sixth and seventh centuries the Irish missionaries who spread Christianity throughout northern Europe described themselves as "exiles for Christ," enduring what was known as "white martyrdom for a man, when for God's sake he parts from everything that he loves." Ironically, among the most famous of these self-exiled pilgrims was the semilegendary St. Brendan, who purportedly sailed west into the uncharted ocean and discovered strange new worlds for God's glory. Yet despite their high calling, the lament attributed to St. Columcille indicated the missionaries' sorrow at leaving their homeland:

> The seagulls of Lough Foyle
> are before me and behind me. . . .
>
> I direct my gaze across the sea
> to the plain of the luxuriant oaks,

> great is the tear of my bright grey eye
> as I look back at Ireland . . .
> it will never again see
> Ireland's men or its women. . . .

> Take my blessing back with you;
> my heart is broken in my breast;
>> if I should happen to meet death,
>> it will be because I have loved Ireland too well.

In short, from earliest times the very act of leaving Ireland, for *any* reason, was perceived sorrowfully in Gaelic culture.[5]

The specific words used by Irish speakers to describe emigration expose the sources of this thought pattern. Words, like all linguistic phenomena, are social facts and do not exist apart from the particular culture which employs them as a means of communication. Scholars such as B. L. Whorf have argued that a careful examination of words, both etymologically and in their relationship with others in the same semantic system, can reveal much about the structure and thought of a given society. Although still controversial, Whorf's hypotheses are especially useful in the present context. It may be very significant that the Irish language had no equivalent for the English word "emigrant," with its voluntary and emotionally neutral connotations. Rather, the Irish word primarily used to describe one who left Ireland has been *deoraí,* the literal meaning of which is "exile." In Old Irish, the form *deoraid* was a legal term referring to a person without property, and, given the intimate relations under the *brehon* laws between property, family, and social bonds (particularly the tangible ties between lords and clients), the word also implied a person without kinfolk or social "place"—an outsider, a stranger, even an outlaw. Also, Irish poets often employed two additional words to describe a person who left Ireland: *díthreabhach,* which meant one who was homeless; and *díbeartach,* meaning one who suffered banishment. Thus, the Irish language, when combined with the poets' interpretation of postconquest Irish history, provided both linguistic patterns and heroic models to predispose the Catholic Irish to regard all those who left Ireland as unwilling and tragic political exiles. Indeed, in the seventeenth century Gaelic bards used even stronger terms—such as *priosáil,* meaning "impressed" or "conscripted"— which linked emigration with coercion.[6]

In addition, the acute yearning of many Irish abroad for their birthplace probably had its roots in *dúchas,* the unusually intimate attachment between Irish-speakers and their native surroundings: topographical, familial, and cultural. In the early nineteenth century, numerous observers remarked upon the strong bonds between the Catholic peasantry and their localities. "They are warmly attached to their native soil, to their cabins, their families, and to old customs and habits," declared an Ulsterman; and in Munster another witness agreed that their affection for "their native land is wonderful, and in banishment or even emigration there is an air of romance thrown around every recollection of the country where they have toiled for mere subsistence." This attachment was expressed in several overlapping categories of popular Gaelic poetry which were still being composed on the Famine's eve: songs in praise of place (*dánta faoi'n dúlraidh*), patriotic verse (*dánta tír ghradh*), and exile poetry. It was also evident in the more recent, published autobiographies by Irish-speakers from west Munster and other coastal districts: "Wherever a person is reared," declared a Blasket Islander, "that's the place he'd rather be." Furthermore, all these literary sources and others such as the *aisling* poems, also evinced a strong and bitterly resentful racial exclusiveness: an "us versus them," of Catholic *Gael* versus Protestant *Sasanaigh,* which intensified from the late sixteenth century on as political and cultural discontinuities became inseparable from religious persecution and economic injustice. Modern Irish nationalism, although expressed largely in English, later corroborated and focused the older attachments and resentments, which survived into the age of mass emigration in a pervasive tendency to blame Protestant superiors and English misgovernment both for the demise of a romanticized Gaelic order and for all the contemporary ills, even the most impersonal, which afflicted Irish society. In the early nineteenth century, such sentiments found expression in compositions by Gaelic poets in all four provinces, as well as in Daniel O'Connell's orations. In all circumstances, however mundane, Irish Catholics were portrayed as "victims" of English and Protestant oppression. Humphrey O'Sullivan, the Kilkenny diarist, was only one of many representative figures who related all these themes to the phenomenon of emigration: "Many a hardship the poor children of the Gael undergo in search of honest bread in strange lands," he lamented, "since the sons of the foreigner chanced to come to Ireland."[7]

By themselves, neither the force of the terms *deoraí* and *díbeartach,* nor the passion of localism in Gaelic culture, nor even the strength of an anti-"foreign" tradition (which included Irish-born Protestants) fully explains the persistence of the exile image or its prevalence among nineteenth-century, English-speaking emigrants. However, the resentment of all discontinuities, and their interpretation in a context of conquest and persecution, found renewed expression in a cult which interpreted emigration as forced exile—as the final, culminating oppression. Cultural predisposition, historic tradition, and contemporary mass migration merged in literary sources as separate as the late-eighteenth-century laments of the poet Donnchadh Ruadh Mac Conmara and the early-twentieth-century novel *Deoraidheacht,* by Pádraic Ó Conaire, who linked emigration with Anglicization, demoralization, and exile. Popular songs such as "Campbell's Exile of Erin," "An Díbeartach ó Éirinn," and "An Díbeartach," all extant in both Irish and English versions, demonstrated how the older traditions shaped the emergent broadside balladry of emigration composed in the conqueror's idiom. Indeed, the direct lineage is so intimate that it is impossible to maintain an artificial distinction between the "authenticity" of Gaelic materials and a supposedly synthetic quality often attributed to their English replacements. For example, the songs of Thomas Moore, although disparaged by later nationalists for their "whining lamentation over our eternal fall," were faithful reflections of the despairing tones of the Gaelic *aislingí*.[8]

More survived than merely a fashion of conceiving expatriation. Despite the waning of the Irish language, certain cultural patterns persisted to produce a native Irish worldview in which the old exile motif had a continuing validity. A wide variety of evidence suggests the existence of a series of basic distinctions which can be "characterized" as being between native Irish Catholic culture and Protestant Irish, British, and American cultures. Such distinctions were often employed for invidious purposes: to justify conquest, institutionalized prejudice, and Protestant social and political ascendancy both at home and abroad. Since the early Middle Ages, English apologists had characterized the Irish as barbaric, and by the nineteenth century the Anglo-American press and stage had created in "Paddy" a figure whose pathetic, comic, or malevolent qualities made him the supposed antithesis of the middle-class Englishman or North American. Nevertheless, despite past abuse, cultural distinctions consonant with recent scholarly findings are useful and valid insofar as they aid explanation of various anomalies in Irish and Irish-American life. George Templeton Strong, a mid-Victorian New Yorker, commented in his diary that the poor Irish in his city were "almost as remote from us in temperament and constitution as the Chinese"—a statement of patrician disdain, yet one which reflected the distance between Protestant American and traditional Irish attitudes and activities. Although many Americans, and some Irish and British Protestants, were notably more sympathetic, they usually believed that any understanding of the Catholic Irish required much effort and forbearance. "I love the Irish for their attachment to the faith and for many amiable and noble qualities," wrote the Yankee convert Orestes Brownson, "but they are deficient in good sense, sound judgement, and manly character."[9]

In broadest terms, much evidence indicates that, in contrast to the Protestants they encountered in Ireland and North America, the Catholic Irish were more communal than individualistic, more dependent than independent, more fatalistic than optimistic, more prone to accept conditions passively than to take initiatives for change, and more sensitive to the weight of tradition than to innovative possibilities for the future. Indeed, their perspectives seemed so premodern that to bourgeois observers from business-minded cultures, the native Irish often appeared "feckless," "child-like," and "irresponsible": inclined to behave or justify behavior in ways which avoided personal initiative and individual responsibility, especially as to livelihood.[10]

In the late eighteenth and early nineteenth centuries, Irish Catholic "character" came under particularly close scrutiny from British and Irish Protestants seeking to explain or ameliorate Catholic poverty and discontent. Although often acknowledging the Penal Laws' debilitating effects, such observers usually attributed Irish destitution primarily to the "heedless improvidence" of the poor Catholics themselves, in contrast to the "character of industry and enterprise" which purportedly animated Protestants in Ulster and elsewhere. Although sympathetic visitors like Arthur Young and H. D. Inglis found praiseworthy such Catholic traits as generous hospitality and cheerfulness in the face of want, they regarded these as inseparable from a pervasive lack of ambition. In the late 1770s Young lamented that rural Catholics in the north midlands "only work to eat, and, when provisions are plenty, will totally idle away so much of their time, that there is scarce any such thing as getting work done." Likewise, over thirty years later Edward Wakefield despaired of Ireland's economic "improvement" as long as its "inhabitants . . . have no desire to push their industry beyond that indolent exertion which procures them the bare necessities of life. . . ." "The Irish peasant is too easily satisfied," declared Inglis in 1834. "The English peasant will work, not only that he may live, but that he may live well and comfortably. The Irish peasant, on the contrary, will generally work only up to the acquirement of mere subsistence. . . ."[11]

Protestant observers attributed Irish "improvidence" to a number of interrelated causes. The shrewdest recognized that ancient communal values and work habits persisted despite commercialization. Caesar Otway argued that the legacy of rundale cultivation still inhibited individual initiative, for under that system "[a] man, if he wanted more tillage ground, could not go beyond the old village enclosure and take in a new spot for himself. No such thing: if he brought in any new piece to cultivation every householder had a right to his ridge therein, as well as the man who made the improvement." Other visitors noted that Catholic smallholders deeply resented individuals who attempted to better their condition, and often showed little regard for modern notions of private property; broken fences were a frequent problem for many landlords who discovered that it was "the habit of the population . . . to throw the ground they occupy into a sort of commonage that is quite inconsistent with any permanent improvement." Similarly, Wakefield observed that "Irish labourers never work singly"; they had "a sympathy of feeling, which makes company necessary," and they tended to labor at the pace set by the slowest member of the gang. In addition, the Catholic lower classes seemed to lack bourgeois concepts of time and deferred gratification: after spending long evenings talking, dancing, and drinking, they rose late in the mornings and looked only to "the benefits of the moment"; "tiresome Irish," exclaimed one exasperated proprietor, "when will you learn that time is valuable?"[12]

Many Protestant observers also blamed Catholic poverty on peasant traits of fatalism and conservatism. In 1812 a sympathetic traveler remarked, "[T]he poor Irishman endures all with fortitude and humility, even with a degree of content. . . . The degradation of the population . . . has endured from time immemorial, and they are themselves somewhat to blame for it. They want an independence of mind, which produces independence of station, and, with too indolent and obsequious a caress, they hug their poverty to their bosoms." "If you expect from them independent volition," warned an English journalist, "where no one has gone before, or enterprise of any kind, you will fail." Most critics believed that centuries-old patterns could be broken only by the "encouragement" of trustworthy, resident superiors: "The lower order have so great a dislike to change," declared an Anglican parson in County Waterford, "that without the exertions of some person possessing influence sufficient to alter the old mode for the better, it is vain to expect any agricultural improvements." However, other observers feared that such guidance only exacerbated Catholic "dependence" upon upper-class benevolence; and the most pessimistic believed that "even the presence of their lord would with difficulty overcome" the "inherent spirit of indolence and obstinacy" which enabled "the lower order of Irish . . . to live without any apparent notion of comfort or even common decency." Furthermore, whenever the Irish did achieve some temporary alleviation of their poverty, instead of investing in permanent improvements, too often they squandered their gains in "reckless" fashion: on lavish wedding feasts and funerals or on "intoxication and riot." And then, when economic disaster struck, the Catholic peasant "curses his stars, leaves the blame of his misfortune upon any body but himself, and with a blanket on his back, sets out to beg, with the consoling reflection, that it was his destiny, and could not be avoided." The result, Protestant critics concluded, was that the poorer Irish seemed, "notwithstanding so many apparent[ly remedial] causes of wretchedness, apparently at ease, and perfectly assimilated to their habitations" of misery. "Are we to set all this down to absenteeism, and pity poor injured Ireland?" asked the English novelist William Thackeray. "Is the landlord's absence the reason why the house is filthy, and Biddy lolls on the porch all day? People need not be dirty if they are ever so idle; if they are ever so poor, pigs and men need not live together." For most British and Irish Protestants, Irish Catholic destitution and dissatisfaction were the inevitable consequences of a simple moral equation: lack of ambition produced idleness; "idleness is the parent of want; want gives birth to discontent, and discontent produces anarchy, resistance to the laws, and rebellion."[13]

Anglo-Irish Protestant strictures were often brutally harsh, but sympathetic visitors from Europe and North America, and many middle-class Catholics themselves, advanced the same criticisms of the rural poor. Asenath Nicholson, a Yankee missionary who loved the native Irish and their culture, made the identical distinctions between them and their Protestant countrymen as did less benign observers. Both the Frenchman La Tocnaye and the German Johann Kohl remarked upon the peasants' stubborn conservatism, and the latter described them as "credulous, child-like," and overly "enthusiastic." In 1790 another French visitor likened Catholic Ireland to "an amiable child full of spirit"—a giddy, careless, mercurial younger "sister" to "steady, thrifty" England. "To deny the vices of the Irish people would be assuredly to contradict all evidence," declared the world traveler Gustave de Beaumont, who proceeded to characterize them as indolent, mendacious, reckless, and improvident. Middle-class Irish Catholics distressfully agreed. Not only converts to Protestantism such as the novelist William Carleton criticized the prevalence in rural Ireland of a "Paddy-Go-Easy" mentality which shunned cleanliness, order, industry, and efficiency. In 1835 the bishop of Kilkenny admitted to another Frenchman, Alexis de Tocqueville, that although Irish Catholics had "all the virtues dear to God," they "basically lack[ed] the civil virtues" preeminent among the English. Would-be political leaders despaired of emancipating a people so volatile, seemingly alternating between listless apathy and outbursts of "barbarous folly"; "how easy it is," observed a Kilkenny schoolmaster, "to induce the children of the Gael towards good or evil, with a little urging." "Our people," lamented a Wexford priest, "still have, and will, for a long time, have many of the vices of slaves."[14]

Finally, when accosted by the pre-Famine traveler or, later, by the folklorist and anthropologist, poor Catholics themselves gave evidence of a premodern mentality which viewed the universe as static and tradition bound, within which they were merely passive recipients of whatever bounties or ills God or fate saw fit to ordain. In the 1840s Mrs. Nicholson noted that " 'We must be patient with what the Almighty puts upon us' " was the peasants' "ready answer when their sufferings were mentioned." Early in the next century, an old woman in west Kerry expressed the same sense of resignation: "the way of the world," she declared, was "the same as God made it in the beginning." "We are under the mercy of the world," sighed another Irish-speaker, "and a poor mercy it is, hard living and little pay and the workhouse and the grave at the end of it all." The peasants found consolation in countless stories and songs which deprecated material achievement and warned that sudden affluence would bring inevitable ruin to its recipients. "As regards the person with most wealth," went a traditional song, "little goes with him to the grave but a little sheet of a shroud and a narrow wooden coffin." Beyond working for subsistence, effort was useless—even suspect and ridiculed—for "[a] man meets what is coming to him and he cannot avoid it." When death or hardship came, the native Irish merely resolved "to meet them with endurance" and to "live as long as we can and die when we can't help it." "We were poor people," remembered one elderly woman, and "[w]e accepted the kind of life that was ours and never wished for any other." In short, many poor Catholics—especially Irish-speakers—regarded themselves not as independent agents but as dependent patients, bound to their communal traditions and subject to the "twists and turns" of fate or to what one Donegal man called *"rotha mór an tsaoghail"* (the great wheel of life).[15]

Thus, whether native or foreign, Catholic or Protestant, sympathetic or critical, the sources concur and by their breadth suggest that much more was involved than a widespread character failure—the Victorian misreading of the evidence cited above. Rather, most Catholic Irish came from a sociocultural framework in which the concept of individuality was less sharply defined and hence less important than in contemporary Protestant frameworks. In abstract terms, both the Irish Catholic and the Anglo-American Protestant worldviews made a clear distinction between stasis (or patience) and action, with all the attendant features of that paradigm: communalism versus individualism, dependence versus independence, authority versus freedom, custom versus innovation, nonresponsibility versus responsibility. The greater Irish Catholic emphases on the first of each of these polarities stemmed from the preeminence they gave to stasis, as against the Anglo-American Protestant emphasis on action—an emphasis shared, albeit to a less pronounced degree, by Irish Protestants. Consequently, given the Irish Catholics' worldview, as well as their historical and literary traditions, it was understandable they would prove more resistant to permanent emigration, and more likely to regard themselves as forced exiles, than Irish Protestants. For emigration ideally demanded all the features or virtues of "action"—individual initiative, personal responsibility, independence from traditional constraints—whereas exile connoted the absence, even the opposite, of those qualities. As Wakefield invidiously put it, Catholics endured "degradation" at home because they lacked the "natural shrewdness and strength of mind" which urged their Protestant countrymen to go abroad.[16]

Of course, a worldview oriented toward stasis was not unique to Catholic Ireland, but was similar to those held by other "traditional" peasant and subsistence-based societies which discouraged individualism and had "a basically collective idea of man." Hence, it could be expected that many poor Protestants in rural Ireland would share at least some features of this premodern outlook and also that many Catholics would react to the commercialization of the Irish countryside by altering patterns of belief and behavior to comport with new realities and perceived opportunities. In short, it could be argued that the worldview, which in the late eighteenth and early nineteenth centuries seemed to most observers both pervasive among and confined exclusively to Irish Catholics, was in fact less a reflection of religion or ethnicity, as was commonly believed, than of economic situation and social class.[17]

To a degree, this was true. Both in the countryside and in towns the lower ranks of Protestants and Catholics shared numerous cultural characteristics: localism and familism; Celtic customs and superstitions; low rates of formal religious observance; an overfondness for whiskey; and strong emphasis on economic security and communal solidarity, which found expression in a variety of organizations, from the Oakboys to the Orange Order, which became active whenever Protestants felt that tenant-right or other communal prerogatives were threatened by landlords or Catholic competitors. Such similarities were most marked in the eighteenth century, before the individualizing influences of industrialization and evangelicalism had taken effect. For example, in the 1770s Arthur Young found little evidence of a "Protestant ethic" at work in many parts of rural Ulster: in heavily Anglican north Armagh, he discovered that "when provisions are very cheap the poor spend much of their time in whiskey-houses," while even master weavers invested in packs of hunting dogs and abandoned their looms whenever the cry of the chase was raised; among the Presbyterians of south Down, "the men do not work more than half what they might do, owing to the cheapness of provisions making them idle, as they think of nothing more than the present necessity"—criticisms identical to those later levied on "improvident" Catholics only.[18]

Conversely, perceptive observers noted that some Catholics exhibited admirably "modern" traits, particularly in south Leinster and other districts long subject to commercial and urban influences. Pre-Famine travelers such as Jacob Venedey found a prosperous, "rising middle class" half-hidden behind a semblance of universal poverty, and recent scholars conclude that strong and middling Catholic farmers were about as responsive to changing market conditions as their purportedly more "rational" counterparts elsewhere in northern Europe. Other observers denied that even lower-class Catholics were inveterately indolent. For example, in 1816 an Anglican pastor in County Armagh noted that in his parish "several of the roman catholics, incited by the prosperity which they saw attend the exertions of their protestant neighbours, have fully equalled them in a regular course of industry, sobriety, and neatness." Even Wakefield admitted that "a salutary change" often came over former rundale cultivators whose landlords "encouraged" them to adopt the "English mode of farming"; and Otway, after seeing how laboriously peasants in west Cork toiled to reclaim potato ground from the rocks and bogs—struggling up steep cliffs with creels of kelp for manure strapped to their backs—declared that "no one witnessing this . . . but must acknowledge that the Irish *can* be industrious." The "want of continuous employment, and of adequate remuneration when employed": this, argued a government commission in 1838, was the real cause of "those habits of lassitude" so common among the "lower Irish." "The poor Irish are only like the rest of the world," agreed a British economist; "they do not work when they get no return." "Often I have heard the peasant reproached for his idleness and drunkenness," wrote the French traveler, La Tocnaye, "but when one is reduced to the danger of dying from hunger, is it not a better thing to do nothing, since the most assiduous work will not hinder the evil from arriving?"[19]

Such evidence would indicate that a premodern Catholic Irish worldview was merely the reflection of a culture of impoverished peasants, perhaps exacerbated by conquest and systematic discrimination but—like similar traits among rural Protestants—destined to disappear rapidly before the spread of commerce, industry, communications, education, and political liberalization. Certainly, many contemporaries, Irish and foreign, believed with Gustave de Beaumont that "six hundred years of hereditary slavery, physical suffering, and moral oppression, *must* have deteriorated a nation, vitiated its blood, and tainted its habits." Even O'Connell characterized his poor followers as "crawling slaves," and observers as disparate as English travelers, Catholic churchmen, and members of the Protestant Ascendancy acknowledged that the poverty enforced by the Penal Laws had reduced most Catholics to a state of hopeless apathy—"patient and resigned to their humble condition in life"—punctuated only by wild outbursts of equally hopeless violence. Indeed, despite brief periods of relative prosperity for a minority of favored tenants, from the sevententh to the mid-nineteenth century most rural Catholics did experience both poverty and the necessity of submission—with psychological impacts traceable in the growing despair of Gaelic poets as well as in pitiful petitions from peasants themselves who complained, "Our heads, long bent beneath a Slavish yoke, require Support & encouragement towards their being raised to a natural Consistency: our mouths Can hardly open to express our humble complaints, being almost locked up in the sullen Spirit which darkens our intellects: Never was a Cause more miserable . . . than ours."[20]

There is little doubt that social status affected outlook among Irish Catholics and Protestants alike. Each society exhibited a range of normative emphases, from more traditional among subsistence cultivators to more "progressive" among urban entrepreneurs. However, the broad distinctions characterized between the two societies were too widely observed and pervasive to be dismissed as merely the product of temporal and material conditions—as simply a consequence of Catholic Ireland's numerical dominance by its impoverished lower classes. Granted that rural Catholics and Protestants displayed certain cultural similarities, that a Catholic middle class grew and prospered, and that the poor native Irish displayed more industry and ingenuity than was commonly recognized: still, the distinctive Irish Catholic attitude toward emigration demands explanation in the context of a worldview which was widely diffused among all social ranks.

What dampened the optimism of many pre-Famine observers was their recognition that middle-class Catholics, both urban and rural, often exhibited the same premodern attitudes as did their poorer coreligionists. An Irish economic historian recently noted the intensely familial and conservative nature of Catholic commercial enterprises in the eighteenth century; and in the nineteenth century travelers frequently contrasted the "improvidence, allied with a love of ostentation," characteristic of Catholic merchants and professionals in Dublin and Cork with the greater shrewdness and thrift displayed by their Protestant counterparts in Belfast and Britain. In 1834 H. D. Inglis lamented that "the Dublin tradesman sets up his car and his country-house, with a capital that a London tradesman would look upon but as a beginning for industry to work upon. . . ." The decayed appearance of many southern towns led visitors such as Thackeray to decry a lack of perseverance and public spirit among the rising native bourgeoisie: "The whole country is filled with such failures," he declared; "swaggering beginnings that could not be carried through; grand enterprises begun dashingly, and ending in shabby compromises or downright ruin." Similarly, other critics charged that affluent Catholic tenants invested neither energy nor capital sufficient to earn maximum possible returns from their holdings. In the 1770s Young argued that the strong farmer's preference for grazing over tillage was due less to relative price levels than to the fact that "cattle . . . will give him an idle, lazy superintendence, instead of an active attentive one." In the early nineteenth century, Wakefield observed that wealthy tenants in Meath were "so wedded to their old habits, that they never contemplate a change" in modes of housing or agriculture; and in 1852 another critic of the large farmers declared, "They will not lay out on the land a single shilling they can keep, never thinking how a shilling will double itself when laid out, while it will breed nothing in the purse. . . ." When asked the source of Ireland's poverty, a Catholic shopkeeper admitted, "Inherent want of enterprise in Irishmen themselves, leading them to hoard money when they should use it in business."[21]

In short, at least certain features of an Irish Catholic worldview emphasizing stasis seemed to transcend social and regional divisions. Moreover, this outlook displayed remarkable continuity over time. Comparing eighteenth-century economic development in Ireland and Scotland, two scholars recently concluded that, although the Irish had their apostles of progress, "the sense of a country vigorously determined to twist its fate to its advantage is peculiarly Scottish." Long after the Famine had wrought massive changes in Ireland's social fabric, both foreign and native observers lamented that many Irish Catholics, especially but not exclusively in the West, still seemed tradition bound, dependent, and nonresponsible compared with their Protestant countrymen. In 1949, nearly thirty years after the establishment of the Irish Free State had eliminated the overt manifestations of "English oppression" in most of the island, a citizen of the new republic lamented that "the Irish, for good or ill, are not a modern people. . . ." And a decade later, the author of *Dialann Deoraí* (Diary of an Exile), the autobiography of an Irish laborer in postwar Britain, reported that many of his fellow navvies still blamed Cromwell and the Penal Laws for Ireland's contemporary problems and for their own involuntary expatriation.[22]

The roots of an Irish Catholic worldview which carried the exile motif down to the present century lay in the secular, religious, and linguistic aspects of Gaelic culture (and in Ireland's Anglo-Norman culture insofar as it had been assimilated to Gaelic norms by the late seventeenth century). Certainly, experiences of conquest, proscription, and pauperization helped confirm cultural traits such as communalism, fatalism, and passivity. However, certain cultural features antedated those experiences and persisted long after subsequent events had mitigated or transcended the practical effects of confiscations and Penal Laws. Examining first the *secular* aspects of Gaelic culture: ideally and, to a great extent, practically, Irish society was hierarchical, communal, familial, and traditional—each quality diminishing the individual's importance in relation to society as a whole. Despite some social mobility, preconquest Gaelic society was basically status bound.

Social rank depended on family and inherited property; although the system of clientage enabled short-term acquisition of cattle or land, even prior to the Norman invasion the position of clients was deteriorating into quasi-serfdom, and afterward patron-client relations became increasingly arbitrary and autocratic. Evidence such as *Páirlimint Cloinne Tomáis* may indicate that conquest actually offered those of low status increased security or opportunity, but such literary sources also demonstrate the harsh strictures levied on those who attempted to rise above ascribed status. Certainly, confiscations and penal legislation debased those of high rank in Gaelic and Old English societies; however, it is probable that the great mass of Catholics experienced substantial continuity of condition from the seventeenth through the early nineteenth century. Save during brief periods of unusual prosperity, sustained amelioration was exceptional; for the vast majority, what fleeting opportunities existed were counterbalanced by rising rents, frequent poor harvests, and the practices of partible inheritance and—under the rundale system—periodic land redistribution. Even the physical configuration of rundale clachans and field patterns, as well as of traditional Irish farmhouses, embodied communal values—summed up by the colloquial term "through-other"—which imposed severe limits on individual activity and privacy. Thus, ambition was thwarted and ideally was inappropriate. The system both denied advancement and supported or "explained" the failure to rise. The individual's duties did not include self-betterment, and ambition or innovation often brought scorn, ridicule, even physical hindrance, from diverse sources such as the *comhar,* or peer group, and the secret agrarian societies.[23]

The preeminence of the family in Gaelic culture also diminished the individual's importance. In *brehon* law an Irishman without a family was legally and socially a nonentity. Hence, the early Gaelic poets placed enormous stress on genealogy, and ordinary folk were deeply anxious to be buried with their ancestors. Moreover, the traditional family itself was authoritarian and patriarchal: sons waiting for inheritances and women in general had limited public personalities; child-rearing practices seem to have been designed to inculcate a sense of duty and emotional dependence rather than individuality or self-reliance; outward shame and internalized guilt seem to have been the primary control mechanisms. In addition, larger social structures—such as the *túatha,* the church, the whole people, and later the secret societies and the nationalists' idealized polity—were all conceived as extensions or analogues of the family. Thus, the inhabitants of a particular village or parish were "children of the one mother"; the members of agrarian societies were "Sieve's children" or "sons to that poor old woman called Terry's Mother"; and the Irish, generally, were "children of the Gael" and, in 1916, "children of the nation" proclaimed on Easter Monday. Such feminine characterization of Irish social units is archaic, and the maternal imagery must have heightened the pressures toward conformity within the community.[24]

Finally, in the secular realm, the traditional nature of Gaelic society also buttressed dependent behavior and curtailed personal innovation. The weight of custom was tremendous. *Brehon* law was regarded as ideally immutable and comprehensive; similarly, Gaelic poets scorned originality which involved deviation from received forms of composition. Moreover, in everyday life the Irish regulated and judged experience by traditional proverbs, thus fitting events and behavior to a preexisting scheme. These received aphorisms stressed continuity and curbed individuality. Many specifically counseled passivity and fatalism: "Holy and blessed is he who is patient"; "What is fated for me is hard to shun"; "Good fortune is better than rising early"; "There is nothing in the world but mist, and prosperity lasts but a short time"—to cite but a few proverbs employed in the last century by Donegal Irish-speakers.[25]

The *religious* aspects of Irish culture reinforced the temporal side of life and sacralized its emphasis on tradition and communalism. In contrast to Florentine Catholicism, with its considerable individualism, medieval and early modern Irish Catholicism may have been shaped in these respects by its secular surroundings. Perhaps it was not merely fortuitous that Catholicism won an easy, bloodless acceptance in Gaelic society or that after the eighth century it was rather perfunctorily observed; for in a thriving secular culture, Catholicism was but a supportive and corroboratory subsystem—merely one of many props of Irish thought and behavior. Not until conquest swept away the old social structure did religion begin to assume its later preeminence. Nevertheless, there were some basic affinities between intrinsic aspects of Catholicism and those of the secular culture. For example, Catholicism is fundamentally collectivist and analogous to the authoritative Irish family. Individual salvation is primarily a consequence of membership in the baptized community and of adherence to essential dogma and rules of worship and conduct which—like the *brehon* laws and proverbs—are regarded as eternal and unalterable wisdom. In certain areas, individuality is inappropriate: the church authoritatively requires uniformity of belief and restricts personal interpretation of central doctrine. Even in the realm of behavior, Catholicism provides a framework which—while it intensifies personal responsibility to obey God's laws as interpreted by the church—limits the field of individuality. Beginning in the late nineteenth century, some Catholics expressed fears that Irish churchmen had overemphasized these constraints and produced among their parishioners an "obedience syndrome." Certainly, Irish Catholicism seems to have promoted a worldview which subordinated what one sociologist has called the "active virtues" of enterprise, initiative, and action to the exigencies of tradition, community, and conformity.[26]

Moreover, certain church teachings specifically reinforced secular emphases on passivity and fatalism. The relationship, if any, between religious belief and economic behavior is extremely controversial, but by the late nineteenth century several Irish and Irish-American Catholics, anticipating Max Weber, were analyzing the admitted differences in what they called "Material Progress" between themselves and their Protestant neighbors.

It was customary to attribute these to "English oppression," but clerical apologists such as Thomas Burke and Michael O'Riordan also cited approvingly their people's relative "spirituality" or unworldliness. Indeed, save perhaps for a brief period in the late eighteenth and early nineteenth centuries, when churchmen themselves fell under the influence of the "spirit of improvement," a deemphasis on striving for material success seems to have been a major theme of Irish Catholic sermons. In the early eighteenth century, Bishop O'Gallagher's popular sermons in Irish counseled humility, charity, and patience and denounced those "avaricious, . . . greedy beings" who procure "the transitory riches of this world, and who . . . forget the salvation of their soul." Nearly two centuries later an Irishman lamented, "The general drift of Catholic sermons, insofar as they deal with money, is not conducive to thrift, but to generosity. . . . the people are constantly reminded of the text that it is harder for a rich man to enter heaven than for a camel to go through the eye of a needle. . . ."[27]

In addition, Catholic teachings seem to have imparted to the Irish a strong sense of sinfulness and dependence on God's grace—perhaps overlapping with archaic concepts of shame, and intensified by historical experiences of defeat and impoverishment. In the Middle Ages, Anglo-Norman observers noted the Irish propensity to blame their defeats on their own moral transgressions—a tendency carried into modern times by Gaelic poets and churchmen such as O'Gallagher, who proclaimed that individual self-seeking and pride were among the worst "sins that brought ruin on the people of Ireland, and have given their estates and properties to other nations." Scholars have argued that eighteenth- and nineteenth-century Irish Catholicism was strongly influenced by Augustinian and Jansenist traditions, which overemphasized man's sinful nature consequent on Adam's fall, severely limited the scope for self-regeneration through reason and "good works," and thus placed primary reliance on negative sanctions ("Thou shalt not . . .") and church-centered devotional practices and penances, rather than on ethical behavior, as means of obtaining grace. For example, in the version of the Salve Regina favored by Irish-speakers in south Ulster, a sense of helplessness before God's judgment seems to have merged with historical and literary traditions of defeat and *díbeartach: "Is Ortsa a sgairteamuid . . ."*—"To you do we cry, poor exiled children of Eve, to you do we send up our sighs, mourning and weeping in this valley of tears. And after our banishment in this life is finished, show to us the blessed fruit of thy womb, Jesus." To Irish Catholics, "exile" had spiritual as well as secular connotations.[28]

Of course, before the late nineteenth century the Irish church lacked the means to fully order, much less to homogenize, Irish Catholicism. However, the peasantry's premodern Catholicism also emphasized passivity and fatalism by stressing the magical and customary elements of religion. Through festivals and other predictive celebrations, the Irish strove to perpetuate their universe and ensure bountiful crops and healthy livestock. Long after the Famine, rural Catholics gave preeminence to mechanical and magical means of expiation—a tendency inadvertently reinforced, perhaps, by their church's emphasis on formal rather than internalized devotion. For example, when a girl on Great Blasket Island stole from a neighbor and feared discovery and punishment, her friend did not counsel repentance or reparation but advised her, "Cut the Sign of the Cross on yourself, . . . and ask God to protect you [from your accuser]." In addition, widespread belief in the fairies—"religious" in its concern for the supernatural—likewise reinforced the inhibitions of Gaelic society; for, like Bishop O'Gallagher's vengeful God, and like the priests—also deemed to possess unearthly powers—the fairies had to be propitiated by rigid adherence to set forms of "worship" and respect.[29]

Thus, in Irish peasant society the religious and secular injunctions against explicit individualism so intertwined that they can scarcely be separated. Distinctions between the resultant outlook and that of Irish Protestants could be very sharp. Jack White, author of a recent work on Irish Protestants, has written, "Deep in the fabric of all Protestants there is a belief in the importance of the Reformation as one of the great liberations of human history. They believe in it as a bursting of the bars, as a triumph of the spirit of the individual over the dead hand of the institution." After Luther's protest, the only spiritual authority was God Himself, and theoretically all Protestants had an equal right to interpret His Word. In short, White concludes, "The Protestant sees his church as an institution created to serve him." Of course, in practice the needs of minority solidarity in the face of "papist aggression" restrained the individualist impact of such convictions—"The boys must all show themselves" in the annual Orange parades, declared one Ulsterman; "else how could we tell whether they are of the right or wrong sort?"—although in Britain and especially in the United States, as Tocqueville observed, they had full play. However, even in Ireland there were fundamental differences. Among Presbyterians, their representative form of church government; their close, contentious scrutiny of the Bible and of their ministers' doctrinal purity; their repeated schisms and secessions; and after 1800, among both Dissenters and Anglicans, their evangelical spirit, reflected in periodic revivals and anguished self-examinations: all led to a fracturing of spiritual authority and an acceptance of religious (if not political) diversity among Protestants in Ireland as in America. The consequences were very alien to Irish Catholics' more traditional patterns of faith and religious expression. For example, Arthur Quin, a poor emigrant from County Tyrone, related to religion much differently than did his Protestant neighbors in upstate New York, lately "burned over" by revivalism, sect formation, and interdenominational rivalry. "There is a great change for the better since we came here," he wrote home in 1873; "it will be our neglect if we dont attend our duty their was only one priest before but now there is two and the[y] have mass every Sunday and the[y] *make* the people attend there duty well. . . ." Quin's wording betrays an outlook worlds removed from the region's special dedication to personal inspiration, associated with leaders such as

Charles G. Finney and Joseph Smith. Both in Ireland and in America, outsiders were amazed, often repelled, to observe that, as a papal emissary wrote in 1853, Irish Catholics "see in their priests not a simple minister of religion, but their father, their magistrate, their judge, their king, their 'papa,' their idol." In short, the weight of authority was preeminent in the religious as well as the secular aspects of Irish culture. Spiritual individualism was associated with Protestantism and condemned by the church as leading to licentiousness and atheism. "I know that Catholics may not lawfully believe or do some things as to which non-Catholics enjoy untrammelled scope for thought and action," declared an Irish cleric. "But, if those things are wrong it is not liberty of thought to assent to them; [nor] . . . liberty of action to do them . . . , but license in both. . . ."[30]

Finally, the semantic structure of the Irish language itself reflected and reinforced an Irish worldview which emphasized dependence and passivity. Although scholars debate whether words and grammars available to speakers predetermine their experienced world, none deny that languages vary widely in the way they "cut up" or classify experience in apparently arbitrary ways. Languages are not predetermined by the structures of the facts with which they must deal; the relationships are neither closed nor given. Languages and the cultures related to them in turn variously influence the received world, and hence the outlook, of their speakers. The categories of a language like Irish may represent one mode—analogous to others, such as law, religion, social organization—whereby society "explains" its values to itself and constitutes its culture. Language thus plays a corroborative role in the formation of a worldview, and a culture can be seen as a structure of conceptual systems, including language, each of which—using its peculiar terms—reinforces the others.[31]

In each of its systems traditional Irish culture draws a careful distinction between "patience" and "action" (or, dependence and independence). Indeed, the opposition between these categories may be regarded as a central element of the Irish worldview. Simply stated, the one category ("action") views the participant in a given event as an "initiator," the other category ("patience") as an "experiencer." The initiator is viewed as exercising control, while the experiencer is regarded as passive. One either causes an event to happen, or an event happens to one. According to the Irish worldview, certain phenomena are marked as appropriate for patient participation; in other words, areas of responsibility and nonresponsibility are clearly delimited.[32]

Irish belongs to a large group of languages which give explicit formal expression to the patience/action opposition. Such languages are known as "stative-active"—as opposed to "nominative" languages such as English, in which the underlying semantic opposition is blurred. For example, the English-speaker says "I eat" and "I am black-haired." Structurally, the two sentences are identical, obscuring the fact that the former is an "active" sentence, expressing agency and independent participation, while the latter is "stative," signifying patient and dependent participation, since, in the natural course of events, "I" has no control over the hair color imposed by nature. Thus, in English the formal opposition between initiator and experiencer (in the first person, for example) is expressed formally by "I" versus "me" (or, as the case may be, by "I" versus "for me" or "to me," and so on). Whenever a formal merger of such underlying semantic opposition takes place in English and other typically nominative languages, it is always in favor of the initiator (the "I"-form). Under such circumstances, the experiencer (e.g., the "black-haired" person) is inevitably colored with a tinge of agency, since the general meaning of the "I"-form is "initiator." In other words, the English language is weighted toward action, control, independence: its speakers will "see" a greater range of phenomena in terms of action than will speakers of a stative-active language such as Irish.[33]

In contrast, the Irish language explicitly recognizes distinctions between action and patience. For example, there are at least two Irish equivalents of the English sentence "I am sad": *tá brón orm* and *táim go brónach.* Both mean "I am sad," but they are not interchangeable, for they express fundamentally different relationships between the participant and his emotional state. The first sentence, *tá brón orm,* is stative; it literally means "sadness exists on me" and might be paraphrased as "I have been subjected to sadness," thus presenting the participant as the passive recipient of whatever "outside" action produced his or her sadness. The second sentence, *táim go brónach,* is essentially active; it says literally "I exist sadly" and presents the participant as *behaving* sadly. There are other Irish variations of "I am sad," but the point is that the Irish-speaker can carefully specify the relationship between the participant and his or her state of being, particularly whether the participant takes an active or passive role in the situation. In other words, the Irish language categorizes experience as either active or stative, and by making the distinction between the categories overt in the structure of sentences, forces an awareness of that distinction upon the Irish-speaker in a much stronger way than does a nominative language such as English, where the distinction remains covert.[34]

Furthermore, in comparison with English, the Irish language puts greater emphasis on passivity and nonresponsibility by classifying a far broader range of phenomena into an area in which action and self-assertion are inappropriate. In this respect, the Irish language provides a close analogue to, and therefore a reinforcer of, the other constituent systems of Irish culture. Although these linguistic oppositions are subtle, they are no more subtle or any less psychologically real than the stative-active oppositions which characterize law, religion, and mythology. For example, while the English-speaker says "I met him on the road," signifying that "I" was in control of the event, the Irish-speaker says *do casadh orm ar an mbóthar é*—literally, "He was twisted on me on the road," indicating passive reception of a fated or chance encounter. Finally, in practical usage Irish-speakers frequently chose a stative over an active way of expressing behavior, thereby demonstrating the interplay among historical tradition, worldview, and the categorical choices which a language offers. For example, when describing the act of emigration, an English-speaker might either say "he went to America" or "he had to go to America," depending upon whether the speaker wished to stress independent volition or passive necessity in the particular instance. The Irish-speaker *can* employ a phrase, *d'imthigh sé go Meirice,* which conveys the sense of purposeful action. However, in terms of the central thesis of this work, it is very significant that by far the most common way for an Irish-speaker to describe his emigration has been *dob éigean dom imeacht go Meirice:* "I had to go to America"; literally, "going to America was a necessity for me." Thus, Irish-speakers chose a patient over an active way of expressing their emigration. In fact, this sentence belongs to a type known in Irish grammar as "impersonal," and the function of such sentences is precisely to downgrade active participation and present inexorable fact. The message of the sentence is entirely consistent with the equally common use of the word *deoraí* (exile) to designate "emigrant," as one subject to imposed pressures. In short, *dob éigean dom imeacht go Meirice* meant that emigration was fate more than choice, necessity rather than opportunity. It was a natural, if perhaps ahistorical, step for a traditionalist people to inflate it by reference to the involuntary exile of banished cultural heroes such as O'Neill and Sarsfield.[35]

Thus, traditional Irish culture was composed of three interlocking subsystems—secular, religious, and linguistic—supporting a worldview which valued conservatism, collective behavior, and dependence and which limited individual responsibility in broad areas. The Irish Catholic's reluctance to emigrate—perhaps common in all peasant societies—and his characterization of emigration as exile were reinforced by historical and literary traditions and by cultural categories which laid unusual emphasis on stasis. In this context, aversion to emigration, even if economically desirable, and a view of emigration as involuntary expatriation were perfectly "rational."

As many of the conditions of life worsened from Tudor times onward, the Irish worldview's archaic constraints took on a new reality in explanation of passively experienced trials and the need for collective endurance. However, as Chapter 2 demonstrated, beginning in the late eighteenth century waves of commercialization and Anglicization swept away much that remained of the old culture and challenged the relevance of a worldview which placed primary emphasis on stasis. Contemporary descriptions of pre-Famine Ireland reflect a society marked by increasing socioeconomic and cultural differentiation, with ever-more distinct regions and classes in various stages of transition to modern ways of thinking and behaving. In the post-Famine decades, change was even more accelerated: death and departures overseas sharply reduced the laboring and subsistence-oriented sectors of the rural population, and by 1901 only 14 percent of the island's inhabitants still spoke Irish. Yet, despite these developments, the widespread persistence of premodern traits occasioned comment by native and by foreign observers from the late eighteenth through the early twentieth century. Nineteenth-century broadside ballads in English showed the same "obsession with failure, and . . . apparent acceptance of misfortune" which had been staples of earlier Gaelic poetry. Post-Famine travelers continued to describe Irish Catholics as obdurately conservative, "desperately afraid of responsibility," and "lamentably deficient in that practical common sense, persevering industry, and taste for the decencies and comforts of life, which constitute . . . 'civilization.' " Visitors to the western remnants of Irish-speaking Ireland were most frequent in their strictures, but others, such as Horace Plunkett, a sympathetic native Protestant, found pervasive both a "lack of moral courage, initiative, independence, and self-reliance" and a habit of blaming England for all Ireland's problems. Aspects of the old worldview continued to the most recent years, as a number of anthropological studies have demonstrated, and as a west Corkman implied when he acknowledged that country people still prefer "anonymity of action" over the assumption or attribution of individual responsibility.[36]

But how could these characteristics have persisted in the face of what recent Irish scholars term the "modernization" of Irish society? Perhaps such scholars, focused primarily on the phenomena of change, have been insufficiently attentive to continuities. Certainly, many of the social institutions and task orientations of the past which underlay archaic traits and outlooks lasted into the twentieth century to permit folklorists to collect a vast body of traditional oral culture and to enable anthropologists and historical geographers to reconstruct premodern patterns from such survivals. Moreover, although the Irish language almost disappeared outside a few western districts, those who abandoned Irish still preserved much of the sense as well as the stative grammatical structure of the old idiom in their Hiberno-English dialects. Recently current phrases such as "death came on him" and "there's a dread on me" (rather than "I am afraid") express the same passive and nonresponsible viewpoint as their older Irish equivalents. Thus, the *categories* of Irish, not the physical act of speaking the language, provided the framework for the traditional worldview; if these were duplicated in the other, nonlinguistic aspects of Irish culture, the old outlook could be translated into another language. Perhaps more important, for most Irish Catholics the objective socioeconomic and political realities of the nineteenth and early twentieth centuries continued to be eminently "explainable" in premodern terms. Despite commercialization and political liberalization, until the early twentieth century crucial economic and political decisions affecting livelihood remained concentrated in the hands of an "alien" minority of Protestant landowners and English legislators and officials. As late as 1912 an English advocate of Irish self-government wrote that "British rule in Ireland is to be condemned . . . not so much for what it has done or has failed to do as for its inevitable and disintegrating influence on the character of the ruled. It has dissipated their sense of responsibility" and "encourages them to rely on external agencies instead of on themselves. . . ." A persistent dearth of economic opportunities also discouraged independence and initiative. Whatever material benefits accrued to Catholic smallholders, cottiers, and laborers during the relative prosperity of the late eighteenth and early nineteenth centuries largely evaporated in the severe depression following the Napoleonic Wars. The fatalism and millennialism of the pre-Famine decades were complementary, and it was understandable that the peasants regarded the Great Famine—itself awful "proof" of the validity of their old worldview—as the will of God. During and immediately after the Famine, the evictions of thousands of tenants and undertenants testified to their dependent and non-responsible status; and wholesale adjustments in post-Famine agricultural and inheritance patterns only debased the condition of laborers and farmers' noninheriting children. Economic stagnation persisted despite the partial achievement of political independence in 1921, and until the urban-industrial growth of the last few decades, a fatalistic attitude toward one's chances for material success—even for marriage—at home was not at variance with the realities faced by those without lands or dowries. In short, while sweeping changes occurred, some fundamental conditions endured.[37]

Of course, the traditional Irish worldview could not prevent commercialization, nor could the conception of emigration as exile preclude a massive Catholic exodus overseas. However, cultural conservatism may have regulated the pace of those developments, and it certainly provided a degree of psychological continuity. The careful distinction in Gaelic culture between stasis and action was conceptual and not necessarily carried over into behavior. That is, the Irish worldview described an *ideal* ordering of things: the ideal did not constrain behavior absolutely, but rather guided it—or, alternatively, "explained" it. Indeed, traditional conceptualization of decidedly nontraditional behavior becomes more necessary in periods of rapid socioeconomic change, as in Ireland from the late eighteenth century onward, to restore the psychic equilibrium between inherited attitudes and current activity. To members of the society concerned, the resultant "compromise" might be fairly satisfying, but to unsympathetic outsiders it might appear irrational, duplicitous, "hypocritical"—as Irish behavior often did appear to non-Catholic observers. Theorists of "cultural lag," the phenomenon described here, argue that such compromises can modify socioeconomic change itself by restricting the uses made of new opportunities, and can also affect the psychological adjustments of the people involved, sometimes very considerably. The result can be a kind of widespread "social sickness" when the changing society is one—like the Irish—which assigns a less significant value to "progress" than do the "modern" societies which it seeks to emulate. In Catholic Ireland, as in similar cultures, the consequent stress generated structures of thought, or ideologies, which had "the character of answers, cures, excuses, or even remorse": the peculiar fate of a colonized, traditionalist society, both jealous and defensive in the face of its conqueror's apparent superiority.[38]

Such explanatory thought structures can function on conscious as well as on unconscious levels. The Irish versions, although perhaps dysfunctional in the long term, certainly assisted as they modulated modernization: they provided a defensive ideological cement for a society faced with profound and potentially disintegrating change; and they moderated the tensions between older pressures for conformity and the thrust to modern, individualistic behavior. By accounting for their often innovative actions in pre-individualist, nonresponsible categories ("it was a necessity . . ."; "the boys have in mind that we all . . . ," as it would be expressed in the *comhar,* or peer group), many Catholic Irish could square their traditional outlook with the practice of a new and broader freedom of action. The very anonymity of such categories cloaked the rising tide of personal calculation in the face of a host of social institutions—for example, family, *comhars,* secret agrarian societies, the church—which could exert diverse degrees of pressure for conformity to communal obligations: shame, ridicule, ostracism, violence, even the threat of eternal damnation.

All these mechanisms sustained a common allegiance, or at least rhetorical obeisance, to the ideological adjustments to change prescribed by the traditional Irish worldview. Certainly, *some* sort of compromise was a psychological necessity. However, it would be naïve to assume that the precise forms of such adjustments were merely spontaneous or that they served no disinterested functions for those who formulated and enforced them. Such ideologies provided cultural and psychic continuity, but they were also instruments of hegemony. It was not fortuitous that the social institutions in Catholic Ireland which emerged preeminent from the wreckage of Gaelic culture were those which were in the forefront of modernization or "improvement" and which also found it most necessary to explain or justify their innovations in traditional contexts to inhibit resentment and conflict arising from those who suffered or felt aggrieved by the resultant discontinuities. At the risk of oversimplification, it could be argued that in nineteenth-century Catholic Ireland, especially in the "New Ireland" of the post-Famine decades, there were three dominant social forces, all closely associated with the growing *embourgeoisement* of Catholic society: first, the strong-farmer *type* of rural Irish family, which became ubiquitous after mid-century; second, the Catholic church, which through its "devotional revolution" in the same period imposed a high degree of homogeneity and moral order on its adherents; and, third, Irish nationalism in both its constitutional and its revolutionary forms, especially the former—commonly associated with strong farmers, urban middle classes, and village entrepreneurs. On the level of personal affiliation these categories often overlapped, as did their ideological affinities, and their influence increased as literacy rates rose and as competing sources of leadership and pressures for conformity—such as landlords, secret agrarian societies, premodern folk beliefs, and the formerly preponderant, traditionalist lower classes—lost potency or withered away during the Famine and its aftermath.[39]

Each of these three institutions—strong-farmer family type, church, and Irish nationalism (especially in its bourgeois aspects)—was both a creation and an agent of modernization. Commercialization created the socioeconomic base for their hegemony; and Anglicization provided their models for emulation as well as the means by which they could impose their ideals on a sometimes apathetic, even hostile populace. However, all three were also "carriers" and exponents of certain traditional attitudes and modes of behavior: functional necessities ensured cultural continuity. For example, the strong-farmer family type, which after the Famine became common among all classes of landholders, was designed to maximize and concentrate capital in the conjugal or stem family: hence, the widespread adoption of impartible inheritance, delayed retirement for household heads, and prolonged adolescence and postponed marriage for children—accompanied by extremely strong sanctions against premarital sex—despite the fact that such practices violated a broader and more traditional kinship ideology associated with the *derbfine,* rundale cultivation, and once-common customs of partible inheritance. In short, the strong-farmer family type upset older ideals of family arrangements, with consequences particularly disruptive in less affluent farm families where fathers lacked the resources to provide noninheriting children with marriage portions or sufficient education or training to enable them to pursue independent careers at home. However, such structural discontinuities made the retention and reemphasis of traditional, authoritarian, and patriarchal ideals of parent-child (especially father-son) relationships more crucial than ever to suppress intergenerational strife and prevent sexual mésalliances. As anthropological studies have shown, in the late nineteenth and early twentieth centuries rural parents continued to demand obedience and stigmatize "boldness" in children through a variety of mechanisms, such as ridicule, thereby producing offspring often characterized by emotional dependence, a strong sense of obligation, and an aversion to innovative behavior which might bring communal censure and "loss of face." Thus, despite some modifications, the patriarchal family persisted both as an ideal and in practice, although the actual degrees of reciprocity which once underlay it had been vitiated by parental responses to changing economic conditions.[40]

The nineteenth-century Irish church was also "modern," in its heavy financial reliance upon the Catholic bourgeoisie to support its educational and church-building programs, as well as in its ultimately successful campaign to replace archaic devotional practices with forms of regular worship prescribed by Rome. Through its dominance of the national primary and, later, secondary school systems, the church implicitly helped erode parochial and traditional attitudes; likewise, the church accepted and vindicated the strong-farmer family arrangements, extolling celibacy and imposing strict clerical sanctions on actual sexual transgressions and on potential "occasions of sin," such as "company-keeping" and traditional crossroads dancing, which threatened parents' careful calculations as to "matches" and inheritances. Also, the church usually gave at least tacit support to Irish nationalists, especially if constitutionalists, in their efforts to secure a greater degree of Irish self-government and, after the Famine, to overthrow landlordism. However, the church also provided continuity, for as the old secular and linguistic subsystems of Gaelic culture withered, the church—with its corroboratory ideal of the proper relationship between the individual and his universe—grew in compensatory cultural strength and importance, commanding increased devotion from a people who were beset by discontinuities and who saw themselves politically and culturally orphaned. In part, this increased devotion was spontaneous: supernatural "explanations" came naturally to a traditionalist people, and Irish Catholics had long regarded religion as a badge of national identity. However, in the early nineteenth century it was churchmen's conscious decision to disavow former accommodationist policies and to link arms with secular nationalists which reestablished the sociocultural dominance of the church itself. By the mid-1830s, Tocqueville remarked on the extraordinary unity between clerics and parishioners, particularly in commercialized counties like Carlow and Kilkenny, as well as on the "note of triumph" and "air of exultation at present or approaching victory" which characterized Irish bishops. A decade later, another traveler expressed concern that, because of increased clerical prestige, "there grows up the habit of the priest interfering in all matters—in extending his views from the church to the forum, and from the forum to the fireside, until at last he is engaged not only with political affairs, but also with domestic concerns, and thus may be induced to think more of his dominion than his doctrine"—a situation realized fully in the post-Famine decades. In several respects, the church's expanded authority helped perpetuate traditional patterns of behavior and outlook, even as it aided the hierarchy's campaign to modernize devotional practices. For example, despite the modernization of political attitudes which occurred in nineteenth-century Ireland, contemporary accounts indicate that tenants often experienced less of an awakening to issue-oriented politics than a transfer of old habits of deference from landlords to Catholic clergy; and by the end of the century, astonished contemporaries claimed that many parish priests had assumed virtually unchallenged authority over the lives and thoughts of their congregations.[41]

Thus, during this period of rapid change, and especially during severe crises such as the Great Famine, the churchmen "explained" events in familiar, traditional terms, upbraiding their parishioners for their supposed deviations from prescribed, collectivist behavior and enjoining humility, charity, obedience, and heightened devotion to and dependence upon spiritual authority for guidance in troubled times. For example, while they offered few practical solutions to the socioeconomic problems of landless laborers and farmers' children, churchmen apothesized the small family farm as the major bulwark of Catholic morality and Irish national identity against the secularism, materialism, and amoral individualism purportedly characteristic of English society and Protestantism. In short, although the church both relied upon and reinforced middle-class hegemony, by criticizing the *ultimate* tendencies of commercialization and by stigmatizing them as "alien," Catholic clerics not only provided psychic solace to the poor but also obscured social differentiation and mitigated class and inter-generational conflicts within the Catholic community. By all accounts the results were impressive: by 1900 Ireland's faithful constituted the most fervent—some said, the most clerically repressed—Catholic people in the world.[42]

Finally, Irish nationalism also combined modern and traditionalist elements. Both in its supralocal organization and in its ideal goal of the nation-state—whether republican or autonomist (e.g., "repeal" and "home rule")—Irish nationalism deviated from Gaelic and peasant political concepts. Originating in urbanized, Anglicized districts in eastern Ireland, its primary advocates were usually commercial farmers and middle-class professionals and entrepreneurs, such as village publicans, traders, and money-lenders who regarded nationalism, like ostentatious piety, both as a faith and as a necessary complement to their economic and social dominance of the countryside. However, on structural as well as ideological levels, Irish nationalism perpetuated traditional patterns of thought and behavior. For example, in most rural areas nationalist politics were intensely localistic and personalistic, allegiances being cemented by familial and patron-client ties—for instance, between creditor-shopkeepers and indebted smallholders—and enforced by traditional modes of intimidation such as peer pressure, socioeconomic ostracism (i.e., "boycotting"), clerical censure, and physical violence. Thus, as one visitor observed, by the early twentieth century Ireland had become "a network of 'organisations,' leagues, societies, factions and cliques. Almost every department of life seems to be on a committee basis," and "individual action and individual opinion are everywhere marshalled in subservience to the interests of this movement or that." Nationalist ideology also reinforced premodern tendencies toward dependence and nonresponsibility, not only by demanding collective obedience and self-abnegation but also by focusing Irish attention on the supposed external causes of all socioeconomic and cultural discontinuities. Of necessity, therefore, as well as by custom, nationalist rhetoric was tradition bound, feeding more on the past than the future: in countless ballads and interminable orations, the primary message was "Remember . . . , Remember . . . , Remember." "Speak to an Irish audience of the practical problems of the present, or of the practical ideals for the future, and it will remain unmoved," wrote an Irish scholar in 1916; but "recite to it the stirring deeds of Brian Boru, and it will thrill with patriotic emotion. Cry out with a tragic intonation 'Remember '98' and, whether it really knows what happened in 1798 or not, it will vow as one man never, never to forget it." In short, although doctrinal rifts among Irish nationalists allowed some latitude for political choices, nationalism—like family and church—stressed the individual's "duty" to conform to modern institutions cloaked in traditional garb. Mutually reinforcing, collectivist ideologies both "explained" and buttressed the hegemony of those who had achieved economic, social, and cultural dominance at the expense of the customs and the interests of a large portion of the Catholic community.[43]

Thus, aspects of the traditional Irish worldview persisted to recent times, and continued emphases upon collectivism, passivity, fatalism, and non-responsibility encouraged retention, by English- as well as by Irish-speakers, of the old perception of emigration as involuntary exile. Moreover, the social forces described above—strong-farmer family type, church, and na-tionalism—specifically perpetuated the exile motif in ways which justified and promoted their social and cultural authority. Representatives of all three institutions regarded emigration with ambivalence. On one hand, emigration was a necessary concomitant of Irish modernization: save in the context of mass migration overseas, bourgeois dominance of rural Ireland could not have been achieved without immeasurably greater tension and conflict within the Catholic community. Like the Great Famine, emigration provided for the rapid attrition of those groups and individuals most resis-tant to new socioeconomic and cultural patterns: especially the tradition-alist and disadvantaged lower classes, and farmers' noninheriting children. Wholesale emigration by these people, particularly during and after the Famine, enabled commercial farmers and graziers to expand and consoli-date their holdings with less fear of retaliatory violence from the land poor and the landless; it allowed rural parents to disinherit the majority of their offspring without severe disruption of domestic stability; it provided church-men with opportunities to impose their influence upon a diminishing but increasingly literate and "respectable" Catholic populace and to gain the glory of spreading the faith abroad via the emigrant stream; and, finally, it enabled bourgeois politicians to pursue nationalist goals largely without hindrance from lower-class-based movements which threatened collective purpose as well as the privileged status of nationalist leaders themselves. Moreover, the establishment of Catholic Irish communities overseas also served the New Ireland's practical needs. Less affluent farm families were dependent on emigrants' remittances from abroad, to finance subsequent departures without draining parental resources as well as to enable those at home to pay rents and shopkeepers' bills and to make "improvements." Likewise, the Irish church solicited money earned by emigrants to help finance church building and education. Finally, nationalists—constitutional-ists and revolutionaries alike—had especial need for aid from emigrants, for only the Irish abroad could generate sufficient capital, diplomatic pres-sure, and, on occasion, arms and trained soldiers to realize nationalist aspi-rations.[44]

On the other hand, however, emigration had its dangers. Wholesale departures by the country's "bone and sinew" seemed to portend the reali-zation of the old English goal of a pacified, pastoral, and largely Protestant Ireland. Furthermore, leaving Ireland—especially for anticipated personal gain—not only violated archaic sanctions but also threatened to mitigate the influence of family, church, and nationalism over the emigrants. To parents the departures of children were often occasions of grief, sometimes of bitter recriminations, for emigrants might withdraw practical as well as emotional sustenance, thereby abandoning parents to an impoverished as well as a lonely old age. To churchmen and nationalists emigration was a matter of equally grave concern, for emigrants freed from communal pressures might forget or forswear spiritual and political obligations. Despite the myth of unanimous emigrant loyalty and devotion to family, religion, and "sacred cause," these dangers were real, particularly if the landless and disinherited recognized that in specific instances their departures were often necessitated more by the calculated ambitions of Catholic parents and "land-grabbers" than by English/Protestant/landlord "oppression."[45]

In short, mass migration had both positive and negative implications for the dominant institutions of Catholic Ireland. Consequently, their spokesmen responded variously, at times encouraging emigration, especially for the most impoverished and disgruntled elements of society, but often adamantly opposing it, arguing that communal obligations and the physical and moral hazards of life abroad outweighed potentials for personal betterment. However, these institutions had helped create the compelling causes for emigration, and as individuals neither parents, clerics, nor bourgeois politicians could constrain what by mid-century had become a flood tide overseas. These realities combined with historic models, literary fashions, and the hegemonic necessities of family, church, and middle-class nationalism to perpetuate an "explanation" of emigration as exile which reconciled that phenomenon with traditional sanctions and contemporary communal exigencies and which fixed responsibility for the exodus on inexorable fate or, more commonly, English malevolence, rather than on Catholic parents and rural bourgeoisie or on the individual emigrants themselves. Thus, emigration, albeit lamented, could continue without challenging either the relevance of the old worldview or the hegemony of the very forces which helped impel departures; indeed, the continued conceptualization of emigration as exile served to buttress that hegemony by heightening popular loyalty to Catholic Ireland's clerical and political defenders against the "alien" elements deemed culpable for emigration as well as for all the other ills afflicting the island since the Norman invasion. Political speeches, sermons, the popular press, and especially emigrants' songs and ballads combined familial, religious, and national themes to portray Ireland's departing children as banished rebels and sorrowful victims of ancient, continuing oppression.[46]

In the early twentieth century, a sympathetic observer declared that in Ireland "coercion, in some form or other, is the rule of life." Certainly, the collective devotion to family, church, and the ideal of Irish nationality displayed by Irish-American Catholics generally—as well as by the letters and memoirs of many individual emigrants—demonstrated that the exile motif helped perpetuate traditional patterns of thought and behavior abroad and at home. Of course, both in Ireland and America, different classes and individuals experienced pressures for conformity in different degrees: some more, some less, which may partly explain their variant responses to emigration as exile or advantage. Even eager emigrants usually conformed publicly to traditional conceptualizations of nontraditional ambitions; however, at one end of the social scale, exceptionally secularized or Anglicized individuals and, at the other end, particularly disadvantaged or alienated smallholders, laborers, and farmers' children sometimes openly regarded emigration as fortuitous escape from intolerable constraints rather than as forced banishment. For some Irishmen and -women the contrast between ideology and reality became too blatant to palliate or ignore. Nevertheless, large numbers were sufficiently influenced by attitudes which prevailed among both traditional and modern sectors of Catholic society to maintain a common worldview which predetermined a discernibly national response to emigration as exile.[47]

TWO

The Patterns of Irish Emigration, 1607–1921

NEITHER IRISH POVERTY NOR American opportunity was alone sufficient to stimulate mass migration across the Atlantic Ocean. Ironically, in absolute terms Irish Catholics were more destitute and oppressed during the eighteenth century, when relatively few emigrated, than during the late nineteenth century, when millions went overseas. Similarly, although annual departure rates fluctuated in response to economic conditions abroad, overall far fewer Irish emigrated in the eighteenth and early nineteenth centuries, when American farmland was cheap and wages high, than later when New World circumstances were less favorable in many respects.

Irish emigration was most responsive to *change* within Ireland: change, real or anticipated, from a previously accepted status quo. Any number of developments could encourage individuals to emigrate, but generally most crucial were those attendant upon the commercialization of agriculture, the decline of rural industry, and the Anglicization of Irish cultures. By the late nineteenth century these developments—ruthlessly accelerated by the Great Famine and the wholesale evictions of 1845–55—had so thoroughly transformed Irish society that emigration had become an integral and essential feature of Irish life. However, these changes affected different groups within Irish society in different ways: notions of what conditions were acceptable, which changes intolerable, were far from uniform, and reactions varied accordingly. Socioeconomic, religious, cultural, regional, and political variables determined responses to emigration as advantage or necessity, as opportunity or exile, and those responses in turn influenced both the changing size and the character of the movements overseas.

Nearly all Irish emigrants shared a nostalgia rooted in the idylls of childhood memories. Thus, even so fabulously successful an emigrant as the financier Thomas Mellon wondered at the poignancy of his recollections of Ulster after sixty years in America, and concluded, "It must not only be true that we learn more in the first five years of life than in any ten years afterwards, but also that we retain whatever we learn in those five years incomparably better than anything we learn at a later date."[1] Nevertheless, Irish perceptions of emigration itself varied enormously, and in general Irish emigrants can be placed in three broad categories according to their attitudes toward departure. First were those most strongly disposed by tradition and/or by circumstances to regard themselves as sorrowful, banished exiles. By the middle of the nineteenth century an increasingly pervasive "official" Catholic/nationalist ideology labeled all Irish emigrants as involuntary expatriates, but for some that outlook reflected more than a superficial adherence to political and clerical rhetoric. A large number of emigrants really did not want to leave Ireland; often their departures were occasions of violent grief, for they and their relatives perceived emigration not primarily as opportunity but as necessity, forced by circumstances beyond their control. Members of several sociocultural groups belonged to this category of self-styled exiles. For example, small in numbers but symbolically important was a minority of politically active Catholics and radical Protestants who despaired of Ireland's ever being free of British rule; a few such men actually suffered legal banishment or fled to avoid punishment for their involvement in rebellions or secret agrarian activities. More numerous and also of symbolic importance were evicted farmers who emigrated after suffering "landlord oppression," and those fugitives from death and destruction during the Great Famine. In addition, many farmers' superfluous sons and daughters, denied inheritances and dowries, both understood and lamented the degree of compulsion involved in their emigrations. Also included was that unknown number who departed under the cloud of some personal disgrace.

In the broadest sense, all Irishmen and -women who perceived themselves as "victims" of the socioeconomic consequences of modernization could also view themselves as involuntary emigrants. However, the largest group of "exiles" was composed of those members of the rural lower classes—smallholders, cottiers, and laborers—who, despite increasing Anglicization, remained steeped in the traditions and inhibitions of Gaelic peasant culture. Among the Irish-speaking peasantry, and among many whose families had recently abandoned the old language but not the worldview it expressed, their culture's emphasis upon stasis combined with the inertia of accepted poverty to restrain emigration from self-sufficient, traditional communities where life was tolerable, even rewarding in nonmaterial ways. Faced with the exigencies of commercialization, these traditional countrymen long struggled to avoid permanent emigration—the most "rational" solution to increasing destitution—through a variety of rent-earning strategies and passive or violent resistance. Eventually, of course, they failed, and as Gaelic culture and subsistence economies steadily and simultaneously disintegrated, so did their resistance to emigration. However, in the most remote and traditional districts, catastrophes such as the Great Famine of 1845–55 and the near-famine of 1879–81 were necessary to discredit that culture and expose its adherents to the full force of commercialization. Even during such crises these emigrants left home more out of panic or despair than calculated ambition, and in the late nineteenth and early twentieth centuries they emigrated because the peculiar evolution of Irish rural society simply gave them no alternatives. Their traditional ways of life were breaking down, but their outlooks on life, on emigration itself, remained basically passive, fatalistic, and nonresponsible. In general, they were not ambitious to emigrate; rather, they submitted to this new but inescapable "fact" of Irish life as their fathers had endured crop failures and poverty; they would have preferred to remain at home, and they often tried to re-create as much of home as possible in their adopted countries. Occasionally, such emigrants repressed emotions with almost frightening thoroughness, but in the main it was the members of this most traditional group who regarded themselves most instinctively as involuntary exiles, or *deoraithe;* moreover, given the richness of their still-extant traditions, they were most prone to conflate their sorrows with those of past victims of *Sasanaigh* tyranny.

At the other extreme were Irishmen and -women who responded to the changes in their homeland by emigrating voluntarily, even eagerly, in order to improve their material condition. Although not necessarily happy to leave childhood homes, they were ambitious for themselves and their children, and they foresaw only limited or declining opportunities in Ireland. In the face of all the difficulties they knew they might encounter, such emigrants made mature, responsible decisions to go abroad. Consequently, although sometimes discouraged or disillusioned after their arrival in North America, rarely did they regard themselves as involuntary expatriates; they had consciously rejected Ireland for a new life abroad, and, if they failed to achieve material success, they usually acknowledged they had only themselves to blame for their decisions. Among such emigrants were those farmers' noninheriting children and those members of the urban and rural laboring classes whose alienation from harshly oppressive social conditions, whose distance from traditional cultural restraints, and whose estrangement from the dominant, bourgeois institutions of their own societies enabled them to make open breaks with ideologies which demanded self-abnegation and self-perception as unwilling exiles. However, most prominent among these consciously voluntary emigrants were Irish Protestants and Anglicized Catholics, particularly those of upper- and middle-class status, who had never been or no longer were bound to the traditional, communalistic constraints of Gaelic peasant culture. In outlook such emigrants were "modern," often entrepreneurial: imbued with the "spirit of improvement" and acquisitive individualism, they made "rational" responses to socioeconomic developments in Ireland and transferred their capital and labor to more remunerative overseas markets. Often they wrote in letters and memoirs that they emigrated to seek what they called an "independence," an ambition which they conceived in terms of opportunities for individual upward mobility. To realize that goal, such emigrants frequently were willing to sacrifice traditional considerations—security, family, friendships—and once in North America they often strove for complete assimilation to bourgeois society in their adopted country. Whenever these emigrants did employ the exile motif, they tended to do so pragmatically, even cynically, to deflate communal criticism of ambition or innovation, or to manipulate other emigrants still susceptible to traditional patterns of thought and behavior.

Finally, there was a third group of emigrants, less easy to define, who made conscious decisions to emigrate, but on grounds which often proved specious. In a sense these emigrants were ambitious, but often they lacked the modern outlook, the degree of individuality or self-reliance, characteristic of those in the second category. In short, they decided to leave Ireland under apprehensions which frequently proved false. In the eighteenth and early nineteenth centuries such emigrants included those who defined their goals of "independence" not in terms of upward mobility and individual acquisitiveness but in traditional contexts of security, self-sufficiency, and community; reflecting such sentiments, they strove, whenever possible, to emigrate and settle in communal or family groups rather than as solitary figures. Among these were both Protestants and Catholics: middling farmers and smallholders, rural and urban artisans, who correctly perceived that their attempts to avoid the inevitable tendencies of Irish economic development to reduce them or their children to what they called "slavery"—the economic dependence characteristic of landless laborers and factory operatives—were doomed to failure. Hence, they projected traditional goals of self-sufficiency across the Atlantic to a land supposedly free of rents, tithes, taxes, and parasitical middlemen. Similar were many post-Famine emigrants, often farmers' adolescent sons and daughters, who left home in large measure because relatives already in America persuaded or enabled them to do so; indeed, without expectations of family and communal shelter and assistance overseas, many would not have dared to emigrate as individuals. Often such farmers' children, particularly those from relatively comfortable backgrounds, emigrated in hope of preserving a privileged status enjoyed at home, and in order to preclude social descent into the ranks of the landless laborers whom their families despised. The point is that the major common denominator among the emigrants in this third category was the belief in a myth of the New World as earthly paradise, as promised land—a compensatory vision which reflected less the realities of North American life, especially in later periods, than the increasing harshness and insecurity of Irish conditions. The dream was common among Irish Protestants, particularly Dissenters, in the eighteenth and early nineteenth centuries, but it proved especially enduring among rural Catholics, in part because their emigrations remained heavily dependent upon Irish-American remittances, which seemed to "prove" the myth's validity, and also because the vision of the *caisleáin óir* (castles of gold) in the New World which persisted in Gaelic peasant cultures continued to blur modern distinctions between myth and reality.

In economic and cultural terms, these emigrants were in transition between traditional and modern patterns of thinking and behaving. They naturally conceived ambitions in communalistic and pre-entrepreneurial terms; they often remained dependent upon kinship ties or other sources of material and psychological "encouragement" (landlords, philanthropists, government assistance) to make possible their departures; and they eagerly embraced a vision of America as earthly paradise which counterbalanced the tradition of emigration as exile. Once in America, if they succeeded in realizing their goals—as many did in the eighteenth and early nineteenth centuries, especially—then they or their children usually completed the transition and assimilated to the bourgeois values characteristic of life in the New World. However, given the rampant commercialization, urbanization, and industrialization of American society in the nineteenth century, and given the often naïve and fabulous nature of their apprehensions, many others suffered deep disappointment when their adopted country, even their Irish-American kinfolk and neighbors, frequently failed to meet their expectations and needs. In general, these emigrants, often mere adolescents, had not anticipated such hardships and insecurities; nor, unlike those in the second category, were they prepared for the degree of self-motivation and -reliance which even survival, let alone success, in America usually demanded. Although most adjusted to their circumstances—sometimes through religious palliatives, sometimes at great psychic cost—others remained disadvantaged in the struggle to achieve a mere competence, much less an "independence," however defined. Such disappointments served to shatter ill-founded ambitions and to confirm the validity of premodern thought and behavior patterns from which these emigrants had never entirely broken. Given their retention of traditionalist outlooks—especially prevalent among rural Catholics—and given the transmission of pre-individualist attitudes by the "official" ideology of nineteenth- and early-twentieth-century Irish and Irish-American Catholic institutions, it was hardly surprising that many disillusioned emigrants reverted to old but seemingly still valid cultural categories which enabled them to skirt responsibility for their decisions to go abroad, and to fall back upon an "explanation" of themselves as involuntary exiles. Indeed, it was among such disillusioned emigrants, perhaps even more than among those who had regarded themselves as exiles *before* their arrival in the New World, that Irish-American nationalism found its most devoted and bitter adherents.

Of course, all three of these categories were represented in all periods of mass emigration. In addition, many, perhaps most, Irish emigrants carried a mélange of emotions and responses to their departures and experiences abroad. "Their outlook," despaired a British consul in Boston, "is a strange jumble of mental characteristics and extremely difficult to analyze."[2] Even the emigrants' personal letters and private journals are not entirely reliable indications of attitude, for historic circumstances and both external and internalized sanctions had for centuries combined to produce what Seán O'Faolain has called an "Irish national genius" for "reservations, loopholes, wordy discrimination . . . —anything on earth and under heaven except a clear statement of simple fact or intent."[3] Nevertheless, the evidence indicates that over time broad changes occurred in what might be called the psychological character of Irish emigration—just as changes in its socioeconomic, cultural, religious, and regional composition occurred which, in turn, reflected changes in the conditions of Irish life which inhibited or encouraged departures. As succeeding chapters demonstrate, all these developments were intimately related, eventually producing a mass movement of self-styled exiles from Ireland.

4

Settlers, Servants, and Slaves:
Irish Emigration
before the American Revolution

Early emigration records are so incomplete that it is possible to achieve only the roughest estimates of the numbers, regional origins, and relative proportions of Catholic and Protestant Irish who sailed to the North American colonies. At best, we can guess that perhaps 50–100,000 left Ireland in the 1600s, and 250–400,000 from 1700 to 1776. The total figure of 300–500,000 Irish emigrants during almost two centuries is small by comparison with the great migrations of the nineteenth century, but relative to Ireland's population—merely 2.3 million in 1754—the exodus was substantial. During the 1600s perhaps three-fourths of the emigrants were Catholics, primarily from the southern provinces; most of the remainder were probably Anglicans, although the last decades of the century witnessed the beginnings of Quaker and Ulster Presbyterian migrations. For the 1700s more information is available, but much is highly contradictory. Most contemporaries testified that Irish emigration in 1700–1776 was overwhelmingly of Ulster origin and Protestant composition. However, after examining shipping records and lists of Irish-American servants, the historian David N. Doyle concluded that a quarter of the Irish emigrants came from southern Ireland and that about one-third of all passengers were Catholics. Doyle's argument that more Irish Catholics went to pre-Revolutionary America than was previously supposed is probably correct, but he may have inflated their numbers by equating Gaelic and Old English surnames with Catholicism—thus underestimating conversions to Protestantism—and by assuming that southern Irish emigration was almost entirely Catholic—thus ignoring evidence of a substantial decline in the Protestant populations of Leinster, Munster, and Connaught during the period. It seems more likely that only one-fifth to one-fourth of the emigrants of 1700–1776 were Catholics, with about another one-fifth Anglicans, and the rest Dissenters, primarly Presbyterians from Ulster. In short, early Irish emigration to North America was highly unrepresentative of the religious composition of Ireland's population.[1]

These migrations reflected the political and socioeconomic dislocations caused by wars, rebellions, and the increasing commercialization of Irish life—as well as the growing attractiveness of North America as refuge and opportunity. Perhaps most important, these first mass movements of Irish overseas helped shape communal attitudes toward emigration which subsequent generations would adopt and perpetuate. Initially, many Protestant as well as Catholic Irish regarded emigration as a species of "exile" occasioned by oppression in Ireland. However, different cultural backgrounds and historical experiences predisposed varying interpretations of that perception and varying responses to the New World. Protestants, especially Dissenters, perceived an element of compulsion in their emigrations, but they regarded their experiences positively in terms of "escape," and they flocked overseas to a land that promised abundance and freedom. Conversely, Catholics perceived emigration as forced banishment, and most remained at home—ignorant of or indifferent, even hostile, to the possibility of removal from Ireland, especially to Protestant-dominated colonies, where they could expect mistreatment and discrimination. Not until the last quarter of the eighteenth century would the American Revolution and the United Irish rising of 1798 effectively, if temporarily, merge Protestant and Catholic Irish attitudes toward emigration and point members of both communities toward an idealized America where all Irishmen—whether eager "emigrants" or sorrowful "exiles"—could find refuge and opportunity.

Even before the American Revolution the contrasts between Irish and American conditions were compelling, as Benjamin Franklin remarked during a visit to Ireland in 1771. Franklin traveled only from Dublin to Belfast, through regions which other contemporary observers such as Arthur Young praised for their comparative prosperity under "improving" landlords. However, Franklin was appalled by "the most sordid wretchedness" and "extreme poverty" which characterized the mass of tenants and laborers, and left thankful for "the happy Mediocrity, that so generally prevails throughout" his own country, "where the Cultivator works for himself, and supports his family in decent Plenty." Unlike most British visitors, Franklin was less than impressed by the consequences of Ireland's expanding market economy: "The chief exports," he wrote, "seem to be pinched off the backs and out of the bellies of the miserable inhabitants"— adding sarcastically that if the American colonists, like "three fourths of the People of Ireland," were willing to "live the year round on Potatoes and Buttermilk, without Shirts, then may *their* Merchants export Beef, Butter, and Linnen." Franklin's comparisons were accurate: renting one acre of Irish land for a single year cost as much as the purchase price of an acre of fertile, if yet uncleared, American soil; in Ireland growing numbers of poor weavers, cottiers, and landless laborers formed a "mudsill" class at the bottom of a highly stratified society, while in the colonies—despite increasing social differentiation—artisans, tenant farmers, and even laborers were often upwardly mobile. In retrospect, the prevalence of Negro slavery takes much of the gloss off colonial society, but for white Europeans America *was* a relative paradise where subsistence cultivators, commercial farmers, aspiring merchants, skilled craftsmen, and industrious laborers could all realize dreams of "independence"—whether defined as self-sufficiency or as improvement—unobtainable at home. Such opportunities abroad were not only theoretically available to impoverished Irishmen, for the economic processes which created pressures for emigration also produced an expanding commerce between Irish and North American seaports, and the colonies' voracious need for labor gave rise to an extensive trade in Irish indentured servants. Consequently, as an old ballad declared, many seventeenth- and eighteenth-century Irishmen knew, "You can emigrate for nothing, boys / You can emigrate for nothing," and so decided not to "toil and starve like slaves," but to "trust [themselves] across the waves, / And emigrate for nothing." Such enthusiasm was actively encouraged by shipmasters and agents who proclaimed in newspapers, handbills, and in person at country fairs that removal to "the Land of Promise" could not fail to bring "freedom, peace, and plenty" to their passengers, whether bond or free, and to their fortunate posterity.[2]

Attracted by such prospects and pushed by distress and insecurity at home, some Irish Catholics did venture to the North American colonies. The great majority were indentured servants who pledged to complete several years of bonded labor in return for free passage and the promise of some material reward when their term of service was over. As early as the 1620s ships were sailing regularly from southern Irish ports such as Cork and Kinsale, laden with provisions, textiles, and Irish servants to exchange for West Indian sugar and Chesapeake tobacco. As a result of this trade, during the 1600s Irish Catholics appeared in every mainland colony, particularly in Virginia and in Maryland, where tracts of land named "New Ireland" and "New Munster" were set aside for Irish settlers and their servants. However, in the seventeenth century the most visible settlement of Irish Catholics took place in the West Indies, partly because Irish-born governors of the Leeward Islands encouraged their countrymen to emigrate. In 1666 the white population of Barbados was about one-fifth Irish, and twelve years later the Irish composed about a third of the free inhabitants of the Leeward Islands. Catholic emigration to the Caribbean continued into the eighteenth century, and in 1731 the governor of Jamaica complained that such "great numbers" had arrived during the preceding decade that they now constituted the bulk of "our servants and lower rank of people." However, the growth of a slave-based economy steadily diminished economic opportunities for freed servants in the West Indies, and during the 1700s most Irish Catholic emigrants went to the mainland colonies. A substantial minority of Catholic servants continued to sail from Munster ports to the plantations of Virginia, Maryland, and the Carolinas, but most now left from Dublin and from Ulster towns such as Newry and Londonderry, bound for Pennsylvania and New York. Their numbers were obscured by the much larger emigrations of northern Protestants, but colonial records and a few contemporary accounts testified to the existence of "an intermixture of wild Irish Roman Catholics" among the Protestant

settlers in the middle colonies. Many were probably farm laborers and servants who accompanied more affluent Presbyterian, Anglican, and Quaker
families to the New World. Finally, in the eighteenth century there was a
sizable migration of Catholics to Newfoundland, primarily from Waterford,
Wexford, and other southeastern counties. In 1776 Arthur Young was astounded "at the number of people who go as passengers in the Newfoundland ships . . . from three to five thousand annually." Most were but temporary sojourners, returning home each winter with £15 to £24 earned
as seasonal laborers in the Grand Banks fisheries. However, a minority
settled permanently: in 1732 an English officer stationed on the island reported that "the greater number of men now there are Irish Romans," and
in 1784 the Catholics in St. John's declared that seven-eighths of the town's
inhabitants hailed from Ireland. Eventually, many of the Newfoundland
Irish made their way to the mainland, as did Irish servants from the West
Indies.[3]

Little is known about the background of most early Catholic emigrants,
or about their reasons for leaving Ireland. In the early seventeenth century
one ship's captain claimed that "lustye and strong boddied" women were
"reddear . . . than men" to leave Munster for the West Indies, but the
great majority of Irish emigrants were single males; for example, in 1678
only a fourth of the adult Irish in the Leeward Islands were women. Most
Irish servants were probably the children of impoverished subtenants and
rural and urban laborers. The upheavals and dislocations of the seventeenth and eighteenth centuries—wars, famines, evictions produced by confiscations, the expansion of grazing, the consolidation of holdings, and the
consequent attrition of common lands and joint tenancies—sundered a large
number of Catholic Irish from their traditional communities. Most roamed
the countryside in search of land and employment, but many swelled the
populations of Irish towns such as Dublin, where in 1773 an English visitor
remarked, "Half the inhabitants are in absolute rags, . . . idle, drunken,
and universally thieves. . . ." Others moved across the Irish Sea, forming
part of the "great multitude of wandering persons" which plagued rural
England, or settling in poverty-stricken urban parishes such as St. Giles-
in-the-Fields in London. In spite of statutory proscription, some enlisted in
the British army and navy and occasionally served overseas in colonies
such as New York, whose governor complained in 1700 that "the very
scum of the army . . . , and severall Irish Papists among 'em, . . . have
stirred up a generall mutiny among the souldiers. . . ." However, others
emigrated to North America as indentured servants; perhaps they were the
most enterprising, or the most desperate, of these impoverished seven-
teenth- and eighteenth-century Irishmen.[4]

If early Catholic Irish emigrants had any common characteristic, it may
have been rootlessness. Most hailed from seaports or the surrounding
countryside where agriculture was highly commercialized. For example, a
substantial proportion of Catholic servants came from County Dublin and
other market-oriented regions where landlords' improvements and farmers'

inheritance patterns early made superfluous a large percentage of the rural population. Such emigrants may have been rootless in a cultural sense as well. Adrift from familial and communal moorings, many may have worn their religion lightly; furthermore, although Irish was spoken in both the West Indies and Newfoundland, runaway-servant advertisements in the mainland colonies indicate that by the eighteenth century nearly all Irish emigrants of that class spoke fluent English, whereas Irish Catholics at home remained predominantly Irish-speaking. Of course, not all Catholic servants were "loose, idle people" from the bottom of Irish society. For example, in the early 1670s poor harvests and livestock disease in Munster caused such widespread distress that, according to the Quaker missionary William Edmundson, "several Families that had lived plentifully, . . . their Corn being spent and Cattle dead, . . . shipped themselves for Servants to the West-Indies, to get food. . . ." Subsequent crises—crop failures in the 1720s and 1760s, general famine in 1740–41, periodic depressions in the woolen and linen industries—probably encouraged similar Catholic families to emigrate overseas.[5]

Finally, a small minority of Irish Catholic emigrants paid their own passages across the Atlantic. During the seventeenth and early eighteenth centuries, most members of the dispossessed Gaelic and Old English gentry looked to Europe for refuge, but some who joined the French and Spanish military saw service in North America and settled there. Others went directly: for example, in the late 1600s the defeated chieftain of the O'Mores left Queen's County for South Carolina, where his son and grandson—Anglicized in name and religion—later served as colonial governors; likewise, Charles O'Carroll of Tipperary, grandfather of a signer of the Declaration of Independence, became Lord Baltimore's attorney general in Maryland. However, the largest migration of this kind was composed of younger sons of the Galway "tribes"—Old English gentry and merchant families such as the Blakes, Darcys, and Kirwans—who established sugar plantations and counting houses on Barbados, Montserrat, and other Caribbean islands in an attempt to recoup family fortunes after the Cromwellian confiscations. Throughout the eighteenth century, a steady trickle of similarly circumstanced young Catholics continued to cross the Atlantic. Irish and Franco-Irish mercantile families sent men such as Thomas FitzSimons and Stephen Moylan to settle in Philadelphia and other American seaports. Well-to-do rural Catholics' custom of impartible inheritance produced talented but disinherited sons who sought adventure and opportunity in the New World. Perhaps typical of such emigrants was Thomas Burke, who in 1772 explained that although he was "born in Ireland of a once affluent Family, . . . some Family misfortunes reduced [him] to the alternative of Domestick Indolent Dependence, or an Enterprising Peregrination" to Virginia.[6]

In retrospect, it seems unsurprising that Catholics emigrated from Ireland during the seventeenth and eighteenth centuries, for—despite overall economic growth—legal proscription, Protestant prejudice, and lack of capital thwarted ambition and kept most Catholics in poverty. In the early

1700s Jonathan Swift observed the expansion of pastureland in the Irish midlands, remarking acidly, "Where the plough has no work one family can do the work of fifty, and you may send away the other forty-nine"— "An admirable piece of husbandry" which forced the rural poor either to emigrate or to cling to the soil by paying ever-rising rents earned from cottage industry, migratory labor, and reduced living standards. Thus, in the 1770s Arthur Young noted that Kerry peasants' "circumstances are incomparably worse than they were 20 years ago," for then "they all had cows," but now they were obliged to spin yarn or become seasonal migrants to England in order to meet their landlords' demands. Similarly, in north Tipperary, Young interviewed a cottier who rented a one-acre plot and whose annual expenses exceeded family income by twenty shillings; "When . . . I demanded how the 20s. deficiency . . . were to be paid, the answer was, that *he must not eat his geese and pig, or else not dress so well,* which probably is the case." In other parts of Munster, cottier-dairymen could no longer afford to consume the milk and butter produced by their own cows, and even in relatively prosperous Wexford population pressures forced thousands of cottiers and farmers' sons to make annual voyages to the Newfoundland fisheries. Irish towns provided few opportunities to such countrymen or to more skilled and educated Catholics; for example, in 1770 "papists" in Armagh town were excluded almost entirely from the ranks of traders, shopkeepers, and craftsmen, confined instead to the most poorly paid, least prestigious occupations.[7]

In view of such conditions, it is singular that so *few* Catholic Irish emigrated to colonial America—a fact which astonished most contemporary observers. In 1669 an emigration agent for the Carolina proprietors despaired of attracting Munster peasants overseas, remarking that they were "loath to leave the smoke of their owne Cabbin if they can but beg neer it." In 1718 the Anglican archbishop of Dublin claimed that "[n]o Papists stir" from northern Ireland, although their Protestant neighbors had begun to flock out of the country. Traveling through heavily Catholic western Ulster in 1759, an Irish magistrate reported that all the region's emigrants were Protestants because an "Irish papist will not leave the kingdom to go to . . . our colonies for any prospect of gain." Even in the 1770s, when Protestant emigration was at its height, Arthur Young believed that "Catholics never went; they seem not only tied to the country, but almost to the parish where their ancestors were born." Of course, Catholic emigration did occur, but contemporaries were correct in remarking its disproportionately low level. For example, in 1740–41 bad weather and harvest failures produced what peasants called *"bliadhain an áir"* (the year of the slaughter), when starvation and disease caused 200–400,000 deaths. However, this catastrophe witnessed no Catholic exodus remotely comparable to that resulting from the Great Famine of 1845–50.[8]

Thus, in spite of distress, during the seventeenth and eighteenth centuries tradition and experience combined to inhibit Irish Catholic emigration to the New World. Throughout this period the great majority of Catholics were Irish-speakers, largely insulated from the impulse to emigrate by the provincialism of Gaelic culture; by its secular, religious, and linguistic biases against individual initiative and innovation; and by literary modes which stigmatized emigration as *deoraí,* or involuntary exile. Maxims dating from the ninth century warned Irishmen not to go abroad and endure "[t]he abbot of a strange tribe over you, estrangement from your family to the day of your death, and foreign earth over you at the end of your road." Later poets had declared, "Only for God should a man stay away from the island of the Irish, and not for the worst hardship, nor for worldly advantage"—injunctions repeated in the eighteenth-century sermons of Bishop O'Gallagher, who condemned those who would "search sea or land . . . for . . . the gain of gold or silver." Also, it was during the 1600s and 1700s that Irish Catholics had before them vivid images of real exiles—the Ulster earls, Sarsfield and the Wild Geese—whom the poets portrayed as sorrowing eternally for their native land. "When awake I am in France," lamented a banished bard, but "When asleep I am in Ireland; / Therefore it is little love I have for wakefulness, / My goal is ever to be asleep."[9]

Such traditions, widely diffused in popular culture, scarcely predisposed Irish-speakers to regard emigration with favor, especially if they enjoyed at least a subsistence living in traditional communities which remained intensely localistic and family oriented. For most Catholics, language constituted an effective barrier to American attractions advertised in English, and emigration remained an unknown or fearful alternative to the relative security of clachan life. Of course, commercialization in various guises was beginning to erode peasants' insularity and security, but their cultural conservatism was so pervasive that in the early eighteenth century Protestant observers claimed that many Irish-speakers refused either to weave linen for the market or to enlist in the British army—preferring instead "their bogs, their misery and their potatoes." By mid-century those inhibitions had largely disappeared, but most Catholics' continued reluctance to "emigrate for nothing" indicates their preference for partible inheritance, cottage industry, seasonal migration, and other poor strategies designed to retain land or employment in Ireland. While increasing numbers of poor Protestants took ship for America, their Catholic counterparts painfully colonized mountain wastelands or bid outrageously high rents for the holdings abandoned by Protestant neighbors who refused to endure conditions which most Catholics found tolerable.[10]

In addition, during the seventeenth and eighteenth centuries the *in*voluntary status of a symbolically important minority of Catholics who did go to North America corroborated traditional perceptions of emigration as exile. From the early 1600s English and Irish Protestant officials regarded the colonies as suitable dumping grounds for rebellious and disorderly "papists." During the reigns of James I and Charles I, the Irish government shipped small numbers of dispossessed Catholics to Virginia as virtual slaves, and under Cromwell's regime several thousands, including women and children, were transported to Barbados, Jamaica, and the mainland colonies. Strictly speaking, however, most Irish deported to North America were not political prisoners but "vagabonds and rogues," as defined by statutes which equated idleness and vagrancy with immorality and crime. Others were petty thieves sentenced to long periods of indentured servitude overseas as alternatives to imprisonment or execution at home. Such deportations continued until the American Revolution: in 1700–1775 at least 10,000 Irish convicts were transported, primarily to Virginia and Maryland. Also, in the late seventeenth century colonial demands for indentured servants—and profits for selling their services—were so great that unscrupulous Irish magistrates, merchants, and shipmasters often resorted to kidnapping to fill the holds of vessels bound for North America. Not infrequently, Irish servants complained to colonial officials that they had been "barbadosed"—"stolen in Ireland, by some of the English soldiers, in the night out of theyr beds . . . weeping and Crying." Even some voluntary Catholic emigrants were exiles in at least a quasi-political sense: for example, in 1765 the military suppression of the Munster Whiteboys caused some to take ship for Newfoundland to avoid prosecution. The result of these experiences was that many native Irish naturally associated going to the New World with banishment and enslavement. Thus, in 1669 the agent Robert Southwell lamented his inability to entice Catholic servants from Munster to South Carolina, even under most generous terms: "I could not obteyne any," he reported, "for the thing at present seems new & forraigne to them, & . . . they have been so terrified with the ill practice of them to the Carib[da] Ileands, where they were sould as slaves, that as yet they will hardly give credence to any other usage. . . ."[11]

Finally, the hardships and discrimination experienced by many Irish Catholics in colonial America reinforced cultural biases which inhibited large-scale emigration. Conditions were particularly harsh during the seventeenth century, when perhaps a third or more of all white settlers in the Caribbean and southern mainland colonies perished on the Atlantic voyage or during the first year's "seasoning"; in 1671 Virginia's governor testified that in the colony's early decades four-fifths of the indentured servants died shortly after their arrival from the effects of disease, climate, or overwork. Irish-born servants may have been less able than their British counterparts to stand the physical rigors of American life; for example, a sample of Irish servants in late eighteenth-century Maryland revealed their average height as a mere 5′ 4″, compared with 5′ 7″ for those born in England. In addition, although mistreatment of colonial servants was common, Irish Catholics seem to have suffered especially severe abuse: partly because of Anglo-Protestant prejudice; partly because many Catholic servants lacked sufficient skills to bargain for favorable treatment; and partly because southern Irish trade routes carried most Catholics to colonies dominated by plantation agriculture. For example, in 1667 an account of Barbados described the Irish there as "poor men, that are just permitted to live, . . . derided by the Negroes, and branded wth the Epithite of white slaves." During their terms of service they worked "in the parching sun wth out shirt, shoe or stocking"—"domineered over and used like dogs," as Barbados' governor admitted in 1695—and when they were free the scarcity of farmland and competition from slave labor condemned most to a wretched hand-to-mouth existence at the very bottom of West Indian society. Abusive treatment was equally common in the southern mainland colonies, especially in eighteenth-century Maryland, where plantation owners—driven by falling tobacco prices and the pressures of debt, greed, and social pretensions—legislated long service terms, imposed savage punishments for running away, and, according to judicial records, combined overwork with inadequate food and clothing. Few Irish Catholic servants in the southern colonies succeeded in becoming yeomen farmers after their service was over; perhaps physically broken or demoralized by their experiences, most remained laborers or wandered about in "poverty, want and misery." Farther north the zealous Protestants of New England were so hostile to "St. Patrick's Vermin" that few Irish Catholics ventured to settle there; even in Newfoundland, Irish servants suffered discrimination and economic exploitation. In the early eighteenth century, English officials frequently remarked that Irish laborers in Newfoundland often had great difficulty in collecting their wages; many were paid in liquor, and remained in an almost perpetual state of drunkenness and debt peonage. Finally, all the colonial governments—even of initially Catholic Maryland and heavily Irish Montserrat—passed legislation to restrict the importation of Irish Catholic servants and prevent them from practicing their religion; even where not always proscribed, as in relatively enlightened Pennsylvania, Catholicism was at best barely tolerated before the American Revolution.[12]

Of course, some Irish Catholics did prosper in colonial America, especially if they arrived as freemen possessing capital, skills, and education. Thus, in 1673 the Montserrat plantation owner Henry Blake wrote to his "loveing Brother" in Galway that he enjoyed "nothing sweeter than a good plentifull liveing," and other affluent Irishmen in the West Indies could spare money to repay family debts, build Catholic churches, and assist the poor at home. On the mainland, eighteenth-century settlers such as Thomas FitzSimons and John Fitzpatrick flourished in trade, the former in Philadelphia and the latter along the Mississippi River. Other talented sons of gentry or strong-farmer origins did equally well; for example, Thomas Burke practiced law, entered politics, and eventually became governor of North Carolina. Less spectacularly successful, but perhaps well satisfied, were those few Catholic Irish settled on colonial farms by wealthy patrons such as Thomas Dongan of Kildare, governor of New York during James II's reign, and William Johnson of Meath, an extensive landowner and Indian trader in the Mohawk valley. Considering their initial poverty, even Irish Catholic servants sometimes made remarkable achievements. For example, in the late seventeenth century some 10 percent of Jamaica's property owners were of Irish extraction, and several—such as Teague Mackmarroe, owner of eight slaves—attained the rank of "middling planter." However, economic opportunities for freed servants were greatest on the mainland, particularly in Pennsylvania, New Jersey, and New York, where flourishing towns, abundant land, family-farm agriculture, and heterogeneous populations offered Irish Catholics chances for a comfortable subsistence, cultural autonomy, even upward mobility rarely experienced elsewhere. Hidden in the eighteenth-century Ulster Protestant exodus to the middle colonies was a significant minority of Catholic servants; and whereas their coreligionists farther south suffered harsh treatment, they seem to have fared relatively well both during their periods of indenture and afterwards—when some succeeded in gaining "the Satisfaction of being Land holders," as New York's governor testified in 1767. For instance, Donald Callagher served his time with a Jersey farmer and later rented land for himself; by 1776 he possessed crops and cattle worth £124. Other Catholic servants accompanied Irish Protestant masters to the frontier, where they took up land when their service ended. Perhaps most fortunate were those skilled servants who were indentured to urban artisans and builders, some of whom were Catholic Irishmen who had begun American careers in like fashion. Philadelphia and New York contained the largest concentrations of urban Irish, but others found success in smaller towns. For example, in 1764 John Hennessy, aged nineteen, landed in Charleston, South Carolina, and was indentured to a carter for four years; in time he acquired his own horses and wagons, and by 1778 his property amounted to £460, including a brick house, furniture, a gold watch, and twelve silver spoons. By the American Revolution, then, Irish Catholic farmers—mostly tenants and backwoods squatters—were scattered in the colonial countryside; and in seaport towns a tiny but visible Irish Catholic middle class of shopkeepers, craftsmen, and building contractors had taken shape above a larger, more amorphous group of Irish-born porters, day laborers, and sailors. Generally, their successes were modest, but they attained far more material comfort and security than their countrymen at home. And a rare few achieved truly impressive upward mobility. For example, in 1754 Connor Dowd arrived in North Carolina unable to read or write and possessing only a few pieces of Irish linen, which he hawked through the southern countryside; however, twenty years later Dowd owned 7,000 acres of land, plus slaves, furniture, and other property worth £10,000.[13]

Nevertheless, it must be reemphasized that such achievements were highly exceptional and that most Irish Catholic emigrants lived short, brutish lives in colonial America: toiling in obscure poverty for harsh taskmasters and afterwards often "wander[ing] up and down from Plantation to Plantation, as vagabonds, refusing to labour . . . , but continuing in a dissolute, lewd, and slothful kind of life, [engaging] in evil practices, thefts, robberies, and other felonious acts, for their subsistency." From the Maritimes to the West Indies, seventeenth- and eighteenth-century colonial records revealed that unhappiness and alienation were characteristic of Irish Catholic servants. Save in the middle colonies, they frequently ran away from their masters and were notorious for drunken and disorderly conduct. In addition, they were often hostile to English authority overseas: on numerous occasions in the late seventeeth and early eighteenth centuries, colonial officials in Newfoundland, Nova Scotia, New York, and the West Indies feared that Irish "papists" were plotting insurrection with Negro slaves or foreign enemies; indeed, Irish Catholics in the Leeward Islands did assist several French invasions. Such "treachery" stemmed partly from resentment born of colonial mistreatment, partly from ethnic and religious antagonisms transplanted from the old country. The Barbados Irishman who received twelve lashes for swearing at dinner that "if there was so much English Blood in the tray as there was Meat, he would eat it," expressed a tribal hatred engendered during the Elizabethan and Crom-wellian conquests—which perhaps he regarded as directly responsible for his present, unhappy "exile."[14]

Furthermore, the very circumstances of seventeenth- and eighteenth-century Catholic emigration combined with colonial prejudices to ensure that most Irish Catholics in North America, whether successful or not, never coalesced into permanent, distinctive ethnic communities which could maintain transatlantic links to attract or facilitate large-scale emigration to the New World. Those Catholics who did leave Ireland during the colonial period seem to have been rootless, restless men, already estranged from the communal, familial, and cultural ties which kept the bulk of their countrymen at home. They emigrated, settled, and often disappeared as solitary individuals. Since the great majority were single males, marriage usually entailed absorption into colonial Protestant family and community networks. In addition, pervasive anti-Catholic and anti-Irish prejudice often demanded a sort of cultural suicide, reflected in the fact that very few colonial Irishmen retained the traditional "O" or "Mac" before their surnames. Finally, the scarcity of Catholic churches and priests in the colonies encouraged large numbers of Catholic Irish, scattered thinly among an overwhelmingly Protestant population, to abandon a faith that was largely customary rather than individualized for some variety of Protestantism more congenial to their new social environment. In 1783, for example, there were only about 25,000 practicing Catholics of all nationalities in the new United States, although since 1700 perhaps three to four times that number had arrived from Ireland alone. The rest had become "name only Catholics," as Bishop John Carroll complained in 1796, or had melted into Protestant denominations; in the early nineteenth century Irish missionary priests reported that the southern states were full of the Protestant descendants of early Irish Catholic settlers who "in nine cases out of ten . . . never had an opportunity of seeing a priest, or assisting at the holy sacrifice, or receiving the holy sacraments of the Church."[15]

Under such circumstances, and considering the ill-treatment many had received at colonial hands, it was understandable that, despite the conspicuous patriotism of a few individuals such as the Wexford-born naval hero John Barry, Irish Catholics *as a group* played a rather obscure and indifferent role in the American Revolution. After all, "No Popery" was a major rallying cry for patriot leaders like Samuel Adams, although once war began the revolutionaries suppressed their antipapist prejudices to encourage Catholic enlistments and win French support. Ironically, some of the most successful Irish Catholic settlers, such as William Johnson's tenants in upstate New York, remained loyal to the crown, but the majority seem to have been at least lukewarm revolutionaries—perhaps because traditional hatreds for England meshed with hopes for achieving an improved status in America through participation in a successful rebellion. Although the patriot leader Thomas Burke proclaimed himself "a passionate Lover of Liberty, and Hater of Tyranny," most Irish Catholics served in the Continental forces for more pragmatic reasons: to Irish indentured servants, enlistment brought an early termination of arduous servitude, as well as promised land grants and other bounties at the war's end. Thus, a British army officer from Dublin was probably correct when, after interviewing Irish Catholic prisoners, he claimed they had joined the Revolution merely for "the sake of a present subsistence, Clothing and plunder; and the prospect of acquiring some property, and becoming men of some substance, in case they are successful."[16]

Of course, the Revolution did improve the legal and social status of Irish Catholics in America, and in time the new United States became a beacon to their coreligionists in Ireland. However, during the colonial period itself—indeed, for several decades thereafter—relatively few native Irish ventured to the New World. Even well-educated Catholics, although chafing under Irish Penal Laws, probably saw little point in exchanging one Protestant Ascendancy for another, less familiar. Among the vast majority—Irish-speaking peasants—culture predisposed and experience confirmed the traditional belief that emigration was exile. Although most Catholics probably had only the vaguest notions of North America, what little they knew was unfavorable: forced transportations, kidnappings, high mortality, hard labor, discrimination, and, perhaps most frightening of all, the high probability of social and cultural oblivion—even for the successful—in the awful vastness of a far-distant, alien land. Some Irish Catholics who did emigrate later returned to give the lie to shipmasters' and colonial agents' claims that the New World was a "Land of Promise" for all. For example, about 1760 an Irish magistrate reported that several years earlier some Munster Catholics had been enticed to the colonies by "advantageous offers of land"; however, many returned "and by acquainting their neighbours how they were deceived by the promises of those who had prevailed upon them to go, . . . put a stop to that emigration." Most dramatically, cultural traditions and negative experiences combined in the forceful injunctions against emigration which were composed by a few Gaelic poets who actually sojourned in North America. For example, in the mid-eighteenth century one of Munster's most popular poets, Donnchadh Ruadh Mac Conmara of County Waterford, sailed to Newfoundland, the "land of fish," where he bewailed his "fate . . . to be a thousand miles away / From the fair hills of holy Ireland," and upon his return vowed, "Never again on a ship they'll find me / Unless by force they take and bind me."

From the other end of Ireland, an anonymous eighteenth-century Ulster composer was more detailed in his description of the New World, and more specific about his reasons for returning home. Upon landing in America, he wrote, he had

> . . . walked twenty miles and never met a Christian,
> A horse, a cow, or a sheep who would graze on the grass;
> But only dense woods and valleys and the roaring of wild beasts
> And men and women without a thread on them.

Appalled by such an unfamiliar environment, the author decided that "it would be a blessed thing if [he] could die in Ireland," where at least he would have family and friends to share his poverty.[17]

The empty lands that frightened this unknown bard represented a paradise of unlimited opportunities to more rootless, individualistically motivated Catholic emigrants such as Thomas Burke, who rejoiced that in Virginia "we have . . . everything of Arcadia but its flocks and Fountains and even these . . . are not wanting in the back parts of our Country." However, despite scanty evidence, it seems that even highly successful Irish Catholics often felt like homesick exiles in the New World. Perhaps the considerable remittances sent home by affluent Irishmen in the West Indies reflected a continued emotional allegiance to Ireland; and at least one of them, Henry Blake, eventually abandoned his "plentifull liveing" in Montserrat and returned to Galway to enjoy the wealth wrung from his slaves and less fortunate indentured countrymen. Even Thomas Burke, "restless revolutionary," wrote self-pitying letters home in which he lamented his "Exile" and expressed desires to return to his "Native Country." His feelings of "Banishment" may have been more attributable to personal circumstances than to cultural influences or broad historical causes, for in Ireland he had been "persecuted with relentless rancour by [his] nearer relations," and he certainly did not allow the "Melancholy anxity" which sometimes beset him to prevent his laboring quite successfully "to supply by Industry the Defects of Fortune." Nevertheless, although Burke was atypical in both his social origins and his Anglicized background, his allusions to himself as a "homesick pilgrim" accurately reflected the deep-seated aversion most Irish Catholics felt toward the prospect of emigration to colonial America.[18]

By the last decades of the 1600s, Irish Protestant emigration to North America probably exceeded that of Catholics, and in 1700–1776 Dissenters and Anglicans together composed some three-fourths of all transatlantic emigrants from Ireland, although they constituted only one-fourth to one-third of the island's population. About 70 percent of the Irish Protestant emigrants were Presbyterians from the northern province of Ulster, and their numerical and cultural dominance largely obscured the movements overseas of Anglicans, other Dissenters, and southern Irish Protestants generally. However, during the eighteenth century Protestant emigration from the three southern provinces may have been substantial in proportion to their numbers. Southern gentry and merchant families probably sent many superfluous sons to seek fortunes abroad, but most southern Protestants were craftsmen, laborers, and small farmers residing in towns or in highly commercialized rural areas, where pressures for emigration were heaviest. After peaking in the early 1700s, the Protestant populations of many southern towns and country districts began to decline because of emigration and conversions. For example, in 1729–30 significant numbers of Presbyterians departed from County Longford; between 1731 and 1800 the Protestant population of County Kilkenny fell by one-third; and in 1760 John Wesley reported that many of the German Palatine Protestants settled in County Limerick during Queen Anne's reign were abandoning rack-rented farms and fleeing to the New World. For southern Protestants economic grievances were worsened by hostility and competition for leases and employment from their "dangerous and unwearied enemies" among the overwhelmingly Catholic majority, growing yearly in strength and "insolence."[19]

Members of the established Church of Ireland probably constituted about a quarter of all Protestant emigrants. Given their control of that church, plus their near monopoly of landownership, political offices, military commissions, entry to the professions, and higher education, it was understandable that relatively few affluent Anglicans went to the New World unless impelled by adventurous spirits or unusual prospects of gain. Genteely bred Anglo-Irishmen such as Warren Johnson found little to attract them in the "Nasty dirty Town[s]" and backcountry of colonial America, where "Flies & Musketoes are troublesome beyond Naming" and where the "weather is . . . soe variable that one Day the Heat is almost intolerable, & next Day the People can hardly bear leaving the fire, tis soe Excessive Cold." However, even a bloated Ascendancy could not provide respectable livings and sinecures for all its sons, and while most went to England to seek their fortunes, others ventured across the Atlantic. The most visible Anglican emigrants were colonial officials and land speculators, such as Governors Arthur Dobbs of North Carolina and William Cosby of New York, whose vast land grants and patronage systems attracted other Anglo-Irishmen, such as William Johnson, a middleman from County Meath. Some were merchants like Robert Pillson from Drogheda, who by 1764 had established himself on the New York quays, invested £300 in a "compleat machine" for cleaning flaxseed, and was shipping that article home in exchange for "Irish Beef," "Mault," and "Coarse linnen Sheeting much Wanted for about 3,000 provincial Troops now raiseing to protect our Frontiers." Still others were discharged military men who remained to settle where they had fought the French and Indians. A significant number of Anglican emigrants may have been individuals or members of families recently converted from Catholicism: both for colonial officials like William Johnson and Joseph Murray and for indentured servants like Daniel Dulany and Matthew Lyon, emigration at once

fulfilled the ambitions which had inspired conversion, and resolved consequent problems of social and cultural marginality endured at home.[20]

A few Anglo-Irish families, such as the Butlers and Lynches, established plantations on the Chesapeake tidewater and Carolina coasts. However, most well-to-do Anglicans sought the cosmopolitan atmosphere and
commercial opportunities offered by Philadelphia, New York, and other
colonial towns. There they founded the first Irish-American societies, gentlemen's clubs such as the Friendly Sons of St. Patrick, but they mingled so
thoroughly with the local political and mercantile elites that they became
almost indistinguishable from their English- or native-born counterparts;
indeed, in 1776 such relationships largely determined whether affluent Anglo-Irishmen became patriots or remained loyalists—as did most of those
linked with the Cosby-DeLancey faction in New York. However, the great
majority of Anglican emigrants were of humble origins: urban artisans and
laborers, tenant farmers and peasants. Most rural Anglicans probably came
from Ulster alongside their Presbyterian neighbors, particularly from overpopulated linen districts like north Armagh. Poor Anglicans generally went
to the colonies as indentured servants. Those with skills and education,
such as Lyon and Dulany, probably fared reasonably well, especially if indentured to urban masters. However, like their wealthier coreligionists,
most became ethnically invisible: in towns merging with native- or English-
born craftsmen and laborers; in the countryside swallowed up by the numerically dominant Ulster Presbyterians. A few—such as George Taylor,
indentured ore shoveler in a Pennsylvania iron furnace, later its owner,
member of the colonial assembly, and signer of the Declaration of Independence—achieved remarkable success; but even fewer remained distinctively Irish, as did the Wicklow-born Matthew Lyon, whose hatred of
England and fierce republicanism linked Irish and American political
radicalism.[21]

Demographically and symbolically, Dissenters were the most important
Irish Protestant emigrants to colonial America. Although Anglicans, like
Catholics, tended to emigrate and assimilate as individuals, Dissenters
transplanted communal and familial networks, retained relatively close ties
to Ireland, and remained culturally distinct. Moreover, although all Irish
Protestants left home for reasons primarily economic, Dissenters often perceived emigration in religious and political terms. The vast majority of Dissenting emigrants were Ulster Presbyterians; however, a steady trickle of
Irish Quakers, Wesleyan Methodists, and members of other sects also went
overseas. Of these, the most significant were the Quakers; between 1682
and 1776 perhaps 3,000 Irish Friends settled in North America, from the
middle colonies south to the West Indies. Most Irish Quakers were of English origin—farmers, tradesmen, artisans, and discharged soldiers who settled in Ireland or converted to Quakerism after the Cromwellian conquest.
In Ulster, Friends played a prominent role in the founding of the linen industry; in Dublin and in Munster towns such as Cork and Limerick, some
Quakers amassed fortunes in transatlantic trade and sent younger sons

abroad to establish branches of family businesses in Philadelphia, New York, Charleston, and other colonial seaports. However, most Irish Quakers were tenant farmers and craftsmen, subject to the same economic pressures which inspired emigration among their Anglican and Presbyterian counterparts. Moreover, in the late seventeenth and early eighteenth centuries, Irish Quakers suffered physical harassment from rebellious Catholics, and legal persecution from the Anglican establishment because of their religious objections to tithes, oaths, and military service. In these circumstances, Irish Quakers responded eagerly to the attractions of William Penn's refuge in the New World, assiduously advertised by Penn's secretary, the Armagh-born James Logan. Consequently, most Irish Quakers settled in Pennsylvania and New Jersey, and the favorable accounts they sent back to Ireland combined with the continued dissatisfaction over tithes to encourage a small but steady flow of Friends to America. For example, in 1725 an Irish Quaker settled on a Pennsylvania farm reported to his sister, "[T]here is not one of the family but what likes the country very well and wod If we were in Ireland again come here Directly it being the best country for working folk & tradesmen in the world. . . ." Despite close association with British Quakers in the colonies, Irish Friends remained somewhat distinct; perhaps because of their Irish experiences, during the American Revolution they seem to have been more "hearty in the good cause of liberty" than their Anglo-American coreligionists.[22]

Both in size and in relative proportion, Ulster Presbyterian emigration far overshadowed all other population movements from Ireland to colonial America. In 1700–1776 at least 200,000 left the northern province—a massive drain from a Presbyterian community that probably numbered only 400–600,000 during the period. Before 1715, small numbers of Presbyterians left northern Ireland for New England and the Chesapeake region, but between 1690 and 1715 Ulster itself was the preferred destination for over 50,000 Scottish Presbyterians who fled poor harvests, rising rents, and religious strife in the Lowlands. Consequently, the first substantial migrations from Ulster to North America did not occur until 1717–20, when the generous leases landlords had granted to attract these newcomers began to expire. Many seventeenth-century leases were held in partnership by Presbyterian families who inhabited clachan settlements and practiced open-field farming. However, when old leases terminated, many proprietors consolidated farms into individual holdings and often doubled, sometimes tripled, rent levels. In the ensuing competition for leases, grazier middlemen and aspiring Catholics frequently outbid Presbyterian tillage farmers. Many of the latter, especially if recent settlers, broke their shallow ties to Ulster and emigrated to New England, claiming that "one reason . . . for their going is the raising of the rent on the land to such a high rate that they cannot support their families thereon with the greatest industry." Moreover, in 1715–20 the raising of rents coincided with religious persecution and a series of natural disasters—bad weather, crop failures, livestock diseases, high food prices, smallpox epidemics—which also encouraged Presbyterian emigration and reportedly left some landlords' estates "all waste the tenants being all gone to New England."[23]

After a brief interlude, Ulster emigration peaked again in 1725–29; some 4,000 departures occurred in 1728 alone, and Protestant officials began to voice fears that northern Ireland was being abandoned to the Catholics. Again, the major causes were higher rents and disastrous harvests. More late-seventeenth-century leases expired, and proprietors commonly doubled rent levels. Furthermore, as the linen industry grew, many landlords inaugurated a century-long trend toward granting shorter leases directly to smallholders and cottier-weavers, a practice which enabled proprietors to bring rent charges into closer alignment with market conditions but which threatened to reduce substantial farmers to "the same abject poverty" formerly endured by their undertenants. Naturally, graziers and strong farmers found such changes "intolerable," and, as a magistrate reported in 1729, "ye richer sort" decided "that if they stay in Ireland their children will be slaves and that it is better for them to make money of their leases while they are still worth something to inable them to transport themselves and familys to America." However, in the late 1720s Ulster's lower classes suffered even greater hardship. So much northern farmland was still devoted to pasture that a series of poor crop yields in 1727–29 caused severe food shortages, drove provision prices beyond the means of the poor, and reduced many smallholders and laborers to a state of "misery and desolation." Thousands "crowded along the roads, scarce able to walk, and infinite numbers starved in every ditch"; some fled to Britain in search of employment, but many others signed on as indentured servants and sailed to North America alongside their more affluent countrymen. Surprisingly, few observers cited the contemporary depression in the linen trade as a major cause for the 1725–29 emigrations. Linen manufacturing was probably not yet central to the North's economy: certainly, reduced incomes from weaving and spinning exacerbated the distress caused by high rents and food prices, but the hardships of the late 1720s probably encouraged landlords and tenants alike to concentrate more heavily on linen production. However, the growth of the linen industry already had altered the patterns of Ulster emigration: beginning in the late 1720s the great majority of Ulstermen traveled to Delaware River ports such as Philadelphia, Chester, and New Castle in the holds of ships which had sailed to Ulster towns to exchange Pennsylvania flaxseed for cargoes of linen cloth, fare-paying passengers, and indentured servants. Indeed, it was during this period that Ulster landlords and officials first complained of shipowners and agents "tempting and ensnareing" unwary emigrants by "promising them liberty and ease" in the New World.[24]

Between 1730 and 1769 perhaps 70,000 northern Presbyterians sailed to the colonies; the movement might have been even greater if the activities of French privateers and news of Indian massacres on the American frontier had not dampened enthusiasm for emigration. The drain of tenant farmers was relatively steady. Some tenants may have reacted positively to the allure of greater profits in a more commercialized Ulster, but many others, such as David Lindsey, resented landlords' demands to modernize their holdings through enclosures, fertilizers, and other means—especially when such expensive "improvements" almost inevitably presaged rent increases. Thus, in 1758 Lindsey complained to his cousin in "Pennsillvena," "[w]e are now oppressed with our lands in two-acre parts and quicking [making hedges], and only two years time for doing it all—yea, we cannot stand more." Other farmers grumbled that rents, tithes, and taxes were so high "that the most exerted Industry scarcely affords a Comfortable Subsistence to their Families." "[H]aving no hopes to obtain better terms by renewal of their Leases when expired," many Ulster tenants responded eagerly to letters from American relatives, the propaganda of shipping agents, and the blandishments of colonial governments and Ulster-born land speculators who sought to lure settlers to the frontiers of Pennsylvania, the southern colonies, even to Nova Scotia. For example, in the 1730s and again in the 1760s the South Carolina and Georgia assemblies successfully encouraged Ulster emigration by offering cheap land, free tools and seed, and temporary maintenance to farmers willing to settle in the southern backcountry. As David Lindsey declared to his American cousin, "The good bargains of your land in that country doe greatly encourage me to 'pluck up my spirits and make redie for the journey. . . ."[25]

In 1730–69 an increasing proportion of Ulster Presbyterian emigrants were of lower-class origin: poor smallholders, artisans, cottier-weavers, and laborers. During the eighteenth century about a third of all harvests were bad, and general crop failures, as in 1740–41 and in 1755–56, reduced employment and created food shortages which compelled the poor to seek relief through emigration. In addition, though it is arguable that the steady expansion of linen manufacturing temporarily inhibited lower-class emigration by increasing employment and enabling subdivision of holdings at home, in the long run the growth of the linen industry created economic and demographic pressures which could find release only in outbreaks of agrarian violence, such as the Oakboy disturbances of 1763–64, or through emigration. At first linen weaving or spinning promised security, even upward mobility, through increased incomes, but such hopes proved illusory as "the price of land . . . kept pace with the linen manufacture to the summit." Dependence upon linen weaving made Ulster's lower classes more subject to market fluctuations, and by mid-century some rural areas were grossly overpopulated with cottier-weavers, whose tiny plots covering the hillsides no longer produced half the food necessary for their families' subsistence. Moreover, the trend toward functional specialization within the industry reduced growing numbers of weavers to the status of landless employees, easily exploited by petty "manufacturers," yarn jobbers, and other middlemen. In such circumstances, prospects of high wages and cheap lands in the colonies proved increasingly irresistible.[26]

However, Ulster's lower classes could rarely afford to pay their own fares to America or to emigrate in family groups. Between 1720 and 1770 an Atlantic passage, including provisions, cost between £9 and £3. 5s., and those who intended to farm in the New World needed at least £10 more for inland transportation, fees to secure land grants, tools and seed, and subsistence until their first harvest. Such sums represented over a year's wages for most weavers and laborers. Consequently, after 1730 at least half of all Presbyterian emigrants went out individually, as either indentured servants or "redemptioners." The difference could be crucial: indentured servants were irrevocably bound to the shipmaster or his assigns for a stipulated term; conversely, redemptioners could purchase their freedom by repaying or "redeeming" the cost of their passage shortly after arrival in the colonies. Of course, if the redemptioner failed to secure the passage money—either from friends or by indenting himself—then he was at the mercy of the shipmaster, who could sell his services to the highest bidder. Despite the gamble, many poor emigrants preferred to chance self-redemption, especially if they had relatives already in America. Alternatively, some poor emigrants indentured themselves to wealthier countrymen who wanted to take laborers with them to the colonies. Thus, Robert Parke, a farmer in Pennsylvania, advised his "old friend Samuel Thornton" to "Procure 3 or 4 Lusty Servants & Agree to pay their passage," for "at this Side he might sell 2 & pay the others' passage with the money." Such strategies enabled a growing number of lower-class Ulstermen to reach the "land of promise."[27]

Finally, in 1770–75, northern Irish emigration peaked as adverse circumstances affecting both strong farmers and peasants coincided to drive some 30,000 Ulster Presbyterians to the New World. For several decades landlord-tenant relations had grown more commercialized: rent levels rose and evictions became common as proprietors increasingly ignored the claims of sitting tenants and canted expired leases to the highest bidders. Such trends, most prevalent in the linen districts around Belfast, climaxed in the early 1770s when Lord Donegall imposed large fines for the renewal of leases on his huge estates in eastern Ulster. This action had a "ripple" effect which united all rural classes in anger and distress and led directly to the Steelboy uprising of 1771–74. Substantial occupying tenants were infuriated when the marquis granted leases to rentier middlemen and speculators rather than to themselves. Without direct leases, strong farmers feared what one called "the melancholy prospect of being turn'd out of their possessions and obliged to remove their numerous families to America." Subsequent evictions did occur, but those injured most were the smallholder and cottier subtenants lowest on the ladder of exploitation; their per-acre rents increased considerably, and they provided the bulk of the membership of the Hearts of Steel. Furthermore, lower-class grievances were exacerbated by a severe depression in the linen industry, which put a third of Ulster's weavers out of employment, and by high food prices caused by poor harvests and the activities of engrossers. The consequent distress alone was sufficient to increase emigration, but official repression of the Steelboys caused thousands more to flee "[t]hrough dread of prose-

cution for the riots which their idea of . . . persecution had occasioned";
one observer declared that "whole villages" embarked for America. Some
emigrants were well-to-do farmers who sold their leases and took several
hundred pounds overseas; however, most were the "poor and unemployed"—
those whom "respectable" contemporaries regarded as "idle and worthless,
and not reckoned any loss to the country."[28]

Thus, in large measure the rapid commercialization of eighteenth-century
Ulster explains the outpouring of northern Presbyterians to colonial America. In addition, it may be, as some scholars argue, that the Calvinist emphasis on the religious "calling" to pursue wealth encouraged Ulster Presbyterians to engage in market-oriented activities at home and to emigrate
abroad when economic adversities thwarted material aspirations. The celebrated industry of Ulster's overseas merchants, and the readiness of poor
Presbyterians to hazard the perils of indentured servitude to reach America's shores, would seem to corroborate the Weber thesis. By contrast,
although Ulster's Catholics were subject to similar economic pressures,
culture and experience combined to inhibit their emigration. The fact that
many Presbyterians, relatively recent migrants from Scotland, lacked the
Catholics' deep roots in Ulster soil may also help explain the great numerical and proportional disparities between their emigrations. Indeed, in the
late nineteenth and early twentieth centuries, Protestant Americans of Ulster descent wove a "Scotch-Irish myth" to distinguish their "race" as
separate from and superior to the native Irish. Apologists as eminent as
Woodrow Wilson alleged that certain modern traits peculiar to the Ulster
Presbyterian heritage, such as "rugged individualism" and entrepreneurial
acumen, had enabled Ulster colonists to achieve remarkable material success and such a thorough assimilation to their new environment that by
1776 they were unanimous in their enthusiasm for the American Revolution. Many reputable scholars have sanctioned elements of this myth: for
example, James Leyburn asserted that because of their outlook Ulster emigrants never endured "minority" status, never were "marginal men" caught
between two cultures, but instead were "full Americans almost from the
moment they took up their farms in the backcountry."[29]

It may be that certain aspects of the Presbyterians' worldview made
them more *predisposed* than Catholics to commerce and emigration. Perhaps the prevalence of "tenant-right" among Ulster Presbyterians not only
facilitated emigration by enabling farmers to sell their leases but also reflected a market ethos which encouraged such sales. Probably, there was a
dialectical relation between worldview and commercial expansion in eighteenth-century Ulster: the increasing marketability of land, the new forms
of social stratification resulting from the growth of the linen industry, the
fluctuations of market prices for crops and manufactured goods, the broadening of horizons consequent upon the expansion of internal and overseas
trade—all had secularizing and individualizing effects on Presbyterian society, sundering its members from traditional relationships and attitudes, and
making emigration an acceptable option. In the late eighteenth century, the

growth of "Moderate" or "New Light" Presbyterianism in relatively urbanized eastern Ulster was one indication of the rationalization of values that accompanied economic expansion. Nevertheless, such influences spread slowly, first among urban dwellers and large farmers, merchants and linen drapers, and it would be incorrect to describe most eighteenth-century Ulster Presbyterians as future-oriented, profit-seeking entrepreneurs. Although a commercial mentality led some large farmers to practice impartible inheritance, thus obliging superfluous sons to emigrate, contemporary observers usually decried the absence of anything resembling a "Protestant work ethic" among the vast majority of Ulster's rural dwellers. This was particularly true of the Presbyterian smallholders and cottier-weavers whose lack of "ambition" Arthur Young criticized in the 1770s, but even relatively well-to-do tenants merely sought what they called a "comfortable subsistence" for themselves and their children. In short, despite Ulster's commercial growth, the goals of most Presbyterians remained traditional in orientation, even if increasingly modern in the means of achievement employed. The validity and force of tradition remained marked, as in most Ulstermen's continued propensity for partible inheritance—a custom which mitigated the felt necessity for emigration. To be sure, the mere fact of 200,000 Presbyterian departures during 1700–1776 indicates the *relative* modernity of northern Irish society, and it is probably true that those who went abroad were less parochial than those who stayed at home. Nevertheless, most Ulster emigrants sought not upward mobility but an "independence" defined as the security enjoyed by the self-sufficient yeoman farmer or self-employed artisan—a security which was becoming increasingly elusive in Ulster. Thus, they departed to escape economic processes and demographic pressures which threatened to reduce them or their children to "slavery"—perhaps landlessness, certainly a greater degree of dependence on market forces manipulated by rack-renting landlords, parasitical middlemen, and exploitative employers. Of course, both in Ireland and in America, novel activities eventually engendered new conceptualizations of purpose, especially when innovations—such as emigration—were rewarded with material gains. However, the image of the ambitious, entrepreneurial Ulsterman or Scotch-Irish American was a more accurate reflection of late-nineteenth-century Belfast or Pittsburgh than of eighteenth-century Ulster or colonial America.[30]

For example, it is significant that Presbyterian spokesmen usually explained or justified emigration as compelled by religious and political persecution rather than by personal, materialistic ambitions. Indeed, Ulster Presbyterian society, religiously based by definition, was characterized by a strong sense of communal solidarity, which constrained overtly individualistic behavior. Divinely ordained and ideally eternal covenants reinforced the natural ties which bound families and neighbors, ministers and congregations, together in the face of external enemies and internal dissension. The church itself enforced social as well as doctrinal discipline through kirk sessions, regional presbyteries, and general synods. Although Ulster

Presbyterianism repeatedly fractured over contending interpretations of Scripture, each fragment zealously preserved the ideals of cohesion and uniformity. In such circumstances, it was understandable that Presbyterian leaders would explain emigration, an action which entailed the disruption of covenanted congregations, as sanctioned only by communal exigencies rather than by individual aspirations. Fortunately for them, Ulstermen had historical precedents which justified a view of emigration as occasioned by religious and political oppression.[31]

Irish Presbyterians believed that their ancestors had struck a sacred bargain with the English monarchy which guaranteed their religious and political "liberties" in return for serving as the king's loyal garrison in the midst of his "papist" enemies. Whenever the king or Parliament broke that compact, as ofttimes happened despite Ulster's fidelity, Presbyterians felt justified in abandoning Ireland for a more congenial environment. The first such effort occurred during the reign of Charles I, when Irish Presbyterians experienced the same High Anglican persecution which stimulated English Puritan emigration. In 1636 some 140 Ulstermen, led by their ministers, left Belfast Lough aboard the biblically named *Eagle Wing* to seek "the public liberty of pure ordinances" in New England. Severe storms and adverse winds persuaded these Irish pilgrims to return to Ulster, but despite its failure the *Eagle Wing* expedition provided a model for subsequent Presbyterian emigration. Later, under Charles II and James II, religious persecution occasioned emigration by a small number of Presbyterian ministers and laymen from western Ulster. Finally, although Ulstermen fought bravely to secure Protestant ascendancy in the "Glorious Revolution" against King James, in Queen Anne's reign the Anglican-dominated Irish Parliament passed penal legislation against Dissenters. The Sacramental Test Act of 1704 barred Presbyterians from civil and military offices; closed their churches, schools, and burying grounds; and prohibited Dissenting clergymen from officiating at weddings or funerals. Penalties could be harsh; in 1713 the Reverend Alexander McCracken of Lisburn was jailed for six months and fined £500 for refusing to conform. Again Presbyterians responded by emigrating, especially to New England, where Puritan clergymen promised Ulstermen "all the Brotherly Assistance that we are capable of giving you." Consequently, much of the exodus of 1717–20 was led by ministers, and its tone was set by the Reverend James McCracken of Aghadowey, whose farewell sermon explained that he and his congregation left home "to avoid oppression and cruel bondage, to shun persecution and designed ruin, to withdraw from the communion of idolators, and to have an opportunity of worshipping God according to the dictates of conscience and the rules of His inspired Word."[32]

Anglican contemporaries scoffed at such pious proclamations and argued that Presbyterian emigrants' alleged religious and political grievances were "only imaginary," merely "some excuse for their goeing." Most historians of Ulster emigration agree, pointing out that during Queen Anne's reign—when persecution was at its height—little emigration occurred, and those who did sail to New England encountered Puritan hostility, not hospitality. Large-scale emigration did not begin until after 1719, when compelled by economic circumstances, but in that year the Irish Parliament passed the first of an annual series of indemnity acts which gave Presbyterians effective toleration until the final repeal of the Sacramental Test Act in 1780. Although Presbyterians remained excluded from government posts until the American Revolution, such disabilities directly affected only an affluent, largely urban minority—not the vast majority of tenant farmers and artisans who left Ulster in family groups or as individuals, rather than in congregations led by persecuted clergymen.[33]

Nevertheless, throughout the eighteenth and even into the nineteenth century, Presbyterian emigration retained the flavor of a communal exodus compelled by religious and political oppression. In 1729 an exasperated magistrate remarked that although Ulstermen no longer experienced persecution, still their "[m]inisters have taken their shear of pains to seduce their poor ignorant hearers, by bellowing from the pulpits . . . that God had appoynted a country for them to dwell in . . . and desires them to depart thence, where they will be freed from the bondage of Egipt and goe to ye land of Cannan. . . ." There were many reasons for the perpetuation of this traditional explanation of what seems, in retrospect, to have been a secularly motivated movement. First, the concerted, albeit ineffective, opposition to Ulster emigration by Anglican landlords and officials—who feared the loss of so many rent-paying Protestants—seemed to substantiate Presbyterians' beliefs that they were indeed fleeing from captivity. Second, Presbyterian leaders, lay and clerical, tried to manipulate Anglican fears by arguing that emigration, purportedly due to proscriptive legislation alone, could be stemmed if the Ascendancy would repeal the Sacramental Test Act. Thus, traditional outlooks merged with pragmatic political considerations to demand that emigration be justified on religious rather than materialistic grounds. For example, although the Reverend Mr. McCracken became a cultural hero, a second Moses leading his flock to a new promised land, a minister such as Isaac Taylor of Ardstraw, who openly admitted that his desire to emigrate stemmed only from "the want of a necessary support" from his impoverished congregation, earned communal opprobrium for his honesty. Third, in spite of general toleration after 1719, incidents of overt persecution still occurred, stimulating emigration and reinforcing traditional attitudes. For instance, in 1764 the Reverend Thomas Clark of Monaghan, several times arrested for refusing to take oaths by kissing the Bible, led his entire congregation to the New World. Fourth, such incidents, coupled with the fact that at best Presbyterianism enjoyed merely a grudging toleration, engendered deep resentment among those who considered themselves both God's chosen people and the king's most faithful subjects. Penal legislation which classed Presbyterians with despised and disloyal "papists" was highly offensive, and Dissenters particularly resented paying tithes to Anglican clergymen, many of whom were notoriously rapacious and indolent. Even the Anglican archbishop William King admitted that his ministers were regarded "as a parcel of men who have invented a trade for our easy and convenient living," and the feelings of most Presbyterians were summed up by one emigrant who remembered the local parson as "an old Boor" who was "possessed of no more religion than the old Gray Mare he rode and which he would if possible rode to the devil of Sunday morning to preach and Receive half a guinea." In addition, tithes, which rose as land valuations increased, constituted a serious economic burden as well as a galling symbol of Presbyterian inferiority; consequently, throughout the eighteenth century Ulstermen claimed that the desire to escape from tithes was a primary motive for emigration. Finally, and most important, Ulster Presbyterians viewed history as if it were a morality play—with themselves in the role of Old Testament Israelites—which would end in the prophesied millennium when they would be delivered from their enemies; consequently, they regarded the secular and the supernatural—economic, political, and religious causation—as inseparable. Presbyterian countrymen saw themselves as "exiles" already in an Ulster where they labored under the harsh authority of Anglican pharaohs, and they interpreted the adverse consequences of commercialization not as the inexorable workings of impersonal market forces but as evidence of a villainous campaign to suppress their civil and religious liberties. Harsh landlords were not only "rack-renters" but also representatives of an evil, heretical Ascendancy; proprietors' policies of canting farms to the highest bidders—often to Catholics—were part of an insidious conspiracy by Tories suspected of "popish," Jacobite sympathies to destroy "true Protestantism" in Ireland. Thus, for Ulster emigrants, and particularly for such as the fugitive Steelboys, economic, religious, and political grievances merged: the flight of Lord Donegall's rebellious tenants in the 1770s seemed but a continuation of earlier migrations inspired by Stuart persecution. However, the prayers of God's chosen were answered, for—as a Presbyterian minister in New York proclaimed to "aw the poor Folk" of Ulster—"God has open'd a Door for their Deliverance" in America.[34]

Ulster Presbyterians conceptualized the New World in material as well as prophetic terms. However, the promotional literature which enticed Ulstermen overseas—the advertisements of shipping agents and land speculators, as well as the letters written by ordinary emigrants—demonstrated the precapitalist outlook of most northern Presbyterians who sailed to colonial America. Even if, as critics charged, emigration promoters employed "Forgery & Lyes" to seduce Ulstermen to leave home, their descriptions of the colonies were designed to appeal to their audience's fondest dreams. In general, those dreams reflected traditional, rural aspirations. Promoters portrayed America as an agrarian paradise, a "new Eden," where every man could enjoy all the "blessings" so lacking in an increasingly commercialized, stratified, and overpopulated Ulster: "liberty and ease" on abundant land, sufficient for both the emigrants and their posterity, unencumbered by the rents, tithes, and taxes which pauperized Irish farmers and drove them to an ever-deeper dependence on market prices for labor and linens. "[F]rom tenants they are become landlords," wrote one agent, describing the security and comfort enjoyed by those his ships had carried to Nova Scotia, and "from working for others they now work for themselves," experiencing an "independence" unattainable at home. Security, safety, and material contentment—these were the goals which promotional literature repeatedly stressed: "we have . . . plenty of good eating and drinking, . . . with good punch, wine, and beer," declared a land speculator in pre-Revolutionary Georgia, adding the clinching enticement that those who purchased slaves could live especially "easy and well." The handful of extant letters written by actual settlers offered similar attractions. Dissenters such as Morris Birbeck and Robert Parke described rural America as a land of incredible plenty: "there are . . . Hazles, wild Roses, Grape Vines in abundance bearing fine Fruit of wch I partook with no small pleasure," wrote Birbeck of his "Rich Land" in "New Garden," North Carolina, in addition to every "Variety of flowering Shrubs, Plumb Trees, Sassafrass & other aromaticks . . . too tedious to enumerate." "This country abounds in fruit," declared Parke from his Pennsylvania farm. "Scarce an house but has an Apple, Peach & cherry orchard," and even farm laborers enjoyed "a pint of Rum beside meat & drink of the best, for no workman works without their Victuals in the bargain." In short, what little of their testimony survives indicates that most Ulstermen viewed America not as a field for untrammeled individualism but as a place where their families could secure "a good and comfortable settlement, free from all those oppressions and impositions which they are subject to" in Ireland. This appealing image made an enormous impact on Presbyterian Ulster, sustaining a steady flow of emigrants.[35]

Finally, the record of the Ulster Presbyterian experience in colonial America refutes the purported uniformity and modernity of the Scotch-Irish myth. That experience was very diverse, as might be expected of an emigration well under way for six decades before the American Revolution; by the time the Steelboys landed in the early 1770s, second- and third-generation Ulster-Americans were settled in towns and on farms from Nova Scotia to Georgia. The character of Ulster emigration varied over time, perhaps becoming more secular by the eve of the Revolution. Different New World environments also precluded social or cultural homogeneity. Although perhaps 50,000 Ulstermen settled in the northern colonies, transatlantic trade routes carried most Presbyterians to the Delaware estuary, especially to Pennsylvania, where Cumberland County became the "cradle" of Ulster settlement. In the 1730s a second wave of emigrants, accompanied by the children of earlier settlers, moved farther west in Pennsylvania and south into the Valley of Virginia. By the 1750s a third movement, now largely composed of the American-born, pushed farther south into the Carolina and Georgia backcountry, there mixing with recent emigrants who had come directly from Ulster through southern seaports such as Charleston and Savannah; by 1790 perhaps 50 percent or more of the settlers on the trans-Appalachian frontier were of Ulster lineage. In addition, during the last pre-Revolutionary decades increasing numbers of Presbyterian emigrants, mostly skilled artisans and indentured servants, settled in colonial seaports such as Philadelphia and New York where earlier arrivals and their children had already attained status and, sometimes, real affluence.[36]

Certainly, many Ulstermen found neither ease nor hospitality in the New World. Emigrants of genteel birth or education found the lack of familiar amenities depressing. For example, John Rea, a land speculator in Georgia, warned his brother that in the colonies "there is not the pleasure of society that there is" at home, nor "the comfort of the gospel preached, nor fairs and markets to go to." Farming uncleared American land was a backbreaking experience, and life on the frontier could be barbaric and demoralizing—as Robert Witherspoon, who in 1734 sailed from Belfast to settle in the South Carolina wilderness—testified in his journal: "we were oppressed with fears, on divers accounts," he wrote, "especially of being massacred by the Indians, or bitten by snakes, or torn by wild beasts, or being lost and perishing in the woods. . . . [M]any were taken with the fever and ague, . . . grew dropsical and died." Presbyterian indentured servants often fared little better than their Catholic peers. After arrival in the colonies, servants and redemptioners who failed to redeem themselves were sold at auction like goods or slaves, often purchased in groups by "soul drivers" who hawked them through the countryside. Although every colonial government provided servants some legal protection against abuse, and promised them "freedom dues" on completion of service, the welfare of individual servants depended ultimately upon their masters' means and character. Like Catholic bondsmen, Presbyterian servants fared worst in the plantation South and best in the middle colonies, especially if they were skilled craftsmen indentured to urban masters, preferably of the same nationality. However, although James Murray of New York wrote to a friend in County Tyrone, "There is servants come here out of Ereland . . . who are now Justices of the Piece . . . ," few Ulster servants ever achieved such high status; even in prosperous Philadelphia, the career of Charles Thomson from Maghera, County Derry, who became secretary to the Continental Congress, was exceptional. Most Presbyterian servants labored in the countryside, and remained there when freed: as tenant farmers or laborers in the eastern districts, or as squatters in the backcountry, where visitors such as the Irish Anglican Charles Woodmason described them as "lazy, dissipated, and poor."[37]

Furthermore, English colonists generally regarded all Irish Presbyterians as alien and inferior. Despite their common Calvinism, New England Puritans despised Ulster emigrants as "uncleanly, unwholesome and disgusting," and even in Pennsylvania—after an initial welcome—Quaker officials soon condemned them as "a pernicious and pugnacious people." Both in Pennsylvania and in the Carolinas, colonial authorities exploited Irish Presbyterians settled on the western frontier, milking them for revenue but according them little political influence and inadequate protection against the Indians. On occasion Ulstermen revolted against such treatment. In 1764 an armed mob of Presbyterian farmers marched on Philadelphia to demand relief from the Quaker-dominated assembly, and between 1766 and 1771 their counterparts in western North Carolina formed the "Regulation" movement to protest official corruption and high taxes; for a time the Regulators virtually ruled large parts of the Carolina backcountry, until colonial troops crushed their "army" and hanged many of their leaders at the battle of Alamance.[38]

Nevertheless, few Ulster emigrants became as alienated from colonial America as the Tyrone-born clergyman James McSparran of Rhode Island, who cautioned Irishmen to remain at home and avowed his own desire "to end my Days nearer to where I began them than I am now." Despite all their difficulties, most Presbyterian colonists succeeded in achieving a greater degree of material comfort than could be realized by any but an affluent few in Ireland. By 1776 Ulster-America was a complex, if widely dispersed, society, able to attract and absorb a continual influx of newcomers of all levels of skills and wealth. At the top of Ulster-America was a growing and influential urban elite of merchants, lawyers, newspaper editors, and professional men, supplemented by a prosperous middle class of shopkeepers, artisans, country traders, and commercial farmers. These men, on the cutting edge of commercialization, prototypes for later myth makers, served as the political and cultural spokesmen for the great majority of Ulster-Americans. That majority, rural rather than urban, was also prosperous compared with those who remained in Ireland. However, its members still pursued an "independence" largely defined in traditional rather than entrepreneurial terms. Some scholars have argued that the prevalence among Ulster-American farmers of scattered homesteads, instead of nucleated settlements, proves that their dominant values were "modern," individualistic, and acquisitive. However, most Ulstermen had lived similarly before emigrating, and in America their marked propensity to congregate in what were known as "the Irish settlements"—ethnically homogeneous townships with names such as Colerain, Donegal, and Fermanagh—suggests a desire to preserve traditional values as well as nomenclature. Most Ulster-American farms were subsistence oriented, with at most one-third of the produce (significantly termed the "surplus") carried to market. Even in market-oriented eastern Pennsylvania, few farmers specialized; their modes and implements of production were highly conservative and resistant to suggested innovations. As in Ireland, Ulster-American farmers chose to settle well-drained hillside soils rather than richer but wetter bottomlands, and their predilection for unfenced cattle grazing reflected an adaptation of the old "outfield" system to a new environment of boundless forests. Likewise, the Ulster-American farmer's reputation for slovenly destitution—a semblance often masking material abundance—perhaps stemmed from the Irish tenant's old reluctance to display wealth before either landlords or jealous neighbors. Despite the superior productivity of colonial soils, old-country patterns of cooperative labor and resource distribution persisted among neighbors and kinfolk—most strikingly in the Ulster-American farmer's continued practice of partible inheritance, even to the point where subdivision made "independence" as self-sufficiency almost impossible. Of course, demographic pressures and rising land prices eventually obliged later generations of Ulster-Americans to abandon long-settled areas and move south and west in search of new lands; however, it would be ahistorical to view such pioneers as frontier capitalists, for, like their emigrant fathers, they generally sought what in 1773 a Presbyterian clergyman called "the enjoyment of independence in their wordly circumstances." In short, traditional goals were pursued and realized in new settings, and even the "moral economy" of the Oak- and Steelboys lived on: for example, in early eighteenth-century Pennsylvania, where Irish squatters refused to pay quitrents, on the grounds that "it was against the laws of God and nature, that so much land should be idle while so many Christians wanted it to labor on and raise their bread"; in western North Carolina, where the Regulators denounced merchant-usurers and lawyers as "parasites" and "upstarts" and asserted their "right" to take possession of vacant land regardless of the claims of distant proprietors and speculators; and, much later, again in Pennsylvania, where in 1794 the so-called Whiskey Rebels took up arms against the same hated excise tax which had oppressed their ancestors in Ireland.[39]

The question whether by 1776 Ulster colonists were still "Irish" or had become "American" cannot be answered simply. Unlike the contemporary Catholic emigration, the Ulster Presbyterian exodus included a large number of whole families and women generally. That fact encouraged endogamous marriage patterns—as obtained even in ethnically mixed areas such as western North Carolina—and enabled the creation of an "Ulster-American" society which displayed certain cultural continuities. However, the degree of cultural transmission or retention depended heavily upon length and place of settlement. Second- and third-generation Ulster-Americans, particularly if located in large towns or highly commercialized rural districts, were largely assimilated to predominantly Anglo-American patterns. Conversely, more recent emigrants, especially if settled in almost exclusively Irish areas, remained culturally distinctive. Thus, during the American Revolution a British general observed of the Steelboy emigrants of 1770–74, "From their numbers . . . national customs were kept amongst them and the pride of having sprung in the old country . . . prevented them from entirely assimilating with the Americans." Indeed, in relatively isolated Ulster-American settlements, some Irish customs survived for generations. For example, in the late eighteenth century the inhabitants of Londonderry, New Hampshire, founded in 1719, still fired guns at wedding celebrations (an archaic triumphal gesture toward disarmed Ulster Catholics) and still spent lavishly on—and drank heavily at—traditional wakes and funeral feasts. Even on the eve of the Civil War, Ulster-American farmers in western Pennsylvania—only a few miles from Pittsburgh, smoky citadel of Scotch-Irish enterprise—still spoke a blend of Lallans and English and combined a rigidly conservative Presbyterianism with beliefs in fairies and in the efficacy of pre-Christian "predictive" celebrations.[40]

However, in at least one important respect assimilation was widespread. Since Ulster Presbyterians defined group identity largely in religious terms, it is ironic that most eighteenth-century Ulster-Americans seem to have strayed from the kirk, despite the prominent role their clergy played in the early stages of emigration. To be sure, colonial Ulstermen built Presbyterian churches, petitioned for clergymen from home, and established colonial academies or "log colleges" to train an American ministry. Nonetheless, Presbyterian clergymen remained scarce in the colonies, particularly in the backcountry, where so many Ulstermen settled. As a result, thousands of Ulster-Americans, "burned over" by the evangelical fires of the first Great Awakening, turned to the Methodists, Baptists, and other denominations for inspiration and solace; by 1800 only 15,000 adult Americans were members of Presbyterian churches, although during the preceding century perhaps twenty times that number had emigrated from Ireland alone. Furthermore, revivalism—the dominant form of American Protestantism after the 1740s—deeply affected Ulster-Americans even if they remained loyal to their fathers' church: in the ensuing competition for souls, regardless of their ethnicity, American Presbyterianism shed many of the customs and doctrines brought from Ulster; even more important, during the revivals those who experienced traumatic "conversions" underwent a psychological reorientation away from the country of their earthly nativity and toward what a later Ulster emigrant called "the land of my second birth." In short, evangelical Protestantism not only submerged Ulster Presbyterianism's ethnocentric millennial tradition in an inclusively American crusade against sin but also—with its emphasis upon *personal* salvation—combined with broadening economic horizons to begin the transformation of communal-oriented Ulstermen into more individualistic "Scotch-Irish" Americans.[41]

In 1776, though, most Irish Presbyterian emigrants and their descendants were still "Ulster-Americans" whose customs and attitudes reflected a practical synthesis of cultural retentions, borrowings, and adaptations. On the level of material culture, for example, Ulster-American farmers cultivated flax, wove linens, and adapted Indian corn to the same multiple uses which oats served at home; they borrowed the ubiquitous log cabin from Swedish and German settlers, but reshaped its dimensions and floor plan in conformity with traditional Ulster farmhouses; even their music was a blend of Ulster Scottish, native Irish, and Anglo-American forms. Perhaps most important, Ulster-America's responses to the American Revolution reflected mixtures of Irish and American, traditional and contemporary, concerns. According to the Scotch-Irish myth, Ulster colonists rallied as one man to the patriot cause: "Call this war by whatever name you may," declared an oft-quoted Hessian officer, "only call it not an American rebellion; it is nothing more or less than a Scotch Irish Presbyterian rebellion." However, a large minority of Ulster-Americans, particularly in the

southern colonies, became Tories or, at best, "tepid patriots." In North
Carolina many defeated Regulators refused to join tidewater planters and
"upstart" entrepreneurs who now proclaimed themselves "champions" of
the people they had so recently helped suppress; and in Georgia some
Ulstermen remained loyal out of gratitude for the free passages and other
assistance received from a paternalistic royal government. As a result, in
the southern backcountry the Revolution quickly degenerated into a savage
civil war among Ulster-American factions. Even the fugitive Steelboys, although generally fierce opponents of English rule on both sides of the Atlantic, contributed a Loyalist regiment to the British army after General
Clinton played upon their "latent seeds of national attachment" and lured
them with the "prospect of returning home without apprehension."[42]

Nevertheless, in general Ulster's political traditions inclined its colonial
sons to be "unfriendly to monarchical government," as one royal official
lamented. Those traditions originated in seventeenth-century notions of
Presbyterian "liberties," guaranteed by the crown, sealed in blood by the
events of 1641 and by the Glorious Revolution, broadened in 1698 by William Molyneux's "bold and pernicious" assertion of Protestant Ireland's
constitutional equality with England, democratized by the radical Whig
teachings of Francis Hutcheson of County Down, and transmitted to America by one of Hutcheson's students, Francis Alison of Donegal, who emigrated in 1735 and at the College of Philadelphia taught Ulster-America's
future Revolutionary leaders—Charles Thomson, Thomas McKean, George
Read, among others—that "[t]he end of all civil power is the public happiness,
& any power not conducive to this is unjust & the People who gave it may
Justly abolish it." Sometimes the transatlantic continuities, personal and
ideological, were remarkable. In 1714 the Reverend Robert Craighead
fled Anglican persecution in Ulster and accepted Cotton Mather's offer of
asylum in Boston; three generations later, his direct descendants inspired
Ulster-American farmers in Mecklenburg County, North Carolina, to declare independence from England. Likewise, when other Ulstermen in the
southern colonies wavered in their allegiance to the Revolution, Philadelphia's Presbyterian clergy appealed to their memories of Irish oppression,
and declared, "If we are now wrong in our conduct, our forefathers that
fought for liberty at Londonderry and Enniskillen in King James' time were
wrong. . . . But we hope that such language will never be heard from the
mouth of a protestant. . . ." Indeed, although Ulster Presbyterianism's
radical strain could flower in an America where fears of "papist" majorities no longer constrained democratic expressions, anti-Catholicism also
linked Ulster-Americans to the patriot cause—in response to the Quebec
Act of 1774, and later to the "scum of the Irish Roman Catholics" who
served in the British forces.[43]

These hereditary sentiments, so compatible with Anglo-Americans' own
grievances and political culture, did inspire Ulster-Americans to play a role
in the Revolution far out of proportion to their numbers. However, this
was particularly true only in the middle colonies, where uniquely Ameri-

can circumstances reinforced Irish Protestant traditions. In Pennsylvania, New Jersey, Delaware, and, to a lesser extent, New York and Maryland a mature elite of Presbyterian merchants, professional men, shopkeepers, and commercial farmers was ready to lead an Ulster-American rising against the local Anglican and Quaker ascendancies, which had long denied them political power commensurate with their economic achievements. Their opposition to "privilege," although born of American aspirations as well as Irish traditions, united them with their poorer coreligionists—artisans, subsistence farmers, laborers—who feared the emergence in the New World of the conditions which had threatened to pauperize them or their fathers in the Old. Thus, in all senses of the word, for Ulster-Americans the Revolution was a struggle to achieve and retain an "independence," and their victory not only added a new gloss to Ulster Presbyterians' perception of America as land of refuge and promise but also enabled Ulster-Americans and their descendants to justly claim the sobriquet of "American"—an achievement which later generations of Irish emigrants suffering nativist prejudice would often envy and attempt to emulate.[44]

In some respects, Irish Catholic and Protestant emigrations to colonial America were similar: economic distress and religious persecution inspired—and the expansion of Irish-American trade facilitated—both movements, and a majority of those in each group were indentured servants and redemptioners; in addition, Catholics and Dissenters alike perceived emigration as an act laden with political and religious significance. However, the differences between early Catholic and Protestant emigrations were more profound, for varying cultures and experiences combined to encourage a disproportionately large number of Protestants to hazard the journey to the New World during a period when the traffic in indentured servants enabled poor Irishmen of all faiths to "emigrate for nothing." Perhaps a Protestant worldview contained the seeds of an individualistic outlook which—nurtured by Irish Protestants' relative economic advantages and by Ulster's accelerated commercial growth—enabled business-minded Protestants to more easily sunder ties to kin and community and seek fortunes in a more fluid social environment. Although most Protestant emigrants sought an "independence" still defined in precapitalist terms—as the security and self-sufficiency enjoyed by yeoman farmers and self-employed artisans—most Catholics retained an outlook best characterized as "dependent," formalized in life-styles associated with clachan settlements and rundale cultivation, and expressed in Irish-speakers' traditional strictures against innovation and self-aggrandizement. Moreover, although during the colonial period most members of both religious groups remained intensely communal oriented, their conceptualizations of community were very different. The group identity of Irish Protestants, particularly of Dissenters, was linked primarily to a religious ideal which could be transferred to another land where conditions for its realization were more favorable; by contrast, Irish Catholic identity, especially of Irish-speakers, was tied to

Ireland itself and was inseparable from historical, cultural, religious, and linguistic associations with their homeland. Thus, at bottom, Irish Catholics' and early Irish Protestants' conceptualizations of emigration as "exile" were quite distinct: for the former, "exile" implied severe sociocultural discontinuities as well as political banishment; for the latter, although "exile" implied compulsion, it also anticipated fulfillment of communal goals and biblical prophecies in a new "promised land"—and, when those goals were realized in the colonies and confirmed in the American war against the English Antichrist, then Irish Protestants were no longer "exiles" but "Americans." Consequently, whereas Catholic emigration was largely a trickle of footloose individuals, culturally or circumstantially divorced from traditional bonds, Protestant emigration—especially Dissenter emigration—was a mass movement, a social exodus. Had Catholic experiences in colonial America been more positive, more departures would perhaps have occurred; certainly the creation of a cohesive and self-satisfied Ulster-America offered inducements to subsequent emigrants which the scattered, submerged, and largely downtrodden Irish Catholics in the New World could not provide. In later decades a more favorable image of America would combine with acute distress and the attrition of Gaelic culture at home to encourage more Catholic emigration. However, before 1776, experiences abroad only served to reinforce a traditional native Irish worldview which stigmatized emigration to America as less desirable than poverty and persecution in Ireland.

5

Liberty, Intolerance, and Profit: Irish Emigration, 1783–1814

The American Revolution interrupted the flow of Irish emigrants to the New World, but from 1783 through 1814 perhaps 100–150,000 crossed the Atlantic. In 1783 roughly 5,000 emigrants left from Ulster ports and from Dublin; in 1784 over 10,000 departed; and during the 1780s and 1790s the annual emigration rate was probably at least 5,000. In retrospect, it is remarkable that so many departures occurred. By destroying the British mercantile empire, the Revolution severely disrupted the old channels of Irish-American trade; after 1783 direct shipping between Ireland and the new United States steadily declined, and although Munster and south Leinster continued to provision the West Indies, that destination had long ceased to attract prospective emigrants. Furthermore, after the Revolution the formerly large traffic in Irish servants also diminished, since British captains could no longer count on American courts to enforce contracts of indenture; in the 1780s Irish merchants still offered to take "a few indentured servants," but by the 1790s such advertisements had virtually disappeared. In addition, between 1793 and 1814 almost continuous war between Britain and France curtailed all transatlantic shipping. Only in 1801–2, a brief interval of peace, did large numbers leave Ireland, and from 1803 to 1805 scarcely 1,000 managed to depart annually. In 1811 emigration from Ulster rose briefly to 3,500, but in 1812 war with the United States completely closed the sea-lanes until 1815.[1]

During wartime would-be emigrants feared not only enemy warships and privateers but also impressment into the undermanned British navy. Irish passengers often suffered impressment in mid-voyage, sometimes within sight of America's shores. Even emigrants of genteel background were not immune, as Wolfe Tone, an exiled leader of the United Irishmen, discovered in 1795 when three British frigates stopped the vessel carrying him to the "land of freedom": "after treating us with the greatest insolence," Tone wrote,

> they impressed every one of our hands save one, and near fifty of my fellow passengers. . . . As I was in a jacket and trowsers, one of the lieutenants ordered me into the boat as a fit man to serve the king, and it was only the screams of my wife and sister which induced him to desist.

Such incidents inspired public outrage in Ireland and probably caused post-ponement of many planned departures. However, the British government—operating under the prevalent mercantilist notion that all British subjects, no matter how humble, were a source of strength to the kingdom—regarded emigration, particularly to the rival United States, as tantamount to trea-son. In addition, Irish officials feared that the drain of skilled Protestants would weaken the Ascendancy at home and lead to the establishment of competing textile industries abroad. Consequently, in 1783 Parliament passed legislation which forbade any attempt to "contract with, entice, per-suade, solicit or seduce any manufacturer, workman, or artificer" to emi-grate. Some historians argue that such measures were ineffectual, since emigrating artisans could easily represent themselves as farmers to the port inspectors. Such evasion undoubtedly occurred, but restrictive legisla-tion caused great consternation in Ulster, where one would-be emigrant from County Tyrone lamented that now it was "a difficult matter to deter-mine on any thing." Even more effective was the Passenger Act of 1803, which regulated steerage conditions, required specific amounts of provi-sions, limited the number of passengers to a fixed proportion of a ship's registered tonnage, and discriminated against American-owned vessels, which had carried the bulk of the traffic. Although ostensibly a humani-tarian measure—and despite subterfuge by shipmasters and passengers alike—the 1803 act fulfilled its real purpose: by sharply raising fares be-yond the means of the poor, it checked departures by artisans and thereby reduced the volume of Irish emigration.[2]

Of those who succeeded in leaving Ireland despite these obstacles, at least two-thirds—some 100,000—were from Ulster, primarily Presbyterians of Scottish ancestry, the remainder being Catholics and Anglicans from the southern provinces. Evidence of the movement's social character is highly contradictory. In 1793 the customs officer at Newry, a port which drew emigrants from backward and religiously mixed south Ulster, declared that embarking vessels contained "no people of real property," but only "the lower order of tradesmen . . . besides numbers of no occupation that went as servants." "[T]he people now offering to go," he concluded, "are almost entirely of a very inferior class." Similarly, in 1796, reflecting upon the recent arrival of a shipload of Ulster emigrants, New York's city coun-cil deplored the "prodigious influx of indigent foreigners" who had become dependent on municipal charity. However, patrician and nativist biases frequently inspired such comments, and although many poor Irishmen did go abroad—for example, as servants to wealthier passengers—the declining servant trade combined with the 1803 Passenger Act to curtail lower-class emigration. Indeed, as surviving ships' manifests indicate, the bulk of the emigrants of 1783–1814 were substantial farmers and artisans—weavers, millwrights, tanners—in middling circumstances; moreover, a significant minority were from business and professional backgrounds—merchants, shopkeepers, clerks, schoolmasters, physicians, and so forth. Such emi-grants paid their own fares and embarked with some capital; large numbers traveled in family groups—a sure indication of relative affluence—while many of the remaining young, single men were probably superfluous, often skilled or educated sons of well-to-do parents who practiced impartible inheritance. (During this period very few single women emigrated, a sign of good marriage prospects in an expanding Irish economy.) Thus, in 1784 the *Belfast News-Letter* reported that that year's exodus was composed primarily of "the yeomanry . . . who . . . take with them from £300 to £700" and of "industrious" linen weavers who had "scraped together a sufficiency" to pay their families' passages. Likewise, seven years later the British consul in New York lamented that disembarking Ulstermen represented "a very great loss to . . . his Majesty's Dominions for they are not servants or redemptioners, but people who paid their passage before they embarked, and immediately on their arrival here went into the country, well-clad and with money in their pockets." In short, although it is probable that lower-class and Catholic emigration was significant during such years of political and agrarian unrest as 1796–98 and 1811–14, overall those who left Ireland in 1783–1814 were Protestants in fairly comfortable circumstances.[3]

However, at first glance this emigration seems surprising, for it took place during a period when Ireland enjoyed relative prosperity. High prices for Irish textile and agricultural products spurred economic growth and increased employment opportunities at home. For example, the linen industry recovered rapidly from the 1770s depression and expanded outside traditional manufacturing areas into southern and western Ulster, north Leinster, and Connaught. By the mid-1780s weavers in eastern Ulster enjoyed full employment; in Westmeath the spinning wheel became "the principle occupation of farmers daughters and a profitable source of revenue"; and even on the remote Mayo and Donegal coasts visitors reported that new income from weaving and spinning enabled once-impoverished peasants to purchase "sattin waistcoats . . . , white silk stockings, silver buckles and ruffled shirts." Moreover, in the late eighteenth century northern artisans and laborers, male and female, gained another source of income as English investors began to promote Irish cotton manufacturing. By 1810 the Belfast region had a dozen cotton mills, equipped with water- or steam-powered spinning frames, which employed about 1,700 operatives plus weavers and bleachers in the countryside. The cotton industry also spread to southern counties such as Louth, Wicklow, Queen's, and Cork—where nearly 2,000 weavers worked in the town of Bandon alone. Perhaps most important, 1783–1814 witnessed a great expansion of agriculture, especially tillage farming, stimulated by increased demand and Irish government bounties. From 1793 to 1814 almost constant war deprived England of European and American foodstuffs and made its people heavily dependent on Irish grain, flour, meat, and dairy products. Consequently, farm prices rose to unprecedented levels, and although landlords, middlemen, and strong farmers reaped most of the benefits, some profits trickled down to formerly destitute smallholders, such as those described

in 1814 by an Anglican parson in the parish of Lismore, County Waterford, as "now full, florid, well cloathed, nay many of them with horses,
boots, saddles; taking their wives behind them on pillions to mass, to fairs,
and to funerals." Inspired by the early fruits of commercialization and
freed from legal restrictions on profit-seeking by the Catholic Relief Acts
of the late eighteenth century, many Catholic as well as Protestant tenants
began to take long leases, improve holdings and farmhouses, and seek educations for their children. Moreover, the expansion of tillage generated
increased employment for farm laborers and for rural artisans such as
blacksmiths, wheelwrights, and masons. Small wonder that after 1814,
when farm prices fell catastrophically, most Irish countrymen remembered
1783–1814 as a "golden age"–particularly the years of the Napoleonic
Wars "when Boney, the Lord speed him! was uppermost."[4]

Yet, despite economic expansion, emigration continued; indeed, save for
the artificial limitations imposed by war and proscriptive legislation, it is
likely that annual departure rates in 1783–1814 would have far exceeded
those of preceding decades. Certainly, much emigration was almost automatic, the result of Ulster-America's continuing attraction to districts and
families in northern Ireland which had sent people overseas for nearly a
hundred years. Thus, large numbers of Ulstermen merely followed in the
wake of relatives who had emigrated before the American Revolution, as
letters written by Ulster-Americans settled on the trans-Appalachian frontier, in the Ohio Valley, and elsewhere amply demonstrate. Moreover, as
was noted above, a large proportion of these emigrants commanded capital, skills, and education; many were well-to-do farmers' sons who were
excluded from inheriting family holdings and who recognized that other
opportunities in even a relatively prosperous Ireland were far less prevalent and potentially lucrative than those in the new American Republic.
"[T]he young men of Ireland who wish to be free and happy should leave
it and come here as soon as possible," advised one Ulsterman settled in
Philadelphia, for "[t]here is no place in the world where a man meets so
rich a reward for good conduct and industry as in America." Enterprising
young Irishmen who followed such advice, desiring "to advance themselves
in life" and to "get independent . . . in a manner not to be done in
Ireland," were not exiles in any sense, but instead voluntary, even eager
emigrants; like John Bell, a medical student who left County Monaghan
before 1811, they listened to what he called the "whisperings of ambition."[5]

The initial emergence of such motivations among emigrants in 1783–
1814 indicates how the accelerated commercialization of Irish society
facilitated departures by disrupting traditional social bonds and subtly transforming older attitudes. Expanding opportunities for profit not only encouraged affluent or aspiring farmers and tradesmen to practice impartible inheritance but also inspired many Irishmen with ambitions for an "independence" which they now conceived more in terms of individual upward
mobility than in traditional contexts of self-sufficiency and security. Thus, for

the first time, a new type of Irish emigrant becomes visible: the young man on the make, imbued with acquisitive, entrepreneurial values. As Edward Wakefield lamented in 1812, from an "improving" landlord's perspective such emigrants constituted "the most valuable part of the community, enterprising individuals, anxious to improve their condition." Many were in occupations on the cutting edge of Irish commercialization: merchants, clerks, skilled tradesmen, and so forth. However, others were farmers such as the countryman in market-oriented County Wicklow who, although "pretty comfortable" at home, wanted to emigrate " '[b]ecause I can never be better as I am.' " In short, economic expansion broadened horizons and engendered materialistic ambitions which could be satisfied only in the New World's more fluid society.[6]

During 1783–1814 the impact of commercialization was felt by all sectors of Irish society. For example, geographical, if not social, mobility became more common, loosening communal and familial bonds: thus, intense competition for short leases forced many smallholders, such as the novelist William Carleton's father in County Tyrone, to change farms three times in twenty years; likewise, the lure of employment persuaded cottier-weavers such as John Doherty of Donegal to migrate first to a cotton mill in east Ulster, later to England, where he became leader of the spinners' union in Lancashire. However, regional, social, and cultural factors combined to determine how Irishmen would react to such changes. As in preceding decades, emigration was heaviest from those districts in Ulster and, to a lesser degree, in southern Ireland where market-oriented agriculture, industrialization, urban growth, improved communications, and Anglicization prevailed to the greatest extent. Moreover, an overwhelming majority of those who now defined "independence" in terms of individual upward mobility were Protestants. Most Catholics—rural Irish-speakers whose culture emphasized virtues of stasis and dependence—still clung to their traditional communities. A sympathetic Scottish traveler attributed Catholics' continued aversion to emigration to their "strong attachment to kindred," while the censorious Wakefield blamed their lack of "industry and enterprise," and the fact that disposition and destitution combined to make them "depressed beyond all conception," willing to "bear their degradation without murmuring or complaint. Familiarized with misery, they have acquired an habitual apathy."[7]

Of course, economic expansion and the rationalization of holdings on many estates engendered new ambitions among many Catholic tenants and broke up old clachan settlements. During 1783–1814 some Catholics did go abroad: several thousands may have fled in the wake of the abortive United Irish rising of 1798—itself dramatic proof that many native Irish did not accept their "degradation"—and affluent Catholic families sent an increasing trickle of ambitious younger sons to become storekeepers, tradesmen, building contractors, and professional men in a United States which had formally abolished religious barriers to economic advancement. However, the latter group represented a highly Anglicized minority from the most commercialized towns and rural districts of eastern Ireland, and even the fugitive rebels of 1798 came from regions long characterized by English-speaking and intense market activities. Moreover, although in 1804 an observer reported that in many areas the "manners of the ancient Irish have been very much done away with by the increase of English commercial civilisation," even Catholics who had abandoned the Irish language, clachan life, and cotillage remained deeply conservative and parochial, still convinced that emigration was exile. Although many now conceptualized economic goals in terms of an "independence," they defined that aspiration as self-sufficiency, not as upward mobility, and in 1783–1814 most merely took advantage of the greater availability of land and employment in an expanding Irish economy to better secure such goals at home.[8]

Even in Ulster, Catholics generally responded to commercialization by accommodation in Ireland rather than by emigration abroad. For example, in the parish of Dungiven, County Londonderry, Catholic smallholders refused to emulate their affluent Presbyterian neighbors who kept farms intact and economically viable by sending superfluous sons to America; instead, they clung fiercely to archaic customs, subdivided farms into minute portions, and earned rent money through cattle droving and seasonal migration to Scotland. Likewise, in County Cavan and elsewhere, Catholic cottiers responded to "the rage for land in the time of the French war" by "rush[ing] in crowds to the landlord or his agent, fawned on them for farms, tempted them with big promises, and got the land at enormous rack-rents": compelling the "old families"—Protestants who "could not, or would not, compete" with "papists"—to emigrate. In short, as long as Catholics could gain a subsistence at home, they were still extremely averse to permanent emigration—at least unless they had what Wakefield called "adventitious assistance" from a "protector . . . to shield them" from the hazards involved. Thus, in 1794 Hugh Hovell Farmer, a member of the Cork gentry who proposed founding an Irish colony in Canada, testified to the "dependent" outlook of most rural Catholics when he requested a land grant so that his prospective Catholic settlers could get "small Farms for their immediate acquisition"; these men, he explained, would emigrate only "under a certainty of getting land from me and being under my protection"; otherwise, they "would not stir," for "[t]he Irish are not over fond of leaving their Country but under certain inducements."[9]

By the late eighteenth century, large numbers of Irish Protestants were sufficiently self-reliant that they had no need for such inducements or guarantees. Nevertheless, it would be incorrect to assume that all Protestant emigrants now perceived their actions in individualistic or entrepreneurial terms. A landlord such as Thomas Talbot of Malahide, County Dublin, who left Ireland in 1803 to found a semi-feudal barony—complete with deferential tenants—on the shores of Lake Erie, was reacting against the increasing rationalization and consequent hostility of landlord-tenant relations at home. More important, Ulster artisans and farmers, such as those who fled Catholic competition in Cavan, obviously found unpalatable the free-market ethos of "improving" Ireland. Indeed, the fact that many northern Protestants emigrated only if they could afford to transport whole families and settle them on American lands demonstrated their traditional attitudes toward kin and community. In short, during 1783–1814 most Irish Protestants still left home, not so much to pursue the main chance, but in an effort to retain status and life-styles which were threatened with erosion in Ireland. For despite prevailing faiths in "progress" and "improvement," the accelerated commercialization of Irish society did not diffuse prosperity or even greater security among many artisans, farmers, or peasants.[10]

For example, in spite of overall expansion, even the Irish linen industry experienced economic fluctuations and structural changes which stimulated emigration. In southern Ireland, linen manufacturing never recovered from the 1770s depression, and large numbers of weavers in Leinster and Munster reportedly moved to Britain and America. In Ulster many artisans went abroad in the early 1780s, before full employment returned; in 1801–2 a sharp recession in the northern linen industry produced about 12,000 emigrants; and in 1810–14 Napoleon's continental blockade ravaged Ulster's economy and caused thousands of unemployed weavers to seek refuge in England. Moreover, the increasing capitalization of Ulster's linen industry provided other, less tangible motives for emigration. By inflating prices for imported flaxseed and provisions, the wars of 1793–1814 increased the economic leverage of merchant capitalists over rural manufacturers and cottier-weavers. Although neither flax spinning nor linen weaving was yet mechanized, the large bleaching firms began to bypass local middlemen and directly employ debt-ridden cottagers for wages. Thus, even as linen manufacturing was spreading into new districts, control over the industry was shifting from the farmers and artisans of the countryside to a small group of merchants and industrialists around Belfast; the former's resentment over their declining independence helped inspire Ulster emigration as well as social and political unrest.[11]

Furthermore, in many parts of Ireland industrial employment was declining as native manufactures succumbed to English competition. For example, in 1783 Dublin's silk weavers were reportedly preparing to emigrate en masse to escape starvation in their rat-infested tenements. More important, in the late eighteenth century the Irish woolen industry began a precipitous decline. By the 1790s rural employment in spinning had contracted by 50 percent, because of the disappearance of the once-flourishing export trade in woolen yarn. Like Ulster's linen industry, woolen manufacturing had enabled the southern Irish peasant to compete for land with rich graziers and to eke out a precarious living on barren soils. Consequently, loss of that income reduced thousands of rural families in south Leinster and Munster to what Lord Fitzgibbon described as "a state of oppression, abject poverty, sloth, dirt and misery not to be equalled in any other part of the world." Other Irish industries, such as brewing and glass-making, succeeded in achieving economies of scale, but only at the cost of reduced employment; for example, in 1770–90 the number of small rural breweries fell sharply as a few large urban firms came to dominate the market. Although Irish manufacturers attempted to produce new commodities—such as hats, gloves, carpets, soap, paper, crockery—most enterprises soon failed in competition with cheaper English imports. In addition, war with France brought high prices for raw materials and heavy taxation which crippled many trades. Thus, in 1811 John Rutherford emigrated from County Tyrone with £100 and a letter of introduction which described him to be

> as good a Currier & Tanner as ever left this Country [but] that business has of late years been so Closed by heavy Duty on leather together with heavy Taxes of every kind that he expects to do better . . . in America as he has been Informed . . . of his trade being a good one there.

Industrial decline not only inspired artisans and laborers to emigrate but also spurred Irish manufacturers and statesmen to launch a legal campaign to destroy trade unions, the alleged causes of native industries' inability to compete with English products. The consequent strife and repression no doubt encouraged additional workers to go abroad in search of high wages and job security.[12]

Moreover, conditions in the Irish countryside were not uniformly favorable between 1783 and 1814. Although prices for farm products rose significantly, rents, tithes, and taxes more than kept pace. Rentier middlemen, "land-jobbers," and farmers on long leases profited from high prices, but tenants and subtenants without formal contracts and those farmers whose leases expired during the period often saw their rents increase as much as fourfold. For instance, in the late eighteenth century middlemen leased Lord Antrim's 173,000 acres for £8,000 per year and then sublet them to the actual occupiers for £64,000; on the Gosford estate in County Armagh, per-acre rents negotiated during the war years rose by 150 percent, and similar increases took place on estates in Wicklow, in Mayo, and elsewhere. Some scholars contend that, even where rent increases occurred, prices were sufficiently high to enable strong and middling farmers to profit; and when rents remained at low prewar levels—as on the generous duke of Devonshire's County Waterford estates—even smallholders could prosper. However, many landlords sought to increase rent rolls by breaking up large farms and canting leases to former subtenants and cottiers who would promise extortionate rents for the privilege of becoming smallholders; other proprietors transformed leaseholders into tenants at will. Thus, letters written during the period by Irish farmers reflect an atmosphere of increasing hardship and insecurity, even for the relatively comfortable. For example, in 1803 James Steele, a strong farmer in east Donegal, complained to his brother in Pennsylvania, "Land here has got very high, [and] good farms will set out at 3 half guineas per acre. Some farms that has been set at 20s per acre has sold for £20 per acre, and but a short leas. . . ." Steele added that even "turf is got exceeding scarce" and that landlords were renting mere boglands for £12 per acre. Seven years later, a tenant in County Tyrone lamented that farmers "cannot by any means pay the demans of Rents and tiths that are Comeing on them if the[y] continue at the present rate for somtime Longer plenty will be forced out of their houses."[13]

In addition, while war with France brought high prices, it also entailed sharply increased taxation, which encouraged Irish farmers to contemplate emigration. "We should all wish to be out of this countrie," cried James Burns of County Armagh, "as every year oppression is growing greater upon account of the war. . . ." "O Dear Brother," lamented James Steele in 1806, "but you are happy that your country is not at war":

> we have had so long a war that has cost so much money that we are loaded with taxes we have hearth and window taxes which cost me £2-4s-6d per year a militia tax 15s per year a county tax £3-s14 per year . . . besides malt tax, whiskey tax and in short all kinds of goods pays have[y] duty.

Another Ulsterman claimed, "[W]e cannot even keep a dog without paying the advanced sum of 3ˢ3ᵈ per year." Indeed, wartime taxation became so burdensome that street singers composed ballads on the subject: "No wonder people grumble at the taxes more and more," for "[t]here never was such taxes in Ireland before." However, as James Burns testified, few dared grumble publicly "at anything that is laid on them, [for] If they do they are counted rebels and hurried away to jail and tried for treason." The wars also brought about a debasement of Irish currency which partially nullified farmers' rising incomes. Thus, a poor farmer in Tyrone complained that "our gold and silver currency hath been greatly depressed of late by reason of a paper circulation and so general a thing is paper money that scarce a Guinea is to be perceived in a year's trading"; but unfortunately, he added, "[b]anknotes (as they are called) will not be taken in payment" for taxes. Moreover, in some parts of Ireland war brought farmers increased labor costs as thousands of the rural poor enlisted in the British army and navy: "Our servants is got very scarce and high," reported James Steele in 1802, "double wages for men by what they were about five years ago." Little wonder that farmers such as Steele sighed "that many is the time I wished I had gone to your country ten years ago where I would have been free from rumors of wars." After all, in America their kinsmen boasted of living on their own lands in "the richest country in the world in every respect," no longer pinched by rising rents, tithes, and taxes. "We are not afraid of the landlord takeing [our livestock] for the rent," declared one Ulster-American farmer in western Pennsylvania; and "[h]ear all we have to pay is our necery taxes which we do with pleashur."[14]

Of course, between 1783 and 1814 rising commodity prices and the general expansion of tillage farming increased opportunities for farmers' sons and the laboring poor to acquire land at home. However, during the same period Ireland's population exploded—from about four million in 1780 to nearly seven million in 1821—and this demographic growth increased competition for tenancies and conacre and kept wage levels significantly below rising rents and provision costs. Consequently, by 1814, smallholders in heavily populated districts were already reaching a point of diminishing returns. For example, in 1821 William Greig, the agent for the Gosford estates in mid-Ulster, reflected on the purported progress and prosperity of the wartime decades. He observed that although "a prodigious rise in the value of land" had taken place, agricultural improvements among "the mere occupying tenants . . . were almost too inconsiderable to be traced"; nor had their "comforts . . . augmented in any considerable degree. On the contrary, it is most certain that in a great proportion of instances they [were] much lessened," for rising rents were only "made up from increased privations and from excessive cropping, and other expedients"—such as subdividing holdings with kinfolk or subletting portions to strangers—"which have only served to entail . . . future loss and inconvenience." Thus, even before the end of the Napoleonic Wars, high rents and the excessive fragmentation of farms were forcing many tenants to fall into debt to village usurers, to depend more exclusively upon a potato diet, and to seek supplementary sources of income through spinning, weaving, migratory labor, or enlistment in the British military. In southern Ireland, where industrial employment was already declining, many impoverished smallholders were reduced "more and more to the situation of cotters, rather serfs, or villains"; the less fortunate descended to the ranks of landless laborers. In Ulster, already overpopulated in many districts at the time of the American Revolution, the ubiquitous linen industry staved off disaster until the postwar depression. However, in 1806 John Kerr described the consequences of the great "encrease of Inhabitants" in south Tyrone:

> as its population increaseth every necessary of life increaseth in proportion, for land at present is become remarkably high and still seems to increase in price and in demand, so that very few are capable of entering on farms which occasions numbers of our Inhabitants to transport themselves to America.

Moreover, high food prices, coupled with periodic crop failures and hoarding by merchants who "amassed wealth by very ignominious means," caused severe hardship for land-poor cottier-weavers and landless laborers who had to purchase provisions on the open market. As one sympathetic Ulster farmer reported in 1801, "everything for Seal is So high that the buyer is ill of[f] & in great distress & the country full of poor people goeing begging." Seven years later, provisions remained "remarkably high, and they who have nought to support themselves but their daily labour are hardly enough dealt withal."[15]

By 1814, observers in Armagh, Tyrone, Derry, and other Ulster counties were reporting that "the population . . . exceeds the means of subsistence, and seems to be the chief cause of the frequency of emigration." However, as was noted earlier, in 1783–1814 the lower classes did not leave Ireland in large numbers; the emigrants from County Tyrone to whom John Kerr referred in 1806 were probably not cottiers or laborers but farmers' sons who despaired of acquiring comfortable holdings of their own. Although in many parts of Ulster the desire to emigrate seems to have been increasing among the poor, before 1815 they were thwarted by legal restrictions, prohibitive fares, and the declining traffic in indentured servants; in these circumstances, Ireland's lower classes could have emigrated only as individuals—not in family groups—and this was something many poor Protestants, as well as most Catholics, refused to do as long as life was bearable at home. However, both in Ulster and elsewhere pressures for increased emigration were mounting steadily, and the end of the Napoleonic Wars would release a flood of farmers, artisans, and laborers. In the meantime, poor countrymen such as John Kerr could only beg their relatives abroad to assist them to reach America: "believe me my dear Uncle," Kerr wrote, "there is nought but trouble and vexation attending our lives in this countery. . . . by some means or other procure me an entrance into that land of happiness."[16]

Prior to the American Revolution, Irish Dissenters perceived the New World as a refuge from tyranny, while Catholics—if they had any concrete images of North America—perceived it as a place of banishment and persecution. However, the creation of an American republic which proclaimed political and religious liberty further embellished and politicized the Irish image of the New World, and made transatlantic emigration more appealing to Catholics as well as to Protestants chafing under an oppressive Ascendancy. In addition, the Revolution inspired Irishmen of all faiths, constitutionalists and radical revolutionaries alike, to greater efforts to reform or abolish that Ascendancy. When those efforts failed, Irishmen of all denominations fled to the United States. Their flight reinforced and modernized Catholics' traditional conception of emigration as involuntary, political exile, but the asylum and opportunity the fugitives found abroad persuaded many Catholics as well as radical Protestants that America was indeed a land of freedom and promise.

The varying Irish responses to the American Revolution partly reflected the nature and strength of the ties which emigration had already forged between Ireland and the New World. Anglicans' response was ambivalent: the Tory landowners who dominated the Irish Parliament voted revenue to support the king's efforts to restore the empire, but the Whiggish middle classes followed Patriot leaders such as Henry Grattan and Charles

Lucas who drew telling analogies between England's "oppression" of
America and her "heavy Yoke of Tyranny" over Irish political and economic life. Thus, the leading Whig newspaper, the Dublin *Freeman's
Journal,* published the writings of John Adams and Thomas Paine and
declared that the Americans had "set us a noble example . . . to show
ourselves men!" and from Athlone the Anglican merchant William Potts
wrote to an American kinsman that while he "feared much for the People
of Boston," he wished "we Could Instill some of their Principles In Our
Own Irish parliment." Irish Dissenters were overwhelmingly supportive
of the American cause. Among Ulster Presbyterians political principles
merged with communal affections, for—as one northern minister declared—
"there is scarcely a protestant family . . . among us, who does not
reckon kindred with the inhabitants of that extensive country." In public
resolutions, private toasts, sermons, songs, and poems, Ulstermen expressed such solidarity with the Revolution that the lord lieutenant reported to London that Irish Presbyterians were Americans "in their
Hearts" and "talking in all companies in such a way that if they are not
rebels, it is hard to find a name for them." Thus, when Hugh Harper of
Belfast learned that his emigrant son was a soldier in the American army,
he exulted over such "a very satisfying account of his character and behaviour." The wartime alliance between the United States and Catholic
France—Protestant Ireland's old nemesis—temporarily complicated Protestant sympathies. However, the ranks of the Irish Volunteers, formed by
Protestants to defend the island from threatened French invasion, quickly
filled with Anglican Whigs and Presbyterians who supported Grattan's
goals of legislative independence, free trade, and parliamentary reform for
Ireland. The Volunteers modeled their program and their tactics on American precedents: they formed "Yankee Clubs," proclaimed their demands
in conventions or "congresses," organized boycotts of English goods, and
threatened revolution if the English government proved recalcitrant. In
1782–83, when Westminster partly acquiesced and renounced its claims to
legislate for Ireland, Grattan happily concluded that "the American war
was the Irish harvest."[17]

Catholic Ireland's initial reaction to the American Revolution was far
more ambiguous. Although in the early 1770s Irish newspapers reported
that affluent "papists" were selling their estates and crossing the Atlantic
in search of religious freedom, most upper- and middle-class Catholics regarded the colonies as bastions of Protestant bigotry and had little or no
sympathy with a revolution partly based on "No Popery" and leveling principles. Thus, conservative Catholic leaders, lay and clerical, only tried to
use the American crisis as an opportunity to prove their loyalty and thereby
coax concessions from the British government. For example, "the principal
Romanists in Cork and Limerick . . . formed Associations and offered
bounties" to persuade lower-class Catholics to enlist in the British military;
and the O'Conor Don, a Roscommon landlord and descendant of the last
ard rí, predicted that after "our Armies" had defeated the colonists a grate-

ful king would reward Catholics' loyalty by renewing their old patent to Maryland: "most probably," he confided, "our [Irish] Masters would rather repeal all Queen Annes Laws relative to us, than admit a general Emigration into that part of the world, where so much would be lost to this nation." Such strategies were partly successful: the British cabinet coerced the Irish Parliament into repealing Penal Laws which restricted Catholic leaseholding and manufacturing, and thousands of lower-class Catholics served in the British army and navy; even Eoghan Ruadh Ó Súilleabháin—the Munster poet, rake, and folk hero—fought under Admiral Rodney and composed an obsequious ode which declared that he and his fellow Irish tars took "delight in the fight" to "vindicate bold England's right / And die for Erin's glory." Another contemporary ballad, which charged that American colonists were "savage blacks" who strove to "banish Irishmen out of America," was even more revealing, for it indicated the depth of ignorance and prejudice which still dominated many Catholics' perceptions of the New World.[18]

However, the Revolution began to alter Catholic Ireland's image of America, if only because the colonists were battling the hereditary enemy. Even at the beginning of the war, an Irish Protestant lamented that although the Catholic gentry and hierarchy were "in the interest of the government, the lower class . . . are, to a man, attached to the Americans, and say plainly that the Irish ought to follow their example." When Catholic Ireland's old allies France and Spain joined the American cause, the new United States became linked to the traditional sources of refuge and succor; by the late 1770s Munster Catholics were reportedly "in hourly expectation" of foreign invasion. Thus, most Catholic enlistments in the British forces resulted not from sympathy but from necessity born of poverty or—in Ó Súilleabháin's case—personal exigencies, and reports in the mid-1780s that Munster Rightboys were marching under the American stars and stripes may indicate the returned soldiers' impact on rural Catholic attitudes. Indeed, Irish-speaking poets even assimilated events in America to old *aisling* traditions, rejoicing—in the words of the Clare schoolmaster Tomás Ó Miodhacháin—that "the arrogant robbers are wounded at last" by "the sturdy Washington," and predicting that "the boors of Britain" would now fall "under the bondage of Louis," that "Ireland will be given to her lawful spouse . . . Charles Stuart," and that "for the lifetime of the eagle, permission to use grass and water shall belong to the Gael" again. The victories of "lively Washington"—as another bard called him—earned the American general a place alongside Brian Ború and Patrick Sarsfield as a source of inspiration for Irish-speaking rebels and agitators. However, most Catholics—still immersed in aristocratic political traditions, as these poems demonstrate—little comprehended the *ideology* of the American Revolution, and many who did were fearful of its egalitarian implications. Nevertheless, a few middle-class, urban Catholics began to explain how colonial theories of representative government were relevant to the plight of their poorer coreligionists. The most notable was the Dubliner Mathew

Carey, a young printer's apprentice whose writings merged Catholic outrage, Dissenter radicalism, Dublin trade unionism, and American revolutionary principles. Persecution from alarmed Catholic conservatives as well as from the government forced Carey to emigrate to "the land of freedom" in 1784. However, his pamphlets helped originate a modernized Catholic nationalism which looked to the secular American Republic, rather than to the Catholic monarchies of Europe, for example and inspiration. In later years, more than one Catholic Irish rebel would avow, "It was the Declaration of Independence that awoke in my heart that idea of liberty which I hope I shall see accomplished" in Ireland.[19]

The success of the American Revolution only magnified the New World's image in the eyes of Irish Protestants. Even before the war's end, Dublin and Belfast printers began to publish Irish editions of works such as Crèvecoeur's *Letters from an American Farmer,* copies of the American state constitutions, Imlay's romanticized *Description of the Western Territory,* and flattering travel accounts by Chastellux and by Brissot de Warville to satisfy a voracious public appetite for more information about the new United States. In private correspondence, Presbyterians on both sides of the Atlantic exchanged opinions about the Revolution, generally agreeing that it "laid the foundation of one of the greatest empires . . . in the world." Irishmen abroad redoubled their encouragement to prospective emigrants: "They are very fond of Irish Emigration here," reported John Joyce from Virginia in 1785, "and it is Given as a Toast often at their Fairs." Joyce added, "Workmen of all Denominations have most enormous prices for their Work . . . [and] in a short time may make fortunes." However, post-Revolutionary America was not merely a land of economic opportunity but also—as correspondents, newspapers, and pamphlets repeatedly stressed—a republic where "Liberty has erected her throne," "holds out a system of equal liberty to mankind, and waits with open arms to receive the emigrants from surrounding nations." No wonder that for idealistic young Irishmen such as William Drennan, the United States became "the promised land I would wish to view before I die."[20]

America's attractiveness further increased when middle-class Whigs and Ulster Presbyterians realized that Grattan's "revolution of 1782" was a sham. The Irish Parliament remained grossly unrepresentative as well as subservient to English interests; "consequently," wrote a disillusioned Hugh Harper in Belfast, "our free trade and the emancipation so loudly talked of are mere names." Some embittered Patriots followed Grattan into semi-retirement or, like Harper, prepared to emigrate to "that happy country where there will be no jarring interests, where unfeigned love and universal benevolence will glow in every breast and the reigning Monarch is in reality the Father of his people." However, in 1791 more-radical reformers in Dublin and Belfast formed the Society of United Irishmen, which at first merely agitated for parliamentary reform, protective tariffs, and total repeal of the Penal Laws but which eventually conspired for complete independence and the establishment of an Irish republic based on universal suffrage. The society's initial appeals were to the rationalism of urban merchants and artisans and to the millennial expectations and anti-Ascendancy resentments of Presbyterian farmers and weavers in east Ulster. However, leaders such as Wolfe Tone advocated an alliance with the dispossessed Catholic peasantry—the "men of no property"—who had gotten no benefits from the Catholic Relief Acts of the late eighteenth century; accordingly, the United Irishmen effected an uneasy merger with the Defenders, the dominant Catholic secret society, and prepared for a general rising to be assisted by a French invasion. The United Irishmen found immediate inspiration in revolutionary France, but their propaganda continued to pay homage to the precedent of America—"It was in you it first began"—and so spread favorable images of the United States among rural dwellers who had known little or nothing about the New World. Indeed, the popular impacts of the American and French revolutions were inseparable, linked by the widely read works of Tom Paine and by the United Irishmen's own revolutionary catechism: "What have you got in your hand?—A green bough. Where did it first grow?—In America. Where did it bud?—In France. Where are you going to plant it?—In the crown of Great Britain." The society's newspaper, the Belfast *Northern Star,* informed its readers that the "lowest" inhabitants of the United States "(unlike those of poor Ireland) [were] well fed, well dressed, and happy. . . . [T]hey stand erect and crouch not before any man . . . due to the enjoyment of liberty in her proper extent"—a condition poor Irishmen could achieve by emulating America's rebellious colonists. Likewise, Wolfe Tone sought to assuage Protestant rebels' fears of Catholic equality by pointing to the United States, where "the Catholic and Protestant sit equally in Congress, without any contention arising, other than who shall serve his country best. So may it be in Ireland!"[21]

However, Tone's analogy—and his dream of an inclusive, secular Irish republic—failed, for American society was very unlike Ireland, where sectarianism poisoned the wellsprings of political action. Protestant conservatives correctly perceived that egalitarian notions applied to Ireland would produce religious as well as political revolution. Irish democracy would inevitably result in Catholic hegemony, and neither the leaders nor the most ardent Protestant followers of the United Irishmen desired that result: middle-class, urban radicals fondly imagined that when the Penal Laws were entirely repealed, "the Roman Catholic religion, or at least the worst part of it, would gradually decay"—dissipated by the light of reason; and millenarian Presbyterians in rural east Ulster, where few Catholics resided, envisioned an apocalyptic upheaval which would free all Irishmen from papal as well as royal tyranny. Even William Drennan, a founder of the United Irishmen, regarded the Irish "Catholic mind" as "churlish soil" which "must be cultivated, or we must emigrate." Indeed, it is likely that the partial repeal of the Penal Laws in the late eighteenth century—the result of British pressure, not Irish Protestant generosity—helped persuade many Protestant families to emigrate to America. Moreover, Irish Protestants were not the only shallow converts to the ideals of fraternity and equality. Despite their alliance with the United Irishmen and their adoption of slogans of the French Revolution, the Catholic Defenders—born in the vicious sectarian strife of mid-Ulster—were often merely rhetorical adherents to nonsectarian republicanism: their members still swore to "sweep clean the Protestants, kill the Lord Lieutenant, and leave none alive"; and most peasants, barely affected by new outlooks, still yearned for the restoration of a pastoral, aristocratic Gaelic past.[22]

Religious strife and government repression aborted the United Irishmen's hopes. In mid-Ulster, where the two denominations were evenly balanced and fiercely competitive, Protestants reacted to the arming of "papists" by forming sectarian secret societies such as the Peep of Day Boys; in 1795, with landlord encouragement, these evolved into the Orange Order, dedicated to preserving Protestant supremacy by disarming United Irishmen and Catholics generally, and by driving perhaps 7,000 of the latter out of Ulster into Connaught. In 1796 the government organized Orangemen and other loyal Protestants into companies of "yeomen" and authorized them to assist the regular army and militia in terrorizing United Irishmen and their sympathizers. "We have had a confused time here since you left Ireland," wrote James Burns of County Armagh to his son in Pennsylvania:

> . . . our government began to fear if the french should invade us, the Liberty men would join them and they made an act to disarm the people . . . and all to come in to the magistrates and take the oath of allegiance . . . and give up their arms. . . . the light horse and yeomen went out thru the countrie and upon the least information of arms or of being united [Irishmen], their houses were burned and they sent to gaol and some shot on the spot.

This "dragooning of Ulster" decimated the United Irishmen in the northern province; in June 1798 the remnants—some 10,000 men, primarily Presbyterians from Antrim and Down—rose in revolt, but British troops, Protestant yeomen, and, ironically, Irish-speaking Catholic militiamen from the politically archaic western counties quickly suppressed them. However, in southeast Leinster the depredations of Orangemen and yeomen served to goad more modernized, English-speaking Catholics into desperate and, for a time, successful rebellion. On the eve of that rising, Walter Devereux, a County Wexford Catholic, described the rebels' sufferings and enthusiasm in a letter to his brother in New York. "Dear John," he wrote,

> it is the greatest happyness to you that you left this Unfortunate Cuntry now the prey of the Orange and Castle Bloodhouns   Almost every county in Poor Old Ireland under Martial Law and the Poor Cuntry Pesants shot or hanged or Basteeled without Law or form of Tryal . . . but thank god that Irish men have Resolution and can Suffer more and Will be free. . . .

Devereux predicted that soon the results of that "Resolution" would "be none [known] and Praised throw the Whole World," but by late June the rebel armies in Leinster had suffered total defeat: peasants armed largely with pikes were no match for disciplined soldiers and grapeshot. Finally, in late August, about 1,100 long-awaited French troops landed in County Mayo—a district least influenced by republican ideas: the few thousand Catholic countrymen who joined the French thought their allies were champions of the pope and the Blessed Virgin! The French were too few and too late; despite initial success, they surrendered within three weeks of their arrival. Thus ended the "year of liberty." In reality, 1798 was a holocaust, replete with massacres and atrocities committed by both sides: contemporary estimates of the dead ranged as high as 100,000, most of them killed "in cold blood."[23]

In the spring of 1798 Walter Devereux had written to his brother, "If the times are not Settled Before Next August I Certainly will then leave this land of tiriney and Seek a land of Liberty. . . ." Whether Devereux escaped the shambles of the Wexford rising is uncertain; as he admitted, "for a man hear to Promise himselfe a Single Day to live would be a Presumption." Nevertheless, a large number of Irishmen, both loyalists and rebels, did flee from the turmoil of the 1790s and settle in North America. For example, "dread of a foreign invasion" and the "utmost disquietude" of the times caused loyal Protestants to yearn for a new world where their kinsmen "enjoy[ed] the blessing of peace in its fullest purity." However, most fugitives were United Irishmen and Defenders. In 1796 a correspondent informed Lord Charlemont that thousands of Ulster Catholics were emigrating to escape Orange persecution; like Bernard M'Kenna of County Tyrone, they fled to the ports "exhausted with fatigue of travelling and want of subsistence. The yeomen made such a stirr through the different villages," he remembered, "that I found it impracticable for me to make any delay without being detected. . . ." Protestant United Irishmen, primarily Presbyterians, also had to flee from "the vengeful malignity" of "their more wealthy & in most cases their inveterate Orange fellow subjects."[24]

The majority of emigrating United Irishmen were probably like the poor farmers and artisans in one vessel bound for New York: "a set of Steerage Passengers ripe for every Species of Disorder particularly while their Whiskey lasted." However, a large proportion of the Protestants especially came from middle- and even upper-class backgrounds. The rebellion crushed and their property confiscated, they were "literally transported from his Britanic Majesty's Dominions under the sentence of a Court Martial, or obliged to fly to avoid instant death by military execution." "That was the time of tryal," recalled an exiled member of the Ulster gentry; "there was a large assemblage of people that partook of the dance in them days, but I know who paid the Music. . . . I was ruined and my property totally destroyed." In short, as one refugee claimed, "[m]any hundreds of persons of rank and property are in a similar situation, and all bent on coming" to America, forming, he boasted, "the most respectable emigration which has taken place to your United States since the settlement of the New-England colonies." The most illustrious exiles were the surviving leaders of the United Irishmen. Several, including Wolfe Tone, spent only brief sojourns in America before they received pardons or, like Tone, returned home to die in a hopeless cause. Others, such as Thomas Addis Emmet, William James Macneven, and William Sampson, won release from British prisons only on condition that they remain abroad permanently. Talented and well educated, these men settled in flourishing seaports such as New York, gained eminence in native American society, and became the acknowledged leaders of the Irish in the United States. Emmet was the most honored, in part for his own considerable ability, in part because in 1803 his brother, Robert, achieved martyrdom on the scaffold for attempting another, ill-fated rising in Dublin.[25]

The events of 1798 exposed and accelerated the deterioration of Protestant-Catholic and landlord-tenant relations which had accompanied economic expansion and rationalization in the late eighteenth century. In south Leinster, priest-led mobs of vengeful Catholics had massacred helpless Protestant prisoners, and the horrors of Wexford bridge and Scullabogue barn revived all the tribal memories and fears of many Protestants who had inclined toward toleration. For example, at first Samuel Rogers of County Cavan could scarcely believe the news from the south: "I cant say that the[y] are ye united irish men," he wrote, "for the[y] are killing all the prodistants"; however, he concluded that "the Romans here had a bad intention if the[y] Could I Suppose the[y] Would Not leve one of us Alive. . . . GOD SAVE THE KING." Such Protestants quickly renounced brief flirtations with ecumenical radicalism and returned to loyalism and the old siege mentality. By 1803 the sister of the United Irishman William Drennan was frightened even by "a singing procession of Catholics": "I begin to fear these people," she wrote, "and think, like the Jews, they will regain their native land." In 1800 the British prime minister William Pitt took advantage of Irish Protestant fears to press for a legislative union between the two islands, arguing that only such a union could secure Protestant Ascendancy in the future. Government bribery reinforced propertied panic, and over Grattan's fervent protests the Irish Parliament voted itself out of existence. In 1801 Ireland's representatives sat at Westminster, Dublin sank to the status of a provincial city, and, appropriately, the Irish Parliament was converted into a bank. Upper- and middle-class Catholics, lay and clerical, did not regret the demise of a government which had always excluded and persecuted them, and they welcomed Pitt's assurances—soon proven false—that repeal of the remaining Penal Laws would shortly follow the Act of Union. The Catholic lower classes cared little for such abstractions: their primary concerns were economic—rents, wages, tithes, taxes, priests' dues—and they returned to the secret societies for self-protection against "improvements" pushed by landlords whose paternalistic pretensions had been shattered by the events of the 1790s. From 1806 through 1814, "night battalions" terrorized parts of Leinster, Connaught, and especially east Munster; even in mid-Ulster, one farmer complained,

"Some are robed on the highway others when in their beds . . . all by a banditry of papist known by the apelation of whitboys."[26]

For several years after the '98 rebellion, Protestant reprisals compelled some Catholics to emigrate. For example, in 1800 a Catholic woman in County Wexford wrote to her son in New York,

> We remain here, but do not know how long it may be a place of residence, as the country is much disturbed by some unknown people who are rioting and burning every night. Our Chapples are burning and tearing down.

She intended to join her son within two years "if we don't get some change for the better," for "[t]his country is almost done away . . . [and] if we don't get some relief the Catholics cannot live here." Six years later a Catholic emigrant lamented that "terror still hangs over our native Country, and there is no one symptom of consolation or of security." However, there is no evidence of substantial Catholic emigration between 1800 and 1814: Connaught's vacant wastelands, even nearby England, were the destinations preferred over America until the postwar depression. Most Catholics still chose to struggle at home, still perceived emigration negatively, and still regarded America as a frightening, alien land. A contemporary ballad—in English, but set to the tune of a song in the Irish language—accurately reflected Catholic peasants' archaic, unfavorable image of the New World and their perception of emigration as a violation of traditional values which stressed community, continuity, and security over individual innovation and acquisitiveness:

> An exile, I fly to the banks of Ohio,
>   Where gloomy dark deserts bewilder my way. . . .
> Where fell snakes are hissing and dire monsters screaming,
>   Where death pregnant lightnings are dreadfully gleaming,
> And direful contagion destruction proclaiming,
>   Infest every vale and embitter each day. . . .
>
> Oh, man! thou art fretful, contentless, and wavering;
>   Thy blessings are countless, but thou mean and vile;
> The hand of Jehovah extended and favouring
>   Peculiarly visits the Emerald Isle.
> Yet outcast of Nature, how blind to true pleasure,
>   Thou bart'rest of enjoyment for base sordid treasure,
> And home thou forsakest, though dear beyond measure,
>   Where friendship and freedom in harmony smile.[27]

However, despite such evidence of substantial cultural continuity, the United Irishmen, their ideals, and their abortive revolution had ultimately profound effects upon Catholic Irish society and Catholics' perception of emigration to America. First, the horrors of '98 became part of the peasants' bitter heritage, modernizing and reinforcing the legends of Elizabethan and Cromwellian persecutions: "Before I was ever able to read a book," remembered a late nineteenth-century Catholic rebel, "I heard stories of Irish women ripped open by English bayonets, and of Irish infants dashed against the walls." Second, through their propaganda the United Irishmen bridged the ideological gulf between Dissenter radicalism and Gaelic tribalism, melding both into a future-oriented and at least theoretically inclusive Irish nationalism couched in the language of American and French republicanism. Thus, the United Irishmen gave Catholics' old anti-*Sasanaigh* traditions a new medium of expression—born in urban, Anglicized Ireland—which could flourish despite the inexorable decline of Gaelic culture. Third, by fleeing abroad after their defeat, the United Irish leaders preserved and perpetuated the Gaelic tradition of emigration as political exile; banished to a foreign land, these first republican nationalists inherited the mantle of O'Neill and Sarsfield, and so established continuity between past and present persecutions. Finally, by making the United States—rather than Europe—their asylum, the United Irishmen helped transform Catholics' hitherto negative perceptions of the New World. Just as the flights of the Ulster earls and the Wild Geese had directed Catholic attention to Spain and France, the experiences of Emmet, Macneven, and countless other fugitives demonstrated that—even if emigration was "exile"—at least the United States was a land of refuge, abundance, and equal opportunity for Irish Catholics as well as Protestants.[28]

Of course, had the Hamiltonian Federalists retained political power in America, their prejudices against the "Wild Irish" republicans—formalized in the Alien and Sedition Acts of 1798—would have dampened Irish enthusiasm for the United States. However, Thomas Jefferson's election in 1800, achieved with overwhelming Irish-American support, validated Irish revolutionary ideals. Now the fugitives could embrace America without forfeiting their Irishness, since both affections were grounded in opposition to English monarchism, reaffirmed by Irish-American patriotism during the Anglo-American war of 1812–15, and even rewarded by political appointments to United Irishmen such as Robert Patterson, who became director of the federal mint. Furthermore, not only did their acceptance and prosperity in Jeffersonian America provide a symbolic model for prospective Irish emigrants but the United Irishmen themselves offered the protection and "encouragement" which a communal-oriented peasantry still needed before they would hazard their future in a strange land. For example, through their influence in the Republican party, the United Irishmen provided political patronage and legal protection to subsequent emigrants; Emmet, Macneven, Sampson, and others were instrumental in founding the first Irish emigrant-aid societies in American cities; and in 1817–18 they petitioned Congress for a land grant in Illinois where poor Irish countrymen could settle and acquire farms. Finally, although the United Irish leaders' own letters expressed complete satisfaction with their adopted land—"this happy country," exulted Emmet, "where Liberty is triumphant & cherished"—they helped perpetuate the exile motif among Irishmen *in* the United States: for that self-image not only justified their own respected status in Irish-American society (despite the fact that some had given evidence during their imprisonment) but also united Irish emigrants into an effective political bloc despite potentially disruptive divisions of creed and class. Indeed, before the rise of organized American nativism in the 1830s, it was expedient for all Irish-Americans to advertise themselves as political exiles from English tyranny. As James Richey, an Ulsterman in fiercely republican Kentucky, reported,

> the Irish in America are particularly well recvd. and looked upon as Patriotic republicans, and if you were to tell an American you had flyd your country or you would have been hung for treason against the Government, they would think ten times more of you and it would be the highest trumpet sounded in your praise. . . .

Sadly, later Irish emigrants would discover that an increasingly Anglophilic, nativist, and evangelical Protestant America no longer considered self-proclaimed Irish exiles to be almost honorary Americans. However, from 1800 through the 1828 election of Andrew Jackson, son of emigrants from County Antrim, a common republicanism largely obscured old antagonisms between Americans and Irishmen, Protestants and Catholics.[29]

Yet, as was noted earlier, despite the positive model the United Irishmen provided, before the postwar depression Catholic Irishmen generally preferred to pursue traditional goals at home. Not until after 1814 would increased Anglicization, acute economic distress, and—by compensation—an enhanced image of the United States as earthly paradise encourage large numbers of Catholics to break communal and familial ties. Nevertheless, even before 1814, Catholics' perceptions of America and of the act of emigration itself were changing and coming to resemble those long held by Irish Dissenters. Letters such as those by Neal Campbell, a Catholic refugee from the '98 rising in County Tyrone, now happily tilling his own soil "under the wide-spreading shade of The tree of genuine liberty," must have made a profound impression upon rack-rented and land-poor countrymen who had become attuned to such radical imagery. The changes in Catholic attitudes can be traced in contemporary ballads, such as one which verse by verse literally transformed "that rude, savage countree / Called Wild Amerikay" into a "Rich Amerikay" of arcadian proportions. Perhaps more typical was an Ulster Catholic song entitled "Paddy's Farewell" in which emigration was still described negatively as a "hard fate," but now was *justified* and explained as a necessary act "forc'd by tyrant knavery" and the adverse consequences of wartime commercialization:

> The Rents are high, and Taxes great, and vict'ling growing dear,
> And riches hurded up in store by those who persevere
> In adding to oppressions weight such laws as curb the poor.
> Which makes me leave my heart's delight and the sweet Shamrock shore.[30]

The United Irishmen's legacy was more ambivalent and divisive for Irish Protestants and their perceptions of emigration. After 1798 commercial and industrial expansion in Ulster and Orangeism and evangelicalism throughout Protestant Ireland combined with fears of resurgent Catholicism to forge the loyal, conservative, bourgeois Protestant Irish "nation" of the nineteenth and twentieth centuries. As a former United Irishman gloomily reported, Irish Protestants had by 1807 become separated "into three divisions, viz: the Lovers of Liberty, the lovers of intolerance, & the lovers of loaves & fishes. The last two seem invariably to unite, & are perhaps now too many for the first." In such an atmosphere, it was not surprising that—judging from the emigrants' letters and political behavior abroad—Irish Protestant emigration to the United States seems for several decades after 1800 to have been dominated by those who refused to forswear the radical republicanism of the 1790s. Most visible in America were those of urban and/or middle-class origins, often Moderate or New Light Presbyterians, who were unable to accept Orange tribalism as a substitute for the egalitarian political implications of modernization. However, many others were rural traditionalists from east Ulster, where the threat of Catholic competition did not exist to deflect traditional resentments against Anglican landlords and parsons and against the increasing stratification of east Ulster society. Men such as John Kerr, whose relatives and friends had fallen "by the userpers sword," could no longer "submit to their despotic government," and for those still steeped in eighteenth-century prophetic traditions, America remained "the land of freedom and of liberty . . . accounted like the land of promise flowing with milk and honey . . . to those labouring under Egyptian bondage." Such idyllic visions could have resulted in bitter disappointments, save in the ebullient political atmosphere and open economy of Jeffersonian America—where even a poor laborer such as John Chambers of County Armagh could, within a few years of his arrival, rent a New Jersey farm and own a horse worth £35 in addition to other valuable livestock. On the expanding frontier, opportunities for acquiring a self-sufficient "independence" were even greater, and at least prior to the American financial panic of 1819 the United States seems to have fulfilled the expectations of radical Irish Protestants. "I have seen many hundreds of their letters" from overseas, wrote John Gamble of early nineteenth-century Ulster emigrants, "and, scarcely with an exception, the comfort most insisted on . . . was that they could there speak to man as man, and that they were not obliged to uncover the head, or to bend the knee, to any stern Lord, arrogant Squire, proud Vicar, or, above all, upstart Agent." Like their pre-Revolutionary predecessors, these self-perceived Protestant exiles found refuge and new identity as Americans in Jeffersonian society. "It's hard to be forced from the land that we live in," sang a contemporary Ulster ballad, but the United States "is the land, boys, for both you and me; / There we'll be happy when we are our own masters, / In that land of plenty and sweet liberty."[31]

Ironically, however, just as Catholic and Protestant emigrants seemed to find common ideological ground in the new American Republic, most Irish Protestants were turning to the British government as guarantor of their hegemony and security. Given the spectacular growth of the Orange Order in the early nineteenth century, it was natural that in the period

1798–1814 Protestants such as William Heazelton and William McCutchan brought loyalist convictions and anti-Catholic prejudices to the United States, where they were quick to condemn "the Lower Order of the Irish" and "the Blagard Runaway United Irish men" among their fellow emigrants. However, during the first several decades of the century, probably only a minority of Protestant emigrants to the United States were self-proclaimed loyalists or political conservatives. Their low departure rates partly reflected lower-class Orangemen's traditionalist, tribal outlook, coupled with the fact that membership in the Orange Order conferred socio-economic and psychic benefits which somewhat mitigated any felt necessity for emigration. But perhaps more important, as the Ulster-American James Richey implied in his letter, Irish loyalists and conservatives realized they would find Jeffersonian America's rampant republicanism uncongenial, even dangerous—as during the Anglo-American war of 1812–15 when American and Irish patriots mobbed and murdered Irish Orangemen in the streets of Baltimore. Consequently, it was not surprising that in the early nineteenth century Irish loyalists began to emigrate to Upper Canada and the Maritimes, where their principles and Orange lodges could flourish under the British flag. Significantly, "The Sash My Father Wore," perhaps Orangemen's favorite ballad, is an emigrants' song; however, its words do not convey a sense of alienated exile, for in Canada (and in a few areas of the United States, such as Scotch-Irish Pittsburgh) the Orange Order provided a fraternal network and patronage system which ensured loyal Irish Protestants they could find security, community, and opportunity overseas. Once begun, Irish Protestant emigration to Canada continued to the present day, but by the 1830s the rise of evangelicalism and anti-Catholicism in the United States enabled Irish conservatives to feel at home in an increasingly bourgeois Protestant America now more fearful of lower-class and "papist" threats to middle-class hegemony than of British emigrants with conservative political convictions. Henceforth, if Irish Protestant emigrants regarded or advertised themselves as exiles, it was usually in reaction to the supposed threat of "Rome rule" in Ireland—a "danger" many native Americans increasingly appreciated.[32]

Finally, however, in 1783–1814 a growing minority of Irish Protestant emigrants felt no need to describe themselves as exiles or to justify their actions in terms of communal exigencies. Whatever their political opinions, they saw the New World primarily in personal, secular, economic terms. Expanding trade and industrial growth, improved education and communications, steadily multiplied the numbers of "lovers of loaves & fishes" who left Ireland voluntarily to pursue an "independence" defined as individual upward mobility. These were the first visibly "modern" Irish emigrants, responding rationally and without exculpatory "explanations" to economic development in the transatlantic world; they accepted the values of an emergent "free market" capitalism and transferred their capital and labor to the land that promised greatest remuneration. To be sure, some young Irish Protestants who had listened to the "whisperings of ambition" later regretted "the social love and unity" left behind—although, unlike most Catholics and still-traditionalist Protestants, they had sundered such bonds with relative ease. At least a few became alienated from their adopted country when they failed to find quick success; in 1800 an Ulster-American reported to his father in highly commercialized east Donegal that "this very fine country . . . is abuset by a class of young men that cums from among you that is too lasey to work at home and is not scholar anuf to get other business and is too proud to work" at manual labor. Perhaps such disappointments could transform naïve, half-educated strong farmers' sons and would-be clerks into self-pitying "exiles," but the burgeoning economy of Jeffersonian America ensured that most ambitious, skilled young emigrants could realize rationally conceived goals in a country which was characterized—as more traditional-minded emigrants sometimes complained—by rampant materialism and social fluidity.[33]

6

From "Emigrants" to "Exiles": The Pre-Famine Exodus, 1815–1844

During the thirty years from the end of the Napoleonic Wars to the beginning of the Great Famine, between 800,000 and 1,000,000 Irish emigrants—about twice the total for the preceding two hundred years—sailed to North America. In its size, composition, and character, pre-Famine emigration differed significantly from earlier movements and anticipated the massive flight which followed the potato crop failures of the late 1840s. Thanks to Ireland's prolonged postwar economic crisis, the "contagion" of emigration spread far beyond Ulster and affected nearly all groups in Irish society. Although in the immediate postwar years the typical emigrants were still relatively affluent Protestant farmers and artisans from the northern province, by the early 1840s a majority were comparatively poor Catholic subtenants, farmers' sons, and laborers from the three southern provinces. Nevertheless, not only did conservative peasants in southern and western Ireland continue to resist the New World's attractions but Irish social and political developments in 1815–44 paradoxically served to revitalize Irish Catholics' ancient perception of emigration as exile even as they helped sever Catholics' ties to their homeland. In addition, pre-Famine voyage conditions did little to assuage traditional Irish fears of emigration, and, more important, contemporary changes in North American societies helped alter the nature of the Irish emigrant experience in ways conducive to the emergence of Irish-American poverty, alienation, and nationalism.

Between 1815 and 1844 the volume, direction, and character of Irish emigration changed markedly in response to British legislation, transatlantic trade patterns, and economic conditions in both the Old World and the New. In 1815 long-awaited peace between Britain, France, and the United States reopened the sea-lanes between Ireland and North America. Although the restraints of the 1803 Passenger Act were still in effect, in 1815–16 some 20,000 Irish crossed the Atlantic. The United States remained the emigrants' preferred destination: some from southeastern Ireland traveled via the Newfoundland fisheries, but most sailed from Ulster directly to Philadelphia or to New York, where their "vast number[s]" astonished earlier settlers. However, after 1816, new British Passenger Acts temporarily reduced the volume and altered the direction of Irish emigration by imposing carriage restrictions on American-bound vessels, which made average fares to the United States more than double the costs of passages to British North America. Consequently, for the next two decades most Irish emigrants sailed in the holds of Canadian timber ships to Quebec or the Maritime provinces. Nevertheless, despite Parliament's intentions, before 1819 relatively few Irish actually settled in Canada: conditions were too primitive, employment was scarce, speculators monopolized much of the available land, and most Irishmen preferred to follow kinfolk who had emigrated earlier to the United States, where farmland was easier to secure and where construction of public works such as the Erie Canal offered relatively steady, well-paid employment. Therefore, in 1817–18 perhaps two-thirds of the Irish who landed at Quebec, and an even higher proportion of those who sailed to Nova Scotia and New Brunswick, continued traveling until they reached the American Republic; indeed, many Irish vessels merely touched at Halifax or St. John before proceeding to New York with their passengers. However, in 1819 the government of Upper Canada (now Ontario) began giving fifty-acre land grants to attract settlers. More important, in the same year reports of financial panic and economic depression in the United States began to reach Ireland: Ulster-American farmers warned that "this Contery is Much poluted with Insolvent Banks and with speckalators," and unemployed artisans declared that "it is almost impossible to get work of any kind . . . all over America." The result was a sharp decrease in Irish emigration to the United States, as would-be emigrants either postponed departures or settled in British North America. There was even a small reverse migration northward; James Buchanan, an Irish-born British consul, alone sent some 3,000 countrymen from New York to frontier settlements in Upper Canada.[1]

The 1815–19 emigrants were very similar in background to those who departed in the late eighteenth century. About two-thirds were from Ulster, primarily Presbyterians and Anglicans. Even the emigrants from southern Ireland were mostly Protestants, causing landlords and officials to voice alarm at the consequent weakening of the Ascendancy. According to most observers, the 1815–19 emigrants were also of a "superior quality": "strong and active farmers," artisans, shopkeepers, tradesmen, and professionals. Ever since the American Revolution the steady decline of the once-flourishing traffic in indentured servants had sharply reduced lower-class emigration. Consequently, although emigrants bound for Newfoundland or the Maritimes needed little capital, the cost of sailing to the United States was beyond the means of most poor Irishmen. For example, in 1819–20 only a fourth of the Irish who disembarked in New York were mere laborers or servants, and during the whole 1815–19 period between one-half and two-thirds of all Irish passengers were sufficiently affluent to travel in family groups, rather than as individuals. As the *Dublin Evening Post* lamented in 1818, "It is a melancholy thing that emigration is necessarily restricted to the class immediately above the labouring poor, who cannot raise the money to pay their passage."[2]

The American financial panics of 1819 and 1837 are useful benchmarks in the history of pre-Famine emigration. Both produced sharp, short-term declines in departures, but, more important, between those crises the traditional patterns of Irish emigration changed dramatically and permanently. At first, in 1820–26, emigration was moderate; not until 1827 did departures exceed the level of 20,000 achieved in 1818. In the early 1820s accounts of a depressed American economy discouraged many prospective emigrants. Ulster-Americans such as Robert McClorg of Philadelphia reported home that "business of every kind is dull . . . and wages very low . . . and many from Ireland cannot get either." The result, McClorg observed, was that "[e]migration to this country . . . has . . . wisely diminished": in 1820 fewer than 10,000 Irish crossed the Atlantic, and only 6,000 the following year. British legislation continued to discriminate against American-bound emigrants, and so most Irishmen sailed in Canadian timber ships rather than pay higher fares for direct passages to the United States. Thus, in 1822–23 about 8,000 Irish sailed to Quebec while only 2,000 went directly to the American Republic; similarly, in 1826 some 14,000 embarked for British North America, while fewer than 5,000 sailed to the States. As in 1815–19 most emigrants to the British provinces pushed on to the United States, although increasing numbers now remained to take up land or seek employment in Canada's rapidly developing economy. Whatever their ultimate destination, in the 1820s most emigrants continued to sail from Irish ports, particularly from Belfast, Londonderry, and Dublin. However, in this decade developments in technology and transatlantic trade began to create new avenues of emigration: the inauguration of steamship traffic between Ireland and Britain eliminated the economic advantages of direct Irish-American trade; and the enormous expansion of commerce in British manufactured goods and American farm products between Liverpool and New York provided more regular, more reliable, and eventually less expensive passages to the New World. Indeed, as early as 1826 one-third of the Irish arrivals in New York had taken ship in Liverpool, and by the mid-1820s the burgeoning Empire City—gateway to the American West via the Erie Canal—had replaced Philadelphia as Irishmen's most popular port of entry in the United States. In short, new streams of Irish emigrants were no longer merely following in the well-worn channels of eighteenth-century Ulster emigration.[3]

Moreover, despite the prevailing high fares, by the mid-1820s a decided shift toward the emigration of poorer classes of Irish seems to have taken place. In the decade's early years, only "people that had some capital left the country," and in 1820 American port officials recording the occupations of arriving Irishmen found that 27 percent were farmers, 22 percent artisans, 10 percent tradesmen and professionals, while only 21 percent were mere laborers. However, in 1826 the passenger lists of vessels landing in New York revealed that now almost 48 percent of the Irish were artisans, over 28 percent were laborers, nearly 10 percent were servants, but fewer than 10 percent were listed either as farmers or as businessmen and professionals. Undoubtedly, many young men listed as "laborers" were actually the sons of farmers rather than from the ranks of cottiers and unskilled laborers. However, over 62 percent of the Irish passengers to New York (two-thirds of whom were males) traveled alone rather than in families—another indication of their relative lack of capital. Considering the nearly unanimous reports in the 1820s that the Irish who sailed to British North America—a "great many" of whom had "little or nothing after paying their passage"—were less affluent than those bound directly for the States, it seems reasonable to conclude that the poorer Irish were already playing a greater role in the movement overseas.[4]

In addition, although a large majority of the 1820–26 emigrants were still Ulster Protestants, Catholic departures were steadily increasing, particularly among small farmers and artisans in the economically depressed cottage textile districts in south Ulster, north Leinster, and east Connaught. In 1821 a visitor to Londonderry declared that Ulster Catholics were so "wedded to the soil" that "not one in a hundred" of those leaving through that port was "of the Catholic persuasion," but in 1826 an Irish-born Canadian official testified that over a fourth of the Londonderry emigrants were Catholics. Furthermore, although declining trade between Waterford and Newfoundland limited the flow of Catholics from southeastern Ireland, in 1823–25 the British government gave an enormous stimulus to southern emigration by providing free passages, land grants in Upper Canada, and other assistance to over 2,500 poor Catholic smallholders and cottiers, primarily from the Mallow and Fermoy districts in north Cork. Despite initial apprehensions, the settlers' letters home expressed complete satisfaction with what they described as a "most delightful country," where "all have plenty and to spare, and no man living willing to work but may live happy." Such reports excited desires to emigrate throughout southern Ireland: in 1825 over 50,000 persons applied for free passages and Canadian farms, and although Parliament terminated the project in that year, during the next decade thousands more petitions for similar assistance swamped the British Colonial Office. However, without such aid Catholic emigration in 1820–26 was limited to those who could pay fares ranging from £4 to £10 per person: primarily "very snug farmers" and the "best mechanics and . . . labourers" who possessed at least "a little capital." Nevertheless, as witnesses before Parliament testified, by the mid-1820s great numbers of poorer Catholics throughout Ireland were now willing to emigrate. Indeed, the Irish-born attorney general of Nova Scotia claimed that Irish emigration would be "immense" if the Passenger Acts, which artificially inflated fares, were repealed: "You might as well talk to [the Catholic poor] of paying ninety or a hundred pounds as nine or ten pounds," he declared, "but when you come to talk of a less sum, they might be able . . . to make it up."[5]

Experience proved the validity of that prediction. In 1827 the British government repealed all restrictions on emigration, and over 20,000 Irish responded to lower fares, prosperity overseas, and deep agricultural and industrial depression at home by flocking to the New World. In the following year Parliament enacted new but less stringent regulations, and between 1828 and 1837 nearly 400,000 Irish emigrated to North America. Overall about 65 percent sailed to the British provinces, primarily to Quebec. However, relaxed regulations and increased trade between Liverpool and American seaports reduced both the general costs of emigration and the differences between fares to Canada and the United States: by 1831 the standard fare from Ireland to Canada was only £1 10s., but a passage from Liverpool to New York now cost merely £2 to £3 and emigrants could bargain for further reductions. Consequently, by the mid-1830s annual departures for Canada only slightly exceeded those for the States. Furthermore, an increasing proportion of those who initially landed in British North America did not remain there. In both 1831 and 1832 a record 65,000 Irish emigrated, primarily to Canada. However, such unprecedented numbers exceeded the capacities of contemporary shippers and the absorptive powers of the Canadian economy; subsequent reports of overcrowded vessels, outbreaks of cholera, shipwrecks, and unemployment after arrival reduced Canada's appeal and caused departures to decline in 1833–34. "There are many tradesmen and labourers going about idle and can't get any work," wrote the recently arrived Ulster artisan Sampson Brady from Montreal in 1832: "The poor emigrants that went up the country . . . are dying in hundreds"; "[t]hose that have money enough are returning to their native homes as fast as possible"; and Brady himself hoped to move his family south to New York, where he had "hopes of doing better." The severe distress which Brady described was short-lived, but the United States–not British North America–remained the "land of promise" for most Irishmen. By 1836 an emigrant in Philadelphia could report enthusiastically, "Thousands are coming yearly to this country [where] there is room for all—employment for all and success for many." In 1837, departures from Ireland rose to nearly 50,000 before the American financial panic and Canadian rebellions of that year brought a temporary halt to the exodus.[6]

Between 1827 and 1832 Ulster still contributed about 50 percent of the Irish emigrants to North America: the Protestant North's century-old ties to the New World encouraged a steady chain migration which was less sensitive than southern emigration to fluctuating economic conditions at home or abroad. Moreover, during these years there was still a sizable emigration of "substantial farmers," primarily Protestants, who left to take up land in the western States or in Upper Canada, where, as Sampson Brady acknowledged, a "farmer that has plenty of cash, good health, and long life may do well. . . ." Thus, in north Leitrim—as in much of Ireland—the "greater proportion of the emigration" remained "from the class of employers rather than from the employed." Many Ulster emigrants carried as much as £100–£500, and most of the remainder had at least £10 left after paying their fares. Conversely, despite lower passage costs, increased landlord assistance, and remittances from North America, the poorest Irish—the overwhelmingly Catholic smallholders, cottiers, and laborers of southern and western Ireland—reportedly still lacked the means to cross the Atlantic. "Few labourers are to be found among the emigrants," testified a witness before Parliament in 1836, for "they are unable to pay the passage; their earnings hardly suffice for their daily maintenance, they cannot save." Although many observers believed that great numbers of impoverished peasants, particularly the young and unmarried, would go to America if assisted to do so, the only passages that many could afford were to England or Scotland. In 1830–35 alone some 200,000 Irish paid the few pence per head for deck passage across the Irish Sea, and by 1841 over 400,000 lived permanently in London, Manchester, Glasgow, and other cities in Great Britain.[7]

Nevertheless, although Irishmen from Ulster and Protestants generally continued to be overrepresented among the emigrants of 1827–37, for the first time since the seventeenth century *relatively* poor Catholics from the three southern provinces constituted a major proportion of the movement overseas. At some point in the early 1830s annual departures by Catholics began to exceed those of Dissenters and Anglicans combined, and over the entire period Catholics composed an estimated 50 to 60 percent of all emigrants. By 1834 the British traveler H. D. Inglis could report that "the disposition to emigrate increases; . . . all of the lower classes who are able to avail themselves of it, do" so, and "the persons who emigrate are chiefly . . . Catholics." Protestant farmers and artisans continued to dominate emigration from parts of Ulster such as Antrim, Down, north Derry, and east Donegal. However, an increasing number leaving the northern province were Catholics, particularly from impoverished and overpopulated counties such as Tyrone, Monaghan, and Cavan; even in eastern Ulster's prosperous Lagan Valley, Catholics constituted about 40 percent of all departures. Furthermore, during 1827–37 perhaps four-fifths of the estimated 200,000 emigrants from southern and western Ireland were Catholics. A list made in 1829 of over 600 Irish canal workers in Upper Canada suggests that only about a third of the recently arrived emigrants came from Munster and Connaught, but in the 1830s a significantly larger proportion of Catholic Irishmen came from the South and West. By 1832, departures from Connaught were sufficient to inspire a firm in Westport, County Mayo, to publish an *Emigrant's Guide,* and in 1834 Inglis remarked on a substantial increase in emigration from the port of Galway. In addition, between 1827 and 1837 most Catholic emigrants—although by no means destitute—were less affluent and skilled than their immediate predecessors. Witnesses on both sides of the Atlantic testified that smallholders, farmers' noninheriting sons, and "the better kind of labourers" now dominated the exodus. Thus, in 1836 almost 60 percent of the Irish arriving at New York were classified as laborers or servants, compared with only 38 percent in 1826; farmers constituted 8.5 percent—only a slight drop since 1826—but the proportions of artisans and professional men had declined steeply, to 27 percent and 3 percent respectively. A contemporary survey of arrivals at the Delaware River ports of Amboy and Wilmington revealed a similar occupational distribution. Of those Irish who paid less to land in British North America, contemporaries charged that growing numbers had little or no capital; during the cholera years of 1831–32 many appeared to be "of the most useless description," if not "mere beggars." Reflecting their lower economic status, most Irish emigrants now traveled alone or with siblings rather than in nuclear families; of those landing in New York about two-thirds were males, usually in their early twenties, although witnesses reported increasing numbers of young women traveling singly.[8]

In 1837–38 financial panic in the United States and political instability in Canada temporarily discouraged Irish emigration. "[T]imes is hard and wages low," wrote one Ulster-American, warning his relatives "that if they do well in Ireland . . . they have no need to come here," where "scarcely any person . . . can find employment." In 1837 over 48,000 Irish crossed the Atlantic, but such reports reduced departures the next year to only 11,000. However, despite the American economy's slow recovery, emigration quickly revived: from 1838 to 1844—the last pre-Famine years—over 351,000 Irish journeyed to North America. After 1838 an average of nearly 56,700 left Ireland annually, and in 1842 an astonished Dublin editor declared, "In no former year do we remember so many persons leaving this country for America." In short, Irish emigration now flowed at a permanent, unprecedentedly high level despite economic stagnation overseas; even before the potato crop failures of 1845–50, emigration had become an integral aspect of Irish life.[9]

Between 1838 and 1844 the trends of the preceding decades became the fixed patterns of nineteenth-century Irish emigration; the necessary channels and preconditions for the massive Famine and post-Famine exoduses were now established. For instance, the Liverpool–New York route had become routine; trade between those ports was so extensive that passage costs to the States were almost as low as fares to Canada. Even relatively poor emigrants could thus reach their preferred destination directly: only in 1840 did departures for the British provinces exceed those for the United States, and over the entire period more than 202,000 sailed to the American Republic compared with 149,000 bound for Canada. Moreover, although Ulster emigration continued "with amazing rapidity," a majority of the emigrants of 1838–44 were now Catholics from the other provinces. Departures from Ulster's predominantly Catholic border counties rose steadily, but the greatest increases took place in southern and western Ireland; more Irishmen now took ship at Cork than at Belfast, and large numbers also left from ports such as Limerick and Sligo. Still, emigration was really popular only in Ulster, Leinster, and certain highly commercialized districts of Munster and east Connaught. However, it was of great future significance that in 1838–44 at least a few people emigrated from nearly every parish in the island. For example, departures from Connaught increased noticeably as "shoals of persons" from the West crossed the Shannon at Athlone bridge "on their way to Dublin for America"; in these years the most remote and primitive areas, such as the Mullet of Mayo, experienced their first departures for the New World. In addition, although poor Protestants and "respectable," "industrious and well-conducted" farmers and tradesmen of both religions continued to emigrate, by the Famine's eve a large majority of those departing were not only Catholics but poor smallholders, farmers' sons, cottiers, and laborers as well: those who often carried "no capital but their manual labor" and were "without acquired skill of any kind." Others were young females, classified by port officials as "servants" or "spinsters," who emigrated in response to letters which claimed that "[y]oung women who can wash and sew well can find plenty of employment" in American cities. Many emigrants were so poor that only remittances or landlord assistance enabled them to leave home: in 1838 money sent from America paid the fares of over half the Irish passengers; and after that year the levying of new taxes to maintain resident paupers gave Irish landlords and leaseholders added incentive to persuade impecunious subtenants and laborers to emigrate. Some poor emigrants were reportedly unprepared or unwilling to leave their homes, and many of them arrived destitute and disoriented. Thus, in the early 1840s a New York emigrant-aid society complained, "Thousands continually land entirely penniless," and in 1843 over half the Irish disembarking in Canada required some form of charity.[10]

Nevertheless, even in 1838–44 most Catholic emigrants were neither destitute nor desperate. In 1841, census takers in County Cavan noted that most emigrants came from the ranks of middling and small farmers, not from the laboring classes. Without assistance the latter could not afford the fares, while the former remained sensitive to changing American employment opportunities. For example, many of the record 93,000 emigrants of 1842 wrote home that they had found few jobs and poor wages: "I have heard of some lately arrived to be working for their board and have seen many looking for employment," warned one Irishman in Pennsylvania, and "there is a poor prospect for any person emigrating to this country at present"; in 1843 the Irish heeded such reports, and departures fell nearly 60 percent. Moreover, many emigrants only *appeared* destitute after long ocean voyages. In 1840, for instance, Canadian port officials described most Irish arrivals as impoverished laborers, but also noted that they had refused low-paid employment on local construction projects and moved great distances in search of better wages. Similarly, a merchant in Cork observed that most emigrants embarking from that port were laborers whose wages had averaged at least 8d. per day; the greater numbers who earned less could not afford to emigrate. Finally, in the poorest and most-archaic districts of southern and western Ireland the largely Irish-speaking peasantry still resisted the lure of emigration. Thus, although both the scale and the character of Irish emigration had changed enormously since 1815, on the Famine's eve Irish officials and landlords continued to lament that emigration was still not ridding Ireland of those they considered its most superfluous inhabitants: "the young, the enterprising and the industrious . . . leave us whilst the old, the impotent, the idle and indolent portions"—"the dregs," one Protestant minister called them—"stay with us." As one Englishman ruefully observed, "The best go—the worst remain." In short, the final solution for Ireland's overpopulation, "backwardness," and poverty still lay ahead, in the holocaust of the late 1840s.[11]

In the pre-Famine decades, as earlier, the glaring contrasts between Irish and North American economic conditions encouraged emigration. However, those contrasts had always existed, and the unprecedented size of the 1815–44 exodus reflected in part the profound structural and psychological effects of commercialization on early-nineteenth-century Irish society. The spread of a cash-based market economy; greatly improved networks of transportation and communications; expanding educational systems and increased literacy: in short, all the "modern improvements" described in Chapter 2 facilitated emigration by providing the necessary means, transport, and awareness of conditions outside Ireland. More important, ever since the mid-eighteenth century the accelerated commercialization of Irish life had weakened older hierarchical and communalistic socioeconomic linkages and transformed popular attitudes to comport with new social realities. An emerging "free market" in land and labor had encouraged the economic rationalization of human relationships. Archaic dependent or interdependent outlooks once compatible with relative economic stagnation, subsistence agriculture, and cotillage eroded as rundale clachans, medieval common lands, and joint tenancies fragmented into enclosed family holdings and as class divisions between farmers and laborers, merchant capitalists and artisans, became more sharply delineated. Communalistic traditions often made way for individualistic or familistic ambitions and actions in new social contexts where emigration now seemed logical, necessary, even desirable.[12]

To be precise, by 1815 increasing numbers of Irishmen were defining goals in entrepreneurial or protocapitalistic terms: as "gaining an Independence," an aspiration which in its two primary connotations represented marked deviations from ideals which had underlain early-eighteenth-century modes of production and social interaction. First, for a growing minority of business-minded, urban-oriented Irishmen, "independence" meant individual upward mobility in a "free market" which demanded and theoretically rewarded acquisitive, competitive attitudes and activities. Among those who fully embraced the ethos of "improvement," capitalist calculations liberated ambitious and, after 1814, increasingly frustrated individuals to emigrate "on speculation" rather than out of necessity. Second, however, for most agriculturists and artisans, "independence" still meant "comfortable self-sufficiency": an ambition reflecting an early, transitory stage of commercialization—a nuclear-household capitalism in which families sought security through *limited* involvement in a market economy. "Independence" so defined was compatible with the retention of some traditional or "peasant" practices and attitudes: conservative farming methods; the *meitheall;* strictures against "upstarts," "parasitical middlemen," and *individual* aggrandizement; and, given sufficient land, partible inheritance. In this sense the goal of "independence" could inhibit emigration when the anticipated degrees of "comfortable self-sufficiency" could be realized at home. However, such realization was always precarious for tenants, artisans, and laborers enmeshed in a market system inherently dynamic and ultimately beyond their control; this was true even before 1815, and, indeed, for landless laborers—the rootless first "victims" of commercialization—achieving "independence" almost inevitably necessitated emigration. Moreover, each social gradation, each household, of farmers and artisans jealously guarded its own relative status and possessed a keen awareness of the point beyond which adverse economic conditions threatened to reduce "independence" to "slavery." After 1814, when great numbers of tenants and artisans reached that point, only two options other than violent resistance were available: household emigration in search of "comfortable self-sufficiency" abroad; or adoption of impartible inheritance, thereby ensuring self-sufficiency or at least survival for the stem family at home, but at the cost of obliging noninheriting children to emigrate as individuals. In the 1700s these had been the choices posed to Protestants in commercially advanced Ulster; by 1815–44 the same alternatives were facing Catholics as well as Protestants throughout Ireland.[13]

Thus, by the end of the Napoleonic Wars, Ireland's socioeconomic development had made increased emigration inevitable if Irishmen were going to pursue widespread ambitions for "independence" at home or abroad. Indeed, between 1815 and 1844, emigrants' and would-be emigrants' letters and petitions repeatedly expressed desires to achieve "independance" in the New World. Aspiring entrepreneurs such as the Ulsterman John King observed with frustration, "In Ireland, unless a young man has capital, or Connections able to assist him, and I may add willing to do so, he may toil all his life and never find an independent feeling occupy his breast"; by contrast, in America "if a young man is industrious and saving he will Eventually succeed." To Samuel Fogarty, son of Quaker merchants in Limerick, "gaining an Independence" meant self-improvement in "my mind, manners and conduct," while for Catholic professional men such as Michael McDermott and Robert Elliott it meant opportunity unfettered by Protestant prejudice. For William Lyster, Anglican clergyman of Wexford gentry stock, "independence" meant the security of an abundant environment: in the 1830s he moved his family into the Michigan forests, for despite "the distance and length of voyage, . . . our own & posterity's attainment of a useful & comfortable, perhaps affluent independence . . . is to be found in perfection in America." For William Lalor, son of a strong farmer in Queen's County, "independence" signified escape from a father who had refused to give him land, while for the Antrim weaver John Mc-

Bride it meant he would no longer have "to stand like a beggar at a manufacturer's door." For distressed tenants such as Timothy O'Connell, Michael Heaton, Pádraig Cúndún, and many others who "from Cheapness of Provisions and the Dearness of Rents is unable to maintain our former independence," the goal was flight from "tyrannous landlords who have no mercy" and from "that Ebb of Poverty" beyond which lay the "Slavery" of wage labor. For those already in that condition, for cottiers and landless laborers such as John Tovil, Hugh Rock, and John Quinlivan—"reduced to a Starving Situation" and "eternally apprehensive of our being expelled from our wretched dwellings"—the dream was for steady employment, enough to eat, and "a place to Stop that I can call my own." In short, like the Ulster farmer Nathaniel Carrothers, all these Irishmen hoped to better "their condishon by coming to america far beyont what it was posible for them to have done had the[y] stoped in Ireland."[14]

After 1815, new emigrants' letters enhanced the New World's already glowing reputation and convinced increasing numbers of Irishmen that "independence" could best be achieved in what one Ulsterman called "the land of freedom and no oppression." Soldiers returning from the Anglo-American war of 1812–15 reported that North America was still an arcadian paradise with "[g]ame of all kinds in the greatest profusion" where "all a man wanted was a gun and sufficient ammunition to be able to live like a prince." Hard-pressed Irish tenants could not but envy emigrants such as Pádraig Cúndún of upstate New York, who owned "outright a fine farm of land": "[N]o one can demand rent of me," he boasted, and "[m]y family and I can eat our fill of bread and meat, butter and milk any day we like throughout the year. . . ." Catholics and Dissenters harassed by tithe jobbers and demands from their own clergy learned of a country where their kinsman had "no established churches nor Popes nor Bishops nor Fryers nor even Rectors to pay Tithes for." Other emigrants informed Irish artisans they "could make a fortune" in America, as one weaver reported that he had purchased a house and lot worth $200 although "I am not three years from home . . . and when I came here I had only half a dollar." Likewise, the lowest classes received encouragement from advertisements of work on American roads and canals, supplemented by private assurances that "the peasant or labourer would find at all times ready and constant employment, good wages and such fare as would surprise him." In Kentucky, declared an Ulster-American, "a fellow that will put his hand to anything . . . can get work . . . Seven days in the week & can earn a Dollar every day he sees"; and from Ohio came the claim that "an industerous Labourer here can live in Every respect as well as the welthiest farmer in the County of Tyrone." Thus, as the Catholic landlord Francis Wyse testified, letters from the New World often "represented emigration to the United States as the panacea for every ill and untoward difficulty in the old country. . . ." No wonder many pre-Famine Irish regarded North America as "the land that flows with milk and hony—the land of work and peace."[15]

Of course, between 1815 and 1844, emigrants' letters also contained cautionary, even negative information and often warned that "independence"—however conceived—was not easily achieved on the "other side." Indeed, during depressions, as in 1819–22 and 1837–43, Irish-Americans frequently penned unequivocal warnings not to emigrate. On a practical level the Irish heeded such advice, adjusting their departure dates and destinations accordingly. However, as an emigrant from County Roscommon recognized, on an ideological level most Irishmen did not want to receive letters which "never contained anything of the marvellous, and [which were] not calculated to make [them] believe that riches grow like grass on this side of the Atlantic." Although disillusioned emigrants could write that "the people of Ireland are sorely mistaken about" the New World, the realistic information sent home could not dampen what the Anglo-Irish diplomat T. C. Grattan described as a widespread "enthusiasm for America" which mingled with peasants' complaints of poverty and oppression. In other words, to a large degree the pre-Famine Irish read emigrants' letters for confirmation of a fabulous, semimythical image of North America as "promised land of plenty." The image had been current among Ulster Dissenters since the early eighteenth century, but after 1814 it grew in both intensity and popularity to compensate for Irishmen's thwarted dreams and gathering despair over the land of their birth. Irish ambitions for "independence"—inspired by economic growth before 1814, but afterward soured by deep, prolonged depression—were now projected abroad to a purportedly idyllic America of "no tyranny, no oppression from landlords, and no taxes"—where, as even a Catholic bishop believed, "the poor require no assistance which the kindness of nature will not sufficiently supply." Like other traditional, religious-based societies adversely affected by rapid change, pre-Famine Ireland was rife with prophecies of doom and millennial expectations of earthly salvation: the growing "rage for emigration" to the New World reflected both popular moods.[16]

In short, despite North America's real advantages, it is doubtful whether so many Irish would have emigrated after 1814 had conditions at home not deteriorated so dramatically. After four decades of economic expansion and relative prosperity, the end of the Napoleonic Wars precipitated severe depression afflicting nearly every region and class. Prices for Irish products fell catastrophically, major industries collapsed, capital investment and urban growth stagnated, per capita income declined, and unemployment and destitution became widespread. Not all Ireland suffered equally—indeed, in eastern Ulster a reorganized linen industry expanded and flourished—and by the mid-1830s the worst of the crisis was over. However, in general, Ireland's pre-Famine economy never recovered its wartime affluence, and rising exports of agricultural goods were a reflection less of increased productivity than of diminished domestic consumption among small farmers and laborers, who often literally starved themselves to pay rents in an intensely competitive land market. Economic deterioration led to increased social conflict: after 1814 agrarian violence and religious and political strife were almost incessant, further estranging rich and poor, Protestants and Catholics. Indeed, even God seemed about to abandon pre-Famine Ireland. In 1816–18 unusually cold, wet weather destroyed the grain and potato crops; their resistance weakened by hunger, one-eighth of the Irish contracted typhus or smallpox and some 50,000 died of starvation or disease. In 1821 the potato failed again in Munster, and people perished of hunger in Cork and Clare. In 1825–29 seasons of alternating drought and excessive rain injured both the potato and the cereal harvests; in 1830 only shipments of Indian meal from North America prevented starvation, but in 1832 there was "stark famine" in parts of Munster and south Leinster. In the early 1830s cholera also ravaged the lower classes, and during the entire decade the potato crop failed on a local or national scale eight out of ten years; the 1841 census estimated that over 112,000 persons had perished of fevers accompanying malnutrition. Then, as if incessant rain were not sufficient affliction, the winter of 1838 brought "the night of the big wind," when snow covered the peasants' cottages and froze the livestock in the fields. Finally, in 1840–44, the potato crops partly failed three more times. Truly, as one historian has written, after 1814 the Irish people staggered toward their ultimate disaster. Not surprisingly, the letters and petitions written by Irishmen in 1815–44 reflect an almost universal pessimism, a conviction that their homeland was doomed: "The cuntery is done," cried one farmer; "the mizerable world seems to be tottering to its centre," wrote another. However, the most accurately phrased epitaph for pre-Famine Ireland was the prophecy of an emigrant from County Tyrone: "there is a Distruction Aproaching to [the people of] Ireland," he wrote, "thire time is nerely at an end." No wonder that many Irishmen, of all creeds and classes, now eagerly anticipated emigration to America as "a Joyful deliverance."[17]

The severity of the postwar economic crisis led affluent as well as poor Irishmen to conclude that "independence" could be achieved or maintained only through emigration; as one of the former lamented, "the present . . . circumstances of ireland are of such a nature as to offer very few opportunities for the exercise of talent and activity." For example, after 1814, Irish merchants and manufacturers immediately suffered from the return of peace. In 1815 Charles Lewis of County Down reported, "Trade never was in my Memory so dull as at present   Failures among our Merchants so common that hardly any are thought secure." Similar complaints came from southern Ireland: in Dublin "three of the principle Houses in the Serge & General Woolen business hav stopped payment," and "Manufacturers in Limerick, as well as in other parts of the Country" were unable to sell their products or pay their creditors. The long wartime boom had persuaded many businessmen that prosperity would be perpetual. For example, during the wars Samuel Smyth was a flourishing Belfast merchant worth £10,000. Just before 1815 he invested heavily in town lots and built four Georgian houses—"one of the worst things I Ever Don," Smyth later recalled, since after "Bonypar's Downfall" his houses could attract neither purchasers nor tenants. Worse, the sudden decline in farm prices bankrupted Smyth's provisioning concern: "At that time I had a large Quantity of Bacon in London laid in at high Rates, it was selling before [Waterloo] at 100ˢ [but] it came Down Dayly to 50 – 40 – 20 [and] the last was sold at 16 to Close Sales." Like many other failed entrepreneurs, Smyth and his family started over in North America. Most retained at least some capital to invest abroad, but some were like Peter Roe of New Ross, County Wexford: a bankrupt brewer once worth £40,000, Roe was reduced to begging the government for a free passage to "distant climes, where our late compeers can not look with contempt on us, for having fallen from our comparative exalted station in life."[18]

For the next three decades ambitious emigrants who conceived "independence" in entrepreneurial terms expressed in letters and petitions the desire to escape from an economic stagnation which stifled opportunities "for making money." Even in the late 1820s Ulstermen despaired, "Trade . . . is every day Geting worse," and although conditions in eastern Ulster eventually improved, in southern Ireland manufacturing and commerce remained chronically depressed. Shortly after Waterloo half the banks in Munster and south Leinster closed their doors, and between 1813 and 1823 the circulation of private banknotes fell by two-thirds. Local investments fell sharply, and Irish capital fled to Britain or was concentrated in the Northeast. Employment opportunities even for educated Irishmen declined since "there is nothin in Ireland but failers bankrups and business gone to nothing"; as Peter Finegan of Carrickmacross, County Monaghan, complained, although he had "received in youth a liberal Education, . . . at present [it] is but of little use." In County Longford even Anglicans considered themselves fortunate to get clerical "situations," but they could earn only "a few Shillings a week by working hard from morning 'till night." In 1842 James Nowlan, a would-be emigrant and unemployed clerk in County Wexford, lamented that the four local flour mills for which he had worked "all had the misfortunes to fail in the short time of five years." Nowlan's brother still had work as a "Shop man," but he, too, planned to emigrate since he wrote, "I am . . . not well paid for my services" and "Its out of young mens power to save money in this country. . . ."[19]

Outside the Northeast nearly all Irish engaged in skilled crafts and manufacturing suffered from low wages, unemployment, and loss of "independence" as cheap British factory goods flooded already-depressed local markets. In Dublin, Cork, and other southern cities, trade unions' efforts to forestall the degradation of their crafts proved unavailing, and many members took advantage of union assistance to emigrate to Britain or America. In country towns and rural districts, competition from British imports, declining incomes, and increased emigration among farmers persuaded large numbers of shoemakers, masons, carpenters, coopers, nailers, and other artisans to follow their former customers to the New World. For example, in 1824 Peter Falvey of Kanturk, County Cork—once an upwardly mobile blacksmith who had raised his large family "above want untill the fealure of the Farmers"—was in "the Greatest Distress for the want of Employment" and petitioned the government for a free passage to Canada. Similarly, in 1843 Christopher Kelly, a young carpenter in County Meath, could not find work since "there is two many of that trade and the[y] are nearly all idel"; three years later Kelly was employed by an Irish building contractor in upstate New York.[20]

The crisis in Irish manufacturing was particularly acute for textile workers. Before 1814, thousands of small farmers, cottiers, and laborers had paid rents and shop bills through weaving and spinning. Already the increased capitalization of textile manufacturing had reduced many once-independent craftsmen to debt-ridden piece- or wageworkers, and after Waterloo spinsters and weavers received even less return for their labor. For example, in 1818 a County Antrim linen weaver complained that he was "in A hard way of Earning [his] Bread"; he wanted to join his brother in South Carolina, "But times is so Bad and wages so Little that all that A man can Doe in this Country will Doe Verry Little for him." In the early 1820s travelers were describing Ireland's cottier-weavers as wretchedly poor, but conditions worsened in 1825–26 when the final removal of Irish tariff protection and the industrial depression in Great Britain encouraged English manufacturers to dump massive amounts of cheap clothing on the Irish market. The effects on the Irish woolen and cotton industries were disastrous and permanent. Woolen manufacturing, concentrated primarily in southern towns such as Kilkenny and Mountmellick, was already in decline, but between 1825 and 1838 Ireland's output of woolen cloth fell by 85 percent. The south Leinster flannel trade became virtually extinct, and the number of Kilkenny blanket weavers fell from 3,000 to 600. By the Famine's eve English woolen imports were underselling even cottage-made garments, and most peasants now wore clothing made abroad. In 1850 only nine woolen mills, employing 553 workers, remained of a once-flourishing industry, and during the preceding decades thousands of distressed weavers, spinners, and wool combers had left the country. Likewise, Ireland's formerly promising cotton industry declined precipitously. Between 1825 and 1833 the number of cotton mills in the Belfast region fell from twenty-one to fifteen. The city's cotton workers went on strike to maintain jobs and wages, but their efforts failed; millworkers and weavers turned to linen manufacturing or emigrated, and at mid-century cotton manufacturing in the entire northern province employed fewer than 3,000 persons. In southern Ireland the industry almost totally disappeared, and in 1829 Cork's cotton weavers begged for relief, claiming,

> We are in the most deplorable state of distress actually famishing for the want of employment, and such as have the fortune to be employed are pining in unparalelled misery . . . all our cloaths are in pawn, bedcloaths we have scarcely any many of us are oblidged to lie on the floor—and expect daily to be turned out on the Street. . . . we are . . . deprived of any hope of existence, and see no prospect but in emigration. . . .[21]

Postwar depression and British competition also staggered Ireland's linen industry. In 1825 John McBride, an emigrant from Antrim, remarked that "the prices of weaving were so low" that he had no "idea how a poor man with a large family of children can support them"; and two years later a small farmer in County Armagh reported that "the linen trade that so many live by . . . has completely failed," and so "a vast number of our neighbours . . . are selling off their little property and emigrating to Canada." However, Belfast's capitalists reorganized their industry to counter English competition. In 1825 James Kay patented the wet-spinning process which made it possible to machine-spin flax fibers into fine yarn. Ulster manufacturers quickly adopted the invention, built new flax mills, and converted cotton factories to flax spinning. Between 1830 and 1850 the Lagan Valley became one of Britain's major industrial centers, and Belfast's population exploded from 50,000 to 100,000. Nevertheless, the linen industry's successful modernization resulted in severe socioeconomic dislocations. Before 1814 cottage weaving and spinning had spread into southern and western Ulster, north Leinster and Connaught, even into parts of Munster. Now, however, manufacturing contracted to the Lagan Valley and north Armagh, areas easily accessible to imported coal for the spinning mills, and cottagers in more remote districts lost vital supplementary income. As one Ulsterman lamented in 1832, "there is So many Spinning Machines Got Into this Country which hurt the women Spinners very much," for machine-spun "Yarn is far Superior for Strength to that of Womans Spining." The social status of rural women, based ultimately on their economic contributions to family incomes, deteriorated with the decline of cottage spinning; in parts of Connaught, cottiers' wives turned to poultry raising; in County Tyrone "many more endeavour to get field labour, but the number of men is so great that the women seldom get any employment." Consequently, marriage rates fell, the average age at marriage rose, and the songs of Ulster's rhyming weavers reflected rural women's sorrow that "Now men hae erected a new ingine, / An' left but little for us to earn." Many females migrated to work in the new mills, but others left Ireland in search of employment and husbands. Moreover, outside the Northeast, cottage weaving—traditionally a male occupation—also declined as weavers in south Ulster, north Connaught, and other regions remote from the yarn factories were unable to compete with those who lived in the Lagan Valley and adjacent districts. Overpopulated counties such as Monaghan and Cavan degenerated into rural slums, and weavers in Louth, Westmeath, Mayo, and elsewhere fell back to subsistence level. Even in the Northeast both the status and the wages of rural weavers deteriorated, and in 1840 an observer noted that "men cannot live for what they get for weaving now. There is a great difference in respect of the appearance of weavers who come to market now and formerly; they are not so well dressed, nor near so comfortable looking: the fine sturdy young men, who once came to the market, have now gone out of the trade, and many have emigrated to America."[22]

In short, for Ulster's lower classes the North's prosperity was largely relative to conditions in southern Ireland, where the collapse of textile manufacturing had catastrophic consequences. In 1827, tradesmen in Mullingar were reportedly "struggling . . . in a state of starvation" on less than 4d. per day. Between 1831 and 1836 the number of textile workers in Drogheda fell by three-fourths, and in 1840 those who remained had only part-time employment. In the latter year the once-bustling linen hall at Westport, County Mayo, was "almost unused," and in Bandon, County Cork, only 150 of the town's 2,000 weavers in 1815 still plied their trade. In a sense, the pre-Famine decades witnessed the de-industrialization of southern Ireland: the number of families supported by nonagricultural occupations fell by over 50 percent, rural incomes declined sharply, and both the physical and the social fabric of southern Ireland deteriorated visibly. For example, emigrants from Dublin and other cities remembered "the numberless number" vainly seeking work; prostitution increased as "many unfortunate females, through necessity, perambulate the streets." Many country towns and villages fell into decay: "bad as this town looked when you seen it," declared a resident of Ballymahon, County Longford, to his emigrant son, "it is fifty times worse now   houses falling out of the face and no sign of . . . any encouragement whatever." When Irish towns did grow, it was often due only to influxes of destitute rural migrants who squatted in "cabin suburbs" or in "alleys where the odours and rags and the darkness are so hideous, that one runs frightened away from them." Some dramatic letters written by a Bandon weaver revealed the effects of industrial depression on Munster. In 1827 Wills Anstis reported that "the weavers in Bandon are in a state of beggary and many of them have turned to begging entirely. And such of them that have work their earning were miserable. . . ." Seven years later the town's "[t]radespeople [were] all in a state of Starvation." His income reduced, Anstis and his family twice suffered eviction from smallholdings. In 1827 they "lost the priviledge of our Cow . . . and the two upper fields" but retained "one field and the house in place of the whole," "a good Crop of potatoes," and "an acre of good barley." By 1834, however, Anstis had fallen further into arrears and was again evicted. He now fell to the level of a mere laborer, without even a "potatoe garden"—"only barely the house and wages which is a Shilling a day   I get that and nothing else and obliged to earn that by [weaving by] Night as well as by Day." Most of Anstis's fellow weavers emigrated to England or America, but Anstis never saved sufficient money; in 1834 he was still begging his brother-in-law for a free passage to New Brunswick.[23]

The postwar industrial crisis condemned most Irishmen to a choice between emigration and a more exclusive reliance on the land for profit or, more likely, bare subsistence. Unfortunately, after 1814 Irish agriculture experienced an equally severe depression as Britain's wartime dependence on Irish foodstuffs lessened, producing a steep decline in the prices received for all farm products. Between 1818 and 1822, grain prices fell by half, beef and pork prices by one-third; although Irish farmers tried to compensate by doubling grain exports, in 1821 the total *value* of all exported cereals was still lower than at the war's end. Agricultural prices rallied in the late 1820s, fell again in the 1830s, and finally stabilized around 1840—but at levels far below those which had prevailed before 1815. Although exports of grain, butter, and live cattle and swine continued to rise, few profits trickled down to the great mass of tenants, cottiers, and laborers.[24]

Indeed, agricultural depression adversely affected *every* class in rural Ireland. Although landlords continued to dominate the countryside, their economic position weakened. In 1816 Richard Edgeworth, a modest proprietor in County Longford, complained, "The value of lands, this last year, in Ireland has sunk amazingly. I have been obliged to reduce several of my rents 20 percent and I should be happy to receive 800 pounds for every 1000 that is due to me." Landlords less business minded than Edgeworth found themselves in desperate straits: wartime prosperity had encouraged many to construct expensive country houses and entertain lavishly; often their incomes were heavily committed to mortgage payments, family settlements, and other debts which could not be honored when their tenants fell into arrears. Some proprietors, unable to relinquish the extravagant habits of the eighteenth century, brought ruin to their families. For example, Richard Boyse Osborne should have inherited property in Wexford worth £80,000; instead, he found himself "ruined by the weakness and delusion" of his father. His lands confiscated for debt, Osborne left Ireland at age nineteen to "join the popular movement of Westward Ho!" More pathetic was the plight of the bankrupt landlord Ralph Gore of County Kilkenny, who vainly petitioned the crown for a new estate in Canada, where he could restore his position "as the head of an ancient and honourable Family enjoying Rank & respectability in these Kingdoms for above 700 Years."[25]

However, with few exceptions—such as Richard Talbot, who in 1818 settled his family and 172 Tipperary Protestants on a land grant in Upper Canada—Irish landlords did not emigrate to the North American wilderness. Instead, most responded to economic crises in ways that prolonged their hegemony but had detrimental effects on their dependents. After 1814, changes of ownership and economic necessities accelerated the transformation of a paternalistic or negligent gentry into a class of landed businessmen. Either in person or through salaried agents, proprietors assumed closer supervision of estate management: efficiency and profits now took precedence over archaic ideals of honor and noblesse oblige. One result was a sharp reduction of investments in beautification projects, local industries, and public works which had formerly provided employment to artisans and laborers. Another was the elimination of middlemen, once invaluable intermediaries between proprietors and peasants, now increasingly regarded as profligate, anachronistic impediments to the rationalization of Irish agriculture. Consequently, after 1814 when middlemen fell into ar-

rears or when their long leases expired, landlords seized the opportunity to
evict them or, at least, to reduce their holdings drastically; by the Famine's
eve this "large and prosperous, albeit parasitic class" had almost disappeared.[26]

By Victorian standards, no doubt, many middlemen deserved extinction.
In later years the son of Robert Armstrong lamented that his "squireen"
father in County Leitrim had displayed "a taste only for eating, drinking,
fishing, and shooting. . . . Like all his class in those days, he thought of
little but hounds and horses by day and mirth and laughter by night."
However, for all their precapitalist habits, middlemen had performed important social and political functions; Protestants, especially, regarded
themselves with some justice as the mortar of the Ascendancy and felt outrage and betrayal over their loss of privileged status. Indeed, the fall of
some middlemen assumed tragic proportions: from "living well and riding
horses . . . in the better rank of society," they were reduced to mere tenants at will, even landless beggars. However, large numbers emigrated, as
did Robert Armstrong, who—when "a change came o'er the spirit of his
dream" of Irish idleness—settled his family on 600 acres in Upper Canada,
where he hoped "to live like a Prince [on] Fat venison and wild turkeys."
Perhaps more typical was the fate of the Andrew Johnston family at Ballymahon, County Longford. In 1834 Johnston led the life of a comfortable
Protestant middleman. He and his relatives partied and hunted foxes with
the gentry; his family vacationed at the seashore or in Dublin, and a private governess tutored his daughters. Although many of his friends had already emigrated, Johnston's position seemed secure: he was a local official
and an Orangeman with influential friends in the Tory administration; he
had even named one son after his landlord! Nevertheless, even in 1834,
falling farm prices threatened his standard of living; "our Markets here are
still very low," he reported, and "every thing the landholder has to Dis-
pose of is low and the landlords not Making any Reduction. . . ." As a
consequence, he was beginning to have difficulties collecting sufficient rent
from his undertenants to meet his own obligations. By 1837 Andrew Johnston had fallen "far behind in paying off his arrears of rent," and his
world was collapsing around him. His now "Heartless Landlord" was
"grinding his tenants to the *dust*" and "after all the thousands that I paid
him had me served with Ejectments for all the holdings I had." Johnston
himself never left Ireland; in 1841 he was struggling "under a *very heavy
rent*" on a worn-out farm in County Fermanagh. However, he managed to
save his children from his own degradation; by the early 1840s at least
seven sons and daughters were making their fortunes in the United States
and Canada.[27]

After 1814, tenant farmers generally found themselves squeezed between falling incomes and fixed or rising costs: substantial tenants saw
profit margins decline sharply, while middling farmers and smallholders
often were reduced to near subsistence level. With the end of the Napoleonic Wars, prices for Irish farm products fell so precipitously that, as

early as autumn 1814, travelers in the countryside noted the consequent "great and general poverty" and heard farmers' declarations that, unless landlords lowered the rents, "[t]he jail, or the road, is before ourselves and families"; by 1819 even Ulster tenant-right was valueless for, as one northerner lamented, prices were so low that "the best farm in Drumconvis would not get a purchaser at any money." On many estates arrears mounted as tenants defaulted on rents based on wartime prices: for example, between 1814 and 1826, arrears on the Fitzwilliam estates rose from just under £3,000 to over £35,000; in the same period arrears on the earl of Leitrim's properties increased sevenfold. Under duress many proprietors forgave arrears and/or reduced rents; the 25 percent abatements which the duke of Devonshire granted tenants on his Cork estates were probably typical. However, such reductions were often insufficient in a period when farm prices fell 30 to 35 percent, and "in general," wrote one critic, "the landlords did not make reduction till the means of the tenant were totally exhausted. . . ." Moreover, landlords granted abatements only to *head* tenants—that is, to farmers and graziers who held leases directly from proprietors—but head tenants rarely passed such reductions down to sublessees, who constituted the great bulk of Ireland's middling and small farmers. Instead, because population pressures coincided with declining cottage manufacturing, competition for land in 1814–44 remained so intense that overall rent levels probably increased despite the fall in farm prices. Finally, although farmers' labor costs remained steady or declined, other costs continued to rise. As one Ulsterman complained, tithes were "a constant drain of money from the poor farmer," especially when computed on a per-acre basis which failed to reflect falling profits; despite the Tithe Commutation Act of 1838, the annual burden on Irish agriculture amounted to more than £8 million. Taxes also increased: in 1818 one resentful emigrant reported that his homeland was "groaning under a most exorbitant taxation . . . to pay the interest on the National debt"; between 1820 and 1840 county cess, another per-acre charge, rose by about 25 percent; and after 1838 both landlords and leaseholders paid poor rates which by 1844 supported over 43,000 paupers in 118 newly constructed workhouses. No wonder large numbers of farmers found themselves "under Such Slavery of Rents Thths and Texes" that they viewed emigration as their only alternative to insolvency.[28]

Caught between crushing debts and shrinking rent rolls, most landlords granted abatements "only . . . from the actual impossibility of levying the larger sum" and generally displayed little sympathy for their hard-pressed tenants. Instead, they moved to assume greater control over their properties in an effort to exact larger, more punctually paid incomes. Prior to 1814, high wartime prices had encouraged landlords and middlemen to allow smallholdings, joint tenancies, and laborers' garden plots to proliferate. Numerous small or inefficient proprietors continued that practice but raised their rent rolls by forcing tenants to bid competitively for leases (a shortsighted strategy, since successful bidders often promised rents they could never pay). However, after Waterloo many other landlords began to rationalize landholdings and modernize farming methods on their estates. Although few were as energetic and successful as Sir John Benn-Walsh, whose ruthless innovations on his west Munster properties more than doubled his income, most made at least some efforts to consolidate inefficient smallholdings and joint tenancies into larger, compact, and commercially viable farms. Landlords pursued this goal in several ways. Most dramatically, they evicted large numbers of defaulted or "superfluous" tenants. After 1816, when new laws passed at landlords' behest made evictions relatively easy and inexpensive, neither once-proud leaseholders nor poverty-stricken squatters were safe from ejection; for example, the earl of Leitrim was not unique when in 1839 he instructed his agent to find grounds for breaking leases of tenants who were *not* in arrears! The exact number of those evicted in 1815–44 is unknown, but the total must have been substantial: perhaps 100,000 families lost their leases after 1829 when Parliament disfranchised the 40s. freeholders, and one source alleged that another 150,000 evictions occurred in 1839–43 alone. Of course, many—perhaps most—of these "evictions" represented mere "notices to quit" and were never actually carried out; moreover, large numbers of evicted families found new holdings on other estates. Nevertheless, evictions caused considerable suffering in pre-Famine Ireland: for instance, in 1826 a witness before Parliament testified that evictions in County Limerick had "throw[n] a great distressed population upon the country"; and the following year a single proprietor in County Kerry admitted evicting 1,100 "surreptitious tenantry" while consolidating common lands into compact farms. Also, landlords strove to prevent the remaining tenants from negating consolidation's effects by subdividing and subletting their holdings to strangers or their own children. After 1814 most new leases contained stringent covenants against subdivision, and in 1826 Parliament passed the Subletting Act, which marshaled the power of the state behind landlords' injunctions. At the same time, in order to gain increased control over their tenants, proprietors accelerated the trend toward shorter leases begun in the late eighteenth century. For example, before 1816 most leases granted on the Downshire estates were of fairly long duration, but afterward when old contracts expired tenants were allowed to hold land only on a year-to-year basis. In northern Ireland some proprietors even challenged the hallowed "Ulster custom" of tenant-right by denying sitting tenants preferential treatment when old leases expired and by forbidding evicted farmers to sell the "interest" in their holdings. In short, on several fronts landlords were moving to create a "free market" in land.[29]

As a result, even strong farmers were increasingly insecure, more subject to their landlords' caprice or rapacity; as Gerald Griffin, a prosperous Limerick grazier, warned, "You [never] know the moment a Landlord may pounce on you, ruin & throw you out." Among farmers, however, it was sublessees and smallholders who suffered most from the "improvements" in pre-Famine agriculture. Indeed, although statistics are unavailable, it is likely that the great majority of families evicted in 1815–44 were ejected by Catholic head tenants, graziers and strong farmers, rather than by Protestant landlords. Aside from the common contention that smallholders were wretched husbandmen who exhausted the soil and were frequently in arrears, proprietors and head tenants had more compelling motives after 1814 for opposing their continuance. Prices for all Irish farm products declined after 1814 but the value of live cattle, butter, and sheep fell less sharply and recovered earlier, and at higher levels, than did prices of flour, meal, or cereals: thus, it soon became obvious that grazing livestock was again more remunerative than tillage farming. However, only tenants with substantial holdings, secure leases, and some capital reserves could afford to build up and maintain large herds; consequently, smallholders suffered severe competitive disadvantages, for although

> rearing young Cattle is the only Commodity that the farmer can make money at, . . . there is a great number labouring under the oppression of new leased lands that is not able to hold but must sell [their calves whenever the rent comes due] to meet the demands of their oppressor.

As a result, the relative profitability of pasture farming over tillage further encouraged proprietors and strong farmers to evict smallholders and replace them with cattle or sheep. From 1821 to 1844 the numbers of Irish livestock increased at a faster rate than the population; cattle exports more than quadrupled; and by 1841 approximately 80 percent of Ireland's arable land was under grass. Admittedly, the spread of pasture was slow and uneven, largely because of smallholders' and cottiers' dogged resistance; in most of the countryside holdings of fifteen acres or less remained typical, and in the North and the West lands were still "Set in Small Divisions" to accommodate growing numbers of land-hungry inhabitants. Nevertheless, in Meath, the north midlands, and the most fertile districts of Munster and south Leinster the proliferation of livestock at the expense of poor tenants was considerable. For example, in 1826 a witness from "the richest part of Co. Limerick" testified to Parliament that "every gentleman of landed property . . . is getting his land as much as possible under pasture" and expelling "the pauper population." Similarly, in 1836, contemporaries reported that subtenants in south Longford faced eviction "before May as the houses . . . are all to be thrown down to add the ground to the green for sheep. . . . Corcorans family [was] turned out . . . last week [and] his things were all sold even the Bed under them." Again, in 1840 the agent on Viscount Midleton's Cork estate ordered that 560 acres occupied by seventeen families "should be laid down to pasture, and kept as sheep walks. All the tenants are under notice to quit in consequence of their bad management and nonpayment of rent." On another tract he decreed, "All the miserable cabins should be destroyed, and the Townland divided into two Farms."[30]

A number of favored tenants benefited from these developments, while many others less fortunate survived despite them. With landlord encouragement, strong farmers enlarged their holdings at their neighbors' expense, expelled subtenants, added more livestock, and generally profited in the midst of distress. Other tenants remained solvent by farming their lands more intensively, increasing grain production to compensate for falling prices; indeed, despite the expansion of pasture, prior to 1845 the total acreage under tillage also increased as farmers and cottiers extended the cultivation of cereals and potatoes onto boglands and up mountainsides. In addition, large numbers of small and middling farmers retained holdings by paying extortionate rents through a combination of supplementary income—for example, from selling *poitín*—and reduced living standards. For instance, in 1834 a witness observed that mid-Ulster's farmers "neither eat drink nor wear as well as . . . they formerly have done," since "[t]hey are obliged to sell the butter, pork, eggs, and poultry" formerly consumed at home in order "to meet the many and pressing demands . . . which they have to encounter."[31]

Nevertheless, the glaring contrast between wartime comforts and postwar deprivation proved too great for many Irish farmers, large and small, persuading unprecedented numbers to emigrate from a country where, as the people complained, "everything was going to the bad." As soon as prices began to plummet in 1814, farmers with capital started to emigrate in search of the "independence" now vanishing in Ireland. Some left because they were unable to maintain living standards and pay high rents negotiated during the French wars; others departed "after the expiration of old leases of farms held by them at a low rent, and of which they could not expect a renewal on the same profitable terms." As population rose while industrial employment declined, competition for land became increasingly intense, and in districts where landlords raised rents through short leases and competitive bidding, every farmer who aspired to "comfortable self-sufficiency" or better knew, as the novelist William Carleton put it, that "the mass of destitution which is so rapidly increasing in every direction must . . . ultimately drag them down" if they remained in Ireland. "I should not like to live," declared one threatened husbandman, "to see [my sons] in menial Situations in a Country where their Ancestors have . . . lived in Independence and Respectability."[32]

Strong-farmer emigrants, most prominent in the first fifteen years or so after Waterloo, left home to maintain life-styles considerably superior to those of most tenants. Even during the halcyon war years, middling farmers and smallholders had experienced far fewer comforts, and after 1814 they faced much greater dangers of absolute destitution. Those who still enjoyed what a group of smallholders in County Limerick called "some little mediocrity in life" sensed that "short leases, rack rents, tythe, taxation, and every other evil with which this unfortunate country is pregnant, would at length overwhelm them." In 1834 the British visitor H. D. Inglis reported that most tenants could not "pay the rents . . . without limiting their diet and their comforts within the bounds prescribed by the absolute necessities of nature"; yet "not withstanding their privations, a large pro-

portion [were] in arrears" and liable to eviction. That was the petty landholder's great fear: to be "left upon the roads, to raise miserable hovels in
the ditches"; to descend into the ranks of common laborers, perchance to
endure the shame of "slavery" to their former peers. To avoid such a fate,
large numbers of middling farmers and smallholders emigrated while they
still possessed the means. For example, in east Galway a traveler spoke to a
farmer with "a large family [who] told [him] he was trying to get off to
America, because he feared that if he staid in Ireland the time might come
when he would be turned on the world." Pádraig Cúndún, a middling
farmer from east Cork, justified emigration in similar terms: "I myself was
cast down," he wrote, "but what could I do? I had seen strong and mighty
men cloathed in rags at work for their masters . . . , often without their
fill of shriveled potatoes to eat. I told myself that I would die before I
put up with that, and [so] I decided to come . . . to America." Many
hard-pressed tenants barely escaped impoverishment: it was not uncommon for farmers to sell their crops and livestock surreptitiously, default on
their rents, and escape their debts by a sudden, unannounced emigration.
However, others waited too long, exhausted their capital in a futile struggle to hold on to their land, and found themselves "in broken circumstances," unable to emigrate without assistance. In 1823–25 the British
government shipped 2,500 such "broken . . . Farmers" to Upper Canada, and in subsequent years it became increasingly common for landlords
themselves to provide ejected tenants with free passages; for example, from
1840 to 1844 the Wandesfordes of north Kilkenny alone sent over 2,000
people to America. Nevertheless, most evicted farmers were not so fortunate: in 1836 a parliamentary commission concluded that the great majority
remained in Ireland, often mired in hopeless poverty.[33]

In the early postwar years, a large proportion of the emigrating farmers
embarked with wives, with children, even with extended kin and servants.
However, during the entire pre-Famine period most emigrants from farming backgrounds left singly or accompanied only by a sibling or a cousin.
Relative poverty provided one explanation for this pattern: a distressed
smallholder who had a "long Weak Family"—that is, numerous small children—could rarely transport his entire household without assistance; consequently, such families often emigrated by stages, sending young adult
members overseas one or two at a time, relying on their remitted earnings
to carry the rest across eventually. However, most farmers' sons and
daughters who emigrated did so because their parents—who had no intention of abandoning Ireland themselves—practiced impartible inheritance
and so provided neither farms nor dowries to the majority of their offspring. Traders, graziers, and strong farmers in market-oriented eastern
Ireland had practiced impartible inheritance for generations, although in
the relatively prosperous 1750–1814 period they could often give noninheriting children sufficient education or training to enable them to find
suitable careers and spouses at home. However, in the depressed postwar
decades even strong farmers' superfluous offspring had few alternatives

more promising than emigration. Moreover, the tendencies of relatively affluent farmers to marry late in life and yet have exceptionally large families made the problem of providing for their children's futures especially acute. Thus, although the widow of Daniel Griffin, a Limerick grazier, found means to provide some of her twelve children with farms, trades, or marriages in Ireland, she could do no better than send the rest overseas with hopes they might acquire "independence" on their own. As one Irish-American aptly noted, such emigrants were "the children of circumstance."[34]

Between 1750 and 1814 the great majority of Irish tenants seem to have practiced partible inheritance, subdividing their farms to allow sons to secure land and marry relatively early. During that period high farm prices, expanded tillage (especially potato) cultivation, and the spread of cottage industry had encouraged tenants and proprietors alike to allow subdivision. Yet even in the prosperous war years excessive fragmentation of holdings had persuaded some tenants in overpopulated areas such as mid-Ulster to curtail subdivision, thereby obliging thousands of farmers' sons to enlist in the British army and navy. As John Tovil, a veteran of the Napoleonic Wars, explained, farmers assumed that the government would provide for sons who wore the king's uniform, and so "when boys [en]lists if their Fathers has any property they will not will it to them if they have any other to give it to." Not surprisingly, after Waterloo many of the 100,000 or more demobilized Irish soldiers and sailors found themselves in a state of landless poverty and desperately petitioned the Colonial Office for free passages and land grants in Canada. More important, however, was that after 1814 impartible inheritance became much more common among middling and small farmers as well as among their more affluent countrymen: collapsing farm prices, contracting industrial employment, and the obvious advantages of pasture farming over tillage made continued subdivision a severe economic liability for tenants as well as proprietors. In part, farmers' increased unwillingness to provide land to all sons was a reflection of new pressures from landlords armed with the 1826 Subletting Act; for example, when a tenant on the duke of Devonshire's County Cork estate tried to give a portion of his farm to each of his married sons, he quickly learned that "this is not allowed and that if one of them does not leave, the property will be taken" away. Before the Great Famine many middling and small farmers resisted such pressures, and in western Ireland most tenants continued to subdivide boggy soils into tiny subsistence farms. Nevertheless, in commercial farming districts large numbers of middling and small farmers adopted impartible inheritance *voluntarily*— both to emulate their relatively prosperous superiors and to avoid the sad examples of peers who had "been broken on their original farms, from the subdivision of it among their children," and who were now "in a state of starvation."[35]

Moreover, as farmers' sons faced shrinking prospects of acquiring land, and as wives' and children's abilities to contribute to the household economy diminished with the decline of domestic industry, marriage practices among middling and small tenants also began to shift toward the standards set by strong farmers and graziers. Marriages among farmers' children became fewer and took place later in life: between 1830 and 1840 the rural marriage rate per 1,000 inhabitants declined by more than a third, while the proportion of men marrying at age twenty-five or younger fell from nearly 40 percent to only 28 percent. Fewer, later marriages resulted in a declining birthrate, which combined with emigration and rising mortality among laborers to cause a drastic reduction in population growth. For example, between 1821 and 1831 Ireland's population rose nearly 15 percent, from 6.8 million to 7.8 million; however, in 1831–41 the rate of growth (to 8.2 million) was a mere 5.25 percent, and in the remaining pre-Famine years the island's population was virtually stagnant. Indeed, by 1844 the population in the most commercialized rural districts of eastern Ireland was beginning to decline at rates comparable to those of the post-Famine decades; only in areas of abundant, if poor, land, as along the western coasts, did subdivision, early marriage, and high birthrates persist together.[36]

These changing inheritance and marriage patterns provided an enormous stimulus to emigration among farmers' sons and daughters. In 1844 a land agent in east Ulster testified that on the several estates he managed all the tenants practiced impartible inheritance and the noninheriting sons "almost invariably" emigrated with compensation from their favored brothers. Even in mountainous mid-Ulster, declared another witness, subdivision had greatly declined since farms of fifteen to twenty acres "are generally considered small enough, and [so] the younger branches of the family go to America . . . rather than make the farms smaller." Increasingly, after 1814 farmers' superfluous offspring faced the alternatives of an aimless, celibate life under the parental roof, reckless marriage accompanied by probable destitution and degradation to the ranks of cottiers or laborers, and emigration in search of the "independence" denied at home. No wonder contemporaries frequently reported that "[t]he unmarried of both sexes [were] the most inclined to emigrate"; "I have 11 brothers and sisters," testified Thomas Buckley, an artisan in County Limerick, "and if they had the means to emigrate they would not stop another day here." Often the expressed willingness of farmers' children to emigrate stemmed more from status anxiety than from actual want. Many farmers' sons were like William Carleton: "a fine well-dressed young fellow . . . from whom great things were expected," and who vowed accordingly that he would "walk over the country, mile for mile, from one end of it to the other," before he would "degrade [him]self to the condition of a day labourer." In truth, Carleton got no farther from his native Tyrone than Dublin, but thousands of similarly circumstanced farmers' children went overseas. The Ulsterman John Gifford King, with his "tolerably good education"; Hugh Quin of County Down, without land but full of "great expectations"; the Corkman Andrew Leary O'Brien, of "wild and speculative mind"; James Cavanagh of County

Kilkenny, raised "in a Comfortable Station of life" but with "no way whatsoever of earning an honest livelihood but that of a common Slave": all
hoped that emigration to the New World would somehow transform them
"from poverty to Independence." Moreover, America promised matrimony as well as possible prosperity. According to the 1841 census, in rural
Ireland 44 percent of the male and 36 percent of the female population
aged twenty-six to thirty-five were still single, but in American cities Irish
emigrants formed families at the same high rate as the native-born. In addition, greater employment opportunities overseas enabled farmers' sons and
daughters to marry partners of their own choosing rather than according to
what the Ulster-American James Richey condemned as "the old Irish rule
to marry for riches and work for love": a rule which too often resulted in
what another emigrant described as "unhappy matches which attend many
to the grave, blunting through life their energies, rendering exertion without object, and success without enjoyment."[37]

The fear of losing "independence" persuaded many farmers to leave
Ireland, but for the majority of pre-Famine Irish emigration represented
the only hope of escape from absolute destitution. For the poorest smallholders and joint tenants, who lived barely at subsistence level, and for the
laboring classes, who constituted over half the rural population, the pre-
Famine decades were an agonizing prelude to disaster. Ironically, unlike
their more prudent, market-oriented superiors, the poorest Irish continued
to marry young: "if I had a blanket to cover her," declared one peasant,
"I would marry the woman I liked; and if I could get potatoes enough to
put into my children's mouths, I would be as happy and content as any
man. . . ." Land for potato ground was still available in districts of poor
soil, remote from markets, where landlords had fewer incentives to "improve" old customs of partible inheritance or even rundale out of existence.
Consequently, in western Ireland smallholders and joint tenants still colonized boglands and partitioned holdings into smaller and smaller fragments
to accommodate their children. As a result, between 1821 and 1841 the
population of the poor western counties rose by more than 30 percent,
pressing ominously on the land's ability to support so many inhabitants.
As early as 1822, poor potato harvests brought starvation to parts of Connaught and west Munster, where the population was "redundant beyond
conception." In 1838 a traveler in east Connaught described the country
between Athlone and Ballinasloe as "an almost continuous village" of
"wretchedly clad people inhabiting wretched houses, and carrying on a
wretched and destructive tillage." Along the windswept, rocky shores of
the Atlantic, the inhabitants were generally even more thickly settled and
impoverished.[38]

Yet, according to most observers, distress among cottiers and laborers in
the middle and eastern counties usually surpassed the poverty of the western peasants. Although the latter suffered periodically from poor harvests,
cottiers and laborers in market-oriented districts had increasing difficulty
even gaining access to sufficient land to grow potatoes. Despite high infant

mortality rates, prior to the Famine the numbers of cottiers and, especially, landless laborers grew steadily, both by natural increase and by the social descent of "broken farmers" and impoverished tradesmen. Competition for land was fierce, and, as the least-efficient and most-undesirable occupants, cottiers, laborers, and rundale cultivators were usually the first to be "cleared" or evicted by "improving" landlords and strong farmers. Those suffered to remain had to pay high rates for kitchen gardens and conacre, and the disparity between rents paid by head tenants and laborers steadily widened. "It is Impossible for such as me to live," complained John Tovil of County Tyrone, ". . . for we are a Class of men that is charged double for house or land as Cotters." In fact, farmers often demanded far more than double: in 1844 leaseholders on one large estate paid per-acre rents of £1 2s. 2d., but they charged their cottiers an average of £4 16s. 5d. per acre. Conacre rents also soared, from an average of £3–£6 per acre in 1800 to £10–£12 by the early 1840s. As one Corkman bitterly observed, although many Catholic farmers may have felt "humbled and exhausted by English oppression," they "pull[ed] the knot as tightly on the poor as the English, or even tighter, [when] they were able."[39]

Furthermore, after 1814 the means by which subsistence cultivators, cottiers, and laborers might pay such rents evaporated. Falling pork and bacon prices meant that the cottiers' ubiquitous pig no longer paid the rent, and the collapse of domestic industry reduced the value of the loom and spinning wheel. In addition, hard-pressed landlords and tenant farmers offered less employment at lower wages. As was noted earlier, proprietors curtailed expenditures on construction, drainage, and beautification projects which had formerly employed local workers. More important, the shift from tillage to pasture not only led to evictions of poor subtenants but also reduced the need for agricultural laborers: when arable land was turned to grazing, over 90 percent of the laborers once needed for planting, weeding, and harvesting became superfluous. Also, even tillage farmers cut labor costs by relying on new tools and/or on unpaid family assistance. Use of the scythe halved the numbers of workers once needed to cut oats and meadow grass with old-fashioned sickles; similarly, breaking topsoil with "Scotch ploughs" enabled six men with two horses to sow an acre of potatoes, formerly the work of thirty spademen. Moreover, as a parliamentary commission reported, small farmers responded to shrinking profit margins by resorting to "every expedient . . . in order to avoid the employment of a single paid laborer." According to most reports, those who were hired usually received shabby treatment, poor wages, and, a group of laborers complained, a "sort of diet inferior to that which we behold given to the Brute Creation." Indeed, due to diminished demand and increased competition for work, farm laborers' wages declined slightly: in 1800–1810 day laborers earned about 5s. per week, but in the late 1830s only 4s. 6d. More significant, however, was that—save for farm servants who slaved for less than £4 per year—steady employment at any wages was almost unknown; in 1836 a government commission estimated that 585,000 laborers, with some 1,800,000 dependents, had no work for at least thirty weeks per year. "[W]e would deem ourselves quite happy could we procure daily labour of the most irksome kind, with any reasonable hire," declared a band of laborers in County Clare, "but our hire is a mere nothing & our work an uncertainty. . . ."[40]

Lack of employment, diminished access to land, high rents, and increasing population predicted a Malthusian scenario of gravely deteriorating living standards among the Irish lower classes. After 1814, fewer cottiers could afford to keep livestock, and outside Ulster former staples such as buttermilk, bread, and oatmeal disappeared from the peasants' regular diet. Later in life an emigrant from pre-Famine Galway remembered the "happy days" before Waterloo when "landlords . . . were very kind" and when "wheaten bread, oatmeal bread, stirabout & eggs Butter & potatoes were abundant," in contrast to the postwar decades when high rents forced the peasants to sell all their produce and "obliged them to live on potatoes herring and dip." Another emigrant, the son of cottiers from east Cork, recalled that in his youth "[p]otatoes were the only food of the people. . . . We had potatoes three times a day. . . ." Fortunately, potatoes were both cheap and nutritious, but the need for high yields per acre caused widespread adoption of the watery "lumper"—a variety highly susceptible to bad weather and blight; thus, between 1816 and 1842 over half the potato harvests were complete or partial failures. Even in years of good harvests, the summer months between crops witnessed widespread suffering among the poor, when grown men would lie "in bed *'for the hunger'*—because a man lying on his back does not need so much food as a person a-foot." "Despair has seized us," cried one group of laborers who "groaned under the galling darts of wretchedness. . . . [W]e are rendered old without age, and our lives are but short of their natural limits from diseases arising out of want": indeed, weakened by malnutrition, thousands fell victim to typhus, dysentery, cholera, and other prevalent "fevers." The more enterprising, or unattached, laborers traveled about in search of employment, but often encountered only the violent hostility of local workers. Others gravitated to towns, where they subsisted by a combination of charity and casual labor. For example, in 1824 John Quinlivan reported that he was "a labouring Man" from Fermoy, "has wandred from place to place in Search of work & can find none, [and so] is now in the Citty of Cork, living on the daily bounty of the humane, in a Starving and hopeless Condition." In 1838 public relief partially supplanted private charity, but discipline in the new Irish workhouses was so severe that even the most destitute usually preferred to take their chances on the roads. Travelers reported that beggars were everywhere: a "mass of filth, nakedness and squalor" that lined the main highways and crowded the market squares. English visitors often regarded mendicants as little better than "vermin," but men such as Hugh Rock of County Westmeath were not so degraded that they lost all hope of self-betterment. In 1823 Rock, "a poor labouring Man having his Father, Mother, Wife and six children to maintain," declared that "by the Extreme badness of the Times [he was] reduced to a Starving Situation (The Farmers not being able to employ labourers)"; however, unwilling to continue *"Begging* on the Road," Rock asked the government for free passages to North America.[41]

Rock's ambition was reportedly widespread among the lower-class Irish. Letters from the 2,500 Munster emigrants given free passages and Canadian farms by the British government in 1823–25 spread the image of North America as promised land among peasants whose "extreme wretchedness" persuaded them "that almost any change, of whatever nature, would be beneficial to them." Landless laborers, especially, seemed receptive to the New World's charms: perhaps partly because their meager wages and scanty diet contrasted so dramatically with advertisements of high pay on American public works and reports that "[i]n every house here there is no meal eaten without fresh meat, and Tea twice a day"; perhaps also because Irish laborers were already more mobile, both physically and socially, than countrymen who still retained any formal or customary claims to land or patronage. Ironically, although laborers rarely handled cash, market conditions affected them more directly and intimately than any other class, shaping attitudes compatible with willing emigration. For example, laborers who had fallen from the ranks of landholders had little desire to stay in Ireland and "work for those who were in the same class of life in which they were" once themselves. The institution of conacre accurately reflected the laborers' tenuous, instrumental relationship to the soil and its owners, and it is significant that an 1836 parish survey seemed to indicate that in southern Ireland the prevalence of conacre and lower-class emigration varied inversely. In short, many landless laborers—particularly in the ruthlessly commercialized, culturally deracinated grazing counties—had little to hold them in Ireland and believed with the Cork laborer Richard Sullivan that assisted emigration "would be the most Charitable grant that could be made to Individuals perishing for want of Means to purchase one Meal of Potatoes in twenty four Hours." For two decades after the 1823–25 assisted emigrations to Canada, thousands of petitions similar to Sullivan's vainly deluged the Colonial Office, and in 1836 witnesses testified before Parliament, "If a free passage to America were offered, almost all the laborers would go,—old, young, married, and single." Without such assistance, most lower-class Irish either could not or would not go overseas. Thousands went instead to Great Britain, where at least a few labored and saved to reach the New World, but the great majority still remained at home, sharing potatoes, subdividing what little land they had. Nevertheless, despite their poverty or inertia the lower classes composed a steadily increasing proportion of pre-Famine emigration. As early as 1826, when fares were high, a member of the Limerick gentry testified that "where the poor labourer is able to amass a sum of money to enable him to go, he takes advantage of it"; and by the early 1840s, when passage costs had fallen, observers in many parts of Ireland reported that emigration was now "chiefly from the class of single labourers . . . who have gone . . . 'to better themselves.' "[42]

Not only was pre-Famine emigration unprecedented in its size and composition but many contemporaries believed that the desire to leave home was so widespread that only a lack of means prevented a tidal wave of eager emigrants from deluging American shores. In 1827 John Foster, MP for County Louth, reported, "The peasantry are . . . quite ready to go, and take all chances of what may await them on the other side": testimony later echoed by priests and parsons, landlords and laborers. In 1845 a proprietor in King's County argued that, if given a free passage to America, even an evicted tenant would "leave the place of his forefathers with as little reluctance as possible." Unquestionably, the processes of commercialization and Anglicization, combined with the deepening contrasts between Irish poverty and American opportunity, not only spurred departures but also inspired positive, even utilitarian attitudes toward emigration, which occasionally surfaced in popular ballads. Although many emigrants' songs still eulogized America as "Land of Liberty," they sometimes justified emigration in terms largely, even purely, materialistic: "The times are looking very hard, / The wages they are small," explained one composer, "So now I'm off to America, / Where there's work and food for all." Indeed, a few songs not only encouraged Irishmen to emigrate to a country where they would "roll in gold and silver" but even implied that leaving Ireland—"that wretched isle"—was no longer a cause for sorrow or regret. Thus, one composer expressed naught but joyful relief at escaping "the rough scourges of despotic sway," for "Though my home I have lost, it's no evil to me, / It's exchanged for the land they call sweet liberty."[43]

However, other observers, such as the French traveler Gustave de Beaumont, believed that most Irishmen were *not* "anxious to better their condition" through emigration, and many emigrants' songs still conveyed the sense of involuntary exile; for example, although one composer entitled his ballad "The Bright Land of Freedom," he avowed, "If I had a home in the land of old Ireland / To go to America would never cross my mind. . . . Sure our people are *forced* to some foreign clime." In short, much of the evidence respecting pre-Famine emigration is contradictory and poses dilemmas of interpretation. To be sure, from 1814 to 1844, departure rates rose steeply, but—given Ireland's profound destitution—why did so many Irish remain at home? If enthusiasm for America was so widespread, why did it not inspire even more departures? For, as one scholar has observed, "when the social condition of pre-famine Ireland is considered, it is the paucity and not the magnitude of the emigration which is astonishing." Although contemporaries often testified that the level of transatlantic fares varied inversely with the level of emigration, poverty was in fact not the only, perhaps not even the most important, factor restraining departures. For example, more Irishmen and -women sailed to

the New World between 1845 and 1850 than in the three preceding decades combined; although many Famine emigrants received assisted passages, most had possessed the means to emigrate *before* that catastrophe
but had been unwilling to do so. Thus, in 1846 Thomas Spring Rice, a
British official and keen observer of Irish emigration, remarked that the
potato blights of 1845–50 caused Irish countrymen to view emigration now
as "release," whereas earlier most had regarded it as "banishment."[44]

To a degree, contradictory assessments of popular attitudes toward emigration reflected contemporary observers' social and political biases. Landlords and strong farmers eager to consolidate smallholdings and reduce
labor costs had reason to hope their former dependents would view emigration favorably, while nationalist politicians striving to mobilize 40s.
freeholders against the Ascendancy counted on the former's proverbial attachment to their homeland. However, in the pre-Famine decades popular
responses to emigration *were* wildly inconsistent, as might be expected in a
society marked by increasing economic differentiation, social fragmentation, and cultural discontinuity: many factors interacted in complex fashion
to determine whether Irishmen and -women viewed emigration as opportunity, necessity, or unacceptable calamity. On the one hand, departure
rates were certainly highest in areas with long-established links to the New
World and in districts characterized by rapid socioeconomic and cultural
change. For example, in 1836 a parliamentary commission's survey indicated that in southern Ireland emigration was common only in parishes
whose inhabitants were primarily or exclusively English-speaking and
which contained or were proximate to market towns and major arteries of
commerce and communications: that is, in regions with cash economies,
capital-intensive farming, strong external and internal pressures against
subdivision and partible inheritance, and high sensitivity to fluctuating
price levels and competition from imported manufactured goods. In short,
deteriorating cottage textile districts and the fertile midlands and river
valleys provided the bulk of the emigrants. In such areas both structural
and attitudinal changes stimulated departures; even some Irishmen at the
bottom of society at least implicitly accepted the "logic" of emigration to
an America where, as one pragmatic songster wrote, "the value of your labour, / With comfort can be found." Indeed, contemporaries were wont to
comment that dynamic local economies often transformed peasants' attitudes "in an incredibly short space of time," making them "active, dili-
gent, . . . laborious," and, by inference, willing emigrants when new ambitions were frustrated at home. In 1841 the census commissioners came to
a similar conclusion when they noted that emigration did "not appear to
be the first step in the march of improvement. It is when a man has already
begun to move upwards that he seeks a more advantageous field than his
native country affords." Put another way, Irishmen who conceived social
goals in terms of "gaining an Independence"—especially if defined as upward mobility—were most likely to leave pre-Famine Ireland: for, like the
artisans John Taylor and John Conway of east Galway, they "wish[ed] to

ameliorate their Situation and to give their families . . . an opportunity of forwarding themselves . . . by permanent and lucrative employment."[45]

However, before the Great Famine most Irishmen still strove to modify the impact of the marketplace by imposing traditional, communal sanctions against landlords, strong farmers, shopkeepers, and even parents who sought to maximize profits at their dependents' expense. Indeed, many districts characterized by high emigration rates were also rife with agrarian violence, as the disadvantaged struggled savagely against the very processes which encouraged or compelled departures. Violent conflict, rural and urban, was endemic in the pre-Famine decades. Occasionally, poor harvests caused such severe distress that food riots broke out; in 1814 mobs in Louth, Limerick, and elsewhere plundered flour mills, bakers' shops, even canal boats carrying food to Dublin. Sometimes neighborly restraints against thievery lost efficacy in the face of starvation; for example, in 1826 one Ulsterman reported that after drought "burent up" all the crops the poor "Was in Such wont . . . that the[y] Stole out of the pits of potatoes . . . and . . . at night . . . Would . . . Break the Windows and Rob the Houses." Far more significant, however, were the fierce conflicts over access to land and employment. As their incomes declined after 1814, many proprietors abandoned all pretenses of paternalism; as one wealthy landlord admitted, "there has not been that kindly intercourse between the owner, and cultivator of the Soil which ought to bind two classes whose interests are really identified with one another." For their part, the "cultivators" in the Rockites, Terry Alts, Whitefeet, and other secret societies fought evictions and other "oppressions" by spreading terror through parts of all four provinces, particularly in districts where market forces had begun to challenge traditional patterns but were not yet triumphant. During the 1820s much of Ireland was in a state of "smothered war": in some areas the gentry lived practically under siege, in barricaded houses, and assassinations became so common that one coroner's jury ruled that a murdered estate agent had died of "natural causes." Violence peaked in the early 1830s when large numbers of countrymen refused to pay rents or tithes; in County Clare, exclaimed one witness, "[l]arge bodies of the Peasantry march through the Country in the open day . . . and take arms with impunity." In 1831 the lord lieutenant concluded, "There exists to the most frightful extent a mutual and violent hatred between the proprietors and the peasantry."[46]

In a sense Lord Anglesey was right: since the Ascendancy had written the rules governing the Irish land system to benefit those who owned the soil, any challenge to those rules ultimately threatened the landlord class and the British state. In most instances, however, immediate, everyday conflicts in pre-Famine Ireland were not between proprietors and peasants but rather between graziers, strong farmers, and what country people called ternybegs (*tiarnaí beaga:* little landlords) on one side and the land poor and the landless—subtenants, laborers, farmers' disinherited sons—on the other. For example, in County Clare cottiers and laborers demanded lower conacre rents and dug up farmers' pastures to render them unfit for any crop but potatoes; in County Meath laborers ordered farmers to increase wages and cease using "Scotch ploughs"; and in County Limerick the landless issued a manifesto "stating that no man should hold more than one farm, [and] that any man who held more . . . should give them up." It was this social conflict that exposed the cleavages between the "modernizing" and "traditionalist" sectors of the rural population, between those who accepted and those who rejected the logic as well as the consequences of "free market" competition in a shrinking Irish economy. For traditionalists, the fight for access to land, employment, low rents, and a living wage represented a struggle to *avoid* the necessity of emigration, otherwise the only alternative to absolute destitution. However, those who found themselves the targets of agrarian violence—"parasitical middlemen," farmers attempting to take the holdings of evicted tenants, artisans and laborers who underbid their rivals, peasants generally who demonstrated what T. C. Croker called "energy and expedience" instead of "herding with [their] own countrymen"—now had more-urgent reasons to emigrate than mere frustrated ambitions. As one historian wrote, the almost "continuous disturbances" of the pre-Famine decades created a climate of tension and insecurity which "slowly drove out of the country, not only the immediate victims, but all who hoped by industry to amass a competence." A common complaint was that the "best" tenants fled while the worst, "who chose to fight," remained. Thus, in 1831 a wealthy merchant reported that in Limerick and Clare "the turbulent followers of Captain Rock" were causing "an extensive Emigration," and "the worst of it is," he lamented, "that those who go are the very people one does not like to lose: Industrious substantial farmers who have accumulated a little property—and who remove to a distant shore in quest of that peace & security which they cannot find at home." Indeed, "industrious" tenants such as Jonathan Brett and Daniel Ryan found themselves squeezed between "a Nocturnal Enemy on the one side—and . . . the tyranny and oppression of land lords . . . on the other"; "there is so much Competition for Land in this Country," complained Ryan from Tipperary, the most "disturbed" county in pre-Famine Ireland, "that there is no geting [a lease] of it and if there was it may Cost a man his Life to take it over any man." For those unwilling to run such risks, and for aspiring countrymen such as the Cork blacksmith Peter Falvey, who proudly declared that he was "no rebel whiteboy or Drunkard But a man that has devoted his time to the Emprovement of his Children Both moral and religious [and in] . . . Arithmethick and Book keeping," emigration to North America held out "a prospect of peace and security for life and property, denied to us in our native land."[47]

By intimidating "improvers" and innovators, the secret agrarian societies no doubt slowed the pace of change in rural Ireland, thus obviating the necessity for more lower-class emigration. Not until the Great Famine decimated and demoralized the ranks of smallholders, cottiers, and laborers would landlords and strong farmers be able to carry out wholesale evictions and consolidations; not until after that catastrophe would most agriculturists eschew subdivision and adopt impartible inheritance. Nevertheless, even before the Famine many who initially "chose to fight" in the secret societies were forced to take refuge in the New World. By the 1830s areas such as County Kilkenny, earlier in the century convulsed by conflicts between farmers and laborers, were relatively tranquil; martial law, paid informers, and farmers' vigilante groups had crushed the secret societies, and the lower classes now turned to emigration instead of overt resistance. In other, imperfectly modernized areas such as northwest Munster and east Connaught, the struggle continued, but even there official repression could be effective; "such is the terror . . . inspired in the offenders" by vigorous prosecutions, exulted the Irish under secretary in 1833, "that many of the worst characters have taken their departure for America." With reason, many such fugitives readily advertised themselves as martyred exiles; farmers who resisted eviction often figured prominently in contemporary emigration ballads. Furthermore, even if America was seen as "promised land," it was understandable that the large numbers who sympathized with the activities and shared the goals of the secret societies should also feel resentment at the conditions which impelled emigration. For example, although often trained since childhood to anticipate emigration as "escape," and although usually constrained from expressing overt resentment, many farmers' disinherited children left Ireland in anger and later bitterly "recollected the time when [my father] could not provide [for] me . . . like his other children."[48]

Thus, among both Catholics and Protestants, degrees of advantage or disadvantage in relation to the marketplace helped determine whether Irishmen would embrace or resist emigration. As Gustave de Beaumont observed, "in general it is not the poorest who emigrate [but] . . . chiefly . . . the middle classes . . . comfortable tradesmen, or small farmers, who, though already possessing some comforts, are anxious to better their condition." However, economic circumstances alone were insufficient to explain the varied responses to pre-Famine emigration, as Beaumont himself implied when he noted that even in the late 1830s those departing were disproportionately Protestant and that "[i]n spite of all her miseries, the [Catholic] Irishman passionately loves his country." To be sure, pre-Famine Catholic emigration was unprecedented in size; however, even in the early 1840s annual Catholic emigration rates (that is, departures in proportion to total numbers) were still lower than comparable rates among Dissenters back in the 1770s. In heavily commercialized County Carlow, a witness in 1825 contrasted the "universal willingness" of Protestants to emigrate with the "great disinclination, on the part of the Roman Catholics"; even in eastern Ulster, where emigration had been habitual for over a century, observers in the mid-1830s discovered that Protestants still constituted an inordinately large share of the exodus. Broad economic differences between Protestants and Catholics can account in part for their different rates of emigration—but only in part—and economics alone cannot explain why Protestant and Catholic *attitudes* toward emigration became, if anything, increasingly distinctive even as Catholic departures rose. Rather, in 1815–44 Protestant and Catholic Irishmen still interpreted social conditions in light of different cultural traditions, religious teachings, and increasingly divergent and mutually antagonistic political experiences, which, to a growing extent, cut across class and generational lines within each religious community to produce two variant responses to emigration.[49]

Between 1815 and 1844, contemporaries in both Ulster and southern Ireland were unanimous in reporting that "Great Numbers" of Dissenters and Anglicans were "leaving this poor Kingdom"—"all that can are determined to go"—and apparently did "not much regret their native land." Of course, Irish Protestants, especially northern Presbyterians, had been departing regularly for over a hundred years, going to a New World where millennial and material expectations merged in a vision of "promised land." However, during the pre-Famine decades two trends within Irish Protestant societies accelerated to affect the pace and character of Protestant emigration. First, Irish Protestantism became increasingly bourgeois in both composition and tone, causing more Anglicans and Dissenters to conceptualize emigration in positive, secular, and individualistic terms. "[G]aining an Independence" defined as personal acquisitiveness, as upward mobility, became an increasingly acceptable and widespread aspiration, thus liberating greater numbers of Irish Protestants to pursue ambitions overseas. Second, during the same period most Irish Protestants became fervently loyal to the union with Great Britain, which meant that even those who still clung to more-traditional economic outlooks (i.e., "independence" as "comfortable self-sufficiency"), and who therefore perceived a degree of compulsion in their emigrations, now rarely blamed British misgovernment for the "necessity" to go abroad. Save for the dwindling minority who yet adhered to a defeated and discredited republicanism, Protestants generally no longer regarded emigration as the United Irishmen, the Steelboys, and the victims of Queen Anne's persecutions had done. During the rest of the nineteenth century, for most Irish Protestants emigration was not "exile" but "opportunity" or, at worst, "escape" to a North America where the paradoxes and ambiguities of Protestant Irish identity could be reconciled under the American or the Canadian flag. Thus, as John Gamble wrote of northern Presbyterians in 1818, they "carry their industry, talents and energy to a distant and happier land and never think of the one they have quitted but with loathing."[50]

In the early nineteenth century the conditions which had encouraged Protestant radicalism ceased to exist or assumed lesser importance. In the 1780s and 1790s Catholics had been relatively quiescent; middle-class Protestantism had been suffused with an ecumenical rationalism which chafed at economic discrimination and political corruption; and Presbyterian farmers and weavers experiencing rapid erosion of economic "independence" had responded with a mélange of millennialism and republicanism which anticipated a tribal victory over an oppressive Ascendancy.

Of course, even after 1798 some Protestant United Irishmen and their descendants, particularly in eastern Ulster, still maintained the "genuine hatred of British intolerance and cruel injustice toward Ireland" that animated "every member" of the family of Thomas Smyth, a Belfast merchant, and probably many of the Presbyterians whom Gamble described. However, most radical Protestants either abandoned their former principles or emigrated to the United States, "where the natural rights of man are cherished," where "the purjured fors[w]orn informer Cannot Exist," and where they could live without fear their ideals would result in either official repression or "papist" domination. After 1815 especially, the experiences and attitudes of those who remained in Ireland began to change rapidly, for the socioeconomic, religious, and political circumstances that made Irish Protestantism both bourgeois and loyal were mutually reinforcing.[51]

Of primary importance, perhaps, was the impact of changing economic conditions. As was noted above, in the early nineteenth century eastern Ulster, always the demographic center of Irish Protestantism, became increasingly urbanized and industrialized: burgeoning Belfast, with its satellite towns such as Ballymena and Lurgan, replaced a stagnating Dublin as the locus of Protestant economic, political, and cultural activity. This development had several major consequences. First, the Northeast's commercial and urban growth resulted in a significant expansion of the region's middle classes, accompanied by an accelerated dissemination of entrepreneurial attitudes in an Ulster countryside which was increasingly oriented, culturally as well as economically, toward Belfast and the outside world. Moreover, the dislocating effects of rapid industrialization, especially the inauguration of large-scale, urban-centered factory production, steadily eroded older, communal outlooks and behavior patterns. In short, both the cultural and the economic preconditions for mass rural-to-urban migration, whether to Belfast or cities overseas, were quickly emerging; Ulstermen increasingly manifested the habits and attitudes associated with the "Protestant ethic," which may always have been latent in their religious traditions. Second, the prosperity of eastern Ulster helped lift its largely Presbyterian manufacturers, merchants, and religious and political spokesmen out of the second-class status they had endured under Anglican/landlord domination in the eighteenth century and demonstrated that Ireland under the union offered ample opportunities for advancement. Although Ulster's entrepreneurs had once regarded England as an oppressive commercial rival, after 1815 the British connection became the only guarantee of the Northeast's continued industrial growth: British coal powered Ulster's new factories; British immigrants brought much-needed capital and expertise; and, most important, the sister island and its overseas empire constituted almost the entire market for Ulster's linens. No wonder the conservative Presbyterian minister Henry Cooke thought Ulstermen of all classes had an unanswerable argument against Catholic demands for repeal of the union: "Look at Belfast and be a Repealer if you can," he exclaimed. "When I was . . . a youth I remember it almost a village. But what

a glorious sight does it now present—the masted grove within our harbour—
our mighty warehouses teeming with the wealth of every climate. . . .
all this we owe to the Union." Moreover, Protestant landlords and merchants in *southern* Ireland also realized how inextricably their fortunes
as well as their social and political hegemony now depended upon maintenance of the tie with England. As southern Ireland's once-extensive trade
with North America and Europe evaporated, Britain became almost the
sole market for Irish agricultural products. For southern merchants like
the Dublin Quaker Thomas Todhunter, the prospect of repeal raised fears
that an autonomous Irish parliament might initiate a tariff war with Britain
and destroy what remained of southern commerce and industry.[52]

Of course, for many Irish Protestants neither Belfast's growth nor the
union with Britain brought tangible economic benefits. The postwar decline of agricultural prices injured Protestant tenants generally, and the
mechanization and consolidation of the linen industry in the Northeast
deprived Protestant farmers and cottiers in outlying districts of vital income. In addition, by eliminating tariff barriers to English manufactured
goods, the union ensured the decimation of most southern Irish industries,
many of which—like cotton manufacturing—had been dominated by Protestant operatives. Many of these Protestant farmers and workers still aspired
merely to self-sufficiency, and while the erosion of their cherished "independence" certainly stimulated emigration, it is not self-evident why their
loyalty to the crown should have intensified. However, in a depressed economy Protestant-Catholic competition for land and employment became
acute in towns and in rural areas with mixed populations such as south
Ulster, east Leinster, and north Connaught where, as one tenant complained, the "landlords now care no more for a Protestant than a Roman
Catholic"—especially when the Catholic, desperate for land and accustomed to lower living standards, was willing to pay rents which Protestant
tenants considered outrageously high. As Caesar Otway observed, "when
a proprietor *cants* away his farms to the highest bidder, the Romanist is
sure to get the land, and the Protestant is forced to emigrate." Indeed, the
"chief source of annoyance" to many a Protestant emigrant who left his
farm "was its being rented to a Catholic." In the 1760s and 1770s, to be
sure, Protestant tenants suffering from rack-renting and other grievances
had embarked on violent campaigns against landlords, tithe jobbers, and
tax collectors; but that was before the Peep of Day Boys and the horrors
of '98. Now—resenting that "they were not better off than the Roman
Catholics"—they either left Ireland, filled with bitterness against their "papist" competitors, or flocked into the anti-Catholic Orange Order.[53]

Orangeism's rapid expansion during the 1820s and 1830s exemplified
the changes within Irish Protestantism. In the late 1790s Protestant liberals and radicals alike had despised the order as a bastion of bloodthirsty
reactionaries—"Sworn," they feared, "to Distroy all Prisbitearans" as well
as "Rommans." However, in the pre-Famine decades the Orange lodges
linked Protestant farmers and urban workers of all denominations to their

Protestant landlords, employers, and, ultimately, the Tory party leaders and the Irish administration in Dublin Castle. In short, the Orange lodges provided much of the institutional infrastructure, as well as the symbolism, of the emerging Irish Protestant "nation." Save in 1835–41, when the Whigs ruled Ireland in alliance with Catholic liberals, the British government extended protection and patronage to Orangemen to foster Protestant loyalty and solidarity. As the son of a United Irishman reported in dismay, the consequence was that Protestants and Catholics no longer could "behold their grievances thro' one focus. . . . The Government have connived at a disunion of the people & they have succeeded to the full extent of their wishes." Every twelfth of July, lamented another critic, huge Orange processions "were led on by Lords and Noblemen actuated by self interest, the Vulgar throng not thinking that they were a Government tool to support oppression or a Cripple leg for the Church [of Ireland] to stand on." However, membership in the Orange Order not only gave the "Vulgar" a spurious sense of community with their exploiters but also provided an armed paramilitary organization, protected by a sympathetic magistracy, with which they could confront the threat of Catholic competition. Thus, in south Ulster and other areas where members of the two religions were evenly balanced, Orangemen and Ribbonmen—their Catholic counterparts—waged fierce sectarian warfare: in counties such as Armagh pitched battles at fairs and "the most cruel and atrocious murders and burnings" became common occurrences.[54]

If economic advantage served as the foundation, and Orangeism as the scaffolding, of nineteenth-century Irish Protestantism, a new evangelical spirit was the mortar holding the structure together. In the late eighteenth century upper- and middle-class Protestants had often held religious beliefs which were rational and ecumenical. Preaching a sober piety and a code of behavior based more on reason than on holy writ, many clergymen—especially Moderate or New Light Presbyterians—had assumed that progress, education, and fair treatment would eventually transform superstitious and turbulent "papists" into enlightened, trustworthy citizens. Thus, in 1784 Belfast's Protestant Volunteers marched to celebrate the opening of that city's first Catholic church, and in 1810 Londonderry Protestants subscribed £300 to renovate the Catholic cathedral. As late as the 1820s the Reverend Henry Montgomery, the leader of the Moderate Presbyterians, campaigned for Catholic emancipation and spoke from Catholic altars. However, Protestant religious opinion had by then turned decisively against rationalism and toleration. Shortly after the Act of Union, conservative Anglican clergy and laymen launched a "New Reformation" designed to join all Irish Protestants in benevolent societies and fervent revivals which would purge Protestant ranks of religious and political radicalism and unite them in a holy crusade to eradicate Catholicism through a militant proselytism. Although spearheaded by Anglicans and Methodists, the movement soon encompassed most Presbyterians. In the late 1820s the Reverend Henry Cooke's evangelical "Old Light" Presbyterians wrested control of the Ulster synod away from Montgomery and the Moderate minority, thus committing most Presbyterians to an Orange-Tory alliance in defense of the union and in opposition to Catholic emancipation and the Roman Antichrist. Interdenominational associations such as the Hibernian Bible Society showered Catholics with millions of Bibles and religious tracts and sent preachers, often trained in Irish, into the countryside to convert the peasantry. "[A]las," cried a Catholic schoolmaster, "no attention is being paid to the fine smooth Irish language, except by wretched swaddlers, who are trying to see whether they can wheedle away the children of the Gael to their accursed religion." Protestant enthusiasts believed that a new era was dawning: "the reformation . . . is going on rapidly," rejoiced a Munster Protestant in 1826. "In Ireland they are every day leaving [the Catholic church]. . . . the Dominion of Babylon is near about being done away for ever   her judgements have overtaken her   her time is at hand."[55]

In fact, the New Reformation produced few converts, in part because Catholic churchmen reacted to the Protestant threat by launching a vigorous counterattack. However, the evangelical crusade had profound and permanent consequences for the shape of Irish Protestant society and for the ways in which its members regarded emigration. First, the New Reformation successfully sublimated denominational and social differences among Irish Protestants, marshaling them in defense of both the Ascendancy and the union with their British coreligionists. However, by emphasizing the exclusively *religious* aspects of group identity, the New Reformation effectively divorced Irish Protestants from the bulk of their countrymen who were demanding repeal of the union under the slogan "Ireland for the Irish." Unable or unwilling to be "Irish" by that definition, yet not really "British" despite their proclamations of loyalty to the crown, Ireland's Protestants were, in a sense, a "nation" bereft of a homeland. Only emigration could resolve the paradox of Irish Protestant identity, and it was no wonder that many could go abroad "without, they say, the slightest regret," and in the New World could express only relief at having left an "Ill fated country" where "religious divisions and broils fomented by superstitious bigotry [will] never have an end." Second, the ministers and financiers of the New Reformation enjoined a "new moral order" upon their adherents which identified Protestant spirituality with bourgeois values such as industry, thrift, cleanliness, sobriety, sexual continence: the supposed keys to upward mobility and respectability, which purportedly distinguished Protestants of all classes from Catholics, whose rejection of the evangelical message thereby "explained" their moral and economic inferiority. However, although this shared value system of deferred gratification ensured bourgeois hegemony and relative class harmony within Protestant Ireland, it also encouraged—even demanded—emigration whenever the material indices of Protestant identity and superiority were unattainable or, worse, threatened by successful "papist" competition. In addition, by stressing moral free agency and the personal relationship between man and Christ, the evangelicals reinforced the atomizing effects of commercialization, urbanization, and industrialization on Irish Protestant society, thus encouraging its members to pursue secular as well as spiritual advantages in whatever climes were best suited to those complementary pursuits. In short, confidence in a personal Saviour could both inspire Protestant emigrants to unremitting industry and offer special consolation in the face of hardship or homesickness. For example, Frances Stewart, suffering the loneliness and drudgery of Canadian frontier life, could write in 1825, "We often talk of 'home,' wishing and hoping that we may return there, . . . [but] we build our hopes and wishes on the real Home above which can never change, where will be no more sorrow nor parting."[56]

Finally, between 1815 and 1844 an aggressive Catholic political resurgence virtually compelled many Protestants, particularly those "uncomfortably situated" in the three southern provinces, to abandon Ireland to get "out of the Reach of Popish Inquisi[t]ion." Although most Catholic leaders were socially conservative and sincere in their professions of loyalty to the crown, and although Daniel O'Connell actively courted Protestant support for Catholic emancipation and repeal of the union, most Anglicans and Dissenters regarded him as a demagogue and feared his and the priests' influence over "their deluded people." Protestant apprehensions partly reflected hereditary bigotry inflamed by Orangeism and evangelical rhetoric; however, their fears had a very practical basis, for—as one Protestant admitted from the safety of America—"because [the Catholics'] property was confiscated in times of Old . . . [we] are afraid they would try to get back their just due." Moreover, although O'Connell and the Catholic bishops tried to keep their people orderly and law-abiding, their crusades for emancipation, abolition of tithes, and repeal excited violent outbreaks of localized resentment among Catholic countrymen who seemed to believe that a bloody fulfillment of Pastorini's prophecies was at hand. Thus, during the emancipation crisis of the 1820s Protestants declared that "life is not safe, even in the broad face of day, from the hands of the hired assassin," and in Munster rumors flew that Catholics were forging pikes and awaiting shipments of foreign arms. Likewise, during the tithe wars of the 1830s Protestants complained of "a combined Systematick persecution from county to county," and in the early 1840s Leinster Anglicans feared that the repeal movement was but a prelude to a reenactment of the massacres of '98. Even when physical dangers seemed remote, the psychological impact of sustained, successful Catholic agitation was devastating for Protestants accustomed to unquestioned dominion and unlimited submission. In former times Anglican landlords had herded docile tenants to the polls, but now "Priests & Money, Perjury & Bribery, Bloodshed & Battery" carried Irish elections. The accompanying changes in social relationships seemed equally disturbing. Expecting deferential behavior from their inferiors, Protestants were dismayed that "a rabble of papists" no longer "rejoiced at having a respectable protestant join them" on social occasions; "the Country is in such a state . . . [that] each now stick to their *party*."[57]

Protestants were especially resentful between 1835 and 1841, when the

Whigs governed Ireland in alliance with O'Connell. The Liberal Irish under
secretary, Thomas Drummond, reversed the policies which had ruled Ireland for over a century: he opened the constabulary to Catholics, dismissed
bigoted magistrates and appointed Catholics in their place, suppressed the
Orange Order, and lectured landlords that "property has its duties as well
as its rights." Meanwhile, Parliament made some concessions to middle-
class Catholic demands by dismantling the most egregious features of the
Anglican establishment, commuting tithes to a fixed rent charge, and abolishing the Protestant monopoly over municipal government. Naturally,
while Catholics rejoiced over these changes, Protestants felt bitterly betrayed and some suffered severely under the Drummond administration.
For example, Andrew Johnston, a County Longford Tory and middleman,
lost several lucrative offices; in early 1837 his sister lamented that "nothing is now given to Protestants but left to the mercy of the Papists who are
ruling them with a rod of iron." Six months later Johnston was attacked
in broad daylight in front of his house by a mob of Catholic "savages"
crying, "[H]ere he is again the Orange rascal now is our time to Masacre
them all." In the ensuing weeks Catholics made further attempts on Johnston's life, but the government, he charged, "looks quietly on at it"; "open
rebellion walks about the Priests command and control, no one to stop
them." No wonder that for Protestants such as the Limerick merchant
Joseph Harvey, the pre-Famine decades were "very awful times": "I cannot but look forward with very gloomy forebodings," he wrote; "I fear the
crisis which now seems impending, will at some period or other arrive, and
then the struggle will be between poverty and property." Harvey begged
"the Almighty [to] avert this Calamity," but—like Andrew Johnston—he
took the precaution to send his younger relatives to America.[58]

Indeed, many Irish Protestants could scarcely contemplate living in an
Ireland where they would no longer be masters. "The polaticks have taken
a queer turn," wrote a farmer in County Cavan to his brother in Cincinnati; "I think popery will rule with a rod of iron ere long; you had a fine
escape out of it. . . ." Consequently, throughout the period Protestants
flocked out of Ireland to avoid "Persecution from the Romish Church";
southern Ireland, especially, lost much of the second layer of the Ascendancy—the magistrates, policemen, estate employees, favored tenants, and
others whose demonstrations of loyalty now became dangerous liabilities.
Thus, in 1832 a Catholic servant girl from County Carlow wrote that most
of her fellow emigrants were "snug . . . Protestants, that found home
growing too hot for them, and that they had better save their four bones
and their little earnings before it was too late." Significantly, many of the
Protestants who sent frantic petitions to the Colonial Office, begging for
free passages and land grants in Canada, had "Catholic" names (Kearney,
Mooney, Costello, Mulloy, etc.), indicating that their families' apostasy
had singled them out for special vengeance: "I have met with great Persecution . . . this ten years past," complained a blacksmith and ex-police-
man in County Mayo, "as I was once A Member of [the Catholic] Church,

and I being a tradsman . . . the priest would allow none of his hearers to Employ me." For Protestants such as these, emigration was "escape," not "exile," and their letters and petitions revealed how eager they were to exchange an Ireland they could no longer call home for either a "land of liberty and toleration" where they would be "far removed from such scenes" or, better still, a Canada where they could live safely under the "fostering shade" of Britain's "Incomparable Constitution which their forefathers defended with their blood in the days of William of Glorious memory."[59]

Catholic attitudes toward emigration are more difficult to analyze, for pre-Famine Catholic opinion, like Catholic society, was an unstable mixture of disparate elements, still in the process of coalescence: rural and urban, peasant and bourgeois, and Gaelic and Anglicized outlooks competed for hegemony. In the years immediately following the Napoleonic Wars, nearly all observers concurred that few Catholics were emigrating and that their attitudes toward leaving Ireland were as pervasively negative as in the preceding century. According to a Dublin newspaper, "the native Irish" still maintained "a vehement and, in many instances, an absurd attachment to the soil on which they were born." Irish-speakers, such as those in the mid-Ulster uplands, were "cut off by the barrier of language from those about them," and their parishes "stood out like little islands in the sea of Ulster emigration." Even in commercialized, English-speaking south Leinster, most Catholics were reportedly "unwilling to leave home on almost any occasion," and only the traditional route to the Newfoundland fisheries provided a small stream of southern Catholic emigrants to the New World. Ignorance of American opportunities was still widespread among rural Catholics; in 1819 an Irishman in St. Louis admitted that his countrymen knew "little of the chances going in this country." Indeed, many Catholics' perceptions of North America remained archaic and profoundly negative: for example, in 1816 a returned emigrant remarked that the peasants in his native Carlow believed all Americans to be *"Black,"* and as late as 1823 Peter Robinson, in charge of government-sponsored emigration from north Cork to free Canadian homesteads, reported that Catholic smallholders and cottiers initially feared the idea and would not leave until he had dissipated "their apprehensions concerning Wild Beasts and the danger of being lost in the Woods." Coupled with ignorance was a profound parochialism and inertia, which reflected a general Catholic worldview emphasizing stasis rather than action: as one Catholic farmer remarked of his countrymen, "if the[y] would only bild A New End to thire house the[y] could not find from thire heart to lave it," believing "it to Be one of the greatest pallices in the world." In addition, for many Catholics poverty and oppression reinforced traditional tendencies toward passivity and fatalism. Thus, in 1819 an Anglican parson in mid-Tyrone observed that the "greatest part" of his impoverished Catholic parishioners "find that their employment depends on so many casualties, that they become indifferent about it, except as it is absolutely necessary for their existence."[60]

Of course, by the late 1820s large numbers of Catholics were leaving Ireland, and by the Famine's eve emigration had become habitual in many Catholic parishes throughout the island. Significantly, absolute resistance to leaving Ireland remained strongest among those Catholics whose culture and circumstances predisposed them to perceive emigration as *deoraí*, forced banishment. On the western coasts and other remote, mountainous regions sheltered from Anglicizing influences, many of the secular, religious, and linguistic props of an ancient Gaelic worldview remained reasonably intact. There Irish-speakers still clung to clachan settlements, rundale and joint tenancies, partible inheritance, and other customs which materially reinforced archaic "dependent" or "interdependent" outlooks, including strong communal and familial inhibitions against individual initiative and improvement. For example, in 1827 a native of Galway reported that he knew of "no petition from the county I reside in, to enable" the people to emigrate, for they were not "at all sensible of their own [impoverished] condition, and of the evils they suffer," and "as to any remedy to be applied to their situation, I believe they never consider it"; indeed, he added, the peasants were so "attached to the place where they are bred" that they were "unwilling to move" even to nearby parishes to secure better land. To be sure, even western Irish-speakers were subject to external pressures for change, and, after 1814, landlords such as Lord George Hill of west Donegal moved to eradicate rundale and clachans and to disperse their former inhabitants onto consolidated farms. Many of the evicted smallholders and cottiers whom the government shipped to Canada in 1823–25 were at least bilingual Irish-speakers, and in 1826 the unassisted emigration of the east Cork poet Pádraig Cúndún demonstrated that by then even complete ignorance of English was no longer an insurmountable barrier to the lure of the New World. Nevertheless, Gaelic conservatism remained profound. Western peasants fiercely resisted proprietors' attempts to destroy the structural underpinnings of their communal culture: on Hill's Gweedore estate peasant resistance shaped new landholding patterns according to local customs rather than scientific abstractions, and even on the Famine's eve most of the land in Mayo and other western counties was still held in common. Moreover, Pádraig Cúndún himself realized that his action was exceptional: more typical, he admitted, was the "poor senseless Irishman [who will] stay behind forever," and his own violation of traditional sanctions led him to write long letters justifying his audacity in terms of circumstances beyond his control. Thus, down to the Famine, contemporaries remarked with astonishment that in Irish-speaking areas along the coasts "[t]here is not at all the anxiety to emigrate . . . that there is in the interior," but instead "such a clinging to the country" that the inhabitants "would live on anything rather than go." "They are not anxious for it—they have not the courage," agreed a cottier in west Cork; few would emigrate even if given free passages, added a priest in County Mayo, because of their "great tenacity for the place of their birth." Western peasants "want . . . a spirit to better their condition," lamented a west Kerry landlord; "[t]hey are easily satisfied," and "as long as they can get a corner in a bog to stick a cabin in, and grow potatoes," they were not disposed to cross the Atlantic. As the Clareman Mathew Milekin, an evicted cottier who had refused an offer of assisted emigration, explained, "I thought it better to stay where I was, where I was used to, than to go to a strange" land.[61]

Furthermore, even in easterly districts characterized by rapid linguistic change and strong socioeconomic pressures for emigration, most Catholics still preferred to seek livelihoods at home. In 1841 the average value of livestock on farms of six to fifteen acres was £22½, and on holdings of sixteen to thirty acres the value was £46; with transatlantic passage costs ranging between £2 and £3 by the 1830s, the bulk of Catholic Ireland's middling farmers and smallholders, and even many cottiers, *could* have sold their animals and transported their families overseas. However, prior to the Great Famine relatively few did so. Despite widespread "improvements," as the British economist J. E. Bicheno remarked, pre-Famine Ireland remained "a country not yet emerged from the ancient territorial relation, and upon which the commercial principle has been grafted with very imperfect success." Indeed, the impact of change should not be overestimated: most rural Catholics inhabited a sort of cultural twilight, translating older attitudes and concepts into a new language but imperfectly understood, coping with a new world they never made or could make work to their own advantage. For many lower-class Catholics, postwar depression did not inspire ambition but rather increased dependence on traditional sources of solace and security. "The poor Irishman," wrote the French traveler Gustave de Beaumont,

> does not seek after enjoyments of which he has never formed a notion . . . ; a great enterprise, undertaken to procure happiness of which he is incredulous, has no charms for him. He remains on the spot of his present misery, . . . and it is some consolation for him to bear the load of life in the country where he was born, where his father and mother lived and died, and where his children will have to live and die.

Moreover, even among those removed from hopeless destitution, communal traditions still constrained individualistic or acquisitive impulses; for example, in decaying linen districts farmers' wives sold eggs and poultry in the greatest secrecy to avoid antagonizing less affluent neighbors. Likewise, hospitality remained a "sacred duty" for farmers and cottiers who "think that the potatoes they have are God's, and that when one of his creatures is in distress, he has as good a right to a share of them as themselves." In short, most Catholics still conceived economic goals conservatively, and aspirations for "independence" defined as "comfortable self-sufficiency" remained compatible with traditional attitudes which discouraged emigration. The general willingness to reduce living standards in the face of declining incomes; the extensive colonization of acidic wastelands, at a rate of over 30,000 acres per year in the 1830s; the prevalence of seasonal migration and *poitín* making in south Ulster and the north midlands; and, most dramatic, the now almost exclusively Catholic agrarian violence which wracked "improving" districts throughout the pre-Famine period: all testified to the desperate measures Catholic tenants and laborers were willing to take in an effort to *avoid* what British officials regarded as the only "rational" solution to Ireland's poverty. In addition, despite landlords' injunctions, among Catholic farmers the subdivision of holdings remained common, thereby diminishing the necessity for emigration; as one farmer testified, "A parent must provide for his children in some way, and he cannot send them all to America."[62]

Thus, much evidence indicates that Catholics throughout Ireland, not just in remote Irish-speaking areas, were much more reluctant to leave home than were their Protestant countrymen. In 1825 a group of impoverished laborers declared that they would be content to remain in Ireland "even if [they] could afford means to Cultivate for provision here to subsist [their] families for [just] one season," and eleven years later a witness before Parliament stated that many emigrants "would have staid at home if they could have got land . . . for a fair rent, such as would have enabled them to enjoy *some* degree of comfort and independence." However, as such testimony implied, despite all expedients and privations the economic deterioration of pre-Famine Ireland made the retention of even a limited measure of "comfortable self-sufficiency" virtually impossible. The result, as an observer of east Leinster's tenants and cottiers noted in 1836, was that "[m]any who have hitherto forborne to emigrate would now accept the offer of a free passage, notwithstanding their great affection for the land of their birth, from their increasing misery and hopelessness of improvement in their condition by any other means." As was noted earlier, postwar destitution and insecurity soon transformed Catholic peasants' customary fatalism into profound despair over Ireland's future, and encouraged a compensatory vision of an American Eden flowing with "milk and hony." After 1823–25, when the British government placed 2,500 impoverished Munstermen in a reportedly blissful state of "independence and happiness" on Canadian farms, thousands of petitions from Catholics begging similar assistance flooded London. Moreover, to avoid eviction or pauperization, increasing numbers of Catholic tenants did adopt impartible inheritance, thereby obliging the disinherited to seek "independence" overseas. Nevertheless, although the New World certainly became an increasingly necessary and attractive option, a close examination of contemporary testimony indicates that many Catholics' purported "enthusiasm" for emigration was both shallow and hedged about with qualifications rooted in customary considerations. For example, although a land agent on the Clanricarde estate in east Galway glibly stated that his tenants had an "extraordinary . . . desire . . . for emigration," he also noted that when joint tenancies were consolidated the former partners cast lots to determine which families would get the new twenty-acre farms and which would have to emigrate; moreover, he added revealingly, the people's willingness to leave home depended entirely upon whether letters from overseas corroborated their fanciful image of America—merely "one discouraging letter will discourage them all." In addition, many Catholics who petitioned the Colonial Office for free passages indicated that lack of individual initiative or "courage," not money, was their primary reason for wishing "to depend [either] on the good faith of the government" or on some member of the local gentry "in whom they would place a confidence, whom they would look up to as a person of a better description," and of whom they could say, "This man is going with us, we will have the benefit of his advice and his counsel, and his respectability. . . ." In short, many petitioners wanted moral as well as material "inCuridgment," a word that appeared continually in their testimonials. They also wanted to eliminate all uncertainties as to their future overseas: "Many more would be willing to go than now are," declared one observer, "if they had any certainty as to what awaits them on the other side of the water"; thousands of supposedly eager emigrants hesitated, reported another, for lack of knowledge that "a certain provision . . . awaited them." Such desires for support and security were easily understandable; not until the Great Famine would large numbers embark without any certainty "that a mode of earning their bread was provided for them on their landing." However, the point is that Catholics' often unrealistic demands for absolute assurances reflected a "dependent" worldview sharply distinct from the sense of purpose and self-reliance which characterized the statements of most contemporary Protestant emigrants.[63]

Also, in their testaments Catholic petitioners often revealed how strong were the familial ties which still bound them to their homeland. The greatest anxiety expressed by the beneficiaries of government paternalism in 1823–25 was whether there was sufficient room in Upper Canada for their "friends" to come and settle beside them. Farmers such as Tery Brady of County Cavan, who could afford to take his own household to America, still requested funds because they were "unwilling to lave thair poor friends be hind them." Similarly, in County Kilkenny the desire to emigrate of "numbers of young people" hinged largely upon whether they "were assured that their aged parents would be provided for." Thus, for many Catholics the New World's appeal was qualified by familial obligations, and before the Famine many who could have afforded to emigrate as *individuals* remained behind rather than abrogate the bonds of kinship. Thousands of others left only after promising that they would remit sufficient money to reunite their relatives in America. Of course, other evidence indicates that acute distress and the impact of the market combined to weaken Irish family relationships during the pre-Famine period. In 1838 testimony that grown children were increasingly unwilling or unable to take care of aged parents helped persuade Parliament to pass the Irish Poor Law. For their part, Catholic farmers became more cautious and domineering toward their offspring. Not only did they turn to impartible inheritance and renewed emphasis upon the dowry system but they also became reluctant to relinquish control of their farms or designate their successors until they were practically at death's door—a practice which condemned farmers' sons to a prolonged, demeaning adolescence under parental authority. The result was increased emigration by thousands of impatient, frustrated young men and women. In a letter written in 1843 to his father, a strong farmer in Queen's County, William Lalor expressed the bitterness felt by many of his generation:

> As to your saying if I return to Ireland you are as willing to divide with me as ever I dont know what you mean—If you mean that when you are dying you would leave me part of your property it is a very poor consolation to me—its like saying Live[,] Horse and you'll get grass— . . . I must say that your opinions and mine as regards the treatment of Children differ very widely— . . . What I mean is keeping your property until you have no one to leave it to but old men   perhaps old Bachelors who can never enjoy any thing—I say it is almost unnatural.

Lalor later achieved his own "independence" on a Wisconsin farm, although his bitterness never abated. However, the significance of this quotation is the indication that as late as 1843 old Denis Lalor's actions which forced his son to emigrate were still viewed as violations of Catholic tradition even in the highly commercialized south Leinster midlands. Not until after the Famine would such family arrangements no longer be regarded as "unnatural" but as perfectly normal and commonplace.[64]

In short, emigration still posed severe social, cultural, and even psychological problems for many Catholics caught between individual necessity or ambition on the one hand and communal customs and obligations on the other. Therefore, as might be expected, their exodus was led by those whom Protestants considered "the most enterprising, industrious, and virtuous part" of the Catholic population: middle-class urban dwellers and strong farmers, largely of Old English rather than Gaelic background, from the most economically and culturally "improved" parts of southern and eastern Ireland. In addition, many members of this class—particularly strong farmers and graziers—shared with landlords a major responsibility for stimulating emigration among the less fortunate: not only through impartible inheritance but also through their efforts to enlarge holdings, rationalize land use, and reduce labor costs. For example, in 1826 the civil engineer Alexander Nimmo testified that in Munster strong farmers were promoting emigration by paying poorer neighbors and subtenants to relinquish their farms and go to America; in areas where secret societies were less active, graziers achieved the same ends through simple coercion. Ironically, however, it was these same middle-class Catholics who provided the secular and the clerical leadership of the emergent Irish Catholic "nation" and in the process resurrected the ancient Gaelic perception of emigration as exile compelled by British/Protestant/landlord oppression. Through their popular crusades for Catholic emancipation, abolition of tithes, repeal of the union, and total abstinence—in addition to their successful struggle to turn back the tide of the New Reformation—lay and clerical leaders forged an aggressive, self-conscious Catholic community largely united both in action and by an "official" ideology which interpreted all contemporary sufferings and disruptions, including emigration, in light of the age-old group conflict with the treacherous *Sasanaigh*. This revitalized "explanation" of emigration as involuntary banishment not only obscured the social and generational conflicts within Catholic society which often precipitated departures but also helped relieve the tensions individual emigrants felt in balancing duty and expediency.[65]

Bourgeois nationalism had a profound impact upon pre-Famine Catholic society. In 1818 an emigrant could truly describe Ireland's Catholics as "the most Degrdeingest people in the world," and seven years later a farmer in Limerick could fairly exclaim, "What a Country this is to live in" where the Catholics "are only breathing, afraid & scarce able to raise their heads." However, the successive crusades for emancipation, abolition of tithes, total abstinence, and repeal taught Irish Catholics to lift their heads and form mass political organizations unprecedented in European experience. Through newspapers, ballads, sermons, interminable speeches, "monster" rallies, and elaborate, centralized associations which linked the smallest parish to the metropolis, O'Connell and his lay and clerical allies succeeded in creating—at least in Leinster and Munster—a "mass national public" which supported their campaigns with enthusiasm and money. Likewise, under the leadership of Father Theobald Mathew millions of Catholics took solemn pledges to abstain from drink; despite Father Mathew's attempt to dissociate his moral crusade from political issues, nationalists seized upon it and marched under the banner of "Sobriety! Domestic Comfort! and National Independence!" Although middle-class nationalists' primary objectives—emancipation, repeal, municipal corporation reform—were of little direct benefit to most Catholics, O'Connell linked those goals to more-popular concerns such as tenant-right and tax relief. Perhaps most important, the peasantry embraced O'Connell and his aims because they interpreted both in the light of traditional hopes and hatreds. Thus, John O'Driscol admitted that most of his coreligionists had not the slightest idea what emancipation meant, but "they were willing to do anything to diminish what they perceived as a Protestant assumption of 'ascendancy.'" Irish-speaking agitators such as the schoolmaster Humphrey O'Sullivan synthesized Gaelic and modern nationalism, and for a people still steeped in history and prophecy O'Connell assumed the stature of a messiah who would deliver the Irish from bondage and usher in the promised millennium when "flowers will bloom and trees will be fruitful," and "the rabble breed" be "banished" or "broken" by the vengeance of the Gael. Similarly, although Father Mathew's temperance movement was designed to make the Irish orderly and law-abiding, "the poor . . . peasants got it into their heads that surely God, through the means of his servant in making them a sober people, was thus preparing the country for that national uprising which they supposed would be imminent should O'Connell's parliamentary tactics fail. . . ." No wonder O'Connell and the priests found it difficult to restrain their followers' yearnings for retribution, for as one Protestant ruefully observed, "the People have been taught their own strength—and now they seem resolved to use it as they see fit, without consulting their Teachers."[66]

On the Famine's eve the middle-class Irish Catholic "nation" was still in the process of creation. Not only was O'Connell's crusade to repeal the union thwarted by British intransigence but many Catholics still clung to traditional consolations or expressed their grievances through violence rather than constitutional agitation. Even some middle-class nationalists were disillusioned by O'Connell's inconsistent policies and political opportunism, and for many lower-class Catholics nationalists' promises and pleas for unity could neither excuse nor obscure the realities of economic exploitation and cultural imperialism which they endured at the hands of their more affluent and Anglicized coreligionists. Moreover, emigration continued to increase, since for many Catholics of all classes leaving Ireland remained both necessity and opportunity. Thus, the impoverished laborers who in 1825 petitioned London for assisted passages to America were perhaps not entirely insincere when they declared that they "set more Value on our Maintenance & the love of our Sovereign than [on] the bellowing nonsense of religious Sectarianism" or on "all the Emancipation Bills that could be passed." If British officials had continued and extended their generous assisted emigration scheme of 1823–25, they might have undermined nationalism's appeal to lower-class Catholics and finally eradicated their prejudices against leaving Ireland. However, parliamentary advocates of economy and laissez-faire terminated the experiment, and assisted emigration was left to Protestant landlords, who often deserved nationalist epithets and popular distrust. Consequently, the influence of bourgeois Catholic nationalism grew steadily, and by the advent of the Great Famine many Irishmen were fully prepared to interpret the massive emigrations consequent on that catastrophe as yet another tragic chapter in the interminable saga of British oppression and forced exile.[67]

Ironically, however, although Gaelic and peasant traditions contained strong biases against leaving Ireland, theoretical as well as pragmatic considerations inclined many Catholic nationalists and their middle-class supporters to look favorably or at least neutrally on emigration. Their commercial-urban outlook, material ambitions, and opposition to penal disabilities and to peasant customs which circumscribed Catholic "progress" naturally biased them in favor of a "free market" system which justified in theory and necessitated in practice wholesale emigration from a rapidly modernizing Ireland. Often, only emigration could fulfill bourgeois desires for self-improvement, just as lower-class emigration was perhaps the only remedy for poverty, agrarian violence, and cultural "backwardness." Indeed, if it was true, as one emigrant suspected, "that our poor country is doomed to long, if not to perpetual distraction & unhappiness & poverty," then emigration was the poor's only hope. This recognition, coupling self-interest with genuine concern for the destitute, may help explain why in the pre-Famine decades middle-class Catholic spokesmen voiced relatively few objections to the act of emigration itself, particularly in comparison with the woeful lamentations and fierce denunciations which became staples of nationalist oratory and clerical admonitions after the Famine. Indeed, Daniel O'Connell, Thomas Wyse, Bishop James Doyle, and others at times even advocated large-scale government-assisted emigration as, in Doyle's words, "a useful, nay, a necessary expedient to relieve our present distress." Realizing, as Richard Lalor Sheil, one of O'Connell's lieutenants, put it, that even "deportation from this island, which for most of its inhabitants is a miserable one, is to many a change greatly for the better," Catholic leaders' primary *practical* concern seemed to be the amelioration of the emigration experience rather than the cessation of departures. Thus, although some Catholic clergymen preached sermons against emigration, others led Irish colonies to America, and most remained neutral, concerned only with the emigrants' physical and spiritual welfare. In 1824 O'Connell announced that part of the money collected by the Catholic Association would be used to train priests for the American mission, and in 1843 he joined with other prominent Catholics to found the Catholic Emigration Society, designed to advise prospective emigrants, protect them from fraud in the embarkation ports, and guide them to clerically supervised farming communities in the western United States. However, while such proposals demonstrated that Catholic leaders were not irrevocably opposed to emigration, the Catholic Emigration Society's quick demise and the failure of Catholic spokesmen generally to push hard or consistently for government aid may indicate their profound ambivalence over the subject. Sheil best expressed that ambivalence in the speech cited above, when he described emigration as a blessed release from bondage yet also portrayed those who left Ireland as homeless, heartsick wanderers forever separated from "the place of their birth, and . . . their fathers' graves." Likewise, Bishop Doyle referred to the emigrants as "exiled countrymen" consigned, in O'Connell's words, "to the inhospitable wilds of America."[68]

Such phrases might command automatic assent from peasant audiences, but men like O'Connell, Doyle, and Sheil were far too urbane to be merely unconscious transmitters of an archaic tradition which conceptualized emigration as sorrowful banishment. Although they hoped to mitigate the hardships and dangers of emigration, they understood that on a practical, individual level going to America often conferred material advantages on both the emigrants and those left behind. However, given Catholics' communal traditions and contemporary sufferings, and given the exigencies of their leaders' efforts to rally them against the Ascendancy, emigration could not be regarded simply as a practical, individual matter. Rather, emigration—like evictions, tithes, and taxes—was a political issue, if for no other reason than that massive departures threatened to vitiate nationalist and clerical influence. Thus, most Catholic spokesmen—and even a few Protestant reformers such as William Sharman Crawford, champion of tenant-right—tried to draw a fine distinction between voluntary emigration and "compulsory expatriation," in effect arguing that whereas the former was natural and beneficial, the latter was artificially induced by landlord "exterminations" and British misgovernment and thus was lamentable and injurious both to the emigrants and to Irish society generally. In practice and in the light of their people's traditions, that distinction was impossible to maintain: in the heat of declamation, all emigrants became "exiles." And so, in a lengthy speech before Parliament in 1834, O'Connell demanded repeal and denounced the government by declaring that English "policy is now scattering [the Irish] over the face of the earth. The Union is banishing them from their native land."[69]

To be sure, such expressions partly reflected O'Connell's and other Catholic spokesmen's habit of blaming English and Protestant malevolence for all Catholic grievances. However, there *was* evidence that at least some Catholic departures could be attributed to circumstances rooted in political and/or religious causes. Contemporary British statesmen and economists made no secret of their conviction that, as one of Lord John Russell's adherents put it, "[e]migration would prepare the way for consolidation of farms in Ireland," and often it appeared that British legislation was designed to produce just that effect. In a real sense the Subletting Act of 1826 and other new laws which strengthened Irish landlords' control over their property made the British government at least indirectly responsible for the evictions and emigrations which resulted from their operations—operations often enforced by British troops. Similarly, the Irish Poor Law of 1838 reportedly stimulated emigration by increasing the taxes burdening leaseholders and by inducing landlords to clear their estates of paupers. Significantly, O'Connell vehemently opposed both the Subletting Act and the Poor Law, and although he was primarily concerned about their injurious effects on strong farmers (for example, he favored state-aided emigration for the poor rather than tax-supported workhouses), his public denunciations focused heavily on the cruel evictions—or "exterminations"—and involuntary emigrations occasioned by that legislation. In addition, many of O'Connell's own middle-class supporters personally experienced what could be interpreted as political and religious pressures for emigration. Before emancipation, Catholic professionals like the architect Robert Elliott and the lawyer George O'Keefe faced such religious barriers to success that they felt compelled to emigrate; as late as 1843 Jasper O'Farrell, later one of San Francisco's leading citizens, left home because "however accomplished as a scholar or a gentleman," an ambitious Catholic found it nearly impossible "to get along or even exist in his native land." Also, in some parts of Ireland prosperous Catholics were threatened when landlords moved to eliminate middlemen and assume direct control over their estates. Indeed, economic, sectarian, and political motives were often indistinguishable when proprietors imbued with the spirit of the New Reformation or angry at Catholic tenants for opposing their political wishes discriminated openly against "papists" when consolidating farms or granting leases. For example, in the wake of the emancipation crisis of the late

1820s vindictive landlords such as Lord Beresford punished defiant 40s. freeholders by carrying out wholesale evictions; others such as Lord Roden and the marquis of Downshire simply made anti-Catholic prejudice an integral feature of estate management. Such policies were not common, but they threatened middle- and lower-class Catholics alike and seem to have been pursued with greatest notoriety in areas such as south Leinster which were O'Connellite strongholds and centers of Catholic agitation. Thus, in 1838 a well-to-do Catholic in County Carlow complained bitterly of "the exclusive, orange system of letting now practiced in this Country"; in 1840 a schoolmaster and Catholic activist left King's County "when a combination, headed by some of the local Orange Magistracy, forced [him] to fly from Ireland"; and a year later John Nowlan, a Wexford shopkeeper, reported that "the people are so divided . . . [that] Landlords are driving their unfortunate Tennants out Especially Roman Catholick."[70]

In fact, it is impossible to determine whether British laws, religious bigotry, or political retaliation produced departures much in excess of those occasioned by the "normal" operations of market forces. Nor is it possible to ascertain whether Protestant landlords were really more directly responsible than Catholic graziers and strong farmers for lower-class emigration, although certainly most peasants' welfare was more immediately affected by the exploitative policies of those who often posed as Catholic champions against landlord oppression. However, the point is not only that some middle- and lower-class emigration could be justly and dramatically attributed to British misgovernment and Protestant prejudice but also that in the emotionally charged climate of pre-Famine Ireland it was both natural and politically expedient for Catholic spokesmen to characterize *all* emigration in light of the current political and sectarian struggle against the hereditary enemies. Thus, the plight of an evicted 40s. freeholder such as Harry Mills of County Louth, whose vote for a proponent of Catholic emancipation against his landlord's wishes necessitated flight to America, became both a cause célèbre and an evocative, if inaccurate, symbol for all pre-Famine emigration.[71]

Perhaps equally important in the recasting of the exile motif for modern usage was that in the course of their agitation nationalist leaders conceptualized an ideal Irish society from which emigration was unnecessary and inappropriate. British legislation for Ireland was based largely on Malthusian economic theory: Ireland's poverty was due primarily to overpopulation, a reflection of Catholic "improvidence"; a superabundance of discontented laborers and petty farmers kept wages at subsistence level and prevented Irish landlords and British investors from rationalizing Irish agriculture and making it profitable. Logically, if population was the problem, then massive emigration was at least part of the solution. Nevertheless, however much some Catholic spokesmen such as O'Connell and Bishop Doyle might favor improved agriculture and state-aided emigration, their oppositional roles obliged them to contend that Irish distress was caused by external and legal factors rather than by overpopulation or any other intrinsic defects in Catholic society. By condemning Malthusian theory as applied to Ireland, nationalist leaders also rejected the only politically neutral justification for Irish emigration and so inadvertently undermined any case for state-financed departures. Moreover, since Catholic leaders rejected British plans for Ireland's future under the union, they had to pose a positive alternative which would not only gratify middle-class Catholic ambitions but also satisfy the more traditional yearnings of their lower-class supporters. This was more difficult than merely denouncing tithes or landlords, and as a consequence nationalists' statements often appeared contradictory. On the one hand, men such as O'Connell, Sheil, and Doyle admired England, and in certain respects wanted Ireland to emulate her prosperity and institutions. O'Connell himself was an apostle of material progress, an advocate of a fluid socioeconomic and political system open to men of talent regardless of creed, and a disciple of the English philosopher Jeremy Bentham, who preached absolute individualism and the sanctity of private property. However, even O'Connell and certainly more-conservative Catholic spokesmen—especially churchmen such as Doyle and Archbishop John MacHale of Tuam—recognized that untrammeled capitalism and its corroborative, utilitarian values were impoverishing, fragmenting, and demoralizing Catholic Ireland. Mass destitution and suffering were self-evident, but equally disturbing was the breakdown of social and moral order, which could be attributed to selfish materialism among the affluent and to desperation coupled with a rudimentary radicalism among the disadvantaged. In short, not only were the Catholic lower classes uninspired by the prospects of a fully commercialized and Anglicized Ireland but many Catholic leaders themselves shrank from what they feared as the social and moral implications.[72]

In response, nationalist spokesmen conceptualized an Ireland free from "English" influences as well as from English political domination. Catholic leaders synthesized English liberalism with what one historian has called "Catholic communitarianism" and hypothesized an ideal organic society which would combine equal opportunity and religious tolerance with strong communal restraints on individualism, materialism, and social conflict. Nationalists' economic notions were especially vague. O'Connell often predicted that repeal of the union would make Ireland England's commercial and industrial rival, as she had purportedly been in the glorious days of "Grattan's Parliament." In general, however, nationalists envisaged a sort of protocapitalist, rural-based economy—in a sense almost frozen in time—of smallholding "yeomen" farmers and cottage manufacturers, the former protected by the legalization of tenant-right, the latter by protective tariffs. The future of the landless laborers was left particularly obscure, but presumably they would achieve happiness through an extensive state-sponsored program of wasteland colonization. Although relatively egalitarian in economic outlines, the ideal Ireland was socially interdependent, even hierarchical. Under the supervision of a paternalistic native government, "good landlords"—resident on their estates and imbued with a "national" spirit—would sponsor their tenants' prosperity while the Catholic church would provide moral guidance through its prescribed devotions and anticipated control over education. However, at this point nationalists split into religious and secular camps. Despite their assurances to fearful Protestants, O'Connell and especially the bishops envisioned an essentially Catholic Ireland in which the church in partnership with Catholic nationalists would impose unity, order, and morality primarily through external constraints: modern political and religious sanctions enforced through traditional communal pressures. However, in the early 1840s a small but influential band of cosmopolitan, urban-oriented Catholic and Protestant nationalists, known as Young Ireland, began to question and challenge that sectarian vision. Although Young Irelanders like Thomas Davis often waxed eloquent over the supposed virtues of peasant life, they hoped that secular and interdenominational education would create an Irish people characterized individually by "self-reliance" but united collectively by a romantic nationalism which would merge Catholic and Protestant differences into a common consciousness based on a synthesis of Gaelic, Old English, and Cromwellian cultures and traditions. As O'Connell's power waned after 1843, the differences among nationalists became more blatant and politically significant. However, the point here is that their collective vision of an organic, self-sufficient society not only hypothesized a future, free Ireland from which emigration would no longer be necessary, but also enjoined models of contemporary thought and behavior which reinforced archaic communal, precapitalist traditions and which at least implicitly rejected as inappropriate, as "un-Irish," those individualistic, business-minded attitudes which justified voluntary emigration for material gain. As Catholic nationalist ideology had developed, by its own internal logic emigration had to be either "treason" or involuntary exile caused by British oppression. Why else would departures occur "from a land which only wants social justice and self-government to give comforts, nay luxuries, to its present inhabitants and their multiplying descendants . . . ?" Viewed in this light, emigration was neither socially nor individually desirable: rather, it was a tragedy for the organic nation bereft of its "bone and sinew," and an unrelieved sorrow for any "true" Irishman or -woman whose primary loyalties were to family, community, church, and "sacred cause."[73]

There is no doubt that the politicization of pre-Famine Ireland had important effects on the *character* of contemporary emigration. For example, although the last wave of pre-Famine emigrants departing in 1838–44 was generally poorer and less skilled than its predecessors, the effects of Father Mathew's crusade caused American observers to comment favorably on the newcomers' relative sobriety and consequent indisposition to engage in the drunken brawls formerly common among Irish-American laborers. On the other hand, the incessant sectarian conflicts in contemporary Ireland heightened religious tribalism and animosity on both sides: most Protestants leaving home after the mid-1820s carried attitudes toward "papists" much more hostile than those shared by earlier emigrants fired by the ecumenical radicalism of the United Irishmen; likewise, Catholic emigrants were equally bitter toward "bloody heretics," Orangemen, and the "anti-Irish host" from "the Black and British north." Further exacerbated by conditions peculiar to the New World, this sectarian legacy exploded in violence on the streets of American cities. Finally, because of O'Connell's campaigns and political organizations—concentrated in Leinster and east Munster, and supplemented by the Ribbon lodges in the Ulster borderlands and many Irish towns—Catholic emigrants, overwhelmingly from those areas, arrived in the New World with an unusual degree of national consciousness and political expertise, which helped to unite them across class and parochial lines and favored their later emergence as a significant and successful force in American politics.[74]

However, it is much more difficult to determine whether Catholic political activity or ideology had any actual effects on the *volume* or *pace* of Catholic emigration. In 1828–29 nationalist newspapers reported that Catholic farmers, "overjoyed with the prospect of living in their renovated country" after the passage of emancipation, were postponing emigration and "willingly forfeiting their passage money." Similarly, Catholic spokesmen later claimed that the more than 58 percent decline in departures between 1842 and 1843 was due to Catholic confidence in O'Connell's pledge that the latter would be "Repeal Year" when, as one emigrant remembered, "all Seem^d to feel that the Great Agitator had only to ask the British . . . for Repeal of the cursed union to have it granted." Such stories may be apocryphal: nationalist dogma prescribed that, since British misgovernment caused Irish emigration, then the hope or realization of self-government must cause it to cease. However, given Catholic countrymen's millennial cast of mind, it is not illogical to assume that peasants who expected to regain "their rightful possessions," or who failed to plant crops because "[t]hey thought O'Connell and Sheil would stream gold into their pockets" after the winning of emancipation and repeal, might also be more likely to focus hopes for earthly salvation on a regenerated Ireland than on an almost equally mythical vision of an American alternative to their present despair. After all, the nationalists' promise to create an Ireland of yeomen farmers and rural artisans perfectly reflected the widespread desire for "independence" as "comfortable self-sufficiency" which lured many Catholics overseas. Moreover, it seems that by the early 1840s the nationalists' attacks upon evictions and landlord-assisted emigration were beginning to take effect. "Emigrate, say the quacks. Exterminate, say the squires. . . . Try it," challenged the nationalist Thomas Davis in one of his essays, and "the people will resist." Of course, emigration continued despite Davis's brave words, but considerable evidence suggests that by the Famine's eve more Catholics *were* resisting. For example, in 1845, proprietors in Munster and south Leinster testified to the Devon commission that their tenants were much more opposed than in the past to giving up their farms in return for free passages overseas—a practice which, under nationalist tutelage, they now regarded as "dumping": "there is a different feeling as to emigration," admitted the Tipperary estate agent Thomas Bolton, and a much "greater determination to hold" on to the land at all costs.[75]

However, other evidence indicates that Irish politicization may have stimulated emigration by exacerbating Catholic dissatisfaction with conditions at home. As one frustrated would-be emigrant exclaimed,

> When looking at the persecution, the plunder, the misrule, the wretched degradation of poor unfortunate Ireland, where the sanctimonious parson robs the people and spills their blood; and the ignorant, bigoted minion of power defeats their rights, blasts the hopes and crushes the energies of her children, I often wished to taste the delights of freedom and independence beyond the Atlantic.

Certainly, when Catholics abandoned deferential habits, they became less willing to remain in Ireland "running after every upstart and hound puppy, with hat in hand, . . . in danger of a severe reprimand for not Saluting every heretic and infidel preacher and every Miscreant Agent in the country." Why, asked one emigrant, should an Irish Catholic "work a long day for a paltry sixpence, and . . . put his hand to his hat whenever his Squireen of an employer may pass by . . . ?" Like Peter Connolly of County Monaghan, many Catholics answered by leaving "humiliation and degradation . . . to those who have the mean hearts and sordid minds to bear such a state of things." In addition, when O'Connell's campaigns failed to bring anticipated results, disillusioned Catholics emigrated rather than return to a now even more intolerable poverty and subordination. "Emancipation has done nothing for us," concluded one peasant. "We must save ourselves." Many nationalists were particularly disappointed when in 1843, capitulating to British military force, O'Connell canceled the monster meeting at Clontarf which was supposed to culminate his crusade for repeal, and when subsequently he asserted that even Irish freedom did not justify bloodshed. "[F]rom the time he utter[ed] this maxim," wrote the emigrant John Burke, "I thought him a humbug. . . . If talk and agitation, speechmaking and begging would free a Country from the grip of her conqueror then Ireland would be entitled to the first Call." Becoming convinced, as were many Young Irelanders, that Britain would listen only to arguments fired "from the Cannons mouth," Burke left Ireland "in disgust" for the shores of America. Finally, even Father Mathew's temperance crusade may have inadvertently increased emigration. Abstemious peasants may or may not have been more industrious and ambitious than their tippling countrymen, but certainly they had more money to spend on passage tickets. Moreover, by crippling the Irish liquor industry, the temperance movement not only shut down half the island's distilleries and many breweries but also sharply reduced the incomes of backyard *poitín* makers and drove thousands of petty publicans out of business. For example, John Nowlan of Newtownbarry, County Wexford, reported that between 1840 and 1841 the number of local public houses fell from thirty-three to only four—"and them doing little good." Although middle-class nationalists could now rejoice that in such towns "you would not See a drunken man or a fight in the last twelve months," perhaps they took less comfort in the emigration between 1840 and 1844 of an estimated 20,000 bankrupt publicans and shopkeepers.[76]

Thus, all the efforts of O'Connell and Father Mathew could not stop the tide of emigration from "that beautiful, but ill-fated miserable, misgoverned Land . . . —Blessed by Nature and Natures God but cursed by Man." However, as that emigrant's lament indicates, nationalism's most important effect on emigration was that it provided a communally acceptable "explanation" for departures which linked archaic traditions with contemporary events and exigencies, and so provided both an evocative device for nationalist rhetoric and a balm for the social and individual tensions which emigration—like other aspects of modernization—exposed within the Catholic community. Ironically, despite their ambitions, pre-Famine nationalism may have had the greatest impact on the self-image of middle-class Catholic emigrants, disposing them to regard, or at least advertise, themselves as political exiles. After all, such men were most likely to be politically conscious and active in O'Connell's campaigns or, in the North, in Ribbonism. Also, emigrants from urban-commercial backgrounds and strong farmers' sons were most likely to be insecure about their social status and most prone to feel the intergenerational and personal conflicts occasioned by the breaking of familial and communal ties. Perhaps most important, despite their distance from Gaelic and peasant traditions, contemporary bourgeois literature both reinforced their sense of national identity and transmitted the imagery of exile. In the nineteenth century's early decades, Thomas Moore's enormously popular *Irish Melodies,* first published in 1807, synthesized Gaelic music with sentimental lyrics approved by polite society. Songs such as "Tho' the Last Glimpse of Erin with Sorrow I See" not only sanitized and popularized Irish nationalism among a Catholic middle class still reeling from the barbarism of '98 but also provided models of proper, patriotic emotion and behavior when young men reared on Moore's *Melodies* went abroad. Later, in the early 1840s, Thomas Davis and the other romantic nationalists in the Young Ireland movement shaped the literary tastes and self-imagery of a new and larger generation of middle-class emigrants through political essays, bombastic orations, and inspiring, albeit mediocre, poems such as Davis's "The Exile" which appeared in nationalist newspapers like the *Nation* and which were admired, emulated, and recited ad nauseam on public occasions and in the clubs and reading rooms which the Young Irelanders established to uplift and politicize their less sophisticated countrymen.[77]

However, if middle-class emigrants such as Hugh Quin of Portaferry and Michael O'Sullivan of Tulamore merely idealized themselves as noble, self-pitying victims of "tyranny and misfortune," more-ordinary Catholic countryfolk already shared historical traditions and contemporary experiences easily corroborated by nationalist rhetoric. As early as 1825 John Rochefort of County Carlow testified before Parliament that in at least a primitive sense the attitudes of rural Catholics toward emigration were already politicized. When asked why "the Catholic peasant was more attached to the country than the Protestant," Rochefort replied that the Catholic considered "himself and his religion indigenous to the land—that he is one of the original inhabitants," that Protestants were only "usurpers . . . that have deprived him and the Catholics at large of their inheritance, and that neither the Protestant nor his religion belong to the soil, but to another country." During the next twenty years constant agitation reinforced inchoate instincts and archaic literary traditions and taught peasants to view even assisted emigration as political banishment; by 1848 an American visitor could remark that, regardless of the real sources of their sufferings, Catholics had "been made to believe" that the English government's sole concern was to "force them to renounce their religion or flee the country and leave it . . . to the Protestants." Of course, during the pre-Famine decades nationalism's influence was still limited, and many poor Catholics did not view emigration in negative terms. Nevertheless, it is significant that emigration ballads increasingly conveyed the message that, although America was still seen as refuge, emigration itself was a matter of political compulsion rather than personal choice. The ballads usually sang of rack-rented tenants, "steeped to the lips in bitter want and woe," or of evicted farmers who heroically resisted heartless landlords and cruel bailiffs until forced to abandon the "dear little cabin at the foot of the mountain." Moreover, the songs often made explicit connections between individual acts of oppression and the national struggle against Protestantism and British tyranny. Indeed, the songs sometimes implied that political and religious persecution alone caused emigration: "Foul British laws are the whole cause of our going far away," sang "The Kilrane Boys" from County Wexford before they "gave three cheers for Ireland that echoed with hurray / And one for Dan O'Connell, then boldly sailed away." Or, "For the sake of my religion / I was forced to leave my native home," claimed another composer, for "I've been a bold defender / and a member of the Church of Rome." In fact, the purported reasons for emigration given by "The Kilrane Boys" and the apocryphal "Patrick Brady" were unlikely; however, in the politically charged atmosphere of pre-Famine Ireland, they could symbolize, justify, even ennoble, present necessities and reconcile them with communal traditions by maintaining at least thematic, if not linguistic, continuities with an archaic literature of sorrow and protest. Indeed, in the life and poetry of Nicholas O'Kearney, Gaelic and modern nationalism, ancient and modern renditions of the exile theme, achieved an ultimate synthesis. In 1843 O'Kearney, one of north Leinster's last Gaelic poets yet also a contributor of English verses to the *Nation,* composed a poem in Irish lamenting O'Connell's surrender at Clontarf:

> The Englishman's hand is strong and harsh—
> > the might of his laws and the slaughter of his victories—
> > his promise is a lie, his blade is bloody,
> > and it's high time for me to flee across the sea.

Alas that they have laid low the arm that accomplished valorous deeds,
Alas that they have destroyed the wound-dealing champion,
My thousand destructions that we are so feeble,
And alas for my journey across the sea.

Will the prophecies of our saints and learned men come true,
Will we always be exiles from our native land?
Will good fortune and prosperity ever come to Ireland?
If I thought so, I would not be going across the sea.

O'Kearney's verses are anachronistic; they could have been written centuries earlier to mourn the defeats of O'Neill or Sarsfield and to explain
their supporters' subsequent flights from Ireland. Nevertheless, O'Kearney's
audience—still locked in what seemed but a continuation of the age-old
combat with the *Sasanaigh*—found them and their popular English imita-
tions yet relevant to contemporary experience.[78]

Reinforcing the natural reluctance of Irish countrymen to leave their
birthplace was their fear of the ocean voyage, of the dangers and difficulties—real and imagined—which they were afraid to encounter. "[*A*]*ll could
not induce me to go*" to America, wrote one Ulsterwoman in 1836; "if it
was any place I could *travel* to by *land* I would not mind it so much . . .
but I feel a kind of *terror* of the *sea.*" Likewise, James J. Mitchell, a later
emigrant from County Galway, admitted that he "dreaded the crossing of
the Atlantic," and, significantly, Catholic peasants consistently exhibited
much greater reluctance and apprehension on that occasion than did Irish
Protestants and middle-class emigrants generally. Irish emigrant songs
dealing with the transatlantic voyage nearly all sang of suffering and disaster, not infrequently warning Irishmen to remain at home rather than venture on the high seas. Anti-emigration propaganda tried to exacerbate such
fears by issuing similar warnings, and even in the late nineteenth century—
when most emigrants traveled swiftly and in relative comfort aboard steamships—rural Catholics going to America still felt constrained to carry talis-
mans to protect them against shipwreck or disease.[79]
Despite such precautions, intense fears of the voyage persisted, although
in many respects pre-Famine passages had become less hazardous and less
uncomfortable since 1815. For example, technological improvements in
sailing ships significantly reduced the duration of the average Atlantic
crossing, from eight to ten weeks in the eighteenth century to only five to
six weeks by about 1830. Moreover, after 1815, Irish emigrants no longer
had to fear impressment by the British navy or interception by pirates or
French and Spanish privateers and warships, dangers which had plagued
their predecessors. In addition, after 1830 most of the vessels which carried Irish passengers to America were specifically constructed for the emigrant trade rather than for cargo, and from 1803 onward the British and,
to a much lesser extent, the American governments at least tried to regulate the traffic for the passengers' benefit. However, the Irish still had good

reasons for apprehension. Not only were the Passenger Acts rarely or laxly enforced but the extinction of the old traffic in Irish indentured servants and redemptioners weakened the direct financial interest of shippers and shipmasters in their passengers' nutrition and general health; indeed, during the eighteenth century most shippers had provisioned even their poorest passengers, but after about 1800 the emigrants usually had to purchase and prepare most of their own food. Also, the much greater volume of emigration in the pre-Famine decades strained the capacity of existing shipping and led to many abuses, while the fact that increasing numbers of Irish emigrants came from the peasant classes meant that their ignorance of shipboard life would create as well as magnify dangers and difficulties. In addition, during the eighteenth century, when emigrants were few and largely illiterate, what knowledge of the ocean voyage existed in rural Ireland consisted primarily of the favorable accounts circulated by self-interested shippers and ticket agents; by contrast, the pre-Famine Irish were increasingly inundated by letters from actual emigrants who usually described the Atlantic passage in highly unflattering and discouraging terms. Finally, the steady decline of direct Irish trade with North America obliged most pre-Famine emigrants to journey first to Liverpool (or, in some cases, to Greenock, in Scotland), a trip itself fraught with perils and inconveniences.[80]

The cross-channel passages from Irish ports to Liverpool usually lasted only fourteen to thirty hours, and deck fares never exceeded 10d. and were usually much less. By all accounts, though, the emigrants' first experience with the sea was particularly miserable. Baggage and livestock had first priority on the Liverpool steamers, and the poor Irish huddled without shelter on the open decks, packed shoulder to shoulder, "holding on to each other, and to anything else they could lay hold on to keep from being washed overboard"; one ship's officer admitted crowding 1,400 emigrants on the deck of a single vessel, and many passengers had to stand during the entire passage. Accidents were common, safety provisions such as life-boats were absent or woefully inadequate, and during heavy seas the passengers were drenched with cold seawater on decks awash with vomit and "animal mire." Seasickness was nearly universal; as one priest reported, "we were sea-sick before we were quite out of sight of Ireland." Even cabin passengers such as Mary Cumming, who awoke in her berth with a dead rat beneath her head, were ecstatic to reach Liverpool, but many deck passengers arrived so ill and weakened they had to be carried ashore.[81]

Unfortunately, neither in the Irish ports nor in Liverpool did the emigrants find temporary havens; instead, they had to run virtual gauntlets of frauds and impositions before embarking for the New World. The Irish countrymen's relative poverty and ignorance made them especially vulnerable to the wiles of ticket agents, shippers, passage brokers, lodging-house keepers, porters or "runners," shipmasters, and sailors. In 1836 the chief emigration officer at Liverpool reported that 90 percent of the frauds perpetrated there involved the Irish: "they show great ignorance and gullibility," he testified, "and indeed appear to want common sense in making a bargain." Ticket agents subjected the Irish to the "most gross and reprehensible delusions," often selling them tickets which proved wholly or partially worthless, sometimes committing the emigrants to sail on old, leaky vessels or on ships bound for ports far from their intended destinations. Shippers frequently advertised that their vessels would embark weeks or even months before their actual sailings, thus forcing emigrants with tickets to subsist in Liverpool in the meantime, depleting their meager savings and consuming the provisions so sorely needed on the voyage ahead. The longer the Irish were delayed in port, the more likely their victimization by the denizens of the waterfront slums. Runners, lodging-house keepers, and passage brokers were usually in collusion and nearly always unscrupulous, especially in Liverpool and Cork. Overcharging was universal, outright robbery was common, and the risk of contracting disease in most lodging houses, often no better than fetid cellars, was appallingly high. In addition, the general ambiance of the dockyard slums was dangerous to naïve and already-homesick emigrants who too eagerly trusted Irish-born saloon-keepers and other "sharpers," often losing through drunkenness and ignorance the few pounds they had saved to carry them to the "land of promise." Liverpool magistrates reported that a large proportion of that city's slum dwellers were brokenhearted emigrants who had squandered or been fleeced of their passage money. In short, the Irish could consider themselves fortunate if they escaped "the Liverpool harpies of embarkation." Safely in America, one Irishman vividly remembered "all the trials, cheats, plots and chicanery of every kind which [he] had to overcome"; "if man had 7 senses," he declared, "[i]t would take 500 senses largely developed to counteract the sharpers of Liverpool."[82]

After days or weeks of delay, it might be expected that emigrants would regard their long-awaited embarkations with joy and relief. Later, during the Great Famine, many Irish were indeed delighted to begin their journeys. However, during the early nineteenth century most accounts indicate that the majority of Irish emigrants, especially rural Catholics, found embarkation a time filled with confusion, apprehension, and homesickness. On Hugh Campbell's vessel, for example, "sorrow for having undertaken the voyage seemed to be universally felt by all," and some passengers begged desperately to be set ashore again; comparing the "many privations & dangers" ahead "with the security & ease they left behind," the Irish were deeply "conscious of being set adrift on a doubtful world." Anglicized, middle-class emigrants consoled themselves with "prospect[s] of happiness and independence" or expressed their homesickness in poignant, if mediocre, verses which emulated those of Thomas Moore or Lord Byron. However, most stared tearfully at the receding coastline or turned to drink "in order to drive away the sorrow which a separation from their native land produced."[83]

Once at sea, beyond the reach of port officials and regulations, the deceits and neglects practiced by shippers and captains before embarkations had their harshest and sometimes deadliest effects. Before the mid-nineteenth century many emigrant ships were small, old, slow, and unseaworthy; this was especially true of the Canadian timber vessels which carried large numbers of poor Irishmen in the 1810s and 1820s. Moreover, the keen competition among Irish, British, and American shippers impelled cost-cutting measures, which resulted in deteriorating ships, poorly trained and undermanned crews, and incompetent or drunken officers. Shipwrecks and ships putting back to port in distress were almost weekly events, and John Doyle was only one of many Irishmen who sailed on a vessel that "leaked through every part" and had to be "pumped . . . into port" by both passengers and crew. In addition, many ships employed in the emigrant trade were not originally designed to carry large numbers of passengers. Hastily converted cargo ships had only primitive and uncomfortable accommodations, and even true emigrant ships, with specially constructed steerage decks, allotted passengers less than two square feet of space apiece; only children had room to stand upright, and each narrow sleeping berth held at least four people. Such vessels usually carried as many passengers as the laws allowed, and often far more. Shippers regularly falsified their vessels' burden or tonnage to deceive the port officials, and in the early nineteenth century the publicly advertised tonnage of Irish emigrant ships was usually between two and three times their actual burden. Some small vessels carried "nearly double the number ever attempted to be stowed in a slave ship of equal burden."[84]

Sailing for six weeks in the holds of such vessels was at best extremely uncomfortable, and during storms, when the hatches were battened down and all ventilation ceased, the sufferings of the frightened passengers became acute. As one Ulsterman reported, at such times the emigrants "can get no cooking done and are shut up in a dark hold without a ray of light and almost no air; the very noise of the poor children is enough to put one deranged at the idea of a steerage passage to America." Moreover, the close, unsanitary confines of the steerage quickly bred disease. Toilet facilities were at best inadequate, and most peasant emigrants knew little and cared less about elementary hygiene. British and Irish Protestant passengers concurred in branding their "papist" companions as lice-ridden, "barbarous dirty scum"—"the Most Ignorant and degraded Mass of human beings with whom I had ever been brought in contact," complained one Ulster Presbyterian. On a few voyages either the ships' officers or the passengers themselves policed and cleaned the steerage, but during most passages the former were indifferent and the latter too ignorant or demoralized to make significant efforts. As a result, "the filthy beds [were] teeming with abominations, . . . [t]he narrow space between the berths . . . breathe[d] up a damp and fetid stench," and many ships arrived with streams of "foul air issuing from the hatches—as dense and as palatable as seen on a foggy day from a dung heap." Genteel passengers were particularly exercised by the sexual immorality which purportedly flourished and by the drunkenness and general disorder which certainly abounded in the foul holds of many vessels. However, a greater danger was from contagious diseases such as smallpox, dysentery, cholera, and typhus. Only a minority of the ships carried medicine, and not one in fifty engaged a physician for the voyage. All things considered, it was remarkable that shipboard mortality rates were usually low, 2 percent or less, with most deaths occurring among infants and small children. Nevertheless, practically every season witnessed a few tragic voyages, and the worst years were replete with horror. Typhus ravaged Irish emigrant ships in 1817–18, as did cholera in 1831–34; during these years shipboard mortality rates of 10 percent were frequent and rates of 25 percent or more were not unknown.[85]

Many emigrant vessels carried insufficient food and water as shippers and captains economized at their passengers' peril; moreover, much of the food was wretched in quality, poorly stored, and unfit for consumption before the voyage was half over; similarly, shippers often stored precious water in leaky or contaminated containers. Throughout the period emigrants' letters testified to their sufferings from inadequate or foul provisions and water, and although most passengers brought food with them, very often their own supplies spoiled or were exhausted before long voyages ended. Indeed, some shipmasters intentionally misrepresented the length of the Atlantic passage so that later they could extort high prices for food from their starving passengers. Most emigrant ships' cooking facilities were also inadequate, and since steerage passengers had to prepare their own food, mealtimes often witnessed fierce struggles for access to the few available stoves. Some of the most untutored peasant emigrants understood neither how to use the stoves nor how to prepare foodstuffs other than potatoes; for example, the assisted cottier emigrants from north Munster in 1823 refused to eat the exceptionally good provisions which the government provided, and instead "called constantly for potatoes."[86]

Between 1803 and 1842 the British Parliament passed a series of Passenger Acts (the American Congress legislated only once on the subject, in 1819) designed to regulate emigration and curb abuses; many of the laws were quite specific, and that of 1834 established a corps of salaried emigration officers stationed in the major ports. However, both British and American administrative machineries were inadequate to their appointed tasks: evasions of the laws were easy and commonplace, for the few customs and emigration officials were overwhelmed by their duties, and once the emigrants were at sea legislative protection effectively ceased. Thus, John Doyle complained that the Dublin customs officers' inspection was "a mere matter of form," and in 1818 Hugh Campbell's captain had little difficulty embarking from Londonderry with more than the legal number of passengers: he merely secreted Campbell and fifteen other emigrants for ten hours within a cavity in the ship's brick ballast, where they lay—"moaning, swearing, vomiting & begging to get out"—until the vessel was safely at sea. Nearly all the Passenger Acts proved insufficient to stem abuses, and emigrants such as Gerald Griffin lamented that it was a great "pity that those who have so much responsibility Cannot be punished severely for their brutal neglect." However, there were no effective means of redress, and most emigrants were too ignorant of their legal rights, too bewildered or intimidated to complain of their sufferings except in their letters home.[87]

Letters such as Griffin's undoubtedly discouraged many departures, especially among recipients who lacked sufficient knowledge of the outside world to put such warnings in perspective. However, extreme, prolonged discomforts or privations were experienced only on exceptional voyages or during years when epidemics occurred. Indeed, many peasant emigrants probably found the food, filth, and suffocating atmosphere of the steerage little worse than what they had been accustomed to in one- or two-room cabins back home. Some pre-Famine emigrants ate more and better food on shipboard than they had in Ireland, and many voyages were so short and devoid of danger that they surprised apprehensive emigrants such as John McBride, who testified that the transatlantic crossing "was not near so unpleasant as [he] thought it would have been." "Its a long way," admitted another Irishman, "but its a much greater difficulty in Idea than it often turns out." In fact, the word which pre-Famine emigrants most commonly used to describe their entire passages was merely "tedious," although that term could signify anything from a voyage's unusual length to the degree of seasickness experienced. Practically all Irish emigrants complained of seasickness: many began "casting up [their] accounts over the side of the vessel" within minutes of embarkation, and though acute nausea usually lasted only a few days, a significant number were "sea sick all the way" and "were worn to perfect weakness" by the time they reached the New World. However, for most emigrants "tedious" was less a reflection of objective realities than of their emotional state. Always alone or among strangers, far from familiar and comforting surroundings, most emigrants experienced periods of profound loneliness and homesickness at sea. One Ulsterman believed that such feelings were particularly strong only during the first few days' sailing; afterward the emigrants became reconciled to their situation "& turned their attention from Lamentations about their friend[s] to enquiries how fast the ship was sailing & how the wind blew." Nevertheless, the great majority of the emigrants' voyage letters indicate that their authors never became accustomed to the solitude and uncertainty of the sea and that their fears and loneliness only exacerbated longings for home and regrets for having left it. "Oh thou spot of earth," exclaimed one emigrant, gazing back to Ireland, "endeared by a thousand tender ties and fond recollections, your receding form but little knows with what sad feelings your unhappy exile bids you his last farewell." Another Ulsterman expressed his longings in verse:

> Let him not say "I love my country" he
> Who ne'er has left it; but what time one hears
> The yell of water ringing in his ears
> And views around him nought but sky and sea
> And sea and sky interminable—then—

Then comes the longing for soft hills and dales
And trees and rivulets and gloomy vales
And the green twilight of the shady lea.

"[S]o great is the hardship & ennui of travelling," concluded a third emigrant, "that I would rather see my friends live poor & penniless in Ireland than ever emigrate for the precarious goods of this earth."[88]

During much of the voyage Irish emigrants were simply bored, so much so, reported one Ulsterman, that "everything attracts attention that varies the monotony of the surrounding expance": icebergs, whales, shoals of porpoises or flying fish—all excited momentary wonder; and "if a solitary sail was seen gliding along the Edge of the horizon our deck would be crowded with the passengers. How interesting to them this fragment of a world hastening to rejoin the great mass of existence!" However, boredom often led to less wholesome diversions, especially among "the wild Irish passengers": drinking, quarreling, the spreading of false rumors born of fear which panicked novice travelers; "some said the captain had lost his reckoning & was taking us lord knows where—others that the ship had sprung a leak . . . and a third swore that the ship was such a clumsy, slow sailing vessel . . . that we would be obliged to eat our shoes before we seen land again." On some voyages "there was scarce a day without a fight or a night without a robery," and faction fights and pitched battles between Irish Catholics, Orangemen, and British Protestant passengers were commonplace—giving the latter "great satisfaction regarding the Roman Catholic religion," since "[t]he damaging behavior of those who profess it," declared a pious Welshman, "showed very clearly the mark of the beast." In addition, the emigrants diverted themselves with music, dancing, games, cardplaying—any "amusements" which "tended . . . to reconcile us to our solitary floating prison." Although Protestant passengers often complained that in the steerage "the voice of prayer is never heard" and that their Catholic countrymen "lacked any regard for the sanctity of the sabbath," on many ships the officers or passengers held regular religious services. However, such occasions often only inflamed the "Spirit of bigotry" among both Protestant and Catholic emigrants.[89]

On nearly every voyage the emigrants' boredom was broken by at least one traumatic episode of real or imagined danger, which later gave dramatic focus to their first letters home. The threat of fires aboard wooden ships was constant, often started in poorly constructed "cookhouses" or by "the thoughtless Irish" who insisted on smoking or lighting candles below decks, oblivious to the warnings of officers and their more "steady" countrymen. However, storms at sea were most common and dangerous: terrible weather seemed ubiquitous in the North Atlantic, and some vessels experienced weeks and even months of continuous gales. Thomas Reilly endured "15 Storms, one greater than another," before his ship finally foundered on a sandbank within two days of New York. Earlier in the century John O'Raw spent five stormy months traveling from Belfast to South Carolina; after his first ship sank off Bermuda, he and his fellow passengers chartered another, but gales nearly wrecked it before the vessel at last limped into Charleston. Other, less fortunate emigrants never reached their destinations. Storms sank some ships in open seas and drove others into the bewilderingly thick fogs and rocky coasts of Newfoundland; such was the celebrated fate of the *Lady of the Lake,* which sailed from Belfast in 1833:

> Our ship was split asunder as you may understand,
> Which left our bodies floating on the banks of Newfoundland.

Although relatively few ships were lost at sea, storms were the emigrants' greatest concern. Only a few middle-class emigrants such as the Derry Protestant Thomas Cathar found the noise of "the timber straining and the wind whistling through the rigging" during strong gales "exulting," or became impressed thereby "with the conviction of *man*'s power" to "make the most unstable elements the slaves of his will." Most Protestant emigrants merely fortified themselves with the faith that "God is as strong on sea as on land." However, traditionalist rural Catholics were denied both those consolations: their outlook on life on *land* was fatalistic and dependent, and their religious faith was usually neither generalized nor internalized, but instead was almost inseparable from archaic customs and landmarks rooted in particular locales now thousands of miles behind them; in addition, the thought of dying far from friends and without a priest's ministrations was to them almost unbearable. This helps explain why even a middle-class Catholic like Anne Griffin had such "a great aversion to crossing the Atlantic," expecting to "die of fear on Such a passage." It also helps explain why Anglicized and traditionalist emigrants often reacted so differently when storms struck their vessels.[90]

Practically all pre-Famine emigrants encountered at least one storm which made them fear for their lives. Since most Irishmen and -women had had no previous experience with the sea (even coastal dwellers rarely engaged in deep-sea fishing), the often sudden, totally unexpected advent of severe gales was especially frightening. For example, one emigrant remembered sitting on deck with her fellow passengers in "weather . . . as calm and beautiful as any day [she] ever saw," but the next moment the captain bellowed orders, the sailors raced up the rigging to furl the sails, and "[b]efore all the passengers could get below deck the waves were rolling over"; other Irishmen were suddenly awakened in their berths "by the dash of a tremendous breaker that streamed like a torrent down every hatchway," while the "furious billows . . . broke like thunder against [their] bows till [their] stout-ship realed and quivered like an aspen bough." Thomas Reilly's vessel "screech[ed] with every stroke of the waves, every bolt in her quaked, every timber writhed, the smallest nail had a cry of its own." Sometimes the huge waves, striking a ship's "bows and sides with the force and noise of a thousand Sledge hammers upon so many anvils," would break a hole in her hull. In such cases, water poured into the hold until the sailors could mend the leak at least well enough that the frantic work of both crew and passengers at the pumps could keep the vessel from foundering. Occasionally, the ship's cargo or ballast would break loose, endangering the hull from the inside and causing the vessel to lurch heavily or even lie on its side in the water. Sheets of water would sweep over the upper deck, smashing bulwarks and lifeboats and threatening to carry the sailors overboard. During the worst storms the frail vessels were entirely at the mercy of the elements. "One moment the vessel seemed swallowed up, immersed in the deep with an insurmountable barrier around us—the next elevated on the foaming surge," mountains high above the lightning-streaked horizon, before again plunging sickeningly into the abyss below. Down in the steerage the scene was equally chaotic. The ship's violent motions would cause boxes, trunks, and passengers to fly back and forth, endangering lives, smashing containers, and ruining provisions and valuable possessions. In some instances the emigrants' berths would collapse, leaving their occupants, "their bedding, and most of their luggage . . . all lying in one confused mass."[91]

The effects of such storms upon the poor emigrants were generally devastating. Protestant passengers like Henry Johnson often claimed that they "took the matter cooly enough," but most of the Irish were terrified: " 'Save Lord, or I perish,' " prayed one Ulsterwoman who thought herself "face to face with death." "Over and over I said it, as Father sat with his arms around me, holding me tight in silent prayer." Tossed about with their belongings in total, suffocating darkness, nauseated and vomiting, completely ignorant of their vessel's ability to withstand the howling wind and crashing waves, the steerage passengers "all expected to meet with a watery grave." As another emigrant remembered, the sounds of the storm "mingled with the groans of the sea sick who cared little whether the ship sunk or swam"; "the noise above and the noise below gave . . . a pretty neat idea of the place of infernal torments." Aboard another vessel the passengers were "quaking with fear, . . . some crying, some cursing and singing, the wife jawing her husband for bringing her into such danger"; "On deck they . . . gathered like sheep in a pen crying on the captain to save them." Most terrified emigrants quickly turned to their gods and "prayed very stoutly." Indeed, some Protestant passengers were disgusted at what they regarded as the sudden and abject piety displayed by Catholic emigrants who in "fair weather . . . feared neither God nor man." Thus, one Ulsterman denounced his "papist" companions as a "cowardly set of hounds" who "in the time of danger . . . would do nothing but sprinkle holy water, cry, pray, cross themselves and all sorts of tomfoolery instead of giving a hand to pump the ship": a bigoted observation, to be sure, but one often repeated and perhaps revealing of fundamental differences in culturally determined behavior. In any case, once the storms abated, all the grateful passengers crawled out of their berths or, if the hatches had been closed for many days, trampled each other in a mad scramble to reach the fresh air on deck. The danger over, some emigrants quickly forgot their fears and resumed their monotonous routines or the various displays of "wickedness" which so upset their more fastidious companions. However, terrifying storms made lasting impressions on many emigrants, reinforcing tendencies toward homesickness and self-pity: after enduring five straight days of gales, Daniel Malony could only long for

> . . . those whom I shall see
> In this fair earth no more,
> And wish . . . in vain for winds to flee
> Back to my native much loved shore.[92]

After long periods at sea, suffering alternately from homesickness, boredom, terror, and in some instances severe privation, many Irish emigrants nearly relinquished hope of ever reaching their destinations. Father Luke Kiernan reported that his fellow "passengers were all with a few exceptions afraid we should never see land," and a later emigrant remembered, "I thought I would never reach my Jurneys end." No wonder, then, that the Irish joyfully greeted the first indications of approaching land: floating driftwood or flights of "[l]and birds . . . were hailed as welcome visitors," and on Hugh Campbell's ship the "cheering news" that they were only three days' sail from New York "revived the passengers' drooping spirits" and "[t]he disenchantment of a tedious voyage was forgotten in the joyful expectance of shortly landing on the shores of the great 'land of promise.' " These first signs of land heightened the emigrants' anticipation, and many now remained constantly on deck, staring eagerly at the western horizon. At last, "shouts of joy went up from the Passengers at the sight of *tera firma":* "the exciting cry of 'Land!' 'Land!' 'Land!' ran through the ship like wild fire," remembered a later emigrant; "such were my feelings vacillating between hope and fear, that I could hardly believe it."[93]

Thankful for their deliverance from the cruel sea, many Irishmen—especially Anglicized and politically conscious emigrants—were equally eager to debark in the idealized American Republic. In 1818 one Ulsterman reported that he felt like Columbus rediscovering the New World, for "[t]he very name of America carried a volume of associations in themselves indescribable." The same year another Irishman, a Leinster Catholic, could scarcely wait to touch "the sacred soil of liberty": "had I not feared the ridicule of my companions," he later wrote, "I would . . . have fallen prostrate saying, 'thus I embrace thee, O land of freedom!' " However, some pre-Famine emigrants fell prostrate involuntarily, too weakened by seasickness, malnutrition, or disease to enjoy their first moments in America. In general, pre-Famine emigrants were superior in health to those who traveled in the "coffin ships" during the Great Famine, but in 1817–18 many Irishmen carried typhus to the New World, and in the early 1830s several thousands perished from cholera after debarkation. For example, when young Mary McLean from Leitrim arrived at Quebec in 1832, she found herself "in a plague-stricken City; where men, women, and children,

smitten by cholera, dropped in the streets to die in agony." Within a day
she fell sick, unconscious, and was carried on a "sick cart" to the crowded
hospital on the city's outskirts. There she found herself in

> a veritable house of torture, where the most appalling shrieks, groans,
> prayers and curses filled the air continually, and, as if in answer to all this,
> day and night, from the sheds outside, came the tap, tap, tap of the work-
> mens' hammers; as they drove the nails into the rough coffins; which could
> not be put together hastily enough for the many whose shrieks, subsided
> into moans, which gradually died away into that silence not to be broken;
> and whose poor bodies were then carried to the dead-house in the hospital-
> yard, coffined, piled on the dead Cart . . . and hurried off to what was
> called the cholera burying ground; where, so great was the mortality at the
> time, corpses were buried five and six deep, with layers of lime between, in
> one grave.[94]

Most pre-Famine emigrants escaped such horrors, commonplace in 1847,
but many arrived less hopeful than demoralized by their voyage experience
and bewildered by their novel surroundings. Some were frightened by the
"vast extent of woodland" along North American shores, quite alien to
Irish experience, others by "the tumult and busy bustle" of the waterfront
areas of cities such as New York, where, as one emigrant warned, "[i]t is
everyone for himself." Another newcomer remembered that he and his
fellow Irish passengers were unceremoniously "dumped on the dock Bag
and Baggage to make out the best we could in this new and strange land."
Most pathetic were those peasant emigrants whose destitution matched their
ignorance. One traveler remarked how "painful" was the sight of many
Irish arrivals: "Squalid, thinly clad, and far from clean, . . . dragging an
ill-packed bundle—their all of worldly wealth—down a plank, and having
drawn it aside on the dock, they hang helplessly around it." Often the newcomers felt a renewed and "painful sense of loneliness" and "a sinking of
the spirits when they actually find themselves in a land of strangers and
strange customs." Although the crowded society of the ship's hold may
have been filthy and disagreeable, yet it was the "last link" which connected them with their common country; now, when this "community of
feeling" forged in suffering dispersed forever, it gave rise to "painful emotions."[95]

Lonely, confused, frightened, many Irish emigrants—especially rural
Catholics—were overeager to meet and trust the fellow countrymen they
met in the port cities. Most fortunate were those newcomers whose relatives either resided in the debarkation ports or could afford to travel great
distances to welcome them there. As one Ulsterman rejoiced in 1825, "you
can scarcely conceive how I felt after escaping the dangers of the Sea, and
on meeting with a Dear brother in a strange land." However, many—perhaps most—pre-Famine emigrants found no kinsmen or friends at the
docks, in part because the great majority of earlier emigrants lived widely
dispersed throughout the country, in part because many pre-Famine emigrants, especially Catholics, were among the first of their families or neigh-

borhoods to venture overseas. Moreover, not until the late 1840s were state officials authorized to meet and protect the newcomers in New York, Boston, and other ports; in the meantime most debarking Irish encountered an unregulated horde of ex-countrymen and "Yankee tricksters" eager to prey upon their ignorance. As early as 1817 a returned emigrant warned that "on the arrival of an Irish ship" in America, "a crowd of poor Irish, who have been in that country for a number of years, are always fond of meeting their countrymen on landing, and of encouraging them to take a share of grog or porter"—and, in effect, to squander the little capital they had carried overseas. Far more dangerous were the rapacious porters, lodging-house keepers, ticket brokers for inland travel, currency exchangers, and employment agents (sometimes pimps for local brothels) who infested the ports and fleeced the unwary. "People may think that if they get safe through Liverpool they are all right," warned a later emigrant, "but I can assure you that there is greater robberies done in New York on emigrants than there is in Liverpool." Back in Ireland such admonitions became part of rural folklore, dampening enthusiasm for the "land of promise"; in America, such experiences often initiated a long process of disillusionment: "I have met with so much deception since we have landed on the shores of the New World," lamented Francis Rankin, "that I am fearful of trusting [anyone]."[96]

Pre-Famine emigration was so heterogeneous in composition, and Jacksonian America so fluid and diverse, that Irish experiences in and responses to the New World were extremely varied. Ambitious entrepreneurs, skilled craftsmen, farm families rich and poor, illiterate laborers and servant girls brought a wide range of aptitudes and outlooks to a North American economy that was dynamic but highly unstable, to a society that was far more egalitarian yet also far more competitive and insecure than the one they had abandoned. Native Americans, themselves increasingly unsure of their country's future as economic growth created new problems of mass poverty and social instability, both welcomed the new arrivals as affirmations of American opportunity and regarded them with suspicion and hostility as harbingers of disorder and as threats to already-eroding traditional values. The rapid commercialization of American agriculture, the mushrooming growth of old seaports and new inland cities, the beginnings of industrialization: all fragmented an increasingly competitive American society along socioeconomic lines. Pre-Famine Irish emigrants, not—as later—overwhelmingly concentrated in any class or occupational groupings, were simultaneously drawn into native society on various levels and yet repelled when religious and ethnic distinctions assumed paramount importance. Consequently, their situation was ambivalent: often unable to achieve full assimilation as individuals, but too widely scattered, divided among themselves, and—with a few urban exceptions—insufficiently numerous to create their own society for self-protection and sustenance. Not until the early 1840s, on the eve of the Famine emigrations, did a new middle class of laymen and clerics emerge to found permanent institutions which could claim to speak to and for Irish-America.[97]

Protestant and Anglicized Catholic Irishmen who possessed capital, education, marketable skills, and strong ambitions for upward mobility usually achieved the greatest degrees of material success and social acceptance overseas, especially if they arrived early in the period, when it seemed, as one Irishman reported, that "any industrious person can get work and may soon become independent." Before the financial panic of 1819 burst the bubble of republican optimism, expanding economic opportunities reinforced egalitarian idealism. "I went up to [a prospective employer] with my hat in my hand as humble as any Irishman," recalled the Ulsterman James Richey of his first experiences looking for work in America, "and asked him if he wanted a person of my description (put on yr hat said he, we are all a free people here   we all enjoy equal freedom & privilages)— he hesitated a little and said I believe I do . . . and we closed our bargain." Like many early emigrants with enterpreneurial backgrounds, Richey found employment in commerce and prospered by trading indiscriminately with peers and customers of native as well as of foreign birth. However, many other emigrants sought to recapture the "independence" eroding in Ireland by establishing themselves as farmers or self-employed artisans. "I have always told you," wrote the Belfast-born James Christie to his wife, while painfully clearing trees from his midwestern farm, "that it was for the sake of our children that I would take upon me the toils of a settlers life, and if God spares them, how much easier will it be for me to die, knowing that they will be independent . . . when I am gone   not as if working in a mill where when you die, it is likely you may leave a legacy of debt to your children, and the same eternal round of slavery which has been your own lot." The same motives drove the Catholic James McCleer to leave his job in a New England carpet factory and walk to Michigan, where he purchased forty acres of thin, marshy soil; life there was so hard and lonely that his wife abandoned the struggle and returned to Connecticut, but his sons were "All agreed in Keeping and staying on this place if Posible for we all think that it is Beter to have a home than to trust to a factory." Other artisans, such as the weaver John McBride and the machinist John Ard, did not desert their trades, but they labored and saved to purchase a little farmland to make them "more independent" of market fluctuations and employers' whims. It is impossible to determine what proportion of pre-Famine emigrants turned to farming on a full- or part-time basis: evidence from the Maritimes and Upper Canada indicates that most Protestant and many Catholic Irishmen engaged in agriculture, and a recent study of Irish canal workers in the United States corroborates impressionistic evidence that a substantial number of emigrants either rented or purchased farmland at some point in their lives. All that can be said with certainty is that the *pre-Famine* Irish-American experience, unlike that of later generations, was not still heavily rural—albeit increasingly urban by the 1830s and early 1840s.[98]

Emigrants who settled in ethnically homogeneous farming communities retained Irish customs compatible with new environments and the demands of American agriculture. Similarly, Irishmen in large cities whose primary socioeconomic or political ties were with fellow emigrants remained self-consciously or at least self-interestedly Irish. However, for many pre-Famine emigrants—especially those who lived in small towns and whose levels of education or skill enabled them to mix with Americans on equal terms—material attainments and social mingling caused a lessening of emotional identification with an often rejected homeland. "I am sure if I had stopped in Ireland till the end of my days I would not have had as much as I will have in a few years," wrote John McBride to his father in County Antrim; therefore, "now I give up all notion of seeing Ireland again, [for] what could I do . . . if I was at home with you—nothing." "I never was sorry for coming," declared another Ulster emigrant, "but ever shall be that I spent so many of my days in Ireland." Irish sojourners in North America such as Edward Talbot and Francis Wyse noted with mixed emotions that when their countrymen confronted new opportunities and exigencies, often "they arouse themselves from all their former and habitual indolence—doff the old man—put on the new," eventually "assume an appearance of importance, and [become] quite ashamed of their former unassuming manners and native customs." The speed with which some emigrants shed old habits and loyalties often surprised and offended newer arrivals and relatives still in Ireland. "George is quite and if possible far more than a Yankee," wrote one Ulsterman of a fellow emigrant; "you would scarcely know a word he speaks." Likewise, lamely apologizing for not having written home in seven years, William Gamble admitted that "when people comes to this country and gets into the way of making money they appear to overlook every object but that." Indeed, many emigrants even abandoned their most distinctive tribal characteristics: American revivalism often swept Irish Presbyterians and Anglicans into the ranks of Baptists, Methodists, and other evangelical sects; and many Catholics who settled far from priests and women of their own religion intermarried with native Protestants and joined their neighbors' churches.[99]

Moreover, for many emigrants an Irish identity seemed perfectly compatible with new loyalties, especially in the early nineteenth century, before religious and ethnic cleavages widened on both sides of the Atlantic. Catholic and radical Protestant emigrants found fellowship in a United States where "all possess a spirit of independence" and where "Jack is as good as his Master except he is [a] Negro." As late as 1843, Irish-Americans such as the liquor dealer Robert Smith saw no reason why political sentiments nurtured in the old country should not win hearty approval, even material rewards, in their adopted land: appointed weighmaster "through my oun merit" in the Philadelphia customhouse, Smith declared, "I owe it to the stand that I have taken in the political field   I am a Democrat out and out and takes the platform for the cause against monarchy and aristocracy   I am for free republick government." After all, wrote another Irish-American politician, "[n]o men Surely can better appreciate the value of Such institutions as this Republic is blest with as the . . . Irish Exiles who have a personal knowledge of the . . . Political and Sectarian bigotry . . . of the Old World." Irishmen who settled in British North America did not have to reconcile past and present allegiances. The Irish Protestants questioned by the Anglican traveler John Godley described Upper Canada as a "fine Protestant country" where Orangemen could have "a great walk on the twelfth"; and despite their clashes with hostile Protestant neighbors, the Catholic Munstermen settled by the British government on Canadian homesteads exclaimed, "[W]e are obligated to the King—God bless him!—for we have been taken from misery and want and put into independence and happiness." Of course, even successful emigrants sometimes found it "very hard to assimilate themselves to the habits manners customs & whims of another" country, and it was not unusual for a young man whose ambitions had driven him far from home and family to declare, "[T]here is scarce a night that I go to Bed but it costs me Tears when I think on Ireland." Nevertheless, material achievements usually obviated the pangs of homesickness. Thus, although the Irish-Canadian farmer William Radcliff admitted that occasionally "an *Irish* day of recollection, sinking the spirits down, down will occur," at such times all he had to do was "look at [his] rich land, unencumbered by rent or taxes, and ask [him]self, if I *were* back again, how could I command such certain *independence*."[100]

However, while North America was certainly a land of opportunity compared with Ireland, economic growth was uneven and halting, and many pre-Famine emigrants discovered that achieving "independence" in the New World was an extremely arduous, sometimes impossible task. "I am alarmed . . . that the Irish is so soft as to think that the[y] will get rich by coming to this country," warned Robert Smith in 1840, "for it is in one out of ten that you will find any improvement": an exaggeration of Irish-American poverty in general, but an accurate reflection of conditions during one of the two great depressions—of 1819–22 and 1837–44—which reduced many pre-Famine emigrants to want and distress. Moreover, the fruits of progress were unevenly distributed, and the native-born possessed inherent advantages over most newcomers. For example, as land values rose with the commercialization of American agriculture, prospective Irish farmers found it increasingly difficult to realize dreams of "purchasing an 'American Estate,'" and many who tried were "obliged to suffer great privations or incure heavy debts before their own labour can be productive"; "the generality of our farmers," reported an Irish visitor to Upper Canada, "are by no means the independent class of men they may be supposed to be." In addition, as industrialization began to erode skilled craftsmen's status and wages, many Irish artisans—unfortunately concentrated in dying or rapidly mechanizing trades such as handloom weaving and shoe-making—lived barely above subsistence level in such working-class slums as Philadelphia's Kensington district; the rise to wealth and political influence of some master craftsmen such as the boss weaver, saloonkeeper, and slumlord Hugh Clark of Philadelphia hardly softened the sting of exploitation suffered by his impoverished Irish pieceworkers. In general, Irish artisans found better conditions in small, inland towns than in major commercial centers, but an expanding network of canals and improved roads brought market fluctuations even to Watertown, New York, where by 1827 the cotton weaver John McBride was having increasing difficulties realizing his dream of homeownership.[101]

Most disadvantaged were the growing numbers of Irish emigrants without skills or education. The rise of a native bourgeoisie opened opportunities for Irish servant girls, and in western states such as Illinois successful emigrants continued to claim that "in this country no kind of Labour is considered disreputable." However, in eastern cities most Irish laborers suffered low wages, frequent unemployment, wretched housing, and—in the eyes of white Americans—social degradation to the level of the free Negroes, with whom they competed and fought bitterly for jobs and living space. Opportunities for upward mobility and property ownership lessened in an increasingly stratified society: "The Irish labourer very rarely attains independence," reported one European visitor, "changing only the nature of his toil, from the hackney coachman to the porter . . . or the hired drudge"; yet "[t]hey toil without ceasing," added another observer, "for it is the only stay between them and absolute want. . . . They are in very truth, . . . the 'hewers of wood and drawers of water.' . . ." Many lived nomadic lives constructing canals and roads or following the agricultural harvests; others settled, permanently or seasonally, in the "Little Dublins," "Paddy Towns," and other disease-ridden slums which disfigured the back alleys and shanty suburbs of many American cities. Their labor—when they had work—was backbreaking, their living conditions highly unsanitary; epidemics, such as cholera in 1832–33, frequently ravaged their quarters, and some observers believed that many perished shortly after arrival. "How often do we see such paragraphs in the paper," exclaimed one middle-class emigrant, "as an Irishman drowned—an Irishman crushed by a beam—an Irishman suffocated in a pit—an Irishman blown to atoms by a steam engine—ten, twenty Irishmen buried alive in the sinking of a bank—and other like casualties and perils to which honest Pat is constantly exposed, in the hard toils for his daily bread." However, many successful Irish-Americans were far less sympathetic to their destitute countrymen. In the century's early decades upper- and middle-class emigrants such as Mathew Carey and the United Irishmen William James Macneven and William Sampson had mixed confidently in native society while simultaneously expressing paternalistic concern for the Irish poor by founding emigrant-aid societies and other charities. However, in the 1820s and 1830s new middle-class arrivals and those who achieved success as house builders, real-estate speculators, shopkeepers, subcontractors on public works—in short, the nouveaux riches whom one older emigrant contemptuously characterized as "a mushroom aristocracy"—were still too insecure to be other than "vain and assuming" toward those they exploited and yet often despised as "the wicked, ignorant, profligate dregs of society." Indeed, it was hardly surprising that poverty and contempt often bred demoralization and that, as one emigrant wrote, some poor Irishmen "Begin to speckalate on some Idle Employ sooner than work   some to gamling   some to follow Women some others to hard Drinking   others to [crime] from whence the[y] are sentenced to the Cells and workhouse for which the[y] are A Disgrace to thire Contery and An Upcast to those that is well behaved." Nor was it remarkable if, as the Irish visitor Francis Wyse believed, "nine tenths of . . . this class of Irish who emigrate to the United States, would gladly return to their country and former homestead, however humble." "I onely wish that I had been sent to a trade while in Ireland," lamented one unhappy emigrant, for "it would [have] saved both Soul and body from Danger and it is good for them [without skills or capital] that never saw America."[102]

Often more than just lack of capital and skills hampered pre-Famine emigrants' hopes of achieving "independence," social acceptance, and contentment overseas. Nearly all contemporary observers made sharp distinctions between Protestant and Catholic Irish emigrants, suggesting that the attitudes and customs of many of the latter proved dysfunctional in their new environment. Even middle-class Catholic emigrants realized that something was wrong: often they advised their countrymen that none should leave home unless "qualified by a . . . disposition to do well . . . by dint of industry," and Irish-American newspaper editors repeatedly urged their readers to "take pattern by the Yankee . . . [and] imitate the energy, patience and prudence of his character." "Look to the Yankee as a model for self-improvement and economic progress," echoed the Connecticut woolen manufacturer John Ryan from Kilkenny. "If we could be seized with a *speculative discontent*," concluded another successful emigrant, "it would be the best thing in the world for us." However, the incessant, embarrassed repetition of such advice alone indicated that a large number of Catholic emigrants were less prepared than their Protestant countrymen to pass successfully what one Irish-American called their "second apprenticeship" in a strange land.[103]

According to contemporary testimony, too many Catholics emigrated "with bright but fallacious dreams of the wealth which they may in a short time easily acquire" in a mythical North America whose image in rural folklore had assumed arcadian dimensions and which had a reputation as a land where emigrants would *not* have to drastically alter customary ways in order to achieve "independence." After all, could they not anticipate "no end to their happiness in this land of sunshine and liberty—'flocks, herds, pigs and poultry, buttermilk and bees, and along with all this, no rint to pay, and the agent and middleman Bedamned, and to hell with the rackrent, and sure isn't it all true? didn't the schoolmaster read it in the Newspaper?' " As the Irish-born British consul T. C. Grattan observed, however, "The expectations of the new comer, romantic rather than reasonable, are too often cruelly checked in the first moments of his arrival." Farmers' sons seemed at least as susceptible to crushing disappointment as their lower-class countrymen, perhaps because of their "too great expectations" and social pretensions, which made them averse to manual labor. For example, Andrew Leary O'Brien, a "spoiled priest" from County Cork, admitted that despite his need for money "I still could not in my native & foolish pride go to hard work with & among those who were raised to work while I was not." "In the name of God," advised another emigrant, "let no respectable farmers' Sons . . . come here alone . . . no education will serve them when they have no trades. . . . they will weep." The disillusioning early experiences of William Lalor were in some respects typical of many pre-Famine emigrants who lacked previously established networks of Irish-American kinfolk: because of "my total ignorance of the ways, manners, customs, prices &c of this Country," Lalor wrote, "I got fooled out of all my money within three months after landing"; then he became sick, "by which I got into debt"; after recovering his health and paying his bills, Lalor made a fresh start but again lost his savings when a native American he had mistakenly trusted proved dishonest; then he begged vainly for money from home, "but when that failed it drove me almost reckless so that for a long time I cared very little what became of me"; by 1843 Lalor was reduced "(greatly against my will) to work on some canal or rail road" merely "for the purpose of earning Clothes" and food. Through perseverance and a fortunate marriage, Lalor eventually overcame these trials. However, he never regained any enthusiasm for his adopted country, and many others succumbed to early disappointments and became permanently "reckless" and impoverished.[104]

Other evidence suggests that many Catholic emigrants, conceiving "independence" in protocapitalistic terms, were less business minded, aggressive, and individualistic than was necessary to compete successfully in a Jacksonian America which idolized the semimythical "self-made" entrepreneur. Protestant as well as Catholic Irishmen often censured the crass materialism, "pride of the purse," and dishonesty in commercial transactions which seemed to characterize native society; the Protestant emigrant Joseph Willcocks even claimed that American parents "give their Children an Education to enable them to be Sharp as they call it and if a Youngster performs a Yankee trick, . . . that is a cheating trick, they say he will do well, there is no fear of him": such child-rearing tactics contrasted sharply with the submissive self-effacement enjoined by Irish parents. However, Catholic emigrants were especially critical of America's " 'go-a-head' system," perhaps because both official church teachings and traditional rural customs subordinated material attainment and individual initiative to spiritual and communal obligations. One middle-class emigrant complained that his countrymen were "too content to 'live from hand to mouth,' " but many Catholics agreed with an Irish schoolmaster in Pennsylvania who argued that "we should be content with a moderate share of the wealth of this world" and should "not be led away by avarice . . . in pursuit of shadows or of filthy trash." Most Irish artisans and laborers effectively expressed the same values in pre-industrial work habits which demon-

strated obvious disdain for the unremitting industry, efficiency, and punctuality demanded by native employers and foremen driven by the competitive pressures of an expanding market economy. Accustomed to sporadic,
seasonal work schedules, frequently interspersed with bouts of social drinking and unofficial holidays to attend wakes and weddings, Catholic emigrants often clashed with American bosses who, as one canal laborer complained, only "give you twenty-one minutes to eat / . . . scream, threaten,
and shout at you / While forcing you back to work."[105]

"I am . . . fully convinced," wrote a Catholic emigrant, "that the family that has a good comfortable way of living together or near each other
at home . . . in Ireland have more real heartfelt enjoyment in that home
than they ever can have by coming to this country *unless* they can bring
. . . plenty of money to . . . establish them on a farm." Again, the statement indicates the preeminence many Catholics gave to familial over individualistic considerations, as well as the attraction of traditional rural
life-styles. However, not only was farmland too expensive for many emigrants but some observers believed that the social isolation characteristic
of much American farm life was repugnant to Catholic countrymen's habits
and outlooks. The Irish were "a social, warmhearted people, with a natural
aversion to solitude or exclusion from society," claimed one emigrant;
they could not "retire into what they look on as a wilderness, and sit down
for life deprived of the society of friends and countrymen . . . which they
enjoy in [American] cities." Before emigrating from Ireland, regretted a
prosperous farmer in Missouri, "I could then go to a fair, or a wake, or a
dance, or I could spend the winter nights in a neighbour's house cracking
the jokes by the turf fire. If I had there but a sore head I would have a
neighbour within every hundred yards of me that would run to see me";
however, in America the farms were so far apart that "they calls them
neighbours that lives two or three miles off—och! the sorra take such neighbours." Indeed, for emigrants such as the Irish-speaker Pádraig Cúndún
the very physical characteristics as well as the loneliness of the American
countryside seemed strange and appalling. "There are no smooth plains,"
lamented Cúndún in one of his poems, "Only woods and trees and great
rough places / . . . Mountains, valleys, and misty regions" filled with
"Wild animals growling defiance / And poisonous snakes slithering in
venom"; even "The heavens rumbling, threatening / The air on fire and
the earth trembling / Thunderbolts in showers cast down to the road" made
a frightening contrast to the gentle, if perpetual, rain of his native land.
Although a sizable minority of pre-Famine Catholic emigrants did settle
on farms, such testimony perhaps helps explain why more did not follow
their example.[106]

"It may be safely observed," wrote T. C. Grattan, "that those Irishmen
who have thriven best in the United States are those who have taken an
independent stand, and, separating themselves from all clannish connexions, have worked their way alone." However, the emerging patterns of
Irish emigration made economic individualism increasingly difficult and,

for many emigrants, decidedly inappropriate. Prior to 1815 the great majority of Irish emigrants were either sufficiently affluent to pay their own passages or else "emigrated for nothing" as indentured servants and redemptioners. However, after that date the impulse to leave Ireland increased dramatically among those Irishmen too poor to finance emigration, while simultaneously the old traffic in indentured servants disappeared almost entirely. Thus, even when entire families were eager to emigrate, financial exigencies usually demanded that only one member—usually the son deemed most likely to succeed—be sent abroad initially, burdened with the obligation to earn enough money to finance the journeys and prepare a home for his parents and siblings. As early as 1816 a Dublin merchant testified that it was already the "general custom" for young men to emigrate first and "then, when they obtain a footing, send for the rest of the family." Likewise, the increasingly prevalent practice of impartible inheritance began to oblige permanent patterns of chain migration, as the first son or daughter to emigrate was duty-bound to send remittances and prepaid passage tickets to his or her other noninheriting siblings and, eventually, to nephews and nieces. By the early 1830s between one-sixth and one-half of the Irish emigrants leaving from Liverpool and the Ulster ports had received their tickets or passage money from America, and by 1840 over half of all Irish emigration was so financed. In addition, some of the money sent from the New World remained in Ireland, a pattern which became commonplace after mid-century: as an elderly woman in County Londonderry admitted, "Were it not that my son and daughter in America occasionally send me some small remittances out of their wages, I would be very badly off."[107]

The fact that a growing proportion of would-be emigrants were not only poor but also Catholic may have contributed to the emergence of chain migration. As was noted above, although purportedly eager to leave pre-Famine Ireland, Catholic peasants demanded "encouragement" to emigrate—both moral and financial—and also some "certainty" of their future in the form of promises of assistance after arrival. Although one emigrant wrote that he hoped "it was the Lord who put courage into my heart to leave Ireland," in a practical as well as a psychological sense, growing numbers of pre-Famine emigrants were more dependent on the relatives who had preceded them. When Irishmen at home failed to receive the expected advice and assistance, they often became sanctimoniously indignant: "How in the name of providence can a man that . . . is of Irish descent . . . shut himself up in a distant nation without showing his love for his friends?" demanded John Nowlan, a shop clerk in County Wexford, while begging passage money from his brother in Nova Scotia. Rural Catholics from traditional backgrounds were even more dependent on American relatives. They "cannot be made to understand that their own hands must build their fortune," lamented John Griffin, a Protestant convert in west Clare: "after all, it is but a natural feeling that of wishing to have some friends in a foreign land—but the great misfortune with our countrymen is that they are willing to depend on any one but themselves and want in a superlative degree the virtue of *Self reliance.*" Indeed, when emigrating twenty-five years earlier, Griffin's own brother had felt "how necessary" it was "to be near [one's] friends for advice" and comfort.[108]

The seeming paradox was that many of the most-successful and best-assimilated pre-Famine emigrants displayed much greater reluctance to "encourage" and assist their kinsmen and friends to emigrate than did the growing numbers of poor peasant arrivals. To be sure, during the eighteenth century and the first two decades of the nineteenth, the New World seemed such a paradise both economically and politically that Irish settlers, primarily Ulster Presbyterians, freely encouraged those at home to partake of America's bounty and freedom. "I wish all the inhabitants of Ireland were in the back woods of America," wrote David Robinson from Kentucky in 1817, "where they could obtain a sufficiency of every thing their heart would wish" on "the millions of uncultivated acres [which] would give employment to all them who wished it." However, after the panic of 1819 the letters written by many emigrants—particularly by Irish Protestants—changed significantly in tone, for their authors were aware that success in the United States was no longer so easily attainable and that their relatives and friends might encounter hardships and disappointments. Furthermore, with the simultaneous collapse of the indentured servant trade, poor would-be emigrants could no longer reach North America without relatives' assistance—assistance which many Irish-Americans found financially harder to give after 1819 and which newcomers were no longer legally obliged to repay. Moreover, the contemporary attrition of the apprenticeship system in America also reduced Irish-American craftsmen's incentives to bring out younger relatives (and when they did so still, the letters written by recipients of such aid often complained that their benefactors were increasingly exploitive). As a result, after about 1820 many Irish-Americans, particularly Protestants who conceptualized their own goals in terms of upward mobility, tried to avoid any personal responsibility for encouraging kinsmen or neighbors to emigrate, warning instead that the latter must have "determination," for they "might meet with many difficulties by coming here." Indeed, caution was a persistent refrain in their letters: for example, in 1826 Robert McClorg would not "advise any of [his] friends to come to this country . . . lest they might be disappointed in their expectations," and in 1831 Edward Robinson decided that he "need not say anything about any of [his] friends coming out to this country, because they might say [he] done wrong to them."[109]

The content and tone of these and similar letters indicate several things. First, it was obvious that the recipients of such missives usually did not *have* to emigrate out of poverty; for them leaving home was still more choice than economic imperative. Second, those who wrote the letters feared that their correspondents had unrealistic and "mistaken notion[s] of this country" and of how easily they might prosper there. Hence, the writers repeatedly warned that emigrants should "be fully resolved to take the world as it comes," for although "a great many think if they can only get to America all their trouble is done, . . . in fact it is only beginning." As James Carlisle later warned, "when a man leaves his home let him bring his views to their lowest standard and then he will be sure to meet with no disappointment." Third, these letter writers were not about to encourage emigration by people who might lack such realistic resolution and self-motivation, for they feared with reason that relatives or friends who emigrated with false expectations and succumbed to disappointments might both blame them personally and burden them financially. Most of these emigrants were simply evasive in their letters, but a few were brutally blunt. For instance, the Ulsterman John McBride would "encourage nobody" to join him in the United States: "don't give anyone letters of recommendation to me," he told his father, "for there are a great deal too many calls on me as it is; let them push their [own] fortune as I have done." "[T]he best freind is do for yourself," wrote another apostle of self-reliance. To be sure, such instrumental attitudes were not universal among Irish Protestant emigrants to pre-Famine America: Quakers, especially, maintained close family ties in the New World, and Ulster-American farmers assisted relatives more readily than their urbanized brethren did, knowing they could always feed and employ the newcomers as laborers on their holdings. Nevertheless, like their British counterparts, ambitious Irish Protestants seemed determined to achieve "independence" even at the sacrifice of the "ties of kindred." Unwilling to allow dependent relatives to retard their economic progress, they sent home long, detailed letters, full of information about America; however, they left their correspondents to interpret that information for themselves and to make their own decisions and financial arrangements as to emigration.[110]

By contrast, most Catholic emigrants were unwilling or unable to sever "clannish connexions" or deny obligations either to assist relatives at home or to bring them to America. The chains of remittances thus established not only enabled much, if not most, Catholic emigration before 1845 but after that date also provided the assistance desperately needed by those suffering from the Great Famine. "[D]ear Mother and Sister," wrote a typical Catholic emigrant from Philadelphia, "do not be fretting for I will have ye comfortable   as long as I can earn a dollar it will be yours." Indeed, although most contemporaries eulogized Irish-American Catholics' self-sacrifice, a few believed that their eagerness to encourage their relatives' emigration caused them to write home "exaggerated" letters which "represent the Country [as] more prosperous and their own exertions [as] more successful than they really are." However, the willingness of Catholic Irish emigrants to impede their own chances for "independence" by assisting kinsmen reflected not only the latter's need for American aid but also the fact that the emigrants themselves retained attitudes toward family and community at marked variance from those displayed by their more individualistic Protestant countrymen. For a still-traditionalist people, the maintenance of close relationships lessened the strangeness and insecurity

of life abroad, as they had cushioned the effects of poverty at home; moreover, they perpetuated comforting continuities between the two worlds.
For the same reasons, many Catholic emigrants also clung to archaic customs which further distinguished them from bourgeois Protestant cultures.
Although middle-class emigrants and Catholic clerics disclaimed and deplored, Irish peasants transplanted boisterous wakes and athletic contests,
faction fights and secret societies, to American cities and work sites. In the
1820s and 1830s British visitors noted with astonishment that the banks of
canals excavated by Irish laborers were congested with shanty towns which
bore a remarkable resemblance to peasant villages in Ireland: "each
shanty," wrote one observer, even "appeared to have those sterling Irish
comforts, a cow, a pig, and a 'praty garden.' " Whiskey drinking, encouraged by subcontractors to keep the Irish tractable, was common on public
works, as were vicious battles over employment and territory among rival
bands of workers from different parts of Ireland and between the Irish
generally and laborers of other nationalities. In cities Irish clannishness
found expression in Irish-American neighborhoods, street gangs, volunteer
fire companies, political clubs centered in Irish grogshops, and mob action
against non-Irish competitors. Middle-class emigrants often encouraged
Irish self-consciousness for political purposes, inventing the annual St.
Patrick's Day celebrations to express interclass ethnic solidarity and political
strength. Likewise, the Catholic church, although institutionally feeble until
after mid-century, promoted its own version of Irish separateness from native society, denouncing mixed marriages, "godless" public schools, and
other interfaith associations (especially trade unions) while simultaneously
condemning wakes and secret societies. As was noted earlier, emigrants
arriving in the 1830s and early 1840s were more aggressively Catholic and
nationalistic than their predecessors, which also created barriers to assimilation in an increasingly Anglophile and evangelical Protestant America. As
Francis Wyse observed of his fellow countrymen, "They carry with them,
in too many instances, . . . the prejudices and dislikes, engendered by
early associations," which make them "obnoxious to the native citizen."[111]
    An extreme but illustrative example of the cultural distance between
rural Irish and native American societies and worldviews was provided by
Pádraig Cúndún of east Cork, a monolingual Irish-speaker and poet who
emigrated around 1826. In the United States he worked on canals, saved
his earnings, and eventually purchased a small farm near Utica, New York.
On the one hand, he was proud of his achievements and wondered at the
"tragic and incomprehensible . . . stupidity" of countrymen who remained
in poverty at home. However, despite his material success, Cúndún was by
no means "modern" in his outlook. He admitted that he had never wanted
to emigrate and that

> the proverb applies to me which says: "Don't be hasty in complaining
> about fate, for in spite of what you think, things usually work out to your
> advantage." That's how it happened to me anyway, for a day never dawned

on me that I thought more sorrowful than the day I left Seanachoill—me and my large, poor family—to make our way far across the sea to an unknown land.

The tone of this passage—its view of life governed by an inscrutable fate and "explained" by traditional proverbs—is much different from that which typically appeared in letters written by Irish Protestants or Anglicized, middle-class Catholics. Furthermore, at bottom Cúndún was unhappy in America and never came to terms with his new environment. He expressed his sadness and alienation in his poems, lamenting that he could not write them as well as he wished, because "the depressing and harassing nature of the frightful, restless life I have here has made a mush of my mind." Indeed, many aspects of American life frightened and offended him, and his poems revealed his distaste for his adopted country and for native Americans, whom he considered "a malicious host" who "spend their lives in sin . . . until death rattles in their throats." His verses also exposed his bitterness toward the *Sasanaigh,* whom he held responsible for Ireland's afflictions and for his own emigration. Of course, in many respects Cúndún was an unusual pre-Famine emigrant; although scattered evidence suggests that some Catholic emigrants were bilingual, very few monolingual Irish-speakers left home before the Famine and those who did were rarely literate, let alone accomplished poets. Nevertheless, Cúndún's compositions reflected a worldview shared by many poor Catholics forced to emigrate by circumstances they regarded as beyond their control, or lured overseas by fabulous dreams, which, when they soured, caused them to lament with Cúndún, "[E]ven if I owned America, there's no place I know of under the sun I'd rather die than in Ireland."[112]

Even if Catholic Irishmen were eager to assimilate to American society, they often found it impossible to do so. In part, the gulf between native and Irish-Americans was a function of socioeconomic and spatial differentiation in a rapidly urbanizing and industrializing society. After 1819, relations became increasingly distant and antagonistic between an emergent, culturally dominant, native bourgeoisie and a working class which, although still predominantly American-born, included most Catholic Irish emigrants. Working-class spokesmen such as Mike Walsh of New York and John Ferrall of Philadelphia, whose Painite radicalism had been shaped by trade unionism prior to emigration, tried to forge workers' alliances across ethnic and religious barriers in defense of vanishing concepts of "independence" and social equality. Their greatest success occurred in Philadelphia in 1833–37 when the General Trades Union—led in part by Ferrall and the Irish cordwainer John Ryan—marshaled some fifty affiliates and over 10,000 Protestant and Catholic, native- and foreign-born workers in a series of successful strikes. In Kensington, Irish Catholic and Protestant handloom weavers united to compel Irish-born entrepreneurs such as Hugh Clark to pay better than starvation wages. However, the Philadelphia experience was unique, and even there working-class unity crumbled in the face of the severe depression of 1837–44 and the accompanying wave of Protestant revivalism and nativism which swept Catholic and Protestant workers into opposite and hostile camps. Of course, American nativism and anti-Catholicism were far older than the Republic itself; so, too, was a deep-seated prejudice against the Irish in particular. "This is an English colony," reminded Charles O'Conor, son of an exiled United Irishman, and its "people inherit from their ancestors the true Saxon contempt for everything Irish." In the nineteenth century's early decades a self-confident Jeffersonian republicanism had obscured those prejudices and embraced the '98 exiles and their largely Protestant followers. However, after the panic of 1819 the republican political consensus began to fragment and the emergent Jacksonian party system divided voters along ethnic and religious lines. As early as 1822 one United Irishman admitted that many Americans viewed the "poor Irish . . . as belonging to a race of savages," and in 1825 William Sampson felt compelled to counter a "fastidious spirit of criticism" by assuring the native-born that Irish emigrants posed no threat to their adopted country. Increasingly, the role of the Irish in American society became a moral and political issue, for the growing numbers of "low Irish" emigrants—poor, Catholic, often boisterous and disease-ridden—heightened all the tensions and anxieties which beset native Americans in the chaotic 1830s and 1840s. Because of their alien religion and peasant habits, all seemingly repugnant to native institutions and bourgeois ideals, Irish Catholics provided easily identifiable targets for middle-class reformers and beleaguered Protestant workers who joined ranks in a second Great Awakening to purge the United States of everything sinful and foreign. Protestant Irish emigrants, often already evangelized in the old country, deserted tenuous political and economic alliances with Irish Catholics and joined their American coreligionists in the Whig party or more overtly nativist associations. Irish Catholic workers, abandoned by their Protestant and native peers, had little alternative to increased reliance on the guidance and protection against nativism provided by Irish Democratic politicians and Catholic clerics, despite the fact that both often opposed the trade unions which were vital to Irish workers' hopes of material betterment. In British North America, Irish Catholics were not so isolated and besieged, for a large, restless Quebecois minority guaranteed a more pluralistic approach to political and social issues, and positioned Irish Catholics in a favorable, intermediate role between Canada's traditional antagonists. However, in the United States the native-Protestant/Irish-Catholic dichotomy was sharp and violent, exacerbated by the emigrants' own sectarian legacies. The sacking of the Charlestown (Boston) convent in 1834 and the great Kensington riots of 1844—both incidents ranging native and Irish Protestants against Irish "papists"—were only the most blatant examples of the religious and ethnic animosities permeating Jacksonian America.[113]

Reflecting on the charred ruins of Kensington, one emigrant exclaimed, "They are worse on the Catholics in this country than . . . they are in

Ireland." That was an exaggeration, for greater economic opportunities, social fluidity, an open political system, and an egalitarian rhetoric which obliged even the bigoted to distinguish individual achievement from ascribed group characteristics prevented the formation of the permanent and impermeable Protestant-Catholic division which prevailed at home. In America there were no legal barriers to Catholic Irish activities, in itself a fact which inspired native Protestant insecurity, and in retrospect it is arguable that the turmoil of the early and mid-nineteenth century represented the painful lurching of a hitherto relatively homogeneous society toward religious and ethnic pluralism. However, as Grattan observed, when a contemporary Irish Catholic emigrant found himself "slighted and despised" by what seemed, in effect, an *American* Protestant ascendancy, he naturally fell back "into the circle of his fellow countrymen." Although he did not entirely "cease to love America," he loved it now only "with a practical and business-like regard"; the social and emotional side of his nature turned back to Ireland, and once-eager emigrants as well as those who had left under duress became self-conscious, often self-pitying "exiles." "The difficulties that are incidental even to his improved condition," agreed Francis Wyse, "the disappointment of every extravagant notion with which he first set out, directs his mind with frequent yearnings to the land of his birth. . . ." "They curse the day they first saw America," wrote one emigrant of his unhappy countrymen; and "although some of them has acquired riches," added another, "it yealds no comfort to them." "I never knew till I left my home," lamented a third, "[h]ow dear it was to my soul." "Every night since I left Ireland," wrote Pádraig Cúndún, "I go home, it seems to me," in dreams; but when "I start awake" and see "it was only a worthless vision / I am sad and despondent."[114]

Such acute homesickness was common. Moreover, disappointments abroad encouraged a Catholic Irish propensity to avoid individual responsibility for innovative actions such as emigration and to fall back on communally acceptable "explanations" embedded in archaic historic and literary traditions and reinforced by modern Irish political rhetoric. When lonely or abused, wrote one emigrant, "then I would sit down and cry and curse him who *made* me leave home": perhaps his own father in truth, but a less likely target for Irish-American recrimination than the landlords, bailiffs, tithe proctors, and other Protestant figures who symbolized British oppression. These emotions formed the basis of popular support among struggling canal diggers and dock laborers for the first, faint stirrings of modern Irish-American nationalism when middle-class emigrants concluded that their own lack of social acceptance abroad stemmed from the degradation of their homeland. "A nation circumstanced as Ireland now is," complained the lawyer Charles O'Conor, "commands no respect from ordinary [Americans]. . . . To make Irish men, as a class, respectable in the eyes of their fellowmen, Ireland must arise from her present state and become a nation." Accordingly, in the late 1820s urban, middle-class Irish-Americans organized Friends of Ireland societies to push for Catholic emancipation, and in the early 1840s they created American repeal associations to aid O'Connell's campaign to restore Irish self-government. Like their counterparts at home, Irish-American leaders and newspaper editors solicited contributions through shopkeepers and priests, played on bitter memories of evictions and rack rents, resurrected the rhetorical imagery of exile, and commanded fealty to the cause of "suffering Erin" in communal and familial terms: "You will soon be called, fellow country men, for your assistance—you cannot—you must not refuse. . . . no Irishman, except a grovelling wretch, will refuse his contribution."[115]

However, compared with later nationalist movements, these early efforts were unimpressive, the amounts of money collected meager. In part, this was because as a cohesive entity "Irish-America" scarcely existed yet; it was still insufficiently urbanized, still divided by great distances and poor communications, riven by parochial and social conflicts. The Irish did not yet dominate American Catholicism, and in the early nineteenth century the church itself was weak and divided by struggles (e.g., the so-called trusteeship controversies) which pitted Irish against Irish as well as against clerics and laymen of other ethnic backgrounds. Likewise, the nationalist societies themselves were fractured by rivalries between "old" and "new" middle-class emigrants. Indeed, unlike the United Irish generation, many of the latter seemed primarily interested in using nationalist appeals for personal gain, to obscure intracommunal exploitation or to marshal Irish-American votes for pragmatic, domestic purposes; thus, during this period once-nativist Tammany Hall emerged as an ostentatious but cynical champion of Catholic rights and Irish freedom. The prominent role played by non-Irish politicians in the American repeal movement, as well as its quick collapse when O'Connell attacked American slavery, testified that Irish-America was not yet sufficiently populous or mature to sustain prolonged agitation without support from native institutions—nor perhaps sufficiently alienated to struggle and sacrifice for Ireland in the face of native indifference or disapproval.

The relative weakness of early Irish-American nationalism may have stemmed in part, from the heterogeneous composition and character of pre-Famine emigration. The apathy or hostility to nationalism of most new Protestant emigrants; the individualistic, pragmatic outlooks of many Anglicized Catholics; the increasingly negative attitudes of all Irish emigrants toward a decaying homeland, not yet adequately countered before their departures by sufficient exposure to or internalization of political "explanations" of emigration—coupled with the fact that a large proportion of pre-Famine emigrants *did* realize material aspirations in the New World: these factors predisposed many Irish-Americans to a relative indifference toward nationalist activities, which diverted time and energy from personal endeavors and threatened to expose them to native disapproval. Furthermore, when leaders like O'Conor merely hoped that Irish-American nationalism would teach "the native American . . . the true character of the natives of Ireland" and thus effect a "closer and well constituted amalgamation of the native and adopted citizens," the grievances and longings of emigrants such as Cúndún and Lalor who *did* feel like exiles abroad were left without an adequate or sympathetic expression. Nevertheless, a pattern had been established, drawing upon and feeding Irish bitterness and American disillusion, and although the unwashed hordes of Famine emigrants would at first overwhelm and appall the Irish already settled abroad, the latter's efforts to provide relief to their stricken homeland would further strengthen Irish-American unity and self-consciousness, while the anger and sorrow of the new arrivals would fuel nationalist fires and fill nationalist coffers for the rest of the century.

7

"Revenge for Skibbereen": The Great Famine and Irish Emigration, 1845–1855

Between 1845 and 1855 the prophesied "Distruction" of Ireland became a reality. From the summer of 1845 through the early 1850s, every harvest of potatoes—practically the only food for most of the island's inhabitants—failed totally or partially, resulting in perhaps a million deaths and precipitating the exodus of another 1.8 million people to North America. Although Irish emigration had increased steadily in the preceding decades, it is unlikely that more than a third that number would have departed in 1845–55 had the social catastrophe caused by the potato blight not occurred. As starvation and disease devastated Ireland, thousands of panic-stricken people embraced emigration as their only escape from destitution and death. A large proportion were poor smallholders, cottiers, and laborers, often Irish-speakers or their children—fugitives from a Gaelic-peasant culture which they might not have abandoned under ordinary circumstances; indeed, many were literally driven from the land as proprietors and strong farmers seized the opportunity to evict thousands of demoralized paupers. Other emigrants, more Anglicized and less poorly circumstanced, regarded blight, famine, and crushing poor rates as final proofs that it was fruitless to remain longer in the hope that Ireland would eventually recover from her long postwar depression. Some Irish Protestants regarded the Famine as God's chastisement of their enemies, while for Catholic peasants the millennial visions inspired by Daniel O'Connell dissipated in the nightmarish realities of mass starvation and epidemic disease. O'Connell himself, decrepit and senile, made a last, pathetic appearance in Parliament to beg assistance for his stricken people. Afterward he departed, dying en route to Rome, leaving behind dissension and demoralization among his former followers. In 1848 one faction, the group of intellectuals and professionals known as Young Ireland, attempted a futile revolt against British rule which ended quickly and ingloriously in a Tipperary cabbage patch. The leaders escaped to the United States or were banished to Australia, eventually joining their comrades in America, but their active adherents were so few that the 1848 "rising"—unlike the bloody defeats of 1798—provided almost no additional stimulus to an emigration that was already massive. However, the Young Irelanders' rhetoric and revolutionary gesture politicized the Famine experience, while their own fate modernized and symbolized old traditions of emigration as exile caused by British oppression. Moreover, in the New World their cry for revolution and revenge inspired embittered and impoverished Irish-Americans to their greatest efforts to free Ireland and wreak vengeance for the horrors they had seen and suffered.[1]

In pre-Famine Ireland partial, even total, failures of potato harvests due to bad weather or plant diseases were common. However, successive annual failures were rare, and the blight that struck in 1845 was caused by a hitherto-unknown fungus, *Phytophthora infestans,* which appeared without warning and destroyed the potatoes so rapidly that it spread terror through the countryside. "Coming on the harvest time of the year 1845, the crops looked splendid," remembered an emigrant from west Munster; "but one fine morning in July there was a cry around that some blight had struck the potato stalks." The leaves turned black, crumbling into ashes when touched, and the very "air was laden with a sickly odor of decay, as if the hand of death had stricken the potato field, and . . . everything growing in it was rotten." Farmers and peasants tried desperately to arrest the disease by cutting off the blackened leaves and stalks, only to discover that the tubers had rotted in the ground. Initially, some thought they had escaped the blight, harvesting thousands of seemingly healthy potatoes which later decayed into inedible putridity. However, in 1845 the blight destroyed only 30 to 40 percent of the potato crop, often sparing some farmers' fields while devastating their neighbors'. As a result, although many suffered in 1845 and early 1846, few starved: relief measures were generally adequate, and country people consumed foodstuffs ordinarily sent to market, sold livestock, or pawned their clothes to purchase food. Nevertheless, their future depended upon a successful crop in 1846, and the mysteriousness of the blight caused widespread foreboding. "This country . . . is greatly alarmed on account of a disease in the Potatoe Crop," wrote a farmer's wife in County Tyrone; "we are feeling the effect of it but God knows but how it will end."[2]

By early August 1846 it was obvious the blight had returned, this time destroying almost the entire potato crop. In late July the temperance crusader Father Theobald Mathew journeyed from Cork to Dublin when the potato "bloomed in all the luxuriance of an abundant harvest," but on his return a week later he "beheld with sorrow one wide waste of putrifying vegetation. In many places the wretched people were seated on the fences of their decaying gardens, wringing their hands and wailing bitterly the destruction that had left them foodless." The blight's sudden, inexplicable recurrence seemed almost supernatural: one day "the potatoes were clean and good," remembered a peasant from Sligo, but that morning a mist rose up out of the sea, and you could hear a voice talking near a mile off across the stillness of the earth. It was the same . . . for three days or more; and then you could begin to see the tops of the stalks lying over as if the life was gone out of them. And that was the beginning of the great trouble and famine that destroyed Ireland.

The 1846 harvest was only 20 percent of its pre-Famine level, and a large proportion of the harvested tubers subsequently rotted. Now the blight afflicted the entire island: as a farmer in Sligo reported, "the potato crop is quite done away all over Ireland. . . . There is nothing expected here, only an immediate famine."[3]

In 1847 the blight abated, but although per-acre yields were high, the demoralized people had planted very few potatoes. Consequently, the harvest was only 10 percent of its 1844 volume, and the poor suffered horribly for lack of food. Unfortunately, the relative healthiness of the 1847 crop revived faith in the potato; in the spring of 1848, farmers and cottiers again sowed it extensively, to the exclusion of other crops. However, by August 1848 the blight had returned in full force, and when the fugitive rebel Michael Doheny fled across the Comeragh Mountains, the countryside below "appeared from sea to sea one mass of unvaried rottenness and decay." Next to 1846, 1848 witnessed the greatest incidence of blight, but disease continued to afflict the potatoes for six more years. In 1849 and throughout the early 1850s, potato harvests were less than 50 percent of their 1844 level: in 1850, farmers in County Meath reported "early potatoes blasted" as well as a failure of the wheat crop, and in Tyrone a farmer's wife wrote to her emigrant son that the "potatoes the[y] ar goaing away again and If you wer hear you woud wonder to see what has com on irland." In 1852 a woman in Queen's County lamented that the potatoes once more fell victim to "the same Distemper," and in 1854 she reported that "the times is Veri Bad as Befor [since] the Potaty Crop is missed as the Last nine years." Not until the following season could farmers such as Michael Donohoe of County Carlow "believe [that] old times are returning to us again."[4]

Except in eastern Ulster, where the poor subsisted largely on oatmeal, Ireland's small farmers, cottiers, and laborers survived almost exclusively on potatoes. Thus, by midsummer 1845 it was obvious that only extraordinary relief measures could avert wholesale starvation. However, although government and private charities made great efforts, relief was woefully insufficient. One problem was Ireland's lack of adequate facilities to meet the crisis. Even the eastern counties had few hospitals, and in the West they were almost nonexistent. Moreover, all the workhouses constructed since the passage of the Irish Poor Law in 1838 could accommodate merely 100,000 persons, and the charity they normally dispensed was harsh and limited by economic and ideological considerations: the law denied relief outside the workhouses, but admittance was as restricted and residence as punitive as their administrators could ensure. Such practices reflected partly the parsimony of landlords and other ratepayers who dominated the local boards of guardians, and partly the negative attitudes toward charity prevailing among British politicians and economists. Indeed, Charles Trevelyan, assistant secretary of the treasury and director of government relief, seemed more concerned that charity might demoralize the Irish than that starvation might kill them. Irish relief also became entangled in British politics and vitiated by anti-Irish prejudices. In 1845 and early 1846 Prime Minister Robert Peel urged the emergency in Ireland as a compelling reason to repeal the Corn Laws restricting food imports to Britain; his opponents countered by minimizing the Famine's dangers and by opposing Irish relief as unnecessary. Equally important, during the preceding decades Catholic spokesmen's seemingly endless recitals of Irish miseries had only alienated British public opinion. Thus, Trevelyan was convinced that Ireland's "great evil" was not famine but "the selfish, perverse and turbulent character of the people"; the abortive 1848 revolution merely provided Britons with further "proof" of Irish treachery and ingratitude. No doubt, British responses in 1845–55 would have been far more generous had famine threatened England's home counties instead of Munster and Connaught.[5]

Nevertheless, official relief and private charity from Britain did save many Irish lives. Ironically, although most Irish Catholics hated Robert Peel, the Tory politician who orchestrated O'Connell's downfall at Clontarf, the British government responded most effectively to Irish distress during his ministry, in 1845 and early 1846. Recognizing the workhouse system's inadequacy, Peel created a special relief commission authorized to purchase and distribute Indian corn from America, thus preventing local merchants from taking advantage of the crisis. Since thousands of Irish peasants had no cash to buy the corn from government depots, Peel's administration also established public works such as road building to employ the poor; by early 1846 the government was paying 10d. per day to 30,000 laborers, thus sustaining about 700,000 people. However, public works provided only a meager subsistence: according to one employee, laborers in County Sligo received merely "two stone of Indian meal for each days labour, to prolong the little money sent out by Government." Moreover, the people knew the ministry's motives were not entirely altruistic but designed "to keep the people from going out to the fields, to prevent slaughtering the cattle, which they are threatening very hard they will do before they starve." In addition, the starving Irish at first refused to eat Indian corn or "yellow male," thinking it poisonous; indeed, since many peasants had no idea how to prepare the corn, they suffered violent dysentery after consuming it raw or half-cooked. Nevertheless, as one farmer admitted, "only for all the Indian corn that is coming in from other countries the one half the population would starve."[6]

In general, Peel's relief measures were successful. However, his Whig successor as prime minister in mid-1846, Lord John Russell, was much less flexible in responding to Ireland's needs. Largely ignorant of Irish conditions and a rigid disciple of laissez-faire, Russell believed that his government should leave relief to the local workhouses and the purchase, importation, and distribution of food to private speculators and entrepreneurs. Accordingly, his administration initially closed all food depots except on the western seaboard, suspended public works, and forbade local relief committees to sell food at less than prevailing prices—which soon soared beyond the means of the suffering poor; in many areas for a time no food was available. Extensive distress soon obliged the Whigs to recommence public works, but for economy's sake each local project now required London's authorization, thus delaying relief in many districts while thousands perished of starvation. By March 1847 the new public works employed over 700,000 workers: however, since food prices were exorbitant, and since many malnourished laborers were too weak to earn full pay, employees often still could not purchase sufficient food for their families; many starved while waiting for their wages. In Rattibarren, County Sligo, laborers complained that "one pound of Indian meal for a full grown person" could scarcely sustain life, "but if we got all that we would be thankful." During the horrible winter of 1846–47 so many deaths occurred that the government was obliged to amend the Poor Law and allow public relief outside the workhouses. By mid-1847 some 2,000 relief committees were distributing free food, usually soup, to over three million Irish— roughly 40 percent of the population. Meanwhile the workhouses filled to overflowing with the starving and diseased. In western towns such as Tralee and Westport local workhouses held thousands of inmates above normal capacity, and by the Famine's end over a million people had spent some time enduring enormous mortality rates and all the horrors of Bedlam in Ireland's prisonlike charity institutions. Fortunately, private alms supplemented public relief. A few landlords such as Richard Martin of Connemara went bankrupt relieving their tenants; Catholic and Protestant clergymen provided material as well as spiritual sustenance; and Irish and British Quakers made extraordinary efforts to feed the poor, primarily through free soup kitchens. In addition, Irish-Americans sent millions of dollars in private remittances and nearly $1 million worth of foodstuffs; "were it not for the america provision," wrote one Irish woman, "half ireland was dead Long since."[7]

Despite every relief effort, the potato blight brought horrible distress to Ireland: "not all the exertions of man," wrote one woman, "have been able to stay the progress of *desolation*." One historian estimates that between 1.1 and 1.5 million persons died of starvation or famine-related disease, and contemporary observers were horrified by scenes of suffering unparalleled in recent European experience. For example, in 1846 the absentee landlord Nicholas Cummins found the cabins on his west Cork estate near Skibbereen inhabited by "famished and ghastly skeletons . . . such frightful spectres as no words can describe." "Their demonic yells are still ringing in my ears," Cummins later wrote, "and their horrible images are fixed upon my brain." In the north midlands another visitor "saw sights that will never wholly leave the eyes that beheld them, cowering wretches almost naked in the savage weather, prowling in turnip fields, and endeavouring to grub up roots . . . little children . . . their limbs fleshless, . . . their faces bloated yet wrinkled and of a pale greenish hue, . . . who would never, it was too plain, grow up to be men and women." In 1847 and 1848 the Quaker philanthropists Jonathan Pim, William Bennett, and Richard Webb reported similar horrors in west Connaught: in northwest Mayo, wrote Bennett, "[t]he scene was one and invariable, differing in little but the number of the sufferers. . . . It was my impression that *one-fourth* of those we saw were in a *dying state,* beyond the reach of any relief that could now be afforded; and many more would follow." In Queen's County as elsewhere, "many familyes . . . liv[ed] on the wild caribs of the fields"; others fed on grass, seaweed and shellfish, rotten potatoes, dead animals, even human corpses. Weakened by malnutrition, thousands fell victim to typhus or "black fever," scurvy, "famine dropsy," cholera, relapsing fever, and dysentery or the "bloody flux." Many simply barricaded themselves in their hovels and waited for death; others wandered about searching for food, spreading disease throughout the island. In towns such as Kenmare, wrote Bennett, "the poor people came in from the rural districts in such numbers, in the hopes of getting some relief, that it was utterly impossible to meet their most urgent exigencies, and therefore they came in literally *to die* . . . in the open streets, actually dying of starvation and fever within a stone's throw of the inn." "I cant let you know how we are suffring," wrote one desperate woman to her emigrant son, "unless you were in Starvation and want without freind or fellow to give you a Shilling But on my too bended Neese fresh and fasting I pray to god that you Nor one of yers may [neither] know Nor ever Suffer what we are Suffering At the present." Truly, one priest declared, "the Angel of death and desolation reigns triumphant in Ireland."[8]

However, death's angel was not impartial. Excess-mortality rates were highest in south Ulster, west Munster, and especially Connaught: areas inhabited by large numbers of petty subsistence farmers, cottiers, and laborers who often resided far from relief centers and who had little or no money to purchase food even when it was made available; in some western counties perhaps one out of five persons died, and most of the rest survived only on charity. Mortality was lower in the midlands and lowest of all in east Leinster and northeast Ulster, where cash economies prevailed and non-agricultural employment was common. Nevertheless, few areas escaped distress entirely: in central and eastern Ireland landless laborers died by the thousands and many comfortable farmers, artisans, and townspeople succumbed to diseases contracted from the lower classes; even in prosperous County Wexford, wrote one shopkeeper, "the young and old are dying as fast as they can bury them, [for] the fever is rageing here at such arate that there are in health in the morning knows not but in the Evening may have taken the infection." Eastern pockets of subsistence cultivators suffered as severely as did their peers in Connaught and west Munster: thus, the Wicklow Mountains, within sight of Dublin; the Irish-speaking districts of north Meath and Louth; and Rathlin Island, off the prosperous Antrim coast—all became virtual wastelands. Even some Protestant districts in eastern Ulster felt the Famine's impact: for example, although distress was slight on Islandmagee, County Antrim, only a few miles away in Antrim town "there is nearly every door closed [and] the people can scarcely live in it the whole cry of the people is the town and country is down." Although cash earned from linen weaving saved many Ulster families from starvation, in Tyrone turnips and cabbages were considered "luxuries," and in Armagh weavers labored day and night to exhaustion "in order, by any means, to procure food." The chronology of suffering also varied greatly from region to region. In east Connaught and the north midlands, most deaths occurred in the Famine's early years, before relief measures became effective. By contrast, in many southern counties wholesale evictions in 1849–50 ensured continued high death rates: thus, in mid-1849 a physician in Clare reported that "still the numbers of poor are daily increasing [and] Each year is worse than the last"; a year later a poor widow in Kilkenny County lamented, "[T]his is the poorest prospect of a winter that ever I had Sence I Began the world without house Nor home . . . Nor a Bit of food to eat." By the early 1850s "famine's wasting breath" had spent its strength, but witnesses in the south midlands reported as late as 1853 hat unemployed laborers were still "prowling about as usual, looking for a turnip, or something to eat" to prevent starvation.[9]

The potato blight was unavoidable, but the Great Famine was largely the result of Ireland's colonial status and grossly inequitable social system. Underrepresented and outnumbered at Westminster, Irish MPs could only beg relief from English ministers who often knew little and cared less about Ireland's condition; although an autonomous Irish parliament would not have been O'Connell's promised panacea for Irish ills, a native legislature would surely have been more responsive to its constituents' distress. The continued exportation of Ireland's grain, cattle, and other foodstuffs to feed British markets while the Irish perished from hunger was an especially poignant example of Ireland's political and economic subservience to British interests; although the exported food could not have compensated for more than a small proportion of the destroyed potato crop, its retention for home consumption might have saved several hundred thousand lives in the dreadful winter of 1846–47, between the exhaustion of the last potatoes and the arrival of new shipments of American meal. Another example of a colonial society's weakness in dealing with crisis was the distracting and debilitating controversy between Irish Protestant and Catholic clergymen over the allocation of famine relief. Protestant philanthropists charged that some priests, especially in western dioceses, were "plundering avaricious Wretch[es]" who misappropriated relief funds or ran away from their stricken parishioners. Catholics countered that Protestant missionaries were proselytizing the starving poor, giving free soup only in return for recantations of "popery." In fact, most clergymen of all denominations labored nobly and disinterestedly in the face of appalling difficulties. Although some conversions did occur, as might be expected in a time of profound social trauma, the virulent controversy over proselytism or "souperism" largely reflected the ongoing contest for religious and political supremacy over a famished people who could scarcely afford such diversionary strife.[10]

Irish colonialism's most lethal legacy was a predominantly alien landlord class which, despite individual instances of benevolence, did little to alleviate and much to exacerbate the crisis. For thirty years prior to the Famine, Irish landlords had striven against popular opposition to rationalize their estates by consolidating farms and evicting insolvent or "superfluous" tenants; the potato blight now provided unique opportunities and added incentives to carry out their designs. By mid-1846, thousands of tenants were in arrears: middling and small farmers could stave off hunger by consuming grain and livestock formerly sent to market, but then they had no money to pay their rents; even large farmers and middlemen frequently fell into arrears as subtenants defaulted, taxes increased, and grain and cattle prices plummeted after the repeal of the Corn Laws. In general, landlords refused to grant abatements, responding instead with distraining orders and eviction notices. Moreover, since proprietors were liable for poor rates on all holdings valued at £4 or less, the Famine gave them an additional compelling reason to clear their estates of pauper tenants and cottiers; consequently, as poor rates soared after 1847—sometimes exceeding the annual rental of entire baronies—so did the numbers of evictions. In mid-1847 Parliament further stimulated clearances by adding the infamous "Gregory clause" to the amended Poor Law. The clause, named for the Irish landlord who proposed it, forbade public relief to any household head who held a quarter-acre or more of land and refused to relinquish possession to his proprietor. Although many peasants tried to evade the law, and some chose to die rather than forfeit their holdings, thousands acquiesced to prevent starvation; after all, evasion was nearly impossible when local Poor Law boards, dominated by landlords or their agents, applied the clause even more ruthlessly than Parliament had intended, often denying relief to wives and children of farmers who refused to give up their land. In all, between 1846 and 1855 perhaps half a million or more persons suffered eviction from their homes, often under especially heartless and brutal circumstances: "All Haggard, half-naked, houseless, hungry, and Clamorous for help" was Richard Webb's description of those evicted "in the depths of Winter" from the Bingham estates in County Mayo; "they crowded into the neighbouring Villages, and filled them with fever and dysentery." Clearances were most common in Munster, Connaught, and north Leinster, but even in County Wexford, one priest reported, "though we are . . . partially exempt from the calamitous suffering of the West of Ireland, we every day behold the cottages of the Poor levelled in the ground, & their inmates sent adrift on the World." Some evicted tenants found new holdings elsewhere; others lingered in the ruins of their leveled cabins until driven away by force; many squatted by the roadsides, burrowing in ditches or erecting rude huts or "sheelings" made of turf and branches; some gave up and entered the workhouses; thousands died of hunger, fever, and exposure. "[W]e are all without a place to lea our head," wrote one of the more fortunate, "And this day we are without a Bit to eat and I wood Be Dead long go only for two Nebours that ofen gives me A Bit for god Sake But little ever I thought that it wood come to my turn to Beg Nomore."[11]

Under such circumstances it was natural that Irish nationalists and clerics portrayed the Catholic community during the Famine as united in suffering at the hands of an avaricious Ascendancy. However, the potato blight also exposed and exacerbated the social divisions *within* Catholic Ireland, and many of the hardships poor Catholics endured came at the hands of their more fortunate coreligionists. Catholic landlords were no more indulgent toward tenants than were Protestant proprietors; indeed, to "a *Catholic* landlord in Tipperary belongs the credit of inventing a machine for the cheaper and more expeditious unroofing and demolishing of tenants' homes." Catholic merchants in cities such as Cork made fortunes speculating in foodstuffs, while in the countryside Catholic shopkeepers and usurers charged extortionate prices and interest rates and showed little reluctance to take starving debtors to court. Regardless of their members' religious affiliation, local relief committees were often negligent or corrupt: in County Mayo, one emigrant remembered, they "received supplies for distribution, favored their friends, and often sold them for their own interests." Cork city's Catholic mayor economized on relief by ordering his magistrates to drive rural refugees from the town; and in rural districts such as north Leitrim many farmers refused to pay poor rates, complaining that outdoor relief gave their laborers "an encouragement to the vice of idleness." Of course, many farmers were desperate, squeezed between demands for rent, threats of eviction, and crushing poor rates on the one hand, and the plights of their poorer neighbors and starving dependents on the other; given the increasing nuclear familism and interclass hostility which had accompanied commercialization in the pre-Famine decades, it was hardly surprising that in a crisis situation most tenants acted to save themselves regardless of the social consequences. Moreover, some tenants even encouraged, if only by their silence, the evictions of neighbors and kinsmen, knowing or hoping their own holdings would be enlarged in consequence; indeed, as one witness testified, many small and middling farmers were ejected "to satisfy the greed of some covetous neighbour who wanted to make room for his sheep and bullocks." Naturally, subtenants fared worse than leaseholders, and it is likely that a large proportion of evicted farmers were sublessees dispossessed not by Protestant landowners but by Catholic graziers and strong farmers who sought thereby both to commercialize land use and to avoid paying poor rates for the maintenance of their former subtenants.[12]

Laborers and cottiers experienced the greatest cruelties—again, usually from employers of their own religion. Farmer-laborer relations had been strained for decades, and the Famine shattered them entirely. Unwilling or unable to feed or employ them, farmers evicted cottiers and discharged laborers and farm servants by the thousands, relying instead on family labor or machinery to work their holdings. "[D]istress stares us in the face more grim than ever," cried laborers in County Sligo, "for we have no sign of employment [since] the farmers is not keeping either boy or girl or workman they can avoid, but are doing the work by their families, though they are not half doing it." In addition, farmers reacted to the repeal of the Corn Laws by accelerating the pre-Famine trend from tillage to pasture farming, thus further reducing their need for labor. As early as 1846 many farmers were refusing to let ground in conacre unless laborers paid at least half the rent in advance—which few could do unless they sold their remaining livestock. Indeed, the Famine witnessed a wholesale transfer of livestock from the poorer to the more affluent sectors of rural society: usually through sales spurred by desperation, but often through seizures for arrears. As for the abandoned, homeless laborers and cottiers, the more fortunate survived the horrors of the workhouse or kept alive on the pittance wages paid by public-works contractors; however, hundreds of thousands perished of hunger and disease. "In times past," recalled one famished worker, "the poor of this country had large gardens of potatoes, and as much conacre as supported them for nearly the whole year"; but now, he lamented, "there are thousands and tens of thousands that has not a cabbage plant in the ground." "I fear the curse of the Almighty will come heavier on this country," he concluded, "the way they are treating the poor."[13]

However, when Famine abated in Ireland, middling and strong farmers, particularly the graziers, found themselves less accursed by God than singularly blessed by the decimation of the less fortunate and the consequent radical restructuring of Irish agriculture. The table below shows the changes that took place between 1845 and 1851.

Number of:	Percentage Change in 1845–51:
Landholdings above 30 acres in size	+16.5%
Landholdings above 15 acres	+ 5.0%
Landholdings between 5 and 15 acres	−38.0%
Landholdings between 1 and 5 acres	−52.0%
All landholdings above 1 acre	−10.0%
Landholdings not exceeding 1 acre	−48.0%
Landless laborers	−28.5%

Put another way, in 1845, farms over fifteen acres and over thirty acres constituted a mere 36 percent and 17 percent, respectively, of all tenancies; however, by 1851 the comparable proportions were 45 percent and 23 percent, and by 1861 they were 49 percent and 26 percent. In short, as a result of death, emigration, eviction, and ruthless consolidation of small-holdings and cottiers' plots, Ireland's commercial farming sector had by the mid-1850s inherited much of the land formerly held by those who before the Famine had struggled tenaciously to retain it for subsistence. In addition, the strong farmers and graziers also inherited the lion's share of the country's valuable livestock: between 1841 and 1861, farmers with thirty or more acres increased their share of Ireland's farm animals from 50 percent to 67 percent. In the same period the total numbers of cattle and sheep increased by 86 percent and 69 percent, respectively, as landlords and graziers transformed their former tenants' and neighbors' tillage lands into pastures and sheep walks. By contrast, the number of pigs—once the sole possessions of cottiers and smallholders—declined with their owners by 22 percent.[14]

In the Famine's early years the first signs of such exploitation engendered familiar patterns of violent social protest as the rural lower classes strove to prevent evictions and to impose price and wage controls on traders and farmers. In 1845–46 food riots were common: crowds descended on towns and poorhouses demanding food or work; when disappointed, they sacked bread shops, provision stores, grain mills, and carts or ships laden with food for export. In Cavan tenants used force to intimidate landlords, in Cork cottiers demanded cash wages, and in Clare smallholders and laborers combined to prevent rich farmers from selling their corn out of the county. However, such activities presumed a degree of social cohesion among the disadvantaged which disintegrated rapidly as the Famine entered its third year. By mid-1847 the peasants were too famished and demoralized to riot or resist eviction; secret societies dissolved and protest degenerated into furtive food stealing, which became so common that farmers mounted armed guards over their herds and fields and demanded that the courts mete out draconian punishments to starving offenders who were often quite willing to exchange the probability of death in Ireland for the certainty of seven to fifteen years in an Australian penal colony. There were numerous other indices of social demoralization. Before the crisis the Irish poor had been remarkable for their abhorrence of the workhouse and their adherence to Father Mathew's temperance pledge: however, the Famine destroyed the peasantry's resistance to the former and fidelity to the latter, and by 1848 Richard Webb could lament, "The good old custom of being drunk on the way home from fair and market is reviving. . . . During my stay in Connaught I saw more whiskey punch made and swallowed than I had seen . . . for the last twenty years." Traditional rural hospitality also vanished, for "[w]hen *sauve qui peut* had resounded throughout a country for three years of alarm and disaster, human nature becomes contracted in its sympathies, and 'every one for himself' becomes a maxim of life and conduct. . . ." Petty rural jealousies, endemic but relatively harmless before the Famine, now had fatal implications: "dear patt," complained a starving widow in Kilkenny County, "Mr.

lowlor wood not give a penny for godSake if I died Dead on the Street Nor [to] one Belonging to me . . . [although her own] huspant Died in preason for det" instead of "Respectable and Desant." Even "the bonds of domestic affection were loosening under the pressure of want," testified one relief worker: reports were common of husbands deserting wives, of grown children turning their parents out on the roads, of fathers and mothers withholding food from offspring; "the parents have become hardened to such a degree, by a long Continuance of extreme distress and Starvation, that they are often not to be trusted with the food intended for their own children." Finally and perhaps most revealing, ancient rural customs surrounding death fell into disuse as the island degenerated into a vast charnel house. Prior to the Famine lavish wakes and funerals were cultural necessities, but by 1847 "there was such . . . hurry and dread on every person, they were burying people they had no hope of, and they with life [still] within them." Wakes disappeared from apathy and fear of contagion, and funerals—when held at all—were sparsely attended. "Many are brought into the workhouse when on the point of death, in order to obtain a parish coffin," wrote Jonathan Pim; but soon coffins and shrouds became impossible to supply, and the reusable "trap-coffin," with a hinged bottom, and the mass grave became ubiquitous. In short, by 1847–48 rural Ireland was in a state of social and moral collapse, and it was hardly surprising that some Catholic peasants responded to proselytizers' offers of food and spiritual assistance to remake the structure of their dying world.[15]

A poor potato harvest had always stimulated a rise in emigration during the following year; therefore, it was to be expected the potato blights commencing in 1845 would encourage a great increase in departures. Nevertheless, the volume of Famine emigration was astonishing: between 1845 and 1855 almost 1.5 million sailed to the United States; another 340,000 embarked for British North America; 200–300,000 settled permanently in Great Britain; and several thousand more went to Australia and elsewhere. In all, over 2.1 million Irish—about one-fourth of the island's pre-Famine population—went overseas; more people left Ireland in just eleven years than during the preceding two and one-half centuries. An entire generation virtually disappeared from the land: only one out of three Irishmen born about 1831 died at home of old age—in Munster only one out of four.[16]

Most Irish emigration normally occurred during spring or early summer, and so the first appearance of blight in late July 1845 had relatively little impact on that year's exodus. Nonetheless, almost 75,000 Irish, more than in any prior season, emigrated in 1845 despite discouraging reports of unemployment and nativism overseas; about 50,000 sailed to the United States, the remainder to Canada. Since the first crop failure was only partial, and since Irish countrymen—accustomed to periodic want—expected subsequent harvests to be plentiful, emigration during the first six months of 1846 was just slightly higher than average. However, the total failure of the 1846 crop had immediate repercussions, and by year's end nearly 106,000 persons had left Ireland, over 64 percent for the American Republic. The exodus now assumed the character of a precipitate flight: thousands risked the perils of a winter voyage, and many embarked without adequate provisions; testimony by emigrants and by contemporary observers suggests that the former were willing to take any chances "save that of remaining in Ireland," now regarded as a "doomed and starving island." This mass, indiscriminate rush to leave continued in 1847: indeed, departures more than doubled as over 214,000 embarked for North America—"running away from fever, and disease and hunger, with money scarcely sufficient to pay passage for and find food for the voyage." Over 117,000 emigrants sailed directly to the United States, but almost 98,000 of the very poorest took the cheaper route to the British provinces, overwhelming the unprepared authorities in Quebec and New Brunswick. Weakened by hunger and ravaged by disease, at least 30 percent of those bound for British North America and 9 percent of those sailing to the United States perished on the "coffin ships" or shortly after debarkation; 30–40,000 who survived the voyage to Canada went south to the American Republic, leaving behind the most helpless and destitute. As one historian has concluded, the 1847 exodus "bore all the marks of panic and hysteria"; it was less an emigration than a "headlong flight of refugees."[17]

In late 1847 and early 1848 the pace of departures slackened, but another total harvest failure that summer produced a tidal wave of panic-stricken emigrants which crested in 1851 and did not subside to pre-Famine levels until 1855. From 1848 to 1851, annual departures steadily increased from 177,000 to a peak of 245,000, slowly falling off thereafter, to 134,000 in 1854 and finally to a mere 63,000 in 1855. However, after 1848 the proportions of emigrants sailing annually to British North America ranged only between 10 and 15 percent—compared with 45 percent in 1847—a sign that the flood of the most destitute had abated. After the crop failure of 1848, farmers who had weathered earlier blights now became convinced that Ireland was hopeless and joined the lower classes in "feeling that come what might, 'they could not be worse off in America.' " Disheartened by bad harvests and low prices, crushed by rents and poor rates, threatened with eviction and the workhouse, thousands of leaseholders gave up the struggle to survive at home. Many farmers emigrated on the proceeds of crop and livestock sales or on compensation from their landlords. However, a large proportion of late Famine emigrants—evicted farmers, cottiers, and laborers—financed departures with remittances which now poured into Ireland from relatives in North America. In the early 1850s many emigrants were wives and children, siblings and aged parents, who had been left behind with neighbors or in workhouses when impoverished families had been unable to finance more than one or two initial departures, usually of their strongest male members deemed most likely to survive and succeed overseas. Remember, "Dear patt," wrote one mother to her emigrant son, "what you promised me to take me and little dickey out for the honour of our lord Jasus christ and his Blessed Mother hurry and take us out of this . . . little Dickey longs and Sighs Both Night and morning untill he Sees . . . his two little Neises And Nephews And . . . the poor child Says I wood not Be hungary if I was Near them." In response to such pathetic pleas, Irish-Americans remitted home in 1850–55 an annual average of over £ 1.2 million, largely in an effort to reunite their relatives in the New World.[18]

To contemporary observers, the Famine emigration seemed unprecedented: a lemming-like march to the sea by Irishmen and -women of all classes and from all parts of the island. To a degree, however, the potato blight merely confirmed already-established patterns of pre-Famine emigration. For example, during the Famine as before, emigration rates were highest in south Ulster, east Connaught, and the Leinster midlands: that is, in districts which were poor but not so generally destitute that relatively few could afford passage overseas. Indeed, in most areas there seems to have been an inverse relation between rates of excess mortality and emigration; thus, population losses in County Cork's commercialized eastern baronies were due primarily to emigration, while in the western, subsistence-oriented regions they were largely the result of appalling mortality among smallholders and cottiers. Similarly, in County Londonderry emigration was greatest from the prosperous northern lowlands, and lowest from the mountainous southern parishes, where starvation and disease ravaged the inhabitants. Only north Connaught experienced extremely high rates of both mortality and emigration: perhaps because Leitrim, Roscommon, and Sligo contained a heterogeneous population of stock farmers who could afford to emigrate and impoverished laborers who could not; perhaps because Irish-speakers in western Mayo clung to their clachans until it was too late, while their peers in the eastern baronies sold their possessions and fled in time. In any case, in 1845–55 the regional patterns of pre-Famine emigration were still discernible.[19]

Moreover, although witnesses in North America frequently described all Famine emigrants as the dregs of humanity, their universally wretched appearance after long, often disease-ridden voyages disguised the fact that many were no more impoverished or unskilled than their immediate pre-Famine predecessors. Craftsmen and petty entrepreneurs constituted a sizable minority; since, as one woman reported, there was virtually "no earning no circulation of mony . . . no trade," tailors, shoemakers, and other artisans "who used to work for the small farmers . . . , and who now have no employment," followed their customers overseas. Strong and middling farmers were also prominent among those departing. In early 1846, contemporaries observed that "comfortable farmers, not the destitute," were leaving: "well-dressed countrymen . . . with baggage and sea store" crowded the Dublin docks, while young families with sufficient belongings to fill several carts and carrying £ 10 to £ 30 in cash followed the roads to Limerick and other ports. Even in "black '47" witnesses such as William Bennett testified, "The obvious strength of the country is departing," and newspapers lamented the loss of the "better class of our population"; "unfortunately for us," wrote a Quaker relief worker, "it is the industrious and enterprising who leave us, . . . in many cases taking out with them considerable sums of money. . . ." Indeed, between 1846 and 1851 the Irish withdrew from banks over £1.2 million in gold, "a large part of which must have gone in the pockets of emigrants." In the late 1840s and early 1850s, an increasing number of emigrants were relatively comfortable farmers fleeing from poor rates; many were "those whom one would wish to keep—farmers with 1 or £200 in their pockets." To amass such sums farmers sold the interest in their holdings and often absconded without paying debts or taxes: "They cut the corn on Sunday, sell it on Monday morning, and are off to America in the evening, leaving the wastelands behind them and the landlords without rent." The pragmatic calculations which such emigrants made were little different from those which had stimulated pre-Famine departures. After 1845 as before, craftsmen and entrepreneurs saw little reason to remain where "there's neither trade nor business of anny sort going on." For many artisans and farmers, the Famine was simply the last straw, final proof after three decades of depression that Ireland was irredeemable. For example, in 1847 an emigrant "came to the conclusion the Country had the dry rot and the sooner she was left to her fate the better for those who had the enterprise enough to leave"; when the potatoes failed twice in succession, he explained, "then the taste of Emigration set in in good earnest as the thinking portion of the country gave up hope of any improvement in their Condition." Comfortable farmers such as James Kiernan did not panic at the first or even the second bad harvest: in early 1847 Kiernan remained on his holding, although his neighbors were "hastening a ways out of the Kingdom"; he declared he would give the land one more try, but added, "If it refuses giving its subsistence this year, as it has done for the last two yrs, our family will strive to go to the New World. . . ." Even later, when emigration reached flood tide, it was still possible to distinguish between purposeful emigrants, "able and calculated to do well," and demoralized refugees who felt they had no alternative. "Let me go to the land of liberty. Let me see no more of the titheman and taxman," was the plea of an emigrant farmer whose desire to avoid pauperization—not fear of death by starvation—was the primary motivation of men of this class.[20]

By contrast, the very poorest Irish, who had barely scraped and begged their way through the pre-Famine decades, could afford to purchase neither sufficient food to stay alive nor passage to North America, the cost of which still ranged from £2 to £5. When the potato failed, the best these paupers could do to avoid death at home was flee to Great Britain in cattle boats and coal barges. Between 1845 and 1855 several hundred thousand of the most destitute Irish—"bringing pestilence on their backs, famine in their stomachs"—inundated British ports and settled permanently in the working-class slums and cellars of Glasgow, Liverpool, London, and other cities. According to frightened middle-class Britons, the migration consisted largely of "men, women, and children with scarcely as much clothing on them as was necessary for the purposes of decency, unable to speak a single word of the English language, and steeped, to all appearances in as hopeless barbarism as the aboriginal inhabitants of Australia." Although some re-emigrated to America as soon as they earned the fare, most either died of fever or found work in British factories and construction sites. By 1861 over 700,000 Irish-born lived in Great Britain, a 58 percent increase since the early 1840s.[21]

Nevertheless, even if comfortable farmers, shopkeepers, and artisans composed a substantial minority of the Famine exodus, and even if the most destitute Irish generally perished or fled to Britain, in many crucial respects the emigrants to North America in 1845–55 were significantly different from their pre-Famine predecessors. For example, statistical as well as impressionistic evidence indicates that Famine emigrants *were* generally poorer and less skilled than those who embarked before the potato blights. Although the Irish who arrived in the United States were reportedly far superior to those debarking in British North America, in 1846 the manifests of ships sailing to New York City classified 75 percent of their Irish passengers as laborers and servants (compared with 60 percent in 1836); of the rest only 12 percent were artisans, 9.5 percent farmers, and 2 percent businessmen or professionals. In the early 1850s the emigrants' lower-class composition became even more pronounced: between 1851 and 1855 Ireland's emigration commissioners reported that the proportion of laborers and servants among all overseas emigrants ranged from 79 percent to 90 percent, while craftsmen and farmers never constituted more than 11 percent and 8 percent, respectively. Moreover, many farmer emigrants—certainly a larger proportion than in any previous period—had suffered eviction, and in general more emigrants than ever before required financial assistance to cross the ocean. Usually, such help came from relatives at home or abroad. Family members often combined their earnings or borrowed to send one son or cousin to the New World; in the poorest districts groups of families banded together for the same purpose: thus, in 1850 a woman in County Meath reported that most of her relatives and neighbors had emigrated by such means, "assist[ing] one another until the[y] get all away." In turn, those who reached the New World were expected to bring out those left behind; indeed, the huge amount of remittances which poured into the stricken island probably financed the great majority of departures, particularly in the early 1850s. Other forms of assistance also existed. American grain ships sometimes carried away small groups of people who begged to be rescued from isolated districts such as Rathlin Island. Stowaways were not uncommon: in 1847 Thomas Garry, a Sligo beggar, hid on board an emigrant ship; he was discovered at sea, but his fellow passengers took pity and collected enough money to pay his fare. Public assistance was significant: in 1847 and 1849 Parliament amended the Irish Poor Law to allow workhouse guardians to finance the emigration of pauper inmates; in the early 1850s some 5,000 annually were sent to North America. Finally, between 1846 to 1855, landlords eager to clear their estates shipped over 50,000 former tenants and laborers across the Atlantic. Most so "assisted" received only their fares, a minority got provisions as well, and a very few got some "landing money." Destitution and disease rendered these emigrants particularly "miserable and helpless," and their wretched appearance shocked North American port officials. For example, although Major Denis Mahon boasted that he had generously spent some £14,000 sending former tenants from Roscommon to Canada, over 25 percent died at sea and the rest arrived at Quebec in conditions resembling those aboard slave ships.[22]

Not only were Famine emigrants generally poorer, less skilled, and more in need of charity than their predecessors, but they were also much less able to fend for themselves abroad. In 1831 an Irishman settled in upstate New York had warned, "[A]ny man that has a weak family . . . would do ill to come here, [and] I hope that no person will come here unless he is healthy. . . ." This was typical, sound advice, and both before and after the Famine the vast majority of Irish emigrants were young men and women, usually traveling alone or with a few siblings, cousins, or friends. However, a sampling from passenger lists of ships docking at New York during the Famine indicates that though the median age of Irish emigrants was only twenty-four (about the same as in previous decades), a much larger number were now traveling in family groups which included middle-aged women, the elderly, and very small children; in 1846, some 49 percent of the Irish shipped to New York in family groups, compared with 41 percent in 1836. This trend continued into the early 1850s, when 42 percent of all Irish emigrants were under twenty or over fifty years old. In addition, women played a larger part in the Famine exodus than in the 1820s and 1830s: among Irish sailing to New York in 1846, the sex ratio was only 1.75 males per female emigrant, compared with 2 to 1 a decade earlier. Moreover, a significant minority of Famine arrivals were permanently incapacitated by physical or mental disabilties, which often stemmed from malnutrition and associated diseases resulting from the potato blights. Among small children the long-term effects of nutritional deficiencies suffered prior to birth or in infancy were often not immediately apparent, but the infirmity of many adult emigrants was obvious. For instance, in 1849 a port official at St. Andrews, New Brunswick, recorded descriptions of some Irish arrivals: Patrick Driscoll was "aged, infirm, and very drunken"; Mary Murphy was an "aged, infirm, incorrigible termagent, [with] sore eyes, now stone blind"; Patrick Coughlin was "insane, now dead"; Ellen Daly was "subject to fits"; and so on through the lists. Perhaps mercifully, thousands so afflicted perished shortly after disembarking; however, the point is that such unusually high proportions of feeble, elderly, and under-aged emigrants meant that large numbers landed in North America unable to provide for themselves—particularly when, as often happened, family heads succumbed to disease, overwork, or industrial accidents overseas.[23]

Also, in terms of religious and cultural background, Famine emigrants differed significantly from their predecessors. Although the proportion of Catholic emigrants had risen steadily since the Napoleonic Wars, not since the seventeenth century had Catholics composed such an overwhelming majority of Irish emigrants as in 1845–55. Although Protestants formed about a quarter of Ireland's population, they probably accounted for no more than 10 percent of the Famine exodus. Most departing Protestants were smallholders and artisans from south Ulster, but perhaps as many as several thousand were only recent converts from Catholicism, "soupers" from mission stations in Connaught and west Munster, whose apostasy made them social outcasts among their former coreligionists. Most important, although in prior decades most Catholic emigrants had come from English-speaking or rapidly Anglicizing districts in eastern and central Ireland, the Famine exodus had a decidedly Gaelic character. Munster and Connaught, where in 1841 over half the inhabitants spoke Irish, contributed at least 50 percent of the Famine emigrants. About 40 percent came from Munster and from Galway, Mayo, and Sligo in Connaught, areas where a large majority were Irish-speakers. Almost 15 percent more left Leitrim and Roscommon in Connaught, Donegal in west Ulster, and Kilkenny and Louth in Leinster—counties where at least a fifth of the inhabitants spoke Irish. In short, about 54 percent of the Famine emigrants had lived in regions where Irish was still the majority, or at least a strong minority, language; in addition, large numbers also left south Ulster and Leinster counties such as Meath and Westmeath, where perhaps 10 percent spoke Irish. Unfortunately, it is impossible to determine precisely how many emigrants from each county were actually Irish-speakers. Common sense indicates that since Irish-speakers were concentrated among the poor and the elderly, they were more likely to perish or migrate to Great Britain than take ship for North America. Nevertheless, it seems certain that a very high proportion of transatlantic emigrants from some districts were Irish-speakers. Using the historical demographer S. H. Cousens's per-county estimates of Famine mortality and emigration rates, together with purposely low calculations of the proportions of Irish-speakers in selected counties in 1841, one can estimate that in the years 1845–51 perhaps 16 percent of the emigrants from Roscommon, 54 percent from Sligo, 74 percent from Cork, and over 90 percent of those leaving Galway, Mayo, and Clare were Irish-speakers. Hazarding the reasonable guess that half the emigrants from Connaught and Munster and 5 percent of the remainder spoke Irish, one then finds that perhaps a fourth to a third of all Famine emigrants—as many as half a million people—were Irish-speakers. Although these estimates are admittedly sketchy, the point is that in comparison with preceding decades a substantial proportion of those emigrating in 1845–55 regarded Irish as their primary, if not only, language. Combined with thousands of other emigrants just one or two generations removed from everyday use of Irish, these Irish-speakers gave Irish-America at mid-century a decidedly Gaelic cast.[24]

Most native Americans overlooked this phenomenon, as have subsequent historians, since Irish-speaking emigrants usually knew or quickly learned at least a little English, and since their Anglicized middle-class spokesmen were generally unwilling to admit the existence of linguistic barriers to full acceptance in American society. However, contemporary evidence substantiates the existence of a Gaelic America. During the late 1840s port officials occasionally remarked on the inability of entire shiploads of emigrants to speak English, while shipping agents touted some shipmasters' fluency in Irish as "a great advantage to Passengers." Likewise, in the early 1850s missionary priests and clerical fund-raisers from Ireland discovered that successful efforts among Irish-American railroad gangs, lead miners, and other laborers depended heavily upon an ability to preach and to administer sacraments in Irish; thus, in 1851 the Clare-born missionary Andrew Talty, after serving Irish construction workers in western Virginia, begged the headmaster of his training college in Dublin to "prevail on every [priest] Coming to this Country to learn some Irish . . . and . . . retain carefully all of it they possess," for "I assure you the Irish wont think anything of them unless they know" the language. Irish-American politicians sometimes admitted the same need: in 1852 the Irish-born David Nagle of New York urged his party's leaders to approach Irish voters only through "[m]en who understand the Irish language and speak it fluently, as it is the language best understood and most applicable to touch the feelings of the Irish heart, and is held in reverence by the great mass of the Catholics located in the" eastern and midwestern states.[25]

Finally, the *motives* governing most Famine emigrants were qualitatively different from those which had inspired earlier departures. In the pre-Famine decades emigrants sought "independence," economic improvement, in a land fabled for opportunity and abundance. During the Famine, however, most emigrants aspired merely to survive: "all we want is to get out of Ireland," testified one group; "we must be better anywhere than here." Old hesitations based on traditional constraints and desires for "certainty" and "encouragement" vanished, and desperate panic fairly screams from the letters and petitions of would-be emigrants begging for assistance to escape the Famine's horrors: "pity our hard case," wrote Mary Rush of County Sligo to her father in Canada, "and do not leave us on the number of the starving poor. . . . For God's sake take us out of poverty, and don't let us die of the hunger." As one historian has written, the Famine departures were characterized by "a note of doom, an air of finality, a sense that a chapter in history has come decisively to a close." From all sides, reported William Bennett, came "expressions of despair . . . such as 'poor Ireland's done,'—'the country's gone forever,'—'it can never again recover.' " Likewise, contemporary ballads sang of death and despair, "For every hope is blighted / That bloomed when first we plighted / Our troth, and were united / *A gradh geal mo chroidhe!*" In short, as another composer lamented, 'twas not ambition but "the blackening of the potatoes / That drove us over the sea / To earn our pay in Baltimore."[26]

There were many indices of desperation which set the Famine emigrations apart from all others. Prior to 1845 most emigrants paid close attention to conditions overseas, sought the safest vessels available, and were reluctant to go unless they could take some capital above the costs of passage and provisions. However, during the Famine emigrants left in the face of discouraging reports; crowded aboard small, unseaworthy ships sailing from nearby but hitherto seldom-used ports such as Westport and Kinsale; embarked "without any money, and with scarcely food and clothing for the voyage"; and often braved the North Atlantic in midwinter, despite the known hazards—"Dear brother," declared one starving laborer, "if you send any thing no matter what part of the year it is with the help of God nothing will stop me of goin to you. . . ." Likewise, before the Famine smallholders, cottiers, and rundale cultivators, especially in the Irish-speaking West, had clung tenaciously to their scraps of land. Now, defeated and demoralized, they offered little resistance to eviction and fled by the thousands to the nearest ports—"a helpless crowd of crushed, dispirited peasants," Lady Wilde called them, "dulled by want, oppression, and despair," often speaking "no other language save the ancient tongue of the primitive Celt, through which no new light of thought has flashed for a thousand years." These men and women had resisted the lure of emigration during the darkest pre-Famine years, and it is unlikely many would have left home after 1845 had it not been for the catastrophe which engulfed them. For example, in 1836 the tenants on the Irvilloughter crown estate in County Galway had refused assistance to emigrate, but ten years later—reduced to eating nettles and diseased potatoes—they begged to be sent to America. Even the peasants' former reluctance to divide their families disappeared when the emigration of a husband or son might be the means of saving the rest from death in the doomed land.[27]

The note of despair pervaded emigration even among families far removed from poverty. For instance, John Solon's father, a strong farmer in east Mayo, initially prospered during the Famine by raising turnips and purchasing his poor neighbors' cattle; however, exhibiting a conscience more tender than that of many of his class, he was depressed by the surrounding destitution, and "being called on to attend from two to four funerals a day caused by fever and starvation . . . fixed his determination to leave the country." By the early 1850s hunger and fever had abated, but evictions continued on a massive scale and the people remained demoralized. "[O]ur fine country is abandoned by all the population," wrote a woman in County Meath in 1850: "the landlords sending them away from the ditch to the cradle . . . or out on the roads." "There is no rest for us here," she noted; "the few that remain on this place is in great need there is no person to employ them"; as for her own family, she wrote, "we were all ejected in March. . . . I think [we] will see you in America before long." Indeed, starvation, disease, and the enormous migrations which had already taken place so decimated many areas that their disheartened inhabitants often felt little desire to remain in what was now but a sorrowing

echo of a once-vibrant society. "The potatoes that failed," lamented one
ballad maker, "brought the nation to agony,

> The poorhouse bare, and the dreadful coffin ship.
> And in mountain graves do they in hundreds lie,
> By hunger taken to their beds of clay.

"There are very few boys left on our side of the country," sighed a woman
in County Wicklow; and "there will be few men soon for they are pouring
out in shoals to America." "[T]he farms that [were] in high life when you
were young," country folk despaired in letters to relatives overseas, "are
now in the poor house"; only "one ile of our Chapel would hold our Congregation on Sunday at present"—"very few to hear the word of God." The
Famine caused such chaos and sweeping change that, in a sense, many
Irish had lost all that meant "home" even before they emigrated. Thus,
when the cottier Edmund Ronayne recovered from the "black fever" which
killed all his relatives, he could scarcely recognize his village in southeast
Cork:

> Every house on our side of the street had been long since torn down,
> most of the people having died and a few managing in some way to go to
> America, but all were gone—their little homes and gardens were levelled,
> trees were planted where they once stood and a high stone wall built in
> front. Our house was the last, and now the landlord was anxious for me to
> leave.

As for thousands of his countrymen, the Famine had severed Ronayne
from his family, his community, even his Irish-speaking culture. Driven
away by circumstances beyond his control, Ronayne spent the rest of his
life wandering spiritually as well as physically through Ireland and North
America, searching for something irretrievably lost in the shambles of his
and his people's past.[28]

The Great Famine seared its survivors with vivid, imperishable memories. Fifty years later one Irishman in America clearly remembered how,
after the potatoes failed, the "weeds had full possession of the soil, and . . .
blossomed beautifully": their "yellow blossoms," he wrote, "rustled by the
gentle breeze, glistening in the sun, . . . made a picture in my mind that
often stands before me—a picture of Death's victory, with all Death's agents
decorating the fields with their baleful laurels." However, it is more difficult to ascertain how the Irish *interpreted* the Famine and its consequent
emigrations. As might be expected in a highly traditional, religiously based
society, one prevalent opinion was that the potato blight itself was God's
judgment on Ireland: "Divine Providence," declared one clergyman, "in its
inscrutable ways has again poured out upon us the vial of its wrath." Since
Irish Protestants generally suffered far less than Catholics, the former believed that God had "interposed his gracious providence to save his people

according to his promises"; thus, the Anglican middleman James Acheson of County Roscommon exulted, that "Popery and Rebellion [were] nearly crushed to pieces" by the Famine, so "we can now Raise our Ebenizer to the Lord and no man to make us afraid." Less self-righteous Irishmen of both religions described the catastrophe as God's "lamentable judgement": as a poor woman in Sligo exclaimed, "the scourge of God fell down in Ireland." Moreover, like the poets Feiritéir and Ó Bruadair in the seventeenth century, and Bishop O'Gallagher in the eighteenth, contemporary Catholic clerics, ballad composers, and peasants often interpreted the Famine as a scourge well deserved—"a calamity with which God wishes to purify . . . the Irish people," as the recently appointed Archbishop Paul Cullen of Armagh put it. For example, to an Irish-speaker from Connaught, blight and fever were "plagues" sent by an angry God to chastise Ireland's Catholics for "their wickedness and . . . animosity against one another." "Sin is the cause of all the woe that Erin's sons do undergo," declared the writer of an emigrants' song, specifically excoriating "the crime of Cain, that frequently our land does stain" as a result of interclass conflict and clerically condemned secret societies. Another composer attributed God's anger to religious indifference: "Oh! when bread did abound! 'Twas little we thought of Thee." Of course, the proper, propitiating response was repentance and renewed dependence on God's grace and clerical authority: "Like the Ninivites of old," sang one balladeer, "we all should join—in penitential works combine, / In hopes for to appease the wrath of Him that rules on high." Such attitudes help explain why more rural Catholics did not "take the soup" during the Famine and why they proved so unusually attentive to clerical admonitions in subsequent decades. They also help explain why country people did not respond more vigorously to the Young Irelanders' cries for rebellion in 1848: peasants whose traditional response to disaster was to petition—"O! King of Glory, . . . From bondage save us, and come to our aid"—made poor revolutionary material, thus enabling British officials to commend the peasants' "orderly and good conduct." Indeed, although letters written during the Famine by ordinary Irish countrymen often complained of individual injustices by landlords, farmers, and relief administrators, they rarely indicted the political *system* as responsible for the holocaust. In 1847–48 the American visitor Asenath Nicholson noted that the starving poor did not curse the government for their suffering but instead thanked God that the "kind English" sent them food; "were it not for the English government that sent all that American Corn," testified a grateful farmer, "there would not be 100 persons alive." Fatalism and passivity seemed especially characteristic of western Irish-speakers, who "melted away . . . like snow before the Sun": "They have made no battle for their lives," observed Richard Webb in County Mayo. "They have presented no resistance to the progress of pinching destitution, except an extraordinary amount of patient endurance. . . ."[29]

Like blight and disease, the massive Famine emigrations could also be regarded as God's will, especially by the devout. After all, wrote one priest,

[t]his Country . . . appears to be one, which the Almighty wishes all men instantly to leave. . . . During the whole course of my life up to the present time, death & exile would be to me equally acceptable, but from the horrors that surround me and seeing the continual tide of the emigration of my people, I occasionally indulge the thought of emigrating with them, and from my former repugnance to such a project sometimes think the thought must come from God.

Indeed, Catholic clerics such as Archbishop MacHale of Tuam quickly formulated a religious rationale for the exodus, explaining that the emigrants had a divine mission to "scatter . . . the blessing of the catholic religion over distant lands," which "will derive fresh accessions of light and virtue from this calamity." Of course, most Famine emigrants had more immediate, material concerns, but they, too, often seemed less bitter than relieved to get "out of this poverty Isle." Observers such as the Quaker philanthropist Jonathan Pim and the American traveler W. S. Balch remarked that "instead of the sorrow usual on leaving their native country," embarking emigrants expressed "nothing but joy at their escape, as if from a doomed land." "There's a curse on ould green Ireland," a poor Ulsterwoman told her children, "and we'll get out of it." The only evidence of "darkness and despair" at the parting scenes, testified Balch, appeared on the countenances of those left behind; the rest fled "like captives escaped from cruel bondage, cheered by the fancied prospect before them, of comfort and competence." American relief and remittances, combined with news of California gold strikes, only fed such fancies of an American arcadia, which contrasted dramatically with the death and poverty in Ireland. "Let Erin's sons and daughters fair now for the promised land prepare," sang one tragically deceptive ballad which pledged, "Employment it is plenty there, on beef and mutton you can fare," and "From five unto six dollars is your wages every day." Likewise, many letters written during the Famine expressed eagerness to leave "the Gulf of Miserary oppression Degradetion and Ruin of every Discription," and those abroad at least initially seemed grateful to reach a "plentyful Country where no man or woman ever Hungerd." *This Country,* I intend to be my home," wrote one Irishman from Ohio; "I have sufficient sense to know when I am well off I do not want to be a fellow sufferer in the ruins of Ireland." "I made a good escape out of it," declared another; "if I had not come the time I did I would have been an inmate of the poor House long before this." Those still in Ireland, who had delayed their departures too long and now lacked the means to emigrate, envied their relatives in North America and lamented their own procrastination. As a farmer's wife admitted to her emigrant niece, "we offin say you had good sucess to leave this unfortunate ireland [and] I often wiched I had gone with you."[30]

According to contemporary reports, even emigrants shipped overseas by landlords and Poor Law guardians were often "cheerful" and "most anxious to leave." Testimony from proprietors and workhouse officials was highly suspect, but statements by "assisted" emigrants themselves sometimes corroborated those of their benefactors. In 1847 a group of Connaught laborers begged their landlord to "be so charitable as to send us to America," promising in return to "bind ourselves to defend the Queen's Right in any place we are sent, and leave it on our children to do the same." Many assisted emigrants seemed grateful to those who sent them to "the best Country in the world," and despite their destitution and the degree of compulsion involved, at least some definitely profited from the change. For example, although Canadian authorities described the assisted emigrants from Lord Palmerston's Sligo estates as especially impoverished and miserable, those who survived quarantine earned enough in twelve months to remit nearly £2,000 to relatives at home. Similarly, in 1848, crown officials sent 253 paupers to Canada from a rundale village on the Boughill estate in County Galway; among them was Michael Byrne, a "very poor" and illiterate Irish-speaker, formerly the occupant of a cabin and a rood of land. Once in America, Byrne dictated a letter to "your Honour," the official who had organized the emigration, informing him, "I am now Employed in the rail road line earning 5s. a day. . . . And instead of being chained with poverty in Boughill I am crowned with glory"; "all the Emigrants of Boughill," he concluded, "send you their best respect and blessing." Byrne's experience was somewhat atypical, since emigration from crown estates proceeded with a minimum of suffering; however, many of the less fortunate "assisted" emigrants from Sir Robert Gore Booth's Sligo estates expressed equally grateful sentiments.[31]

Nevertheless, despite this wholesale and purportedly eager flight overseas, traditional resistance to emigration was still evident, especially among western Irish-speakers who could scarcely contemplate life beyond their parish boundaries. For example, when crown officials initiated assisted emigration from the Ballykilcline estate in County Roscommon, the tenants deluged them with pathetic, semiliterate petitions, pleading they be allowed to "die in the land of their forefathers and their birth." Likewise, relief workers in Cork and Galway expressed amazement that "those creatures called tenants" clung "to their huts with the greatest tenacity, and seem better pleased to perish in the ruins than surrender what they call their last hope of existence." As was noted earlier, many farmers and cottiers made extraordinary efforts to retain their holdings, even rejecting public relief when the Gregory clause presented them with a choice between life and land. In County Mayo, Richard Webb reported "instances in which Cottiers had buried potatoes, with the View of preserving them for Seed—and . . . had actually allowed members of their Families to perish of want and had Suffered the sorest extremities of hunger themselves, sooner than betray their cherished hoard." Moreover, many who did emigrate left reluctantly, not joyfully; for example, in 1847 Michael Foarde, a smallholder in County Sligo, petitioned his estate agent for sufficient compensation for his land and crops to enable him to emigrate—adding, however, that he "would never go if he could over come the Calamity that Surrounds the country." The Limerick landlord Francis Spaight, who sent over

2,000 former tenants to Canada, readily admitted, "I could not have got rid of them by any means, if it had not been for the failure of the potato crop." In addition, at least some emigrants' departures were strategically designed to enable families to retain holdings and survive *in* Ireland until the blight abated. For instance, when the Famine struck western Mayo, Michael and John O'Mally, brothers and subsistence farmers, sold a cow and went to the United States. Michael found work in a Pennsylvania coal mine and remitted his earnings to his wife and children; the money paid the rent while his family subsisted on shellfish and seaweed. After three years, when the potato crops recovered, Michael returned permanently to Ireland. His brother's family was less fortunate: John O'Mally disappeared in America without a trace, and his wife and children starved to death in their cabin.[32]

Despite their desperate situation, it would have been remarkable if at least some Irish countrymen had not regarded the Famine emigrations in traditional, negative terms: as *deoraí,* exile, compelled by forces beyond individual control. Indeed, given the unusually high proportion of emigrants who were Irish-speakers, evicted tenants, and others who probably would not have left home under ordinary circumstances, such attitudes were probably more widespread in 1845–55 than in any previous period. Moreover, although traditionalist countrymen could attribute blight and fever to God's inscrutable will, they fully understood that parsimonious and inequitable relief distribution, sweeping clearances of helpless paupers, and many consequent deaths and departures were due to human greed and cruelty. "No work of God's are these deeds accursed," declared the composer of *"Amhrán Na bPrátaí Dúbha"* (The Song of the Black Potatoes): "Oh pity the proud ones, all earth possessing," he warned, "That for these distresses must surely pay, / Oh, sad their fate, who the poor oppressing / Do richer grow by their moans each day." In addition, for decades prior to the Famine, Catholic nationalists, lay and clerical, had sought to broaden and modernize such traditional resentments by "explaining" all Irish grievances, including evictions and assisted emigration, as caused by landlord tyranny, Protestant malevolence, and British oppression.[33]

However, nationalism's impact on pre-Famine Ireland had been partial and uneven, never wholly supplanting the more parochial and intracommunal-conflict-oriented secret societies, and exerting little influence in Connaught and west Munster—home of many Famine casualties and emigrants. In addition, the early Famine years were so devastating and demoralizing that abstract national issues seemed virtually meaningless beside more-immediate, personal concerns of sheer survival. Moreover, the crisis itself often obscured sectarian and political divisions. When the "kind English" sent food which local Catholic relief committees misappropriated; when Protestant landlords publicly condemned Catholic strong farmers for turning their laborers and servants out on the roads; when Protestant missionaries gave soup to starving recipients whom Catholic clerics "earnestly emplore[d] the Almighty to take . . . to Himself [rather] than permit them to become apostates"; when, in the face of unprecedented misery and social dislocation, Archbishop Paul Cullen could declare that Ireland's greatest problem was "the schools system": then the strict lines which na- tionalists tried to draw between the people's "champions" and "enemies" sometimes became dangerously blurred. Thus, inchoate resentments at first remained vaguely focused, as in the ambiguous message of *"Amhrán Na bPrátaí Dúbha":* "the proud ones" were not identified as either Protes- tant landlords or Catholic graziers; nor was it clear whether their "sad . . . fate" would be the result of divine or human vengeance. In short, although the Famine and its emigrations did inspire some anger and resistance early on, such emotions were at first imperfectly assimilated to the sharp, ideal dichotomies of modern Catholic nationalism. "[G]azing hopelessly into in- finite darkness and despair . . . , stalking by with a fierce but vacant scowl," the famine-striken Irish, reported one observer, "realized that all this ought not to be, but knew not whom to blame."[34]

However, the Irish at home and abroad soon blamed England for their sufferings; by 1848 an American traveler noted that Irish countrymen set "all their misfortunes and misery . . . to the account of English interfer- ence—high rents, heavy taxes, potato rot, and all." Indeed, the Famine it- self became the ultimate symbol of British tyranny, while the mass flights of 1845–55 permanently enshrined the now-imperishable interpretation of emigration as exile forced by English oppression. In the post-Famine de- cades, observers as disparate as the nationalist politician John Francis Ma- guire and the unionist historian W. E. H. Lecky agreed that it was pri- marily the Famine evictions and emigrations that engendered "the savage hatred of England that animates great bodies of Irishmen on either side of the Atlantic." Even some nationalists found this depth of feeling remark- able: although Justin McCarthy regarded his people's "intense hostility to British rule" as a "very natural result of the famine," his fellow politician A. M. Sullivan wondered that "the burning memory of horrors . . . seems to overwhelm all other recollection, and the noble generosity of the En- glish people appears to be forgotten in a frenzy of reproach against the En- glish government."[35]

In a sense, such animosity was well founded in tradition and bitter ex- perience. Gaelic poets as well as contemporary nationalists had usually blamed the treacherous *Sasanaigh* for all Irish ills, and, as Sullivan himself admitted, "more prompt and competent action on the part of the ruling au- thorities might have considerably averted" the Famine's horrors. Most im- portant, the wholesale clearances of grieving paupers, carried out as they were under British laws and often enforced by British troops, inextricably linked the government to the cruelest actions of the Irish landlord class. However, subtler psychological processes were also at work. As one his- torian has noted, the disintegrations of personal relationships and the so- cial dislocations (including panic emigration) which occurred during the Famine reflected not just a failure of the potato crop but "a failure of morale as well." Already weakened by decades of commercialization and

Anglicization, many of the ties and constraints binding Irish Catholics together were dissolved by hunger and disease. Panicked and demoralized, often able to save themselves only at the expense of neighbors and kinsmen, desperate countryfolk frequently displayed what one observer called "the most unscrupulous mendecancy, knavery, cunning & falsehood." During and especially after the Famine, it was natural that those who survived the crisis would feel tremendous shame for such extensive violations of communal mores and that they would seek "explanations" for what had occurred which would project responsibility and resentment upon "outsiders." "*If* for our sins we pay this penalty," prayed an Irish-speaking balladeer, then "Open our hearts, that they may be cleansed"; however, such a burden was too enormous to be internalized entirely, even by the most devout. Thus, it was also natural that the Irish, faced with the failures of traditional predictive celebrations and secret societies to avert the catastrophe, turned more attentively to Catholic clerics and nationalist politicians who not only represented those modern, commercialized, and Anglicized sectors of Irish society which best survived the Famine but who also offered an embracing "explanation" for the crisis which obviated personal guilt, obscured intracommunal conflict, and generalized individual grievances into a powerful political and cultural weapon against the traditional antagonist. As a result, Catholic Ireland and Irish-America emerged from the Famine's terrible crucible more vehemently and unanimously opposed to Protestant England and its Irish representatives than ever before.[36]

At first, Famine and mass emigration had seemed beyond political interpretation, even by clerics and professional agitators. Many individual churchmen such as Father Mathew reluctantly accepted emigration as their people's only hope, rationalizing the exodus as God's plan to disseminate the faith. Lay nationalists were not only distracted by the extent of the crisis but also thrown into confusion and conflict by the early death of the Young Ireland spokesman Thomas Davis in 1845; by Daniel O'Connell's meandering policies, rapidly advancing senility, and eventual demise in 1847; and by internecine struggles for his mantle of leadership. However, by 1847–48 Catholic clerics and nationalists of all persuasions were beginning to question, then attack British actions toward Ireland, and to stigmatize Famine emigration as forced exile; for example, during this period Dublin's leading Catholic newspaper, the *Freeman's Journal,* moved from acquiescence in emigration to near-hysterical hostility. Among nationalists, Young Irelanders such as the Protestant firebrand John Mitchel were most violent in attributing Famine deaths and departures to British malevolence: in editorials and orations Mitchel and his peers raged at Irishmen so supine as to regard the Famine as "a visitation of Providence" instead of "a visitation of English landlordism—as great a curse to Ireland as if it was the archfiend himself had the government of the country." "The Almighty, indeed, sent the potato blight," Mitchel concluded, "but the English created the Famine." Young Ireland was a minority in its revolutionary response to the crisis, but by the early 1850s Catholic political and clerical opinion was virtually unanimous in blaming the British government for Irish suffering and in denouncing emigration as "a devilish plot to exile the bone and sinew of the country"—as a conspiracy formulated by Ireland's "hereditary oppressors . . . who have made the most beautiful island under the sun a land of skulls, or of ghastly spectres."[37]

The reasons for such attacks were both obvious and subtle. For decades all nationalists and most churchmen had believed and preached that Westminster was irrevocably opposed to Irish interests, that most Protestants were at best untrustworthy, and, as one priest declared, that "Landlordism is the Monster evil of Ireland." For such politically minded Irishmen, the government's niggardly relief measures, its failure to stem food exports or curb speculation, and its passage of the fateful Gregory clause not only corroborated preexisting suspicions but also seemed to form a pattern, not of mere indifference or incompetence but of systematic "extermination" and recolonization. Indeed, by 1848 the London *Times* and other leading British journals were supplying ostensible "proof" of the government's evil design by openly "embrac[ing] the idea that the Irish Famine, if properly availed of, would prove a great blessing"—a "valuable opportunity for settling the vexed question of Irish misery and discontent." The *Times* actually advocated the expulsion of impecunious Irish tenants and their replacement by "thrifty Scotch and scientific English farmers; men with means, men with modern ideas," who would pay higher rents, pay them punctually, and not agitate or join secret societies. Viewing the mass evictions and emigrations which followed the enactment of the Gregory clause, the *Times* positively exulted, "In a few years more, a Celtic Irishman will be as rare in Connemara as is the Red Indian on the shores of Manhattan." No wonder that dedicated nationalists such as Mitchel became filled with "a sacred wrath" against England and that ordinary Irishmen and Irish-Americans—who first learned of such callous statements through nationalist channels—soon became equally convinced that their sufferings were intentional, their emigration exile.[38]

However, the gathering nationalist/clerical outcry against England and emigration had sources other than genuine rage. A few radicals such as James Fintan Lalor and Mitchel understood that their people's helplessness and suffering had economic as well as political causes—simple repeal of the union would be insufficient; consequently, they advocated social revolution to destroy landlordism and redistribute Irish land to "a secure and independent agricultural peasantry." "Ireland her own," demanded Lalor, "from the sod to the sky. The soil of Ireland for the people of Ireland, to have and hold from God above who gave it." However, although such appeals accorded well with peasants' precapitalist notions, most Irish nationalists—whether Young Irelanders or more conservative O'Connellites—were thoroughly bourgeois in their reverence for property rights and fear of social upheaval. For example, the Catholic landlord Sir Thomas Wyse, once a leader in the struggle for Catholic emancipation, now urged the government to complete Ireland's "Permanent regeneration" by financing mass emigrations of "superfluous tenants." Likewise, Archbishop Cullen, obsessed with fear that "Civil war and revolutions destroy religion," was most concerned that "the clergy . . . be able to keep the people quiet" despite their sufferings. Even some Young Irelanders such as the journalist A. M. Sullivan privately regarded the Famine clearances as "unfortunately unavoidable" in an unquestioned capitalist context, and later rejoiced that the catastrophe had imprinted bourgeois habits of "Providence, forethought, economy . . . , and punctuality . . . on the sorely shattered nation." In short, institutional and class biases helped shape clerical and nationalist reactions to Famine and emigration. For instance, it may be significant that public criticisms of government policy and emigration became ubiquitous only in the Famine's latter years—*after* decimation of the lower classes—when once-comfortable tenants began to flee en masse from crushing poor rates and when the continued flood tide overseas began to seriously threaten Catholic strong farmers, shopkeepers, and clergymen with a loss of cheap labor, valuable customers, and devout parishioners. In general, the Catholic middle classes—always the backbone of constitutional nationalism—did not want rebellion, much less social revolution, and the primary function of their spokesmen's attacks on English misgovernment and emigration was not to inspire violence but to articulate popular outrage in ways that would reunite the remnants of the fractured Catholic "nation" behind bourgeois leadership and reconsolidate Catholic opinion against English "tyranny" to better realize the pragmatic middle-class and clerical goals which dominated Irish politics in the 1850s: legalization of tenant-right (a non-issue for cottiers and laborers); and church control over Catholic education. Of course, hegemony should not be equated with conscious conspiracy. In a commercialized, Anglicized Catholic society—now rapidly becoming more "modern" than ever, thanks to the deaths and departures of millions of lower-class traditionalists—it was only natural that middle-class laymen would identify the general welfare with their own and that churchmen would seek to marshal their parishioners against the renewed threat of proselytism. Moreover, the nationalist ideology formulated prior to the Famine had conceptualized an organic society which now could best be reconstituted by an attack on its traditional enemies. Thus, just as the official Catholic mythology surrounding "souperism" prescribed that apostasy could result only from Protestant malevolence, so *all* Famine emigration had to be interpreted as forced exile: in neither case would a "good Catholic" break communal bonds unless under durance vile.[39]

Ironically, it was the Young Irelanders' futile but symbolically crucial revolt against British rule—a revolt opposed both by churchmen and by O'Connellite politicians—that ensured the future credibility of nationalist interpretations of Famine and emigration. Since O'Connell's capitulation at Clontarf in 1843, the interdenominational band of young professionals, journalists, and romantic poets who called themselves Young Ireland had slowly but steadily diverged from O'Connell's more opportunistic and clerically influenced policies. Although Young Ireland's weekly, the *Nation,* was the country's most popular newspaper, by mid-1846 O'Connell—angling for a renewed alliance with English Whigs—determined to rid himself of such idealistic and insubordinate allies. He demanded that all members of the Repeal Association agree that under no circumstances were the Irish, or any other oppressed people, justified in shedding blood to gain independence. At that time the Young Irelanders had no thought of armed rebellion, despite their bombastic orations and martial poetry glorifying warrior-patriots from Brian Ború to the United Irishmen. Nevertheless, declining to adopt O'Connell's sweeping renunciation of force, they withdrew from the association and in early 1847 formed their own organization, the Irish Confederation. However, once outside the Catholic nationalist mainstream, subject to charges of being "infidels" and betrayers of the dying O'Connell, they found their influence much reduced. Moreover, bereft of Thomas Davis's leadership, the Young Irelanders soon split among themselves. William Smith O'Brien, Protestant landlord and nominal leader of the confederation, and Charles Gavan Duffy, Davis's Catholic successor as editor of the *Nation,* were conservative, albeit secular, nationalists: neither desired rebellion or social revolution; both dreamed instead of a patriotic landlord-peasant, Protestant-Catholic alliance which would somehow pressure Britain into granting repeal. By contrast, Mitchel preached violent hatred of landlords and England alike, Lalor urged agrarian revolution and creation of a vaguely defined independent republic, and young orators such as Thomas Francis Meagher demanded recourse to "the sword." In early 1848 the confederation's governing council, dominated by Smith O'Brien and Duffy, refused to adopt Lalor's proposal for a general rent strike; subsequently, Mitchel resigned in disgust, started his own newspaper, the *United Irishman,* and openly advocated armed uprising. However, by early summer the outbreak of revolutions all over Europe healed the breach between conservative and radical Young Ireland. News from Paris, Berlin, Budapest, and elsewhere created such euphoria in Dublin that anything, even a successful Irish rebellion, now seemed possible; fired with enthusiasm, the *Nation's* columns soon became almost as inflammatory as those in the *United Irishman.* Alarmed, the British government arrested Mitchel, suppressed his newspaper, and sentenced him to fourteen years' imprisonment in Tasmania. In July the government struck again, arresting Duffy, seizing the *Nation's* offices, and banning the confederation. Desperate in the face of repression, the Young Irelanders "stumbled" into a vain attempt to raise a popular insurrection for which they had made no practical preparations. Only about seventy confederation clubs, with some 20–30,000 members, existed; almost half were in Dublin and none were equipped for revolution. Demoralized by Famine, dissuaded by their priests, and perhaps disappointed that the genteel rebel Smith O'Brien promised only glory—not confiscated estates—if they rose in revolt, Irish countrymen in south Leinster and east Munster gave three cheers for Young Ireland and then disappeared, leaving O'Brien and a small band of followers to surrender at Ballingarry, County Tipperary, after a brief skirmish with police.[40]

As revolution, Young Ireland's 1848 effort was a pathetic farce; however, as Irish revolutionary *theater* it was a grand, if hopeless, gesture against death and despair, evictions and emigration, and against overwhelmingly superior military force. As Mitchel later wrote, the Young Irelanders "could endure the horrible scene no longer and resolved to cross the path of the British car of conquest, though it should crush them to atoms." Crushed they were, but the sacrifice—courage in defeat ennobling its ludicrous aspects—reanimated a seemingly irrelevant nationalist cause and raised Young Ireland, hitherto dwarfed by O'Connell's enormous prestige, to center stage. Politicians who had opposed the rising soon hastened to identify themselves with the lost cause, and after their release from prison Young Irelanders like Duffy, John Martin, and A. M. Sullivan remained prominent in Irish politics for decades, despite their chastened reconversions to nonviolent, constitutional agitation; those like Mitchel, who remained intransigent rebels, became virtual folk heroes. In terms of political culture, Young Ireland's subsequent influence was enormous. The revolt itself, in the name of a future republic, reestablished nationalist links to the United Irishmen which O'Connell and the hierarchy had tried to break; likewise, Lalor and Mitchel had brought the formerly forbidden issue of landownership into the political arena, albeit too late to help Wolfe Tone's "men of no property," most of whom lay in Famine graves or were sailing away to America. Finally, although their revolt occasioned few additional departures among their countrymen, the defeated Young Irelanders' personal experiences gave them special authority to interpret all emigration as exile. Many, including Michael Doheny, Thomas D'Arcy McGee, and Richard O'Gorman, evaded capture and escaped to the United States. James Stephens and John O'Mahony, later cofounders of the Fenian movement, fled to Paris. Smith O'Brien, Thomas Francis Meagher, Terence Bellew McManus, and others were arrested, found guilty of treason, and sentenced to join John Mitchel in Tasmania. In the early 1850s Mitchel, Meagher, and McManus escaped to the United States, where they received heroes' welcomes and, along with the earlier refugees, engaged in Irish-American journalism and politics, agitated and plotted for Irish freedom, and dramatically personified their own contention that emigration was forced banishment.[41]

Even before the Famine's end, Young Ireland's rhetoric and rebellion had discernible effects on the ways Irishmen regarded contemporary emigration. Their greatest immediate impact was on urban emigrants such as the young Dubliner Thomas Reilly, weaned on Davis's romantic poetry and Mitchel's hate-filled essays, who sailed to the New World praying that "the atlantic ocean be never so deep as the hell which shall belch down the oppressors of my race." Young Ireland's successful politicization of Famine sufferings may also be evident in the frequent accounts of rural emigrants swearing vengeance on the English government as well as on their land-lords; for example, as they embarked for America, some evicted tenants from County Kildare reportedly declared, "[O]ur graves may be in a for-eign land, but our children may yet return to Ireland, and when they do we hope it will be with rifles on their shoulders." Such stories may have been apocryphal, but they conformed to nationalist models of experience and emotion which gained increasing credibility and currency after the '48 rising. For example, ballads composed in the Famine's latter years, such as "A New Song on Skibbereen," no longer attributed Irish distress to divine providence or even individual proprietors, but instead indicted the British government and warned that "we may some day remember, / If we're wanted by the Queen, / That hundreds patiently lay down / And starved in Skibbereen." Moreover, the Young Irelanders' ideological influence long outlived the crisis which precipitated their revolt. Their bitter interpreta-tions of the causes of Famine, evictions, and emigration—enshrined in a host of mediocre poems and a few minor masterpieces such as Mitchel's venomously anti-English *Jail Journal*—provided much of the nationalist catechism for the post-Famine generation. Thus, later emigrants, who never experienced the Famine or its ambiguities, faithfully learned from birth "how Erin's children [were] butchered, starved, and ground by the iron heel of the robber Saxon, till worn and broken, the decimated rem-nant fled their homes and country, to find peace and a grave in a foreign land." Significantly, post-Famine emigrants' songs, unlike those of the early nineteenth century, rarely conceded that leaving Ireland could be volun-tary or beneficial: from 1848 onward, "Poor Pat *Must* Emigrate" as, al-most without exception, ballad composers ignored the ambiguities of late-nineteenth-century emigration and portrayed the departed as sorrowing, dutiful, and vengeful exiles.[42]

Young Ireland's greatest influence was on the Irish in America, particu-larly on the Famine emigrants and their children. Although townsmen such as Thomas Reilly and some evicted tenants such as the vindictive Kildare men cited above were politicized before their departures, and although Jeremiah O'Donovan, an itinerant poet and bookseller from Cork, was partly right when he claimed that Irish-American nationalists had only to "arouse an original hatred" in the emigrants' hearts, most of those who left home in 1845–55 needed the perspectives of time and distance before they could translate their personal sufferings into nationalist terms. However, once in the New World the Famine emigrants proved especially receptive to nationalist interpretations of their experiences. One reason was that so many of those who departed during the crisis were Irish-speakers and im-perfectly Anglicized rural dwellers who shared a communal culture which devalued individual initiative and improvement. Indeed, among tradition-alists emigration itself remained *deoraí*—necessity and banishment—a re-flection of a premodern worldview which their helplessness in the face of blight, disease, and ruthless evictions had too clearly corroborated. To be sure, they had escaped death through emigration, but unlike the majority of pre-Famine emigrants, the Famine refugees had not made calculated, responsible decisions to seek "independence" overseas. Rather, they had merely fled in panicked desperation, compelled by fear and by forces beyond their understanding or powers of resistance. Some were literally transported abroad by landlords and Poor Law guardians. Others were lured by remittances, trusting blindly in relatives overseas, hoping naïvely that the New World was still the "promised land" of legend. Under such circumstances, emigration itself did not challenge passive, dependent outlooks, but instead validated traditional tendencies to skirt individual responsibility for actions which violated customary communal mores. Thus, Irishmen who initially regarded the Famine as God's chastisement for their sins, who felt guilty for their demoralized and antisocial behavior during the crisis, and who emigrated because internalized sanctions momentarily crumbled in the face of death—all these had a cultural and psychological need for the examples and exhortations of the Young Ireland leaders who ceaselessly blamed England, the perennial enemy, for forcing the Irish to leave their homes and to endure the shame and "degradation into which hunger and want will reduce human nature." In short, the Young Irelanders both validated and modernized traditional self-perceptions and resentments by "explaining" that the Famine emigrants, like themselves, were in truth nonresponsible "exiles" who had been "driven out of Erin" by "insufferable political tyranny." Moreover, like the Gaelic poets of the seventeenth century, Irish-American nationalists offered a redemptive solution as well as an explanation for Irish suffering: if the Famine emigrants rose above self-pity, renewed communal fealty, and united behind nationalist leadership, then they might expunge their shame, win freedom for Ireland, and take bloody revenge against those responsible for the Famine graves and the coffin ships. Mid-century Irish-American ballads prescribed the ideal emigrant response and prophesied the glorious consequences: "O father dear," promised one famous song,

> . . . the day will come when vengeance loud will call,
> And we will rise with Erin's boys to rally one and all.
> I'll be the man to lead the van beneath our flag of green,
> And loud and high will raise the cry "Revenge for Skibbereen!"[43]

Doubtless the fires of late-nineteenth-century Irish-American nationalism would have burned less intensely if the Famine emigrants' overall experiences in the New World had been less impoverished and embittering. To be sure, the initial reactions of pauper emigrants such as the Galway cottier Michael Byrne and the Cork laborer Daniel Guiney were often euphoric reflections of their joy at escaping death in Ireland and their delight over North America's comparative material abundance. Irish laborers who had slaved at home for a few pence per day were astounded to learn that they could earn one dollar a day—"equal to 4 Shillings British"—constructing American railroads and that even servant "Boys living with farmers can get from 20 to 30 pounds British per year." Likewise, Irish smallholders and cottiers, accustomed to eating meat only on rare occasions, found it incredible that on American farms "there is nothing but kill slay and eate mutton beef . . . pork and fowls in any quantity"—for, as an Ulster-Canadian explained, "we can raise it and not under the nesesety to sell it for the rent." Many recent arrivals also rejoiced that in the New World they were free at last from "landlord oppression" and crippling taxation; thus, Margaret M'Carthy, daughter of a west Cork smallholder, wrote home that she was "proud and happy" to be far "away from where the County Charges man or the poor Rates man . . . would have the satis-faction of Impounding my cow or any other article of mine." In 1853 an Ulster emigrant summed up the seeming advantages of American life: "plenty of work and plenty of wages   plenty to eat and no landlords   thats enough   what more does a man want."[44]

For some emigrants, sustained success overseas only led to an increased appreciation of the New World. The Ulsterman William Kerr recognized the potentially debilitating effects of homesickness on Irish emigrant achieve-ment, but from personal experience believed that "that soon wears away and [the Irish] begin to look at the right side of affairs, and see that this is the best country in the world for a man who has to depend on his labour for a living." Another northern Protestant, William Porter from County Down, experienced the same attitudinal changes: writing home from Chi-cago in 1852, two years after emigrating, Porter avowed a nostalgic desire to return someday to Ireland, but his later letters—written from a prosper-ous Illinois farm—evinced an increasing satisfaction with his adopted coun-try and a corresponding alienation from Ireland; "we would never think of going back to live in that misruled land again," he concluded in 1868, "for here you can hold up your head and not take off your hat to any man." In-deed, the Famine emigrations provided some impressive examples of up-ward mobility which promoted contentment abroad. For instance, Peter Shields, once an inmate of the Poughkeepsie, New York, almshouse, rose in community esteem to become deputy sheriff of Dutchess County and president of the local literary society. Similarly, Patrick Many of Lewiston, Maine, advanced from the ranks of unskilled labor to become a contractor, tenement owner, and racetrack proprietor worth $25,000 by the mid-1870s. Far more spectacular were the successes of Fair, Flood, Mackay, and O'Brien—the "Bonanza Kings" of Virginia City, Nevada—and of Mar-cus Daly from County Cavan, who rose from being a telegraph messenger in New York and farm laborer in California to become a fabulously rich mine owner and racehorse breeder in the Montana copper fields.[45]

However, while the records of such achievements filled the pages of the Cork nationalist John Francis Maguire's *The Irish in America,* an 1868 eulogy of the Famine emigrants' "progress," even relatively modest achieve-ments like those of Shields and Many were in fact atypical of Irish-American experiences in 1845–70. Both pioneer immigrant historians such as Oscar Handlin and Robert Ernst and more recent scholars armed with the latest quantitative methods for analyzing census and tax records concur that the great majority of Famine emigrants—semi- and unskilled laborers and servants—seldom rose from the bottom of American urban society. Moreover, emigrants' letters as well as recent studies of the Irish in Pittsburgh, Worcester, Jersey City, Sacramento, and elsewhere indicate that nearly all those who *did* achieve entrepreneurial or even skilled blue-collar status in the New World had been raised in the most commercialized and urbanized sectors of Irish society and possessed exceptional advantages of capital, education, skills, and/or family connections to prosperous pre-Famine emigrants. Thus, the members of Pittsburgh's post-Famine Irish Catholic elite were generally the sons of Irish merchants, professionals, strong farmers, village shopkeepers, or artisans; and even the petite bourgeosie—grocers, saloonkeepers, butchers, subcontractors—who dominated working-class Irish neighborhoods usually had enjoyed at least a slightly higher status before emigration than had the bulk of their customers and employees. Likewise, the relatively few Irish-American farmers produced by the Famine generation were probably Ulstermen who had realized substantial capital from selling tenant-right, or men such as Hugh Derham of Athboy, County Meath, whose £200 brought from Ireland enabled him to homestead on the Minnesota frontier. Even those Irish emigrants who by the late 1860s were prominent in the American labor movement had atypical origins: few were of peasant background, and many had been born or raised in England—the sons of Famine refugees too poor to move directly to the New World—and thus had prior experience of factory labor and trade union activity before coming to America. In short, the great majority of Famine emigrants who attained status and respect abroad were exceptionally well prepared by experience, by material circumstances, and, perhaps most important, by temperament and outlook for a successful adjustment to a highly commercialized and rapidly urbanizing and industrializing American society. Thus, although the Protestant Corkman and engineer William Cleburne admitted, "The manners of this country are very strange to one just arriving," within four months of landing at New Orleans he had "got so well used to them that [he could] hardly fancy it could be otherwise." Describing New York City in 1857, Richard O'Gorman—Young Irelander, lawyer, and eventually Tammany judge under William M. ("Boss") Tweed—best expressed the comparative ease of assimilation for middle-class emigrants: "For myself, I like it extremely," he wrote, "because I suppose, it likes me."[46]

In 1853 another middle-class emigrant wrote home from Pittsburgh, "A poor man here if industrious can hope to place his family in a position of comfort & independence." In fact, however, most Famine Irish in the New World never achieved "independence," whether defined as upward mobility or as comfortable self-sufficiency, but instead lived and labored in impoverished, insecure, "dependent" circumstances. Typical was the 1849 report of an Irish missionary in Newburyport, Massachusetts: "There is not in the town now . . . one Irishman or Catholic who is not utterly dependent for his support on his days wages . . . many cannot even find employment owing to the crowds that have come from Ireland this year, and many of the latter arrive in such a needy helpless utterly destitute state that it requires the utmost effort which their friends or countrymen can make to keep them from starving. . . ." Of course, within North America, regional economic and social conditions differed considerably, offering even unskilled newcomers various degrees and kinds of opportunities. Emigrant-aid societies frequently advised the Irish to desert overcrowded eastern seaports for inland destinations where labor was more in demand; indeed, recent studies of Detroit and San Francisco in 1850–80 indicate that Irish-Americans generally achieved greatest success in relatively new, rapidly expanding urban environments. Another analysis of the Irish in Philadelphia during the same period demonstrates how local factors such as economic diversity, abundant land space, and the presence of a relatively successful pre-Famine Irish settlement could promote occupational mobility and homeownership among the Famine refugees. Even the availability of factory labor in Troy's iron foundries or Lowell's textile mills represented possibilities for economic security and working-class organization which were superior to those experienced by day laborers or artisans in dying crafts. In addition, new research on the Irish in Ontario, and in Canada generally, suggests that a majority of Famine emigrants who remained in British North America, Catholic as well as Protestant, took up farming rather than urban occupations, as did many who settled on the Wisconsin frontier in the same era.[47]

Nevertheless, the great bulk of Famine emigrants in 1850–70 were concentrated in the urban-industrial centers of the New England, Middle Atlantic, and midwestern states; even in Ontario, Irish Catholics were much more urbanized than their Protestant countrymen and composed the largest—and poorest—ethnic group in that province's five largest cities. Moreover, despite regional variations, nearly all studies of the Irish in mid-century North America exhibit a deadening and depressing sameness. Whether in large eastern seaports like Boston and New York, in small industrial centers like Lawrence and Poughkeepsie, in midwestern cities like South Bend and Milwaukee, even in frontier towns like Denver and Sacramento: in all these, Irish emigrants were disproportionately concentrated in the lowest-paid, least-skilled, and most dangerous and insecure employment; with few exceptions, they also displayed the highest rates of transience, residential density and segregation, inadequate housing and sanitation, commitments to prisons and charity institutions, and excess mortality. Upward occupational mobility was usually slight, even for those who remained settled in one locale for several decades, and the frequent necessity of sending children to work at early ages often precluded *their* chances to advance much beyond their parents' status. There were some bright spots in an otherwise gloomy picture of Irish-American deprivation: urban-industrial economies gave emigrant women more earning power and encouraged earlier marriages than prevailed in the Irish countryside;

and a significant number of ex-peasants exhibited a grim but successful determination to purchase real estate—usually just a lot and wooden house, but sometimes a tenement or a small shop. However, often property ownership was achieved only at the expense of children's opportunities for education, and in general the Famine Irish experience in the New World was one of poverty and hardship or, at best, gradual and painfully achieved improvement which was often halted or even reversed by wage cuts, sickness, industrial accidents, frequent bouts of localized unemployment, or national economic downturns, as in 1857–58, 1861–62, and 1867–69.[48]

The Famine emigrants' harsh experiences, chronicled in their own letters and diaries as well as in official documents and the testaments of contemporary observers, often resulted in disappointment with, even alienation from, their adopted, once-promised land. The average emigrant, wrote one Irish sojourner in America, "toils on, year after year, under a burning sun in summer, and an intense cold winter, to earn a miserable subsistence, and is not so happy in his position as he would be in his own country with a single acre to raise potatoes for himself and family." Disillusion and demoralization began early among the significant minority who endured agonizing voyages abroad "coffin ships" ridden with typhus, dysentery, or cholera. In "black '47" the vessels carrying Irish emigrants to Canada "literally reeked with pestilence": at least 20,000 died en route to British North America or shortly after arrival, and of those bound for the States between 8,000 and 9,000 perished. Thousands died in the "fever sheds" on Grosse Isle, near Quebec; others escaped cursory medical inspections and spread disease and death up the St. Lawrence River; some 6,000 more expired in Montreal; and farther west, at Lachine, the dying Irish crawled through the streets, vainly begging shelter from the frightened inhabitants. Similar scenes were reenacted in St. John, New Brunswick, in Boston, in New York, in New Orleans, and along inland travel routes. Mortality rates fell sharply after 1847, but certain voyages were still replete with horrors, and during the cholera epidemic of 1853 about 10 percent of the Irish passengers died.[49]

Of those who survived the voyage and the dreaded quarantine hospitals, many were widows and helpless orphans; others were so demoralized, deranged, or physically weakened by their experiences that they sank into permanent poverty or threw themselves "listlessly upon the daily dole of government." Even those still healthy and energetic found little shelter or employment in the debarkation ports. For example, Bryan Clancy, an "assisted" emigrant from the Gore Booth estates in County Sligo, reported from St. John that he and his sister were "very uneasy for ever coming to this country": "this place is Different to our opinions at home," he wrote, and "any new pasengers except the[y] have friends before them are in Distress"; many of his companions were already dead or dying, and Clancy concluded that he "offten wished to be at home again   Bad and all as we were [in Ireland] we offten wished we never Seen St. John." Kealing Hurley from County Clare, another 1847 emigrant to New Brunswick, survived three relapses of fever and worked his way south to Boston, where he nearly starved for want of employment: "I . . . boarded at a yankee house for some days expecting every day to get something to do untill my money was all expended but O! it fails me absolutely to recount the affliction that I felt . . . involved in such destitution & misery." Illness contracted on shipboard could ruin the plans of even relatively affluent emigrants. For instance, Anne Browne, sister of a Franciscan friar in County Wexford, lamented, regarding her family's arrival in New York, "We were determined . . . to proceed to some of the Western States but from sickness and disappointments we were obliged to remain in this City, which have nearly exausted our little Capitol, [since] employment is impossible to be found. . . ." Especially disadvantaged were the large numbers who arrived in winter, when bad weather suspended public works on railroads, canals, and building sites. "I worked about 15 days" on such employment, wrote one recently landed Irishman in New England, "but in consequence of the severity of the winter the work was dispended as the greater part of it was runing through a swamp." Likewise, with the onset of winter many recent arrivals, who had gone into the countryside in an often vain effort to find work as farm laborers, drifted helplessly back to the seaports. According to contemporary witnesses, a large number of such emigrants, without money or even adequate clothing, settled into a condition of permanent destitution, huddled in waterfront slums not far from their points of initial debarkation.[50]

In fact, however, most Famine emigrants were almost constantly on the move for at least several years after their arrival, searching for relatively secure, well-paid employment. This was especially true of young single men who lacked established networks of Irish-American kin, but it was also true of many poor married men who left their wives and children in American cities from spring through autumn while they wandered about, looking for work in the countryside. The rambles of Edward McNally, a Catholic artisan, were typical in extent: after landing in Philadelphia in June 1850, he "Remained there for the space of 10 days Constantly Looking for work but no Chance"; by the time McNally penned an account of his experiences, a year after leaving Philadelphia, he had journeyed to Pittsburgh, Cincinnati, western Virginia, and finally back to Pennsylvania, where "on last Christmas day i travelled 38 miles [on foot] and it Snowing and blowing through the Drarey wilds of this distant Land"; despite several bouts of unemployment and a narrow escape from cholera, he had worked as a farm laborer, stevedore, and twice as a railroad navvy before at last finding congenial employment in a machine shop where "the wages is one Pound 1 Shilling Per week and Boarding is 9 Shillings Per week and if the Job Stands a few months it will serve mee." McNally's ramblings ended on a happy note, but, as another Irishman admitted, "if some are successful, there are many who are not, and who wander about, from state to state, without bettering their condition." Historians have discovered that the names of most Irish emigrants rarely appeared in city directories, since, as a New York Irish newspaper lamented in 1859, "the immense majority are as yet but a mere floating population, migrating from place to place, wherever they may find a market for their labor." Such chronic impermanence bred anxiety and homesickness, and even the successful McNally sorrowed that he "never felt so uneasy lonsuming for home."[51]

Often without capital or skills, unaccustomed to work practices in their adopted country, the Famine Irish usually entered the American work force at the very bottom, competing only with free Negroes or—in the South—with slave labor for the dirty, backbreaking, poorly paid jobs that white native Americans and emigrants from elsewhere generally disdained to perform. Even if they aspired to higher status, most Irish males probably worked at least part of their lives in North America as canal, railroad, building-construction, or dock laborers. Those who later rose to more remunerative or respectable employment remembered bitterly that as "Labouring men" they were "thought nothing of more than *dogs* . . . despised & kicked about" in the supposed land of equality. "I commenced working in digging Cellars," reported James Dever, a farmer's son from Donegal, "and may heaven save me from ever again being compelled to labour so severely, up before the Stars and working till darkness, nothing but driven like horses . . . a slave for the Americans as the generality of the Irish out here are." For Dever, such unaccustomed hardships heightened ambition: "If I must live here . . . along the Canals and in the Cellars & on the public Sewars & Streets," he feared, "I would [sooner] be dead. . . ." However, large numbers never escaped such drudgery and eventually lost all hope of self-betterment. For example, after a decade of vicissitudes abroad, the Dubliner Charles Locke was only a teamster for Canadian railroad contractors. His pay was one dollar per day, but he pocketed merely twelve dollars per month after his employers deducted the rest for board. In return, Locke wrote, "I am up at four a clock every morning   out and feed my teems then to breakfast and off to the working ground   it is mostly eight O Clock before my worke is over [and] I am often so tired that I wish God in his mercy would take me to himself"; "as a labouring man I find I can never rise," Locke concluded, "in fact I have lost all ambition   poverty soon humbles pride."[52]

Among Irishwomen the work experience comparable to day labor was domestic service, a nearly universal part of the life cycle for young, unmarried girls. The next most common female occupations included unskilled labor in the textile factories, sweatshop garment manufacturing, and domestic piecework in the needle trades; among the poorest Irish families, women continued to labor in these occupations even after marriage, especially if—as was all too common—they were widowed or deserted by their husbands. Like their menfolk, Irish immigrant women worked in oppressive, often dangerous conditions and usually received miserably low wages; during economic depressions, many in New York, Philadelphia, and elsewhere turned to prostitution. Consequently, although many Irishwomen found relative economic "independence" in the New World, others were bitterly disappointed: "it is not so very easey to get Muney heer as we all [thought] when [we] were to home," lamented Bridget Tunney to her friends in Cork; "you have to work hard to make one pound."[53]

To be sure, by 1870 Irish-American society had attained relative stability and maturity after the dire poverty of the 1850s, and many Famine emigrants had had sufficient skill, luck, and perseverance to find fairly secure employment as bricklayers, carpenters, miners, factory workers, even building contractors and small proprietors. Nevertheless, in 1870 some 40 percent of the Irish-born in the United States still toiled as unskilled laborers or domestic servants. Moreover, according to contemporary observers, a significant number of Famine emigrants *failed to survive* until 1870. "It is a well established fact," reported one Irish-American, "that the average length of life of the emigrant after landing here is six years; and many insist it is much less": perhaps an exaggeration, but one which reflected alarmingly high mortality rates from disease, exposure, accidents, and sheer overwork. "A man who labours steadily for 10 to 12 years in America is of very little use afterwards," wrote another emigrant from personal experience, for "he becomes old before his time and generally dies unheeded." The grossly overcrowded and unsanitary housing conditions that prevailed in most working-class slums helped contribute to high Irish mortality. In the predominantly Irish Fifth Ward of Providence, Rhode Island, in 1850 an average of nearly nine persons, 1.82 families, were packed into one- or two-room dwellings; in New York City almost 30,000 people, primarily Irish, lived below ground level in cellars often flooded with rainwater and raw sewage. Living conditions were little better for laborers in the countryside. In 1860 Patrick Walsh reported that Irish railroad workers in upstate New York lived through the winter in " 'shanties' (. . . huts made of rough boards), with the fierce wind howling through them": in one shanty, occupied by a family of five who lacked "sufficient clothing to protect them against this terrible climate, . . . stood a vessel filled with water the night before, and, though within four feet of the fire, it was frozen solid."[54]

Bishop John Hughes of New York was in part correct when he admitted that Irish "abode[s] in the cellars and garrets" of that city were "not more deplorable nor more squalid than the Irish hovels from which many have been 'exterminated.' " However, inadequate sanitation had potentially more lethal consequences in densely crowded, working-class wards such as the "Bloody Ould Sixth" than in the rural hamlets of Hughes's native Tyrone. Furthermore, as Hughes and his fellow churchmen well knew, the conditions of Irish-American working-class life bred or exacerbated severe social problems such as drunkenness, crime, violence, and insanity which both reflected and reinforced economic deprivation and uncertainty.[55]

Of course in large measure Irish emigrants simply transplanted traditional drinking patterns to American settings, and ownership of saloons, grogshops, or jerry-built "shebeens" on public-works sites provided Famine Irishmen with one of their few opportunities to escape the rigors of manual labor. However, it is probable that American conditions only increased Irish propensities to drink. For example, many of the Irish emigrants arrested at mid-century for public drunkenness in Pittsburgh attributed their habit to the uncongenial weather, to a lack of proper food and clothing, or to a need to assuage both the physical pain caused by work accidents and the psychological anxieties stemming from unfamiliar situations. Whatever their causes, drunkenness and alcoholism in America led in turn to economic failure, pathological family relationships, public violence, and crime. Given Irish-American poverty, it was not surprising that Irish emigrants dominated crime statistics and prison populations in most states and cities; for example, in New York criminal convictions among the Irish-born in the 1850s were five times those for native- or German-born citizens. Although most Irish arrests stemmed from want or drink, and although peasant behavior in Ireland had been notoriously turbulent, Irish violence in the New World differed in both extent and quality from that at home. "The people here can far beat your country killing one another," wrote one emigrant to a friend in County Antrim. "The people here think as little of killing others as you would of killing the mice in a cornstack. . . . Theirs no such thing as men fighting here as they would about a Saintfield fair for if ever you get into a fight here you must either kill or be killed [with] . . . pistols and large knives which they use instead of fighting with their fists."[56]

Beset with insecurity, a significant minority of Famine emigrants drifted into the relative haven of insanity. In 1855 an official Massachusetts report on insanity blamed the high proportion of Irish-born in the state's lunatic asylums on the unsettling nature of the emigrants' experiences: "Their lives are filled with doubt, and harrowing anxiety troubles them, and they are involved in frequent mental, and probably physical suffering." Indeed, even Irish-Americans with relatively well paid employment endured constant threats of wage cuts, unemployment, and—especially during and immediately after the Civil War—rampant inflation of food and housing costs. Thus, commenting on the Irish he met during a tour of North America in the late 1860s, the British traveler John White reported, "The cost of living seems frightful to people who have lived on so little at home. A waiter at a monster hotel, where all the waiters were Irishmen, told me what wages they were getting, naming a very high figure. When I congratulated him upon their wealth, he looked round the room and whispered, 'I doubt whether half the Irishmen in this room could pay their way back to Ireland to-morrow. Everything is so dear here.'"[57]

The failure of the Famine Irish to achieve a greater degree of material success and psychic contentment overseas was due to several interrelated causes. Pre-Famine emigrants had usually advised their countrymen to remain in Ireland unless they possessed marketable skills "and plenty of money"; however, most Famine emigrants had little of either, and many arrived penniless. Equally important was that in some respects North American society at mid-century was less fluid and offered fewer opportunities for upward mobility than had been the case a generation or two earlier. "Some twenty years ago," wrote an Irish traveler in 1852, "there was an opening for industry in America; but its sea-board—nay, three or four hundred miles inside it, is now satiated with labor." Perceptive emigrants agreed: "this country is overburdened with our countrymen and women," warned one Boston Irishman in 1855. By the 1850s prices for farmlands in the eastern and old midwestern states had risen beyond most Irish emigrants' abilities to purchase, and both the costs and the prospects of homesteading uncleared soils farther west were too formidable for former cottiers and laborers accustomed solely to spade cultivation. Opportunities for artisans to achieve "independence" had also diminished. In the early nineteenth century even poorly skilled craftsmen could prosper in rural or small-town settings, but by mid-century—save in still-remote areas like western Arkansas where, one emigrant alleged, "a *Common Tinker* that could make a tin *Cup* or *Can* would make a fortune"—such men faced devastating competition from cheap urban manufactures shipped by river, by canal or, increasingly, by rail. Indeed, the relative prosperity of San Francisco's working-class Irish during this period owed much to that city's comparative isolation from other manufacturing centers; however, in the late 1860s the completion of the transcontinental railroad plus imported Chinese laborers inaugurated a decade of economic dislocation and political unrest among the Bay Area's Irish. In general, increased capitalization and mechanization in the nation's intensely competitive small-manufacturing sector (most industries averaged fewer than thirty workers per establishment) continued to reduce most artisans and journeymen to the status of pieceworkers or machine tenders—who were easily replaceable and subject to frequent layoffs and whose wages lagged behind food and fuel costs. Save for Irish workers in a handful of industries—textile and iron manufacturing, for example—the relative security of large-scale factory employment lay in the future, as did the possibility of effective labor union organization.[58]

Moreover, not only were chances for upward mobility within or from the laboring ranks diminishing when the Famine Irish arrived but the Irish-American entrepreneurial class thrown up by the pre-Famine migrations was still too small, insecure, or indifferent to extend paternalistic assistance to the newcomers in the forms of steady employment or decent wages. Although elderly Ulster radicals such as James McConnell of Illinois welcomed these "Brave but unfortunate people" as fellow victims of English tyranny, most Protestant Irish who had prospered in pre-1845 America evinced little concern for the overwhelmingly Catholic flood of 1845–55. As for established Irish-American Catholics, too often they also remained aloof or else exploited their less fortunate countrymen in their roles as subcontractors, petty manufacturers, tenement owners, and saloonkeepers. Not until the last third of the century would a rising class of Irish-American entrepreneurs, urban politicians, factory foremen, and labor leaders be able and eager to absorb newly arrived emigrants into relatively secure socioeconomic and political structures; in the meantime, conflicts between contemptuous "narrowbacks" and despised "greenhorns" were occasionally as bitter as those between Protestant nativists and Irish Catholics generally.[59]

Diminished opportunities for upward mobility reflected an overall hardening of class lines in an increasingly urbanized and stratified society; for example, in 1860 about 1 percent of Philadelphia's inhabitants owned 50 percent of the city's real and personal property, while the lower 80 percent of the population owned but 3 percent; in western cities such as Chicago, the gap between rich and poor was equally vast. Frightened by the growth of what seemed to be a permanently impoverished proletariat, the nation's upper and middle classes adopted increasingly harsh attitudes toward unskilled laborers, whose failure to rise in a purportedly open and egalitarian society could now be "explained" conveniently by reference to their predominantly Irish origins, Catholic religion, and intemperate and unruly habits. Cultural antipathies often so reinforced economic cleavages as to preclude even the most elemental forms of justice or charity. For example, in the winter of 1851–52 railroad contractors in upstate New York advertised liberal wages and jobs for twice the number of workers actually needed; when the latter, almost all Irish, were assembled, the contractors reduced wages to fifty-five cents per day and called in the state militia to force their terms on the protesting men. "[T]here was no recourse for the unfortunate people," remembered one Irish-American, for "the country presented nothing to the view but a frozen wilderness of ice and snow, and what was to be done? They proposed to work for the reduced wages, and drag out life on it until something better might offer; but a few over half were allowed to stay; the rest were pronounced troublesome, and driven off, with their families, to perish . . . in the midst of a fearful American winter." Revealingly, he added, "these things were noticed as mere items of news in the papers, without any comment, as no concern was felt in their case, being Irish."[60]

Such incidents were not uncommon, nor were more institutionalized forms of injustice such as company stores, crooked weighmasters (as in the Pennsylvania anthracite fields), and wages paid in overpriced goods, in devalued currency, or, at times, not at all. In 1859, Irish navvies in Jersey City barricaded the railroad tracks they had just constructed to protest not receiving their promised wages: in return the city's elite condemned them as *"animals"*—as a "mongrel mass of ignorance and crime and superstition" who were "utterly unfit for . . . the common courtesies and decencies of civilized life"; after a massive show of unnecessary force, six Irishmen received two-year prison terms for their affront to property and order. Although middle-class emigrants sometimes claimed that "a perfect system of republican equality" still prevailed away from the Atlantic seaboard, conditions for Irish laborers were in fact no better farther west. For example, in Illinois, strikes by Irish coal miners in 1863 prompted the state legislature to pass the "LaSalle Black Laws," which virtually outlawed labor unions; in 1867 Chicago's captains of industry called in the state's militia to repress Irish strikers in Bridgeport, a suburb dominated by packinghouses, rolling mills, and workers' shanties. In short, as one outraged emigrant declared, the life of an Irish laborer in mid-century America was often "despicable, humiliating, [and] slavish": there "was no love for him—no protection of life—[he] can be shot down, run through, kicked, cuffed, spat on—and no redress, but a response of served the damn son of an Irish b— right, damn him."[61]

Moreover, although native American animosity usually focused on the Irish lower classes, Protestant prejudices embraced Irish-American Catholics generally. "The great majority of the American people are, in heart and soul anti-Catholic, but more especially anti-Irish," lamented a middle-class emigrant in 1860; "everything Irish is repugnant to them." During the 1850s anti-Irish Catholic feelings, exacerbated by social and political tensions, reached a crescendo with an outbreak of virulent nativism which was institutionalized in the American Protestant Society, the short-lived Know-Nothing party, and, to a lesser degree, in the new Republican party. Prejudice was greatest in Yankee New England, along the Atlantic seaboard, and in the upper Midwest, where most Famine Irish settled. It was also especially strong in areas such as western Pennsylvania which contained large numbers of Irish Protestant emigrants and their descendants; in 1851 Bishop O'Connor of Pittsburgh attributed the virulence of local nativism to the "large number of Orange Irishmen" resident, who "persecute Catholics with relentlessness and without shame." Even in comparatively tolerant San Francisco, the activities of the second Vigilance Committee in 1856 assumed the character of an anti-Irish Catholic pogrom, which drove the Irish out of city politics for a decade. Orangeism and anti-Irish Catholicism also flourished in the Maritime Provinces and in Ontario, especially in Irish Protestant–dominated Toronto, known as the "Belfast of America," in part for the frequency of local Orange-Green confrontations. However, despite the Canadian Orange Order's growing strength, Canadian nativism was in general a pale reflection of its American counterpart, which inspired brutal mob violence and, in Massachusetts, legislation designed to curb Catholicism and discourage Irish immigration.[62]

Such prejudices adversely affected nearly all Irish-American Catholics, regardless of social status. Unskilled workers and servants, especially, encountered the ubiquitous "No Irish Need Apply" notices when they searched for jobs in Boston, New York, and other major cities. Likewise, skilled workers such as the carpenters Charles Dwyer and Patrick Taggart reported that—when they found work despite their religion and nationality—their employers often treated them in an "insulting manir" and that, "where they are strong enough," Protestant fellow workers "are not slow in coming out with their Scarlous attacs on our creed and Country." Even well-educated, middle-class Irish Catholics experienced religious barriers to success and respect: "Although in this country all religions enjoy perfect equality *before* the *law*, in society it is far otherwise," lamented the Young

Ireland exile John Blake Dillon. "In this latter respect, this country may be said to be eminently protestant, and the inconveniences to which persons of strong Catholic convictions are subjected are neither few nor inconsiderable." Consequently, by the mid-1850s even prosperous emigrants were warning their countrymen to remain in Ireland: "if people can live comfortable there they ought to remain there," wrote the merchant James Dixon to relatives in County Wexford, for "[a]ffairs are becoming fearful in this Country"; "the Know-Nothings have murdered a number of Irishmen . . . and destroyed their property and [if] feeling continue as it is . . . an Irishman will not get to live in this Country"; even "if people are poor in Ireland," he concluded, at least, "they will be protected from Murderers."[63]

In the late 1850s nativism abated before the gathering storm of sectional conflict, and in 1861 middle-class Irish-Americans tried to persuade themselves that the advent of Civil War had "banished . . . rancorous bigotry" and united Irish- and native-born citizens "in an eternal bond of generous brotherhood." In fact, however, anti-Irish Catholic prejudice remained blatant even in wartime, manifested in the military draft's inequitable application to working-class Irish wards, in the mistreatment of Irish-American conscripts and soldiers, and—some Irishmen felt—in the unnecessary, if not intentional, waste of Irish regiments in hopeless combat situations. As a result, suspicion and resentment were prominent themes in the letters of Irish soldiers in the Union armies: "An Irishman, particularly a Catholic, has a devilish hard road to travel when not in an Irish regiment," testified an Irish-born captain in Tennessee. In a letter to Colonel James Mulligan, commander of an all-Irish Illinois regiment, another soldier trapped in a native American company begged Mulligan, "[I]f you can possibly do it, . . . get us transferred to you, where we can be with and amongst our own race and people." Despite Irish loyalty and sacrifice, lamented Private Peter Casey, "That Black abolishism is potent . . . they will not give us a Chance . . . the Negro and not the welfare of the Country is what most Engrosses their minds and perhaps when all is over they will turn their attention to the burning of Convents and Churches as the[y] have done before"; "the Irish Catholic so bravely fighting for the country will get no thanks when peace will be proclaimed," Casey predicted, for "this has always been the case heretofore and we need not expect anything better for the time to Come   the enemies of our Race and Religion are numerous every where yet." Unfortunately, Casey was largely correct. In towns such as Worcester native American elites belittled Irish war contributions, excluded or minimized Irish participation in victory celebrations, and cited the New York draft riots of 1863 as continued proof of Irish disloyalty and barbarity. As late as 1870 the British visitor John White declared, "In no part of the world are the virtues of the Irish so little appreciated; . . . in no part is the name of Irishman a greater obstacle to a man's success." Police bullets and baton charges—the official responses of New York's ruling classes to an Irish anti-Orange protest in

1871 and to a predominantly Irish strike for shorter hours in 1872—amply demonstrated that the guardians of property and Protestantism were as arrogant and unyielding as ever.[64]

American nativism, reinforcing a legacy of colonialism and social inferiority, made most Irish Catholic emigrants almost morbidly sensitive: John White observed that "if you ask a man, whose speech has betrayed him, whether he is not an Irishman, you can see that he winces under the question," too often returning "a defiant self-assertion"—" 'Yes—and I'm none the worse for that!' "—or a "half-guilty, half-resentful expression" which revealed the psychic scars of prejudice and proscription. In response, some emigrants—such as the "family of Yankified Irish who don't like to pass for Irish" that the Dublin cleric Father Pius Devine encountered near Pittsburgh in 1870—strove to erase the stigma by changing their accents, their names, even their religion. How many Famine and post-Famine emigrants abandoned Catholicism is unknown, but contemporary churchmen such as Bishop John Lynch of Toronto believed the number alarmingly large. More common, however, were attempts to adopt or ostentatiously display bourgeois habits which might allay prejudice without sacrificing creed or country. Both sympathetic native critics, such as the New England convert Orestes Brownson, and Anglicized, middle-class emigrants, such as William Dever and Bartholomew Colgan, advised working-class Irishmen to imitate Yankee models of thrift, sobriety, industry, and individualism. In scathing letters Dever and his brother condemned "the poor drunken Irish" for their poverty and suffering—"much of this is their own fault" since "very few of them are anything but hard workers"—and counseled that "good conduct & perseverance will elevate men here." Likewise, Colgan, a strong farmer's son from County Carlow, warned in 1854 that "liveing in Citys" and along public-works sites "ruines a great portion of our fine Countrymen": "Company is good and I like company," he admitted, "but too much is not the best—[for] we ought to make the hay while the sun shines [and] while we have the youth we ought to lay up something for the rainy day." J. Fitzgerald of Columbus, Ohio, was more analytical: America *is* a land of opportunity, he wrote, with "no Aristocracy or rank but what money and talent establish"; however, "[e]very man must depend . . . upon his own individual efforts. He must be active . . . up with the Times and away ahead of them for . . . Progress, cents and dollars are the watchwords of the day." In conclusion, he wrote, if an Irishman abroad "be quick, active, enterprising, disposed to labor hard, get rid as soon as possible of National peculiarities and set himself down to adopt the ways and customs of the people he is certain to succeed. . . . But if he cannot divest himself of his old way of doing things, if he cannot flow into the great current of American life he will never succeed."[65]

Such admonitions too clearly exposed the enormous cultural gap between modern American and traditionalist Irish societies—"All things nearly," Fitzgerald warned, "are done in this country in a different way from . . . Ireland"—and they also indicated how extremely difficult, if not impossible, it would be for most Famine emigrants to follow these prescriptions for success. Not only poverty and lack of skills prevented most Irishmen from heeding advice to go west and farm where their families could "grow up prosperous and industrious removed from the pestilential examples and practices of city life." Many Famine refugees were temperamentally as well as economically less prepared than their predecessors for material achievement and assimilation abroad. In 1850 an Irish-American journalist in New Orleans observed, "The Irish of the present day . . . whom we see landing on our levees seem to be a different race of the Irish ten, 15, or 20 years since"; "Dire wretchedness, appalling want and festering famine have tended to change their characters." However, more crucial than the effects of hunger and disease was the fact that in 1845–55 an unprecedented proportion of the Irish emigrants were traditionalist peasants, often Irish-speakers, who might never have emigrated under normal circumstances and who carried to the New World premodern attitudes and behavior patterns diametrically opposed to those which Fitzgerald characterized as typically American. Non-Irish observers such as Brownson, George Templeton Strong, and John White recognized that in many respects modern American and traditional Irish Catholic worldviews were antithetical, even "mutually repugnant"—a perception also shared by many emigrants: "Had I fallen from the clouds amongst this people," declared one Irishman, "I could not feel more isolated, more bewildered. . . ." "This is a fast country in which our lot has been cast," another lamented. "With the ideas of old movements, still clinging to us, like the memories of childhood, we can scarcely keep pace with it." "We are a primitive people," confessed a third emigrant, "wandering wildly in a strange land, the Nineteenth Century."[66]

Even Irish-American newspaper editors—bourgeois, Anglicized men who ceaselessly urged their readers to adopt entrepreneurial attitudes—often acknowledged that the typical Famine emigrant was a cultural conservative, "a bundle of habits and associations, [with] a number of unanswerable longings, likings, and propensities which stay in his nature though he change his place." For example, despite injunctions to individual enterprise, Irish-American work and residential patterns usually demonstrated, as a native philanthropist complained, that the Irish "love to clan together" and "are content to live together in filth and disorder, and enjoy their balls and wakes and frolics without molestation." Non-Irish contemporaries lamented that "the huddling together of the Irish" constituted the "great bar to quick denationalization," for in working-class slums and shantytowns the emigrant was "lost in the crowd of his countrymen," thus enjoying few "glimpses of American manners, morals, and religion." In fact, many emigrants had far too many glimpses of native prejudice, and so huddled together for mutual protection; in addition, such settings more nearly replicated the social atmosphere of pre-Famine rural Ireland, especially the crowded coasts and glens of the South and West. Indeed, evidence from urban tax records indicates that within Irish districts emigrants from the same areas in Ireland, often sharing the same surnames, tended to congregate in discrete neighborhoods, where they could perpetuate traditional social patterns, including boisterous wakes and "Paddy funerals," in comparative isolation from censorious middle-class contemporaries, both native and Irish, lay and clerical.[67]

What upset genteel observers even more than Irish drunkenness or cultural retentions such as fairy belief was the embarrassing fact that many Famine emigrants seemed oblivious, even antagonistic, to bourgeois ideals and leadership. For example, nonpracticing or "anonymous" Catholics from southern and western Ireland probably dominated the peasant exodus of 1845–55, and large numbers rarely or never observed formal religious obligations in the New World. Thus, during the 1850s and 1860s at least half the Irish in New York City's Sixth Ward, including a great majority of the unskilled laborers, hardly ever attended mass; in Ohio, one priest lamented, "scarcely one out of ten of our Irish on the railroad goes to his duty   one half are grown up to 20–25 years & never made their first communion [and] know nothing of their catechism." Nor were many Famine emigrants more respectful of lay authority, whether native or Irish-American: "deep-rooted prejudices of early training," reinforced by sectarian conflicts, promoted "a spirit of antagonism toward strangers"; and traditional economic notions led ex-peasants to regard employers and foremen as "grasping, money-making person[s]" more deserving of resentment and reprisal than emulation or respect. Consequently, to the despair of pragmatic politicians and labor leaders, working-class emigrants faced with discrimination or injustice usually reacted by combining in militant, ethnic-based associations reminiscent of secret societies at home. Sometimes Irishmen fought each other, as in the faction fights between "Corkonians" and "Far-downs" which convulsed canal routes and railroad camps; however, by the end of the period, Irishmen were combining despite different regional origins, as in Prince Edward Island's Irish Tenant League and the more-notorious Molly Maguires, who temporarily ruled Pennsylvania's anthracite fields through intimidation and violence. Finally, to middle-class emigrants the most embarrassing example of the alienation of lower-class Irish-Americans was the New York draft riot of 1863, when thousands of "[s]trange, wretched, abandoned creatures . . . flocked out of their dens and lairs" to wreak vengeance on the symbols of property, propriety, and Protestantism.[68]

To be sure, even middle-class Catholics often found aspects of American life alien and uncongenial—widespread "immorality" and the natives' "habits of cursing" offended genteel emigrants such as James Butler of County Kildare—and many responded to the strangeness of the New World by reading Irish-American newspapers which "left the impression that the United States was a suburb of Ireland rather than a different country." Likewise, the Ulsterman Wilson Benson's pathetic autobiography demonstrates that some Irish Protestants also failed to make successful adjustments to American exigencies. "You have no idea how I hate this Country," wrote another dissatisfied Protestant; "if I was to make a million pounds here I would never adopt the Country as my own." Nevertheless, it was the cultural as well as the socioeconomic gulf between peasant Ireland and bourgeois America which at mid-century seemed almost insurmountable and which threatened to expose even respectable Catholic emigrants to a common opprobrium. After all, admitted one of the latter, "to judge of Ireland and Irishmen from the *enchantillon* which the United States presents, one would be forced to regard the former as the fruitful home of incorrigible ignorance and incurable superstition." For aspiring emigrants who either could not or would not conceal their Irishness, the best hope of resolving these tensions was to guide their fellow countrymen to respectability and power.[69]

Stricken with poverty, besieged by prejudice, unable or unwilling to assimilate to American society, most Famine Irish were thrown back on their own resources. For large numbers, the parochial comforts of corner saloons, urban street gangs, congenial workmates, and the proximity of transplanted neighbors and kinfolk were sufficient expressions of social action and solace. For many, however, desires for greater security or stature also necessitated some participation in either specifically ethnic or Irish-dominated *national* institutions. The prevalence of Irish-American affiliation with such institutions in 1845–70 should not be overstressed, for Irish dominance of national labor unions and the creation of national benevolent and self-help associations did not begin until the very end of this period, when Irish-American society was more matured and socially stratified. Nevertheless, it was the Famine Irish who first erected a national, institutional framework for Irish-America: their sheer numbers, concentrated in urban centers, enabled the establishment or the appropriation of such institutions as their desperate needs demanded; and the exigencies of Irish-American life broke down parochial barriers between emigrants who realized that, at least in nativist eyes, they were not Dubliners or Kerrymen, cottiers or strong farmers' sons, but merely despised Irishmen who therefore must needs unite on the basis of broadly shared characteristics and experiences.[70]

In 1845–70 the three institutions which embodied pragmatic as well as ideal aspirations for most Irish-American Catholics were the Democratic party, the Catholic church, and Irish-American nationalism, particularly the Fenian movement. Although most Irish emigrants were loyal to all three, relations between these institutions were largely utilitarian and competitive, sometimes hostile. Moreover, although each institution served to insulate emigrants and traditional Irish values from nativist hostility, each also provided a bridge to modern industrial culture, with its opposing values, and to an ultimately fuller participation in "the great current of American life." This assimilationist thrust was most obvious in the Democratic party and Catholic church; it was much less so in Irish-American nationalism, save in sociological retrospect, which can appreciate the mere creation of formal organizations, regardless of avowed purpose, as evidence of modernity. Although primarily working-class in membership, these institutions were led by middle-class emigrants or emigrants' sons whose ethnicity was often less instinctual than functional and whose desires to organize and influence their fellow countrymen partook of various measures of altruism and ambition, both based on convictions that only through union could Irishmen achieve status and respect. Nevertheless, it can be argued that these affiliations only diverted working-class Irish-Americans from more-practical or fundamental remedies to economic grievances; indeed, in America as in Ireland, Protestant proscription corroborated cultural predispositions (e.g., toward conformity to communal symbols) to unite poor, traditionalist Catholics with more-affluent, Anglicized countrymen who wanted to mold them for "common" purposes or "higher" goals defined in modern and sometimes practicably irrelevant terms. At best, most Irish-Americans got only vicarious or cathartic benefits in return for their fealty and enthusiasm. However, in the context of Irish emigrant life at mid-century—when it seemed to one bishop that his people were too "dispersed, beaten, [and] discouraged . . . to unite"— Irish-American efforts and rewards were perhaps far greater than apprehensive sympathizers might have anticipated.[71]

Of course, neither the Democratic party nor the American Catholic church was a specifically *Irish* organization, and both predated the massive emigrations of the mid-nineteenth century. However, as they attracted the overwhelming majority of Famine emigrants, they were both to a degree transformed into Irish institutions. Irish Catholic attachment to the Democratic party was based partly on historic alliances between United Irish exiles and the followers of Jefferson and Jackson, partly on antagonism to the strong evangelical Protestant and anti-Irish Catholic strains which ran through opposing political organizations (Whigs, Know-Nothings, and Republicans), and partly on pragmatic considerations. In return for Irish votes, Democratic politicians—especially on municipal levels—offered charity, jobs, opportunities for upward mobility in party ranks, protection against discriminatory legislation and law enforcement, symbolic recognition of Irish culture and nationalism (e.g., bombast and green flags at Tammany Hall on St. Patrick's Day), and a sense of belonging to a powerful, *American* institution. Despite these benefits, however, in 1845–70 the Democratic party still generally excluded Irishmen from elective offices; when they *were* nominated for minor posts, native Protestant Democrats often "scratched" them from their ballots: in short, Irish-American dominance of urban and state Democratic machines still lay in the future. In addition, those few Irish-Americans who did attain political power during this period—for example, Richard Connolly and Peter Sweeney, who rode to fortune and ruin with New York's Boss Tweed in the 1860s— were generally exceptional in background: either second-generation Irish-Americans or emigrants of atypical education and skill; even lesser party functionaries were usually saloonkeepers, contractors, slumlords, and other petty entrepreneurs whose relations with their constituents smacked of exploitation as well as paternalism. In nearly all instances, commitments to capitalist values and personal aggrandizement precluded more than rhetorical challenges to established wealth. Thus, the great mass of Irish Democrats, as in New York City, had to be content with jobs shoveling dirt in Central Park, with baskets of food during hard winters, with an occasional foot on the lower rungs of the civil-service ladder, and with whatever psychic satisfaction came from watching party leaders outrage Protestant propriety, as when Tweed secured a short-lived tax support for Catholic schools. Finally, as the Tammany stalwart and former Young Irelander Richard O'Gorman admitted, Democratic party politics at mid-century was "a filthy pool of shabbiness, falsehood and corruption," and Irish participation in the political trough (e.g., as "repeater" voters or as "shoulder-hitters" bullying native voters away from polling places) did nothing to dispel Irish reputations for untrustworthiness and violence.[72]

Nevertheless, with few exceptions (as in Philadelphia, where Irish building contractors were tied into a Republican machine of unusual longevity and corruption, or as in Massachusetts during the late 1860s, when the Republican Ben Butler flirted with Fenianism and the labor movement), Catholic Irishmen remained staunchly Democratic. Two examples will suffice to demonstrate the psychological and material bases of working-class Irish support for the Democracy. Patrick Dunny from County Carlow was one Irish emigrant who fully appreciated the United States for a social and political egalitarianism which contrasted strongly with the rigid class divisions and enforced deference which prevailed in Ireland: "poeple that Cuts a great dash at home," he wrote in 1856, "when they come here the[y] tink it strange for the humble Class of poeple to get as much respect as themselves [but] when they come here it wont do to say i had such and was such and such at home [for] strangers here the[y] must gain respect by there conduct and not by there tongue." In great measure, Dunny's new self-esteem was based on his (admittedly illegal) participation in the American political process: "i know poeple here from [Ireland] . . . that would not speak to me [there] if the[y] met me on the public road [but] here i can laugh in there face when i see them [because] . . . i am not here 2 years until next spring and [yet] i had the honor of voteing at the last too Elections . . . through the very best of interest." His former social superiors, meanwhile, had to wait five years for legal naturalization. Moreover, for Dunny the Democratic party was both a bulwark against nativist attacks on the equality he enjoyed and a means by which the Irish generally could attain status in their adopted country: "James Buchannon is Elected President on the Democratic ticket by an overwhelming Majority," he exulted; "there never was [such] excitement . . . before at an Elections nor the [nativist] Americans neverr got a home blow before the Irish Came out victorious and now Clame as good right here as americans themselves. . . ." The second example was Dennis Morgan, a bricklayers' assistant from County Monaghan whose poem "The Hodman's Lament" expressed the naïve faith many New York Irish had in the protection and largesse of Boss Tweed. Morgan perceived the mechanization of his own trade—which "cut our wages down so small a poor man can scarce live at all"—and Tweed's fall from power and subsequent imprisonment as mutually reinforcing evidence that employers and nativists had conspired to degrade Irish workingmen and subvert democratic institutions. "Long life and health to you, Bill Tweed," Morgan wrote. "For you always helped the poor in need when you were Senator":

> . . . if e'er you should come back again you'll
> meet the help of honest workingmen.
> For no matter who may you condemn, you were
> poverty's best screen. . . .
> Tho' you robbed the rich you fed the poor,
> and never acted mean.

Morgan was correct in suspecting that Tweed's genteel enemies regarded "good government" as inseparable from propertied, Protestant rule; nevertheless, the tragedy of his and other emigrants' pathetic dependence on such rapacious champions of "the poor man's cause" was that Gilded Age America offered the Irish so few alternative sources of charity and secular guidance.[73]

The other native institution which commanded Irish fealty was the Catholic church: "We have changed the clime," declared one emigrant, "but not the faith. . . ." However, Famine Irish loyalty to Catholicism in the New World was by no means automatic. As was noted above, in 1845–55 many emigrants, especially Irish-speakers, were merely nominal or customary Catholics, with religious notions and practices so inseparable from parochial, premodern contexts that they were in danger of disintegrating in unfamiliar environments; as a priest in New York lamented, "half of our Irish population here is Catholic merely because Catholicity was the religion of the land of their birth." For large numbers of transplanted peasants, with a faith at best imperfectly internalized, an American church led by clerics who rarely could speak Irish, and who were often not of Irish birth or descent, was an alien institution. The American practice of charging pew rents was also an unpleasant novelty, and perhaps a major reason why so few lower-class Irish-Americans were regular communicants. In addition, some ambitious emigrants may have suspected, as nativists claimed, that Catholicism was inimical to democratic institutions, the pursuit of opportunity, and the spirit of rational progress—and thus had best be abandoned. Indeed, many observers believed that exposure to American values made Irish emigrants less deferential to clerical authority, if not "heretics and atheists." Perhaps most important, in the late 1840s the American church was totally incapable of ministering to the emigrant hordes: for example, although in Ireland the ratio of priests to parishioners was only 1 to 3,000 (a source of grave concern to Irish churchmen), in New York City at mid-century the ratio was 1 to 4,500, and in western parishes it was an overwhelming 1 to 7,000. Existing physical facilities were equally inadequate, and not until the last quarter of the century was the church capable of caring for most emigrants' spiritual needs; by most accounts, tens of thousands of Irish-Americans in the meantime drifted into indifference or apostasy.[74]

Nevertheless, the great majority of Irish Catholic emigrants not only remained loyal to the church but eventually became more faithful practitioners than they had been at home. One reason was that in 1845–70 the American hierarchy, led by New York's John Hughes and other bishops of Irish birth or descent, made massive efforts to church the emigrants, bolster and modernize their faith, and insulate them from Protestant scorn and proselytization. Although accomplishments fell far short of perceived needs, by the end of the period hundreds of new churches and cathedrals had been built, thousands of priests and members of teaching and charitable orders were trained or imported from Ireland, the foundations of parochial education were laid, and a greater degree of centralized discipline was imposed on priests and parishioners alike. Irish emigrants' reactions to these efforts were overwhelmingly favorable. Although some newcomers undoubtedly resented clerical offensives against traditional customs, habits of deference to spiritual authority usually prevailed. After all, emigrants trained to believe, as one Irishwoman counseled, that "you Will not fret for bng in A strange Country [if] you . . . mind your duty to god and go to your priest A[nd] consult with him" would be more prone to intensify than to neglect their religion abroad. Like Democratic ward bosses, educated priests were vitally necessary protectors and intermediaries between illiterate "greenhorns" and an unfamiliar, often hostile environment. Moreover, as the clerical personnel of the American church became progressively more Irish in composition, the church itself seemed more familiar, a link rather than a break with home. For example, in 1870 an Irish missionary in western Pennsylvania received a delirious welcome from a settlement of Donegal emigrants: "In a short time the word was spread that an Irish priest had arrived—all the villages forthwith came to see me & hear about the old country. How delighted they were & what an affection they have for every thing Irish." Indeed, in circumstances which demanded abandonment of so many indices of nationality, such as the Irish language, Catholicism itself became the primary expression of Irish-American identity, a development parallel to that taking place in Anglicizing Ireland. Thus, in 1872 an Irish priest visiting the United States declared, "Take an average Irishman—I don't care where you find him—and you will find that the very first principle in his mind is, 'I am not an Englishman, because I am a Catholic.' "[75]

However, the leaders of the Irish-*American* church were deeply sensitive to nativist charges that being Irish and Catholic was also incompatible with becoming American or respectable. As a result, the church assiduously promoted American patriotism, bourgeois values, and upward mobility among its adherents. Some clerics even demanded that emigrants

Anglicize "unpronounceable" Gaelic names—a reflection both of assimilationist desires and of the dominance of churchmen from eastern Ireland, of Hiberno-Norman descent, among the Irish-American clergy. More generally, Catholic clerics and newspaper editors vigorously denounced emigrant violence and drunkenness, lauding instead Irish-American sacrifices in wartime and instances of individual success. To nativist criticism they countered that Irish Catholics in fact made the *best* American citizens: because they came to the New World seeking religious liberty, exiled by the same tyrannical government that had driven the Pilgrims overseas, and because conservative Catholic values were necessary to protect American democracy from the anarchic, anti-institutional reform spirit which endangered sectional and class harmony. Likewise, church teachings, as reflected in sermons and parochial school readers, commanded emigrants and their children to industry, thrift, sobriety, and self-control—habits which would not only prevent spiritual ruin but also shape good citizens and successful businessmen. Although in 1870 most Irish-Americans remained mired in the lower classes and although evidence of continued emigrant intemperance and turbulence abounded, by then newly formed, church-sponsored associations of upwardly mobile Irish-Americans were avidly seeking prosperity through piety and self-help. The late draft rioters still loomed largest in nativist eyes, but the future of Irish-America belonged to devout, aspiring workingmen such as Patrick Taggart, who proudly avowed "abstainance from those mixtures which destroys health, ruins the constitution and debases men lower than the beast"; "a man cannot have a good reputation," he concluded, "without soberiety." For Taggart and others, nativist hostility had certainly intensified ethnic and religious identification; however, his striving to be a "good" Irish Catholic, a credit to his church and people, put him on the road to ultimate cultural assimilation.[76]

Nevertheless, the Irish-Catholic road to respectability was a track separate from, albeit parallel to, that followed by native Protestants; and for most impoverished Famine emigrants the church's primary function was to insulate them from native animosity and from despair engendered by their own deplorable condition. To emigrants who failed to achieve "independence," the church offered spiritual consolation: sermons and textbooks idealized a medieval, hierarchical version of society compatible with peasant outlooks, a society in which poverty was part of God's plan, to be endured with patience and resignation; piety outweighed material attainments, themselves the results of chance and fate. Likewise, while the church sought to bolster the emigrants' shattered pride in their Irishness, it perpetuated a traditional, fatalistic conceptualization of Irish history: the Irish were the "martyr nation," akin to the Jews of the Old Testament, and had suffered "seven centuries of British oppression"—culminating in famine and exile—for the sake of their religion. Parochial history texts, sometimes imported from Ireland, offered a sanitized, sanctified rendition of Irish history, dominated by saints and martyrs, but minimizing or excluding mention of secular heroes like Wolfe Tone or "Captain Rock" who had striven for clerically condemned goals.[77]

However, the church did not counsel passivity in the face of threats to religion. Bishop Hughes, especially, sought to forge Irish emigrants into an ethnically exclusive, militantly Catholic body under conservative clerical leadership: he denounced not just nativism but Protestantism generally, as well as "godless" public education, "mixed" marriages, priests who mingled with "heretics," Irish-American leaders purportedly tainted with "red republicanism," and even fellow bishops who dared suggest that the emigrants move west, where, Hughes feared, they might be too free from clerical influence. Many of the Irish missionary priests brought to America were equally strident, their scornful intolerance of even friendly Protestants reflecting the harsher sectarianism which prevailed at home. Not all Irish-Americans approved of their clergy's militancy: "Ere long," one emigrant feared, "if their sentiments increase in virulence and charitable hatred of Protestantism as it has latterly, a Catholic will be unable to meet a neighbour but with a dagger in belt or a pistol on cock. Don't they feel that the hatred of heretics which they seek to disseminate and strengthen, will be met by a similar feeling on the other side?" Likewise, many working-class Irish resented clerical denunciations of Catholic parents too poor to send their children to parochial rather than public schools. However, for most emigrants weaned on the bitter milk of religious and ethnic animosity, the church militant was a familiar and welcome institution.[78]

In a sense, the American church *had* to be militant in defense of its adherents, just as Democratic party politicians had to wave the green flag on election day, for both faced stiff competition for the emigrants' loyalty from an Irish-American nationalism which required separate institutional expression. Although organized emigrant opposition to British "tyranny" had existed since the early nineteenth century, the Famine generation created modern Irish-American nationalism, with its mass-based, national societies and radical goals rooted in the republicanism of Young Ireland and the bitter memories of "black '47." In the early Famine years the old American repeal associations were largely moribund, but in early 1848 news of the successful revolution in France combined with growing outrage over the Famine itself to radicalize and unite warring American factions in expectation of an imminent Irish rising under Young Ireland's leadership. Enthusiastic Irish-Americans established a national directory in New York, held monster rallies, raised money, purchased arms, and formed militia companies for anticipated service overseas. So widespread was the excitement that even conservative bishops such as New York's John Hughes felt obliged to lend oratorical and financial support. However, Smith O'Brien's ignominious defeat shattered Irish-American hopes and unity: many middle-class emigrants, former O'Connellite moderates, withdrew in embarrassment, while others squabbled over the deposition of unused funds. Internecine strife assumed ideological dimensions when fugitive Young Irelanders like Thomas D'Arcy McGee and John Mitchel blamed Irish priests for counseling their parishioners not to fight. Such anticlericalism from secular competitors for emigrant loyalties was too much for American churchmen like Hughes and Boston's Bishop Fitzpatrick, and within a few years their denunciations of "atheistic," "red republicanism" forced most bourgeois Irish-Americans to desert revolutionary leadership and drove McGee's and Mitchel's newspapers out of business. Chastened by his experiences, McGee began his spiritual pilgrimage from freethinker to devout Catholic, and from ardent Irish revolutionary to loyal Canadian politician—a transformation provoking the contempt of former comrades and his eventual assassination in Montreal.[79]

However, most Irish-American spokesmen did not desert nationalism in the 1850s but merely employed it in more practical and profitable ways. Many former Young Irelanders drifted into Democratic politics, using their talents and reputations to cement emigrant loyalties to the party of Jackson. Even most Catholic churchmen and newspaper editors continued to make vague noises supporting "justice" for Ireland while simultaneously condemning revolutionary violence and secret conspiracies. Nevertheless, a staunch minority of former rebels resisted financial allurements and clerical pressures and continued to agitate and organize for revolution. Mitchel and Michael Doheny were especially prominent in creating new revolutionary societies and Irish-American militia companies; although most societies died in infancy and most companies did little more than add martial flavor to St. Patrick's Day parades, hopes again ran high in 1854–56 that Britain's involvement in the Crimean War might provide another opportunity for rebellion. However, the Russian defeat dashed emigrant enthusiasm once more, and in the late 1850s the British spy Thomas Doyle reported that although three-fifths of Irish-Americans had strong "sympathies . . . in unison with those who would compass a revolution in Ireland," they were "convinced this is not practicable in the present state of the world, &, therefore do not take part in a movement . . . from which they expect no other result but mischief."[80]

However, Doyle also noted that another 10 percent of the Irish-Americans, by "far the most energetic," so hated "British dominion in Ireland, & especially . . . the landlord class," that they "would not hesitate to do anything in their power to destroy both." In 1858 three such irreconcilable "exiles" established a transatlantic revolutionary organization which eventually united most emigrants in support of Irish independence. The major figures were James Stephens and John O'Mahony, Young Irelanders who had initially fled to Paris, where they studied the art of conspiracy under more experienced, continental radicals. By 1856 O'Mahony had moved to New York and joined forces with Michael Doheny, and in 1858 they reestablished contact with Stephens, now back in Ireland. Stephens proposed to establish a secret, mass-based revolutionary society at home, while O'Mahony and Doheny agreed to found a similar organization in America which would supply money, arms, and trained soldiers for a forthcoming rebellion. Stephens's Irish society was officially called the

Irish Republican Brotherhood (IRB), but O'Mahony's romantic name for the American organization—the Fenian Brotherhood, an attempt to link modern nationalism to Gaelic antiquity's legendary heroes—became generally used on both sides of the Atlantic. Success in America was initially slow: in 1859 O'Mahony complained it was "hard to get the mass of the Irish . . . to believe that any one can be serious who speaks of freeing Ireland," although he hoped "[t]rue men are beginning to see that we are really in earnest." By 1860 O'Mahony was publishing his own, extreme nationalist newspaper, and Fenian "circles" were established in most areas of Irish-American settlement. Nevertheless, total membership and financial contributions remained small; as Thomas Doyle reported, most emigrants were too poor and preoccupied with everyday struggles for mere subsistence to spare time or money for "filibustering theories and military organization." However, the Civil War freed many emigrants from financial concerns and provided a ready-made military framework for Fenian recruitment and training: over 150,000 Irish-Americans served in the Union armies, many in Irish companies easily converted into Fenian circles. At the war's end Fenianism had about 50,000 actual members, many of them trained soldiers, and hundreds of thousands of ardent sympathizers; in just seven years, and despite clerical condemnation, Fenianism had become the most popular and powerful ethnic organization in Irish-American history.[81]

However, Fenianism's fall was equally meteoric, and by the early 1870s the movement collapsed into pitiful fragments. Fenian hopes, ofttimes encouraged by the Lincoln administration, that following Union victory the federal government would either go to war with Britain or at least support Fenian operations in gratitude for Irish wartime sacrifices, proved illusory. In addition, rapid demobilization after Appomattox forced many poor Fenians back into the labor market during a period of wage cuts and price inflation. Perhaps most important, the British arrest of Stephens and other IRB leaders in September 1865 led to fatal divisions within the American movement. O'Mahony's supporters remained dedicated to an eventual rising at home, but a larger faction, led by William R. Roberts, an Irish-born dry-goods merchant in Brooklyn, instead advocated immediate use of Fenian soldiers to attack the British Empire in Canada. Although several hundred Irish-American officers did cross the Atlantic and took leading roles in an abortive IRB rising in early 1867, the American split dissipated most Fenian energies in equally unsuccessful, comic-opera invasions of Canada in 1866 and 1870. After the last failure, Irish-American nationalism temporarily dissolved in acrimony and despair: "Ah, but we are sorry revolutionists," exclaimed one heartbroken Fenian.[82]

To E. M. Archibald, British consul in New York, and to Irish-Canadian loyalists such as D'Arcy McGee and Nicholas Davin, Irish-American nationalist leaders were mere "schemers and demagogues who derive a pecuniary profit" from "the lower and more ignorant classes of Irish," whose hatred for England was, by the 1860s, hopelessly anachronistic, ignoring the "improved condition" and "present and prospective prosperity" of post-Famine Ireland which an unsuccessful rebellion might jeopardize or destroy. In a variation on this theme, recent historians have argued that Irish-American nationalism was primarily a means to ultimate assimilation, dominated as it was by middle-class emigrants and emigrants' sons whose ambitions for upward mobility and respect were thwarted by American prejudice and who therefore sought Irish freedom to promote group status and personal success in their adopted country. It was certainly true that Irish-American notions of conditions at home remained frozen in time, fixed at the point of their embarkations. It was equally true that many nationalist spokesmen were self-serving "professional ethnics" like Thomas Francis Meagher and Richard O'Gorman, whom Doheny characterized as "sharp as a chisel and equally keen in his race for money." Many Fenian leaders, such as Roberts and Patrick Collins of Boston, also used nationalism to promote careers in mainstream politics. In some areas Fenian circles were no more than local auxiliaries of the Democratic party, and in Wisconsin, as elsewhere, middle-class Irish politicians often employed nationalist symbols to divert working-class emigrant attention from controversial economic issues which threatened bourgeois interests and ethnic solidarity. In addition, there is no doubt that many nationalists were less concerned to free Ireland from British rule than to free Irish-Americans from nativist scorn and proscription. Only if Ireland were independent and prosperous, argued Meagher's New York *Irish News,* would her exiled "children [be] honored or respected"; only then, claimed another nationalist journal, could emigrants meet native Americans "without being inflamed with feelings of . . . shame." Indeed, mere devotion to nationalism would promote habits conducive to improved status, for "true" Irishmen should be "frugal, sober, and industrious" to achieve political as well as personal goals. Certainly, ambitious Irish-Americans found such arguments persuasive: frustrated by prejudice from employers and workmates, the Fenian sympathizer Patrick Taggart hoped "that ere long Irish men will have a flag of their own to shelter and protect them" from such aspersions. For second-generation Irish-Americans, and for emigrants such as the Galway-born Patrick Ford, who came to the New World so young that he claimed, "I brought nothing with me from Ireland . . . to make me what I am," ethnic self-consciousness was largely a reaction to *American* disadvantages, as was Ford's conclusion that "it was necessary for everyone of Irish blood to do all in his power" to elevate the Irish abroad by liberating the Irish at home.[83]

Irish-Americans who perceived nationalism largely as a bridge to acceptance and material success overseas faced a major problem: how to promote Irish revolution while residing in a nation whose government was at peace with Ireland's oppressor and whose Protestant citizens generally regarded Irish-American agitation as foolish or criminal. In 1857 an American judge in Cincinnati posed the dilemma starkly when he warned twelve naturalized Irishmen that their dreams for Ireland "ought not to be indulged . . . at the hazard of the interest and peace of the country of [their] adoption. . . . There can be no such thing as a divided national allegiance." This was current native opinion, and most nationalists felt obliged to make tortuous rhetorical efforts to reconcile Irish and American interests, lamely insisting that common ideals and a shared history of struggle against English "tyranny" united Irish and native traditions—or, as the editor Patrick Lynch baldly put it, "The strongest and best hater of England is sure to prove the best American." Certainly, Fenian designs on Canada reflected desires to merge Irish national goals with traditional American aspirations to conquer that valuable "speculation" in northern "real estate," but the most contrived and tragic attempt at self-serving synthesis occurred in the Civil War's early years, when ingenious nationalists such as the would-be military hero Thomas Francis Meagher urged ordinary emigrants to join the slaughter in anticipation of wider war against an English government which purportedly favored southern secession. "Every blow that . . . clears the way for the Stars and Stripes," he glibly proclaimed, "deals to this English aristocracy a deadly mortification . . . and thus so far avenges and liberates" Ireland. No wonder that the IRB leader James Stephens, who blamed his own considerable failings on inadequate American aid, condemned Irish-American nationalism in the 1850s and 1860s as "a wind-bag or a phantom" whose "sum total" consisted of "[s]peeches of bayonets, gala days and jolly nights, banners and sashes . . . bunkum and fulsome filibustering": while emigrant soldiers died by the thousands fighting under alien flags, and while Irish rebels at home rotted in prison or perished on the gallows, Irish-American "patriots" such as Meagher and O'Gorman "sang songs and responded in glowing language to glowing toasts on Irish National Independence over beakers of fizzling champagne."[84]

However, Stephens was only partly accurate, and his contemptuous characterization of Irish-American nationalism—like the functionalist interpretations of later historians—only trivialized the fierce dedication and depths of emotion which animated many nationalist leaders and most of their followers. Although some nationalist agitators were charlatans and parasites, those who inspired the greatest devotion and posthumous respect were men such as John Mitchel, Michael Doheny, and John O'Mahony— single-minded fanatics who cared little or nothing for either their adopted country or opportunities for self-advancement. Perhaps significantly, although most former Young Irelanders were of bourgeois, urban, Anglicized Catholic backgrounds, Doheny, O'Mahony, and Mitchel shared important traits with their poorest followers: Doheny was a fluent Irish-speaker, son of a poor cottier in Tipperary, and, despite his law degree, still "peasant" enough to pummel the apostate nationalist D'Arcy McGee on the streets of New York; O'Mahony, also an Irish-speaker, was immersed in Gaelic literature, and before his flight had been a paternalistic landlord on the eighteenth-century model, able to "call out" 2,000 armed dependents to fight for Smith O'Brien; Mitchel, son of an Ulster Protestant minister, was the only seeming anomaly, but his ancestors had been United Irishmen, and his hatred for landlords and the English government ran as deep as that of any evicted tenant. For men like these, obsession with nationalist activities usually precluded material success, as one critic acknowledged when he condemned them for "wast[ing] precious hours and priceless energies which might have been devoted to elevating their own position." "The Fenian is not that reasoning creature which his critics in England have called him," observed a sympathetic British visitor; "a calculation of profits is not among his leading motives." Rather, "[h]e is that much more unreasonable animal, a dreamer, an enthusiast, a poet. Instead of making himself a career in the new country, he dreams of what he can be doing for the old." Nationalists such as Doheny were incorrigible "exiles," with emotional attachments to Ireland which obscured perceptions of American advantages: "I would like to be gay and happy," wrote Doheny from New York, "but I cannot. . . . [H]ope is fast disappearing, and a dark horizon closing in. . . . Oh! it is a sad thing to be . . . so far away from the sympathies that fired one's youth. It is a terrible thought that one must lie down to sleep at last in foreign soil." O'Mahony was similarly self-sacrificing, dying penniless in an unheated garret, cheered only by his translations of Gaelic sagas. Perhaps the period's quintessential exile was John Mitchel, who "had a sort of feeling that Ireland was his natural home, and that nowhere else could he find peace."[85]

Imbued with such sentiments, men like Mitchel and O'Mahony made few efforts to reconcile nationalist aspirations with native American opinions; indeed, they soon ceased all pretense of speaking to Americans as well as to their own people. At bottom they were implacable romantics, obsessed with Ireland, but their indifference to non-Irish opinion also stemmed from their ruthless analyses of the harsh, hostile realities of Irish-American life which neither the bombast of St. Patrick's Day nor the lace curtains of the nouveaux riches could obscure or alleviate. For example, when Mitchel first landed in New York, he declared his intention to be a "true and thorough American," for like his United Irish predecessors he believed initially that "America will not hold it disloyal to her if we Irish-Americans look anxiously out for an opportuny" to free Ireland. However, disillusioned by emigrant poverty and nativist prejudice, Mitchel soon viewed the United States only as a training field for Irish revolution, and he urged his countrymen to *use* America as the "very stamping ground prayed for by Archimedes, whereon they may plant a lever that shall move the world." The curious interlude when Mitchel supported southern secession was another reflection of his emergent abhorrence of the crass materialism and hypocrisy which he believed characteristic of a rejected American society. The Fenian leader John O'Mahony was equally disdainful—"I am sick of Yankee-doodle twaddle, Yankee-doodle selfishness, and all Yankee-doodle-dum!" he exclaimed—and he argued publicly that Irishmen owed nothing to their adopted land. "We give the country more than we get," he wrote, and "we claim nothing but that to which we have a right"–the right to maintain "our inflexible attachment" to Ireland. Nationalists such as Mitchel not only rejected America and made "no peace with England" but were also barely willing to compromise with the exigencies or even the existence of *Irish*-America: "the phrase I have heard of late, 'a new Ireland in America,' conveys no meaning to my mind," Mitchel admitted; "Ireland without the Irish–the Irish out of Ireland–neither of these can be our country." Consequently, such men ignored or discouraged assimilationist pressures and desires, seeking instead to kindle the same longings and resentments which inflamed their own hearts. "Remember Limerick!" Mitchel demanded; "remember Skull and Skibbereen! And oh! remember the long, bitter years of exile, and think of that beautiful land, the home of your childhood and your affections, where rest the ashes of your fathers, and the martyrs of your race. . . ." Remain faithful, the nationalists enjoined, and "take the vow, that should God in our lifetime light the day when Ireland's freedom must be struck for, our arms shall be ready to strike the blow." And, as one Fenian "martyr" prophesied, if the "exiles" remained true to their "Jerusalem," one day they might leave the land of bondage and return to a free and prosperous homeland.[86]

Such rhetoric touched responsive chords among ordinary Famine emigrants. Visitors to North America as disparate as the Englishmen John White and William Russell and the Irishmen John Francis Maguire and the O'Conor Don were fully sensible of Irish-American nationalism's mass appeal and its adherents' sincere devotion. The London journalist Russell "came away" from a New York Irish rally "regretting deeply that so many natives of the British Isles should be animated with a hostile feeling towards England. . . . Their strong antipathy is not diminished by the impossibility of gratifying it. They live in hope. . . ." More approving was the Cork politician Maguire, who wrote of the American Fenians that "never did martyrs more joyfully approach the stake, in which they beheld the gates of Paradise, than would these Irish exiles and their descendants march to battle in a cause that gratified the twin passions of their souls–love and hate." Although most emigrants struggled for mere subsistence, they opened their hearts and meager purses to those who refused to compromise with reality. Their loyalty to a seemingly hopeless cause was rooted in heritage and experience. Although Patrick Ford proclaimed that his own attitudes stemmed entirely from American circumstances, such was not the case for most Famine emigrants–and probably untrue even for such as Ford. In 1845–70 Irish-Americans either transported from the old country or learned at their fathers' knees in the new all the old traditions, songs, and personal memories of sectarian bitterness, landlord cruelty, and English perfidy. Perhaps sentiments were more sharply politicized for young middle-class emigrants such as Thomas Reilly, schooled on Young Ireland's romantic nationalism: in self-conscious, stylized letters Reilly declared himself "a Slave in the land of liberty" and announced his intention of joining an Irish-American militia company "preparing . . . to invade Ireland." "Perhaps I will return with the green flag flying above me," he wrote, "I care not if it becomes my shroud. I have no regard for life while I am in exile." Although peasants were less prone to such posturing, emigrants rooted in Gaelic traditions were at least as susceptible to feelings of antipathy and exile.[87]

Of equal importance, a large proportion of Famine emigrants, whether Gaelic or Anglicized, had personally experienced instances of landlord or English oppression which directly corroborated anti-*Sasanaigh* legacies and lent credence to beliefs that emigration was forced banishment. For example, in the late 1860s the Irish traveler Maguire met a fellow countryman in America whose conscience would not allow him to attend mass, "because he could not stamp out of his mind the hatred of, and passion for revenge against, the landlord who had evicted his family in Ireland and smashed their cabin"; likewise, another Famine emigrant, an evicted tenant from Meath, saw his wife die of fever on Grosse Isle and vowed on her grave to return someday to Ireland and shoot the landlord who had "murdered" her. These were extreme, although not atypical, cases, but even the British spy Thomas Doyle testified that the Famine emigrants' vivid memories of the "horrifying cruelties of the Crowbar Brigade" inspired their desire to "wreak vengeance on the persecutors of their race and creed." Such burning recollections help explain why Irish-American perceptions of Anglo-Irish relations remained fossilized, impervious to evidence of subsequent amelioration, and tainted with an unreasoning hatred. "Many of my informants seemed to be bright and quick-witted men," wrote the British traveler John White of his interviews with Irish emigrants. "On any other subject, at all within their range, they would talk, not merely sanely, but sensibly. It was only on the relations between England and Ireland, that the wonderful Irish monomania blazed out. Touch on that topic; and they began literally to rave."[88]

Moreover, even if Famine emigrants had left home voluntarily, without attributable compulsion, cultural characteristics not easily shed predisposed them to view their departures in conformity with communal traditions and nationalist motifs. As was noted earlier, suppressed resentments against fellow Irish Catholics—parents or "landgrabbers," often the proximate causes of emigration—could be subsumed and sublimated in acceptable anger against the "common enemy." Such was the case of William Lalor who, in his earliest letters home, blamed his father for forcing him to emigrate, but who over twenty years later blamed the English and avowed his burning desire to return to Ireland in the ranks of the Fenian army. More generally, as White observed, although Irish-Americans might improve material conditions overseas, "a more home-sick people cannot be": ironically, "[a] hard fate has singled out for an expatriation the most wholesale in modern history the people most attached to old places, and that suffers most sorely in exile. . . It is this sentimental home-sickness that is the well-spring of Fenianism in America." Longings for "the hills, streams, and valleys . . . of childhood" affected prosperous as well as poor emigrants; even a pragmatist like Richard O'Gorman could admit, "Still, I remember my old home and there comes sometimes a sting, and I dream of old times." Indeed, homesickness could cripple ambition and impede material achievement, as for Bartholomew Colgan, by 1862 no longer the well-adjusted emigrant of ten years earlier, but a self-proclaimed "exile" and Fenian sympathizer who admitted, "I could do very well in this country if I only could be contented and conclude to live and die hear: but since I left old Ireland I have a desire to return and untill I do I believe I never will be contented." However, impoverished Irish-Americans were most home-sick and most attracted to the nationalist dream: partly because such emi-grants were most likely to share archaic outlooks rooted in peasant paro-chialism and Gaelic traditions; partly because American experiences of poverty and proscription corroborated such outlooks and alienated affec-tions from their adopted country. In short, for most ordinary nationalists Irish heritage and New World circumstances were mutually reinforcing, shaping political "explanations" for present miseries which found release in visions of returning home. After all, the nationalists told them that per-fidious Albion was "the persecution, the crippling fetter, the recurring fam-ine, the pervading blight, the social cancer, and the rank source of our poverty and slanders" on both sides of the Atlantic. More specifically, En-lish tyranny was the reason why the emigrants were "exiles" like "the chil-dren of Israel."[89]

Acute homesickness conducive to nationalist dreams was prominent among genteel emigrants who failed to achieve naïve ambitions and instead sank to the bottom of Irish-American society. One such failure was Henry Hunt, "[d]escended from one of the most Honoured families" in Leinster, who by 1852 was a self-admitted "absolute pauper," begging money for a return passage to "poor hapless tyrant ridden Ireland." Another was Anne Browne from County Wexford, whose social degradation in America pro-voked deep regrets that her family ever came to "this land of Exile and of the Stranger." However, by all accounts alienation and nationalism were most pervasive among working-class emigrants: the former smallholders, cottiers, and laborers who inhabited North America's urban slums, mining camps, and shantytowns, enjoying few or no prospects for upward mobil-ity or social acceptance, yet still largely untouched by the Catholic church's institutionalized consolations. Thus, although John White reported meeting some affluent Irish-Americans and Irish-Canadians who ridiculed or con-demned Fenianism, he declared that "of the masses of the Roman Catholic Irish, the millions of workers and wage-earners, [he] never met any who condemned it, and seldom any who did not sympathise warmly." Working-class emigrants such as Daniel Rowntree soon had their fill of the "prom-ised land." "I have suffered more than I thought I could endure," Rown-tree wrote, "in a strange Country far from a friend, necessitated to go on public works from four oClock of a Summer Morning until Eight at Night enduring the hardships of a burning Sun, then by Sickness losing what I dearly earned"; "for my short time in this Country," Rowntree concluded, "I have experienced a great deal which may serve me in the remainder of my days." "We don't like this country very well," wrote another day laborer; "I think as soon as possible we will come home to old Ireland." The letters of such men usually revealed no assimilationist desires, no attachment to their adopted country. Indeed, by the late 1850s William Smith O'Brien, now released from Australian capitivity, reported after a visit to the New World that poverty and nativism had rendered the emigrants "so uncomfortable that they would willingly have left the United States if their circumstances had enabled them to quit that country without great loss." Although politicians often hailed Irish participation in the Civil War as a harbinger of ultimate acceptance, by mid-1863 emigrant newspapers were admitting that "the Irish spirit for the war is dead"—destroyed in senseless battles, under incompetent officers such as Meagher, and in the blood-stained streets of riot-torn New York. As one Irish-American concluded, "So hopelessly irksome do our people find their condition in this country that . . . hundreds of thousands . . . would ask no greater boon from Heaven at this side of the grave, than an opportunity to Stake their lives to regain a foothold on their native soil." Realistically, of course, as John White observed, relatively few ever returned to their homeland—"for, as they tell you, 'it's no place for a poor man.' " Despite their unhappiness they remained in North America, for at least there they could usually find work, feed their families, and hope their children might do better; besides, most emigrants reportedly never had funds sufficient to go home, and "by the time the fortunate are in a position to return, they have formed so many ties in America, that a return seems no longer what it seemed." Nevertheless, White added, "a return is looked forward to by the poor," and Irish-American nationalism—especially Fenianism—promised at least a vicarious realization of such longings.[90]

In terms of mass involvement and its avowed goal to transport thousands of disaffected, armed emigrants back to Ireland, Fenianism was unique in Irish-American nationalism. Although popular enthusiasm and financial contributions for Irish causes ran high in the early 1880s and in 1916–21, qualitatively these subsequent movements were different: by comparison with the Famine emigrants, later generations were less alienated from American society, more integrated into Irish-American socioeconomic, political, and religious institutions which promoted relative security and contentment. Nevertheless, the Famine exodus and its nationalist fervor left a permanent mark on Irish as well as American society, influencing future developments on both sides of the Atlantic. As the IRB leader John O'Leary testified, it was Fenianism that first demonstrated "what a powerful factor in *Irish* politics the Irish in America had become": in the early nineteenth century Irish leaders such as O'Connell had paid little regard to Irish-America; however, from the 1860s onward nationalists at home were heavily dependent on Irish-American approbation and funds. On the American side, nationalist interpretations of the Famine enshrined a now-permanent model for Irish emigration, to which all emigrants, present and future, had to conform. For example, John Burke, who left Westmeath in "black '47," did so not on compulsion but from "disgust" at inadequate opportunities; he was eager to reach the "land of plenty," and he prospered there. However, when Burke completed his memoirs, he asserted that his own migration, like that of his fellow "exiles," had been caused by English oppression; forty years afterward, he had tailored his story to communal tradition and Irish-American rhetoric. In addition, the Famine emigrants and their nationalist spokesmen passed down a legacy of lasting bitterness and unfulfilled dreams to their American-born children: "keep bright in your mind the story of Ireland," demanded one ex-Fenian of his young son, "and should God send the opportunity during your life [to] aid by voice or means the great struggle which is but postponed, then I charge you in your manhood to act as becometh your race."[91]

"Revenge for Skibbereen"—for "The *tears* your *mothers* shed"—was a terrible burden for innocents to bear. However, for their emigrant fathers neither time nor success had dulled recollections of the years "when gaunt hunger and death stalked abroad" and when thousands of evicted peasants perished in the ditches or sailed in floating charnel houses to a land of false promises. Thirty years after such events had precipitated his own emigration, an Irishman in Minnesota still remembered and hated "the cursed government and the odious way the laws are administered" in Ireland: "Why don't you in the name of God," he asked his cousin in County Carlow, "just shake the dust from your feet and leave your curse upon the system that exiled . . . all . . . good honest and faithful Irishmen from their native land."[92]

8

The Last "Exiles": Ireland
and Post-Famine Emigration
1856–1921

Between 1856 and 1921 the last great waves of Irish emigration broke on American shores, and during this period more Irishmen and -women left their native land than in the preceding two and a half centuries. They departed largely for economic reasons: attracted by New World opportunities and the examples of earlier emigrants, but primarily repelled by developments in Irish agriculture and industry which made life at home untenable. Indeed, by the late nineteenth century the peculiar evolution of Irish society had made mass emigration a permanent institution. Many emigrated eagerly or at least without protest, either alienated from a society impoverished in more than economic respects, or conditioned to join relatives abroad whose letters and remittances promised advantages unavailable in Ireland. However, a large number still left reluctantly, sometimes bitterly, and even many who welcomed or accepted emigration still conformed to old patterns, at least occasionally, by interpreting departure as involuntary exile. In part the persistence of that traditional perception reflected important continuities in Irish Catholic society and culture, especially in western Ireland, as well as continued conflicts with landlordism and British officialdom, epitomized by the Land War of 1879–82 and subsequent campaigns for Irish self-government. However, in large measure it was also a response to the profound changes taking place in post-Famine Ireland—changes which threatened to fragment Catholic society and erode its traditional defenses against internal dissension and external enemies. In that context the exile motif remained essential, for it served as an ideological bridge between past and present, uniting social groups and reconciling personal impulses which were inherently conflicting and logically contradictory. Likewise, although in late-nineteenth- and early-twentieth-century America the pressures and incentives to discard transplanted attitudes were great, Irish-Americans also needed traditional symbols which gave unity and meaning to the diversity and fluidity of immigrant life. Ironically, in a sense Irish-America still needed Ireland and its "sacred cause" almost as much as Ireland and the Irish leaders of that cause still needed Irish-American dollars. Perhaps by 1921 Irish-America, by then composed overwhelmingly of the American-born, was sufficiently mature and secure to stand on its own. But by then the exile motif's imperative had been fulfilled: after a last great infusion of Irish-American money and enthusiasm, Ireland—three-fourths of it, at least—was finally free of the British misgovernment which had purportedly exiled so many of her faithful and vengeful children.

Section 1. The Outlines of Post-Famine Emigration

In 1845–55 Ireland's population fell from about 8.5 million to around 6 million, as a result of starvation, disease, and, especially, emigration. Ordinarily, demographic catastrophes such as the Great Famine only temporarily retard population growth; however, Ireland's mid-century crisis was not an anomaly, but rather a tragic, accelerating symptom of the island's integration into a maturing international market system as a dependent and subordinate supplier of raw materials, specialized manufactured goods, and cheap labor to the world's dominant industrial nations. Consequently, although famine abated, Ireland's population continued to decline, from 5.8 million in 1861 to less than 4.3 million in 1926. This phenomenon was the central fact of post-Famine Irish experience and a major focus of contemporary political debate. However, belying nationalists' prophecies, the establishment of the Irish Free State in 1921 failed to reverse the downward trend: ironically, it was the six northern Irish counties, which after 1921 remained an integral part of Great Britain, which experienced a slight, subsequent growth in population, while that of the new southern Irish nation continued to fall until the 1960s.[1]

Emigration was the major reason for Ireland's declining population. The registrar general's annual returns, based on reports furnished by police at the principal Irish ports, reflect a total Irish emigration between 1856 and 1921 of 3.6 million. However, the most recent students of Irish emigration statistics argue convincingly that that figure represents almost exclusively *overseas* movements and that at least 500,000 (perhaps as many as one million) additional, unrecorded emigrants moved to Great Britain. Of the overseas migrants, the vast majority—some 3,054,000—moved directly to the United States, while about 209,000 sailed to Canada. An additional 289,000 emigrated to Australia and New Zealand, and 60,000 more went to South Africa, Argentina, and other destinations. Moreover, a large but unknown proportion of the Irish who initially settled in Britain (or who were born there of emigrant parents) eventually re-emigrated to the United States, as did some who originally embarked for Canada, Australia, and elsewhere. Thus, in 1856–1921 Ireland lost between 4.1 and 4.5 million inhabitants, of whom perhaps 3.5 million ended their travels in North America, primarily in the United States. Indeed, by 1900, more Irishmen and -women (including second-generation Irish-Americans) were living in the United States alone than in Ireland itself.[2]

According to the registrar general's reports, between 1856 and the outbreak of World War I, annual emigration overseas never fell below 23,300 and was rarely less than 35,000. Over the entire period the annual average was at least 54,000 (62–68,000 if the estimated, unrecorded outflow to Britain is included), and in peak years the annual total exceeded 100,000. In short, emigration was such an integral part of post-Famine Irish society that a substantial stream flowed continuously. However, as in the pre-Famine decades (and as Tables 1–6 in the Appendix demonstrate), the tide of emigration fluctuated in response to specific economic and, to a lesser extent, political conditions at home and abroad. For example, on the basis of official (albeit suspect) reports, it appears that in the years 1856–60 nearly 250,000 Irish sailed to the United States (compared with 734,000 in 1851–55)—a total which reflected continued rural adjustment to the Famine experience (plus a sharp decline in handloom weaving in east Ulster), tempered by the depletion of those age groups and classes most prone to emigration and by reports of widespread unemployment, poverty, and prejudice encountered in the New World. The annual average of America-bound emigrants in 1856–60 was nearly 50,000, although in 1858 news of the American financial panic of the preceding year reduced departures to 31,500. In 1861–62 the outbreak of the Civil War and consequent economic dislocations in the United States caused emigration to fall to an average of less than 31,000. However, in 1863–64 poor harvests, rural distress, and political unrest in Ireland combined with voracious American demands for soldiers and wartime laborers to inspire a dramatic resurgence of departures; in each year over 94,000 Irish sailed to the United States. Thanks to continued economic expansion in America, coupled with industrial depression at home, after the Civil War Irish emigration to the United States remained at high levels—averaging about 72,000 per year—until the American financial crisis of 1873 sharply reduced departures the following season to only 48,000. The years 1874–78 were unusually prosperous ones for Irish agriculture, while the United States was mired in economic depression and torn by industrial strife: consequently, emigration to America fell to the lowest levels since 1838; departures averaged under 26,500 per year, and in 1877 fewer than 14,000 Irish went to the United States. However, in the late 1870s and the 1880s poor harvests, evictions, agrarian turmoil, and, most important, steep price declines for Irish farm products combined with renewed economic growth in the United States to produce a new wave of departures: in 1879 emigration to America rose to 30,100, and in 1880 and again in 1883 about 83,000 embarked for the "land of promise"; the annual average over the entire decade was 65,751. Emigration declined somewhat in subsequent years, but despite periodic American economic crises (as in 1893–97 and 1907–8), continued Irish adjustments to economic exigencies—highlighted by sporadic crop failures and industrial recessions—ensured a steady flow of departures until the onset of war in mid-1914. In the 1890s over 427,000 journeyed to the United States, followed by nearly 419,000 in the next decade and by 125,000 in the four immediate pre-war years; from 1890 to 1913 annual emigration ranged from 31,000 to 53,000, averaging about 43,000 per year. During the war departures fell sharply—from 24,100 in 1914 to only 980 in 1918—but recovered strongly by 1920–21, when almost 43,000 sailed to the United States. Curiously, it was only during this later period, 1901–21, that Irish emigration to Canada formed a significant proportion of the post-Famine transatlantic movement. During the Famine years nearly one-fourth of the Irish emigrants to the New World had landed in British North America, but in 1856–60 the proportion fell to 5 percent and averaged less than that for the rest of the century; between 1856 and 1900, annual embarkations for Canada averaged fewer than 3,000—only once, in 1883, exceeding 10,000. Affluent emigrants intending to farm now preferred Australia or New Zealand, while remittances and reduced transatlantic fares made it possible for poor Irishmen to sail directly to the United States. However, in 1901–10 the Canada-bound proportion of transatlantic emigration rose to 8.4 percent and in 1911–21 to nearly 16 percent, and annual departures over the period 1901–21 (excluding 1915–18) averaged nearly 4,000: perhaps reflecting the lure of Canada's prairie provinces, coupled with Irish Protestant emigrants' desires to settle under the British flag.[3]

Tables 2–14 (see Appendix) also indicate the composition of post-Famine emigration: its peculiar characteristics, which reflected precipitating conditions in Ireland, helped shape prevailing Irish attitudes toward the exodus and—in conjunction with earlier emigrants and their descendants—determined the structure and character of late-nineteenth- and early-twentieth-century Irish-American society. However, one must use the departure statistics in Table 2 (and the compilations based largely on those statistics: Tables 3–10) with caution, especially when drawing conclusions therefrom on the nature of Irish emigration to *North America*. For example, the official figures in Table 2 purportedly represent *total* Irish emigration, to Britain, Australia, and so on, as well as to the New World. Also, as was noted above, they may omit a considerable number of emigrants to Britain, perhaps as many as one million. Moreover, on the basis of age-cohort depletion rates, the historians Cormac Ó Gráda and David Fitzpatrick have argued that the official figures seriously underestimate departures from Connaught and, to a lesser extent, from Ulster and Leinster, while overestimating Munster emigration. Nevertheless, for purposes of this analysis these problems are not insuperable. If the great majority of British-bound emigrants indeed went unrecorded, then the official figures must largely represent overseas emigration, the bulk of which was to North America. The question of inaccurate regional origins data is more crucial, but may be alleviated by several considerations. First is Ó Gráda's informed suggestion that most of the "hidden emigrants" from Connaught, Ulster, and Leinster went to Great Britain rather than to the New World. Second is the fact that Connaught and Munster shared certain socioeconomic and cultural characteristics which shaped their emigrants' experiences and outlooks; in that respect, therefore, the alleged discrepancies in the official emigration figures for the two provinces somewhat counterbalance each other, preventing undue distortion of the general backgrounds of post-Famine emigration.[4]

According to the official statistics, between 1 January 1856 and 31 December 1920 over 3,590,000 emigrants left Ireland. Of these, 16.1 percent (577,000) departed from Leinster, 29.9 percent (1,073,000) from Ulster, 33.4 percent (1,163,000) from Munster, and 17.8 percent (637,000) from Connaught. Thus, whereas in the pre-Famine decades departures from Ulster and Leinster had predominated, in 1856–1920 over 51 percent of the Irish emigrants left the southern- and westernmost provinces. Also, in proportion to their respective populations, and in proportion to their provinces' shares of the total Irish population during the period, emigration from Munster and Connaught was significantly greater than that from Leinster and Ulster. For example, in 1856–1910 the average annual emigration rates (the number of departures per 1,000 inhabitants) for Munster and Connaught were 15.6 and 13.8 respectively, while in Leinster and Ulster the comparable rates were only 7.5 and 10.3. In addition, although together Munster and Connaught contained only 40 percent of Ireland's mean population in 1856–1910, during the period they contributed over half the total exodus; by contrast, Leinster with 25.2 percent and Ulster with 33.3 percent of Ireland's inhabitants sent forth proportionately fewer emigrants. Furthermore, after 1880 the emigrants' geographical origins shifted farther south- and westward: in 1856–1880 only 45.6 percent of the recorded Irish emigrants left Munster and Connaught, while Ulster alone contributed one-third the total; by contrast, in 1881–1910 nearly 59 percent of the exodus was from Munster and Connaught, while Ulster sent forth only 26.6 percent and Leinster merely 14.9 percent of the total. Taking another perspective, considering decadal emigration as a proportion of the population in the census year beginning each decade, one then finds that during every ten-year period from 1861 to 1910 Munster and Connaught each lost at minimum 10 percent of their populations through emigration: Munster during the 1860s, 1880s, 1890s, and Connaught during the latter two decades, saw at least 15 percent of their inhabitants depart; conversely, in the 1890s only 5 percent of Ulster's and 4 percent of Leinster's 1891 populations left the country. Finally, although total Irish emigration between 1856–80 and 1881–1910 declined by 18 percent, emigration from Munster declined by less than 13 percent (compared with 28 percent and 32 percent declines in Leinster and Ulster), and emigration from Connaught *increased* by nearly 53 percent. By the last decades of the nineteenth century, nearly all the Irish counties experiencing unusually heavy emigration were located on the western seaboard: Counties Clare, Cork, and especially Kerry in Munster; Donegal in Ulster; and all the Connaught counties, particularly Galway and Mayo. The exceptions were three especially impoverished mid-Ulster and north Leinster counties: Cavan, Tyrone, and Longford. (See Tables 2–6.)

Although the data base is admittedly imprecise, the above percentages derived therefrom support several general conclusions. First, the post-Famine exodus was overwhelmingly Catholic. Even if we assume that in 1856–1920 the Protestant proportion of Irish emigration equaled Protestant shares of Ireland's provincial populations (e.g., in 1881), Protestant departures numbered no more than about 746,000 (560,000 from Ulster), or less than 21 percent of the total. Only in 1856–60, 1871–80, and 1901–20—periods of relatively low overall emigration, when Ulster contributed an above-average share of departures—did Protestant emigration probably exceed one-fifth of the total. Indeed, it is highly likely that in 1856–1920 Protestant emigrants numbered fewer than 746,000, since during the period the Protestant proportion of Ulster's population steadily increased (from 49.5 percent in 1861 to 56.3 percent in 1911), indicating a disproportionately high Ulster Catholic departure rate: an impression strengthened by the fact that the four counties (Antrim, Armagh, Down, and Londonderry) which contained about three-quarters of Ulster's Protestants (75.2 percent in 1881) did not contribute a disproportionately greater share of Ulster emigrants than did the province's predominantly Catholic counties. In the three southern provinces the pattern was different: there the Protestant population in 1861–1911 fell in both absolute and relative terms (e.g., from 6.2 percent to 6.0 percent in Munster), indicating a higher rate of Protestant than of Catholic departures. However, southern Irish Protestants were so few that their disproportionately greater emigration rate made little impact on what was, overall, a predominantly Catholic exodus.[5]

Second, a large proportion of the post-Famine emigrants were not only Catholics but also Irish-speakers (albeit usually bilingual) and their imperfectly Anglicized children. Unfortunately, port officials did not inquire whether post-Famine emigrants spoke Irish, but Tables 9 and 10 (see Appendix) indicate that Irish-speakers alone constituted a significant minority, particularly after 1880. As late as 1891, Irish was still a living language in ten counties where it was spoken by over 10 percent of the population: in 1856–80 44 percent, and in 1881–1910 over 55 percent of Irish emigrants came from those counties. Moreover, between 1881 and 1910 almost one-fourth of all departures took place from counties where in 1891 from 41 to 59 percent of the inhabitants spoke Irish. If the proportion of Irish-speaking emigrants equaled the Irish-speaking shares of Ireland's county populations, then during the 1890s (a decade when that hypothesis might be most valid, given the high departure rates from Connaught and west Munster) Irish-speakers constituted nearly one-quarter of the total emigrants (see Table 10). From these tables it is possible to infer that perhaps one-fourth to one-third of all post-Famine emigrants spoke Irish (the historian David N. Doyle suggests 28 percent) and that perhaps about another fourth were the children of Irish-speakers: educated in English, discouraged by their parents and teachers from speaking Irish, perhaps ashamed to admit even partial fluency to the census takers, yet still familiar with the native idiom and the concepts and traditions it expressed.[6]

Third, post-Famine emigrants came largely from more-impoverished backgrounds, and consequently possessed fewer skills and less capital, than their pre-Famine predecessors. Tables 4 and 7 (see Appendix) indicate that in general those Irish counties which were least urbanized, contained the smallest proportions of inhabitants engaged in nonagricultural occupations, and exhibited the poorest farmland and, to a lesser degree, the worst rural-housing conditions were the counties which experienced the highest emigration rates and together produced a majority of the post-Famine exodus. (The two most striking exceptions to these patterns, Counties Cork and Donegal, can be explained by their extraordinary size and diversity: in socioeconomic and cultural terms, west Cork and western Donegal are analogous to west Kerry and Mayo, while their eastern districts correspond in affluence to Kilkenny and Antrim.) Table 8 also suggests the post-Famine emigrants' relative destitution. Beginning in 1891 Parliament designated Ireland's most wretchedly poor regions as "congested districts" eligible for special government assistance: in 1856–1910 over 28 percent of all Irish emigrants departed the seven western counties which had a substantial proportion of their areas so designated; between 1881 and 1910 over 35 percent of the emigrants came from those counties. On the other hand, it is certain that post-Famine emigrants were much more literate than those who had preceded them. Between 1851 and 1901 the proportion of Ireland's inhabitants over age five who could neither read nor write fell from 47 percent to only 14 percent. However, this improvement was somewhat mitigated by disproportionately high illiteracy rates among Catholics generally (16.4 percent in 1901) and especially among the inhabitants of those western counties which, after 1880, had the highest departure rates; for example, in 1881, 38 percent of Connaught's people could neither read nor write, and in 1901 the comparable figure was still 21 percent. Admittedly, illiteracy was much less prevalent among the age groups (fifteen to twenty-four) most likely to emigrate, and in 1897 one American official noted that less than 5 percent of the Irish arriving at New York were unable to read and write. Nevertheless, the *officially* recorded illiteracy among Irish emigrants was still higher than that among their English and Scottish counterparts, and a large number of western Irish emigrants (and many laboring-class emigrants from eastern Ireland) were at best imperfectly literate. Moreover, if emigrant illiteracy declined in the post-Famine decades, so did the proportion of emigrants possessing skills or trades. In 1836 ships' captains classified over 27 percent of the Irish passengers debarking at New York as artisans and craftsmen, but in 1856 only 18 percent were so classified, compared with 73 percent who described themselves as laborers and servants. From Table 14 it is evident that in the period 1875–1910 unskilled emigrants were even more predominant: in 1875 over 78 percent of all recorded emigrants were classified as laborers and servants, and in 1900 the comparable figure exceeded 91 percent. Undoubtedly, a large number of these "laborers" and "servants" were not actually from working-class backgrounds, but instead were the sons and daughters of petty and middling farmers. Nevertheless, their official occupational designations were probably accurate indications of their levels of marketable skills: "It is to be feared," wrote the American consul in Belfast in 1883, "that most of such emigrants are without means, and, what is worse, without skill in trades or other occupations, and with so little money as to afford no promise of any respectable support on their arrival in America." Indeed, as late as 1900 the average emigrant landed in the United States with only £2 15s. capital, and remittances from the New World had to finance the vast majority of post-Famine departures. Contemporaries observed that few late-nineteenth-century Irish emigrants traveled on their own resources, and one scholar estimates that in 1850–1900 prepaid passage tickets (only one form of remittances) paid for over 75 percent of all Irish emigration to the New World.[7]

Finally, Tables 11, 12, and 13 (see Appendix) indicate that the typical post-Famine emigrant was younger and more likely to be female and unmarried than her or his pre-Famine counterpart. Before the Famine the median age of the Irish arriving in New York City had been about 24, but between 1852 and 1921 the median age for all male emigrants was 22.5, for females only 21.2. By the 1890s female emigrants' median age was under 20, and during the entire post-Famine period the proportion of emigrants in their teens and early twenties steadily increased. For example, in the years 1861–70 and 1901–10 the proportion of male emigrants aged fifteen to twenty-four rose from 42 percent to 54 percent, while the proportion of similarly aged female emigrants increased from 47 percent to 65 percent; indeed, by 1901–10 over a fourth of all female emigrants were merely fifteen to nineteen years old. In addition, relatively few post-Famine emigrants were married or apt to travel in family groups. There were exceptions: crop failures and evictions in the early 1860s and 1880s inspired some family emigration (often assisted by public or private charities), and periods of exceptionally high Protestant emigration (e.g., the 1870s and 1911–21) witnessed many departures by entire families. Nevertheless, after mid-century the proportion of married emigrants rarely exceeded 16 percent, and the proportions of children under fifteen and adults over thirty-four steadily diminished. Moreover, a surprisingly high proportion of post-Famine emigrants was female. Prior to 1845 about two-thirds of the Irish disembarking at New York were males, but between 1851 and 1910 the sex ratio for all emigrants was about equal. In none of the post-Famine decades did females compose less than 45 percent of the departing Irish, and after 1880 they constituted a majority. Among the four Irish provinces, only Ulster retained any semblance of the male-dominated pre-Famine emigration patterns; by contrast, in 1881–1910 almost four females left Connaught for every three males. This was a uniquely Irish pattern, for males overwhelmingly predominated among the southern and eastern Europeans who flocked to the United States during the same period.[8]

In short, between 1856 and 1921, and particularly after 1880, the majority of Irish emigrants were Catholics from the three southern provinces, especially Munster and Connaught, and from the poorest rural districts where peasant folkways and an attenuated Gaelic culture survived. In terms of marketable skills, most were mere laborers and servants who carried little, if any, capital and whose emigrations were financed by remittances from abroad. In addition, most were quite young, in their teens or early twenties; about half were female; few were married or traveling with parents. Thus, by the last decades of the nineteenth century, all the patterns of Irish emigration slowly emerging during the pre-Famine period had become dominant and permanent, in turn reflecting the conditions which inspired and impelled the exodus.

Section 2. Emigration as "Escape": Modernization and the
Causes of Post-Famine Emigration

In the late nineteenth and early twentieth centuries, Irishmen on both sides of the Atlantic persistently asked the question raised in 1874 by a County Limerick emigrant, Maurice Wolfe, when he "wonder[ed] what is the cause of So many people leaving Ireland?": improved facilities for emigration, the attractions of North America, or compelling conditions in Ireland itself? Certainly, post-Famine Ireland was rife with alluring inducements to emigrate, circulated by those who had direct economic interests in encouraging departures. For example, in the last quarter of the nineteenth century, fiercely competitive transatlantic steamship companies conducted intensive advertising campaigns and employed shipping agents and ticket brokers in the remotest districts. In the 1890s the five largest firms alone employed several thousand agents and brokers, usually shopkeepers, publicans, or auctioneers—who thereby gained a personal interest in stimulating or at least facilitating emigration. In addition, American and Canadian railroad and land companies, as well as state and provincial governments, employed Irish agents, advertised in newspapers, issued handbills, and published pamphlets to lure Irishmen and -women to their respective climates, soils, and labor markets. The Canadian government was particularly assiduous in recruiting Irish emigrants, especially Protestants. Indeed, the Canadian Orange Order seems to have functioned almost as Ontario's official emigration society, encouraging the Ulster " 'brethren' "—as one Catholic complained—"to go there and make a second Belfast of the whole province."[9]

The relative ease and cheapness of the transatlantic voyage during most of the post-Famine era also encouraged as it facilitated departures. Beginning in 1855 both the British Parliament and the American Congress passed comprehensive legislation which regulated deck and berth space per passenger and which demanded relatively high standards of diet, sanitation, and medical facilities. In addition, the British legislation required that passage brokers and shipcaptains post high bonds for good behavior, licensed and registered all the runners and lodging-house keepers in the embarkation ports, and gave the emigration commissioners the power to issue orders-in-council affecting virtually all aspects of the emigrant trade. Later in the century the American government demanded that emigrants undergo stringent medical examinations before embarking. However, although well-intentioned, most of these new laws were as ineffective as their predecessors. They were impossible to enforce at sea: thus, although shipboard mortality in the late 1850s fell below 1 percent, reports of overcrowding, unsanitary conditions, poor treatment, and frauds remained common—especially in the immediate post-Famine decades, when Irish public opinion was periodically outraged by salacious newspaper accounts of unchecked drunkenness and sexual immorality aboard what one "excitable imagination" called "Floating Brothels." Moreover, since the American and British governments never coordinated their legislation or enforcement procedures, aggrieved passengers had no redress other than to warn future emigrants against particular shippers and captains by inserting notices in the Irish or Liverpool newspapers.[10]

Dramatic improvements in voyage conditions came only with the inauguration of transatlantic steamship traffic. In the late 1850s the Cunard and Allan steamship lines (both British) already carried a small proportion of Irish emigrants; in 1863, 45 percent—in 1866, 81 percent—of the Irish emigrants traveled by steam, and after 1870 only a handful of Irishmen still journeyed by sail. The steamships themselves became larger, faster, and more comfortable. The early Cunard liners were relatively small, constructed of wood, propelled by paddles, and capable of speeds of eight to twelve knots; however, steamships launched in the 1880s were up to 500 feet in length, built largely of iron and steel, driven by screw propellers, and capable of doubling previous speeds; by the early twentieth century vessels such as the White Star liner *Oceanic* could carry 2,000 passengers (over 1,000 in steerage) at speeds commonly in excess of twenty-five knots. Voyage length was the single most important factor affecting passengers' safety and comfort: the earliest steamships reduced what had been a normal voyage length of five to six weeks to a mere fortnight, and voyages of less than ten or twelve days had by 1900 become commonplace. In addition, the new steamships provided even steerage passengers with amenities unimaginable to their predecessors: separate beds with mattresses, blankets, and pillows; tiled washrooms where emigrants could bathe regularly; cooked meals served thrice daily; even smoking rooms. Moreover, intense competition for passengers forced the steamship companies to ameliorate the entire process of emigration. For example, after 1858, Irishmen no longer had to travel to Liverpool or Glasgow to board a transatlantic vessel. In that year efforts to establish a new steamship line between Galway and North America forced the major British companies to make regular calls at Queenstown (in Cork harbor), Moville (near Londonderry), Belfast, Galway, and other Irish ports to pick up passengers; after 1870 Queenstown and Moville replaced Liverpool as the major embarkation ports for emigrants bound for the United States or Canada. In addition, the steamship companies brought relative order and honesty out of the chaos and fraud which had formerly characterized the embarkation ports: now salaried company agents supplanted independent passage brokers, met the emigrant trains and cross-channel streamers, transported baggage, directed the emigrants to licensed (sometimes company-owned) lodging houses, and generally protected them until they were on shipboard. Finally and perhaps most important, although initially steamships charged higher fares than sailing vessels, by the late nineteenth century companies were slashing rates drastically to attract passengers: in 1894 an Irishman or -woman could travel to the New World for as little as £1 16s. or $8.75.[11]

Of course, some discomforts persisted, particularly in the immediate post-Famine decades, when steamships were still relatively slow and cramped, and emigrants' complaints often belied the steamship companies' glowing advertisements. For example, in 1870 L. B. Sheil, an emigrant from Wexford, could still lament "the bad air of our Cabin . . . next [to] the Water Closets," and in 1873 F. McCosker from Drogheda complained that his ship was "officered . . . by the scum of the cities" who treated the passengers like "paupers instead of the travelling public" and "burst [their luggage] to smithereens . . . and no redress." Even twenty years later an emigrant who sailed from Moville reported that his berth was as hard and narrow as a coffin and that "the food put down before us" consisted largely of "a few sea-biscuits that were as hard as a ram's horn." In addition, some voyage conditions were impervious to change: seasickness still plagued passengers such as the Corkman Denis Hurley, who spent his passage "below by the bunks with a heavy heart and an upset stomach puking," and heavy storms and icebergs remained profound inspirations to the emigrants' wonder, fear, and desperate prayer. From their privileged vantages on the upper decks, first-and second-class passengers such as the affluent emigrants James Greene and Pat McCarthy could afford to despise the southern and eastern Europeans, who by the 1890s constituted the bulk of steerage or third-class passengers; however, poor Irishmen who still had to travel in steerage found practical discomforts only accentuated by enforced proximity to those Greene called "a filthy collection of human beings." Despite its brevity, the ocean voyage still seemed "tedious" to many Irish emigrants, and the continued efforts by some "wild irish men" to relieve monotony by drinking, by singing nationalist songs and otherwise taunting non-Irish Catholic passengers, or by fighting among themselves with "hammer, tongs, and shillalahs"—as one disgusted English emigrant reported in 1886—only caused unnecessary hardships. Homesickness remained another perennial of the voyage experience: "I have to struggle to keep my mind away from home," wrote one emigrant in mid-ocean, "for the thought inevitably calls up a copious flood of blinding tears and quite unnerves me." However, by comparison with what the pre-Famine and the Famine emigrants had accepted and endured, the later complaints of steamship passengers such as the Ulsterman Martin Beatty—who whined that the ship's stewards were too slow in serving admittedly excellent food—seem ludicrously insignificant. True, third-class steamship accommodations were not sumptuous, and their exposed pipes and girders compared unfavorably with the true luxury of first-class staterooms. Nevertheless, in quality they were worlds removed from the foul holds of the coffin ships and probably superior to both the Irish cottages left behind and the Irish-American slum tenements which generally lay ahead. Indeed, after about 1870 the great majority of the Irish emigrants either testified by their silence that they had found their short passages unremarkable, undeserving of complaint or comment, or else declared in letters home that they had enjoyed a "very pleasant voyage." In fact, by the 1890s the largest steamship companies were striving to eliminate passenger boredom as well as discomfort by organizing regular concerts, church services, dances, and games. No wonder, then, that unsophisticated young emigrants like Mary Ann Landy wished that such splendid experiences would never end, and that most Irish recipients of accounts such as hers no longer shared their forefathers' fears of the transatlantic crossing.[12]

In addition, not only were ocean fares relatively low in the post-Famine decades but those Irish still too poor to pay their own passages enjoyed increased access to public and private assistance. Between 1856 and 1906 the Irish Poor Law boards of guardians financed the emigration of about 25,000 paupers, primarily to the United States and Canada, and in 1882–83 Parliament passed legislation which subsidized transportation for over 54,000 more. Also, between 1847 and 1870 the colonial land and emigration commissioners sent out 116,500 Irish emigrants, nearly all to Australia. Passage money also came from landlords, charitable and friendly societies, and private philanthropists such as Vere Foster and James Hack Tuke, who together financed about 30,000 departures during the 1880s, largely from the poor western counties to North America. Moreover, enormous amounts of money arrived from overseas to subsidize and encourage emigration. During the American Civil War, Union agents and consuls in Ireland allegedly distributed free passage tickets and other inducements, and between 1864 and 1885 Congress encouraged the importation of contract laborers from Ireland and elsewhere: for example, in 1863 some 250 Irishmen left Dublin for the United States with fares paid by the Alton and Chicago Railroad; in 1883 a Nashua, New Hampshire, cotton manufacturer contracted the services of sixty-five female inmates of the Limerick poorhouse; and in the following year a traveler in County Galway complained that American agents were signing large numbers of prospective emigrants to labor contracts, "dazzl[ing] the Irish workers by statements of the amounts that might be earned by labouring an indefinite time." In fact, however, relatively few Irish emigrated as contract laborers: unskilled workers generally were too plentiful in America for businesses to risk investments easily lost if the Irish evaded their obligations after disembarking; besides, Irish emigrants' ability to speak English, plus their reputation for contentiousness, made them less attractive employees than were the more dependent and docile members of non-English-speaking groups. Thus, the most common contractual arrangements involving Irish emigrants were small-scale, private affairs, as when H. T. Lawlor and Francis Aglionby, affluent Irish-Americans living in southern states, contracted for the services of a few countrymen from home to replace "the wretched negroes" as plantation workers and house servants. Finally, of course, remittances from the now-large established Irish-American and Irish-Canadian communities financed the great majority of post-Famine emigrations. Prior to mid-century, channels for sending home money or prepaid passage tickets had been varied but often troublesome and uncertain; however, during and after the Famine more-secure ways to remit money emerged, and organizations such as Patrick Donohoe's Boston *Pilot* newspaper and New York's Irish Emigrant Industrial Savings Bank became major conduits of remittances. Also, in 1871 the American and British governments signed an international postal-money-order agreement, which greatly facilitated the transmission of funds overseas. The level of remittances fluctuated annually in response to American business cycles, Irish-American prosperity, and the relative degrees of Irish need. But overall between 1848 and 1900 the North American Irish sent home over £52 million ($260 million), a yearly average of £1 million ($5 million); over 90 percent of this money came from the United States, about 40 percent in the form of prepaid passage tickets.[13]

Many contemporaries believed that it was this flood of money and the accompanying letters from America—not the poverty and social inadequacies of Irish society—which inspired most post-Famine emigrants to take the now-brief, comfortable passage to the New World. Certainly, favorable reports of American conditions remained important stimulants to Irish emigration. As an American correspondent for the London *Daily News* reported in 1864, "What brings such crowds to New York by every packet-ship is the letters which are written by the Irish already here to their relations in Ireland"—relations who often waited eagerly, as one prospective emigrant wrote, for the Irish-Americans' "views Ideas and prospects" of opportunities abroad. Many emigrants no doubt sent home encouraging accounts of America during the post-Famine decades. For example, Irish-American farmers such as William Porter in Illinois and William Austin in Nebraska drew telling contrasts between the position of Irish tenants subjected to rents, taxes, and enforced subservience and their own happier status in a country where "the rod of the Landlord is not still a holding over your head and what you acquire is your own." Likewise, Irish-American skilled workers, such as the Detroit carpenter who now enjoyed a monthly salary 350 percent higher than the one he had earned in Ireland, transmitted reports of such encouraging experiences. Even a semiliterate, unskilled laborer like James Glover could declare that American cities were "gret ples[es] fur . . . blast frnises and Rolen milles" and conclude happily that "this is awelth[y] Cuntery." And young Irishwomen were similarly heartened to learn, as from Philadelphia in 1894, that "there is always a demand for them as few native girls care to go out as house Servants" or factory workers. Such letters also remained important in directing would-be emigrants to specific locations. For example, in 1890 the Protestant Ulster-American N. Shanks informed his brother in County Antrim that Canada now offered prospective farmer emigrants greater opportunities than the thickly settled American Midwest; during the next two decades his relatives heeded such advice and emigrated to northern Ontario and Saskatchewan.[14]

Nevertheless, the primary causes of post-Famine emigration were the changing economic conditions, social structures, and cultural patterns of contemporary Ireland. Although remittances and favorable reports from North America, coupled with the ease of transatlantic travel, made possible and encouraged departures, the fact that most emigrants' letters written in the post-Famine decades contained not flattering but cautionary or negative information about New World conditions indicates the primacy of Irish over American stimulants to emigration. During economic depressions abroad, Irish-Americans' letters were especially discouraging. For example, after the financial panics of 1857 and 1873, emigrants often warned of "the deplorable state of business caused by the wholesale knavery and universal swindling prevalent here." "The times are very hard in this country," wrote another Irish-American in the early 1870s, for "there is no money afloat, manufactories are all stopped . . . as are the majority of Government works, throwing thousands of men and women out of employment." The later crises of 1883–85, 1893–97, and 1907–8 provoked a spate of similar warnings: "work is dull all over . . . no work to be got except by chance or influence," lamented Owen O'Callaghan in 1883–84. "This is a very bad country for the Irish just now," testified Patrick Burdan in 1894, "thousands unemployed"; "stay at home," advised a typical emigrants' letter in 1907. However, although such injunctions temporarily reduced Irish emigration, especially in the mid-1870s, large numbers persisted in departing even in the worst of times; indeed, in the depression-ridden 1890s Irish emigration levels seemed less responsive to American business cycles than at any earlier period, save the desperate Famine years. Moreover, even during times when American economic conditions were ostensibly favorable (e.g., 1878–82, 1885–90, 1898–1902), most Irish emigrants' letters still disparaged the United States and either implicitly or explicitly tried to discourage further departures. "Man & B[oy is] very lookey to get work to do," warned the Corkman James Chamberlain in 1880, "for the centers is crowded [with laborers] from all nations"; "the parks and squares . . . are filled with [Irish] men," reported another emigrant in 1901, "idle and unable to get employment." In short, throughout the late nineteenth and early twentieth centuries the great majority of Irish emigrants strove to convey the same basic messages: "this America is not what it used to be," and "any person who can make a fair living at home are better Stay theire." In the face of such admonitions, the continuing flood tide overseas made manifest the fact that millions of young men and women could not earn (or believed they could not earn) even "a fair living" in post-Famine Ireland.[15]

Patterns of Irish emigration during the American Civil War of 1861–65 dramatically demonstrate that exigencies at home were sufficiently powerful to offset even the dangers of conscription and death overseas. During the first two wartime years, departures declined 40 percent, perhaps in response to letters such as those of the Ulster-American William McSparron, who reported in August 1861 that "the times is miserable in this contery . . . [since] this rebelion has stoped all publick works and men is going about in thousants that cant get any thing to Do." For McSparron, as for many other poor Irishmen *already* settled in the United States, there were few alternatives to enlistment, because, as a Corkman in Boston lamented, "the business of the Country is wholly prostrate . . . , and all the people who have lived by their labour and only from hand to mouth . . . are going to the War"—"actuated," the New York *Herald* suspected, more by "the desire of preserving . . . the union of their own bodies and souls" than by the wish to preserve "the union of the states." Initially, however, the Irish *at home* evinced little desire to join the fight, perhaps heeding Irish-American injunctions *"not* [to emigrate], whatever way you may live where you are, while the North and South continue slaughtering one another." Moreover, Irish public opinion—at least as expressed by newspapers, politicians, and clergymen of nearly all persuasions—sympathized with the Confederacy and condemned wartime emigration, especially after December 1862, when New York's Irish-American brigade suffered virtual annihilation at Fredericksburg; "driven to mere slaughter," claimed the Irish press, by incompetent generals and nativist politicans. Anti-American sentiment only intensified as emigrants sent home accounts of having been tricked or coerced into the Union army and afterward grossly mistreated; one such soldier lamented he was "[s]orry to the heart that [he] should become the dupe of a Federal agent." But he added, "I am not the only one . . . to believe the falsifying statements. . . . They are enlisting young men every day, and the moment they land they are drafted to the battlefield. . . ." Even the period's popular Irish ballads displayed growing hostility to the "cursed Yankees" and "savage blacks" in whose cause Irish "blood in rivers ran . . . / And wounded men did loudly cry with pain. . . ." By mid-1863 even William B. West, the American consul at Galway, admitted that the Irish countryside was filled with thousands of bereaved households, bitterly "bewailing the loss of Brothers, sons and Husbands in our disastrous war."[16]

Yet, despite all the warnings and accumulating sorrows, Irish emigration to war-torn America not only continued but between 1861–62 and 1863–64 tripled in volume. To be sure, many of these later emigrants neither intended to fight nor in fact did fight in the Civil War. Indeed, the American

consuls in Ireland were inundated with demands for draft-exemption certificates from would-be emigrants responding only to the North's now-
booming wartime labor market and to letters such as that from the Ulsterman Stewart Bates, who claimed that in Chicago "there is . . . plenty
of demand for working men & they can easily earn from one to two dollars
per day." Nevertheless, the dangers of overt or covert conscription were
great, and whether by design or coercion large numbers of those who left
Ireland in 1863–64 fought and died from Gettysburg to Appomattox: in
all, at least 200,000 Irishmen served in the Civil War, the vast majority in
the Union forces. Why did so many Irishmen emigrate to fight for a foreign
flag? No doubt some were idealists: dedicated Fenians hoped to gain martial skills and the federal government's support for the coming struggle
against England; others, such as the radical Ulster Presbyterian Abraham
Irvine, fought for "the champions of Liberty" to save "the free, the glorious
institutions of this great land." Others were romantic adventurers like Myles
Keogh, who left his native Carlow and enlisted to "carr[y] out at least some
of the visionary fancies" he and his brothers had "indulged in . . . days
of long ago." However, probably the great majority were men who cared
little "whether puritanical North or slave-holding South carried off the
laurels of victory" but whose destitution at home contrasted so starkly
with the lucrative bounties which the federal and northern state governments offered to prospective soldiers that they were willing to risk death
to escape hopeless poverty. The early 1860s were especially bad years for
rural Ireland: unusually wet weather ruined pastures, cash crops, potatoes,
and turf, thus injuring graziers, commercial tillage farmers, subsistence
cultivators, and laborers alike. In 1861–64 evictions were 65 percent more
numerous than in the preceding four years, and the poor inhabitants of
many midland and western counties endured near-famine conditions. Between 1861–62 and 1863–64 male emigration from these "wretchedly impoverished" districts increased markedly: for example, by 309 percent from
Donegal; by 336 percent from Longford; by 350 percent from Kerry; and
by 374 percent from the province of Connaught, led by a 422 percent increase from County Galway, where, according to the resident American
consul, "there are many thousands of strong young men . . . who sigh
for food & employment in the US, and wo^d gladly embrace *any* opportunity
of removal from the misery & starvation they are enduring here." Indeed,
in 1862–64 hordes of poor Irishmen besieged the American consulates,
begging for free passage tickets in return for enlisting in the Union forces;
as Confederate agents in Britain despaired, Irish poverty—coupled with
ignorance of or indifference to the issues involved in the American conflict—
was so great among "that class that the temptation of a little ready money
. . . would lead them to go anywhere." Such destitution also induced
other emigrants, who originally had not intended to join the Union army,
to enlist shortly after their arrival. One such emigrant, Thomas McManus,
assured his relatives that he had not been *"forced* to list up." However,
McManus wrote, "by 'Gor' the bounty was very tempting, and I enlisted

the first day I came here" for $700 (more than ten years' wages for an Irish laborer), over half of which he immediately remitted home to his parents. Thus, in 1863–64 the welfare, even the survival, of many of Ireland's people—those who remained at home as well as those who emigrated—depended upon thousands of such often fatal speculations. Uncounted numbers of Irish-American soldiers and sailors never lived to enjoy what were, in effect, the wages of death, and, as West, the U.S. consul, reported in 1867, the war left rural Ireland with thousands of "starving and bereaved widows and widowed mothers" of husbands and sons who had perished on southern battlefields, often before they had been able to remit home the rewards of their sacrifice.[17]

In the face of such want, it was ironic that contemporaries often remarked on the growing "prosperity" and "progress" of post-Famine Ireland. In a similar vein, some recent historians have described the period as one of "modernization." In economic terms, modernization implies expansion of trade and communications, commercialization of agriculture, industrialization, and urbanization. In social contexts, the concept connotes the rationalization of human relationships according to the impersonal operations of the marketplace: resulting in increased functional specialization, social differentiation, occupational and geographical mobility, and the growth of supralocal, voluntary associational activities (economic, political, religious, etc.) and of bureaucratic forms of organization. In cultural and psychological terms, modernization is deemed synonymous with the primacy of cosmopolitanism over localism, "rational" over "supernatural" belief systems, acquisitive individualism over communal constraints, and meritocratic principles over claims to ascribed status. In theory the modernization process is beneficial to the society in question, producing overall economic growth, equality of opportunity, and the means and outlook necessary to achieve individual as well as societal goals.[18]

To a degree it is arguable not only that modernization took place in post-Famine Ireland but also that it conferred benefits. Certainly, some Irish economic indices improved markedly: exports of both agricultural and industrial goods rose in volume and value; commercial transactions, banking and credit facilities, and savings deposits multiplied; per capita income may have tripled; imports and consumption greatly increased; and popular diet and housing improved significantly. Likewise, urbanization and literacy increased, while a marked decline in popular deference coupled with a growing political sophistication enabled the Irish to realize previously unattainable goals: the abolition of landlordism and the achievement of self-government.[19]

However, to interpret post-Famine Ireland's history simply in terms of triumphant modernization would be grossly superficial, for certain traditional socioeconomic and cultural features not only survived but in large measure even determined and delimited the peculiar evolution of contemporary Irish society—a seeming paradox whose causes and consequences are examined in the next section of this chapter. More important in the present context is the disturbing fact that the economic, social, and cultural modernization which *did* occur in post-Famine Ireland not only failed to prevent massive emigration but was in reality its primary cause.

The harsh truth is that post-Famine Ireland was little more than an inferior appendage of British capitalism and imperialism which, in rivalry and later in partnership with their American counterparts, dominated an expanding international market system. This was the crucial, colonial context in which Irish modernization occurred, determined and distorted by the priorities and tastes of the sister island. Consequently, Ireland's economic development, its further integration into world capitalism, was highly uneven, specialized, and dependent. Although certain economic enterprises and social groups flourished, other important and much larger sectors atrophied. Domestic employment declined, and preexisting social and sectarian divisions, themselves the legacies of colonialism, were exacerbated. Not only were the overall economic gains noted above inequitably distributed—inordinately concentrated in certain regions and classes—but, more important, they at best accrued only to those who were able to remain in Ireland. In fact, Ireland's social adjustments to the exigencies of colonialism and world capitalism—adjustments dictated by external pressures and by internal inequities—mandated massive, sustained emigration. Put bluntly, emigration became a societal imperative of post-Famine Ireland: in reality less a choice than a vital necessity both to secure the livelihoods of nearly all who left and most who stayed and to ensure the relative stability of a fundamentally "sick" society which offered its lower classes and most of its young people "equal opportunities" only for aimless poverty at home or menial labor and slum tenements abroad. Ironically, post-Famine Ireland could not—or would not—even finance most emigration from its own internal resources, and had the "victims" of modernization remained at home, the general destitution and social unrest would very likely have exceeded even pre-Famine experience. Only their convenient disappearance, coupled with their generous remittances, enabled those who stayed in Ireland to enjoy a misleadingly high average per capita income and to realize in part the bourgeois aspirations for a "modern" Ireland. Thus, emigration was a "safety valve" for a society which condemned a great majority of its members to institutionalized superfluousness.[20]

In short, the human costs of Irish modernization were enormous, for the island's alleged "progress" was both cause and consequence of the exodus of between 4.1 and 4.5 million people. Given the intimate relation between British imperialism and Irish social structure, these developments were inexorable, barring *social* as well as political revolution. However, the Great Famine had already undercut that remote possibility by decimating those traditionalist and subsistence-oriented sectors which had previously proved most resistant to economic rationalization. Indeed, by the early twentieth century Ireland had become so thoroughly commercialized and colonized that the successive terminations of Irish landlordism and direct British rule had minimal structural consequences, but involved merely the transferal of local property and power from an "alien" elite to a native bourgeoisie which remained inextricably bound to a system which, albeit *personally* profitable, was ultimately both beyond their control and subversive of the general welfare. As a result, Irish emigration did not cease after 1921, for the compelling structural imperatives remained unchanged.

Specifically, the evolution of post-Famine Irish society mandated or at least encouraged emigration through a variety of complex, interrelated processes. Certain economic and social developments virtually obliged wholesale departures. First, Ireland's political integration to a "free trade" system dominated by England and, to an increasing degree, by the United States dictated the continuing de-industrialization of southern Ireland, flooded by cheap imported manufactured goods, and the consequent emigration of rural and urban artisans, craftsmen, and would-be factory workers. Second, competitive exigencies and technological developments mandated the further mechanization and contraction around the Lagan Valley of Ulster's linen industry, thereby reducing employment and income among the North's cottage manufacturers, most of whom could not be absorbed in Belfast's growing but highly specialized and viciously sectarian economy. Third, the increasing commercialization of Irish agriculture more deeply tied the farming classes to specialized market production, with consequently greater and (especially for middling and small farmers) ultimately damaging exposure to the perils of international competition, fluctuating or permanently declining prices, indebtedness, and crop failures. Fourth, beginning in the late 1870s these dire possibilities converged to wreak particular havoc on the fragile economies of western Ireland, ravaging societies still based largely on potato cultivation for subsistence. Fifth, the attractions or exigencies of market production persuaded or obliged all farming classes to adopt inheritance and marriage patterns which consigned most farmers' children to the emigrant ships. Sixth and perhaps most important, changing market conditions dictated pronounced shifts from tillage to pasture farming, and from the employment of paid farm labor to that of machines or family assistance; consequently, agricultural laborers' access to land and opportunities for employment declined sharply, while wages failed to keep pace with rising living costs, thus presenting most laborers with no viable alternatives to emigration.[21]

More broadly, all these economic developments, coupled with improvements in communications and education, further encouraged emigration by altering traditional social relationships and outlooks which had formerly served to stem the tide of emigration, even in the desperate pre-Famine years. Consequently, despite the social compulsion involved, many Irishmen and -women now regarded emigration favorably, as opportunity or even escape, rather than as exile. Irish nationalists and clerics condemned such attitudes as evidence of what they called Anglicization, but while they correctly identified the pervasive influence of British (and American) capitalism on post-Famine Irish culture, their efforts to check that influence not only were superficial but may inadvertently have prompted more departures. Finally, the very process of post-Famine emigration developed its own dynamic, in symbiosis with other social institutions, until by the end of the century emigration appeared to be both a self-perpetuating phenomenon and an integral, automatically accepted feature of Irish life.

The de-industrialization of rural Ireland, especially the southern provinces, had been under way for decades. However, during and after the Great Famine the process accelerated: between 1841 and 1891 the proportion of Ireland's population engaged in manufacturing and building fell from 29 percent to 20 percent, and by the latter date the "industrial classes" constituted merely 14 percent and were concentrated overwhelmingly in a few highly urbanized eastern and northeastern counties. The changing structure of Irish agriculture, the improved transportation and distribution networks, and the increased availability of factory-made goods were the primary causes of this decline. Prior to the Famine thousands of rural and village craftsmen still eked out precarious livings and paid rents by serving the local needs of small farmers and agricultural laborers. However, in 1845–55 large numbers of both craftsmen and poor customers died or departed, and in subsequent decades continued depopulation coupled with the shift from tillage to pasture farming sharply reduced local markets for cottage manufactures; thus, in 1861 when an unemployed artisan in Boston contemplated returning to Ireland, he sadly concluded, "[T]here is no chance for me at home in consequence of the famine . . . [since] the sole & staple dependence of the Mechanic . . . was in the farmer"—and since those farmers who did prosper in the post-Famine era increasingly preferred factory products. At the same time improved transportation and trade facilities rapidly broke down parochial markets for locally made goods and services. Between 1845 and 1914 Ireland's railroad system grew from 65 to 3,500 miles of track, supplementing the island's already-extensive road and canal network and facilitating the specialization of labor and the penetration—unhindered by protective tariffs—of cheap, mass-produced goods from Britain and the United States. Consequently, during the same period the value of Irish imports rose from £15 million to £75 million; retail shops multiplied in villages and towns; and traveling salesmen for large commercial houses superseded country peddlers. Rural tailors, shoemakers, blacksmiths, nailers, and other craftsmen could not compete with the lower prices and purportedly superior quality and "modernity" of factory products; their numbers thus fell steadily—especially in the 1870s, when depressed British industries dumped huge quantities of low-cost goods on the Irish market, and in the 1880s, when agricultural distress sharply reduced farmers' purchasing power. In short, thousands of rural and village craftsmen departed once self-sufficient districts and followed their vanishing customers overseas. As one old man later reminisced, in his Donegal townland formerly "there were masons, carpenters, coopers, thatchers and every kind of tradesman you could name . . . [but t]hey all went into strange and distant lands and never returned since."[72]

"Strange and distant lands"—because with few exceptions, primarily in east Ulster, post-Famine Ireland's cities and towns offered little employment to displaced or disinherited refugees from the countryside; indeed, those towns situated in what eventually became the Irish Free State could not even absorb their own inhabitants' children. Ironically, in the late nineteenth and early twentieth centuries both population and available employment in southern towns stagnated or shrank, while their overall demographic and socioeconomic importance grew significantly. Between 1851 and 1911 most major cities outside Ulster lost population: Limerick's fell by 21 percent, Kilkenny's by 31 percent, Galway's by 34 percent; in 1861 Cork city had reverted to its 1820 level of 80,000 inhabitants, and by 1911 it had fewer than 77,000. Among large southern cities, only Dublin and Waterford grew in numbers (by 24 percent and 20 percent), and those increases came entirely after 1891; prior to that date even Dublin lost population, partly through emigration and partly through upper- and middle-class flight to tax-sheltered suburbs such as Rathmines and Kingstown. In smaller towns population declines were equally precipitous, sometimes catastrophic: by 1881, towns which before the Famine had 3–5,000 inhabitants had lost an average of 27 percent of their people, and some towns had declined by half. However, Ireland generally was becoming a relatively urbanized society, although outside the Northeast this was obviously a result of rural decline rather than of urban growth. Between 1851 and 1911 the proportion of Irish living in towns of 2,000 or more people rose from 17 percent to 33.5 percent, the greatest increase taking place after 1891. As before the Famine, Leinster remained the most urbanized province (47 percent), Connaught the least (8 percent), while Ulster (38 percent) overtook Munster (26 percent) for second place.[23]

Southern Ireland's cities, towns, and crossroads villages assumed a crucial economic significance as retail, financial, and service centers for an increasingly commercialized countryside. As Padraic Colum noted, in the early twentieth century, "The farmers sell everything they produce, and buy everything they consume"—often on credit. Indeed, beginning in the 1850s even the poorest western peasants supplemented potato diets with imported cornmeal purchased in small towns and villages where prior to the Famine retail stores had scarcely existed. As a result, while agricultural and industrial employment declined, Irishmen and -women working in commerce and service increased both numerically and proportionately. Between 1841 and 1891 the proportion of the population employed in commerce rose from 2.6 percent to 5.4 percent: by 1881 the numbers of "shopkeepers" and "dealers" had grown by 20 percent, the numbers of publicans and innkeepers by 116 percent; by 1911 the number of traders in Ireland had risen by 102 percent. Equally significant, between 1851 and 1891 Irish banking offices increased 230 percent. Occupations subsidiary to trade and finance also expanded: for example, between 1841 and

1891 the proportion of Irishmen employed in public services and liberal professions rose from 1.6 percent to 5.8 percent; meanwhile, the proportion in domestic service to this growing middle class increased from 9.4 percent to 12.2 percent. Concentrated overwhelmingly in towns, these burgeoning occupational groups and their activities increasingly dominated Irish urban society: for example, in 1841 persons engaged in trade constituted merely 15 percent of the inhabitants of towns with 1,500 or more people, but by 1901 the comparable figure was 32 percent. More important, the urban bourgeoisie increasingly dominated Irish rural society: socially, politically, and culturally, as well as economically. Thus, although often exploitive, relations between town and country were much closer and more frequent than before the Famine: for example, in addition to normal trade and credit arrangements, townsmen often invested or speculated in land or cattle; conversely, farmers' sons constituted a large proportion of urban traders, publicans, shopkeepers, and shopkeepers' assistants, while farmers' daughters frequently migrated to towns and served as shopgirls and domestic servants.[24]

Thus, at least the specialized economic growth of southern towns served to *stem* Irish emigration and prevent urban population levels from falling even more precipitously, as would have occurred without constant replenishment from the countryside; it was no coincidence that in the four provinces urbanization and emigration rates varied inversely. However, trade and credit expansion created relatively few urban employment opportunities, especially since shrinking populations of rural and urban customers placed limits on the retailing classes' growth and prosperity. Indeed, bankruptcies among traders and shopkeepers were remarkably common, no doubt contributing to the petite bourgeoisie's proverbial parsimony and insecurity, as well as to the high population turnover characteristic of market towns such as Navan. In short, Ireland's new urban middle class was relatively undynamic and unstable. It was also relatively exclusive, especially in its upper levels. As late as 1914, Protestants still dominated or held a disproportionately large share of positions in finance and insurance, the professions, the more lucrative branches of trade (e.g., auctioneers, chartered accountants), and the higher grades of civil service. Also, while Irish primary education made great strides after 1856, public secondary schools and scholarships (save for aspirants to the priesthood) were so few that only a handful of poor farmers' or laborers' children acquired sufficient education even to aspire to such elevated positions. The close kinship ties between affluent farmers and urban retailers indicate that even entry to the shopkeeper and publican ranks was governed more by family connections than by individual merit. Furthermore, young men and women who did find situations as shopkeepers' assistants or shopgirls often became discontented and emigrated: as one critic observed, "There is no chance for them economically," and so "[t]he girl behind the counter in a little shop gets dissatisfied with her meagre wage" and "her employer's pettiness," and "[i]n a while, as she herself says, she 'hoists her sails for America.' " Female domestic servants were even more exploited, suffering the aspersions of the nouveaux riches. Of course, much better opportunities were available in the expanding educational and civil service bureaucracies, for example, as National School teachers and Royal Irish Constabulary. However, Irish teachers' salaries were poor (50 percent lower than in England) and clerical supervision oppressive. Likewise, members of the RIC often found that severe discipline, limited possibilities for promotion (especially for Catholics), and unpopular or distasteful duties more than offset their comparative security; thus, Myles McDermott eventually decided that laboring in Minnesota for only £9 per month, plus room and board, was "Infinitely better" than his former post of "Royal Irish Pig Driver . . . under the lash of the tyrants who rule that department."[25]

More important, the expansion of urban Ireland's middle class only slightly offset the effects of southern towns' declining manufacturing sectors. Since 1815, southern cities had offered little industrial employment, and after 1856 the situation only worsened as major manufacturing concerns either collapsed or stagnated in the face of British or American competition. In the mid-1850s a returned emigrant to Kilkenny found woolen mills closed, "business crushed, industry paralyzed, not a ray of hope around." In 1884 a visitor to Galway saw the old port in total decay: the "great warehouses near the wharves" were "spectral in their desolation," and imported American flour had made useless the local mills which once ground Irish grain. Even in Dublin, between 1851 and 1911 the proportion of the work force engaged in manufacturing fell from 35 percent to 22 percent. The major industries which did survive—for example, brewing, distilling, food processing—were capital, not labor, intensive; confined almost entirely to the export trade, they generated few tertiary enterprises. Moreover, rationalization of production reduced employment in the most successful southern industries: in brewing, for instance, between 1901 and 1920 the number of firms fell by 42 percent; since 1837 the decline was 90 percent. In the small manufacturing sector, employment among urban artisans and journeymen also contracted, almost as sharply as among their rural counterparts. For example, in post-Famine Cork cabinetmaking, coopering, brush and hat manufacturing, the leather trades, and all textile-related industries declined dramatically: between 1851 and 1901 the number of local weavers fell from 160 to 3, that of shoemakers from 1,216 to 510. Journeymen suffered worst of all, often replaced, as in the tailoring trade, by unskilled laborers using American sewing machines. Even in trades which remained relatively unmechanized, relations between struggling master craftsmen and their journeymen and apprentices became increasingly exploitive. Although skilled-trade unions were common, and although violent strikes convulsed Cork in the early 1870s, during most of the post-Famine period union activities were muted and generally unsuccessful. Trade union militancy was weakened by the close physical proximity still extant in most shops between masters and employees; by parochial and sectarian divisions among the work force; and by the pragmatic conservatism displayed by most union leaders, reinforced by bourgeois and clerical admonitions for conformity to class-collaborationist, nationalist or unionist orthodoxies. Partly as a result, wages for Irish artisans remained low, inspiring thousands to emigrate to Britain or the New World. Ironically, one strength which Irish trade unions did retain—their ability to demand lengthy and expensive formal apprenticeships from prospective craftsmen—only further encouraged departures. As one Kerryman declared, "to sign up to learn any of the trades which required five or six years of apprenticeship without any pay and not enough to eat much of the time, that . . . was out of the question," and so instead he emigrated to America. Even "if your boys should get trades," warned another Irish emigrant, "after proficiency its [only] one out of five hundred that ever Makes more than a living"; in post-Famine Ireland's depressed condition, "force of circumstances will oblige them to leave." By contrast, in the United States apprenticeships were relatively short and remunerative, and subsequent employment opportunities infinitely greater. "I am very glad you did not bind him to a trad in Ireland," wrote the Irish-Philadelphian John Fleming of his recently arrived nephew, "for he Can Save more [money] here [while] learning his trade than ther after his time being Served."[26]

In short, southern Irish cities and towns offered few opportunities to rural migrants, save to those so lacking in money, skills, or ambition that they were at least temporarily content to swell southern cities' growing ranks of unskilled slum dwellers. Conditions in Dublin were particularly appalling, but the social structures and problems of Cork, Limerick, and other southern towns differed only in scale. By 1900, unskilled, casual, and unemployed laborers constituted 70 percent of Dublin's work force. Transportation, construction, and the export trade provided some work for unskilled males, but the dearth of factory employment for women meant that in 1910 most Dublin families earned less than 20s. per week, scarcely enough to pay rents and buy food even when all ablebodied members had work; moreover, at any time at least one-fifth of such families were entirely unemployed. At best unskilled workers' families subsisted largely on oatmeal and potatoes; at worst they starved: in the early twentieth century Dublin's working classes were so malnourished, stunted, and diseased that about one-third of the city's applicants failed to pass the British army's none-too-stringent medical examination. Housing conditions were equally wretched. Speculators subdivided decaying Georgian homes and warehouses into tenements, and by 1901 over 21,000 families—about 40 percent of the city's population—were living in unheated, rat-infested, oneroom apartments whose crumbling walls reeked with damp and decay; as late as 1926, 28 percent of Dublin's inhabitants lived in rooms which housed four or more people. Tuberculosis was rampant and sanitation and sewage grossly inadequate, and by 1900 Dublin's mortality rates were the highest in western Europe; infant mortality alone was nearly 20 percent. The huge available pool of under- and unemployed meant that Dublin's workers were easily exploited. In 1905–12 Dublin laborers' wages were only 54 percent of those paid in London, although food costs in Dublin were 7 percent higher: in themselves sufficient causes for emigration or working-class militancy. In fact, Dublin's workers were generally submissive until 1908, when James Larkin, born in Liverpool of Irish working-class parents, moved to Dublin and organized the National Union of Dock Laborers. A socialist, syndicalist, and powerful orator, Larkin inflamed Dublin's masses with his own outrage against the employing classes and their bourgeois and clerical allies. In 1911, following a wave of successful strikes, Larkin and James Connolly, another British-born Irishman and working-class socialist, formed the Irish Transport and General Workers Union (ITGWU). However, in 1913 the employers, led by the transport and press mogul William Martin Murphy, struck back with a citywide lockout of ITGWU members, precipitating a great general strike, which ended in partial defeat when Britain's more conservative labor leaders refused Larkin adequate support; the ITGWU remained unbroken, but its starving members drifted back to work, and the discouraged Larkin emigrated to America.[27]

Dublin's unskilled workers were never able to translate their newfound militancy into a successful bid for political power. Before the Local Government Act of 1898, high property qualifications confined urban voting and office holding to Dublin's upper and upper-middle classes. After 1898 the franchise was more democratic, but working-class transience and apathy, coupled with clerical and bourgeois nationalist denunciations of "atheistic socialism," allowed the city corporation to fall into the hands of representatives of the Catholic lower-middle classes—small employers, real-estate speculators, publicans, shopkeepers—whose vociferous enthusiasm for Irish self-government, or "home rule," was perhaps grounded as much in desires to obscure class conflicts and to insulate Irish employers from twentieth-century British social legislation (e.g., factory safety, minimum wage, unemployment insurance acts) as in disinterested patriotism. Circumscribed by a shrinking tax base, by the proliferation of independent, middle-class suburbs, and by politically inspired parliamentary limitations on public borrowing, Dublin's aldermen could only exploit, not ameliorate, working-class Dublin's wretchedness. It was no coincidence that the slumlords who dominated corporation policy did little to alleviate the city's tremendous housing shortage: self-interest easily blended with solicitation for the ratepayers into pious devotion to the sanctity of private property and to home rule as the supposed only "real" solution to Dublin's economic stagnation. In short, like other southern cities, Ireland's decaying metropolis was no haven for the countryside's unemployed; at best it was an embarkation point, at worst a "strumpet city" whose foul embrace compelled escape or revolution as the only logical alternatives to poverty, disease, and exploitation.[28]

Ulster was the only province in post-Famine Ireland to experience sufficient industrialization and urban growth to absorb a significant proportion of rural migrants. Between 1851 and 1911 the proportion of Ulster's inhabitants living in towns of 2,000 or more people rose from 12.6 percent to 38.4 percent. Urbanization in Ulster's eastern counties was even more pronounced: by 1911, 55 percent of the populations of Counties Antrim, Armagh, Down, and Londonderry were living in towns and cities. Belfast experienced phenomenal growth, based on textile manufacturing, shipbuilding and related industries, and food processing. Between 1851 and 1911 Belfast's population mushroomed by 296 percent, from 98,000 to 387,000 inhabitants; by 1891 the northern metropolis had surpassed Dublin in both size and economic importance; for example, in 1906 Belfast's harbor receipts were 150 percent greater than Dublin's. Londonderry city, with its shirt-making industry and shipping, was northwest Ulster's commercial center and the province's second-largest town; in 1851–1911 Londonderry's population rose by 107 percent, from 20,000 to 41,000. Belfast's economic importance and the expansion of Ulster's railroad network stimulated the growth of other northern communities: of industrial towns such as Lisburn, Ballymena, Lurgan, and Portadown; of middle-class suburbs like Bangor and Hollywood; and of seaside resorts such as Portrush and Bundoran. Even inland market towns such as Cookstown, Omagh, and Monaghan grew slightly, in contrast to their southern counterparts. In short, Ulster's urban-industrial expansion generated employment opportunities unavailable elsewhere in post-Famine Ireland; indeed, in their dynamism, economic linkages, social structures, even physical appearances, Belfast, Londonderry, and Ulster's other industrial towns were much closer to their British counterparts than to southern Ireland's stagnant communities.[29]

Nevertheless, between 1851 and 1911 Ulster's population fell 21 percent, and the population of the North's four most urbanized counties fell by 10,000, since not even Belfast's dramatic growth could compensate entirely for a 32 percent population decline in the rest of the region. In counties farther from Belfast the decline was still more precipitous: in 1851–1911 the populations of Cavan, Fermanagh, Monaghan, and Tyrone all fell by 40 to 44 percent. Thus, although post-Famine Ulster's emigration rate was only 10.3 per 1,000 inhabitants (vs. Munster's 15.6 and Connaught's 13.8), the northern province's urban-industrial infrastructure lacked the capacity to retain at least 1,073,000 Ulstermen and -women who sought employment and new homes overseas. Indeed, the largest *numbers* of Ulster emigrants (57 percent of the total) left the four most heavily urbanized counties (nearly 400,000 in 1856–1910 from Antrim and Down alone), although in proportion to population emigration was generally heavier from southern and western Ulster: for example, the departure rates from Armagh and Down were only 9.5 and 9.1, while comparable rates from Monaghan and Cavan were 10.2 and 13.3. Religious data for Irish emigrants do not exist, but the different rates of population decline among Ulster's three major denominations in 1861–1911 (Catholics minus 29 percent, Presbyterians minus 16 percent, Anglicans minus 6 percent) suggest that Catholics and Presbyterians constituted the bulk of the Ulster emigrants, Catholics probably a clear majority.[30]

Otherwise, Ulster emigration differed from southern Irish patterns in several important respects. First, in terms of occupational distribution, although in 1883 the American consul indicated that most emigrants leaving Belfast were poor and unskilled, at least by the early twentieth century Ulster was contributing a larger proportion of middle-class and skilled working-class emigrants (farmers, shopkeepers, artisans, etc.) than any other province: thus, in 1911 only 57 percent of Ulster emigrants were classified as laborers, compared with 63 percent of those leaving Leinster and 84 to 87 percent of those from Munster and Connaught. Second, Ulster emigration was preponderantly male: in 1851–1910 the ratio of male to female emigrants was 1.23 to 1, in contrast to 1.02 to 1 in the southern provinces. Male dominance was greatest among east Ulster emigrants: among those from Antrim and Down the sex ratios were 1.31 to 1 and 1.50 to 1, while in counties such as Tyrone and Cavan the proportions were nearly equal. Third, a much larger minority of Ulster than of southern Irish emigrants went to Canada or Great Britain rather than to the United States; indeed, emigrants to Canada alone often constituted a majority of those leaving Antrim and Down, as in 1901–10. Evidence from Canadian sources suggests that Ulster Anglicans and Methodists were disproportionately likely to emigrate to British North America, while Catholics and Presbyterians still preferred the United States. Finally, and perhaps most revealing, the rhythms of Ulster emigration varied inversely with those in the rest of the island. Ulster emigration rates were high (as in 1856–60, 1871–80, 1901–10) when departures from southern Ireland were in decline; conversely, peaks of southern emigration (as in 1861–70 and 1881–1900) coincided with relatively low emigration from the northern province. For example, between 1851–55 and 1856–60 total Irish emigration declined by 44.5 percent, but Ulster emigration fell by only 8 percent and in Antrim and Down increased by 114 percent and 36 percent, respectively. From the 1860s to the 1870s total Irish emigration fell by 27 percent, while departures from Ulster rose by 19 percent, led by 61 percent and 149 percent increases in Londonderry and Donegal. To complete the pattern, between 1891–1900 and 1901–10 total Irish emigration declined 20 percent, but rose in Ulster by 22 percent and in Antrim and Down by 119 percent and 95 percent. In short, Ulster's urban-industrial society did not stop northern emigration, but to a degree it did produce a different kind of Irish emigrant, one who marched to the beat of a drummer different from that heard by his southern peers.[31]

The very nature of Ulster's industrial expansion stimulated far more rural-to-urban migration than the North's towns and factories could absorb. In part, the stimulus was cultural and psychological, as economic growth and the shift from rural to urban-industrial production modes and life-styles combined with the region's fervent evangelicalism to foster and justify more individualistic and cosmopolitan outlooks. Thus, for William Irvine of Antrim town, son of an impoverished Anglican cobbler and alcoholic mother, secular ambitions and religious visions mutually reinforced desires for improvement and "self-mastery" which could be realized only through emigration. However, more obviously important was the impact on rural Ulster of structural changes in the North's linen industry. As in southern Ireland, the Ulster countryside after the Famine was subject to economic pressures favoring shifts from subsistence to commercial agriculture, tillage to pasture farming, small to large holdings, partible to impartible inheritance, and hired labor to mechanization or family assistance. A thickly settled society composed largely of smallholders, cottiers, and laborers, rural Ulster was particularly vulnerable to such pressures, despite the cushion of tenant-right. Only the proceeds of cottage industry, primarily linen spinning and weaving, had enabled most northern families to pay rents and survive crop failures. However, in the 1820s and 1830s the mechanization of spinning and the concentration of spinning mills in the Lagan Valley initiated the de-industrialization of rural Ulster, especially the counties farthest from Belfast. The mechanization of spinning sharply reduced earning power among northern cottiers' wives and daughters, although many young women found employment in the new mills. Moreover, although prior to the Famine handloom weaving still flourished in eastern Ulster, employing thousands of rural males, after 1845, labor shortages caused by deaths and emigration persuaded Ulster's manufacturers to adopt steam-powered looms and factory weaving in an effort to reduce costs. By the eve of the American Civil War, which caused cotton shortages and a consequent boom in linen production, power looms had inaugurated "a second era in the history of the trade": both the prosperity of the 1860s and the depression of subsequent decades accelerated the trend toward factory weaving, as lures of increased profits alternated with falling prices and heightened competition to inspire greater degrees of mechanization and centralization of production near imported coal supplies. Thus, in the post-Famine period all phases of Ulster's linen industry were increasingly divorced from agriculture and confined to factories in Belfast and adjacent towns: handloom weaving declined by at least 75 percent, and by 1900 two-thirds of Ireland's linen weaving was taking place in Belfast alone. Cottage industry survived only in western Ulster, where Londonderry city's clothing manufacturers employed peasant women in the poor, mountainous districts of Donegal, south Derry, and Tyrone to finish shirts, sew embroidery, and knit stockings. This remnant of a once-extensive rural industry was grossly exploitive: at best a woman might earn 2½ d. for a pair of stockings which retailed for 1s. 6d.; local shopkeepers, who distributed the yarn and unfinished cloth, often paid wages only in overpriced store goods. One final development in the linen industry also reduced rural incomes and employment. Prior to the American Civil War, flax was often the Ulster smallholder's most valuable cash crop, while in winter cottiers and laborers commonly found work in local flax-scutching mills. However, after 1864, manufacturers began importing cheaper flax from Russia and Belgium, and the number of Irish acres planted in flax began a slow but inexorable decline; by the early twentieth century, the vanished profitability of flax production was an oft-cited cause for poverty and emigration among Ulster's small farmers.[32]

Once bereft of income from cottage industry and flax production, Ulster's smallholders and cottier-weavers were no longer insulated from pressures to rationalize farm-size, land-use, and inheritance patterns. Mid-Antrim's Braid Valley, surrounding the town of Ballymena, provides a clear example of the consequent transformation. In the 1850s tiny farms and cottage industry were still characteristic; tenants spent half the year weaving linen, and so the land was poorly tended; drainage and crop rotation were virtually unknown, and most farmers subdivided holdings when their sons married. Although power spinning dominated the Lagan Valley, only thirty miles distant, the roads were so poor that local markets for homespun yarn and handwoven cloth still flourished. However, after 1870 the advent of power looms and the coming of the railroad decimated cottage industry in the Braid Valley. By 1884 Ballymena's linen market was nearly deserted, and many smallholders—unable to exist by farming alone—migrated to factory towns or left the country; the farmers who survived curtailed subdivision, obliging their disinherited children to join the exodus. Consolidation of holdings into commercial farms and pasturage proceeded until by 1944 over half the valley's holdings were between 30 and 100 acres. Linked by rail to Belfast, Ballymena itself became a major manufacturing town with factories able to absorb at least a small proportion of the district's excess rural population. However, other areas in Ulster were less fortunate: distant communities such as Belturbet and Ballyshannon, mere market centers for a depressed and depopulated countryside, saw their populations fall by a third or more. Without railroad connections, even once-prosperous towns close to Belfast, such as Newry and Downpatrick, stagnated demographically and economically; although their declines were less precipitous than those commonly experienced by southern Irish towns, their capacity to attract and hold migrants from the surrounding area was minimal.[33]

In a letter written to his emigrant brother in 1901, the farmer Thomas Kells remarked on the depopulation of rural Armagh: "the labouring class," he wrote, "is nearly all gone to the towns," swelling the populations of Belfast, Lurgan, and Portadown. Certainly, Ulster's industrial cities provided viable alternatives to emigration. For example, in the 1860s and 1890s, when expatriation from Ulster was particularly low, Belfast experienced its highest rates of decadal growth, 46 percent and 36 percent, respectively. In contrast to Dublin's, Belfast's economy was more balanced and provided employment opportunities to migrants of both sexes. Although female workers dominated textile manufacturing and domestic service, shipbuilding, machine shops, and related industries—as well as rough, unskilled work—were all-male preserves. Indeed, between 1870 and 1900 it was the enormous expansion of shipbuilding and other male-dominated industries which gave Belfast a dynamic economy: in 1881–90 the city's shipyards constructed vessels totaling 435,000 tons, nearly quadruple the production of the preceding decade; in the 1890s output exceeded one million tons, and Belfast's largest shipyard alone employed 9,000 men. Belfast also contrasted favorably with Dublin in other important respects. Working-class housing was ample and relatively inexpensive, thanks to overconstruction during the linen boom of the 1860s and to the comparatively high wage levels for skilled workers, which encouraged speculators and house builders to construct more rows of single-family dwellings in subsequent decades. Between 1871 and 1891 the number of houses in Belfast increased by an average of 2,000 per year; in Dublin the total of new housing units for the entire period was less than 1,900. As a result, whereas in Dublin 43 percent of all families inhabited one-room dwellings in 1881, only 1.6 percent of Belfast's population lived in such cramped quarters. In 1884 the American consul reported that Belfast working-class families could rent small, two-story houses for less than $1.00 per week, and even the joys of homeownership were available to the highest-paid shipyard workers, such as riveters and iron molders, whose wages averaged between $7.66 and $8.21 per week. Moreover, although no paradise, Belfast was by 1900 also a much healthier city than Dublin, enjoying mortality rates which were among the lowest in urban Britain.[34]

Nevertheless, although Ulster's economic linkages with Great Britain brought urban-industrial growth, they also ensured that the North would fully experience British industrial crises as well as share to a degree in southern Ireland's rural distress. By 1900 only 25 percent of east Ulster's work force remained in agriculture, and one consequence of the province's economic integration with Britain was clearly evident in the emigration statistics: although Ulster's emigration patterns were quite distinct from those of southern Ireland, they were almost identical to those in England and Scotland. Sometimes Ulster's industrial orientation was advantageous: in the 1860s and again in the 1880s and 1890s, southern Ireland suffered severely from crop failures and/or low farm prices, while east Ulster enjoyed unparalleled prosperity based on linen production in the 1860s and shipbuilding in the century's latter decades. However, at other times the North suffered: in the 1870s Ulster's linen industry was mired in depression while southern farmers fattened on high cattle prices; likewise, after 1900 all the North's major industries experienced, together with Britain, sharp fluctuations in demand and employment, while in southern Ireland farm prices stabilized or rose. In short, during these depressions Ulster's urban-industrial sector stagnated or grew relatively slowly, and in these periods the North's excess rural population, as well as its cities' distressed inhabitants, had to look overseas for relief. Thus, in the depressed 1870s east Ulster's mill villages experienced significant emigration, and later the U.S. consuls in Belfast reported that many northern "mechanics" ("Boiler

Makers, Painters, Machinists, Flax Spinners") either emigrated permanently, "aided by Trade Societies of which they are members," or migrated seasonally across the Atlantic. Countless others merely drifted back and forth across the Irish Sea, working alternately in Belfast, Glasgow, Manchester, and elsewhere.[35]

Moreover, even in ostensibly prosperous periods, working-class conditions in Belfast and other northern industrial towns were far from uniformly attractive. This was especially true in the industry which generated the largest amount of employment, for after the American Civil War linen manufacturing experienced little growth. In the mid-1880s male linen operatives earned about £1 per week; their families subsisted largely on bread, potatoes, and tea, eating meat (the poorest cuts of beef or sausage) only on rare occasions. Even the thriftiest mill workers had few savings and little opportunity for upward mobility; indeed, one observer noted that "most men worked all their lives in the mills and died with almost nothing; many had to be buried at their employers' expense." However, female operatives dominated linen manufacturing and were most exploited and dissatisfied, confined to the lowest-skilled and poorest-paid sectors of the trade. For example, in 1884 Belfast's female flax spinners earned on the average only $1.88 per week; twenty-five years later their wages had risen a mere thirty cents. At best, when the mills were fully operating, working conditions were hazardous, unhealthful, and oppressive; "a ruthless system of fines" punished the slightest violations of work discipline. At worst, when markets were poor and the operatives working only half-time, as in 1907–8, distress was so great that many turned to prostitution. Conditions for child laborers were even worse: in 1909, factory inspectors discovered children seven years old working twelve-hour shifts; many were malnourished, permanently stunted, or crippled from factory accidents. According to one report, although the better-paid male operatives sometimes escaped mill work through emigration, the women found it impossible to save sufficient funds: instead, "they are tied to the wheel. . . . What their lot is today it will be tomorrow. No prospect presents itself but a life of toil with scant remuneration, with limited pleasures, with want never far off, and with the possibility or even the probability, of the workhouse in old age." In short, for those James Connolly called "the Linen Slaves of Belfast," only quiet prayers or orgiastic revivalism could relieve oppression and monotony; however, their cheerless examples no doubt persuaded many of their rural sisters to search for better futures across the ocean.[36]

Whether Ulster's bankrupt tenants, disinherited farmers' children, and unemployed rural artisans and laborers emigrated to North America or migrated to northern industrial towns such as Belfast depended on a host of related factors. Relative economic conditions were important considerations, as in the 1890s, when severe depression in the United States contrasted unfavorably with Belfast's booming economy. Also crucial were the prospective migrants' financial resources: travel costs to Belfast were minimal, but without remittances many poor Ulstermen and -women still could not afford the transatlantic passage. Equally important was the fact that Ulster's urban-industrial centers offered many more employment opportunities to females than to males: for example, Londonderry city's shirt making exclusively employed women in all but a few, highly skilled branches of the trade. To be sure, Belfast's shipbuilding and related industries were male dominated. However, those jobs employed only a small, elite proportion of Belfast's work force, and the levels of necessary skills combined with nepotism to deny most rural migrants entry to the city's labor aristocracy; indeed, skilled immigrants, trade union members, from Britain were more likely than rural Ulstermen to find lucrative employment in Belfast's shipyards and machine shops. Access to the linen mills was much easier, but about 75 percent of the jobs in Belfast's textile industry were reserved for women; in handkerchief making, females constituted over 80 percent of the work force. As a result, in 1911 the sex ratio among Belfast's unmarried males and females aged fifteen to thirty-four (the age of most emigrants) was 1 to 1.12; by contrast, Dublin's ratio was 1 to 0.94. In short, to rural Ulster*men* without capital, skills, or connections, Belfast and the North's other industrial communities were far less attractive destinations than the New World: combined with the survival of cottage industry among west Ulster*women,* this situation ensured the North a male-dominated emigration unique in post-Famine Ireland.[37]

However, other considerations also determined choices between emigration and internal migration. As was noted earlier, despite their relative poverty Ulster Catholics chose to emigrate in numbers disproportionate to their share of the North's population. Concurrently, Catholics migrated to Belfast much less frequently than Protestants: as a result, between 1861 and 1911 the city's Catholic population rose only 125 percent, while the number of Protestants increased 266 percent; during the same period the Catholic share of Belfast's population fell from 34 percent to 24 percent. To a degree, rural Protestants' easier access to Belfast helps account for this pattern: between 1856 and 1911 Counties Antrim, Armagh, and Down contributed a large majority of Belfast's new residents, and this hinterland was about two-thirds Protestant (67 percent in 1881). However, more was involved than mere physical proximity: for example, in the pre-Famine decades Belfast had been a mecca for poor rural Catholics, and prior to mid-century their share of the city's population had grown steadily; by contrast, in the early twentieth century Catholics in the Mourne Mountains and Antrim Glens (both less than fifty miles from Belfast) reportedly considered Ulster's metropolis to be at least "as strange a land as America" and much preferred the latter destination. Ulster's rural Presbyterians also seem to have preferred the New World over Belfast, despite the latter's reputation as a "Presbyterian city," while rural Anglicans disproportionately chose internal migration over emigration. Thus, in 1861–1911 the North's Presbyterian population declined by 16 percent, but the number of Anglicans fell by only 6 percent. Concurrently, Belfast's Anglican population rose by 293 percent, and their share of the city's inhabitants increased from 24.6 percent to 30.5 percent, but Belfast's Presbyterian population rose by only 207 percent and their share declined from 35.2 percent to 33.7 percent. Since Antrim and Down, the counties adjacent to Belfast, were predominantly Presbyterian, not Anglican, proximity to Belfast could not have been a decisive factor. Indeed, rural Presbyterians seem to have preferred emigration over migrating even the shortest distances to local industrial towns. For example, in 1901 only 15 percent of the linen-mill operatives in Gilford, County Down, were Presbyterians, compared with 50 percent Anglicans, despite the fact that 72 percent of the workers hailed from Down itself, a county whose Protestant population was 57 percent Presbyterian, only 23 percent Anglican.[38]

Variations in social background and socially determined aspirations partly account for these patterns. In general, Ulster's rural Presbyterians enjoyed greater status or "independence" than the province's rural Anglicans. Although nearly all northern landlords were Anglicans, as were many rich farmers in sparsely populated County Fermanagh, most Ulster farmers were Presbyterians, while Protestant laborers and landless weavers were predominantly Anglican. Consequently, the "Ulster custom" of tenant-right benefited rural Presbyterians more often than Anglicans, giving the former an "interest" which could be sold or mortgaged to finance overseas travel. Likewise, perhaps greater social pretensions made Presbyterian farmers and farmers' children less willing than Anglican laborers to admit economic failure by seeking employment in Ireland as "dependent" mill workers; certainly, any Ulsterman who aspired to regain "independence" through farming would direct his ambitions to the New World, not to Belfast. By contrast, for most Anglican migrants, factory labor in a northern industrial town involved changes in venue but not in status. In addition, membership in the Orange Order, generally more common among rural Anglicans than among Presbyterians, gave the former relatively easy access to employment and a sense of working-class Protestant community in an urban Ulster which replicated the countryside's sectarian institutions and strife. Thus, social class may have merged with religious and political outlooks in determining choices between emigration and internal migration. Rural Presbyterians, most of whom voted Whig or Liberal—not Tory—until the mid-1880s, may have been less prone than Anglicans to embrace the province's increasingly dogmatic and militant conservatism, instead opting for emigration to what one Presbyterian called "a land of freedom wher you can worship God as you think proper and no one to ask you to what church you belong or any." Also, such considerations may have helped determine choices of destination *outside* Ireland, at least until the late 1880s, when Ulster Protestants began to unite almost solidly in Tory-led Unionist associations and in a revitalized Orange Order against the threat of a Catholic-dominated "home rule" government in Dublin. For example, the Protestant emigrant George Pepper recalled that when he left east Ulster in the 1850s his conservative coreligionists went to British North America while those who, like himself, were "republicans . . . gravitated to the more

congenial atmosphere of the United States." However, by the early twentieth century virtually unanimous and self-conscious loyalty to the British
flag, coupled with aggressive recruitment by the Canadian government, directed nearly all Protestant emigration to a land which boasted opportunities which the United States no longer, or never, offered: free homesteads
in the prairie provinces and, especially in Ontario, a skilled labor market
which largely welcomed Irish immigrants only when they carried transfer
certificates proving membership in the Orange Order. By 1914 nearly all
the Presbyterian emigrants from the Braid Valley, as well as their Anglican
counterparts from north Fermanagh, were going to Canada: no wonder
when some Toronto department-store and factory owners virtually guaranteed employment to loyal Protestants born in Ballymena.[39]

Ulster Catholics' disproportionately high population decline and their
decided preference for emigration over internal migration also reflect religious and political, as well as economic, circumstances. Indeed, these patterns were part of a more general "sorting out" of Ulster's post-Famine
population along geographic and denominational lines which prefigured
the province's political partition in 1920–21. Between 1861 and 1911 the
Protestant population of the six counties which became Northern Ireland
declined by only 2 percent, while the number of Catholics fell 25 percent;
in 1911, Catholics composed only 34 percent of the area's inhabitants,
compared with 41 percent in 1861. By contrast, in the same period the
Protestant population of the three Ulster counties which became part of
the Irish Free State fell 44 percent, whereas the Catholic decline was only
34 percent; in 1861–1911 the Catholic share of the three counties' population increased, from 76 percent to 79 percent. Within the future Northern Ireland, Catholic declines were largest in Antrim and Down, counties
which in 1861 already had the heaviest Protestant majorities; conversely,
in evenly balanced counties such as Tyrone and Fermanagh, Catholic and
Protestant depletion rates were nearly identical. The same sorting-out process also took place on local levels: for instance, in the late nineteenth century north County Down became more predominantly Protestant, while
south Down became more heavily Catholic. The explanation for these patterns seems obvious. The increasing commercialization and de-industrialization of the Ulster countryside only heightened competition for land and
rural employment. Such competition had always been fought primarily on
sectarian lines, and, despite occasional instances of interdenominational
cooperation against landlords (as in 1879–82), the Fenian and home rule
movements of the late nineteenth and early twentieth centuries only confirmed and politicized the North's traditional tribalism. In short, economic,
religious, and political motivations were inextricable, and Catholics found
themselves "squeezed out" of Protestant-majority districts, while Protestants experienced the same fate in Catholic-dominated areas.[40]

The same discriminatory patterns militated against Catholic migration
to Belfast (and, to a lesser degree, against Protestant emigration to Londonderry city). Although in 1848 Belfast's population was 43 percent

Catholic, thereafter the tide turned as Protestant workers, especially in shipbuilding and other skilled crafts, united against Catholic competition for jobs and housing. Skilled workers' natural hostility to cheap, unskilled labor combined with inveterate anti-Catholic prejudices to convince working-class Protestants that their relatively favorable status was attributable to their moral superiority and fidelity to militant Protestantism and the British connection, and therefore to their ideological and economic affinities with Protestant employers, who naturally did little to discourage sentiments which so conveniently precluded working-class unity. Protestant working-class exclusiveness was manifested by periodic outbursts of anti-Catholic violence and sacralized by militant street preachers such as "Roaring" Hugh Hanna, who told his listeners that their "blood-bought cherished rights were imperilled by the audacious and savage outrages of a Romish mob." Sporadic waves of religious revivalism, as in the "year of grace" 1859, only heightened Protestant self-consciousness and hostility to the Lord's enemies. Thus, between 1852 and 1886 at least four major sectarian riots convulsed Belfast, replicated on smaller scales in Londonderry, in Portadown, and elsewhere. In 1886 Belfast's worst riots left 32 dead and over 400 wounded. Thereafter, "respectable" Protestants strove to channel their coreligionists' animosities into formal Unionist associations, but after Parliament passed a home rule bill in 1912, sanctioned violence against Belfast's "fenian bastards" became endemic. To be sure, occasionally working-class Protestants rebelled against their genteel spokesmen's failures to protect labor's interests, and occasionally, as in 1907, organizers like James Larkin and James Connolly succeeded in uniting Protestant and Catholic workers against commonly experienced exploitation. However, such moments were anomalous. Maverick Protestant organizations like the Protestant Workingmen's Association in the late 1860s and the Independent Orange Order of the early twentieth century merely reflected a working-class Orange populism which Ulster's Protestant elites could easily co-opt by raising their levels of anti-Catholic rhetoric. Similarly, inter-denominational labor unions quickly foundered on the rocks of sectarianism, especially when politicians and clerics of all stripes moved to denounce (e.g., as "socialistic") and destroy such unholy combinations, which threatened bourgeois hegemony on both sides of the religious divide; it was no coincidence that in 1912–14 both the Orange Order and its Catholic counterpart, the Ancient Order of Hibernians (Board of Erin), assaulted Connolly's radical, nonsectarian mill workers' union even more vehemently than they attacked each other.[41]

In such an atmosphere, Catholics in Belfast and other industrial towns found themselves confined to the lowest-paid, least-secure occupations and to the worst housing in embattled ghettos such as Belfast's Falls Road and Londonderry's Bogside district. In 1900, Catholics accounted for 47 percent of Belfast's barefoot female spinners, but only 29 percent of the "superior" women weavers; 41 percent of the unskilled dock laborers were Catholics, but only 7 percent of the elite shipyard workers. Catholics composed 32 percent of the city's general laborers, compared with 13 percent of its commercial clerks; in the public sector, where Orange influence was strongest, Catholics suffered even greater discrimination. As a result, despite the slow growth of a small middle class (inordinately dominated by priests, publicans, and small grocers), Belfast's Catholic community was generally impoverished; in 1900, Catholics made up 46 percent of the city's workhouse inmates (compared with 48 percent in 1853), although they were now less than a quarter of the general population. In these circumstances it was no wonder most rural Catholics bypassed Belfast, preferring to leave a land where, as one emigrant correctly prophesied, "Religion shall cause bloodshed to the Judgement Day." Indeed, the slow growth of Belfast's Catholic population suggests that many of its more ambitious or frustrated residents joined the exodus overseas. Finally, heightened self-consciousness and alienation among Ulster Catholics may have helped influence their choices of destinations abroad. Despite efforts by the British government and by the apostate nationalist Thomas D'Arcy McGee to direct Irish emigrants to Canada, Catholics in Ulster, as in the southern provinces, seemed increasingly convinced that British North America was "but a second England," with all "the ear-marks of slavery" present in the old country: an impression which Canada's powerful Orange Order and its even more rabidly anti-Catholic Protestant Protective Association did nothing to dispel. Thus, while early-twentieth-century emigration from predominantly Protestant north Fermanagh flowed largely to Canada, in heavily Catholic south Fermanagh emigrants overwhelmingly favored the United States.[42]

In the absence of significant urban growth or industrial employment, the commercialization of Irish agriculture and the consequent rationalization of land-use and inheritance patterns always mandated emigration by rural Ireland's "superfluous" inhabitants. Prior to the Famine large numbers had resisted the "logical" alternative to pauperization at home, but the holocaust of 1845–55 created what "improving" landlords and British legislation had been unable to accomplish: a market-oriented rural society dominated by commercial farmers and graziers instead of by an entrenched and intransigent subsistence sector composed of laborers, cottiers, and petty tillage farmers. In 1861 about half a million landless laborers still constituted one-quarter of rural Ireland's population, but otherwise the structure of agrarian society had changed radically. For example, in 1861 farms under fifteen acres in size composed only 47 percent of all holdings larger than one acre, although prior to the Famine they had constituted nearly 78 percent; between 1845 and 1861, smallholdings and cottiers' plots between one and five acres had declined 53 percent, and by the latter year they accounted for a mere 14 percent of all farms. Numerically, holdings between fifteen and thirty acres had also declined, by 5 percent, but their proportion of the total had risen from 23 percent to 25 percent. Significantly, farms over thirty acres increased both numerically (by 23 percent) and proportionately (from 20 percent to 28 percent), and in 1861 over 15 percent of all holdings exceeded fifty acres in size. The consolidation of farms had advanced furthest in southern and eastern Ireland: in 1861 nearly 44 percent of the holdings in Munster and 30 percent of those in Leinster were over thirty acres, compared with only 18 percent in Ulster and 17 percent in Connaught. The Famine years also had produced a great expansion of cattle and sheep farming at the expense of tillage: between 1841 and 1861 the number of cattle rose 86 percent and that of sheep by 69 percent, and by the latter date about 70 percent of Irish land was in pasture or meadow. Although the average value of livestock per holding had increased most rapidly on farms under thirty acres, by 1861 two-thirds of the total value was concentrated among the minority of farmers who held over thirty acres. Thus, in 1861 Irish rural society finally approximated the long-standing British ideal: gone were the families of 200,000 landless laborers and of 160,000 cottiers and smallholders; however, still present and now numerically as well as economically dominant were nearly 300,000 commerical or semicommercial farmers, almost 158,000 of whom held at least thirty acres devoted primarily to the production of livestock for the British market. "Ireland's famine was the punishment of her imprudence and idleness," concluded the Anglo-Irish novelist Anthony Trollope in 1862, "but it has given her prosperity and progress."[43]

Moreover, in the post-Famine period these indices of "progress" only continued at a steady, albeit much less dramatic, pace. Between 1861 and 1911 the number of landless laborers fell by 200,000, and by the latter date such laborers and cottiers together constituted less than one-third the adult males engaged in agriculture; by contrast, in 1911 farmers composed 39 percent and farmers' sons and other assisting relatives made up another 20 percent. In addition, not only did farmers increase their dominance of rural society but among landholders the balance continued to shift in favor of strong farmers and graziers. In 1861–1911 the total number of agricultural holdings above one acre in size declined 14 percent, led by a 37 percent fall in one-to-five-acre holdings and a 24 percent decline in five-to-fifteen-acre farms; by 1911 holdings of one to fifteen acres composed only 40 percent of all Irish farms, compared with 47 percent half a century earlier. Medium-sized holdings of fifteen to thirty acres also declined, by 8.5 percent, although their share of all farms remained stable at about 25 percent. However, farms above thirty acres increased by 3 percent, led by a 5.5 percent rise in holdings above fifty acres and an 18 percent increase in farms above one hundred acres. As a result, by 1911 holdings above thirty acres constituted 33 percent of all farms, compared with 28 percent in 1861; during the same period the proportion of farms over fifty acres rose from 15 percent to 18.5 percent, and that of farms over one hundred acres increased from 5.5 percent to 7 percent. The greatest structural changes took place in northern and western Ireland: between 1861 and 1911 holdings under thirty acres declined 24 percent in Ulster, 15.5 percent in Connaught. However, large farms remained most characteristic of Munster and

Leinster, where in 1911 some 45 percent and 33.5 percent of all holdings
exceeded thirty acres, compared with 25 percent in Ulster and merely 19.5
percent in Connaught. The movement from tillage to pasture farming also
continued: in 1876 nearly 80 percent of Ireland's arable land was grass or
meadow, and by the middle of the next century the comparable figure was
85 percent. Meanwhile, the number of cattle rose 43 percent, from 3.5 million in 1861 to 5 million in 1914, and the number of sheep increased by a
third. Correspondingly, acreage under cereals and green crops steadily declined; between 1861 and 1886 land planted in wheat, oats, or barley fell
nearly 40 percent. Potato cultivation drastically diminished, from 2.5 million acres in 1845 to 1 million in 1876; by 1897 only 677,000 acres were
planted in potatoes, and per-acre yields were two-thirds less than before
the Famine.[44]

Apologists for Ireland's union with Britain regarded these trends with
satisfaction, as promoting further prosperity for post-Famine agriculture.
Certainly, conditions in rural Ireland had improved significantly since mid-
century. Between 1850 and 1914, Irish cattle exports quadrupled, savings
deposits rose from £9.6 million to over £60 million, and imports increased from £15 million to £75 million, indicating comparable gains in
rural purchasing power. Between 1861 and 1881 the number of one-room
rural hovels declined 54 percent, and in 1893 one observer noted that the
remainder were "disappearing fast." Nevertheless, such apologists either
ignored or callously applauded the fact that these salutary developments
reflected massive emigration by tillage farmers, smallholders, farmers' children, cottiers, and laborers whose homes were leveled and whose fields were
consolidated into the large farms and grazing ranches whose relative prosperity so delighted both their holders and British observers. Moreover, rural Ireland's increasing commercialization only made most farmers, as well
as laborers, more vulnerable to declining prices, credit squeezes, poor harvests, and livestock diseases—as in the 1880s, when all four factors combined to cause widespread distress and a 24 percent increase in emigration.
Equally important, even among the landholding sector post-Famine "prosperity" was distributed very inequitably. Between 1861 and 1914 both land
and livestock were increasingly concentrated among a small minority of
farmers; although by the latter date the Irish poor were fewer in number
and generally less destitute, the *gap* between rich and poor was at least as
wide as, probably wider than, before the Famine.[45]

In the mid-nineteenth century Dublin Castle authorized for tax purposes
a detailed valuation of Irish farmland, and although imperfect the results
provide a reasonably accurate picture of the distribution of rural wealth. In
1911 holdings valued under £4 averaged 9.3 acres in size and were ten-
anted by smallholders and cottiers; holdings valued between £4 and £15
averaged 24.1 acres, corresponding to the tenancies of middling farmers;
and farms valued above £15 ranged from 30 to over 600 acres (averaging 110 acres) and were held by strong farmers and graziers. A few
years earlier, the economist Moritz Bonn had noted that all the holdings

valued under £4, plus "a large number" of those valued between £4 and £15, were "uneconomic": "too small to support, even according to the low Irish standard of life, the families living on them, and to supply them with food, clothing, education, and occupation." Despite all of post-Famine Ireland's "progress," in 1911 some 30 percent of all Irish farms were still valued at less than £4, and although these smallholdings constituted merely 12.5 percent of Ireland's farmland, they were occupied by 26 percent of the country's rural families. Moreover, another 40 percent of Irish farms were rated between £4 and £15; these holdings maintained 37 percent of the island's rural families but occupied only 27 percent of its agricultural land. In short, by Bonn's definition about 200,000 farms, over 40 percent of the total, were "uneconomic" or "deficit holdings," while another 100,000 were marginal at best, highly susceptible to declining markets or natural disasters. Deficit holdings were most prevalent in Connaught, where in 1911 about 82 percent of the population occupied holdings valued below £15 (34 percent on farms below £4); by contrast, in Munster and Leinster only 47 percent and 53 percent, respectively, occupied farms rated below £15; in Ulster the comparable figure was 56 percent. At the other end of the social scale, although only 78,000 farms—representing 30 percent of all holdings and 39 percent of rural families—were rated above £15, they occupied over 60 percent of all Irish farmland and a significantly higher proportion of the island's richest soil. Indeed, less than 3 percent of all Irish farms—valued above £100 and averaging 245 acres apiece—engrossed nearly one-fifth of the country's farmland. As might be expected, large and prosperous holdings predominated in Leinster and Munster, where 13 percent and 10 percent, respectively, of all farms were rated above £50 (averaging 152 acres apiece); in Ulster the comparable figure was 5 percent, in Connaught less than 3 percent. As these statistics suggest, the benefits of post-Famine consolidations and commercialization accrued to a relatively small sector of the rural population, primarily to strong farmers and graziers who, thanks to landlords' policies and their own superior capital resources, were best able to compete in the Irish land market. Consequently, when lands became untenanted—whether through voluntary sale, bankruptcy, eviction, or emigration—the unoccupied fields generally served only to enlarge the pastures of already-affluent tenants rather than to make viable the holdings of petty or middling farmers. Moreover, although prior to the 1870s small farmers had extended their cattle herds at a faster rate than their wealthy neighbors had, after about 1874 that process was reversed: subsequently, only the large graziers significantly extended their herds, and so wealth measured in livestock as well as land was increasingly concentrated at the top of rural society. As a result, noted one visitor, post-Famine rural Ireland exhibited not uniform amelioration but rather "cultivation and high prosperity on the one hand, struggling poverty and sad sterility on the other."[46]

After the Famine as before, Irish farmers and nationalist politicians usually blamed landlordism and the British government for both the depopulation and the still-prevalent poverty of rural Ireland. Biased legislation, high rents, insecurity of tenure, and a variety of oppressive restrictions and petty tyrannies: all purportedly left Irish tenants "at the mercy of a parcel of bloodsuckers" and mandated wholesale emigration. Certainly, Irish landlords emerged from the crisis of 1845–55 in a much stronger position relative to their remaining dependents, for the Famine had given proprietors an unexpected but eagerly seized opportunity to rationalize their estates by eliminating bankrupt middlemen, by virtually eradicating rundale settlements, and by evicting about half a million impecunious farmers and cottiers. As a result, and despite the lasting bitterness thereby engendered, by 1856 Irish landlords enjoyed greater control over their properties than at any time since the conquest. Moreover, at the behest of landlords and economists, the British government passed more legislation designed to fully commercialize Irish agriculture by creating a totally "free" land market. In 1849 Parliament passed the Encumbered Estates Act to facilitate the sale of overmortgaged, now-bankrupt estates to new and presumably more-solvent and business-minded proprietors. During the next few years about one-seventh of Ireland's estates changed hands, often at bargain prices. For the landlord class as a whole the change was invigorating, but for bankrupt scions of the old order it was traumatic: "people of the first distinction are only too glad to get a pittance," lamented one member of a once-wealthy family, and some got even less; for example, the last representative of the Martins of Ballynahinch, once virtual lords of Connemara, died penniless in New York, her vast estates sold for less than the enormous debts accumulated by her profligate sires. As for the new purchasers, although the act's authors anticipated a flood of British investors, and although a few large properties, such as the Martin estate, passed under the control of London-based corporations, in fact over 95 percent of the 7,500 new proprietors were not British but Irish, often Catholics, mainly solicitors, merchants, and other townsmen who had always sought land for both symbolic and mercenary motives. Nevertheless, popular opinion generally condemned all the new owners as "upstarts," if not "aliens," and regarded them as far more avaricious and ruthless than their predecessors. Many such accusations doubtless were well deserved, particularly in western Ireland, where many former landlords' proverbial laxity contrasted favorably with new owners' capitalistic outlooks and "improvements" which mandated evictions, the consolidation of holdings, the fencing of former common lands, and the abrogation of peasants' customary grazing and turbary rights. When new landlords invited English and Scottish sheep ranchers to displace starving tenants, as in western Mayo, popular resentment was especially keen. No wonder, then, that farmers in west Munster, Connaught, and Donegal often sighed nostalgically for a pre-Famine "golden age" or that emigrants such as James Mitchell of County Galway implied that all subsequent evils were attributable to new "English" proprietors who had usurped the authority without assuming the duties of "ancient and honored" families. In fact, however, these new owners merely symbolized and epitomized a shift from paternalistic to instrumental models of landlord-tenant relations which, although culminating in the mid-nineteenth century, had been under way for decades. Indeed, in this context Parliament's passage of the Deasy Act in 1860 was the more significant development, for it climaxed over two centuries of pro-landlord legislation. By explicitly denying legal status to all noncontractual landlord-tenant arrangements, the act eradicated the last legal traces of Irish feudalism and gave proprietors virtually absolute control over their tenants, especially the great majority who lacked formal leases. Theoretically, at least, after 1860 unless written leases specifically allowed claims for tenant-right, not even that hallowed custom could impede landlords' freedom of action.[47]

To be sure, once the Famine had abated, most Irish landlords did not press their advantages to the fullest extent. Indeed, as the historian L. P. Curtis, Jr., concludes, despite the infusion of new owners, proprietors generally still "cared more about preserving status than maximizing profit," and so continued to tie up a large portion of their income in family settlements and mortgage payments; as a result, Irish landlords remained encumbered by debts, and in 1880 the debt burden on all estates averaged 27 percent of the annual income, being much higher on small and medium-sized properties. Yet in spite of such financial pressures, most post-Famine landlords sought accommodation, not conflict, with their tenantry. The formerly common practice of canting tenancies to the highest bidder became rare, and in the years 1855–75 rents generally increased by only 20 percent, lagging far behind a 40 to 50 percent rise in the value of total farm output, which reflected price increases of 87 percent for livestock and 61 percent for livestock products (beef, butter, pork, etc.). Thus, during the immediate post-Famine period many farmers enjoyed unusual prosperity: "The price of farm produce have been so good . . . that the country is in a much more prosperous state," declared the Ulster tenant Art McConnell; and as a result, he boasted, "we have got the parlour ceiled papered & carpeted & a new fireplace in the Kitchen." Consequently, on most estates the enormous arrears accumulated during the Famine rapidly evaporated, and after 1855 evictions were relatively few. Between 1856 and 1878, evictions averaged only about 800 per year (compared with 10,000 per year in 1849–55), and landlords probably readmitted about a third of the evicted as tenants or caretakers. In short, all but the most intransigently insolvent tenants enjoyed considerable security. As a result, in the period 1856–78 agrarian outrages were far less frequent and widespread than before the Famine, generally occurring only in response to especially obnoxious estate agents or wholesale clearances in specific districts, as in south Ulster in the mid-1850s and the north midlands in 1869–71. Indeed, during this period Irish landlords even experienced a renaissance of political power, enjoying more deference and electoral influence over their tenantry than at any time since O'Connell's Catholic emancipation crusade in the 1820s.[48]

Nevertheless, most farmers still regarded landlords with fear and aversion, if not overt hostility. As one observer noted, "The present relations between landlords and tenants seem to be universally felt . . . as a great evil." The Tenant League of the 1850s, Fenianism in the 1860s, the farmers' clubs and the home rule movement of the 1870s, and the Land League of 1879–82: all represented, directly or indirectly, attempts to weaken or eradicate Irish landlordism. Although exacerbated by the Famine and politicized by decades of agitation, some causes for poor landlord-tenant relations were perennial. Despite growing numbers of new Catholic landlords, most proprietors remained Protestant, alienated (outside east Ulster) by religion, politics, and culture from the vast majority of their tenants. Absenteeism also remained common; in 1870 about a third of Ireland's landlords lived outside the country. In addition, after the Famine, landlord-tenant relations became increasingly distant, formal, and utilitarian, symbolized by the growing numbers of salaried estate agents. The changes can be traced even in contemporary literature: the late-nineteenth-century Ascendancy novels of Edith Sommerville and Violet Martin (who used the pseudonym Ross) portray a rigidly segmented society, with little intercourse between the "Big House" and the tenantry, a radical contrast to the paternalistic, if irresponsible, eighteenth-century squirearchy depicted in Maria Edgeworth's *Castle Rackrent*. Increasingly, the deference and political influence which landlords enjoyed was due to fear or calculated self-interest, not respect, and after the passage of the Secret Ballot Act in 1872 their ability to command voter allegiance rapidly declined. Landlords still retained an inordinate degree of political power, especially on the local level: they dominated the Poor Law boards of guardians until the 1880s, and the county grand juries, magistracy, and justices of the peace until much later. In 1880 a Donegal priest remarked disgustedly that it was common to see a "landlord browbeating a judge [himself a proprietor or estate agent] to such an extent that every decision given by that judge . . . was against the tenants and for that landlord"; as late as 1911, Protestants still constituted 62 percent of the justices of the peace, although (save in east Ulster) by then they had lost influence over local elected bodies. That the British government felt it necessary to maintain a minimum of 24,000 troops in post-Famine Ireland, in addition to the Royal Irish Constabulary, vividly demonstrated that the landlords' authority now derived almost exclusively from Westminster, not from tenant deference.[49]

To be sure, in the years 1856–78 Irish proprietors rarely used their power in tyrannical fashion, but in times of relative prosperity they could extract rents without resort to overt coercion. What rankled tenants during this period was, first, that landlords performed so few positive actions for their dependents and, second and more important, that legally proprietors could be tyrannical with impunity. The former deficiency left tenants without feelings of obligation to those they regarded as mere rent receivers and parasites, while the latter implied threats which made all farmers anxious and insecure. "Even where no unfairness has been shown, and no wrong perpetrated," noted one critic, "the mere feeling of the insecurity, the simple consciousness that the law, if put in force, will authorise what is a virtual wrong,—act on the feelings and the judgement, like tyranny and oppression." Whether residents or absentees, landlords spent very little of their gross incomes on their estates, even less on drainage or other projects beneficial to tenants. When proprietors did take active roles in estate management, too often these were manifested by restrictive lease covenants or rationalizations of holdings which many tenants viewed as constricting, demeaning, or oppressive. In addition, although rent levels in 1856–78 were generally moderate, they still absorbed between 25 and 40 percent of tenants' gross incomes. Although the period's inflated livestock prices enabled prosperous graziers to pay such rents easily, contemporary prices for cereals and flax declined 39 percent and 49 percent, respectively, which meant that tillage farmers (primarily small and middling tenants) struggled to meet their landlords' demands. Moreover, considerable evidence suggests that per-acre rents were higher on tillage land than on pastures, and highest of all on the wretched potato plots which cottiers and "reclamation tenants" had colonized from boglands and mountain wastes. Little wonder, then, that contemporaries argued that, despite *generally* moderate rents, "[t]he small farmers are in as bad a position as they were forty years ago," or that a modern economic historian concludes that most tenants' net incomes were little, if any, higher than before the Famine. Also, while *overall* rent increases lagged behind rising prices, the increases which actually occurred seemed highly arbitrary in both their timing and their choice of targets. Unlike their Scottish peers, Irish landlords never correlated price and rent levels, and consequently rents varied widely from estate to estate and even from tenant to tenant on the same estate. Some proprietors never increased pre-Famine rents, whereas others such as William Bence Jones and the notorious (and eventually assassinated) Lord Leitrim constantly raised rents to force their tenants to greater exertions. Most landlords increased rents sporadically and haphazardly, as did Lord Kenmare to finance construction of his lavish Killarney mansion, but such capricious policies engendered at least as much uncertainty and resentment among tenants as did Bence Jones's more consistent and predictable rack-renting.[50]

Finally, the greatest grievance of Irish farmers was their lack of guaranteed compensation for improvements and of fixity of tenure. The two issues were intimately related but had varying connotations for different classes of farmers. For example, compensation for improvements was a valid concern among reclamation tenants whose arduous toil had created viable homesteads out of formerly useless wasteland; however, in fact, most tenants made few or no improvements, quite the reverse, but if successful their claims would serve to deter landlords from carrying out evictions. At the other end of the social scale, compensation for improvements translated into a demand for "free sale": graziers and other affluent farmers wanted guaranteed compensation not because they feared eviction but because such claims would give them a marketable equity or "interest" in their holdings. Correspondingly, wealthy farmers were less interested in fixity of tenure, for that principle, if institutionalized, would rigidify an otherwise "free" land market in which they enjoyed competitive advantages. However, small and middling farmers were vitally interested in fixity of tenure, especially because prior to 1870 about three-quarters of Irish farmers were yearly tenants or tenants at will, without formal leases. To be sure, tradition dictated that yearly tenancies were usually perpetual, and both compensation for improvements and fixity of tenure were pillars of the "Ulster custom" of tenant-right, which prevailed throughout the island in varying degrees. Also, as was noted above, in 1856–78 evictions were relatively uncommon, usually enforced only when tenants were hopelessly in arrears. Nevertheless, the Famine had cruelly demonstrated the vulnerability of yearly tenancies, and in its aftermath proprietors armed with the Deasy Act had shown increasing hostility to claims for tenant-right. As a result, farmers' demands for legalization of the Ulster custom became so strident that in 1870 Prime Minister William Gladstone, frightened by the recent Fenian uprisings, persuaded Parliament to reverse centuries of antitenant legislation by passing a new Irish Land Act, which guaranteed evicted tenants compensation for "disturbance" and improvements. However, landlords effectively nullified the act by restricting free sales of tenant interest and by imposing new written leases which forced tenants to contract out of the law's benefits or prohibited tenant investments which might require future compensation. Thus, although revolutionary in intent (especially the "Bright clauses," which provided opportunities for tenants to purchase their own holdings), the 1870 Land Act quickly became a dead letter; whether because of ignorance, high legal costs, or fear of retaliation, few tenants dared go to court to challenge their landlords' authority. The point is not that this failure caused evictions to increase but rather that despite the law proprietors' powers to evict remained virtually unchanged. Granted that in 1856–78 evictions were few, averaging under one ejection per 500 tenants; nevertheless, *threats* to evict—formal "notices to quit"—were alarmingly common, and every actual eviction was a socially traumatic, often highly publicized and politicized experience, symptomatic of all tenants' relative powerlessness. Moreover, when harvests were poor and farm prices low, all tenants, rich and poor, were susceptible to ejection. During the bad years of the early 1860s, annual evictions exceeded 1,000, approaching 2,000 in 1863 and 1864. In the late 1870s the halcyon post-Famine decades ended abruptly when a run of poor harvests coincided with sharp price declines for all Irish farm products. Graziers and tillage farmers alike fell deeply into arrears, and landlords were generally unsympathetic to pleas for abatements. As a result the number of evicted persons climbed steadily—from 4,600 in 1878 to 10,600 in 1880 and to 26,800 in 1882—until it appeared to many frightened tenants that the Famine clearances were on the verge of reenactment; in all, between 1878 and 1886 some 132,000 persons, over 26,000 families, suffered eviction.[51]

Unlike tenants in the Famine years, however, Irish tenants in 1879 and afterward refused to starve patiently or endure evictions quietly; instead, they organized and resisted, thereby revealing that Irish landlords, although seemingly at the zenith of their power, were in fact fatally weakened by their now almost exclusive reliance on Britain to sustain their authority. In 1879–82 Irish tenants joined the newly formed Irish National Land League, under the leadership of the ex-Fenian Michael Davitt, the home rule MP Charles Stewart Parnell, and a host of local agitators. Subsidized by Irish-American dollars, the league terrorized landlords and their supporters, resisted evictions, demanded rent reductions, and raised such an effective popular outcry against the whole landlord system that in 1881 Gladstone and Parliament felt obliged to pass a historic Land Act, which rendered inevitable that system's ultimate demise. The act fully legalized the "3 Fs" of tenant-right: "free sale" (or compensation for improvements); "fixity of tenure" (i.e., undisturbed occupancy, provided the tenant met his obligations); and, most important, a "fair rent," to be determined not by landlords but by a government-appointed land commission. The act deprived Irish proprietors of several fundamental "rights" of property ownership: they could no longer freely choose or evict their tenants; nor could they charge competitive, "free market" rents, for the commission's land courts imposed statutory rent reductions which averaged 18 to 20 percent below pre-1879 levels. Nevertheless, many tenants remained unsatisfied: the 1881 act excluded leaseholders (perhaps one-third of all farmers with more than one acre) from statutory rent reductions, and it made no provision for the estimated 100,000 smallholders who faced eviction because of inability to pay off *past* arrears; in addition, tenants *already* evicted, for whatever cause, had no means of redress, and many farmers argued that even reductions of 18 to 20 percent were insufficient, especially in the mid-1880s, when renewed price declines and poor harvests caused a second round of agrarian distress, evictions, and organized tenant resistance in the form of a "Plan of Campaign" against landlords who refused further rent reductions. Although Irish proprietors raged at Britain's "betrayal" of landlord interests, Parliament continued to buckle under tenant pressure. Thus, in 1882 Gladstone's Liberals amended the 1881 act, arbitrarily canceling half the smallholders' arrears (some £2 million), and in 1887 a Parliament dominated by Conservatives passed a new Land Act, which admitted leaseholders to the land courts and, more significant, imposed additional rent reductions averaging another 19 percent. Already-evicted tenants languished until 1907, when the government provided their reinstatement on new holdings, but together the 1881–82 and 1887 Land Acts created a revolutionary system of dual ownership which made landlordism economically untenable.[52]

As proprietors' rent rolls declined with statutory reductions, so also fell the value of their estates and their ability to meet their own financial obligations. From their standpoint, as from that of British politicians eager to "pacify" Ireland, acquiescence to popular demands for peasant proprietorship appeared the only rational solution to an increasingly intolerable situation. Accordingly, between 1885 and 1909 Parliament passed a succession of Land Purchase Acts to encourage and subsidize the sale of Irish estates on terms favorable to both landlords and tenant purchasers. As a result, by the end of World War I about 85 percent of all Irish farms, over 400,000 holdings, were sold or in the process of sale to their former tenants; the great majority of holdings changed hands after passage of the 1903 Wyndham Act, and by 1921 a mere 70,000 farms remained to be transferred under the aegis of the new Irish Free State and Northern Ireland governments. In addition, Tory politicians sought to "kill home rule with kindness" by benefiting rural Ireland in other ways. For example, in 1889 the Irish chief secretary Arthur Balfour provided government financing for "light railway" lines designed to spur economic development in the impoverished western counties. In 1891 Parliament created the Congested Districts Board with authority to improve western farming methods and livestock breeds; promote local industries such as fishing and lace making; construct new roads, bridges, and harbor facilities; and, most important, eradicate uneconomical farms by redistributing and amalgamating existing holdings. In 1908 the board acquired power to purchase western estates by compulsion (outside the Congested Districts, estate sales remained voluntary), and by 1921 nearly 1,000 estates had been acquired and their holdings rationalized and resold on easy terms to the occupants. Finally, in 1899, Parliament established the Irish Department of Agriculture and Technical Instruction; between 1900 and 1907 the department worked with the Tory philanthropist Sir Horace Plunkett's Irish Agricultural Organization Society to promote cooperative creameries and other "self-help" enterprises among Irish farmers.[53]

In 1903, during debate over passage of the Wyndham Land Purchase Act, the Irish nationalist leader John Redmond prophesied that by abolishing landlordism Parliament would create "wealth from poverty" and give "to the Irish people a new field at home for their industry, instead of driving them, generation after generation, as [Britain has] done in the past," to emigrate to other lands. However, events proved Redmond wrong: despite the late-nineteenth-century Land Acts, despite the Congested Districts Board, despite even the creation of peasant proprietorship, the exodus overseas not only continued but flowed most heavily from the very western counties targeted for maximum government assistance. In part, persistent emigration reflected the Land Purchase Acts' specific inadequacies. For example, the acts confirmed only *present* tenants as owners of their *existing* holdings, despite the facts revealed in the 1911 census that at least 40 percent of these farms were too small and poor to support decent livings, while a mere 7 percent (valued over £50 and averaging 155 acres) engrossed a third of all Irish farmland. Even the Congested Districts Board's authority was inadequate to make western smallholdings economically viable: the population was too great relative to available arable land, and the board lacked power to expropriate and parcel out the cattle and sheep ranches leased by wealthy graziers. Consequently, for most small and many middling farmers, ownership did not preclude struggling poverty. Moreover, the Land Purchase Acts made no provisions for those without tenancies, and so, lacking alternative employment, agricultural laborers and farmers' noninheriting children still faced a Hobson's choice of landless destitution at home or emigration abroad.[54]

Even more important than these specific deficiencies, and also their root cause, was the fact that all the Irish land legislation together could not touch, indeed was purposely designed *not* to touch, the basic source of rural Ireland's socioeconomic "sickness" and consequent emigration: Irish agriculture's integration into an international market system in which most Irish farmers suffered increasing competitive disadvantages. The main reason for Irish rural distress after 1878 was not bad weather and poor harvests, although these dramatized and exacerbated the farmers' plight, but rather falling prices caused by foreign competition in the British market for foodstuffs. Most Irish farmers, 70 percent of whom held fewer than thirty acres in 1911, could not compete favorably with the technologically advanced, highly mechanized, and heavily capitalized agriculture of foreign countries: Irish grain could not compete in price with cereals from the North American and Argentinian prairies; Ulster flax could not compete with Russian and Belgian products; Irish butter could compete neither in price nor quality with continental European butter and butter substitutes. And, although prices remained *relatively* remunerative, even Irish livestock had difficulty competing with North and South American beef and pork, and with mutton and wool from Australia and New Zealand. As a result, one observer noted, "To-day the competition of the trust-owned farms of the United States and the Argentine Republic is a more deadly enemy to the Irish agriculturist than the lingering remnants of landlordism or the bureaucratic officialdom of the British Empire," for "after the Irish agriculturist has gathered his harvest and brought it to market, he finds that a competitor living three thousand miles away under a friendly flag has undersold and beggared him." In short, the destruction of Irish landlordism merely removed a small group of major capitalists to make way for a mass of petty ones, most of whom were too impoverished to profit from the few economic advantages implicit in Ireland's dependent and competitively inferior position. To be sure, the island's full exposure to the vagaries of international trade conferred certain benefits even on the poorest Irish; for example, the availability of imported cornmeal ensured that potato crop failures no longer entailed starvation. However, critics noted with heavy irony that "nothing more forcibly shows the abnormal condition into which the country has sunk than the fact that the Irish farmer exports his own superior bacon in order to make enough money to be able to import and eat inferior American bacon."[55]

It is arguable that the creation of a peasant proprietorship delayed Irish agriculture's full commercialization by entrenching a multitude of small and middling farmers on their holdings. However, the authors of the Land

and Land Purchase acts did not intend that consequence; otherwise the acts would not have forbidden subdivision and would have taken steps to break up the large grass farms and provide smallholdings to the landless. According to Parnell himself, the Land Acts were designed to create a "free" land market in which only efficient farmers would prosper and survive. By conferring a mortgageable equity or "interest" in their holdings, the laws encouraged tenants to take out loans, using their farms as security; the need to repay such loans with interest, like the annuities which incipient farm owners paid under the Land Purchase schemes, served the same basic functions as the old rent charges, driving farmers to produce a marketable surplus, practice impartible inheritance, and cut labor costs. Thus, James Connolly argued that "the recent Land Acts, acting contemporaneously with the development of trans-Atlantic traffic, are converting Ireland from a country governed according to the conception of feudalism into a country shaping itself after capitalistic laws of trade." In fact, the conversion had begun long before and continued long afterward—perhaps nearing its logical consequence, destruction of the small- and medium-sized "family farm," only in the present decade. Nevertheless, the Land Acts confirmed and, for the Irish people, legitimized a system in which relatively few rural dwellers could prosper even at the time. *If* the large grazing ranches had been broken up into viable smallholdings; *if* the landlords' estates had been confiscated outright and given to the peasantry; or *if,* as Michael Davitt and Connolly proposed, all Irish land had been nationalized and utilized for broad social purposes: then rural Ireland's destiny might have been different. However, the British government would not allow, and Irish leaders were not willing to fight for, land confiscation or the breakup of the grazing ranches; and neither the government, nor the Irish bourgeoisie, nor the land-hungry tenants themselves were willing to countenance land nationalization. Consequently, given the dearth of nonfarm employment, the conditions promoting mass emigration remained inherent in the very structure of post-Famine Irish agriculture.[56]

The only sectors which benefited greatly from the increased commercialization of Irish agriculture were the urban and rural middle classes, especially the former: the merchants, traders, bankers, shopkeepers, and usurers of post-Famine Ireland's cities, towns, and villages. "Of all the various classes in Ireland," wrote the French visitor L. Paul-Dubois in 1908, "only those connected with the distribution of wealth are increasing, and their parasitic earnings merely lead to the impoverishment"—and emigration, he might have added—"of the class by whom wealth is directly produced." Certainly, Ireland's new economic middlemen siphoned off a significant portion of gross national income and provided a web of credit which fatally enmeshed poor farmers who found such arrangements initially attractive or necessary but often ultimately disastrous. Thus, even during the economically depressed early 1860s and 1880s, travelers remarked how the bustling prosperity of towns such as Kilrush and Ennis contrasted dramatically with the poverty and deprivation in the surrounding countryside. After passage of the Land Acts, financiers, traders, and shopkeepers pressed loans and credit purchases on farmers, some of whom sought to expand acreage and livestock herds; others strove thereby to improve the meager quality of their lives—or "to *look* at least as good as their neighbours," while still more needed credit merely to survive in periods of declining tillage prices and alternative income sources. However, when severe depression struck, as in the 1880s, or when peasant proprietorship failed to engender the promised prosperity, as among western smallholders, then loans dried up, creditors demanded repayment, and many farmers faced bankruptcy, forced sales of property to creditors or wealthier neighbors, and the likelihood of emigration. Thus, in 1887 John Moriarty, an emigrating tenant from County Cork, declared bitterly that all the Land Acts were "disastrous in the end, because they allow one to [mortgage] his tenant-right at a discount." "You believe that it will set you up," he concluded, "and it is the very stone that makes you sink. The banks are our ruin. Once they have taken hold of their man, they don't let him out before they have skinned him." Even more predatory than branch banks were the village shopkeepers and usurers, or "gombeen-men,'" who charged exorbitant interest rates for small loans and credit purchases. In 1862 one traveler noted, "The extortions of the usurers . . . press very severely on the unfortunate people whose necessities force them to have recourse to those harpies" and who are so "ignorant of the commercial value of money [that] . . . they do not really know how atrociously they have been 'fleeced' " by interest rates ranging from 50 to 100 percent. By the early twentieth century extended banking facilities and competition among increased numbers of retailers had lowered interest rates generally, but in the far western counties, where local and familial obligations reinforced economic clientage, "a plague of small shopkeepers" and gombeen-men still commanded inordinate influence: interest rates remained extortionate, shop goods were overpriced, and "the debtors [were] often unable to transfer their custom to another shop, through fear that such a step would be followed by immediate prosecution for the amounts" owed. Despite their ostentatious patriotism, the dramatist John Millington Synge believed that village retailers and publicans were at least as ruthless "exterminators" as the former landlords: "they're swindling the people themselves in a dozen ways," he wrote, "and then buying out their holdings and packing whole families to America."[57]

The other generally prosperous group comprised strong farmers, especially graziers who held several hundred acres or more. Livestock rearing was a capital-intensive and highly speculative enterprise: consequently, many graziers had merely an instrumental relationship to the soil, and a large number were townsmen—"upstarts" and "coarse parvenus" such as cattle dealers, butchers, and shopkeepers—who never resided on their holdings. Graziers occupied an intermediate and ambivalent position between landlords and the majority of tenant farmers. They desired a highly flexible land market which they could dominate through superior capital resources and which would allow them to expand or contract investments according to prevailing livestock prices. Before and during the troubled 1880s, graziers maintained an uneasy alliance with other tenants in opposition to landlords who imposed long leases and high rents which curtailed their ability to respond quickly to fluctuating prices; thus, graziers and strong farmers assumed disproportionately prominent roles in contemporary tenants' movements, such as the Land League and Plan of Campaign in the 1880s. However, graziers also opposed most tenants' ultimate goals—fixity of tenure or peasant proprietorship—because these, too, reduced land-market elasticity and the graziers' competitive advantages. In 1881 Parliament benefited both landlords and graziers by exempting the rental of grasslands for *less* than twelve months from the provisions of that year's Land Act. This led to the emergence of the "eleven-month system," which enabled proprietors to charge full market rents for pastureland but which also freed graziers from long-term capital commitments and created a land market more favorable to their needs. Subsequently, many graziers and strong farmers became more conservative politically, and their always-implicit conflicts with less affluent tenants and peasants became overt as the latter began to realize that their former allies were "land-" or "grass-grabbers" and that the issue of land redistribution was at least as critical as that of landownership.[58]

Antigrazier resentment was widespread among small and middling farmers, but most intense in Connaught, north Leinster, and parts of Munster where wholesale Famine clearances to create grazing ranches were still fresh in popular memory and where large numbers of poor and land-hungry smallholders and laborers still inhabited nearby wastelands and the fringes of great estates. Perhaps the most valid complaint against graziers was that, directly or indirectly, they were responsible for much post-Famine emigration; "it is the grabber on the eleven-month system," declared a group of laborers' representatives in County Meath, "that is keeping the emigration vessel floating with the youth of Ireland." Certainly, the graziers' successful competition for land kept rents high, encouraged poor farmers to sell their holdings, curtailed opportunities for the land poor and the landless to acquire acreage, and, by shoring up the tottering landlord class through the eleven-month system, made proprietors less eager to part with their estates. Moreover, grazing itself caused emigration by reducing employment for farmers' sons and agricultural laborers. Indeed, many Irishmen thought graziers responsible for the social and cultural desolation which seemed to accompany depopulation in large districts of central and western Ireland: "the best land is given up to bullocks and the worst to men," lamented one critic, and a once-vibrant countryside had become "little more than a ranch for the rearing of cattle"; to another observer, Meath's rich farms only "spelt waste and loss and loneliness and vanished people." Nevertheless, despite growing demands for land redistribution and sporadic outbursts of antigrazier agitation (such as the "Ranch War" of 1906–8 in the north midlands), the graziers reigned supreme and emigration continued. By the late nineteenth century livestock constituted some three-fourths of Ireland's agricultural exports, and the grazing system had become ubiquitous, ineradicable without severe economic dislocations even for western peasants and cottier-dairymen who desperately needed the small profits derived from selling calves and yearlings to the more affluent grass farmers. Moreover, despite their ambivalent attitude to home rule, the graziers' economic power translated into political influence which, united with that of their shopkeeper allies, effectively stemmed radical impulses within mainstream Catholic nationalism. As James Connolly admitted, "sheep and cows paid better than men and women, and hence despite the unpopularity of the grazier he stayed and waxed fat and prosperous, and the Irish men and women came to America. . . . As long as cattle raising pays better than raising Christian men and women, it will flourish in Ireland as elsewhere."[59]

By contrast, the great majority of Irish farmers, those with holdings valued under £15 and, especially, under £4, profited little from the increased capitalization of post-Famine agriculture. Despite an initial surge in tillage crop prices during the mid-1850s, after the Crimean War prices for wheat, oats, and barley—the smallholders' staple crops—steadily declined, with flax prices following suit by the end of the 1860s. Consequently, as one tenant reported, "all our farmers or men of capital . . . are turning their land to grass as there is nothing else paying," or instead investing in horse-drawn farm machinery to cut labor costs. However, such expedients were possible only for large tenants who could command or safely borrow sufficient capital, and most middling and small farmers either lacked personal access to such funds or put themselves deeply, often fatally, in debt to secure the requisite credit. Moreover, outside east Ulster most small- and medium-sized tenants still deserved a dubious reputation as "inefficient, stubborn, and lacking in vision": more prone to display meager earnings in conspicuous consumption or to hoard them in savings accounts or under mattresses than to invest them in the improvement of farms or farm methods. Thus, after the Famine as before, critics still lamented fields infested with weeds, livestock poorly bred and neglected, unsanitary conditions which rendered Irish dairy products inferior to European competitors, and so forth. As a result, even during relatively prosperous periods, middling and small farmers increased their productivity and incomes only marginally, and so remained heavily burdened by rents and fears of eviction. Peasants with holdings valued under £4 still faced the perennial choice— "Rent for the landlord or food for the child"—and often managed to avert bankruptcy only through supplementary but now-vanishing sources of income such as cottage manufacturing. Middling tenants also found rent levels onerous, and many must have heeded advice from emigrant relatives such as William Porter, who admonished his brother in County Down, "[I]t is foolishness in you to be working yourself out there to pay rent and all other demands," for "when you will have done . . . your family will have nothing." Such pressures only exacerbated and embittered tenants' normally harsh, incessant struggles with Irish soil and climate, for even during generally "good years" farmers' letters were replete with complaints of personal or localized disasters which threatened narrow profit margins and precarious livelihoods: "So you See," reported one farmer, "there is scarcely a year passing over that there is not a Mishap in something. . . ." No wonder, then, that even a relatively comfortable farmers' son, such as Maurice Wolfe of County Limerick, readily concluded that he "would be easier in [his] mind in [America] than to be 'pulling the Devil by the Tail' in Cratloe."[60]

To be sure, some periods—such as the mid-1850s, late 1860s, and early 1870s—were so favorable for Irish agriculture that practically all farmers experienced some gains in income and purchasing power. However, such prosperous interludes were anomalous and only served to enmesh tenants more deeply in webs of market and credit arrangements, raise false expectations of continued amelioration, and thereby make subsequent hard times more difficult to bear, both financially and psychologically. "They riz above themselves entirely, and that's why they are so pinched now," gloated one elderly tenant over his neighbors' straitened circumstances in the depressed early 1860s. "Nothing would do them but they should buy fine clothes for their wives and daughters, and now they find it hard to pay for them." Indeed, when crop failures, livestock diseases, and sharp price declines simultaneously occurred in 1859–64 and more severely in 1879–88, the ephemeral prosperity of preceding years quickly vanished, and the negative consequences of Irish farmers' dependence on an international price system became painfully evident. Each depression stimulated a wave of emigration partially composed of bankrupt or evicted farmers: thus, in the early 1860s, when constant rain transformed farmers' fields into "so many inland seas," many tenants lost "hope of doing well in Ireland" and fled abroad; similarly, in the early 1880s accumulating disasters inspired such despair that, as W. E. Forster, the Irish chief secretary, observed, "[t]he poor cottier tenants are beginning to see that their only hope is in emigration." The more fortunate, "spirited and enterprising" tenants left early: "finding their capital diminishing," they "sell out their interest in their holdings before it is too late"; however, many others tarried too long and either emigrated without surplus capital or found themselves dependent on relatives' remittances, private philanthropy, or public charity to finance escape overseas. Although such periods of distress also brought suffering and occasional emigration to graziers and strong farmers, their superior resources usually enabled them to weather such crises and emerge with their holdings and herds enlarged at their poorer neighbors' expense. Moreover, their dominant economic position generally allowed them to pass the greatest hardships on to their impoverished inferiors: for example, when Irish butter prices collapsed because of foreign competition in the late 1870s, Munster graziers dispossessed thousands of cottier-dairymen, consolidating their plots into large pastures for stock raising. Thus, both in good times and in bad, the gaps between rich and poor farmers steadily increased, and despite attrition through emigration—and despite the effects of the Land and Land Purchase acts—most farms remained too small and unproductive to sustain much more than a subsistence living. Even in the relatively prosperous years immediately prior to World War I, observers noted that in the Ulster highlands, the south midlands, and elsewhere, most farmers still led a spartan existence, dining largely on potatoes, porridge, bread, and overbrewed tea. Indeed, the sheer survival of many smallholders depended on American remittances to pay rents, land-purchase annuities, or shopkeepers' bills—for they were "loaded with debt, and if the shopkeeper refuse [further credit] there is nothing before them but the emigrant ship or the workhouse." No wonder many farmers continued to abandon a struggle made more intolerable by the bitter knowledge that peasant proprietorship alone brought little respite from grinding poverty: they sold their last crops, "disposed of . . . their holdings to Neighboring tenants who required large Acreage to sustain increased stock," and emigrated across the ocean.[61]

Decline and emigration among Ireland's small farmers were most dramatic in those parts of the island where the population still depended heavily on potato cultivation. Such districts included the mid-Ulster highlands, east Ulster's Antrim Glens and Mourne Mountains, and scattered areas in Leinster and east Munster, such as County Louth's Carlingford peninsula. However, potato-based economies remained most prevalent in the counties along the Atlantic seaboard, from west Cork, Kerry, and Clare north to Connaught and Donegal. During the Famine these districts suffered exceptionally high rates of mortality, evictions, and emigration, but, except for the depression of 1859–64, between 1856 and 1878 conditions in western Ireland seemed markedly improved, and travelers in west Kerry, Mayo, Donegal, and elsewhere noted their inhabitants' increased income and consumption of store-bought clothes, food, tobacco, tea, and other items once considered unattainable "luxuries"; in the late 1870s one visitor to Mayo concluded that "the general rise in the scale of comfort" had been "simply enormous." Demographic data seemed to reflect economic improvement. For example, in the 1870s the total Irish population fell 4.4 percent, but most western districts experienced substantially lower losses; County Mayo lost only a handful of inhabitants, and County Kerry's population actually increased by 2.3 percent. Moreover, according to official records, with few exceptions (e.g., Donegal, whose eastern baronies responded to Ulster's depressed linen industry) in the 1870s the western counties enjoyed emigration rates below the national average. Pre-Famine emigration patterns seemed to reemerge: for example, in County Londonderry emigration was once more confined largely to the more prosperous, lowland parishes, and departures from impoverished west Cork were proportionately lower than from the county's affluent eastern districts. As was noted earlier, some recent scholars question the accuracy of contemporary records and contend that emigration from Connaught and other western areas continued at high levels throughout the immediate post-Famine decades. However, their argument sharply contradicts contemporary observations, both official and unofficial; moreover, even if it is true, most unrecorded western emigrants apparently went to Great Britain, not North America or Australia: in part a reflection of their poverty, but perhaps also an indication that a disproportionate number of westerners still preferred not to preclude the hope of returning home permanently by making an irreversible move across the Atlantic.[62]

The West's economic improvement and comparative resistance to overseas emigration were due to several related circumstances. Merely by eradicating a large proportion of the region's poorest families, and thereby alleviating the hitherto-intolerable demographic pressure on the land, the Famine ameliorated the condition of its surviving inhabitants. In terms of mitigating pressures for subsequent emigration, the results of this thinning-out process were twofold. The reduced population allowed the inhabitants of remote, primitive coastal and mountain areas to resume traditional social patterns (e.g., rundale and its associated customs) which—given sufficient land—precluded heavy emigration. However, in the western counties *generally,* the Famine's attrition of laborers and subsistence farmers helped promote the region's conversion to commercial agriculture, with consequent—if temporary—rises in income and living standards which also dampened enthusiasm for further emigration. The commercialization of western agriculture was most pronounced in areas of relatively good soils, such as central Connaught and parts of west Munster, but it prevailed to some degree throughout the region. After all, the late tragedy had demonstrated clearly that western peasants could no longer rely on potato plots alone; in addition, rents still had to be paid, and cottage textile manufacturing no longer provided the requisite cash. Given high cattle prices, the unsuitability of local soils for wheat or barley, and the prominence of large grass farms in the area, it was almost inevitable that western farmers would become linked more closely to the island's expanding grazing economy, if only as suppliers of calves and yearlings to more-affluent store graziers, as was common practice in Connaught and Donegal. Likewise, in west Munster peasants profited from selling dairy products to the Cork butter market. To a large extent it was the proceeds from such sales, combined with relief from pre-Famine congestion, which temporarily blessed western smallholders with increased income and purchasing power.[63]

However, as one acute observer remarked, even in 1856–78 "it must be remembered that the [West's] improvement [was] only relative" to the extreme and near-universal destitution which had formerly prevailed. The western counties remained the most impoverished in Ireland: in 1861 nearly 80 percent of Connaught's farms contained fewer than fifteen acres and over a fifth were below five acres; most farmers still inhabited one- or two-room thatched cabins with little furniture, and still subsisted primarily on potatoes and corn- or oatmeal. Whenever potato crops failed because of blight or bad weather, as in 1859–64, famine again threatened and emigration soared. Even during ostensibly "good years" poverty and unemployment inspired a desire to emigrate; for example, in 1873 a native of County Galway remarked that many local Catholics "would *gladly* embrace any pecuniary assistance that would take them *anywhere* they could make a living." Moreover, what improvements *did* occur in 1856–78 ironically contained the seeds of the West's future destruction. The region's high rates of natural population growth, from three to five times those in Leinster, ensured that by the late 1870s population pressure on available resources was in many areas nearly as severe as before the Famine. In addition, the commercialization of western economies proved a very mixed blessing. Increased incomes often resulted in increased rents, which only necessitated further concentration on market production, greater vulnerability to price fluctuations and international competition, increased indebtedness to branch banks or gombeen-men, and further dependence on supplementary cash-earning strategies. Between 1856 and 1878 such strategies proliferated, a sure indication that for many western farmers high cattle and dairy prices alone were woefully insufficient to pay rents and shopkeepers' bills. Along the western coast farmers gathered tons of seaweed for the kelp market; in Connaught farmers' wives and daughters raised chickens and sold eggs to local dealers, while in Donegal they knitted stockings to exchange for shop goods. Most important was the seasonal migration of men and boys, especially from north Connaught and Donegal, to plant crops and gather harvests in Great Britain and eastern Ireland. At its height, in the mid-1860s, over 100,000 crossed the Irish Sea to work in British agriculture: their earnings averaged only £5–£6, but for western peasants seasonal migration "was a means of avoiding full proletarianization" and its logical concomitant, permanent emigration.[64]

Marginal at best, the western peasant's world, and his already-weakened resistance to emigration, collapsed in the 1880s when both the subsistence and the commercial props of his fragile society eroded beyond recovery. Thanks to bad weather and recurring blight, between 1879 and 1886 the harvests of potatoes—still preeminent in the western farmers' diet—failed nearly every season; for example, in 1879 per-acre yields were 60 percent below normal, producing near starvation in parts of Donegal, Connaught, and west Munster. Mortality rates rose, but deaths directly attributable to malnutrition were few: partly because Irish-American and British relief money flooded the island; and, more important, because the West now had a network of retail outlets which sold imported cornmeal. Nevertheless, shop purchases presumed that western peasants still had access to cash and credit, while in fact both were fast disappearing. Excessively cold, wet weather not only ruined potatoes but also engendered livestock diseases and destroyed cash crops and cattle fodder; in addition, the dearth of potatoes sharply reduced pig and poultry numbers, causing severe financial losses to smallholders. More important, crop failures coincided with steep price declines for Irish farm products: in 1879 butter fell 50 percent in value; grain crops declined 30 percent; and cattle prices fell 12 percent.

Prices recovered somewhat by 1884, but plummeted again in 1885–86; even livestock values never regained the buoyant levels of the mid-1870s. Furthermore, not only did western peasants' incomes from selling calves and dairy products decline but their sources of supplementary cash evaporated as well. The kelp market collapsed because of German discoveries of vast potassium and iodine deposits, and, more crucial, agricultural depression and widespread adoption of mechanical harvesters in Great Britain sharply reduced the sister island's demand for Irish farm laborers: in 1880 only 38,000 Irishmen migrated to the British harvests, in 1890 merely 23,000.[65]

This multifaceted crisis had dire consequences. Inadequate or imbalanced diets, plus a scarcity of dry turf as a result of incessant rain, produced outbreaks of typhus, pellagra, and other diseases. The precarious economic gains of prior decades quickly vanished, and visitors remarked that most western farmers were now "miserably poor." The philanthropist James H. Tuke noted a typical example in Connemara: "H.B., aged thirty-five; wife thirty; five children. . ·. . Rent £15 a year, jointly with another. Twelve years ago had several head of cattle and sheep; was then worth £200 or more. Had sold his last cow for £6 10s., and had now no milk to give his children, no meal whatever . . . children in rags." Another traveler, initially skeptical of alarming reports, soon conceded "there can be no falsehood in their gaunt, famished faces, no fabrication in their own rags and the nakedness of their children." Western smallholders faced an impossible dilemma: their need for food necessitated more shop purchases, but their lack of cash forced them to sell their remaining livestock at bargain prices; after those meager earnings were gone, the peasants went hopelessly into debt, but still lacked sufficient money to pay rents. In general, landlords were unsympathetic to pleas for abatements: by 1881 at least 100,000 tenants, largely in western counties, were in arrears, and between 1879 and 1881 nearly 7,000 families suffered eviction. In 1879 western distress, demands for lower rents, fears of impending wholesale clearances, and dreams of peasant proprietorship inspired the creation of the Irish National Land League and the subsequent Land War against recalcitrant landlords. However, pragmatic politicians and rural bourgeois interests dominant in eastern Ireland largely shaped Land League policies, and the 1881 Land Act bitterly disappointed western smallholders: statutory rent adjustments were insufficient, and tenants in arrears were excluded from the land courts until the 1882 Amending Act; by then it was too late for many tenants, as over 5,000 were evicted in that year alone. Conditions improved only slightly during the rest of the decade, and between 1883 and passage of the 1887 Land Act another 14,500 families lost their holdings.[66]

In these circumstances western farmers' resistance to emigration crumbled, and even local priests—normally opposed to emigration—began to promote it as their parishioners' only hope: "The holdings are so small, the land so sterile, that these people will be always steeped in poverty," despaired a pastor in west Galway; "I wish to God half the people of this barren territory would emigrate somewhere," he concluded, for "[p]enal servitude would be a paradise . . . compared to their present condition." Despair only deepened when the 1881–82 Land Acts failed to bring significant improvement. By 1884, travelers in west Munster, Connaught, and west Ulster were reporting "a positive rage for emigration," a "contagion" which "even spread to the Galway fishermen . . . as home-loving a set of people as are to be met with anywhere." Not all the emigrants were destitute: many were still "well off" by western standards, but realized, "[I]f we wait the workhouse is our certain doom." However, large numbers of western emigrants, perhaps a substantial majority, could not afford to pay their own passages: James H. Tuke discovered that in Connemara all the evicted tenants and at least one-tenth of those who still had farms were unable to finance emigration for even one family member, even if they sold everything they still possessed; a parish priest in Donegal reported that in the Rosses district most young men could not afford passage to the Scottish harvests, much less to America. Consequently, most emigrated with money sent from the New World. However, many western Irish, especially in remote districts where prior emigration was uncommon, still lacked relatives in North America and so were obliged to depend on public or private charity. Between 1881 and 1885 Poor Law boards of guardians paid passages for 7,500 pauper emigrants, including some workhouse inmates whose allegedly "indolent, vicious, crippled" condition (a few from the Cahirciveen workhouse were unwed mothers and prostitutes) outraged genteel Irish-American opinion. More fortunate were about 30,000 poor emigrants, primarily young women from Connaught and Donegal, sent overseas by the philanthropists Tuke and Vere Foster.[67]

In all, between 1881 and 1890 about 400,000 emigrants left western Ireland, over half the total exodus. Departures from Connaught were 88 percent higher than in the preceding decade, and both that province's and Munster's population fell 12 percent (compared with 7 percent declines in Ulster and Leinster). Moreover, unlike the earlier crises of 1845–55 and 1859–64, the 1879–88 depression made emigration a permanent, pervasive feature of western life: henceforth, the counties along the Atlantic coast contributed a disproportionately large share of Irish departures. By 1911 Connaught's population had declined nearly 26 percent, and in the years 1891–1910 emigrants from the areas designated as Congested Districts constituted over 40 percent of the total. Once fairly begun, western emigration became a self-generating process as the emigrants of the 1880s sent home "cheering reports" and remittances to finance subsequent departures; for example, in the early twentieth century the Clifden district in west Galway received £10,000 annually from North America. Significantly, however, over half such money was spent *in* Ireland: to pay rents, land purchase annuities, and shop bills—or, for the more fortunate, to enlarge holdings and livestock herds or improve farmhouses. Thus, American dollars could discourage as well as encourage emigration. Also, after 1891 the British government made concerted efforts to improve local agriculture, create viable farms, and promote native industries: all designed to increase western incomes and preclude departures. Nevertheless, despite certain indications of economic improvement, emigration continued at the highest rates in the island.[68]

The basic problem was that by the late nineteenth century western small-holders (and their peers in other regions) were too dependent on market prices for farm products and labor to be self-sufficient, and yet the prices they received were too low to sustain a decent livelihood or allow them to escape a still-heavy reliance on their annual potato harvests. In short, fatal deficiencies in both the subsistence and the commercial aspects of the West's economy spurred continued emigration. Sporadic potato crop failures—as in 1890, 1897, and 1904—still brought malnutrition, famine fever, evictions, bankruptcies, and emigration; as the dramatist John M. Synge noted, although western farmers depended totally on cash earnings to meet their obligations, "yet the failure of a few small plots of potatoes [brought] them literally to a state of starvation" and precipitated more departures. Seasonal migration to Great Britain, formerly the most important source of supplementary income, continued to decline. Earnings from calf rearing and dairying also remained low, and most western farms remained too small to allow an expansion of productivity. As a result, in districts such as Gweedore, Achill Island, Connemara, northwest Clare, and the Kerry and Cork peninsulas, annual expenditures regularly exceeded incomes, mandating constant indebtedness and abject dependence on remittances from abroad. As the poet and cooperatives advocate George Russell lamented, western peasants remained "men who were born in debt [and] who were rarely if ever free from it." Ironically, the British government's efforts to promote further commercialization of western economies merely precipitated or at least facilitated more emigration. Light railways destroyed local markets and further exposed western smallholders to the diseconomies of small-scale agriculture. Through its policy of purchasing and consolidating rundale plots and petty farms, the Congested Districts Board eroded clachan social bonds and subsidized departures. Revitalized fisheries generated increased incomes, but by introducing motorcraft the board made redundant about 60 percent of the men formerly employed on the old fishing boats. Even the board's lace schools, ostensibly started to keep western girls at home, only provided another "means of earning money enough to pay for their passage." Synge attributed these anomalies to the West's "diseased state": "normal remedies produce abnormal results," he believed. However, as the Irish chief secretary and architect of the Congested Districts Board, Arthur Balfour, himself admitted, in the prevailing economic context the flood of western emigrants to overseas labor markets was perfectly normal, while their former resistance had been the most "abnormal" evidence of western peasants' "irrationality" and backwardness. Thus, the crisis of the 1880s finally confirmed for western Ireland what Karl Marx had sardonically prophesied as the entire island's "true destiny, that of an English sheepwalk and cattle pasture."[69]

Although periods of special distress witnessed considerable departures of bankrupt or evicted farm families, the great majority of emigrants from the farming classes consisted of their noninheriting offspring, single men and women in their teens and early twenties. Before the Great Famine partible inheritance and early marriage helped preclude emigration outside the most heavily commercialized farming areas of eastern and southern Ireland. Although graziers and strong farmers had long practiced impartible inheritance and delayed marriage, even in the south midlands such customs still seemed novel and "almost unnatural" to disinherited young emigrants such as William Lalor. Resistance to change persisted even after the Famine, most strongly among smallholders in subsistence-oriented and culturally archaic regions such as the Ulster highlands and western counties where alternative income sources (cottage industry, seasonal migration, fishing) offset the cash value of land. Thus, from the mid-1850s through the early 1880s western peasants' propensity to "divide and subdivide whatever little property they have" continued, and landlords and estate agents in west Munster, Connaught, and west Ulster complained frequently, "The minute subdivision of land is . . . still carried out here to such an extent as to interfere materially with the full development of the agricultural resources of the country." For "improving" landlords the solution was obvious: "You ought [to] send your sons and daughters into the world and retain your farms unbroken," exclaimed one exasperated west Cork proprietor to his unheeding tenants, "instead of trying, as you do now, [to see] on how small a plot of earth you can contrive to exist."[70]

Nevertheless, despite such resistance, after the Famine impartible inheritance became increasingly commonplace, and by the early twentieth century it was almost universal. Since matrimony among the farming classes had always been predicated on access to land, one major consequence of the shift to impartible inheritance was a sharp decline in opportunities to marry, or at least to marry early. Thus, between 1845 and 1914 Ireland's annual marriage rate fell from 7 per 10,000 inhabitants to only 4, while the average age at marriage for males rose from twenty-five to thirty-three, for females from twenty-one to twenty-eight; by 1926 the average nuptial age in the new Irish Free State was thirty-five for men, twenty-nine for women. Celibacy rates soared: between 1851 and 1911 the proportion of females aged forty-five to fifty who had never married rose from 12 percent to 26 percent, and by 1936 over one-third of the Free State's male citizens aged forty to forty-nine remained unmarried. Correspondingly declining birthrates, coupled with emigration and increased longevity, transformed post-Famine Ireland into "an old man's country": between 1841 and 1901 the proportion of the population over age sixty increased from 6 percent to 11 percent. These social and demographic changes first occurred in eastern Ireland, where, by the early twentieth century, smallholders and laborers had the lowest marriage rates and highest marriage ages—a dramatic reversal of pre-Famine patterns. However, after the Famine the same changes began to take place in western Ireland, at first in more-commercialized districts such as north Kerry in the 1870s, but eventually throughout the entire region. For example, as late as 1871 only 10 percent of the adult women in Connaught and 15 percent of those in Munster were unmarried, compared with 25 percent and 50 percent in Ulster and Leinster, respectively. However, during the next quarter-century the farmers and peasants of western Ireland adopted impartible inheritance wholesale and began to assimilate to the marital practices and demographic configurations which prevailed in the East. Indeed, although the transition was slow and belated, it was eventually and drastically thorough: by the middle of the twentieth century average ages at marriage and celibacy rates were significantly *higher* in the western counties than elsewhere in the island.[71]

These shifts toward impartible inheritance and postponed (or denied) marriage had several related causes. The Great Famine itself had dramatically altered Irish social structure, obliterating by death or emigration nearly three million of the island's poorest and most "reckless" inhabitants, those formerly most likely to subdivide holdings and marry early. By contrast, a disproportionate number of the survivors of that crisis were strong and middling commercial farmers whose cautious, acquisitive instincts had long predisposed them to impartible inheritance, delayed marriage, and the dowry system. After the Famine the remaining rural lower classes either left Ireland or eventually conformed to the inheritance and marriage customs of the bourgeoisie. It may be, as contemporaries suggested, that the Famine years taught smallholders and peasants such terrible, traumatic lessons in the dangers of subdivision and early marriage that many resolved to eschew such "improvidence" thereafter. Believing themselves somehow responsible for the crisis, peasants may have become more repentant and attentive to priests who condemned their parishioners' former "recklessness" and preached the redeeming virtues of sexual restraint, chastity, and deferred gratification. However, Famine memories and clerical admonitions merely reinforced and justified pragmatic responses to economic exigencies. For example, in the immediate post-Famine decades many landlords redoubled their efforts to prevent subdivision and partible inheritance among their tenantry. However, more important than fear of eviction were farmers' own reactions to the increasing commercialization of post-Famine agriculture, especially the renewed emphasis on extensive grass farming. As times of relative prosperity alternated with periods of economic disaster, farmers and peasants experienced both positive and negative inducements to maximize farm size, maintain holdings intact, and exercise strict control over their children's inheritance and marriage prospects. Such necessities became blatant even in western Ireland with the crisis of 1879–88, as the increasing importance of land for grazing, the declining availability of supplementary earnings, and the growing dependence on shop purchases all combined to push western smallholders into conformity with their economic superiors. In short, as James Connolly noted, the spread of capitalist agriculture necessitated new family arrangements and, in the absence of alternative employment for noninheriting children, "the continual dispersion of Irish families" through emigration. As a result, " 'The home-nest could eventually maintain but one, and the hard road for the others' was a constant saying" in post-Famine Ireland.[72]

Without access to land or dowries, most farmers' children were destined to become emigrants. This was especially true for small and middling farmers' offspring, for their fathers could rarely afford for them adequate education or training for nonfarm careers: as one Irish-American advised his brother, an east Ulster smallholder, "force of circumstance will oblige [your sons] to leave [since] your place is not sufficient to give more than one a living." Consequently, many farmers' children eagerly awaited their inheriting brother's marriage, for his wife's dowry helped to finance their departures overseas. Social and psychological considerations only reinforced economic exigencies. In theory, most noninheriting sons could have remained living under their parents' roofs, but without land or independent sources of income their fathers and the general community treated them contemptuously as mere "boys," regardless of their age, forbade them to marry, and considered them incompetent to handle money or do other than drink with similarly frustrated bachelors. Even those sons chosen to inherit farms often endured demeaning periods of prolonged adolescence as fathers and widowed mothers became increasingly reluctant to relinquish control of holdings. The consequences were bitterness and strife, both between parents and children and among competing offspring, as well as increased alcoholism and mental illness when religious consolations proved inadequate. In these circumstances, it was hardly surprising that farmers' sons flocked overseas when they learned from emigrants' letters that in America "you can be your own master a gooddeal sooner" than in Ireland; for in the New World's more fluid economy, wrote another, "[w]hen Children gets 21 years of age . . . the[y] work for themselves and are what we call their own Boss."[73]

If farmers' noninheriting sons tried to break from parental control *without* emigrating, their efforts usually entailed social descent from the landholding to the laboring classes, a decline in status so severe that few dared chance the consequent criticism and disgrace. Equally disastrous was the danger of marriage for love rather than for strictly economic considerations. Earlier emigrants had long noted "the old Irish rule to marry for riches and work for love" which prevailed among strong farmers, and after the Famine one contemporary observed that even the proverbially "reckless" western peasant "takes unto himself a mate with as clear a head, as placid a heart and as steady a nerve as if he were buying a cow at Ballinasloe Fair." Indeed, by the early twentieth century farmers in western Ireland may have become more fanatically attached to the "match" and more disdainful of romance than their more affluent eastern peers; "beauty didn't boil the pot" was a familiar proverb in west Kerry, where farmers "cared for nothing but their own satisfaction even if that meant having the son troubled in his mind and tied to a good-for-nothing slattern for the rest of his days." Such arranged marriages often resulted in unhappy mésalliances which, although usually endured with patient resignation, sometimes culminated in desertions and emigration: thus, the "ne'er-do-well" George Griffin, "*fond of cards* and other games of chance," "bitterly disgusted" his long-suffering wife before disappearing across the ocean. However, those who dared defy the now-ubiquitous "match" and dowry systems risked poverty, parental displeasure, communal contempt, and loss of caste. These perils were not imaginary, as the emigrant Margaret M'Carthy knew when she rejoiced to her father in Cork, "The Lord had not it destined for [me] to get married to Some Loammun or another at home and after a few months he and I [might have been] an Incumberance upon you or perhaps in the poor house." Love-struck adolescents could escape such dangers only through "runaway matches" and emigration; as the emigrant Margaret Cleland wrote of herself and her new husband, "if we had not been in so big a hurry [to marry] we might a been in Ireland yet," waiting for land and their parents' grudging approval. Other farmers' children emigrated not in order to marry already-chosen sweethearts but to pick spouses in the freer social atmosphere of the New World. In post-Famine Ireland parents and priests closely regulated social contacts between unmarried men and women, vigorously denouncing unsupervised occasions for "company-keeping." No wonder emigrants such as Joseph Hewitt "greatly prefer[red] the American way of sparking (as it is called here)" which gave courting couples "the best chances to talk sentimentalism or soft nonsense, without danger of being interrupted."[74]

The rationalization of Irish family relationships particularly stimulated emigration among farmers' daughters. The status of women in rural Ireland had never been high: derogatory proverbs contrasted harshly with stylized love poetry, and the early-nineteenth-century traveler Edward Wakefield had noted that Irishwomen worked "more like slaves than labourers." Nevertheless, after the Famine their social status deteriorated as the decline in domestic manufacturing and the shift from tillage to pasture farming reduced the value of women's contributions to household economies. Moreover, as arranged marriages became near universal, women lost even the freedom to choose their own mates, while the dowry system transformed them from independent personalities into a species of closely guarded property. Before marriage farmers' daughters were totally subordinate to fathers and brothers; their chastity and reputation—that is, their marketability— were matters of constant scrutiny by relatives, neighbors, and priests. Their education inculcated docility and submission, for all most could hope for were dowries and arranged marriages, sometimes to complete strangers. About a fourth of those who remained in Ireland never married, and many of the rest wedded men considerably older than themselves: prior to the Famine only about 20 percent of all Irish wives were ten or more years younger than their husbands, but by the early twentieth century the comparable figure was 50 percent. Consequently, many marriages were loveless "May-December" matches, and young wives frequently became middle-aged widows who projected frustrated affections on sons and bitter jealousy on daughters and prospective daughters-in-law. Despite their dowries, married women merely exchanged their fathers' for their husbands' domination: the latter controlled the family income, and if they proved improvident, drunken, or brutish, communal mores dictated that wives patiently suffer the results of "God's will." Family work allotments were also discriminatory: among smallholders women were expected to help with strenuous outdoor work, but their menfolk disdained to assist with equally arduous chores, such as churning, traditionally stigmatized as "women's work." It was even common for wives and daughters to delay eating meals until the men had finished, which meant that women frequently got short rations although their heavy work regimen and childbearing "duties" demanded at least equivalent nutrition. As a result, in post-Famine Ireland life expectancy for men and women was roughly equal, despite the fact that women are biologically predisposed to live longer—and did so in contemporary England and North America.[75]

One index of Irishwomen's deteriorating status was a great increase in female emigration: between 1856 and 1921 about half of the Irish emigrants were women, and from Connaught and west Munster—where farm life was especially harsh and nonfarm employment practically nonexistent—females constituted a majority of the exodus. Large numbers of emigrating women were farmers' superfluous daughters: as James Connolly wrote, "Laws made by men shut them out of all hope of inheritance in their native land; their male relatives exploited their labour and returned them never a penny as reward, and finally, when at last their labour could not wring sufficient from the meagre soil to satisfy the exertions of all, these girls were incontinently packed across the ocean. . . ." Their primary reasons for emigration were economic: except for a favored few who could aspire to become national schoolteachers, the only employment opportunities for rural women were in domestic service; but that "was regarded as so low in status that no parent or girl would consider it" except under "dire necessity." However, "no disparagement attached to any kind of employment" in America, where, as one emigrant typically reported, "Good girls to do house work in Respectable families can readily get from one and a half to two Dollars per week and good Board and food." More broadly, female emigrants hoped that in America steady employment and decent wages would translate into personal independence: thus, the west Kerrywoman Peig Sayers eagerly awaited the remittances which would transport her to a land where she hoped to "be free from the power of slavery and . . . be independent of everyone." In fact, Irish-American women's work was often hard and poorly paid. However, throughout the late nineteenth century Irish emigrants expressed the belief that a "girl has a good time of it here" compared with her life in Ireland: "It would be considered a wonder to see a woman in the States Carry water or milk Cows," claimed one emigrant at mid-century; and in 1894 a Philadelphia laborer swore that even working-class women dressed so well that, in contrast to the situation in his native Belfast, "you can scarcely distinguish a [factory] girl going to her work from a prosperous merchants wife or daughter."[76]

In addition, although economic motives predominated, many a farmer's daughter emigrated in hope of finding a husband. In many parts of post-famine Ireland, females far outnumbered males, and many of the latter were less-than-attractive marriage prospects, in either an economic or a romantic sense. As one lonely woman in Roscommon complained, there were "[a]ll chrisenings and no marriage here"; "there is no fun in Ireland atall," lamented another, "the times are very lonesome . . . there are no one getting married." Even affluent farmers' daughters often despaired of bleak and celibate futures under their parents' roofs: "Dreary discontent crept over me," wrote Sissy O'Brien of County Limerick. "Must I for ever oversee the maids, regulate the wayfarers, visit the sick, make butter? Could this be called *living?* I asked myself if I should ever marry and if not, why . . . ?" Eventually, Sissy O'Brien made a loveless match with a dull, decent man, but girls without dowries—and those less submissive to parental pressures—frequently escaped overseas: "Anyplace in the world only here," wrote the desperate Julia McCullough, begging her uncle for passage money. A significant minority, especially from the western counties, emigrated specifically to scrimp and save their own "fortunes" in order to return home and attract respectable mates, "tempting the boys with their chains and their rings." However, the great majority found husbands in America and remained there. According to the *Cork Examiner,* "Every servant-maid thinks of the land of promise where . . . husbands are thought more procurable than in Ireland." Indeed, girls such as Mary Brown from County Wexford seem to have found overseas the self-importance and affection denied them in Ireland. Enraptured by New York, she bragged to a friend back home, "You would not think I had any beaux, but I have a good many . . . about half a dozen now. I have become quite a Yankee and [if] I was at home the boys would be all around me." In closing, she advised her friend to join her in "the country where thers love and liberty," an injunction which fairly summarized the frustrated dreams of women in post-Famine Ireland.[77]

Sadly, a small proportion of farmers' daughters and other Irishwomen made the mistake of seeking "love and liberty" *in* Ireland, without parental approval or benefit of clergy, and so were forced to emigrate to escape a damaged reputation, sanctimonious outrage, or the disgrace of unwed motherhood. In the early nineteenth century premarital sex had been common and had almost inevitably led to marriage. Although peasants in a few remote areas, such as Tory Island, still regarded illegitimate children as no hindrance to a respectable marriage, in post-Famine Ireland generally chastity signified a woman's marketability as well as her personal virtue, and so unchastity became an unpardonable sin against the family economy and rural social stability, as well as against an unforgiving bourgeois God. Even the suspicion of impropriety could destroy a girl's marriage prospects, and unwed mothers faced only the barracks brothel, the workhouse, or, at best, the hoped-for anonymity of America. Thus, in 1870 Annie Sproule, probably a victim of Victorian Ireland's double standard of morality, stole away from her Londonderry home with a "brokenheart": "unknown to her mother and all, [she] took all the money she could leaving not the price of a loaf in the house, and started by the . . . steamer for Philadelphia." In short, while the parental and clerical guardians of post-Famine Ireland's virtue ensured the island Europe's lowest illegitimacy rates, the system's sacrificial examples helped form what one scholar has called the tragic "underworld" of Irish emigration.[78]

The commercialization of post-Famine agriculture produced the greatest hardships and the highest emigration rates among rural laborers. As a result, both numerically and proportionately, the ranks of agricultural laborers steadily declined. For example, as measured by the attrition of one-acre plots, between 1845 and 1911 the number of cottier subtenants—ubiquitous before the Famine—declined by 60 percent. Likewise, between 1861 and 1911 the number of landless laborers, already eroded a third by the Famine, fell another 40 percent, from about 500,000 to 300,000. The numbers of farm servants also declined rapidly, for example, from 77,000 males to 62,500 in 1901–11 alone.[79]

Arguably, living standards for the remaining laborers improved to a degree. Their diminishing numbers created seasonal labor shortages which, coupled with inflation, caused weekly wages to triple between 1850 and 1912. As a result, laborers' clothing and diet improved somewhat: by 1900, male laborers generally wore shoes, and milk was no longer an unattainable luxury. However, in other crucial respects conditions remained unchanged or even worsened. In general, employment opportunities for rural workers shrank more rapidly than the labor supply, partly because "the Gentry are coming down and keeps so few Servants," as a Kilkenny milkmaid lamented, but more because of the contemporary shift from labor-intensive tillage farming to capital-intensive livestock raising. As a visiting American priest noted in 1863, "the immense tracts of land taken from cultivation for pasturage has deprived great numbers of employment, who are not needed for herding as they were for farming purposes." Consequently, laborers fled in droves from grazing districts such as north Leinster, east Connaught, and north Munster; between 1841 and 1891 the number of farm workers in County Cork alone fell 77 percent. Moreover, even tillage farmers curtailed their labor costs: prosperous landholders reacted to rising wages and labor shortages by adopting horse-drawn machinery, while small farmers turned almost exclusively to family assistance. In the mid-1850s Edward Donohoe reported from heavily commercialized south Leinster that "the farmers here now do no work but what they do with their servant boys and horses, even the t[h]rashing they nearly all have Machines for. . . ." By the end of the century, labor-saving devices were common throughout the island: even in western Mayo the scythe was replacing the sickle, and in County Armagh "the labour is nearly all done with horses now," as the farmer Thomas Kells boasted in the 1890s: "We have machines to mow, reap, thrash, and churn, so we can do with very little men."[80]

More broadly, post-Famine agricultural laborers were increasingly proletarianized, divorced from the land. Diminished needs for labor and desires to increase per-acre productivity persuaded farmers to curtail sharply the formerly common practice of paying workers in potato ground. Consequently, cottier subtenants became relatively rare, especially after supplementary income sources—such as dairying in Munster and cottage industry in Ulster—collapsed in the 1870s and 1880s. Equally important, after the Famine farmers usually refused to rent land in conacre, thus forcing laborers to depend on food purchased from shops at inflated prices which largely canceled contemporary wage gains. During periods of crop failure, when employment declined and food prices soared, laborers experienced near starvation, but even in ostensibly prosperous times most farm workers lived barely above subsistence level. In the early 1870s the farm laborers' union organizer Peter O'Leary described Munster's agricultural workers as "the worst-fed, the worst-clad and worst-housed probably in Europe," and other observers believed that those in north midlands counties such as Meath were even more destitute and hopeless. Despite increases, Irish laborers' wages remained pathetically below American and even British standards; their diet consisted almost entirely of cornmeal and potatoes; their children went barefoot, received little education, and had virtually no prospects for upward mobility. Their housing remained almost as wretched as before the Famine, confined largely to the one-room mud hovels which even smallholders had abandoned. Not until after 1882 did a succession of Labourers' Housing Acts begin to provide decent accommodations for a minority of rural workers, and most of these were not built until the eve of World War I.[81]

Most laborers emigrated to find work and decent wages: "Sure you [k]now that I have no money nor Cant Earn it for there is nothing dewing in this Country," wrote Tom Grant from County Kildare, begging for an assisted passage, as most farm workers were obliged to do. However, emigrant agricultural laborers—like farmers' disinherited children—sought more than mere employment. Although their material condition was marginally superior to what it had been before the Famine, Irish laborers were much more dissatisfied with their lot: "I don't like the work on the land," declared one laborer in 1894. "It is very laborious and does not lead to anything." Such alienation stemmed partly from an increased awareness of greater opportunities abroad: "their education is much better," testified a farm worker from Clonakilty in 1881, "and there is aspiration and ambition to be better off than when I was young, when people were entirely illiterate." However, at least equally important was the laborers' recognition that their status in rural Ireland was inexorably declining, as epitomized by the farmers' contemptuous refusal to rent them land. Relations between farmers and laborers had never been good, but prior to the Famine farm workers had been able to overawe their employers through the secret agrarian societies and by sheer force of numbers; moreover, before mid-century the large classes of cottiers and petty farmers with less than five acres (together constituting 40 percent of all tenants in 1845) had provided a social bridge between the landless and their employers. However, in the post-Famine period social divisions between landholders and laborers became increasingly sharp, just when the latter were becoming a comparatively powerless minority: for example, in 1841 County Limerick had contained 15,000 farmers and 54,000 laborers and farm servants, but by 1911 nearly 11,000 farmers clearly dominated the remaining 5,000 agricultural workers. In these altered circumstances, farmers could be exacting and scornful of their employees with relative impunity. The farmers "had a line drawn and a hedge about them" remembered one elderly laborer from Westmeath, and they "were so cocked up with vulgar pride, they never lost an opportunity of belittling boys and girls that were working faithfully for starvation wages." "[I]f a farmer in Ireland made 3 or 4 thousand dollars in a Year you couldnt walk the road with them," declared an emigrant from County Limerick. "You would have to go inside the fence or they would ride over you." Intermarriage between farm workers and even the poorest smallholders became extremely rare, and the contempt in which farmers held laborers permeated all rural society; for example, the east Cork emigrant Timothy Cashman bitterly recalled how the local schoolmasters and priests "confined [their] beatings to the laboring man's child," while "petting" the offspring of strong farmers and shopkeepers. Live-in servant girls probably endured the most relentless scorn, for in addition to an endless and arduous work regimen, the "farmers' wives . . . and their children . . . would always be reminding her of the gulf that lay between their respectability and hers. What wonder then that that girl would save and scrape until she could get to America." What wonder either that emigrant farm laborers such as J. F. Costello would declare vehemently, "[S]ooner than I would work for a farmer in Ireland, I would cut off my good right hand."[82]

Post-Famine laborers deeply resented such treatment from those they termed "mean devils [who] . . . give you spuds and milk and put you to the hardest work, and eat plenty of meat themselves and do the lightest." For example, their contemporary ballads urged laborers to "not let the farmer your wages cut down," and denounced employers who lay "snug in bed" while their servants slaved from before dawn to after dark. In the early 1870s British organizers affiliated discontented Munster farm workers to the National Agricultural Labourers' Union, and in the 1880s laborers from the same province struck for higher wages, destroyed mowing machines, and demanded that the farmers' self-serving slogan "The land for the people" be applied to their own needs. More than a few farm laborers strongly suspected that, in the words of one ballad, the nationalist agitation of the late nineteenth-century was "human humbug," and in 1885 a mob of farm workers even broke up a nationalist rally at Mitchelstown, County Cork, crying, "Cheers for landlordism, down with machines." However, the laborers' poverty, falling status, and declining numbers paralleled a cultural impoverishment and loss of self-confidence which precluded effective organization and left them unable to withstand the blandishments of their social superiors. Thus, nationalist leaders often marshaled the laborers' land hunger to frighten Parliament into making concessions to farmers' demands; however, the subsequent Land and Land Purchase acts did nothing for landless workers who found their grievances shelved and forgotten. For example, during the Land War farmers' spokesmen pacified aggrieved Munster laborers by belatedly incorporating demands for land redistribution in Land League speeches; however, redistribution remained an unfulfilled aspiration, and even the Labourers' Housing Acts of 1882–85 proved an initial mockery when the "patriotic" farmers who now controlled the locally elected Poor Law boards refused to tax themselves to carry out the laws' provisions. Indeed, some farmers even evicted laborers to avoid building them new cottages: "They'd let a labourer lie in the ditch," rather than see him housed decently, swore an outraged farm worker from Tipperary. Ironically, although only British pressure after 1907 forced Irish local government bodies to construct substantial amounts of rural workers' housing, laborers continued to furnish much of Irish nationalism's rank and file, vainly hoping that the next turn of the wheel of revolution would somehow resolve their own grievances. However, in such paradoxical circumstances, emigration was the farm workers' best chance, and most of them knew and seized it: as a laborer's ballad admitted, "T'would be better for us . . . to be tramping the highways, . . . Than to be miserable slaves without strength or hope." In the end, all the laborers' alternatives to emigration proved abortive: even the National Agricultural Labourers' Union, originally designed to improve rural workers' condition at home, concluded its brief career by advocating wholesale departures as the only solution to unemployment, poverty, and despair.[83]

Given these changes in post-Famine Ireland's economy and social structure, and given the consequent dearth of available land and employment, the philanthropist Vere Foster was correct in observing that from a purely economic standpoint it was "as natural and desirable for young people to emigrate as for young bees to swarm." Equally important, the modernization of Irish society not only mandated emigration to sustain livelihoods but also encouraged departures more subtly by eroding the customary social ties and traditional perspectives which had formerly either constrained the impulse to go abroad or obliged that such moves be interpreted tragically. Consequently, a large proportion of those leaving Ireland in 1856–1921 were no longer self-perceived exiles but eager, ambitious emigrants seeking material and personal enhancement in the New World. As always, such attitudes seemed especially prevalent among Ulster Protestants such as James Harold of Belfast, who carried overseas his society's more explicit injunction "above all [to] strive and make money . . . for the glorious privilege of being Independent." However, growing numbers of Irish Catholics expressed similarly individualistic and hedonistic goals; moreover, such avowals were not confined to middle-class or urbanized Catholics but became common among the poorest sectors of rural society as well. Reflecting such positive attitudes, contemporary ballads often described emigration as opportunity, and the Cork clergyman Canon Patrick Sheehan lamented that many embarking Catholics "no longer" displayed "sad weeping and melancholy farewell, but buoyancy and cheerfulness, and hope," while "the crowds on shore look with envy at the more fortunate friends who are escaping." In short, post-Famine emigration became more than a socioeconomic imperative: in the words of the French visitor L. Paul-Dubois, it became "fatally fashionable," an eagerly anticipated alternative to life in an Ireland where "[m]any people live in the hopes of seeing or in the regret of never having seen that land of promise, America."[84]

Rural Ireland's increasing commercialization was itself sufficient to produce attitudinal changes conducive to emigration. In 1877 A. M. Sullivan contrasted the old with the "New Ireland" and rejoiced that in the post-Famine countryside "Providence, forethought, economy are studied and valued as they never were before. There is more method, strictness, and punctuality in business transactions. There is a graver sense of responsibility on all hands," and "[f]or the first time the future seems to be earnestly thought of. . . ." By 1919 another observer, the Ulsterman James Hannay, believed the transition complete: in 1850, Hannay wrote, the average Irish rural dweller had been a peasant, but "[t]o-day he is a capitalist." Although Hannay's assertion ignored the weight of tradition on the Irish countryside, still considerable even in 1919, the contrast with 1850 remained valid. Economically, socially, and culturally, post-Famine Ireland was dominated by a rural bourgeoisie whose comparatively instrumental attitudes toward land, work, and human relationships permeated society and altered traditional outlooks in ways which promoted emigration—just as their specifically profit-motivated activities mandated departures by the landless and unemployed.[85]

While static, subsistence-oriented economies had demanded a high degree of cooperation and inculcated a conservative outlook, post-Famine Ireland's commercialization and economic growth—halting and uneven though it was—engendered novel expectations of material progress and aspirations for *individual* improvement. Even relatively minor ameliorations, as in housing, could have profound psychological consequences, "for if a man's house be neat, clean, and comfortable, it consciously tends to elevate his ideas, raise his standards of personal comfort, and increase his *self*-respect." As a result, observed the American consul at Londonderry, by 1883 those "means of domestic and personal comfort" which "ranked in former times as objects of irrational desire" were "now . . . set down as among the reasonable necessities of life"; even in the Ulster highlands,

414   EMIGRANTS AND EXILES

he wrote, "[a] diet of potatoes, and a cabin of one room and a floor of clay . . . have ceased to be satisfactory." Consequently, when thwarted by chronically inadequate resources or, more dramatically, by catastrophic price or crop failures, most Irishmen no longer responded passively and fatalistically but instead either projected aspirations abroad or else mobilized politically to demand material betterment at home. "My father could pay the rent . . . because he was content to live so he could pay it," testified a Tipperary farmer during the Land War of 1879–82: "He sat on a boss of straw, and ate out of a bowl. He lived in a way in which I don't intend to live, and so he could pay the rent. Now, I must have, and I mean to have, out of the land, before I pay the rent, the means of living as I wish to live; and if I can't have it, I'll sell out and go away; but I'll be ——— if I don't fight before I do that same." Such fierce tenacity was not uncommon during the 1880s, but emigration was at least an equally logical and common response to frustrated ambitions. " 'You can't rise in Ireland,' that is the dominant feeling," reported L. Paul-Dubois: "In order to succeed you must begin by leaving the country." Thus, although lacking the Tipperaryman's bravado, more typically utilitarian was the reaction of John Flanagan, a farmer in County Louth: "Looking at the [discouraging] state of affairs at home" in 1880, he wondered, "[W]hat *business* have I remaining here? Some years ago there was pleasure and comfort at home but now there is none"; however, he concluded, "if I go away I may be able to make a living for myself and might sometime become independent."[86]

Similarly, the "commercial spirit" pervading post-Famine Ireland encouraged emigration by making social relationships more instrumental and overtly competitive. In an "Irish world . . . peopled by communities dissevered the one from the other as the pieces in a kaleidoscope," an almost amoral familism characterized a fragmented society in which shopkeepers and farmers jealously guarded precarious gains from both peers and inferiors. "Such social well-being as there is here is only grudgingly shared," wrote Padraic Colum in the early twentieth century: "Those who have acquired money here would never think of benefiting anyone except an immediate relation. . . ." The holdings of graziers and strong farmers who could afford to dispense with neighborly assistance became bastions of propriety, while in areas where excess population and limited resources flouted newly engendered ambitions, the necessity for continued economic cooperation among smallholders coexisted uneasily with a vicious, albeit usually covert, competitiveness which found poisonous expression in bitter envy, incessant gossip, and obsessive attention to the most minute indices of comparative status or respectability. In such a context, even the slightest diminutions of material well-being could be intolerable compulsions to emigration; after all, as one Ulsterwoman declared, "it is not the easiest thing in the world to stand and see your neighbors triumphing over you."[87]

Moreover, the increasing social differentiation between farmers and disinherited children, and between rural employers and their proletarianized laborers, not only necessitated emigration but often so estranged the dispossessed that they departed eagerly to escape institutionalized inferiority. When bleak prospects of inheriting land effectively mocked patriarchial authority's traditional rationale, many farmers' sons concluded with the emigrant Myles McDermott "that 'tis far more creditable for a man to fight his way to independence in a foreign land than to stay at home dependent on a Father." Indeed, emigration became a sort of *rite de passage* for repressed Irish youths whose economic ambitions were inseparable from desires for personal liberty: "Be a *man* and go Where you can get a living," one emigrant advised a brother facing perpetual adolescence under a tyrannical father back home in Kinsale; "it is to Bad to have you killing your-Self and geting no thanks [or wages] for it." Often manners of departure revealed both the personal tensions and the cash nexus which underlay post-Famine family relationships, as it was not uncommon "for a farmer's son to drive off some of his father's stock to a neighbouring town . . . , sell the stock and clear off to America." Farmers' daughters emigrated even more willingly than their brothers, and their dreams of "love . . . liberty" and economic opportunities abroad often merged with deep resentment against parents ("many tis the battle we used to have," recalled one bitter emigrant) and communities which offered little except servitude and celibacy. "There was nothing in Ireland," declared Bridget Fitzgerald. "Thanks be to God I got out of it." Landless laborers were especially eager emigrants, just as they were the most rootless and exploited group in the countryside: their "incentive was great," reported one elderly informant, "taking into account the little home-life had to offer them." In short, while members of more-favored groups (including many comfortable farmers' sons) often left Ireland to *preserve* status, and thus felt some qualms over abandoning relatively pleasant situations, the victims of commercialization—especially farmers' daughters and laborers—knew they had little or nothing to lose. Usually, their aspirations were minimal, soberly realistic, and so less prone to disappointment overseas. Emigrants such as Julia Lough, whose "highest ambition" was to become a seamstress, and Michael Kinney, who willingly exchanged the unpaid drudgery of his parents' farm for a Pittsburgh steel mill, conceptualized goals in the most elemental terms: as freedom to marry for love or to work for wages at jobs of their own choosing; at most, as the possibility of homeownership. Their consciousness that post-Famine society precluded fulfillment of even such limited aspirations enabled these young men and women to leave Ireland with comparatively few regrets.[88]

Of course, the New World had always offered to Ireland's poor a variety of economic opportunities unavailable at home. However, more was involved here than comparative assessments of Irish and American economic conditions, for in several respects New World opportunities for the poor and unskilled were more limited in the late nineteenth and early twentieth centuries than they had been fifty or one hundred years earlier, when emi-

gration had been relatively exceptional and more widely perceived in negative terms. Ironically, prior to the Famine the poorest sectors of rural
Catholic—and Protestant—societies had been most resistant to emigration,
in large part because a rich, vibrant, and intensely localized traditional
culture had complemented intricate networks of affective social relationships and so had helped mitigate material deprivation and insulate Irish
countrymen from the New World's attractions. Indeed, in southeast Cork
during the 1870s and 1880s, what Timothy Cashman called "the simple
life of the country people" still helped offset the poverty, exploitation, and
"fearful sway of the parish priest" which his parents and fellow Irish-
speaking laborers otherwise endured "without a murmer." "One of the
pleasantest features of country life in those days," he wrote, was "the
gathering of neighbors to one another's fireside during the long winter's
evenings" for singing and "story-telling of Ireland's past" and of "the
legends of Fionn McCumhal's warriors." Likewise, on "Sunday afternoons
in summer time the boys and girls congregated at a crossroads . . . and
danced away the time until sundown. A piper came . . . to supply the
music" and "all kinds of sports were indulged. . . ." Like his neighbors,
Cashman "knew the haunts of the Banshee, the fairies and all . . . the
ghosts of the countryside." In short, he concluded, he "was deeply interested in the locality": bound to its interwoven human, historical, and
cultural associations in an intimate, emotional relationship which Irish-
speakers called *dúchas*—parochial patriotism.[89]

However, even Cashman's deep attachment to place could not preclude
his departure for America, and both the sheer magnitude and the greater
popular acceptance of post-Famine emigration indicated that the traditional cultural as well as social fabric of rural Catholic Ireland was rapidly
unraveling. Indeed, by the 1870s Cashman's and his neighbors' attachment
to old customs and to the Irish language was exceptional in eastern and
midlands counties, where the traditional vernacular and its associated folkways were generally disused and discredited; by 1900 both were in retreat
even in their last strongholds on the western coast. For example, between
1851 and 1901 the proportion of Irish-speakers in the island's population
fell from 23 percent to 14 percent, and throughout the period contemporaries not only noted the widespread attrition of traditional music and
dancing, storytelling and fairy belief, wakes and keening, but also remarked
a growing popular disinterest in, even aversion to, such customs. By the
early twentieth century L. Paul-Dubois characterized rural Ireland as suffering from "a mental famine" as well as a dearth of secular opportunities,
and Sir Horace Plunkett lamented that younger generations "without culture or knowledge of literature or of music have succeeded a former generation who were passionately interested in these things." The consequent
encouragements to emigration were profound, Plunkett concluded, for
"[t]he national customs, culture, and recreations which made the country a
pleasant place to live have almost disappeared, and with them one of the
strongest ties which bind people to the country of their birth."[90]

The Great Famine itself had been a major cause of cultural change, loosening the ties which bound rural dwellers to Ireland. After the crisis the people were reportedly "changed" and "brokenhearted": they no longer "look upon Erin as they once did," observed one newspaper, but "view it now as a pest-spot, as a widowed mother would gaze upon the turf that covers the ashes of a child." It may be that the catastrophe chastened rural dwellers and discredited archaic customs by corroborating long-standing clerical warnings that "rustic festivities" and pre-Christian, "predictive celebrations" either provoked God's wrath or, at least, were useless in stemming blight, plague, and mass starvation. More certain is that the Famine transformed much of Ireland into a social and cultural desert by thinning the ranks of traditionalist peasants, Irish-speakers, and elderly custodians of old customs and beliefs. The result was a "great silence": a generational and cultural gap that severed many young Irishmen from traditional, communal associations and gave them a dubious freedom to seek salvation overseas. By 1851 only 300,000 monoglot Irish-speakers remained on the island, and four years later the folk-musicologist George Petrie lamented that " 'The land of song' was no longer tuneful": instead, an "awful, unwonted silence . . . almost everywhere prevailed," and "if a human sound met the traveller's ear, it was only that of the feeble and despairing wail for the dead." Famine mortality, evictions, and emigration made much of rural Ireland "very lonely" for those who remained. For example, when John Solon's parents left Mayo "there was a good deal of lamentation," for his family "was the life of the neighborhood, the boys nearly all being musicians. It was the head center for neighborhood festivities, and now that the head was going never to be seen again they could appreciate their great loss." Large districts of eastern and central Ireland never recovered either demographic or cultural vitality: four decades after the holocaust an old man in east Leinster sadly remembered "when you'd see forty boys and girls . . . on a Sunday evening, playing ball and diverting themselves; but now all this country is gone lonesome and bewildered, and there's no man knows what ails it."[91]

This decline of traditional customs coincided with an increasing emulation of Anglo-American social norms and cultural values. For fifty years, wrote one observer in 1908, "Anglicisation has reigned supreme," and English middle-class standards of dress and speech, popular literature and music, sports and pastimes, flourished in a post-Famine Ireland which "seemed little more than a province in the empire of Victorian taste." As traditional customs, beliefs, and values reflecting precapitalistic life-styles no longer appeared functional, Irishmen looked abroad for cultural standards more compatible with new realities. "Every incentive comes from abroad," lamented the journalist D. P. Moran, and "the Irish nation so deeply despises itself that it has ceased to develop by force of its own vitality." One major index of this process was a growing popular alienation from the Irish language, despite the Gaelic League's efforts to arrest its decline. Indeed, the bitter statements of former Irish-speakers themselves revealed the material bases for their communities' linguistic apostasy. "Irish will get you nothing and nowhere," declared a countryman from north Louth, especially when economic contacts with English-speakers (as purchasers of local products, as employers of seasonal migrants, even as tourists) were vital necessities. "Only for England we couldn't live," he concluded, while by contrast—as one old man in western Ireland asked rhetorically—"Who has Irish but the wretches of the world?"[92]

Similarly, many Irishmen grew "so accustomed to thinking that nothing good can come out of Ireland" that they preferred to purchase imported over native products, even when the latter were cheaper and qualitatively superior. At the same time, English music-hall songs displaced traditional ballads in popularity, despite one critic's lament that "there is all the difference in the world between the new tunes and the old"—"as much difference . . . as between giggling and natural laughter, as between maudlin sentimentalism and the passion of despair." Indeed, many contemporaries decried the superficiality, if not the "moral depravity," of the new ersatz culture, but the more thoughtful foresaw a consequent erosion of social bonds and a loss of national identity which would lead inevitably to more emigration. "Has Ireland adopted the better features of the Anglo-Saxon character, those which are most worthy of respect?" asked L. Paul-Dubois. "No," he answered, "but she has taken from it precisely what is lowest and most vile": the crass materialism and utilitarianism of an avaricious, untutored bourgeoisie—those values most corrosive of Irish countrymen's traditional attachments to place and kin. Thus, he concluded, "emigration is not solely due to the vices of the land system, not even to the need of industries in Ireland; it is due also to the contagion of Anglicisation. . . ."[93]

Anglicizing influences spread through many specific channels: increased economic transactions, improved communication networks, the proliferation of cheap newspapers filled with foreign news and advertisements—all helped expose formerly sheltered districts to a greater awareness of a seemingly more prosperous and exciting outside world. Many Irishmen who lamented the countryside's cultural deracination and demographic decline particularly blamed the National School system for producing generations of half-educated students who knew little and cared less about their native land or its vanishing linguistic and cultural heritage. According to critics as diverse as Horace Plunkett and Patrick Pearse, Irish education was an intellectual and cultural "murder machine" which "dulled the intelligence of the people, impaired their interest in their own surroundings, [and] stimulated emigration by teaching them to look on other countries as more agreeable places to live in." Certainly, Irish primary schools facilitated emigration by raising popular levels of literacy and familiarity with foreign lands—"study American history and American geography," enjoined one schoolmaster, "for 'that's where the most of ye will be going' "—but in fact they only corroborated more-fundamental processes which made emigration seem attractive as well as imperative.[94]

Anglicization was merely a logical concomitant of contemporary economic and social changes, a reflection of the fact that post-Famine Ireland's commercialization and consequent *embourgeoisement* took place in a colonial context. Just as rural Ireland became increasingly dependent on local urban, British, and American markets for goods and labor, so also did it become more emulative of life-styles prevailing in the urban sources of wealth—in Irish country towns, in Belfast and Dublin, and ultimately in London and, to a lesser degree, in American cities. Ironically, noted one Irish critic, "[w]hile we have shouted" about mere *political* freedom, "our economic centre of gravity has steadily shifted to England, shifting our national centre of gravity along with it."[95]

Thus, while middle-class Catholics often decried Anglicization and denounced English imperialism, the Catholic bourgeoisie itself bore major direct responsibility for the Anglicization of the countryside. "From one end of Ireland to the other," reported L. Paul-Dubois, "one sees, in towns and villages alike, a class of people who, while they remain Nationalist politically and preach fervently against English tyranny, have no other ambition than to become *West Britons":* slavish imitators and eager disseminators of Victorian fashions and notions of respectability. While such emulation stemmed naturally from increased contacts with their more affluent English counterparts, the Catholic bourgeoisie's newly adopted lifestyles also served to reinforce and sharpen the desired social distance from their economic inferiors. For example, when strong farmers abandoned wakes and harvest festivals for exclusive tea parties and piano recitals, they were not only mirroring middle-class English society but also intentionally terminating customs which had once united rural communities across class lines. However, while members of the Catholic bourgeoisie certainly "had a line drawn and hedge round them," they made strenuous efforts to propagate their tastes and values among the lower classes. In part, their motives were positive and benevolent, based on the desire to "uplift" the masses both for their own good and in order to better mobilize them for the attainment of bourgeois-defined political and religious goals. However, in part their aims were negative and at least implicitly repressive, for the existence of precapitalist outlooks threatened vital bourgeois interests at several points. On the most intimate level, for example, peasant attitudes toward sex and marriage—as expressed in Gaelic folkways, songs, stories, and aphorisms—were not only too frank and earthy for newly refined sensibilities but, when brought into strong farmers' homes by servants and laborers, threatened to subvert the repressive chastity which parents strove to impose on frustrated and potentially rebellious adolescents. More overt was the problem of social control over laborers, for cultural dissonance exacerbated socioeconomic conflicts and reinforced the lower classes' resistance to those they regarded as "shoneens" (Anglicized snobs) as well as harsh employers. In short, the Irish bourgeoisie had direct interests in remolding rural culture in its own synthetic image. In large measure its influence was naturally contagious, for despite popular resentment the middle classes constituted Catholic Ireland's new "aristocracy" and, as such, provided obviously successful models for emulation in an increasingly materialistic society. However, cultural hegemony was far from automatic, and the Irish bourgeoisie used economic sanctions as well as social prestige to induce conformity. For example, strong farmers such as Sissy O'Brien's parents in County Limerick forbade their servants to speak Irish in the house and prohibited their attending wakes or other peasant festivals where "drinking and noise and the strange old games . . . were usually part of the ceremony"; as a result of such pressures, local wakes soon became so "gloomy and religious" that, as one servant obediently reported, "the misthress herself could attend and take no harm." Irish schools only corroborated such parents' goals by enlisting their children in the cultural crusade: "The nuns say we must never miss a chance of curing people of pagan superstition," declared Sissy O'Brien, never realizing that her youthful essays in cultural imperialism only helped rivet her own shackles to an oppressive cult of respectability.[96]

As O'Brien's statement suggests, although Catholic clergymen often denounced Anglicization and lamented post-Famine emigration, the church itself helped erode the cultural cement which bound rural dwellers to their homeland. Religious strictures reinforced and sacralized middle-class lifestyles as the church—itself staffed largely by a pious bourgeoisie's superfluous sons and daughters—successfully promulgated a "devotional revolution" among a decimated and demoralized peasantry. Under the initial leadership of Archbishop, later Cardinal, Paul Cullen, the post-Famine church professionalized the clergy (e.g., by mandating the Roman collar and surplice), enforced tighter hierarchical discipline, and launched a vigorous campaign to conform the faithful to Roman prescriptions of belief and practice. Hundreds of newly constructed cathedrals, parish churches, convents, and other costly edifices contrasted so starkly with the poverty of their surroundings that they compelled admiration from overawed peasants, many of whom—as those in Enniskillen—had never before "witnessed benediction of the Blessed Sacrament [or] . . . seen incense rise from a thurible," but who now "streamed out of their huts in such numbers that the Protestants marvelled." The influence of parish priests over their flocks correspondingly increased, in part because formerly competing sources of wisdom and authority either vanished (e.g., Gaelic poets and storytellers) or lost popular confidence (e.g., landlords and Anglican parsons) in an increasingly nationalistic and sectarian age. For example, prior to the famine local priests and hedge-schoolmasters had often clashed over political or cultural issues, but in the late nineteenth century the church gained effective control over Catholic education, and, as managers of the National Schools, priests now enjoyed virtually unlimited authority over teachers and over the moral content of education. Most crucial, however, was that after the Famine growing numbers of clergy could more easily dominate a declining Catholic population: in 1840 the ratio of priests to parishioners had been a disheartening 1 to 3,000, but by 1900 the comparable proportion was 1 to 900, and the ratio of nuns to lay Catholics had risen to 1 to 400.[97]

In such favorable circumstances, a dynamic church played a major role in the formation of an eminently Victorian Irish Catholic culture. Trained in rigidly conservative seminaries, most Irish priests reflected both their church's concerns for order, authority, and spiritual conformity and their middle-class parents' compatible obsessions with social stability and their children's chastity. Often "distorting humanity in the twisted mirror of a prurient puritanism," as one critic charged, they condemned traditional wakes, fairy belief, sexually integrated education, crossroads dancing, and all other practices which threatened either clerical or bourgeois hegemony. Irish Protestants and foreign travelers were often appalled at the consequences: it was "a strange phenomenon," "a depressing sight," they reported, "to witness lads and lasses. . . walking on opposite sides of the road and incurring the ban of the priest if they talk to one another." This "iron morality" helped make the post-Famine Irish the world's most faithfully practicing and sexually controlled Catholics, but in the process it crushed many old customs which had given color and vitality to peasant life; as a Munster farmer wistfully explained, there were "fairies in the old time, but it is long since the priests got the upper hand of them, and there are no fairies in the world today." However, it seemed that Ireland's youth was literally vanishing along with the fairy hosts, for "[n]o man can get into the confidence of the emigrating classes," declared Sir Horace Plunkett, "without being told by them that the exodus is largely due to a feeling that the clergy are . . . taking innocent joy from the social side of life."[98]

Of course, Catholic clerics vehemently denied charges that their activities were destroying the social life of a "priest-ridden" people. Indeed, it is arguable whether clerical influence and pressures for Anglicization were any greater or more oppressive in post-Famine Catholic than in Protestant societies. For example, in 1908 the ratios of Anglican parsons and Presbyterian ministers to their flocks were 1 to 363 and 1 to 554, respectively, while the contemporary ratio of priests to lay Catholics was only 1 to 891. In addition, a fervent and frequent revivalism characterized both major Protestant denominations, exhorting adherents to conform to middle-class standards of thrift, industry, sobriety, and sexual continence. Trinity College–trained Anglican parsons reputedly were at least as puritanical as their counterparts from Maynooth, and Presbyterian clergymen enjoined a rigid Sabbatarianism and condemned dancing, cardplaying, and "other neutral pleasures" as "enticements to mortal sin." Thus, religion sanctified bourgeois values on both sides of Ireland's sectarian divide, and one critic suggested that young Ulster Presbyterians were at least as eager to escape the resultant stifling atmosphere as were their Catholic counterparts.[99]

More to the point, however, is that Irish clergymen and the middle classes generally (both Catholic and Protestant) aimed not to devitalize rural society but rather to restructure and mobilize it in pursuit of various socioeconomic, political, and religious goals. To do so, they strove to substitute purportedly "rational" and cosmopolitan belief systems and forms of social action for older, parochial patterns deemed inadequate to such purposes. The result was a complex of specialized, supralocal organizations and activities which both structured local life and linked each parish to ostensibly "larger" concerns centered on Dublin, Belfast, Westminster, Rome, or even beyond. For example, the post-Famine Catholic church not only expanded its physical plant and the numbers of its clergy but also encouraged the faithful to engage in a wide variety of spiritual exercises and church-centered associations: local priests and visiting missionaries stimulated popular adherence to devotions such as the Way of the Cross and the veneration of the Sacred Heart; parish altar societies, sodalities, confraternities, and temperance associations abounded; and national organizations such as the Pioneer Total Abstinence Association (1901–present) and urban-based periodicals such as the *Messenger of the Sacred Heart* and the *Catholic Bulletin* diffused a common worldview and united laymen with clerics in moral crusades to reform individuals, purify Ireland, and convert the heathen. Likewise, Irish political life achieved an unprecedented degree of organizational sophistication and permanence. For example, James Stephens's conspiratorial Irish Republican Brotherhood was preeminently modern in its bureaucratic complexity, centralization, and remarkable persistence, bearing little resemblance to the ephemeral secret agrarian societies of the early nineteenth century. Far more important in molding an organized body politic were new, mass-based, legal or quasi-legal associations such as the Irish Land and National leagues which mobilized nationwide Catholic support against landlordism and for Irish self-government. Similarly, their loyalist counterparts such as the Orange Order and the Ulster Unionist Council were equally effective in marshaling Irish Protestants in militant opposition to Catholic goals. More-specialized political and semipolitical societies also flourished: for example, the Gaelic Athletic Association organized Catholic sports along nationalist lines; the Gaelic League strove to reanimate the island's traditional language; and Sinn Féin promoted Irish economic and political self-sufficiency.[100]

Most of these associations, religious and secular, had large or even predominantly rural memberships, and often they pursued goals which seemingly ran counter to commercializing and Anglicizing trends. However, the organizations themselves, their structures and methods, were nontraditional. For example, however large their rural base or nostalgic their programs and rhetoric, all these associations were urban oriented, with leadership cadres recruited disproportionately from among middle-class town dwellers (merchants, professionals, clerks, artisans) as well as from among affluent farmers with close urban ties. Also, most of these organizations published their own newspapers, thereby providing an increasingly literate public with mental nourishment which, however nationalistic in tone, was largely emulative of British literary tastes. Likewise, mass-produced collections of patriotic songs, poems, and *Speeches from the Dock*—plus popular histories, devotional literature, and sentimental fiction such as Charles Kickham's interminable *Knocknagow*—filled the void left by the vanishing Gaelic poets and ballad singers with properly Victorian, if often xenophobic, sentiments. In short, whether in competition or cooperation, together these associations permeated the countryside, bridged regional and social (but not sectarian) divisions, and complemented contemporary economic processes by reordering social life and homogenizing popular culture.[101]

Ironically, then, while many of these organizations denounced emigration, at least indirectly they may have encouraged the movement overseas. Supralocal societies not only helped orient Irish countrymen toward the outside world but through their ties to affiliated organizations in North America associations such as the Orange Order and its Catholic counterpart, the Ancient Order of Hibernians (Board of Erin), facilitated their members' departures and mitigated fears of loneliness in unfamiliar surroundings. Moreover, subtly or overtly, such organizations helped inspire material ambitions unattainable at home. For example, the church's grand new buildings and solemnly impressive ceremonies indirectly aroused parishioners' acquisitive and competitive instincts when the "Sunday suit" and "-dress" became social necessities in communities which perceived piety and respectability as inseparable. Likewise, to a degree all Irish political organizations promised that material gains would accrue from electoral or martial success, yet not only did these movements fail to deliver anticipated prosperity but their middle-class leaders in fact had no programs adequate to solve the economic problems of those who composed the bulk of the exodus. Most important, while these associations could mobilize Irishmen on *national* levels, given their cosmopolitan, instrumental, and at least theoretically voluntary nature they could not entirely substitute for the rich, intricate fabric of affective relationships and traditional customs which had once bound Irish peasants to kinsmen and neighborhoods. In short, it seemed that the "New Ireland" was merely "a bad copy of another social order," still lacking "the possibilities for recreation, education, culture, [and] advancement" which half-Anglicized emigrants had come to expect. By contrast with the feverish vitality of William Carleton's countryside, post-Famine Ireland "suffered grievously from dullness." Sheer boredom exacerbated material deprivation and spurred desires to escape, especially when, as Sir Horace Plunkett suggested, the now-dominant social institutions themselves seemed at least partly responsible for "the mortal melancholy" of rural life. "The best men will face toil and perhaps privation" in Ireland, wrote another observer, but "[t]hey will not willingly resign themselves to years of unrelieved stupidity . . .": "The young, the vigorous, and the active are tolerant of anything rather than monotony," and consequently "[t]he city, with its promise of companionship, with its bright lights and varied interests, lures men [and women] from the countryside . . . across the Atlantic."[102]

Thus, desires for excitement mingled with material aspirations for young emigrants such as Augustine Costello and James J. Mitchell, who in his memoirs recorded the impact of literacy and communications on his hitherto-sheltered parish: "Having read and heard much of other places and People," he wrote, yet "never been more than thirty miles from home, I was very anxious to see the 'sights.'" And sometimes emigrants' experiences fulfilled dreams of adventure and romance—"God, Peg, I never knew I was alive till I got out here and woke up," wrote James Quinn from southern California, America's reputed lotusland—while such letters home only encouraged further dissatisfaction and departures. "I often laughf at how green I was [in Carlow]," wrote Ellen Wogan from Philadelphia; "a mere child here of 6 years old has more sence than I had then. Dear Tommy," she told her brother, "if only you were to stop [in America] for 3 months it would learn you how to live."[103]

Finally, emigration itself played a key role in restructuring and reorienting rural society and culture in ways that produced more emigration. Most broadly, the structural changes in post-Famine Irish society developed *in tandem with* emigration; they were mutually reinforcing as well as self-perpetuating phenomena. For example, while it is fair to cite the commercialization of Irish agriculture as emigration's root *cause,* it is equally true that that process—involving the engrossment of grassland, the switch to impartible inheritance, and the proletarianization of rural labor—could not have occurred so rapidly and thoroughly except as a *result* of mass emigration. Likewise, the growing instrumentalism of parent-child relationships in rural families must have been a consequence as well as a cause of constant emigration. In short, these processes were circular and interdependent: commercialization produced social and cultural changes which mandated and encouraged an emigration which facilitated more commercialization and changes which in turn promoted more emigration, *et cetera.*

More specifically, emigration undermined the vitality of rural life, thereby eroding the social and cultural ties which bound to their homeland those who had not yet emigrated. "The more the peasants emigrate," wrote one observer, "the more is social life destroyed in the country districts; hence a fresh reason for emigrating." Steady departures by relatives and neighbors engendered loneliness and depression among those left behind. "We are here on this side of the world a mere figment of what our family once was," lamented an Ulsterman, while to the south a Munster Catholic despaired when he "brought to mind the happy & joyous days I spent with those who were now lying in the cold dark vault" or living in America. Among the peasantry, the resultant "Solitude or dearth of kinsmen" only exacerbated material deprivations: "Ah, Avourneen," exclaimed a would-be emigrant in the Wicklow glens, "did you ever see the like of the place we live in? . . . the poorest, wildest, lonesomest, dreariest bit of a hill a person ever passed a life on?" In such circumstances, it was only natural that those who could followed relatives and neighbors across the ocean rather than remain in an empty, cheerless land; after all, "the greater the number of Irish in America, the more complete is the social life they find in their *new* home." Ironically, then, emigration so fragmented Irish families and communities that it often seemed to those still at home that only through *more* emigration could broken social ties be reunited. Thus, when the west Kerryman Maurice O'Sullivan contemplated emigration to America he envisioned "the boys and girls who were once [his] companions walking the street, laughing brightly and well contented." "I see my brother Shaun and my sisters Maura and Eileen," fancied O'Sullivan, and "it seemed to me now that Maura was raising her fist to me and saying aloud, '. . . come out here where your own people are, for if you [do not] you will never see any of your kinfolk again.' "[104]

Emigration's self-perpetuating dynamic operated in other ways as well. In the late nineteenth and early twentieth centuries, the Irish abroad—more literate than their predecessors—flooded Ireland with letters and remittances. Most obviously, many letters directly encouraged departures through either the promises they conveyed concerning American opportunities or the prepaid passage tickets they often contained. More broadly, by encouraging emigration through letters and remittances, Irish-Americans inadvertently furthered the circular processes noted above—facilitating structural changes in Irish society which in turn mandated yet additional departures. This was an ironic development, for while many post-Famine emigrants were making heroic efforts to liberate Ireland politically, their simultaneous promotion of more emigration only ensured their homeland's closer integration into and subordination to British capitalism. Moreover, incessant communications from abroad eroded their recipients' cultural and psychological ties to Ireland. For example, many Irish countrymen grew so familiar with conditions overseas that they came to regard the United States "as if it were not a foreign country at all," but rather "their second native land." Indeed, western peasants often knew far more about Boston or New York than about Dublin, Cork, or even parts of their own counties. Thus, when Horace Plunkett asked a girl from County Galway why she refused to join relatives on a farm thirty miles distant and instead preferred emigrating to New York City, she "replied in so many words, 'because it is nearer.' " In addition, Irish-Americans not only sent home enormous sums of money but also deluged relatives with presents such as clothes and with consumer-oriented materials: newspapers, glossy magazines, mail-order catalogs, and even photographs of themselves proudly attired in stylish new garments. The Irish reaction, especially in more-impoverished, less-sophisticated, and hitherto-isolated communities, was predictable—astonishment, admiration, envy, and, ultimately, shame and contempt for their own and their society's comparative deficiencies: "Is this fashionably attired lady [in the photographs] the Bridget they knew? Ballybog never provided hats like that, never pictured such elegance in its wildest dreams."[105]

By the end of the nineteenth century, all these communications provided the major sources of cultural nourishment and material standards to many rural communities, which almost lived vicariously with the emigrants overseas. They not only prompted specific additional departures but directly or indirectly also encouraged the Irish to despise and reject traditional habits now deemed inferior by American norms and even dysfunctional for those eager to enter the purported "land of promise." For example, "the American letter helped anglicize this country," reported one elderly Kerryman, for "nearly every letter that came from America urged and exhorted the parents to try and teach English to the children." Consequently, most Irish-speaking parents collaborated with schoolmasters in forcing their offspring to learn the language of progress and opportunity—"lest we should find the world awkward later on," as one emigrant remembered. After all, once their children reached the nearest railroad station, "they won't hear a word of Irish or meet anyone who'd understand it; so what good," they asked, "is a man who hasn't got the English and plenty of it?"[106]

Lastly, an estimated 10 percent of the post-Famine emigrants returned to Ireland, and though many returned impoverished or chastened by their experience, those who had been successful in America also promoted more emigration: for example, by the material evidence of their accomplishments and sometimes by direct admonitions. "If I had remained at home as you are doing," they would tell their poor countrymen, "I would still be here in rags, working in dirt and mud, and with nothing to show for it." More subtly, successful returned emigrants were agents of broad cultural changes which encouraged emigration. The self-assertiveness, habits of industry, and lack of respect for convention and ascribed status which they had learned in America often proved infectious and helped erode the deference and resignation which had formerly inhibited overt dissatisfaction, ambition, and emigration. Indeed, returned emigrants' purported influence and the consequent changes in popular attitudes evoked concern and criticism from a variety of conservative sources: from landlords and strong farmers who detested "independence" among tenants and employees; from churchmen such as Cardinal Cullen who feared that returned emigrants contaminated their flocks with "infidelity" and ideas of "excessive liberty"; from Irishmen, generally, who felt threatened by hardworking, "close-fisted" servant girls whose dowries earned in American kitchens enabled them to pick their own husbands; and from British officials who warned that "the spirit of unrest" during the Land War was fomented largely by Irish-Americans who "returned to their country impressed with democratic ideas." Thus, prosperous returned emigrants personified broader modernizing processes, and in 1883 the Corkwoman Charlotte O'Brien exulted that "the strength and independence begotten of American thought is to-day springing like new blood through the veins of Ireland." However, Ireland's hardened social arteries obliged most "new blood" to flow outward to America, and the successful returned emigrants' influence on Irish culture merely provided another anticoagulant.[107]

Section 3. Emigration as "Exile": Tradition and Expediency in Post-Famine Ireland

By the early twentieth century, some observers regretfully concluded that the processes of commercialization and Anglicization had so changed Irish outlooks that "[t]o go to America no longer convey[ed] the same idea of exile or expatriation" as it had before the Great Famine. In fact, however, Irish attitudes concerning post-Famine emigration and its causes were highly contradictory, and the predominant interpretations remained remarkably traditional and, from a strictly economic viewpoint, "irrational." Considerable public and private testimony, from both sides of the Atlantic, indicates that many, perhaps most Irishmen still regarded emigration as tragic, involuntary exile compelled by circumstances beyond individual control, most especially by overt British oppression. For example, according to the U.S. consul Edward Brooks, the Irish who left from Queenstown in the early 1880s perceived their departures as flight "from 'hated British rule,' " and later in the decade another observer claimed that "each one of the emigrants who leaves Ireland for America carries away with him a bitter hatred of [England]": "England be damned!" exclaimed the Wexford emigrant Dennis O'Rourke, who blamed his departure on the British misgovernment which had made Ireland "rotten to the core."[108]

Such nationalistic interpretations of emigration were especially pronounced during periods characterized by high rates of agrarian and political strife. However, negative and politicized perceptions were commonly expressed in a variety of ways throughout the era. Thus, the heartrending scenes when emigrants left home and when they boarded ships testified to the profound sorrow felt on such occasions, while emigration ballads specifically linked such emotions to feelings of compulsion and political causation. "After a poor fella got his passage," remembered one informant, "you would see him getting sadder and sadder as the time for going got close. Before that the same one might be going about singing from morning 'till night, but the thought of going to America took the singing out of his heart and left a hole that was never filled." "'Tis no for the want of gold and silver, that my darlin left his native shore," ran one ballad which explicitly absolved emigrants of self-motivation, "But only for loving his country, as his ancestors loved it before . . . ," thus linking personal exigencies to communal traditions of expropriation and expulsion. Other songs specifically attributed emigration to evictions or political and religious oppression, and promised that although "Time may roll o'er me its circles uncheering, . . . the exile shall never forget thee, loved Eire. . . ." Such ballads were as common in America as in Ireland and, whether commercial or personal compositions, conveyed similar sentiments. Indeed, travelers as diverse as the Irish missionary Michael Buckley, the Anglo-Irish landlord Sir Horace Plunkett, and the unsympathetic English journalist Philip Bagenal testified to the extraordinary persistence of acute homesickness and Anglo-phobia among the emigrants abroad. "The Irish in America, rightly or wrongly, believe that the vast immigration of their race into that continent is owing to English rule," Bagenal lamented. "They believe themselves to have been 'frozen out' of their native land," and consequently they entertain "an unreasoning and yet solid feeling of inextinguishable hostility to the English system of government." Such sentiments found expression in the various nationalist movements which exercised Irish-America in the late nineteenth and early twentieth centuries, and also in the comparatively high rates of return migration which characterized the period. Although contemporary claims that most post-Famine emigrants left *intending* to return are very dubious, the relative cheapness and ease of steamship travel now certainly enabled an unprecedentedly large number of emigrants to indulge longings for home and, on occasion, even desires for revenge against the British authority deemed responsible for their unhappy and involuntary "exile."[109]

Of course, the interpretation of all post-Famine emigrations as unwilling and attributable to British coercion hardly squared with either social reality or the contradictory statements of many emigrants. Although a small minority of post-Famine emigrants were fugitive rebels or evicted tenants who could blame departures on British "tyranny" with some justification, the great majority left home for mundane reasons rooted in the dynamics of a socioeconomic system whose basic premises most Irish nationalists accepted without question: "For many years," admitted the Catholic journalist D. P. Moran, "the Irish nation has been breaking up before the inexorable forces of political economy." Thus, even a 1909 nationalist tract entitled *The Irish in America* acknowledged that while emigrants might have "feelings of discontent" against England, "those thoughts cannot be consistently advanced as the real causes of the regrettable exodus." However, the fact that they *were* advanced, both publicly and privately, albeit inconsistently, tells much about post-Famine Irish society and culture—about the contradictory nature and consequences of a "modernization" which paradoxically allowed and even encouraged the retention of traditional behavior and attitudes such as those concerning emigration.[110]

Indeed, the historian Joseph Lee has argued that Irish misperceptions of emigration and its causes merely exemplified and epitomized "the wide failure of Irish thought to grapple with the social realities of the modern world." Although it remains to be seen whether post-Famine Ireland's "social realities" were in fact as "modern" as Lee suggests, much evidence certainly indicates that despite commercialization and Anglicization a traditional Irish Catholic worldview—with its emphases on communalism as opposed to individualism, custom versus innovation, conformity versus initiative, fatalism versus optimism, passivity versus action, dependence versus independence, nonresponsibility versus responsibility—remained prevalent and continued to shape attitudes toward social phenomena such as emigration. As was noted in Chapter 3, throughout the late nineteenth and early twentieth centuries, observers as disparate as Horace Plunkett and James Connolly lamented their Catholic countrymen's alleged lack of "manly independence," "self-reliance," and "moral courage." Regardless of the critics' nationality, religion, or political sympathies, their strictures were not only similar to each other but virtually identical to those levied in the pre-Famine period. For example, according to the U.S. consul Louis Richmond, the Irish remained incorrigible conservatives whose "spirit . . . leans rather toward contentment with things as they are rather than toward the adoption of anything new." Likewise, a host of critics claimed that the Catholic Irish still lacked industry, thrift, foresight, efficiency—in short, what the agrarian reformer P. H. Kenny called "industrial character"— deficiencies manifest in the slovenly state of Irish agriculture. Other observers still noted an Irish Catholic propensity to avoid personal responsibility and subordinate self-expression to the exigencies of group conformity: "More often than not," wrote L. Paul-Dubois, ". . . the Irish . . . go in groups, in cliques, in separate leagues; . . . individualism has not yet come forth from its Limbo, and the community is still the dominant fact." Finally, critics lamented that, despite all British efforts to improve Anglo-Irish relations, Irish political culture was still narrowly parochial and "largely retrospective," while the time-honored habit of blaming England for all Irish ills remained nearly ubiquitous.[111]

In short, the persistent interpretation of emigration as exile was more than a hackneyed or situational response to evictions or specific conflicts with British authorities, although such instances certainly reinforced and politicized the image. Rather, that perception was only one of many expressions of a traditional Irish Catholic worldview which continued to deprecate innovation, initiative, and the assumption or attribution of personal responsibility. But how could such a worldview still prevail in post-Famine Ireland? Theoretically, at least, the processes of modernization should have discredited or made irrelevant traditional outlooks, just as they eroded the traditional social structures and relationships which had fostered those outlooks. Indeed, as we have seen, commercialization and Anglicization in post-Famine Ireland did engender in many individuals a novel ambition for self-improvement and an alienation from new or now-intolerable forms of exploitation, both of which in turn encouraged willing, if not always eager, emigrations. Nevertheless, the weight of evidence indicates that such modern, economically "rational" attitudes—concerning emigration as well as other aspects of life—were only inconsistently held or expressed, and that whether commonly or occasionally, sincerely or calculatingly, most Irish Catholics still relied on traditional categories of thought to interpret or justify their situations and actions.

The paradoxes of post-Famine Irish Catholic thought derived from the contradictory nature and consequences of Irish Catholic society's contemporary development. Although it is broadly and retrospectively accurate to describe post-Famine Ireland in terms of *overall* "progress" or modernization, in some crucial respects the rates of contemporary change were remarkably slow, allowing substantial continuities in social structures and attitudes. For example, despite increasing urbanization and market pressures for consolidation of farms, as late as 1911 not only did Ireland remain an overwhelmingly agrarian society but in addition almost 70 percent of all farms were still under thirty acres in size, nearly 46 percent under fifteen acres. After rapid, forced attrition during the Great Famine, between 1861 and 1911 the number of Irish holdings under thirty acres fell by only 17.5 percent; by contrast, in roughly the same period the number of French farms of comparable size declined by 40 percent. These small and medium-sized Irish holdings were still "family farms," conforming to what the Irish sociologist Damian Hannan has called the "peasant model": characterized by "a familial economy, where farms are owned or securely rented and are large enough to support a family but not large enough to employ labour" on a regular basis; and by "a subsistence economy, where production for the market is not the dominating purpose of production," where "use values rather than exchange values are dominant," and where the perpetuation of the family holding itself rather than profit is the overriding goal. Indeed, in 1911 over half these family farms were "deficit holdings" *incapable* of generating profits, and as late as 1955 Irish farms under thirty acres were still heavily subsistence oriented.[112]

Given the post-Famine decline in nonfarm employment and the overall downward trends of agricultural prices, it was understandable that despite their straitened circumstances most occupiers clung tenaciously to these family farms and remained conservative and parochial in farming practices and outlooks. Both geographic and upward social mobility within rural Ireland remained very limited, and most parishes were characterized by what Hannan has called "a highly localized communal system in which the mutual aid arrangements of family and kinship groups mitigated, if not controlled, class-differentiating tendencies." Likewise, the slow growth of Ireland's post-Famine economy, itself limited by the prevalence of semi-subsistence family farming, circumscribed expansion and modernization in the urban sector, which, beyond Dublin and the industrialized Northeast, was dominated by petty shopkeepers who experienced high degrees of economic insecurity and intimate socioeconomic, cultural, and familial ties with the farming community. In such marginal circumstances most rural and urban dwellers tempered aspirations for "improvement" with anxious, even obsessive concerns for a security which could best be retained through traditional means such as the possession of land and the continued cultivation of close communal and familial relationships. Indeed, opportunities to acquire land or employment on the open market remained too limited to undermine entirely most Irishmen's customary fatalism, or to challenge effectively the old "peasant" notion that competition and social fluidity threatened communal survival and violated purportedly immutable status relationships: hence, the popular resentment of—and occasional violence against—"outsiders," "upstarts," and "land-" and "grass-grabbers." Similarly, the subsistence orientation of most Irish farmers—their consequent dependence on the weather and the avoidance of crop and livestock diseases—encouraged the retention of deeply religious outlooks, while prior to 1903 the prevalence of landlordism and the possibility of eviction reinforced patterns of social dependence. In short, during the post-Famine era most Irishmen's economic situation remained compatible with the guidelines and constraints of their traditional worldview.[113]

Thus, the changes wrought by commercialization were distributed unevenly across the social spectrum: concentrated primarily at its extremes—among the *haute bourgeoisie* and among proletarianized artisans and farm laborers—while limited in their effects on the great majority of rural dwellers and the petite bourgeoisie of Ireland's small market towns and villages. Moreover, modernization was distributed unevenly among regions as well. Industrialization occurred only in the Northeast, and the consolidation of farmsteads proceeded much more rapidly in eastern than in western Ireland. For example, in 1861–1911 the number of farms between one and thirty acres in size fell 25 percent in Leinster but only 12 percent in Connaught; indeed, during the same period farms between fifteen and thirty acres actually increased 10 percent in Connaught while declining 13 percent in Leinster. Similarly, quantifiable rates of cultural change also varied enormously from region to region. Thus, in 1861–91 the number of Irish-speakers in Leinster fell 62 percent but in Connaught only 33 percent. Even in 1901, 38 percent of Connaught's inhabitants and 26 percent of Munster's still spoke Irish, while most of the rest conversed in Hiberno-English dialects which still purveyed the stative thought patterns and grammatical structures of the traditional language.[114]

Paradoxically, not only did the dilatory and uneven development of Ireland's post-Famine economy *allow* traditional social structures and attitudes to survive but many of the socioeconomic changes which occurred most pervasively actually *caused* or exacerbated Irish "backwardness." Most broadly, to the despair of nationalists who preached economic as well as political "self-reliance," Irish commercialization reduced the island's economic autonomy, forcing all classes and regions into greater dependence on foreign markets, products, and finance. Ireland's fuller integration into world capitalism had other contradictory consequences: such as de-industrialization outside the Northeast, which made Ireland a more agrarian society in 1900 than in 1850; such as the nationwide expansion of commercial grazing, which enabled impoverished family farms to avert bankruptcy by supplying calves to wealthy graziers. Emigration also reinforced rural conservatism: for example, by enabling semisubsistence farms to survive economically; by increasing the proportion of Ireland's elderly while reducing the numbers of "spirited and enterprising" young people at home; and, most important, by removing the human evidence of social differentiation. Thus, the contradictory nature of Irish "modernization" both increased social differentiation and mitigated its expected consequences within Ireland itself, instead creating new or confirming old patterns of social dependence and thereby encouraging deferential or "dependent" outlooks among those who remained at home. For example, whereas pre-Famine Ireland had witnessed open class warfare, ranging journeymen and rural laborers against their employers, after mid-century members of both groups became increasingly powerless to assert themselves *except* by leaving the country; meanwhile, their proletarianization and rapidly diminishing numbers obliged those who stayed in Ireland to cultivate kinship attachments, patron-client ties, and ostentatious piety and patriotism to secure employment and credit from a Catholic bourgeoisie that demanded loyalty and docility in return. Similarly, the spread of the grazing system throughout rural Ireland made land-hungry smallholders more hesitant to challenge the graziers who purchased their calves and yearlings, while the expansion of commerce and credit networks enmeshed poor farmers in virtually unbreakable webs of debt and dependence on village traders and usurers. Ironically, in some respects commercialization actually strengthened rural family ties even as it mandated impartible inheritance and emigration. For instance, market pressures and inflated labor costs obliged most farmers to rely exclusively on their children's assistance, while fathers' powers to choose their successors and dowried daughters—coupled with the dearth of employment caused by rural de-industrialization and the expansion of grazing—enforced at least a sullen obedience on their offspring; even emigrating children usually were forced to rely on family connections to finance their passages overseas.[115]

Furthermore, Irish "modernization" failed to promote social fluidity or political dialogue across sectarian lines. Rather, commercialization's class-differentiating tendencies widened extant socioeconomic gaps between Protestants and Catholics, as in Ulster, while heightened competition for land and employment only intensified religious tribalism. In addition, expanding civil service, religious, and political bureaucracies established new or more efficient systems of social control. For example, the bureaucratization of Irish education reduced the independence of teachers and parents as well as of students, while official programs such as the Congested Districts Board and the Old-Age Pension system exerted pervasive influences over rural life—in both cases subsidizing traditional family farms while forging new links of dependence on external authorities. Likewise, more-elaborate institutional structures and the use of new mass media techniques enabled both the Catholic church and organized nationalism—themselves highly traditional in ideology—to impose unprecedented degrees of conformity on Irish thought and behavior. For instance, although the local statures of parish priests and publican-patriots still depended heavily on kinship and clientage, their increasingly tangible links to cosmopolitan power structures greatly augmented their personal authority while simultaneously increasing both their and their constituents' ultimate dependence on and subordination to supralocal institutions. Consequently, on parochial as well as national levels Irish Catholic society became more authoritarian and disciplined.[116]

In short, the development of late-nineteenth- and early-twentieth-century Irish society was an extremely complex process. Traditional attitudes and customs were themselves "social facts" which conditioned the pace and directions of change, and as a result many of the "modern" institutions and relationships which prevailed in post-Famine Ireland were in fact synthetic adaptations of old values and patterns to contemporary conditions. Consequently, the "new" institutions and relationships perpetuated the traditional outlooks and concerns which had helped shape them, making those outlooks still seem relevant to altered but not unfamiliar circumstances. For example, although the leaders of the Catholic church and of organized nationalism hoped their adherents would internalize religious and political ideals, in practice they relied heavily upon customary beliefs and communal sanctions—such as "boycotting"—which exacted conformity at the expense of rational, voluntary, and individualized conviction. Indeed, perhaps that result was inevitable, given not only the persistent strengths of localism and familialism in rural society but also the fact that clerical and political ideals and rhetoric were themselves rooted in archaic traditions and antimodernist impulses. Likewise, "peasant" notions of proper behavior were instrumental in determining the character of ostensibly "rational" market relationships, as between village shopkeepers and rural customers. Thus, despite commercialization post-Famine society scarcely resembled the "meritocracy" prophesied by modernization theorists; rather, as Moritz Bonn lamented in 1906, Ireland was still "a land where nothing can be accomplished by principles, but where personal address" and family connections "mean everything."[117]

Most important in this context, it was not ambition for profits but rather the traditional idealization of the family holding as providing subsistence, security, and generational continuity that was the primary determinant of most farmers' responses to new market pressures. Although commercial graziers desired a more fluid and exploitable land system, family farmers pursued goals which ran counter to market trends: fixity of tenure, lowered rents, peasant purchase on easy terms, and the breakup and redistribution of grass farms. Consequently, although the Land Acts of the 1880s created a theoretically free land market, family farmers seized upon those provisions, such as judicially lowered rents, which weakened landlord pressures for commercial production; likewise, prior to the 1903 Wyndham Act the same farmers refused to purchase their own holdings on terms which would have obliged greater market involvement. Significantly, after 1881, contemporaries often complained that neither fixity of tenure, reduced rents, nor peasant proprietorship made Irish farmers generally more efficient or productive. Indeed, they seemed less inclined to take risks or make investments than before their legal victories: indicating that in their eyes security of tenure had never been a means to the "greater" end, "improvements," predicted by tenant-right's middle-class advocates, but rather had always been itself the family farmers' primary, if not only, goal. Moreover, in this light it would be misleading to interpret family farmers' adoption of impartible inheritance, delayed marriage, and emigration as unambiguous evidence of rural modernity. For although these family arrangements replicated those long practiced by the rural bourgeoisie and were, from an economic perspective, purely "rational," if not ruthless, in the case of most farmers it is more accurate to view them as necessary adaptations to market imperatives designed to ensure traditional goals—namely, the perpetuation of the family farm and the continuity of generations on the ancestral hold-ing. In this sense, impartible inheritance and emigration were analogous to former (and, in some areas, still extant) strategies such as cottage manu-facturing, *poitín* making, and seasonal migration. Indeed, in a few remote regions such as west Donegal and the Mourne Mountains, where cottage manufacturing and seasonal migration survived, partible inheritance and aversion to emigration prevailed even in the early twentieth century. How-ever, in western Ireland as a whole there was a direct correlation between the decreasing efficacy of traditional strategies and the belated adoption of impartible inheritance and emigration, for after 1880 these were the only means by which most family farmers could hold the line against the in-evitable tendencies of commercialization. To be sure, family farmers were obliged to redraw that line, to adjust their behavior radically and force their noninheriting children into the "modern" world. However, the conse-quent friction within families would have been unbearable had not these innovations been justified and imposed in a traditional context; otherwise, the willingness of the disinherited to remit millions of pounds in support of the households which had expelled them would be inexplicable.[118]

Nevertheless, if post-Famine Ireland was not yet fully "modern," it was far from wholly "traditional." Although mitigated, change was real and, in some respects, rapid and traumatic. Commercialization *did* produce drastic rationalizations of social and familial relationships, and while wholesale departures by the dispossessed and disinherited eventually siphoned off most of the resultant alienation and potential for internecine conflict, in-stitutionalized mass emigration was itself a novel and unsettling phenome-non, especially in western Ireland. Moreover, as was noted in the preced-ing section, altered social relationships *did* promote overt expressions of increasingly instrumental and individualistic attitudes, while greater expo-sure to foreign, urban-industrial life-styles *did* produce cultural changes which critics stigmatized as "Anglicization." Yet, paradoxically, these very innovations, so pregnant with social disruption and demoralization, them-selves encouraged greater popular reliance on traditional outlooks which could relieve the tensions consequent on rapid transition. In order to en-sure social and psychic equilibrium in such situations, changes *had* to be interpreted in customary, comforting ways. Thus, although most Irishmen and -women reacted "rationally" to new economic exigencies or oppor-tunities and sometimes openly admitted their active roles in these processes, the great majority usually fell back on traditional categories of thought to "explain," justify, exculpate, or obscure causation and accountability, often projecting responsibility for change on uncontrollable "alien" or "outside" forces. To cite but one example, it became customary to blame post-Famine evictions on the special ruthlessness of new "English" landlords who purchased estates under the Encumbered Estates Act, despite the fact that the great majority of these rural entrepreneurs were Irish and primarily Catholic.[119]

Indeed, sometimes the disjunctions between reality and interpretation were so great as to make post-Famine Ireland appear an almost schizophrenic, if not hypocritical, society. However, the fact that the society's primary institutions—family farm, Catholic church, and organized nationalism—were themselves syntheses of traditional and modern ideals and processes served to promote outlooks which obscured those disjunctions. In fact, the very need to resolve social and psychic tensions encouraged an increased popular reliance on these institutions which offered seeming continuities and comforting identifications with traditional symbols. Consequently, as alternative or competing role models, social activities, and cultural phenomena withered or were abandoned, family, church, and nationalism assumed a pervasive importance. Moreover, for their parts the very dynamics of these institutions—their culpability in the processes of change as well as their hegemonic imperatives—obliged them to purvey traditionalist outlooks and generate obscurantist "explanations" of change which served to reduce the intracommunal conflicts consequent on modernization and to bind their adherents across generational, class, and regional lines. In short, it was both traditional and expedient for family farmers, Catholic clergymen, and nationalist politicians not only to promote the persistence of a general worldview which enjoined unity and self-sacrifice but also to explain emigration—perhaps the most radical disjunction between ideal and reality—within the context of that worldview, in ways which obscured or, even better, externalized causation and thereby cemented their adherents' allegiance to the self-proclaimed "defenders" of Catholic society. And, in turn it was both customary and convenient for ordinary Irish Catholics to accept interpretations and allegiances which offered such neat, if superficial, resolutions of the psychic and social conflicts which underlay the seeming unity and continuity of Catholic Ireland.[120]

In conclusion, then, what might be called the "traditionalization" of post-Famine Ireland was—like "modernization," its paradoxically necessary complement—a circular and self-perpetuating process. Consequently, although Ireland's religious and political institutions, and their "official" explanations of change, were themselves reflections of contradictory socioeconomic and cultural realities, their crucial roles in interpreting those realities assumed preponderant importance in a pervasively religious and politicized society. Thus, without forgetting the primacy of socioeconomic conditions, the next part of this section will examine church and nationalism in post-Famine Ireland, demonstrating how their internal dynamics and complex relationships to Irish society generated the "official" explanations of emigration which proved most appropriate and acceptable to a people in transition.

One might have expected that the increasing interdependence of the

English and Irish economies and cultures, as well as the substantial British concessions to Ireland after 1867, might have lessened Catholics' desire for self-government and their age-old animosity toward England during the post-Famine period. In fact, however, the impacts of commercialization and Anglicization only heightened Irish Catholic nationalism. "Hatred of England still exists in Ireland," reported L. Paul-Dubois in 1908; indeed, he added, the "people . . . have never been more disloyal than they are at the present day."[121]

Irish resentment and nationalism increased for several interrelated reasons. First, archaic traditions of defeat, despoliation, and proscription—reinforced by fresher memories of famine and mass evictions—still provided frames of reference for interpreting contemporary suffering. Thus, late in the nineteenth century one observer lamented that Catholic peasants still perceived themselves as "the oppressed descendants of kings and saints, plundered of their natural heritage of prosperity, and persecuted through the ages for their steadfast devotion to a form of religion which they judged essential to the salvation of their souls." Second, post-Famine Ireland's economic development—slow, halting, and subordinate to British capitalism—generated more frustration than achievement, while increased exposure to England's obviously superior wealth and power only intensified Irish jealousy and hostility. Third, both commercialization and Anglicization produced in Ireland severe socioeconomic and cultural crises, ranging from the disastrous price failures and evictions of the 1880s to the more subtle but equally threatening loss of national identity. In other words, both frustrated Irish aspirations for "progress" and the felt need to protect Irish society from the adverse consequences of *too much* "progress" combined effectively, if paradoxically, to range different groups within Catholic Ireland against British economic, cultural, and political domination. Finally but perhaps equally important, Irish nationalism—like its complement, increased popular devotion to Catholicism—arose out of the tensions and social conflicts which modernization generated within Catholic society itself. Organized nationalism—aided by its clerical auxiliaries—both mobilized and mitigated those internal tensions, projecting blame and its followers' frustrations upon the traditional enemy. Consequently, the history of post-Famine nationalism at once reflected and offered seeming resolutions of the conflicts and contradictions within Catholic Ireland.[122]

Prior to the Great Famine the Catholic nationalism forged by Daniel O'Connell had been based on broad coalitions between a rising urban bourgeoisie and strong-farmer and clerical allies marshaling a large mass of enthusiastic, if potentially disruptive, peasants. However, the Famine years witnessed the peasantry's decimation, O'Connell's death, and Young Ireland's defeat and dispersal, and for the next three decades representatives of the shattered alliance's major constituents struggled vainly to regain leadership of a united body politic. In this effort, two problems were paramount. First, the existing political system hampered independent Irish political activity in several respects. Prior to 1885 only one out of six adult males could vote, and before 1872 they had to cast their votes publicly—a situation which usually assured landlord domination of parliamentary and local elections alike. Moreover, even if Irish MPs so elected were patriotically inclined, their degree of influence and patronage at Westminster depended entirely on their loyalty to one or the other of the British political parties, which made independent action on behalf of purely Irish concerns seem dysfunctional as well as futile. Such obstacles to constitutional nationalism were not insuperable, as O'Connell had shown: they could be overcome by focusing public attention on a single issue, such as Catholic emancipation or repeal, which was sufficiently emotive and inclusive in its perceived benefits to unite Catholics across class lines, mobilizing them for election victories in the very face of landlord intimidation. However, the second major problem facing would-be nationalist leaders was that the Famine had so fragmented and demoralized Catholic society that in its immediate aftermath no single issue had sufficiently broad appeal to serve as a basis for reunion. Thus, at worst, post-Famine political life degenerated into local factionalism and power brokerage; at best, it was characterized by movements which foundered on Catholic Ireland's internal divisions.[123]

For example, during the 1850s and 1860s the most politically active elements in Catholic society were the strong farmers, the church, and the Fenians: their different aspirations and social bases not only precluded cooperation but even generated mutually damaging antagonism. Strong farmers, particularly in south Leinster and east Munster, wanted Parliament to legalize tenant-right, a demand made by the short-lived Tenant League of the early 1850s and by the various farmers' clubs which proliferated at county levels during the late nineteenth century. Strictly speaking, the tenant-right movement was not nationalistic, although the Tenant League was led initially by the ex–Young Irelander Charles Gavan Duffy and enjoyed a brief "national" alliance with northern Presbyterian farmers made desperate by landlords' efforts to abolish the "Ulster custom." Meanwhile, under Cardinal Paul Cullen's leadership the post-Famine church moved to complete its "devotional revolution" and regain its due preeminence in Irish society, especially through the disendowment and disestablishment of the Church of Ireland, and by securing complete control of Catholic primary and secondary education. Again, except in the sense that most bishops assumed that church and Ireland were synonymous and detested England for historical and religious reasons, the church's program was not nationalistic, depending as it did on the British Parliament's approval; moreover, the Vatican itself opposed Irish nationalism and pursued rapprochement with England, even at "faithful" Ireland's expense. However, the Fenians of the Irish Republican Brotherhood, founded in 1858, were wholehearted and extreme nationalists. They aimed at nothing less than total Irish independence and the establishment of a vaguely defined republic, to be achieved through organized conspiracy, Irish-American aid, and eventual mass uprising. Many IRB leaders, such as Charles Kickham

and John O'Leary, were of bourgeois orgin and conservative in social outlook. However, Fenianism had greatest appeal among the urban lower-
middle and working classes (clerks and shopkeepers' assistants, artisans
and journeymen) and to a lesser degree among small farmers, farmers'
sons, and agricultural laborers. Disadvantaged and disfranchised, melding
trade union radicalism with smoldering agrarian discontent and St. Columcille's spurious prophecies of deliverance, Fenianism's adherents knew
that redress of their grievances could come only through successful revolution.

Cooperation among these three groups was minimal, open hostility or
suspicion common. Strong farmers—indeed, the propertied classes generally—loathed Fenianism, partly from fear of the violence and repression
which hopeless rebellion would occasion, partly from opposition to the exploited but hitherto-submerged social elements which composed the bulk
of IRB membership. For their part, although in theory Fenian leaders appealed for all-class unity against England and urged postponement of divisive social issues until after independence, in practice Fenianism was conditioned by the 1859–64 depression, its adherents' desperate circumstances,
and bourgeois opposition. In response Fenian spokesmen formulated a
harsh critique of post-Famine society, attacking graziers and strong farmers
as well as landlords for exploiting the peasantry and opposing Irish freedom. As for the church, with few exceptions bishops and priests vigorously
condemned Fenianism, in part for the same reasons which inspired attacks
from the middle classes, in part because Cullen and other churchmen regarded the IRB as tainted with "atheism" and continental radicalism. In
fact, most Fenians were devout Catholics, but denunciations from Catholic
altars provoked IRB leaders to anticlerical outbursts which only further
convinced the pious that Fenianism was synonymous with the "red republicanism" currently besieging the Italian Papal States. Ironically, the church's
relations with the moderate tenant-right movement were also poor, in part
because Cardinal Cullen deeply distrusted all lay initiatives, especially
those which agitated issues deemed socially divisive or threatening to property rights. Nevertheless, initial prospects for an alliance between the
church and strong farmers had seemed promising. In mid-1851 the Tenant League joined forces with the newly formed Catholic Defense Association, an organization uniting clerics and Catholic Whig MPs in support of
church interests. Together the two groups established the Independent Irish
party, and although the party's Catholicity drove Ulster Protestants from
the Tenant League, the party successfully contested the 1852 parliamentary
election on a platform linking farmers' and church goals. However, the alliance quickly disintegrated, in part because two CDA leaders accepted lucrative appointments from the new Whig administration, in part because
Cullen distrusted the Tenant League and withdrew essential clerical support, hoping instead to win concessions for the church through direct negotiations with Westminster. The church did not return to active politics until
1864 when, in response to rural distress and the threat of Fenianism, the

bishops and Catholic Whigs organized the National Association of Ireland to agitate for reforms and influence Irish elections. Again, however, the demand for tenant right was muted, largely a device to undercut Fenianism's rural appeal, and was subordinated to church-centered issues such as disestablishment and denominational education. In the opinion of Fenians and many later nationalists, the church was bartering Irish nationality for a self-serving mésalliance with William Gladstone's Whig party. However, given the hopelessness of rebellion, the restrictive Irish franchise, and the conservatism of Irish MPs and of Parliament generally, denouncing the IRB and embracing Gladstone's promise of "justice to Ireland" appeared a soundly pragmatic policy, which reaped a partial reward in 1869 when the Whigs finally dismantled the Anglican establishment.

Despite this limited triumph, the potential components of Irish nationalism seemed as disunited and dispirited as before. In 1867, British troops easily crushed the long-anticipated Fenian uprising, as most countrymen obeyed their priests' injunctions and their own premonitions of disaster by staying home. The urban upper-middle classes, the posturing remnants of Young Ireland, had opposed the IRB but were themselves discouraged and without followers. The strong farmers' hopes for concessions from Parliament were dashed when the 1870 Land Act excluded substantial farmers from its meager and illusory benefits. Even the church's victory proved temporary, since its demand for denominational education was basically incompatible with British Whigs' antipapist prejudices and commitment to nonsectarian schooling. Thus, when the bishops rejected Gladstone's Irish universities bill of 1873 as a recipe for "godless" "mixed education," the church-Whig alliance crumbled in mutual acrimony and the National Association of Ireland—already split over the 1870 Land Act's acceptability—disintegrated.

In fact, conditions were now propitious for a renaissance of constitutional nationalism: threats from the revolutionary "left" had abated; the Whig alliance—and thus the British connection—had proved unsatisfactory to both the church and the propertied classes; and the Secret Ballot Act of 1872 largely removed the danger of landlord intimidation at the polls. The government itself provided the first unifying issue: its harsh treatment of Fenian prisoners—especially the 1867 execution of the three so-called Manchester martyrs—inspired widespread public resentment and enabled both middle-class politicians and clergymen to reassume "patriotic" prominence as leaders of a nationwide amnesty movement. As for the Fenians themselves, although most remained committed to rebellion and total independence, at the grass-roots level they began to infiltrate Ribbon lodges, farmers' clubs, and secret societies, and to forge pragmatic alliances with agrarian reformers and constitutional nationalists. As a result, by the early 1870s IRB influence had spread beyond its original bases in south Leinster and Munster to Connaught and the north midlands, merging with peasant grievances into what British officials termed "Ribbon Fenianism"—what recent historians have labeled neo-Fenianism. In addition, "pure" or "physical-force" Fenian sentiments remained very strong among the Irish in North America and especially in Great Britain.

Most important, in 1870—when the twin failures to secure amnesty and tenant-right publicly exposed the shallowness of the English Whigs' commitment to Irish "justice"—the Dublin barrister Isaac Butt launched his Home Government Association to agitate for an autonomous Irish parliament. Butt was a Protestant and former Tory, now turned constitutional nationalist through admiration for the Young Ireland and Fenian prisoners he had defended in court. However, Butt remained deeply conservative: self-government to him was a desirable expression of Irish nationality, but it was also a necessary expedient to prevent violent revolution and social upheaval, to secure propertied interests and the essential integrity of the British empire. Indeed, Butt originally envisioned a Tory-led Irish democracy, in which landlords would resume the patriotic leadership forfeited in 1800, and in its early stages his Home Government Association was an incongruous alliance of Protestant conservatives (temporarily alienated from Britain because of Anglican disestablishment), upper-middle-class Catholic Whigs, and pragmatic neo-Fenians. Nevertheless, although "home rule" proposed a degree of self-government considerably more limited than O'Connell's old demand for repeal of the union, Butt's slogan proved an evocative, if vague, symbol for Irish aspirations, and between 1870 and 1874 his movement (reconstituted in 1873 as the Home Rule League) won nine of fourteen by-elections. In the process, the league attracted support from strong farmers and younger bishops such as Thomas Croke of Cashel; both hoped that an autonomous Irish legislature might grant concessions which the British Parliament had refused, and clerics such as Croke felt the church must needs reunite with grass-roots nationalism or risk alienating the people. However, by endorsing its new allies' demands for tenant-right and denominational education, the Home Rule League forfeited landlord and Protestant support, thus losing its slim chance of creating a nonsectarian nationalism. Within Catholic Ireland, Butt's popularity peaked at the 1874 general election. At first, the results seemed revolutionary: outside Ulster the Whig party's Irish wing was all but obliterated as fifty-nine pledged home rulers went to Parliament and formed what came to be known as the Home Rule party or, variously, the Irish Parliamentary party, the Irish Nationalist party, or simply the Irish party. Equally startling was the sharp reduction in the numbers of landlord and Protestant MPs, and their replacement by upper-middle-class Catholics—lawyers, merchants, newspaper proprietors—as well as the first representatives from the strong-farmer/shopkeeper ranks. Thus, Butt's movement not only reanimated Irish nationalism but also gave the Catholic bourgeoisie its first taste of power. However, Butt's victory proved disappointing: most home rule MPs were conservative "closet Whigs," with only a shallow commitment to self-government or tenant-right. Moreover, Butt's gentlemanly tactics were inadequate either to enforce party discipline or to impress Irish demands against a solid wall of British hostility and indifference. Consequently, by the late 1870s home rule seemed a forlorn cause, and in 1879 Butt himself died unhappy and discredited.

However, as Butt's popularity and health declined, three closely related developments combined to make Irish nationalism a permanent and seemingly irresistible political force: the rise to prominence within the home rule movement of Charles Stewart Parnell, rural economic disaster, and Irish and Irish-American radicals' tactical decision to support agrarian revolt and parliamentary agitation. Parnell had an unusual background for a nationalist leader: a member of the Wicklow Protestant gentry, of striking presence but frigid personality, Parnell entered Parliament as a home ruler in 1875 and allied himself with a small band of Irish MPs who, despairing of Butt's ineffectiveness and British intransigence, had begun a policy of systematically obstructing normal parliamentary operations to gain hearings for Irish grievances. Obstructionism alone could not achieve home rule, but it goaded the British to hysterical displays of anti-Irish prejudice and reanimated Irish and Irish-American enthusiasm for the home rule cause. Equally important, Parnell's leading role in obstruction, and his obvious contempt for British institutions, catapulted him to fame both at home and abroad, especially among more-radical nationalists. In 1877 the IRB-dominated Home Rule Confederation of Great Britain rejected Butt's leadership and elected Parnell president. Although Butt remained in control of the Irish Home Rule League until his death, Parnell's star was clearly ascendant when rural Ireland's short-lived prosperity came to an end in the late 1870s.

Coupled with sharply falling prices, the disastrous harvest of 1879 brought severe distress to all sectors of the rural population, especially to western smallholders; eviction rates soared, and threats of ejection and bankruptcy hung over the entire island, affecting alike farmers, laborers, and townsmen dependent on rural customers. In past decades, such calamities had engendered merely despair or sporadic Whiteboyism; since the Famine, however, increased literacy, rural-urban contacts, and, not least, the grass-roots activities of neo-Fenians, such as Matthew Harris and Thomas Brennan in Connaught, had laid the foundations for a radical politicization of tenant grievances. However, the key organizational initiatives came from John Devoy and Michael Davitt, both of whom had spent years in prison for Fenian activities during the 1860s. On his release in 1871, Devoy had emigrated to New York City, and assumed leadership of the Clan na Gael, or United Brotherhood, an extreme nationalist society linked to the IRB and designed to supplant the squabbling remnants of American Fenianism. Devoy himself was a "pure" physical-force nationalist who scorned parliamentary politics and subordinated social issues to the winning of independence. However, responding both to news of Irish distress and to competition for emigrant loyalties from the more socially radical Irish-American journalist Patrick Ford, Devoy shrewdly concluded that agrarianism and home rule could serve as stalking-horses for revolution, and that Irish tenants' and Irish emigrants' hatred of landlordism, if properly mobilized and led, could provide the mass base for ultimate insurrection which the IRB and Clan currently lacked. Davitt was the son of poor Mayo cottiers who fled to England during the Famine; radicalized by his experiences in Lancashire factories (he lost an arm in a mill accident), Davitt joined the Fenians and spent most of the 1870s in British prisons. On his release in 1877, Davitt toured Connaught to familiarize himself with rural conditions and then traveled to the United States under Clan na Gael auspices. Together Devoy and Davitt worked out what became known as the New Departure, a proposed alliance between physical-force nationalism on both sides of the Atlantic, agrarianism, and Parnell's wing of the Home Rule party. Under its terms, Irish-American money would support tenant resistance to evictions and create a mass organization which, under IRB guidance, would demand such radical changes in the land system—the abolition of landlordism to create a peasant proprietary—that the anticipated British rejection and attempts at coercion would create a revolutionary situation. Ideally, Parnell would at that point demand home rule, withdraw from Parliament when refused, and establish in Dublin an Irish government which an organized populace would defend with arms shipped from the United States. To begin the work, Davitt returned to Ireland and in 1879 established the Land League of Mayo, which by October evolved into the Irish National Land League. Supplied with Irish-American money and propaganda, the league mobilized rural discontent into the Land War which convulsed the Irish countryside through early 1882.

By many standards, the Land League and the Land War were resounding successes: they mobilized and politicized rural Ireland to an unprecedented degree, enlisting remote regions and submerged classes to an extent never achieved by O'Connell or the IRB, and laid both the emotional and the institutional foundations of an independent Irish Catholic state. However, they did not achieve the New Departure's envisioned aims. Devoy had assumed that the demand for peasant proprietorship would lead inevitably to revolution, so sure was he that the British government would never grant it. However, while peasant proprietorship, the abolition of landlordism, was an evocative slogan for embittered Famine emigrants in America, it compelled much less than universal enthusiasm in Ireland, where specific remedies for rural grievances evolved pragmatically from widely varying material interests and local conditions. For example, farm laborers, disinherited farmers' sons, and many smallholders in Connaught, the north midlands, and elsewhere realized that without land redistribution—especially of the large grazing ranches—tenant ownership would merely perpetuate existing injustices. Consequently, some Land League spokesmen, especially in Connaught, where neo-Fenian influence was strongest, fulminated against graziers and land speculators more vehemently than they attacked landlordism. Michael Davitt soon went even further: not only did he estrange Devoy by subordinating revolutionary goals to social issues but, influenced by Patrick Ford and by Henry George's *Progress and Poverty* (1879), he began to champion land nationalization as a radical alternative to merely transferring the soil to a new set of petty landlords. At the other end of the social spectrum, peasant proprietorship was even more unappealing to strong farmers and graziers in less distressed regions of Munster and Leinster. More affluent and cautious than their western brethren, feeling threatened by assaults from below, these classes were more than willing to settle for legalized tenant-right and reduced rents, and had little taste for ultimate confrontation with Britain. As a result, they joined the Land League hesitantly and pragmatically, more to deflect popular criticism, influence league policies, and share in its benefits than out of commitment to radical ends.

Significantly, in their conservatism the strong farmers found allies in both Parnell and the Catholic clergy. Despite his sincere detestation of England, Parnell remained a constitutional nationalist. Although differing from Butt in his willingness to harness radical forces to the home rule chariot, and although more than willing to accept and even stimulate Irish-American contributions by promising to break Ireland's "last link" with Britain, Parnell never endorsed the New Departure and, in fact, abhorred even the Land League's agrarian violence, much more the prospect of revolution. Moreover, despite his occasional gestures toward land redistribution and his real contempt for the Catholic bourgeoisie, Parnell remained a social conservative who naïvely hoped that, once tenant ownership diffused rural class warfare, landlords such as he could resume paternalistic roles and guide Ireland to self-government. However, Parnell was playing a dangerous game, for although nominal leader of the Land League and (since 1880) chairman of the Home Rule party, he could not control the turbulent forces loose in the countryside. Consequently, and despite his personal distaste for "priests in politics," he encouraged the church to participate in the Land League, both to help enlist the reticent strong farmers and to serve as a counterweight to the neo-Fenians and the more radical demands of the dispossessed. Although Cardinal Cullen had died in 1878, many bishops—as well as the Vatican—still opposed both home rule and the Land League. However, most parish priests and younger bishops such as Croke recognized the dangers of opposition and joined the agitation to guide the movement and so "keep the godless nobodies in their place," as Bishop McEvilly of Galway delicately put it.

As a result of these accretions of support, the Land League became a national movement, at least outside east Ulster, where Orangemen condemned it as a Trojan horse for home rule. However, the unity of radical purpose which Devoy had desired was lost. League leaders vacillated between policies to help evicted peasants and measures designed to benefit strong farmers, and when Gladstone persuaded Parliament to pass the 1881 Land Act, thousands of tenants deserted the league and flocked to the new land courts to seek rent reductions. Parnell now faced a dilemma: the Land Act stopped far short of peasant proprietorship and did nothing for leaseholders, for farmers in arrears, or for already evicted tenants; radicals at home and abroad demanded he reject it, while strong farmers and

Catholic clerics demanded he accept it and call off the Land War. Fortunately for Parnell, Gladstone's government arrested him, thereby conferring martyrdom, and embarked on a ruthless campaign to crush the league through coercion, thereby relieving Parnell of the necessity to disband it. From prison, Parnell basically reached a compromise with Gladstone, the so-called Kilmainham treaty of 1882: Parnell agreed to quell the remaining agitation in return for Gladstone's promise to suspend coercion, release political prisoners, and pass an amending act to relieve the tenants in arrears (the 1882 Arrears Act). Both sides abided by the agreement, and by the middle of the year the Land War was over.

The Kilmainham treaty bitterly disappointed Davitt and league officials in Connaught, but the mid-1882 assassinations in Dublin of the Irish chief secretary and under secretary by the Invincibles, an IRB splinter group, discredited physical-force nationalism, drove the IRB back underground, and ensured Parnell's continued ascendancy. In 1883 Parnell established a new organization, the Irish National League: although based on the Land League's infrastructure, the INL was merely an electoral machine for the Irish Parliamentary party (IPP), and its major goal was home rule, not land reform. Whereas the Land League had been uncontrollably democratic, the INL was highly centralized and authoritarian, dominated by Parnell and the other party leaders, most notably John Dillon, Tim Healy, and William O'Brien. The party itself was tightly disciplined: a façade of popular selection at county conventions masked the fact that the party elite carefully screened and chose parliamentary candidates, who were required to take oaths of absolute allegiance to IPP directives in return for subvention from party funds, largely collected through the INL's affiliated organizations in North America, Australia, and Britain. Some nationalists chafed under party discipline, but the results were unquestionable. In 1885 Parliament enfranchised a majority of Irish adult males, and in that year's general election the IPP won eighty-six seats—a formidable voting bloc in a legislature often closely divided between Liberals and Conservatives. In a sense, the INL/IPP already constituted a political framework for an independent Irish state, now dominated by the Catholic bourgeoisie who rode to power under Parnell. Of the new party MPs, most came from the ranks of strong farmers, shopkeepers, traders, and the lower professions; simultaneously, representatives of the same classes conquered the Poor Law boards of guardians under the home rule banner. In short, outside Ulster the Protestant Ascendancy had finally lost political control of Ireland.

However, if dead politically, Irish landlordism was still alive economically, and so Parnell and the INL/IPP could hardly disavow further land reforms, especially when another run of poor harvests and falling prices afflicted the countryside in the mid-1880s. Nevertheless, by formulating the so-called Plan of Campaign—a scheme by which farmers would refuse rents and instead place the money in escrow to aid evicted tenants—Dillon, O'Brien, and other IPP leaders ensured that henceforth the party would control agrarian agitation and gain popular credit whether the government responded with coercion or, as in 1887, with a new Land Act which granted further rent reductions and admitted leaseholders to the land courts. Moreover, Parnell both counterbalanced agrarianism and sacralized his embryo state by making what amounted to a formal concordat with the Catholic hierarchy. In effect, the bishops—led by Croke and the new archbishop of Dublin, William J. Walsh—embraced Irish nationalism and disavowed the Vatican's policy of conciliating England. In return, the IPP promoted church interests—especially educational—at Westminster and allowed substantial clerical influence over the selection of its parliamentary candidates and local INL officials. Consequently, in 1888 when Pope Leo XIII condemned the Plan of Campaign at England's behest, the bishops—although themselves less than enthusiastic over agrarian conflict—ignored the papal rescript, preferring to maintain the nationalist alliance rather than risk alienating their parishioners. Finally, since Parnell's ultimate goal was Irish self-government, the capstone of his policy was Gladstone's celebrated conversion to that aim and his subsequent introduction of the first home rule bill. The 1886 bill failed to pass the House of Commons and caused serious defections from the Liberal ranks. However, for the first time a British party had endorsed the principle of Irish nationalism, and it seemed likely that the Liberal-IPP alliance would ultimately prevail.

In 1889 Parnell seemed triumphant, but the very extent of his successes boded ill for the future. Despite Parnell's immense popularity as Ireland's "uncrowned king," his diverse constituencies strained under his coldly imperious sway. Socially minded politicians resented his disdain for agrarianism and trade unions, while neither the church nor the Catholic bourgeoisie was comfortable with Parnell's Protestantism and gentry antecedents; moreover, some bishops chafed at their subsidiary role in the nationalist-clerical alliance, and feared the IPP-Liberal compact threatened to corrupt the party and Catholic society generally through too close an association with "alien" interests and values. Indeed, Parnell's "union of hearts" with Gladstone had several unhappy consequences. Gladstone's embrace of home rule not only split the English Liberals but also destroyed his party's credibility in Ulster, where it had formerly served as a moderate alternative to Orange militancy. Thereafter, Irish political life was almost entirely divided on sectarian lines, as Ulster Protestants of all backgrounds united in militant, organized opposition to a home rule which, they feared, presaged Catholic domination. Their intransigence was encouraged by Conservative party leaders such as Randolph Churchill, who in 1886 urged Ulstermen to "fight" rather than accept "Rome rule." Strengthened by Liberal defections, the Conservative party itself formally changed its name to Unionist, thereby symbolizing its alliance with Protestant Ulster in defense of the empire. These portentous developments, although blithely ignored by most nationalists, severely weakened their chances for ultimate success. More immediately, the IPP-Liberal compact also circumscribed Parnell's freedom of action, for the union of hearts had effectively reduced Irish nationalism to a position dependent on Gladstone and British Liberal opinion. This weakness became dramatically evident in 1890–91, when Parnell was destroyed by the very forces he had created. In November 1890 Parnell's long-standing, adulterous relationship with Katharine O'Shea became public knowledge as the result of a divorce suit by her estranged husband, a former Irish party MP. Initial Irish reaction was muted, but the Liberal party's powerful nonconformist constituency in Britain obliged Gladstone to demand that Parnell resign his Irish party chairmanship or forfeit the Liberal alliance. On December 6, after a week of acrimonious debate, Irish party MPs removed Parnell from leadership. However, Parnell refused to accept demotion, rallied a loyal minority of MPs, and appealed to the country in a series of parliamentary by-elections which ranged Parnellite and anti-Parnellite candidates in bitter opposition. Parnell posed the question in nationalist terms, accused his opponents of subservience to England, and made overtures to the IRB and to social groups, such as trade unionists and farm laborers, which formerly he had largely ignored. However, his opponents made telling use of the moral issue, received overwhelming support from Catholic clergy and the strong-farmer/shopkeeper classes, and crushed Parnell's candidates in campaigns marred by violence and intimidation.

Parnell ruined his health campaigning and died in late 1891, but the Irish Parliamentary party remained divided between an anti-Parnellite majority and a Parnellite minority for the rest of the decade. Not even Gladstone's introduction of a second home rule bill in 1893 brought the warring factions together, and when the House of Lords vetoed the bill after it passed the Commons, public disenchantment with Irish politics became acute and Irish-American contributions almost evaporated. Even within the anti-Parnellite majority, discipline vanished in a welter of rivalries for leadership (eventually won by John Dillon), and real power devolved to constituency levels where local elites and clerical influence held sway. By 1897 the situation was desperate: the Liberals were out of power and the post-Gladstone leadership was indifferent to home rule; the Unionist government was striving with some success to kill the demand for home rule through ameliorative legislation, such as the Congested Districts Act; the Catholic bishops were distant and domineering; and Irish party coffers were virtually empty. However, in 1898–1900 the home rule movement's fortunes revived dramatically. The centenary of the 1798 rebellion and popular opposition to Britain's imperialist role in the Boer War (1899–1902) gave Irish politicians new opportunities to posture and lead. Also, the Local Government Act of 1898 created a host of elective offices and patronage possibilities on which the party faithful could fatten while awaiting the greater but illusive rewards promised by home rule. In addition, increasingly bitter Protestant-Catholic relations in northern Ireland helped stimulate the rise of the Belfast politician Joe Devlin's Ancient Order of Hibernians (Board of Erin), a sectarian-nationalist outgrowth of the old Ribbon lodges and later a highly effective, if somewhat thuggish, grass-roots electoral machine for the Irish party. Last but most important were William O'Brien's successful efforts to revive constitutional nationalism through reunion with agrarian grievances, especially those of Connaught smallholders, farmers' noninheriting sons, and landless laborers. In 1898 O'Brien launched the United Irish League, ostensibly to agitate for peasant proprietorship and the breakup and redistribution of the grazing ranches, but in reality to provide a popular basis for a rejuvenated home rule movement. The strategy worked, although not quite as O'Brien envisioned. Tired of strife and fearful of the UIL's growing popularity, the two Irish party factions reunited in 1900 and successfully co-opted O'Brien's creation as the party's new electoral organization. John Redmond, the former Parnellite leader, became chairman of both the reconstituted IPP and the UIL, and henceforth—as in Parnell's day—agrarianism was largely manipulated to the party's advantage: sometimes encouraged, as in 1900–3 when the Unionists were in power, to create fresh martyrs, incite public indignation against the government, and stimulate Irish-American contributions; at other times sharply curtailed, as after 1906 when the Liberals took office, to conciliate British opinion for home rule's sake.

Thus, after 1900 the Irish Parliamentary party seemingly recovered its former authority and promise. Once again the IPP constituted a formidable political machine, virtually unbeatable outside Ulster, and the party's elite—primarily Redmond, Dillon, and Devlin—reimposed strict discipline on back-bench MPs and local constituencies. The working alliance between party and church was resumed, and in 1908 Parliament finally satisfied the bishops' educational goals by creating a church-controlled Irish university. In addition, the party benefited from popular acclaim for the 1903 Wyndham Act, which established the financial basis for wholesale land purchase by tenants. Most important, a united Irish party was again in position to demand home rule as the price of Liberal alliance whenever the Liberals found themselves dependent on Irish votes. In 1906 the Liberals regained control of Parliament, but their majority was so huge that the leadership offered only a "devolution" scheme of expanded local government, which Redmond rejected. However, Redmond's opportunity came in 1909 when the Unionist majority in the House of Lords violated constitutional precedent and rejected Chancellor of the Exchequer David Lloyd George's "people's budget," which imposed high income, inheritance, and land taxes to finance old-age pensions and health, unemployment, and employer's liability insurance. Determined to break the Lords' veto power, the Liberals appealed to the country, but after two general elections in 1910 the Liberals and Unionists had exactly 273 seats apiece. The IPP now held the balance of power, and Redmond demanded that Prime Minister Henry Asquith, a Liberal, both reform the House of Lords and legislate home rule in return for Irish support. Accordingly, in 1911 Parliament limited the Lords' veto to a suspensory power of two years, and in early 1913 the government passed the third home rule bill. The degree of self-government thereby granted Ireland was very limited: Britain retained control of police and tax collection; the proposed Irish legislature had a government-appointed senate and was forbidden to conduct foreign policy, impose tariffs, or legislate in religious matters. Moreover, the Lords' veto ensured the act's suspension for two years. Nevertheless, immediate reaction in Catholic Ireland was ecstatic, and it seemed that both the Irish party and the principle of constitutional nationalism had triumphed.

However, Redmond's victory proved hollow, in large measure because of Unionist intransigence and Liberal pusillanimity, but also because the Irish party itself had already lost the loyalty of much of the Catholic population. Dominated by an aging leadership, absorbed in the details and perquisites of Westminster politics, lulled into a sense of false security by its near-automatic election victories in southern Ireland, the IPP had largely ignored or opposed the social and cultural issues which had captured the younger generation's attention. Concentrating entirely on the political question of home rule, the party had paid only superficial heed to the larger question of the future *nature* of Irish society once self-government was won. Prior to 1890 Parnell's commanding personality and the immediacy and intensity of the agrarian struggle had largely obscured these issues; however, Parnell's fall and the abatement of rural distress and agitation had produced a vacuum which allowed other questions and interests to compete for hegemony.

For example, both the Catholic church and the "Irish-Ireland" movement were determined to create a society distinctly and oppositionally "Irish" in reaction against what bishops and journalists such as D. P. Moran perceived as crassly utilitarian and demoralizing English influences. Churchmen wanted a "holy Ireland," rooted in an unquestioning Catholic faith and an idealized peasant-family system which would safeguard the nascent state's morality and social stability. Hence their determined opposition to secularism, materialism, class conflict, and especially "godless" socialism, all stigmatized as English imports. Hence, also, their desire to control and shape Catholic education; their struggle to dominate the Gaelic Athletic Association, the Gaelic League, and other sociocultural organizations; and their efforts to inculcate sobriety and morality among Ireland's future voters and leaders through societies such as the Pioneer Total Abstinence Association. Because of their vision of what Ireland should be, the bishops' relations with the Irish party grew increasingly tense. While churchmen supported home rule as a means of insulating Ireland from pernicious Albion, many never fully trusted the IPP—believing it tainted by association with British liberalism—and so systematically undermined its credibility with the pious, repeatedly accusing it of "selling-out" to expediency or Unionist pressure. In fact, however, the IPP's usual subservience to church interests not only alienated many young nationalists who defined "Irishness" in other than exclusively religious terms but also torpedoed party leaders' efforts to reach compromises with Ulster Protestants which might have prevented future bloodshed and partition.

"Irish-Ireland" was a generic term, coined by D. P. Moran, which characterized a broad and diverse movement to expunge English influences and reconstruct Irish society and culture on traditional bases. Its quintessential expression was the Gaelic League, founded in 1893 by the Gaelic scholars Eoin MacNeill and Douglas Hyde and dedicated to restoring Irish as the national vernacular; in the early twentieth century the league grew spectacularly, from 107 branches in 1899 to nearly 400 by 1902. Although most Irish-Irelanders were young, middle-class townsmen, primarily in eastern and southeastern Ireland, they idealized a sanitized vision of the western peasant as the prototypical citizen of the future Ireland. However, they often applauded "pagan" aspects of peasant society which conflicted with clerical ideals. Indeed, Irish-Ireland was extremely vague and inclusive, and its adherents ranged from conservative clerics and businessmen who hoped the Irish language would insulate Catholics from secularism and socialism, to Anglo-Irish writers such as W. B. Yeats who wanted to weave Gaelic traditions into an inclusive, nonsectarian nationalism, to revolutionaries such as Patrick Pearse who hoped Ireland's youth would emulate the martial deeds of legendary Celtic heroes, and to social radicals such as George Russell and W. P. Ryan who dreamed of translating Gaelic society's communitarian ethos into a program of social reform. At times, Irish-Irelanders clashed bitterly with churchmen over control of local Gaelic League branches and over Irish-language instruction in the schools. However, both were similar in their moral absolutism, disdain for "mere politics," and contempt for the Irish Parliamentary party. Indeed, the Gaelic League, like the Gaelic Athletic Association, served as a sort of "school" for many of the young nationalists who overthrew the IPP after 1916.

The Irish party also faced challenges on economic and political fronts. Although local UIL elites tied into the Wyndham Act's land purchase arrangements—making league membership and party loyalty helpful, if not indispensable, for aspiring farm owners—the IPP's neglect of agrarian grievances after 1906 alienated the land poor and the landless. For example, the party virtually ignored the antigrazier "Ranch War" of 1906–8, thereby forfeiting popular affection in west Munster, east Connaught, and other areas which later became hotbeds of physical-force nationalism. Moreover, while the party at least gave lip service to its agrarian traditions, it paid little or no attention to urban working-class conditions and opposed trade unions which it could not co-opt. James Connolly's socialist movement and his and James Larkin's Irish Transport and General Workers' Union were anathema to the party's bourgeois leaders, who regarded the great Dublin strike of 1913 as an intolerable diversion of public attention from home rule. Although most urban workers remained staunch nationalists, as did even their most radical leaders such as Connolly, the IPP's indifference to their plight made them highly receptive to more extreme forms of political activity. A more significant threat than the nascent labor movement was Arthur Griffith's Sinn Féin, a loose-knit propagandist organization which combined political, economic, and cultural themes into a thorough critique of IPP strategy and Irish society generally. Sinn Féin was the most prominent of several associations which Griffith, a Dublin journalist, founded in the early twentieth century. Its name, roughly translated as "ourselves alone," reflected Irish-Ireland's general conviction that Irish society and particularly the IPP were too dependent on England. Griffith elaborated that idea into a specific political and economic program, demanding that Irish MPs withdraw unilaterally from Westminster and, after passive resistance overcame British opposition, establish an independent (or autonomous—Griffith wavered between republican and dual-monarchist models) government whose primary duty would be the creation of a self-sufficient, industrialized economy behind high protective tariffs. Griffith abhorred socialism, and his was essentially a petty-bourgeois vision of corporate state capitalism; however, at least Sinn Féin was concerned about urban problems, and so got fair support from Dublin's skilled workers and captured several town corporation and county council seats. Prior to 1916 Sinn Féin never constituted a serious threat to Irish party rule, but as the only extant political alternative it benefited immeasurably from the IPP's subsequent dishonor and disintegration. Ultimately, the greatest challenge to the Irish party came from the "pure" physical-force nationalists of the Irish Republican Brotherhood. After languishing for decades, the IRB was after 1900 reorganized and reinvigorated by Thomas Clarke, a veteran of English prisons and master conspirator, and it soon attracted some of the most vigorous and idealistic of Ireland's younger generation, men such as Patrick Pearse and Sean MacDermott who were disillusioned by parliamentarianism and by what they perceived as an Anglicized and morally corrupt society which could be redeemed only through bloody revolution. By 1913 the IRB had successfully infiltrated the Gaelic League, the Gaelic Athletic Association, and Sinn Féin and linked arms with Dublin's small Irish Citizen Army, which James Connolly had formed to protect striking workers against policemen and company thugs.

Nevertheless, the IRB numbered only about 1,500 men, and all the various criticisms and challenges from bishops and dissident nationalists together could not have shaken the IPP's grip on the country had it not been for developments which the party could not control or, in some cases, even foresee. The Home Rule Act's suspension alone was bound to cause the party embarrassment, for it gave Griffith and other critics two years to expose its inadequacies. Far more serious, however, was Protestant Ulster's adamant refusal to accept Parliament's decision. Under the leadership of Edward Carson and James Craig, the Ulster Unionist Council and the Orange Order obtained 471,000 Protestants' signatures to a "Solemn League and Covenant" which pledged them to use force, if need be, to resist home rule. Carson then created a shadow government, raised an army of Ulster Volunteers, and began smuggling arms from Germany. British Unionists, ordinarily staunch defenders of law and order, rallied to Carson's support, in part out of genuine concern for the empire's integrity, in part to discredit the reforming Liberal administration. Meanwhile, the Liberals' loyalty to their Irish party allies crumbled, especially when it became evident that the

British army was totally unreliable in the crisis, so sympathetic were its officers to Ulster unionism. In November 1913, correctly perceiving that peaceful implementation of home rule was impossible, the IRB and other physical-force nationalists created their own armed force, the Irish Volunteers, as a counterweight to Unionist militancy. Irish party leaders, their hard-won victory slipping from their grasp, quickly co-opted the Irish Volunteers, both to dilute IRB influence and to strengthen Redmond's hand in negotiations with Carson and the vacillating liberals. Carson, a Dubliner who hoped to save all Ireland from home rule, made impossible demands, primarily the exclusion of all nine Ulster counties from Dublin's rule. Redmond was willing to countenance temporary exclusion, but not of all Ulster, and when World War I broke out, in mid-1914, civil war over home rule seemed imminent.

England's entry into the European war produced a face-saving compromise: home rule became law to satisfy Irish nationalists, but it was suspended for the war's duration to appease Ulster Unionists. However, Redmond then made the gravest mistake of his political career: before Parliament he pledged Ireland's total support in the war against Germany and offered the Irish Volunteers for service overseas. Immediately, about 12,000 IRB-led Volunteers, largely from midland and western counties, refused to fight for England. Moreover, although at first most Catholic laymen and clerics supported Redmond's prowar policy, and although Britain's demand for Irish foodstuffs and soldiers brought rural prosperity and full employment, by early 1916 many Irishmen were thoroughly disenchanted with both the war and the Irish party's involvement. The carnage alone was appalling, but in addition the British army demonstrated systematic disdain for Irish Catholic recruits, and when Asquith invited Carson and other implacable Unionists to join a coalition government, it seemed that the Irish were being asked to die for their bitterest enemies. By late 1915, Irish enlistments had declined significantly, and even bishops were heaping scorn on the IPP and its much-vaunted nonaccomplishment—home rule. However, the fatal stroke to both the Irish party and constitutional nationalism came without warning. On Easter Monday 1916 a force of 1,500 IRB-led Irish Volunteers and Citizen Army members—commanded by Patrick Pearse, James Connolly, and Thomas Clarke—seized the center of Dublin and proclaimed the establishment of an Irish republic. The rebellion lasted only six days, and at first the Catholic clergy and most laymen joined Redmond and other IPP spokesmen in condemning it. However, summary British executions of Pearse, Connolly, and thirteen other participants, plus the imposition of harsh martial law and the arrest and transportation to English prisons of over 2,000 Sinn Féiners and other nationalists, many of them innocent, caused a dramatic reversal of public opinion. By the time Lloyd George, now prime minister, released the internees in early 1917, Pearse and his fellow rebels had been publicly canonized as the latest martyrs to British tyranny, and those who now returned from prison—especially Eamon de Valera, the only Easter-rising commandant to escape execution—were acclaimed as heroes. Arthur Griffith, who had also been interned (in his case, unjustly), turned Sinn Féin over to de Valera's leadership; consequently, Sinn Féin became the Irish Volunteers' political organization, and its candidates proceeded to rout the Irish party in a series of by-elections. Redmond's desperate efforts to secure immediate implementation of home rule foundered on the rocks of Lloyd George's duplicity and the issue of partition; indeed, his futile attempts at compromise only further alienated public opinion, and by the war's end Redmond was dead and his party fast disintegrating as both bishops and former adherents, out of sincerity or expediency, concluded that Sinn Féin represented the future of Irish nationalist politics.

In the December 1918 general election, Sinn Féin captured nearly the whole of southern Ireland, although its strength was greatest among young voters and in the western half of the island. Following Griffith's policy, the successful Sinn Féin candidates refused to go to Westminster and instead assembled in Dublin, where they formed a parliament called Dáil Éireann and began to rule Ireland in the name of the republic founded by Pearse on Easter Monday. De Valera, the republic's nominal president, embarked for the United States to raise funds and solicit diplomatic recognition. Meanwhile, the IRB leader Michael Collins, who emerged as the nascent republic's dominant figure, melded the Irish Volunteers and the IRB into a new fighting force, the Irish Republican Army. Although the Dáil vainly hoped to win Irish independence at the Versailles peace conference, by early 1919 the IRA was engaged in full-scale guerrilla warfare with the British army and later with the "Black and Tans," ex-British soldiers recruited as police auxiliaries, who became infamous for their vicious reprisals on civilians. The Anglo-Irish war quickly deteriorated into what one participant called "a lawless and savage duel between rage and revenge." Indeed, not only did sectarian murders become rampant in several parts of the island but the conflict also exposed the countryside's hitherto-suppressed social and factional conflicts. For example, in parts of Munster, Connaught, and north Leinster, where IRA forces were strongest, the land poor and the landless began seizing and redistributing the holdings of strong farmers and graziers deemed "disloyal" to the republic. In fact, those accusations were often correct, but such pressures from below only hastened the propertied classes' conversion to republicanism, and so Sinn Féin soon became as bourgeois and socially conservative as its predecessors, moving swiftly and effectively to check its poorer followers' agrarian impulses.

Despite its bravery the IRA could not defeat the British army, yet despite its superior resources the British government could not crush the IRA, at least not without further inflaming an already-hostile world opinion. Consequently, by mid-1921 both sides were ready for peace talks. In December, after months of agonizing negotiations with Lloyd George in London, Collins, Griffith, and other Dáil representatives signed a treaty which established the Irish Free State, with dominion status similar to that enjoyed by Canada and other self-governing former colonies. However, the new state included only twenty-six of Ireland's counties; the other six counties, all in Ulster, remained an integral part of the United Kingdom, but with their own parliament to legislate local matters and ensure Protestant domination of the region's unhappy Catholic minority. Despite partition and its denial of the republican dream, the treaty's terms were perhaps the best that Catholic Ireland could hope for. Irish bishops, who had never been keen about an Irish republic containing Ulster Protestants, eagerly endorsed it, as did the propertied classes and all those weary of war. However, the treaty occasioned bitter debates in the Dáil, and a minority led by de Valera refused to accept anything less than Pearse's republic. The IRA quickly split between pro- and antitreaty forces; negotiations between the two sides broke down; and from June 1922 to May 1923 Ireland was convulsed by civil war. Despite the purely political rhetoric employed by both sides—Irish Free State versus Irish republic—again there was a covert social dimension to the conflict. To the propertied classes and clergy, the Free State represented order and security; while to the rural poor, especially in Connaught and west Munster, where the antitreaty forces were strongest, the idealized republic seemed to represent their last chance to realize their material aspirations at the bourgeoisie's expense. If chance it was, however, it was lost when de Valera ordered his weary troops to surrender. The conflict over, Catholic Ireland had finally become what one wag called "three-quarters of a nation once again."

After de Valera's surrender the more or less obligatory departures overseas of several thousand defeated republicans gave immediate notice that even the achievement of most nationalists' political goals would not halt emigration. More disconcerting evidence came later in the century—for example, between 1946 and 1961, when more than half a million people left the country, bound mostly for England. Likewise, during the post-Famine period itself nationalist agitation had actually stimulated emigration: not only by reinforcing general modernizing and Anglicizing trends, as was explained in the preceding section, but also by dividing the population along political and sectarian lines, thus creating small but significant streams of refugees from parts of the island where minority status became untenable. Such division was particularly evident in northern Ireland, where, as was noted earlier, emigration patterns in 1861–1911 largely prefigured the island's eventual partition. Although the Land League made great efforts to attract Protestant tenants in the Ulster border counties, ironically the league's very success in legalizing tenant-right removed Protestant farmers' last major grievance against the Ascendancy, while Parnell's subsequent emphasis on home rule ratified Orange warnings of a "papist" conspiracy. Similarly, R. Lindsay Crawford's later attempt to transform his Independent Orange movement into a nonsectarian, working-class alliance foundered on the rocks of religious tribalism, and Crawford himself felt obliged to emigrate to Canada. Meanwhile, Protestants left the three southern provinces in disproportionate numbers, in part out of fear of the Catholic majority. In the mid-1860s the threat of Fenianism made Protestants such as John Griffin of west Clare feel very "unsafe"— "at the mercy . . . of the ignorant peasantry should a rising take place"— and by the early twentieth century a southern Unionist reported a general "process of squeezing out Protestants . . . by a system of gentle boycott." Indeed, between 1919 and 1923 that process was far from gentle as some southern Catholics, under the pretext of patriotism, launched mini-pogroms seemingly designed to erase the Protestant presence; as one Cork-woman rejoiced, "every Protestant church in the county has been burned down, Thanks be to God." Partly as a result of such persecution, between 1911 and 1926 the Protestant population of what became the Irish Free State fell by nearly a third (compared with a 2 percent Catholic decline) as large numbers migrated to Northern Ireland or emigrated to England, Canada, and elsewhere in the empire. Ironically, many of the displaced felt the loss of their homeland as keenly as any earlier Catholic rebel and "still look[ed] back on the country with deep affection": "for we exiles who have been driven to cast anchor in . . . English havens," lamented one former royal official, "there seems little prospect of a return to the land of our birth. Ireland for us is the Isle of Long Ago."[124]

Nevertheless, since neither the efforts nor the achievements of Irish nationalists halted emigration, the crucial question remains, How did they "explain" that phenomenon? With respect to that issue, some basic patterns emerge from post-Famine Ireland's complex political history. First, with few exceptions, such as James Connolly's Irish Socialist Republican party, Irish nationalist organizations reflected primarily the aspirations of middle-class Catholic farmers and townsmen. Even ostensibly "peasant" movements, such as the Land League, were solidly bourgeois in leadership, bureaucratic structure, and specific political goals. Second, however, such organizations could not achieve the mass base necessary for either electoral or martial success without strong support from disadvantaged social groups—land-hungry smallholders, farmers' disinherited sons, artisans, rural and urban laborers. Third, in order to mobilize that support, it was necessary for middle-class nationalists to persuade the disadvantaged that their economic problems would be solved through the achievement of some form of self-government, a task facilitated by Catholics' customary attribution of mundane sufferings to English oppression. Fourth, nevertheless, at some point in the history of nearly every nationalist movement, it became obvious that bourgeois and "peasant" or proletarian material interests, economic ideologies, and political goals were in fact antithetical. At that point the disadvantaged felt "betrayed" or "abandoned" by their middle-class leaders, at least until the next round of agitation or until a new, purportedly more "sincere" and "extreme" nationalist organization arose to capitalize on lower-class disenchantment with its predecessors. However, the immediate results of each successive movement were the same—disillusionment and internecine conflict, epitomized by the 1922–23 civil war. Fifth, in

order to mitigate, obscure, and postpone such conflicts, bourgeois nationalists had to utilize traditional rhetoric and techniques of social control which
reinforced customary Catholic tribalism. In this sense, an alliance with the
Catholic church was essential, despite the fact that such an alliance imposed certain tactical and ideological constraints on middle- as well as
lower-class nationalists. Thus, in its uneasy syntheses of the secular and
spiritual, modern and traditional, and of divergent social interests and outlooks, Catholic nationalism mirrored the tensions within Catholic society.
No wonder, then, that Catholic Ireland's "official" spokesmen, lay and
clerical, characterized or "explained" post-Famine emigration in very contradictory ways as they groped for resolutions of their society's internal
paradoxes and conflicts.

A few Catholic leaders were sufficiently realistic to acknowledge that
their people's "irredeemable poverty" made at least some emigration "absolutely necessary." For example, although Bishop Duggan of Clonfert
prophesied that emigration would "ruin" Ireland, he admitted that "for
the individual himself . . . it may be a blessing." "What prospect of anything but misery have these emigrants if they stay in Ireland?" asked a
parish priest in west Clare: emigration's "doctrinaire" opponents "have
never had the experience of living in a one room . . . cabin as a member
of a family of ten, and on a budget of some £20 a year," he charged. "If
they had they would be . . . in as much a hurry to seek a means of livelihood in America as the 1,500 Clare boys and girls that yearly rush to the
emigrant ship." "[I]f I were a working man," added Fr. Walter McDonald,
a Maynooth professor, "I should certainly leave for America. . . ." Thus,
many churchmen resigned themselves to their parishioners' departure and
merely tried to ensure the emigrants' physical and spiritual welfare, either
through personal ministrations or through agencies such as the Society of
St. Vincent de Paul and All Hallows College, Dublin, which prepared
priests for overseas service.[125]

However, emigration was too important a phenomenon to be treated
realistically or accepted with resignation. As the central experience of post-
Famine Irish life, it demanded interpretation in political and religious contexts. On the one hand, for example, Catholic spokesmen took great pride
in the emigrants' accomplishments and, when lauding the past and present
glories of "the Irish race," made sure to include the "nation beyond the
seas," the "Greater Ireland" of the diaspora, whose members had proven
what Irishmen could accomplish when unfettered by landlordism and
British oppression. Clerics were especially given to describing emigration as
divine "destiny": "God's hand is upon them," wrote one churchman, for,
like the sixth- and seventh-century Irish saints, contemporary emigrants
had a "holy mission" to spread inseparable Catholicism and Irishness to
distant lands. Thus, while England's overseas empire was merely temporal,
based on force and greed, the faithful, long-suffering Irish had created a
far greater "spiritual empire," which would endure forever. Even the socialist James Connolly could not resist the religious metaphor, although

clerics must have shuddered at his "hope that Irish apostles of Socialism will ere long be privileged to carry the message of that grander civilisation of the future to the masses lost in the dark ages of capitalist bondage."[126]

On the other hand, however, negative characterizations of emigration overwhelmingly predominated, and throughout the late nineteenth and early twentieth centuries Catholic clergymen and nationalists of all stripes were united in condemning emigration as an evil. For Ireland, emigration was seen as tragic because it deprived the island of its young men and women and threatened ultimate depopulation. As the result of emigration, declared one nationalist journal, "ruin was extending its dark arms all over the country," and "[o]nce populous districts scarcely now rejoice in the sound of a human voice." Churchmen such as Archbishop Croke also regarded emigration as "the greatest scourge in Irish rural life": "I am opposed to emigration for the sake of the general welfare of the country," testified Bishop Duggan; "it is a shame and a reproach to the country to see the bone and sinew going away from it." Likewise, critics also charged that emigration was tragic and potentially disastrous for the emigrants themselves. Clerics, especially, espoused this line of argument, at first primarily emphasizing the hazards of the transatlantic crossing and the poverty and physical dangers which awaited most emigrants in the New World. For example, the two most popular post-Famine emigrants' guidebooks, both written by Irish priests, warned of the "poverty, misery, and wretchedness" prevalent among Irish-Americans, and in 1860 Cardinal Cullen predicted that emigrants were likely to "find a watery grave upon the ocean, or to perish in the swamps of America"; "one-half of the workmen who left Ireland," he asserted, "were generally in their graves within twelve months after their arrival in America," while many of the rest ended their unhappy days in the poorhouse. As late as 1902, the Irish hierarchy's standing committee declared that it was "utterly reckless on the part of the vast majority of male emigrants to the United States and Canada to quit Ireland in the present state of the American labour market." Increasingly, however, churchmen went further and stigmatized the United States itself as a vicious, materialistic, "godless" society, which corrupted the emigrants' morals and destroyed their religious faith. According to priests such as Peter O'Leary, Joseph Guinan, and Patrick Sheehan, America was *"Tír Mhí-Nadúrtha"* (An Unnatural Land)—"a country that does not suit the nature of the Irish," where "there is no such thing as neighborliness," for "everyone . . . loves [only] money," and where "rosy-faced, fair young girls, so pure, so innocent, so pious," would be "dragged down to shame and crime, and to an early and a dishonoured grave." It were far better, urged many clergyymen, for Irish youth "to save their souls in Holy Ireland than to hazard them for this world's goods among American heretics"— better to endure "one meal a day of potatoes and salt in Ireland than face the sin and horrors of American city life"—for emigration was "a fate far worse than death—a fate compared with which the poverty, hunger and rags of an Irish hovel would be very heaven." From a radically different perspective, James Connolly basically agreed with clerical strictures, decried the United States as a crassly materialistic and selfishly individualistic society, and lamented the sad fate of those forced "to venture upon the cold world of capitalist America." Thus, in the early twentieth century churchmen and extreme nationalists combined to form an anti-emigration society, designed to discourage further departures.[127]

Nevertheless, although nationalists and clerics generally agreed that emigration was lamentable, they were very inconsistent in assigning blame for its prevalence. Some Catholic spokesmen charged that the emigrants themselves were culpable. The most charitable interpretation was that naïve Irish youths who "haven't any sense" were deluded by visionary fancies of America, often inspired by glowing, but false, accounts circulated by ticket brokers, letters, and returned emigrants. However, by the nineteenth century's last decades it was not unusual to condemn the emigrant as a "coward," "sordid churl," and "lucre-loving wretch that flees his land for greed," as Fanny Parnell charged in her Land League poem "Hold the Harvest," of 1880. "Let us plainly tell the emigrant that he is a traitor to the Irish State," declared Patrick Pearse in the Gaelic League journal *An Claidheamh Soluis:* "a large proportion of them . . . are deserters who have left their posts. . . ." Moreover, not only had Irish-Americans "abandoned" their homes for material gain but their "interest in Ireland is chiefly manifested in their efforts to induce the remnant of the population . . . to leave it." Thus, as another nationalist charged in 1910, "[e]migration is the most pleasant-seeming form of national treachery."[128]

Yet, despite these animadversions, it was far more common to blame emigration on landlordism and British oppression and to characterize the emigrants as sorrowing, vengeful "exiles." Richard O'Brien, archdeacon of the Limerick diocese, spoke for most Catholic clergymen when he declared in 1864 that English law and "mere brute force, compels us to work like slaves for unfeeling landlords, or to be expatriated like felons." According to priests such as Thomas Burke and Joseph Guinan, the emigrants were victims of religious persecution and of "tyrants who drove us from our happy home," while the emigrants themselves were consumed with "one absorbing passion, . . . their love for Ireland" and were "eating away their hearts with longing to set eyes again on the 'fair hills of holy Ireland,' and to breathe once more the peat-scented air of their native valleys." Likewise, in their speeches and public writings, nearly all nationalists characterized the exodus as "reluctant emigration" and described the emigrants as "exiles": "Our people have been exterminated by the robbers," declared a local speaker at a Mayo Land League meeting, echoing sentiments widely voiced by leaders like Parnell, Davitt, and Thomas Brennan. In the early twentieth century the exile theme was common in the popular historical dramas performed at the Gaelic League's *oireachtas* and *feiseanna,* or assemblies and festivals, and one of Arthur Griffith's avowed purposes was "[t]he rooting of the whole Irish people in Ireland, the weakening of every force and influence that tends to drive them into exile. . . ." Thus, the Irish in America were the "sea-divided Gael," mother Erin's exiled "children," as Patrick Pearse called them in 1916, and emigration would cease only when Ireland was independent and so able to provide prosperity and employment for all. "Ireland has resources to feed five times her population," Pearse—like all preceding nationalists—asserted; and "[a] free Ireland would not, and could not, have hunger in her fertile vales and squalor in her cities."[129]

Such contradictory attributions of blame for emigration reflected nationalists' and clerics' tortuous efforts to reconcile traditional social ideals and their own hegemonic imperatives with a social reality which violated those ideals and yet paradoxically both sustained and threatened that hegemony. On the one hand, many Catholic spokesmen realized that only massive lower-class emigration had created the relatively commercialized, urbanized, and bourgeois-dominated "New Ireland," which had been a precondition for the success of disciplined nationalist movements and the church's devotional revolution. For example, without wholesale emigration the consolidation of many strong farmers' and graziers' holdings would have been much more difficult, if not impossible, and these groups were vital support sources for both church and constitutional nationalism. Likewise, emigration stabilized the family farm, helped preclude overt social and generational conflicts over land, and prevented the subdivision and pauperization which had characterized the pre-Famine decades. In addition, Catholic spokesmen also understood that emigration brought specific material benefits to some key elements in Irish society as well as, they hoped, to the emigrants themselves. For instance, publicans and shopkeepers—usually vociferous nationalists—often profited from the selling of passage tickets, while much of the £1 million in annual remittances found its way to the retailers' coffers and the priests' collection boxes. During the post-Famine period, Catholic missionaries regularly visited the United States seeking alms from affluent emigrants for new churches and schools which their parishioners at home could not afford to build. Most important, Irish nationalists—both constitutional and physical-force—relied heavily on Irish-American contributions to finance party activities and insurrections. Michael Davitt estimated that in the last quarter of the nineteenth century Irishmen in the United States subscribed £500,-000 to the nationalist cause, and in 1900–1910 additional contributions probably totaled £70,000. Much of the money came regularly from Irish-American nationalist organizations, but a great deal resulted from special collecting missions; thus, in 1880 Parnell's tour of the United States netted the Land League some $200,000, and in 1910 a visit by Redmond and Devlin collected about £40,000. Even those nationalists who most vigorously denounced emigration and preached the virtue of "self-reliance" depended on overseas donations. Both Arthur Griffith and Patrick Pearse begged American money for their respective projects, and between 1913 and 1916 the Clan na Gael sent the IRB over $100,000 to help finance the Irish Volunteers and the Easter rising. Finally, in the years 1919–21 Irish-

Americans sent over £1 million to relieve Irish distress and subvent the Dáil's war against Britain. In short, then, Catholic clergymen and nationalists alike had good reasons to praise the emigrants and rationalize the exodus as the "Divine Mission of the Irish Race."[130]

However, Irish nationalists had to denounce emigration for other reasons. Emigration connoted depopulation, and ever since the early nineteenth century, when British economists had urged wholesale removal of Ireland's "surplus" inhabitants to rationalize agriculture, the question of Irish population had been charged with politics and emotion. Given the recent experiences of Famine clearances and of contemporary mass evictions, as in 1879–82, it was logical that Catholic spokesmen would equate emigration with "extermination" and vehemently deny British contentions that the reduction of post-Famine Ireland's population had brought real prosperity to the island. Moreover, emigration endangered nationalists' hopes for Ireland's future and threatened their efforts to oppose British power and Anglicizing influences. For example, the nationalists' proposed rejuvenation of the island's economy could not take place as long as potential entrepreneurs, workers, and purchasers of Irish goods fled overseas; strong farmers in Meath and elsewhere already complained of a dearth of laborers, and, as one witness lamented in 1885, "everyone who leaves the country is . . . a customer lost." Similarly, many Irish leaders feared that mass departures were undermining Catholic Ireland's religious and political bulwarks. In 1864 the bishop of Ardagh reported that "the effects of this state of things are becoming plainly visible in our Churches and Chapels & in the ruin of a large number of trading and mercantile classes in our principle towns." "Emigration will soon leave us . . . without any Catholic population at all," despaired the president of St. Colman's College, almost implying that the exodus was more a Protestant plot than an economic phenomenon. For their part, Unionists often accused Catholic clergymen of opposing emigration for selfish reasons, in order to prevent a "diminution of their 'dues' "; such accusations were typical, but in 1882 one priest admitted, "[S]urely we ought to be as anxious to preserve our dioceses as foreign bishops are to create theirs." Likewise, lay nationalists feared that emigration was a safety valve for discontent which otherwise could be mobilized against British rule. Thus, in 1920 the Dáil's minister of defense issued a manifesto warning that the British government was attempting to stimulate emigration and thereby weaken the national struggle: "The young men of Ireland must stand fast," he demanded. "To leave their country at this supreme crisis would be nothing less than base desertion in the face of the enemy." Finally, Catholic leaders were apprehensive lest emigration deprive them of political and religious influence over the emigrants, especially those who left home for "selfish," materialistic reasons. For example, one observer lamented that the emigrants of the 1880s did "not carry with them . . . one single reminder of their nationality, not a shamrock, not a ribbon, as if they were casting off all allegiance to the motherland." Similarly, most churchmen were deeply concerned about the danger of

apostasy or "spiritual ruin" among emigrants who became "lost to morality, to Society, to religion, and, finally to God."[131]

In short, their self-assumed roles as Ireland's champions obliged Catholic spokesmen to denounce emigration. As Bishop George Butler of Limerick put it in 1864, in a letter to fellow churchmen, "The depopulation
of our Country is progressing at an awful pace and *we must not appear to
be taking it too easy.*" To be sure, their opposition to emigration was sincere, and a surprisingly large number of post-Famine Ireland's prominent
men—including Parnell, John Dillon, Arthur Griffith, D. P. Moran, Thomas
Clarke, James Connolly, and the churchmen Thomas Croke, Patrick Sheehan, and Joseph Guinan—had spent considerable time abroad and had
either personally endured poverty, prejudice, or homesickness or were so
unfavorably impressed by Irish emigrant conditions that they returned
home determined to oppose emigration and mitigate its causes. Thus, after
a lengthy visit in 1871 Parnell concluded the United States was a "barbar-
ian country" and "expressed . . . vivid delight at being home again,"
while Father Guinan felt in "exile" during his mission to Liverpool's Irish
slums and "longed and sighed for the pure bracing air and green fields"
of "dear old Ireland." "I have seen the scattered children of our race in
almost every land that the sun shines upon," declared Archbishop Croke,
"and I have no hesitation whatever in saying that an Irishman's fittest and
happiest home is in Ireland."[132]

Nevertheless, Bishop Butler's private remark, made in response to Fenian attempts to capitalize on agrarian discontent, revealed a profound
ambiguity in the nationalist position. Bourgeois nationalists, whether con-
stitutionalist or physical-force, *had* to address emigration and its socioeconomic causes because those issues—not mere political abstractions—were
the ones which most concerned the discontented elements of Irish society
whose mass support the nationalists wanted and needed. As one observer
remarked on a visit to Connaught in 1880, "Very few [countrymen] . . .
seem to take any account of Home Rule. . . All [the peasant's] . . .
ideas are dominated by the single one of land. He knows and cares for very
little else." In 1892 another traveler heard similar sentiments from a north
midlands cottier: "My host's discourse was practical; he cared little for
theorizing. . . . He cared little for politics. A law that would give him a
bit of good ground cheap was all he cared about." In short, grass-roots
pressures forced nationalists to link political goals (repeal, home rule, republic) to practical aspirations, more specifically to promises of fundamental socioeconomic changes which would obviate the need for mass emigration. By all accounts, nationalists were successful in doing so. For example,
recent historians' profiles of rank-and-file Fenians in the 1860s and IRA
soldiers in 1919–21 indicate that nationalism's staunchest supporters were
members of precisely those groups most threatened by economic displacement and the necessity of emigration: artisans, journeymen, and shopkeepers' assistants in south Leinster's and Munster's decaying towns in the
1860s; landless laborers and small- to medium-sized farmers' noninherit-

ing sons in 1919–21, who had been prevented from emigrating by travel restrictions during World War I. However, the issues which mobilized such adherents were potentially dangerous, for if thwarted in their material aspirations by their leaders' concessions to British power or entrenched local interests, these men might either disrupt nationalist unity (e.g., by attacking middle-class "patriots") or—more likely, given Irishmen's traditional propensity to translate class interests into political symbols—switch allegiance to more-extreme varieties of nationalism. The latter happened in 1922–23 when smallholders' sons and laborers in Connaught and west Munster joined the antitreaty forces and rejected the Free State as an inadequate expression of inseparable political and material goals. Because of these dangers, nationalist leaders were of conflicting minds on emigration: mass departures by the discontented and dispossessed would vitiate nationalist movements, but their presence threatened to disrupt the movements or to divert them into unacceptable channels. The dilemma was most clearly stated during the Anglo-Irish war when the Dáil's defense minister urged Ireland's sons to "stand fast," while its minister of agriculture warned that the "[t]housands of young men" who "had been forced to remain in Ireland" during the Great War would now "in their dire need . . . swarm . . . on to the land as their only hope."[133]

The basic source of this dilemma was that most nationalist and clerical leaders, bourgeois products of an increasingly commercialized society, had little or no desire to take the really radical measures necessary to restructure that society and so halt emigration. Most "established" nationalist leaders, on both national and local levels, were middle-aged to elderly men of comfortable, middle-class origins; on the national level, most were from eastern Ireland. The point is that the members of these elites had either grown up in eastern counties, where post-Famine pressures for emigration were least (judging from relative departure rates), or had enjoyed in their youth sufficient money and opportunities at home to enable them to ignore or withstand those pressures. Now, when their prominence enabled them to define political goals and implement policies, they had long since passed in years and success beyond the point where emigration was a personal threat which demanded social redress. But above all, now these men had risen to the top of an Irish Catholic society whose very shape and stability depended to a large degree on emigration's continuance; indeed, their very affluence and authority derived from existing socioeconomic structures which could not flourish or perhaps even survive if emigration ceased. By contrast, throughout the post-Famine era most young men, especially those of humble origin, particularly those from the western counties, always faced the prospect, if not the probability, of emigration and so had to be cognizant of its root causes. Thus, different attitudes toward emigration and its sources may help account for the generational, regional, and social differences between adherents of "moderate" versus "extreme" forms of nationalism: for example, Catholic Whigs and tenant-righters versus Fenians; Buttite versus Parnellite home rulers; IPP/UIL versus Sinn Féin/

IRB; protreaty versus antitreaty IRA. Indeed, as was noted above, many of the young nationalists who challenged IPP hegemony in 1890–1916 (Griffith, Moran, Connolly, W. P. Ryan) actually had emigrated, and not only did their experiences abroad give them somewhat of an outsider's critical perspective on Irish society but the mere fact that the pressures impelling emigration proved effective in their cases forced them to face some unpleasant social realities which they might otherwise have ignored or rationalized.[134]

Whatever light such analysis sheds on the patterns of Irish political history, the unpleasant fact remains that *no* Irish Catholic leaders advocated or implemented measures sufficient to stop emigration once they had achieved national prominence or power. After all, Irish nationalism itself was a bourgeois ideal which obscured internal conflicts in the name of all-class unity against the English foe. Moreover, nationalist and clerical leaders alike were financially dependent on—when they were not synonymous with—Catholic society's entrenched interests: strong farmers and graziers, shopkeepers and traders, the local cliques dominated by "the groggy-patriot-publican-general shopman who is married to the priest's half sister" that Synge found ruling western villages in the 1890s. Such men were deeply opposed to land redistribution, land nationalization, socialism—in short, to any fundamental changes in a society which had permanently institutionalized lower-class emigration. For example, during the Land War one observer noted that although Munster laborers' "sufferings have made an excellent stalking-horse for the farmers," the latter "look with anything but favour upon a scheme for raising the poor peasants above the necessity of working for them by giving them a stake in the country." Likewise, it was revealing that not even in Orange Belfast did the socialist James Connolly meet such a violently hostile reception as in Queenstown, southern Ireland's major port, whose "decent people" fed parasitically upon an unceasing emigrant stream.[135]

As a result of either affinity with or pressures from such sources, nationalist leaders repeatedly ignored or opposed policies which might have stemmed emigration. For example, under conservative criticism Parnell quickly repudiated his earlier suggestion that Irish land hunger might be relieved through internal migration and settlement of western peasants on the north Leinster grasslands, falling back instead on the old chimera of western wasteland reclamation. Also, while Parnell and, later, Arthur Griffith, realized that self-government was useless without economic independence, both retreated from their advocacy of protective tariffs to stimulate native industries and provide employment. Catholic Ireland's major export-import sectors—graziers and traders—opposed any disruption of their profitable economic links to England, and so Parnell (also under strong pressures from English Liberals) dropped his demand that home rule include the power to enact tariff legislation. Likewise, four decades later the Free State government, which Griffith helped found, catered to the same interests and pursued free-trade policies throughout the 1920s. Similarly, in the early twentieth century IPP leaders and churchmen denounced Sir Horace Plunkett's Irish Agricultural Organization Society as a Unionist plot, in large measure because local traders—"the backbone of nationality in Ireland"—feared competition from cooperative enterprises.[136]

Thus, caught between their poor followers' demands that they support radical measures to halt emigration, and their affluent adherents' and their own aversion to such steps, bourgeois nationalists and churchmen had to formulate "explanations" of emigration in ideological contexts which would ignore or obscure post-Famine Ireland's economic realities and social conflicts. As a result, Catholic spokesmen's interpretations of emigration were integrally related to their idealization of a semimythical "holy Ireland" which could be defended against both external assault and internal schisms. In the early nineteenth century Catholic politicians and clerics had tried to conceptualize a semitraditional, protocapitalist Irish society insulated from damaging change. By the late nineteenth and early twentieth centuries most nationalist and especially clerical rhetoric and literature had a profoundly antimodernist thrust, as the papacy's contemporary crusade against secularism and liberalism—coupled with the sentimental romanticism prevailing in bourgeois culture—only reinforced Irish leaders' increasingly strident reactions against the more pervasive influences of British capitalism and the consequent social differentiation and Anglicization of Irish society. In response, they conceptualized a fortress Hibernia, an ideal and purportedly "traditional" Catholic Ireland which was antithetical to their images of England and America and to the "modern" and supposedly "alien" tendencies within Ireland itself. For example, according to Catholic leaders, especially churchmen, Irish Catholics were distinct from and superior to the English and to all Protestants because of their relative indifference to material wealth and the false idols of urban-industrial civilization: "the trend of their minds is religious," wrote Father Guinan, "and their abiding concern is to 'mind the things that are above, not the things that are upon the earth.' " Because of such unworldliness, the Irish were alleged to be deeply conservative, content to live simple lives at home under clerical guidance and in intimate, harmonious relationship with family, neighbors, and their natural environment. The ideal Irish society was static, organic, and paternalistic, a divinely ordained hierarchy devoid of internal conflicts, insulated by faith from potential "contamination." Likewise, to ensure stability and continuity "holy Ireland's" economy needs be overwhelmingly agricultural: its fundamental social unit was the peasant family, also paternalistic and static, tilling the soil in secure contentment, hard by the parish church where its ancestors were buried. There were several variations on this theme. Nationalists regarded the Irish party or the IRB as coguardians with the church of the people's traditions, and Parnell hoped that a patriotic landlord class might play a guiding role. Urban-oriented nationalists such as Arthur Griffith envisioned a partnership between Irish agriculture and industry, while Gaelic Leaguers desired the idealized peasant-citizen to be Irish-speaking as well as pious. However, similarities of vision outweighed the differences, for clerics and nationalists of almost every hue conceptualized an organic, tradition-based society which would be able to support a maximum number of people in frugal comfort.[137]

Clerical and nationalist rhetoric sometimes implied that this model society was still in the process of creation, at other times indicated that it was already in being. In either case, its perceived enemies—landlordism, Protestantism, materialism, atheism, and socialism—were legion, and so "holy Ireland" needed constant and vigorous defense: thus, the church's support for Irish self-government, its assiduous efforts to control Catholic education, its eternal vigilance against its foes. Similarly, the church's espousal of agrarian reforms despite implied threats to otherwise-sacred property rights—its slow progress from grudging approval of tenant-right in the 1850s to enthusiastic advocacy of peasant proprietorship in the 1880s—should be seen not only as pragmatic concession to popular demands but also as the result of churchmen's realization that only sweeping changes in landlord-tenant relations could root the peasantry in the soil and so create "holy Ireland's" secure social and moral foundation. Thus, in 1881 Bishop Nulty of Meath declared that "the land of every country is the common property of the people of that country," given to them by God for their subsistence; and in 1900 the bishops even gave hesitant, qualified approval to the demands of the land poor and landless that the "great grass farms" be broken up and redistributed.[138]

Moreover, within this ideological framework clerics and nationalists could both oppose emigration and harshly condemn the emigrants themselves. For although the notion of a divinely ordered society could reinforce churchmen's sometime claim that its pious emigrants were furthering God's work overseas, the more prevalent imagery of "holy Ireland" struggling for birth against the forces of evil implied that mass departures constituted an intolerable weakening of its ranks. In addition, the very ideal of "holy Ireland" made emigration seem highly inappropriate, if not treacherous. If, as many Catholic spokesmen claimed by the 1890s, the ideal Irish society was already substantially created—thanks to the devotional revolution, the Land Acts, and the Liberals' promise of eventual home rule—then continued emigration was an ominous indication that subtle and subversive forces were at work internally. Since clerics and nationalists had conceptualized "holy Ireland" in static, traditional, and communitarian terms and had created or sanctified the socioeconomic, religious, and cultural institutions which purportedly obviated emigration's further necessity, then by the logic of their vision any departures which still occurred implied the emigrants' self-willed or self-deluded repudiation of the organic nation as family and their violation of the sacralized "peasant" ethos on which the nation was supposedly based. After all, even if America did still offer superior opportunities, which many Catholic spokesmen were no longer willing to admit, Irish Catholics were, supposedly by definition, too selfless and unworldly to succumb to such lures. Thus, the emigrants must be either "traitors" or "fools" (Pearse stigmatized them as both), and in either case—since outside "holy Ireland" there was no salvation—they were destined at best for a harsher poverty than they had known at home, at worst for sin, shame, and eternal damnation.

Of course, "holy Ireland" imperfectly reflected only the traditional aspects of post-Famine society's complex realities and contradictory impulses. Indeed, in the sense that it ignored, obscured, or denied the real and often ruthless effects of commercialization, "holy Ireland" was at best an appealing self-delusion, at worst a pious fraud. Even Catholic churchmen, those most responsible for propagating the image, failed at crucial times to use their influence to make reality match the dream of an organic, rural society capable of sustaining all its people. To be sure, the bishops supported home rule and landlordism's abolition, but neither measure addressed emigration's root causes, and the hierarchy refused to countenance more-radical steps. Thus, although Bishops Nulty and Croke echoed Davitt's cry of "The land for the people," their anger when Davitt tried to use their pastorals and sermons to justify land nationalization revealed that by "people" the bishops—like most lay nationalists—meant current tenants only. Similarly, despite their ideal advocacy of peasant proprietorship and their qualified endorsement of grasslands redistribution, in practice the bishops often undermined those goals in order to advance the church's institutional interests. For example, in 1902 alone they almost sabotaged comprehensive land purchase because they feared the huge expense would reduce government subvention for Catholic schools; and they forced the IPP to end its temporary abstention from Parliament (a tactic in support of the UIL's antigrazier campaign) in order to vote for bills benefiting the church. More important, even conceptually the notion of "holy Ireland" was grievously flawed with respect to emigration. In large measure it was merely a cloak, woven of medieval dogmas and Victorian pieties, masking a petty bourgeois society whose vaunted stability and sacralized family farm both mandated and depended on constant emigration by the disinherited and dispossessed. Furthermore, the concept not only ignored Irish Protestants (thereby encouraging cultural, if not political, partition) but also failed to make any concession to the need for cities and industries as outlets for the countryside's surplus population; Ireland must remain rural, churchmen demanded, for in contrast to the idealized peasant world, cities and industries connoted secularism and social fragmentation, the "full sewerage . . . of Anglicization" and the "black devil of Socialism." Thus, in light of these glaring anomalies, the demands by Father Guinan, Pearse, and other spokesmen that Catholic emigrants not desert "the holy peace of home" for the fleshpots of America smacked of willful blindness, even gross hypocrisy.[139]

In short, the ideological problem remained. If "holy Ireland" was more cause than hindrance to emigration, then how could its apologists explain continuing mass departures without either admitting their ineffectiveness or exposing the concept's inadequacies and contradictions, and without thereby alienating the emigrants from the society left behind? To be sure, nationalists and clerics could redouble their denunciations of the emigrants as "fools" and "traitors," but such epithets not only violated realities too grossly but also threatened to engender in their targets the very bitterness or indifference which Catholic Ireland's guardians wanted to avoid. Or, they could resort to the old religious rationalization "that God in his inscrutable wisdom and methods had intended and used the Irish race to carry Catholicism to the ends of the earth." However, that interpretation also had its dangers, for as John Leslie, working-class spokesman for Scotland's Irish slums, pointed out, "the Irishman who accepts this teaching cannot any longer lay the misfortunes of his country upon the shoulders of the British government." In the end, then, the only, the most logical, and indeed the most prevalent recourse was to fall back on the oldest "explanation" of all, that emigration was "exile" forced by British oppression. That interpretation implied no criticism of "holy Ireland" but postponed any embarrassing social questions until after independence was won, and in the meantime, Ireland's apologists hoped, deflected what Father Guinan called the emigrants' "fierce rage and fury" against "the system of misgovernment, which renders [emigration] . . . inevitable in a land capable of supporting twice its present population." Nor did that interpretation imply criticism of the emigrants themselves, for they were merely "victims" whose all-absorbing hatred of England and love for Ireland—assiduously inculcated by priests and politicians before they departed—inspired unceasing devotion and donations to the staunch defenders of "holy Ireland."[140]

To be sure, there were voices of dissent from both "holy Ireland" and its facile approaches to emigration: "We have sung and prayed, 'God Save Ireland,' " wrote P. H. Kenny, "and still Ireland dies by 40,000 a year." Anglo-Irish writers like Synge and Lennox Robinson tried to dramatize the realities of what Patrick Kavanagh later called "the normal barbaric life of the Irish country poor." A few Gaelic Leaguers such as D. P. Moran and W. P. Ryan denounced mainstream nationalist rhetoric as "bucketfulls of trash," criticized churchmen who helped make "Irish local life a dreary desert," and suggested that the "resulting dullness and deadliness . . . drove not a few of the young folk to America." James Connolly ridiculed a "Church [which] curses the Protestant Reformation . . . [but] blesses capitalism—its parent," and heaped scorn on the bourgeois nationalist who would "rear [his] child up to love its country" but "support a social system which declares that the child has no right to the country, but must pay for permission to live on it as it is the property of private individuals." And perhaps the most eloquent, if silent, dissent came from those emigrants who refused to conceptualize their actions in prescribed ways, for despite "the triumph of empty rhetoric," wrote L. Paul-Dubois, "[i]t is easy to understand how it is that the utilitarians and the realists turn to where life and success are real. . . ." However, Connolly was largely ignored when alive, canonized and devitalized after his martyrdom in 1916, and although his influence moved Pearse's own republicanism distinctly leftward, the latter's "democratic programme" for an equitable Irish society was never implemented by his idolaters. Likewise, the Gaelic League's remedy for emigration—the creation, through compulsory education in Irish, of a truly Gaelic "atmosphere [which] would act as a barrier . . . by tying the people's hearts to the country"—was pathetically superficial and foundered on the rock of economic realities and the seemingly irreversible tide of Anglicization. In the end, Irish-Ireland merely became a linguistic complement to "holy Ireland," as insular and authoritarian as Maynooth itself, for Moran's proclaimed "battle of two civilizations" demanded absolute conformity to the Gaelic peasant ideal, and so he eagerly joined clerics and Irish Parliamentary party hacks in denouncing Anglo-Irish plays which exposed the tensions and hypocrisies of Irish life. Finally, whether by instinct or by design, most Catholic emigrants adhered to the exile motif and remained emotionally or at least publicly loyal to the "old land."[141]

To a degree, it is easily understood why ordinary Irishmen usually accepted the official interpretation of emigration as exile. Archaic historical and literary traditions, reinforced by famine, failed rebellions, and early-nineteenth-century rhetoric, had long predisposed Irish Catholics to blame all ills, including emigration, on English oppression. Consequently, the exile imagery was rooted so deeply in both traditional and modern protest literature that even radical nationalists of lower-class origin such as Davitt and Connolly, who knew better, employed it automatically. Likewise, in Douglas Hyde's exile ballads and in Pearse's translations of seventeenth-century exile poetry, modern nationalism came full circle from its Anglo-Irish and urban origins to embrace formally the archaic patriotism of a dying Gaelic literature. Moreover, by the late nineteenth century the impact of nationalist and religious literature on the Catholic population was intense and pervasive, much more so than on earlier, less literate, and less mobilized generations. As a result, the Irish were more exposed from childhood to rhetoric and literature which corroborated earlier traditions by blaming British malevolence for poverty and emigration. By most accounts the impression was widespread and profound. For example, Bourke Cockran, who left County Sligo in 1871, remembered, "The songs I heard when a boy . . . helped to render indestructable the spirit of Irish nationality"; over a decade later, at age twelve Hugh O'Daly from Monaghan first "grasped the curse that foreign rule was to [his] country" from newspaper accounts of Parnell's speeches; while less sophisticated emigrants spent their "tedious" days en route to America singing current nationalist songs and in old age still blamed their "exile" upon highly distorted "memories" of England's baleful effects on Irish society.[142]

Furthermore, present as well as past British policies and landlord actions seemed to confirm nationalists' claims that post-Famine emigration was still planned "extermination," particularly when Unionist journals continued to urge Catholic departures as the "natural remedy" for the "unhealthy state of our social system"; when Tory MPs such as Goldwyn Smith in 1883 announced that the native Irish were a "weaker race" whose farms "nature has designed for grazing lands"; and when in 1881–87 British officials and parliamentary commissions often seemed more eager to finance assisted emigration to the colonies than take measures to keep the Irish at home. In addition, the frequent movement to America of real political exiles still served to dramatize the entire exodus. The banishment of Fenian leaders such as John Devoy and Jeremiah O'Donovan Rossa in the early 1870s, the escapes from arrest of local Land League and National League activists in the 1880s, the flights of Invincibles and IRB terrorists: all served as models for an increasingly politicized people, especially for the embittered evicted farmers of the 1860s and 1880s.[143]

Nevertheless, given the fact that the real causes of most post-Famine emigration were rooted in the dynamics of Catholic society itself, it is doubtful whether ordinary Irish people would have been so receptive to the "official" interpretation of emigration had the exile motif and the "holy Ireland" concept not been such natural and logical expressions of the traditional worldview which still prevailed in Catholic Ireland, condemning innovation and selfish individualism while externalizing responsibility for unsettling change. Thanks to the uneven and contradictory development of post-Famine Ireland, "holy Ireland" was at least a partially valid metaphor for a society still centered on the family farm and parish church; and, even more important, "holy Ireland" was a wholly accurate and systematic expression of what a people in transition desperately needed and wanted to believe was still entirely true about their society and themselves. Likewise, although nationalist literature and selective contemporary evidence could formalize and corroborate the image of emigration as exile, its fundamental appeal lay in its symbolic resolution of the discrepancies between the reality of social fragmentation and the ideal of organic community. After all, if England could yet be blamed for emigration's causes, for the inability of "holy Ireland" to support all her children, then both the emigrants and those who profited by their departures could be absolved of culpability, while the consequent resentments against England could themselves reinforce the traditional outlooks and allegiances which held Catholic Ireland together in the face of the disintegrative and demoralizing effects of commercialization and Anglicization.

Thus, the hegemonic imperatives of Catholic church and organized nationalism perfectly coincided with their adherents' social and psychic needs for comforting "explanations" and symbolic resolutions. Moreover, since "traditionalization"—like "modernization"—was a circular process, both institutions greatly strengthened as they drew upon and refracted the traditional outlooks which underlay "holy Ireland" and the exile motif. As was noted earlier, church and nationalist movements synthesized customary local pressures for conformity with supralocal social-control mechanisms to ensure both parochial and national unanimity against external foes and internal divisions and subversions. Even the most mundane factional rivalries among local Gaelic Athletic Association clubs were resolved by boycotts, violence, and accusations that one's opponents were "traitors to Ireland"—"men who try to prove that Irishmen are not worthy of self-government." From such evidence, recent historians have concluded that "Irish freedom" meant *corporate* rather than individual liberty and that the "characteristic spirit" which animated nationalist organizations such as Sinn Féin was not "self-reliance," Arthur Griffith's constant injunction, but popular "sheepism"—as reflected, for example, in most Irishmen's instinctive desire to confer "unquestioning allegiance" on whichever movement was ascendant. Thus, modern and traditional, imposed and voluntary, practical and ideological, impulses toward communal conformity converged to control and obscure the real conflicts and discontinuities within Catholic Ireland. Consequently, when in 1887 a traveler asked a Tipperary farm laborer whether his exploited fellow workers subscribed to Irish nationalism, the man replied that although "[t]hey hate the farmers, . . . *they love Ireland, and they all stand together for the country.*" And, mystified by an imagery which both mitigated and externalized their resentments, such men to an astonishing degree blamed England when they left home seeking the dignity and decent wages denied them by the "pathriotic" farmers and shopkeepers of "holy Ireland."[144]

In short, then, the demands for conformity by those who claimed to speak for what Patrick Pearse called "the Sovereign People" would not have been so compelling had not the ordinary Irish themselves felt a need for politicized and sacralized traditions which mirrored their self-image and mitigated their social and psychological tensions. As the concluding parts of this section will demonstrate, although such spurious "explanations" were most necessary and appropriate in the twilight world of western Ireland, the ambiguities and contradictions surrounding emigration prevailed in rural families throughout the island, thus obliging their members' interpretations of emigration as nonresponsible and sorrowful "exile" from a multitude of microcosmic "Mother Irelands."[145]

The interpretation of emigration as exile was commonly accepted throughout Catholic Ireland. Even urban-born Catholics, such as the Dubliner Patrick Pearse, whose father was English, learned from grandparents and other relatives the songs and stories which combined Gaelic and contemporary nationalist themes and attributed emigration to British misgovernment. Likewise, Ulster Catholics—composing perhaps 20 percent of all Catholic emigrants in 1856–1921—may have been especially prone to politicize emigration, given their province's increasing sectarian conflict and the bitter growth of the Ancient Order of Hibernians. Thus, by ten years of age Joseph McGarrity of County Tyrone had imbibed a "hatred of the landlord, of the police, and of the soldiers" which informed his emigration in 1892 and his subsequent labors in the Clan na Gael.[146]

However, much evidence indicates that Catholic emigrants from Ireland's western districts—making up at least 40 percent of the total Catholic exodus in 1856–1921, over 50 percent after 1880—were the *most* likely to perceive emigration negatively, as forced banishment. There were several reasons for this tendency. First, throughout the post-Famine period the

West's greater incidence of parochial subsistence economies, of customary social relationships, and of archaic cultural expressions tied to the Irish language strongly encouraged the retention of a traditional value system which condemned emigration generally and of old oral traditions which blamed such innovations specifically on *Sasanaigh* tyranny. Second, after 1878 commercialization and Anglicization had effects on western Ireland which were at once more rapid and traumatic, but also more uneven and contradictory, than elsewhere. Consequently, although they produced massive emigration and widespread alienation, they also created striking social and cultural anomalies which in turn both allowed and demanded a further reliance on traditional outlooks which could lessen the dangers of total communal disintegration and demoralization. Third, after 1878 the western Irish sought resolution of their districts' economic problems and social tensions in organized nationalist movements, thus transforming the West from the island's least to its most politicized region, and thus exposing its inhabitants to the "official" interpretations of contemporary developments, such as emigration as exile. Finally, since in many respects western communities still resembled the "holy Ireland" of nationalist mythology, and since those same communities were nonetheless experiencing such rapid and destabilizing change, it was both natural and expedient for their inhabitants to accept such interpretations, which coincided with their traditional beliefs and which seemingly "explained" both the continuities and the discontinuities of western life.

As was noted in Section 1, prior to 1880 permanent emigration from Ireland's western-most counties was still relatively rare, a response to specific crises such as the Great Famine or the near famine of 1859–64 rather than a social institution. Before 1880 a traditional worldview which inhibited *desires* to emigrate suitably reflected traditional social arrangements which lessened economic *pressures* to emigrate. In much of Connaught, in west Munster, and in west Ulster, life remained primitive, centered on potato cultivation for subsistence; economic transactions were few, largely through barter, and cash was scarce. "Hardly more than two people in the whole parish had a clock," remembered Michael MacGowan of west Donegal, "and if they had to look to being punctual—which was seldom—they relied on the sun or the moon." Most of these districts' inhabitants were petty farmers who still practiced partible inheritance, while seasonal migration, fishing, kelp harvesting, knitting, and other income sources served to supplement the land's meager resources. Even clachan communities, rundale, and joint tenancies remained common in many areas. Moreover, the exigencies of peasant agriculture demanded retention of corroborating customs and conservative outlooks which helped cement loyalties to place and kin. Thus, although poverty was ubiquitous—"The people were as poor as poor could be," declared one westerner—yet "there was friendship and charity among them; they helped one another in work and in trouble, in adversity and in pain and it was that neighborliness which, with the grace of God, was the solid stanchion of their lives." Likewise, in these regions traditional music, crossroads dancing, old wake customs and religious festivals, storytelling, and even remnants of formal *aisling* poetry still flourished or survived, while the church's authority remained relatively limited. "You would hear no word of English in Dingle that time," recalled Tomás Ó Crohan of his west Kerry boyhood, "but Irish only spoken through all the streets and houses. The country was full to the lid of songs and stories, and you would not put a stir out of you from getting up in the morning to lying down at night but you would meet a poet, man or woman, making songs on all that would be happening." The prevalence of the Irish language, high illiteracy rates, and poor transportation and communications both reflected and reinforced western peasants' relative insulation from American attractions or "any convulsions in the great world outside them." Consequently, prior to 1880, observers often remarked the aversion to emigration common in areas such as County Mayo—where "the people . . . cling to their inhospitable mountains as a woman clings to a deformed or idiot child"—as well as the "heartrending scenes" and comparatively high return rates which characterized the emigration that did occur.[147]

Of course, even in the 1870s the sociocultural patterns which inhibited western emigration were weakening. As John M. Synge later perceived, "part of the misfortune of Ireland" was that "nearly all the characteristics which give colour and attractiveness to Irish life are bound up with a social condition that is near to penury." While habitual deprivation could be accommodated and justified as "God's will," relative economic improvements alternating with exceptional distress could lessen even western peasants' submission to "the Great Wheel of Life." In the 1870s high livestock and butter prices; the spread of shops, cash transactions, and credit arrangements; increased consumption of shop goods: all helped persuade inhabitants of the western coasts that "life does not remain equally and unalterably hard on poor people for ever." Similarly, participation in wider economic networks brought exposure to urban and Anglicizing influences; even seasonal migration, although a defense against the need for permanent emigration, reflected eroding self-sufficiency and entailed increased awareness of the outside world. Thus, by the decade's end commercialization had already wrought significant changes, especially in east Connaught and parts of west Munster, and the consequent spread of grazing and of impartible inheritance inevitably heightened pressures for permanent emigration.[148]

However, had it not been for the catastrophic potato crop failures, price declines, supplementary-income losses, and wholesale evictions of the 1880s, the effects of commercialization on western Ireland might have been far less dramatic and traumatic. Travelers remarked that the psychological effects of the crisis were similar to those which the Great Famine had produced thirty years earlier: "There is no merriment in Kerry," reported one visitor. "The old dances at the crossroads are danced no more. The pipe of the piper is played out." Although at first some observers testified that many peasants were "so rooted to the country" they remained amazingly "indifferent" to emigration, severe distress coupled with the collapse of expectations raised in the prosperous 1870s soon produced such a flood of departures that it appeared "as though the people were flying from a doomed city. The full conviction had come upon them that it was impossible to struggle longer with the depth of poverty by which they had been surrounded." Likewise, although peasant family ties remained strong, government and private assistance which enabled entire families to emigrate broke down resistance among "a people who follow a lead very readily," while favorable reports and remittances from the first to depart encouraged others to do the same. America was "the best place from Heaven," declared one emigrant to his relatives in bleak Connemara, so "don't delay one day": "It is not starving with the hunger you will be here." Consequently, attachments to home dissolved in frantic desires to escape, and philanthropists such as James Hack Tuke were besieged by requests for assisted passages: "Send us, your honour, where you like," they cried, "only let us go."[149]

The desperate panic of 1879–82 was short-lived, but the economic crisis of those years—reinforced in subsequent decades by further crop failures and price declines—initiated the last, lingering era of Gaelic peasant Ireland's existence and institutionalized permanently high rates of emigration from the western counties. However, examined carefully, the short-term consequences of the West's sudden "modernization" were extraordinarily uneven and traumatic. As a result, western Irish attitudes toward, and explanations of, emigration were extremely contradictory.

On the one hand, much evidence indicates that after 1880 commercialization rationalized western peasants' attitudes toward emigration as well as their economic and social relationships. The western Irish who survived the depressed 1880s and 1890s did so largely through increased dependence on commercial agriculture, primarily grazing, and on village traders, shopkeepers, and usurers. In turn, this commercialization entailed the abandonment of clachan settlements, cotillage, and subdivision, and the adoption of consolidated farmsteads and, most important, impartible inheritance: trends imposed by the Congested Districts Board as well as by market realities. Consequently, in western as in eastern Ireland, social relationships became more instrumental and emigration became a structural imperative: "one son will stay at home and keep on the farm," as a west Kerryman declared, "and the others will go away because they must go." Simultaneously, Anglicization accompanied commercialization, eroding western peasants' cultural ties to their homeland and thereby facilitating departures mandated by structural changes. Between 1881 and 1901 the number of Irish-speakers in Munster and Connaught fell by a third, while literacy rates in English increased commensurately. In the transition, much of the traditional music and folklore conveyed in the Irish language was lost. Now his neighbor had "books and newspapers," an old man in west Kerry explained, "and he reads them to me, and the little tales one after another, day after day, . . . have driven the old stories out of my head." He added significantly, "But maybe I'm little the worse for losing them." Ironically, efforts to alleviate the West's distress—for example, through the Land and United Irish leagues and the Congested Districts Board—only entailed further exposure to cosmopolitan influences. Similarly, emigration both resulted from and promoted cultural change, for letters and gifts from abroad inspired dissatisfaction with customary life-styles, while the steady drain of young people weakened traditional communities and cultures. "[I]n the old times it's many a piper would be moving around through those houses . . . , playing his pipes and drinking poteen and the people dancing around him," recalled an elderly Connemara man in the 1890s, "but now there is no drinking and singing in this place at all, and most of the young people is growing up and going to America."[150]

In great measure this commercialization and Anglicization had profound and logically predictable effects on the ways western peasants viewed emigration. In those regions which remained destitute, Synge lamented, the people go "because they are unable to keep themselves at home; but in places where there has been much improvement the younger and brighter men and girls get ambitions which they cannot satisfy in this country, and so they go also. Again, where there is no local life or amusements they go because they are dull, and when amusements and races are introduced they get the taste for amusements and go because they cannot get enough of them." Indeed, some westerners now exhibited brutally pragmatic attitudes toward emigration—"God ordered us to help ourselves," one asserted—and although enthusiasts from eastern Ireland hoped that the Gaelic League might revitalize the West and stem emigration, Synge admitted that many peasants regarded the league's missionaries as "busybodies" and the old language itself as merely a hindrance to their children's "progress" overseas.[151]

On the other hand, while traditional western society and culture seemed "like a sea on ebb," many customary features remained despite or even because of the contradictory effects of rapid change. In turn, these residual relationships and outlooks continued to generate or reinforce traditional attitudes toward emigration. As was noted earlier in this section, although increased dependence on grazing, retail, and credit networks entailed the *ultimate* destruction of peasant agriculture, in the short run such involvement shored up the semisubsistence family farms which still dominated the impoverished western landscape. Likewise, judicially reduced rents, low land purchase annuities, and government improvement projects gave family farmers time to adjust to market conditions in ways designed to realize traditional, "peasant" goals. Many of these adjustments—particularly impartible inheritance and obligatory emigration for the disinherited—were radical innovations in western contexts, but the goals themselves were decidedly conservative: generational continuity, relative self-sufficiency, and security on the family holding. Thus, emigration, like seasonal migration formerly, served highly conservative functions in western Ireland, for the departures and remittances of "superfluous" youngsters precluded felt necessities for even greater changes among those who remained at home. Similarly, despite Anglicization, cultural continuities in western communities remained sufficient to provide gold mines of information to twentieth-century anthropologists, folklorists, and Celtic scholars from Dublin and abroad. Along the western seaboard Irish was still the primary medium of expression, the language of childhood which helped shape attitudes later translated imperfectly into Hiberno-English after the few years of primary education which constituted the full extent of schooling for most western youths. Moreover, despite clerical condemnations and alternative sources of wisdom and entertainment, fairy belief and magic still underlay an imposed formal Catholicism, while archaic songs, stories, poems, and proverbs yet constituted the basic oral culture of a marginally literate people.[152]

In short, western Ireland after 1880 was a very unevenly "modernized" society. In regional terms, for example, commercial grazing and farm consolidation were much further advanced in central than in western Mayo, in north Kerry than on the Dingle and Iveragh peninsulas. Indeed, in a few remote areas, such as Achill Island, off the Mayo coast, rundale persisted until very recently. Likewise, rates of linguistic and cultural change varied sharply from district to district. For example, between 1901 and 1911 the number of Irish-speakers in County Roscommon fell 34 percent while in Mayo they declined only 11 percent. Within Mayo itself declension rates varied from 17 percent in the Swinford district to only 3 percent around Castlebar; in the Far West, on the Mullet of Mayo, the number of Irish-speakers actually rose 4 percent. North and west Kerry exhibited equally striking contrasts. Moreover, in terms of their inhabitants' general outlook or worldview, these regional social and cultural variations merely exemplified the profound discrepancies which prevailed throughout the West, in every district and community in transition. For while antimodernists such as Synge and George Russell lamented what they perceived as the West's social fragmentation and cultural decline, apostles of "progress" such as the Congested Districts Board inspectors (and, fifty years later, Bord na Gaeltacht officials) who visited the same coasts and glens complained of their inhabitants' seemingly intransigent conservatism. Thus, although Synge noted that western peasants now "sit together and talk with endless iteration of . . . the price of kelp," government officials despaired to teach them "the virtue of self-reliance." "The problem of improvement is a difficult one to solve," wrote an inspector in west Donegal, for "[t]he people are slow to grasp any new idea and suspicious of all movement from the old lines along which they and their fathers have moved for generations. Individually, they are amenable and teachable, but collectively they are as unmovable and adverse to change as anything can be, and the individual units who would rise are held down by the weight of old custom and prejudice." "The readiness to accept new ideas and to engage on new enterprises is precisely the characteristic most wanting in the population," generalized Arthur Balfour, the Irish chief secretary. "If it were not so they would long have refused to squat generation after generation on the bogs and mountains of the inclement West."[153]

Indeed, although western Ireland now exhibited the island's highest over-all emigration rates, the remarkable persistence of these traditionally oriented social institutions and their correspondingly conservative outlooks still served to inhibit emigration from a few remote districts and, more important, continued to validate customary, negative attitudes toward emigration. Both demographic and literary evidence indicates that many western peasants still preferred to squat on their bogs and mountains rather than emigrate. For example, the remote areas which remained most traditional in socioeconomic and cultural respects were also remarkably resistant to emigration. Thus, although in 1881–1911 the population of County Donegal fell 18 percent, that of the Rosses district actually rose slightly; similar increases took place in County Galway's Oughterard district and on the Belmullet and Dingle peninsulas of Mayo and Kerry. Moreover, census analysis reveals that throughout the West traditional impulses to stay at home remained unusually strong, in striking contrast to the novel and equally powerful pressures for emigration. For instance, western farmers' sons who *inherited* land were much more likely to stay at home and marry than were their counterparts elsewhere in Ireland, despite the fact that the holdings which westerners inherited were generally much smaller and poorer than in the eastern counties. Until after World War II the western counties had the island's highest marriage rates and the youngest average ages at marriage; also, the smaller the western farms, the higher their occupants' marriage rate, while in eastern Ireland the reverse was the case. In other words, despite severe economic pressures, western peasants who remained in Ireland did not alter their marriage patterns in conformity to those prevailing in the more commercialized East. Instead, they still pursued and realized traditional communal goals: persistence on the land and early marriage.[154]

To be sure, western peasants' adoption of impartible inheritance meant that such traditional goals were now unattainable for *non*inheritors. After 1881 their marriage opportunities declined dramatically and their emigration rates soared; in fact, noninheritors in western Ireland were more likely to emigrate than were their counterparts in the East, reflecting the almost complete absence of nonfarm employment in the former region. However, even among noninheritors *preferences* to remain at home seemed unusually strong in western Ireland. On the average, for example, western farm families supported much larger numbers of dependent relatives—postponing or avoiding emigration—than did eastern families. Thus, although Peig Sayers, a young farm servant on the Dingle peninsula, expressed eagerness to escape from "slavery," her attachment to locale and family remained so strong that she rejected a free passage to America, concluding that she would be "better off and more favored with grace" if she stayed to comfort her mother's old age. Likewise, the intense parochialism of some western peasants, especially Irish-speakers, inspired a reluctance to leave familiar surroundings. Again, for Peig Sayers even a short journey from her native parish to the town of Dingle, population under 2,000, "filled [her] with wonder" and fear of the "Grand tall buildings" and crowds of English-speakers. Moreover, the western Irish who *did* emigrate seem to have been much more likely than their eastern peers to return to Ireland and purchase farms and marry. Indeed, in many western communities the emigrants' eventual return seems to have been commonly expected. For instance, in County Mayo when a family emigrated it was usual for kinsmen or neighbors to take a piece of burning turf from the last fire in the abandoned house and place it on their own, never-quenched fire: at least a symbolic refusal to accept the probable finality of most departures—the harsh fact that even in the West relatively few emigrants would actually return to relight their fires and so restore the broken continuities of western life.[155]

In short, western Ireland was an almost schizophrenic society, where strikingly novel social processes and outlooks coexisted uneasily with others which remained obdurately conservative. In turn, the duality of western society—epitomized by the remarkable variations in emigration rates among regions and within families—generated or validated sharply opposed attitudes toward emigration: as "opportunity" for individual achievement or as "exile" from traditionally oriented communities. Indeed, the mere fact that so many western Irish were raised in Irish-speaking homes almost guaranteed that they would conceptualize emigration as *deoraí* and its impulses in terms of necessity or compulsion.[156]

However, while these contrasting attitudes were logical reflections of the West's social and cultural duality, that very duality—itself the product of extraordinarily sudden change—generated social, cultural, and psychological tensions which were so severe that they largely precluded constructive resolutions. Instead, they inspired widespread demoralization, alienation, and insecurity—for change was too rapid, exposure to radically different and purportedly superior life-styles too sudden, and the discrepancies between tradition and innovation, ideal and reality, were too profound to be assimilated or explained "rationally." Consequently, many western peasants simply lost faith in themselves, their way of life, the traditional benchmarks of their identities, and by the beginning of this century the region exhibited much the same "culture of despair" which had characterized transitional areas of eastern Ireland in the pre-Famine decades. For example, the dichotomies between ideals (e.g., family farm) and means (e.g., impartible inheritance) were now so sharp that they produced feelings of guilt and shame: "I am not as good a man as my father was," lamented one west Kerryman, "and my son is growing up worse than I am"—a statement reflecting the inability of many westerners to rationalize deviations from custom. Ironically, the very rapidity of change—taking place within contexts of crop failures, price declines, and mass emigration—not only inspired pervasive fears that western Ireland was doomed but also obliged the region's inhabitants to fall back on familiar explanatory categories, which themselves fed the growing demoralization. For instance, economic catastrophes seemed to corroborate Irish-speaking peasants' ingrained fatalism and apocalyptic tendencies: "even the sea is failing us now," declared a western fisherman. "Isn't it in the prophecy," he warned, "that the sea will be a dry cow a little before the world's end?" Thus, while western peasants increasingly scorned their traditional language and its associated customs, linguistic and cultural attrition only exacerbated demoralization and despair: "when the people realize," Synge predicted, that any "hope of restoring a lost language is a vain one, the last result will be a new kind of hopelessness and many crowded ships leaving Queenstown and Galway."[157]

Reflecting its schizophrenic origins, the demoralization of western society engendered two radically different perceptions of emigration and, especially, of most emigrants' destination, the United States. On the one hand, for example, unsophisticated Irish-speakers—who had never been wont to make clear distinctions between what outsiders might call "myth" and "reality"—now responded to letters, remittances, presents, and well-heeled returned emigrants sporting the proverbial gold watches by concluding that America was a veritable paradise whose fabulous cities were what the Donegal novelist Séamus Ó Grianna called *caisleáin óir*, castles of gold. Thus, when would-be emigrants such as the young west Kerryman Maurice O'Sullivan "look[ed] west at the edge of the sky where America should be lying and . . . slipped back on the paths of thought," they envisioned American cities "with . . . fine streets and great high houses, some of them so tall that they scratched the sky; gold and silver out on the ditches, and nothing to do but to gather it." And, by contrast, they regarded western Ireland as a wretched, hopeless place: "isn't it a queer thing to be sitting here," asked an aspiring emigrant in Connemara, "on this bit of a rock that a dog wouldn't look at, where the pigs die and the spuds die, and even the quality do lower our rents when they see the wild Atlantic driving in across the cursed stones?" In light of such images, it was no wonder that "[a]t night beside the fire" the boys and girls of west Kerry "talked of nothing else" but emigration and that their peers in west Connaught were "delighted when their passage arrived," while western peasants too old to leave envied the emigrants' good fortune and exclaimed, "Pity I didn't go there—pity I spent my life here," for America "must be a wonderful country," judging from "the fine dacent clothes that comes from it."[158]

Yet, on the other hand, profound fears of emigration and extremely negative images of the United States were equally widespread. Thus, a woman about to leave west Kerry feared she wouldn't "be alive a month in the place we're going . . . [for] there's no view of the sea and the strand is too far away." "I'm afraid," she avowed, "for moving to a strange place is always an extremely chancy thing." Such apprehensions reflected more than parochialism, for if the western Irish sometimes perceived America as a land of gold, they also viewed it as "the Land of the Snakes" or "the land of sweat"—as "a hard, merciless, self-seeking country" where emigrants commonly perished prematurely from overwork, disease, or immorality, or simply because by emigrating they had deviated too sharply from traditional norms: " 'Twas the shame of emigration / Laid you low, my Noreen Bawn," as one song declared.[159]

Certainly, there were many valid reasons for western peasants to fear emigration, for their poverty and lack of marketable skills, their unfamiliarity with the demands of urban-industrial societies, often their illiteracy and imperfect or nonexistent command of English—all made them much poorer candidates for success abroad than their more sophisticated peers from eastern Ireland. "What would I do if there was not a word of English on my lips?" wondered a west Kerryman traveling eastward by train. "Wouldn't I be a public show? Where is the man or woman who would give me an answer?" Indeed, Synge was right when he remarked that poor Connemara peasants formed "probably the worst kind of emigration" and when he predicted that "the sufferings of these families, who are suddenly moved to quite different surroundings, must be very great." Although many of the western emigrants assisted by Tuke and Vere Foster in the early 1880s seem to have prospered under careful, clerical guidance, most westerners faced years of privation in urban slums and mining towns. As a result, relatives at home and returned emigrants often reported that a "big number of our boys and girls died of a broken heart" in America, or at least "lived to rue the day they abandoned their happy homes in old Ireland—poor though they were there—for the chimera of the golden west."[160]

However, although much evidence suggests that western Irish-speakers *were* disproportionately unsuccessful and homesick in the New World, western images of emigration and of America were less reflective of realities than of the fact that the region's inhabitants were largely incapable of making informed comparisons of the relative advantages of life at home and abroad. Testimony collected by the Irish Folklore Commission indicates that while Irishmen in Meath or Wexford (Anglicized districts with long experiences of impartible inheritance and emigration) assessed America rationally as a land where hard work brought "opportunity," western peasants commonly held the grossly inflated and highly contradictory notions described above: "land of gold" *versus* "Land of the Snakes." The negative perception nicely corroborated clerical warnings of emigration's likely consequences, but both images were rooted primarily in western Ireland's profound contradictions and crumbling self-confidence. For western peasants, especially Irish-speakers, America was something totally novel, beyond experience or received wisdom: it was *An tOileán Úr,* the New Island, and whether positively or negatively perceived it represented everything that western Ireland was not. On the one hand its fabulously favorable image mirrored westerner's growing self-contempt, their belief that any place must be better than home. On the other hand the equally marvelous negative image reflected their inability to comprehend an urban-industrial society which seemed so unfamiliar, so dramatically different from that which they clung to so fearfully.[161]

These mythical images were so irreconcilable that they only further exposed and exacerbated the dualities and demoralization of western society. In fact, they were positively dangerous, for the myth of the *caisleán óir* threatened the West with total demographic and cultural deracination, while the fears inspired by the opposing image threatened to prevent the mass departures which were vitally necessary to secure the region's relative stability. In the last analysis, these conflicting perceptions—like the tensions which they reflected and intensified—could only be "resolved" or obscured by the maintenance of the archaic fiction that all emigration was nonresponsible exile, attributable neither to the emigrants themselves nor to the dynamics of their contradictory society. Indeed, mystified as they were by these mythical images of America, western peasants could justly conclude that their emigrants were in truth exiles in the sense that they were completely "lost" to the world left behind, so drastically would they have to alter customary behavior and values in conformity to such a radically different society. Thus, while Irishmen in eastern counties generally welcomed successful returned emigrants for their energy and innovative ideas, westerners simultaneously coveted their reputed wealth and scorned them for any marks of individuality or deviations from traditional customs. Only if they divested themselves of all traces of their American experience would they be reaccepted in western communities, and even then they and their Irish-born children would always be known as "the Yanks"—a half-envious, half-contemptuous appellation which accurately reflected western peasants' deeply ambivalent feelings toward both America and themselves.[162]

In short, throughout the West—but especially in Irish-speaking districts— both the remarkable persistence of traditions and the impact of unsettling change made it at once more natural and more necessary than elsewhere for emigration to be perceived as *deoraí,* as sorrowful exile compelled by uncontrollable forces. Only that perception could simultaneously dampen the enthusiasm for the *caisleáin óir* which threatened to disintegrate western society and reconcile those fears of "the Land of the Snakes" which threatened to stem departures. Thus, the Blasket Islander Peig Sayers insisted that her emigrating son "was deeply attached to his country and to his native language and . . . never had any desire to leave Ireland." "But," she explained, "that's not the way events turned out for he too *had* to take to the road like the others, his heart laden with sorrow." Occasionally, the discrepancies between independent volition and communal convention became obvious, but self-abnegation and passivity remained predominant. For instance, another woman from west Kerry, about to emigrate, initially admitted to neighbors that "it isn't hunger or thirst that's putting us out, but when we see all the people leaving we want to do the same." That statement alone carefully balanced selfish desire and conformist exigencies, but in the next breath she lamented, "[I]sn't it a hard world when we are going to *have* to leave our own little cot at last, after all the affection we had for it." Finally, she and her friends concluded that her departure was "fated": "I can't be convinced," she declared, "that all these things aren't laid out for us from the day we come into the world until the day we leave it." Such fatalism was comforting, both to the emigrants and to those left behind: it absolved community members of responsibility for actions which violated every inherited notion of community; and while it may have vitiated self-reliance among those who departed, it helped them

stoically endure a future which they were unable or unwilling to conceptualize realistically. They could "remember when there was no thought of
America," convince themselves that those "were fine happy days," and yet
resign themselves to the knowledge that now they or their children "had to
go": it was "the way of the world" and "even if it is the cause of your
death, welcome it." "I shall be alone at the end of my life," sighed one
poor woman who had sent all her children abroad. "But it is God's
will . . . , and we must not complain."[163]

In fact, however, the western Irish complained bitterly, as was shown by
the desperate grief which still characterized final parting scenes along the
Atlantic seaboard. In part such complaints reflected western peasants' traditional attachments to family and place, exacerbated by fears born of insularity and demoralization, but they also indicated that since the Famine
western perspectives had been sufficiently modernized that passive acceptance of "God's will" was no longer entirely adequate to explain why "exile" was necessary. Consequently, alternating with fatalism was the growing
conviction that England, its government and its Protestant Irish adherents,
was really responsible for western poverty and emigration. Of course, this
was modern nationalist dogma, and its acceptance and reiteration by western peasants in large measure reflected their increasing politicization, especially after the Land War's inception. In many respects it was perfectly
logical for the western Irish to seek a resolution for their region's economic
and social problems in nationalist movements. Memories of the Great
Famine and its consequent mass evictions and emigrations were especially
vivid in western Ireland, and resentments against their new, allegedly "English" landlords spawned in the Encumbered Estates Court ran deep among
peasants who still clung to the margins of vast pasturelands which their
immediate ancestors formerly tilled. The crisis of 1879–82 intensified these
old grievances and created new ones of compelling urgency, while the leaders of the Land League and, later, the United Irish League, Sinn Féin, and
the antitreaty republicans were assiduous in linking western anxiety and
land hunger to broader political offensives against British rule. Ireland
must be free, they argued, for British exploitation and misrule were responsible for destroying Ireland's economy and so undermining its ability
to support its inhabitants at home.[164]

For most Irishmen but especially for western peasants, the key issue was
the inadequacy or injustice of the existing land system. As a Connaught
Irish-speaker declared, specifically linking emigration to political oppression, "If we had each of us a bit of ground that would keep him and his
family decent and comfortable, there would not be half of the wandering
fit on the people." However, it was not entirely logical or just to blame all
the land system's inequities on "British tyranny," especially by the early
twentieth century, when Parliament was abolishing Irish landlordism with almost unseemly haste and pouring money into western revitalization schemes.
Although W. P. Ryan believed that western farmers' anger and aversion to
emigration was inspired largely by the sight of vast, untenanted grasslands

in the north midlands and the Shannon estuary, their consequent envy and resentment were more appropriately directed against Catholic graziers and "grass-grabbers" than against British officials or the tottering landlord class. Moreover, under the impact of commercialization many western farmers were no longer content with "a bit of ground": rather, they were as eager as their more affluent eastern peers to enlarge their existing holdings at their neighbors' expense, and as reluctant to share the earth's bounty with the landless and disinherited. However, while western peasants were increasingly involved in the marketplace, with all its implications for their social relationships, the very novelty of their situation ensured that the responsibility for the conflicts and tensions produced by their consequent violations of peasant mores would be projected outward on the perceived agents of change: on local graziers and gombeen-men, certainly, but ultimately on the British exploitation traditionally deemed responsible for all detrimental or unsettling innovations. Arguably, such projections were most natural and instinctive for western Irish-speakers: in part because western Ireland, still dominated by peasant farm and parish church, at least superficially resembled the "holy Ireland" of nationalist and clerical mythology more closely than did rural society elsewhere; and, perhaps most important, because in the Irish-speaking West perception of the *Sasanaigh* as eternal foes was not merely learned from modern nationalist literature but instead was deeply rooted in still-vibrant oral traditions, shaping interpretations of contemporary sufferings which could yet be blamed on those who—as a seventeenth-century poem still extant in west Munster put it—"have ceaseless comfort and ease unending" because "Poor Ireland . . . has been ripped and shred to thin ribbons." Thus, in western Ireland especially—in districts which contributed half the Catholic exodus—an archaic cultural and linguistic heritage, recent historical experience, and the profound contemporary tensions between tradition and modernity: all combined to corroborate and intensify nationalist and clerical interpretations of emigration as bitter exile.[165]

Finally, throughout Catholic Ireland—in eastern, Anglicized regions as well as in the Gaelic West—the tensions and conflicts within Irish farm families epitomized those in "holy Ireland" generally and so facilitated, even demanded that emigration be "explained" in involuntary, nonresponsible, and politicized terms. For ironically, if western peasants' traditional outlooks inhibited departures by disinherited children, the more modern, instrumental attitudes common among their eastern peers could also make the latter unwilling to obey parental injunctions that they emigrate to ensure the profitability or viability of the family holding.

Despite post-Famine commercialization, a persistent lack of scope for individual enterprise within Ireland confirmed the Irish farm family's position as the dominant socioeconomic and cultural unit. Family bonds still took precedence over all other associational ties, and religious teachings sacralized authoritarian parent-child relationships and the cooperative ethos mandated by the exigencies of small-farm agriculture. Most farmers still depended heavily on their children's unpaid labor and also relied on the latter's willingness to support parents in old age. In general, children were trained to be dutiful, submissive, and self-effacing—to subordinate individual motives and desires to customary notions of family welfare and status. Again, clerical strictures reinforced child-rearing methods; for example, at Sissy O'Brien's convent school the nuns did "[l]ittle . . . to encourage self-reliance and independence. Rather the reverse." Emotional bonds between mothers and sons were proverbially close, at times smotheringly so, as frustrated farmers' wives—often trapped in loveless marriages to men much older than themselves—lavished compensatory affection on male offspring, who welcomed relief from their fathers' stern demeanor and general refusal to allow sons any degree of responsibility until they left home or married with parental approval.[166]

The family's importance, its close-knit relationships and socialization patterns, produced highly ambivalent attitudes toward emigration among parents and offspring alike. On the one hand, emigration threatened family integrity, physically sundered ties to birthplace and kin, and violated customary notions of proper behavior. Sir Horace Plunkett was one of many observers who remarked "the Irish love of home"—the strong "sense of human neighbourhood and kinship" felt by those raised in relatively sheltered, parochial communities. "The Irish are distinguished for love of their kindred," wrote the U.S. consul at Londonderry in 1883, "and that love has hitherto acted as a check to the obvious motives that induce them to leave their homes." Parents—especially mothers—often reacted to their children's impending emigration with opposition or desperate grief. For example, when Mary Jane Hill married Robert Anderson, a landless laborer, her mother was deeply distressed because she realized the young couple would have to go to America: "Mary Jane," she cried, "if I had all the world to choose a son-in-law from, it would be Robert, except that he is taking you away where I shall never see you again." Parents especially feared that their children's departure condemned them to a comfortless old age and a lonely death: "God help the old people," exclaimed one Kerryman. "There will be none left to bury them with the haste that is on the world." Sometimes parental protests successfully prevented or at least postponed their children's emigration; thus, John Flanagan of County Louth wrote wistfully that he had "been often tempted to leave this country altogether and would have long since tried my fortune in the New World, but for my father." Although in most instances ambition or financial exigencies overcame parental objections, emigrants generally felt deep sorrow at leaving childhood homes and kinsmen: "it is a hard thing to leave our native soil and leave all our loved ones behind us," testified Bartholomew Colgan. "It was a great trial to me on account of leaveing a poor old hartbroken mother behind me." Indeed, many letters and memoirs indicate that parents as well as emigrants often mourned their separation for many years, sometimes until death. "My Dear Son," wrote one Ulsterwoman, "You havent been absent from my Mind long for the last 16 or 17 Years"—emotions reciprocated by Irish-Americans like P. J. Ryan: "You know, dear mother, that you are the world to me. . . . Though far, far away from me I always feel that you are near me, and watching over me like my Angel Guardian. . . ."[167]

On the other hand, despite much evidence of mutual grief, there is no doubt that many emigrants were eager to leave home, both to fulfill ambitions and to escape parental repression; it is equally certain that many, if not most, parents either explicitly or implicitly urged their children's departure as a vital necessity to preserve social stability and improve the material welfare of those who remained at home. Given the dearth of non-farm employment, farmers' near-universal adoption of impartible inheritance made emigration mandatory for the great majority of sons and daughters who would receive neither land nor dowries and whose continued presence threatened intrafamilial and social strife. Moreover, many parents wanted money from the children sent abroad, both to finance further emigration and to bolster Ireland's small-farm economy. Although the inheriting son's dowry acquired at marriage often financed his less fortunate siblings' departure, whether from poverty or parsimony most parents relied on American remittances to pay their children's passage. Usually, an uncle or aunt in the New World financed the initial departure of an eldest son or daughter, who in turn was expected to send prepaid passage tickets and promise further assistance (e.g., a place to live, help in finding employment) to his or her younger brothers and sisters. In addition, Irish parents wanted children to remit money for other purposes: to pay rents and shop bills, purchase holdings, enlarge acreage and livestock herds, or improve housing and living standards generally. For example, in 1907 one witness before a parliamentary commission testified that increased savings bank deposits, so often cited as evidence of rural Ireland's "prosperity," were in fact "largely earned abroad"; "throughout the West of Ireland," wrote L. Paul-Dubois a year later, "the landlord's rents are often merely a tax levied on the filial piety of child emigrants. . . ."[168]

In short, "holy Ireland" and its basic social unit, the family farm, both mandated emigration and fed vampirelike upon the meager resources its victims earned abroad: a contradiction which outraged the urban socialist James Connolly, who urged, "Those who prate glibly about the 'sacredness of the home' and the 'sanctity of the family circle' would do well to consider what home in Ireland to-day is sacred from the influence of the greedy mercenary spirit . . . ; what family circle is unbroken by the emigration of its most gentle and loving ones." Indeed, emigration at once reflected and reinforced an increasing instrumentalism in family relationships which defied traditional norms and prescribed emotions. For example, although family bonds were probably closest in the one- and two-room cabins of western Ireland, even there economic considerations born of poverty quickly predominated. Thus, when Paddy Gallagher's family in west Donegal received an offer from a cousin in Philadelphia to pay his sisters' fares to America, his parents at first wept loudly at the prospect of "breaking up . . . the family." However, a neighbor, hearing the commotion, reassured them: "You may thank God," he admonished, "that the door is going to be opened for your children going to America. Look at our children that sent us twenty pounds at Christmas. Thank God, we were able to pay our debt and raise our heads." Indeed, parents eventually grew accustomed to the loss of children; for instance, an old woman on Great Blasket Island remembered that she "gave fifteen days crying and pining" when her eldest son emigrated. "But from that day out," she added, "I wasn't as lonely after any member of the family."[169]

However, Irish parents'—especially fathers'—calculating attitudes toward their sons' and daughters' departure had potential dangers which threatened the very interests which their emigration was designed to promote or secure. Impartible inheritance, fathers' arbitrary selection of male heirs and dowried daughters, postponed marriage even for the fortunate, emigration or social sterility for the rest: all exacerbated the intergenerational tensions normally expected in periods of rapid cultural change. Moreover, for various reasons a large proportion of farmers' children did not want to emigrate: in part because of extreme youth, inexperience, and strong attachment to relatives and familiar scenes; in part because of child-rearing practices which encouraged dependence and portrayed the outside world as "dangerous and hostile." The point is that, whether emigrants left home eagerly or reluctantly, *if* they perceived and resented the explicit or implicit compulsion which parents and neighbors had exerted upon them, then they might refuse to render either the emotional or the material homage which parents demanded. These dangers were real, for not only did contemporary Irish dramatists such as Synge (*Playboy of the Western World*) and T. C. Murray (*Birthright*) expose the murderous intrafamilial passions surrounding land inheritance (much to the outrage of clerics and bourgeois nationalists) but even some popular emigrants' ballads characterized departures as resulting from capricious decisions by "cruel . . . parents." Irish mothers, especially, felt aggrieved when emigrants such as Mary O'Hanlon displayed "cold & hardhearted" behavior at their departure, and the fact that Julia Lough, a seamstress in Connecticut, felt obliged to assure her mother, "[Y]ou need not ever be afraid . . . we will ever say you were the cause of sending us away," indicated parents' awareness of their children's potential resentment. Indeed, although contemporary eulogists and Irish countrymen themselves claimed that nearly all emigrants dutifully remitted money home—"a testimony of generosity and self-denial unparalleled in the world"—in fact a large number rarely or never did so. In 1888 a priest in west Donegal admitted, regarding those who went abroad, "We hear of two out of ten perhaps." He added, "The rest disappear, and are never heard from again." Likewise, an elderly informant from County Mayo later testified that although "[t]here were many requests for financial help from home, . . . it can be truthfully said, that not even half these importunate letters were answered much less complied with." Of course, the failure to write and send remittances stemmed from many causes, including poverty and consequent shame exacerbated by the emigrants' knowledge that "american letters is no use in ireland without money in them." Also, many ill-educated emigrants still found writing a difficult, if not impossible, chore, as did Richard Rourke who excused his "not haven Riten . . . for the Last four yers" with the self-evident plea "you can Sea iam Not a nexpert At the Buissnes." Nevertheless, while those at home could rage that "black hell would seize them that never wrote three words," many "neglected" parents could justly blame themselves for their children's "ungratitude": at worst they had compelled emigration, at best they had helped rationalize family relationships; in the first case they often inspired lasting resentments, while in the latter they undermined the traditional and emotional bases of their own authority and implicitly encouraged their children to demonstrate a comparable pragmatism.[170]

In these circumstances, it was necessary for Irish parents—indeed, for rural society as a whole—to develop perceptions of emigration which would obscure causation and responsibility, which would at once encourage departures yet neither inspire their children's indignation nor allow them to become so self-motivated or "independent" that they would foreswear or forget filial obligations. Logically, the consequent popular notions were highly contradictory; however, they not only mirrored current clerical and nationalist views but also functioned with considerable success in assimilating emigration to both the traditions and the modern exigencies of rural life. The discrepancies between customary expectations and emigration, the resultant grief and bitterness, were most blatant in districts where partible inheritance and mass emigration were but recently institutionalized. Very rapidly, however, emigration itself became a custom, with its own corroborating folkways. For example, as was noted earlier, through much of the countryside it was commonly believed that the New World was a paradise and that by contrast Ireland was "a Purgatory, where the Irish must suffer in patience before going to America." The origins of the notion that America was a land of gold are problematical, perhaps traceable to archaic myths concerning *Tír na nÓg* (the Land of the Young) and other legendary places supposedly located in the west Atlantic, or to sixteenth-century tales of the Spanish Indies told by Iberian merchants or Elizabethan soldiers. However, until the nineteenth century Catholic peasants' negative images of the New World more than counterbalanced the alluring vision, and in the present period many Irishmen and Irish-Americans charged that emigrants' letters and returned "Yanks" were primarily responsible for disseminating a false picture of American bounty which deluded the Irish at home and resulted in their bitter disillusionment when they went abroad. To be sure, in relatively isolated and economically primitive districts where emigration was novel, such as the Far West, the first influxes of letters and, especially, remittances from America made a tremendous impression on peasants unused to handling or even seeing such sums. For example, an Irish-American railroad engineer testified that although his laborers—almost all Kerrymen—often had to beg to accumulate the money they sent home, "[w]hen this money reached Kerry in so short a time after their arrival in America, of course it raised a furor all over the country, and the next thing was 'Hurrah for Amerikey!' " However, contrary to popular belief, most emigrants' letters did not contain highly colored, fictitious accounts or descriptions, and one would have expected that after a few years a steady influx of realistic, cautionary, even derogatory information about the New World would have dampened popular fancies, especially when many emigrants such as T. J. Kelly specifically warned, "It is all very fine for people in Ireland to think that if a man is in America he has nothing to do but pick up gold in the streets, but I can tell you that there is as much suffering in New York today as there is in any part of Ireland, and it is a great mistake for nineteen in twenty who come here." Likewise, most returned "Yanks" were poor advertisements for emigration: either because they came home defeated and impoverished, broken in body and spirit, or because—even if successful abroad—they refused to encourage others to emulate their example. As one informant testified, the great majority of returned emigrants did not describe America as "the land of promise"; rather, "[t]here was no man so guarded in that respect as the man who was there": "I didn't care for America," declared Michael MacGowan, who returned to Donegal with a small fortune, "and I often said to myself that if I ever had a family, I'd never let one of them go there. I'd rather have seen them gathering rags."[171]

Given this wealth of easily available information, reinforced by the negative image of America purveyed by Catholic clergymen and politicians, one can conclude only that the persistent belief that the New World was a land of gold was due far less to Irish-American efforts to delude the Irish at home than to the latter's efforts to delude themselves. In general terms, the fabulous image of America reflected Irish countrymen's diminishing faith in their own society, coupled with attempts to project traditional rural aspirations (e.g., for "independence" as comfortable self-sufficiency) on an inadequately comprehended urban-industrial society: since the New World was obviously no longer the rural arcadia it had seemed in the late eighteenth century, the peasants' compensatory vision for Irish poverty and insecurity was translated into a mythical urban setting where "The houses were all jasper / And the streets were paved in gold. . . ." However, the fact that this vision survived the impact of mass public education, much contradictory information, and the Irish countryman's proverbial skepticism suggests that belief in the *caisleán óir* served practical functions vital to the families which composed rural society. For example, in many parts of Ireland interfamilial relationships were characterized by a jealous and secretive competitiveness. Emigration played a role in this rivalry, because in order to maintain its own petty status each family that sent children to America carefully guarded the news that came home and always pretended that its offspring were doing well; many families burned their children's letters as soon as they read them, and the receipt of an "empty American letter" (i.e., one which contained no money) was never admitted. Thus, given endemic rural jealousy, every family's pretense that its own children were prospering overseas naturally encouraged the common notion that America was so rich that *anyone* could prosper there: in every household, the feeling was that "if such lazy, worthless creatures as the neighbor's children could afford to send home £10 every month, then America must truly be a land where gold can be picked up off the streets." Furthermore, since all young emigrants would be expected to at least equal this spurious standard of achievement, it was only natural that parents would ignore letters which described America realistically or which pleaded poverty as an excuse for not sending remittances. "They might not have bothered sending their pictures," exclaimed the angry father of emigrants from Roscommon, "for we know well what they look like. The pictures I would like to see are a few of Abraham Lincoln's."[172]

However, the most important function of America's alluring mythical image was in assuaging the bitterness of departure for potentially reluctant young emigrants. Given the abundance of contradictory information, Irish child-rearing practices must have been crucial in transmitting that image from generation to generation; parents who knew that their own decisions would inevitably consign most of their children to America could try to forestall any resentment by holding the fabulous vision of the New World before their youthful imaginations. As L. Paul-Dubois remarked, "Children are brought up with the idea of probably becoming emigrants"— "trained to regard life 'in the country' as a transitory matter, merely a period of waiting until the time shall come for them to begin life 'over there.'" Indeed, even Canon Michael O'Riordan, one of the staunchest defenders of "holy Ireland," admitted parental culpability when he wrote, "Children learn from their childhood that their destiny is America; and as they grow up, the thought is set before them as a thing to hope for. . . ." Thus, whereas traditional proverbs—vital instruments of socialization—formerly enjoined loyalty to birthplace, new aphorisms suited to new social realities stigmatized Irish life as hopelessly impoverished, and condemned stay-at-homes as lazy or weak. Given such upbringings, reinforced by Irish youngsters' own perceptions of Ireland's real inadequacies and America's real attractions, it was no wonder that travelers in south Donegal as elsewhere reported that "the lads of fourteen and fifteen are all growing up with the determination to bid adieu for ever to their native land."[173]

The vision of the *caisleáin óir* must have struck a responsive chord in many Irish youths. Certainly, it must have had a strong appeal to those who feared or resented the "necessity" to leave home, for the prospect of a promised land, with "gold and silver out on the ditches and nothing to do but to gather it," made that imperative much easier to fulfill. Ironically, that image may also have been useful for would-be emigrants who faced parental opposition, for if the United States was the paradise it was reputed to be, then they would be fools not to go there—and, once abroad, they could send back enough of that proverbial gold to stem their parents' tears. As was noted in the preceding part of this section, in cultural and regional terms the vision of the *caisleáin óir* enjoyed greatest credence in the Gaelic West. In social terms, America's mythical image may have had special appeal for farmers' disinherited *sons* and may have had more credibility among them than among their sisters or the children of landless laborers. As the sons of landholders, however petty, these young men had grown up accustomed to a certain degree of ascribed status and maternal indulgence, and so had been relatively free from the drudgery and discrimination endured by their sisters and their peers in the laboring classes. However, without prospects of inheriting land, they faced an adulthood of socioeconomic and personal dependence. Since nonagricultural opportunities were limited, and since most farmers' sons seem to have abhorred the possibility of descending to the ranks of landless laborers, their only alternative was emigration to American cities where they might recover the "independent" status and relatively comfortable life-styles they had enjoyed at home. Of course, in reality most farmers' sons faced years of hard, manual labor in the United States, with slight chances of ever attaining "independence" as traditionally defined. However, because of their social background and their prejudices, they preferred to ignore that probability and to believe instead in a vision of America which promised them the quick and easy realization of their goals. Thus, the available evidence indicates that while most laborers' children, and female emigrants generally, regarded America fairly realistically—as a land of arduous toil but superior opportunities—farmers' sons often emigrated with naïve expectations which soon shattered on the rocks of experience.[174]

Nevertheless, the complementary images of a fabulously alluring America and a hopeless Ireland helped preclude young emigrants' potential resentment, for even those who became disillusioned abroad usually blamed their fallacious expectations on the allegedly "lying accounts" of their predecessors, not on their parents. However, before the emigrants left Ireland, those images had to be carefully balanced by parental and communal sanctions against individualism and materialism. Otherwise, there was the danger that emigrants who eagerly rejected Ireland for the land of gold might also reject Irish associations and obligations (familial, religious, political, etc.) in their lust for wealth and excitement. In 1978 the anthropologist Robin Fox noted the consequent paradox still extant on remote Tory Island: although a child who does not emigrate is "lazy," one who does is "disloyal." In other words, although Irish parents encouraged emigration, they demanded that departures take place not from hedonistic ambition but only out of familial obligations to relatives at home or already abroad. Thus, on the one hand parents condemned emigrants as "selfish," "ungrateful," and "disloyal" for "abandoning" them; yet, on the other hand, they made clear that emigration for the family's sake was a duty which could not be ignored. Eager emigrants, enraptured by their vision of the *caisleáin óir,* were warned that "it's not wealth and riches that make a person satisfied," constantly reminded of the lonely misery their "deserted" parents would endure, yet also admonished to depart in order to relieve burdens at home and to remit money: "Confound you," people would say, "what's the use of spending your life here—Would it not be better for you to go to America and earn something for your father and mother?" Such conflicting messages placed would-be emigrants in an extremely difficult position: it was "a shame" to emigrate, but also "a shame" to remain at home. However, while "selfish" emigration threatened family welfare and psychic peace, emigration undertaken in a proper, "dutiful" spirit promised to mitigate all conflicts: in short, sufficient expressions of sorrow (often truly felt) and, most important, steady and ample remittances (often willingly sent) constituted the "price" which many emigrants paid to resolve the tensions between desire and duty.[175]

Clerical and nationalist strictures against "selfish" emigration and materialism in general served to reinforce parental injunctions—persuading, for example, the emigrant Thomas Garry not to "delay in Relieving [his family in Ireland] as it is a duty Encumbered on me by the laws of Church." Again, however, traditional child-rearing practices were probably crucial insofar as they stigmatized "boldness," enjoined conformity to authority and communal opinion, and inspired the felt need to avoid individual responsibility. Moreover, the very process of chain migration both reflected and corroborated such tendencies: one's ability to emigrate usually depended on family ties stretching across the Atlantic in the forms of letters and remittances, and the fact that most post-Famine emigrants at least initially joined relatives overseas made departures seem much less acts of *self*-assertion than of conformity to established custom—much less disruptions of family bonds than of a process of reunion whose continuance depended on the new emigrants' persistent devotion. "Ask one of the crowd" at the docks why he is leaving Ireland, explained the *Cork Examiner,* "and he would probably tell you of 'relatives in America'—as if he had none at home." In addition, if youthful socialization was not sufficient to instill grief and guilt, highly ritualized leave-taking ceremonies known as "American wakes" seemed almost purposely designed to wring the last drops of sorrow and self-recrimination from the intending emigrant and to impress upon the departing a sense of eternal obligation to those left at home. As a result, while emigrants such as James Mitchell might strive to be "stern and resolute," the parting scenes usually broke down all defenses, obliterated all resentments: "It is impossible," Mitchell wrote later, "for any one not experienced to have an adequate idea of the effect of a *last* look from a Father or Mother." Furthermore, once the emigrants were overseas, parents and other relatives deluged them with letters, either pitifully entreating or imperiously demanding that those in America remit some of that reputedly plentiful gold: "was there ever so ungrateful Children as his to A grateful father," they whined; "we had ye so much to heart . . . and how did ye forget us ye that we loved so dear"? While many emigrants ignored such requests, many more fulfilled their "duty"—often at great sacrifice—and sent home the money which financed further emigration and "kept Ireland alive": "I suppose," testified one elderly Kerryman, "it would buy Ireland a dozen times over, all the money which has come from America."[176]

Finally, underlying and resolving all other "explanations" was the key perception that emigration was exile—an enforced process for which neither parents nor their children were ultimately responsible. Even if departure was desirable because of the supposedly enormous gulf between Irish poverty and American prosperity, even if it was obligatory to preserve the family farm and sustain living standards at home: in the last analysis the emigrants "had to go" because past oppression and contemporary misgovernment by England had ruined Ireland and, in Canon O'Riordan's words, made emigration an "economic necessity . . . artificially made." This politicization of emigration was natural, given historical and literary traditions—corroborated and familiarized by pervasive nationalist agitation—which "explained" all discontinuities and offered such an appealing resolution of the conflicts and injustices within Irish Catholic society. Thus, as a United Irish League official testified in 1908, although rural parents' attitude toward emigration was "the more children in America the better," the emigrants themselves "attribute[d] their being in exile to landlordism and the support given it in the past by the . . . Government": a perception which ensured that the departed remained emotionally tied to a beloved and beleaguered homeland whose families and farms, religion and nationalism—all inseparable in memory—still deserved the exile's devotion and dollars. Through such fidelity, as one popular ballad put it, Ireland's "banished children" would "prove their worth wheresoever they roam / True to their country, their God, and their home."[177]

Of course, some emigrants refused to conform to the prescribed perception of emigration as political exile, for whether they left home bitterly or joyfully they clearly recognized the proximate causes of their departure, the sources of socioeconomic and personal repression which made Irish life untenable or unbearable. "Let writers write and talkers talk," declared one informant, "the youth of this country . . . looked forward to the day when they could leave off for the U.S.A. as eagerly as if it was the day they would inherit a house and home." Indeed, most had no chance to acquire house or home in Ireland, and, as was noted earlier, Irish laborers and women generally seemed the most consciously self-motivated emigrants, largely reflecting their blatantly inferior status at home. As another witness testified in 1881, although emigrating "farmers could not pay the rents and *had* to go, . . . the labourers were trying to *better* themselves": farm work "is not the life for me," declared one young emigrant, and "Dark Rosaleen has nothing to offer me but a spade." Moreover, ambitious Irish youths from all classes often realized that traditional Irish attitudes toward individual endeavor and success—the entrenched, peasant-bred hostility to "upstarts" who aspired to something higher than ascribed social "place," the malignant gossip which "warped . . . human growth" in what W. B. Yeats called "this blind and bitter land"—necessitated the removal to more-fluid environments as much as, if not more than, did Ireland's actual dearth of opportunities. Thus, more than a few emigrants found it "a Matter of Much gratification" to be "at such a distance of five thousand miles from the Slander and talk" of former neighbors, fulfilling one critic's prediction that "as soon as Irishmen leave Ireland and breathe an atmosphere free from fears, they become openly, as they are, like other men." Finally, at least a few Irishmen not only emigrated willingly but also explicitly rejected the mawkish sentimentalism and obscurantist mythology which permeated official views of Ireland and Irish emigration. Ironically, while Irish-speakers were most instinctively attached to their homeland, the very archaism of their worldview enabled some to perceive clearly the gross discrepancies between the harsh realities and the "idolatrous self-image" of "holy Ireland." Thus, the east Cork laborer Daniel Cashman wrote scathing poems mocking priests who advised the poor "to be satisfied / With your position in this world, working quietly . . . with your heads bowed down and your prayers offered up," denouncing such sermons as "lies, . . . poison and hypocrisy" designed to keep "the people under chastisement and slavishness" to their employers. Likewise, Seaghan ar Fan, an anonymous west Clare poet, "depressed by this rotten lonely, starving place" where "poverty and piety [were] vying with one another," sighed for the vanished vibrant world of the eighteenth-century poet Eoghan Ruadh Ó Súilleabháin, damned modern Ireland as "Leabadh an Chaca" (Shit Bed), and declared his desire to "sell this whole place for a half-crown." In a sense, emigration perhaps came easier to an intransigent traditionalist such as Seaghan ar Fan, for, like his seventeenth- and eighteenth-century peers, he was already an exile in a bourgeois Ireland which had reduced its Gaelic heritage to a set of sanitized slogans.[178]

However, most post-Famine emigrants were neither alienated nor self-assertive enough to defy communal demands that they deemphasize individual motivation and perceive emigration in negative, compulsory terms— especially when such attitudes and perceptions had been internalized from birth and reinforced by every institution which shaped rural life. In short, for the emigrants themselves, as well as their parents, the interpretation of emigration as exile was both traditional and expedient. Fortunately for eager emigrants, the process of chain migration permitted a reinterpretation of independent action as passive acquiescence. As a result, it was common for post-famine emigrants to make the highly dubious claim that they never had the slightest notion of leaving Ireland until the purportedly unexpected arrival of supposedly unsolicited prepaid passage tickets from America confronted them with an inescapable "fate." Thus, while clerics and nationalists might denounce emigrants as "traitors" to the "cause," the very process of emigration enabled young Irishmen to circumvent such injunctions in terms which validated traditional, dependent outlooks. For example, an elderly man in Mullingar mistakenly "remembered" that in the early 1880s, during the Land War, "[e]*xcept* when pre-paid sailing tickets came, emigration was over, [for] all were wanted at home to carry on the fight"; however, "when pre-paid sailing tickets came," eager young emigrants could then argue that they simply *"had* to go," while nationalists could claim that such excused and supposedly exceptional departures implied no renunciation of communal loyalties.[179]

However, the conflicts which emigrants found most difficult and painful to resolve were those in their own minds. In his short story significantly entitled "Going into Exile," the Irish novelist Liam O'Flaherty convincingly and movingly portrayed a young girl's contradictory emotions on the night before her departure for America: at one moment she was filled with "thoughts of love and of foreign men and of clothes and of houses where there were more than three rooms and where people ate meat every day," yet in the next instant "she was stricken with horror at the thought of leaving her mother and at the selfishness of her thoughts. . . . that made her hate herself as a cruel, heartless, lazy, selfish wretch." Even the obligatory grief and promises expressed at the American wakes did not fully erase or alleviate such tensions between desire and duty. For example, in a letter from New York the emigrant Anne Flood oscillated between self-assertion and self-destruction as her internalized conflicts threatened her psychic well-being. She began her letter boldly, telling her mother—who wanted her to return to County Meath—that she was "happy and contented . . . and never enjoyed better health" in her life. "I never once thought of going home," she admitted, and "you know when I was home I often wished myself in this Country and now to return I think would be quite a folly." However, she faltered, *"I would say more on this subject but I feel so nerves I do not know from what effect,"* and so terminated the letter abruptly, in handwriting whose increasing unsteadiness showed the effects of growing strain. In fact, few recently arrived emigrants dared to be as "bold" as Anne Flood, and whether sincerely or calculatingly it was thus much easier—and, perhaps, kinder to all concerned—to obscure motivation by claiming or at least implying that emigration was fated and unwilling exile.[180]

*Section 4. Exile's Last Hurrah: The Post-Famine
Emigrants in America, 1870–1921*

Between 1870 and 1921 Irish-America emerged from the near-ubiquitous poverty and crippling prejudice of the Famine decades. The process was slow, halting, incomplete even by 1921, and fraught with considerable pain and anxiety, but by the early twentieth century Irish-America was a relatively mature and exceptionally diverse society, enjoying some real prosperity, far greater security than in 1850–70, and inordinate influence in politics and organized labor. The high proportion of females in the Famine and especially in the post-Famine emigrations, for example, imparted a degree of social and psychic stability as yet unknown by the heavily male and more-transient "new immigrants" from Sicily, Poland, or Greece, and after 1880 the Irish-born no longer constituted a majority of Irish-America's population. Of the nearly five million Irish-Americans in 1900, about two-thirds had been born in the United States, and by World War I the Famine emigrants' grandchildren were coming to maturity. Moreover, cruel though the Irish emigrants' experience at mid-century had been, their initial concentrations in American cities, factories, construction, and transportation gave them uniquely favorable opportunities to benefit from the enormous urbanization and industrial expansion of the late nineteenth and early twentieth centuries. Consequently, the Irish were poised to take advantage of the rise of trade unions and the tremendous growth of urban government, public services, and managerial and white-collar occupations. Even new Irish emigrants were relatively favored by high literacy rates, and even more so by the existence of well-established Irish-American networks—familial, socio-economic, political, religious—whose absorptive capacities lessened the insecurities and strangeness of immigrant life. Back in 1868 the Cork politician John Francis Maguire had predicted such progress, but his had been an unjustifiably rosy portrait of contemporary conditions. However, by the early twentieth century Irish visitors such as the Anglican canon James Hannay (pseud., George Birmingham) and Sir James Power, Dublin's lord mayor, could be truly impressed by Irish-American affluence and acceptance. Contrary to what he had feared, wrote Power in 1903, "[t]he Irishman in America" was no longer "merely a hewer of wood and a drawer of water"; instead, such drudgery and degradation was now more commonly associated with Italians, Poles, Chinese, and blacks, while "Irishmen," Power claimed, "are universally respected, and are found occupying many of the respectable positions in the country."[181]

Despite these accomplishments, Irish-Americans remained in figurative, if not literal, "exile," increasingly divorced from Ireland by time and circumstance, eagerly embracing the opportunities which the New World afforded, yet still remarkably estranged from the dominant culture of their adopted country. For many middle-class Irish-Americans, the scars of poverty and proscription—theirs or their parents'—ran too deep to be palliated by success, especially when recurrent prejudice threatened or demeaned their achievements. Likewise, for working-class Irish-Americans, the skilled majority as well as the yet sizable unskilled minority, acute anxiety and even severe deprivation were still things endured rather than remembered. Moreover, not only did millions of youthful and elderly emigrants alike suffer from a collective, almost institutionalized homesickness but Irish-Americans of all ranks and generations, from Catholic bishops to humble laborers just arrived from Donegal and west Kerry, often sensed urban-industrial America's moral and human inadequacies for men and women shaped by customs and values attuned to older, less overtly competitive life-styles. In such circumstances, Irish-Americans often wondered whether full assimilation was possible or even desirable. "How shall we preserve our identity?" asked Patrick Ford in 1872. "How shall we preserve our faith and nationality, through our posterity, and leave our impress on the civilization of this country as the puritans have?" Twenty years earlier Thomas D'Arcy

McGee had blithely predicted that "while the Irish would become more American, . . . America in temperament would become insensibly more Irish." In 1850–70 poverty, nativism, and the Fenian reaction dashed such hopes (and drove McGee to Canadian refuge), but in the decades thereafter Irish emigrants and their sons strove to synthesize Irish traditions and American opportunities in ethnic associations and activities and, less successfully, in ideologies which would be uniquely "Irish-American," ideally embracing the duality of their situation and outlook.[182]

However, although persistent ambivalence intensified Irish-American spokesmen's need for collective identification and purpose, the extreme diversity of Irish-American society usually precluded such unity on domestic issues. For example, despite notable exceptions, such as the minister George Pepper and the editor E. L. Godkin, that "society" did not include Irish Protestants who distinguished themselves sharply from their Catholic countrymen and strove for acceptance and assimilation on a separate track as Protestant, British-Americans: the more genteel gloried in what one critic called the "Scotch-Irish myth" of America's origins, while the less educated often played prominent roles in anti–Irish Catholic agitations, as in the 1890s and early 1920s. "I hate Home Rule," declared a typical Ulster-American in 1890, advising his relatives to shun Irish Catholic–dominated American cities for Canada's more congenial Orange atmosphere. More to the point, Catholic Irish-America itself was deeply divided in a variety of ways: for example, between Irish- and American-born generations; among different waves of emigrants, in different stages of affluence and adaptation; between the English-speaking majority and the half-million or so who still spoke Irish as their primary or only language; and even between men and women, for as Hasia Diner has demonstrated, American conditions reinforced the gender segregation characteristic of the post-Famine countryside, and Irish-American females enjoyed markedly greater upward mobility and more successful adjustment to American society than their male peers. Perhaps most important, Irish-America was divided by class, for despite considerable mobility the growing social fragmentation and stratification of urban-industrial America generally confirmed and exacerbated the relatively small but crucial differences in skills, education, and capital which the children of strong farmers, smallholders, and laborers had brought from widely varying regions of Ireland.[183]

To be sure, group loyalty to the Catholic church, the Democratic party, and, in a lesser degree, to Hibernian self-help and fraternal societies could mitigate Irish-America's fissiparous tendencies, and communal self-consciousness would ultimately be largely submerged in domestic religious and political identifications. However, in 1870–1921 intracommunal conflict born of diversity was often paramount, for Irish-America, like the host society, was still insufficiently bourgeois in condition and outlook to rationalize or ignore the painful realities of immigration and working-class life. Paradoxically, only the increasingly anachronistic rhetoric of Irish-American nationalism could unite and impel to concerted action Irish-America's diverse constituencies, and yet its emphases heightened questions of identity and exposed its adherents to nativist charges of having divided loyalties. Far less alienated from their environment than the Fenians had been, Irish-American nationalists in 1870–1921 made sincere but tortuous efforts to reconcile competing allegiances and identify Irish freedom with native American traditions and interests. For Irish purposes, their aspirations were ultimately successful, but in an American context their efforts were fraught with perils and contradictions. Ironically, in 1914 President Woodrow Wilson's gratuitous attack on Irish-American "hyphenism" demonstrated that WASP champions of "100% Americanism" remained unsatisfied, whereas in 1920 Eamon de Valera's disillusionment with his Irish-American hosts reflected how irretrievably "American" most of the latter had become.[184]

In the early 1870s Irish-America began to emerge from the destitution and discrimination which had characterized the preceding quarter-century. A small but increasingly visible Irish-stock upper and upper-middle class now vacationed at Saratoga Springs, while a growing petite bourgeoisie of "lace curtain" Irish furnished parlors with pianos and strove to keep the still omnipresent "shanty" and "tenement" Irish at arm's length. With the development of cheap public transportation in the 1880s and 1890s, even those with modest pretensions to respectability could escape working-class slums for suburban refuges such as Brooklyn and South Boston. Irish-America's growing political influence was first reflected by the succession of "Honest John" Kelly to the leadership of Tammany Hall, a success duplicated in most American cities outside the Deep South by the century's end. Likewise, in the 1870s the gothic spires of the newly completed St. Patrick's Cathedral, towering above New York's fashionable Fifth Avenue, symbolized the Irish-dominated Catholic church's increased solvency and self-confidence. By the 1880s literate immigrants and their children supported at least one Irish-American newspaper in nearly every major city in the North and Midwest (New York alone boasted five), and by the early twentieth century a higher proportion of Irish-American youths were attending college than were those of WASP parentage. Most remarkable of all, despite the crippling depressions of 1873–78 and 1893–97, as David N. Doyle has shown, by 1900 Irish-America (the Irish-born and their children) had achieved "relative occupational parity with native white America": that is, roughly the same proportions of male Irish-Americans were engaged in white-collar or farming (35 percent), skilled (50 percent), and unskilled (15 percent) laboring occupations as were white Americans of native birth and parentage. The principal difference was in the farming sector, where Irish-Americans were minimally represented—perhaps to their ultimate advantage, considering the contemporary travails and consequent attrition of American agriculturists. Irish economic progress was

greatest in the Far West and Midwest, least in stagnant and rigidly stratified New England, but considerable in New York and Pennsylvania, where
35 percent of all Irish-Americans lived in 1900.[185]

Moreover, whereas in the 1870s most middle-class Irish-Americans had
based their success largely on advantages (education, skills, capital)
brought from Ireland, by the early twentieth century the Irish-American
bourgeoisie was primarily the product of upward mobility from the laboring ranks. On occasion the Irish-born experienced dramatic social ascent,
frequently through political channels or connections, as for building contractors. For example, by the 1890s Patrick Collins—Famine emigrant,
former Fenian, and labor leader—had become a wealthy businessman, influential politician, member of exclusive clubs, and in 1901 mayor of Boston. However, Collins was exceptional: most Irish emigrants ended their
American careers as manual laborers or at best as small proprietors, and
it was their children who took fullest advantage of the mushrooming growth
of corporate and public-service bureaucracies. For instance, whereas only
10 percent of Boston's Irish-born inhabitants held white-collar jobs in
1890, 40 percent of the second-generation Irish eventually did so; similarly,
in 1900 one-third of Detroit's American-born Irish engaged in nonmanual
labor, compared with one-fifth of the Irish-born. Perhaps a typical success
story was that of John Kearney's family in Poughkeepsie, New York: an
unskilled Famine emigrant, Kearney himself never became more than a
laborer, junk dealer, and owner of a small frame house; however, his eldest
son progressed from the job of grocery clerk to the post of inspector of the
city's waterworks, and another son rose from a post office clerkship to being superintendent of city streets. Daughters in such families often became
secretaries, stenographers, nurses, or schoolteachers; for instance, by 1900–
1910 one-fifth of all public-school teachers in northern cities—one-third in
Chicago—were Irish-American Catholics. Finally, at the very peak of Irish-
American society was a handful of millionaires—men such as the California
oilman Edward L. Doheny and the shipping magnate William R. Grace,
New York's first Catholic mayor—flanked by a growing number of affluent
lawyers, doctors, real-estate speculators, and second-tier businessmen and
corporate executives.[186]

Irish-American success often astounded recently arrived emigrants such
as Annie Gass from Armagh, delighted to discover that her kinsmen in
Indiana lived in large houses "all Carpeted with ritsh Carpet," with "all
mehogny furniture," and "silver dishes nives and forkes" on well-stocked
dinner tables. Similarly, the Irish rise to respectability helped assuage native American fears, predominant at mid-century, that Irish Catholic immigrants constituted a dangerous, unassimilable, and permanent proletariat.
In 1887 a Boston Brahmin declared, "What we need is not to dominate
the Irish but absorb them. . . . We want them to become rich, and send
their sons to our colleges, to share our prosperity and sentiments." Only
nine years later the prestigious *Atlantic Monthly* rejoiced that such goals
were nearly achieved, that "the Irish will, before many years are past, be

lost in the American and . . . there will be no longer an 'Irish question' or an 'Irish vote,' but a people one in feelings, and practically one in race." A graphic symbol of Irish-American acceptance in 1870–1921 was their changing cartoon caricature, from Thomas Nast's brutal, half-simian Fenian to George McManus's comic portrayal of "Maggie and Jiggs," vulgar but harmless lace-curtain Irish striving for respectability. Indeed, when middle-class Irish-Americans—politicians, priests, and policemen—upheld "law and order" and property rights against socialist agitators and exploited "new immigrants," as in the great textile strike of 1912 in Lawrence, Massachusetts, it was understandable why Yankee aristocrats and advocates of immigration restriction like Henry Cabot Lodge enlisted the Irish as honorary Anglo-Saxons in defense of the socioeconomic and cultural status quo.[187]

Of course, Lodge was at best condescending toward the Irish, and most middle-class Irish-Americans were painfully aware that their status in native society remained marginal. For example, a significant proportion of bourgeois Irish-Americans—publicans, shopkeepers, building contractors, local politicians—remained economically dependent on a working-class Irish clientele and often lived among their customers. Consequently, they could hardly ignore working-class Irish-America's persistent problems, nor could they afford overt indulgence in social pretensions, however much their wives wished to emulate their native American peers. However, problems of social and cultural marginality may have been even greater for middle-class Irish-Americans who mixed in WASP society. Although upper-middle-class Irishmen—merchants, proprietors, professionals—catered primarily to downtown, non-Irish customers, and although they usually lived in ethnically mixed suburban neighborhoods, save in exceptional environments such as San Francisco they remained seriously underrepresented in their respective fields and generally excluded from financial, manufacturing, and professional elites; this was as true in relatively fluid urban societies like Detroit as in stagnant Yankee fiefdoms like Boston. As for the lower-middle classes, although clerks, sales personnel, and secretaries enjoyed higher status than manual workers, they were economically dependent and insecure, and they often earned considerably lower wages than skilled laborers in unionized trades. During late-nineteenth- and early-twentieth-century America's frequent depressions, their struggles to purchase homes often proved unavailing, and even the successful usually were burdened with second mortgages on modest frame or brick houses located precariously in "zones of emergence" or inner suburbs, little removed in time or distance from the slum tenements only recently abandoned. Constantly in contact with native Protestant employers and peers, these middle-class Irish-Americans still endured irritating, if not economically damaging, slights and prejudices. For instance, when Peter Murphy worked in downtown Chicago, he learned quickly that "some bigotry toward Catholics" was "taken for granted"; at times prejudice was virulent, as in the 1890s when members of the temporarily powerful American Protective Association pledged not to employ, work with, or vote for Irish Catholics. Even

Irish-American political triumphs were circumscribed or at least conditioned by nativism. For example, in 1870 the New Jersey state legislature
abolished elective government in Jersey City after Irish Catholics were
elected to municipal office; similarly, in 1885 the Massachusetts legislature
stripped Boston's police force from city control when Hugh O'Brien became the town's first Irish Catholic mayor. Ironically, Irish dominance of
the Democratic party in states such as Rhode Island was facilitated by mass
defections of Yankee Democrats who switched party allegiance rather than
associate with the sons of former servants.[188]

In short, underrepresentation in native power structures, the precariousness of status in rapidly changing, bureaucratized economies, unwelcome
proximity to the less successful, and perhaps most important, WASP non-
recognition of Irish-American accomplishments embittered the Irish middle
class and kept old, inherited wounds fresh. Thus, James Michael Curley,
defiant champion of Boston's Irish, many times city mayor, and once governor of Massachusetts, never forgot what he learned as an Irish-speaking
boy in Roxbury—that he "belonged to an Irish-Catholic minority who were
despised socially and discriminated against politically." "[O]ften unconscious of their too frequent vulgarity," as one critic alleged, the Irish-
American bourgeoisie tended to be morbidly sensitive to real or imagined
snubs, invariably attributed to Protestant prejudice, and to any perceived
threats to their tenuous grasp on respectability. "What will the neighbors think!" became lace-curtain Irish-America's secular catechism. Thus,
throughout the early twentieth century the Ancient Order of Hibernians
bewailed a half-imagined "wave of bigotry and intolerance . . . sweeping
over the land" and counterattacked by launching a crusade to purge newspapers, theaters, and libraries of material deemed defamatory—including
William Carleton's fictional accounts of pre-Famine peasant life and John
M. Synge's *Playboy of the Western World,* as well as true examples of the
"stage Irishman" genre. Less dramatic but more crippling was the reality
that many successful Irish-Americans never overcame deep-seated feelings
of inferiority and insecurity: having learned too young what Eugene O'Neill
called "the value of a dollar and the fear of the poorhouse," they sometimes
became compulsive hoarders or rack-renting slumlords, "more American
than the Americans," as Alice Stopford Green put it. However, others
came to wonder whether the game was worth the candle. For example, the
affluent Irish Californian Michael Flanagan lamented that "in the midst of
haste and hurry" in America, secular concerns "monopolise a man . . .
body and soul, to the banishment of every vestige of . . . what the ideal
Christian man should be." Likewise, even John Boyle O'Reilly—ex-Fenian,
fugitive from Australian prisons, but by the 1880s editor of the Boston
Pilot, spokesman for "respectable" Irish-Americans, and recipient of honors as Yankee Boston's "token Irishman"—poured forth his private alienation in poems denouncing a society which held that "the meaning of life is
to barter and buy." Generally, such conflicts were internalized, mitigated
through religious devotion or later expressed in autobiographical fiction

such as O'Neill's *Long Day's Journey into Night*. However, they often assumed self-destructive dimensions: rarely in actual suicides, although O'Reilly seems to have seized that resolution after years of compulsive overwork and insomnia; sometimes in cultural suicide or apostasy; more often in chronic drinking. The historian John Duffy Ibsen speculates that "the tensions sewn into the lace curtain," as well as "the putridity of the shanty," reinforced Irish propensities to drink; and many Irish emigrants' journals, such as Michael Kilcran's account of Chicago in 1880–90, portray an Irish-American petite bourgeoisie whose aspirations and achievements were ravaged by an alcoholism born of crippling self-doubt.[189]

On the eve of World War I, most Irish-Americans remained in the working classes; however, their overall situation was much improved since the mid-nineteenth century, and their circumstances were extremely varied. In 1900 about 1.2 million male Irish-Americans (Irish-born and their sons), 65 percent of the total employed, were blue-collar workers. The great majority, some 930,000, were skilled workers, disproportionately concentrated in the best-paid, most highly unionized trades; only in Massachusetts did unskilled outnumber skilled Irish laborers, a dramatic change since 1850, when 60 to 80 percent of all Irish emigrants held semi- or unskilled jobs. For example, although in 1900 Irish-Americans constituted only one-thirteenth (7.5 percent) of the total male work-force, they composed almost one-third of the plumbers, steamfitters, and boilermakers; one-fifth of the stonecutters, leather tanners, wire workers, brass workers, skilled textile operatives, paper mill workers, roofers, and street rail workers; and one-sixth of the teamsters, iron- and steelworkers, and masons. Also, within heavy industries such as iron making, steel making, and mining, Irish-Americans dominated blue-collar managerial positions such as foreman and pit boss; for instance, between 1890 and 1910, Slavs, Hungarians, and Italians largely displaced Irish workers in Pennsylvania's anthracite mines, steel mills, iron foundries, and railroad yards, pushing the latter up the occupational scale into better-paid skilled and supervisory posts.[190]

Nevertheless, in 1900 another 270,000 Irish-American males (25 percent of the Irish-born and 17 percent of the second generation) continued to labor in unskilled, poorly paid occupations. In 1880 nearly half the Philadelphia Irish (including 30 percent of the American-born) were unskilled workers; in 1890 some 65 percent of Boston's and 34 percent of Chicago's Irish-born inhabitants occupied low manual jobs; and in 1900 about 56 percent of Detroit's Irish-born and 27 percent of second-generation Irish remained semi- or unskilled workers. As late as 1904, Irish-Americans still made up a disproportionately high percentage (11 percent) of the nation's casual laborers, including 45 percent of such workers in Massachusetts. Moreover, although fewer Irish-American women were obliged to work in 1900 than at mid-century, Irish-born females remained heavily concentrated in domestic service, laundry work, and the least-remunerative branches of the textile industry. For example, in 1900, 54 percent of the Irish-born women were house servants (compared with 19 percent of the second generation), and another 6.5 percent were laundresses; Irishwomen composed a majority of all servants in New England and 40 percent or more of those in New York, Philadelphia, and other eastern cities. In addition, although even Irish-born women usually retired from paid labor on marriage, in New England, especially, their children still entered the work force at an early age; as late as 1908, Irish-American children in Fall River, Massachusetts, contributed 45 percent of their families' income, largely through labor in the local textile mills.[191]

Thus, in 1870–1921 the conditions and experiences of working-class Irish-Americans varied enormously, although overall trends were encouraging. In the 1870s Irish predominance in factory labor, construction, and transportation proved highly advantageous as those sectors expanded in subsequent decades. For example, as early as 1870 nearly a fifth of the nation's building contractors were Irish-born: such men naturally preferred Irish subcontractors and employees, and the intimate connections between Irish-dominated municipal politics, the Catholic church's ambitious building program, and mushrooming urban construction generally gave full scope to what the historian Dennis Clark has called the "Irish ethic" of intracommunal patronage. Moreover, by 1900 the skilled trades in which Irish-Americans were best established were also those most highly unionized, thanks largely to efforts by the Irish themselves, especially by those already experienced in British unions. In the 1870s and 1880s Irish-Americans such as Terence Powderly played leading roles in the Knights of Labor, and in 1890–1921 the Irish were "incredibly dominant" in the craft unions affiliated with the American Federation of Labor, which then accounted for 75 percent of all organized workers; Irish-Americans were also prominent in the United Mine Workers and in the Western Federation of Miners. Such unions not only protected the relatively decent wages and working conditions which skilled Irish-American workers enjoyed but their ubiquitous nepotism and other restrictive practices also transmitted similar opportunities to members' sons and newcomers from Ireland. Other ethnic associations such as the Catholic Total Abstinence Union, the Ancient Order of Hibernians, and even the Clan na Gael provided networks which facilitated employment and upward mobility for their members. Finally, even unskilled emigrants from western Ireland benefited from preexisting Irish-American kinship networks and more generally from "urban villages" of Mayo- or Kerrymen which by 1900 provided a wide range of socioeconomic, political, educational, and charitable institutions, usually centered on local parish churches. Consequently, as Canon Hannay observed, by the late nineteenth and early twentieth centuries most Irish emigrants began their American careers with comforts and advantages which their predecessors had lacked. Emigration was no longer "like going into a City where you dont know anybody," wrote a typical Irish-American laborer to a relative at home: "Should your Brother Paddy Come to america . . . he can rely on his Cousins to promote his interests in Procuring work." No wonder beneficiaries of such aid and influence could often boast, "I am just the same . . . [in America] as if I were at home . . . surrounded by friends here and those that would wish me well."[192]

Partly because of these developments, many working-class Irishmen and -women did well in 1870–1921. Although the iron puddler William Murphy probably exaggerated his family's ability to "save twice 40 pounds A year" in the depression year of 1874, certainly wages in the United States were significantly higher than in Ireland, and for ex-farm laborers' and small farmers' children almost any jobs in America connoted improvements in status and condition. Thus, Michael Kinney rejoiced that, by contrast to his farmer employers in Kerry, his new bosses in a Pittsburgh steel mill "paid [him] what was coming to [him]"; similarly, the railroad yardman Owen O'Callaghan found his working "hours are short from seven to six" compared with the endless regimen of farm labor in his native Waterford. Even more fortunate was the Galway emigrant Matthew Murray, "tickled to death" to escape farm work, who through familial and political connections secured a lifetime job with Boston's Metropolitan Transit Authority. Some emigrants achieved exceptional upward mobility: for instance, David Lawlor, who left County Waterford with his parents in 1872, labored in Fall River's textile mills from age seven to seventeen but read assiduously in the public library, devoured Horatio Alger's inspirational novels, attended night school, and eventually left the mills for a successful career in the business world. Lawlor's rise from unskilled factory worker to advertising executive was unusual, but many post-Famine emigrants advanced to skilled blue-collar status or small proprietorships by the end of their careers: "I am getting along splendid and likes my work," wrote the apprentice seamstress Julia Lough in 1891; "it seems like a new life [for] I will soon have a trade and be . . . independent." Moreover, even unskilled Irish-Americans were usually able to provide their children with superior educational and occupational advantages. Thus, the textile worker Owen Mangan, son of a cattle drover in County Cavan, saw at least one of his eleven children graduate from college; likewise, although the Ulsterman Patrick McKeown never rose from the ranks of casual labor during forty years in Philadelphia, his children became plumbers, steamfitters, stenographers, and elevator operators. Even Irish emigrants who remained un- or semiskilled workers were often able to purchase property and become small rentier capitalists. For example, the Irish-American matriarch Ellen Quin, mother of five and wife of a laborer who earned less than $4 per week, worked twelve hours a day as a laundress, kept "all her earning to herself," and not only paid her relatives' passages to America but eventually "purchased a house and lot that cost her fourteen hundred dollars and . . . built a [second] house on it that brings her in six dollars a month." Such acquisitions conferred a modicum of gentility as well as security, as Irish missionaries realized when they visited working-class Irish-American neighborhoods and discovered that, despite their plain exteriors, "the little wooden houses had each a parlor & a carpet into which nobody got entrance except very respectable visitors."[193]

Given these overall improvements, it is at first glance remarkable that most surviving letters and memoirs written by working-class Irish emigrants in 1870–1921 reflect a pervasive dissatisfaction with urban-industrial life in their adopted country. Although most Irish-Americans offered assistance to impending emigrants, sending passage tickets to relatives at home, only rarely did they encourage further departures by praising America's economic opportunities, as had been common during the eighteenth and early nineteenth centuries. Instead, as was noted earlier, most letters written during the period conveyed cautionary or negative information about the United States and the newcomers' likely prospects. In large part, such letters accurately reflected the harsh realities of working-class life in a generally expanding but highly unstable, ruthlessly competitive, and even physically brutal industrial economy. Frequent financial panics and crises of overproduction brought wage cuts and severe unemployment which temporarily—and, in many cases, permanently—reversed the precarious gains of prior years and precipitated savage confrontations between capital and labor. Skilled as well as unskilled Irish-Americans suffered grievously during economic depressions. "[O]ur hopes become tinctured with despair . . . [and] we feel as if there was no use further to struggle," wrote the Belfast-born Frank Roney, an unemployed iron molder in San Francisco, during the dark winter of 1875–76. "This country has seen its happiest days," concluded another emigrant in 1875, "working men can hardly live in it now." During the crisis of 1893–97 over a fifth of the entire work force was unemployed, including 55 percent of the building tradesmen, 44 percent of the miners, and 30 percent of the textile workers—fields where Irish-Americans were heavily concentrated. The consequent misery and social dislocation in working-class Irish neighborhoods, such as Bridgeport on Chicago's South Side, became acute in the mid-1890s, reflected in the black despair and barely suppressed rage which characterized Finley Peter Dunne's "Mr. Dooley" sketches of contemporary Bridgeport life. Likewise, in the aftermath of the 1907 stock market crash, wages fell 15 to 20 percent, unemployment again soared, and to emigrants such as James Connolly the ubiquitous breadlines in New York, Chicago, and other cities seemed the only typically "American" institutions.[194]

Even during ostensibly "good times" the lives of Irish-American workers were fraught with insecurity: "life in America was very trying on a person's nerves," recalled one returned emigrant, for "there was always the fear that one might lose his position and become destitute, and destitution in America made life unbearable." Indeed, after forty years laboring in New England factories, the Corkman Timothy Cashman concluded, "There never was good times for the ordinary *honest worker.*" Although wages in the United States were considerably higher than in Ireland, so were American living costs—as Irish emigrants repeatedly warned relatives at home: between depressions and inflation it was "the same [in America] as in Ireland," wrote the railroad worker James McFadden; "every year something new comes up to make the rich man richer and the poor man poorer." Competition for jobs was fierce, exacerbating ethnic and religious hostilities: in the strife-ridden 1890s Irish Catholics such as Michael Kilcran lost jobs or promotions through nativist prejudice, and another emigrant lamented, "If a man to-day in America . . . doesn't belong to a secret order of society, such as the Odd Fellows [or] the Masons . . . he can get nothing." Although in retrospect it appears that the flood of "new immigrants" in 1880–1924 elevated Irish-Americans' status, its effects seemed entirely negative to Irishmen such as Michael Kearney, James Chamberlain, and Patrick Mc-Keown, who complained in 1904 that his trade of street paving was now monopolized by Italians and Slavs who "work cheaper & are more submissive than the English-speaking working man." Union cards provided some protection to skilled Irish-Americans, but even their gains were constantly under assault as employers sought to reduce costs through wage cuts, mechanization, speedups, fraudulent measures for piecework, and union-busting tactics such as blacklists, scab labor, court injunctions, and outright intimidation by company thugs, Pinkerton detectives, or state and federal troops. Willingly or reluctantly, Irish employers and what Frank Roney called "lick-spittle" foremen often helped exploit their own countrymen: thus, despite his conviction that "to deprive the laborer of his wages" was the "one sin which cries to the Holy Ghost for vengeance," fear of losing his own job forced the young David Lawlor to help cheat his fellow mill workers in Fall River. Although Irish-American leaders of American Federation of Labor–affiliated craft unions generally deserved their conservative reputations, the sheer magnitude of labor unrest in late-nineteenth- and early-twentieth-century America (in 1880–1905 the building trades alone engaged in over 9,500 strikes) indicated how tenuous was the status of Irish-America's blue-collar elite. Defensive exigencies, if not working-class solidarity, propelled Irish-Americans to the forefront of most major business-labor confrontations during the period, from the "great upheaval" of 1877 to the national steel strike of 1919, which launched William Z. Foster, slum-bred son of Carlow emigrants, on his career in America's Communist party. Significantly, workers lost most of these dramatic battles, and the persistent gap between poverty and plutocracy convinced many Irishmen that "Ireland and America is much all a like. . . . ther is People to be los[t] in both Places and ther is anuff be hind."[195]

Those Irish-Americans who remained in unskilled occupations suffered the greatest hardships and exploitation. In 1880, unskilled workers still constituted about half of all Irish-American males and perhaps a third of Irish emigrants' sons, and during the 1880s the proportion of unskilled probably remained fairly stable as a renewed flood of peasants and laborers from southern and western Ireland offset progress and attrition among the earlier arrivals and their children. Even in 1900 one-seventh of all Irish-American males and a fourth of those born in Ireland remained unskilled workers, as did about two-thirds of all Irish-born working women. Lack of marketable skills alone was a serious disadvantage in America's highly competitive and uncertain economy. Thus, in 1877 the young Mary

Malone, an Irish-born scrubwoman, lamented she could earn no more than "1 Dolard a week": "I am not capble of as earning big wages [*sic*] like other girls who can cook and [do] the large washings and fine ironings," she explained, for "I was not brought [up] to anny such thing [but] . . . was sent away from my Mother when young to the farmers to work out in the fields and I never got much in sight about house keeping or to be handy to sew. . . ." Although they were rarely so pathetic as Mary Malone, a high proportion of post-Famine emigrants—landless laborers and small farmers' children—had nothing but brawn to market abroad. Moreover, although post-Famine emigrants' literacy rates were significantly higher than in previous periods, in terms of social experience and cultural background many were no better prepared than their predecessors for an increasingly complex urban-industrial society which demanded work patterns and outlooks antithetical to those prevailing in Connaught and west Munster: most west Kerrymen "had no business in America," testified one returned emigrant, for "[t]hey had no experience at keeping watch on a clock or at the kind of work that was there, and consequently a lot of them came home again." In addition, despite Ireland's expanding educational facilities, a significant minority of post-Famine emigrants remained functionally illiterate; as late as 1910 a fifth of the Irish in north Philadelphia's Schuylkill district, most of them Irish-speakers, could neither read nor write.[196]

Lacking skills and sophistication, usually without even the frail protection which unions afforded craft workers, unskilled Irish-Americans were easily exploited in factories, mines, and domestic service, sharing travails similar to those of the "new immigrants" from southern and eastern Europe. Wages for unskilled workers remained abysmally low. In 1880 an Irishman in Philadelphia needed about $650 per year to support a family of five at subsistence level; however, half that city's Irish-Americans earned less, making up the difference through the earnings of working wives and children, by taking in boarders, or through systematic self-privation. Despite such strategies, about a third of Philadelphia's Irish endured chronic poverty: after thirty years of paving streets and digging ditches, emigrants such as Patrick McKeown were unable to save even the $9 cost of a passage ticket home; many others who did return were like Tomás Ó Crohan's brother, who came home a broken man, without "a red farthing in his pocket . . . [t]hough he had not had a day out of work all those long years." In the early twentieth century between a fourth and a fifth of male Irish-Americans still earned less than family-subsistence wages. Poverty bred impermanence: although most unskilled Irish women were rooted to particular locales as servants or textile workers, unmarried men without skills drifted about searching for work as harvesters, miners, or factory hands. Between 1880 and 1890 some 50 percent of Boston's predominantly Irish low manual workers left town; between 1910 and 1920 the comparable figure was 66 percent. In 1902 Eóin Ua Cathail reported from Michigan that the typical Irish laborer might "get work for a month or two, [but] then he'll have to go elsewhere . . . [and b]efore he gets work again, his money will be gone"—the prevalent experience of the west Kerryman Séamus Ó Muircheartaigh, who spent long years in America "Going from place to place, with no company at my side; / When night would come it was cold and wet; / Often I lay stretched out in the woods."[197]

Moreover, the jobs which unskilled Irish-Americans found were often extremely dangerous. Mortality and accident rates in American mills, mines, and building sites were the world's highest: an estimated third of all workers suffered crippling injuries, and disability insurance was practically nonexistent. Irishmen such as David Lawlor, Michael Kilcran, and Seán Ruiséal noted how employers' insensitivity to their laborers' lives and safety brutalized workers who grew accustomed to replacing killed or injured workmates on assembly lines and pit crews without pause or murmer. Other health hazards were more subtle but equally damaging over time. The west Kerryman Ruiséal remembered the choking dust of Montana's copper mines—"so deep in the ground

> That you'll never see the sun or the moon,
> But only the light of the dim little candle in your hand
> At the break of day

—while Lawlor and Seán Ó Gormain reported how the damp air and incessant noise of New England's textile mills produced tuberculosis, permanent deafness, and worse. "Their knees are broken and there's no strength in their backs," wrote Ó Gormain of Irish mill girls in the early twentieth century:

> Their heads are empty of sense and their ears are deaf
> From continually standing and tying knots
> Until they lose their minds and run amuck.

A second hand in the spool room of a Fall River textile factory, Lawlor carried 5,000 pounds of warps per day, and in a year his weight fell from 175 to 133 pounds: "the job was hell," he remembered. Ironically, promotion to assistant overseer in the weave room only worsened his health and brought him to "the verge of nervous prostration." "The sudden change from the quiet of the spool room to the thousand looms striking 240 times a minute was too much for me," he wrote, for "[a]ll night long the looms all assembled under my pillow and through the night they banged, banged, banged . . . [until] I resolved to quit the mill forever."[198]

Less hazardous but equally galling, especially to former peasants from western Ireland, was the strict discipline imposed by American employers. Irish-speaking miners such as Ruiséal and Ó Muircheartaigh bitterly resented the imperious "boss" and "the lean foreman" who "think . . . you're only an ass to be beaten with a stick" and who drove "all the wretches to work / At the break of day," while the English-speaker David Fouhey chronicled the plight of an Irish streetcar conductor, "hunched with his hand on the brake / Afraid of his life not one word to spake." In the 1890s the Corkman Timothy Cashman migrated from factory to foundry, from Boston to Chicago and back again, in an effort to escape "tyrannical 'Boss[es]' " and "slave drivers" who demanded "cringing submission" from workers, before he finally found employers who paid small wages but "treated the employees fairly." Likewise, Irish domestic servants such as Elizabeth Dolan chafed under "hard mistresses" who "want girls on tap from six in the morning to 10 or 11 at night" and "boss . . . you ever-lastingly." "Whatever you do, don't go into service," they advised their daughters. "You'll always be prisoners and always be looked down upon." In such circumstances, many unskilled Irish emigrants agreed with James Connolly's observation, if not with his radical remedies: "Immigration does not bring the Irish worker from slavery to freedom," he wrote in 1908, "It only lands him into a slavery swifter and more deadly in its effects."[199]

Given the persistent poverty of a large minority of Irish emigrants and their children, it was not surprising that descriptions of lower-working-class Irish-American neighborhoods in the 1890s–1920s were often strikingly reminiscent of the destitution and demoralization observed at mid-century. Both residents' and outsiders' accounts of Irish slum life in Boston, New York, Philadelphia, Chicago, and other cities revealed societies ravaged by chronic unemployment, alcoholism, and disease. In the late nineteenth and early twentieth centuries, Irish-Americans still contributed a higher propor-tion of the nation's paupers than did any other white ethnic group: for ex-ample, in 1891 the Irish-born constituted 66 percent of New York City's almshouse inmates, only a slight drop since 1870, and in 1900 the Irish in Boston's North and West End neighborhoods received a proportion of pub-lic relief far exceeding their percentage of the population. Mortality rates, especially from tuberculosis, remained appallingly high: in 1915 the Irish death rate in New York City was 34.0 per 1,000, highest in the city and twice that of contemporary Ireland. Infant mortality assumed frightening proportions: after a visit to New York in 1882, Charlotte O'Brien claimed that 75 percent of the children born "among the poor Irish die." "It would keep you poor burying your children," one woman told her. Excessive drinking was common among Irish slum dwellers—in part because they "could not stand the work," as a Pittsburgh Irishwoman testified of her al-coholic husband—and brutally mistreated or abandoned wives and children accounted for the largest number of Irish-American paupers. Likewise, Irish emigrants still composed a disproportionately large percentage of pa-tients in public mental institutions: many suffered the effects of chronic drinking, but even more from schizophrenia—ironically symbolic of both the extreme disparities in Irish-American society and the still-enormous gap between new emigrants' naïve expectations and the often unpleasant realities they encountered.[200]

How did post-Famine emigrants react to the varied circumstances of Irish-American life in the late nineteenth and early twentieth centuries? How did their experiences alter or confirm expectations and outlooks brought from Ireland? Certainly, their first exposures to the harsh landscape of urban-industrial America shocked many rural emigrants. "The port of Boston was our disembarking place," remembered one Corkman who arrived in 1893, "and the wharf of East Boston where we landed was of a miserable forbidding aspect. Dire poverty was to be seen all round, such wretched, horrible tenements with ragged, hungry looking dirty children playing in the ash-heaps of a nearby railroad. . . . Thinks I to myself:—'Is this the great country of "peace and plenty" there is so much talk about?' " Equally startled were the Connaughtmen who journeyed to the steel mills and coalfields of Pennsylvania: "And you mean to tell me . . . ," they often exclaimed, gazing in astonishment at the Irish shanty towns illuminated by the lurid glow of smoldering slag heaps—"Do you mean to tell me that *this* is America?"[201]

However, the prospect and eventual achievement of material improvements helped many such emigrants overcome initial disappointments and recognize that, as Elizabeth Lough put it, "we are better off than if we stayed in Ireland." Such sentiments were commonest among emigrants from especially disadvantaged backgrounds, among whom acute misery or blatant exploitation had severed emotional ties with home. For example, although other evidence suggests that Irish-speakers from western Ireland often suffered crippling homesickness, the impoverished Connaught refugees assisted by James Hack Tuke in the early 1880s expressed unfeigned joy over steady jobs and ample diets in the New World: "this is a splendid country," wrote one Mayo emigrant from Minneapolis, "I can sit at a table as good as the best man in Belmullet   thank God that I left that miserable place." Likewise, former agricultural laborers fully appreciated that although "you have got to work hard in America, and work to the clock . . . there is work to be got, and when you do it, you get paid." "[Y]ou need not wright to me abought goying back" to Ireland, wrote one emigrant from California, "I will not go back   that country wood not do with me now   I stead to long in it . . . [for] from the first day I landed in California my pocket never wanted money [but] when I was in Ireland I could not say that anny day." Female emigrants seemed especially prone to make realistic assessments of America's comparative advantages, less likely than husbands or sons to cling to old customs or romanticize the society left behind. "Maggie is well and likes this Country," wrote Thomas McCann of his emigrant sister; "she would not go back to old Ireland for anny money. . . . she sayes she had to work to hard when she was there and had nothing for it." "I like this Country real well," wrote Minnie Markey—like the equally happy Mary Brown, an emigrant for "love and liberty"—"it is the loveliest place I think on earth."[202]

Successful emigrants frequently exulted in the fluidity of American society, "where labor is prized and rewarded, and where every man is the equal of his fellows" as one affluent Irish-American put it. "I tell you America is a going to lift up the poor man and put him on a level with the so called gentleman," declared another emigrant, who could not understand how his countrymen could endure to *"bow* and *scrape . . . Yes your Honour No your Honour"* before landlords and employers back home. Such eulogies were reminiscent of pre-Famine emigrants, and later arrivals were usually less sanguine about the possibilities of dramatic upward mobility from the laboring ranks. However, at a minimum, post-Famine emigrants generally realized that the New World offered their American-born children opportunities unattainable at home: "my children is doying first rate," declared one transplanted Ulsterman, but "if the[y] were back there [in Ireland] what wood the[y] be"? Moreover, Irish visitors to the United States such as the priests Michael Buckley (1870) and Walter McDonald (1900 and 1908) noted that even working-class Irish-Americans were characterized by a "manly independence" which contrasted so favorably with the "absurd . . . aristocratic spirit at home, . . . and the cringing respect with which those of the lower rungs of the social ladder regard those above them."[203]

However, while "a residence under the wings of the American Eagle soon makes people think for themselves," as one emigrant declared, the promptings of their own ambitions and the exigencies of American life often obliged Irish-Americans to alter traditional attitudes and behavior patterns in ways which were less than entirely constructive. Nearly all emigrants quickly assimilated to American norms in superficial matters of speech, dress, and diet, easily persuaded that such adjustments were both means to and symbols of improved status. For example, Tuke's Connemara emigrants in Minnesota rapidly exhibited a "more developed 'acquisitiveness' " by purchasing white bread, first-quality tea, and fashionable clothes from storekeepers who easily exploited their eagerness "to get . . . into 'the hang' of the country." "I learned about ice cream sodas and . . . how to tie my hair with a big bow and . . . I began to feel like a real Yankee," wrote Margaret McGuinness of her first weeks in New York in 1905, "and that to me was a real accomplishment." Likewise, "there are very few Irish people who do not pick up the American accent and . . . form of speech," observed Father Buckley in Boston, and although some Irish-speakers such as the west Kerryman Jerry O'Connor later regretted abandoning their native language, others took pride in acquired abilities to speak English "grandly" which belied their humble origins. More significantly, as James McCauley of Donegal remembered, the Irish in America not only had "to forget a good many of their Irish habits" but also had to *"mind their own business"* abroad: "I guess," advised returned "Yanks," "if you are prepared to wake up and work hard, and keep your mind to yourself, you will do well in America." In other words, behavior and outlooks compatible with traditional, close-knit peasant societies were often dysfunctional in a ruthlessly competitive and individualistic America which obliged a successful emigrant such as Michael MacGowan "to do a lot of things against his will in trying to make a livelihood." Naïve young emigrants frequently had great initial difficulties adjusting to the demands of urban-industrial society, but relatives and workmates long settled in America usually subjected "greenhorns" to a sometimes brutal process of socialization, often showering the newcomers with pitiless ridicule. Thus, Patrick Campbell from Fermanagh was in Philadelphia less than twenty-four hours when his brother denounced him for idling about, saying, "[I]f that's what I came to this country to do I might go home again. . . ." Similarly, when Michael Kilcran returned from his first day's work at a Chicago slaughterhouse, his back aching and his hands bleeding from burst blisters, his fellow boarders only taunted him, called him " 'a big baby,' " and told him life would only get worse: "you must work or starve," one Irishman advised him. "This is not Ireland, this is America and there is no bread for idlers here."[204]

Kilcran swore he would not be "as heartless . . . after being ten years in America" as his tormentors, but he eventually learned—as another emigrant admitted—that "a man's mind changes a good deal in this country." Both calculated ambition and the need for sheer self-preservation obliged many emigrants to become "hard hearted and selfish," for in America, they reported, "it was a case of 'every man for himself,' " and anyone who failed to develop self-reliance "got it in the neck." "Every man you meet," advised another returned emigrant, "take him for a rogue." Significantly, post-Famine emigrants complained less of harsh treatment from native Americans, from whom indifference or exploitation was perhaps expected, than of such treatment from fellow countrymen. "Irishmen who own tenement houses I find the stingiest & most inhospitable," reported a visiting Irish missionary; "I suppose it is because they get accustomed to screw down their poor tenants for rent that they lose all ideas of charity or pity." "[A]n Irishman was the worst boss you could have there," declared the Leitrim emigrant Líam O'Brian, "slave-driving all the time." Even more disillusioning for many "greenhorns" was the realization that "[a] man Cant depend on any friend in this Country, as the whole of them (however near in Kin) would try to get your last Dollar. . . ." Similar complaints had been made in the early nineteenth century, but they increased in frequency during the post-Famine decades. For example, contrary to the expectations raised in his American relatives' letters, Jeremiah Cahill found them too poor to assist him and so joined the U.S. Army, concluding sadly that "it is a poor thing to trust to a friend for any thing." Other emigrants found kinsmen who were financially able to give assistance but unwilling to do so. Owen Mangan's "rich relatives" exploited his labor and refused to lend him the money to bring his wife and children to Philadelphia, self-righteously declaring that "every tub has to stand on its own bottom in this country." "That settled me with my relations," Mangan wrote, and similar experiences taught other newcomers the same bitter lessons in "rugged individualism." Consequently, the guiding philosophy of many Irish-Americans such as Jim Bredin became "look out for N° 1"—"it does not pay to have to many . . . friends . . . in this country": advice echoed by tough-minded women such as Mary Sheehan, who summed up the wisdom of twenty-eight years in America as "the dollar is your only friend not your relations." Indeed, some emigrants complained that Irish-American children cared nothing for their emigrant parents, despite the latters' considerable sacrifices: "old people are very little thought of in this country," lamented Patrick McKeown in 1904; "not Even there own families have any regard for them when they become played out from age and my own is no Exception as I could not get 1 penny from any of mine but what I can Earn myself" digging ditches at sixty-three years of age.[205]

Many post-Famine emigrants' letters also indicate that the obligatory ties which stretched across the ocean back to Ireland were finally beginning to fray and break: in part because some "un-Irish" emigrants—"of an uncouth, vulgar, brazen, ignorant type," as one traditionalist called them—were alienated from or indifferent to those left behind; in part because the circumstances of American life often encouraged emotional distance from the old country. "Duties" to assist newcomers, remit passage tickets, and support relatives at home were onerous burdens for struggling or ambitious emigrants, who grew increasingly hardened to kinsmen's incessant pleas and angered at their obstinate assumptions that all emigrants were "on the pig's back since they were on the other side." "You know how things is with you in ireland," wrote Michael Corr to his sister in Tyrone, "but what Do you know how the[y] are with me." "[B]ecause I am in america," he admonished, "Dont you for A moment Doubt but I have my own Difficultys to work through." Despite his objections, Corr continued to "run [his] life and soul out," "[a] slave in simpathy" for his Irish relatives, but other emigrants grew more calculating over time. For example, although in her first letters home the servant girl Annie Carroll of Chicago cheerfully remitted large sums to enable her parents to pay the landlord, after two years of sacrifice she announced her unwillingness "to be sending that old rent . . . any longer" and demanded that her kinsmen abandon the farm and join her in America: "thair is now use in trying to live in that country at all," she declared, "the people do not like to send money to ireland   it is all lost." Similarly, the emigrants Thomas O'Brien and Francis Higgins eventually concluded that their Irish relatives were "cringing beggars" whose "powers of absorption were boundless," and either stopped sending money or sent it via parish priests to ensure that it would not all end up in the publicans' tills. Moreover, not all post-Famine emigrants were as willing as Annie Carroll to assist relatives to join them in the United States. Although few were as alienated as Michael and Ellen Connor, who hoped their parents' ship would sink en route, many wished to avoid responsibilities for aged relatives and naïve "greenhorns" whose incapacities might drain hard-earned savings. Also, ambitious and assimilation-oriented emigrants such as Joseph Hewitt feared association with intemperate kinsmen who might "disgrace . . . any Civilized Community" and jeopardize their own precious "Character for Industry and Sobriety": "I would rather than £100 Sterling," wrote Hewitt of his alcoholic uncle and aunt, "that neither of them had never come [to] the part of the Country where I am."[206]

In 1883 Alexander Sullivan of Chicago, president of the Irish National League of America, demanded that the U.S. government curtail further pauper emigration from Ireland and declared that the $5 million in annual remittances had become an intolerable burden—"compulsory and of the nature of a tax"—on Irish-Americans and their adopted country. Sullivan couched his statements in traditionally nationalistic terms—asserting that British oppression caused Irish poverty and that further emigration and remittances merely shored up British misrule—but his line of argument accurately reflected the growing distance between Irish-America and Ireland, between contemporary lace curtains and embarrassing memories of famines and evictions. By 1880 over one-half—by 1900 two-thirds—of all Irish-Americans had been born in the United States and so lacked immediate ties to their parents' homeland. Although contemporaries sometimes stated that American-born Irishmen were as devoted as the emigrants to Irish nationalism, the paucity of surviving correspondence indicates that the second generation rarely maintained personal ties to Irish relatives. Other evidence suggests that James T. Farrell's fictional Studs Lonigan—a child of American mass culture, bereft of historical consciousness and identity—was a far more typical post-Famine emigrant's son than William Lomasney, the Cincinnati-born Fenian who vaporized himself while attempting to dynamite London Bridge. Indeed, many emigrants purposely avoided telling their children anything about Ireland: "the second generation here are not interested in their ancestors," admitted Agnes Kelly, for "we have never told them of the realities of life . . . over there, and would not encourage any of them to visit. . . . When we left there, we left the old world behind, we are all American citizens and proud of it."[207]

For emigrants such as Agnes Kelly, pride in their adopted country, shame for Irish poverty and "backwardness," and conscious suppression of acute homesickness combined to shape decisions not to pass on their own ambivalent feelings to American offspring. Others were so deeply alienated from impoverished, repressive backgrounds, or so impressed with the necessity to alter totally their personalities in America, that they contemptuously rejected Ireland and Irish ways. Thus, in the early 1870s a visiting priest from Dublin was disappointed to find that his own brother, like most "money-making countrymen" in America, "thoroughly despise[d] our do-nothing and gain-nothing system of going on in the Old Country"; "their Is I think no people as Ignorant In Any part of the world as they people . . . from where I was raised," declared Minnie Markey from the safety of Chicago, "they are to fond of drinking to be any good." Such emigrants rarely even wrote to Ireland—"since I left I forgot all about the past," stated one woman—except to vent old hatreds and display their newfound superiority to those left behind. Mary Sheehan of Roxbury, for example, could neither forget her humble origins nor forgo the bitter pleasure of writing home venomous letters disparaging Ireland and boasting that her own children were "Irish *Americans*"—one of them married to "a real American"—who "dont know anything about Ireland"; "I am glad they dont," she added, for "I know too much about it." Needless to say, few such emigrants expressed nostalgic desires to return home, save perhaps as "American tourists": "Dear Mary you would like I to go home," exclaimed Annie Carroll, amused at her sister's ludicrous request; "I do not care any thing at all about gone home." "I was born in old ireland," admitted Thomas McCann, "but I am quite happy sometimes I never think I was in old Ireland at all I never [even] think of it . . . for I do not entend ever to see it."[208]

However, for most emigrants emotional disengagement from Ireland was less a matter of conscious rejection than of time's inexorable process. Many remained attached to relatives at home, especially to mothers, but when those kin died or emigrated and when the emigrants married and begat families of their own, their centers of emotional gravity almost inevitably shifted to the scenes of new ties and responsibilities. Thus, James Butler, a Famine emigrant and widower from Kildare, felt "very lonesome" and longed for "the green land of Erin" until he remarried and settled psychologically as well as physically in the New World. By the time the emigrants were reaching old age, as millions were doing in 1870–1921, attachments to their adopted country had long since become paramount: "we have too many loved ones in the Cemetary here to leave them," explained the elderly Jane Crowe to her brother in Roscommon. "We have been here a long time—and it is home to use now." Their Irish youth was now but a distant, albeit vivid, dream, and while aged emigrants might fondly hope

> . . . the Breeze of Death shall waft that Dream among
> The hills of Ireland lost when I was young,

most were reconciled to dying where they had spent all their adult lives.[209]

Although a significant proportion of post-Famine emigrants thus embraced American opportunities and either consciously rejected or gradually abandoned Irish habits, outlooks, and loyalties, the surviving evidence indicates that a very large number still regarded themselves as homesick, involuntary exiles. For most individuals that self-perception was not consistent, but neither was it invariably situational—sometimes reflecting, but often conflicting with, objective circumstances—and it stemmed from complex interactions between transplanted Irish outlooks and American experiences. For many late-nineteenth- and early-twentieth-century emigrants, the exile imagery was merely rhetorical or ceremonial, a label of communal identification but not personally internalized. For others, probably the majority, it was a personalized but transitory image, deeply felt at certain stages of the emigrants' life cycle or on particularly emotive occasions, but otherwise suppressed or irrelevant. However, for a large minority of post-Famine emigrants, especially for western Irish-speakers and others whose backgrounds ill fitted them for urban-industrial life, feelings of unhappy exile were so ingrained that they helped shape the emigrants' "reality" by affecting their responses to American conditions.

Acute homesickness pervaded the letters and journals of most post-Famine emigrants. "Ah Nora," wrote one woman to her sister in east Galway. "It makes my very heart break when I think right of home, . . . oh Nora I hate to think of it [because] I do be that homesick and lonely."

Usually such feelings were most intense during the emigrants' first months or years abroad. For example, despite his eagerness to escape Irish farm labor, Michael Kinney was "very lonesome" during his initial year in Pittsburgh, "but then [he] settled down." However, others such as Margaret McGuinness and Patrick McKeown retained "that longing" for home throughout their lives and deeply regretted their inability to return as promised. Often homesickness was largely attributable to poverty, the rootlessness experienced by transient laborers, the lack of relatives and friends nearby, and, perhaps, the emigrants' marriage customs; for while the post-Famine Irish in America married earlier and more often than their relatives at home, whether from desires for "independence" or security they still married later and less frequently than any other native- or foreign-born group. Consequently, although those emigrants who did marry had exceptionally large numbers of children, the unusually high proportion of bachelors and spinsters in Irish-American society not only gave rise to publicly expressed fears of imminent "race suicide" but may also have contributed to the loneliness and homesickness which characterized so many emigrants' letters and songs. Thus, poor Mary Malone, slaving as an underpaid scrubwoman, was "verry lonseom and down hearted" and wished that her sister Margaret was with her, while Seán Ruiséal, a self-described *"Spailpín Fánach"* (itinerant laborer), complained of "wandering . . . like a helpless cripple / Without a woman to love me" through the mining districts of the Far West. Likewise, the traveling mechanic Samuel Buchanan and the Canadian lumberjack Alexander Robb felt desperately "isolated"—"thousands of miles" from anyone "who would care two straws if I were dead and buried tomorrow," Robb lamented; "there has not even been a day or hour," wrote Buchanan, "but the love of home and all earthly things that I have left behind always come to my mind." On the other hand, many emigrants who were comfortably situated, happily married, surrounded by kinsmen and neighbors, expressed similar sentiments. For all his success and fame, John Boyle O'Reilly "long[ed] to lie down in the clover fields of [his] boyhood," and although Maurice Wolfe admitted that America more than satisfied his material needs, he could "never forget home . . . [a]s every Irishman in a foreign land can never forget the land he was raised in." "It isnt but I have everything I want," acknowledged a woman who nevertheless felt "terrible" in the New World.[210]

Most Irish emigrants tempered nostalgia with reason. For instance, Tom Brick was desperately homesick for west Kerry but the girl he had loved there was now "married to a farmer and raising a family." That "put a crimp in my idea of ever going back," Brick wrote, "whatever the future had in store for me." Similarly, although J. F. Costello, a farm laborer in the Pacific Northwest, considered Ireland "the dearest spot in the world," he rationalized that "home sickness is something that's natural": "I often get a relapse of it," he admitted, "but somehow there seems to be no cure only to stand it. I often thinks that I would give $200 for to be at home again for the short space of one day. But when you cannot have what you like, you must learn to like what you have"; after all, he concluded, "I still think I am in as good a country as there is in the world to day for a poor man." Nevertheless, for some emigrants chronic homesickness crippled ambition and paralyzed exertion, as among those Irish-speakers in Chicago whom Michael MacGowan characterized as having "only one wish and that was to get back to the old country"; "many who would never see the green land of Ireland again," he wrote, "spent two-thirds of the day nostalgically recalling to themselves the places where they first saw the light." Indeed, however dubious the prevailing tradition in western Ireland that "a big number of our boys and girls died of a broken heart" or "of thinking long in America," there is no doubt that homesickness sometimes assumed pathological proportions. Many emigrants were tormented nightly by vivid dreams of home—sometimes by "sweet illusion[s]" but often by unnerving (and frequently accurate!) premonitions of the death of loved ones. Thus, Cathy Greene, a Brooklyn servant, became "heart sick fretting" for news from her family in Kilkenny: "I cannot sleep the night and if I chance to sleep I wake up with the most frightful dreams"; "I feel so nervous," she concluded, that "I faint often into a swoone" from "an[x]iety about ye." Likewise, Mary Ann Rowe could scarcely bear to write home. "I do feel so bad," she wrote, that "I dont be the better of it for a long time": at night plagued by dreams of her brother's death, by day she could "not banish the thought of home out of [her] mind"; "no matter where I go is equal to me," she cried, "nothing could cheer and Strange to say I am growing worse every day."[211]

In short, Irish emigrants' homesickness was both a consequence and a contributing cause of the difficulties experienced abroad, and it resulted from the interaction of characteristics and outlooks brought from Ireland with conditions and situations encountered in the New World. Although J. F. Costello was correct in asserting that homesickness was "natural" for nearly all emigrants, it was perhaps especially so for the post-Famine Irish because of their still-remarkable unpreparedness for urban-industrial society. Thus, recalling his family's emigration to Chicago, Peter Murphy remembered "how inept we were, how unfitted to battle for a living in a foreign country. . . . We were babes in the woods." Late-nineteenth- and early-twentieth-century America was "a surging workshop, displaying incredible marvels at worlds fairs with its spider webs of electricity, its dynamos, its cranes, its transmissions of power, leading to perpetual upheavals and revisions," but what perplexed the Kilkenny emigrant Francis Hackett—despite his bourgeois origins—was his and his countrymen's "lack of preparation for all this."[212]

Although the exiled nationalist Jeremiah O'Donovan Rossa believed that elderly emigrants, "brought over from Ireland by their children," were the most bewildered and "melancholy" Irish in American cities, a disadvantage peculiar to the majority of post-Famine emigrants was their extreme youth. Most were in their teens or early twenties, and many—particularly farmers' children—were even more socially than physically immature. However, now they were obliged to endure the tensions of adolescence and emigration simultaneously, and while many welcomed their new freedom from prior restraints, others lamented their inexperience and lost innocence and comforts. "I was too young to know what was good for me / When I left lovely Ireland," admitted a west Kerry Irish-speaker, now wandering alone through the wilds of Montana "without a penny in the bottom of my purse." In addition, despite the modernization of Irish cultures, most young emigrants—especially those from the western counties—still came from close-knit, parochial communities, and although an increasing minority evinced some alienation from relatives or the society left behind, most remained almost pathetically attached to parents, neighbors, and childhood scenes. Separation anxiety was particularly evident in the emigrants' initial letters, but longings for parents—especially mothers—often continued for years thereafter. "I never knew the good of a Father or Mother to I had left them," lamented Patrick Campbell, "but I never lost that hope nor never will, to be back with them again." "There is no friend that takes the place of mother," declared P. J. Ryan. "Who is so kind, so thoughtful . . . ? What attaches and keeps our thoughts continually centered on home? . . .— Mother." In reality, of course, "Father" could be an undemonstrative tyrant and "Mother" a nagging shrew, but distance, immaturity, and childhood training combined to induce acute nostalgia and emotional dependence. Thus, William Mullen thought "the time long as [he was] all alone," far from his parents' hearth; a "heartbroken, homesick" young Michael Kilcran wept copious, self-pitying tears when he tried to write home; and Eóin Ua Cathail reported that whenever an emigrant was ill or impoverished, "[a]las, that's the time he'll think of his mother."[213]

However, Irish emigrants lamented more than distance from parents. As Sir Horace Plunkett observed, an Irish countryman had a much broader concept of "home" than a middle-class Englishman, one which transcended the nuclear family to embrace an entire "social order"—the human and physical landscapes with which rural dwellers, especially Irish-speakers, had such intimate, organic relationships: "these are the things to which [an Irishman] clings in Ireland," Plunkett wrote, "and which he remembers in exile." Conveniently forgetting the drudgery and spitefulness of rural life, many emigrants expressed deep nostalgia for the physical beauties and social amenities of their native parishes, creating in memory a "holy Ireland" which comported with official rhetoric. "I can picture everything so vividly as I write," sighed one emigrant: "the hills and the fields, the bogs and the turf combined with a charming simplicity and hospitality which is not to be equalled any place in the world. I miss it very much and pray to God to hasten the day when I may go back once more." One emigrant who did return, Batt O'Connor of east Kerry, later explained, "To leave Ireland does not make one love Ireland more, but it does make one aware of the strength of that love. While we are at home, Ireland is a part of ourselves. Its landscape is as familiar as the face of father and mother. We take it for granted, and are not conscious of the strong hold it has upon us. But when we are withdrawn from the familiar horizon and find ourselves in a new setting, we realize that however fine and splendid it is, it is not home. It has no associations."[214]

The fact that urban-industrial America was startlingly different from rural Ireland only heightened emigrants' natural homesickness. Thus, the servant girl Anastasia Dowling felt "very lonesome here" because "the ways of this place is so different from home," and Seán Ruiséal lamented, although "I walked every village and city / From Boston to Coral Street / I never saw a place like the village / I left at the break of day." Plunkett believed that Irish-American propensities for urban life were attributable largely to "the fact that the tenement house, [for] all its domestic abominations, provided the social order which [the emigrants] brought from Ireland," but transplanted rural dwellers often complained of the relative anomie of American cities. "You might be here for five long years / Before a friend you'd chance to meet / Or a neighbour to talk to / Whilst walking in the street," warned one post-Famine ballad, echoing complaints of emigrants such as the Irish Philadelphians Ellen Wogan and Owen O'Callaghan: "there is not one here that I know," lamented Wogan in 1870, and "if we went out in the morning and walked all day we would not meet one face we know"; "he was a good hearted boy," wrote O'Callaghan in 1884 of a fellow emigrant who had returned to County Waterford, "too much so for this country" for "there's no fun at all here except walking round the park . . . quite different from home [where] it was so easy getting up an evening's fun any time among the neighbours."[215]

Similarly, as for Pádraig Cúndún and others in the early nineteenth century, post-Famine emigrants' avowed antipathy to the American climate symbolized the profound sense of discontinuity felt by many displaced peasants. Thus, while a few emigrants such as Patrick Burden were pleased to exchange Ireland's perpetual damp for the ovenlike atmosphere of a New York tenement in summertime, others found the climatic contrasts harsh and oppressive. "There's been a good deal of talk" that in America "you won't be bothered by rain or wind [for] There's only bright sunshine," declared the scornful Seán Ruiséal. "But I saw plenty of snow there and heard the rattle of heavy rain / And frozen candlesticks beside the bed / At the break of day." "The summer is as hot as hell, and the winter as cold as the north of the world," warned Eóin Ua Cathail from Michigan, and "I'm telling you . . . if you know this country, it would be better for you to stay in [Ireland] where there is neither cold nor heat."[216]

In 1872 the emigrant William Porter warned his brother in Ulster, "[N]ever come to this Country while you are undecided whether it would suit you better than Ireland, for no body prospers Here that thinks they could do better at home. When you make up your mind to leave Ireland, do it for good and all. . . ." However, a large proportion of young post-Famine emigrants never made such mature, calculated decisions to leave home, but instead merely followed the established chains of relatives and remittances to the New World. Many were reluctant emigrants who submitted passively and fatalistically to the exigencies of Irish life, while others who left eagerly did so with naïve expectations based on fallacious visions of the *caisleán óir*. When those visions almost inevitably proved false, and when even the emigrants' American kinsmen proved less "friendly" and helpful than anticipated, the frequent result was sorrow and regret. "Alas that I ever came to this land," wrote Séamus Ó Muircheartaigh, "And that I left my beloved Ireland behind," but

> I got a letter from a relation
> Telling me to hasten across the sea,
> That gold was to be found in plenty there
> And that I'd never have a hard day or a poor one again. . . .
>
> Naïvely I went abroad
> With my bag on my shoulder, praying to God
> To bring me safe to land through storm and wind,
> Where I'd be a gentleman for the rest of my days.
>
> Alas, when I landed
> I made for the city without delay;
> But I never saw gold on the street corners—
> Alas, I was a poor aimless person cast adrift.[217]

As was noted earlier in this chapter, although farmers' daughters and working-class emigrants of both sexes generally left Ireland with realistic and minimal goals which made them less prone to suffer disappointment abroad, comfortable farmers' and shopkeepers' sons often had grossly inflated notions of their future prospects and so were easily disillusioned. "It is a great pity," wrote Patrick Kearney, "to see all the young Irishmen . . . [who] come here from the old country, where they had places as clerks, store or shop keepers, living a good life—thinking they can do better. But they are mistaken. . . ." Frequently, such youths had to work hard for the first time in their lives, often on equal terms with the working-class Irish whom they had despised at home. Thus, the Ulster-American John Hall admitted that "this is a good place for men who do manual labour and never feasted on anything better than 'Indian Buck,' " but he lamented that for clerks such as himself he could "see neither comfort nor pleasure" in America. "Ah, Jimmy," complained another pretentious emigrant, "dacent people and priests' brothers, there's no respect for them over there!" In addition, emigrants of pious upbringings and genteel backgrounds were as distressed as Irish clerics by the "degradation and dissipation . . . profanity and immorality" they encountered in the New World. Maurice Wolfe in 1863, William Downes in 1887, and Thomas Waldron in 1907—all described American cities as "the most wicked place[s] . . . for Cursing Blasphemy and other immoral habits": "OH!," exclaimed the sanctimonious Downes, a fervent temperance crusader, "when I think of the innocence existing in Ireland, compared to this Country, it makes me shed tears."[218]

However, the myth of America as land of gold was so widely diffused in Irish rural culture that even emigrants from impoverished backgrounds often suffered bitter disillusionment. For example, when in 1883 the New York immigration authorities asked a poor widow why she had left Ireland with her children, she replied "with some warmth" that "she was like many other fools in that country who were led to believe they would pick up money in the streets of America." Although Irish-Americans repeatedly warned that "America is not what you people in Ireland have it cracked up to be," Irish country people persisted in what one newspaper called their "pitiable ignorance" and their notions that the United States was "a mutual-assistance-doing-unto-others-as-you-would-be-done-by society, in which every man's duty is to lend a helping hand to his fellow." Like Frank Roney, many soon discovered that their "exalted ideal of man's equality in the American republic was rather mythical," and although few emigrants embraced James Connolly's socialist solutions for America's ills, their letters and memoirs reflected the same encounters with "industrial tyranny, breadlines, cold charity, and exploitation"—and the same consequent estrangement from

> . . . this western land, so cold
> Where the throbbings of the human heart are weak and unavailing,
> And human souls are reckoned less than gold.[219]

Indeed, for several reasons emigrants of peasant origins, and particularly western Irish-speakers, were the most likely candidates for disillusionment abroad. Unskilled and poorly educated, such Irishmen and -women were especially vulnerable to nativist prejudice and the insecurities of life at the bottom of a society where "[a]nything you get . . . , you sweat blood for." For emigrants from western counties problems of adjustment were exacerbated by the inability to speak English. For example, the west Kerryman Tom Brick had obtained what he considered "a fair knowledge of the English language from the schoolbooks at Bally Ferriter" before he left there in 1902; "never the less," Brick admitted, "it was difficult for me to hold a conversation in the English language," and even after two years in America "I [still] had to translate my words from Gaelic to English, before expressing myself." The "broken English" which many western emigrants spoke, even the "Irish brogue" of English-speaking emigrants, remained objects of ridicule among native Americans; and as the historian Dennis Clark has observed, "For most native speakers, to have come from a society in which the language of their childhood, with its potent emotions and memories, was subtracted from their environment was a cultural wound"—one which remained raw despite their frequent claims to ignorance of a vernacular associated with poverty and shame.[220]

Perhaps the most formidable barriers to adjustment were cultural and psychological. Although inured to hardship, peasant emigrants—particularly Irish-speakers—were generally naïve and unsophisticated, most attached to kinsmen and familiar scenes, most likely to have emigrated passively rather than purposely, and least prepared by training or outlook for the "ruthless efficiency" of urban-industrial society. Thus, at the turn of the century Frederick Bushee observed that the Irish of Boston's South End seemed "severely out of touch with the American cultural environment to which they were at the same time so vulnerable": " 'It cannot be said,' " Bushee admitted, " 'that the ordinary Irishman is of a provident disposition; he lives in the present and worries comparatively little about the future. He is not extravagant in any particular way, but he is wasteful in every way; it is his nature to drift when he ought to plan and economize. This disposition, combined with an ever-present tendency to drink too much, is liable to result in insecure employment and a small income.' " Of course, Bushee was typically Victorian in blaming poverty on the moral inadequacies of the poor themselves, but his Irish emigrant contemporary Francis Hackett drew the same cultural distinctions when he admitted that American employers "were full of business enterprise, while unenterprise was much more our specialty." "The Irish in New York could patrol the sidewalks, work on the railroads, put out the fires, carry the hod. Their hands and feet were adaptable," Hackett observed, "but there was this mind lag. . . . [T]hey were scientifically backward."[221]

The point here is not that Irish emigrants' cultural legacies predetermined failure abroad, although the cold and "unnatural" ruthlessness which "greenhorns" decried among many Irish-Americans indicated the drastic personality changes which success often demanded, but rather that these transplanted outlooks shaped attitudes toward America and the emigration experience which contradicted myths of the *caisleáin óir* and which reinforced or revived old perceptions of emigration as unhappy exile. "Dear Mother," post-Famine emigrants frequently wrote, "this country is not what I thought it was," for "life here is not a bit romantic—it is painfully real." In such circumstances, expressed desires to return home were commonplace: among skilled English-speakers like James Connolly, filled with "burning desire" to "get out of this cursed country," as well as among Irish-speakers like Ruiséal and Ó Muircheartaigh who longed for the remembered securities of village childhoods. "Go back to Ireland, my modest young girl," counseled Ó Muircheartaigh,

> Listen to me, little lad and head for home,
> Where you'll have a pound and sixpence on fair day
> And freedom for a carefree dance together on the dew.

Indeed, impressionistic evidence suggests that post-Famine emigrants did return home permanently in unprecedented numbers, in part a reflection of the cheapness and rapidity of steamship travel which made Ireland "not seem so far away" as in earlier periods, but in part also a result of the negative impact of American economic depressions and urban-industrial life, generally, on Irish-speakers such as Sarah Doherty who were "never happy" in American cities and who "never got up a morning in it, but . . . thought how nice it would have been to be rising in Ballighan and seeing the sun" rise over their native mountains.[222]

Nevertheless, the great majority never returned: some, like the protagonist of Frank O'Connor's story "Uprooted," because they realized that childhood's idealized and timeless past was irretrievable; others, like Colm Cháit Anna, Máirtín Ó Cadhain's fictional Connemara emigrant, because of lifelong poverty. "[I]f I had the money I would go Back Home again. . . . In fact I would have been as well if I had never left it," admitted one of Ó Cadhain's nonfictional models, "but I suppose that will be more than I can ever do." Many turned to drink for solace, in barrooms awash with broken dreams of lost childhood homes, but most struggled on resignedly against American odds; "still I hope," wrote Frank Roney in the depression winter of 1875–76, "and still will hope while life remains to me." In this instance at least, post-Famine Ireland's devotional revolution served her emigrants well, for an internalized faith saved young Irishmen like Michael Kilcran and James Hagan from debilitating homesickness and self-pity, as well as from more secular temptations. Thus, Kilcran took solace in reflecting that the sun which shone on the Chicago stockyards was "just the same sun as used to shine in Ireland, under the guidance and control of the same One God . . . Ruler of my destiny," and although Hagan longed to see his native Ulster, he rationalized that "come what may we must all be satisfied with God's holy will" and with the hope that, as another emigrant prayed, "the brightness of heaven will shine on us someday when we meet where there will be no more sorrow."[223]

Fragmented by generation, class, and culture, torn between the New World's opportunities and the Old World's real or imagined securities, Irish-America in the late nineteenth and early twentieth centuries expressed its needs for community and identity in diverse but interrelated patterns of social interaction and institutional affiliation which linked past and present, communal ideals and divergent realities, in tenuous yet creative resolution. As in the past, newly arrived emigrants of peasant origin relied heavily for maintenance and comfort on informal and personal networks which reinforced customary ties even as they promoted contentment abroad. For example, the continued willingness of most Irish emigrants to remit money and assist new arrivals reflected satisfactory conjunctions of traditional obligations with pragmatic solutions to the poverty and insecurity experienced by individuals in unfamiliar, urban-industrial societies. Thus, while competitive exigencies could undermine familial relationships, they could also strengthen dependence on kinsmen and emotional bonds with home. "[W]e will stick together in this country . . . [and] form a sort of family commune," pledged Patrick Callaghan to his emigrating siblings; "each for himself and all for one another is the nearest way I can tell how to get on." Usually, strong ties to relatives in America and in Ireland were complementary, as for James Hagan, who both welcomed his sister to the New World and promised his parents in Ulster to "pay the head rent [him]self every year"; "it would be a sad thing to see the old sod leaving our hand," he declared, *"I wont forget you."*[224]

However, although familial bonds remained crucially important, as most post-Famine emigrants' letters gratefully attested, by their novelty and diversity the circumstances which Irish emigrants encountered abroad also obliged reliance on new, wider, yet still highly personal relationships based on broadly common characteristics, environments, and situations: for instance, shared regional origins, urban neighborhoods, occupations and work places, or ties of clientage to local community figures. New bonds were strongest when Old and New World affinities overlapped. Thus, when Owen Mangan's relatives in Philadelphia failed him, his former workmates from England (Famine refugees to Lancashire who, like Mangan, made a second move to America in the late 1860s and early 1870s) invited him to Fall River, found him work in the textile mills, and lent him money to bring over his wife and children. As Michael MacGowan wrote of his fellow Irish-speaking miners in Montana and Alaska, "Our bit of money was getting scarce, . . . but that didn't worry us . . . because . . . every person help[ed] the next." Likewise, the Irish working-class neighborhoods described by Finley Peter Dunne (Chicago, 1890s), Alvan Sanborn (Boston, 1890s), Barbara Mullen (Boston and New York, 1910–30), and John Healy (Holyoke and Springfield, Massachusetts, 1950s) were characterized by a high degree of informal cooperation and charity as poor families pooled meager resources and held raffles to aid each other in times of distress. Such environments provided staging grounds for ultimate assimilation but also reinforced both practical and emotional links to Ireland: in the former case through peer pressure to send remittances and support Irish causes, in the latter by replicating social networks and cultural patterns analogous to those left behind. When sufficient numbers allowed, new emigrants tended to reside and socialize primarily with others from the same counties or districts. Thus, in 1884 an Ulsterman in Philadelphia reported, "[T]here is scarcely a day or night passes that we have not some person from Dungannon or the neighborhood in with us," and "there is nothing happens in or about Dungannon that we dont hear the next week afterwards." Similarly, a later emigrant to New York City rejoiced to find himself in "a little Dublin," and in Holyoke the Kerry Irish were so widespread that they compartmentalized themselves socially by village of origin: some "were Dingle men in everything but geographical location," observed one Irish visitor. "They had their Kerry dances, their Kerry legends, the Kerry *meitheal* when someone was in trouble, and they made regular pilgrimages to Kerry itself to renew the faith, as it were."[225]

Indeed, some linguistic and cultural traditions were more assiduously conserved by emigrants in such environments than by the Irish at home. For example, in the 1880s a priest reported that the impoverished Connaught and Donegal Irish who lived in the Point neighborhood of Pittsburgh "[n]early all spoke Irish" and could "hardly make themselves understood in English" after twelve years or more in America—an observation later made of certain neighborhoods in Philadelphia, in Boston, and elsewhere. Likewise, belief in fairies persisted in eastern textile cities and western mining towns, and by the early twentieth century traditional Irish music was more popular and less compromised by modern influences in Irish-American New York and Chicago than in Ireland itself. Such retentions both reflected and reinforced emigrants' ties to an idealized homeland, and while familiar songs provided a cultural continuity which eased the strangeness of life abroad, they also evoked profound melancholy or bitter anguish among their homesick audiences: "My thousand sorrows that I am not near it today," cried a distraught west Kerryman on hearing the landscape of his native parish eulogized by a ballad singer in New York City.[226]

However, by the late nineteenth and early twentieth centuries, relatively few Irish-Americans inhabited insular and ethnically or even socially homogeneous neighborhoods. Dale Light's recent historical research on Philadelphia in 1880 confirms the findings of Robert Hunter's 1901 survey of Chicago tenements, namely, that the great bulk of Irish-Americans (80 percent in Philadelphia) lived in areas where they constituted a minority of the inhabitants. Although studies by Sam Bass Warner indicate that residential segregation among *new* arrivals from western Ireland remained as marked in 1930 as it had been in the mid-nineteenth century, on the whole Irish-Americans were dispersing throughout the typical industrial metropolis, their residential patterns determined more by economic than by ethnic considerations. Even more rare were Irish neighborhoods overwhelmingly dominated by emigrants from one or two counties or even a single province. Pittsburgh's Point district was unusual in that respect, partly reflecting its geographical isolation and abysmally poor economic attractions, and more typical were that city's West and South Side districts whose Irish residents more precisely reflected emigrations' diverse regional origins.[227]

Moreover, contemporary and recent studies alike have demonstrated that Irish "working-class" neighborhoods were as a rule highly fluid and internally differentiated environments. For example, during the 1890s Boston's and Chicago's predominantly Irish districts experienced rapid demographic change as both the successful and the failures moved out in search of better housing or steady jobs; Turley Street, in Boston's North End, witnessed an almost total population turnover every seven years. In addition, in most instances it is only superficially accurate to speak of Irish *working-class* districts, as if that phrase indicated either social homogeneity or cultural solidarity. Most such districts were leavened by the presence of saloonkeepers, grocers, subcontractors, and other small entrepreneurs and employers, and while these men were often former factory or even unskilled laborers themselves, and while they often supported strikes by local residents and customers, their functions and life-styles oriented such neighborhoods toward cosmopolitan socioeconomic and political structures and values which ultimately vitiated both proletarian and parochial identities. Working-class Irish emigrants' ambivalent attitudes toward the Irish-American policemen in their midst—admiration for their status mingling with contempt for their social apostasy—symbolized such neighborhoods' vulnerability, cultural and political; and the fact that many emigrants' children and grandchildren scorned manual labor for the lowest rungs on the white-collar ladder both reflected their elders' attitudes toward "working-class community" and promoted its eventual disintegration. As David N. Doyle has noted, although early twentieth-century Irish-America remained predominantly blue-collar in occupation, "most Irish American families were fluid in their kinship and communal status relationships: the railroad worker, switchman or maintenance worker, would have a cousin a grocer, a brother a small official, a son a teacher or a traindriver." Consequently, "[h]e did not identify with a closed community based on occupational uniformity, and slight, marginal chances for improvement, whatever the facts of his personal prospects. He identified with a quasi-middle class subsociety. . . ." Although more applicable, for example, to the New York Irish in the 1910s than in the 1880s, and less true in New England mill towns during any period than elsewhere, Doyle's argument does not preclude Irish-Americans' alienation but again highlights the ambiguities and tensions inherent in their situation and outlook.[228]

Given the increasing maturity, variety, and fluidity of Irish-American society, it was perhaps inevitable that its identity and aspirations would find expression in formal and specialized associations. In the late 1860s and early 1870s began what the historian Dale Light has called Irish-America's transition from "neighborhood society to ethnic society": the latter based on overlapping institutional networks which linked local parishes to cosmopolitan programs and ideals as defined primarily by an Irish-American bourgeoisie—merchants, professionals, churchmen, and politicians—although often in conjunction with skilled trade union leaders. For example, studies of Irish communities in Philadelphia, Pittsburgh, Chicago, and New England mill towns demonstrate that the late 1860s and early 1870s generally witnessed the first flowering of permanent religious, political, and sociocultural institutions on the parish level, as well as the establishment of national ethnic- and religious-based organizations which (unlike the Fenians) were explicitly assimilation oriented. Both on national and on local levels, these associations were usually dominated by middle-class Irishmen, often of American birth. However, it would for several reasons be misleading to interpret these institutions as merely green-tinged facsimiles of their native, Protestant-American counterparts or simply as purveyors of Victorian values which harmonized precisely with those of the mainstream culture. Although bourgeois-dominated, these were designedly ethnic and/or Catholic—not class-specific—associations, and as such they claimed to, and perforce had to, reflect the enormous range of Irish and Irish-American experiences, outlooks, and traditions which often conflicted with those of the native American middle class. The competition and co-optation which often characterized relations among Irish-American institutions, and the diverse and even contradictory policies and ideologies which various associations pursued, continued to reflect Irish-America's still-ambivalent socioeconomic and cultural status and also generated needs and desires for some kind of overarching unanimity of communal purpose and self-defense.[229]

Moreover, in the 1870s and 1880s many, perhaps most, working-class Irish-Americans found primary expression of both ethnic and social identities not in bourgeois institutions but in militant labor unions and, to a lesser extent, in radical politics which linked Irish protest traditions to American urban-industrial conditions and grievances: sometimes subterraneously, as in the Molly Maguires of the Pennsylvania coalfields (1870s); openly but regionally, as in Denis Kearney's Workingmen's Union and party in California (late 1870s); nationally and climactically in the Irish-dominated Knights of Labor and the Union Labor party, which attained peak strength in the mid-1880s, the latter nearly victorious in mayoralty elections in New York and Chicago. As Michael Gordon, Victor Walsh, and other scholars have demonstrated, in this period labor organizations dominated associational activity in working-class Irish neighborhoods such as Woods Run, near Pittsburgh, where common employment and suffering in local iron and steel mills reinforced ethnic bonds. Admittedly, by 1900–1921 the class-collaborationist and assimilationist policies of the American Federation of Labor had come to characterize most *organized* Irish-American workers, but militant traditions persisted: regionally among "new" Irish emigrant miners in the Far West, individually among both expatriate and American-born radicals such as James Larkin and James Connolly of the radical Industrial Workers of the World, and Elizabeth Gurley Flynn and William Z. Foster of the nascent American Communist party. Consequently, the still-desperate condition of many Irish-American workers combined with the vague alienation of newly arrived peasants to oblige most middle-class Hibernian spokesmen, themselves often sensitive to past poverty and contemporary scorn, to voice criticism of native institutions and support for distinctively Irish aspirations which their Anglo-Protestant peers considered harsh and disloyal.[230]

In short, like their constituency, late-nineteenth- and early-twentieth-century Irish-American institutions were Janus-faced, divided between bourgeois aspirations and proletarian realities, torn by conflicting loyalties to the United States and Ireland. Paradoxes were especially evident in those institutions which were only partially and circumstantially Irish-American—namely, the Democratic party and Catholic church, which embraced both Irish and non-Irish citizens as well as Irish-Americans of all classes and stages of adaptation.

The Irish relationship to the Democratic party was intimate, often dominant on local and state levels by 1900, but more ambivalent and conditional than critics who complained of the "Irish Conquest of Our Cities" generally realized. Despite the charity, employment opportunities, and other patronage parceled out to voters by local and state "machines," as a *group* Irish-American workers received few benefits from Irish-stock politicians such as John Kelly or Richard Croker of Tammany Hall, whose primary concern was to loot city coffers in league with equally unscrupulous native and Irish businessmen. Irish-stock advocates of "good government," such as San Francisco's James D. Phelan, were even less sympathetic to the Irish poor, their "reforms" consisting primarily of budget cuts and model charters which promoted corporate and injured working-class interests. As a consequence, both as workers and as Irishmen—the two identities conflated by a sense of economic and ethnic persecution—Irish-Americans occasionally revolted against the Democratic party, forming or flirting with radical alternatives, as in Massachusetts in 1866–76, in California in 1877–80, in New York, Chicago, and elsewhere in the mid-1880s, and in San Francisco in 1901–5. Indeed, on at least two occasions only massive voter fraud thwarted the efforts of New York City's working-class Irish to overthrow Tammany hegemony: in 1870 when a banished Fenian, Jeremiah O'Donovan Rossa, apparently defeated Boss Tweed himself for election to the state senate; and again in 1886 when Tammany regulars "counted out" the land reformer Henry George, who ran for mayor with overwhelming support from Irish labor. To be sure, by the early twentieth century a more prosperous and politically integrated Irish-America was almost automatically Democratic, local dissensions now expressed merely in personal, intraparty feuds between rival bosses. Also, by this time Irish-stock political leaders were more assiduous in cultivating working-class loyalty, for example, by perfecting informal service networks on neighborhood levels, by forging pragmatic alliances with Irish-stock bishops and AF of L leaders, and by hesitant support of various Progressive reforms (e.g., tenement-house regulation, factory-safety laws) which both appeased proletarian discontents and expanded opportunities for patronage and graft. However, the earlier revolts should be remembered, for while they helped push Irish-stock politicians leftward, at least superficially, they also indicated how narrow were the allowed choices of political expression which Irish-Americans (and workers generally) enjoyed in a system designed to obscure conflict and contain or if necessary crush working-class challenges to business rule.[231]

Moreover, although Democratic party affiliations and activities ultimately promoted Irish-American assimilation, in the short term they also reinforced ethnic identities and exclusiveness. Ward-based patronage systems, centered on local saloonkeepers, served insulating and protective as well as integrative functions, stabilizing and perpetuating patterns of "village" relationships and consciousness. In addition, given the social tensions described above, it was both natural and expedient for Irish-stock and other Democratic bosses to cement voter allegiance by emphasizing specifically Irish themes and interests, especially those symbolic rather than substantive and those furthest removed from local realities and responsibilities, such as nationalist causes. Of course, "twisting the British lion's tail" for Anglophobic audiences was a cynical game played by politicians of both parties; however, Democrats could play it best, in part because of the usual ethnic affinities between Democratic orators and auditors, in part because anti-Irish Catholic prejudice remained a powerful, if sometimes

embarrassing, Republican party constituent. Foreign observers as disparate
as Horace Plunkett and James Connolly adjudged Democratic politicians'
espousals of Irish nationalism as superficial or insincere. Certainly, on the
national level the party gave little practical aid to Ireland's cause, and on
the local level nationalist clubs were merely stepping-stones to power for
aspiring politicos such as Boston's James Michael Curley. "[T]he local issue
is the Dago Rinaldo," declared the Tammany candidate Tim Campbell of
his Republican opponent. "He is from Italy, I am from Ireland. Are you in
favor of Italy or Ireland?" It was a crude appeal but nonetheless effective
for many Irish-American voters, especially new emigrants, who perhaps
still viewed St. Patrick's Day parades and the hoisting of Irish flags over
city hall more as symbols of triumphant tribalism—as WASP reformers
feared—than as indications of compatible loyalties or eventual amalgamation, the rationalizations made contemporaneously by middle-class Hibernians sensitive to nativist strictures, and subsequently by social and political scientists.[232]

Like the Democratic party, the American Catholic church both reflected
and formulated Irish-America's varied interests and outlooks. In the late-
nineteenth- and early-twentieth-century United States, as in Ireland, Catholicism became the central institution of Irish life and the primary source
and expression of Irish identity. In part this was due to religious and
political developments in Ireland itself: thanks to the devotional revolution
wrought by Cardinal Cullen and his successors and to the successful efforts
of churchmen such as Croke and Walsh to merge Irish Catholicism and
nationalism, post-Famine emigrants generally were more faithfully practicing Catholics than their predecessors and more likely to perceive formal
religion and Irishness as synonymous. Moreover, the emigration experience
often completed Irish processes of sociocultural modernization which reduced the importance of alternative identifications (e.g., provincial or linguistic), just as the insecurities of a strange environment promoted the
newcomers' increased reliance on a traditional and comforting faith. At
least equally important were changes in the American Catholic church. As
churchmen of Irish stock or birth became increasingly predominant in the
American hierarchy and priesthood, Irish emigrants were less likely to
experience the alienation from non-Irish pastors which had disturbed the
church in the early nineteenth century. More crucial, with the aid of a
more settled and prosperous laity, bishops and priests made heroic and
ultimately successful efforts to provide the physical facilities for devotion
and religious instruction so lacking at mid-century. Thus, whereas in 1864
an emigrant to New York City could justly complain that "the Roman
Cathlick Religion is not carried to its full extent here as in old Ireland,"
only nine years later an Irishman in an upstate New York town could rejoice that, thanks to new facilities and resident priests, "we can mind our
duty as well here as we can do in Ireland if it is not our own fault." Between 1870 and 1921 the church constructed thousands of cathedrals,
churches, rectories and convents, parochial schools, colleges, and semi-

naries, and in 1889 the official Catholic University, in Washington, D.C. Nationally, for example, between 1880 and 1920 the number of parochial schools increased from 2,246 to 5,382, and their combined enrollment rose from 400,000 to 1.7 million, faster even than the enormous rise of the nation's Catholic population, from 6.1 to 17.7 million. Locally, the experience of the working-class Irish parish of St. Andrew's, in greater Pittsburgh, was probably typical: the parishioners received their first permanent church and priest in the late 1860s, an additional pastor in 1873; their donations built a parochial school in 1877, a convent for the teaching nuns in 1880, and a large rectory in 1890; by 1892 parish church properties were worth $100,000, and annual collections from the faithful averaged $8,000. Given their and their church's mid-century poverty, such accomplishments were considerable, and Irish-Americans naturally pointed with pride to these edifices as proof of their rising fortunes and respectability in native society. However, like the local Democratic clubs, parish churches and other religious institutions both linked the faithful to and insulated them from a wider world.[233]

Between 1870 and 1921, especially in 1880–1900, American Catholic churchmen were divided over the ideal relationship between the church and American society. In part the debate on this side of the Atlantic reflected Rome's broader efforts to defend the faith in an increasingly secular, urban-industrial world. However, in North America the issue was compounded by Catholicism's minority status and by the fact that its adherents were disproportionately concentrated in the urban working class (rather than in agriculture, as in Europe) and were largely of foreign birth or parentage, as were the major disputants themselves. The controversy in the American church reflected this peculiar situation and, more specifically, the tensions and crosscurrents within Catholic Irish-America. It was not coincidental that nearly all the churchmen prominent in debate on all sides were of Irish birth or background, thereby mirroring their people's diverse situations and viewpoints. Likewise, although Rome ultimately decided the issues involved, their specific resolutions owed much to Irish traditions and influences.[234]

The general questions which agitated Irish-American clerics were, first, their church's ideal posture toward a Protestant-dominated society, its secular institutions and individualistic values; second, the church's proper attitude toward current socioeconomic conditions and trends; third, the church's relationship to the mass of its adherents in their roles as *workers,* often in conflict with employers and legal authorities; and, fourth, issues of assimilation versus ethnic integrity which arose from the faithful's overwhelmingly foreign origins. Out of these emerged specific controversies over labor unions, Catholic membership in "secret" or non-Catholic associations, education, the laity's role in the church, and ethnic exclusiveness. Nevertheless, although their stands on these issues varied widely, all the disputants shared certain fears: of nativism; of violent conflict, whether based on religion or on class; and, perhaps most important, of "leakage" from the church to Protestantism, religious indifference, or, worst of all, "atheistic socialism." Viewed positively, Irish-American clerics were unanimous in devotion to their church's institutional interests and primary mission, the salvation of souls in a materialistic age. Moreover, in varying degrees all were critical of at least the economic and moral *consequences* of industrial capitalism: indeed, their controversies' immediate origins lay in churchmen's varied responses to the economic crises and conflicts of the late 1870s and 1880s, more specifically to their acute embarrassment over the Molly Maguire trials and executions of 1876, the great strikes of 1877, and the subsequent rise of the Knights of Labor—all events in which Irish Catholics played predominant roles, thereby provoking renewed nativist charges of Irish Catholic disloyalty.

By the mid-1880s Irish-American churchmen had divided into three identifiable groups: radicals, liberals (or "Americanists"), and conservatives. The radicals comprised merely a handful of priests, centered in New York City, the most prominent and outspoken of whom was Dr. Edward McGlynn. Appalled by the poverty and exploitation afflicting their working-class parishioners, the radicals denounced plutocracy and Tammany, championed organized labor, and formulated a comprehensive critique of Gilded Age capitalism based on a synthesis of Henry George's contemporary writings with antimonopolist and egalitarian traditions rooted in Irish nationalism, earlier trade unionism, and the New Testament. Their ideals were formalized in McGlynn's Anti-Poverty Society and, most dramatically, in his strong support for George's mayoral candidacy in 1886. The radicals' aim was to place the church in the forefront of the social changes they believed necessary and inevitable; the alternative, they feared, would be the apostasy of the laboring masses, as was occurring in continental Europe. In short, McGlynn wanted a confrontational church, opposed to contemporary elites and economic orthodoxies, allied with the most advanced advocates of social democracy. He believed Catholic cooperation with like-minded Protestants essential, and considered parochial schools a wasteful diversion of Catholic resources. McGlynn's economic heresies and his defiance of episcopal authority aroused fierce conservative opposition, both within and without the church, and after George's defeat Tammany and New York's Archbishop Michael Corrigan mounted a counteroffensive to reassert their mutually reinforcing influences over the faithful. McGlynn suffered excommunication, and his clerical allies were suppressed or exiled to remote, upstate parishes. Thereafter, clerical advocates of radical change were extremely rare and summarily treated; for example, Father Tom Haggerty received instant excommunication for his part in the founding of the IWW in 1905.

The liberals, led by Archbishop John Ireland of St. Paul and Cardinal James Gibbons of Baltimore, were sympathetic to McGlynn, *not* for his radical doctrines, but because they opposed his conservative persecutors and, more important, because they feared his suppression would both alienate Irish workers from the church and fuel nativist charges that Catholicism was un-American in its authoritarianism. Largely for the same pragmatic reasons, the liberals also opposed conservatives' condemnations of the Knights of Labor, radical Irish nationalist societies, and quasi-Masonic friendly associations, such as the Odd Fellows, which had large Catholic memberships. Although analogous to Protestant Progressives in their attitudes toward trusts and political corruption, the liberals did not criticize capitalist America but instead almost embraced it and its individualistic, democratic values. They believed that the United States had a mission to spread progress, democracy, and bourgeois civilization throughout the world (and among the immigrant working class) and that the church should help lead that uplifting crusade, guiding Catholics and society generally between the Scylla of poverty and ignorance and the Charybdis of gross materialism and religious indifference. The liberals advocated an internalized faith which would guide Catholics' active lives, and they deprecated mere formalism and the "passive" Christian virtues so dear to conservatives—humility, obedience, fatalism; instead they preached a "gospel of success" through industry, self-reliance, thrift, and temperance. They favored dialogue with Protestants and lay initiatives (as in the Catholic lay congresses of 1889 and 1893), and they opposed both Catholic and ethnic insularity. Consequently, liberals demanded rapid assimilation for immigrants (especially for non-English-speakers such as midwestern German Catholics, their bitterest opponents) and were indifferent or hostile to parochial schools. Liberal influences dominated much of the American church during the 1880s and early 1890s. However, after 1893 a resurgence of vitriolic nativism discredited their accommodationist approach to Protestant America, and by the decade's end the conservatives had mounted a successful counterattack culminating in papal condemnation of "Americanism" in 1899.

Led primarily by Archbishop Corrigan of New York, by Bishop Bernard McQuaid of Rochester, and after 1907 by Cardinal William O'Connell of Boston, the conservatives favored everything which radical and liberal churchmen considered dysfunctional and reactionary. Clinging to medieval visions of church and society, the conservatives revered tradition, order, and authority, both religious and secular. They equated the current social crises in the United States with the pope's losing struggle to retain the Papal States, and they regarded the American church—like the pope in Rome—as besieged by hostile, infidel forces. In their view, Catholicism represented America's last bulwark against physical chaos and moral decadence. Deeply suspicious of lay initiatives and of anything that smacked of ecumenism, the conservatives opposed lay congresses and urged Rome to condemn wholesale any intellectual currents (e.g., George's *Progress and Poverty*) or secular associations which might weaken Catholics' faith or which were beyond church control. Often trained in Rome, conservative prelates naturally inclined to ultramontanism, a tendency reinforced by their dependence on papal authority for condemnation of McGlynn and Americanism generally. Ironically, however, the very archaism of their ideals led conservative churchmen to criticisms of American society almost as harsh as those made by McGlynn. They viewed the United States as ruthlessly exploitative and crassly materialistic; skeptical of American pretensions to virtue, they opposed jingoistic imperialism, especially when directed against Catholic Spain, as in 1898. In short, unlike the liberals, conservatives perceived the church and its adherents as antagonistic to urban-industrial America and its dominant values. However, with a few exceptions such as San Francisco's labor champion Peter Yorke, clerical conservatives could not formulate their insights into a comprehensive critique of corporate capitalism. Instead, their fears of socialism and devotion to order led them into pragmatic alliances with the most reactionary elements of native society. Likewise, their refusal to attribute social and spiritual ills to any source other than "Anglo-Saxonism" (their synonym for Protestantism and materialism) impelled conservatives to segregate their flocks behind rigid ideological and institutional barriers. Consequently, they preached a "gospel of resignation" and obedience to authority, supported comprehensive parochial education, and allied with German-stock bishops' efforts to protect their parishioners' cultural integrity. By the early twentieth century the conservatives' triumph over clerical liberalism had produced what the historian Robert Curran has called the "Catholic ghetto," inhabited by "bifurcated Catholics": loudly proclaiming their American patriotism (equated with staunch moral and economic orthodoxy), yet firmly inclosed within an *imperium in imperio,* a comprehensive network of Catholic parish organizations which ensured a separate educational, social, and religious life—and political as well, insofar as local religious and Democratic party structures were often interdependent and mutually reinforcing.

The clerical disputants in 1870–1921 both reflected and appealed to Irish-America's diverse interests and outlooks, and in part the conservatives' victory was attributable to a successful synthesis of their and their people's interpretations of Catholicism and Irishness. By all accounts, Dr. McGlynn received overwhelming support from New York's working-class Irish, and a large number may have followed Elizabeth Gurley Flynn's family out of the church in anger at his suppression. However, despite his enthusiastic support for the Land League, what McGlynn considered uniquely laudable in the Irish was neither their Catholicism nor their devotion to Irish nationalism, but rather what he called their abstract "love of liberty"; like his allies Davitt and George, McGlynn wished to channel that impulse into streams of universal, not merely Irish, reform, and he declared openly that home rule was irrelevant and superficial compared with the international struggle against plutocracy. In short, McGlynn addressed his adherents primarily as exploited workers, secondarily as persecuted Irishmen; his appeal in the Irish-American community therefore had limitations. When economic conditions improved, when more Irish-Americans achieved bourgeois status or relative security as members of labor's organized aristocracy, and as Irish (and Irish-American) nationalism became less economically oriented and more respectable, McGlynn's brand of radical Catholicism seemed not only inexpedient in an America where just being Catholic and Irish caused problems but also less relevant to improved conditions and ethnic identity. To be sure, a minority strand of Irish-American radicalism persisted, but, as James Connolly lamented, such men usually spurned Irish nationalism for "internationalism" and became "more anti-Christian than the devil," thus rejecting both secular and religious aspects of Irishness.[235]

Popular support for liberal churchmen seems to have come primarily from upper- and middle-class Irish-Americans, and also from some skilled workers who espoused temperance and appreciated (and exaggerated) the liberals' benevolent neutrality toward labor. Their strength was greatest in the Midwest and generally in cities and small towns where Irish-Americans were neither heavily concentrated nor the dominant foreign-stock group, but instead well integrated in native society. A typical, if especially prominent, lay liberal was Chicago's William James Onahan, a success in business, a mugwump in politics, an ostentatious patriot and ubiquitous leader of Catholic societies, and, despite his sincere interest in Irish culture and history, a proponent of Irish assimilation who opposed stopping city business on St. Patrick's Day.[236]

Onahan's characteristics indicate the limitations of liberal Catholicism's appeal to many Irish-Americans. Irish Democratic politicos naturally resented liberals' condemnations of corrupt bossism and their frequent affiliation with the Republican party. Also, on economic issues the Americanists were too conservative for the working-class Irish who had followed McGlynn and George, yet too radical for members of the *haute bourgeoisie,* whose devotion to property and authority in the turbulent 1890s turned them toward the conservative apostles of law and order. Moreover, in cultural terms liberalism was probably unsatisfying, an inadequate resolution of ethnic tensions and traditions. For example, in the face of persistent bigotry, middle-class Irish-Americans' efforts to embrace bourgeois America often led to harsh rebuffs and heightened ethno-religious consciousness: in such events, the alternative responses seemed either a retreat to the conservatives' Catholic ghetto or a denial of religious as well as ethnic identities; in either case the result was the attrition of liberal support. Consequently, after their disillusionment in the 1890s most ambitious Irish-American parents favored parochial education for their children, although they insisted that church schools provide the same opportunities for upward mobility as the public systems. Perhaps most important, liberal clerics were not natural spokesmen for many of the Irish who emigrated in 1880–1920. Raised in the church militant and in an atmosphere surcharged with nationalism, often from highly traditional and impoverished backgrounds, and thus easily exploited and stigmatized as poor Paddies, such newcomers found Americanist injunctions to self-reliance and assimilation both uncongenial and unrealistic. Likewise, while Americanist churchmen made the usual St. Patrick's Day speeches and protected the Clan na Gael and the Ancient Order of Hibernians from conservative condemnation, their drives for acceptance and amalgamation precluded full identification with their adherents' nationalist yearnings. Bishops Ireland and John Lancaster Spalding of Peoria believed that the Irish had a divine mission, not to free their homeland, but to diffuse throughout and Catholicize American society, a dream formalized in their Irish Catholic Colonization Society (1879–84). After 1900 the nationalism of most liberals extended no further than sympathy for John Redmond and his eminently respectable Irish Parliamentary party. "[F]irst and always . . . American," as his biographer describes Cardinal Gibbons, the liberals in 1914 welcomed Redmond's support for Britain's war and in 1916–21 recoiled in horror from the events in Ireland which so thrilled their Irish parishioners.[237]

Strongest in large, eastern cities with heavy Irish populations, Irish-American loyalty to a conservative church stemmed from many sources: Tammany stalwarts such as Richard Croker; affluent and socially conservative Irishmen such as Bourke Cockran and the members of New York's elite Catholic Club; middle-class Irish-Americans on defense against nativism, proud to associate their own aspirations with the church's rising power and respectability; pious emigrants frightened by American immorality, who wondered "if the priest has no influence what would guide the people"; working-class Irish bereft of alternative leadership since McGlynn's suppression, their choice made easier after 1900 by the church's tacit alliance with the more conservative AF of L; and bewildered new arrivals from western Ireland who found the "gospel of resignation" and the "Catholic ghetto" appropriate reflections of peasant traditions, childhood training, and current needs.[238]

Moreover, impelled by the desire to insulate their people from contamination, conservative churchmen not only supported the establishment of ethnic parishes but also buttressed Irish group consciousness by coming to terms with an Irish-American nationalism which obscured social conflict and exalted the primacy of religious identification. In the 1880s conservatives had been deeply suspicious of an American Irish Land League tainted by social radicalism and association with clerically proscribed revolutionaries in the secret Clan na Gael, and as late as 1891 Bishop McQuaid perceived most specifically Irish societies, such as the American branch of the Ancient Order of Hibernians, as synonymous with the Clan. However, only three years later McQuaid formally accepted the AOH as "Catholic," ostensibly because of changes in the order, but more likely because of conservative churchmen's desire to close Catholic ranks against both the contemporary nativist revival and liberal assimilationism generally. Bishops such as McQuaid now understood that a clerically recognized and tamed Irish-American assertiveness could strengthen rather than subvert a conservative church. They also understood that the potential dangers of this strategy could be mitigated if clerics in America, as in Ireland, interpreted Irishness in predominantly religious terms. Ironically, it had been the liberal (and non-Irish) Bishop Spalding who had pointed the way in his 1880 colonization tract, *The Religious Mission of the Irish People,* when he lauded the Irish as the "great martyr-nation" and characterized them as instinctively devout, patient, long-suffering, and otherwordly—that is, as the quintessential Catholics of the conservatives' dreams. In subsequent decades, just as churchmen across the Atlantic were creating an image of "holy Ireland," their American counterparts were propagating its replica in the New World. Both served the same purposes, to insulate the faithful from Anglo-Saxon and socialist corruptions and to ground Irish identity in Catholicism. Thus, in 1904 Bishop Shahan of Catholic University rejoiced that Irish-Americans were "highly spiritual and unmaterial," and in 1912 Bishop Carroll of Montana (a state racked by labor strife between Irish miners and employers) appealed to the AOH to condemn socialism and to ensure their children's piety by studying "Irish history and literature in your homes . . . not because it is Irish" but because "it is thoroughly Catholic." For churchmen such as Cardinal O'Connell, himself still resentful against Protestant prejudice he had endured as a New England youth, Irishness and Catholicism were inseparable; and for emigrants raised in "holy Ireland" and suffering in Yankee-owned textile mills and shoe factories, that synthesis provided comfort and continuity in the present and twin hopes for spiritual and political redemption in the future.[239]

In addition to specifically political and religious organizations, by the last quarter of the nineteenth century Irish-America exhibited a rich variety of formal, ethnic associations which catered to their members' social, economic, and cultural needs. In 1874 an exiled nationalist in New York City complained that existing Irish societies were "all money-making concerns," unwilling to lend the newcomer "a dollar or a helping hand." However, already nationwide associations such as the Irish Catholic Benevolent Union (1869), the Ancient Order of Hibernians (reorganized 1871), and the Catholic Total Abstinence Union (1872) were well established, and by 1884 a working-class emigrant in Philadelphia could rejoice that "Irishmen are pretty well organized here under the principle of Brotherly love & Christian Charity": "this is a great place for societies," reported Owen O'Callaghan, and "90 per cent of the population belong to some order." The variety of available associations reflected Irish-American diversity, but together they provided the formal infrastructure which linked Hibernians across regional, generational, and social lines; indeed, lists of officers and members often overlapped on both national and local levels. The societies which enjoyed the greatest longevity and largest *permanent* memberships were national fraternal and self-help organizations such as the ICBU, CTAU, AOH, and Knights of Columbus (1881) which provided insurance benefits as well as camaraderie in an economically uncertain age; the largest of these, the AOH (including its ladies' auxiliary), claimed nearly 200,000 members in 1908. Other associations, such as the elite Friendly Sons of St. Patrick and the various county clubs which flourished in large cities, were predominantly social organizations, while the Philo-Celtic societies (1873), the American Irish Historical Society (1897), and the Gaelic League of America (1898) were dedicated to cultural pursuits. In addition, a number of associations (discussed below) were designed specifically to promote or conspire for Irish nationalist causes.[240]

All of the beneficial societies (including the AOH after about 1890) were closely tied to the Catholic church, often enjoying hierarchical patronage, and the CTAU and the K of C were officially and inclusively "Catholic" (albeit Irish-dominated) associations. The leaders of these organizations were predominantly middle class, often second generation, and the bulk of their members were either of bourgeois or of skilled-worker status. In certain respects, these societies seemed merely Irish-Catholic replicas of native Protestant institutions, proclaiming American patriotism, urging uplift and assimilation, and promoting eminently Victorian habits of industry, discipline, thrift, and sobriety. All were morbidly sensitive to nativist prejudice and sought to improve Irish-Americans' image in diverse but complementary ways: the AOH by combatting the "stage Irishman" while providing American flags for every parochial schoolroom in the country; the AIHS by producing historical "evidence" of America's glorious Irish origins; the K of C by being conspicuously patriotic in wartime; and the CTAU by encouraging total abstinence from alcohol. "[T]he Irish people should never touch liquor or Beer in America . . . if they are desirous of becoming good Citizens," declared the Limerick-born temperance crusader William Downes; "total abstinence . . . is the golden lever which will guide our weak machinery to a successful goal." Even learning the Irish language was justified in terms of uplift and assimilation, to make Irishmen "more respected as American citizens," a dramatic reversal of conventional wisdom.[241]

However, it would be misleading to view Irish-American organizations as simply bourgeois and assimilationist. Although some societies, such as the Knights of Father Mathew in St. Louis, were exclusively upper and middle class in composition, most had large numbers of working-class members and others (clerks, bartenders, small proprietors) on the ragged edge of respectability; for example, in 1893 Philadelphia's AOH had a slight majority of working-class members, a substantial number of whom were unskilled laborers. Often such members used middle-class means for proletarian goals: thus, the iron and steel workers who dominated CTAU locals in Pittsburgh espoused temperance as a necessary precondition for successful strikes as well as individual upward mobility. Moreover, although these organizations naturally attracted more-ambitious laborers and oriented them toward their leaders' bourgeois goals, the substantial presence of working-class adherents prevented those leaders from ignoring proletarian concerns. For example, although at Bishop Carroll's insistence the 1912 national AOH convention issued a perfunctory denunciation of socialism, the delegates revealed their origins and sympathies by "condemn-[ing] with *equal* earnestness the selfish greed and the intolerable industrial conditions" which inspired radicalism, and concluded by recommending that their "members do everything in their power to advance the claims of men and labor whenever they come in conflict with those of money and concentrated capital." The AOH was more proletarian in composition than other beneficial societies, but similar statements came from the eminently respectable delegates to the Catholic lay congresses and even from the Knights of Columbus.[242]

In addition, although membership in these institutions certainly aided emigrants such as the disenchanted Timothy Cashman to become "reconciled to American ways," these were specifically *Irish-Catholic* organizations whose very separateness indicated their ultimately defensive posture toward a suspicious, if not hostile, society and which perforce both drew on and in the process reinforced peculiarly Irish traditions, experiences, and consciousness, however loudly they proclaimed their compatibility with American ways. To be sure, organizations such as the CTAU and the K of C presaged the "triple melting pot," dissolving ethnicity in predominantly religious-based variations of bourgeois culture, but despite its theoretical inclusiveness the CTAU was in the late nineteenth century a determinedly Irish association and both it and the K of C were informed by the prevalent notion that history, racial character, and "divine mission" made Irish-Americans the nation's quintessential Catholics. Furthermore, although most fraternal and self-help associations avoided strong, specific political statements, they commonly employed Irish nationalist rhetoric to stir their members and cement their ranks. For example, despite its ethic of self-reliance, the CTAU's spokesmen regularly interpreted the temperance issue in traditional, communal terms: blaming Irish-Americans' embarrassing propensity for drink on "the English laws which drove them from their homes," and urging them to embrace sobriety as an essential prerequisite for successful efforts to liberate their homeland—"Irish-America sober is Ireland free," paraphrasing the pleas of temperance crusaders across the Atlantic. Likewise, the AOH was so Irish-oriented that in 1884 it split over whether to admit American-born Irishmen to membership. Demographic imperatives and the waning of emigration obliged the adoption of inclusive policies in 1897, yet ironically about the same time the order entered its most militantly Irish phase: launching aggressive attacks on defamatory literature; assiduously promoting the study of Irish history in parochial schools; richly endowing the Gaelic League and a chair of Gaelic at Catholic University; and in 1906 swinging away from an easy allegiance to Redmond's respectable Home Rule party to support for Sinn Féin, physical-force nationalism, and total Irish independence. Neither that shift nor the order's simultaneous formal alliance with German-American societies in opposition to British-American détente was designed to appease an Anglophile native middle-class whose leading spokesman, Woodrow Wilson, responded with charges of Irish disloyalty.[243]

In short, to the amazement and consternation of British ambassadors and pro-English Americans, in the late nineteenth and early twentieth centuries Irish nationalism still stirred Irish-America's soul. To be sure, large numbers of Irish-Americans cared little or nothing about either home rule or the Irish republican dream. Most Protestant Irishmen in North America were strongly opposed to any measure of Irish self-government; Robert Lindsay Crawford, the radical ex-Orangeman now a Canadian journalist, was exceptional, and his Protestant Friends of Irish Freedom society (1919–21) attracted few adherents save among men such as New York's Thomas Addis Emmet, namesake and descendant of the exiled rebel of 1798. Catholic Irish-Americans were rarely hostile to Irish nationalism, but many were indifferent—in some cases because of personal alienation from a repressive homeland or apprehension that Irish self-government would merely legitimize the dominance of local elites and former employers. Thus, in 1920 the embittered Mary Sheehan admitted her lack of sympathy "for the irish people," answering her American-born daughters' criticism by declaring, "If they only knew some of them as I do they would not care to talk on ireland." Other emigrants lost interest in the "Irish Question" after they came to the United States. For example, on assuming American citizenship, the former Fenian Frank Roney stated, "By that act I dissolved all future participation in hostility to England [for] . . . I believed it my duty to subordinate [anti-British] sentiments to those in keeping with the policy of my adopted country." Many emigrants simply grew cynical after repeated pleas for money by Irish-American and visiting Irish nationalists failed to produce promised results. "[I]f the [Irish] People are getting all the money that is sent to them from this Country they Ought to be rich," wrote a skeptical Irish-Philadelphian in 1880, wearied of seemingly interminable requests for American aid. Eventually, emigrants such as Roney and Maurice Wolfe concluded that most Irish-American nationalists were "unprincipled 'grafters' " and self-seeking politicians, while others such as Thomas O'Brien and Thomas Waldron wondered whether Irish politicians at home were using American money as the donors intended or, indeed, whether its recipients were even worthy of self-government. "I think that they have become a race of spongers," declared the wealthy lawyer John Quinn, son of Famine emigrants, recoiling from "the painful spectacle" of Irish "envoys" ceaselessly besieging Irish-American wallets. Finally, many emigrants became too devoted to personal striving to concern themselves with Irish politics. Dedicated nationalists believed this was especially true of affluent Irish-Americans who thought nationalism "vulgar" and embarrassing: thus, ex-Fenians such as Thomas McCarthy Fennell and Jeremiah O'Donovan Rossa wrote bitterly of "respectable" emigrants who cared "very little for the cause of the green sod . . . [once] their shamrocks have blossomed into diamonds."[244]

Certainly, much Irish-American nationalism *was* "vulgar"—grossly sentimental and superficial. From their perspective, true nationalists such as Michael Davitt and E. P. St. Clair were justified in condemning "the accursed Yankee Irish politicians" as "men wholly unworthy of the name of Irish, . . . whose sole motive [was] selfishness," and for whom "Ireland . . . [was] a mere catchword for American political parties." Likewise, although young, Irish-born priests were often fervent nationalists, most high-ranking Irish-American churchmen were lukewarm and ambivalent, fearing nationalism's radical potential yet recognizing, as Archbishop Riordan of San Francisco admitted in 1892, that clerical expressions of "sympathy with the national aspirations of the race" helped cement Irish loyalties to the church. Few bishops were as overtly duplicitous as Boston's Cardinal O'Connell, who in 1916–21 made vigorously nationalistic and anti-British speeches in public while privately assuring English diplomats that he meant no harm and did so only to maintain control of his head-strong flock; however, all churchmen realized implicitly that for Irish-American Catholics hatred of Protestant England was "necessary to true religion and the maintenance of due religious fervour," as the British ambassador Thomas Spring Rice wryly observed in 1917. Under mainstream political and clerical influence the annual St. Patrick's Day celebrations became increasingly tame and hollow affairs, so much so that some nationalists tried to substitute an observance of November 22, the anniversary of the Manchester martyrs' execution, as Irish-America's primary holiday. Similarly, the rich raciness of pre-Famine peasant culture was sanitized for bourgeois consumption into green shamrock wallpaper and popular songs such as "When Irish Eyes Are Smiling" (1899) which mocked and minimized the tragic realities of the Irish emigrant experience. In short, many Irish-Americans quickly learned that Irish group consciousness could be profitable not only to politicians and saloonkeepers but also to suppliers of fraternal regalia and the volumes of Thomas Moore's *History of Ireland* which adorned middle-class parlors, and to travel agents such as Lawrence's Duncan Wood who not only arranged cheap sentimental journeys back to the "old country" but in an 1883 newspaper advertisement commercialized Irish emigrants' most vulnerable emotions, exhorting them,

> Remember the Promise You Made to Father or Mother When Leaving the Old Country and Receiving *Their Blessing:* "God bless you! I will never *forget you.*" You can Now Redeem That Promise By Sending Some Article as a *Xmas Present* I am Now Prepared To Forward Small Parcels From Lawrence to Your Home at *Very Low Rates.* . . . Make the Hearts of the Old Folks at Home *Rejoice* Picture Your Good Old Mother or Father opening a Parcel from You in this Country, and exclaiming With Tears of Joy in their eyes "God Bless Them. I knew *they would not forget me.*"[245]

Deluged by such crass appeals, by sentimental rhetoric so remote from either past or present realities, many Irish-Americans not surprisingly compartmentalized and reduced Irish attachments to meaningless, ceremonial proportions: "With a few drinks in," wrote Frank O'Connor, "they sang sentimentally of 'the valley near Slievenamon' or 'the hills of Donegal,' but next morning saw them return cheerfully to office and shop." Indeed, after Rossa's thwarted victory over Boss Tweed in 1870, Irish-Americans henceforth voted with their stomachs rather than their hearts, repeatedly rejecting nationalist pleas to desert and punish the Democratic party for its indifference or hostility to Irish freedom; thus in 1916, less than seven months after the British suppression of the Easter rising in Dublin, Irish-Americans loyally reelected President Wilson, perhaps in gratitude for a few crumbs of prolabor legislation, but willfully ignoring his obvious contempt for Irish nationalism. Nevertheless, among those same millions of Irish-Americans nationalism was genuine and, when aroused by Irish events and focused on Irish—rather than on domestic—political questions, passionate and unreasoning, as British diplomats ruefully attested. Moreover, however superficial or tawdry in retrospect, St. Patrick's Day ceremonies and other symbolic expressions of Irishness had more personal and poignant significance for ordinary Irish emigrants than for their politically or piously motivated organizers and purveyors. Numerous letters testified to the collective pride and nationalist yearnings which St. Patrick's Day celebrations inspired among their emigrant participants. Thus, in 1893 the homesick Kerryman Batt O'Connor marched in procession in Providence, Rhode Island, and later testified, "[I]n the emotion I felt, walking as one of that vast crowd of Irish emigrants celebrating our national festival, I awoke to the full consciousness of my love for my country." Few emigrants so affected returned home to fight for Irish independence as O'Connor did, but their devotion and dollars sustained Irish and Irish-American nationalism from the despairing early 1870s to the eventual, if partial, triumph of 1921.[246]

Organized Irish-American nationalism resonated in response to both Irish and American, political and economic, conditions. The 1870s was a decade of relative inactivity, reflecting Irish rural prosperity and political quiescence under Isaac Butt's genteel sway, and Irish-Americans' preoccupations with economic success and survival during the industrial depression of 1873–78. When John Devoy, Jeremiah O'Donovan Rossa, John Boyle O'Reilly, and other ex-Fenians arrived in the United States in 1870–71, they found that the abortive Canadian invasions of 1866 and 1870 had factionalized and discredited Irish-American nationalism. Initial attempts at reunification proved fruitless, and nationalists divided into four broad groups: the conservatives and the radicals, more attuned to Irish-*American* than to Irish circumstances, and the followers of John Devoy's Clan na Gael and O'Donovan Rossa's United Irishmen, joined in emphasis on Irish freedom and physical-force principles, but clashing over tactics and personalities.[247]

The conservatives, led by O'Reilly, editor of the Boston *Pilot,* and the Massachusetts politician Patrick Collins, supported constitutional nationalism (home rule) for Ireland and uplift and assimilation for Irish-America. Speaking for "the calm, rational, and respectable Irish Catholics of America," as well as for the church and most mainstream politicians, O'Reilly eschewed revolution and urged his fellow exiles to forget the past and devote themselves to progress and self-improvement: "Work for yourself," he advised Devoy. "It pays best in the end." Although equally concerned with the emigrants' status in American society, the radicals led by Patrick Ford offered a working-class road to assimilation via an Irish-American nationalism which stressed fundamental social and economic reforms on both sides of the Atlantic. Ford's *Irish World and Industrial Liberator,* the nation's most popular Irish weekly, spoke to and for struggling emigrant workers, attacked plutocracy and economic monopoly—especially in land—and supported labor unions, strikes, and radical third parties. In Ford's eyes the Irish tenant's fight against his landlord was synonymous with the Irish-American laborer's battle against land speculators and slumlords in the United States. By contrast, the "pure" nationalists in the Clan na Gael and the United Irishmen considered both Irish and American economic issues secondary to their single goal of Irish independence. Founded in 1867, the Clan became under Devoy's leadership a tightly-knit, secret conspiratorial society, linked to the IRB at home. During the 1870s the Clan had only about 10,000 members, primarily working class, but in 1875 it gained widespread respect for its successful rescue of Fenian prisoners from Australia. Otherwise, however, the Clan remained surreptitious, hoping for war between Britain and Russia, sponsoring John Holland's efforts to build workable submarines to raid British shipping, and waiting for developments in Ireland more propitious for revolution. The Clan's relative inactivity generated support among Anglophobic emigrants for the United Irishmen, an ephemeral organization which reflected O'Donovan Rossa's unstable and often inebriated personality. In 1875 Rossa declared that the Clan's work was "too slow" and began to solicit emigrants' contributions for a "Skirmishing Fund" to finance a dynamiting campaign against English cities. Respectable Irish-Americans were horrified; even Devoy disapproved, not of the idea itself, but of Rossa's unprofessional approach. Nevertheless, by 1877, contributions to the fund totaled nearly $50,000, although little of the money was used for the purposes intended.[248]

In 1879–80 events in Ireland reinvigorated and temporarily united most Irish-American nationalists. Rural distress caused by disastrous potato harvests and collapsing farm prices produced massive American relief efforts, while evictions and agrarian violence inspired emigrants' outrage and bitter memories of the Famine clearances. Recognizing the situation's revolutionary potential, Devoy and Michael Davitt formulated the New Departure, a scheme to mobilize Ireland and Irish-America behind demands for the abolition of landlordism—demands which, when thwarted by the British government, might lead to armed rebellion supported by American money and arms. However, in the United States as in Ireland, socioeconomic divisions and political considerations frustrated Devoy's dreams. A few *enragés* broke with the Clan and gravitated to Rossa, disillusioned by Devoy's tactical alliance with mere land reformers and home rulers. Nevertheless, Clan membership rose to 40,000, and more damaging were the divergent policies pursued by middle-class and clerical conservatives such as O'Reilly and Collins, and by radical working-class spokesmen such as Patrick Ford and, eventually, Davitt. Although supporting both violent rebellion and Irish independence, Ford subordinated Devoy's goals to the destruction of landlordism; moreover, under Henry George's influence both Ford and Davitt moved beyond peasant proprietorship to embrace land nationalization, a step which Devoy considered divisive and diversionary. For their part, the conservatives wanted only reform, not revolution—whether political or social; their hero was the eminently respectable Parnell, whose lineage and bearing commanded admiration from native as well as Irish-Americans, and they distrusted Devoy's motives and abhorred Ford's "pernicious doctrines of communism." When the Irish National Land League of America was established, in mid-1880, to support the Irish movement, Clan and conservative delegates united to minimize Ford's influence, and the second INLLA convention of 1881 ratified conservative control by electing Collins president. Nevertheless, for a time Ford was embarrassingly indispensable, for his "Spread the Light" campaign in the *Irish World* collected nearly double the money contributed to Parnell via the American Land League, and his paper's circulation in the United States and Ireland increased enormously. At its peak, in 1881, the INLLA may have had over half a million members organized in some 1,500 branches, many of them dominated by Ford's disciples, and in 1879–82 Irish-Americans publicly remitted over $5 million to relieve Irish distress, sustain evicted tenants, and finance the Land War.[249]

However, Irish-America's tenuous unity foundered on the 1881 Land Act and Parnell's Kilmainham treaty with Gladstone. Ford denounced both, vainly demanded a national Irish rent strike, and henceforth channeled his efforts into Irish-*American* working-class crusades such as the George-McGlynn New York mayoralty campaign of 1886. By contrast, conservatives and clerics rejoiced at the Land War's moderately successful conclusion, and for the rest of the decade eagerly supported Parnell's home rule movement through elite associations such as the Irish Parliamentary Fund. In early 1883 they also helped establish the Irish National League of the United States, successor to the American Land League and intended to be the Irish-American complement to Parnell's Irish party organization. However, the INLUS quickly became dominated by the Clan na Gael, which itself fell under the sway of a clique of Chicago nationalists led by Alexander Sullivan, a brilliant but ruthless and unscrupulous lawyer of Irish parentage. Sullivan tried to retain middle-class Irish-American support by fulminating against Irish pauper emigration (embarrassing to "respectable" Hibernians); at the same time he tried to appease the militants by dynamite attacks on British cities. However, most conservatives outside Chicago balked at both violence and Sullivan's unsavoriness, while Clan members loyal to Devoy accused the "Chicago Triangle" of graft and of reducing the Clan to a mere auxiliary of the Republican party. By the mid-1880s the Sullivan and Devoy factions were openly at war, culminating in the 1889 assassination of one of Sullivan's critics. Both Clan and INLUS membership dwindled, as did Irish-American nationalist enthusiasm, generally, after 1886, when Parliament rejected the first home rule bill. Parnell still enjoyed immense personal popularity, especially among conservatives, but in 1890–91 his divorce scandal and the IPP's violent rupture only exacerbated divisions and demoralization among Irish-American nationalists.[250]

Save for a brief flurry of rallies in 1893, when Gladstone's second home rule bill was before Parliament, organized Irish-American nationalism in the 1890s seemed moribund. Conservative home rulers, now including the chastened Patrick Ford, vainly urged reunion on the Irish Parliamentary party, while otherwise channeling their energies and donations to Catholic American causes. Working-class Irish-Americans were largely preoccupied with economic concerns stemming from the 1893–97 depression, and the Clan na Gael remained factionalized until it reunited in 1900 under the leadership of Devoy and the American-born Daniel Cohalan, a leading Tammany politician and New York supreme court judge. However, recent historical research by Timothy Meagher suggests that, in America as in contemporary Ireland, Irish nationalism was in ferment during the 1890s, especially on local levels and in its nonpolitical aspects. An influx of new Irish emigrants shaped by late-nineteenth-century Ireland's ubiquitous Catholic nationalism; the revival of nativism by the American Protective Association; the decline of *social* radicalism among Irish-American workers, in part a reflection of the APA's assault on their ethnicity and religion; and the simultaneous rise of an Irish-American church militantly opposed to nativism, clerical Americanism, and "Anglo-Saxonism": all combined to heighten Irish-America's group consciousness as asserted, for example, in the AOH's new aggressiveness, popular enthusiasm for the transplanted Gaelic Athletic Association and Gaelic League (the latter closely linked to the Clan as well as to the AOH), vociferous support for the Boers against Britain in 1899–1902, and even renewed pride and participation in local St. Patrick's Day celebrations. In short, by the century's end Irish-America was primed to welcome William O'Brien's renaissance of Irish agrarian agitation and, in 1900, the Irish Parliamentary party's reunion under John Redmond.[251]

Distrusting the militancy of both the Clan and the American AOH, while on a fund-raising tour in 1901 Redmond founded the United Irish League of America to generate donations and popular support for the home rule movement. The UILA attracted members primarily among upper- and middle-class Irish-Americans of moderate views, such as the lawyers Bourke Cockran and Michael J. Ryan, later UILA president. However, Redmond deliberately blurred distinctions between home rule and Irish independence and, like Parnell before him, made speeches sufficiently militant to attract a wide spectrum of Irish-American support; in 1902 the UILA had over two hundred branches and by 1910 had remitted over £50,000 to Ireland. Meanwhile, the Clan struggled to survive, unable to attract followers either through the insurance benefits which helped popularize the AOH or through the quick, tangible results—such as the 1903 Wyndham Act and home rule—which the UILA promised. Bound to oppose home rule, which Clan loyalists considered a "betrayal of everything national," the Clan subsidized Arthur Griffith's and W. P. Ryan's Dublin newspapers, as well as the IRB, established the still-born Sinn Féin League of America in 1908, and, along-side the AOH, agitated against proposed Anglo-American arbitration treaties. However, despite a newly vigorous branch in Philadelphia, led by the recent Tyrone emigrant Joseph McGarrity, by early 1913, when Parliament passed the third home rule bill, the Clan seemed as terminal as the UILA was triumphant.[252]

Nevertheless, despite its success and respectability, many Irish-Americans found the home rule movement less than satisfying. In the United States, as in Ireland, home rule failed to excite the younger generations: as was noted earlier, in 1906–8 the AOH repudiated Redmond and endorsed Sinn Féin; ordinary emigrants such as Thomas Waldron suspected the IPP's fiscal integrity and fidelity to Irish nationalism; and affluent Irish-Americans such as Cockran and Thomas Fortune Ryan were alarmed at Redmond's alliance with the "socialism" of Lloyd George's Liberals. However, it was the rise of Protestant Irish militancy and Redmond's temporizing with Carson and the Unionists which reanimated physical-force nationalism and gave new life to the Clan na Gael. The Clan dominated American fund-raising for the IRB-led Irish National Volunteers, and although wealthy Irish-Americans still held aloof, even former UILA leaders such as Michael J. Ryan deserted Redmond when he avowed Irish loyalty to England at the outbreak of World War I. Hoping as always that England's difficulty would prove Ireland's opportunity, most Irish-American nationalists abandoned the discredited UILA and joined with the Clan and AOH in alliances with German-Americans equally intent on preventing American support for the British war effort. While subsidizing IRB preparations for the Easter rising, in March 1916 the Clan sponsored an Irish Race Convention in New York, out of which emerged the Clan-dominated Friends of Irish Freedom, "the most efficient and effective propaganda and activist organization in Irish-American history"; at its peak the FOIF had 275,000 regular and associate members. News of the Easter rebellion and, more crucial, of its leaders' executions stunned and outraged Irish-America, all but destroyed what remained of UILA support, and marshaled Irish-Americans almost unanimously behind the FOIF and physical-force nationalism: "an outburst of lyrical anger swept through the continent from New York to the Golden Gate"; conservative bishops such as Boston's O'Connell joined with the anathematized Clan in establishing the Irish Relief Fund for the prisoners' families; and even Irish-Americans who still supported Britain's war against Germany publicly denounced "[t]he vilest murders ever committed in Irish history." However, neither the FOIF nor its German-American allies could prevent President Wilson's reelection in 1916 or Congress's declaration of war against the Central Powers in April 1917.[253]

Threatened by charges of disloyalty and government harassment, the FOIF lay low while the war lasted, uttered suitably patriotic noises, and made plans to oblige Wilson to apply his celebrated principle of "self-determination for captive nations" to Ireland at the war's end. Bolder spirits with socialist leanings formed the Irish Progressive League and commenced agitation in late 1917, while conservatives vainly prayed that Redmond might still salvage home rule through negotiations. However, the British government's announcement in April 1918 of its intention to apply conscription to Ireland, followed by Sinn Féin's overwhelming election victory in December, completed the UILA's destruction and threw all Irish-America into the FOIF's hands. As soon as the war ended, Cohalan and Devoy focused on the self-determination issue and organized a series of mass meetings to pressure Wilson into supporting Irish independence at the Versailles peace conference. In effect, by challenging Wilson to apply his vaunted democratic principles to Ireland, something intelligent nationalists knew he neither could nor would do, the FOIF was setting the stage for a Wilsonian "betrayal" of his own professed war aims which would allow Irish-Americans both to oppose his administration and to give all-out support to Sinn Féin without risking renewed charges of treason. In February 1919 another FOIF-orchestrated Irish Race Convention announced its opposition to any peace treaty which ratified British rule over Ireland, and thenceforth the FOIF was allied with Senate Republicans in their ultimately successful campaign to repudiate Wilson's cherished League of Nations.[254]

In June 1919 the Dáil Éireann president, Eamon de Valera, arrived in the United States seeking Irish-American funds and diplomatic recognition for the embryo Irish republic. De Valera traveled throughout the country and spoke before enormous, enthusiastic crowds, but otherwise his visit—which lasted until December 1920—was not a particularly happy one. Almost immediately, de Valera became embroiled in bitter disputes with Cohalan and Devoy over control of FOIF policy and Irish-American donations. Cohalan, whose influence over both the FOIF and the elderly Devoy was nearly supreme, wanted to retain control of Irish-American opinion and use the FOIF and its considerable treasury primarily for Irish-*American* purposes, especially to defeat Wilson, his personal bête noire. By contrast, de Valera cared nothing for American politics and blithely assumed that all Irish-Americans should fulfill their obligations to the Irish republic without hesitation. By the presidential election campaign of 1920 the vicious public quarrels between de Valera and the FOIF leaders gave both American political parties an excuse to ignore the Irish question, but on the eve of his departure de Valera circumvented Cohalan and, with the aid of dissident Clansmen such as Joseph McGarrity, formed a rival organization, the American Association for the Recognition of the Irish Republic. Stimulated by dramatic news of Black and Tan atrocities and of fatal hunger strikes by republican prisoners, plus de Valera's enormous personal popularity among ordinary Irish-Americans, the AARIR rapidly eclipsed the FOIF. At its peak the AARIR claimed 800,000 members, and by late 1921, when the Anglo-Irish war ended, Irish-Americans had subscribed over $5.5 million in Irish republic bond-certificates, plus at least another $5 million in relief funds. Despite de Valera's disappointments, Mother Ireland's "exiled children" had done their duty well. "We have fought the good fight," declared one elderly emigrant, "we have kept the faith, we have loved our God and dear old IRELAND."[255]

The extent of individual Irish-Americans' emotional and practical involvement in nationalist movements reflected both their situations in the New World and their experiences in and perspectives transplanted from the Old. Several historians, notably Thomas N. Brown and Michael Funcheon, have argued that late-nineteenth- and early-twentieth-century nationalism was an emotion primarily learned abroad, a product of the emigration experience which dissolved parochial loyalties and expanded particularistic identities into a broader group consciousness. The nationalists Patrick Ford and Batt O'Connor gave evidence to support that interpretation, as did Irish visitors to America such as Canon Hannay, who noted in 1914, "If you live in Ireland you are aware of a lot of men working very sensibly in a number of ways . . . [seemingly un]connected with each other except by ordinary ties of friendship, rivalry, or community of interest." However, he added, "When you get a long way off from Ireland you lose sight of all these funny, busy little men and see instead Cathleen ní Houlihan. . . ." Brown and Funcheon also argue that upwardly mobile and middle-class Irish-Americans were especially enthusiastic, seeing Irish-American nationalism as an avenue to individual success and acceptability in American society. Interestingly, however, frequent statements by active nationalists such as Devoy and O'Donovan Rossa contradict that hypothesis, charging instead that affluent Irish-Americans either "lost sight of their homes and buried all sympathy for Ireland" or were merely shallow or insincere "patriots," wallowing sentimentally in fancied historical and cultural glories of bygone ages or, more likely, cynically exploiting nationalist rhetoric and organizations for selfish purposes. "Did ye iver see a man that wanted to free Ireland th' day afther to-morra that didn't run f'r aldherman soon or late?" asked the fictional Mr. Dooley, echoing warnings by Clan na Gael leaders of the "politicians and nice, fat, conniving business men" who strove to infiltrate and deflect the movement. Despite his socialism, James Connolly got on well with men such as Devoy and Rossa, perhaps because all shared his opinion of most Irish-American politicians as "descendants of the serpents St. Patrick banished from Ireland."[256]

Certainly, for Irishmen seeking advancement *within* the Irish-American community, at least rhetorical obeisance to Irish freedom was as necessary to success as conspicuous mass attendance. However, for men preoccupied with amassing wealth or intent on mobility and respectability in *native* society, deep or obvious devotion to Irish-American nationalism could be more liability than leverage. As Devoy's friend and Clan associate William Carroll noted in 1879, serious commitment to Irish independence "must cost a good man serious hours of trial and despondency, to say nothing of wreck of life or fortune." Thus, in his Irish emigrants' guide Father Stephen Byrne warned, "The retrospective view of Ireland, of her wrongs and sufferings, sometimes interferes . . . with . . . our opportunities in the land of our adoption," a danger realized in Thomas Kelly's lament that "every Irishman out of employment who has ever had anything to do with the national movement has almost invariably made a demand on my purse." Moreover, vigorous nationalist agitation almost inevitably provoked nativist backlash and charges of disloyalty from increasingly Anglophile American Protestants who no longer remembered their own struggles against England but "now imitate the practices and crave the position of the British titled aristocracy," as Charles O'Conor decried in 1883. As a British journalist had observed a year earlier, although many native Americans admired Parnell and sympathized with Irish distress, the social and political implications of both the Land War and Irish separatism frightened the members of a reactionary bourgeoisie who feared for their own property during that turbulent period and whose suppression of revolutionary secession in their own country was still fresh in memory. The later convergence of home rule agitation, the rise of Ulster unionism, and the emergence of the APA may not have been merely coincidental, and certainly during and after World War I there was a direct correlation between Irish-American nationalist activities and the vicious anti-Catholicism which peaked in the early 1920s. Few Irish-Americans were so financially secure or self-assured that they could afford the true revolutionary's perspective of William Carroll: "the subject of 'respectability' . . . is . . . not worth losing sleep about," he wrote to Devoy in the seemingly hopeless mid-1870s. "We shall all be 'respectable' if we succeed, and certainly never will be . . . until we do."[257]

Nevertheless, many middle- and even upper-class Irish-Americans did participate, often prominently, in late-nineteenth- and early-twentieth-century nationalist movements. Recent research on Irish-American nationalism in Philadelphia, Pittsburgh, St. Louis, and Denver substantiates Brown's hypothesis insofar as it demonstrates that leadership cadres, citywide membership lists, and delegations to national conventions were disproportionately dominated by men of white-collar status, including affluent businessmen and professionals as well as small proprietors and clerks; this was true both of constitutional nationalist organizations (e.g., the American Land and National leagues) and of more extreme societies (e.g., the Clan na Gael and the FOIF). Likewise, second- and even third-generation Irish-Americans often played leading roles—from Philadelphia's Martin I. J. Griffin, indefatigable organizer of American Land League branches, to the California oil magnate Edward L. Doheny, president of the American Association for the Recognition of the Irish Republic—thus corroborating the observations of visitors such as William Bagenal and Sir Horace Plunkett who were amazed to find virulent Anglophobia "deeply rooted" in Irish-Americans "who had themselves never known Ireland." The sources of such emotions were mixed. For men such as Doheny, nephew of a Young Ireland exile, and Illinois's Governor Edward F. Dunne, grandson of a leading Fenian, family tradition and training—perhaps reinforced in Irish-oriented parochial schools—may provide a partial explanation. Similarly, Jeremiah O'Leary, whose anti-British activities during World War I earned him a stiff jail sentence, imbibed Irish patriotism from his emigrant grandfather; and Elizabeth Gurley Flynn, who broadened and systematized her inherited resentments, remembered that the atmosphere of her childhood home was suffused with "a burning hatred of British rule" which emanated more from her second-generation Irish father than from her Galway-born mother.[258]

However, in the late nineteenth and early twentieth centuries most middle-class Irish-American Catholics, whether Irish- or American-born, had been weaned on similar traditions, yet proportionately few were active participants in nationalist movements, and, according to men such as Devoy and Rossa, many cared little or nothing about Irish freedom. Among those who did care, at least ostensibly, other motives were at work besides inherited resentments; as Patrick Ford put it, "every man with Irish blood in his veins" had an "*interest* to subserve, as well as a vengeance to gratify, in keeping up the fight against England." The perceived "interest" of many middle-class nationalists grew out of their ambiguous socioeconomic, cultural, and even psychological status in American society. As Thomas N. Brown has suggested, their unease resulted in part from a felt lack of equal acceptance and respect commensurate with material achievements, a situation potentially rectified once Irish-Americans had a free homeland which would be a source of pride, not shame. Even Irish nationalists indifferent to American opinion recognized and appealed to that yearning: Do "[y]ou want to be honoured among the elements that constitute this nation . . . to be regarded with the respect due you"? Michael Davitt asked a New York Irish audience; if so, then "that you may thus be looked on, aid us in Ireland to remove the stain of degradation from your birth." In addition, not only might nationalist activities bring Irish independence, an event "conducive to the honor of the Irish race in all lands," but the effort itself would also help uplift and unite Irish-Americans, thus fulfilling more-immediate bourgeois goals. Ideally, for example, Irish-Americans must be "faithful, be Catholic, be practical, be temperate, be industrious, be obedient to the laws," if they wished to make Ireland a "glorious and unfettered nation." More crassly, as in Denver in 1879–82, a nationalist movement directed by upper-middle-class Irishmen could mitigate and obscure sharp socioeconomic conflicts within local Irish-American communities and marshal otherwise class-conscious workers to vote for their harshest exploiters.[259]

However, bourgeois Irish-American nationalism reflected more than material interests or assimilative ambitions. It also reflected a crisis of identity which stemmed partly from thwarted attempts to embrace native society, but partly from a widespread, if subtle, alienation from that society—a feeling fed by rejection, but existing separately. His violent devotion to Ireland helps explain why O'Donovan Rossa felt himself "a stranger" after thirty years in America. Less easily explicable was the destructive, subconscious estrangement of an apostle of uplift such as John Boyle O'Reilly; or the fierce conviction of the eminently successful James Shields, thrice U.S. senator, that his children should be raised "as Irish as if born" in his native Tyrone; or the quixotic urge of the west Kerryman Jerry O'Connor to relearn the Irish language through the Gaelic League after forty years' disuse on a South Dakota farm. In short, the "self-indulgent communal morbidity" which characterized bourgeois Irish-America in the late nineteenth and early twentieth centuries reflected not only an externally imposed precariousness of status but also an internalized ambivalence—a yearning for things lost as well as unattained—which found expression in a staunch, ethnocentric Catholicism and, often inseparably, in Irish-American nationalism: mutually reinforcing bulwarks against a rapacious and decadent "Anglo-Saxonism."[260]

Nevertheless, although "Anglo-Saxonism" was a cultural and religious symbol of the industrial capitalism which disquieted the members of the Irish-American bourgeoisie, in the United States, as in Ireland, their material interests and social position forbade them the ruthlessly critical perspective of a James Connolly. Moreover, their contradictory, yet convergent, desires for ethnic solidarity on the one hand and respect and acceptance from their native Protestant peers on the other naturally biased them against internally divisive or dangerously "un-American" issues. Indeed, for many, perhaps most, middle-class (and skilled working-class) Irish-Americans, ethnicity was more safely absorbed in a devout Catholic consciousness, public expressions of which threatened to eclipse in popularity more specifically *Irish* celebrations by the early twentieth century. By contrast, Irish-American nationalism too often clashed with mainstream society or bourgeois aspirations, for example, in its foreign policy and sometimes radical social implications, even in its rhetoric of "exile" implying a group alienation from the land of adoption. Consequently, it was no wonder that—with notable exceptions such as John Devoy, who "respectfully decline[d] the honour of being classed as an 'American,' " and the prosperous Philadelphia Clansman William J. Bradley, who boldly signed himself *"Éireannach Éigin"* "Exile Irishman"—most middle-class Irish-Americans who were active nationalists eschewed both physical force and social radicalism, adhering instead to parliamentary agitation and, as Connolly scornfully observed, to the goal of a bourgeois Ireland "patterned after . . . America."[261]

Such desires for respectability help explain the enormous popularity of the Protestant landlord Parnell among affluent Irish-Americans, as well as their abhorrence of both Davitt's land nationalization scheme and the Clan's thirst for revolution. It also helps explain their dogged devotion after 1900 to Redmond and the slowness of their conversion to physical-force nationalism until events (the Easter rebels' executions, Sinn Féin's 1918 election victory, Black and Tan atrocities) overwhelmed cautious instincts. Even then, as before, middle-class nationalists made tortuous efforts to reconcile Irish freedom with American traditions and interests, a task increasingly difficult as the American government moved ever closer to a tacit alliance with Great Britain in 1900–1917. Fortunately, Wilson's pledge of self-determination for captive nations and, later, the Republican party's own opposition to the League of Nations gave Irish-American nationalists a last opportunity to synthesize Irish and American loyalties, to pretend at least that the "true" interests and ideals of both old and adopted countries could be served simultaneously. De Valera's arrival upset the facile equation (Cohalan feared that even the term "Irish *Republic*" had too-radical connotations in the aftermath of the Bolshevik revolution) since, in effect, de Valera appealed to Irish-Americans as vengeful "exiles." They responded manfully, partly in hopes of laying the burdensome and embarrassing "Irish Question" to rest forever, but in the face of a gathering storm of anti-Irish Catholicism, the end of the Anglo-Irish war came for them none too soon.[262]

Despite the prominence of affluent Irish emigrants and American-born Irishmen, most evidence indicates that the major support for Irish-American nationalism came from recently arrived Irishmen, and primarily from working-class rather than middle-class emigrants. Moreover, the types of men who favored the more extreme varieties of nationalism, both socially radical and physical-force, were overwhelmingly proletarian and Irish-born. Thus, in 1881 the *New York Times* sneered, "The money that has kept the Land League together has come mostly from the day laborers and servant maids of America," and in 1887 John Fitzgerald, president of the Clan-dominated Irish National League of the United States, declared that long experience had "forced [him] to the conviction that in the future as in the past, Ireland must depend not upon those whom God has blessed with wealth, but on the dollars of those who though they can least afford it are ever the readiest to give support and sustenance to the Irish Cause." As Eric Foner, Michael Gordon, and Victor Walsh have demonstrated, in 1879–82 Irish-American donations to sustain the Land War, especially those made through Patrick Ford's radical *Irish World,* were heaviest from among working-class emigrants in urban industrial neighborhoods like Pittsburgh's Woods Run, factory towns like Troy and Lawrence, the Pennsylvania anthracite fields, and far western mining communities like Leadville and Virginia City. Likewise, research by Dale Light and Timothy Meagher suggests that working-class Irish predominance in the Clan na Gael and the increasingly militant AOH continued at least through the early 1900s, and comments by British diplomats in 1916–22 indicate that lower-middle- and laboring-class Irish-Americans were still the most virulently anti-British. Furthermore, proletarian emigrants provided most of the donations to Rossa's Skirmishing Fund, and remained embarrassingly enthusiastic for terrorists such as the Invincibles who horrified middle-class nationalists. The fact that Philadelphia's Luke Dillon, a Clan dynamiter who spent fourteen years in a Canadian jail, and not Martin I. J. Griffin, that same city's highly successful and respectable INLLA and temperance leader, became the subject of a popular Irish-American ballad suggests which of the two styles of agitation captured the hearts of ordinary emigrants.[263]

Indeed, the historians Foner and Gordon have argued that in the 1880s, at least, there existed "a symbiotic relationship" between Irish-American nationalism and radical trade unionism, each informing and reinforcing the other. For example, the two efforts overlapped considerably in leadership, personnel, tactics, and ideology: Patrick Ford, Father Edward Mc-Glynn, Henry George, and Terence Powderly (head of the Knights of Labor and the Scranton branch of the Clan na Gael) were prominent in both movements; rank-and-file support for the Land War was strongest in areas with a high degree of labor organization and industrial strife; both Irish nationalists and Irish-American workers (e.g., in New York City) employed the boycott extensively against landlords, employers, and "scabs"; and both efforts were significantly influenced by the programs of George and Michael Davitt and, more generally, by Irish emigrants' resentment of exploitation, broadened by Ford's insistence and their own growing realization that landlordism and imperialism were international oppressions and that "[t]he cause of the poor in Donegal is the cause of the factory slave in Fall River." As Elizabeth Gurley Flynn put it, an Irish peasant heritage was excellent preparation for social militancy, for "[w]hen one understood British imperialism it was an open window to all imperialism." Throughout the period Irish-American labor leaders such as Powderly and the English-born Robert Blissert drew analogies between Irish rural and American industrial experiences and goals, their success exemplified by the poetry of the Irish-born worker David Fouhey, whose crude verses written in Massachusetts during the early 1880s synthesized the struggles of American laborers and Irish tenants. Of course, Irish-American working-class radicalism waned rapidly after 1886, and the demise of the Knights of Labor in 1886–1893 paralleled that of the General Trades Union in 1837–44, both movements fragmenting along sectarian lines and culminating in heightened ethnic and religious consciousness which obscured social conflicts. However, despite the growing *embourgeoisement* of both Irish-America and Irish-American nationalism, connections between the latter and militant labor did not entirely disappear, maintained not only by lonely figures such as Connolly and Larkin but also by Father Peter Yorke in San Francisco and by the Irish Progressive League in New York City. Ironically, contemporary nativists and crusaders for "100% Americanism" were more adept at sensing that continued relationship than subsequent historians have been, as both the APA and later the American Legion perceived anti-Irish Catholicism, union-busting, and repression of radicalism as inseparable goals.[264]

Nevertheless, the intimacy of that relationship should not be overstated. It is unlikely that many Irish-American labor leaders were any more sincere in their espousals of Irish freedom than were their adversaries in Tammany Hall and the Catholic hierarchy, as the wily Fenian John Devoy suspected and as AF of L leaders demonstrated during their 1894 convention when they cynically resurrected Davitt's land nationalization scheme to defeat a socialist motion calling for collective ownership of the means of production. As its success in 1913–21 indicates, Irish-American nationalism had a life of its own, and the most that can be said with certainty is that working-class emigrants' experiences in urban-industrial America both facilitated nationalist organization and heightened extant hatred of England and devotion to Irish independence. For example, there is no doubt that the bonds forged in steel mills, pit crews, and working-class neighborhoods among Irish-American laborers heightened ethnic as well as class consciousness, facilitated their mobilization in nationalist movements, and inclined them to more-extreme forms of nationalism which reflected not only a social radicalism derived from contemporary labor agitations but also a proletarian culture of masculinity which exalted physical force as a means of redressing or revenging both personal and communal injuries. In addition, the fact that (at least in the 1880s) such environments were as yet unleavened by the substantial presence of either the church or an Irish-American bourgeoisie meant that extreme nationalism could flourish with little local opposition. For instance, in Philadelphia during the late 1880s less than a tenth of the members of the city's leading home rule association were workers (all of them skilled), while by contrast 93 percent of the members of Clan na Gael local no. 246 were working class, over three-fourths of them unskilled laborers. That the Clan's strength in Philadelphia (as in Worcester) drew disproportionately from such working-class neighborhoods was demonstrated by the city's delegations to contemporary national Clan conventions: almost half the delegates were skilled or unskilled workers. Moreover, there is no doubt that harsh exploitation in American factories, mines, and building sites reinforced nationalist hatreds and yearnings: sometimes directly, as for the workers John Purcell and William Cannon, who drew easy analogies between English-born foremen in the United States and Orangemen in Ireland; sometimes more subtly, as for the servant Bridget Fitzgerald, who blamed her social immobility in America on English-enforced Irish poverty, and for the clerk Francis Hackett, who resented the "wounding manners" of Yankee employers "through the twisted windowpane that looks back on conquest." Father Yorke understood the connection, for his own feelings of "exile" in America were shaped not only by his Irish background but also by his anger "that an Irishman is compelled to fight so hard for a square deal in this land of ours!"[265]

In short, American experiences and Irish legacies converged to mold Irish-American consciousness and nationalism, and though it is difficult to evaluate their respective influence, it is arguable that great numbers of post-Famine emigrants landed in America already predisposed by training and outlook to perceive emigration as forced exile and to respond to unpleasant situations abroad with resentments and desires easily translated into nationalist expressions and activities. For example, the emigrants of 1856–1921 were weaned on memories or nationalist interpretations of "black '47" and the Famine clearances, and many of the letters written in the 1870s and 1880s expressed burning hatreds of landlordism and English rule directly traceable to those events. Thus, Michael Flanagan remembered "the rich gluttons"—"the Devils clothed in purple and fine linen"—"who drove the population into the Poorhouse or across the Atlantic" and "who will receive a just reward for their oppression." Likewise, Patrick O'Callaghan prayed for "the day of retribution," and John Cronin vowed that the "exiles" eagerly awaited an opportunity "to go back again with a double undying vengeance to hurl the vile Saxon oppressor from the shores of Erin." "For the love of Ireland and the hate of England," Joseph Cromien begged Patrick Ford, "strike out, strike out strong."[266]

Of course, by 1900 those Irish-Americans who had actually experienced the Famine's horrors were old and few, but the tradition persisted, coloring emigrants' perceptions of all subsequent Irish events; as the British consul Frederick Leahy lamented in 1917, Irish-Americans' "minds hark back to the past, and their mental picture is based upon an Ireland of seventy-five to one hundred years ago." Leahy presumed that more-recent Irish emigrants appreciated the great improvements which subsequent British legislation had wrought in Ireland, but he overlooked the fact that the post-Famine generations were the most effectively politicized, Catholicized, and nationalized in history: heirs not only of transmitted Famine memories but also of Fenianism, of the Land War, of the mass mobilizations of the Irish National and United Irish leagues, and of the pervasive, multifaceted Irish-Ireland movement. As a result of such training, no doubt many post-Famine emigrants were like H. O'C. McCarthy, "[o]ne of those enthusiastic Irish youths who seem to live, move, and have their being in the memories of Sarsfield, Emmet, Fitzgerald, [and] Tone." Indeed, significant minorities of late-nineteenth-century emigrants had been active participants in Fenianism or the agrarian agitations of 1879–90 and 1898–1907—or had been evicted farmers as in 1879–82, equally prone to perceive emigration in involuntary, political terms, to cry with the departing William Dermady, "[A]dieu to the land of Land Lord tireny and Oppression." Thus, an elderly informant from Westmeath contrasted the "slave mind" characteristic of earlier emigrants with the sturdy, assertive patriotism of those leaving in the 1880s, after political baptism in the Land War. Similarly, Francis Hackett's youthful impressions of Parnell's speeches "were to live with" him in America, "to feed the flame of imagination, the flame of a free Ireland"; less dramatically, when late-nineteenth-century emigrants such as Patrick Ryan remembered their Irish villages, images of relatives, neighbors, church, and local nationalist clubs merged in inseparable memories.[267]

No wonder, then, that when interviewed decades after their departures, elderly emigrants would automatically relate emigration to British oppression; or that when emigrants so trained met poverty and prejudice in America, they concluded with Hackett that "England had crippled the Irish deliberately," unfitting them for success abroad while obliging their exodus. "My predicament . . . was highly complicated," wrote Hackett of his first, unpleasant experiences in New York, for "[u]nless I ascribed guilt to England, I could not excuse the Irish for all those failings that made the English [and Yankee employers] feel superior." "Was I to take them as my natural enemies?" he wondered—a question many less reflective emigrants answered automatically and affirmatively. To be sure, large numbers of post-Famine emigrants recognized that the disadvantages of their Irish background and the circumstances of their departure owed far more to decisions by "cruel parents" or exploitation by "grass-grabbers" and employers than to British misgoverment. However, many such emigrants— J. F. Costello, Timothy Cashman, Bridget Fitzgerald, for example—conformed to tradition and translated resentment of Ireland's social inadequacies into hatred for England and, at least in Cashman's case, into more extreme varieties of Irish-American nationalism which seemingly promised social as well as political revolution.[268]

Moreover, the post-Famine exodus's unique regional and sociocultural origins combined with pervasive political and religious influences to predispose the emigrants to strong nationalist sentiments. Current research indicates that in the 1890s and in the early twentieth century recently arrived Irish emigrants tended to be the most vociferous Irish-American nationalists. A partly sufficient explanation may be that, of all Irish emigrants in 1880–1910, some 15 percent came from middle and west Ulster counties, where sectarian strife between Orangemen and the Irish AOH inflamed nationalist emotions, and nearly 44 percent from Connaught, west Munster, and north Leinster counties, where peasants and farm laborers most strongly supported the Land War's more radical manifestations, the antigrazier agitation of the 1890s and early 1900s, Sinn Féin, and the antitreaty republicans. In short, these emigrants left regions not only where nationalism was in ferment but also where socioeconomic conditions or sectarianism inspired the disadvantaged to support extreme, or at least strongly anti-Protestant, varieties of nationalism as means of redressing their grievances. Moreover, since such extreme political resolutions were widely perceived as necessary to stop emigration from these districts, it was logical that those obliged to depart would both interpret emigration in political terms and, once in the New World, gravitate to equally extreme varieties of Irish-American nationalism. Again, this seems to have been true of Cashman, the Cork laborers' son who despised bourgeois home rulers on both sides of the Atlantic and who hoped that the Clan na Gael and Sinn Féin would create a socially equitable as well as politically independent Ireland.[269]

Significantly, Cashman's ideal Ireland was also to be Irish-speaking, as had been the east Cork district whence he had emigrated in 1893. Indeed, more subtle but perhaps equally important in predisposing post-Famine emigrants to Irish-American nationalism was the fact that, as their regional origins suggest, so many came from a peasant and/or Irish-speaking background, from a culture whose worldview still counseled conservatism, patience, and nonresponsibility. As was noted earlier, such emigrants were most prone to have negative or ambivalent feelings concerning their departure, or, alternatively, most likely to be deluded by mythic images of a paradisaical America. Given their inadequate skills, capital, education, even ability to speak English, they were also most likely to suffer disappointments abroad which either corroborated initial apprehensions or shattered naïve expectations, in either case often producing acute homesickness and self-perceptions as involuntary exiles readily politicized. Unsophisticated young emigrants were also most prone to accept uncritically the injunctions to duty, often couched in parent-child analogies, which remained Irish-American nationalists' stock appeals. The emigrant who would forswear or neglect his obligation to Mother Ireland, declared O'Donovan Rossa, would also consign his own mother to the poorhouse: a telling argument for emigrants trained since childhood to feel guilty for "abandoning" heartbroken parents—and to exorcise that guilt through financial sacrifice.[270]

Finally, it may be crucial that such an unusually high proportion of post-Famine emigrants were either Irish-speakers or at most barely removed from a traditional Gaelic-peasant culture where archaic anti-*Sasanaigh* traditions remained firmly rooted, reinforced by contemporary agitations and corroborating the now-official interpretation of emigration as exile. To be sure, western peasant outlooks could be so passive and parochial that emigrants from Connaught and other bleak regions could evince in America no interest in political developments beyond their reconstructed urban villages, as Victor Walsh has demonstrated of the Galway and Donegal emigrants isolated both geographically and socially in Pittsburgh's impoverished Point neighborhood during the early 1880s. Again, the interaction between Irish legacies and American experiences was often decisive, for in other working-class districts of greater Pittsburgh, Connaughtmen joined with emigrants from more politicized and culturally enriched, yet still Irish-speaking, areas of Munster to form large and vigorous nationalist associations. Even after 1880 western emigrants' nationalist expressions tended to be specific, parochial, and archaic. For example, when the Kerryman Batt O'Connor remembered his homeland, he recalled the "places where [he] played and romped as a child . . . the smell of the turf, . . . the streams in which [he] went fishing, and . . . the bareness and narrow limits of [his] old home." Likewise, in some of his verses the west Kerryman Seán Ruiséal sang not of "Ireland" but of his native parish, "bright, lovely Ventry" on "the borders of Dingle"—rich in historic and literary associations with the legendary Fianna of pre-Christian times and with the "gallant" Pierce Ferriter, seventeenth-century poet and Cromwellian martyr.[271]

However, it was that very intimacy with their birthplace, their physical environment, their archaic association with a living past, which often made western peasants and Irish-speakers feel so alien in America and which provided such a firm basis for a broader and deeper Irish nationalism which could transcend both the limits of parochialism and the shallowness of the ubiquitous "holy Ireland" cant. The premodernism of western Irish nationalism was also its strength, for its persistent millennial cast conflated history and compelled extreme solutions. Thus, Ruiséal's verses written in 1900–1910 purposely confused "independence and Home Rule" and lamented that O'Connell and Parnell were "decaying in the grave, . . . With no one alive now but miserable dregs / Unworthy to send to Parliament"—a characteristic condemnation of Irish parliamentarians whose goals and tactics seemed unworthy in Ruiséal's cultural context.[272]

In short, when men such as Ruiséal and Séamus Ó Muircheartaigh left Ireland, they often naturally interpreted their emigration in traditional terms, casting themselves as *deoraithe* in heroic, sorrowing, anti-*Sasanaigh* roles. Thus, their anguish in urban-industrial America and their longing to return home were inseparably associated with nationalist sentiments. "My hope lies again with the King of Heaven / And with the gentle Virgin," prayed Ruiséal,

> That the Milesians will again raise their heads
> To strike a blow to their enemies;
> The English-speaking wretches will yet be scattered
> From Patrick's holy island
> And the Gael admonished by their own laws—
> That's the hope that keeps the *Spailpín Fánach* going.

Essentially, it would seem, the dream of the western Gaels was still the same vision that had inspired the eighteenth-century *aisling* poets and, to a degree, the mid-nineteenth-century Fenian "exiles." As Ruiséal's fellow west Kerryman Ó Muircheartaigh put it, the hope was to "Go back to Ireland" so that

> When the day comes and the sky is alight
> And the hosts march under the green banner of the Gael,
> That day you'll be glorious in the battle
> Which will scatter the cursed English across the sea.

In fact, Ó Muircheartaigh died in San Francisco, and few post-Famine emigrants followed Batt O'Connor back to fight for Irish freedom. However, the worth of the dream was not in its explicit fulfillment but in the impetus it gave to Irish-American nationalism and, equally important, in its power to sustain unhappy "exiles" in the New World. "Your heart is broken and your health as well," wrote Eóin Ua Cathail, addressing the plight of the Irish-speaking laborer in the United States; "you hope that the next year will be better," but it isn't, "and so you will be pulling the devil by the tail as long as you live." For Irish-speakers such as Ua Cathail, Ruiséal, and Ó Muircheartaigh, the vision of a victorious return to a free Ireland was "the hope that ke[pt them] going" and that fanned the dying embers of Irish-American nationalism.[273]

In retrospect, Irish-American nationalists such as John Devoy were very fortunate that in the end, in 1916–21, they finally succeeded in helping to free most of Ireland politically through Irish-American financial support. For essentially they were fighting what had appeared a losing battle against time, dwindling numbers of new emigrants, and the powerful forces working for ideological as well as behavioral assimilation in America. The image of the Irish-American as exile was extremely useful in holding together the increasingly disparate and contented Irish-American community, but at bottom it ran counter to the Irish being regarded, or regarding themselves truly, as full-fledged Americans. Already great numbers had lost interest, and for many others Ireland, its ways of life, and its traditional loyalties and worldview were better forgotten or repressed except on occasions when nationalist agitators or the old folks at home still played upon the heartstrings of duty or guilt. And finally, as time passed, the emigrants who had gone out in the great waves of the 1840s and 1850s, even of the 1880s, simply got older and fewer, and the nostalgia of old age was tempered by their having spent most or all of their adult years abroad. If nothing else, time alone had brought them to terms with America, and the parents and friends they had left in Ireland were usually now dead or had long since emigrated themselves; and so they knew that if they tried to return, they would only endure the disillusionment of now being "exiles" in the land of their birth. Thus, in 1898 the elderly Clareman Patrick Kane longed for "that home in Old Ireland," dreamed of his boyhood scenes, yet sadly realized

> . . . that it all now is altered,
>   My friends and companions are gone,
> That home is replaced by another,
>   Beside which the Shannon rolls on;
> And if I should revisit that Island,
>   That cottage which once I called home,
> There is none who would now recognize me,
>   A stranger around there I'd roam.[274]

In short, the Irish and Irish-American nationalists were lucky that the Easter rising and the Anglo-Irish war occurred just before the well of Irish-American memories, duty, and guilt ran dry—just before the old Irish worldview became in America nothing more than a shell of largely meaningless clichés. The years 1916–21 witnessed the "last hurrah" for the image of the Irish emigrant as "exile" in America, for both the image and the activities it inspired evaporated almost entirely with Irish-America's happy relief over the Anglo-Irish treaty and with its subsequent confusion and embarrassment over the Irish civil war. To be sure, the disappointment of Al Smith's crushing defeat in 1928 and the traumatic setback of the Great Depression of the 1930s still lay ahead, but those were entirely *American* concerns. By 1923, except for the continuing trickle of embittered Catholic emigrants from Northern Ireland, the long, dark winter of Irish exile in America was over. The golden summer of Irish-American tourism was about to begin.[275]

Conclusion

The central thesis of this book has been that Irish-American homesickness, alienation, and nationalism were rooted ultimately in a traditional Irish Catholic worldview which predisposed Irish emigrants to perceive or at least justify themselves not as voluntary, ambitious emigrants but as involuntary, nonresponsible "exiles," compelled to leave home by forces beyond individual control, particularly by British and landlord oppression. In premodern times Gaelic culture's secular, religious, and linguistic aspects expressed or reinforced a worldview which deemphasized and even condemned individualistic and innovative actions such as emigration. Although Gaelic Ireland withered from the blasts of conquest and change, not only did certain real continuities remain to justify the retention of archaic attitudes and behavior patterns but in fact those institutions—family, church, and nationalism—which dominated modern Catholic Ireland strove to perpetuate old outlooks which both minimized the demoralizing impacts of change and cemented communal loyalties in the face of internal conflicts and external enemies. Thus, tradition and expediency merged, and emigration remained forced banishment—demanding political redress and the emigrants' continued fealty to sorrowing Mother Ireland.

All these themes, attitudes, and social pressures were epitomized by the emigrants' leave-taking ceremonies, commonly known as "American wakes." Archaic in origin yet adapted to modern exigencies, the American wakes both reflected and reinforced traditional communal attitudes toward emigration. Indeed, these rituals seemed almost purposely designed to obscure the often mundane or ambiguous realities of emigration, to project communal sorrow and anger on the traditional English foe, to impress deep feelings of grief, guilt, and duty on the departing emigrants, and to send them forth as unhappy but faithful and vengeful "exiles"—their final, heart-rending moments at home burned indelibly into their memories, easily recalled by parents' letters, old songs, or the appeals of Irish-American nationalists.

The American wake seems to have been a peculiarly Irish custom, unknown in Britain or continental Europe. Most extant evidence of the practice dates from the post-Famine decades, but Asenath Nicholson witnessed an American wake in County Kilkenny in 1844, and similar ceremonies—called living wakes—were common in late-eighteenth- and early-nineteenth-century Ulster, where they were held by Presbyterians as well as by Catholics. Nevertheless, the American wake seems to have been primarily a Catholic peasant custom carried on most persistently and in its original forms in areas which were still, or in recent memory, Irish-speaking. Thus, by the late nineteenth and early twentieth centuries, American wakes were most common in west Munster, Connaught, and west and mid-Ulster, while in the midlands and eastern counties the custom had either become disused or lost many of its traditional features. In short, like its model—the wake for the dead—the American wake was a product of Gaelic culture, and both customs eventually disappeared with the routinization of emigration and the westward advance of Anglicization. However, as late as 1901, American wakes were still common throughout most of Catholic Ireland, and one newspaper lamented that the entire island had become "one vast 'American wake.'" The name given the custom differed from area to area. Although the term "American wake" was most common, peasants in the Golden Vale called the ceremony a "live wake," while in east Ulster it was a "convoy." In Connaught Irish-speakers referred to "the farewell supper" or "feast of departure," those in Donegal to the "American bottle night" or "bottle drink." In especially Anglicized counties with long experience of emigration, such as Meath and Wexford, the leave-taking occasion was called the "parting spree," indicating the attrition of its once-tragic connotations.[1]

Nevertheless, despite regional variations of nomenclature, save in east Leinster the custom remained substantially similar throughout the island, and its most common name—the American wake—best reflected its character and tone. Of course, in traditional wakes for the dead, the relatives and neighbors of the deceased sat through the night and watched the corpse until burial. Among Catholic peasants the custom was a seemingly incongruous mixture of sorrow and hilarity, with prayers for the dead and the mournful keening of old women alternating with drinking, dancing, and mirthful games. Although real deaths did not occasion American wakes, the choice of name was significant since Catholic countrymen at least initially regarded emigration as death's equivalent, a final breaking of earthly ties. Such attitudes were rooted deep in Irish folklore, for example, in voyage tales which symbolized death or banishment and in popular beliefs which equated going west with earthly dissolution. In the mists of the west Atlantic, in the direction of America, lay the mythical isles which ancient traditions held to be abodes of the dead. Westward travelers, even peasants who added west rooms to their cottages, were believed fated for early demise; likewise, west rooms in farmhouses were traditionally reserved for aged parents who had relinquished control of farms to sons and daughters-in-law. More concretely, in emigration's early decades, when money was scarce, travel slow and perilous, illiteracy widespread and mail service highly uncertain, and destinations only vaguely perceived, the departure for North America of a relative or neighbor represented as final a parting as a descent into the grave. Indeed, given the high mortality rates which afflicted Irish emigrants in both colonial Virginia and early-twentieth-century New York City, associating emigration and death was not illogical, as churchmen warned and as peasants' own observations of consumptive "returned Yanks" seemed to verify, ironically corroborating ancient tales of *Tír na nÓg,* the mythical western Land of the Young, whence no traveler returned except to wither and die. In addition, for the politically minded the American wake seemed a proper commemoration of a process that was bleeding Ireland of its young men and women. As the Irish-Irelander Robert Lynd observed in 1909, it was "not without significance that so funereal a name should be given to the emigration ceremonies, for the Irish emigrant is not the personification of national adventure, but of something that has the appearance of national doom." Given such traditions and attitudes, it was not unnatural for Irish countrymen to hold wakes for departing emigrants. Even in the late nineteenth century, traditional countrymen "made very little difference between going to America and going to the grave," and as one elderly informant remembered, when you left home, "[i]t was as if you were going out to be buried."[2]

The American wakes resembled the traditional deathwatches in their outward characteristics as well as in their symbolic significance. Both were held to gather together relatives and neighbors to honor the "departed," to share and assuage the grief of the bereaved, and to express at once communal sorrow and a reaffirmation of communal continuity in the face of potentially demoralizing disruptions. The American wakes usually took place in the home of the prospective emigrant and generally lasted from nightfall until early morning of the next day, when the "Yankee"—as he or she was called in west Munster—made the final departure. During the week preceding the American wake, the intending emigrant visited relatives and neighbors to bid them personal farewells and invite them to attend. Priests seem to have been rarely or only briefly present at these affairs (perhaps because traditional wakes generally were clerically proscribed occasions of sin), but by the late nineteenth century it was customary for the "Yankee" to make confession and take communion on the Sunday before departing, and also to pay an obligatory visit to the parish priest's house, there receiving his blessing, presents of prayer books, scapulars, and holy pictures and medals, "as well as much excellent advice and warnings as to the dangers to faith and morals to be met with by those who leave the Catholic atmosphere of holy Ireland." Through these rituals churchmen both sanctioned and, they hoped, retained some control over a process which they opposed but could not halt. Meanwhile, the women of the emigrant's house were busy baking, cooking, and cleaning in preparation for the American wake. Unless times were very bad or the community exceptionally poor, either the emigrant's parents or the guests supplied liberal amounts of food and refreshments, including large quantities of whiskey or, later, porter and stout. While their elders sat around the hearth, the young folk danced to the music of fiddles, flutes, pipes, or melodeons. Between dances the guests cried, sang songs, told stories, and drank away the night.[3]

Thus, like their more gruesome counterparts, the American wakes combined elements of gaiety and grief, but all the evidence indicates that the latter emotion predominated. This was particularly true in the earliest American wakes, held in areas which had witnessed little previous emigration and in traditional or Irish-speaking districts generally. Dancing and singing were often absent at such early wakes, and the participants passed the night with sighs and somber conversation, in an atmosphere laden with gloom and foreboding. Frequently, as in real wakes, the emigrant's mother or another old woman raised a keen over the "dead" one. These were long, sorrowful elegies which alternately praised the emigrant's virtues and descanted upon the sufferings which his or her loss would inflict on parents and community. Indeed, both the traditional keens for the dead and these stylized lamentations over emigration often bitterly reproached their subjects, thus projecting parental and communal responsibility and guilt upon the "departed." "Why did you leave us? had you not every comfort that heart could wish? were you not beloved by your parents and friends?" sang a keener for the dead in 1817: sentiments replicated later in the century by an emigrant's mother in Kilkenny—"O mavourneen, and why do ye break the heart of her who raired ye? Was there no turf in the bog, no praties in the pit, that ye leave the hairth of yer poor ould mother?"—and still later by another in Connemara—"Is there anything so pitiful as a son and a mother / Straying continually from each other? I who reared him without pain or shame / And provided food and good clean sauce for him. . . . Isn't it little my painful disease affects him / And the many sorrows that go through my heart?" Likewise, about 1900 a Kerry priest recorded the desolate keen of an Irish-speaking mother about to part with a beloved child: "You were my love and my treasure," she cried,

> You were lively and handsome
> Going down the road. . . .
> I will not pass a gate
> From the Maigue to Youghal
> Or from Tralee of the yellow gold
> To Ardnagoshragh
> Without talking of you. . . .
> Alas, my woe
> That you are leaving me to make your fortune
> In the bloom of youth.
>
> Alas, my bitter lament
> And my sorrow that I could not describe;
> This day is painful
> And sorrowful for your mother. . . .
>
> Alas, my destruction, . . .
> Will you leave me
> Alone behind you
> With death calling me
> Every day of my life?

Regardless of the emigrant's ambitions or the real roles parents may have played in obliging departure, the effects of such laments, delivered in shrill, piercing wails, were irresistible and devastating. Before long, "with tears rolling down worn cheeks and feeble old men tearing their gray hair," a chorus of wailing women and weeping men, including the emigrant, joined the old keener in her despair. No wonder that participants in such starkly primitive American wakes described them as "harrowing affairs" displaying "naked grief" and "elemental emotions." No wonder, either, that participants, especially the emigrants themselves, would seek to relieve the tensions of such occasions by making elaborate promises to return or send remittances and by excusing their actions as involuntary, nonresponsible "exile."[4]

Even the later American wakes were anything but joyful affairs, despite the singing and dancing which had become common. For example, when Maurice O'Sullivan's sister left the Great Blasket Island in the early twentieth century, her relatives and neighbors had already experienced several generations of such departures. Nevertheless, at her American wake—although "music and songs, dancing and mirth were flying in the air"—"there was a mournful look on all within." "No wonder," wrote O'Sullivan,

> for they were like children of the one mother, the people of the Island, no more than twenty yards between any two houses, the boys and girls every moonlight night dancing on the Sandhills or sitting together and listening to the sound of the waves from Shingle Strand; and when the moon would wane, gathered together talking and conversing in the house of old Nell.

It would seem that in such remote, traditional villages those gathered at the American wakes lamented not only the emigration of a relative or friend but also the inexorable disintegration of old communities and the decline of traditional ways of life which emigration epitomized. However, in nearly all these ceremonies, in English- as well as Irish-speaking districts, "the veneer of merriment was at best a paper-thin cover for the strong undercurrent of sadness." The grief of the emigrant's parents was particularly obvious, and often their sorrow or self-pity broke through the merriment or their affected reserve to infect the emigrant and the rest of the company. Thus, an old woman recalled that at a "bottle drink" in Donegal a father turned to his son and said, " 'Get up here son and face me in a step for likely it will be the last step ever we'll dance.' " "At that," she remembered, "there wasn't a dry eye in the house."[5]

Perhaps the most telling indicators of the spirit prevalent in the American wakes were the songs which the participants sang. These were a mixture of folk compositions, broadside ballads, and—increasingly by the late nineteenth century—songs published in popular periodicals such as *The Nation's Penny Readings* or in cheap collections like *The Harp of Tara Song Book*. The later published ballads were almost invariably nationalistic, interpreting emigration in political terms, but in fact it is often difficult, if not impossible, to distinguish "genuine" folk compositions from commercial productions, so similar were their themes and so frequently did authors of both kinds of songs borrow images and phrases from each other and from the earlier formal-song traditions. To be sure, the great majority of the emigrants' ballads were unoriginal, clumsily worded and rhymed, and replete with mawkish sentimentality. However, their sheer number and immense popularity on both sides of the Atlantic (many songs current in late-nineteenth-century Ireland had been composed in America) indicate that they both reflected and reinforced conventional Irish perceptions of emigration, and were so deemed highly appropriate to express communal sentiments at the American wakes.[6]

That such sentiments were nevertheless not entirely unambiguous is demonstrated by a significant minority of songs which conceptualized emigration in other than political or negative terms. For example, several ballads portrayed emigration unhappily but realistically depicted its usually mundane causes. Thus, the author of "The Emigrant's Farewell to Donegal" lamented, "My father [held only] five acres of land / it was not enough to support us all, / Which banished me from my native land, / to old Ireland dear I bid farewell." A few songs went further and blamed emigration on parental decisions regarding inheritances and marriage prospects: "How cruel it was of my parents to send me / Away o'er the dark rolling waves of the sea," cried "Barney, the Lad from Kildare," now alone, "out of work, and without a red penny" on the cold streets of urban America. In addition, a number of ballads actually celebrated emigration as a blessed release from poverty or oppression, and predicted that the emigrants would enjoy prosperity and liberty in "The Glorious and Free United States of America." "If you labour in America," promised that song's composer, "In riches you will roll, / There's neither tithes nor taxes there / Nor rent to press you down; / It's a glorious fine free country, / To welcome every man, / So sail off to America, / As soon as e'er you can." Some songs were positively joyful, portraying emigration as an exciting adventure best undertaken by footloose "playboys" such as "The Rambling Irishman," "The Wild Irish Boy," and the author of "Muirsheen Durkin," who declared he was "sick and tired of working" and so was "off to California, where instead of diggin' praties / I'll be diggin' lumps of gold." Likewise, "The Irishman now going to America" told the rollicking story of an Irish canal laborer who fought and wooed his way into the heart and purse of an American widow with $2,000 and a well-stocked farm. That song's composer, like many others, urged his listeners to reject Irish poverty and follow his example. More extreme was the atypical ballad "The Green Fields of America," whose unsentimental author declared, "[It's] little I'd care where my bones should be buried," and cursed those so supine as to remain willingly in Ireland.[7]

Songs which described emigration and America positively seem to have been most common in the late eighteenth and early nineteenth centuries, and most popular then and later in Anglicized districts whose relatively advantaged inhabitants had had long and generally favorable experiences with emigration. For example, most of the emigrants' ballads sung in Counties Meath and Wexford around 1900 were optimistic, promising opportunity and even "independence" in a still-idealized America. Coinciding as they did with the Great Famine's horrors, the 1848 California gold strikes at least temporarily reinvigorated the old image of America as a land of easy riches; even in traditional Kerry, songs promising freedom and happiness in the United States (especially to the unmarried) were popular in the late nineteenth and early twentieth centuries. Such songs certainly served useful purposes, for as rhymed renditions of the *caisleáin óir* myth they assuaged many of the fears and tensions surrounding emigration. However, theirs remained a *minority* viewpoint, especially in the post-Famine period, when emigration became at once more intensely politicized and most prevalent in hitherto-traditional or Irish-speaking districts. Moreover, despite their undoubted popularity such songs were generally inappropriate at American wakes, for those occasions were designed not to celebrate departures but to lament them, not to extol the emigrant as an ambitious or carefree individual but rather to impress upon him or her the full burden of a communal opinion which demanded grief, duty, and self-abnegation as the price of departure. Thus, although a number of songs praised the "Land of Liberty" as a refuge, usually this was in the context of politicized exile from a beloved Ireland rather than a simple eulogy of America's abstract attractions. More typical was a composition entitled "My woe be to Columbus who first found out the way," and even in the early nineteenth century the majority of emigration ballads were profoundly melancholic. Indeed, one elderly woman later recalled, "All the songs that ever I heard about going away to America were sad. . . ."[8]

Taken together, the great majority of ballads sung at American wakes represented a stylized dialogue between the emigrants and those who remained in Ireland—a dialogue which fully and dramatically expressed the central elements of the traditional Irish worldview in its conventional applications to the emigration experience. For example, among the saddest and most popular songs were those which, like the traditional keens, reproached and reminded the emigrants how lonely and miserable their parents would be after their departure. "Where are our darling children gone," asked one song heard in County Kerry; "Will they nevermore return, / . . . To their fathers and their mothers, / They have left in misery?" Replete with parents' self-pity, songs of this genre seemed intended to inspire guilt in departing children:

> God keep all the mothers who rear up a child,
> And also the father who labors and toils.
> Trying to support them he works night and day,
> And when they are reared up, they then go away.

These ballads scarcely reflected an accurate picture of emigration's practical causes or of Irish family relationships, but, given their childhood training, neither ambitious nor resentful emigrants could help feeling remorse and guilt for leaving home when they heard such songs. However, the emigrants' tears shed in response were not sufficient recompense for their communal apostasy—"ye go to sarve yourselves, and why do ye bawl about the thing that's yer own choosin'," exclaimed one reproachful father—and other songs composed from the parents' perspective made clear the continued obligations which the emigrants were enjoined to fulfill. "Good-bye Johnny dear," sang one apocryphal mother, "when you are far away,

> Don't forget your poor old mother,
> Far across the sea,
> Write a letter now and then,
> And send me all you can,
> But don't forget where'er you roam,
> that you are an Irishman.

Similarly, related songs warned of the dire consequences of *not* sending remittances home. Thus, in "The Three Leaved Shamrock" a young Irishwoman begs a traveler to carry a tragic message to her brother in the United States—their aged mother has been evicted:

> Tell him since he went away how bitter was her lot,
> And the landlord came one winter's night and turned
>   us from our cot.
> Our troubles they were many and our friends they
>   were but few,
> And brother dear our mother used to ofttimes talk of you,
> Saying darling son come back again, she often
>   used to say,
> 'Till at last one day she sickened, aye, and soon
>   was laid away,
> Her grave I watered with my tears, it's where these
>   flowers grew,
> This is all I've got now and them I send to you.

"Imagine," exclaimed an old woman from Donegal, "if you were going away the next morning and hear a song like that: wouldn't it put you out of your mind with longing!"[9]

The natural counterparts to such ballads were the many songs which dramatized the emigrants' own sorrow for leaving and predicted their unhappiness in North America. Of course, the fact that many young Irishmen and -women left home eagerly, if often naïvely, contradicted the ballads' messages, but the songs accurately reflected young emigrants' frequent regrets and self-pity for their lost childhood as well as the reactions of those who stayed behind and projected their own loneliness on their children overseas. Even more important, such songs allowed the emigrants to exorcise guilt and responsibility for breaking familial and communal ties, because their dominant theme was that all Irish emigrants were really grief-stricken and involuntary "exiles," compelled to leave home against their will. For example, many ballads—such as this original composition by a west Ulster emigrant—described the "exile's" feelings at the moment of departure:

> Gazing back through Barnes Gap on my own dear native hills
> I thought no shame (Oh! who could blame?) 'twas there I cried my fill,
> My parents kind ran in my mind, my friends and comrades all,
> My heart did ache, I thought 'twould break in leaving Donegal.

Most songs of this genre emphasized that "Poor Pat *Must* Emigrate," that young Irishmen and -women were all, in the words of one emigrant composer, *"forced* to rove abroad far from the Shamrock shore, / And leave the land which gave me birth, and her whom I adore." However, as might be expected, only rarely did they attribute causation to "cruel parents," Catholic "land-grabbers" or employers, or even to abstract poverty and natural disasters, but instead they almost invariably projected responsibility on Catholic Ireland's historic oppressors, thus portraying the emigrants as "exiles" for faith and country, as victims of landlord or British/Protestant tyranny. Highly politicized emigration ballads were most common in the late nineteenth century, when they reflected the Land League's and home rulers' efforts to propagandize and mobilize the countryside. For example, a popular Land League ballad sung at contemporary American wakes declared defiantly, "We want no emigration / Or coercion of our nation," while "Home Rule and Freedom" described the emigrants as "driven away from the home of their childhood." Likewise, in another "New National Ballad" of the period, the singer laments, "From my cabin I'm evicted and alas compelled to go, / And leave this sainted island where the green shamrocks grow." However, "exile" was hardly a novel theme in Irish popular literature: the Gaelic poetry of the sixteenth and seventeenth centuries; the *aisling* verses and traditional keens of the eighteenth century; and the ubiquitous broadside ballads of the pre-Famine decades—all blamed Catholic Ireland's sorrows and discontinuities on British oppression and depicted emigration as analogous to political banishment. In short, for emigrants compelled to self-exculpation, historical and literary traditions, cultural and psychological predisposition, contemporary expedience, and continued communal conflicts with landlords and British officialdom merged to perpetuate in song the image of emigration as forced "exile."[10]

Moreover, although some late-eighteenth- and early-nineteenth-century emigration/exile ballads promised the emigrants happiness in the "land of plenty and sweet liberty," the majority of songs heard at American wakes prophesied only poverty and homesickness in the "land of the stranger," where the Irish would wander "lonely . . . in sorrow and fear, / Not a hand that can sooth, nor a smile that can cheer." Thus, "The Irish Labourer" and "The Honest Irish Lad" foretold unemployment and prejudice in America, while "The Irish Emigrant's Lament" expressed the anguish of traditional personalities adrift in an alien and ruthlessly competitive country: "They say I'm now in freedom's land, / Where all men masters be," cried that song's composer, "But were I in my winding-sheet / There's none to care for me." In part, these dire predictions accurately reflected the harsh and uncertain conditions of Irish-American life, especially at mid-century. However, their prevalence in song at the American wakes indicated the strength of conventional outlooks, which persisted throughout the period whether corroborated by or conflicting with the realities to be encountered overseas. Logically, if emigration was reluctant and sorrowful "exile," then the Irish going to America should not—indeed, could not—find happiness there, separated as they would be from their ancestral homes and beloved country. If truly "Exiles from Erin" (*An Díbeartach ó Éirinn*), then they could never be content abroad. As the author of "Song of an Exile" declared, although "cold," "senseless," ambitious emigrants might forget "the loved isle of sorrow," "the heart of the patriot—though seas roll between them— / Forgets not the smiles of his once happy home": thus,

> Time may roll o'er me its circles uncheering,
>   Columbia's proud forests around me shall wave,
> But the exile shall never forget thee, loved *Eire*
>   Till, unmourned, he sleep in a far, foreign grave.[11]

In effect, by declaring in verse that their lives in America, as well as their departures from Ireland, were or would be unhappy—riven with inconsolable homesickness—the emigrants further satisfied the demands of the exile convention and effectively deflected both communal and self-accusations of selfish and nontraditional behavior. In addition, many ballads sung at American wakes specifically promised parents not only that the emigrants would never forget them "In the land I'm going to" but also that they would fulfill their duties to those left behind. Thus, the composer of "Farewell to Ireland" swore to "write to all relations" and "send my savings home to keep / My mother, dear, alive." Indeed, by the late nineteenth century American remittances had become so customary and obligatory that a number of emigration ballads were written in the form of letters from cheerfully self-sacrificing emigrants who thus provided the participants at American wakes with models for future emulation. "Dear Mother, I take up my pen to write you these few lines," sang one composition,

> Hoping to find you well, and close on better times,
> I send home a ten-pound note [!] to my brothers Mick and Joe,
> And that's all I can afford till the champions grow. . . .

At least equally gratifying both to apprehensive emigrants and to loved ones at home were those songs which in a sense completed the "exile" cycle by predicting that someday the homesick emigrant would "Once . . . more return to my dear native home, / And from that old farm ne'er again will I roam." Finally, not a few ballads sung on both sides of the Atlantic promised not only that the emigrants would remit money and, if possible, return to their parents but also that they would always remember and someday wreak vengeance on those deemed responsible for their country's sufferings and their own unhappy "exile." Thus, the composer of "Evicted" demanded that Irish-Americans never forget "the homeless ones tonight who lie on Irish soil,

> Where British red-coats ruthlessly their sacred homes despoil
> Where mothers, bent and worn with age, are turned abroad to die,
> While from a thousand breaking hearts, there comes this wailing cry:

> Torn from the home that has shelter'd us, home of our joys and tears,
> Thrust from the hearth where the laugh and songs gladden'd us many years,
> Homeless we wander tonight, under the moonlit sky.
> England may break the Irish heart, but its spirit will never die.[12]

In short, despite the dancing and drinking, these sad and angry ballads expressed the essence of the American wake experience. As one elderly returned emigrant recalled, "On the night of the Bottle Drink . . . you would think that they were trying to see who could sing the oldest and saddest songs . . . and if you were going away yourself and hear them it would break your heart." Inspiring profuse weeping and bitter lamentations, the ballads helped make the American wake an occasion the emigrants would never forget, filling them with memories associated with intense sorrow and regret—memories easily evoked whenever they gathered in America to sing and hear the old songs from home.[13]

When at last dawn broke, the emotionally draining American wake itself came to an end, but the poignant rituals surrounding the final parting continued until the last terrible moment. Among Catholic emigrants the parish priest again appeared to sanction and sacralize the event, often sprinkling holy water on the heads of the departing while invoking God's and the church's reluctant blessing on their enterprise. Then came the emigrant's last look around his old house and, perhaps, his last farewell before he started on foot or by horse cart to meet the stagecoach or the train which would carry him to Queenstown or some other port. At such moments "[t]he last embraces were terrible to see; but worse were the kissings and the claspings of the hands during the long minutes that remained." When Maura O'Sullivan left her mother's cottage, the old women of the village raised a last mournful keen: "Oh, musha, Maura, how shall I live after you when the long winter's night will be here and you not coming to the door nor your laughter to be heard!" Their testimony indicates that even the most stoic of emigrants were shaken by these last good-byes. For example, James Greene recalled, "The parting Shake hands . . . brought tears to my eye & an ache to my heart," and years later an elderly Ulster-American remembered, "The last thing I saw was Father, Mother, and the children standing at the gate. I never saw them again. . . ." "I took my seat [in] the Jaunting car," wrote another; "the whip was applied, and amidst the waving of hats and handkerchiefs I took a last and lingering look at that little town where I spent some of my happiest days."[14]

However, in many districts it was customary for parents and friends to prolong the agony as much as possible by accompanying or "convoying"

the emigrant for a certain distance from home. One historian argues that the "convoys" were intended to "cheer" the emigrants, but contemporary descriptions indicate that usually the practice was anything but cheerful. Peig Sayers remembered that when her neighbors left west Kerry, at first some people in the convoy were "crying and others were laughing," but "[b]y the time we moved up the Well Road one would think that it was a funeral procession." In 1863 the *Nation* reported, "Every other night a wailing cry passes over the roads of the country from the friends of the emigrants conveying them to the different railway stations, and lamenting their departure. . . . It is melancholy to hear this mournful lament before daybreak in the silent country." Sometimes relatives and friends would walk only a short distance with the emigrant, perhaps to some traditional and appropriate landmark such as "the Rock of the Weeping of Tears" in west Clare. There the emigrant and his "mourners" would take their last sight of one another and say their last good-byes; it was a "sorrowful sight, for parted they were from that day forward as surely as if they were buried in a grave." However, if the railroad station was near, the peasant Irish had no compunctions about enacting their last scenes of grief among strangers. Such leave-takings were especially tumultuous and traumatic:

> A deafening wail resounds as the station-bell gives the signal of starting. . . . [G]ray-haired peasants so clutch and cling to the departing child at this last moment that only the utmost force of three or four friends could tear them asunder. The porters have to use some violence before the train moves off, the crowd so presses against door and window. When at length it moves away, amidst a scene of passionate grief, hundreds run along the fields beside the line to catch yet another glimpse of the friends they shall see no more.

Nevertheless, at last the final break with home had come, and the emigrants were now on their way to North America.[15]

"The final break with home"? Not really, save in a physical sense, for the significance of the American wake and, indeed, of the entire Irish leave-taking ritual was that it both reflected and reemphasized in an extremely forceful fashion all of the conventional Irish attitudes toward life in general and toward emigration in particular. For most young Irishmen and -women leaving home was in some respects a traumatic initiation into adulthood, because emigration literally expelled them from the confines of childhoods passed in largely parochial and still-traditional societies. However, the parting ceremonies reinforced old patterns in such a dramatic manner that they ensured that all but the most "cold" and "senseless" emigrants carried away burning memories and burdensome emotional obligations—that despite their physical departure, they would not break totally away from the values and behavior demanded by tradition and by parents, priests, and nationalist politicians. In a very tangible sense, these heart-wrenching scenes and songs constituted the emigrants' final overt exposure in Ireland to the values and symbolism of a traditional worldview which "explained" and justified emigration only in terms of involuntary "exile." Perhaps revealing were the promises which many emigrants, under the stress of these moments, gave to return someday to Ireland, convincing those who remained behind that "[n]early every Irish person that went to America had the intention of coming back . . . and settling down at home." Of course, such promises were unrealistic and rarely fulfilled. However, the fact that they were made, remembered, and cherished and that their failure was regretted on both sides of the Atlantic served to keep Irish-Americans emotionally oriented to their childhood homes. Furthermore, even if they enjoyed material prosperity in the New World, their guilt about promises unfulfilled reinforced internalized obligations to ensure that most emigrants would send remittances and that at least occasionally they would still regard or portray themselves as involuntary "exiles." "For God's sake and for ours," begged one harassed emigrant of his parents at home, "endeavor to shake off your sorrow and do not leave us to accuse ourselves of bringing down your grey hairs with sorrow to the grave by leaving you when we should have stayed by you. Our intentions were good and still continue—and, if God prosper our endeavors, we will soon be able to assist and cheer you." Finally, the same guilt, refracted through the stark memories of the American wakes, provided fertile ground for the appeals of Irish-American nationalists that the emigrants "do something" for Mother Ireland. Images of their mothers' tears, their fathers' graves, their parents' hypothetical sufferings from poverty, English oppression, or their children's alleged "ingratitude": all these were the nationalists' stock-in-trade, just as they had been the prevalent themes of the songs sung at the moment when the emigrants had been most vulnerable. Freeing Ireland, declared one orator, "is a debt we owe to nature and nature's God, and until it is discharged, all who call themselves Irishmen . . . cannot be at peace"—and, he might have added, would not be left at peace.[16]

Appendix

Table 1. Number of Overseas Emigrants from Ireland, classified by destination, 1851–1921

	1851–55	1856–60	1861–70	1871–80	1881–90	1891–1900	1901–10	1911–21	1851–1921
United States	740,216	249,618	690,845	449,549	626,604	427,301	418,995	191,724	3,794,852
British North America	104,844	13,274	40,079	25,783	44,505	10,648	38,238	36,251	313,622
Australia, New Zealand	53,801	47,740	82,917	61,946	55,476	11,448	11,885	17,629	342,842
Other Overseas	2,298	4,428	4,741	5,425	7,890	11,885	16,343	9,691	62,701
TOTAL OVERSEAS	901,159	315,060	818,582	542,703	734,475	461,282	485,461	255,295	4,514,017

SOURCE: *Commission on Emigration and Other Population Problems* . . . (Dublin: Ministry of Social Welfare, 1954), 309–11, based on Reports of the Colonial Land and Emigration Commissioners, 1851–72, and on Board of Trade Returns, 1873–1921.

Table 2. Total Irish Emigration, 1851–1920

	1851[1]–55	*1856–60*	*1861–70*	*1871–80*	*1856–80*
Carlow	8,157	2,482	5,396	5,450	13,328
Dublin	13,991	11,205	30,996	19,592	61,793
Kildare	9,123	3,054	7,366	5,873	16,293
Kilkenny	25,000	8,748	12,476	9,178	30,402
King's	15,765	5,102	12,177	8,754	26,033
Longford	10,609	3,825	13,504	11,450	28,779
Louth	12,503	4,401	10,200	5,803	20,404
Meath	17,515	5,618	15,406	10,671	31,695
Queen's	15,334	4,396	9,643	9,080	23,119
Westmeath	13,455	4,931	11,377	7,345	23,653
Wexford	21,081	5,883	15,917	13,258	35,058
Wicklow	8,668	2,485	5,336	4,592	12,413
LEINSTER	171,201	62,130	149,794	111,046	322,970
Clare	37,368	12,315	31,758	18,736	62,809
Cork	90,552	55,870	119,603	73,978	249,451
Kerry	39,520	14,963	40,445	26,898	82,306
Limerick	44,423	17,217	46,667	22,026	85,910
Tipperary	59,597	20,622	47,686	26,499	94,807
Waterford	25,071	12,891	19,904	12,731	45,526
MUNSTER	296,531	133,878	306,063	180,868	620,809
Antrim[2]	24,039	51,490	55,034	59,960	166,484
Armagh	14,898	14,159	17,775	19,327	51,261
Cavan	23,893	12,247	22,385	19,391	54,023
Donegal	26,437	11,504	12,088	29,959	53,551
Down	19,998	27,237	28,156	31,322	86,715
Fermanagh	10,878	6,279	10,966	10,452	27,697
Londonderry	15,844	11,667	16,719	26,876	55,262
Monaghan	16,651	9,866	15,079	13,342	38,287
Tyrone	22,513	16,665	23,782	29,674	70,121
ULSTER	175,151	161,114	201,984	240,299	603,397
Galway	37,609	12,744	38,839	23,578	75,161
Leitrim	10,154	6,274	14,167	12,591	33,032
Mayo	21,204	7,676	27,468	24,614	59,758
Roscommon	19,831	7,492	21,599	13,801	42,892
Sligo	8,911	4,216	11,986	11,706	27,908
CONNAUGHT	97,709	38,402	114,059	86,290	238,751
County Unspecified	7,407	19,895	77,936	5,430	103,261
IRELAND	747,999	415,419	849,836	623,933	1,889,188

[1] Beginning 1 May 1851.
[2] Including Belfast until 1911–20, when emigrants from that city were distributed between Antrim and Down.

1881–90	1891–1900	1901–10	1881–1910	1856–1910	1911–20	1856–1920
8,090	2,629	2,417	13,136	26,464	1,112	27,576
24,816	10,959	9,479	45,254	107,047	5,557	112,604
8,337	2,145	2,602	13,084	29,377	1,771	31,148
13,215	4,894	3,407	21,516	51,918	1,531	53,449
12,465	3,749	3,315	19,529	45,562	1,273	46,835
11,833	5,084	5,056	21,973	50,752	2,458	53,210
6,939	2,826	3,007	12,772	33,176	3,510	36,686
11,301	4,432	3,422	19,155	50,850	1,525	52,375
13,707	4,481	2,539	20,727	43,846	1,082	44,928
9,757	3,418	2,579	15,754	39,407	962	40,369
11,982	3,988	2,918	18,888	53,946	1,041	54,987
6,220	1,771	1,749	9,740	22,153	1,130	23,283
138,662	50,376	42,490	231,528	554,498	22,952	577,450
32,492	18,156	13,636	64,284	127,093	5,228	132,321
82,780	77,456	44,551	204,787	454,238	12,294	466,532
50,721	38,718	23,340	112,779	195,085	8,449	203,534
33,166	14,537	11,287	58,990	144,900	4,022	148,922
32,889	19,084	12,403	64,376	159,183	3,599	162,782
19,491	10,059	7,133	36,683	82,209	2,629	84,838
251,539	178,010	112,350	541,899	1,162,708	36,221	1,198,929
46,094	14,927	32,665	93,686	260,170	17,439	277,609
20,951	7,311	8,373	36,635	87,896	5,190	93,086
21,786	12,094	9,389	43,269	97,292	4,426	101,718
29,511	13,067	12,559	55,137	108,688	6,307	114,995
23,963	7,889	15,384	47,236	133,951	10,949	144,900
10,232	5,472	3,537	19,241	46,938	2,059	48,997
23,442	8,228	9,233	40,903	96,165	4,256	100,421
13,536	5,351	4,319	23,206	61,493	2,235	63,728
29,130	12,682	10,521	52,333	122,454	5,117	127,571
218,645	87,021	105,980	411,646	1,015,043	57,978	1,073,021
51,345	36,852	26,578	114,775	189,936	9,854	199,790
21,127	9,937	8,302	39,366	72,398	3,823	76,221
42,494	40,835	29,970	113,299	173,057	12,043	185,100
23,252	16,298	11,123	50,673	93,565	3,710	97,275
23,642	14,197	9,160	46,999	74,907	4,175	79,082
161,860	118,119	85,133	365,112	603,863	33,605	637,468
0	0	71	71	103,332	0	103,332
770,706	433,526	346,024	1,550,256	3,439,444	150,756	3,590,200

SOURCE: W. E. Vaughn and A. J. Fitzpatrick, eds. *Irish Historical Statistics: Population, 1821–1971* (Dublin, 1978), 261–353, based on the Returns of the Emigration Commissioners to the Registrar General.

Table 3. Percentage Changes in Irish Emigration, 1856–1910

	1856–60 (% change since 1851–55)	1861–70 (since 1851–60)	1871–80 (since 1861–70)	1881–90 (since 1871–80)	1891–1900 (since 1881–90)	1901–10 (since 1891–1900)	1881–1910 (since 1856–80)
Carlow	−69.6	−49.3	+0.1	+48.4	−67.5	−8.1	−1.4
Dublin	−19.9	+23.0	−36.8	+26.7	−55.8	−13.5	−26.8
Kildare	−66.5	−39.5	−20.3	+42.0	−74.3	+21.3	−19.7
Kilkenny	−65.0	−63.0	−26.4	+44.0	−63.0	−30.4	−29.2
King's	−67.6	−41.6	−28.1	+42.4	−69.9	−11.6	−25.0
Longford	−63.9	−6.4	−15.2	+3.3	−57.0	−0.6	−23.6
Louth	−64.8	−39.7	−43.1	+19.6	−59.3	+6.4	−37.4
Meath	−67.9	−33.4	−30.7	+5.9	−60.8	−22.8	−39.6
Queen's	−71.3	−51.1	−5.8	+51.0	−67.3	−43.3	−10.3
Westmeath	−63.4	−38.1	−35.4	+32.8	−65.0	−24.5	−33.4
Wexford	−72.1	−41.0	−16.7	−9.6	−66.7	−26.8	−46.1
Wicklow	−71.3	−52.2	−13.9	+35.5	−71.5	−1.2	−21.5
LEINSTER	−63.7	−35.8	−25.9	+24.9	−63.7	−15.7	−28.3
Clare	−67.0	−36.1	−41.0	+73.4	−44.1	−24.9	+2.3
Cork	−38.3	−18.3	−38.1	+11.9	−6.4	−42.5	−17.9
Kerry	−62.1	−25.8	−33.5	+88.6	−23.7	−39.7	+37.0
Limerick	−61.2	−24.3	−52.8	+50.6	−56.2	−22.4	−31.3
Tipperary	−65.4	−40.6	−44.4	+24.1	−42.0	−35.0	−32.1
Waterford	−48.6	−47.6	−36.0	+53.1	−48.4	−29.1	−19.4
MUNSTER	−54.9	−28.9	−40.9	+39.1	−29.2	−36.9	−12.7
Antrim	+114.2	−27.1	+9.0	−23.1	−67.6	+118.8	−43.7
Armagh	−5.0	−38.8	+8.7	+8.4	−65.1	+14.5	−28.5
Cavan	−48.7	−38.1	−13.4	+12.4	−44.5	−22.4	−19.9
Donegal	−56.5	−68.1	+147.8	−1.5	−55.7	−3.9	+3.0
Down	+36.2	−40.4	+11.2	−23.5	−67.1	+95.0	−45.5
Fermanagh	−42.3	−36.1	−4.7	−2.1	−46.5	−35.4	−30.5
Londonderry	−26.4	−39.2	+60.8	−12.8	−64.9	+12.2	−26.0
Monaghan	−40.7	−43.1	−11.5	+1.5	−60.5	−19.3	−39.4
Tyrone	−26.0	−39.3	+24.8	−1.8	−56.5	−17.0	−25.4
ULSTER	−8.0	−39.9	+19.0	−9.0	−60.2	+21.8	−31.8
Galway	−66.1	−22.9	−39.3	+117.8	−28.2	−27.9	+52.7
Leitrim	−38.2	−13.8	−11.1	+67.8	−53.0	−16.5	+19.2
Mayo	−63.8	−4.9	−10.4	+72.6	−3.9	−26.6	+89.6
Roscommon	−62.2	−20.9	−36.1	+68.5	−29.9	−31.8	+18.1
Sligo	−52.7	−8.7	−2.3	+102.0	−40.0	−35.5	+68.4
CONNAUGHT	−60.7	−16.2	−24.3	+87.6	−27.0	−27.9	+52.9
IRELAND (including "County Unspecified")	−44.5	−27.0	−26.6	+23.5	−43.7	−20.2	−17.9

SOURCE: Vaughn and Fitzpatrick, 261–353.

Table 4. County and Provincial Proportions of Irish Emigration Compared with Population, 1851–1920

| | 1851–55 | | 1856–60 | | 1861–70 | | 1871–80 | | 1856–80 | |
	A	B	A¹	B	A	B²	A	B	A³	B
Carlow	1.0	1.1	0.6	1.0	0.6	0.9	0.9			0.7
Dublin	6.2	1.9	2.7	7.0	3.6	7.5	3.1			3.3
Kildare	1.5	1.2	0.7	1.6	0.9	1.5	0.9			0.9
Kilkenny	2.4	3.3	2.1	2.2	1.5	2.0	1.5			1.6
King's	1.7	2.1	1.2	1.6	1.4	1.4	1.4			1.4
Longford	1.3	1.4	0.9	1.2	1.6	1.2	1.8			1.5
Louth	1.6	1.7	1.1	1.6	1.2	1.6	0.9			1.1
Meath	2.1	2.4	1.4	1.9	1.8	1.8	1.7			1.7
Queen's	1.7	2.1	1.1	1.6	1.1	1.5	1.5			1.2
Westmeath	1.7	1.8	1.2	1.6	1.3	1.5	1.2			1.3
Wexford	2.7	2.8	1.4	2.5	1.9	2.5	2.1			1.9
Wicklow	1.5	1.2	0.6	1.5	0.6	1.5	0.7			0.7
LEINSTER	25.5	22.9	15.0	25.1	17.6	24.7	17.8	25.2	17.1
Clare	3.2	5.0	3.0	2.9	3.7	2.7	3.0			3.3
Cork	9.9	12.1	13.4	9.4	14.1	9.6	11.9			13.2
Kerry	3.6	5.3	3.6	3.5	4.8	3.6	4.3			4.4
Limerick	4.0	5.9	4.1	3.7	5.5	3.5	3.5			4.5
Tipperary	5.1	8.0	5.0	4.3	5.6	4.0	4.2			5.0
Waterford	2.5	3.4	3.1	2.3	2.3	2.3	2.0			2.4
MUNSTER	28.4	39.6	32.2	26.1	36.0	25.7	29.0	26.8	33.0
Antrim[5]	5.3	3.2	12.4	6.5	6.5	7.8	9.6			8.8
Armagh	3.0	2.0	3.4	3.3	2.1	3.3	3.1			2.7
Cavan	2.7	3.2	2.9	2.7	2.6	2.6	3.1			2.9
Donegal	3.9	3.5	2.8	4.1	1.4	4.0	4.8			2.8
Down	4.9	2.7	6.6	5.2	3.3	5.1	5.0			4.6
Fermanagh	1.8	1.5	1.5	1.8	1.3	1.7	1.7			1.4
Londonderry	2.9	2.1	2.8	3.2	2.0	3.2	4.3			2.9
Monaghan	2.2	2.2	2.4	2.2	1.8	2.1	2.1			2.0
Tyrone	3.9	3.0	4.0	3.6	2.8	4.0	4.8			3.7
ULSTER	30.7	23.4	38.8	33.0	23.8	33.9	38.5	32.4	31.9
Galway	4.9	5.0	3.1	4.7	4.6	4.6	3.8			4.0
Leitrim	1.7	1.4	1.5	1.8	1.7	1.8	2.0			1.7
Mayo	4.2	2.8	1.8	4.4	3.2	4.5	3.9			3.2
Roscommon	2.7	2.7	1.8	2.7	2.5	2.6	2.2			2.3
Sligo	2.0	1.2	1.0	2.2	1.4	2.1	1.9			1.5
CONNAUGHT	15.4	13.1	9.2	15.7	13.4	15.6	13.8	15.6	12.6
County Unspecified		1.0	4.8		9.2		0.9			5.5

A = % of Total Irish Population in Each County and Province (at beginning of time period)

B = % of Total Irish Emigration from Each County and Province

1 Based on 1851.

2 Ó Gráda's revised estimates for 1861–70: Leinster, 20.5%; Munster, 29.3%; Ulster, 30.3%; Connaught, 19.9%. See C. Ó Gráda, "Some Aspects of 19th-Century Irish Emigration," in L. M. Cullen and T. C. Smout, eds., *Comparative Aspects of Scottish and Irish Economic and Social History* (Edinburgh, 1977), 68–71.

| 1881–90 | | 1891–1900 | | 1901–10 | | 1911–20 | | 1881–1910 | | 1856–1910 | | 1856–1920 | |
A	B	A	B	A	B[4]	A	B	A[3]	B	A[3]	B	A[3]	B
0.9	1.0	0.9	0.6	0.8	0.7	0.8	0.7		0.8		0.8		0.8
8.1	3.2	8.9	2.5	10.1	2.7	10.9	3.7		2.9		3.1		3.1
1.5	1.1	1.5	0.5	1.4	0.8	1.5	1.2		0.8		0.9		0.9
1.9	1.7	1.9	1.1	1.8	1.0	1.7	1.0		1.4		1.5		1.5
1.4	1.6	1.4	0.9	1.3	1.0	1.3	0.8		1.3		1.3		1.3
1.2	1.5	1.1	1.2	1.1	1.5	1.0	1.6		1.4		1.5		1.5
1.5	0.9	1.5	0.7	1.5	0.9	1.5	2.3		0.8		1.0		1.0
1.7	1.5	1.6	1.0	1.5	1.0	1.5	1.0		1.2		1.5		1.5
1.4	1.8	1.4	1.0	1.3	0.7	1.2	0.7		1.3		1.3		1.3
1.4	1.3	1.4	0.8	1.4	0.7	1.4	0.6		1.0		1.1		1.1
2.4	1.6	2.4	0.9	2.3	0.8	2.3	0.7		1.2		1.6		1.5
1.4	0.8	1.3	0.4	1.4	0.5	1.4	0.7		0.6		0.6		0.6
24.7	18.0	25.2	11.6	25.9	12.3	26.5	15.2	25.2	14.9	25.2	16.1	25.4	16.1
2.7	4.2	2.6	4.2	2.5	3.9	2.4	3.5		4.1		3.7		3.7
9.6	10.7	9.3	17.9	9.1	12.9	8.9	8.2		13.2		13.2		13.0
3.9	6.6	3.8	8.9	3.7	6.7	3.6	5.6		7.3		5.7		5.7
3.5	4.3	3.4	3.4	3.3	3.3	3.3	2.7		3.8		4.2		4.1
3.9	4.3	3.7	4.4	3.6	3.6	3.5	2.4		4.2		4.6		4.5
2.2	2.5	2.1	2.3	2.0	2.1	1.9	1.7		2.4		2.4		2.4
25.7	32.6	24.9	41.1	24.1	32.5	23.6	24.0	25.0	35.0	26.0	33.8	25.7	33.4
8.6	6.0	10.0	3.4	12.2	9.4	13.2	11.6		6.0		7.6		7.7
3.2	2.7	3.0	1.7	2.8	2.4	2.7	3.4		2.4		2.6		2.6
2.5	2.8	2.4	2.8	2.2	2.7	2.1	2.9		2.8		2.8		2.8
4.0	3.8	3.9	3.0	3.9	3.6	3.8	4.2		3.6		3.2		3.2
4.8	3.1	4.8	1.8	4.6	4.4	4.7	7.3		3.0		3.9		4.0
1.6	1.3	1.6	1.3	1.5	1.0	1.4	1.4		1.2		1.4		1.4
3.2	3.0	3.2	1.9	3.2	2.7	3.2	2.8		2.6		2.8		2.8
2.0	1.8	1.8	1.2	1.7	1.2	1.6	1.5		1.5		1.8		1.8
3.8	3.8	3.6	2.9	3.4	3.0	3.2	3.4		3.4		3.6		3.6
33.7	28.4	34.4	20.1	35.5	30.6	36.0	38.5	34.5	26.6	33.3	29.5	33.7	29.9
4.7	6.7	4.6	8.5	4.3	7.7	4.2	6.5		7.4		5.5		5.6
1.8	2.7	1.7	2.3	1.6	2.4	1.4	2.5		2.5		2.1		2.1
4.7	5.5	4.7	9.4	4.5	8.7	4.4	8.0		7.3		5.0		5.2
2.6	3.0	2.4	3.8	2.3	3.2	2.1	2.5		3.3		2.7		2.7
2.2	3.1	1.9	3.3	1.9	2.6	1.8	2.8		3.0		2.2		2.2
15.9	21.0	15.4	27.2	14.5	24.6	13.9	22.3	15.3	23.6	15.5	17.6	15.3	17.8
	0.0		0.0		0.02		0.0		0.005		3.0		2.9

[3] Percentage of mean total population.
[4] Ó Gráda's revised estimates for 1901–10: Leinster, 12.8%; Munster, 29.7%; Ulster, 31.6%; Connaught, 25.9%. See Ó Gráda, "Some Aspects. . . ."
[5] Including Belfast.

SOURCE: Vaughn and Fitzpatrick, 261–353.

Table 5. Average Annual County and Provincial Emigration Rates, 1851–1910 (pe
1,000 inhabitants at the beginning of each period)

	1851–55	1856–60 (estimated)	1861–70	1871–80	1856–80	1881–90	1891–1900	1901–10	1881–1910	1856–1910
Carlow	24.0	8.3	9.4	10.6	9.7	17.4	6.4	6.4	10.1	9.9
Dublin	6.9	5.5	7.6	4.8	6.1	5.9	2.6	2.1	3.5	4.7
Kildare	19.1	6.8	8.1	7.0	7.4	11.0	3.1	4.1	6.1	6.7
Kilkenny	31.5	13.1	10.0	8.4	10.0	13.3	5.6	4.3	7.7	8.8
King's	28.1	10.7	13.5	11.5	12.1	17.1	5.7	5.8	9.5	10.7
Longford	25.8	10.4	18.8	17.8	16.7	19.4	9.7	10.8	13.3	14.9
Louth	23.2	9.3	11.2	6.9	9.1	8.9	4.0	4.6	5.8	7.3
Meath	24.9	9.4	14.0	11.2	12.0	12.9	5.8	5.1	7.9	9.8
Queen's	27.5	9.2	10.6	11.4	10.6	18.7	6.9	4.4	10.0	10.3
Westmeath	24.2	10.2	12.5	9.4	10.8	13.6	5.2	4.2	7.7	9.1
Wexford	23.4	7.6	11.1	10.0	10.0	9.7	3.6	2.8	5.4	7.5
Wicklow	17.5	5.5	6.2	5.8	5.9	8.8	2.9	2.9	4.9	5.3
LEINSTER	20.5	8.2	10.3	8.3	9.1	10.8	4.2	3.7	6.2	7.5
Clare	35.2	13.9	19.1	12.7	15.5	23.0	14.6	12.1	16.6	16.1
Cork	27.9	19.3	22.0	14.3	18.4	16.7	17.7	10.2	14.9	16.5
Kerry	33.2	14.4	20.0	13.7	16.4	25.2	21.6	14.1	20.3	18.5
Limerick	33.9	15.2	21.5	11.5	16.2	18.4	9.1	7.7	11.7	13.8
Tipperary	35.9	15.2	19.1	12.2	15.6	16.5	11.0	7.7	11.7	13.5
Waterford	30.6	18.0	14.8	10.3	13.6	17.3	10.2	8.2	11.9	12.7
MUNSTER	31.9	16.7	20.2	13.0	16.6	18.9	15.2	10.4	14.8	15.6
Antrim	13.9	27.4	14.5	14.3	17.0	10.3	3.2	6.0	6.5	11.3
Armagh	15.2	14.7	9.4	10.8	11.0	12.8	5.1	6.7	8.2	9.5
Cavan	27.5	15.5	14.5	13.8	14.4	16.8	10.8	9.6	12.4	13.3
Donegal	20.7	9.6	5.1	13.7	9.4	14.3	7.0	7.2	9.5	9.5
Down	12.5	17.5	9.4	11.3	11.8	9.7	3.5	7.5	6.9	9.1
Fermanagh	18.7	11.6	10.4	11.3	11.0	12.1	7.4	5.4	8.3	9.5
Londonderry	16.5	12.5	9.1	15.5	12.3	14.2	5.4	6.4	8.7	10.3
Monaghan	23.5	15.1	11.9	11.6	12.4	13.2	6.2	5.8	8.4	10.2
Tyrone	17.6	13.7	10.0	13.8	12.3	14.7	7.4	7.0	9.7	10.9
ULSTER	17.4	16.5	10.6	13.1	12.8	12.5	5.4	6.7	8.2	10.3
Galway	23.4	9.0	14.3	9.5	11.3	21.2	17.2	13.8	17.4	14.6
Leitrim	18.1	11.8	13.5	13.2	13.0	23.4	12.6	12.0	16.0	14.7
Mayo	15.4	6.0	10.8	10.0	9.5	17.3	18.6	15.0	17.0	13.6
Roscommon	22.9	9.4	13.7	9.8	11.3	17.6	14.2	10.9	14.2	12.9
Sligo	13.9	6.8	9.6	10.1	9.2	21.2	14.5	10.9	15.5	12.7
CONNAUGHT	19.3	8.2	12.5	10.2	10.7	19.7	16.3	13.2	16.4	13.8
IRELAND (including "County Unspecified")	22.8	13.8	14.7	11.5	13.2	14.9	9.2	7.8	10.6	11.8

SOURCE: Vaughn and Fitzpatrick, 3–16, 261–353.

Table 6. Irish Emigration per Decade As a Percentage of the Population at the Last Preceding Census: Provinces and Selected Counties, 1851–1910

	1851–55	*1856*–60	*1861*–70	*1871*–80	*1881*–90	*1891*–1900	*1901*–10
LEINSTER	10.2	3.7	10.2	8.3	10.8	4.2	3.7
Dublin	3.5	2.8	7.6	4.8	5.9	2.6	2.1
Kilkenny	15.7	5.5	10.0	8.4	13.3	5.6	4.3
Longford	12.9	4.6	18.8	17.8	19.4	9.7	10.8
Meath	12.4	4.0	14.0	11.3	12.9	5.8	5.1
Queen's	13.7	3.9	10.6	11.8	18.7	6.9	4.4
Wexford	11.7	3.3	11.1	9.1	9.7	3.6	2.8
MUNSTER	16.0	7.2	20.2	13.0	18.9	15.2	10.4
Clare	17.6	5.8	19.1	12.7	23.0	14.6	12.1
Cork	13.9	8.6	22.0	14.3	16.7	17.7	11.0
Kerry	16.6	6.3	20.4	13.7	25.2	21.6	14.1
Limerick	16.9	6.6	21.5	11.5	18.4	9.2	7.6
Tipperary	18.0	6.2	19.1	12.3	16.5	11.0	7.7
Waterford	15.3	7.9	14.8	10.4	17.3	10.2	8.2
ULSTER	8.7	8.0	10.6	13.1	12.5	5.4	6.7
Antrim	6.9	14.8	14.5	14.3	10.3	3.5	6.0
Cavan	13.7	7.0	14.8	13.8	16.8	10.8	9.6
Donegal	10.4	4.5	5.1	13.7	14.3	7.0	7.2
Down	6.2	8.5	9.1	10.7	8.8	3.3	7.5
Tyrone	8.8	6.5	10.0	13.8	14.7	7.4	7.0
CONNAUGHT	9.6	3.8	12.5	10.2	19.7	16.3	13.2
Galway	11.7	4.0	14.3	9.5	21.2	17.2	13.8
Leitrim	9.1	5.6	13.5	13.2	23.4	12.6	12.0
Mayo	7.7	2.8	10.8	10.0	17.4	18.6	15.1
Roscommon	11.4	4.3	13.7	9.8	17.6	14.3	10.9
Sligo	6.9	3.3	9.6	10.2	21.2	14.5	10.9
IRELAND	11.4	6.3	14.7	11.5	14.9	9.2	7.8

* Census years.

SOURCE: Vaughn and Fitzpatrick, 3–16, 261–353.

Table 7. Rankings of Irish Counties

	Emigration Rates per 1,000 Inhabitants, 1856–1910 (from highest to lowest)	Percentage Living in Towns (2,000+ people), 1891 (from lowest to highest)	Valuation of Land per Person, 1891 (from lowest to highest)	Proportion of Persons in Commercial Occupations, 1891 (from lowest to highest)	Proportion of Persons in Industrial Occupations, 1891 (from lowest to highest)	Proportion of Families in Third and Fourth Class Housing, 1891 (from highest to lowest)
Kerry	1	12	3	15	8	4
Cork	2	28	12	28	22	23
Clare	3	9	8	6	7	14
Longford	4	7	13	3	9	20
Leitrim	5	1	4	1	2	14
Galway	6	13	6	12	4	5
Limerick	7	25	21	25	23	11
Mayo	8	4	1	5	1	1
Tipperary	9	23	25	20	14	25
Cavan	10	2	7	4	6	13
Roscommon	11	6	11	2	3	8
Sligo (tie)	12	14	5	16	5	7
Waterford	12	26	18	30	25	27
Antrim	*14*	31	*15*	31	32	32
Tyrone	15	11	9	11	*26*	10
King's	16	19	24	19	17	18
Queen's (tie)	17	15	26	14	13	19
Londonderry	17	27	10	26	28	14
Monaghan	19	5	16	7	10	17
Carlow	20	18	27	17	18	30
Meath	21	9	32	13	19	3
Fermanagh (tie)	22	8	17	10	11	22
Donegal	22	2	2	9	21	2
Armagh	22	24	14	22	30	24
Down (tie)	25	29	19	27	31	31
Westmeath	25	17	31	8	12	21
Kilkenny	27	16	28	18	16	27
Wexford	28	22	22	23	20	26
Louth	29	30	20	29	27	9
Kildare	30	20	30	21	24	12
Wicklow	31	21	29	24	15	29
Dublin	32	32	23	32	29	6

(Italicized numbers indicate county ranks approximately equal national averages.)

SOURCE: T. W. Grimshaw, *Facts and Figures about Ireland* (Dublin, 1893).

Table 8. Irish Emigration, 1851–1910, from Counties Having a Substantial Proportion of Their Area Designated as "Congested Districts"

County	Emigration 1851–55	% of Total*	Emigration 1856–80	% of Total*	Emigration 1881–1910	% of Total*	Emigration 1856–1910	% of Total*
Clare	37,368	5.0	62,809	3.5	64,284	4.1	127,093	3.8
Donegal	26,437	3.6	53,551	3.0	55,137	3.6	108,688	3.3
Galway	37,609	5.1	75,161	4.2	114,775	7.4	189,936	5.7
Kerry	39,520	5.3	82,306	4.6	112,779	7.3	195,085	5.8
Leitrim	10,154	1.4	33,032	1.8	39,366	2.5	72,398	2.2
Mayo	21,204	2.9	59,758	3.3	113,299	7.3	173,057	5.2
Sligo	8,911	1.2	27,908	1.6	46,999	3.0	74,907	2.2
Total	181,203	24.5	394,525	22.1	546,639	35.3	942,067	28.2

* Total excluding "County Unspecified" emigrants.

SOURCE: Vaughn and Fitzpatrick, 261–353.

Table 9. Irish Emigration, 1856–1910, from Counties with at Least 10% Irish-Speaking Population in 1891

% of Irish-Speakers in 1891	Emigration 1856–80	% of Total*	Emigration 1881–1910	% of Total*	Emigration 1856–1910	% of Total*
Over 40% Irish-Speaking in 1891						
Galway (58.5%)	75,161	4.2	114,775	7.4	189,936	5.7
Mayo (50.4%)	59,758	3.3	113,299	7.3	173,057	5.2
Waterford (46.9%)	45,526	2.5	36,683	2.4	82,209	2.5
Kerry (41.4%)	82,306	4.6	112,779	7.3	195,085	5.8
Total 40+%	262,751	14.7	377,536	24.4	640,287	19.2
Over 30%						
Clare (37.7%)	62,809	3.5	64,284	4.1	127,093	3.8
Donegal (33.4%)	53,551	3.0	55,137	3.6	108,688	3.3
Cork (31.0%)	249,451	14.0	204,787	13.2	454,238	13.6
Total 30–40%	365,811	20.5	324,208	20.9	690,019	20.7
Total 30+%	628,562	35.2	701,744	45.3	1,330,306	39.9
Over 20%						
Sligo (21.8%)	27,908	1.6	46,999	3.0	74,907	2.2
Total 20+%	656,470	36.8	748,743	48.3	1,405,213	42.1
Over 10%						
Limerick (13.1%)	85,910	4.8	58,990	3.8	144,900	4.3
Roscommon (10.4%)	42,892	2.4	50,673	3.3	93,565	2.8
Total 10–20%	128,802	7.2	109,663	7.1	238,465	7.1
Grand Total 10+%	785,272	44.0	858,406	55.4	1,643,678	49.3

* Total excluding "County Unspecified" emigrants.

SOURCE: Vaughn and Fitzpatrick, 261–353; and B. Ó Cuív, *Irish Dialects and Irish-Speaking Districts* (Dublin, 1971), 77–93.

Table 10. Estimated Irish-Speaking Emigrants in 1851–55 and 1891–1900 (based on the proportions of Irish-speaking inhabitants in 1851 and 1891)

	% Irish-Speaking Inhabitants, 1851	Est. Irish-Speaking Emigrants, 1851–55	% Irish-Speaking Inhabitants, 1891	Est. Irish-Speaking Emigrants, 1891–1900
Carlow	0.4	33	0.3	8
Dublin	0.9	126	0.7	74
Kildare	0.5	46	0.5	11
Kilkenny	15.0	3,750	4.5	218
King's	0.4	63	0.5	19
Longford	1.8	191	0.5	25
Louth	20.7	2,588	3.8	107
Meath	6.4	1,134	1.9	83
Queen's	0.2	31	0.3	13
Westmeath	0.8	108	0.5	17
Wexford	0.4	84	0.3	12
Wicklow	0.1	9	0.3	5
Antrim	1.2	289	0.4	60
Armagh	7.0	1,043	2.4	173
Cavan	7.5	1,792	3.0	361
Donegal	28.7	7,587	33.4	4,364
Down	0.4	80	0.3	24
Fermangh	2.3	250	0.8	43
Londonderry	2.8	444	1.8	147
Monaghan	7.7	1,282	3.3	175
Tyrone	5.0	1,126	3.9	491
Clare	59.8	22,346	37.7	6,798
Cork	47.2	42,740	27.3	21,040
Kerry	61.5	24,305	41.4	15,980
Limerick	31.4	13,949	10.7	1,544
Tipperary	18.9	11,264	7.1	1,353
Waterford	55.4	13,889	38.1	3,832
Galway	69.1	25,988	62.2	22,902
Leitrim	13.4	1,361	7.2	708
Mayo	65.6	13,910	50.4	20,514
Roscommon	26.7	5,295	10.4	1,699
Sligo	38.3	3,413	21.8	3,066
Total Irish-Speaking Emigrants		200,516		105,866
% of Total Emigration*		27.1%		24.4%

* Total excluding "County Unspecified."

SOURCES: Vaughn and Fitzpatrick, 261–353; and Ó Cuív, 77–93.

Table 11. Age Distribution of Irish Emigrants, 1852–1921

	0–14	15–19	20–24	25–29	30–34	35–54	55+	?
Males								
1852–54*	22.5%	14.7%	28.1%	21.2%		12.2%	1.1%	0.1%
1861–70	13.7	8.4	33.7	20.1	9.0	9.8	0.9	4.2
1871–80	15.7	17.9	33.8	20.9	10.4	11.8	1.3	0.1
1881–90	13.7	15.1	38.3	15.5	6.4	9.5	1.3	0.1
1891–1900	8.5	11.0	41.6	23.4	6.2	7.9	1.4	0.0
1901–10	9.1	11.6	42.1	21.3	7.8	7.2	1.0	0.0
1911–20	9.2	12.7	41.7	28.1		7.5	0.8	0.0
1921	11.4	12.0	39.8	28.3		7.3	1.2	0.0
Total	13.7	11.7	35.5	27.0		9.9	1.1	1.1

Male Median Age: 22.48

	0–14	15–19	20–24	25–29	30–34	35–54	55+	?
Females								
1852–54*	22.0%	18.8%	28.4%	16.8%		12.7%	1.3%	0.1%
1861–70	16.1	13.1	34.0	13.3	6.9	10.8	1.2	4.5
1871–80	15.7	17.9	33.8	13.7	7.5	10.0	1.4	0.1
1881–90	13.8	26.0	35.5	10.0	4.8	8.5	1.2	0.1
1891–1900	7.3	22.1	44.1	14.1	4.6	6.7	1.1	0.0
1901–10	8.8	25.2	39.5	14.0	5.1	6.2	1.2	0.0
1911–20	8.8	26.5	39.2	18.4		6.1	0.9	0.0
1921	7.2	25.9	42.6	16.6		5.9	1.8	0.0
Total	14.2	20.4	35.6	18.3		9.3	1.2	1.0

Female Median Age: 21.2

* Four-year period only.

SOURCE: *Commission on Emigration and Other Population Problems,* 320.

Table 12. Males and Females Aged 15–24 As a Proportion of Total Irish Emigration, 1852–1921

	Females	*Males*	*Total 1852–1921*
1852–54*	23.6%	21.4%	45.0%
1861–70	21.1	23.3	44.4
1871–80	23.3	23.0	46.3
1881–90	30.0	27.4	57.4
1891–1900	35.4	24.5	59.9
1901–10	32.5	26.7	59.2
1911–20	32.6	27.4	60.0
1921	41.8	20.2	62.0
Total	27.0%	24.4%	51.4%

* Four-year period only.

SOURCE: *Commission on Emigration and Other Population Problems,* 320.

Table 13. Sex Ratio of Male to Female Irish Emigrants, 1851–1910, and for 1851–1880 and 1881–1910, by Provinces

	Males	*Females*	*Ratio*
1851–1910			
IRELAND	2,175,641	2,011,802	1.08 : 1
Leinster	381,848	343,851	1.11 : 1
Ulster	657,038	533,156	1.23 : 1
Munster	743,334	713,905	1.04 : 1
Connaught	329,655	371,917	0.89 : 1
1851–1880			
IRELAND	1,406,476	1,230,711	1.14 : 1
Leinster	257,968	236,203	1.09 : 1
Ulster	441,510	337,038	1.31 : 1
Munster	476,306	441,034	1.07 : 1
Connaught	168,926	167,534	1.00 : 1
1881–1910			
IRELAND	768,965	781,091	0.98 : 1
Leinster	123,880	107,648	1.15 : 1
Ulster	215,528	163,118	1.10 : 1
Munster	267,028	272,871	0.98 : 1
Connaught	160,729	204,383	0.77 : 1

SOURCE: Compiled from "Emigration Statistics of Ireland," in *GBPP*, 1861 [1275], LXII, 376–89; 1871 [239], LXIII, 645; 1872 [465], LXIII, 626. 1880 in *IUP-BPP, Emigration,* vol. 25 (Shannon, 1972), 660–61; 1890 in ibid., *Emigration,* vol. 27, p. 5; 1900 in *GBPP,* 1901 [531], LXXXVIII, 677; 1910 in *GBPP,* 1911 [5607], IX, 701.

Table 14. Occupational Distribution (%) of Irish Emigrants, 1851–55 and 1875–1910

	1851	*1852*	*1853*	*1854*	*1855*	*1875*	*1880*	*1885*	*1890*	*1895*	*1900*	*1905*	*1910*
Professional	2	*	*	*	*	0.7	0.3	0.4	0.6	0.5	0.3	1.3	1.9
Entrepreneurial						1.3	1.0	0.9	1.2	0.8	0.5	1.3	1.2
Skilled	11	8	7	9	11	13.3	7.6	9.5	7.6	11.7	6.2	13.4	18.1
Farmers	8	4	3	6	1	5.1	5.7	4.8	4.6	5.5	0.9	2.1	3.6
Common laborers	79	87	90	84	87	50.9	60.4	53.8	54.9	27.2	37.7	27.8	26.5
Farm laborers						0.3	0.2	—	—	—	4.6	4.0	9.2
Servants						27.1	24.4	29.6	30.5	52.4	48.9	48.9	37.7
Miscellaneous						1.1	1.0	0.9	1.2	0.8	0.5	1.3	1.2
Not stated						0.2	0.002	0.1	0.02	—	—	—	—

* Less than 1.0%.

SOURCES: P. Blessing, "West among Strangers" (Ph.D. diss., UCLA, 1976), 70; B. Thomas, *Migration and Economic Growth* (Cambridge, 1973 ed.), 384.

Notes

ABBREVIATIONS

Serial Titles

ABS	*American Behavioral Scientist*
AHR	*American Historical Review*
A-IS	*Anglo-Irish Studies*
ANLHB	*Analecta Hibernica*
AQ	*American Quarterly*
B-ÉSB	*Bulletin: The Éire Society of Boston*
BMOHS	*Bulletin of the Missouri Historical Society*
CAH	*California History*
CATHHR	*Catholic Historical Review*
CDB	*Congested Districts Board* (Reports of)
CH	*Church History*
CHR	*Canadian Historical Review*
CLREC	*Clogher Record*
COLMAG	*Colorado Magazine*
CPRH	*Canadian Papers in Rural History*
CRSA	*Canadian Review of Sociology and Anthropology*
CSSH	*Comparative Studies in Society and History*
CWH	*Civil War History*
ECONHR	*Economic History Review*
ECSOR	*Economic and Social Review*
EHR	*English Historical Review*
É-I	*Éire-Ireland*
ESS	*Economic and Social Studies* (Dublin)
GBPP	*Great Britain, Parliamentary Papers*
HC	*House of Commons Papers* (in *GBPP*)
HJ	*History Journal*
HS	*Historical Studies*
IECCR	*Irish Ecclesiastical Record*
IESH	*Irish Economic and Social History*
IHN	*Immigration History Newsletter*
IHS	*Irish Historical Studies*
IRGEO	*Irish Geography*
IUP-BPP	*Irish University Press Series of British Parliamentary Papers*
IUR	*Irish University Review*
J.	*Journal*
JAH	*Journal of American History*
JAIHS	*Journal of the American Irish Historical Society*
JCH	*Journal of Contemporary History*
JCHAS	*Journal of the Cork Historical and Archaeological Society*
JECONH	*Journal of Economic History*
JFH	*Journal of Family History*
JGAHS	*Journal of the Galway Archaeological and Historical Society*
JHG	*Journal of Historical Geography*

JKHS	*Journal of the Kerry Historical Society*
JPCUL	*Journal of Popular Culture*
JPS	*Journal of Peasant Studies*
JRSAI	*Journal of the Royal Society of Antiquaries of Ireland*
JRSS	*Journal of the Royal Statistical Society*
JSH	*Journal of Social History*
JSSISI	*Journal of the Social and Statistical Inquiry Society of Ireland*
JUH	*Journal of Urban History*
LH	*Labor History*
LIMAY	*Limerick Annual Yearbook*
L/LT	*Labour/Le Travailleur*
M-A	*Mid-America*
MEHQ	*Maine Historical Quarterly*
MHPC	*Michigan Historical and Pioneer Collections*
MOHR	*Missouri Historical Review*
MP	*Marxist Perspectives*
MYREV	*Maynooth Review*
NEQ	*New England Quarterly*
NHI III	*A New History of Ireland, Volume III*
NYH	*New York History*
ONTH	*Ontario History*
ORLH	*Oral History*
PAH	*Perspectives in American History*
PAPS	*Proceedings of the American Philosophical Society*
PCSM	*Proceedings of the Colonial Society of Massachusetts*
PENNH	*Pennsylvania History*
P&P	*Past & Present*
PRIA	*Proceedings of the Royal Irish Academy*
PROHS	*Papers and Records of the Ontario Historical Society*
PS	*Population Studies*
R.	*Review*
RACHSP	*Records of the American Catholic Historical Society of Philadelphia*
REH	*Research in Economic History*
RIH	*Rhode Island History*
RKHS	*Register of the Kentucky Historical Society*
RPE	*Research in Population Economics*
RPOL	*Review of Politics*
SH	*Studia Hibernica*
SWES	*Southwest Economy and Society*
T&P-IBG	*Transactions and Papers of the Institute of British Geographers*
UF	*Ulster Folklife*
USCR	*United States Consular Reports*
VS	*Victorian Studies*
VTH	*Vermont History*
WMQ	*William & Mary Quarterly*
WPHM	*Western Pennsylvania Historical Magazine*

Archives, Manuscript Collections, Etc.

ACIS	American Committee for Irish Studies
AD	Archives Department (in UCD)
AHA	American Historical Association
AIAH	Albany Institute of Art and History, Albany, New York
AIS-UP	Archives of Industrial Society, University of Pittsburgh
AS	Professor Arnold Schrier, University of Cincinnati. From the collection of . . .
BDB	Professor Bruce D. Boling, Brown University. Translated by . . .
BI	Balch Institute for Ethnic Studies, Philadelphia
CAC	Cork Archives Council, Cork, County Cork
CAHS	California Historical Society, San Francisco
CHS	Cincinnati Historical Society

CHHS	Chicago Historical Society
CO	Colonial Office Papers (in PRO)
CUL	Cornell University Library, Ithaca, New York
D.	Document (as cataloged in PRONI)
DIF	Department of Irish Folklore (in UCD)
DUL	Duke University Library, Durham, North Carolina
DWL	Dr. Williams' Library, London
ERRG	Professor E. R. R. Green, Queen's University, Belfast. From the collection of the late . . .
FL	Franciscan Library, Dun Mhuire, Killiney, County Dublin
FO	Foreign Office Papers (in PRO)
FP/PR	Fenian Papers, Police Reports (in SPO)
GASA	Georgia State Archives, Atlanta
HL	Huntington Library, San Marino, California
HO	Home Office Papers (in PRO)
ILSHS	Illinois State Historical Society, Springfield
INHS	Indiana Historical Society, Indianapolis
INSL	Indiana State Library, Indianapolis
JD	John Dillon Papers (in TCD)
KFLC	Kentucky Foreign Language Conference, Lexington
KRM	Kinsale Regional Museum, Kinsale, County Cork
KSRL/UKS	Kenneth Spencer Research Library, University of Kansas, Lawrence
KYHS	Kentucky Historical Society, Frankfort
LC	Library of Congress, Washington, D.C.
LIHS	Long Island Historical Society, Brooklyn, New York
LSFL	Library of the Society of Friends, London
LWCL	Longforth-Westmeath County Library, Mullingar, County Westmeath
MDA	Meath Diocesan Archives, Mullingar, County Westmeath
MDHS	Maryland Historical Society, Baltimore
mf	microfilm
MIC	Microfilm (as cataloged in PRONI)
MIHC	Michigan Historical Collections, University of Michigan, Ann Arbor
MNHS	Minnesota Historical Society, St. Paul
MOHS	Missouri Historical Society, St. Louis
Ms. Mss.	Manuscript Manuscripts
MTCL	Metropolitan Toronto Central Library, Toronto, Ontario
n	negative microfilm (as cataloged in NLI)
n. nn.	note notes
NA	National Archives, Washington, D.C.
NCSA	North Carolina State Archives, Raleigh
NLI	National Library of Ireland, Dublin
NUI	National University of Ireland, Dublin
NY	New York
N-YHS	New-York Historical Society, New York City
NYPL	New York Public Library, New York City
O'CD	O'Conor Don Papers, Clonalis House, Castlerea, County Roscommon
O'DR	Jeremiah O'Donovan Rossa Papers (on mf in CUA)
OMC/AHC	Overseas Missionary Correspondence, All Hallows College, Drumcondra, Dublin (on mf in NLI)
OS	Ordnance Survey Papers (in RIA)
p	positive microfilm (as cataloged in NLI)
PAC	Public Archives of Canada, Ottawa, Ontario
PRO	Public Record Office of Great Britain, London
PROC	Public Record Office of Canada, Ottawa
PROI	Public Record Office of Ireland, Dublin
PRONI	Public Record Office of Northern Ireland, Belfast
QUB	Queen's University of Belfast, Northern Ireland
RIA	Royal Irish Academy, Dublin
RJP	Dr. Richard J. Purcell Papers (in CUA)
RSFL	Religious Society of Friends Library, Dublin
SCL/USC	South Caroliniana Library, University of South Carolina, Columbia

SHC	Southern Historical Collections (in UNC-CH)
SPO	State Paper Office, Dublin
SSHA	Social Science History Association
STPCR	St. Paul of the Cross Retreat, Mt. Argus, Dublin
T.	Transcript (as cataloged in PRONI)
tc	tape-recorded conversation
TCD	Trinity College, Dublin
ts	typescript
TSLA	Tennessee State Library and Archives, Nashville
UCB	University of California, Berkeley
UCD	University College, Dublin
UCLA	University of California, Los Angeles
UNC-CH	University of North Carolina, Chapel Hill
UNDA	University of Notre Dame Archives, South Bend, Indiana
USCR	United States Consular Reports (on mf in NA)
UWVL	University of West Virginia Library, Morgantown
WISHS	Wisconsin State Historical Society, Madison
WJSML	W. J. Sweeney Memorial Library, Kilkee, County Clare
WSO'B	William Smith O'Brien Papers (in NLI)

Introduction

1. The only published works by North American scholars which treat the emigrants' backgrounds adequately are W. F. Adams, *Ireland and the Irish Emigration to the New World from 1815 to the Famine* (New Haven, 1932); A. Schrier, *Ireland and the Irish Emigration, 1850–1900* (Minneapolis, 1958); J. G. Leyburn, *The Scotch-Irish: A Social History* (Chapel Hill, 1962); and J. Mannion, *Irish Settlements in Eastern Canada* (Toronto, 1974). Schrier used several hundred emigrants' letters, as did the Irish historian E. R. R. Green, "Ulster Emigrants' Letters," in Green, ed., *Essays in Scotch-Irish History* (London, 1969), and the Australian scholar P. O'Farrell, "Emigrant Attitudes and Behaviour as a Source for Irish History," *HS*, 10 (1976).

2. F. E. Gibson, *Attitudes of the New York Irish toward State and National Affairs* (NY, 1951), 26; C. Wittke, *The Irish in America* (Baton Rouge, 1956), 161; E. Abbott, ed., *Historical Aspects of the Immigrant Problem* (Chicago, 1926), 413, 438; T. N. Brown, "Origins and Character of Irish-American Nationalism," *RPOL*, 18 (July 1956), 329.

3. J. O'Donovan, *Brief Account of the Author's Interview with His Countrymen . . .* (Pittsburgh, 1864), 151; O'Sullivan's speech, 1883, clipping in HO 45/9635/A29278 (PRO); C. S. Rice, 16 June 1916 (FO 115/2073, PRO).

4. Schrier, 94; Ms. 1411, p. 93 (DIF/UCD); R. L. Wright, ed., *Irish Emigrant Ballads and Songs* (Bowling Green, Ohio, 1975), 40, 184–85; J. N. Healy, ed., *Irish Ballads and Songs of the Sea* (Cork, 1967), 95–96; M. A. Gordon, "Studies in Irish and Irish-American Thought and Behavior in Gilded Age New York City" (Ph.D. diss., Univ. of Rochester, 1977), xxxiii.

5. M. Wolfe, 1869 (p3887, NLI); M. McG. Elliott memoir (A. L. McGuinness, Hampton Bays, NY); A. McDonald, 3 Feb. 1868 (T. McMahon, Monaghan); Rev. J. O'Hanlon, *Irish Emigrant's Guide to the United States* (1851; rev. ed. by E. J. Maguire, NY, 1976), 9–14, 232–33; M. MacGowan, *Hard Road to Klondike* (London, 1962), 136; M. R. Fallows, *Irish Americans* (Englewood Cliffs, 1979), 83; M. Carroll (tc, San Francisco, 1977).

6. Gibson, 98; G. R. Gilkey, "The United States and Italy: Migration and Repatriation," *J. Developing Areas*, 2 (1967); T. Saloutos, *They Remember America* (Berkeley, 1966); L. G. Tedebrand, "Remigration from America to Sweden," in H. Runblom and H. Norman, eds., *From Sweden to America* (Uppsala, 1976).

7. D. N. Doyle, *Irish-Americans, Native Rights, and National Empires, 1890–1901* (NY, 1976), 36–90, 187–88, 226, 334.

Part One. The Making of the Emigrants' Ireland

1. F. H. A. Aalen, *Man and the Landscape in Ireland* (London, 1978), 25–26; T. W. Freeman, *Ireland* (NY, 1950), 45–52, 65–72; A. R. Orme, *Ireland* (Chicago, 1970), 38–42.

2. E.g., see Aalen 1–39, for a geographical determinist interpretation of Irish history recently challenged by J. Mokyr, *Why Ireland Starved: A Quantitative and Analytical History*

of the Irish Economy, 1800–1850 (London, 1983), 151–94. The quotation is from E. Barker, *Ireland in the Last Fifty Years* (Oxford, 1917), 9.

Chapter 1. Conquest: Exiles in Erin

1. P. Colum, ed., *Anthology of Irish Verse* (NY, 1972), 261–63.
2. J. C. Beckett, *Short History of Ireland* (NY, 1968), 16–18.
3. Ibid., 10–17; R. Kee, *The Green Flag: History of Irish Nationalism* (NY, 1972), 9–14.
4. G. Mac Niocaill, *Ireland before the Vikings* (Dublin, 1972), 49–69; D. Ó Corráin, *Ireland before the Normans* (Dublin, 1972), 41–48.
5. Ó Corráin, 28–42; D. Ó Corráin, "Nationality and Kingship in Pre-Norman Ireland," *HS*, 11 (1978), 1–36; L. M. Cullen, *Life in Ireland* (London, 1968), 15–16.
6. Mac Niocaill, 42–49; Ó Corráin, *Ireland*, 65, 74–89; M. Dillon, "The Archaism of Irish Tradition," ACIS reprint no. 5 (Chicago, 1969), 6–28; D. Ó Corráin, "Women in Early Irish Society," in M. Mac Curtain and Ó Corráin, eds., *Women in Irish Society* (Dublin, 1978), 1–11; F. H. A. Aalen, *Man and Landscape in Ireland* (London, 1978), 100–104; R. Flower, *The Irish Tradition* (Oxford, 1947), 3–4; E. Knott, *Irish Classical Poetry* (Cork, 1973).
7. Ó Corráin, *Ireland*, 48–58, 66–67, 72–73; Aalen, 69–71, 81–99, 107–8.
8. Beckett, 15–25; Aalen, 109–11, 117–21, 128–29; R. H. Buchanan, "Field Systems of Ireland," in A. R. H. Baker and R. A. Butlin, eds., *Studies of Field Systems in the British Isles* (London, 1973), 608–11; I. Leister, *Peasant Openfield Farming and Its Territorial Organization in County Tipperary* (Marburg, 1976), 44–46.
9. Beckett, 21–33; K. Nicholls, *Gaelic and Gaelicized Ireland in the Middle Ages* (Dublin, 1972), 29–45, 68–71, 82–84, 91–113; J. Watt, *The Church in Medieval Ireland* (Dublin, 1972), 181–202; Aalen, 111–14; Knott, 67; S. O' Faolain, *The Irish* (NY, 1949), 46.
10. Beckett, 38–48; B. Bradshaw, *Irish Constitutional Revolution of the 16th Century* (Cambridge, 1979), 3–257.
11. Beckett, 38–48.
12. Ibid., 48–63; Watt, 215–17; K. S. Bottigheimer, "Kingdom and Colony: Ireland in the Westward Enterprise, 1536–1660," in K. R. Andrews et al., eds., *The Westward Enterprise* (Liverpool, 1980), 46–51; B. Bradshaw, "Sword, Word, and Strategy in the Reformation in Ireland," *HJ*, 21, no. 3 (1978); N. P. Canny, "The Ideology of English Colonization: From Ireland to America," *WMQ*, 30 (1973), 575–98; D. B. Quinn, *The Elizabethans and the Irish* (Ithaca, 1966), 20, 32; M. Hechter, *Internal Colonization: The Celtic Fringe in British National Development, 1536–1966* (Berkeley, 1974), 59–67.
13. Beckett, 48–63; Kee, 9–14; Bradshaw, *Irish,* 258–63; Bradshaw, "Sword," passim; Bottigheimer, 50; B. Bradshaw, "Native Reaction to the Western Enterprise: A Case Study in Gaelic Ideology," in Andrews et al., 75–77; N. Canny, "Formation of the Irish Mind: Religion, Politics and Gaelic Irish Literature, 1580–1750," *P&P*, no. 95 (1982), 91–104; P. J. Corish, *Catholic Community in the 17th and 18th Centuries* (Dublin, 1981), 41–42.
14. Beckett, 48–63; A. Clarke, "The Irish Economy, 1600–60," in T. W. Moody et al., *NHI III: Early Modern Ireland, 1534–1691* (Oxford, 1976), 168–86; R. Mitchison, "Ireland and Scotland: The 17th Century," in T. M. Devine and D. Dickson, eds., *Ireland and Scotland, 1600–1850* (Edinburgh, 1983), 3–9.
15. M. Mac Curtain, *Tudor and Stuart Ireland* (Dublin, 1976), 190; P. J. Corish, "Origins of Catholic Nationalism," in Corish, ed., *History of Irish Catholicism*, vol. 3, pt. 8 (Dublin, 1968), 23–31; N. P. Canny, "Dominant Minorities: English Settlers in Ireland and Virginia," in A. C. Hepburn, ed., *Minorities in History* (London, 1978), 60–63; Bradshaw, "Sword," 502; J. C. Beckett, *Anglo-Irish Tradition* (Ithaca, 1976), 28–30.
16. Beckett, *Short*, 55–56; J. G. Leyburn, *The Scotch-Irish . . .* (Chapel Hill, 1962), 93–94; Aalen, 143; M. Perceval-Maxwell, *Scottish Migration to Ulster in the Reign of James I* (London, 1973), 229–51; W. Macafee, "Colonization of the Maghera Region of South Derry during the 17th and 18th Centuries," *UF*, 23 (1977), 70–85; A. T. Q. Stewart, *The Narrow Ground: Aspects of Ulster, 1609–1969* (London, 1977), 39.
17. Perceval-Maxwell, 30–45; Macafee, 70–85; Aalen, 144–45; P. Robinson, "Irish Settlement in Tyrone before the Ulster Plantation," *UF*, 22 (1976), 68; P. Robinson, "British Settlement in Co. Tyrone, 1610–66," *IESH*, 5 (1978), 19–26; G. B. Adams, "Dialects of Ulster," in D. Ó Muirithe, ed., *English Language in Ireland* (Cork, 1977), 57; D. McCourt, "Dynamic Quality of Irish Rural Settlement," in R. H. Buchanan et al., eds., *Man and His Habitat* (London, 1971), 142–43.
18. Beckett, *Short*, 67–80; Kee, 15–16; J. C. Beckett, *Making of Modern Ireland, 1603–*

1923 (NY, 1966), 82–103; T. C. Croker, *Researches in the South of Ireland* (London, 1824), 11.

19. Beckett, *Making*, 104–15; Kee, 15–17; A. R. Orme, *Ireland* (Chicago, 1970), 130–31; P. J. Corish, "The Cromwellian Regime, 1650–60," in Moody et al., 369; T. C. Barnard, *Cromwellian Ireland* (London, 1975), 90–112, 173–81, 298–99.

20. Beckett, *Making*, 122–49; E. MacLysaght, *Irish Life in the 17th Century* (Shannon, 1969), 278–311.

21. Beckett, *Making*, 150–66; Kee, 18–20; Orme, 130–31.

22. Canny, "Dominant," 52; T. Newenham, *Statistical . . . Inquiry into . . . the Population of Ireland* (London, 1805), 307–18; L. M. Cullen, *Emergence of Modern Ireland, 1600–1900* (Dublin, 1983), 87; M. Mac Curtain, "Rural Society in Post-Cromwellian Ireland," in A. Cosgrove and D. McCartney, eds., *Studies in Irish History Presented to R. Dudley Edwards* (Dublin, 1979), 131; Corish, "Cromwellian," 373; R. B. McDowell, *Public Opinion and Government Policy in Ireland, 1801–1846* (London, 1952), 110–11.

23. Beckett, *Making*, 48–63; M. Wall, "Catholics in Economic Life," in L. M. Cullen, ed., *Formation of the Irish Economy* (Cork, 1969), 48–49; W. Nolan, *Fassadinin: Land, Settlement and Society in Southeast Ireland, 1600–1850* (Dublin, 1979), 89, 100, 118; J. Brady and P. J. Corish, "The Church under the Penal Code," in Corish, ed., *History*, vol. 4, pt. 2 (Dublin, 1971), 62; Corish, *Catholic*, 93; Mac Curtain, "Rural," 126–27; L. M. Cullen, "Economic Trends, 1660–91," in Moody et al., 535; A. de Blácam, *Gaelic Literature Surveyed* (Dublin, 1929), 251–52, 322–23; Beckett, *Anglo-Irish*, 65; Barnard, 180–81; for evidence of conversions, see petitions dated 14 and 29 Dec. 1817 (CO 384/1, PRO) and 17 Feb. 1830 (CO 384/23, PRO).

24. L. M. Cullen, "Merchant Communities, the Navigation Acts, and Irish and Scottish Responses," in Cullen and T. C. Smout, eds., *Comparative Aspects of Scottish and Irish Economic and Social History, 1600–1900* (Edinburgh, 1976), 165–76; Brady and Corish, 30–49; L. M. Cullen, *Economic History of Ireland since 1660* (London, 1972), 7–49; Mac Curtain, "Rural," 126–27; B. Ó Cuív, "Irish Language in the Early Modern Period," in Moody et al., 527, 541–42; A. Bliss, "Development of the English Language in Early Modern Ireland," in Moody et al., 546; Blácam, 350–51; O'Faolain, 88–91; Cullen, *Emergence*, 250–51.

25. W. E. H. Lecky, *History of Ireland in the 18th Century*, abr. and ed. L. P. Curtis, Jr. (Chicago, 1972), 43; A. W. Hutton, ed., *Arthur Young's Tour in Ireland* (London, 1892), I, 114, and II, 65–66; D. Dewar, *Observations on the Character . . . of the Irish* (London, 1812), 19–22, 59–60; M. Wall, "Whiteboys," in T. D. Williams, ed., *Secret Societies in Ireland* (Dublin, 1973), 13–18; T. C. Croker, *Keen of the South of Ireland* (London, 1844), xxv–xxvii; M. N. Hennessy, *The Wild Geese: The Irish Soldier in Exile* (London, 1973); Canny, "Formation," 104–16; D. Corkery, *Hidden Ireland: A Study of Gaelic Munster in the 18th Century* (Dublin, 1967 ed.), 130, 142, 206, and passim; Ó Cuív, 536, 541–45; P. Ua Duinnín, ed., *Dánta Phiarais Feiritéir . . .* (Dublin, 1903), 11–12 (trans. BDB); C. O'Rahilly, ed., *Five 17th-Century Political Poems* (Dublin, 1952), 98–99 and passim (trans. BDB); Blácam, 259, 273–75, 307.

Chapter 2. Change: Ireland before the Great Famine

1. P. E. Razzell, "Population Growth and Economic Change in 18th- and Early 19th-Century England and Ireland," in E. L. Jones and G. E. Mingay, eds., *Land, Labour and Population in the Industrial Revolution* (London, 1967), 279; G. de Beaumont, *Ireland, Social, Political and Religious* (London, 1839), I, 264–65.

2. E. Estyn Evans, *Irish Heritage* (Dundalk, 1967), 48; D. McCourt, "Dynamic Quality of Irish Rural Settlements," in R. H. Buchanan et al., eds., *Man and His Habitat* (London, 1971).

3. Evans, 48–54; E. Estyn Evans, *Personality of Ireland* (Cambridge, 1973), 59–62; J. E. Pomfret, *Struggle for Land in Ireland, 1800–1923* (NY, 1969 ed.), 18.

4. M. Hechter, *Internal Colonialism . . .* (Berkeley, 1974), 80–81; S. Clark, *Social Origins of the Land War* (Princeton, 1979), 44–45; R. H. Buchanan, "Field Systems of Ireland," in A. R. H. Baker and R. A. Butlin, eds., *Studies of Field Systems . . .* (London, 1973), 598–606.

5. L. M. Cullen, *Economic History of Ireland . . .* (London, 1972), 7–49, 67–71; W. Nolan, *Fassadinin . . .* (Dublin, 1979), 53–55, 86–88; K. H. Connell, *Population of Ireland, 1750–1845* (Oxford, 1950), 25; L. A. Clarkson, "Irish Population Revisited, 1687–

1821," in J. M. Goldstrom and Clarkson, eds., *Irish Population, Economy, and Society* (Oxford, 1981), 25–27; S. Daultrey, D. Dickson, and C. Ó Gráda, "18th-Century Irish Population: New Perspectives from Old Sources," *JECONH,* 41 (Sept. 1981), 621–28.

6. Cullen, 54, 95, 109, 126; *Second Report of the Commissioners Appointed to Consider and Recommend a General System of Railways for Ireland, GBPP-HC* (145), 1837–38, XXXV, 492; J. Carr, *Stranger in Ireland* (London, 1806), 67; T. W. Freeman, "Irish Towns in the 18th and 19th Centuries," in R. A. Butlin, ed., *Development of the Irish Town* (London, 1977), 101–4; W. Bennett, *Narrative of a Recent Journey . . . in Ireland* (London, 1847), 7–8; H. D. Inglis, *Tour throughout Ireland in . . . 1834* (London, 1835), II, 316–17; F. H. A. Aalen, *Man and the Landscape in Ireland* (London, 1978), 193–94, 278–80; P. Lynch and J. Vaizey, *Guinness's Brewery in the Irish Economy, 1759–1876* (Cambridge, 1960), 7–10; L. Barrow, "Use of Money in Mid-19th-Century Ireland," *Studies,* 59 (Spring 1970), 68–80.

7. Cullen, 50–99; W. H. Crawford, "Rise of the Linen Industry," in L. M. Cullen, ed., *Formation of the Irish Economy* (Cork, 1968), 23–27.

8. Cullen, *Economic,* 40–41, 50–99; Connell, 25, 51, and passim; M. Drake, "Marriage and Population Growth in Ireland, 1750–1845," *ECONHR,* 16 (Dec. 1963), 301–13; J. Lee, "Marriage and Population in Pre-Famine Ireland," *ECONHR,* 21 (1968), 283–95; V. Morgan, "Case Study of Population Change over Two Centuries: Blaris, Lisburn, 1661–1848," *IESH,* 3 (1976), 15–16; Clarkson, 25–27, 30–35; J. Lee, "On the Accuracy of the Pre-Famine Irish Censuses," in Goldstrom and Clarkson, 46, speculates that Irish population in 1821 was 7.2 million; Nolan, 161; E. Almquist, "Mayo and Beyond: Land, Domestic Industry, and Rural Transformation in the Irish West" (Ph.D. diss., Boston Univ., 1977), 4–8.

9. R. B. McDowell, *Ireland in the Age of Imperialism and Revolution, 1760–1801* (Oxford, 1979), 9–10; Aalen, 160–62; A. W. Hutton, ed., *Arthur Young's Tour in Ireland* (London, 1892), I, 73, 106–14, 259–83; R. H. Buchanan, "Enclosures in Lecale, Co. Down," *IRGEO,* 5 (1965), 38–39; Almquist, 26–50, 132–35; W. H. Crawford, "Landlord-Tenant Relations in Ulster, 1609–1820," *IESH,* 2 (1975), 19.

10. D. H. Akenson, *Between Two Revolutions: An Ulster Community, Islandmagee, Co. Antrim, 1798–1920* (Hamden, Conn., 1979), 91–95; Aalen, 195–96; McDowell, 17–19, 23–24; Crawford, "Rise," 27–30; H. D. Gribbon, "The Irish Linen Board, 1711–1828," in L. M. Cullen and T. C. Smout, eds., *Comparative Aspects of Scottish and Irish . . . History* (Edinburgh, 1976), 77–87.

11. Aalen, 160–67, 258–61; G. O'Brien, *Economic History of Ireland in the 18th Century* (Dublin, 1918), 36–37; "The Rosses, Co. Donegal, in 1753–4," *UF,* 20 (1974), 20–23; *Second Report . . . Commissioners . . . of Railways,* 553; J. Venedey, *Ireland and the Irish during the Repeal Year, 1843* (Dublin, 1844), 336–37.

12. Inglis, I, 79–81.

13. R. Bell, *Description of the Condition and Manners of the Peasantry of Ireland* (London, 1804), title p. and passim; Hechter, 9–10; Cullen, *Economic,* 93, 99, 106; J. Lee, "Dual Economy in Ireland, 1800–50," *HS,* 8 (1971), 196–97; J. S. Donnelly, Jr., *Land and the People of 19th-Century Cork* (London, 1975), 43.

14. Buchanan, "Enclosures," 38–39; Buchanan, "Field," 606–7; W. Greig, *General Report on the Gosford Estates in Co. Armagh, 1821* (Belfast, 1976), 89; Donnelly, 43; K. A. Miller, "Emigration and Society in Pre-Famine Ireland" (Paper, AHA convention, NY, 1979).

15. Lee, "Dual," 196–97; Greig, 89; Aalen, 182; Clark, 53; Cullen, *Economic,* 48; Almquist, 72–75; T. Newenham, *Statistical . . . Inquiry into . . . the Population of Ireland* (London, 1805), 15; Miller.

16. Freeman, 116–17; M. Drake, "Irish Demographic Crisis of 1740–41," *HS,* 6 (1968), 123–24; Venedey, 229; W. S. Mason, ed., *Statistical Account, or Parochial Survey of Ireland* (Dublin, 1814–19), II, 16; K. H. Connell, *Irish Peasant Society* (Oxford, 1969), 1–49; Inglis, II, 110, 295; B. M. Kerr, "Irish Seasonal Migration to Great Britain, 1800–38," *IHS,* 3 (Sept. 1943), 371–73; J. H. Johnson, "Harvest Migration from 19th-Century Ireland," *T&P-IBG,* 41 (June 1967), 100–103; N. R. Burke, "Some Observations on the Migration of Labourers from the South of Ireland to Newfoundland . . . ," *JCHAS,* 76, (July–Dec. 1971), 104–5; K. H. Connell, "Colonization of Waste Land in Ireland, 1780–1845," *ECONHR,* 3 (1950), 44–71; J. H. Andrews, *Paper Landscape: The Ordnance Survey in 19th-Century Ireland* (Oxford, 1976), 151; J. S. Donnelly, Jr., "Journals of Sir John Benn-Walsh . . . ," *JCHAS,* 80 (July–Dec. 1974), 93.

17. Freeman, 104–5, 130–32; W. E. Vaughn and A. J. Fitzpatrick, eds., *Irish Historical Statistics: Population, 1821–1971* (Dublin, 1978), 27–41; P. Connell, *Changing Forces Shaping a 19th-Century Irish Town: . . . Navan* (Maynooth, 1978), 7–8, 12–17; McDowell, 34; J. Whitelaw, *Essay on the Population of Dublin . . .* in 1798 (Dublin, 1805), 52; W. Griffin, "Enquiry into the Mortality among the Poor of . . . Limerick," *JRSS*, 3 (1841), 320.

18. Aalen, 203–4, 227; Inglis, I, 312–16, 338; P. Connell, 12–17.

19. L. Kennedy, "Regional Specialization, Railway Development, and Irish Agriculture in the 19th Century," in Goldstrom and Clarkson, 173–93; E. Wakefield, *Account of Ireland, Statistical and Political* (London, 1812), I, 322–30; Cullen, *Economic*, 87–88; J. M'Parlan, *Statistical Survey of the County of Sligo* (Dublin, 1802), 14.

20. Le Chevalier de La Tocnaye, *Frenchman's Walk through Ireland, 1796–97* (Belfast, 1917 ed.), 126; T. W. Freeman, *Pre-Famine Ireland* (NY, 1957), 15, 25, 169–70.

21. T. J. Hughes, "Society and Settlement in 19th-Century Ireland," *IRGEO*, 5 (1965), 81–87; Aalen, 169–82, 213; F. H. A. Aalen, "Enclosures in Eastern Ireland," *IRGEO*, 5 (1965), 209–21; Hutton, II, 13–15; Inglis, I, 295; Clark, 127.

22. Hughes, 90–92; Freeman, *Pre-Famine*, 168–70; Cullen, *Economic*, 111–12; E. Willes, 1760 (T.2368, PRONI), Hutton, II, 30; H. C. Brookfield, "Microcosm of Pre-Famine Ireland: Mallow District, 1775–1846," *JCHAS*, 57 (1952), 7–10.

23. Hughes, 88–90; T. J. Hughes, "East Leinster in the Mid-19th Century," *IRGEO*, 3 (1958), 227–41; Hutton, II, 30; Wakefield, II, 775–77; Inglis, I, 40–46.

24. Freeman, *Pre-Famine*, 203–68; Hughes, "Society," 93–94; Aalen, *Man*, 183–90, 254–55; F. H. A. Aalen, "Some Historical Aspects of Landscape and Rural Life in Omeath, Co. Louth," *IRGEO*, 4 (1962), 256–78; McCourt, 140–41; Almquist, 125; J. G. Simms, "Connacht in the 18th Century," *IHS*, 11 (1958), 120–21; W. H. Maxwell, *Wild Sports of the West* (1832; East Ardsley, 1973 ed.), 190, 312–13; T. C. Foster, *Letters on the Condition of the People of Ireland* (London, 1847), 396–97; W. M. Thackeray, *Paris Sketch Book; Irish Sketch Book . . .* (London, 1889 ed.), 326.

25. T. W. Moody and J. C. Beckett, eds., *Ulster since 1800: Political and Economic Survey* (London, 1954), 40–41; E. R. R. Green, *Lagan Valley, 1800–1850* (London, 1949), 125; Freeman, *Pre-Famine*, 269–307; Akenson, 43–44, 189n; J. G. Kohl, *Ireland, Scotland, and England* (London, 1844), 194–97; E. Willes, 1759 (T.2368, PRONI).

26. Wakefield, II, 735; Aalen, *Man*, 190–91; A. Gailey, "Scots Element in North Irish Popular Culture," *Ethnologia Europaea*, 8, no. 1 (1975), 2–22.

27. Crawford, "Landlord-Tenant," *passim*; E. D. Steele, *Irish Land and British Politics* (Cambridge, 1974), 7–8, 28; Moody and Beckett, 40–49; Akenson, 44–48; Cullen, *Economic*, 113–14.

28. Freeman, *Pre-Famine*, 269–70; Crawford, "Rise, 30–31; C. Maxwell, *Country and Town in Ireland under the Georges* (Dundalk, 1949), 230–31; Crawford, "Landlord-Tenant," 13–17; W. H. Crawford, "Economy and Society in South Ulster in the 18th Century," *CLREC*, 8 (1975), 253–55; J. Mogey, *Rural Life in Northern Ireland* (London, 1947), 18–19.

29. Freeman, *Pre-Famine*, 146–47; P. J. Duffy, "Irish Landholding Structures and Population in the Mid-19th Century," *MYREV*, 3, no. 2 (Dec. 1977), *passim*; T. Reid, *Travels in Ireland in the Year 1822* (London, 1823), 230.

30. J. Carty, *Ireland from Grattan's Parliament to the Great Famine* (Dublin, 1965), 2; T. W. Moody and J. C. Beckett, eds., *Ulster since 1800: Social Survey* (London, 1958), 22–23.

31. E. Larkin, "Economic Growth, Capital Investment and the Roman Catholic Church in 19th-Century Ireland," *AHR*, 72 (Apr. 1967), 882; E. Willes, 1760 (T.2368, PRONI).

32. P. B. Ellis, *History of the Irish Working Class* (NY, 1973), 61–62; L. M. Cullen, "Cultural Basis of Modern Irish Nationalism," in R. Mitchison, ed., *Roots of Nationalism* (Edinburgh, 1980), *passim*.

33. Clark, 21–22, 33–34; Hutton, II, 54; G. Ó Tuathaigh, *Ireland before the Famine, 1798–1848* (Dublin, 1972), 147; W. Maxwell, 17–85; D. Corkery, *Hidden Ireland* (Dublin, 1967 ed.), 25; Inglis, I, 346; R. L and M. Edgeworth, *Memoirs of Richard Lovell Edgeworth* (1820; Shannon, 1969 ed.), II, 31–40; McDowell, 41–45, 53–54; J. E. Bicheno, *Ireland and Its Economy* (London, 1830), 140; A. Plumptre, *Narrative of a Residence in Ireland during . . . 1814 and 1815* (London, 1817), 339, 351–52; M. Edgeworth, *Castle Rackrent* (1800; NY, 1965 ed.), 10, 55.

34. H. B. Staples, Jr., *The Ireland of Sir Jonah Barrington* (Seattle, 1967), 6, 37; Bell,

34–37; J. H. Whyte, "Landlord Influence at Elections in Ireland, 1760–1885," *EHR*, 80 (1965), 746; Thackeray, 310, 541.

35. Bell, 36–37; J. S. Donnelly, Jr., *Landlord and Tenant in 19th-Century Ireland* (Dublin, 1973), 5; A. P. W. Malcomson, "Absenteeism in 18th-Century Ireland," *IESH*, 1 (1974), 16–28; A. J. Bliss, "Emergence of Modern English Dialects in Ireland," in D. Ó Muirithe, ed., *English Language in Ireland* (Cork, 1977), 15–18; McDowell, 143–46; G. Christianson, "Landlords and Land Tenure in Ireland, 1790–1830," *É-I*, 9, no. 1 (Spring 1974), 33, 56; J. C. Beckett, *Anglo-Irish Tradition* (Ithaca, 1976), 10; C. Maxwell, *Dublin under the Georges, 1714–1830* (London, 1936), 83, 255.

36. E. Willes, 1764 (T.2368, PRONI); W. A. Maguire, *The Downshire Estates in Ireland, 1801–45* (NY, 1973), 29; D. Large, "Wealth of the Greater Irish Landowners, 1750–1815," *IHS*, 15 (1966), 28–29; Maxwell, *Country,* 17–65, 188.

37. Staples, 6; Wakefield, I, 244, and II, 754, 763–64; McDowell, 47–49; Plumptre, 352–53; W. Maxwell, passim; Donnelly, "Journals," 88; Donnelly, *Land,* 57; Cullen, *Economic,* 115.

38. Whyte, 752–53; Donnelly, *Land,* 62–63; D. Thomson and M. McGusty, eds., *Irish Journals of Elizabeth Smith, 1840–50* (NY, 1980), xviii, 6; H. Dutton, *Statistical Survey of the County of Galway* (Dublin, 1824), 340; R. B. McDowell, *The Irish Administration, 1801–1914* (Toronto, 1964), 19–26; Maguire, 52–54; Bicheno, 164–65; S. Palmer, "Paddy and Peeler: Peasant Violence and Police Terror in Ireland, 1827–32" (Paper, Midwest ACIS conference, Madison, Wis., 1979).

39. Donnelly, *Land,* 9–13; D. Dickson, "Middlemen," in T. Bartlett and T. W. Hayton, eds., *Penal Era and Golden Age: Essays in Irish History, 1690–1800* (Belfast, 1979), 169–75; Nolan, 100; A. de Tocqueville, *Journeys through England and Ireland* (London, 1958), 158–59.

40. W. E. H. Lecky, *History of Ireland in the 18th Century,* abr. and ed. L. P. Curtis, Jr. (Chicago, 1972), 84, 87; C. Maxwell, *Stranger in Ireland* (London, 1954), 171; Dickson, 176–81; Nolan, 103–4; Hutton, II, 26–28; C. Otway, *Tour in Connaught* (Dublin, 1839), 127; L. M. Cullen, *Emergence of Modern Ireland* (Dublin, 1983), 99–106 and passim.

41. Donnelly, *Landlord,* 5–9; C. Maxwell, *Country,* 115; Dickson, 179–84; Crawford, "Landlord-Tenant," 19.

42. K. H. Connell, *Population,* 66; O'Brien, 83–85; Nolan, 103–4.

43. Cullen, *Emergence,* 42; R. D. Crotty, *Irish Agricultural Production* (Cork, 1966), 306–7; Ó Tuathaigh, 147–48; L. M. Cullen, *Life in Ireland* (London, 1968), 106–7; P. M. A. Bourke, "Agricultural Statistics of the 1841 Census of Ireland," *ECONHR*, 18 (1965), 380; C. Ó Gráda, "Supply Responsiveness in Irish Agriculture during the 19th Century," *ECONHR*, 28 (1975), 315; Hutton, II, 22; Donnelly, *Land,* 48–49, 62–63; Clark, 32–33, 38; Akenson, 54.

44. E. R. R. Green, "Agriculture," in R. D. Edwards and T. D. Williams, eds., *The Great Famine* (NY, 1957), 92; Cullen, *Life,* 80, 106–7; Freeman, *Pre-Famine,* 148–49; Bourke, 380; Clark, 34–35; Akenson, 54; Mogey, 18–19; P. M. A. Bourke, "Use of the Potato Crop in Pre-Famine Ireland," *JSSISI*, 21 (1967–68), 78–80.

45. J. Mokyr, *Why Ireland Starved* (London, 1983), 19; Bourke, "Agricultural," 380; P. M. A. Bourke, "Uncertainties in the Statistics of Farm Size in Ireland, 1841–1851," *JSSISI*, 20 (1959–60), 21; Otway, 553; Mason, I, 555–56; Wakefield, I, 580; Akenson, 54; Cullen, *Economic,* 110; R. N. Salaman, *History and Social Influence of the Potato* (Cambridge, 1949), 197; C. Maxwell, *Country,* 122–23; E. Estyn Evans, *Irish Folk Ways* (London, 1957), 1; T. C. Croker, *Researches in the South of Ireland* (London, 1824), 221–22; J. Forbes, *Memorandums Made in Ireland in . . . 1852* (London, 1853), II, 98–100.

46. Steele, 5; Bourke, "Use," passim; Nolan, 127; *Second Report . . . Commissioners . . . of Railways,* 554–55.

47. Inglis, I, 33; Bourke, "Use," 81–83; Clark, 36–38, 114; Cullen, *Life,* 118–19; Edgeworth and Edgeworth, II, 19–29; C. Ó Danachair, "Farmer and Laborer in Pre-Famine Co. Limerick," *LIMAY 1978* (Limerick, 1978), 34; M. R. Beames, "Cottiers and Conacre in Pre-Famine Ireland," *JPS*, 2 (1975), 352; *Third Report of the Select Committee on Emigration from the United Kingdom, 1827,* in *IUP-BPP, Emigration,* vol. 2 (Shannon, 1968), 257–61; Wakefield, I, 507–11.

48. Newenham, 15; Ó Danachair, 37; Donnelly, *Land,* 18–19; *Second Report . . . Commissioners . . . of Railways,* 553–56; Clark, 36–38, 114; Pomfret, 8; A. L. Bowley, "Statistics of Wages in the United Kingdom . . . , (Pt. III) Agricultural Wages—Ireland," *JRSS*, 62 (June 1899), 396, 400–401; W. S. Balch, *Ireland As I Saw It* (NY, 1850), 231;

J. B. O'Brien, "Agricultural Prices and Living Costs in Pre-Famine Cork, *JCHAS*, 82 (1977), 7–10; Green, "Agriculture," 93–95; Beames, 352; P. M. A. Burke, "Extent of the Potato Crop in Ireland at the Time of the Famine," *JSSISI*, 20 (1959), 7, 11–12; Bennett, 7–8.

49. Cullen, *Economic*, 110–11; C. Maxwell, *Country*, 127–29; Salaman, 197, 264–65, 285; Bourke, "Use," 81–83; Donnelly, *Land*, 23–25; Hutton, II, 43–45; T. W. Grimshaw, "Statistical Survey of Ireland," *JSSISI*, 9 (Nov. 1888), 333; Beaumont, I, 273; Kohl, 112–16.

50. Inglis, I, 284; Evans, *Irish Heritage*, 12; A. Humphries, "Family in Ireland," in M. F. Nimkoff, ed., *Comparative Family Systems* (Boston, 1965), 243; Clark, 43–45.

51. See nn. 2–3 above; R. Fox, *Tory Islanders* (Cambridge, 1978), 99–103; Clark, 45–47; Mason, I, 60–61, 134–35, 160–61, 208, 309, and II, 16, 113–14, 361, 460, and III, 28–29, 243, 455, 495, 620; Duffy, 11; *Third Report . . . on Emigration . . . 1827*, 269; Humphries, 244–46; Inglis, I, 46, 129; Wakefield, II, 798; Otway, 251–52; Plumptre, 358; Croker, 230.

52. M. Anderson, *Family Structure in 19th-Century Lancastershire* (Cambridge, 1971), 81–91; Inglis, I, 109; D. Hannan, "Kinship, Neighborhood and Social Change in Irish Rural Communities," *ECSOR*, 2 (July 1972), 169; I. Weld, *Statistical Survey of the Co. of Roscommon* (Dublin, 1832), 660; C. M. Arensberg and S. T. Kimball, *Family and Community in Ireland* (Cambridge, Mass., 1968 ed.), 72–75; Croker, 252.

53. Hannan, 171–72; E. Leyton, *One Blood: Kinship and Class in an Irish Village* (St. Johns, Newfoundland, 1975), 3; Evans, *Personality*, 93–105; Evans, *Irish Heritage*, 51; Mason, I, 604, and II, 385, and III, 105–6; J. Healy *Nineteen Acres* (Galway, 1978), 119–20.

54. Arensberg and Kimball, 58 and passim; Humphries, 244–47; P. Gibbon and C. Curtin, "Stem Family in Ireland," *CSSH*, 20 (1978), 429–53; Ó Tuathaigh, 147–48; Cullen, *Life*, 106–7; C. Ó Gráda, "Some Aspects of 19th-Century Irish Emigration," in Cullen and Smout, 67–68; K. H. Connell, *Population*, 58; W. McDonald, *Reminiscences of a Maynooth Professor* (London, 1925), 15–16.

55. Cullen, *Economic*, 81; Aalen, *Man*, 213; Cullen, "Cultural," 97–98; Duffy, 11–12; Akenson, 66–68; Leyton, 3; Clark, 55–56.

56. Cullen, *Emergence*, 95–97; K. H. Connell, *Population*, 25, 57, and passim; Almquist, 6–8, 95–96, 222; Wakefield, I, 512, and II, 801; Evans, *Irish Folk*, 290–91; R. Twiss, *Tour in Ireland in 1775* (Dublin, 1776), 103–6; Tocqueville, 179; S. J. Connolly, "Illegitimacy and Pre-Nuptial Pregnancy in Ireland before 1864," *IESH*, 6 (1979), passim; Cullen, *Economic*, 100–33; Inglis, I, 247; W. H. Maxwell, 83; Mason, III, 620.

57. Clarkson, 26, 30–35; see works cited in n. 8 above; J. Mokyr, "Malthusian Models and Irish History," *JECONH*, 40 (May 1980), 163; Tocqueville, 121.

58. Donnelly, *Land*, 52, 61; Greig, 89; K. H. Connell, *Population*, 57; Lee, "Marriage," 283–89.

59. Crotty, 39–41; K. H. Connell, *Population*, 25, 33–40; Lee, "Marriage," 283–85; S. H. Cousens, "Restriction of Population in Pre-Famine Ireland," *PRIA*, 65, sec. C (1966), 98–99; F. J. Carney, "Pre-Famine Irish Population: Evidence from the Trinity College Estates," *IESH*, 2 (1975), 35–45; F. J. Carney, "Aspects of Pre-Famine Irish Household Size," in Cullen and Smout, 42–44; K. O'Neill, "Agricultural Change and Family Structure in Pre-Famine Cavan" (Paper, Midwest ACIS conference, Madison, Wis., 1979); Anderson, 94–95; Inglis, I, 286–89.

60. Clark, 66–67; S. Palmer, "Rebellion, Emancipation, Starvation: Dilemma of Peaceful Protest in Ireland, 1798–1848," in K. Philp and B. Lackner, eds., *Essays in Modern European Revolutionary History* (Austin, 1977), 10, 17–19; G. Broeker, *Rural Disorder and Police Reform in Ireland, 1812–36* (Toronto, 1970).

61. Clark, 74–78; Croker, 231; D. Neeson, 19 Sept. 1824 (Neeson Mss., UWVL); P. O'Donnell, *Irish Faction Fighters of the 19th Century* (Tralee, 1975), 24–28, 50, 133–74; P. E. W. Roberts, "Caravats and Shanavests . . . ," in S. Clark and J. S. Donnelly, Jr., eds., *Irish Peasants: Violence and Political Unrest, 1780–1914* (Madison, Wis., 1983), 64–101.

62. G. C. Lewis, *Local Disturbances in Ireland* (1836; Cork, 1977 ed.), 35 and passim; Clark and Donnelly, 25–139; M. R. Beames, *Peasants and Power: Whiteboy Movements and Their Control in Pre-Famine Ireland* (NY, 1983); A. T. Q. Stewart, *Narrow Ground . . .* (London, 1977), 116–17.

63. In addition to works cited in n. 62 above, see J. S. Donnelly, Jr., "Whiteboy Movement," *IHS*, 21 (Mar. 1978), 22–24; M. Wall, "Whiteboys," in T. D. Williams, ed., *Secret Societies in Ireland* (Dublin, 1973), 13–25; J. S. Donnelly, Jr., "Irish Agrarian Rebellion:

Whiteboys of 1769–76," *PRIA*, 83, sec. C, no. 12 (1983), 293–331; J. S. Donnelly, Jr., "Oakboys and Steelboys" (Paper, 1977); M. R. Beames, "Peasant Movements: Ireland, 1785–95," *JPS*, 2, no. 4 (1975); J. S. Donnelly, Jr., "Rightboy Movement," *SH*, 17–18 (1977–78); M. J. Bric, "Priests, Parsons and Politics: Rightboy Movement in Co. Cork, 1785–88," *P&P*, no. 100 (1983), 100–123; J. S. Donnelly, Jr., "Rockite Movement, 1821–24" (Paper, ACIS conference, Pittsburgh, 1981); Lewis, 7, 26–27, 72–73; Ellis, 61–62; Crawford, "Landlord-Tenant," 11; M. R. Beames, "Rural Conflict in Pre-Famine Ireland: Peasant Assassinations in Tipperary, 1837–47," *P&P*, no. 81 (1978), 89; Bell, 26; E. P. Thompson, "Moral Economy of the English Crowd in the 18th Century," *P&P*, no. 50 (1971).

64. J. Lee, "Ribbonmen," in Williams, ed., 26–35; Lewis, 80; G. Foster, cited in E. Kane, *Last Place God Made: Traditional Economy and New Industry in Rural Ireland* (New Haven, 1977), III, 706–7 (also see I, 227, and II, 363–64); Wakefield, II, 786; D. S. Jones, "Agrarian Capitalism and Irish Landlordism," in A. E. C. W. Spencer, ed., *Dependency: Social, Political and Cultural* (Belfast, 1979), 48; C. Otway, *Sketches in Ireland* (Dublin, 1839 ed.), 200, 292; U. J. Bourke, ed., *Sermons in Irish-Gaelic by the Most Rev. James O'Gallagher, Bishop of Raphoe* (Dublin, 1877), 69, 249.

65. *Second Report . . . Commissioners . . . of Railways*, 556; Donnelly, "Oakboys and Steelboys"; Donnelly, "Rightboy," 199–202; Ellis, 61–62; T. Bartlett, "End to Moral Economy: Irish Militia Disturbances of 1793," *P&P*, no. 99 (1983), 41–64; M. McGrath, ed., *Diary of Humphrey O'Sullivan* (Dublin, 1937), III, 5; Lewis, passim; Palmer, "Rebellion," 10, 17–19; Lee, "Ribbonmen," 32; Beames, "Rural," passim; R. Ó Foghludha, ed., *Pádraig Phiarais Cúndún* (Dublin, 1932), 95–96 (trans. BDB).

66. Clark, 70–73; Donnelly, "Rockite"; Lewis, 9, 58–61, 152–54, 196–97; Croker, 326–27; Lee, "Ribbonmen," 26–29; Ó Danachair, 37–39; Roberts, 64–101; Beames, *Peasants*, esp. chaps. 2–3; V. E. Powers, "Invisible Immigrants: Pre-Famine Irish Community in Worcester, Mass., 1826–60" (Ph.D. diss., Clark Univ., 1976), 198; Donnelly, *Land*, 18; Ó Foghludha, 95–96 (trans. BDB).

67. D. A. Chart, *Ireland from the Union to Catholic Emancipation* (London, 1910), 44–45; C. Maxwell, *Dublin*, 33, 230–33; D. N. Doyle, *Ireland, Irishmen and Revolutionary America, 1760–1820* (Cork, 1981), 176; A. Boyd, *Rise of the Irish Trade Unions, 1729–1970* (Tralee, 1972), 1–32; M. O'Connell, "Class Conflict in a Pre-Industrial Society: Dublin in 1780," *Duquesne R.*, 9, no. 1 (Fall 1963), passim; F. d'Arcy, "Artisans of Dublin and Daniel O'Connell, 1830–47," *IHS*, 17 (1970–71), 228–32, 237; McDowell, *Ireland*, 23–24; J. D. Clarkson, *Labour and Nationalism in Ireland* (NY, 1925), 65, 94–96.

68. Beames, "Peasant," 503; Lee, "Ribbonmen," 33; Powers, 88; Beames, "Rural," 77–78; Lewis, 128–44; O'Connell, 47–48; Doyle, 168; D. Bowen, *Protestant Crusade in Ireland, 1800–70* (Dublin, 1978), 12; McDowell, *Ireland*, 200–201; Boyd, 43–45; d'Arcy, 227–29, 236–37.

69. D. W. Miller, "Presbyterianism and 'Modernization' in Ulster," *P&P*, no. 80 (1978), 70–72; J. S. Donnelly, Jr., "Pastorini and Captain Rock: Millenarianism and Sectarianism in the Rockite Movement of 1821–4," in Clark and Donnelly, 103–39; d'Arcy, 222; P. Gibbon, *Origins of Ulster Unionism* (Manchester, 1975), 35; J. S. Donnelly, Jr., "Propagating the Cause of the United Irishmen," *Studies*, 69 (Spring 1980), 7–8 and passim.

70. Lewis, 55.

71. D. W. Miller, *Queen's Rebels: Historical Interpretation of Ulster Unionism* (Dublin, 1978), 53, 77–78; Palmer, "Rebellion," 7; Cullen, *Emergence*, 56–57, 110–11, 204–9, 252–53; D. W. Miller, "The Armagh Troubles, 1784–95," in Clark and Donnelly, 155–91.

72. Cullen, "Cultural," 95–100; D. W. Miller, *Queen's*, 53–56; see relevant chaps. of J. C. Beckett, *Making of Modern Ireland* (NY, 1966), and R. Kee, *The Green Flag* (NY, 1972).

73. W. B. Kennedy, "Irish Jacobins," *SH*, 16 (1976), 109–21; Cullen, "Cultural," 95–100; idem, *Emergence*, 210–33; T. J. Powell, "Background to the Wexford Rebellion," *IESH*, 2 (1975), 61–63; idem, "An Economic Factor in the Wexford Rebellion of 1798," *SH*, 16 (1976), 140–57; Beames, "Peasant," 504–6; idem, "Ribbon Societies: Lower-Class Nationalism in Pre-Famine Ireland," *P&P*, no. 97 (1982); T. Garvin, "Defenders, Ribbonmen and Others: Underground Political Networks in Pre-Famine Ireland," *P&P*, no. 96 (1982); Chart, 200–201; Broeker, 12–15; Lewis, 112.

74. Cullen, *Life*, 139; S. de Fréine, *The Great Silence* (Dublin, 1965), 125–29; B. Ó Cuív, *Irish Dialects and Irish-Speaking Districts* (Dublin, 1971), 19–22; Twiss, 41; Ó Muirithe, 7–87; Mason, II, 16; Otway, *Sketches*, 312–13; D. Dewar, *Observations on the Character . . . of the Irish* (London, 1812), 88.

75. Dewar, 34–35; D. H. Akenson, *The Irish Education Experiment* (Toronto, 1970), 376; Freeman, *Pre-Famine*, 133; Akenson, *Between*, 130; M. J. Murphy, *At Slieve Gullion's Foot* (Dundalk, 1976 ed.), 141–42.

76. A. and B. Rees, *Celtic Heritage: Ancient Tradition in Ireland and Wales* (London, 1961), 105–6; R. Flower, *Irish Tradition* (Oxford, 1947), 100–104; A. de Blácam, *Gaelic Literature Surveyed* (Dublin, 1929), 77–78; Fox, 31–33; Kohl, 29; Mason, II, 364–65; D. Corkery, *Fortunes of the Irish Language* (Dublin, 1954), 98–105; L. M. Cullen, "Hidden Ireland: Reassessment of a Concept," *SH*, 9 (1969), 31–34; F. O'Connor, *Short History of Irish Literature* (NY, 1968), 99, 111; E. Costello, *Traditional Folk Songs from Galway and Mayo* (London, 1919), 59, 90; Gibbon, 55; Gailey, 16.

77. D. Kennedy, "Education and the People," in R. B. McDowell, ed., *Social Life in Ireland* (Dublin, 1957), 65; Kohl, 38–39, 185–90; R. B. Walsh, "Later Gaelic Tradition: Language, Literature and Society" (Paper, Yeats Summer School, Sligo, 1972); A. Nicholson, *Ireland's Welcome to the Stranger* (London, 1847), 74–75; T. Campbell, *Philosophical Survey of the South of Ireland* (Dublin, 1777), 135–36; S. Ó Súilleabháinn, *Irish Folk Custom and Belief* (Dublin, 1967), 31, 82–91; Evans, *Personality*, 53; R. P. Jenkins, "Witches and Fairies: Supernatural Aggression and Deviance among the Irish Peasantry," *UF*, 23 (1976), 33–56; Otway, *Tour*, 142–43, 189; Mason, III, 206–8; E. Ronayne, *Ronayne's Recollections* . . . (Chicago, 1900), 25–26; S. Ó Súilleabháinn, *Irish Wake Amusements* (Cork, 1976); Evans, *Irish Folkways*, 290–91; Croker, 166–69, 176.

78. T. C. Croker, *Keen of the South of Ireland* (London, 1844), xxii–xxiii; D. W. Miller, "Presbyterianism," 70–72; idem, "Catholic Religious Practice in Pre-Famine Ireland," *JSH*, 8 (1975), 84–87; P. J. Corish, *Catholic Community in the 17th and 18th Centuries* (Dublin, 1981), 107–8; S. J. Connolly, *Priests and People in Pre-Famine Ireland, 1780–1845* (Dublin, 1982), passim; idem, "Religion and History," *IESH*, 10 (1983), 69–71; R. E. Burns, "Parsons, Priests, and People: Rise of Irish Anti-Clericalism, 1785–89," *CH*, 31 (1962), 159; E. Larkin, "Devotional Revolution in Ireland, 1850–75," *AHR*, 77 (June 1972), 635; idem, "Church and State in Ireland in the 19th Century," *CH*, 31 (1962), 300; Croker, *Researches*, 277–83; Plumptre, 356–57; C. Maxwell, *Stranger*, 197–98; Ó Súilleabháinn, *Irish Folk*, 38; La Tocnaye, 136, 141; Mason, II, 181–82; L. Kennedy, "Profane Images in the Irish Popular Consciousness," *ORLH*, 7, no. 2 (Autumn 1979); Otway, *Sketches*, 236–37, 253.

79. Mason, II, 146; Blácam, 350–51; Bell, 18; E. Willes, 1760 (T.2368, PRONI); H. Robinson, *Further Memories of Irish Life* (London, 1924), 157; Corkery, *Hidden*, 184–223; B. Kiely, *Poor Scholar: Study of . . . William Carleton* (Dublin, 1972 ed.), 13, 46; D. J. O'Donoghue, *Life of William Carleton* (London, 1896), I, 82; Otway, *Tour*, 122–23; Wakefield, II, 810; Roberts, 68, 70–71, 80.

80. McDowell, *Ireland*, 8; Mason, III, 160; R. Lynd, *Home Life in Ireland* (London, 1909), 90–91.

81. Doyle, 69, 168–75; D. W. Miller, "Presbyterianism," 66–67, 76–77; Larkin, "Church," 300; Wakefield, II, 625–28; Mason, I, 41, 584–97, and II, 369, 544; Otway, *Sketches*, 282–84; McDowell, *Ireland*, 194; R. Stivers, *Hair of the Dog: Irish Drinking and American Stereotype* (University Park, Penn., 1977), 38–44; H. F. Kearney, "Fr. Mathew: Apostle of Modernization," in A. Cosgrove and D. McCartney, eds., *Studies in Irish History* . . . (Dublin, 1979), passim; M. Wall, "Rise of a Catholic Middle Class in 18th-Century Ireland," *IHS*, 11 (Sept. 1958), 110–11; D. Rushe, *Edmund Rice: Man and His Times* (Dublin, 1981); G. Ó Tuathaigh, "Gaelic Ireland, Popular Politics and Daniel O'Connell," *JGAHS*, 74 (1974–75), 23–24.

82. Mason, I, 5, 124, 184–85, 330, and II, 16, 404, and III, 28, 625; Wakefield, II, 775; S. Ní Chinnéide, "New View of 18th-Century Life in Kerry," *JKHS*, 6 (1973), 98; E. Malcolm, "Popular Recreation in 19th-Century Ireland," in O. MacDonagh et al., eds., *Irish Culture and Nationalism, 1750–1950* (NY, 1983), 47.

83. Cullen, *Emergence*, 23–24; C. Maxwell, *Country*, 169–70; Ó Tuathaigh, *Ireland*, 99–100; F. S. L. Lyons, *Ireland since the Famine* (London, 1971), 70–72; Mason, I, 157–58, 208–9, 597–99, and III, 625; McDowell, *Ireland*, 93; O'Donoghue, 95–96, 171; Croker, *Researches*, 326; H. O'Daly, *Life History* (Fr. P. Daly, Monaghan); M. McDermott, *Memoirs* (#2-15-100, LC).

84. Hutton, I, 259; S. Ní Chinnéide, "New View of Cork City in 1790," *JCHAS*, 78 (Jan.–June 1973), 3; Gibbon, 22–42; Mason, III, 106–9, 322–23; Kohl, 13; Nicholson, 139.

85. Fréine, 125–29, 139–41, 154–64; T. N. Brown, "Nationalism and the Irish Peasant, 1800–1848," *RPOL*, 15 (1953), 403–4; D. W. Miller, "Presbyterianism," 68–69; idem,

Queen's, 58–59; Mason, I, 624, and II, 97; O'Donoghue, 7–8; W. R. LeFanu, *Seventy Years of Irish Life* (London, 1914 ed.), 300; G. B. Adams, "Emergence of Ulster as a Distinct Dialect Area," *UF,* 4 (1958), 69; M. Wall, "Decline of the Irish Language," in B. Ó Cuív, ed., *View of the Irish Language* (Dublin, 1969), 81–87.

86. R. P. Breatnach, in C. Ó Síocháin, *Man from Cape Clear* (Cork, 1975), vii; O'Donoghue, passim; Kiely, 12–15; Reid, 228, 248; Mason, I, 95, 584–97, and II, 103–8; D. Hyde, *Literary History of Ireland* (Dublin, 1903), 633; Inglis, I, 41–42, 61–62, and II, 110; J. R. Barrett, "Why Paddy Drank: Social Importance of Whiskey in Pre-Famine Ireland," *JPCUL,* 11 (1977), 155–66; B. W. Noel, *Notes of a Short Tour through the Midland Counties of Ireland in . . . 1836* (London, 1837), 9, 13.

87. Beckett, *Making,* 213–14, 230, 248–49.

88. C. Maxwell, *Stranger,* 197–98, 294, 309; J. Brady and P. J. Corish, "Church under the Penal Code," in Corish, ed., *History of Irish Catholicism,* vol. 4, pt. 2 (Dublin, 1971), 10–30; Corish, *Catholic,* 77; Connolly, "Religion," 69–70; P. Carey, "Voluntaryism: An Irish Catholic Tradition," *CH,* 48 (Mar. 1979), 50; U. J. Bourke, 28–29.

89. Brady and Corish, 62–67, 72–73, 80–83; Larkin, "Church," 301–2; idem, "Economic," 856.

90. Tocqueville, 174; Inglis, I, 337–40; J. A. Murphy, "Support of the Catholic Clergy in Ireland, 1750–1850," *HS,* 5 (1965), 109, 114; Larkin, "Devotional," 627, 630–34; Brady and Corish, 66; Ellis, 61–62; D. A. Kerr, *Peel, Priests and Politics: Sir Robert Peel's Administration and the Roman Catholic Church in Ireland, 1841–46* (Oxford, 1982), 1–67; E. Toner, 7 June 1818 (Ms. 2300, NLI).

91. Burns, 153–60; Murphy, 111, 116–17; Corish, *Catholic,* 122, 128–29; Beames, *Peasants,* 190–93; G. Stockman, *Irish of Achill, Co. Mayo* (Belfast, 1974), 97; Donnelly, "Rightboy," 163–75; Larkin, "Church," 298; Doyle, 173–74; P. O'Farrell, "Millennialism, Messianism and Utopianism in Irish History," *A-IS,* 2 (1976), 47.

92. Corish, *Catholic,* 119–29; Beames, *Peasants,* 190–97; Burns, 153; Doyle, 14, 169–75; O. MacDonagh, "Politicization of the Irish Catholic Bishops," *HJ,* 18, no. 1 (1975), 38; MacDowell, *Ireland,* 195–97; Bowen, 3–9.

93. Tocqueville, 141; MacDonagh, 38–41; Larkin, "Devotional," 626–27, 631; Inglis, I, 125–26; Burns, 161–62; Mason, I, 9, 420, and II, 181–82, 312, 367–69; McDowell, *Ireland,* 195–98; Connolly, "Illegitimacy," 75–76; Ó Foghludha, 87 (trans. BDB); Bowen, 146, 148–56.

94. Clark, 87–88; O'Connor, 128–29; J. C. Molony, *Riddle of the Irish* (London, 1927 ed.), 3.

95. See relevant chaps. in Beckett, *Making;* Kee; McDowell, *Ireland,* E. Strauss, *Irish Nationalism and British Democracy* (1951; Westport, Conn., 1975 ed.); and D. G. Boyce, *Nationalism in Ireland* (Baltimore, 1982).

96. Ibid.

97. Ibid.; S. Cronin, *Development of Irish Nationalist Ideology* (Dublin, 1980), 49; M. Elliott, *Partners in Revolution: United Irishmen and France* (New Haven, 1982).

98. See works cited in n. 95 above. D. W. Miller, *Queen's,* 43–86; H. Senior, *Orangeism in Ireland and Britain, 1795–1836* (London, 1966); I. d'Alton, "Contrast in Crises: Southern Irish Protestantism, 1820–43 and 1885–1910," in A. C. Hepburn, ed., *Minorities in History* (London, 1978), 72–76; Bowen, 67–80; I. Hehir, "The Bible in Ireland, 1800–25" (Paper, ACIS conference, Pittsburgh, 1981); D. N. Hempton, "Methodist Crusade in Ireland, 1795–1845," *IHS,* 22 (Mar. 1980), 33–48; D. W. Miller, "Presbyterianism," 75–90; Clark and Donnolly, 147–51; J. Hill, "Protestant Response to Repeal: Case of the Dublin Working Classes," in F. S. L. Lyons and R. A. J. Hawkins, eds., *Ireland under the Union: Essays in Honour of T. W. Moody* (Oxford, 1980), 35–68.

99. Wall, "Rise," 112–13; Strauss, 90; Beckett, *Making,* 274–76.

100. Clark, 87–100; F. O'Ferrall, "Growth of Political Consciousness in Ireland, 1824–1848," *IESH,* 6 (1979), 70; J. A. Reynolds, *Catholic Emancipation Crisis in Ireland, 1823–29* (New Haven, 1954), 8, 65; Wall, "Catholics," 49; Strauss, 97–100; K. T. Hoppen, "Politics, the Law, and the Nature of the Irish Electorate, 1832–50," *EHR,* 92 (Oct. 1977), 774–75.

101. Tocqueville, 158–59; Nolan, 121, 131–42; Maguire, 130–33; Clark, 32–33, 91–94; R. B. McDowell, *Public Opinion and Government Policy in Ireland, 1801–46* (London, 1952), 126.

102. Reynolds, 51–53; MacDonagh, passim; Kerr, 68–110; Connolly, *Priests,* passim.

103. Clark, 90–100.

104. Walsh, 29–30; Corkery, *Hidden*, 24, 35; P. Sayers, *Peig: Autobiography of Peig Sayers of the Great Blasket Island* (Syracuse, 1974), 112; Fox, 85; P. B. Snyder, "Milk of the Mountain: Meaning of Place in the West Coast of Ireland" (Ph.D. diss., Cornell Univ., 1975), passim; Blácam, 171–72; M. O'Sullivan, *Twenty Years A-Growing* (NY, 1933), passim; Ó Síocháin, 60–89; T. Cashman, Memoirs (P. Clancy, Youghal, Co. Cork).

105. Cullen, "Hidden," 24–25; S. O'Faolain, *King of the Beggars: Life of Daniel O'Connell* (1938; Dublin, 1970 ed.), 33–35; Corkery, *Hidden*, 32; R. L. Wright, ed., *Irish Emigrant Ballads and Songs* (Bowling Green, Ohio, 1975), 70–71; Croker, *Keen*, xx, xliii, 103; Otway, *Tour*, 308–9; McGrath, I, 199.

106. O'Farrell, 58; P. O'Farrell, *England and Ireland since 1800* (London, 1975), 2–4; Corkery, *Hidden*, 145; J. O'Donovan Rossa, *Rossa's Recollections, 1858–98* (Mariner's Harbor, NY, 1898), 81–83; Kohl, 29; Otway, *Sketches*, 21–22; Kee, 14; N. Mansergh, *The Irish Question, 1840–1921* (London, 1965 ed.), 27–28; Inglis, I, 344–45.

107. M. Doheny, *The Felon's Track* (Dublin, 1851), 250; McGrath, passim; B. Ó Cuív, "Irish Language in the Early Modern Period," in T. W. Moody et al., *NHI III: Early Modern Ireland, 1534–1691* (Oxford, 1976), 542; Blácam, 298–99, 319; Mason, III, 625–26; Dewar, 34–35, 89–90; C. Maxwell, *Stranger*, 212, 309; idem, *Country*, 172; Rossa, 75–77.

108. J. White, *Minority Report: Protestant Community in the Irish Republic* (Dublin, 1975), 32; Ó Tuathaigh, "Gaelic," 27–30; Sayers, 46; Dewar, 99–100; Lynd, 3; P. O'Farrell, *Ireland's English Question: Anglo-Irish Relations, 1534–1970* (NY, 1971), 10; Bowen, 138; Ó Síocháin, 16; Doyle, 6–7; Ronayne, 27–28; Maxwell, *Country*, 288.

109. Inglis, II, 18–19; Otway, *Sketches*, 70–71; Palmer, "Rebellion," 5; W. S. Trench, *Realities of Irish Life* (1868; London, 1966 ed.), 119.

110. Donnelly, "Pastorini," 103–39; W. B. Kennedy, 18–19; O'Donoghue, 52–53; Donnelly, "Propagating," 15–19; Bowen, 63–64; G.-D. Zimmermann, *Songs of Irish Rebellion* (Dublin, 1967), 19–30, 76–80; G. Ó Dúghaill, "Ballads and the Law, 1830–32," *UF*, 19 (1973), passim; M. Murphy, "Ballad Singer and the Role of the Seditious Ballad in 19th-Century Ireland: Dublin Castle's View," *UF*, 25 (1979), 84, 89–91; Kohl, 132; Mason, III, 236–37.

111. *Cork Constitution*, 7 May 1825 (clipping in CO 384/13, PRO); Brown, 423–26; Corkery, *Hidden*, 130; McGrath, IV, 143; Croker, *Researches*, 328–29; T. MacMahon, 8 June 1826 (CO 384/14, PRO); La Tocnaye, 106; Inglis, I, 286; Ó Síocháin, 110.

112. Reynolds, 136–60, 171n; D. Hyde, *Songs Ascribed to Raftery* . . . (Shannon, 1973 ed.), 281.

113. Clark, 88–100; Reynolds, 28–29, 58–59, 101–9 and passim; O. MacDonagh, "Contribution of O'Connell," in B. Farrell, ed., *Irish Parliamentary Tradition* (Dublin, 1973), 164–65; Palmer, "Rebellion," 11; Strauss, 92–93; Inglis, I, 158–59; Venedey, 164–66.

114. Palmer, "Rebellion," 13; Kohl, 148–49; Tocqueville, 164–65; Otway, *Tour*, 74; Balch, 214; d'Arcy, 239–42; E. Malcolm, "Temperance and Irish Nationalism," in Lyons and Hawkins, 75–82; Bowen, 19.

115. See relevant chaps. of Beckett, *Making*; Kee; Ó Tuathaigh, *Ireland*; Strauss; and Boyce. O'Farrell, *Ireland's*, 88–89; D. O. Madden, *Ireland and Its Rulers* (London, 1843), 4–7; Kohl, 109; MacDonagh, "Politicization," 51–53; Reynolds, 51–54; K. B. Nowlan, "Catholic Clergy and Irish Politics in the 1830s and '40s," *HS*, 9 (1974), 132; Inglis, I, 102; J. H. Whyte, "Influence of the Catholic Clergy on Elections in 19th-Century Ireland," *EHR*, 75 (1960), passim; D. Fitzpatrick, "Geography of Irish Nationalism," *P&P*, no. 78 (Feb. 1978), 134.

116. Whyte, "Landlord," 752–53; Ó Tuathaigh, "Gaelic," 34; Blácam, 340–41; Clark, 79–80; Tocqueville, 165; Forbes, II, 53; M. Murphy, "Repeal, Popular Politics, and the Catholic Clergy of Cork, 1840–50," *JCHAS*, 82 (Jan.–Dec. 1977), 57–62; Beames, *Peasants*, 186–97; Connolly, *Priests*, passim.

Chapter 3. Continuity: The Culture of Exile

1. J. Mokyr, "Malthusian Models and Irish History," *JECONH*, 40 (May 1980), 159–60; R. D. C. Black, *Economic Thought and the Irish Question* (London, 1960), 88, 210–11, and passim.

2. *Third Report of the Select Committee on Emigration from the United Kingdom, 1827,* in *IUP-BPP, Emigration,* vol. 2 (Shannon, 1968), 277. See below, Chapters 4–8.

3. D. Corkery, *Hidden Ireland* . . . (Dublin, 1967 ed.), 119; R. Flower, *Irish Tradition* (Oxford, 1947), 167–68; B. Ó Cuív, "Irish Language in the Early Modern Period," in T. W.

Moody et al., *NHI III: Early Modern Ireland, 1534–1691* (Oxford, 1976), 526; A. de Blácam, *Gaelic Literature Surveyed* (Dublin, 1929), 139–40, 158, 276; P. Colum, ed., *Anthology of Irish Verse* (NY, 1972), 192; G. Murphy, ed., "Poems of Exile by Uilliam MacBaruin Dealbhna," *Éigse*, 6 (1948), 11–15; B. Bradshaw, *Irish Constitutional Revolution of the 16th Century* (Cambridge, 1979), 285–87.

4. C. Cruise O'Brien, *States of Ireland* (NY, 1972), 309; T. F. O'Rahilly, ed., *Measgra Dánta* (Cork, 1927), II, 146 (trans. BDB); T. C. Croker, *Keen of the South of Ireland* (London, 1844), 4, 8; D. Dewar, *Observations on the Character . . . of the Irish* (London, 1812), 339.

5. G.-D. Zimmermann, *Songs of Irish Rebellion* (Dublin, 1967), 33–34; R. L. Wright, ed., *Irish Emigrant Ballads and Songs* (Bowling Green, Ohio, 1975), 205–38; J. O'Donovan Rossa, *Rossa's Recollections . . .* (Mariner's Harbor, NY, 1898), 6; W. V. Shannon, *American Irish* (NY, 1963), 133; J. Savage, *Fenian Heroes and Martyrs* (Boston, 1868), 283–84; T. N. Burke, *Lectures on Faith and Fatherland* (London, n.d.), 118–19; J. Cardinal Gibbons, "Irish Immigration to the United States," *IECCR*, 4th ser., 1 (1897), 109; S. de Fréine, *Great Silence* (Dublin, 1965), 25; C. O. Sauer, *Northern Mists* (Berkeley, 1968), 163–65; O'Rahilly, I, 126–28 (trans. BDB).

6. K. A. Miller, with B. D. Boling and D. N. Doyle, "Emigrants and Exiles: Irish Cultures and Irish Emigration to North America," *IHS*, 22 (Sept. 1980), 97–125; B. L. Whorf, *Language, Thought, and Reality* (Cambridge, Mass., 1956). Critiques of Whorf's hypotheses include D. Hymes, ed., *Language and Culture in Society* (NY, 1964), 115–63; H. Hoijer, ed., *Language in Culture* (Chicago, 1954); and P. Henle, ed., *Language, Thought, and Culture* (Ann Arbor, 1958).

The neutral Irish equivalent of "emigrant," *eisimirceach,* is a recent coinage. For the older terms, see M. E. Byrne and M. Joynt, *Contributions to a Dictionary of the Irish Language, Degra-Dodelbtha* (Dublin, 1959), 27–28, 69–70; and P. de Brún et al., *Nua-Dhuanaire 1* (Dublin, 1971), 31. It is notable that even the Irish terms for "journeying," *aistrech* and *aistriugad,* also carried the connotations of "restless" and "unsteady"; see the later volume of *Contributions,* vol. A, fasc. 1, by A. O'Sullivan and E. Quinn (Dublin, 1964), 250. For these and other insights and references, I am grateful to Drs. Bruce D. Boling, Brown Univ., and David N. Doyle, UCD.

7. A. MacDougall, 30 Mar. 1830 (CO 384/28, PRO); T. C. Croker, *Researches in the South of Ireland* (1824; Shannon, 1968 ed.), 14. Key Irish texts include C. O'Rahilly, ed., *Five 17th-Century Political Poems* (Dublin, 1952); J. C. MacErlean, ed., *Duanaire Dháibhidh Uí Bruadair,* vols. 1–3 (London, 1910–17); and P. Ó Duinnín, ed., *Eoghan Rua Ó Súilleabháin* (Dublin, 1923). Corkery, 24; P. Sayers, *Peig . . .* (Syracuse, 1974), 26. Examples of early-19th-century poetry include D. Hyde, *Poems Ascribed to Raftery* (Dublin, 1903), 285–321; N. Williams, *Riocard Bairéad: Amhráin* (Dublin, 1978); T. Ó Fiaich, ed., *Art MacCumhaigh: Dánta* (Dublin, 1973); and B. Ó Buachalla, ed., *Peadar Ó Doirnín: Amhráin* (Dublin, 1969). M. McGrath, ed., *Diary of Humphrey O'Sullivan* (Dublin, 1937), I, 119, and IV, 143; N. R. Burke, "Some Observations on the Migration of Laborers from the South of Ireland to Newfoundland . . . ," *JCHAS,* 76 (July–Dec. 1971), 95.

8. R. Ó Foghludha, ed., *Donnchadh Ruadh Mac Conmara, 1715–1810* (Dublin, 1933), 31–32; P. Ó Conaire, *Deoraidheacht* (Dublin, 1910); E. Costello, *Traditional Folk Songs from Galway and Mayo* (London, 1919), 148–49; S. Clandillon and M. Hannigan, eds., *Songs of the Irish Gaels* (London, 1927), 9–10, 15–16; Wright, 107–428; Zimmermann, 76–77.

9. L. M. Cullen, *Life in Ireland* (London, 1968), 27; L. P. Curtis, Jr., *Anglo-Saxons and Celts: A Study of Anti-Irish Prejudices in Victorian England* (Bridgeport, Conn., 1968), 53; idem, *Apes and Angels: Irishman in Victorian Caricature* (Newton Abbot, 1971), passim; D. T. Knobel, "Paddy and the Republic: Popular Images of the American Irish, 1820–60" (Ph.D. diss., Northwestern Univ., 1976); A. Nevins and M. H. Thomas, eds., *Diary of George Templeton Strong* (NY. 1962), I, 348; O. S. Brownson, undated Ms. (#I-3-d, Brownson Mss., UNDA).

For admissions of emigrant inadequacies by Irish-American politicians and clerics, see T. D'A. McGee, *History of the Irish Settlers in North America* (Boston, 1855), 194–235; Rev. S. Byrne, *Irish Emigration to the United States* (NY, 1873), 12, 27, 35, 41, 52; and Rev. J. O'Hanlon, *Irish Emigrant's Guide to the United States* (1851; NY, 1976 ed.), 217–35.

10. Miller, with Boling and Doyle. passim.

11. *Second Report of the Commissioners Appointed to Consider and Recommend a Gen-*

eral System of Railways for Ireland, GBPP-HC (145), 1837–38, XXXV, 83; E. Wakefield, *Account of Ireland* . . . (London, 1812), I, 262–63, and II, 735; A. W. Hutton, ed., *Arthur Young's Tour in Ireland* (London, 1892), I, 213, and II, 146–47; H. D. Inglis, *Tour throughout Ireland in* . . . *1834* (London, 1835), I, 109, 156.

12. C. Otway, *Tour in Connaught* (Dublin, 1839), 352; Wakefield, I, 517, and II, 755, 767, 778, 786–87; *Third Report* . . . *on Emigration* . . . *1827*, 409; M. Edgeworth, *Castle Rackrent* (1800; NY, 1965 ed.), 80; D. Thomson and M. McGusty, eds., *Irish Journals of Elizabeth Smith, 1840–50* (NY, 1980), 8.

13. J. B. Trotter, *Walks through Ireland in* . . . *1812, 1814, and 1817* (London, 1819), 17–18; T. C. Foster, *Letters on the Condition of the People of Ireland* (London, 1847), 292; W. S. Mason, *Statistical Account* . . . *of Ireland* (Dublin, 1814–19), II, 118; Wakefield, I, 698, and II, 262–63, 764; Croker, *Researches*, 103; D. W. Miller, *Queen's Rebels* . . . , (NY, 1978), 52; A. Atkinson, *Ireland Exhibited to England* . . . (London, 1823), I, 159; J. Whitelaw, *Essay on the Population of Dublin* . . . *1798* (Dublin, 1805), 54–55; W. M. Thackeray, *Paris Sketch Book; Irish Sketch Book* . . . (London, 1889 ed.), 369.

14. A. Nicholson, *Ireland's Welcome to the Stranger* (London, 1847), 441 and passim; Le Chevalier de La Tocnaye, *Frenchman's Walk through Ireland, 1796–97* (Belfast, 1917 ed.), 157; J. G. Kohl, *Ireland* . . . (London, 1844), 144, 180; S. Ní Chinnéide, "Frenchman's Impressions of Co. Cork in 1790, Part 2," *JCHAS*, 79 (1974), 24; G. de Beaumont, *Ireland* . . . (London, 1839), II, 19–25; B. Kiely, *Poor Scholar* . . . (Dublin, 1972 ed.), 110–12; Fr. P. Devine, Journal of a Voyage to America, 1870 (STPCR); A. de Tocqueville, *Journeys to England and Ireland* (London, 1963), 141; McGrath, III, 155–57; Fr. W. Purcell, 10 Dec. 1848 (#II-4-k, Bishop Purcell Mss., UNDA).

15. A. Nicholson, *Lights and Shades of Ireland* (London, 1850), 3; C. Otway, *Sketches in Ireland* (Dublin, 1839), 200, 292; R. Flower, *Western Island, or The Great Blasket* (NY, 1945), 58, 134; E. Kane, *Last Place God Made* . . . (New Haven, 1977), III, 227; E. Cross, *Tailor and Ansty* (Cork, 1970 ed.), 90; T. Ó Crohan, *Islandman* (London, 1934), 261–62; J. O'Donoghue, *In Kerry Long Ago* (NY, 1960), 106; idem, *In a Quiet Land* (London, 1957), 107; Sayers, 110, 211; M. MacGowan, *Hard Road to Klondike* (London, 1962), 134–35, 150.

16. K. A. Miller, with Boling and Doyle, passim; Wakefield, II, 735–36.

17. L. Dumont, *Homo Hierarchus: Caste System and Its Implications* (London, 1972), 42.

18. D. H. Akenson, *Between Two Revolutions* . . . *Islandmagee* . . . (Hamden, Conn., 1979), 88–137; A. Gailey, "Scots Element in North Irish Popular Culture," *Ethnologia Europaea*, 8, no. 1 (1975), 15; Hutton, I, 127, 132.

19. J. Venedey, *Ireland and the Irish during the Repeal Year* . . . (Dublin, 1844), 336–40; C. Ó Gráda, "Supply Responsiveness in Irish Agriculture during the 19th Century," *ECONHR*, 28 (1975), 313–15; Mason, II, 82; Wakefield, II, 754; Otway, *Sketches*, 239; *Second Report* . . . *Commissioners* . . . *of Railways*, 83; J. E. Bicheno, *Ireland and Its Economy* (London, 1830), 21; La Tocnaye, 127–28.

20. Beaumont, II, 21–22; Dewar, 19–22; Tocqueville, 141; W. E. H. Lecky, *History of Ireland in the 18th Century*, abr. and ed. L. P. Curtis, Jr. (Chicago, 1972), 43; J. Martyn, 1825, and T. MacMahon, 1825 (CO 384/11, PRO).

21. L. M. Cullen, *Emergence of Modern Ireland* . . . (Dublin, 1983), 128; idem, "Merchant Communities Overseas . . . ," in Cullen and T. C. Smout, eds., *Comparative Aspects of Scottish and Irish* . . . *History* (Edinburgh, 1976), 165–76; Inglis, I, 10–13; Thackeray, 324; Hutton, II, 22; Wakefield, II, 780; J. Forbes, *Memorandums Made in Ireland in* . . . *1852* (London, 1853), I, 156, and II, 102–3.

22. L. M. Cullen and T. C. Smout, "Economic Growth in Scotland and Ireland," in Cullen and Smout, 9; H. Coulter, *West of Ireland* . . . (London, 1862), 83–89, 184; B. Becker, *Disturbed Ireland* (London, 1882), 50, 81–117; A. I. Shand, *Letters from the West of Ireland* (London, 1885), 166–67; *CDB Inspectors' Confidential Reports* (1891–95), 106–7 and passim (TCD); H. Robinson, *Further Memories of Irish Life* (London, 1924), 25 and passim; A. Ussher, *Face and Mind of Ireland* (London, 1949), 77–78; D. MacAmhlaigh, *Irish Navvy: Diary of an Exile* (London, 1966 ed.), 39–42; and the recent essays by T. M. Devine, R. H. Campbell, and S. J. Connolly in Devine and D. Dickson, eds., *Ireland and Scotland, 1600–1850* . . . (Edinburgh, 1983), 12–29, 220–34, 335–46.

23. See Chapter 1; R. H. Buchanan, "Field Systems of Ireland," in A. R. H. Baker and R. A. Butlin, eds., *Studies of Field Systems* . . . (London, 1973), 587; F. H. A. Aalen,

Man and the Landscape in Ireland (London, 1978), 250; Cullen, *Emergence,* 126–27, 250–51; B. Hutchinson, "On the Study of Non-economic Factors in Irish Economic Development," *ESS,* 1 (Apr. 1970), 509–20.

24. For the family as reflected in *brehon* law and early Irish poetry, I have relied on information provided by Dr. B. D. Boling, Brown University. For 19th-century attitudes and practices, see Otway, *Tour,* 122–23; and E. Estyn Evans, *Irish Folk Ways* (London, 1957), 294. Recent studies of the family in Ireland and/or Irish-America include C. Arensberg and S. T. Kimball, *Family and Community in Ireland* (Cambridge, Mass., 1968 ed.); A. J. Humphries, "Family in Ireland," in M. F. Nimkoff, ed., *Comparative Family Systems* (Boston, 1965), 232–58; R. E. Kennedy, Jr., *The Irish: Emigration, Marriage, and Fertility* (Berkeley, 1975); E. Leyton, *The One Blood* . . . (St. Johns, 1975); E. Kane, "Man and Kin in Donegal: Study of Kinship Functions in a Rural Irish and Irish-American Community," *Ethnology,* 7 (July 1968), 245–58; R. Fox, *Tory Islanders* (Cambridge, 1978); D. Hannan and L. Katsiaouni, *Traditional Families* . . . (Dublin, 1977); D. Hannan, *Displacement and Development* . . . (Dublin, 1979); P. Gibbon and C. Curtin, "Stem Family in Ireland," *CSSH,* 20 (1978), 429–53; N. Scheper-Hughes, *Saints, Scholars, and Schizophrenics* . . . (Berkeley, 1979); D. Fitzpatrick, "Irish Farming Families before the First World War," *CSSH,* 25 (1983), 339–74; and H. R. Diner, *Erin's Daughters in America* (Baltimore, 1983). Unpublished Ph.D. dissertations include K. O'Neill, "Family and Farm in Pre-Famine Cavan" (Brown Univ., 1979); J. C. Russell, "In the Shadows of Saints: . . . Family and Religion in a Rural Irish Gaeltacht" (Univ. of California, San Diego, 1979); M. E. Connors, "Their Own Kind: Family and Community in Albany, 1850–1915" (Harvard Univ., 1975); M. C. Mattis, "Irish Family in Buffalo, NY, 1855–75" (Washington Univ., 1975); and A. G. Mitchell, "Irish Family Patterns in 19th-Century Ireland and Lowell, Massachusetts" (Boston Univ., 1976).

For familial and feminine characterizations of Irish social units, see G. Mac Niocaill, *Ireland before the Vikings* (Dublin, 1972), 34; McGrath, III, 155–57; J. M. Synge, *Aran Islands and Other Writings* (NY, 1962), 104–5; A. T. Q. Stewart, *Narrow Ground* . . . (London, 1977), 117; "Proclamation of the Irish Republic," in V. Mercier and D. H. Greene, eds., *1000 Years of Irish Prose* (NY, 1961), 245–46.

25. B. D. Boling, "Irish Language and Behavior" (KFLC, Lexington, 1978); A. and B. Rees, *Celtic Heritage* . . . (London, 1961), 105–6; F. J. Byrne, "Senchas: Nature of Gaelic Historical Tradition," *HS,* 9 (1974), 140–41; Flower, *Irish,* 95–96, 147, 152; É. Ua Muirgheasa, ed., *Seanfhocla Uladh* (Dublin, 1907), 58, 68, 78 (trans. BDB).

26. Humphries, 249–50; B. F. Biever, *Religion, Culture, and Values: Native Irish and American Catholicism* (NY, 1976), 491, 383–93, 673–88; W. Herberg, *Protestant, Catholic, Jew* (Garden City, NY, 1960), 149.

27. D. N. Doyle, *Irish-Americans, Native Rights, and National Empires* (NY, 1976), 55, 187–99; Burke, 108–9, 113, 117; Rev. M. O'Riordan, *Catholicity and Progress in Ireland* (London, 1906), 56–58, 61, 124, 135–98, 215; U. J. Bourke, ed., *Sermons . . . by the Most Rev. James O'Gallagher* . . . (Dublin, 1877), 249; P. Ó Healaí, "Moral Values in Irish Religious Tales," *Béaloideas,* 42/43 (1973–74), 176–212; T. P. O'Neill, "Catholic Church and the Relief of the Poor," *ANLHB,* no. 31 (1973), 132–45; M. J. F. McCarthy, *Irish Land and Irish Liberty* (London, 1911), 356; Hutchinson, 509–29, balanced by J. Mokyr, *Why Ireland Starved* . . . (London, 1983), 197–228.

For Irish-American clerical assessments of Catholic-Protestant achievement differentials, see Fr. J. Hand, "Prosperity of Ulster Compared with the Rest of Ireland," *Donohoe's Magazine* (Boston), 48 (1902), 453–56; and T. Shanahan, "Catholicism and Civilization," *Catholic University Bulletin,* 4 (1898), 467–80, which anticipates the conclusions of K. Samuelsson, *Religion and Economic Action* (NY, 1961 ed.).

28. P. O'Farrell, "Millennialism, Messianism, and Utopianism in Irish History," *A-IS,* 2 (1976), 54; Bourke, 28–29, 275–77, 345, 373–87; Biever, 496–97, 515; Humphries, 246–50; T. S. MacCionaith, ed., *An Paidirín Páirteach agus Urnaighte eile in gCanamhain Bhreifne* (Cavan, 1921), 8 (trans. courtesy of Dr. David N. Doyle, UCD).

29. D. W. Miller, "Catholic Religious Practice in Pre-Famine Ireland," *JSH,* 8 (1975), 81–98; Sayers, 35, 137.

30. J. White, *Minority Report* . . . (Dublin, 1975), 62; T. Reid, *Travels in Ireland in . . . 1822* (London, 1823), 189; A. de Tocqueville, *Democracy in America* (NY, 1969 ed.), 46–47, 288, 293, 528–30; A. Quin, 22 Sept. 1873 (D.1819/4, PRONI; emphasis added); P. E. Johnson, *Shopkeeper's Millennium* (NY, 1978); W. R. Cross, *Burned-Over District* (Ithaca, 1950); J. T. Ellis, ed., *Catholic Priest in the United States* (Collegeville, Minn.,

1971), 307; O. Handlin, *Boston's Immigrants* (NY, 1972 ed.), 125–35; Burke, 128–29; O'Riordan, 64.

Recent studies of Catholic-Protestant differences in Ireland, the U.S., and elsewhere include R. Rose, *Governing without Consensus* (Boston, 1971); G. Lenski, *The Religious Factor* (NY, 1961); G. Golde, *Catholics and Protestants* (NY, 1975); and S. N. Eisenstadt, ed., *Protestant Ethic and Modernization* (NY, 1968). On Irish Protestants, see White, and D. W. Miller, "Presbyterians and Modernization in Ulster," *P&P*, no. 80 (1978), 66–90. Anguished spiritual self-examinations are common in Irish Protestant emigrants' letters and memoirs, rare among Irish Catholics'.

31. See linguistic studies cited in n. 6 above. Boling; C. Levi-Strauss, "Introduction . . . ," in M. Mauss, *Sociologie et anthropologie* (Paris, 1966); C. Geertz, "Ritual and Social Change," in his *Interpretations of Cultures* (NY, 1973), 144–45.

32. Miller, with Boling and Doyle.

33. Ibid.; Boling.

34. Ibid.

35. Ibid.; see E. Sapir, "Psychological Reality of Phonomes," in D. G. Mendelbaum, ed., *Selected Writings of Edward Sapir . . .* (Berkeley, 1963), 46–60.

36. Zimmermann, 11; Robinson, 25; Coulter, 83; H. Plunkett, *Ireland in the New Century* (London, 1904), viii. See anthropological studies cited in n. 24 above; see also Kane, *Last Place*, I, 132–34, 232–34, and III, 657, 663–65, 682, 693–700; as well as T. Young, "Dingle Commercial Fishermen: Analysis of the Economic Action of an Irish Fishing Fleet" (Ph.D. diss., Univ. of Pittsburgh, 1975); and J. Halpern, "Working in the Factory: Resistance to Industrialization in Rural Ireland" (Ph.D. diss., Univ. of Pittsburgh, 1978). Interview with D. Wholley (Berkeley, 1977).

37. J. Lee, *Modernisation of Irish Society, 1848–1918* (Dublin, 1973), preface; B. Almquist, "Irish Folklore Commission," *Béaloideas*, 45–47 (1977–79), 6–26; P. L. Henry, "Anglo-Irish and Its Background," in D. Ó Muirithe, ed., *English Language in Ireland* (Cork, 1977); P. L. Henry, *Anglo-Irish Dialect of North Roscommon* (Dublin, n.d.), 148; Boling; S. Brooks, *Aspects of the Irish Question* (Dublin, 1912), 73–74; R. J. McHugh, "Famine in Irish Oral Tradition," in R. D. Edwards and T. D. Williams, eds., *The Great Famine* (NY, 1957), 407–13. For Irish economic conditions, 18th to early 20th century, see Chapters 2 and 4–8 of this work; on the Irish economy since 1920, see the appropriate chaps. of L. M. Cullen, *Economic History of Ireland . . .* (London, 1972); F. Litton, *Unequal Achievement* (Dublin, 1982); and M. Peillon, *Contemporary Irish Society* (Dublin, 1982). Recent economic trends indicate at least a partial return to older patterns of diminished opportunities, coupled with increased social inequalities and, perhaps, emigration.

38. C. Levi-Strauss, *Structural Anthropology* (NY, 1963), 241.

39. A. M. Sullivan, *New Ireland* (Dublin, 1877); on family structure, see works cited in n. 24 above; on 19th-century Irish Catholicism, see in Chapter 2, n. 78, the cited works by Larkin, D. W. Miller, Connolly, etc., plus E. Hynes, "Great Hunger and Irish Catholicism," *Societas*, 8 (1978), 135–56. On bourgeois aspects of Irish nationalism, see E. Strauss, *Irish Nationalism and British Democracy* (London, 1951); S. Clark, *Social Origins of the Land War* (Princeton, 1979); T. Garvin, *Evolution of Irish Nationalist Politics* (Dublin, 1981); and, contemporaneously, Brooks, 43–45, 120–21—in analytical terms replicated in the fiction of Brinsley MacNamara, e.g., *Valley of the Squinting Windows* (Dublin, 1918).

40. See Chapter 2 this work, and n. 24 above.

41. E. Larkin, "Devotional Revolution in Ireland, 1850–75," *AHR*, 77 (June 1972), 625–52; K. H. Connell, *Irish Peasant Society* (Oxford, 1968), 137–45; see Chapter 2 this work; Tocqueville, *Journeys*, 130, 140, and passim; Venedey, 164–66; S. O'Faolain, *King of the Beggars . . .* (1938; Dublin, 1970 ed.), 226–31; Fr. P. O'Leary, *My Story* (1915; Cork, 1970 ed.), 114–15; C. Ó Siocháin, *Man from Cape Clear* (Cork, 1975), 110–12; J. O'Shea, *Priests, Politics and Society in Post-Famine Ireland* (Dublin, 1983).

42. D. W. Miller, "Catholic"; Hynes; Connell, 113–61; G. Birmingham, *Irishmen All* (London, 1914), 184; S. O'Faolain, *The Irish: A Character Study* (NY, 1949), 129–46.

43. See works on nationalism cited in n. 39 above; also D. Fitzpatrick, "Geography of Irish Nationalism," *P&P*, no. 77 (1978), 113–44; idem, *Politics and Irish Life, 1913–1921* (Dublin, 1977); E. Rumpf and A. C. Hepburn, *Nationalism and Socialism in 20th-Century Ireland* (Liverpool, 1977); P. Gibbon and M. D. Higgins, "The Irish 'Gombeenman' . . . ," *ECSOR*, 8 (July 1977), 313–19; and for contemporary descriptions of relations between

local economic and political power, see Brooks, 43–45, 120–21; Becker, 49–50, 123–24; Plunkett, 69–83; R. Lynd, *Home Life in Ireland* (London, 1909), 264–65; and P. Gallagher, *Paddy the Cope: An Autobiography* (NY, 1947). Zimmermann, 69; W. A. Phillips, Report on the State of Ireland, 1916 (FO 115/2244, PRO).

44. For an elaboration of the issues discussed here, see Chapter 8, Section 3, below.

45. Ibid.; and see Conclusion, this work.

46. Ibid.

47. Brooks, 47.

Part Two. The Patterns of Irish Emigration, 1607–1921

1. M. T. Mellon, ed., *Selections from Thomas Mellon and His Times* . . . (1885: Belfast, 1968 ed.), 1–2.

2. F. P. Leahy, 11 Dec. 1916 (FO 115/2244, PRO).

3. S. O'Faolain, *De Valera* (Harmondsworth, 1939), 69–70.

Chapter 4. Settlers, Servants, and Slaves: Irish Emigration before the American Revolution

1. H. A. Gemery, "Emigration from the British Isles to the New World, 1630–1700 . . . ," *REH*, 5 (1980), 180, 204–5; J. J. Silke, "Irish Abroad, 1534–1691," in T. W. Moody et al., *NHI III: Early Modern-Ireland, 1534–1691* (Oxford, 1976), 599–604; D. N. Doyle, *Ireland, Irishmen and Revolutionary America, 1760–1820* (Cork, 1981), 59–61, 70; L. A. Clarkson, "Irish Population Revisited . . . ," in J. M. Goldstrom and Clarkson, eds., *Irish Population, Economy, and Society* (Oxford, 1981), 26; T. Newenham, *Statistical . . . Inquiry into . . . the Population of Ireland* (London, 1805), 307, 313–15. Prior to Doyle's study, most scholars agreed that Catholics composed a mere 5 percent of the 1700–1776 emigration; e.g., see T. W. Moody, "Irish and Scotch-Irish in 18th-Century America," *Studies*, 25 (1946), 88.

2. O. D. Edwards, "American Image of Ireland . . . ," *PAH*, 4 (1970), 236; Doyle, 15–18; F. G. James, "Irish Colonial Trade in the 18th Century," *WMQ*, 20 (Oct. 1963), passim; R. L. Wright, ed., *Irish Emigrant Ballads and Songs* (Bowling Green, Ohio, 1975), 103; R. J. Dickson, *Ulster Emigration to Colonial America, 1718–1775* (London, 1968), 17.

3. Silke, 600–603; A. Lockhart, "Some Aspects of Emigration from Ireland to the North American Colonies . . ." (M.Lit. thesis, TCD, 1971; since published, NY, 1976), 2–7, 10, 102; A. E. Smith, *Colonists in Bondage* . . . (Gloucester, 1965 ed.), 63–64, 172; H. J. Ford, *Scotch-Irish in America* (Princeton, 1915), 262; W. N. Sainsbury et al., eds., *Calendar of State Papers, Colonial Series, America and West Indies*, vol. 14 (London, 1910), 349, vol. 33 (1938), 292, and vol. 34 (1939), 96; O. Patterson, *Sociology of Slavery . . . in Jamaica* (London, 1965), 45; R. S. Dunn, *Sugar and Slaves . . . in the English West Indies* (NY, 1973), 124–25, 127, 130; Doyle, 57–69; H. A. Fergus, "Montserrat, 'Colony of Ireland': Myth and Reality," *Studies*, 70 (1981), 325–40; A. W. Hutton, ed., *Arthur Young's Tour in Ireland* (London, 1892), I, 87–92; N. R. Burke, "Some Observations on the Migration of Laborers from the South of Ireland to Newfoundland . . . ," *JCHAS*, 76 (July–Dec. 1971), 104–5; G. O'Brien, *Economic History of Ireland in the 18th Century* (Dublin, 1918), 171; D. Corkery, *Hidden Ireland* . . . (Dublin, 1970 ed.), 245.

4. Silke, 601; Dunn, 127; Doyle, 61–62; O. D. Edwards, "Impact of the American Revolution on Ireland," in R. B. Morris, ed., *Impact of the American Revolution Abroad* Washington, D.C., 1976), 131; L. H. Lees, *Exiles of Erin: Irish Migrants in Victorian London* (Ithaca, 1979), 45; R. B. McDowell, "Ireland in the 18th-Century British Empire," *HS*, 9 (1974), 61; Sainsbury, vol. 13 (1910), 622–23.

5. Doyle, 65–70, 150; in the 1770s Arthur Young reported no emigration from inland counties but some from the vicinities of southern seaports such as Waterford, Sligo, Limerick, and Galway, see Hutton, I, 238, 276, 294, 402; see Chapter 2, this work, pp. 70–71; W. Edmundson, *Journal of the Life . . . of . . . William Edmundson* (London, 1774), 78.

6. I. Neu, "From Kilkenny to Louisiana: 18th-Century Irish Emigration," *M-A*, 49 (1967), 101–14; Silke, 602; A. Gwynn, "Documents Relating to the Irish in the West Indies," *ANLHB* (Oct. 1932), 273–77; McDowell, 51; Doyle, 47–48, T. Burke, 25 Apr. 1772 (Thomas Burke Mss., mf 1–653, UNC-CH).

7. F. O'Connor, *Short History of Irish Literature* (NY, 1968 ed.), 123; T. Bartlett, "O'Haras of Annaghmore, c.1600–c.1800: Survival and Revival," *IESH*, 9 (1982), 34–52;

Hutton, I, 87–92, 369, 444–45; H. C. Brookfield, "Microcosm of Pre-Famine Ireland: Mallow District, 1775–1846," *JCHAS,* 57 (1952), 7–8; L. A. Clarkson, "Anatomy of an Irish Town: Economy of Armagh, 1770," *IESH,* 5 (1978), 32.

8. Smith, 61–62; E. M. Johnston, *Ireland in the 18th Century* (Dublin, 1974), 31; E. Willes, 1759 (T.2368, PRONI); M. Glasgow, *Scotch-Irish in Northern Ireland and in the American Colonies* (NY, 1936), 158–59; M. Drake, "Irish Demographic Crisis of 1740–41," *HS,* 6 (1968), 121 and passim.

9. See Chapter 3 above, pp. 114–21; O'Connor, 20; D. Greene, "Professional Poets," in B. Ó Cuív, ed., *Seven Centuries of Irish Learning* (Cork, 1971), 47; U. J. Bourke, ed., *Sermons . . . by the Most Rev. James O'Gallagher . . .* (Dublin, 1877), 249; J. Carty, ed., *Ireland from the Flight of the Earls to Grattan's Parliament* (Dublin, 1966 ed.), 172 (trans. BDB).

10. W. H. Crawford, "Economy and Society in South Ulster in the 18th Century," *CLREC,* 8 (1975), 246; R. B. McDowell, *Ireland in the Age of Imperialism . . .* (NY, 1980), 61; C. Ó Gráda, "Seasonal Migration and Post-Famine Adjustment in the West of Ireland," *SH,* 13 (1973), 49; D. McCourt, "Dynamic Quality of Irish Rural Settlement," in R. H. Buchanan et al., eds., *Man and His Habitat* (London, 1971), 140–41; J. G. Simms, "Connacht in the 18th Century," *IHS,* 11 (1958), 120–21; Hutton, I, e.g., 87–92, 115–20.

11. R. N. Salaman, *History and Social Influence of the Potato* (Cambridge, 1970), 194; Gwynn, 157; J. W. Blake, "Transportation from Ireland to America, 1653–60," *IHS,* 3 (March 1943), 268–69, 281; Silke, 601; Dunn, 69; Smith, 61–62, 134, 162–67; Lockhart, 89–93; J. S. Donnelly, Jr., "Irish Agrarian Rebellion: Whiteboys of 1769–76," *PRIA,* 83, sec. C, no. 12(1983), 315; T. C. Croker, *Keen of the South of Ireland . . .* (London, 1844), xxxvii.

12. Lockhart, 89–93, 129–43; Smith, 134, 220, 254; Gemery, 187–88; C. G. Steffen, "Pre-Industrial Iron Worker: Northampton Iron Works, 1780–1820," *LH,* 20 (Winter 1979), 92; Gwynn, 250; Sainsbury, vol. 14 (1910), 349, vol. 22 (1928), 312, and vol. 39 (1969), 237; J. Sheppard, *"Redlegs" of Barbados* (Millwood, N.J., 1977), passim; Doyle, 94, 97–100, 105; Burke, 103–4.

13. Dunn, 130, 174; McDowell, "Ireland," 51–52; Doyle, 47–48, 57, 70, 95–97, 104–5; M. F. Dalrymple, *Merchant of Manchac: Letterbooks of John Fitzpatrick* (Baton Rouge, 1978), 3:25; J. S. Watterson, *Thomas Burke: Restless Revolutionary* (Washington, D.C., 1980); Silke, 602–3; M. W. Hamilton, *Sir William Johnson* (Port Washington, N.Y., 1976), 3–7; C. Crary, "Humble Immigrant and the American Dream," *JAH,* 46 (1959), 59–61.

14. Lockhart, 104–5; Smith, 171–72; Gwynn, 236; Doyle, 182–83; Sainsbury, vol. 2 (1880), 547, vol. 8 (1901), 73, 79, 112, vol. 13 (1910), 622–23, vol. 20 (1924), 554, and vol. 23 (1928), 55; Dunn, 69.

15. Doyle, 71–73, 184; M. G. Kelly, "Irish Catholic Colonies and Colonization Projects in the United States, 1795–1860," *Studies,* 29 (1940), 96; *7th Report of All Hallows College . . .* (Dublin, 1855), 59.

16. F. G. James, *Ireland in the Empire, 1688–1770 . . .* (Cambridge, Mass., 1973), 302; J. F. Duff, *Irish in the United States* (Belmont, Calif., 1971), 74; C. Metzger, *Catholics and the American Revolution* (Chicago, 1962), passim; W. N. Nolte, "Irish in Canada, 1815–1867" (Ph.D. diss., Univ. of Maryland, 1975), 4–5; Crary, 59–61; Doyle, 142–44; T. Burke, ca. 1771 and n.d. (Thomas Burke Mss., mf 1-653, UNC-CH).

17. Doyle, 181–86; E. Willes, 1760 (T.2368, PRONI); Corkery, 248, 253; É. Ó Muirgheasa, ed., *Céad de Cheoltaibh Uladh* (Dublin, 1915), 139–40 (trans. BDB).

18. T. Burke, ca. 1771; Gwynn, 273.

19. T. J. Barron, "Presbyterian Exodus from Co. Longford in 1729," *Breifne,* 5, no. 18 (1977–78), passim; Newenham, 313–14; T. W. Freeman, "John Wesley in Ireland," *IRGEO,* 8 (1975), 89; Dickson, 35.

20. M. W. Hamilton, ed., *Papers of Sir William Johnson,* vol. 13 (Albany, 1962), 181–84; James, *Ireland,* 303; Arthur Dobbs Mss. (NCSA); Doyle, 38–39, 57–59; R. Pillson, 5 Apr. 1764 (Ms. 10,360, NLI); C. Lee, 15 Dec. 1777 (Lord Charlemont Mss., RIA).

21. Doyle, 57–59; E. P. Alexander, ed., *Journal of John Fontaine . . .* (Charlottesville, 1972), 19; R. C. Murphy and L. J. Mannion, *Society of the Friendly Sons of St. Patrick in . . . New York* (NY, 1962), 44–75; W. H. Crawford, "Landlord-Tenant Relations in Ulster, 1609–1820," *IESH,* 2 (1975), 13–17; Crary, 47; A. Austin, *Matthew Lyon* (University Park, Penn., 1980), 3–13 and passim.

22. A. C. Myers, *Immigration of the Irish Quakers into Pennsylvania* (Swarthmore, 1902), 32–37, 42–49, 53–61, 82; W. H. Crawford, "Origins of the Linen Industry in North Armagh

and the Lagan Valley," *UF*, 17 (1971), 43–46; Doyle, 47–48; Edmundson, 130–60, 200–221; S. and J. Morton, 4 Apr. 1769 (D.1044/178, PRONI).

23. J. G. Leyburn, *The Scotch-Irish* . . . (Chapel Hill, 1962), 160–64; Dickson, 19–31; W. Macafee, "Colonization of the Maghera Region of South Derry during the 17th and 18th Centuries," *UF*, 23 (1977), 70–85; Crawford, "Landlord," 13; E. Kaine, 17 Mar. 1718 (T.2739/6, p. 310, PRONI).

24. Johnston, 31; Leyburn, 170–71; Dickson, 32–47; E. Stewart, 25 Mar. 1729 (D.2092/1/3, PRONI); C. K. Bolton, *Scotch-Irish Pioneers in Ulster and America* (Boston, 1910), 47–48; W. H. Crawford and B. Trainor, eds., *Aspects of Irish Social History, 1750–1800* (Belfast, 1969), 67; E. R. R. Green, "'Strange Humors' That Drove the Scotch-Irish to America," *WMQ*, 12 (1955), 118.

25. Dickson, 13, 48–59; Leyburn, 172–73; D. Lindsey, 1758 (T.2539, PRONI); E. R. R. Green, "Queensborough Township: Scotch-Irish Emigration and the Expansion of Georgia, 1763–76," *WMQ*, 17 (1960), 191–92.

26. Dickson, 9–12, 52; Crawford, "Economy," 254; D. Miller, *Queen's Rebels . . .* , (NY, 1978), 50–51; P. Gibbon, *Origins of Ulster Unionism* (Manchester, 1975), 28–29; W. H. Crawford, "Change in Ulster in the Late 18th Century," in T. J. Bartlett and D. W. Hayton, eds., *Penal Era and Golden Age . . .* (Belfast, 1979), 190–91; Hutton, I, 120, 150–51.

27. Dickson, 84–88; D. Lindsey, 1758 (T.2359, PRONI); C. A. Hanna, *The Scotch-Irish* (Baltimore, 1968 ed.), I, 67.

28. Dickson, 61–80; Leyburn, 173; O'Brien, 83; L. M. Cullen, *Economic History of Ireland . . .* (London, 1972), 62; J. S. Donnelly, Jr., "Steelboy Movement, 1769–72" (Paper, 1979); W. A. Maguire, "Lord Donegall and the Hearts of Steel," *IHS*, 21 (Sept. 1979), 351–76; K. G. Davies, ed., *Documents of the American Revolution, 1770–83* (Dublin, 1976), XV, 227–29.

29. M. Weber, *Protestant Ethic and the Spirit of Capitalism* (NY, 1958 ed.), and see works cited in Chapter 3, nn. 27 and 30. T. W. Moody, "Ulster Scot in Colonial and Revolutionary America," *Studies*, 34 (1945), 85–86. For expressions of the "Scotch-Irish myth," see *Proceedings and Addresses of the Scotch-Irish Society of America*, 10 vols. (Nashville, 1890–1900); Hanna; and Glasgow. Leyburn, 271–72.

30. See above, pp. 39–41 and 111–12.

31. D. W. Miller, "Presbyterianism and 'Modernization' in Ulster," *P&P*, no. 80 (1978), passim; Miller, *Queen's*, passim; K. M. Boyd, *Scottish Church Attitudes to Sex, Marriage, and the Family* (Edinburgh, 1980), 1–24.

32. Miller, *Queen's*, 1–86; Dickson, 19–26; Green, "'Strange,'" 114; Hanna, I, 618–19; Bolton, 109; Leyburn, 166.

33. Dickson, 38–39, 123–24; E. Stewart, 25 Mar. 1729 (D.2092/1/3, PRONI); Hanna, II, 16; Bolton, 109–26.

34. E. Stewart, 25 Mar. 1729; Dickson, 27–28, 35–39, 191–200; E. R. R. Green, "Scotch-Irish Emigration: An Imperial Problem," *WPHM*, 35 (Dec. 1952), 193–209; Notes re migration of an entire congregation from Ireland to Salem, New York, in 1764 (T.1791, PRONI); Bolton, 68; D. Armstrong, 1 Aug. 1828 (D.682/38, PRONI); Crawford and Trainor, 26–27; Hanna, II, 69; E. G. Swem, ed., *Letter of James Murray . . .* (Metuchen, 1925), 2.

35. Hanna, II, 65–67, 69; Dickson, 17, 41, 44; Green, "Queensborough," 186–87; M. Birbeck, 28 Nov. 1773 (Fennell Mss., RSFL); Green, "'Strange,'" 118.

36. Doyle, 56–57; Leyburn, 186n, 199–219, 236–55; W. F. Dunaway, *Scotch-Irish of Colonial Pennsylvania* (Chapel Hill, 1944), passim; E. Estyn Evans, "Scotch-Irish: Their Cultural Adaptation and Heritage in the American Old West," in E. R. R. Green, ed., *Essays in Scotch-Irish History* (NY, 1969), 75; F. and E. S. McDonald, "Ethnic Origins of the American People, 1790," *WMQ*, 37 (Apr. 1980), 195–99; T. L. Purvis, "Ethnic Descent of Kentucky's Early Population . . . 1790–1820," *RKHS*, 80 (1982), 260.

37. Green, "Queensborough," 186–87; Hanna, II, 28; Smith, 239–40; Dickson, 95–96; Swem, 6.

38. Leyburn, 191, 231, 237, 302–3, 328–34; Evans, 75–76; A. R. Ekirch, "North Carolina Regulators, 1766–71," *PAH*, 11 (1977–78), passim; J. P. Whittenburg, "Backwoods Rebels: North Carolina Regulators" (Ms., 1981).

39. J. McSparran, *America Dissected . . .* (Dublin, 1753), title p., 38; Doyle, 80–92; J. T. Lemon, *Best Poor Man's Country: Geographical Study of Early Southeastern Pennsylvania* (NY, 1976), xv, 6–7, 27–31, 43, 87–110, 116, 149–85; R. W. Ramsey, *Carolina*

Cradle . . . *1747–62* (Chapel Hill, 1964), 117–29; Evans, "Scotch-Irish," 73–75, 80–81, 84; E. Estyn Evans, "Culture and Land Use in the Old West of North America," *Festgabe für Gottfried Pfeifer: Heidelberg Geographische Arbeiten*, 15 (1966), 72, 79; J. A. Henretta, "Families and Farms: Mentalité in Pre-Industrial America," *WMQ*, 35 (Jan. 1978), 3–32; F. McDonald and G. McWhiney, "The South from Self-Sufficiency to Peonage," *AHR*, 85 (Dec. 1980), 1105–11; Hanna, II, 63, 84–85; Ekirch, passim; Whittenburg; L. D. Baldwin, *Whiskey Rebels* . . . (Pittsburgh, 1939).

40. Whittenburg; Davies, XV, 227–29; Ford, 242–43; J. W. Dinsmore, *Scotch-Irish in America* (Chicago, 1906), 80–95, 198, 246–50.

41. E. Wright, "Education in the American Colonies: Impact of Scotland," in Green, *Essays*, 24–25; Leyburn, 273–95; Doyle, 59–60; E. I. Nybakken, "New Light on the Old Side: Irish Influences on Colonial Presbyterianism," *JAH*, 67 (Mar. 1982), 813–32; N. Wightman, 4 July 1845 (D.1771, PRONI).

42. E. Estyn Evans, "Scotch-Irish," 79–81; idem, "Culture," 72, 79; idem, "Scotch-Irish in America: Atlantic Heritage," *JRSAI*, 35 (1965), 45–48; idem, "Cultural Relics of the Ulster Scots in the Old West of North America," *UF*, 11 (1965), 33–37; Doyle, 84; Leyburn, 305–7; Lockhart, 162–63; E. R. R. Green, "Scotch-Irish and the Coming of the Revolution in North Carolina," *IHS*, 7 (1950), 80–82; Green, "Queensborough," 197–99; J. O. Carr, ed., *The Dickson Letters* (Raleigh, 1901), 11–23; Davies, XV, 227–29.

43. Davies, VIII, 228; J. C. Beckett, *Making of Modern Ireland* . . . (NY, 1960), 156; Doyle, 114; Green, "Scotch-Irish and the Coming," 83–84; Lockhart, 167; M. R. O'Connell, *Irish Politics and Social Conflict in the Age of the American Revolution* (Philadelphia, 1966), 32–34; M. Duncan, 17 Dec. 1774 (D.1140/2, PRONI).

44. Doyle, 109–24, 186–87.

Chapter 5. *Liberty, Intolerance, and Profit: Irish Emigration, 1783–1814*

1. M. A. Jones, "Ulster Emigration, 1783–1815," in E. R. R. Green, ed., *Essays in Scotch-Irish History* (NY, 1969), 48–49, 52–54, 59, 62–63; H. I. Cowan, *British Emigration to British North America* . . . (Toronto, 1961), 34; R. B. McDowell, *Ireland in the Age of Imperialism* . . . (NY, 1980), 137.

2. J. O'Raw, 1 Apr. 1809 (ERRG); W. T. W. Tone, ed., *Life of Theobald Wolfe Tone* (Washington, D.C., 1826), II, 130; W. F. Adams, *Ireland and the Irish Emigration to the New World from 1815 to the Famine* (NY, 1967 ed.), 15; J. Kerr, 22 Mar. 1806 (McNish Mss., #2086, CUL); Jones, 56–59.

3. Jones, 50–52, 56, 60; C. Ó Gráda, "Across the Briny Ocean: Some Thoughts on Irish Emigration to America, 1800–50," in T. M. Devine and D. Dickson, eds., *Ireland and Scotland, 1600–1850* . . . (Edinburgh, 1983), 118–30; D. Mageean, "Pre- and Post-Famine Migrant Families: Patterns and Change" (Paper, SSHA conference, Nashville, 1981); M. Wildes, 29 Oct. 1838 (N-YHS); A. McGraw, 12 July 1871 (McGraw Mss., #2355, CUL); Adams, 34–35; E. R. R. Green, "Ulster Emigrants' Letters," in Green, 94.

4. L. M. Cullen, *Economic History of Ireland* . . . (London, 1972), 62–63, 66–67, 86–87, 90–94, 100–101; W. H. Crawford, "Economy and Society in South Ulster in the 18th Century," *CLREC*, 8 (1975), 247–55; J. Burke, Reminiscences (N-YHS); "The Rosses, Co. Donegal, in 1753–4," *UF*, 20 (1974), 22–23; F. Geary, "Rise and Fall of the Belfast Cotton Industry," *IESH*, 8 (1981), 30–35; A. Redford, *Labour Migration in England, 1800–50*, rev. ed. (Manchester, 1976), 37–38; R. D. Crotty, *Irish Agricultural Production* . . . (Cork, 1966), 17–19; G. Ó Tuathaigh, *Ireland before the Famine, 1798–1848* (Dublin, 1972), 158; C. Gill, *Rise of the Irish Linen Industry* (Oxford, 1925), 238–40; J. C. Beckett, *Making of Modern Ireland* . . . (NY, 1966), 243–44; W. S. Mason, *Statistical Account* . . . *of Ireland* (Dublin, 1814–19), I, 4–5, 47–73, 198, 553; C. T. Bowden, *Tour through Ireland in 1790* (Dublin, 1791), 250; T. Newenham, *Statistical* . . . *Inquiry into* . . . *the Population of Ireland* (London, 1805), 179–96; K. H. Connell, *Population of Ireland, 1750–1845* (NY, 1950), 87–88; W. H. Maxwell, *Wild Sports of the West* (London, 1850), 305.

5. See Crockett family letters (AS); McClorg Mss. (T.1227, PRONI); and McNish and Stevenson Mss. (#2086, CUL). J. Dunlop, 12 May 1785 (T.1336/1/27, PRONI); J. Richey, 13 Aug. 1819 (ERRG); J. Bell, 12 July 1834 (Bell Mss., #1200, TSLA); J. Wright, 12 Nov. 1801 (Wright Mss., RSFL).

6. E. Wakefield, *Account of Ireland* . . . (London, 1812), II, 808; J. B. Trotter, *Walks through Ireland in* . . . *1812, 1814, and 1817* (London, 1819), 21.

7. D. J. O'Donoghue, *Life of William Carleton* (London, 1896), 38; Redford, 41–42;

D. Dewar, *Observations on the Character . . . of the Irish* (London, 1812), 34–35; Wakefield, I, 698, and II, 735–36, 763–64, 775.

8. See above, pp. 31–32; T. J. Powell, "Background to the Wexford Rising," *IESH*, 2 (1975), 61–63; D. Clark, *Irish in Philadelphia* (Philadelphia, 1973), 10–17; J. A. Beadles, "The Syracuse Irish, 1812–1928" (Ph.D. diss., Syracuse Univ., 1974), 85–86; R. Bell, *Description of . . . the Peasantry of Ireland* (London, 1804), 17.

9. Mason, I, 235–41; R. McCollum, *Sketches of the Highlands of Cavan . . .* (Belfast, 1856), 46–47; H. H. Farmer, 28 Feb. 1794 (Hugh Hovell Farmer Mss., PAC).

10. N. MacDonald, *Canada, 1763–1841: Immigration and Settlement* (Toronto, 1939), 129–44; McCollum, 46–47.

11. W. H. Crawford, "Rise of the Linen Industry," in L. M. Cullen, ed., *Formation of the Irish Economy* (Cork, 1969), 30; Adams, 69–70; M. Elliott, *Partners in Revolution: United Irishmen and France* (New Haven, 1982), 353–54; Gill, 264–80; Mason, I, 258–59, 271–73; Cullen, *Economic*, 75, 93.

12. R. B. McDowell, *Irish Public Opinion, 1750–1800* (London, 1944), 87; Cullen, *Economic*, 64–66, 91–92, 119; Beckett, 243; D. Dickson, "Taxation and Disaffection in Late 18th-Century Ireland," in S. Clark and J. S. Donnelly, Jr., *Irish Peasants* (Madison, Wis., 1983), 37–63; D. Crockett, 21 Feb. 1807 (AS); J. Orr, 1 June 1811 (T.1336, PRONI); A. Boyd, *Rise of the Irish Trade Unions . . .* (Dublin, 1972), 22–29.

13. Crotty, 23; D. Dickson, "Middlemen," in T. Bartlett and T. W. Hayton, eds., *Penal Era and Golden Age* (Belfast, 1979), 183–84; W. Greig, *General Report on the Gosford Estates . . .* (Belfast, 1976), 23–25; E. Almquist, "Mayo and Beyond . . ." (Ph.D. diss., Boston Univ., 1977), 132–35; Trotter, 16–23; W. H. Crawford, "Landlord-Tenant Relations in Ulster, 1609–1820," *IESH*, 2 (1975), 13; Mason, I, 553; J. Steele, 6 June 1803 (Ephraim Steele Mss., #3876, SHC/UNC-CH); J. Kerr, 22 Mar. 1806 (McNish Mss., #2086, CUL).

14. Dickson, "Taxation," 37–63; J. Burns, 12 Nov. 1796 (J. F. Burns, Gainesville, Fla.); J. Kerr, 24 Apr. 1806, 22 Mar. 1806, and W. Stevenson, 10 Apr. 1795 (McNish Mss., #2086, CUL); R. L. Wright, ed., *Irish Emigrant Ballads and Songs* (Bowling Green, Ohio, 1975), 83; J. Steele, 20 May 1802, 24 Apr. 1806 (Ephraim Steele Mss., #3876, SHC/UNC-CH); G. Crockett, 29 Jan. 1807, and J. G. Crockett, 11 Nov. 1810 (AS).

15. Connell, 25; L. M. Cullen, *Life in Ireland* (London, 1968), 118–19; G. O'Brien, *Economic History of Ireland in the 18th Century* (Dublin, 1918), 87–89, 393–94, 408; Greig, 89; Mason, I, 256; B. M. Kerr, "Irish Seasonal Migration to Great Britain, 1800–1838," *IHS*, 3 (Sept. 1943), 372; R. B. McDowell, "Ireland in the 18th-Century British Empire," *HS*, 9 (1974), 58, 61; Trotter, 16–17; J. Kerr, 22 Mar. 1806; J. Steele, 30 May 1801 (Ephraim Steele Mss., #3876, SHC/UNC-CH).

16. Mason, I, 120; Wakefield, II, 723–24; J. Kerr, 27 May 1808 (McNish Mss., #2086, CUL).

17. M. B. Kraus, "America and the Irish Revolutionary Movement in the 18th Century," in R. B. Morris, ed., *Era of the American Revolution* (NY, 1965), 334–36, 341, 346–48; W. Potts, 1774? (Potts Mss., DUL); McDowell, *Irish*, 42–44; Connell, 28; H. Harper, 23 Oct. 1784 (D.1140/13, PRONI); D. N. Doyle, *Ireland, Irishmen and Revolutionary America . . .* (Cork, 1981), 161, 167.

18. A. Lockhart, "Some Aspects of Emigration from Ireland to the North American Colonies . . ." (M.Lit. thesis, TCD, 1971), 55–56; C. Cruise O'Brien, *States of Ireland* (NY, 1972), 37; M. R. O'Connell, *Irish Politics and Social Conflict in the Age of the American Revolution* (Philadelphia, 1966), 32–34; Doyle, 169–71; C. O'Conor Don, Oct. 1777 (#8.4:143, O'CD); O. D. Edwards, "Impact of the American Revolution on Ireland," in R. B. Morris, ed., *Impact of the American Revolution Abroad* (Washington, D.C., 1976), 132–33, 138; Wright, 436.

19. G. L. Kitteredge, "An Irish Song Relating to Washington," *PCSM*, 13 (1910–11), 256–58; M. McGrath, ed., *Diary of Humphrey O'Sullivan* (Dublin, 1937), IV, 109, 141; Doyle, 171–72; Kraus, 341; R. E. Burns, "Parsons, Priests, and People: Rise of Irish Anti-Clericalism, 1785–89," *CH*, 31 (1962), 155; Edwards, 139–40, 147; M. R. Beames, "Ribbon Societies . . . ," *P&P*, no. 97 (1982), 137; M. Doheny, report of speech, 1860, in Subinspector T. Doyle, Report #96, 23 Nov. 1860 (FP/PR/SPO).

20. Doyle, 165–66; J. O. Carr, ed., *Dickson Letters* (Raleigh, 1901), 37–38; J. Joyce, 24 Mar. 1785 (ERRG); McDowell, *Irish*, 41; O'Connell, 29–30.

21. H. Harper, 8 Apr. 1784 (D.1140/12, PRONI); R. Kee, *The Green Flag . . .* (NY, 1972), 31, 46–53; Beckett, 246–48; D. W. Miller, "Presbyterianism and 'Modernization' in Ulster," *P&P*, no. 80 (1978), 76–84; J. S. Donnelly, Jr., "Propagating the Cause of the

United Irishmen," *Studies,* 69 (Spring 1980), 13; Doyle, 166–67, 178; McDowell, *Ireland,* 134; Kraus, 348. The best recent study of the United Irishmen is M. Elliott, *Partners in Revolution.*

22. W. H. Drummond, ed., *Autobiography of Archibald Hamilton Rowan* (Dublin, 1840), 130–31; McDowell, *Irish,* 12, 70, 183, 185–86; Miller, 83–84; D. W. Miller, "The Armagh Troubles, 1784–95," in Clark and Donnelly, 155–91; Cruise O'Brien, 39; Kee, 70.

23. Kee, 71, 109–45; J. Burns, 18 Oct. 1797 (J. F. Burns); C. Lewis and J. D. Kernan, *Devereux of the Leap . . .* (St. Bonaventure, NY, 1974), 71–72; Beckett, 261–66; T. Packenham, *Year of Liberty . . .* (London, 1972), passim.

24. Lewis and Kernan, 71–72, 28; G. Crockett, 2 June 1797 (AS); J. Willcocks, 24 Nov. 1800 (Joseph Willcocks Mss., MTCL); A. H. Haliday, 26 June 1796 (Lord Charlemont Mss., RIA); B. M'Kenna, 15 Sept. 1811 (Ms. 2300, NLI); J. Caldwell, 27 Oct. 1842 (I.436, R. R. Madden Mss., TCD).

25. ? to G. Ivie, 1 Aug. 1797 (Rebellion Mss., carton 620/72, #4, SPO); "Letter From An Irish Emigrant . . ." (D.1759/3B/8, PRONI); J. Caldwell, 27 Oct. 1842; D. Armstrong, 1 Aug. 1826 (D.682/38, PRONI); Packenham, 407–8; Kee, 149–50; R. B. McDowell, *Public Opinion and Government Policy in Ireland, 1801–46* (London, 1952), 50–51; Beckett, 285.

26. S. Rogers, 24 July 1798 (Kemper Mss., CHS); Cruise O'Brien, 41–42; Kee, 149–60; Beckett, 274–76; H. Butler, "The Country House . . . ," in R. B. McDowell, ed., *Social Life in Ireland, 1800–45* (Dublin, 1957), 28–42; J. Kerr, 10 May 1810 (McNish Mss., #2086, CUL).

27. Lewis and Kernan, 29–31; W. Sampson, 15 Oct. 1806 (William Sampson Mss., mf #13,611, LC); Wright, 124–25.

28. Kee, 127; J. O'Donovan Rossa, *Rossa's Recollections . . .* (Mariner's Harbor, NY, 1898), 115; see Wright, 205–46 for exile ballads *re* United Irish refugees in America.

29. O. D. Edwards, "American Image of Ireland . . . ," *PAH,* 4 (1970), 244; Doyle, 196–202, 214–18; R. Cassirer, "United Irishmen in Democratic America," *Ireland Today,* 3 (Feb. 1938), 131–37; T. A. Emmet, 1 June 1805 (D.1759/3B/6, PRONI); J. Richey, 26 Sept. 1826 (ERRG).

30. N. Campbell, 30 Oct. 1819 (Ms. 2300, NLI); Wright, 417–18, 177.

31. J. Chambers, 17 June 1807 (D.1739/3B/6, PRONI); Cruise O'Brien, 42. Remnants of Ulster Presbyterian radicalism are traceable in G. W. Pepper, *Under Three Flags . . .* (Cincinnati, 1899), 18–21; and I. B. Cross, ed., *Frank Roney . . . Autobiography* (Berkeley, 1931), 1–8. J. Kerr, 10 May 1810, and M. Wright, 27 May 1808 (McNish Mss., #2086, CUL); J. and J. Chambers, 20 Mar. 1796 (N-YHS); J. Gamble, *View of Society and Manners in the North of Ireland* (London, 1819), 367; Wright, 138.

32. W. Heazelton, 29 May 1814 (D.592/13, PRONI); K. P. McCutchan, *From Then till Now: History of McCutchanville* (Indianapolis, 1969), 17–18; J. Richey, 26 Sept. 1826 (ERRG); I. Weld, *Travels through the States of North America* (London, 1800), 39–40; P. A. Gilje, "Baltimore Riots of 1812 and Breakdown of Anglo-American Mob Tradition," *JSH,* 13 (Summer 1980), 551 and passim; C. J. Houston and W. J. Smyth, *Sash Canada Wore: Historical Geography of the Orange Order in Canada* (Toronto, 1980), 2, 16–18, and passim; H. Senior, "Genesis of Canadian Orangeism," in J. K. Johnson, ed., *Historical Essays on Upper Canada* (Toronto, 1975), 242; R. A. Billington, *Protestant Crusade, 1800–60* (Chicago, 1964 ed.); D. Montgomery, "Shuttle and Cross: Weavers and Artisans in the Kensington Riots of 1844," *JSH,* 5 (1972), 411–39.

33. J. Bell, 12 July 1834 (Bell Mss., #1200, TSLA); J. Horner, 3 June 1803 (T.1592/15, PRONI); J. Crockett, 30 Jan. 1800 (AS); J. S. Hull, *Remarks on the United States of America* (Dublin, 1801), 19–20, 40; T. W. Tone, 25 Oct. 1795 (Thomas Russell Mss., TCD).

Chapter 6. From "Emigrants" to "Exiles": The Pre-Famine Exodus, 1815–1844

1. W. F. Adams, *Ireland and Irish Emigration . . . 1815 to the Famine* (NY, 1967 ed.), 71, 85–102; H. I. Cowan, *British Emigration to British North America . . .* (Toronto, 1961), 66–67; J. J. Mannion, *Irish Settlements in Eastern Canada . . .* (Toronto, 1974), 18–19; D. Robinson, 4 May 1817 (D.2013/1, PRONI); N. MacDonald, *Canada, 1763–1841 . . .* (Toronto, 1939), 249; E. Toner, 21 Jan. 1819 (Ms. 2300, NLI); J. McBride, 8 Aug. 1819 (T.1613/2, PRONI); R. McClorg, 15 Nov. 1819 (T.1227/4, PRONI);

H. Senior, "Genesis of Canadian Orangeism," in J. K. Johnson, ed., *Historical Essays on Upper Canada* (Toronto, 1975), 242–43.

2. Adams, 102–27; Cowan, 67–68; D. Mageean, "Pre- and Post-Famine Migrant Families . . ." (Paper, SSHA conference, Nashville, 1981); C. Ó Gráda, "Across the Briny Ocean," in T. M. Devine and D. Dickson, eds., *Ireland and Scotland, 1600–1850* (Edinburgh, 1983), 118–30.

3. Adams, 141–54; R. McClorg, 18 and 20 June 1820 (T.1227/8-9A, PRONI); Mageean; Ó Gráda, passim; statistics of Irish arrivals in New York City in 1826 and 1836 were computed by the author from a 1 percent sample of emigrant ships' passenger lists, on mf at NLI.

4. Adams, 142–45; N. Nolan, "Celtic Exodus, or the Irish Emigration" (Ph.D. diss., NUI, 1933), 66; computed from passenger lists, mf in NLI; *Report of the Select Committee on Emigration from the United Kingdom, 1826* (hereafter cited as *Emigration Committee, 1826*), in *IUP-BPP, Emigration*, vol. 1 (Shannon, 1968), 170.

5. Adams, 140–41; Neeson Mss., 1824–30 (UWVL); S. H. Cousens, "Regional Variations in Emigration from Ireland between 1821 and 1841," *T&P-IBG*, 37 (1965), 21–29; T. Reid, *Travels in Ireland in . . . 1822* (London, 1823), 217; *Emigration Committee, 1826*, 38–46, 71–72, 130, 170, 175–76, 196; J. Mannion, "Waterford Merchants and the Irish-Newfoundland Provisions Trade, 1770–1820," in D. H. Akenson, ed., *CPRH*, vol. 3 (Gananoque, Ontario, 1982), 178–203; R. D. C. Black, *Economic Thought and the Irish Question, 1817–70* (London, 1960), 208–9; P. Robinson, n.d. (1824?), and C. O'Brian, 20 Feb. 1824 (Sir R. W. Horton Mss., mf 7-2167, PAC); W. A. Carruthers, *Emigration from the British Isles* (London, 1929), 64–72; H. L. M. Johnston, *British Emigration Policy, 1815–30* (Oxford, 1972), 69–90; *Third Report of the Select Committee on Emigration from the United Kingdom, 1827* (hereafter cited as *Emigration Committee, 1827*), in *IUP-BPP, Emigration*, vol. 2 (Shannon, 1968), 299, 338, 386, 410.

6. Adams, 160–61, 204–5; S. Brady, 17 Sept. 1832 (T.3028, PRONI); F. D., 9 July 1836 (Box 45, RJP/CUA); W. M. Nolte, "Irish in Canada, 1815–67" (Ph.D. diss., Univ. of Maryland, 1975), 24–25.

7. Adams, 161–62, 192–93, 196, 204–5, 413–14; from passenger lists, mf at NLI; Nolte, 24–25; S. Brady, 17 Sept. 1832; *Appendix F, First Report of the Commissioners Inquiring into the Condition of the Poorer Classes in Ireland* (hereafter cited as *Poor Inquiry Commission*), in *GBPP-HC* (38), 1836, XXXIII, 133, 137, 424–819; E. R. R. Green, *Lagan Valley . . .* (London, 1949), 160; J. H. Johnson, "Population Movements in Co. Derry during a Pre-Famine Year," *PRIA*, 60, no. 3 (1959), 149; M. F. Dillon, Irish Emigration, 1840–55" (Ph.D. diss., UCLA, 1940), 88; J. A. Jackson, *Irish in Britain* (Cleveland, 1963), 9.

8. H. D. Inglis, *Tour throughout Ireland in . . . 1834* (London, 1835), II, 32, 310; *Poor Inquiry Commission*, 134–39, 424–819 passim; J. E. Vinyard, "Pre-Famine Generation: Emigration from Northern Ireland in the 1830s, Derry and Antrim" (Paper, AHA convention, NY, 1979); Adams, 158, 188–95; Johnson, 141–45, 150, 154–62; computed from passenger lists, mf in NLI; Green, 160; *Emigrant's Guide . . .* (Westport, 1832), 67–136; O. MacDonagh, "Irish Emigration to the United States of America and the British Colonies during the Famine," in R. D. Edwards and T. D. Williams, eds., *Great Famine . . .* (NY, 1957), 332.

9. Adams, 413–14; R. Smith, 3 Aug. 1837 (D.1828/7, PRONI).

10. Dillon, 114, 118, 125; Adams, 214–35, 413–14; K. O'Mally Toole testimony (Ms. 1410, DIF/UCD).

11. Adams, 219–20, 225–26; Dillon, 102, 138–39; C. Ó Gráda, "Some Aspects of 19th Century Irish Emigration," in L. M. Cullen and T. C. Smout, eds., *Comparative Aspects of Scottish and Irish . . . History . . .* (Edinburgh, 1976), 66–67; J. Kerr, 16 June 1843 (MIC.144/1/1, PRONI); *Evidence Taken before the Commissioners Appointed to Inquire into the Occupation of Land in Ireland* (hereafter cited as *Devon Commission*), pt. 1, 1845, in *GBPP-HC* (606), XIX, 897.

12. T. W. Freeman, *Pre-Famine Ireland . . .* (NY, 1957), 137; F. H. A. Aalen, *Man and the Landscape in Ireland* (London, 1978), 227; S. de Fréine, *Great Silence* (Dublin, 1965), 128–29, 146; see above, pp. 27–79.

13. See above, pp. 171–73; S. N. Fogarty, 4 Mar. 1839 (AS); Vinyard.

14. J. King, ? Sept. 1832 (King Mss., ILSHS); S. N. Fogarty, 4 Mar. 1839; M. McDermott, Recollections (Ms. 2-15-1000, LC); "Memoir of . . . Richard R. Elliott," *MHPC*, 37 (1909), 644; W. N. Lyster, 4 July 1839 (Lyster Mss., MIHC); W. Lalor, 12 May 1843

(Ms. 8567, NLI). T. O'Connell, 29 Jan. 1824; J. H. Montgomery, 18 Jan. 1824; and J. Quinlivan, 11 Sept. 1824 (CO 384/10, PRO). M. Heaton, 26 Mar. 1822 (CO 384/8, PRO); R. Ó Foghludha, *Pádraig Phiarus Cúndún* (Dublin, 1932), 85 (trans. BDB); J. Tovil, 16 Apr. 1842 (CO 384/69, PRO); H. Rock, 30 Nov. 1823 (CO 384/9, PRO); T. MacMahon, n.d. (1825) (CO 384/11, PRO); J. McCuddan, 1 Nov. 1819 (CO 384/5, PRO); N. Carrothers, 5 Dec. 1853 (AS).

15. J. Richey, 15 Sept. 1826 (ERRG); C. Armstrong, "Typical Example of Immigration into Upper Canada in 1819," *PROHS,* 25 (1929), 6; Ó Foghludha, 85 (trans. BDB); R. Crockett, 23 Dec. 1825 (AS); N. Campbell, 30 Oct. 1819 (Ms. 2300, NLI); J. McBride, 24 Feb. 1822 (T.2613/6, PRONI); J. Costello, 20 Nov. 1833 (Costello Mss., BI); J. Richey, 13 Aug. 1819 (ERRG); F. Wyse, *America: Its Realities and Resources* (London, 1846), III, 3–4; T. Johnston, 12 May 1837 (Peyton Johnston Mss., HL).

16. R. E. Kennedy, "Irish Emigration, Marriage, and Fertility" (Ph.D. diss., UCB, 1967; since published as *The Irish* . . . [Berkeley, 1973]), 56; B. Garahan, 19 Dec. 1817 (#9.1:098, O'CD); T. C. Grattan, *Civilized America* (London, 1859), II, 3–4; K. A. Miller, "Irish Emigration and the Popular Image of America in Ireland," in J. Lee, ed., *Emigration: Irish Experience* (Cork, forthcoming); *Devon Commission,* pt. 2, 1845 (616), XX, 965; J. Doyle, *Letters on the State of Ireland* . . . (Dublin, 1825), 321; R. S. Fortner, "Culture of Hope and Culture of Despair . . . ," *É-I,* 13, no. 3 (Fall 1978), 35 and passim; J. S. Donnelly, Jr., "Pastorini and Captain Rock . . . ," in S. Clark and Donnelly, eds., *Irish Peasants* . . . (Madison, Wis., 1983), 103–39; S. J. Connolly, " 'Blessed Turf': Cholera and Popular Panic in Ireland, June 1832," *IHS,* 23 (May 1983), 214–32.

17. F. S. L. Lyons, *Ireland since the Famine* (London, 1971), 24–25; L. M. Cullen, *Economic History of Ireland* . . . (London, 1972), 101–9; G. Christianson, "Population, the Potato and Depression in Ireland, 1800–1830," *É-I,* vol. 7, no. 4 (Winter 1972), 82; E. Larkin, "Economic Growth, Capital Investment, and the Roman Catholic Church in 19th-Century Ireland," *AHR,* 72 (Apr. 1967), 882; M. E. Daly, *Social and Economic History of Ireland since 1800* (Dublin, 1981), 13; J. D. Post, *Last Great Subsistence Crisis in the Western World* (Baltimore, 1977), 15, 47–59, 124–31; K. H. Connell, *Population of Ireland* . . . (NY, 1950), 221–37; R. N. Salaman, *History* . . . *of the Potato* (Cambridge, 1949), 604–7; Adams, 184–5; E. Ronayne, *Ronayne's Reminiscences* . . . (Chicago, 1900), 32; M. McGrath, ed., *Diary of Humphrey O'Sullivan* (Dublin, 1937), I, 51, and II, 291–93; F. Thompson, 4 May 1833 (Kemper Mss., CHS); J. and S. Greeves, 10 June 1837 (O'Brien Mss., Lt. Col. J. R. A. Greeves, Belfast); E. Toner, 21 Jan. 1819 (Ms. 2300, NLI); C. Murray, 9 Aug. 1826 (CO 384/14, PRO).

18. J. Boyce, 6 Jan. 1819 (CO 384/4, PRO); C. Lewis, 29 May 1816 (D. McDowell Mss., SCL/USC); J. Nevitt, 16 Mar. 1816 (AS); T. Smyth, *Autobiographical Notes, Letters, and Reflections* (Charleston, 1914), 343–44; F. Stewart, *Our Forest Home* (Montreal, 1902), 1; P. Roe, 27 Apr. 1817 (CO 384/1, PRO).

19. D. Polin, 2 June 1818 (BI); J. Greeves, 3 Mar. 1827 (O'Brien Mss.); S. Greer, 8 Apr. 1829 (MG24 I133, PAC); Cullen, *Economic* . . . , 102, 129; P. Finegan, 1827 (CO 384/16, PRO); A. Welsh, 15 Sept. and 9 May 1837 (Peyton Johnston Mss., HL); J. Nowlan, 20 Dec. 1841, 31 Mar. 1842, and J. Nowlan, Jr., 2 Aug. 1844 (Nowlan Mss., PAC).

20. E. R. R. Green, "Industrial Decline in the 19th Century," in L. M. Cullen, ed., *Formation of the Irish Economy* (Cork, 1969), 96; A. Boyd, *Rise of the Irish Trade Unions* . . . (Tralee, 1972), 32–38; Daly, 63; *Poor Inquiry Commission,* 139; P. Falvey, 7 June 1824 (CO 384/10, PRO); P. Kelly, 24 Feb. 1843, and C. Kelly, 27 Oct. 1846 (Kelly Mss., Mrs. P. Shaw, San Francisco).

21. J. McCormick, 5 July 1818 (SCL/USC); Reid, 154–60, 200–204, 239, 262–318; Daly, 64–65, 87; Cullen, *Economic,* 105–6, 119; C. Maxwell, *Country and Town in Ireland Under the Georges* (Dundalk, 1949), 236–38; A. R. Orme, *Ireland* (Chicago, 1970), 158, 161; C. Otway, *Tour in Connaught* (Dublin, 1839), 57; C. Gill, *Rise of the Irish Linen Industry* (Oxford, 1925), 243; Adams, 137; F. Geary, "Rise and Fall of the Belfast Cotton Industry," *IESH,* 8 (1981), 38; J. Mokyr, *Why Ireland Starved* . . . (London, 1983), 151–94; J. Curtin et al., 23 June 1829 (CO 384/22, PRO).

22. J. Greeves, 13 Apr. 1819 (O'Brien Mss.); J. McBride, 5 Mar. 1825, 9 Jan. 1820 (T.2613/11 and /3, PRONI); A. Burns, 9 Apr. 1827 (J. F. Burns, Gainesville, Fla.); Gill, 316–25; Orme, 158–61; E. R. R. Green, "Beginning of Industrial Revolution," in T. W. Moody and J. C. Beckett, eds., *Ulster since 1800: Political and Economic Survey* (London, 1954), 32–33; D. and M. McCullogh, 25 June 1832 (McCullough-Hutchinson Mss., DUL); Inglis, II, 100; *Poor Inquiry Commission,* 141; P. Gibbon, *Origins of Ulster Unionism*

(Manchester, 1975), 55; G. Ó Tuathaigh, *Ireland before the Famine* . . . (Dublin, 1972), 124–27; W. H. Crawford, "Economy and Society in South Ulster in the 18th Century," *CLREC*, 8 (1975), 256; P. E. Razzell, "Population Growth and Economic Change in 18th- and Early 19th-Century England and Ireland," in E. L. Jones and G. E. Mingay, eds., *Land, Labour and Population in the Industrial Revolution* . . . (London, 1967), 278.

23. P. Casserly, 16 Mar. 1827 (CO 384/16, PRO); Cullen, *Economic*, 119–20; Ó Tuathaigh, 119; Otway, 277–78; Inglis, II, 99; Kennedy, 37–38; Christianson, 82; J. Costello, 20 Nov. 1833 (BI); A. Johnston, 30 Jan. 1834 (Peyton Johnston Mss., HL); L. M. Cullen, *Life in Ireland* (London, 1968), 134–37; Freeman, 200–201; W. and L. Anstis, 29 July 1827, 6 Apr. 1834 (CAC).

24. Lyons, 24–25; Cullen, *Economic*, 101–3, 109; Daly, 13; *Second Report of the Commissioners Appointed to Consider and Recommend a General System of Railways for Ireland*, in *GBPP-HC* (145), 1837–38, XXXV, 492.

25. E. E. MacDonald, "American Edgeworths . . ." (1970; Paper in SCL/USC); R. B. Osborne, Diary, I, 23–24 (Ms. 7888, NLI); R. Gore, 2 Mar. 1819 (CO 384/4, PRO).

26. N. MacDonald, 246–47; Cullen, *Economic*, 114–16; Christianson, 90.

27. Armstrong, 5–10; e.g., Peyton Johnston Mss. (HL), esp. 20 Dec. 1837; Christianson, 89–90; A. F. McCutchan-Johnston, 29 Mar. 1829 (INHS); J. S. Donnelly, "Land and the People of 19th-Century Cork" (Ph.D. diss., Harvard Univ., 1970; since published, same title [London, 1975]), 93–97.

28. J. B. Trotter, *Walks through Ireland* . . . (London, 1819), 219–20, 305; J. Duff, 31 Mar. 1819 (T.2252/2, PRONI); S. Clark, *Social Origins of the Land War* (Princeton, 1979), 29–33; Cullen, *Economic*, 113; Donnelly, *Land* (published version), 48–49; W. S. Crawford, *Defence of the Small Farmers of Ireland* (Belfast, 1839), 88–89; S. Clark, "Political Mobilization of Irish Farmers," *CRSA*, 12 (1975), 489; J. McMahen, 27 July 1832 (McMahon Mss., MIHC); D. Polin, 2 June 1818 (BI); Freeman, 131.

29. W. S. Crawford, passim; J. S. Donnelly, Jr., "Journals of Sir John Benn-Walsh . . . ," *JCHAS*, 80 (July–Dec. 1974), 88–89; Clark, *Social*, 29–33, 487; J. E. Pomfret, *Struggle for Land in Ireland* . . . (NY, 1969 ed.), 14–15; *Emigration Committee, 1826*, 126; *Emigration Committee, 1827*, 407–9; W. A. Maguire, *Downshire Estates in Ireland* . . . (NY, 1973), 129–30; Donnelly, "Land," 110; Moody and Beckett, 42–43.

30. G. Griffin, 24 Nov. 1825 (L. N. Whittle Mss., GASA); R. D. Crotty, *Irish Agricultural Production* . . . (Cork, 1966), 36, 59; Adams, 164; C. Montgomery, 10 Oct. 1834 (McCullough-Hutchinson Mss., DUL); Lyons, 28; Cullen, *Economic*, 112–13; D. Neeson, 2 Aug. 1825 (Neeson Mss., UWVL); *Emigration Committee, 1826*, 126–29; A. Welsh, 29 Oct. 1835 (Peyton Johnston Mss., HL); Donnelly, "Land," 98–99.

31. Donnelly, *Land*, 32; K. H. Connell, "Colonization of Waste Land in Ireland, 1780–1845," *ECONHR*, 3 (1950), 44–71; Notes on Dungiven (Box 39, OS, RIA).

32. W. Carleton, *Emigrants of Ahadarra* (NY, 1979 ed.), 58, 88–89, 266; J. Richey, 13 Aug. 1819 (ERRG); *Emigration Committee, 1827*, 386; Vinyard; *Poor Inquiry Commission*, 133; Cullen, *Economic*, 112–13; Connell, *Population*, 116–17; Black, 8–9; G. Hamilton, 5 June 1835 (CO 384/37, PRO).

33. J. Martyn et al., 1825 (CO 384/11, PRO); Inglis, I, 294–95; *Emigration Committee, 1826*, 143; *Poor Inquiry Commission*, 133; Ó Foghludha, 24–30 (trans. BDB); Earl of Kingston, 19 June 1825 (CO 384/11, PRO); Donnelly, "Land," 101; W. Nolan, *Fassadinin* . . . (Dublin, 1979), 205; Connell, *Population*, 182.

34. P. Duffy, n.d. (#9.x:038, O'CD); G. Griffin, 29 Jan. 1826, and A. Griffin, 4 Aug. 1826 (L. N. Whittle Mss., GASA).

35. See above, pp. 54–60; R. B. McDowell, "Ireland in the 18th-Century British Empire," *HS*, 9 (1974), 61; *Emigration Committee, 1827*, 309; J. Tovil, 16 Apr. 1842 (CO 384/69, PRO); Post, 64–65; P. Hughes, 5 June 1818 (CO 384/3, PRO); J. Doyle, n.d. (1819) (CO 384/4, PRO); M. Gill, 8 Apr. 1822 (CO 384/8, PRO); Connell, *Population*, 33–40, 51–56; Crotty, 57; J. Lee, "Marriage and Population in Pre-Famine Ireland," *ECONHR*, 21 (Aug. 1968), 283–85; S. H. Cousens, "Restriction of Population Growth in Pre-Famine Ireland," *PRIA*, 65, sec. C (1966), 98–99; Donnelly, "Land," 110; *Emigration Committee, 1826*, 206.

36. Crotty, 39–41; Connell, *Population*, 25; F. J. Carney, "Pre-Famine Irish Population . . . ," *IESH*, 2 (1975), 40; but see J. Lee, "On the Accuracy of Pre-Famine Irish Censuses," in J. M. Goldstrom and L. A. Clarkson, eds., *Irish Population, Economy, and Society* (Oxford, 1981), 54–56.

37. *Devon Commission*, pt. 1, 710, 889; *Poor Inquiry Commission*, 133, 135, 138; D. J.

O'Donoghue, *Life of William Carleton* (London, 1896), I, 117–18, 156; J. G. King, 23 Apr. 1827 (CO 384/16, PRO); Hugh Quin, Jr., Journal (T.2874/1, PRONI); A. L. O'Brien, *Journal of Andrew Leary O'Brien* (Athens, Ga., 1946), 10; J. Cavanagh, 15 Apr. 1837, and D. Ryan, 27 Sept. 1838 (CO 384/51, PRO); L. H. Lees and J. Modell, "Irish Countryman Urbanized . . . ," *JUH*, 3 (Aug. 1977), 392–93; J. Richey, 12 Nov. 1822, and 15 Sept. 1826 (ERRG); J. Carswell, n.d. (J. F. Alexander, Belfast).

38. Orme, 151; Connell, *Population*, 51–52; Cullen, *Economic*, 100–133; Clark, *Social*, 53; E. L. Almquist, "Mayo and Beyond . . ." (Ph.D. diss., Boston Univ., 1977), 103, 123–24; Reid, 271–318; J. Martin, 18 Sept. 1823 (CO 384/9, PRO); Otway, 117–18.

39. J. Tovil, 16 Apr. 1842; Cullen, *Life*, 120; Ó Foghludha, 97 (trans. BDB).

40. Donnelly, *Land*, 23; Connell, *Population*, 181–82; J. Healy, *19 Acres* (Galway, 1978), 119–20; Donnelly, "Land," 69–70; E. R. R. Green, "Agriculture," in Edwards and Williams, 102–3; *Second Report . . . Commissioners . . . of Railways*, 554–56; C. Ó Danachair, "Farmer and Labourer in Pre-Famine Co. Limerick," *LIMAY 1978* (Limerick, 1978), 39; T. MacMahon, 1825 (CO 384/11, PRO); A. L. Bowley, "Statistics of Wages in the United Kingdom . . . ," *JRSS*, 62 (June 1899), 398–401; Ó Tuathaigh, 108; B. W. Noel, *Notes of a Short Tour through . . . Ireland in . . . 1836* (London, 1837), 49–50; J. B. O'Brien, "Agricultural Prices and Living Costs in Pre-Famine Cork," *JCHAS*, 82 (1977), 9–10.

41. Adams, 18–20; M. McDermott, Recollections (Ms. 2-15-1000, LC); Ronayne, 54; Connell, *Population*, 137–38, 226–37; W. M. Thackeray, *Paris Sketch Book; Irish Sketch Book* . . . (London, 1889 ed.), 326; T. MacMahon, 1825; M. Drake, "Population Growth and the Irish Economy," in Cullen, *Formation*, 70–71; C. Maxwell, *Stranger in Ireland* (London, 1954), 243–44, 260; Cullen, *Life*, 121–22; J. Quinlivan, 11 Sept. 1824 (CO 384/10, PRO); Freeman, 131–32; H. Rock, 30 Nov. 1823 (CO 384/9, PRO).

42. Petitions to CO, 1825–44 (CO 384/10-75, PRO); *Emigration Committee, 1826*, 125–26, 193; *Emigration Committee, 1827*, 410–11; Ó Foghludha, 24–30 (trans. BDB); J. Costello, 20 Nov. 1833 (Costello Mss., BI); W. Williamson, 3 July 1843 (T.2680/2/2, PRONI); see above, pp. 00–00; Earl of Kingston, 19 June 1824 (CO 384/11, PRO); *Poor Inquiry Commission*, 135, 424–819; R. Sullivan, 23 June 1824 (CO 384/10, PRO); A. L. Bowley, *Wages in the United Kingdom in the 19th Century* (Cambridge, 1900), 47; T. Coleman, *Going to America* (Garden City, NY, 1973), 140; Jackson, 7; Dillon, 228–29, 268; J. E. Handley, *Irish in Scotland, 1798–1845* (Cork, 1945), 145–46; R. B. McDowell, "Ireland on the Eve of the Famine," in Edwards and Williams, 5; K. O'Mally Toole testimony (Ms. 1410, DIF/UCD); *Devon Commission*, pt. 3, 1845 (657), XXII, 798.

43. *Emigration Committee, 1827*, 337–38; *Poor Inquiry Commission*, 133, 135–36, 138–40; *Devon Commission*, pt. 3, 648; R. L. Wright, ed., *Irish Emigrant Ballads and Songs* (Bowling Green, Ohio, 1975), 140, 491–92.

44. G. de Beaumont, *Ireland* . . . (London, 1839), II, 167–69; Wright, 118; O. Mac-Donagh, "Irish Famine Emigration to the United States," *PAH*, 10 (1976), 393, 407.

45. Adams, 214–35, 413–14; Cousens, "Regional," 21–22; Wright, 491; *Second Report . . . Commissioners . . . of Railways*, 84; N. Nolan, 67; J. Taylor and J. Conway, 3 June 1834 (CO 384/34, PRO).

46. See above, pp. 60–69; J. Lough, 26 Jan. 1817 (T. Moore Mss., DUL); V. B. Law-less, 11 July 1830 (H. W. Paget Mss., DUL); Post, 72–73; D. Neeson, 28 Apr. and 29 May 1827 (Neeson Mss., UWVL); J. Harvey, 13 Apr. 1831 (Harvey Mss., TCD); Adams, 129–30; J. C. Beckett, *Making of Modern Ireland* . . . (NY, 1966), 292; W. Shannon, *American Irish* (NY, 1963), 17; Black, 9; M. R. Beames, *Peasants and Power* . . . (NY, 1983), 111–39.

47. See above, pp. 60–69; T. Garvin, *Evolution of Irish Nationalist Politics* (NY, 1981), 54; J. Harvey, 13 Apr. 1831; Beckett, 310; Adams, 30, 173–74; Freeman, 141; J. Lee, "Ribbonmen," in T. D. Williams, ed., *Secret Societies in Ireland* (Dublin, 1973), 28–29; G. C. Lewis, *Local Disturbances in Ireland* (Cork, 1977 ed.), 158–59; T. C. Croker, *Researches in the South of Ireland* (NY, 1969 ed.), 13; J. Brett, 2 Mar. 1825 (CO 384/11, PRO); D. Ryan, 27 Sept. 1838 (CO 384/51, PRO); P. Falvey, 7 June 1824 (CO 384/10); J. Brett, 24 Feb. 1835 (CO 384/37, PRO).

48. J. Lee, "Patterns of Rural Unrest in 19th-Century Ireland . . . ," in L. M. Cullen and F. Furet, eds., *Ireland and France, 17th–20th Centuries* . . . (Ann Arbor, 1980), 224–25; Adams, 30; G. Broeker, *Rural Disorders and Police Reform in Ireland, 1812–36* (Toronto, 1970), 175–216; E. Toner, 7 June 1818 (Ms. 2300, NLI); Cowan, 213; J. Anderson, 28 June 1847 (T. 1664/1/5, PRONI).

49. Beaumont, II, 167–68; J. S. Rochfort, testimony in *Cork Constitution*, 7 May 1825

(clipping in CO 384/13, PRO); Vinyard; Notes on Counties Antrim and Down (OS, RIA).

50. J. Huston, 24 Mar. 1826 (CAC); A. F. McCutchan-Johnston, 29 Mar. 1824 (INHS); Johnson, "Population," 154; D. N. Doyle, *Ireland, Irishmen and Revolutionary America* . . . (Cork, 1981), 213.

51. Smyth, 4; D. Polin, 2 June 1818 (BI); N. Campbell, 30 Oct. 1819 (Ms. 2300, NLI).

52. D. G. Boyce, *Nationalism in Ireland* (Baltimore, 1982), 135; F. O'Ferrall, *Daniel O'Connell* (Dublin, 1981), 86; T. H. Todhunter, 25 Sept. 1832 (Harvey Mss., TCD); Moody and Beckett, 22.

53. *Poor Inquiry Commission,* 134, 140; C. Otway, *Sketches in Ireland* (Dublin, 1839), 244–46; J. Bell, 12 July 1834 (Bell Mss., TSLA); see above, pp. 60–69.

54. J. McBride, 24 Feb. 1822 (T.2613/6, PRONI); Broeker, 5, 14–15; J. Steele, 15 May 1797 (Ephraim Steele Mss., Acc. #3876, SHC/UNC-CH); D. Polin, 2 June 1818 (BI); J. McMahen, 27 July 1832 (McMahon Mss., MIHC); D. and M. McCullogh, 17 Oct. 1829 (McCullough-Hutchinson Mss., DUL).

55. T. W. Moody and J. C. Beckett, eds., *Ulster since 1800: Social Survey* (London, 1958), 175; Ó Tuathaigh, 58–59; R. B. McDowell, *Public Opinion and Government Policy in Ireland, 1801–46* (London, 1952), 29–31; D. A. Chart, *Ireland from the Union to Catholic Emancipation* (London, 1910), 141–42; D. Bowen, *Protestant Crusade in Ireland* . . . (Dublin, 1978); D. N. Hempton, "Methodist Crusade in Ireland, 1795–1845," *IHS,* 22 (Mar. 1980), 33–48; I. Hehir, "Bible in Ireland, 1800–25" (Paper, ACIS conference, Pittsburgh, 1981); McGrath, I, 55; J. Heuston, 29 July 1827 (CAC).

56. J. Bell, 12 July 1834; J. McBride, 24 Feb. 1822; Hehir, D. W. Miller, "Presbyterianism and 'Modernization' in Ulster," *P&P,* no. 80 (1978), 84–90; Stewart, 82.

57. J. S. Rochefort clipping (CO 384/13, PRO); G. Valentine, 3 Oct. 1819 (CHS); J. Acheson, 22 Apr. 1839 (R. Schrode, Charleston, W.Va.); J. Harvey, 12 Nov. 1830 (Harvey Mss., TCD); J. Heuston, 31 Dec. 1828 (CAC); R. Crockett, 23 Dec. 1825 (AS); J. Brett, 24 Feb. 1835 (CO 384/37, PRO); M. Clarke, 1832 (CO 384/29, PRO); W. N. Lyster, 16 May 1844 (Lyster Mss., MIHC); T. Harvey, 2 June 1841 (Harvey Mss.); A. Welsh, 22 June 1835 (Peyton Johnston Mss., HL).

58. Beckett, 311–19; McDowell, *Public,* 177–203; Peyton Johnston Mss. (HL), esp. letters from 8 Feb. to 20 Dec. 1837; J. Harvey, 12 Nov. 1830.

59. F. Thompson, 4 May 1833 (Kemper Mss., CHS); H. Gordon, 1830 (CO 384/23, PRO); J. Martin, 18 Sept. 1823 (CO 384/9); T. W. Magrath, *Authentic Letters from Upper Canada* (Dublin, 1833), 99; R. Talbot et al., 29 Dec. 1817 (CO 384/1, PRO); J. Tully et al., 17 Feb. 1830 (CO 384/23); J. McBride, 24 Feb. 1822 (T.2613/6, PRONI); A. McEwen, 1826 (CO 384/14, PRO).

60. Adams, 102–27; Cowan, 67–68; W. S. Mason, *Statistical Account . . . of Ireland* (Dublin, 1814–19), III, 174, 409–11; A. Doyle, 31 May 1819 (MOHS); E. Thomas, 15 Feb. 1816 (Corbet Mss., TCD); P. Robinson, 2 Apr. 1824 (CO 384/12, PRO); E. Toner, 21 Jan. 1819 (Ms. 2300, NLI).

61. *Emigration Committee, 1827,* 274, 277; E. Estyn Evans, *Personality of Ireland* . . . (Cambridge, 1973), 85–105; Ó Foghludha, 24–30 (trans. BDB); Almquist, 103; *Devon Commission,* pt. 1, 397, and pt. 2, 535, 657–61, 719–20, 890, 901, 965, 971.

62. Cullen, *Economic,* 112; S. J. Connolly, *Priests and People in Pre-Famine Ireland* . . . (NY, 1982), 16–17, 20; see above, pp. 69–79; Beaumont, II, 167–69; Inglis, II, 100; A. de Tocqueville, *Journeys to England and Ireland* (London, 1963 ed.), 164–65; M. Anderson, *Family Structure in 19th-Century Lancastershire* (Cambridge, 1971), 86; P. M. A. Bourke, "Agricultural Statistics of the 1841 Census of Ireland . . . ," *ECONHR,* (1965), 391; C. Ó Gráda, "Demographic Adjustment and Seasonal Migration in 19th-Century Ireland," in Cullen and Furet, 189; McDowell, "Ireland," 5.

63. T. McMahon, 1825 (CO 384/11, PRO); *Poor Inquiry Commission,* 133–35; B. Hall, *Travels in North America in . . . 1827 and 1828* (Philadelphia, 1829), I, 150; *Devon Commission,* pt.2, 560; *Emigration Committee, 1826,* 207; T. Brady, 12 Mar. 1824 (CO 384/10, PRO).

64. P. Robinson, 2 Apr. 1824 (CO 384/12, PRO); T. Brady, 12 Mar. 1824; *Poor Inquiry Commission,* 135; *Emigration Committee, 1827,* 299; Anderson, 94–98; W. Lalor, 12 May 1843 (Ms. 8567, NLI).

65. *Devon Commission,* pt. 1, 897; V. E. Powers, " 'Invisible Immigrants': Pre-Famine Irish Community in Worcester . . ." (Ph.D. diss., Clark Univ., 1976), 20–21; *Emigration Committee, 1826,* 194; see above, pp. 88–101.

66. See above, pp. 88–101; E. Toner, 7 June 1818 (Ms. 2300, NLI); G. Griffin, 30 May

1825 (L. N. Whittle Mss., GASA); Beckett, 299–326; McDowell, *Public,* 127; O. Mac-Donagh, *Ireland* (Englewood Cliffs, 1968), 45; O'Ferrall, 48–51, 54, 61; Clark, *Social,* 87–100; H. F. Kearney, "Fr. Mathew: Apostle of Modernization," in A. Cosgrove and D. McCartney, eds., *Studies in Irish History* . . . (Dublin, 1979), 164–75; Connell, *Population* . . . , 100; J. Burke, Reminiscences (N-YHS); J. Nowlan, 20 Dec. 1841 (Nowlan Mss., PAC); J. G. Kohl, *Ireland* . . . (London, 1844), 52–57; A. MacIntyre, *The Liberator: Daniel O'Connell and the Irish Party, 1830–47* (London, 1965), 267; Bowen, 63–64, 134; Garvin, 18; Ó Tuathaigh, 67; E. Larkin, "Devotional Revolution in Ireland, 1850–75," *AHR,* 78 (June 1972), 649; L. M. Cullen, "Hidden Ireland: Reassessment of a Concept," *SH,* 9 (1969), 22; G. Ó Tuathaigh, "Gaelic Ireland, Popular Politics and Daniel O'Connell," *JGAHS,* 74 (1974–75), 34; Ronayne, 74–75; J. Harvey, 13 Apr. 1831 (Harvey Mss., TCD).

67. See above, pp. 88–101; T. MacMahon, 1825 (CO 384/11, PRO).

68. Clark, *Social,* 87–88; J. Chambers, 12 Feb. 1822 (D.1759/3B/6, PRONI); N. Nolan, 71; M. F. Cusack, *Speeches . . . of the Liberator* (Dublin, 1875), I, 502–3, 512–13; J. J. Auchmuty, *Sir Thomas Wyse* . . . (London, 1939), 187; W. J. Fitzpatrick, ed., *Life . . . of Rt. Rev. Dr. James Doyle* . . . (Dublin, 1890), II, 4, 44; M. W. Savage, ed., *Sketches . . . by Richard Lalor Sheil* (London, 1855), I, 271–74; J. O'Connell, ed., *Select Speeches of Daniel O'Connell* (Dublin, 1954), II, 62, 296–97; G. McDonald, *History of the Irish in Wisconsin in the 19th Century* (NY, 1976 ed.), 24–25; Adams, 65, 223; M. G. Kelly, *Catholic Immigration Projects in the United States, 1815–60* (NY, 1939); O. Mac-Donagh, "Irish Catholic Clergy and Emigration during the Great Famine," *IHS,* 5 (Sept. 1947), 289–90.

69. Cusack, I, 431; W. S. Crawford, 4.

70. N. Nolan, 57, 65; Cusack, I, 87–88; O. Handlin, *Boston's Immigrants* (NY, 1968 ed.), 44; J.-E. McN. Vinyard, *Irish on the Urban Frontier: Detroit, 1850–80* (NY, 1976); J. O'Farrell, 24 June 1863 (O'Farrell Mss., CAHS), cited in P. J. Blessing, "West among Strangers: Irish Migration to California, 1850–80" (Ph.D. diss., UCLA, 1977), 142; Hibernicus [pseud.], *Hibernicus; or, Memoirs of an Irishman Now in America* . . . (Pittsburgh, 1828), 20–30; W. Nolan, 121–42; Auchmuty, 136; Inglis, I, 158–59; Maguire, 130–33; Noel, 64–65; W. G. Nolan, 10 Aug. 1838 (J. Dowling Mss., INHS); M. L. O'Sullivan, 8 Sept. 1870 (Br. W. P. Allen, Dublin); J. Nowlan, 20 Dec. 1841 (Nowlan Mss., PAC).

71. W. Nolan, 121–42; G. Potter, *To the Golden Door: Story of the Irish in Ireland and America* (Westport, Conn., 1973 ed.), 211.

72. Black, 88, 210–11; J. Mokyr, "Malthusian Models and Irish History," *JECONH,* 40 (May 1980), 159–60; see citations in n. 73 below.

73. My analysis of pre-Famine Catholic nationalist thought is informed by Black, 23–30, 91–102, 140; Boyce, 169–74; Connolly, passim; S. Cronin, *Development of Irish Nationalist Ideology* (Dublin, 1980), 67–68, 74, 79, 82; Garvin, 2–3, 7, 44–46; J. Hill, "Nationalism and the Catholic Church in the 1840s . . . ," *IHS,* 19 (1975), 371–95; idem, "Protestant Response to Repeal . . . ," in F. S. L. Lyons and R. A. J. Hawkins, eds., *Ireland Under the Union* . . . (NY, 1980), 35–68; Kearney, 166–74; D. A. Kerr, *Peel, Priests and Politics* . . . (Oxford, 1982), 68–110; O. MacDonagh, "Contribution of O'Connell," in B. Farrell, ed., *Irish Parliamentary Tradition* (Dublin, 1973), 163–67; McDowell, *Public,* 125–26; E. Malcolm, "Temperance and Irish Nationalism," in Lyons and Hawkins, 70–76; O'Ferrall, passim; Cusack, I and II, passim; Fitzpatrick, I and II, passim; P. MacSuibhne, *Paul Cullen and His Contemporaries,* vol. 5 (Naas, 1977), 307–9; W. T. McCullagh, ed., *Memoirs of . . . Richard Lalor Sheil* (London, 1854), I and II, passim; J. O'Connell, I and II, passim; M. O'Connell, *Correspondence of Daniel O'Connell,* vol. 3 (Dublin, 1975), 406; B. O'Reilly, *John MacHale, Archbishop of Tuam* (NY, 1890), I, passim; T. W. Rolleston, *Prose Writings of Thomas Davis* (London, 1889), passim; Savage, I, 322–23, and II, 27–30, 231, 257. Also see W. S. Crawford, 4, 101–8, and passim; and M. T. Sadlier, *Ireland: Its Evils and Their Remedies* . . . (London, 1829), passim.

74. Adams, 215; J. Nowlan, 20 Dec. 1841 (Nowlan Mss., PAC); J. Venedey, *Ireland and the Irish during the Repeal Year* . . . (Dublin, 1844), 164–66; Connolly, 12–13; J. Burke, Reminiscences (N-YHS); Shannon, 15; E. M. Levine, *Irish and Irish Politicians* (South Bend, 1966).

75. P. O'Donoghue, "Causes of Opposition to Tithes, 1830–8," *SH,* 5 (1965), 21–28; N. Nolan, 46, 63–64; J. Burke, Reminiscences; Inglis, II, 18–19; J. A. Reynolds, *Catholic Emancipation Crisis in Ireland* . . . (Westport, Conn., 1970 ed.), 74n; Broeker, 191; A. Nicholson, *Ireland's Welcome to the Stranger* (London, 1847), 90–91, 114–15, 433; Rolleston, 58; Donnelly, *Land,* 55–57; *Devon Commission,* pt. 3, 281, 387, 406, 849.

76. W. G. Nolan, 10 Aug. 1838 (J. Dowling Mss., INHS); P. Connolly, 11 May 1848 (Lassarine Morris, Raheny, Co. Dublin); G. R. C. Keep, "Irish Migration to North America in the Second Half of the 19th Century" (Ph.D. diss., TCD, 1951), 46; N. Mansergh, *Irish Question, 1840–1921* (London, 1965), 36–37; Beckett, 326–27, J. Burke, Reminiscences; Adams, 215; J. Nowlan, 20 Dec. 1841 (Nowlan Mss., PAC); K. H. Connell, *Irish Peasant Society* (Oxford, 1969), 100.

77. W. Lalor, 12 May 1843 (Ms. 8567, NLI); H. Quin, Jr., Journal (T.2874/1, PRONI); M. L. O'Sullivan, 8 Sept. 1870 (Br. W. P. Allen); Garvin, 41–42; T. de V. White, *Tom Moore* . . . (London, 1977), 67–83, 172; T. Moore, *Irish Melodies* (any ed.), passim; M. Brown, *Politics of Irish Literature* . . . (Seattle, 1972), 3–84; G. A. Hayes-McCoy, "Sir Walter Scott and Ireland," *HS*, 10 (1976), 107; T. Wallis, ed., *Poems of Thomas Davis* (London, 1889), 207–8 and passim.

78. F. D., 9 July 1836 (Box 45, RJP, CUA); J. Rochefort (clipping in CO 384/13, PRO); W. S. Balch, *Ireland As I Saw It* . . . (NY, 1850), 214–15; "Song of an Irish Emigrant in North America," *Dublin Monthly Magazine,* Apr. 1840, p. 398; Wright, 40–41; Ms. 1408, pp. 288–90 (DIF/UCD); Ó Tuathaigh, "Gaelic," 30; T. Ó Fiaich, "Ulster Poetic Tradition in the 19th Century," *Léachtaí Cholm Cille 1972 Litríocht an 19ú hAois* (Maynooth, 1972), 25–31 (trans. BDB).

79. J. Greeves, n.d. (1836?) (Lt. Col. J. R. A. Greeves, Belfast); J. J. Mitchell, Journal (N-YHS); D. H. Akenson and W. H. Crawford, *James Orr* . . . (Belfast, 1977), 28–29, 103; Wright, 104, 314; A. Schrier, *Ireland and the American Emigration, 1850–1900* (NY, 1970 ed.), 91–92.

80. C. Wittke, *We Who Built America* . . . (Cleveland, 1967 ed.), 6–7; E. F. Guillet, *Great Migration: Atlantic Crossing by Sailing Ship since 1770* (Toronto, 1963 ed.), 50–51. Descriptions of Irish emigrants' voyages to colonial America include R. J. Dickson, *Ulster Emigration to Colonial America* . . . (London, 1966), 205–20, 289–90; C. A. Hanna, *Scotch-Irish* (Baltimore, 1968 ed.), II, 26; W. Edmundson, *Journal of the Life . . . of . . . William Edmundson* (London, 1774), 80–81, 332–34; R. J. Hunter, "Dublin to Boston, 1719," *É-I*, 6, no. 2 (Summer 1971), 18–24; K. Sudbury, Diary (mf p1560, NLI); M. W. Hamilton, ed., *Papers of Sir William Johnson,* vol. 13 (Albany, 1962), 180; J. Moore, Journal (T.3165/2, PRONI); W. Henshaw, 20 Jan. 1769 (D.1044/165, PRONI); A. Chesney, Diary (T.1095/3, PRONI); T. Wright, 26 June 1773 (D.1044/373, PRONI). Since voyage conditions and Irish emigrants' reactions to them remained similar during the era of the sailing ship, in the following paragraphs I have occasionally used Ms. sources written by emigrants who sailed slightly earlier or later than the period 1815–44.

81. O. MacDonagh, *Pattern of Government Growth: Passenger Acts and Their Enforcement, 1800–60* (London, 1961), 32; P. Taylor, *Distant Magnet: European Emigration to the U.S.A.* (NY, 1972), 133; Dillon, 389–91; A. L. O'Brien, 12–13; A. Blenkinsop, *Paddiana* . . . (Dublin, 1847), I, 12–15; Rev. D. Malony, 20 May 1845 (OMC/AHC, mf NLI); R. Smith, 18 Apr. 1841 (D.1828/20, PRONI); M. Cumming, 30 Aug. 1811 (T.1475/2, PRONI).

82. MacDonagh, *Pattern,* 22–23, 33, 38–39, 42–43; Adams, 236–37; E. F. Niehaus, *Irish in New Orleans, 1800–60* (Baton Rouge, 1965), 134; J. Kerr, 5 June 1847 (MIC 144/1/9, PRONI); T. Coleman, *Going to America* (London, 1972), 63–67, 77; Taylor, 108–9; Dillon, 398; T. Reilly, 24 Apr. 1848 (Ms. 10,511, NLI).

83. Coleman, 80–84; J. Carrothers, 14 June 1847 (AS); G. R. Brooks, "Journal of Hugh Campbell," *BMOHS,* 23 (1967), 243, 249–50; Magrath, 31; J. J. Mitchell, Journal (N-YHS); S. Harvey, Journal (Maureen McVea, Newtownards, Co. Down).

84. MacDonagh, *Pattern,* 47–49; "Letter of John Doyle," *JAIHS,* 19 (1912–13), 198–99; Coleman, 87–96; M. A. Jones, "Ulster Emigration, 1783–1815," in E. R. R. Green, ed., *Essays in Scotch-Irish History* (NY, 1969), 57; W. McElroy, Diary (AIAH).

85. Anon., Journal (D.280, PRONI); McElroy, Diary; A. Conway, ed., *Welsh in America* (Minneapolis, 1961), 38; C. Erickson, *Invisible Immigrants: Adaptation of English and Scottish Immigrants in 19th-Century America* (Coral Gables, 1972), 149, 313; Hibernicus, 147; W. J. Foster, *John Dobbin of Connagher* (Schenectady, 1936), 75–82; S. de Vere, 1 Dec. 1847 (Ms. 5075a, TCD); G. R. C. Keep, "Irish Migration to Montreal" (M.A. thesis, McGill Univ., 1948), 17; Jones, 53–54; J. Lawlor, 14 Jan. 1845 (Teresa Lawlor Mss., CAHS); MacDonagh, *Pattern,* 50–51, 162, 279–80; J. Griffin, 22 Apr. 1830 (L. N. Whittle Mss., GASA); Adams, 80.

86. "Letter of John Doyle," 199; H. Quin, Jr., Journal (T.2874/1, PRONI); W. Williamson, 22 May 1843 (T. 2680/2/1, PRONI); H. Johnson, 18 Sept. 1848 (McConnell Mss.,

MTCL); Dillon, 96–97; Anon., Journal; Guillet, 56; J. McBride, 16 June 1819 (T.2613/1, PRONI); Taylor, 137–38; A. Collins, ? Nov. 1853 (T.2889/2, PRONI); P. Robinson, Memorandum, n.d. (1823–25) (Sir R. W. Horton Mss., mf 7–2167, PAC).

87. MacDonagh, *Pattern*, 58–59, 67–68, 75–78, 88–90, 115, 148–51, 293–97; Adams, 88–89, 143–45, 160–61, 229–35, 267–68; Taylor, 114–16; "Letter of John Doyle," 198, Brooks, 248; G. Griffin, 24 Nov. 1825 (L. N. Whittle Mss., GASA).

88. Brooks, 345; J. Horner, 18 Aug. 1801 (T.1592/2, PRONI); J. McBride, 16 June 1819 (T.2613/1, PRONI); J. Willcocks, 18 Feb. 1799 (Willcocks Mss., MTCL); M. Doyle, *Hints on Emigration to Upper Canada* (Dublin, 1833), 72–74; R. McClorg, 15 Nov. 1819 (T.1227/4, PRONI); W. Graves, Diary (MG24 H7, PAC); J. Coulter, Journal (MG24 H11, PAC); E. McNally, 8 June 1851 (T.1488, PRONI); R. Smith, 18 Apr. 1841 (D.1828/20, PRONI); S. Harvey, Journal (Maureen McVea); Anon., Journal (D.280, PRONI); D. Malony, 20 May 1845 (OMC/AHC, mf NLI).

89. Brooks, 350–52; J. Coulter, Journal; F.D., 12 Aug. 1835 (RJP, CUA); S. Harvey, Journal; Anon., 1 Aug. 1797 (Carton 620/32, #4, Rebellion Papers, SPO); R. Smith, 3 Aug. 1837 (D.1828/7, PRONI); Hibernicus, 143; Conway, 16, 21, 24–25, 38; Magrath, 101–3; Foster, 78; W. N. Lyster, 4 Oct. 1845 (Lyster Mss., MIHC); S. de Vere, 1 Dec. 1847 (Ms. 5075a, TCD); J. Carrothers, 14 June 1847 (AS); D. Malony, 20 May 1845, and L. Kiernan, 13 May 1856 (OMC/AHC, mf in NLI).

90. T. Reilly, 24 Apr. 1848 (Ms. 10,511, NLI); Guillet, 78, 125–26; J. O'Raw, 1 Apr. 1809 (ERRG); Wright, 314; T. Cathar, *Journal of a Voyage to America in 1836* (London, 1955), 13; J. Horner, 10 Dec. 1803 (T.1592/14, PRONI); J. Richey, 15 Sept. 1826 (ERRG); see above, pp. 91–92 and 107–21; A Griffin, 23 June 1828 (L. N. Whittle Mss., GASA).

91. M. J. H. Anderson, Memoirs (MNHS); F.D., 12 Aug. 1835 (RJP, CUA); D. Armstrong, 1 Aug. 1826 (D.682/38, PRONI); T. Reilly, 24 Apr. 1848; H. Johnson, 18 Sept. 1848 (MConnell Mss., MTCL); R. Smith, 3 Aug. 1837 (D.1828/7, PRONI); W. Graves, Diary (PAC); J. Coulter, Journal (PAC); J. Richey, 22 Sept. 1818 (ERRG).

92. H. Johnson, 18 Sept. 1848; R. Smith, 3 Aug. 1837; T. Reilly, 24 Apr. 1848; D. Malony, 20 May 1845 (OMC/AHC, mf in NLI); Conway, 38; M. J. H. Anderson, Memoirs.

93. L. Kiernan, 13 May 1856 (OMC/AHC, mf in NLI); A. Dowling, 20 Jan. 1870 (AS); J. J. Mitchell, Journal (N-YHS); Brooks, 256; [W. Smith], *Emigrant's Narrative: or, A Voice from the Steerage* (NY, 1850), 23.

94. Brooks, 256; Hibernicus, 160; M. McL. Walsh, Memoirs (Ms. 11,428, NLI).

95. A. L. O'Brien, 16; J. Fields, 11 Nov. 1844 (Pádraig Ó Droighneain, Navan, Co. Meath); J. Burke, Reminiscences (N-YHS); Guillet, 155; *Wiley & Putnam's Emigrant Guide* (NY, 1844), 93.

96. R. Wray, 26 Mar. 1825 (T.1727, PRONI); C. Burleigh, "Advice to Emigrants to America," *Belfast News-Letter*, 25 Apr. 1817; Guillet, 158, 162, 190; Niehaus, 137; Coleman, 180; R. Ernst, *Immigrant Life in New York City, 1825–63* (Port Washington, NY, 1965 ed.), 28–29; Taylor, 124; Wittke, 116–18; R. J. Purcell, "New York Commissioners of Emigration and Irish Immigrants, 1846–60," *Studies*, 37 (1948), 33; T. Kelly, ed., "Letters from America," *Carloviana*, 1, no. 1 (Jan. 1947), 25–26; F. Rankin, 8 May 1848 (WISHS).

97. Readings on the pre-Famine Irish experience in America include Adams, esp. 334–409; J. A. Beadles, "Syracuse Irish, 1812–1928" (Ph.D. diss., Syracuse Univ., 1974); S. M. Blumin, *Urban Threshold* . . . (Chicago, 1976); D. Clark, *Irish in Philadelphia* (Philadelphia, 1973); K. N. Conzen, *Immigrant Milwaukee, 1836–1860* . . . (Cambridge, Mass., 1976); J. P. Dolan, *Immigrant Church: New York's Irish and German Catholics, 1815–65* (Baltimore, 1975); D. N. Doyle, *Ireland, Irishmen and Revolutionary America* . . . (Cork, 1981), 181–230; D. N. Doyle and O. D. Edwards, eds., *America and Ireland, 1776–1976* . . . (Westport, Conn., 1980); R. Ernst, *Immigrant Life in New York City;* C. and S. Griffin, *Natives and Newcomers: Ordering of Opportunity in . . . Poughkeepsie* (Cambridge, Mass., 1977); O. Handlin, *Boston's Immigrants;* D. T. Knobel, "Paddy and the Republic: Popular Images of the American Irish, 1820–60" (Ph.D. diss., Northwestern Univ., 1976); B. Laurie, *Working People of Philadelphia, 1800–50* (Philadelphia, 1980); D. B. Light, Jr., "Class, Ethnicity, and Urban Ecology in a 19th-Century City: Philadelphia's Irish, 1840–90" (Ph.D. diss., Univ. of Pennsylvania, 1979); T. T. McAvoy, *History of the Catholic Church in the United States* (Notre Dame, 1969); D. Montgomery, "Shuttle and the Cross . . . ," *JSH*, 5 (1972), 411–46; T. F. Moriarty, "Irish-American Response to Catholic Emancipation," *CATHHR*, 66 (July 1980), 353–73; E. F. Niehaus, *Irish in New Orleans;* G. Potter, *To the Golden Door;* V. Powers, "Invisible Immigrants"; C. Wittke, *Irish in America*

(NY, 1970 ed.). For pre-Famine Irish in Canada, see D. H. Akenson, "Ontario: Whatever Happened to the Irish?" in Akenson, ed., *CPRH*, vol. 3 (1982), 204–56; M. Cross, "Shiners' War: Social Violence in the Ottawa Valley in the 1830s," *CHR*, 54 (Mar. 1973), 1–26; C. J. Houston and W. J. Smyth, *Sash Canada Wore* . . . (Toronto, 1980); M. Liquori, "Impact of a Century of Irish Catholic Immigration in Nova Scotia, 1750–1850" (Ph.D. diss., Univ. of Ottawa, 1961); J. J. Mannion, *Irish Settlements in Eastern Canada;* W. N. Nolte, "Irish in Canada"; T. M. Punch, "Irish in Halifax, 1836–71 . . ." (M.A. thesis, Dalhousie Univ., 1976); H. Senior, "Genesis of Canadian Orangeism"; G. J. Stortz, "Irish Immigration to Canada in the 19th Century," *IHN*, 9, no. 2 (Nov. 1979).

98. G. Unthank, 16 Feb. 1822 (MNHS); J. Richey, 13 Aug. 1819 (ERRG); J. Christie, 3 Feb. 1847 (MNHS); R. E. Stack, "McCleers and Birneys—Irish Immigrant Families . . ." (Ph.D. diss., St. Louis Univ., 1972), 129 and passim; J. McBride, 30 June 1822 (T.2613/8, PRONI); J. Ard, 8 Apr. 1871 (T.1597, PRONI); Akenson, "Whatever," 231–35; Powers, 20–22; M. Wyman, *Immigrants in the Valley: Irish, German, and Americans in the Upper Mississippi Country, 1830–60* (Chicago, 1984), 101; J. A. King, *Irish Lumberman-Farmer* . . . (Lafayette, Calif., 1982).

99. Mannion, *Irish*, passim; J. McBride, 29 Apr. 1821 and 24 Feb. 1822 (T.2613/5–6, PRONI); N. Carrothers, 5 Dec. 1853 (AS); J. R. Godley, *Letters from America* (London, 1844), II, 38–39; Potter, 356–57; "Story of Melrose [New Brunswick]" (pamphlet, n.d., from J. J. Morrissey, Palo Alto, Calif.); e.g., see priests' laments for Irish-American apostasy in OMC/AHC (on mf in NLI); W. Graham, 21 Oct. 1828 (T.2613/15, PRONI); W. Gamble, n.d. (1830s) (AS); E. Talbot, *Five Years' Residence in the Canadas* (London, 1824), II, 10–11; Wyse, III, 29–30.

100. D. Robinson, 4 May 1817 (D.2013/1, PRONI); J. J. Dwyer, 8 May 1845 (Lassarine Morris, Raheny, Co. Dublin); R. Smith, 14 Aug. 1844 (D.1828/25, PRONI); D. M. Nagle, 4 Jan. 1842 (L. Bradish Mss., N-YHS); Godley, I, 191–92; Hall, I, 150; A. Richey, 12 Mar. 1838 (ERRG); J. Wray, 3 Apr. 1817 (T.1727/PRONI); Magrath, 110.

101. R. Smith, 7 Apr. 1840 (D.1828/15, PRONI); J. Fitzwilliam, 7 Feb. 1844 (CO 384/75, PRO); W. Simpson, 6 June 1836 (Ms. 20,340, NLI); Laurie, 11–29; J. McBride, 8 Jan. 1827 (T. 2613/14, PRONI).

102. J. McConnell, 8 Sept. 1849 (McConnell Mss., ILSHS); R. Beaufoy, *Tour through Parts of the United States and Canada* (London, 1828), 46; Potter, 165; E. F. Niehaus, "Irish in New Orleans, 1800–60" (Ph.D. diss., Tulane Univ., 1961), 61–63; W. Lalor, 12 May 1843 (Ms. 8567, NLI); E. Toner, 21 Jan. 1819 (Ms. 2300, NLI); Wyse, III, 54; R. Smith, 17 June 1838 (D.1828/8, PRONI).

103. F.D., 9 July 1836 (RJP, CUA); Potter, 172, 282; J. Fields, 11 Nov. 1844 (Pádraig Ó Droighneain).

104. St. Patrick's Society, St. Johns, N.B., 2 July 1831 (CO 384/27, PRO); J. Fitzwilliam, 7 Feb. 1844 (CO 384/75, PRO); Grattan, II, 7; W. Lalor, 12 May 1843 (Ms. 8567, NLI); H. Quin, Jr., Journal (T.2874/1, PRONI); A. L. O'Brien, 33; W. Dever, 12 Sept. 1848 (A. Timoney, Clontarf, Co. Dublin).

105. G. Unthank, 16 Feb. 1826 (MNHS); W. Stavely, 1 May 1844 (D.1835/27a/3/2, PRONI); J. Willcocks, 3 Nov. 1800 (Willcocks Mss., MTCL); Wyse, II, 270–71; Potter, 172; F.D., 9 July 1836 (RJP, CUA); Laurie, 56–66; H. Gutman, "Work, Culture, and Society in Industrializing America, 1815-1919," *AHR*, 78 (June 1973), 531–88; Ó Foghludha, 40–44 (trans. BDB).

106. F.D., 9 July 1836; T. Gunning, 26 Jan. 1832 (Ms. 20,328, NLI); Adams, 341–42; Ó Foghludha, 40–44 (trans. BDB); Akenson, "Whatever," passim.

107. Grattan, II, 30, 40–41; Adams, 96, 109, 180–82, 226; C. McLean, n.d. (1842?) (McMullen Mss., DUL).

108. See above, pp. 236–41; M. Doyle, 73; J. Nowlan, 2 Aug. 1844 (Nowlan Mss., PAC); J. Griffin, 22 June 1849, and G. Griffin, 30 Nov. 1825 (L. N. Whittle Mss., GASA).

109. D. Robinson, 4 May 1817 (D.2013/1, PRONI); J. Carlisle, 30 Jan. 1851 (MIC 143, PRONI); G. Nicholl, 1 Aug. 1842 (ERRG); R. Smith, 13 June 1845, and J. Smith, 4 June 1846 (D.1828/28, 33, PRONI); R. McClorg, 13 Feb. 1826 (T.1227, PRONI); *The Emigrant's Guide* (Westport, 1832), 129–30; J. Anderson, 26 Mar. 1837 (D.1859/2, PRONI); C. Bacon, 26 July 1843 (T.1639/5, PRONI); H. Hutcheson, 30 Sept. 1845 (Alison Hutcheson, Armagh); T. Kelly, 26–27.

110. J. McBride, 24 Feb. 1822, 6 June 1822, and 5 May 1824 (T.2613, PRONI); J. Carlisle, 30 Jan. 1851; J. Horner, 14 Oct. 1801, 23 Oct. 1801, 1 Jan. 1802, and 10 Dec. 1803 (T.1592, PRONI); J. Anderson, 8 June 1849 (D.1859/9, PRONI); for Quakers, see J. Bell,

15 Oct. 1820 (AS), S. Fogarty, 4 Mar. 1839 (AS), and Jacob Harvey Mss. (TCD); J. Mc-Connell, 22 July 1848 (McConnell Mss., ILSHS); Erickson, 36–37; J. Lough, 20 Mar. 1817 (Thomas Moore Mss., DUL).

111. J. Fleming, 26 Dec. 1842? (Robert Humphreys Mss., CUL); W. Simpson, 6 June 1836 (Ms. 20,340, NLI); Wyse, I, 59–60, III, 2–5; Grattan, II, 30, 40–41; Potter, 318–42, 357–70; *Niles' Register*, 25 June 1825, p. 261; F. Marryat, *Diary in America* (Bloomington, Ind., 1960 ed.), 92–93; F. Trollope, *Domestic Manners of the Americans* (NY, 1949 ed.), 290–91; Dolan, 116–17.

112. Ó Foghludha, 40–44 (trans. BDB); W. Myler, *Reminiscences of a Trans-Atlantic Traveller* (Dublin, 1835), 20; T. Dublin, *Women at Work: Transformation of Work and Community in Lowell, Massachusetts, 1826–60* (NY, 1979), 147.

113. Potter, 245, 252–63, 311–16, 406–29, 438–46; Laurie, 74–131; R. A. Billington, *Protestant Crusade, 1800–60* (Chicago, 1964 ed.), 1–237 and passim; P. E. Johnson, *Shopkeeper's Millennium: Society and Revivals in Rochester, New York, 1815–37* (NY, 1978); M. Berger, "Irish Emigrant and American Nativism as Seen by British Visitors, 1836–60," *Dublin Review*, 219 (Oct. 1946), 174–86; C. O'Conor, 13 Nov. 1844 (#9.2:131, O'CD); e.g., see L. Benson, *Concept of Jacksonian Democracy* . . . (Princeton, 1961 ed.), and R. P. Formisano, *Birth of Mass Political Parties: Michigan, 1827–61* (Princeton, 1971); J. Chambers, 12 Feb. 1822 (D.1739/3B, PRONI); "Meeting of Irishmen in New York: To the People of Ireland" (pamphlet; NY, 1825), unpag.; *NY Irish Shield*, 1 (June 1829); Knobel, 8 and passim; Nolte, 185–255; Montgomery, passim; Gutman, 581; J. Reford, 15 May 1844 (T.3028/B4, PRONI).

114. Grattan, II, 8–9; Wyse, III, 54; W. Dever, 14 Sept. 1848 (A. Timoney); R. Smith, 17 June 1838 (D.1828/8, PRONI); J. Reilly, ? Feb. 1841 (AS); Ó Foghludha, 40–44 (trans. BDB).

115. This and the following two paragraphs are from Adams, 342; C. O'Conor, 13 Nov. 1844 (#9.2:131, O'CD); Moriarty, 354, 366, and passim; Potter, 207–13, 226–27, 231, 264–65, 388–403; Niehaus, "Irish," 48–50, 366–71; G. Osofsky, "Abolitionists, Irish Immigrants, and the Dilemmas of Romantic Nationalism," *AHR*, 80 (Oct. 1975), 889–912.

Chapter 7. "Revenge for Skibbereen": The Great Famine and Irish Emigration, 1845–1855

1. *Commission on Emigration and Other Population Problems* . . . (Dublin, 1954), statistical app., table 26; O. MacDonagh, "Irish Famine Emigration to the United States," *PAH*, 10 (1976), 405–6; J. Mokyr, "Deadly Fungus: Economic Investigation into the Short-term Demographic Impact of the Irish Famine . . . ," in J. L. Simon, ed., *RPE II* (Greenwich, Conn., 1980).

2. R. N. Salaman, *History and Social Influence of the Potato* (Cambridge, 1970 ed.), 603; J. O'Donovan Rossa, *Rossa's Recollections* . . . (Mariner's Harbor, NY, 1898), 108; J. S. Donnelly, Jr., *Land and the People of 19th-Century Cork* (London, 1975), 76; J. C. Beckett, *Making of Modern Ireland* . . . (NY, 1966), 338; M. Sproule, 21 Dec. 1845 (Sproule Mss., Acc. #1877, SHC/UNC-CH); C. Kelly, 21 June 1846, and P. Kelly, 23 Feb. 1846 (Patricia Shaw, San Francisco); P. M. A. Bourke, "Extent of the Potato Crop in Ireland at the Time of the Famine," *JSSISI*, 20 (1959), 11.

3. C. Woodham-Smith, *Great Hunger* . . . (London, 1962), 91; J. M. Synge, *Aran Islands and Other Writings* (NY, 1962), 183–84; Donnelly, 76–77; F. O'Reilly, 23 Dec. 1846 (Henry O'Reilly Mss., N-YHS); J. Nowlan, 30 Sept. 1847 (Nowlan Mss., PAC); ? Lawless, 30 July 1846 (T.2345/2, PRONI); W. Dunne, 25 Apr. and 16 Nov. 1846 (Curtis Mss., BI); K. P. McCutchan, *From Then till Now* . . . (Indianapolis, 1969), 41; *Further Papers Relative to Emigration to British North America*, in *GBPP-HC* (824), 1847, XXXIX, 12–13.

4. Beckett, 341–42; Donnelly, 76–77; M. Doheny, *Felon's Track* (Dublin, 1951 ed.), 205; Bourke, 11; M. Masterson, 4 Oct. 1850 (Masterson Mss., KYHS); A. Kelly, 12 July 1850 (Patricia Shaw); M. Sproule, 12 Aug. 1850 (Sproule Mss., SHC/UNC-CH); J. Forbes, *Memorandums Made in Ireland in . . . 1852* (London, 1853), 78–89; J. Phelan, 14 May 1850, 24 Jan. 1851, 27 July 1852, 16 Apr. 1854, 5 Sept. 1854 (Teresa Lawlor Mss., CAHS); E. Donohoe, 2 Mar. 1853, and M. Donohoe, 20 Feb. 1855 (Donohoe Mss., AIS-UP).

5. P. M. A. Bourke, "Use of the Potato Crop in Pre-Famine Ireland," *JSSISI*, 21 (1967–68), 78–79; K. H. Connell, *Population of Ireland* . . . (NY, 1950), 203–4; T. P. O'Neill, "Organization and Administration of Relief . . . ," in R. D. Edwards and T. D. Williams, eds., *Great Famine* . . . (NY, 1957), 209; Beckett, 337, 350.

6. O'Neill, 212–21; Donnelly, 82–83; *Further Papers* . . . , 12–13; A. I. Shand, *Letters from the West of Ireland* (London, 1885), 114; J. Kiernan, 14 Apr. 1847 (LIHS).

7. O'Neill, 223–52; Donnelly, 84–86; T. W. Freeman, "Irish Towns in the 18th and 19th Centuries," in R. A. Butlin, ed., *Development of the Irish Town* (London, 1977), 132; L. M. Cullen, *Economic History of Ireland* . . . (London, 1972), 132; W. A. Carruthers, *Emigration from the British Isles* (London, 1929), 188–89; *Transactions of the Central Relief Committee of the Society of Friends during the Famine* . . . (Dublin, 1852), 50, 219, 256; T. J. Sarbaugh, "Moral Spectacle: American Relief and the Famine," *É-I*, 15, no. 4 (Winter 1980), 6–14; J. Phelan, 24 Jan. 1851 (Teresa Lawlor Mss., CAHS).

8. A. E. Pilkington, 3 Mar. 1847 (Ms. 13,093, NLI); Mokyr, 246–48; J. S. Donnelly, Jr., "Land and the People of Nineteenth-Century Cork" (Ph.D. diss., Harvard Univ., 1970), 151–52; J. Phelan, 23 May 1849 (Teresa Lawlor Mss., CAHS); S. MacManus, *Story of the Irish Race* (NY, 1944), 607; *Transactions* . . . , 254–55; R. D. Webb, Narrative of a Tour through Erris . . . in . . . 1848 (LSFL); W Bennett, *Narrative of a Recent Journey . . . in Ireland* (London, 1847), 28–29, 128–29, and passim; W. P. MacArthur, "Medical History of the Famine," in Edwards and Williams, 264–72, 305–6; Mrs. Nolan, ? Oct. 1850 (T. 2054/1, PRONI); J. Nowlan, 30 Sept. 1847 (Nowlan Mss., PAC); Fr. W. Purcell, 18 Oct. 1849 (Bishop John Purcell Mss., UNDA).

9. Mokyr, 250–51, 269–73; S. H. Cousens, "Regional Variation in Mortality during the Great Irish Famine," *PRIA*, 63, sec. C (1963), 146–48; J. H. Johnson, "Population of Londonderry during the Great Irish Famine," *ECONHR*, 10 (1957–58), 273–85; Cullen, 132; MacArthur, 277–79; J. Nowlan, 30 Sept. 1847; D. H. Akenson, *Between Two Revolutions: . . . Islandmagee, Co. Antrim, 1798–1920* (Hamden, Conn., 1979), 66–69; J. Johnson, 11 Apr. 1849 (McConnell Mss., MTCL); F. O'Reilly, 23 Dec. 1846 (Henry O'Reilly Mss., N-YHS); T. W. Moody and J. C. Beckett, eds., *Ulster since 1800: Social Survey* (London, 1958), 36–37; T. J. Hughes, "East Leinster in the Mid-19th Century," *IRGEO*, 3 (1958), 239 and passim; Ms. 1365, p. 86 (DIF/UCD); J. C. Messenger, *Inis Beag, Isle of Ireland* (NY, 1969), 15; R. Fox, *Tory Islanders* . . . (Cambridge, 1978), 23; J. Griffin, 22 June 1849 (L. N. Whittle Mss., GASA); Mrs. Nolan, ? Oct. 1850; R. L. Wright, *Irish Emigrant Ballads and Songs* (Bowling Green, Ohio, 1975), 46; E. Donohoe, 2 Mar. 1853 (Donohoe Mss., AIS-UP).

10. P. M. A. Bourke, "Irish Grain Trade, 1839–48," *IHS*, 20 (Sept. 1976), 156–69; D. Bowen, *Protestant Crusade in Ireland* . . . (Dublin, 1978), 177–256; idem, *Souperism: Myth or Reality?* (Cork, 1970), passim; Webb, Narrative (LSFL).

11. M. Beames, *Peasants and Power* . . . (NY, 1983), 211–17; O'Neill, 239–40, 252–53; J. E. Pomfret, *Struggle for Land in Ireland* . . . (Princeton, 1969 ed.), 38; Donnelly, *Land,* 98–113; J. Phelan, 23 May 1849 (Teresa Lawlor Mss., CAHS); J. Griffin, 22 June 1849 (L. N. Whittle Mss., GASA); A. MacDowall, *Facts about Ireland* . . . (London, 1888), 18; M. E. Daly, *Social and Economic History of Ireland since 1800* (Dublin, 1981), 24; Webb, Narrative (LSFL); A. M. Sullivan, *New Ireland* (London, 1882 ed.), 122; Fr. W. Purcell, 22 May 1849 (Bishop John Purcell Mss., UNDA); Mrs. Nolan, ? Oct. 1850 (T. 2054/1, PRONI).

12. Beames, 211–17; Sullivan, 119, 122; Bennett, 7–8; D. Thomson and M. McGusty, eds., *Irish Journals of Elizabeth Smith, 1840–50* (NY, 1980), 132; *Transactions,* 275, 307; Woodham-Smith, 378; Donnelly, *Land,* 75–81, 84–86; D. Thomson, *Woodbrook* (London, 1974), 156–72; D. S. Jones, "Agrarian Capitalism and Rural Social Development in Ireland" (Ph.D. diss., QUB, 1977), 20–21.

13. Donnelly, *Land,* 74–81, 84–86; Jones, 20–21; E. Donohoe, 2 Mar. 1853 (Donohoe Mss., AIS-UP); Carruthers, 188–89.

14. J. Lee, *Modernisation of Irish Society, 1848–1918* (Dublin, 1973), 2; P. M. A. Bourke, "Agricultural Statistics of the 1841 Census of Ireland . . . ," *ECONHR*, 18 (1965), 380; *Census of Ireland, 1851, pt. 2, Returns of Agricultural Produce,* in *GBPP-HC* (1589), 1852–53, XCIII, iii–xv; *Agricultural Statistics, Ireland, 1861,* in *GBPP-HC* (3156), 1863, LXIX, 356–69.

15. J. Lee, "Patterns of Rural Unrest in 19th-Century Ireland," in L. M. Cullen and F. Furet, eds., *Ireland and France, 17th-20th Centuries* . . . (Ann Arbor, 1980), 226–28; Donnelly, *Land,* 88–91, 111–12; R. McCollum, *Sketches of the Highlands of Cavan* . . . (Belfast, 1856), 18–21; M. F. Dillon, "Irish Emigration, 1840–55" (Ph.D. diss., UCLA, 1940), 205; J. W. Hurst, "Disturbed Tipperary, 1831–60," *É-I,* 9, no. 3 (Autumn 1974), 50; Sullivan, 62–68; Forbes, 90–91, 104; Webb, Narrative (LSFL); Daly, 23; Mrs. Nolan, ?

Oct. 1850 (T.2054/1, PRONI); *Transactions,* 254; Bennett, 130; M. Durey, *Return of the Plague* (Dublin, 1979), 164–65; J. D. Willigan, "Famine and Structural Adaptation in Mid-19th-Century Ireland" (Ph.D. diss., UNC-CH, 1977), 417–18; Synge, 183–84; J. White, *Minority Report* . . . (Dublin, 1975), 47.

16. Bourke, "Agricultural," 382; *Commission on Emigration,* statistical app., table 26; Dillon, 247–55; MacDonagh, 405–6; D. W. Fitzpatrick, "Study of Irish Population, 1840–1900" (Paper, Economic and Social History of Ireland conference, Cork, 1977), 14–15.

17. O. MacDonagh, "Irish Emigration to the United States of America and the British Colonies during the Famine," in Edwards and Williams, 319–31; *Transactions,* 258; C. Ó Gráda, "Irish Emigration to the United States in the 19th Century," in D. N. Doyle and O. D. Edwards, eds., *America and Ireland, 1776–1976* . . . (Westport, Conn., 1980), 93–104; MacDonagh, "Irish Famine Emigration," 410–11.

18. MacDonagh, "Irish Emigration," 319–31; idem, "Irish Famine Emigration," 405–6; J. P. Costello, 27 Dec. 1852 (Costello Mss., BI); J. Phelan, 24 Jan. 1851 (Teresa Lawlor Mss., CAHS); Forbes,78–89, 277; Mrs. Nolan, ? Oct. 1850 (T.2054/1, PRONI); H. Lynch, 21 Apr. 1847 (Curtis Mss., BI); A. Schrier, *Ireland and the American Emigration* . . . (NY, 1970 ed.), 167.

19. W. F. Adams, *Ireland and the Irish Emigration* . . . *1815 to the Famine* (NY, 1967 ed.), 391–92; F. O'Reilly, 23 Dec. 1846 (Henry O'Reilly Mss., N-YHS); Donnelly, *Land,* 120–31; Johnson, 273–85.

20. J. Phelan, 23 May 1849 (Teresa Lawlor Mss., CAHS); *Transactions,* 253, 277; Thomson and McGusty, 131; Woodham-Smith, 214; MacDonagh, "Irish Emigration," 321–26; Dillon, 379–84; L. Barrow, "Uses of Money in Mid-19th-Century Ireland," *Studies,* 59 (Spring 1970), 83; MacDonagh, "Irish Famine Emigration," 409–15; Bennett, 53; H. Donnan, 2 Apr. 1848 (D.2795/5/11, PRONI); J. Nowlan, 30 Sept. 1847 (Nowlan Mss., PAC); C. Kelly, 21 June 1846 (Patricia Shaw); J. Burke, Reminiscences (N-YHS); J. Kiernan, 14 Apr. 1847 (LIHS); J. P. Costello, 27 Dec. 1852 (Costello Mss., BI).

21. MacDonagh, "Irish Emigration," 361–62; Dillon, 207, 247–55; J. A. Jackson, *Irish in Britain* (Cleveland, 1963), 9; J. E. Handley, "Scotland," in P. J. Corish, ed., *History of Irish Catholicism,* vol. 6, pt. 1 (Dublin 1968), 24; R. Lawton, "Irish Immigration to England and Wales in the Mid-19th Century," *IRGEO,* 4 (1959), 38, 43.

22. Compiled from a 1 percent sample of Irish passengers landing at New York (lists on mf in NLI); C. Ó Gráda, "Across the Briny Ocean . . . ," in T. M. Devine and D. Dickson, eds., *Ireland and Scotland, 1600–1850* . . . (Edinburgh, 1983); P. J. Blessing, "West among Strangers: Irish Migration to California, 1850–80" (Ph.D. diss., UCLA, 1977), 70; J. and E. Taylor, 6 June 1847 (ERRG); A. Kelly, 12 July 1850 (Patricia Shaw); W. N. Lyster, 6 Mar. 1846 and 8 June 1850 (Lyster Mss., MIHC); MacDonagh, "Irish Emigration," 332–35, 340; O. MacDonagh, "Poor Law, Emigration, and the Irish Question, 1830–55," *Christus Rex,* 12, no. 1 (1958), 12–14.

23. NY passenger lists (mf, NLI); *The Emigrant's Guide* (Westport, 1832), 134; MacDonagh, "Irish Emigration," 328–29; Willigan, 137–38; H. I. Cowan, *British Emigration to British North America* . . . (Toronto, 1961), 217.

24. MacDonagh, "Irish Famine Emigration," 429; H. Montgomery, *Hugh Montgomery: or, Experiences of an Irish Minister* . . . (NY, 1883), 13–19; White, 47–48; Forbes, 281; see above, pp. 193–201; S. H. Cousens, "Regional Pattern of Emigration during the Great Irish Famine, 1846–51," *T&P-IBG,* 28 (1960), 121; B. Ó Cuív, *Irish Dialects and Irish-Speaking Districts* (Dublin, 1951), 77–94; Donnelly, *Land,* 218–20; D. Gwynn, "England and Wales," in Corish, 37–38.

The following illustrates the method used to estimate the proportion of Irish-speaking emigrants from Roscommon and other counties. The 1841 Irish census listed 253,591 persons in Roscommon, but failed to enumerate Irish-speakers. However, the 1851 census listed 173,436 inhabitants and enumerated 46,296 Irish-speakers (mono- and bilingual), or 26.7 percent of Roscommon's 1851 population. If we assume that in 1841 about 30 percent of Roscommon's inhabitants spoke Irish (surely an underestimation; see Ó Cuív, 93), then, using that percentage, we can estimate 76,077 Irish-speakers among Roscommon's 1841 inhabitants, compared with 46,296 in 1851: a decline of at least 29,781 Irish-speakers in 1841–51. What happened to nearly 30,000 Irish-speakers? S. H. Cousens (in "Regional Variation in Mortality," 139) estimates that 28,000 Roscommon inhabitants perished during the Famine. Elsewhere (in "Regional Patterns of Emigration," 121), he estimates that between 20 and 22 percent of Roscommon's 1841 inhabitants emigrated during the Famine, or between 50,718 and 55,790 emigrants (median figure, 53,254, used below).

Overestimating that as many as 75 percent of the 28,000 Famine deaths in Roscommon were of Irish-speakers accounts for the disappearance of only 21,000 Irish-speakers in 1841–51. However, on the basis of our purposely low estimates for 1841 and the enumerations of the 1851 census, we know that at least 29,781 Irish-speakers vanished from Roscommon during the decade. This leaves 8,780 Irish-speakers unaccounted for. I assume they emigrated, thus forming 16.5 percent of the median figure of 53,254 Roscommon emigrants. (Admittedly, this is merely enlightened guesswork. However, see Appendix, Table 10, which estimates numbers of Irish-speaking emigrants in 1851–55 simply on the basis of the percentage of Irish-speakers resident in 1851. The two methods produce comparable results.)

25. Information on Irish-speaking ships' passengers and captains, courtesy of Prof. Mark Wyman, Illinois State Univ.; Rev. A. Talty, 25 Jan. 1851 (OMC/AHC, on mf in NLI); Dr. J. Donnelly, Journal entry, 21 May 1853 (DIO[RC]1/11B/3, PRONI); D. M. Nagle, 24 July 1852 (L. Bradish Mss., N-YHS).

26. MacDonagh, "Irish Emigration," 319–31, esp. 329; *Further Papers*, 12–13; Bennett, 53; Wright, 46; Ms. 1409, pp. 30–31 (DIF/UCD).

27. J. Hunter, 6 June 1842 and 16 Jan. 1843 (Ms. 20,329, NLI); *Evidence Taken before the Commissioners Appointed to Inquire into the Occupation of Land in Ireland (Devon Commission)*, pt. 3, 1845, in *GBPP-HC* (657), XXII, 849; *Transactions*, 224, 258, 277; J. & E. Taylor, 6 June 1847 (ERRG); Lady J. F. S. Wilde, *American Irish* (Dublin, 1877), 5; E. Ellis, ed., "Letters from the Quit Rent Office . . . ," *ANLHB*, no. 22 (1960), 334, 348–53; Dillon, 377.

28. J. Phelan, 23 May 1849 and 24 Mar. 1850 (Teresa Lawlor Mss., CAHS); A. Kelly, 12 July 1850 (Patricia Shaw); Wright, 91–92; Thomson and McGusty, 250; E. Ronayne, *Ronayne's Reminiscences . . .* (Chicago, 1900), 101, 132–438.

29. Rossa, 112; B. Kiely, *Poor Scholar . . .* (Dublin, 1972 ed.), 131; Ronayne, 85; J. Acheson, 27 Dec. 1848 (Russell Schrode, Charleston, W.Va.); A. E. Pilkington, 3 Mar. 1847 (Ms. 13,093, NLI); *Further Papers*, 12–13; P. MacSuibhne, *Paul Cullen and His Contemporaries . . .*, vol. 2 (Maynooth, 1962), 23; Synge, 183–84; Wright, 91–92, 180–82; e.g., K. H. Connell, *Irish Peasant Society* (Oxford, 1968), 113–61; Dillon, 205; Hurst, 50; A. Nicholson, *Lights and Shades of Ireland* (London, 1850), 8–9; J. Nowlan, 30 Sept. 1847 (Nowlan Mss., PAC); Webb Narrative, (LSFL).

30. Fr. W. Purcell, 22 May 1849 (Bishop John Purcell Mss., UNDA); O. MacDonagh, "Irish Catholic Clergy and Emigration during the Great Famine," *IHS*, 5 (Sept. 1947), 293; *Further Papers*, 12–13; *Transactions*, 255; W. S. Balch, *Ireland As I Saw It . . .* (NY, 1850), 136–37, 201–2; "Story of an Irish Cook," *Independent*, 30 Mar. 1905, p. 715; Wright, 180–82; Ellis, 390–93; W. Cleburne, 22 Apr. 1850 (Ms. 15,588, NLI); W. Johnson, 16 June 1851 (Allen Hamilton Mss., INSL); J. Phelan, 23 May 1849 (Teresa Lawlor Mss., CAHS).

31. W. Nolan, *Fassadinin . . .* (Dublin, 1979), 206; MacDonagh, "Poor Law," 13–14; Carruthers, 188–89; *Appendix, Minutes of Evidence before Select Committee on Colonization from Ireland, Submitted by Sir Robert Gore Booth, 1849* (hereafter cited as *Gore Booth Letters*), in *IUP-BPP, Emigration*, vol. 5 (Shannon, 1968), 128 and 122–32 passim; Cowan, 217; Ellis, 354, 394.

32. MacDonagh, "Irish Emigration," 337–38; Dillon, 184–85, 377; Ellis, 334, 348–53; Webb, Narrative (LSFL); M. Foarde, 1847 (Ms. 20,376, NLI); K. O'Mally Toole, Testimony (Ms. 1410, DIF/UCD).

33. Wright, 91–92.

34. See above, pp. 137–38 and 198–201; Sr. M. T. Collis, 27 July 1847 (Diocese of New Orleans Mss., UNDA); MacSuibhne, III, 98–101; Wright, 91–92; MacManus, 607.

35. Balch, 214; Forces, 53; J. F. Maguire, *Irish in America* (NY, 1868), 590–624; Pomfret, 41; Beckett, 349–50; J. McCarthy, *Irishman's Story* (London, 1905), 67; Sullivan, 58.

36. Sullivan, 58; MacDonagh, "Irish Emigration," 329; Webb, Narrative (LSFL); Wright, 91–92.

37. MacDonagh, "Irish Catholic," 291–94; Beckett, 334–35; R. B. McDowell, *Public Opinion and Government Policy in Ireland, 1801–46* (London, 1952), 234–35; R. Kee, *Green Flag . . .* (NY, 1972), 243–55; Rossa, 110, 122; M. Brown, *Politics of Irish Literature . . .* (Seattle, 1973), 105.

38. Fr. W. Purcell, 11 Nov. 1847 (Bishop John Purcell Mss., UNDA); Brown, 103–6; Sullivan, 118–19, 136.

39. D. G. Boyce, *Nationalism in Ireland* (Baltimore, 1982), 174; J. J. Auchmuty, *Sir Thomas Wyse . . .* (London, 1939), 195–96; MacSuibhne, III, 46; Sullivan, 68, 117; Mac-

Donagh, "Irish Famine Emigration," 414–16; M. McNeill, *Vere Foster* (University, Ala., 1971), 88–94; see above, pp. 241–47; Bowen, *Protestant,* 177–256.

40. Beckett, 332–35; McDowell, 125–27, 231–35; K. B. Nowlan, *Politics of Repeal* (London, 1965), passim; F. S. L. Lyons, *Ireland since the Famine* (London, 1971), 95–98; Kee, 243–55, 270–89; Doheny, 294.

41. Brown, 106; Lyons, 99–101; Doheny, 302–16 and passim.

42. T. Reilly, 19 July 1848 (Ms. 10,511, NLI); G. Potter, *To the Golden Door . . .* (Boston, 1960), 508; Wright, 64, 184–85; Lyons, 99–101; M. A. Gordon, "Studies in Irish and Irish-American Thought and Behavior . . ." (Ph.D. diss., Rochester Univ., 1977), xxiv; see below, 550–52.

43. J. O'Donovan, *Brief Account of the Author's Interview with His Countrymen . . .* (Pittsburgh, 1864), 17, 151; Rossa, 110; F. E. Gibson, *Attitudes of the New York Irish . . . 1848–92* (NY, 1951), 88; Wright, 54.

44. Ellis, 387–94; N. Carrothers, 5 Dec. 1853 (AS); T. B. Delany, 29 Aug. 1853 (AS); T. Kelly, ed., "Letters from America . . . ," *Carloviana,* 1, no. 1 (Jan. 1947), 26; A. Greenlees, 27 May 1853 (T.2046, PRONI).

45. W. Kerr, 27 Oct. 1850 (MIC.144/1, PRONI); W. Porter, 3 Mar. 1852, 3 Mar. 1855, and 30 Dec. 1868 (D.1152/3/3,17–18, PRONI); C. and S. Griffin, *Natives and Newcomers . . .* (Cambridge, Mass., 1977), 48–49; M. J. Buker, "Irish in Lewiston, Maine . . . ," *MEHQ,* 13 (1973), 10; H. Quigley, *Irish Race in California . . .* (San Francisco, 1878), passim; E. E. O'Daly, *History of the O'Dalys* (New Haven, 1937), 503–12.

46. Maguire, passim. Studies of the Irish in North America in 1845–70 include D. H. Akenson, "Whatever Happened to the Irish?" in Akenson, ed., *CPRH,* vol. 3 (Gananoque, Ontario, 1982), 204–56; J. A. Beadles, "Syracuse Irish, 1812–1928" (Ph.D. diss., Univ. of Syracuse, 1974); J. K. Benson, "Irish and German Families and the Economic Development of Midwestern Cities, 1860–95" (Ph.D. diss., Univ. of Minnesota, 1980); M. Berger, "Irish Emigrant and American Nativism . . . ," *Dublin Review,* 219 (Oct. 1946), 174–86; P. J. Blessing, "West among Strangers . . ."; S. M. Blumin, *Urban Threshold . . .* (Chicago, 1976); W. G. Broehl, *Molly Maguires* (NY, 1968); T N. Brown, "Origins and Character of Irish-American Nationalism," *RPOL,* 18 (July 1956), 327–58; idem, *Irish-American Nationalism, 1870–90* (Philadelphia, 1966); M. J. Buker, "Irish in Lewiston, Maine"; R. A. Burchell, *San Francisco Irish, 1848–80* (Berkeley, 1980); A. N. Burnstein, "Residential Distribution and Mobility of Irish and German Immigrants in Philadelphia, 1850–80" (Ph.D. diss., Univ. of Pennsylvania, 1975); D. Clark, *Irish in Philadelphia* (Philadelphia, 1974); idem, *Irish Relations: Trials of an Irish Immigrant Tradition* (East Brunswick, N.J., 1981); D. B. Cole, *Immigrant City: Lawrence, Massachusetts, 1845–1921* (Chapel Hill, 1963); M. E. Conners, "Their Own Kind: Family and Community in Albany, 1850–1915" (Ph.D. diss., Harvard Univ., 1975); K. N. Conzen, *Immigrant Milwaukee, 1836–60 . . .* (Cambridge, Mass., 1976); A. G. Darroch and M. D. Ornstein, "Ethnicity and Occupational Structure in Canada in 1871 . . . ," *CHR,* 61 (Sept. 1980), 305–33; J. P. Dolan, *Immigrant Church . . .* (Baltimore, 1975); D. N. Doyle and O. D. Edwards, eds., *America and Ireland, 1776–1976 . . .* ; T. Dublin, *Women at Work . . .* (NY, 1979); K. Duncan, "Irish Famine Immigration and the Social Structure of Canada-West," *CRSA,* 2 (Feb. 1965), 19–40; H. E. Egan, "Irish Immigration to Minnesota, 1865–90," *M-A,* 12 (July 1929); R. Ernst, *Immigrant Life in New York City, 1825–63* (NY, 1949); D. R. Esslinger, *Immigrants and the City . . .* (Port Washington, NY, 1975); E. F. Feinstein, *Stamford in the Gilded Age* (Stamford, Conn., 1973); F. E. Gibson, *Attitudes of the New York Irish;* H. M. Gitelman, "Waltham System and Coming of the Irish . . . ," *LH,* 8 (Fall 1967); idem, "No Irish Need Apply . . . ," *LH,* 13 (Fall 1972); idem, *Workingmen of Waltham . . . 1850–90* (Baltimore, 1974); L. A. Glasco, "Life-Cycles and Household Structures of American Ethnic Groups . . . ," *JUH,* 1 (1975), 339–64; idem, *Ethnicity and Social Structure . . . of Buffalo, New York, 1850–60* (NY, 1980); P. K. Good, "Irish Adjustment to American Society . . . Portrait of an Irish-Catholic Parish, 1863–86," *RACHSP,* 86 (Mar.–Dec. 1975), 7–23; M. A. Gordon, "Studies in Irish and Irish-American Thought and Behavior"; C. and S. Griffin, *Natives and Newcomers;* C. Groneman, "Working-Class Immigrant Women in Mid-19th-Century New York: Irish Woman's Experience," *JUH,* 4 (May 1978); idem, "She Earns as a Man . . . ," in M. Cantor and B. Laurie, eds., *Sex, Class, and the Woman Worker* (Westport, Conn., 1977); O. Handlin, *Boston's Immigrants . . .* (NY, 1968 ed.); C. Houston and W. J. Smyth, "Orange Order and Expansion of the Frontier in Ontario, 1830–1900," *JHG,* 4 (1978), 251–64, idem, *The Sash Canada Wore . . .* (Toronto, 1980); W. L. Joyce, *Editors and Ethnicity: History of the Irish-*

American Press, 1848–83 (NY, 1976); M. B. Katz, *People of Hamilton, Canada West* (Cambridge, Mass., 1975); B. Laurie, "Immigrants and Industry: Philadelphia Experience, 1850–80," *JSH*, 9 (Winter 1975), 219–48; idem, *Working People of Philadelphia, 1800–50* (Philadelphia, 1980); S. J. Leonard, "Irish, English, and Germans in Denver, 1860–90," *COLMAG*, 54 (Spring 1977); E. M. Levine, *Irish and Irish Politicians* (South Bend, 1966); D. B. Light, Jr., "Class, Ethnicity, and the Urban Ecology . . . : Philadelphia's Irish, 1855–75" (Ph.D. diss., Univ. of Pennsylvania, 1979); G. MacDonald, *History of the Irish in Wisconsin . . .* (NY, 1976); A. P. Man, Jr., "Irish in New York in Early 1860s," *IHS*, 7 (Sept. 1950), 87–108; M. C. Mattis, "Irish Family in Buffalo, . . . 1855–75" (Ph.D. diss., Washington Univ., 1975); D. Merwick, *Boston's Priests, 1848–1910 . . .* (Cambridge, Mass., 1973); W. W. Millet, "Irish and Mobility Patterns in Northampton, Massachusetts, 1846–83" (Ph.D. diss., Univ. of Iowa, 1980); A. G. Mitchell, "Irish Family Patterns in 19th-Century Ireland and Lowell, Massachusetts" (Ph.D. diss., Boston Univ., 1976); E. F. Niehaus, *Irish in New Orleans, 1800–60* (Baton Rouge, 1965); W. M. Nolte, "Irish in Canada, 1815–67" (Ph.D. diss., Univ. of Maryland, 1975); G. J. Parr, "Welcome and Wake: Attitudes in Canada West toward Irish Famine Migration," *ONTH*, 66 (June 1974), 101–13; G. Potter, *To the Golden Door*; V. E. Powers, "'Invisible Immigrants': Pre-Famine Irish Community in Worcester . . . 1826–60" (Ph.D. diss., Clark Univ., 1976); D. P. Ryan, "Beyond the Ballot Box: Social History of Boston Irish, 1845–1917" (Ph.D. diss., Univ. of Massachusetts, 1979); H. Senior, *Orangeism: Canadian Phase* (Toronto, 1972); C. Shanabruch, *Chicago's Catholics . . .* (Notre Dame, Ind., 1980); D. V. Shaw, *Making of an Immigrant City . . . Jersey City* (NY, 1976); W. J. Smyth, "Irish in Mid-19th-Century Ontario," *UF*, 23 (1977), 97–106; S. Thernstrom, *Poverty and Progress: Social Mobility in a 19th-Century City* (NY, 1969 ed.); J. E. McN. Vinyard, *Irish on the Urban Frontier: Detroit, 1850–80* (NY, 1976); D. J. Walkowitz, *Worker City, Company Town: Iron and Cotton Workers in Troy and Cohoes, New York, 1855–84* (Urbana, 1978); J. P. Walsh, ed., *San Francisco Irish, 1850–1976* (San Francisco, 1978); V. A. Walsh, "'Across the Big Wather': Irish-Catholic Community of Mid-19th-Century Pittsburgh," *WPHM*, 66 (Jan. 1983); M. P. Weber, "Occupational Mobility of Ethnic Minorities in 19th-Century Warren, Pennsylvania," in J. Bodnar, ed., *Ethnic Experience in Pennsylvania* (Pittsburgh, 1977); R. A. Wheeler, "Fifth Ward Irish: Immigrant Mobility in Providence, 1850–70," *RIH*, 32 (May 1973), 52–61; C. Wittke, *Irish in America* (Baton Rouge, 1956).

This paragraph derived specifically from Powers, 286–429; V. A. Walsh, diss. on Irish in Pittsburgh (Univ. of Pittsburgh), in progress; Shaw, 51–52, 152–54; Blessing, xiii–xiv and passim; Egan, 140. On Irish-American labor leaders, see D. Montgomery, *Beyond Equality: Labor and the Radical Republicans, 1862–72* (NY, 1967), 199–204. W. Cleburne, 22 Apr. 1850 (Ms. 15,588, NLI); R. O'Gorman, 17 May 1857 (WSO'B, Ms. 455, NLI).

47. W. D. Riddle, 30 Nov. 1853 (D.1859/12, PRONI); Rev. H. Lennon, 22 Oct. 1849 (OMC/AHC, mf NLI); Vinyard, 71–74 and passim; Burchell, 54–71 and passim; Clark, *Irish in Philadelphia*, 40–58, 74–87, and passim; Walkowitz, 22–95 and passim; Dublin, 139–55 and passim; Akenson, 230–39; MacDonald, passim.

48. Darroch and Ornstein, 312–29; Katz, passim; Nolte, 166–70; on Irish in Boston, New York, Lawrence, Poughkeepsie, South Bend, Milwaukee, Denver, and Sacramento, see works cited in n. 46 by Handlin, Ernst, Dolan, Cole, Griffin and Griffin, Esslinger, Conzen, Leonard, and Blessing. On women and marriage patterns, see the two articles by Groneman; also Light, 8; Glasco, "Life Cycles," 339–64; and a new work by H. Diner, *Erin's Daughters in America . . .* (Baltimore, 1983). On real-property acquisition, see Thernstrom, 100–56; Clark, *Irish in Philadelphia*, 40–58; Wheeler, 60; Esslinger, chap. 5; Blumin, 90–93; Griffin and Griffin, 47–48, 103–21; Conzen, 75–79, 102–20; Vinyard, 90; and Burchell, 41–49.

49. P. Mulligan, "Irish in America," *Nation*, 15 May 1852 (citation courtesy of AS); O. MacDonagh, *Pattern of Government Growth . . .* (London, 1961), 50–51, 80–81, 170–71, 183–87, 212–13, 266–67, 279–80; Woodham-Smith, 238; G. R. C. Keep, "Irish Migration to Montreal, 1847–67" (M.A. thesis, McGill Univ., 1948), 21; Dillon, 306; T. Coleman, *Going to America* (Garden City, 1973), 145, 151–52, 291–92, and passim; C. Wittke, *We Who Built America . . .* (Cleveland, 1967 ed.), 113–14; E. C. Guillet, *Great Migration . . .* (Toronto, 1963), 155 and passim; [J. O'Hanlon], *Life and Scenery in Missouri . . .* (Dublin, 1890), 141.

Contemporary accounts of the Famine voyage include A Cabin Passenger [R. Whyte], *The Ocean Plague: or, Voyage to Quebec in an Irish Emigrant Vessel* (Boston, 1848); [W. Smith], *Emigrant's Narrative: or, Voice from the Steerage . . .* (NY, 1850); D. Begley,

"Journal of an Irish Emigrant to Canada," *Irish Ancestor,* 6 no. 1 (1974), 43–47; S. de Vere, 1 Dec. 1847 (Ms. 5075a, TCD); W. N. Lyster, 29 Dec. 1848 (Lyster Mss., MIHC); H. Johnson, 18 Sept. 1848 (McConnell Mss., MTCL); J. Burke, Reminiscences (N-YHS); S. Harvey, Journal (Maureen McVea, Newtownards, Co. Down); P. and C. MacGowan, 25 Dec. 1847, in *Gore Booth Letters,* 125–26.

50. S. de Vere, 1 Dec. 1847; Fr. P. Dowd, 25 Oct. 1850 (Sr. A. Matthews, Maynooth, Co. Kildare); B. Clancy, 17 Nov. 1847, *Gore Booth Letters,* 126; L. O'Connell, "Kealing Hurley's Scrip Book . . . ," *É-I,* 15, no. 2 (Summer 1980), 107–9; A. Browne, 31 July 1851 (Fr. C. Reville Mss., FL); *Transactions,* 324; Parr, 110–12; E. F. Niehaus, "Irish in New Orleans, 1800–60" (Ph.D. diss., Tulane Univ., 1961), 336–38.

51. E. McNally, 8 June 1851 (T.1448, PRONI); P. Mulligan in the *Nation,* 15 May 1852; *New York Phoenix,* 4 June 1859, in Subinspector T. Doyle, Reports, 1859–61 (Fenian Papers, SPO), hereafter cited as Doyle Reports.

52. W. Dever, 1 Sept. 1851, and J. Dever, 29 Nov. 1853 (A. Timoney, Clontarf, Co. Dublin); C. Locke, 27 Nov. 185? and 15 Nov. 185? (Locke Mss., NLI).

53. D. M. Katzman, *Seven Days a Week: Work and Domestic Service in Industrializing America* (NY, 1978), 80; Groneman, "Working-Class"; idem, "She Earns," passim; W. W. Sanger, *History of Prostitution* (NY, 1859), 475–9, 584; Clark, *Irish Relations,* 167; Diner, 70–105 and passim; B. Tunney, 24 Aug. 1855 (E. Binchy, Charleville, Co. Cork).

54. D. Montgomery, "Irish in American Labor Movement," in Doyle and Edwards, 206–7; P. K. Walsh, letter in *Cork Examiner,* 11 June 1860 (AS); T. B. Delany, 29 Aug. 1853 (AS); Wheeler, 56; Ernst, 49.

55. Dolan, 37.

56. Potter, 518–20; V. A. Walsh, "Drowning the Shamrock . . ." (Paper, AHA convention, NY, 1982); P. Simpson, "Drunk and Teetotaler . . ." (Graduate Paper, Univ. of Pittsburgh, 1976; copy in AIS-UP); Ernst, 56; W. Murphy, 6 May 1874 (D.2795/15/2/7, PRONI).

57. E. Abbott, ed., *Historical Aspects of the Immigration Problem . . .* (Chicago, 1926), 615; J. White, *Sketches from America* (London, 1870), 369–70.

58. F.D., 9 July 1836 (Box 45, RJP, CUA); P. Mulligan in the *Nation,* 15 May 1852; T. McIntyre, 27 Aug. 1855 (T.2722/1, PRONI); P. Connolly, 11 May 1848 (Lassarine Morris, Raheny, Co. Dublin); Burchell, 48, 148–53; Montgomery, *Beyond,* 28–37; Laurie, *Working,* 138–39.

59. J. McConnell, 12 Jan. and 8 Sept. 1849 (McConnell Mss., ILSHS); Dolan, 36–37; Powers, 286–429.

60. Clark, *Irish Relations,* 170; P. K. Walsh in *Cork Examiner,* 11 June 1860; R. Bleasdale, "Class Conflict on the Canals of Upper Canada in the 1840s," *L/LT,* 7 (Spring 1981), passim; M. Wyman, *Immigrants in the Valley . . .* (Chicago, 1984), 178–81.

61. Broehl, 73–101; Shaw, 77–82; W. Cleburne, 22 Apr. 1850 (Ms. 15,588, NLI); Montgomery, *Beyond,* 98, 308–11; M. J. Adams, letter in *Cork Examiner,* 10 Aug. 1860 (AS).

62. J. Fitzgerald, 21 Aug. 1860 (A. Kennedy, Castletroy, Co. Limerick); R. A. Billington, *Protestant Crusade, 1800–60 . . .* (Chicago, 1964 ed.), 238–436; M. F. Holt, *Forging a Majority: Republican Party in Pittsburgh, 1848–60* (New Haven, 1969); V. A. Walsh, diss. on Pittsburgh Irish, in progress; Burchell, 129–36; I. R. Robertson, "Highlanders, Irishmen and the Land Question in 19th-Century Prince Edward Island," in L. M. Cullen and T. C. Smout, eds., *Comparative Aspects of Scottish and Irish . . . History* (Edinburgh, 1976), 234–36; Senior, 47, 63–64; Nolte, 179–82, 269–84; G. S. Kealey, *Toronto Workers Respond to Industrial Capitalism, 1867–92* (Toronto, 1980).

63. Potter, 466–69; C. Dwyer, 3 Oct. 1853 (Anne F. Dwyer Mss., INHS); P. Taggart, 14 June 1869 (Robert Humphreys Mss., CUL); J. B. Dillon, 12 Dec. 1852 (WSO'B, Ms. 445, NLI); J. Dixon, 5 Sept. 1855 (AS).

64. Man, 103; D. Baum, "'Irish Vote' and Party Politics in Massachusetts, 1860–76," *CWH,* 26 (June 1980), 122; Gibson, 158–59; W. L. Burton, "'Title Deed to America': Union Ethnic Regiments in the Civil War," *PAPS,* 124 (1980), 461–62; Capt. R. F. Farrell, 8 Feb. 1853, and P. Casey, 23 Mar. 1863 (Col. J. H. Mulligan Mss., CHHS); H. O'Mahoney, Reminiscences (Bridget Lynch, Berkeley, Calif.); Powers, 286–429; Montgomery, *Beyond,* 308–11, 330; A. Cook, *Armies of the Street . . .* (NY, 1975); White, *Sketches,* 353; Gordon, 2–352.

65. White, *Sketches,* 355; Fr. P. Devine, Journal (STPCR); [Bishop J. Lynch], "Evils of Wholesale and Improvident Emigration from Ireland" (Toronto, 1864), citation courtesy of Prof. E. Larkin, Univ. of Chicago; W. Dever, 14 Sept. 1848, and J. Dever, 29 Nov. 1853

(A. Timoney); B. Colgan, 20 Dec. 1854 (AS); J. Fitzgerald, 21 Aug. 1860 (A. Kennedy).

66. J. Fitzgerald, 21 Aug. 1860; Dolan, 132–33; Niehaus, "Irish," 63; White, *Sketches,* 354, 360–62; "A Young Man," letter in *Cork Constitution,* 12 Mar. 1857 (AS); NY *Phoenix,* clipping, n.d., in Doyle Reports #91 (13 Oct. 1860); Gordon, xx–xxi.

67. Joyce, 131–32; NY *Irish News,* 25 Dec. 1858; Woodham-Smith, 267–68; White, *Sketches,* 371–72; Duncan, passim; Montgomery, "Irish," 208; V. A. Walsh, diss. on Pittsburgh Irish, in progress.

68. E. Hynes, "Great Hunger and Irish Catholicism," *Societas,* 8 (1978), 145; Dolan, 52–53, 57–58; Fr. J. Brummer, 18 May 1854 (Bishop J. Purcell Mss., UNDA); J. D. Burns, *Three Years among the Working-Classes in the United States* (NY, 1865), 18; Bleasedale, 30 and passim; Shaw, 77–82; P. Mulligan in the *Nation,* 15 May 1852; Robertson, 233; Broehl; M. Griffith, 27 July 1863 (Mary Estlin Mss., DWL).

69. J. Butler, ? Nov. 1849 and 11 Nov. 1850 (M. J. Kelly, Celbridge, Co. Kildare); Ernst, 125–29; W. Benson, *Life and Adventures of Wilson Benson . . .* (Toronto, 1876), for a synopsis of which, see Katz, 94–105; G. B. O'Reilly, 19 Oct. 1852 (Ms. 3412, TCD); "A Young Man," in *Cork Constitution,* 12 Mar. 1857.

70. The recent doctoral dissertations by Dale Light, Vincent Powers, and Victor Walsh (cited above) are excellent on these issues.

71. Ibid.; citation from Walsh, diss. on Pittsburgh Irish, in progress.

72. White, *Sketches,* 47; A. B. Callow, *Tweed Ring* (NY, 1969); Shaw, 51–52, 152–54; Powers, 286–429; P. M. Green, "Irish Chicago . . . ," in P. d'A. Jones and M. G. Holli, eds., *Ethnic Chicago* (Grand Rapids, 1981); MacDonald, 131–34; R. O'Gorman, 1 Jan. 1859 (WSO'B, Ms. 445, NLI).

73. Clark, *Irish in Philadelphia,* 121–23; Baum, passim; P. Dunny, 30 Dec. 1856 (AS); Gordon, 387–88.

74. Dolan, 51–53, 66, 116; T. T. McAvoy, *History of the Catholic Church in the United States* (Notre Dame, 1969), 123–225; Joyce, 107; White, *Sketches,* 351–52; P. Mulligan in the *Nation,* 15 May 1852; E. Larkin, "Devotional Revolution in Ireland, 1850–75," *AHR,* 77 (June 1972), 626–27; Ernst, 35–36.

75. McAvoy, 163–225; Clark, *Irish in Philadelphia,* 95–97; Light, 172–76; Dolan, 7–8; J. Phelan, 24 Jan. 1851 (Teresa Lawlor Mss., CAHS); Laurie, *Working,* 159; Fr. P. Devine, Journal (STPCR); Larkin, 649. See D. Guiney, 9 Aug. 1850, in Ellis, 387, for evidence of rapid linguistic change: "as to the girls that used to be troting on the bogs at home to hear them talk English would be of great astonishment to you."

76. Powers, 460–63; Joyce, 107; see files of NY *Freeman's Journal* and NY *Metropolitan Record,* 1840s–1870s; Dolan, 114–29; Ryan, 12–15, 36–42, 69, and passim; Light, 165–78; J. M. Donohoe, *Irish Catholic Benevolent Union* (Washington, D.C., 1953); J. Bland, *Hibernian Crusade: Catholic Total Abstinence Union of America* (Washington, D.C., 1951); P. Taggart, 14 June 1869 (Robert Humphreys Mss., CUL).

77. Dolan, 18–26; C. J. O'Fahey, "Reflections on the St. Patrick's Day Orations of John Ireland," *Ethnicity,* 2 (Sept. 1975), 244–57.

78. Potter, 364–65, 412–13; Dolan, 135; J. R. Hassard, *Life of the Most Rev. John Hughes . . .* (NY, 1886), passim; R. Gorman, *Catholic Apologetical Literature in the United States* (Washington, D.C., 1939), 108–10; D. Callahan, *Mind of the Catholic Layman* (NY, 1963), 31–42; *All Hallows College Annual Report, 1854* (Dublin, 1855), 31–42; J. P. Collins, 28 June 1853 (Col. J. H. Mulligan Mss., CHHS).

79. Potter, 495–508; Handlin, 137–53; Joyce, 49–67; I. Skelton, *Life of Thomas D'Arcy McGee* (Gardenville, Ontario, 1925).

80. Joyce, 84; Potter, 557–63; Summary, Doyle Reports (Larcom Papers, Ms. 7697, pp. 4–6, NLI).

81. Summary, Doyle Reports, 4–6. On Fenianism, see Beckett, 358–92; Kee, 299–347; W. M. D'Arcy, *Fenian Movement in the United States, 1858–86* (Washington, D.C., 1947), 180–81, 210, and passim; W. S. Neidhardt, *Fenianism in North America* (University Park, Penn., 1975); H. Senior, *Fenians and Canada* (Toronto, 1978); P. M. Toner, " 'Green Ghost': Canada's Fenians and the Raids," *É-I,* 16, no. 4 (Winter 1981); B. Jenkins, *Fenians and Anglo-American Relations during Reconstruction* (Ithaca, 1969); L. Ó Broin, *Fenian Fever: An Anglo-American Dilemma* (NY, 1971); J. Savage, *Fenian Heroes and Martyrs* (Boston, 1868); J. Devoy, *Recollections of an Irish Rebel* (Shannon, 1969 ed.); and Rossa, 300–304.

82. See works on Fenianism cited above. Clark, *Irish Relations,* 109.

83. E. M. Archibald, 19 Jan., 21 Mar., and 14 June 1859 (HO 45/o.s.6877, PRO); N. F.

Davin, *Irishman in Canada* (London, 1877), 549, 655; see works by T. N. Brown cited in n. 46 above; on Meagher, R. G. Athearn, *Thomas Francis Meagher* . . . (Boulder, 1949); M. Doheny, 20 Aug. 1858 (WSO'B, Ms. 446, NLI); Neidhardt, 129; Montgomery, *Beyond,* 212–13; Toner, passim; MacDonald, 131–34; NY *Irish News,* 17 Apr. 1858; NY *Phoenix,* clipping, n.d., in Doyle Reports #47, 28 Oct. 1859; Hibernicus, *Address to the Irish* . . . (Columbia, S.C., 1848), 12; P. Taggart, 14 June 1869 (Robert Humphreys Mss., CUL); Brown, *Irish-American Nationalism,* 21–22; J. P. Rodechko, *Patrick Ford and His Search for America* . . . (NY, 1976), 56.

84. MacDonagh, "Irish Emigration," 382; Joyce, 77; T. D'A. McGee, *History of the Irish Settlers in North America* (Boston, 1851), 173, 180, and passim; NY *Freeman's Journal,* 4 July 1846; NY *Irish News,* 25 Dec. 1858; Montgomery, *Beyond,* 133; Man, 104; Burton, 456–57; NY *Metropolitan Record,* 7 Sept. 1861; Kee, 307.

85. Davin, 549; White, *Sketches,* 369; M. Doheny, 20 Aug. 1858 (WSO'B, Ms. 446, NLI); Neidhardt, 129; W. Dillon, *Life of John Mitchel* (London, 1888), 61.

86. Gibson, 203; Kee, 307; Doyle Reports #53, 9 Dec. 1859; J. Mitchel, *Jail Journal* (Dublin, 1913 ed.), 357; Abbott, 475–76; *Celebration of St. Patrick's Day, 1863, by the Sons of the Emerald Isle* . . . (San Francisco, 1863), 3–4; Savage, 283–84.

87. W. Russell, *My Diary North and South* (London, 1863), 27; Maguire, 590–624; C. O'Conor Don, *Impressions of Journey through the States of America* (#9.3:249, O'CD); T. Reilly, 24 Apr. 1848 (Ms. 10,511, NLI).

88. Maguire, 590–624; Potter, 46; Woodham-Smith, 225; Doyle Reports #40, 26 Aug. 1859; White, *Sketches,* 364–69.

89. W. Lalor, 12 May 1843, 4 July 1867, and 10 Feb. 1868 (Ms. 8567, NLI); White, *Sketches,* 369–70; R. O'Gorman, 17 May 1857 (WSO'B, Ms. 455, NLI); B. Colgan, 13 June 1861 (AS); Montgomery, *Beyond,* 127, 130–31; NY *Metropolitan Record,* 7 Sept. 1861; R. Glanz, *Jew and Irish: Historic Group Relations* . . . (NY, 1966), 134–35.

90. H. Hunt, 17 June 1852 (John Dowling Mss., INHS); A. Browne, 13 Feb. 1855 (Fr. C. Reville Mss., FL); Montgomery, *Beyond,* 127, 130–31; Cole, 45–46; Nolan, 285–325; Toner, 29; White, *Sketches,* 362, 369; D. Rowntree, 23 Mar. 1852 (AS); J. Reford, 15 July 1849 (T.3028/B5, PRONI); W. S. O'Brien, *Lectures on America* . . . (Dublin, 1860), 16; Baum, 122; P. K. Walsh in *Cork Examiner,* 11 June 1860.

91. J. O'Leary, *Recollections of Fenians and Fenianism* (London, 1896), II, 240; J. Burke, *Reminiscences* (N-YHS); J. P. Carbery, book inscription (25 June 1870), in S. Colton, ed., *Catalogue of the Everett D. Graff Collection of Western Americana* (Chicago, 1968), 388.

92. Gordon, xxxiv; M. McAuley, letter in *Fermanagh Reporter,* 5 Apr. 1878 (ERRG); T. Kelly, ed., "Letters from America (II)," *Carloviana,* 1, no. 2 (Jan. 1948), 87.

Chapter 8. The Last "Exiles": Ireland and Post-Famine Emigration, 1856–1921

1. W. E. Vaughn and A. J. Fitzpatrick, eds., *Irish Historical Statistics: Population, 1821–1971* (Dublin, 1978), 3–4.

2. Ibid., 261–63; C. Ó Gráda, "Note on 19th-Century Irish Emigration Statistics," *PS,* 29 (Mar. 1975), 143–49; idem, "Some Aspects of 19th-Century Irish Emigration," in L. M. Cullen and T. C. Smout, eds., *Comparative Aspects of Scottish and Irish* . . . *History* (Edinburgh, 1977), 68–71; *Commission on Emigration and Other Population Problems* . . . (Dublin, 1954), 309–11; D. Gwynn, "England and Wales," and J. E. Handley, "Scotland," in P. J. Corish, ed., *History of Irish Catholicism,* vol. 6, pt. 1 (Dublin, 1968), 12, 24–26; *Historical Statistics of the United States,* pt. 1 (Washington, D.C., 1975), 116–17.

3. Vaughn and Fitzpatrick, 261–65; *Commission on Emigration,* 309–11; R. E. Kennedy, Jr., *The Irish: Emigration, Marriage, and Fertility* (Berkeley, 1975), 112; D. Fitzpatrick, "Irish Emigration in the Later 19th Century," *IHS,* 22 (Sept. 1980), 131–34; J. M. Mogey, *Rural Life in Northern Ireland* (London, 1947), 83, 143, 229.

4. Ó Gráda, "Some," 69–70; Fitzpatrick, 131–34; D. W. Fitzpatrick, "Study of Irish Population, 1840–1900" (Paper, Economic and Social History of Ireland conference, Cork, 1977), 14–15.

5. Religious estimates based on Vaughn and Fitzpatrick, 51–68. Also, see Kennedy, 112; J. White, *Minority Report* . . . (Dublin, 1975), 9–10; and Mogey, 83, 143, 229.

6. B. Ó Cuív, *Irish Dialects and Irish-Speaking Districts* (Dublin, 1951), 77–94; D. N. Doyle, *Irish Americans, Native Rights and National Empires* (NY, 1976), 32.

7. D. H. Akenson, *Irish Educational Experiment* (Toronto, 1970), 376–77; D. Swiney,

"Emigration from Ireland," in *USCR*, 57, no. 213 (June 1898), 235; 1826 and 1856 occupational statistics from a 1 percent sample of passenger lists of ships arriving at New York (on mf at NLI); E. A. Merritt, "Irish Distress and Emigration," in *USCR*, IX, 30 (Apr. 1883), 636; P. Higgins and F. V. Conolly, *Irish in America* (London, 1909), 40; A. Schrier, *Ireland and the American Emigration, 1850–1900* (NY, 1970 ed.), 110–11, 167–68.

8. Schrier, 4–5; B. Thomas, *Migration and Economic Growth . . .* (Cambridge, 1973 ed.), 74.

9. M. Wolfe, 8 Jan. 1874 (mf p3887, NLI); P. Taylor, *Distant Magnet: European Emigration to the U.S.A.* (NY, 1972), 68–80. Promotional literature includes T. Mooney, *Nine Years in America . . .* (Dublin, 1850); Hibernian Benevolent Society of Omaha, *Immigration to Nebraska Territory* (NY, 1866); California Labor Exchange, *Facts for Emigrants to California* (San Francisco, 1869); and Ministry of the Interior, *What Irishmen Say of Canada* (Ottawa, 1911). C. Houston and W. J. Smyth, "Orange Order and Expansion of the Frontier in Ontario, 1830–1900," *JHG*, 4 (1978), 251–64; N. Macdonald, *Canada: Immigration and Colonization, 1841–1903* (Aberdeen, 1966), 33–35; C. J. Sheil, 10 Mar. 1873 (John O'Donohoe Mss., PAC).

10. O. MacDonagh, *Pattern of Government Growth . . .* (London, 1961), 162, 293–97, 304–13; T. Coleman, *Going to America* (Garden City, 1973), 288–90; R. Pigott, 18 July 1866, and W. Grigsby et al., "Inside View of an English Emigrant Ship" (#9.3:183 and -337, O'CD); E. Rowntree, 26 Aug. 1851 (AS).

11. E. C. Guillet, *Great Migration . . .* (Toronto, 1963), 50–51; Coleman, 87–91; Taylor, 94, 116–20, 145–64; H. C. Brookfield, "Ireland and the Atlantic Ferry . . . ," *IRGEO*, 3 (1955), 71–74; J. B. Taney, 30 July 1894 (USCR, mf T-368, NA).

12. M. A. Jones, "Immigrants, Steamships and Governments . . . ," in H. C. Allen and R. Thompson, eds., *Contrast and Connection: Bicentennial Essays in Anglo-American History* (Athens, Ohio, 1976), 179; L. B. Sheil, 13 Nov. 1870 (Fr. C. Reville Mss., FL); F. McCosker, 14 Sept. 1873 (ERRG); M. MacGowan, *Hard Road to Klondike* (London, 1962), 52; D. Hurley, 24 June 1873 (Hurley Mss., CAC); J. M. Clancy, Diary (Ms. 21,666, NLI); J. Greene, ? Aug. 1902 (Greene Mss., AD/UCD); P. [McCarthy], 26 Oct. 1906 (ERRG); M. Hanlon, 27 Sept. 1870 (D.885, PRONI); W. Murphy, 25 Apr. 1873 (D.2795/5/2/1, PRONI); P. Ryan, Diary (WJSML); Guillet, 78; A. Conway, *Welsh in America* (Minneapolis, 1961), passim; M. Beattie, Diary (MG29 C59, PAC); H. Kennedy, 6 May 1912 (T.3152/6, PRONI); W. Bell, 18–20 Apr. 1905 (A. Hodgson, Derriaghy, Co. Antrim); M. A. Landy, [1885] (Mrs. E. McKenna, Balbriggan, Co. Dublin; courtesy of Drs. Jo-Ellen Vinyard and Francis Blouin, Immigration History Project, Univ. of Michigan).

13. *Royal Commission on Congestion in Ireland* (hereafter cited as *Congestion Commission*), vol. 1, in *GBPP-HC* (3267), 1906, p. 1018; N. Nolan, "Celtic Exodus, or the Irish Emigration" (Ph.D. diss., NUI, 1933), 100; M. McNeill, *Vere Foster* (University, Ala., 1971), 204; J. H. Tuke, *Reports and Papers relating to . . . "Mr. Tuke's Fund" . . .* (Dublin, 1883), passim; H. E. Egan, "Irish Immigration to Minnesota, 1865–90," *M-A*, 12 (July 1929), 234–41; Emigrants' Register Book, Girls' Friendly Society, 1890–1921 (D.648/9, PRONI); C. P. Cullop, "Unequal Duel: Union Recruiting in Ireland, 1863–64," *CWH*, 13 (1967), 106–9; J. M. Hernon, Jr., *Celts, Catholics, and Copperheads: Ireland Views the American Civil War* (Columbus, 1966), 17; U.S. Recruiting in Ireland, 1861–5 (Ms. 16,765, SPO); C. Erickson, *American Industry and European Immigrants, 1860–85* (Cambridge, Mass., 1957); H. B. Hammond, 23 Apr. 1863 (USCR, mf T-199, NA); Merritt, 633–35; A. I. Shand, *Letters from the West of Ireland, 1884* (London, 1885), 148–49; F. Y. Aglionby, 29 June and 22 July 1868 (F. Y. Aglionby Mss., DUL); H. T. Lawler, 16 May 1880 (Ms. 8567, NLI); Schrier, 104–9.

14. London *Daily News*, 9 Sept. 1864 (citation courtesy of AS); E. Donohoe, 12 June 1857 (Donohoe Mss., AIS-UP); W. Porter, 25 Mar. 1872 (D.1152/3/24, PRONI); W. Austin, 10 Mar. 1874 (Ms. 18,236, NLI); J. McN. Vinyard, *Irish on the Urban Frontier: Detroit, 1850–80* (NY, 1976), 146; J. Glover, 4 Apr. 1870 (T.1347B, PRONI); P. McKeown, 22 Apr. 1894 (AS); N. Shanks, 8 Feb. 1890 (D.2709/1/57, PRONI).

15. J. Kirwan, in *Kilkenny Journal*, 1 Dec. 1875 (AS); N. Carrothers, 15 June 1858 (AS); J. Sample, 1 Nov. 1878 (T.2722/3, PRONI); M. Wolfe, 7 Nov. 1873 (mf p.3887, NLI); O. O'Callaghan, 5 Dec. 1883 and 2 Nov. 1884 (Eugene O'Callaghan, Kilmacthomas, Co. Waterford); J. Chamberlain, n.d. [1880?] (AS); Anon. letter, *Kilkenny Journal*, 25 Sept. 1904 (AS); A. Heggarty, 19 July 1884 (AS); S. Buchanan, 30 June 1894 (Buchanan Mss., NLI); C. Connor, 18 Mar. 1907 (T.2085, PRONI). Also see M. Malone, 24 Jan. 1877 (AS); F. Woolsey, 18 June 1877 (AS); M. Kenny, 21 Aug. 1881, 19 Apr. 1889, and

9 Mar. 1890 (AS); T. Sample, 12 Sept. 1887 (T.2722/12, PRONI); P. McKeown, 11 Aug. 1889, 8 Dec. 1901, and 24 June 1905 (AS); J. McFadden, 17 Oct. 1897 (AS); A. Wilson, from 12 Oct. 1899 to 24 Feb. 1901 (D.1921/3/13,18,22-3, PRONI); and W. H. Downes, 23 Mar. 1913 (William O'Shaughnessy, Pallaskenry, Co. Limerick).

16. W. McSparron, 6 Aug. 1861 (T.2743/3/1, PRONI); M. Sexton, 24 Nov. 1861 (AS); A. P. Man, Jr., "Irish in New York in Early 1860s," *IHS,* 7 (Sept. 1950), 105–6; anon. letter in *Kilkenny Journal,* 18 Oct. 1862 (AS); Hernon, 7–8, 15–18, 108; E. Donohoe, 5 July 1862 (Donohoe Mss., AIS-UP); U.S. Recruiting in Ireland, 1861–5 (Ms. 16,765, SPO); H. O'Mahoney, Reminiscences (Bridget Lynch, Berkeley, Calif.); A. MacLochlainn, "Three Ballads of the American Civil War," *Irish Sword,* 6, no. 22 (Summer 1963), 28–33; R. L. Wright, *Irish Emigrant Ballads and Songs* (Bowling Green, Ohio, 1975), 459, 464–65; W. B. West, 23 May 1863 (USCR, mf T-570, NA).

17. E. Eastman, 27 Aug. 1863 (USCR, mf T-196, NA); H. B. Hammond, 23 Apr. 1863 (USCR, mf T-199, NA); S. Bates, 1 July 1863 (AS); Hernon, 7–8, 11; see J. O'Donovan Rossa, *Rossa's Recollections . . .* (Mariner's Harbor, NY, 1898), for letters concerning Irish Fenians' emigration and enlistments; A. Irvine, 4 June 1864 (T.2135, PRONI); M. W. Keogh, 30 Nov. 1867 (Ms. 3885, NLI); L. M. Cullen, *Economic History of Ireland . . .* (London, 1972), 137–38; J. S. Donnelly, Jr., "Irish Agricultural Depression of 1859–64," *IESH,* 3 (1976), 33–54; Vaughn and Fitzpatrick, 269–353; W. B. West, 26 May and 11 Oct. 1862, 15 Aug. 1863 (USCR, mf T-570, NA); E. Eastman, 7 Dec. 1863 (USCR, mf T-196, NA); H. B. Hammond, 31 July, 28 Aug., and 11 Sept. 1862 (USCR, mf T-199, NA); Rev. J. Bannon, 17 Nov. 1863 (Rev. John Bannon Mss., SCL/USC); Cullop, 108; T. McManus, 17 Mar. 1864, and E. Cummins, 23 Mar. 1864, in W. B. West, 20 Apr. 1864, and W. B. West, 6 July 1867 (USCR, mf T-199, NA).

18. J. Lee, *Modernisation of Irish Society, 1848–1918* (Dublin, 1973), preface. On "modernization" generally, see R. Grew, "Modernization and Its Discontents," *ABS,* 21 (Nov./Dec. 1977), 289–312; R. D. Brown, *Modernization: Transformation of American Life,* 1600–1865 (NY, 1976), esp. 3–22.

19. Lee, preface; Cullen, 167 and passim; E. Larkin, "Economic Growth, Capital Investment, and the Roman Catholic Church in 19th-Century Ireland," *AHR,* 72 (Apr. 1967), 882; L. Kennedy, "Roman Catholic Church and Economic Growth in 19th-Century Ireland," *ECSOR,* 10 (Oct. 1978), 50; M. Hechter, *Internal Colonialism . . .* (Berkeley, 1974), passim; L. M. Cullen and T. C. Smout, "Economic Growth in Scotland and Ireland," in Cullen and Smout, 13.

20. Hechter, passim.

21. Fitzpatrick, "Irish Emigration," 127.

22. T. W. Grimshaw, *Facts and Figures about Ireland* (Dublin, 1893), 19 and statistical tables; A. MacDowell, *Facts about Ireland . . .* (London, 1888), 30–31; L. Paul-Dubois, *Contemporary Ireland* (Dublin, 1908), 334; M. Sexton, 24 Nov. 1861 (AS); Lee, 13–15; Cullen, 144–47, 156; L. Kennedy, "Regional Specialization, Railway Development, and Irish Agriculture in the 19th Century," in J. M. Goldstrom and L. A. Clarkson, eds., *Irish Population, Economy, and Society* (Oxford, 1981), 173–93; K. T. Hoppen, "National Politics and Local Realities in Mid-19th Century Ireland," in A. Cosgrove and D. McCartney, eds., *Studies in Irish History . . .* (Dublin, 1979), 191–95; R. McHugh, "Famine in Irish Oral Tradition," in R. D. Edwards and T. D. Williams, eds., *The Great Famine . . .* (NY, 1957), 435.

23. T. W. Freeman, "Irish Towns in the 18th and 19th Centuries," in R. A. Butlin, ed., *Development of the Irish Town* (London, 1977), 133; F. H. A. Aalen, *Man and Landscape in Ireland* (London, 1978), 196–97, 284; Vaughn and Fitzpatrick, 27–41; M. Murphy, "Economic and Social Structure of 19th-Century Cork," in D. Harkness and M. O'Dowd, eds., *Town in Ireland* (Belfast, 1981), 125; J. V. O'Brien, *"Dear Dirty Dublin": City in Distress, 1899–1916* (Berkeley, 1982), 14–15.

24. S. Clark, *Social Origins of the Land War* (Princeton, 1979), 126–38; idem, "Political Mobilization of Irish Farmers," *CRSA,* 12 (1975), 490–91; P. Colum, *Road Round Ireland* (NY, 1926), 33–34; J. Forbes, *Memorandums Made in Ireland in . . . 1852* (London, 1853), 90; Donnelly, 50; Paul-Dubois, 334–35; L. Kennedy, "Farmers, Traders, and Agricultural Politics in Pre-Independence Ireland," in S. Clark and J. S. Donnelly, Jr., *Irish Peasants . . .* (Madison, Wis., 1983), 339–73; P. Connell, *Changing Forces Shaping a 19th-Century Irish Town . . .* Navan (Maynooth, 1978), 29–47; E. Barker, *Ireland in the Last Fifty Years* (Oxford, 1917), 42–43.

25. Murphy, 132–36; White, 56, 159–60; Lee, 28–31; Colum, 43–44; M. McDermott, 22 Feb. 1871 (JD, Ms. 6844, TCD).

26. Cullen, 144–48, 156–59; J. Denieff, *Personal Narrative of the Irish Revolutionary Brotherhood* (Shannon, 1969 ed.), 7–9; S. Glacken, 10 Feb. 1868 (Teresa Lawlor Mss., CAHS); Shand, 154; M. Daly, "Late 19th- and Early 20th-Century Dublin," in Harkness and O'Dowd, 221–26; A. C. Davies, "Roofing Belfast and Dublin," 1896–8: American Penetration of the Irish Market for Welsh Slate," *IESH,* 4 (1977), 26–35; Murphy, 125–54; M. Murphy, "Fenianism, Parnellism, and the Cork Trades, 1860–1900," *Saothar,* 5 (1979), 28–32; A .Boyd, *Rise of the Irish Trade Unions* . . . (Tralee, 1972), 59–60 and passim; S. Daly, *Cork, A City in Crisis: History of Labour Conflict and Social Misery, 1870–2* (Cork, 1978); L. Richmond, 15 Dec. 1877 (USCR, mf T-196, NA); C. D. Greaves, *Life and Times of James Connolly* (NY, 1971 ed.), 247; T. Brick, Memoirs (Doncha Ó Conchúir, Ballyferriter, Co. Kerry); H. O'Mahoney, Reminiscences (Bridget Lynch); E. Hanlon, 4 Mar. 1871 (D.885, PRONI); J. and M. Fleming, 26 Dec. ? (Robert Humphreys Mss., CUL).

27. L. M. Cullen, *Life in Ireland* (London, 1968), 147–48, 167–69; Cullen, *Economic,* 164–66; M. Daly, 221–52; O'Brien, 21–36, 95–100, 156–62, 200–225, and passim; E. Larkin, *James Larkin: Irish Labour Leader, 1876–1947* (London, 1965); Greaves, 247 and passim.

28. M. Daly, 221–52; O'Brien, 70–100 and passim; J. A. MacMahon, "Catholic Clergy and the Social Question in Ireland," *Studies,* 70 (1981), 263–86; I. d'Alton, "Contrast in Crises: Southern Irish Protestantism, 1820–43 and 1885–1910," in A. C. Hepburn, ed., *Minorities in History* (London, 1978), 78; Murphy, "Fenianism," 31–36; H. Robinson, *Further Memories of Irish Life* (London, 1924), 204–10; J. Plunkett, *Strumpet City* (London, 1969).

29. Cullen, *Life,* 168, and *Economic,* 159–60; Freeman, 133–34; Aalen, 203–4; S. Gribbon, "An Irish City: Belfast, 1911," in Harkness and O'Dowd, 205, 215; Vaughn and Fitzpatrick, 36–39.

30. Vaughn and Fitzpatrick, 10–16, 51–68, 311–32; see Appendix, Tables 2, 3, and 5.

31. Merritt, 633–35; see Appendix, Table 13; Fitzpatrick, "Irish Emigration," 129–31; Mogey, 83, 143, 229; A. G. Darroch and M. D. Ornstein, "Ethnicity and Occupational Structure in Canada in 1871," *CHR,* 61 (1980), 312; C. J. Houston and W. J. Smyth, *Sash Canada Wore* . . . (Toronto, 1980), 105; see Appendix, Tables 2, 3, and 5.

32. P. Gibbon, *Origins of Ulster Unionism* (Manchester, 1975), 44–65; A. Irvine, *From the Bottom Up* (NY, 1910), 3–23, 59–60; C. Gill, *Rise of the Irish Linen Industry* (Oxford, 1925), 322–33; T. W. Moody and J. C. Beckett, eds., *Ulster since 1800: Social Survey* (London, 1958), 42–43; E. J. Riordan, *Modern Irish Trade and Industry* (London, 1920), 115–16. T. Frean, 16 Nov. 1859; J. Young, n.d. [1863]; T. A. King, 4 Feb. 1869; A. B. Woods, 10 Jan. 1884 and 8 Jan. 1885 (USCR, mf T-368, NA). Cullen, *Economic,* 151, 160; Shand, 49; R. Lynd, *Home Life in Ireland* (London, 1909), 239–42; Guardian of the Poor, *The Irish Peasant—A Sociological Survey* (London, 1892), 106–7; Paul-Dubois, 326; *Congestion Commission,* vol. 6 (3784), 1908, pp. 98–99, 185; B. M. Walker, *Sentry Hill: Ulster Farm and Family* (Belfast, 1981), 112; J. Graham, "Disappearance of Clachans from South Ards, Co. Down, in the 19th Century," *IRGEO,* 6 (1969), 269.

33. Mogey, 125–26; Vaughn and Fitzpatrick, 36–39; Freeman, 133–34; D. H. Akenson, *Between Two Revolutions* . . . *Islandmagee, Co. Antrim, 1798–1920* (Hamden, Conn., 1979), 72–73.

34. T. Kells, 18 Dec. 1901 (Kells Mss., M7075, PROI); Vaughn and Fitzpatrick, 36–37; Cullen, *Life,* 168; idem, *Economic,* 148, 159–60; Riordan, 101, 110–11; O'Brien, 23, 27; A. B. Woods, 29 Nov. 1884 (USCR, mf T-368, NA).

35. Cullen, *Economic,* 148. Compare the fluctuations of late-19th- and early-20th-century Ulster emigration in Tables 2 and 4, Appendix, with contemporary British emigration, as in *Historical Statistics of the United States* (Washington, D.C., 1961), 56–57. D. S. MacNeice, "Industrial Villages of Ulster, 1800–1900," in P. Roebuck, ed., *Plantation to Partition: Essays in Ulster History* . . . (Belfast, 1981), 184–85; G. W. Savage, 2 June 1886 (USCR, mf T-368, NA); "Report on Enforcement of Alien Contract Labor Laws," *USCR,* in *House Exec. Docs.,* 52d Cong., 1st sess. (1892; serial no. 2957, #235, pt. 1), 208–11.

36. A. B. Woods, 29 Nov. 1884 (USCR, mf T-368, NA); H. B. Miller, "Report on Irish Wages, 1909," *USCR,* in *House Exec. Docs.,* 61st Cong., 2d sess. (June 1910; serial no. 5794, v. 91, #162), 130–31; Lynd, 228–35; Greaves, 293–94.

37. Cullen, *Economic,* 159–60; idem, *Life,* 168; Riordan, 97–99. In 1901, 10 percent of

Belfast's inhabitants had been born outside Ireland, primarily in Great Britain; see A. C. Hepburn and B. Collins, "Industrial Society: Structure of Belfast, 1901," in Roebuck, 220–21. Vaughn and Fitzpatrick, 149, 155; see Appendix, Table 13.

38. Vaughn and Fitzpatrick, 5–16, 51–68; Hepburn and Collins, 220–21; S. E. Baker, "Orange and Green Belfast, 1832–1912," in H. J. Dyos and M. Wolff, eds., *Victorian City: Images and Realities* (London, 1973), II, 793; *Congestion Commission,* vol. 6 (3784), 1908, pp. 114, 151–53; MacNeice, 185–86.

39. On political developments in post-Famine Ulster, see Gibbon, 67–146; D. W. Miller, *Queen's Rebels* . . . (NY, 1978), 60–121; P. Buckland, *Irish Unionism 2: Ulster Unionism* . . . (Dublin, 1973); P. Bew and F. Wright, "Agrarian Question in Ulster Politics, 1848–87," and B. M. Walker, "Land Question and Elections in Ulster," in Clark and Donnelly, 192–268; B. M. Walker, "Party Organization in Ulster, 1865–92 . . . ," in Roebuck, 194 and passim; J. R. B. McMinn, "Liberalism in North Antrim, 1900–14," *IHS,* 23 (May 1982), 17–29. On the Orange Order in Belfast, see H. Patterson, *Class Conflict and Sectarianism: Protestant Working Class and Belfast Labour Movement, 1868–1920* (Belfast, 1980).

W. Porter, 15 June 1873 (D.1152/3/26, PRONI); G. W. Pepper, *Under Three Flags* . . . (Cincinnati, 1899), 62; Macdonald, 33–35; Houston and Smyth, *Sash,* 17 and passim; Houston and Smyth, "Orange Order," 251–64; H. Senior, *Orangeism: Canadian Phase* (Toronto, 1972), 73, 81–82; Mogey, 83, 143. Ulster Protestants' letters enticing remove to Canada include E. Flemming, 7 Aug. 1899 (T.1850/9, PRONI), and A. M. Galbraith, 9 Mar. 1914 (T.2722/29, PRONI).

40. Demographic patterns were computed from Vaughn and Fitzpatrick, 49–68; R. W. Kirkpatrick, "Origins and Development of the Land War in Mid-Ulster, 1879–85," in F. S. L. Lyons and A. J. Hawkins, eds., *Ireland under the Union* . . . (Oxford, 1980), 201–35; information on Co. Down is from Dr. Líam Kennedy, QUB

41. Baker, 793–96, 808; Gibbon, 16–17, 67–140, and passim; Lee, 50–53, 131–33; Moody and Beckett, 164–66; Greaves, 269–70; F. S. L. Lyons, *Culture and Anarchy in Ireland, 1890–1939* (NY, 1979), 125–26; Larkin, *James Larkin,* passim; A. T. Q. Stewart, *Narrow Ground* . . . (London, 1977), 150–53; Buckland, 1–67; Miller, 92; H. Patterson, "Independent Orangeism and Class Conflict in Edwardian Belfast," *PRIA,* 80, no. 1 (1980), 4–27; idem, *Class Conflict,* passim; McMinn, 17–29; R. D. Edwards, *James Connolly* (Dublin, 1981), 101–2.

42. Baker, 796–802; Hepburn and Collins, 220–22; A. C. Hepburn, "Work, Class, and Religion in Belfast, 1871–1911," *IESH,* 10 (1983), 33–50; idem, "Catholics in the North of Ireland, 1850–1921: Urbanization of a Minority," in Hepburn, *Minorities,* 88–89; *Congestion Commission,* vol. 4 (3509), 1907, p. 123; J. Nugent, 18 Sept. 1864 (Alice Timoney, Clontarf, Co. Dublin); R. B. Burns, "D'Arcy McGee and the Fenians," in M. Harmon, ed., *Fenians and Fenianism* (Dublin, 1968), 83–90; A. Perraud, *Ireland under English Rule* (Dublin, 1864), 230; Denieffe, 148; Senior, 81–82; Mogey, 83.

43. Lee, 2; *Census of Ireland, 1861,* pt. 5, *General Report,* in GBPP-HC (3204-IV), 1863, LXI, vii (hereafter cited as *1861 Irish Census*); *Agricultural Statistics, Ireland, 1861,* in GBPP-HC (3156), 1863, LXIX, 547–69 (hereafter cited as *1861 Irish Ag. Stats.*); P. M. A. Bourke, "Uncertainties in the Statistics of Farm Size in Ireland, 1841–51," *JSSISI,* 20 (1959–60), 21, 55; idem, "Agricultural Statistics of the 1841 Census of Ireland . . . ," *ECONHR,* 18 (1965), 380; A. Trollope, *North America* (NY, 1951 ed.), 513.

44. Lee, 2; *Census of Ireland, 1911, General Report,* in GBPP-HC (6663), 1912–13, LXX, 10–21, 431–38 (hereafter cited as *1911 Irish Census*); E. R. Hooker, *Readjustments of Agricultural Tenure in Ireland* (Chapel Hill, 1938), 221; Clark, *Social Origins,* 108; Aalen, 208; M. E. Daly, *Social and Economic History of Ireland since 1800* (Dublin, 1981), 29; McDowell, 8–9; P. M. A. Bourke, "Extent of the Potato Crop in Ireland at the Time of the Famine," *JSSISI,* 20 (1959), 11.

45. Daly, *Social,* 29; Kennedy, "Roman," 50; Cullen, *Economic,* 155–56; Lee, 14; T. W. Grimshaw, "Statistical Survey of Ireland, from 1840 to 1888," *JSSISI,* 9 (Nov. 1888), 333; W. R. LeFanu, *Seventy Years of Irish Life* (London, 1898), 297.

46. M. Bonn, *Modern Ireland and Her Agrarian Problem* (Dublin, 1906), 48–50; *1911 Irish Census,* 434–38; J. S. Donnelly, Jr., *Land and the People of 19th-Century Cork* . . . (London, 1975), 234; W. E. Vaughn, "Agricultural Output, Rents, and Wages in Ireland, 1850–80," in L. M. Cullen and F. Furet, eds., *Ireland and France, 17th–20th Centuries* . . . (Ann Arbor, 1980), 88–89; W. E. Vaughn, "Farmer, Grazier, and Gentleman: Edward Delany of Woodtown, 1851–99," *IESH,* 9 (1982), 53–72; Shand, 89.

47. W. Porter, 30 Dec. 1868 (D.1152/3/18, PRONI); D. McCourt, "Dynamic Quality of Irish Rural Settlement," in R. H. Buchanan et al., eds., *Man and His Habitat* (London, 1971), 145; Clark, *Social,* 171–75; Lee, 36–38; J. North, 1 May 1850, 17 Dec. 1851, and 5 Jan. 1853 (Ms. 13,093, NLI); F. S. L. Lyons, *Ireland since the Famine* (London, 1971), 14–15; Larkin, "Economic," 862–63; Shand, 128–29; H. Coulter, *West of Ireland* (London, 1862), 94–95 B. Becker, *Disturbed Connaught* (London, 1882), 19–25, 89–95, 216–21; M. Houston, *Twenty Years in the Wild West* (London, 1879), 27, 55–56, and passim; J. J. Mitchell, Journal (N-YHS); B. L. Solow, *Land Question and the Irish Economy, 1870–1903* (Cambridge, Mass., 1971), 3 and passim.

48. L. P. Curtis, Jr., "Incumbered Wealth: Landed Indebtedness in Post-Famine Ireland," *AHR,* 85 (Apr. 1980), 360, 365–66; Clark, *Social,* 153–55, 182–86; W. E. Vaughn, "Landlord and Tenant Relations in Ireland between the Famine and the Land War, 1850–78," in Cullen and Smout, 217–19; Vaughn, "Agricultural," 85–86; Solow, 57–77; A. McConnell, 31 Jan. 1856, and M. Hunter, 20 Jan. 1859 (McConnell Mss., MTCL); MacDowell, 18; Lee, 36–38; Cullen, *Economic,* 139–40; W. S. Trench, *Realities of Irish Life* (London, 1869); K. T. Hoppen, "Landlords, Society, and Electoral Politics in Mid-19th-Century Ireland," *P&P,* no. 75 (1977), passim; J. H. Whyte, "Landlord Influence at Elections in Ireland, 1760–1885," *EHR,* 80 (1965), 749–54.

49. Forbes, II, 266; Clark, *Social,* 155–64, 182–93; Akenson, *Between,* 31; W. Nolan, *Fassadinin . . .* (Dublin), 1979), 163–73; e.g., E. Somerville and M. Ross, *The Real Charlotte* (London, 1948 ed.); Hoppen, "Landlords," passim; Perraud, 9–12, 26–31; Whyte, 755–56; W. L. Feingold, "Tenants' Movement to Capture the Irish Poor Law Boards, 1877–86," *Albion,* 7 (Fall 1975), passim; idem, "Political Triumph of the Irish Large Farmer, 1870–86" (Paper, AHR convention, Washington, D.C., 1976); idem, "Land League Power: Tralee Poor-Law Election of 1881," in Clark and Donnelly, 285–310; J. McFadden, 11 Nov. 1880 (Ms. S254, LSFL); D. Fitzpatrick, *Politics and Irish Life, 1913–21* (Dublin, 1977), 55–56; D. N. Haire, "In Aid of the Civil Power, 1868–90," in Lyons and Hawkins, 115–47.

50. Clark, *Social,* 155–71; W. E. Vaughn, "Assessment of Economic Performance of Irish Landlords, 1851–81," in Lyons and Hawkins, 175–81, 190–9; Vaughn, "Landlord and Tenant," 217–18, 221–23; Forbes, II, 266; C. Ó Gráda, "Agricultural Head Rents, Pre-Famine and Post-Famine," *ECSOR,* 3 (1974), 390–91; Shand, 85; P. Bew, *Land and the National Question, 1858–82* (Dublin, 1979), 7–33 and passim; Donnelly, *Land,* 187–200.

51. Bew, 21–23; D. S. Jones, "Agrarian Capitalism and Rural Social Development in Ireland" (Ph.D. diss., QUB, 1977), 32–69; Vaughn, "Landlord and Tenant," 218; Solow, 7, 125–46; E. D. Steele, *Irish Land and British Politics: Tenant Right and Nationality, 1865–70* (Cambridge, 1974), 7–8, 16, 28; Clark, *Social,* 175–79, 225–29; Donnelly, *Land,* 200–18; MacDowell, 18; Cullen, *Economic,* 148–51.

52. Clark, *Social,* 236–40, 334–49, and passim; Solow, 168–94; Bew, 144–65; Donnelly, *Land,* 378; Pomfret, *Struggle for Land in Ireland, 1800–1923* (NY, 1969 ed.), 162–309 passim.

53. Solow, 168–94; Pomfret, 162–309; Lyons, *Ireland since,* 201, 214–15; Cullen, *Economic,* 152–53; L. P. Curtis, Jr., *Coercion and Conciliation in Ireland, 1880–92: Study in Conservative Unionism* (Princeton, 1963), 358–61; Lee, 123–25; C. Ehrlich, "Sir Horace Plunkett and Agricultural Reform," in Goldstrom and Clarkson, 275–76 and passim.

54. Pomfret, 288–89; see Appendix, Table 5; M. E. Daly, *Social,* 56; C. J. Dolan, "Congested Districts," *Irish Year Book, 1909* (Dublin, 1909), 133–40.

55. Cullen, *Economic,* 134–70; Donnelly, *Land,* 148–51, 308–13; C. Ó Gráda, "Beginnings of the Irish Creamery System, 1880–1914," *ECONHR,* 30 (1977), 287–88; J. Connolly, *Labour in Ireland* (Dublin, n.d.), 166–68; Bonn, 152; A. Livermore, 15 May 1878 (USCR, mf T-368, NA); Lynd, 206.

56. F. S. L. Lyons, "Economic Ideas of Parnell," *HS,* 2 (1959), 65–66; Connolly, 166–68; T. W. Moody, *Michael Davitt and Irish Revolution, 1846–82* (NY, 1982), 384–85, 413–14, 517–21; Pomfret, 162–66; Clark, "Political Mobilization," 487; Shand, 85–86; G. Pellew, *In Castle and Cabin* (London, 1888), 9–10 and passim.

57. Paul-Dubois, 334–35; Coulter, 23, 57–58; Shand, 85–86, 166–67; Becker, 210–14; Clark, "Political Mobilization," 487; Pellew, 10; Guardian of the Poor, 41–43; P. Daryl, *Ireland's Disease . . .* (London, 1888), 193; P. Gibbon and M. D. Higgins, "Irish 'Gombeenman': Re-incarnation or Rehabilitation?" *ECSOR,* 8 (July 1977), 313–15; L. Kennedy, "Skeptical View on the Reincarnation of the Irish 'Gombeenman,' " *ECSOR,* 8 (Mar. 1977), 216–19; idem, "Retail Markets in Rural Ireland at the End of the 19th Century," *IESH,* 5 (1978), 46 and passim; P. Gallagher, *Paddy the Cope: Autobiography* (NY, 1942),

passim; W. L. Daniels, "AE and Synge in the Congested Districts," *É-I*, 9, no. 4 (Winter 1976), 18.

58. D. S. Jones, "Cleavage between Graziers and Peasants in the Land Struggle, 1890–1910," in Clark and Donnelly, 374–417; idem, "Agrarian Capitalism," 18–113; Ms. 1408, pp. 65, 83–84, 139–40 (DIF/UCD); Bonn, 41, 90–91; E. Barker, *Ireland in the Last Fifty Years* (Oxford, 1917), 33, 42–43; S. Gwynn, *Holiday in Connemara* (London, 1909), 110; Guardian of the Poor, 144–45; Bew, 22, 87, and passim; Becker, 246; Clark, "Political Mobilization," 494–95; idem, *Social*, 338–49.

59. D. S. Jones, "Agrarian," 1–17, 80–274 (esp. 239–66); M. E. Daly, *Social*, 55; S. Brooks, *Aspects of the Irish Question* (Dublin, 1912), 56–57; W. P. O'Ryan [Ryan], *Plough and the Cross: Story of New Ireland* (Dublin, 1910), 136; Lee, 10–11; Bonn, 39–41; Feingold, "Political,"; J. V. O'Brien, *William O'Brien and the Course of Irish Politics, 1881–1918* (Berkeley, 1976), 105–37; Clark, *Social*, 326–31, 342; L. Kennedy, "Farmers, Traders," passim; D. Ryan, ed., *The Workers' Republic: Selection from the Writings of James Connolly* (Dublin, 1951), 54–55.

60. E. Donohoe, 3 July 1862 (Donohoe Mss., AIS-UP); Schrier, 164; Ó Gráda, "Beginnings," 287–88; M. E. Daly, *Social*, 51, 58; Donnelly, *Land*, 169–72; Solow, 150–51, 199–200; Ehrlich, 272–73; "Pat" [P. D. Kenny], *Economics for Irishmen* (Dublin, 1906), 8 and passim; Vaughn, "Assessment," 186–87; idem, "Agricultural Output," 88–90; Bew, 27–33; C. Ó Síocháin, *Man from Cape Clear* (Cork, 1975), 23; W. Porter, 30 Dec. 1868 (D.1152/3/18, PRONI); Sproule family letters, 1860s–1870s (Acc. #1877, SHC/UNC-CH); E. Donohoe, 28 Nov. 1859 (Donohoe Mss., AIS-UP); M. Wolfe, 25 Jan. 1875 (mf p3887, NLI).

61. Coulter, 22; Donnelly, "Irish," passim; Clark, *Social*, 225–29; Solow, 121–46; Donnelly, *Land*, 144–45, 228, 308–13 E. Carroll, 31 Jan. 1862 (John Dowling Mss., INHS); J. Young, 20 Apr. 1864 (USCR, mf T-368, NA); Bew, 224–25; J. J. Piatt, "Report on Irish Emigration," in *USCR*, 22, no. 76 (1887), 565; Bonn, 44–50; Lynd, 205; *Congestion Commission*, vol. 6 (3784), 1908, pp. 89–97, 100–101, 173, 222, 239–53; E. Eastman, n.d. [1868], and J. J. Piatt, 15 Sept. 1883 (USCR, mf T-196, NA); A. Livermore, 31 July 1883, and J. B. Taney, 30 July 1894 (USCR, mf T-368, NA).

62. *Congestion Commission*, vol. 6 (3784), 1908, pp. 89–97, 151–53, 173–85, 219; F. H. A. Aalen, "Some Historical Aspects of . . . Omeath, Co. Louth," *IRGEO*, 4 (1962), 270–71; see above, pp. 293–97; Cullen, *Economic*, 150–51; Akenson, *Irish*, 376; E. L. Almquist, "Mayo and Beyond . . ." (Ph.D. diss., Boston Univ., 1977), 267–68; Coulter, 22–23, 78–79, 182–83; Shand, 114, 193–94, 202–3; Lee, 71; Vaughn and Fitzpatrick, 5–16; see Appendix, Table 5; J. H. Johnson, "Population of Londonderry during Great Irish Famine," *ECONHR*, 10 (1957–58), passim; Donnelly, *Land*, 219–24, 230–31; Ó Gráda, "Some Aspects," 69–70; Fitzpatrick, "Study," 14–15; idem, "Irish Emigration," 127–30.

63. Coulter, 9, 30, 113–14, 200; Shand, 32–33, 36, 114; B. S. MacAodha, "Clachan Settlement in Iar-Connacht," *IRGEO*, 5 (1965), 20–28; F. H. A. Aalen and H. Brody, *Gola: Life and Last Days of an Island Community* (Cork, 1969), 66; Almquist, 18; Jones, "Agrarian," 1–17; Donnelly, *Land*, 132–72; D. Jordan, "Regional Development and Post-Famine Politics in Co. Mayo" (Paper, Midwest ACIS conference, Chicago, 1982); Clark, *Social*, 111–12.

64. Shand, 36; *1861 Irish Ag. Stats.*, 556; Coulter, 110–11, 189–90; Cullen, *Life*, 160; K. O'Mally Toole, testimony (Ms. 1410, DIF/UCD); Gallagher, 1–3; MacGowan, 3; Donnelly, "Irish," 46–47; see Appendix, Tables 2, 3, and 5; C. J. Sheil, 10 Mar. 1873 (John O'Donohoe Mss., PAC); Clark, *Social*, 229–36; Cullen, *Economic*, 135; Lee, 82–83; S. H. Cousens, "Regional Variations in Population Changes in Ireland, 1861–81," *ECONHR*, 18 ((1964–65), 277–85; B. M. Walsh, "Perspective on Irish Population Patterns," *É-I*, 4, no. 3 (Autumn 1969), 10–11; Gallagher, 5; Becker, 111; J. H. Johnson, "Harvest Migration from 19th-Century Ireland," *T&P-IBG*, 41 (June 1967), 104; C. Ó Gráda, "Post-Famine Adjustment: Essays in 19th-Century Irish Economic History," *IESH*, 1 (1974), 65–66; idem, "Seasonal Migration and Post-Famine Adjustment in the West of Ireland," *SH*, 13 (1973), 55; idem, "Demographic Adjustment and Seasonal Migration," in Cullen and Furet, 189.

65. Cullen, *Economic*, 135, 148–49; idem, *Life*, 152; Lee, 65–66, 70, 79–83; Pomfret, 246–47; T. Barrington, "Review of Irish Agricultural Prices," *JSSISI*, 15 (1927), 252; Clark, *Social*, 225–29; Solow, 121–46; Becker, 101–2; Ó Gráda, "Seasonal," 57, 66.

66. E. M. Crawford, "Indian Meal and Pellagra in 19th-Century Ireland," in Goldstrom and Clarkson, 124–33; Shand, 202; Tuke, 10; Becker, 105–7; Bew, passim; MacDowell, 18.

67. MacNeil, 202–4; Bew, 224–25; Jordan; Shand, 114–15, 148–52; Tuke, 21–22, 24–25, 142–45; Rev. B. Walker, 29 June 1886 (Ms. S254, LSFL); *Congestion Commission,* vol. 1 (3267), 1906, p. 1018; J. J. Piatt, 25 July 1883 (USCR, mf T-196, NA); Misc. documents on assisted emigration, early 1880s (HO 45/9635/A29278, PRO); Egan, 234–41.

68. See Appendix, Tables 2–6 and 8 (assuming that half of Cork's post-1881 emigration left the West Riding, probably an underestimate); Vaughn and Fitzpatrick, 5–16; Tuke, 19–21 and passim; Paul-Dubois, 305; Schrier, 112–22; Cullen, *Economic,* 152–53; Curtis, *Coercion,* 358–61; Lee, 123–25; Pomfret, 309–11.

69. A. J. Reid, "Report on Irish Agriculture," in *USCR,* 34, no. 120 (1890), 45–50; Greaves, 101–5; J. M. Synge, *Aran Islands and Other Writings* (NY, 1962), 317, 329, 332–33; Ó Gráda, "Seasonal," 57; Lynd, 31–32; *CDB Inspectors' Confidential Reports, 1891–5* (TCD), 80–81, 88–89, 482–500, 632–37, and passim (hereafter cited as *CDB Reports*); Aalen and Brody, 60–63; Gallagher, 1–3, 279–80; Cullen, *Life,* 162; *Congestion Commission,* vol. 1 (3267), 1906, p. 686; R. Fox, *Tory Islanders . . .* (Cambridge, 1978), 153–54; Pomfret, 253–54; Almquist, 271–72.

70. See above, pp. 58–59 and 239–40; Cullen, *Economic,* 135; Cousens, 316–20; Walsh, 10–11; Coulter, 30; Donnelly, *Land,* 160; *Preliminary Report of the Royal Commissioners of Agriculture, with Minutes of Evidence (Part 1), 1881,* in *IUP-BPP, Agriculture,* vol. 15 (Shannon, 1969), 612 (hereafter cited as *Report on Agriculture, 1881*); Becker, 117–18; *Congestion Commission,* vol. 6 (3784), 1908, p. 126.

71. Lee, 4–6, 82; J. A. O'Brien, *Vanishing Irish: Enigma of the Modern World* (NY, 1953), 25, 28; Akenson, *Between,* 70–71; Fitzpatrick, "Study," 12; E. E. McKenna, "Age, Region, and Marriage in Post-Famine Ireland . . . ," *ECONHR,* 31 (May 1978), 256 and passim; S. H. Cousens, "Popuplation Trends in Ireland at the Beginning of the 20th Century," *IRGEO,* 5 (1965–68), 389–401; D. F. Hannan, "Peasant Models and the Understanding of Social and Cultural Change in Rural Ireland," in P. J. Drudy, ed., *Irish Studies 2. Ireland: Land, Politics and People* (Cambridge, 1982), 150–52; D. Fitzpatrick, "Irish Farming Families before the First World War," *CSSH,* 25 (Apr. 1983), 359–60.

72. K. H. Connell, *Irish Peasant Society* (Oxford, 1968), 113–61; J. O'Donoghue, *In a Quiet Land* (London, 1957), 174; Lee, 4–6; R. E. Kennedy, Jr., 172; Donnelly, *Land,* 160–63; Almquist, 272–76; Connolly, 225; Ms. 1407, p. 310 (DIF/UCD).

73. E. Hanlon, 4 Mar. 1871 (D.885, PRONI); Lee, 6; C. M. Arensberg and S. T. Kimball, *Family and Community in Ireland* (Cambridge, Mass., 1968 ed.), 58–59, 126; B. Colgan, 20 Dec. 1854 (AS); R. Stivers, *Hair of the Dog: Irish Drinking and American Stereotype* (University Park, Penn., 1977), 94–95, 100; J. Henry, 25 July 1887 (T.1450, PRONI).

74. Ms. 1403, pp. 100–101 (DIF/UCD); J. Richey, 15 Sept. 1826 (ERRG); Lee, 5; McKenna, 256 and passim; P. Sayers, *Autobiography of Peig Sayers . . .* (Syracuse, 1974), 90–91; A. Griffin, 18 Mar. 1851 and 18 Feb. 1858 (L. N. Whittle Mss., Acc. #777, SHC/UNC-CH); S. Buchanan, 16 Feb. 1870 (Buchanan Mss., PC 431, NLI); E. Ellis, "Letters from the Quit Rent Office . . . ," *ANLHB,* 22 (1960), 390; B. MacAodha, "Letters from America," *UF,* 3 (1957), 64–69; M. Donohoe, 7 Oct. 1857 (Donohoe Mss., AIS-UP); M. Carbery, *Farm By Lough Gur* (Cork, 1973), 46–47; J. Hewitt, 12 July 1856 (Joseph Hewitt Mss., INHS).

75. E.g., see proverbs in "An Seabhac" [P. Ó Siochfhradha] ed., *Seanfhocail Na Muimhneach* (Dublin, 1926); F. O'Connor, *Short History of Irish Literature* (NY, 1968 ed.), 32; E. Wakefield, *Account of Ireland, Statistical and Political* (London, 1812), I, 517–18; J. Lee, "Women and the Church since the Famine," in M. Mac Curtain and D. Ó Corrain, eds., *Women in Irish Society . . .* (Dublin, 1978), 37–39; H. Brody, *Inishkillane: Change and Decline in the West of Ireland* (NY, 1973), 110–12; R. E. Kennedy, Jr., 51–54, 84.

76. See Appendix, Tables 12–13; Connolly, 226; Ms. 1409, pp. 278–79 (DIF/UCD); J. McConnell, 8 Sept. 1849 (McConnell Mss., ILSHS); Sayers, 134, 149; J. Dyer, 8 May 1845 (Lassarine Morris, Raheny, Co. Dublin); B. MacAodha, 64–69; H. Diner, *Erin's Daughters in America . . .* (Baltimore, 1983), 1–42.

77. E. Leighton, 26 June 1855 (Russell Schrode, Charleston, W.Va.); S. Connolly, 5 June 1898 (Alice L. McGuinness, Hampton Bays, NY); Carbery, 252–53; J. McCullough, 24 Feb. 1887 (Kells Mss., M7075, PROI); Synge, 320–21; Lynd, 45–46; *Cork Examiner,* 6 June 1860 (AS); M. Markey, 23 Oct. 1889 (Kathleen MacMahon, Martinstown, Co. Louth); M. Brown, 11 Mar. 1858 and 20 Jan. 1859 (AS).

78. Ms. 1403, pp. 100–101 (DIF/UCD); K. H. Connell, 51–62, 77, 84–86; Fox, 160–61; Arensberg and Kimball, 208–9; J. V. O'Brien, *Dear,* 172; A. Sproule, n.d. [1870] and

24 July 1870 (Sproule Mss., Acc. #1877, SHC/UNC-CH); A. Patterson, 10 July 1852 (D.1441/6, PRONI); Akenson, *Between,* 71; G. R. C. Keep, "Irish Migration to North America in the Second Half of the 19th Century" (Ph.D. diss., TCD, 1951), 203.

79. See above, pp. 289–90; Lee, 2; R. Breen, "Farm Servanthood in Ireland, 1900–40," *ECONHR,* 36 (Feb. 1983), 88.

80. D. Fitzpatrick, "Disappearance of Irish Agricultural Labourer, 1841–1912," *IESH,* 7 (1980), 68–82; Donnelly, *Land,* 228–29, 234–36; A. L. Bowley, "Statistics of Wages in the United Kingdom . . . ," *JRSS,* 62 (June 1899), 400–401; Cullen, *Life,* 159–60, and *Economic,* 156; Brooks, 53; B. MacManus, 24 Dec. 1850 (Masterson Mss., KYHS); Rev. J. Bannon, 22 Nov. 1863 (Rev. John Bannon Mss., SCL/USC); J. Young, n.d. [1863] (USCR, mf T-368, NA); E. Donohoe, 2 Mar. 1863 (Donohoe Mss., AIS-UP); G. Dillon, 24 Dec. 1869 (Ms. 8567, NLI); J. Healy, *Nineteen Acres* (Galway, 1978), 119–20; Akenson, *Between,* 72–73; T. Kells, 25 Nov. 1892, 6 Mar. 1896, and 18 Dec. 1901 (Kells Mss., M7075, PROI).

81. Fitzpatrick, "Disappearance," 68–82; P. O'Leary, *Travels and Experiences in Canada, the Red River Territory and the United States* (London, n.d.), 3–4; Guardian of the Poor, 107–16; M. E. Daly, *Social,* 33.

82. T. Grant, 6 Jan. 1852 (AS); Lee, 8–9; Schrier, 74–75; Steele, 18–19; Clark, *Social,* 113–20; C. Ó Danachair, "Farmer and Labourer in Pre-Famine Co. Limerick," *LIMAY 1978* (Limerick, 1978), 37; Breen, passim; Ms. 1408, pp. 83–84, 119–20 (DIF/UCD); J. F. Costello, 11 Jan. 1883 (AS); T. Cashman, Memories (Patrick Clancy, Youghal, Co. Cork); [Kenny], 148.

83. Donnelly, *Land,* 236–42, 246, 322–25; Wright, 98–99; P. Horn, "National Agricultural Labourers' Union in Ireland, 1873–9," *IHS,* 17 (Mar. 1971), 341–49; Fitzpatrick, "Disappearance," 68–80; Bew, passim; J. V. O'Brien, *William,* passim; N. Glassie, *Passing the Time in Ballymenone . . .* (Philadelphia, 1982), 693; Guardian of the Poor, 14; M. E. Daly, *Social,* 33; W. H. Hurlbert, *Ireland under Coercion* (Edinburgh, 1888 ed.), II, 251–57; D. Cashman, "Lady Day in Ireland" (Patrick Clancy).

84. McNeill, 59; J. Harold, 17 June 1869 (James Harold Mss., UWVL); Wright, 159; Ms. 1408, pp. 319–28 (DIF/UCD); P. O'Farrell, "Emigrant Attitudes and Behaviour as a Source for Irish History," *HS,* 10 (1976), 111; Schrier, 15–16; Paul-Dubois, 359.

85. A. M. Sullivan, *New Ireland,* 15th ed. (London, n.d.), 68; G. Birmingham [J. O. Hannay], *Irishman Looks at His World* (London, 1919), 201–2.

86. Coulter, 304; A. Livermore, 31 July 1883 (USCR, mf T-368, NA); T. Garvin, *Evolution of Irish Nationalist Politics* (Dublin, 1982), 70–71; Paul-Dubois, 358; J. Flanagan, 26 Apr. 1880 (Peter & Mary Flanagan, Clogherhead, Co. Louth).

87. J. C. Molony, *Riddle of the Irish* (London, 1927), 4; on Irish families, see Chapter 3, n. 24; Colum, 42–43; Lynd, 11; Ms. 1408, pp. 65, 100, and Ms. 1410, pp. 130–32, 338–39 (DIF/UCD); J. McCullough, 23 Aug. 1886 (Kells Mss., M7075, PROI).

88. M. McDermott, 22 Feb. 1871 (JD, Ms. 6844, TCD); J. J. Murphy, 24 Jan. and 24 Feb. 1883 (Murphy Mss., KRM); Ms. 1408, p. 263 (DIF/UCD); H. O'Daly, Life History (Rev. Patrick Daly, Monaghan); Colum, 43–44; M. Brown, 11 Mar. 1858 and 20 Jan. 1859 (AS); M. [Murphy?], n.d. [1921?] (Murphy-O'Hara Mss., ERRG); J. Morrison and C. F. Zabusky, *American Mosaic: Immigrant Experience in the Words of Those Who Lived It* (NY, 1980), 41–42, 45–46, 48–49. Ms. 1407, p. 310; Ms. 1408, pp. 83–84, 99; and Ms. 1409, pp. 278–79 (DIF/UCD). J. Lough, 18 Jan. 1891 (AS).

89. T. Cashman, Memories (Patrick Clancy).

90. Ó Cuív, 77–94; LeFanu, 296–99; Lynd, 112–13; Paul-Dubois, 398; H. Plunkett, *Ireland in the New Century* (London, 1904), 152–55.

91. Keep, 116; *Roscommon Journal,* 18 Oct. 1851 (AS); Akenson, *Irish,* 378–80; E. Hynes, "Great Hunger and Irish Catholicism," *Societas,* 8 (1978), 139–52; M. Murphy, "Ballad Singer and Role of the Seditious Ballad in 19th-Century Ireland . . . ," *UF,* 25 (1979), 84–85; D. W. Miller, "Catholic Religious Practice in Pre-Famine Ireland," *JSH,* 8 (1975), 91–92; S. de Fréine, *Great Silence* (Dublin, 1965), 147; O'Connor, 137; E. Leighton, 16 Jan. 1855 (Russell Schrode); J. Solon, Reminiscences (WISHS); Synge, 178–79.

92. Paul-Dubois, 399, 434; Lyons, *Culture,* 8; D. P. Moran, *Philosophy of Irish Ireland* (Dublin, 1907), 16–17; Aalen, "Some," 271–72; M. O'Sullivan, *Twenty Years A-Growing* (NY, 1933), 298.

93. Lynd, 206, 275; Paul-Dubois, 399, 434.

94. Plunkett, 152–53; Lee, 142; T. Brick, Memoirs (Doncha Ó Conchúir).

95. [Kenny], 105.

96. Paul-Dubois, 396–98; Akenson, *Between,* 145–48; Ms. 1408, pp. 83–84 (DIF/UCD); Lee, "Women," 40; Guardian of the Poor, 144–45; Carbery, 158–69; W. McDonald, *Reminiscences of a Maynooth Professor,* abr. ed. (Cork, 1967), 13–21.

97. E. Larkin, *Making of the Roman Catholic Church in Ireland, 1850–60* (Chapel Hill, 1980), 488–89 and passim; Lee, *Modernisation,* 13, 28; E. Larkin, "Devotional Revolution in Ireland, 1850–75," *AHR,* 77 (June 1977), 626–67, 644–51; idem, "Church, State, and Nation in Modern Ireland," *AHR,* 80 (Dec. 1975), 1244–76; E. Hosp, "Redemptorist Mission in Enniskillen, 1852," *CLREC,* 8 (1975), 269–70.

98. J. O'Shea, *Priests, Politics and Society in Post-Famine Ireland: Study of Co. Tipperary, 1850–90* (Dublin, 1983), 13–14, 308; K. H. Connell, 132–44; G. Birmingham [J. O. Hannay], *Irishmen All* (London, 1914), 184; Lynd, 112–13; Rev. J. Guinan, *Scenes and Sketches in an Irish Parish . . .* (Dublin, 1906), 3; R. Flower, *Western Island . . .* (NY, 1945), 132; Plunkett, 117.

99. Rev. M. O'Riordan, *Catholicity and Progress in Ireland* (London, 1906), 271–93; Paul-Dubois, 510; Lee, "Women," 39–40; Lynd, 147–49, 212–13.

100. M. Tierney, *Croke of Cashel: Life of Archbishop Thomas William Croke, 1823–1902* (Dublin, 1976), 95; P. O'Farrell, *Ireland's English Question . . .* (NY, 1971 ed.), 223–41; Lyons, *Culture,* 79–82; E. Malcolm, "Temperance and Irish Nationalism," in Lyons and Hawkins, 107; idem, "Catholic Church and Irish Temperance Movement, 1838–1901," *IHS,* 23 (May 1982), 1–16; W. F. Mandle, "Gaelic Athletic Association and Popular Culture, 1884–1924," in O. MacDonagh et al., eds., *Irish Culture and Nationalism, 1750–1950* (NY, 1983), 104–21.

101. See Clark, *Social,* 246–305 and passim; Garvin, 53–134 and passim; and D. G. Boyce, *Nationalism in Ireland* (Baltimore, 1982), esp. 246–48.

102. Most Irish nationalist (and Unionist) organizations had North American affiliates, see below, pp. 533–44. Lee, *Modernisation,* 48; Colum, 42–44; Paul-Dubois, 434; Birmingham, *Irishman Looks,* 182–83; *Cork Examiner,* 6 June 1860 (AS).

103. A. E. Costello, 9 July 1891 (O'Hegerty Mss., KSRL/UKS); J. J. Mitchell, Journal (N-YHS); J. Quinn [alias T. O'Brien], 8 Feb. 1823 (Mrs. M. Cregan, Belfast); E. Wogan, [1864?] (AS).

104. Schrier, 111; Paul-Dubois, 359; J. Wright, [1861?] (Wright Mss., RSFL); P. Griffin, 20 Jan. 1851 (L. N. Whittle Mss., GASA); Rossa, 6; O'Sullivan, 239.

105. *Nation* (Dublin), 3 May 1851 (AS); Paul-Dubois, 359; Plunkett, 56; G. W. Russell, "Photographs and Emigration" (1910), in H. Summerfield, ed., *Selections from Contributions to The Irish Homestead by G. W. Russell—A.E.* (Gerrards Cross, 1978), I, 213–14.

106. Ms. 1407, pp. 34, 279 (DIF/UCD); Synge, 218; O'Donoghue, 19.

107. Ms. 1409, pp. 15–17, 295, and Ms. 1408, pp. 315–16 (DIF/UCD); *Report on Agriculture, 1881,* 665, 1013, 1018; Sommerville and Ross, 221; P. Mac Suibhne, *Paul Cullen and His Contemporaries . . .* (Naas, 1978), IV, 108, 110; D. N. Doyle, "Unestablished Irishmen: New Immigrants and Industrial America," in D. Hoerder, ed., *American Labor and Immigration History, 1877–1920s . . .* (Urbana, 1983), 214; M. t'Hart, " 'Heading for Paddy's Green Shamrock Shore': Returned Emigrants in 19th-Century Ireland," *IESH,* 10 (1983), 96.

108. Paul-Dubois, 359; E. P. Brooks, 3 Mar. 1881 (USCR, mf T-196, NA); Shand, 224; Daryl, 195.

109. O'Farrell, "Emigrant," 109; on leave-taking scenes, see Conclusion, this work; Ms. 1411 (DIF/UCD); "Shane O'Farrell's Wedding in America" (emigrant's song, from J. Bredin, Birmingham, England); Wright, 192; J. McCue, untitled emigrant's song (Mrs. M. Bayers, High Glen, Co. Donegal); Rev. M. Buckley, *Diary of a Tour in America* (Dublin, 1889), 50–51; Plunkett, 53–55; P. H. Bagenal, *American Irish and Their Influence on Irish Politics* (London, 1882), 218–19; on Irish-American nationalism, see below, pp. 535–55. For evidence of returning emigrants, use USCR, especially reels 11–12 (1890–1906) for Cork (mf T-196, NA), and reels 11–12 (1890–1906) for Dublin (mf T-199, NA). For alleged general eagerness to return, see Ms. 1410, p. 303 (DIF/UCD). t'Hart, 96–97.

110. Moran, 21; Higgins and Conolly, 43.

111. Lee cited in O'Farrell, "Emigrant," 109; Lee, *Modernisation,* passim; Plunkett, 10, 16, 22, and passim; Connolly, xii; Coulter, 83–91, 184; L. Richmond, 15 Dec. 1877 (USCR, mf T-196, NA); [Kenny], 8, 45, 103, and passim; Lynd, 125, 190–91; C. Ó Gráda, "Beginnings," 287–88; M. E. Daly, *Social,* 51, 58; Becker, 50; Robinson, 25, 67, 185, 205–10; Paul-Dubois, 160–61, 166–78; W. A. Phillips, Report on the State of Ireland . . . 1916 (FO 115/2244, PRO); Malony, 28.

112. *1861 Irish Census,* vii; *1861 Irish Ag. Stats.,* 547–69; *1911 Irish Census,* 10–21, 431–38; Bonn, 48–50; G. Wright, *Rural Revolution in France: Peasantry in 20th Century* (Stanford, 1964), 25–26, 212, 214; Hannan, 142–44, 146; Fitzpatrick, "Irish Farming," passim.

113. Hannan, 141–42.

114. *1861 Irish Census,* vii; *1861 Irish Ag. Stats.,* 547–69; *1911 Irish Census,* 10–21, 431–48; D. H. Akenson, *Irish Education Experiment* . . . (London, 1970), 378–80.

115. M. E. Daly, *Social,* 71; Fitzpatrick, "Disappearance," 68–80; Murphy, "Fenianism," 28–32; L. Kennedy, "Farmers, Traders," 339–73; M. D. Higgins and J. P. Gibbons, "Shopkeeper-Graziers and Land Agitation in Ireland, 1895–1900," in Drudy, 93–118.

116. On education, see Akenson, *Irish,* and E. B. Titley, *Church, State, and the Control of Schooling in Ireland, 1900–44* (Toronto, 1983). On nationalism, see Garvin, esp. 1–14, 53–134; and Fitzpatrick, *Politics,* passim.

117. Garvin, 53–134; Bonn, 64–65.

118. Solow, passim; Hannan, passim; Fitzpatrick, "Farming Families," passim; M. A. G. Ó Tuathaigh, "Land Question, Politics, and Irish Society, 1922–60," in Drudy, 167; *Congestion Commission,* vol. 6 (3784), 1908, p. 126.

119. Shand, 128–29; Coulter, 94–95; Becker, 19–25, 89–95, 216–21; Houston, 27, 55–56; J. J. Mitchell, Journal (N-YHS).

120. L. M. Cullen, *Emergence of Modern Ireland, 1600–1900* (Dublin, 1983 ed.), 135–39.

121. Paul-Dubois, 173, 177–78.

122. Molony, 28; Hechter, 6–43 and passim; P. O'Farrell, *England and Ireland since 1800* (London, 1975 ed.), 14–15, 130.

123. The descriptive analysis of post-Famine political and religious history contained in this and subsequent paragraphs is based on the following works (specific pages cited for actual quotations only):

J. C. Beckett, *Anglo-Irish Tradition* (Ithaca, 1976); idem, *Making of Modern Ireland* . . . (NY, 1966); P. Bew, *Land and National Question;* idem, *C. S. Parnell* (Dublin, 1980); D. G. Boyce, *Nationalism in Ireland;* A. Boyd, *Rise of Irish Trade Unions;* P. Buckland, *Ulster Unionism;* idem, *Irish Unionism 1: Anglo-Irish and the New Ireland, 1885–1922* (Dublin, 1972); H. V. Brasted, "Irish Nationalism and British Empire in Late 19th Century," in O. MacDonagh et al., *Irish Culture and Nationalism;* S. Clark, "Political Mobilization"; idem, *Social Origins of the Land War;* idem with J. S. Donnelly, Jr., *Irish Peasants;* R. V. Comerford, "Anglo-Irish Tensions and Origins of Fenianism," in Lyons and Hawkins; idem, "Patriotism as Pastime: Appeal of Fenianism in Mid-1860s," *IHS,* 22 (Mar. 1981), 239–50; C. Cruise O'Brien, *Parnell and His Party, 1880–90* (Oxford, 1960); L. P. Curtis, Jr., *Coercion and Conciliation;* R. P. Davis, *Arthur Griffith and Non-Violent Sinn Féin* (Dublin, 1974); M. Davitt, *Leaves from a Prison Diary* (Shannon, 1972 ed.); idem, *Fall of Feudalism in Ireland* (Shannon, 1970 ed.); J. Devoy, *Recollections;* J. S. Donnelly, Jr., *Land and People of 19th-Century Cork;* R. D. Edwards, *James Connolly* (Dublin, 1981); idem, *Patrick Pearse: Triumph of Failure* (London, 1977); W. L. Feingold, "Tenants' Movement"; idem, "Political Triumph of Irish Large Farmer"; D. Fitzpatrick, "Geography of Irish Nationalism," *P&P,* no. 78 (1978), 113–44; idem, *Politics and Irish Life;* D. Ford, "Church, State and Irish Christianity," in P. J. Drudy, ed., *Irish Studies 1* (London, 1980); T. Garvin, *Evolution of Irish Nationalist Politics;* P. Gibbon, *Origins of Ulster Unionism;* D. Greaves, *James Connolly;* W. E. Hall, *Shadowy Heroes: Irish Literature in the 1890s* (Syracuse, 1980); M. Harmon, ed., *Fenians and Fenianism;* M. D. Higgins and J. P. Gibbons, "Shopkeeper-Graziers and Land Agitation"; K. T. Hoppen, "National Politics and Local Realities"; idem, "Landlords, Society, and Electoral Politics"; J. P. Huttman, "Fenians and Farmers: Merger of Home-Rule and Owner-Occupancy Movements in Ireland, 1850–1915," *Albion,* 3, no. 4 (Winter 1971), 182–97; P. Jalland, *Liberals and Ireland: Ulster Question in British Politics to 1914* (Brighton, 1980); idem, "Irish Home-Rule Finance: Neglected Dimension of the Irish Question, 1910–14," *IHS,* 23 (May 1983), 233–53; D. S. Jones, "Agrarian Capitalism and Rural Social Development"; idem, "Cleavage between Graziers and Peasants"; D. Jordan, "Land and Politics in the West of Ireland: Co. Mayo, 1846–82," *IESH,* 10 (1983), 94–96; R. Kee, *Green Flag* . . . (NY, 1972); L. Kennedy, "Farmers, Traders, and Agricultural Politics"; idem, "Early Response of Irish Catholic Clergy to Co-operative Movement," *IHS,* 21 (Mar. 1978), 55–74; J. Lee, *Modernisation of Irish Society.* E. Larkin, "Church, State, and Nation"; "Devotional Revolution"; *James Larkin; Roman Catholic Church and Creation of the Modern Irish State, 1878–86* (Philadelphia, 1975); *Roman Catholic Church and Fall of Parnell, 1888–91* (Chapel Hill, 1979);

Roman Catholic Church and Plan of Campaign in Ireland, 1886–88 (Cork, 1979); *Making of the Roman Catholic Church;* "Roman Catholic Hierarchy and Fall of Parnell," *VS,* 4 (June 1961), 315–56; "Socialism and Catholicism in Ireland," *CH,* 33 (1964), 462–83. F. S. L. Lyons, *Charles Stewart Parnell* (London, 1977); *Culture and Anarchy;* "Decline and Fall of the Nationalist Party," in O. D. Edwards and F. Pyle, eds., *1916: Easter Rising* (Dublin, 1968); "Economic Ideas of Parnell"; *Ireland since the Famine; Irish Parliamentary Party, 1890–1910* (Westport, Conn., 1975 ed.); *John Dillon* (Chicago, 1968); and *Fall of Parnell, 1890–1* (Toronto, 1960).

J. A. MacMahon, "Catholic Clergy and Social Question in Ireland," *Studies,* 70 (1981), 263–88; P. Mac Suibhne, *Paul Cullen and His Contemporaries;* E. Malcolm, "Temperance and Irish Nationalism"; idem, "Catholic Church and Irish Temperance Movement"; W. F. Mandle, "Gaelic Athletic Association and Popular Culture"; idem, "I.R.B. and the Beginnings of the Gaelic Athletic Association," *IHS,* 20 (Sept. 1977); L. J. McCaffrey, *Ireland: From Colony to Nation State* (Englewood Cliffs, 1979); idem, *Irish Federalism in the 1870s . . .* (Philadelphia, 1962); D. W. Miller, *Queen's Rebels;* idem, *Church, State, and Nation in Ireland, 1898–1921* (Pittsburgh, 1973); T. W. Moody, *Davitt and Irish Revolution;* D. P. Moran, *Philosophy of Irish Ireland;* M. Murphy, "Fenianism, Parnellism, and Cork Trades"; E. R. Norman, *History of Modern Ireland* (Coral Gables, 1971); idem, *Catholic Church in Ireland in Age of Rebellion, 1859–73* (London, 1965); J. V. O'Brien, *William O'Brien;* W. O'Brien and D. Ryan, eds., *Devoy's Post Bag, 1871–1928,* 2 vols. (Dublin, 1948, 1953); S. O'Faolain, *De Valera* (Harmondsworth, 1939), quotation on p. 81; P. O'Farrell, *England and Ireland since 1800;* idem, *Ireland's English Question;* J. O'Leary, *Recollections of Fenians and Fenianism* (London, 1896); J. O'Shea, *Priests, Politics and Society in Post-Famine Ireland;* M. A. G. Ó Tuathaigh, "Land Question, Politics and Irish Society"; idem, "19th-Century Irish Politics: Case for Normalcy," in P. J. Drudy, ed., *Anglo-Irish Studies 1* (Bucks, England, 1975); L. Paul-Dubois, *Contemporary Ireland;* W. P. Ryan, *Pope's Green Island* (London, 1912); E. Rumpf and A. C. Hepburn, *Nationalism and Socialism in 20th-Century Ireland* (NY, 1977); Rev. F. Shaw, "Canon of Irish History—A Challenge," *Studies,* 61 (Summer 1972), 116–53. E. D. Steele, *Irish Land and British Politics;* "Gladstone, Irish Violence, and Conciliation," in Cosgrove and McCartney, *Studies in Irish History;* and "Cardinal Cullen and Irish Nationality," in Mac Suibhne, *Paul Cullen . . . ,* vol. 5 (Naas, 1977), 263–88 (originally pub. in *IHS,* 19 [Mar. 1975], 239–60). A. T. Q. Stewart, *Ulster Crisis* (London, 1967); E. Strauss, *Irish Nationalism and British Democracy* (Westport, Conn., 1975 ed.); D. Thornley, *Isaac Butt and Home Rule* (London, 1964); M. Tierney, *Croke of Cashel;* E. B. Titley, *Church, State, and Control of Schooling;* B. M. Walker, "Party Organisation In Ulster, 1865–92 . . . ," in Roebuck, *Plantation to Partition;* idem, "The Irish Electorate, 1868–1915," *IHS,* 18 (Mar. 1973), 359–406; M. Waters, "Peasants and Emigrants: Social Origins of the Gaelic League," in D. J. Casey and R. E. Rhodes, eds., *Views of the Irish Peasantry, 1800–1916* (Hamden, Conn., 1977), 150–77. J. H. Whyte, "Landlord Influence at Elections"; "Influence of Catholic Clergy on Elections in the 19th Century," *EHR,* 75 (1960), 239–59; *Independent Irish Party, 1850–9* (London, 1958); and *Tenant League and Irish Politics in the 1850s* (Dundalk, 1972). C. J. Woods, "General Election of 1892: Catholic Clergy and Defeat of the Parnellites," in Lyons and Hawkins; C. Younger, *Arthur Griffith* (Dublin, 1981).

124. T. P. Coogan, *The I.R.A.* (London, 1970), 40, 114; Vaughn and Fitzpatrick, 266; see above, pp. 378–80; Kirkpatrick, 201–35; Miller, *Queen's,* 76–78; G. Bell, *Protestants of Ulster* (London, 1976), 76–78; O'Brien and Ryan, II, 394–95; J. Griffin, 26 Nov. 1865 (L. N. Whittle Mss., GASA); W. Hanna, 5 Oct. 1869 (T.2193, PRONI); d'Alton, 76–80; W. A. Phillips, Report . . . (FO 115/2244, PRO); White, 9–11, 83–90; Beckett, *Anglo-Irish,* 129–30; Boyce, 325; Fitzpatrick, *Politics,* 78–79; G. [Dougherty?], 17 Aug. 1917 (ERRG); Robinson, 10, 260–61.

125. Fr. P. Sheehan, "Effect of Emigration on the Irish Church," *IECCR,* 3d ser., 3 (1882), 613; *Report on Agriculture, 1881,* 500; *Congestion Commission,* vol. 6 (3784), 1908, p. 272; W. McDonald, *Reminiscences of a Maynooth Professor,* unabr. ed. (London, 1925), 221–23; O. MacDonagh, "Irish Emigration to the United States . . . during the Famine," in Edwards and Williams, *Great Famine,* 300–301; P. F. Murray, "Calendar of Overseas Missionary Correspondence of All Hallows College, Dublin, 1842–77" (M.A. thesis, UCD, 1956; on mf, p2782, NLI), xii–xiii.

126. T. Brown, *Ireland: Social and Cultural History, 1922–79* (London, 1981), 35; O'Farrell, "Emigrant," 113; Rev. T. N. Burke, *Lectures on Faith and Fatherland* (London,

n.d.), 212–13; Rev. M. O'Connor, "Destiny of the Irish Race," *IECCR*, 1 (Nov. 1864), 79; J. Cardinal Gibbons, "Irish Immigration to the United States," *IECCR*, 4th ser., 1 (1897), 109; C. and A. B. Reeve, *James Connolly and the United States* . . . (Atlantic Highlands, 1978), 173.

127. G. R. C. Keep, "Some Irish Opinions on Population and Emigration, 1851–1901," *IECCR*, 5th ser., 84 (1955), 377–81; *Wexford People,* cited in M. Cusack, "Introduction," to Cusack, *Speeches . . . of the Liberator* (Dublin, 1875), I, xxvii–xxviii; Tierney, 80; *Report on Agriculture, 1881,* 500; Rev. J. O'Hanlon, *Irish Emigrants' Guide to the United States* (Boston, 1851), 10–13; Rev. A. J. Peyton, *Emigrants' Friend: or, Hints on Emigration to the United States* (Cork, 1853), ix, 5–6, 15, 21–23, 47; see also, The Nun of Kenmare [M. F. Cusack], *Advice to Irish Girls in America* (NY, 1872); Steele, "Cardinal Cullen . . . ," in *IHS*, 243–45; Mac Suibhne, III, 289, and IV, 108; Keep, "Irish Migration to North America," 373–74; Miller, *Church,* 70–71; R. D. Cross, *Emergence of Liberal Catholicism in America* (Chicago, 1968), 19; Peregrinus, "Falling Off of Irish Catholicism in the United States and Its Causes," *IECCR*, 3 (June 1867), 434; Fr. P. O'Leary, *Sgothbhualadh* (Dublin, 1907), 107–9 (trans. BDB); Guinan, 43–45, 118–19; and Fr. J. Guinan, *Soggarth Aroon* (Dublin, 1905); Sheehan, 602–15; M. P. Linehan, *Canon Sheehan of Doneraile* (Dublin, 1952), 38, 75; Shand, 114–15; K. H. Connell, 135; Reeve and Reeve, 83; Greaves, 151–53; Paul-Dubois, 361 n. 15; Higgins and Conolly, 41.

128. P. O'Leary, 107–9 (trans. BDB); Guinan, *Scenes,* 118–19; R. F. Foster, *Charles Stewart Parnell: Man and His Family* (Atlantic Highlands, 1976), 250–52, 323–25; O'Farrell, "Emigrant," 115–16; R. D. Edwards, *Patrick Pearse,* 78–79.

129. O'Farrell, "Emigrant," 114–15; O'Brien citation, courtesy of Prof. Emmet Larkin, Univ. of Chicago; T. N. Burke, 228–31; Guinan, *Scenes,* 43–44, 118–19; Reeve and Reeve, 17; Davitt, *Fall,* xi, 68, 117, 171, 271, 410; W. P. Ryan, *Pope's,* 300–301; Younger, 20; R. D. Edwards, *Patrick Pearse,* 183; T. Brown, 13; A. M. Sullivan, "Why Send More Irish Out of Ireland?" *Nineteenth Century,* 14 (July 1883), 131–44.

130. Taylor, 68–80; Davis, 69; Fr. P. Devine, Adventures and Misadventures . . . (STPCR); O'Riordan, 37; Ms. 1409, pp. 211–12 (DIF/UCD); Cruise O'Brien, 266–68; Lyons, *Irish Parliamentary,* 201–17; M. V. Hazel, "First Link" Parnell's American Tour, 1880," *É-I,* 15, no. 1 (Spring 1980), 22; O'Brien and Ryan, II, 350, 412–13; M. V. Tarpey, *Role of Joseph McGarrity in Struggle for Irish Independence* (NY, 1976), 63–64; R. D. Edwards, *Patrick Pearse,* 224; A. Ward, *Ireland and Anglo-American Relations* (Toronto, 1969), 218.

131. A. M. Sullivan, "Why Send," 131–44; McNeill, 197; N. Nolan, 103, 200–202; Bew, *Land,* 7–33; Norman, *Catholic,* 2–4; Ms. 1408, pp. 315–16 (DIF/UCD); Ardagh bishop and St. Colman's College president citations, courtesy of Prof. Emmet Larkin; Schrier, 60–61; Sheehan, 613; O'Farrell, "Emigrant," 115, 128–29; K. H. Connell, 135; Guinan, *Scenes,* 54–55.

132. Butler citation, courtesy of Prof. E. Larkin; Foster, 110–11; Guinan, *Soggarth,* 3; Tierney, 80, 102, 133; Waters, 166–67, 171–74.

133. Becker, 85–86; Guardian of the Poor, 14; Commerford, "Patriotism," 240–42; Hoppen, "National Politics," 191–95; Rumpf and Hepburn, 35–68; Fitzpatrick, *Politics,* 222–31; Garvin, 110, 122; Strauss, 147; D. Fitzpatrick, "Class, Family, and Rural Unrest in 19th-Century Ireland," in Drudy, *Irish Studies 2,* 48–49.

134. The generational analysis is borrowed from Miller, *Church,* passim; see works cited in n. 123 above; Waters, 171–74.

135. See above, pp. 124–30; Daniels, 18; Becker, 246–47; Greaves, 254–56; R. D. Edwards, *James Connolly,* 86–87.

136. Lyons, "Economic," 67–73; Bew, *C. S. Parnell,* 49; Davis, 127–44; Cullen, *Economic,* 164; T. Brown, 15–16; L. Kennedy, "Early," 58, 64–73; idem, "Farmers," 339–73; Ehrlich, 278–81; Daniels, 22–23; Barker, 77–78.

137. O'Farrell, *Ireland's English,* 189–207, 212–41; idem, *England and Ireland,* 14–15, 127–30; Lyons, *Culture,* 79–82 and passim; L. Kennedy, "Early," 57, 70–73; Miller, *Church,* 70–76; MacMahon, 263–68 and passim; Guinan, *Scenes,* iv, 3, and passim; idem, *Soggarth,* 15–20 and passim; O'Riordan, 47–135, 227, and passim; Linehan, 66–119 and passim; Carbery, 201–8; Bew, *C. S. Parnell,* 11–15; Davis, 91–98; Younger, 26–27.

138. Norman, *Catholic,* 388–90; Tierney, 100–56; O'Brien and Ryan, II, 118–19; Miller, *Church,* 74–75; L. Kennedy, "Early," 57; O'Riordan, 56, 124, 215; R. D. Edwards, *Patrick Pearse,* 78; Guinan, *Scenes,* 44–45.

139. Tierney, 100–56; O'Brien and Ryan, II, 118–19; Miller, *Church,* 76–94; L. Kennedy,

"Roman," 56–57; MacMahon, 263–86; Larkin, "Socialism," 462–83; Lyons, *Culture,* 96; O'Farrell, *Ireland's English,* 270–71; Guinan, *Scenes,* 43.

140. Greaves, 52; Guinan, *Scenes,* 46.

141. [Kenny], 5; S. Heaney, "Tale of Two Islands: Reflections on Irish Literary Revival," in Drudy, *Irish Studies 1,* 15 and passim; Moran, 29–30, 36, and passim; W. P. Ryan, *Pope's,* 32–33, 78, and passim; O'Ryan [W. P. Ryan], *Plough,* 55, 121; Reeve and Reeve, 243; O. D. Edwards and B. Ransom, eds., *James Connolly: Selected Writings* (NY, 1974), 363–64; Paul-Dubois, 166–67; R. D. Edwards, *Patrick Pearse,* 322–44; Lyons, *Culture,* 60–70, 98–101; T. Brown, 45–69.

142. R. D. Edwards, *Patrick Pearse,* 201–3; Lyons, *Culture,* 87; Hoppen, "Landlords," 88; Boyce, 246–47; J. McGurrin, *Bourke Cockran: Free Lance in American Politics* (NY, 1978 ed.), 1–10; H. O'Daly, Life History . . . (Rev. Patrick Daly, Monaghan): J. M. Clancy, Diary (Ms. 21,666, NLI); P. Ryan, Diary (WJSML); M. R. Fallows, *Irish Americans: Identity and Assimilation* (Englewood Cliffs, 1979), 83; J. Namias, *First Generation: In the Words of 20th-Century American Immigrants* (Boston, 1978), 14–20; R. H. Derham, "Oral History of Irish Immigrants" (Seminar Paper, UCB, 1976).

143. Schrier, 55–56; G. Smith, "Why Send More Irish to America?" *Nineteenth Century,* 13 (June 1883), 913–19; Solow, 147–67; Pomfret, 251–57; N. Nolan, 100–103; Macdonald, *Canada,* 138–40; Rossa, 258–59; C. U. O'Connell, 1 May 1862 (O'DR, on mf at CUA); W. D'Arcy, *Fenian Movement in the United States . . .* (Washington, D.C., 1947), 62–63; S. Ó Súilleabháin, "Iveragh Fenians in Oral Tradition," in Harmon, 36–38; Wright, 205–38; Ms. 1407, pp. 209, 264, and Ms. 1408, pp. 110–11, 268–70 (DIF/UCD); Special Correspondent of 'The Times,' *Letters from Ireland, 1886* (London, 1887), 99–100.

144. Plunkett, 102–5; B. Biever, *Religion, Culture, and Values . . .* (NY, 1976), 776–803; L. Kennedy, "Profane Images in the Irish Popular Consciousness," *ORLH,* 7, no. 2 (Autumn 1979); Brooks, 43–48; Garvin, 2–7, 44–45, 70–78; 179; Mandle, "I.R.B.," 428–29; Clark, *Social,* 305–26; Fitzpatrick, *Politics,* 251, 232–80 passim; idem, "Geography," 114, 123; Hurlbert, II, 257.

145. R. D. Edwards, *Patrick Pearse,* 257–58.

146. Ibid., 8; Tarpey, 23–32.

147. MacGowan, 2–3; R. McIlwaine, *Memories of Three Score Years and Ten* (NY, 1908); A. Machochlainn, "Social Life in Co. Clare, 1800–50," *IUR,* 2 (1972), 55–78; Gallagher, 5, 19, 26, 43–45; Flower, 18.

148. Synge, 282; Ó Síocháin, 80; Aalen and Brody, 62–63; see above, pp. 349–53 and 397–99.

149. Becker, 305–6; J. H. Tuke, "With the Immigrants," *Nineteenth Century,* 12 (July 1882), 152–53; *Report on Agriculture, 1881,* 90–91, 666, 679, 741–42; Tuke, *Reports,* 9.

150. Synge, 218, 282; Akenson, *Irish,* 379–80; Flower, 71.

151. Synge, 332–33; Birmingham, *Irishman Looks,* 167–69; Colum, 41, 170–71; Flower, 18.

152. Flower, 18; J. N. H. Douglas, "Emigration and the Irish Peasant," *UF,* 9 (1963), 9–19.

153. *Census of Ireland, 1911: Province of Connaught,* in *GBPP-HC* (6052), 1912–13, LXIX, 168, and *Province of Munster,* in *GBPP-HC* (6050), 1912–13, LXVII, 162; C. Ó Gráda, "Supply Responsiveness in Irish Agriculture during the 19th Century," *ECONHR,* 28 (1975), 315; Curtis, *Coercion,* 356–57, 368, 373–79; *CDB Reports,* 106–7, 459, 500 (TCD); *Congestion Commission,* vol. 4 (3509), 1907, p. 69.

154. Aalen and Brody, 66, 109; Fox, 18; E. Kane, *Last Place God Made . . .* (New Haven, 1977), II, 247; S. H. Cousens, "Population Trends in Ireland at the Beginning of 20th Century," *IRGEO,* 5 (1965–68), 389–91; *Congestion Commission,* vol. 2 (3319), 1907, pp. 28, 107–8, 159, and vol. 4 (3509), 1907, p. 27; Hannan, 148–53; Fitzpatrick, "Irish Farming," 359–60.

155. Hannan, 149–50; Fitzpatrick, "Irish Farming," 353–55; Sayers, 67, 134, 149; Healy, 115–16.

156. Hannan, 152–53.

157. Flower, 62, 134; Synge, 230, 332–33.

158. "Máire" [S. Ó Grianna], *Caisleáin Óir* (Dundalk, 1924); O'Sullivan, 239; P. Ua Duinnín, *Muinntear Chiarraidhe Roimh an Drochsaoghal* (Dublin, 1905), 54–61 (trans. BDB); Synge, 291; Ms. 1409, pp. 4–5, 11–32, and Ms. 1407, pp. 45–46 (DIF/UCD).

159. M. Ó Gaoithín, *Beatha Peig Sayers* (Dublin, 1970), 86–90 (trans. BDB); Ms. 1408, pp. 148, 188, 319–28, and passim (DIF/UCD); Wright, 626.

160: O'Sullivan, 258; Synge, 73, 317; Robinson, 89–93; Plunkett, 40n. Ms. 1409, pp.

104–7, 240–43, 303–27, and passim; Ms. 1410, pp. 105, 119; and Ms. 1411, pp. 245–47, 258–59, 349 (DIF/UCD).

161. See DIF/UCD ms. citations from nn. 159–60 above.

162. Ibid.

163. Sayers, 185; Ó Gaoithín, 85–86; O'Sullivan, 220–21; J. O'Donoghue, *In Kerry Long Ago* (NY, 1960), 14; M. Ó Gaoithín, *Is Truagh Ná Fannan An Óige* (Dublin, 1953), 85–86 (trans., BDB); Flower, 60, 62.

164. See above, pp. 397–402.

165. See Conclusion, this work; Gwynn, 296; W. P. Ryan, *Pope's* 281–84; Becker, 19–25, 85–95, 216–21; D. S. Jones, "Agrarian," 307–20; Robinson, 78–79; Ó Síocháin, 16, 41–49, 76, 96–98.

166. Fitzpatrick, "Class," 57–58; A. Humphreys, "Family in Ireland," in M. F. Nimkoff, ed., *Comparative Family Systems* (Boston, 1965), passim; Carbery, 38, 92, 140; W. McDonald, *Reminiscences*, abr. ed., 13–14; Sayers, 187; Arensberg and Kimball, 58.

167. Plunkett, 53–55; A. Livermore, 31 July 1883 (USCR, mf T-368, NA); M. J. H. Anderson, Memoirs (MNHS); O'Sullivan, 220–21; J. Flanagan, 5 July 1889 (Peter & Mary Flanagan); B. Colgan, 18 Dec. 1854 (AS); Synge, 73; T. Ó Crohan, *The Islandman* (London, 1934), 68; J. Watt, 5 Aug. 1884 (Kells Mss., M7075, PROI); Rev. P. J. Ryan, 9 Sept. 1931 (Sgt. Robert Maher, Holycross, Co. Tipperary).

168. Arensberg and Kimball, 111–12; Schrier, 104–15; R. E. Kennedy, Jr., 51–64; *Congestion Commission*, vol. 5 (3630), 1907, p. 466, and vol. 6 (3784), 1908, pp. 89–97, 114, 222, 229; Robinson, 89–90; Paul-Dubois, 305.

169. Connolly, 226; Gallagher, 62–63; Sayers, 160.

170. Fitzpatrick, "Class," 62–65; J. C. Russell, "In the Shadows of Saints: Aspects of Family and Religion in Rural Irish Gaeltacht" (Ph.D. diss., Univ. of California, San Diego, 1979), 268–70; A. M. Dalsimer, "Players in the Western World: Abbey Theatre's American Tours," *É-I*, 16, no. 4 (Winter 1981), 79 and passim; Wright, 12–13; M. A. Gordon, "Studies in Irish and Irish-American Thought and Behavior . . ." (Ph.D. diss., Univ. of Rochester, 1977), 388; M. O'Hanlon, n.d. [1871] (D.885/13, PRONI); J. Lough, 20 Oct. 1891 (AS); Keep, "Irish Migration to North America," 147–48; *Freeman's Journal* (Dublin), 22 July 1853 (AS); McNeill, 78; Schrier, 108–9; Hurlbert, I, 94–95; Ms. 1410, p. 129 (DIF/UCD); M. Ó Cadhain, *An Braon Broghach* (Dublin, 1948), 7–32 (trans. BDB); A. B. McMillan, 4 May 1895 (D.1195/5/41, PRONI); J. Kells, 18 Nov. 1883 (Kells Mss., M7075, PROI); R. Rourke, 5 May 1893 (Martin J. Kelly, Celbridge, Co. Kildare); Ms. 1407, p. 281 (DIF/UCD); Synge, 193.

171. Paul-Dubois, 359; K. A. Miller, "Irish Emigration and Popular Image of America in Rural Ireland," in J. Lee, ed., *Emigration: Irish Experience* (Cork, forthcoming); J. Hewitt, 14 Oct. 1853 (Joseph Hewitt Mss., INHS); F. Langan, 20 June 1874 (Gerald Perry, Tara, Co. Meath); J. Henry, 25 July 1887 (T.1450, PRONI); *Kilkenny Journal,* 25 Sept. 1901 (AS); J. O'Donovan Rossa, *Rossa's Prison Life* (NY, 1874), 433; Ms. 1409, pp. 16–17, 32–33 (DIF/UCD); *Cork Examiner,* 20 Apr. 1859 (AS); J. Fleming, 3 May 1853 (D.1047/1, PRONI); J. Dever, 2 Jan. 1868 (Alice Timoney); T. J. Kelly, 24 Mar. 1876 (Ms. 18,437, NLI); J. Hall, 27 Nov. 1888 (D.2041, Bundle 13, PRONI); P. Henry, 12 July 1926 (Ms. 21,570, NLI); Synge, 13, 63, 321; Schrier, 129–43. Ms. 1408, p. 148 and testimony of Joseph Wade, passim; Ms. 1410, K. O'Mally Toole testimony; and Ms. 1411, p. 349 (DIF/UCD); MacGowan, 145.

172. K. A. Miller, passim; C. Mac Mathuna, "Song of the Exile," *Irish Times,* 16 Dec. 1976; J. Bradley, n.d. (Mrs. L. Bradley, Maghera, Co. Derry); J. J. Murphy, 24 Jan. 1881 (Murphy Mss., KRM); Ms. 1407, pp 36–37, and Ms. 1409, p. 297 (DIF/UCD).

173. Paul-Dubois, 359; O'Riordan, 292; Ms. 1407, pp. 45–46 (DIF/UCD); Coulter, 287–88.

174. Ms. 1403, pp. 100–101; Ms. 1407, pp. 43–44; Ms. 1408, 83–84, 147–48, and passim; Ms. 1410, pp. 130–32; and Ms. 1411, pp. 388–89 (DIF/UCD).

175. Fox, 29; Ó Gaoithín, *Beatha,* 86–90 (trans. BDB); Ms. 1409, pp. 45–46, 60 (DIF/UCD); Brody, 165–66.

176. *Gore Booth Letters,* 129 (see Chapter 7, n. 31); E. Hanlon, 11 Dec. 1870 (D.885, PRONI); Arensberg and Kimball, 72–75; Brody, 132; *Cork Examiner,* 11 June 1860 (AS); on "American wakes," see Schrier, 84–91, and Conclusion of this work; J. J. Mitchell, Journal (N-YHS); J. Phelan, 24 Jan. 1851 and 27 July 1852, and S. Glacken, 10 Feb. 1868 (Teresa Lawlor Mss., CAHS); J. A. Reford, 28 June 1856? (T.3028, PRONI);

M. Kelly, 11 Dec. 1896 (Martin J. Kelly); S. Connelly, 26 Mar. 1901 (Alice L. McGuinness).

177. O'Riordan, 292; *Congestion Commission*, vol. 7 (3748), 1908, p. 811; Gwynn, 296; P. Ryan, Diary (WJSML); Schrier, 100.

178. Ms. 1408, p. 58 (DIF/UCD); *Report on Agriculture, 1881*, 512; Brody, 7–16; O'Donoghue, *In a Quiet*, 207; P. J. Blessing, "West among Strangers: Irish Migration to California . . ." (Ph.D. diss., UCLA, 1977), 127; B. MacNamara, *Valley of the Squinting Windows* (Dublin, 1973 ed.), 51; O'Connor, 176–77; A. Patterson, 10 July 1852 (D.1441/6, PRONI); M. Headlam, *Irish Reminiscences* (London, 1947), 223–32; M. Sheehan, 18 June 1920 (M. Hayes Mss., KRM); Lee, "Women," 43; D. Cashman, "Lady Day in Ireland" (Patrick Clancy); Seaghan ar Fan, 25 Dec. 1902 (K. Nilsen, Cambridge, Mass., trans. BDB. In my article "Emigrants and Exiles . . . ," *IHS*, 22 [Sept. 1980], 120, I mistakenly assumed this was an emigrant's letter, but further study convinces me it was sent from Clare to Massachusetts).

179. T. Cashman, Memories (Patrick Clancy); Ms. 1408, p. 130 (DIF/UCD).

180. L. O'Flaherty, "Going into Exile," in V. Mercier and D. H. Greene, eds., *1000 Years of Irish Prose* (NY, 1952), 369–78; A. Flood, 5 Feb. 1853 (Pádraig Ó Droighneain, Navan, Co. Meath).

181. D. N. Doyle, "Irish and American Labour, 1880–1920," *Saothar*, 1 (1975), 44; J. F. Maguire, *Irish in America* (NY, 1868); G. A. Birmingham [J. O. Hannay], *From Connaught to Chicago* (London, 1914), 263–64; Sir J. Power, *Mayor's Holiday* (Dublin, 1903), 24–25.

182. Doyle, *Irish Americans*, 187–88, 204–5, 226, 291–335; D. V. Shaw, *Making of an Immigrant City* . . . (NY, 1976), 2; T. D'A. McGee, *History of Irish Settlers in North America* (Boston, 1851), 180; D. B. Light, Jr., "Class, Ethnicity, and Urban Ecology in a 19th-Century City: Philadelphia's Irish, 1840–90" (Ph.D. diss., Univ. of Pennsylvania, 1979).

183. D. N. Doyle, "Conclusion: Some Further Themes," in Doyle and O. D. Edwards, eds., *America and Ireland, 1776–1976* . . . (Westport, Conn., 1980), 324–25; see Chapter 4, pp. 156–57; J. Higham, *Strangers in the Land: Patterns of American Nativism, 1860–1925* (NY, 1971 ed.), 62–63, 80–87; E. Cuddy, "Irish Question and Revival of Anti-Catholicism in 1920s," *CATHHR*, 67 (Apr. 1981), 242, 246; N. Shanks, 8 Feb. 1890 (D.2709/1/57, PRONI); Diner, passim.

184. J. O'Dea, *History of Ancient Order of Hibernians* . . . (Philadelphia, 1923), III, 1482–86; F. M. Carroll, *American Opinion and Irish Question, 1910–23* (NY, 1978), 156–62.

185. J. P. Dolan, *Immigrant Church* . . . (Baltimore, 1975), 167–68; P. Gleason, "Immigration and American Catholic Higher Education," in B. J. Weiss, ed., *American Education and European Immigrant, 1840–1940* (Urbana, 1982), 163–64; T. N. Brown, "Origins and Character of Irish-American Nationalism," *RPOL*, 18 (July 1956), 348–49; Doyle, *Irish Americans* . . . , 48–49, 59–63; J. McN. Vinyard, *Irish on Urban Frontier: Detroit, 1850–80* (NY, 1976), 315.

186. For analyses of Irish-American social stratification and occupational distribution/ mobility in 1870–1920, see the works cited in Chapter 7, n. 46, by Benson, Blessing, Buker, Burchell, Clark, Cole, Conners, Esslinger, Feinstein, Gitelman, Griffin and Griffin, Leonard, Light, Millet, Ryan, Shanabruch, Shaw, Thernstrom, Vinyard, Walkowitz, J. P. Walsh, V. A. Walsh, and M. P. Weber.

Also see S. Thernstrom, *Other Bostonians: Poverty and Progress in American Metropolis. 1880–1970* (Cambridge, Mass., 1973); P. T. Silvia, "Position of Workers in a Textile Community: Fall River in Early 1880s," *LH*, 16 (1975), 230–48; A. Coelho, "Row of Nationalities: Life in a Working Class Community . . ." (Ph.D. diss., Brown Univ., 1980); J. T. Cumbler, *Working-Class Community in Industrial America: Work, Leisure, and Struggle in Two Industrial Cities, 1880–1930* (Westport, Conn., 1979); J. P. Hanlan, *Working Population of Manchester, New Hampshire, 1840–86* (Ann Arbor, 1981); M. Morgan and H. H. Golden, "Immigrant Families in an Industrial City: . . . Households in Holyoke, 1880," *JFH*, 4 (1979), 59–68; T. Hershberg, ed., *Philadelphia: Work, Space, Family, and Group Experience in the 19th Century* (NY, 1981); J. Bodnar, *Immigration and Industrialization: Ethnicity in an American Mill Town, 1870–1940* (Pittsburgh, 1977); H. P. Chudacoff, *Mobile Americans: Residential and Social Mobility in Omaha* (NY, 1972); M. F. Funcheon, *Chicago's Irish Nationalists, 1881–90* (NY, 1976); and O. Zunz, *Changing Face of In-*

equality: Urbanization, Industrial Development, and Immigrants in Detroit, 1880–1920 (Chicago, 1982).

This paragraph is specifically from D. Montgomery, *Beyond Equality: Labor and Radical Republicans, 1862–72* (NY, 1967), 212–13; Thernstrom, *Other*, 111–27, 131–33; Zunz, 221; G. and S. Griffin, *Natives and Newcomers: Ordering of Opportunity in Mid-19th-Century Poughkeepsie* (Cambridge, Mass., 1977), 216; Doyle, "Conclusion," 322; J. W. Sanders, *Education of an Urban Minority: Catholics in Chicago, 1833–1965* (NY, 1977), 130–31.

187. A. Gass, 8 Jan. 1872 (T.1396, PRONI); K. Donovan, "Good Old Pat: Irish-American Stereotype in Decline," *É-I*, 15, no. 3 (Fall 1980), 6–14; J. J. Appel, "From Shanties to Lace Curtains: Irish Image in *Puck*," *CSSH*, 13 (Oct. 1971), 367–72; M. Keller, *Art and Politics of Thomas Nast* (NY, 1968), 159–75; D. B. Cole, *Immigrant City: Lawrence, Massachusetts, 1845–1921* (Chapel Hill, 1963), 88, 95, 165–66; Coelho, 284 and passim.

188. V. A. Walsh, diss. on Pittsburgh Irish (Univ. of Pittsburgh), in progress; Vinyard, 315; Funcheon, 13–15; Zunz, 214; Thernstrom, *Other*, 111–27, 131–33; A. Kessler-Harris, *Out to Work: History of Wage-Earning Women in the United States* (NY, 1982), 135–37; A. Wilson, 12 Oct. 1899, 11 Feb. 1900, 13 Nov. 1900, and 24 Feb. 1901 (D.1921/3/13, 18, 22–3, PRONI); S. B. Warner, *Streetcar Suburbs: Process of Growth in Boston, 1870–1900* (Cambridge, Mass., 1962), passim; M. J. Buker, "Irish in Lewiston, Maine . . . ," *MEHQ*, 13 (1973), 18–20; T. L. Philpott, *Slum and Ghetto: Neighborhood Deterioration and Middle-Class Reform* (NY, 1978), chap. 1; P. Murphy [alias F. Conlan], 23 Apr. 1954 (Frank Conlan Mss., CHHS); Higham, 62–63, 80–87; Shaw, passim; R. Lane, *Policing the City: Boston, 1822–85* (NY, 1975 ed.), 199–219; J. D. Buenker, *Urban Liberalism and Progressive Reform* (NY, 1978 ed.), 7.

189. Doyle, *Irish Americans*, 187–88, 305; J. M. Curley, *I'd Do It Again: Record of All My Uproarious Years* (Englewood Cliffs, 1957), 32; T. Beer: *Mauve Decade: American Life at the End of the 19th Century* (NY, 1960 ed.), 111–16; M. S. Seller, ed., *Immigrant Women* (Philadelphia, 1981), 298–302; O'Dea, III, 1286, 1452–53, 1470–71, 1487; Donovan, 13; J. D. Ibsen, "Will the World Break Your Heart? Historical Analysis of Dimensions and Consequences of Irish-American Assimilation" (Ph.D. diss., Brandeis Univ., 1976), 56, 106–20, 214, 304–5, and passim; A. S. Green, draft essay on Irish in America (Ms. 10,445, NLI); M. Flanagan, 14 Apr. 1877 (Peter & Mary Flanagan); M. Kilcran, Journal (John & James Kilcran, Carrick-on-Shannon, Co. Leitrim).

190. Doyle, *Irish Americans*, 60–61, 65; idem, "Irish and American Labour," 42–43; D. Montgomery, "Irish and American Labor Movement," in Doyle and Edwards, 211–12; C. Golab, *Immigrant Destinations* (Philadelphia, 1978), 35–40; Bodnar, *Immigration*, 36–38; M. P. Weber, "Occupational Mobility of Ethnic Minorities in 19th-Century Warren, Pennsylvania," in J. Bodnar, ed., *Ethnic Experience in Pennsylvania* (Harrisburg, 1978), 168.

191. Doyle, "Unestablished," 195–203; Light, 55–58; Thernstrom, *Other*, 111–27, 131–33; J. R. Green and H. C. Donohue, *Boston's Workers: Labor History* (Boston, 1979), 53–57; Funcheon, 13; Zunz, 221; D. M. Katzman, *Seven Days a Week: Women and Domestic Service in Industrializing America* (Oxford, 1978), 66–67, 70; D. E. Sutherland, *Americans and Their Servants* (Baton Rouge, 1981), 45–62; Diner, 70–105 and passim; D. Clark, *Irish Relations: Trials of Irish Immigrant Tradition* (East Brunswick, 1981), 42–43; Cumbler, 218–27.

192. Doyle, "Irish and American Labour"; Montgomery, "Irish," 211–13; D. Clark, "Irish Ethic and Spirit of Patronage," in S. Cummings, ed., *Self-Help in Urban America: Patterns of Minority Business Enterprise* (Port Washington, NY, 1980), passim; D. Light, "Social Bases of Community: Patterns of Participation in Irish Ethnic Associations in 19th-Century Philadelphia" (Paper, AHA convention, Washington, D.C., 1982); P. K. Good, "Irish Adjustment to American Society . . . Portrait of an Irish-Catholic Parish, 1863–86," *RACHSP*, 86 (Mar.–Dec. 1975), 18–20; Healy, 91–92; Kane, II, 323–24; A. Sanborn, *Moody's Lodging House and Other Tenement Sketches* (Boston, 1895), 97–161; Birmingham, *Connaught*, 264; J. J. Harte, 21 Apr. 1922 (Nuala Simon, Boyle, Co. Roscommon); M. Wolfe, 19 Nov. 1873 (mf p3887, NLI).

193. W. Murphy, 6 May 1874 (D.2795/5/2/7, PRONI); Vinyard, 146; Morrison and Zabusky, 48–49, 61–62; O. O'Callaghan, 17 Sept. [1883?] (Eugene O'Callaghan); D. S. Lawlor, *Life and Struggles of an Irish Boy in America* (Newton, Mass., 1936), 25–36 and passim; see studies of occupational mobility and property acquisition cited in n. 186 above; J. Lough, 18 Jan. 1891 (AS); O. P. Mangan, Memoir (G. A. Fitzgerald, New York City);

P. McKeown, 8 Dec. 1901 (AS); M. Quin, n.d., and A. Quin, 18 July 1875 (D.1819/3,5, PRONI); Anon., "Irish Catholics in a Yankee Town: Report from Brattleboro, Vt., 1847–1898," *VTH*, 44 (Fall 1976), 189–97; Clark, *Irish Relations*, 17; Philpott, chap. 1; Fr. P. Devine, Adventures . . . (STPCR).

194. See above, pp. 358–59; Doyle, "Irish and American Labour," 45; N. L. Shumsky, "Frank Roney's San Francisco—His Diary: Apr. 1875–Mar. 1876," *LH*, 17 (Spring 1976), 256; J. Shields, 16 May 1875 (mf n5225, NLI); C. Fanning, *Finley Peter Dunne and Mr. Dooley: Chicago Years* (Lexington, 1978), 67–104 and passim; idem, "Mr. Dooley in Chicago: Finley Peter Dunne as Historian of Irish in America," in Doyle and Edwards, 151–64; Reeve and Reeve, 116; Greaves, 208.

195. Ms. 1409, p. 303 (DIF/UCD); T. Cashman, Memories (Patrick Clancy); J. McFadden, 17 Oct. 1897 (AS); M. Kilcran, Journal (John & James Kilcran); P. Kearney, 21 Dec. 1890, in S. de Burca, *Soldier's Song* (Dublin, 1957), 250–53; J. Chamberlain, n.d. [1880?] (AS); W. H. Downes, 23 Mar. 1913 (William O'Shaughnessy); P. McKeown, 11 Sept. 1904 (AS); I. B. Cross, ed., *Frank Roney: Irish Rebel and California Labor Leader: Autobiography* (Berkeley, 1931), 187; Lawlor, 25–26; Doyle, "Irish and American Labour," 46–47; F. Woolsey, 18 June 1877 (AS).

196. Doyle, "Unestablished," 195–203; Katzman, 66–67; Kessler-Harris, 125–27; M. Malone, 24 Jan. 1877 (AS); Ms. 1407, pp. 157–88 (DIF/UCD; trans. BDB); Clark, *Irish Relations*, 54–55.

197. E. Glassberg, "Work, Wages, and Cost of Living, Ethnic Differences, and Poverty Line, Philadelphia, 1880," *PENNH*, 46 (Jan. 1979), passim; Light, "Class," 55–58; P. McKeown, autumn 1892 (AS); Doyle, "Unestablished," 196; idem, "Irish and American Labour," 45; Thernstrom, *Other*, 168–75; E. Ua Cathail, letter in *An Claidheamh Soluis*, 4, no. 7 (Dublin, 26 Apr. 1902), 124–25 (trans. BDB); S. Ó Dúbhda, ed., *Duanaire Duibhneach* (Dublin, 1933), 132–33 (trans. BDB).

198. Doyle, "Irish and American Labour," 45; Clark, *Irish Relations*, 41, 46–55; Montgomery, "Irish," 213; Lawlor, 25–39; Ó Dúbhda, 130–35 (trans. BDB).

199. M. Kilcran, Journal (John & James Kilcran); Ó Dúbhda, 130–35 (trans. BDB); D. Fouhey, Poetry (John M. Tivnan, Woodbridge, Va.); T. Cashman, Memories (Patrick Clancy); Morrison and Zabusky, 44–45; Katzman, 8–9, 38–39, 241; Reeve and Reeve, 81.

200. Sanborn, 97–161; B. Mullen, *Life Is My Adventure* (NY, 1937), passim; William Z. Foster, *Pages from a Worker's Life* (NY, 1970), 15–20; Clark, *Irish Relations*, 54–55, 172–73; M. Kilcran, Journal (John & James Kilcran); Fanning, *Finley*, 67–104; Doyle, "Unestablished," 197–98, 215; J. P. Rodechko, *Patrick Ford and His Search for America* (NY, 1976), 12; Funcheon, 13; V. A. Walsh, "Drowning the Shamrock: Catholic Total Abstinence Movement in Pittsburgh during Gilded Age" (Paper, AHA convention, Washington, D.C., 1982); Diner, 53–62, 106–19; Ibsen, 57–58, 229, 286–90.

201. T. Cashman, Memories (Patrick Clancy); Ms. 1410, pp. 123–25 (DIF/UCD).

202. E. Lough, 29 Oct. 1891 (AS); Tuke, *Reports*, 158 and passim; Ms. 1409, p. 280 (DIF/UCD); J. S. Sinclair, n.d. [1883?] (D.1497/1/2, PRONI); T. N. Brown, *Irish-American Nationalism, 1870–90* (Philadelphia, 1966), 23; P. L. Henry, "Anglo-Irish and Its Irish Background," in D. Ó Muirithe, ed., *English Language in Ireland* (Cork, 1977), 23; T. McCann, 18 Oct. 1884 (T.1456/2, PRONI); M. Markey, 23 Oct. 1889 and 15 Nov. 1891 (Kathleen McMahon).

203. Buckley, 143–44, 170, 280; W. Austin, 10 Mar. 1874 (Ms. 18,236, NLI); J. S. Sinclair, 14 Dec. 1883 (D.1497/1/3, PRONI); W. McDonald, *Reminiscences*, unabr. ed., 209.

204. F. McCosker, 14 Sept. 1873 (ERRG); J. S. Tuke, "News from Some Irish Emigrants," *Nineteenth Century*, 25 (Mar. 1889), 432–33; M. McG. Elliott, Memoir (Alice L. McGuinness, Hampton Bays, NY); Buckley, 151–52; J. O'Connor, 14 Sept. 1932 (Doncha Ó Conchúir); Ms. 1411, p. 349, and Ms. 1409, pp. 300–303 (DIF/UCD); MacGowan, 130; P. F. Campbell, Journal (Paul Maguire, Ederney, Co. Fermanagh); M. Kilcran, Journal (John & James Kilcran).

205. M. Kilcran, Journal; M. Wolfe, 12 May 1867 (mf p3887, NLI); Ms. 1407, p. 56 (DIF/UCD); MacGowan, xii; Fr. P. Devine, Adventures (STPCR); Ms. 1409, p. 327 (DIF/UCD); J. Cahill, 23 June 1889 (AS); O. P. Mangan, Memoir (G. A. Fitzgerald); J. Bredin, 18 Nov. 1887 (James Bredin, Birmingham); M. Sheehan, 4 Aug. 1914 (M. Hayes Mss., KRM); P. Murphy [alias F. Conlan], 13–14 May 1954 (Frank Conlan Mss., CHHS); P. McKeown, 8 Dec. 1901 and 24 June 1905 (AS).

206. T. Cashman, Daily Journal of Observations during Trip to Ireland, 1925 (Timothy D. Cashman, Los Angeles); Ó Crohan, 227; M. Corr, 9 Dec. 1892 (AS); A. Carroll,

26 Oct. 1888, 10 May 1890, and ? Apr. 189? (Kathleen McMahon); T. S. O'Brien, n.d. [1902–4?] (MDA); T. Higgins, 16 May 1916 (J. S. Higgins, Longford); E. A. Aglionby, 22 Sept. 1869 (Francis Yates Aglionby Mss., DUL); J. Hewitt, 26 June 1860 (Joseph Hewitt Mss., INHS).

207. A. Sullivan cited in newspaper clipping (HO 45/9635/A29278, PRO); A. Douglas, "Studs Lonigan and Failure of History in Mass Society," *AQ*, 29 (Winter 1977), 487–505; M. McG. Elliott, Memoir (Alice L. McGuinness); A. Kelly, 7 June 1967 (Martin J. Kelly); J. Heffernan, 15 Jan. 1978 (letter to author).

208. Fr. P. Devine, Adventures (STPCR); M. Markey, 23 Oct. 1889 (Kathleen McMahon); M. [Murphy?], n.d. (Murphy-O'Hara Mss., ERRG); M. Sheehan, 4 Aug. 1914, 18 June 1920, and 5 Apr. 1921 (M. Hayes Mss., KRM); Tuke, "News," 432; A. Carroll, 28 Apr. and 23 Sept. 1897 (Kathleen McMahon); T. McCann, 18 Oct. 1894 (T.1456/2, PRONI).

209. B. Colgan, 20 Dec. 1854 (AS); J. Butler, ? Nov. 1849, 11 Nov. 1850, 2 Mar. 1852, 2 May 1853, and 5 Jan. 1874, and J. K. Crowe, 10 Nov. 1959 (Martin J. Kelly); F. Carlin, *My Ireland* (NY, 1918 ed.), 92; P. Kane, "Reflections of Irish Emigrant," Chicago *New World*, 19 Nov. 1888 (courtesy of Dr. D. N. Doyle, UCD).

210. ? [Murphy?], n.d. [1921?] (Murphy-O'Hara Mss., ERRG); Morrison and Zabusky, 48; M. McG. Elliott, Memoir (Alice L. McGuinness); P. McKeown, fall 1892 and 15 Oct. 1905 (AS); Diner, 43–69; T. J. Meagher, " 'Lord Is Not Dead': Cultural and Social Change among Irish in Worcester, Mass." (Ph.D. diss., Brown Univ., 1982), 105–46; J. Wilcox and H. H. Golden, "Prolific Immigrants and Dwindling Natives? Fertility Patterns in Western Massachusetts," *JFH*, 7 (Fall 1982), 265–88; M. Malone, 24 Jan. 1877 (AS); Ó Dúbhda, 127–29 (trans. BDB); S. Buchanan, n.d. [1870s] (Samuel Buchanan Mss., NLI); A. Robb, 24 Feb. 1872 and 8 July 1873 (T.1454/6/8-9, PRONI); Ibsen, 119; M. Wolfe, 1869 (mf p3887, NLI).

211. T. Brick, Memoirs (Doncha Ó Conchúir); J. F. Costello, 11 Jan. 1883 (AS); MacGowan, 138; Ms. 1410, pp. 104–5, and Ms. 1411, pp. 93, 245 (DIF/UCD); H. J. Walsh, *Hallowed Were the Gold Dust Trails: Story of Pioneer Priests of Northern California* (Santa Clara, 1946), 22; C. Greene, 1 Aug. 1884 (Greene Mss., AD/UCD); M. A. Rowe, 29 Oct. 1888 (Mrs. B. Galway, Thomastown, Co. Kilkenny); C. Rush, 17 Nov. 1872, and J. Durkin, 9 Jan. 1889 (JD, Ms. 6893, TCD).

212. P. Murphy [alias F. Conlan], 21 Apr. 1954 (Frank Conlan Mss., CHHS); F. Hackett, *American Rainbow: Early Reminiscences* (NY, 1971), 89–90.

213. Rossa, *Rossa's Recollections*, 143; Ó Dúbhda, 127–29 (trans. BDB); P. F. Campbell, Journal (Paul Maguire); P. J. Ryan, 9 Sept. 1931 (Katherine Crowe, Thurles, Co. Tipperary); W. Mullen, 28 Oct. 1883 (AS); M. Kilcran, Journal (John & James Kilcran); E. Ua Cathail, as in n. 197 above.

214. Plunkett, 53–55; Fr. Gregory, 5 July 1938 (Mrs. M. Colby, Clondalkin, Co. Dublin); M. McG. Elliott, Memoir (Alice L. McGuinness); ? [Murphy?], n.d. [1921?] (Murphy-O'Hara Mss., ERRG); B. O'Connor, *With Michael Collins in Fight for Irish Independence* (London, 1929), 14–15.

215. A. Dowling, 20 Jan. 1870 (AS); Ó Dúbhda, 130–31 (trans. BDB); Plunkett, 53–55; Ms. 1409, pp. 88–89 (DIF/UCD); E. Wogan, 2 Sept. 1870 (AS); O. O'Callaghan, 27 May 1884 (Eugene O'Callaghan).

216. See above, pp. 270–75; P. Burden, 5 Sept. 1894 (LWCL); E. Ua Cathail, as in n. 197 above.

217. W. Porter, 25 Mar. 1872 (D.1152/3/24, PRONI); Ó Dúbhda, 132–33 (trans. BDB).

218. See above, pp. 487–88; P. Kearney, in de Burca, 250–53; J. Hall, 27 Nov. 1888 (D.2041/Bundle 13, PRONI); Ms. 1407, pp. 43–44 (DIF/UCD); M. Wolfe, 25 Sept. 1863 (mf p3887, NLI); W. H. Downes, 13 Oct. 1887 (William O'Shaughnessy); T. Waldron, 17 Sept. 1907 (Patrick Waldron, Rathmines, Dublin).

219. Keep, "Some," 385–86; P. Henry, 12 July 1926 (Ms. 21,570, NLI); Blessing, 128; I. B. Cross, 181; Edwards and Ransom, 371; Reeve and Reeve, 176.

220. A. Kelly, 22 Sept. 1937 (Martin J. Kelly); T. Brick, Memoir (Doncha Ó Conchúir); E. Ua Cathail, as in n. 197 above; P. Murphy [F. Conlan], 23 Apr. 1954 (Frank Conlan Mss., CHHS); Clark, *Irish Relations*, 226–28.

221. Ibsen, 227–28; Hackett, 86–90.

222. C. Mullen, 28 Dec. 1883 (T.1866/9, PRONI); J. Hall, 27 Nov. 1888 (D.2041/Bundle 13, PRONI). Similar letters include F. Langan, 20 June 1874 (Gerald Perry);

J. Chamberlain, n.d. (AS); O. O'Callaghan, 5 Dec. 1883 (Eugene O'Callaghan); T. Sample, 12 Sept. 1887 (T.2722/12, PRONI); J. Thompson, n.d. (T.1866/12, PRONI); and Charles ?, 18 Mar. 1907 (T.2085, PRONI). Reeve and Reeve, 182; Ó Dúbhda, 127–29, 132–33 (trans. BDB); E. Flemming, 10 Dec. 1897 (T.1850/2, PRONI); Clark, *Irish Relations,* 80; Ms. 1403, pp. 108–9, and Ms. 1411, p. 93 (DIF/UCD).

223. R. Sherry, "Frank O'Connor and Gaelic Ireland," in Drudy, *Irish Studies 1,* 47–48; M. Ó Codhain, "Tnúthán an Dúthchais," in Ó Codhain, *An Braon Broghach* (Dublin, 1948), 7–32 (trans. BDB); A. B. McMillan, 10 Apr. 1894 (D.1195/5/39, PRONI); Shumsky, 256; M. Kilcran, Journal (John & James Kilcran); J. Hagan, 3 Oct. 1884 (MIC 181/33, PRONI); E. Lough, 7 Mar. 1876 (AS).

224. P. Callaghan, 17 Aug. 1883 (Eugene O'Callaghan); J. Hagan, 29 Oct. 1883 (MIC 181/28, PRONI); M. Nolan, 1 May 1886 (AS); J. Carroll, 1 Mar. 1885 (Kathleen McMahon); P. McKeown, 13 Dec. 1889 (AS); M. Kelly, 8 Mar. 1894 and 11 Dec. 1896 (Martin J. Kelly); H. O'Daly, Life History (Rev. Patrick Daly).

225. O. P. Mangan, Memoir (G. A. Fitzgerald); MacGowan, 71, 75–76, 121–22; Fanning, *Finley,* passim; Sanborn, 97–161; Mullen, passim; Healy, 91–92; J. Hagan, 28 Jan. 1884 (MIC 181/30, PRONI); ? Nolan, 26 May 1891 (Mary Nolan, Crumlin, Dublin).

226. V. A. Walsh, " 'Fanatic Heart': Cause of Irish-American Nationalism in Pittsburgh during Gilded Age," *JSH,* 15 (Dec. 1981), 190; Ms. 1408, pp. 239–40 (DIF/UCD); H. G. Gutman, "Work, Culture, and Society in Industrializing America," *AHR,* 79 (June 1973), 563; W. H. A. Williams, "Irish Traditional Music in United States," in Doyle and Edwards, 279–94; L. E. McCullough, "Irish Music in Chicago: Ethnomusicological Study" (Ph.D. diss., Univ. of Pittsburgh, 1978); O'Sullivan, 179.

227. Light, "Class," 29–32; Philpott, chap. 1; S. B. Warner and C. Blake, "Cultural Change and Ghetto," *JCH,* 4 (1969), 173–87; V. A. Walsh, " 'Fanatic,' " 190, 195–96.

228. Sanborn, 97–161; Fanning, *Finley,* 67–104; V. A. Walsh, " 'Fanatic,' " 195–96; Doyle, "Irish and American Labour," 50–51.

229. Light, "Class," 172 and passim, and more specifically in his AHA Paper, "Social Bases of Community"; Good, 12; Funcheon, 22 and passim; Cole, 45–61, 142–52; Fallows, 39–41; Sr. J. M. Donohoe, *Irish Catholic Benevolent Union* (Washington, D.C., 1953); Sr. J. Bland, *Hibernian Crusade: Story of Catholic Total Abstinence Union of America* (Washington, D.C., 1951); V. A. Walsh, "Drowning the Shamrock."

230. E. Foner, "Class, Ethnicity, and Radicalism in the Gilded Age: Land League and Irish America," *MP,* 1 (Summer 1978), 6–55; M. Gordon, "Studies in Irish and Irish-American Thought and Behavior," idem, "Labor Boycott in New York City, 1880–86," *LH,* 16 (1975), 184–229; Montgomery, "Irish," passim; Reeve and Reeve, on Connolly in America; E. Larkin, *James Larkin;* W. Z. Foster, *Pages;* and E. G. Flynn, *Rebel Girl: An Autobiography* (NY, 1973 ed.).

231. W. Bocock, "Irish Conquest of Our Cities," in J. P. Walsh, ed., *The Irish: America's Political Class* (NY, 1976). On Irish-American urban politics generally, see H. P. Chudacoff, *Evolution of American Urban Society* (Englewood Cliffs, 1981), 141–65; W. Riordan, *Plunkitt of Tammany Hall* (NY, 1963 ed.); and E. M. Levine, *Irish and Irish Politicians* (Notre Dame, 1966). On Phelan, see W. A. Bullough, "Chris Buckley and San Francisco: Man and the City," in J. P. Walsh, ed., *San Francisco Irish, 1850–1976* (San Francisco, 1978), 27–38. On voting frauds in the Rossa and George campaigns, see F. E. Gibson, *Attitudes of New York Irish . . .* (NY, 1951), 253–56; and S. Bell, *Rebel, Priest and Prophet: Biography of Dr. Edward McGlynn* (NY, 1937), 39. On Church-Tammany relations, see R. E. Curran, *Michael A. Corrigan and Shaping of Conservative Catholicism in America, 1878–95* (NY, 1978). On urban/ethnic "liberalism" in early twentieth century, see Buenker, *Urban Liberalism;* and idem, "Edward F. Dunne: Urban New Stock Democrat as Progressive," in J. P. Walsh, *The Irish,* 3–21. On formation of an Irish-American Catholic power elite, see J. A. Tarr, "J. R. Walsh of Chicago: Case Study in Banking and Politics, 1881–1905," in J. P. Walsh, *The Irish,* 452–66; and Green and Donohue, *Boston's Workers,* 72–93, for taming of Irish working-class radicalism.

232. See J. P. O'Grady, *Irish-Americans and Anglo-American Relations, 1880–88* (NY, 1976); A. Ward, *Ireland and Anglo-American Relations, 1899–1921* (Toronto, 1969); and F. M. Carroll, *American Opinion and Irish Question, 1910–23* (NY, 1978), for indications of Irish-American influence (or lack of influence) on Democratic party and U.S. government policy. On the persistent ethnoreligious bases of late-19th-century American politics, see P. Kleppner, *Cross of Culture: Social Analysis of Midwestern Politics, 1850–1900* (NY,

1970). Citations from Plunkett, 71–74; Reeve and Reeve, 264–65; J. M. Allswang, *Bosses, Machines, and Urban Voters: American Symbiosis* (Port Washington, NY, 1977), 74; B. O'Connor, 14–15.

233. Not until the late 19th century did Irish *Catholic* emigrants refer frequently in their letters to religious devotions, corroborating E. Larkin, "Devotional Revolution." J. Nugent, 18 Sept. 1864 (Alice Timoney); A. Quin, 22 Sept. 1873 and 18 Sept. 1876 (D.1819/4,8, PRONI); on the American Catholic church's institutional expansion in 1870–1920, see relevant chaps. of J. Hennessey, *American Catholics: History of Roman Catholic Community in the United States* (NY, 1981); T. T. McAvoy, *History of Catholic Church in the United States* (Notre Dame, 1969); and H. Buetow, *Of Singular Benefit: Story of Catholic Education in the United States* (London, 1970), 179. Good, 12.

234. This and the following paragraphs on (Irish-) American Catholicism in 1870–1920 are based on these works: S. Bell, *Rebel, Priest;* H. J. Browne, *Catholic Church and Knights of Labor* (NY, 1976 ed.); D. Callahan, *Mind of the Catholic Layman* (NY, 1963); D. Clark, "Irish Catholics: Postponed Perspective," in R. M. Miller and T. D. Marzik, eds., *Immigrants and Religion in Urban America* (Philadelphia, 1977); J. F. Connolly, *History of Archdiocese of Philadelphia* (Philadelphia, 1976); R. D. Cross, *Emergence of Liberal Catholicism;* R. E. Curran, *Michael Augustine Corrigan;* idem, "The McGlynn Affair and Shaping of New Conservatism in American Catholicism, 1886–94," *CATHHR,* 66 (Apr. 1980), 184–204; J. P. Dolan, *Immigrant Church;* idem, *Catholic Revivalism in America* (Notre Dame, 1978); D. N. Doyle, *Irish Americans, Native Rights;* idem, "Conclusion: Some Further Themes," in Doyle and Edwards, eds., *America and Ireland.* J. T. Ellis, *American Catholicism* (Chicago, 1956); idem, *Life of James Cardinal Gibbons: Archbishop of Baltimore, 1834–1921* (Milwaukee, 1952); and idem, ed., *Catholic Priest in the United States* (Collegeville, Minn., 1971). J. Hennessey, *American Catholics;* J. P. Gaffey, *Citizen of No Mean City: Archbishop Patrick Riordan of San Francisco* (Hawthorne, Calif., 1976); E. R. Kantowicz, "Cardinal Mundelein of Chicago and Shaping of 20th-Century Catholicism" *JAH,* 68 (June 1981), 52–68; F. MacDonald, *Catholic Church and Secret Societies in the United States* (NY, 1946); S. Malone, *Dr. Edward McGlynn* (NY, 1918); D. Merwick, *Boston's Priests: Study of Social and Intellectual Change* (Cambridge, 1973); P. Messbarger, *Fiction with a Parochial Purpose: Social Uses of American Catholic Literature, 1884–1900* (Boston, 1971); J. H. Moynihan, *Life of Archbishop John Ireland* (NY, 1953); D. O'Brien, *Renewal of American Catholicism* (NY, 1972); J. E. Roohan, *American Catholics and Social Question* (NY, 1976); D. Ryan, "Beyond the Ballot Box: Social History of the Boston Irish, 1845–1917" (Ph.D. diss., Univ. of Massachusetts, 1979); C. Shanabruch, *Chicago's Catholics: Evolution of an American Identity* (Notre Dame, 1981); D. F. Sweeney, *Life of John Lancaster Spalding: First Bishop of Peoria, 1840–1916* (NY, 1965); F. J. Zwierlein, *Life and Letters of Bishop McQuaid* (NY, 1926). Additional sources and specific quotations cited in nn. 235–39.

235. Flynn, 41–44; Malone, 100; Bell, 32–33; Greaves, 179, 214.

236. Sr. M. S. Pahorezki, *Social and Political Activities of William James Onahan* (Washington, D.C., 1942), passim.

237. H. Weisz, "Irish-American Attitudes and Americanization of English-Language Parochial School," *NYH,* 53 (1972), 157–76; J. L. Spalding, *Religious Mission of Irish People and Catholic Colonization* (NY 1880), 251; Sr. M. E. Henthorne, *Irish Catholic Colonization Association of the United States* (Champaign, 1932); J. P. Shannon, *Catholic Colonization on the Western Frontier* (New Haven, 1957); J. O'Grady, "Irish Colonization in the United States," *Studies,* 19 (Sept. 1930), 387–407; Ellis, *Life of . . . Gibbons,* II, 224–27.

238. P. Flanagan, 16 Aug. 1891 (Peter & Mary Flanagan). On relations between the church and the AF of L, see M. Karson, *American Labor Unions and Politics, 1900–18* (Carbondale, 1958), 212–84.

239. J. G. Green, "American Catholics and Irish Land League, 1879–82," *CATHHR,* 35 (Apr. 1949), passim; Zwierlein, II, 462; F. MacDonald, 203–4; Spalding, 62–63, 226, 251; O'Dea, III, 1316–26, 1448–50; W. Cardinal O'Connell, *Recollections of Seventy Years* (Boston, 1944), 1–45; W. Wolkovich-Valkavicius, *Immigrants and Yankees in Nashoba Valley, Massachusetts* (West Groton, 1981), passim.

240. Rossa, *Rossa's Prison Life,* 434. See Donohoe on the ICBU; O'Dea and F. MacDonald on the AOH (1908 membership figures in O'Dea, III, 1381, and 1106–7 for promotion of U.S. flags in schools); and Bland on the CTAU. O. O'Callaghan, 12 Dec. 1884

(Eugene O'Callaghan). On the K of C, see C. J. Kauffman, *Faith and Fraternalism: History of Knights of Columbus* (NY, 1982); Light, "Social Bases"; on Philo-Celtic Societies, see T. N. Brown, "Origins and Character of Irish-American Nationalism," 344–45; on the AIHS, see J. J. Appel, "New England Origins of American Irish Historical Society," *NEQ,* 33 (Dec. 1960), 462–75; on Gaelic League in America, see J. J. Ford, "Some Records of Irish Language in Boston Area," *B-ÉSB,* 32 (1972), and N. Ó Gadhra, "Language Report, 1981," *É-I,* 16, no. 4 (Winter 1981), 109.

241. W. H. Downes, 13 Oct. 1887 (William O'Shaughnessy); Shaw, 2.

242. Light, "Social Bases"; M. J. Sullivan and M. G. Towey, "Knights of Father Mathew: Parallel Ethnic Reform," *MOHR,* 75 (1981), 174. Information on Philadelphia AOH, courtesy of Prof. Dale Light, East Carolina Univ. V. A. Walsh, "Drowning the Shamrock"; O'Dea, III, 1451; Pahorezki, 124–29, 149–51; Kauffman, 228–31.

243. T. Cashman, Memories (Patrick Clancy); W. Herberg, *Protestant, Catholic, Jew* (Garden City, 1960 ed.), on "triple melting pot" thesis. E.g., on the aggressive Irishness of the CTAU in Wisconsin, see G. McDonald, *History of Irish in Wisconsin in 19th Century* (NY, 1976 ed.), 223–36. Bland, 109–10; Shaw, 191–92; Sanders, 60; O'Dea, III, 1065–67, 1131, 1214–15, 1221–23, 1376–1422, 1452–1505.

244. J. W. Boyle, "Fenian Protestant in Canada: Robert Lindsay Crawford, 1910–22," *CHR,* 52 (1971), 173–74; T. A. Emmet, *Incidents of My Life* (NY, 1911). For reports on Protestant Irish-American political sentiments, see the British ambassadorial and consular reports, e.g., for 1916–22 (FO 115/2073–751, PRO). M. Sheehan, 18 June 1920 (M. Hayes Mss., KRM); I. B. Cross, 264–65; P. McKenna, 14 Feb. 1880 (Mrs. L. Bradley, Maghera, Co. Derry); M. Wolfe, ? Nov. 1868 and 20 Oct. 1879 (mf p3887, NLI); T. S. O'Brien, n.d. [1903?] (MDA); T. Waldron, 28 Sept. 1910 (Patrick Waldron); B. L. Reid, *Man from New York: John Quinn and His Friends* (NY, 1968), 122, 212; O'Brien and Ryan, II, 250–51; Rossa, *Rossa's Prison Life,* 437.

245. O'Brien and Ryan, I, 42–43, 456, 478; Gaffey, 144; on Cardinal O'Connell, see C. Barclay, 10 Nov. and 12 Dec. 1918 (FO 115/2398, PRO); C. S. Rice, 22 Jan. 1917 (FO 115/2244, PRO); M. F. Funcheon, "Irish Chicago . . . 1870–1900," in P. d'A. Jones and M. G. Holli, eds., *Ethnic Chicago* (Grand Rapids, 1981), 18; H. O'Daly, Life History (Rev. Patrick Daly); Donevan, 12; Sanborn, 97–161; Cole, 99–100.

246. F. O'Connor, *Short History,* 193–97; O'Brien and Ryan, II, 150–53, 252; W. M. Leary, "Woodrow Wilson, Irish-Americans, and Election of 1916," *JAH,* 54 (June 1967); Doyle, "Irish and American Labour," 51–52. Emigrants' references to St. Patrick's Day celebrations include O. O'Callaghan, 26 Mar. 1883 (Eugene O'Callaghan); A. Hagan, 21 Mar. 1885 (MIC 181/36, PRONI); A. Carroll, 12 May 1893 (Kathleen McMahon); and S. Owens, 19 Mar. 1900 (Christopher Fox, Skerries, Co. Dublin). B. O'Connor, 14–15.

247. T. N. Brown, *Irish-American Nationalism,* passim.

248. O'Brien and Ryan, I, xxxi–xxxii, 5, 41, 141–43, 182, 207–11; Gibson, 335–36; W. L. Joyce, *Editors and Ethnicity: History of Irish-American Press, 1848–83* (NY, 1976), chap. 6; Ibsen, 108–11; Rodechko, passim; T. N. Brown, *Irish-American Nationalism,* 66, 70–73; D. C. Lyne and P. M. Toner, "Fenianism in Canada, 1874–84," *SH,* 12 (1972), 27–76.

249. For related developments in Ireland, 1870–1921, see above, pp. 439–53; T. N. Brown, *Irish-American Nationalism,* 85–115; Foner, passim; Green, passim; Rodechko, 49 and passim.

250. T. N. Brown, *Irish-American Nationalism,* 117–77; Foner, 38–42, 46–47; Joyce, 170–73; Funcheon, *Chicago's Irish Nationalists,* 28–55. On the Parnell scandal, see M. Nolan, n.d. [1890–91] (T.2340, PRONI); H. O'Daly, Life History (Rev. Patrick Daly); and P. Flanagan, 16 Aug. 1891 (Peter & Mary Flanagan).

251. Ward, 8–69; Carroll, 7–28; Doyle, *Irish Americans,* 195–268; Meagher, esp. chaps. 9–10; J. S. Brusher, *Consecrated Thunderbolt: Father Yorke of San Francisco* (Hawthorne, N.J., 1973), 16–83; J. V. O'Brien, *William O'Brien,* 97–111.

252. Ward, 12–69; J. McGurrin, *Bourke Cockran . . .* (NY, 1978 ed.), 219–25; Lyons, *Irish Parliamentary Party,* 216–17; O'Brien and Ryan, II, 350, 365–66, 402–5, 412–13; Davis, *Arthur Griffith,* 84; see Tarpey on McGarrity.

253. Ward, 72–140; Carroll, 23–24, 33–38, 48–53, 63–65, 78–79, and passim; T. Waldron, 28 Sept. 1910 (Patrick Waldron); J. V. O'Brien, *William O'Brien,* 194, 203–4, 215–16; Reid, 185–86; J. E. Cuddy, "Irish-American Propagandists and American Neutrality," in J. P. Walsh, ed., *The Irish,* 252–75; Tarpey, 63–64; McGurrin, 235–36; J. E. Cuddy, "Irish-Americans and Election of 1916," in J. P. Walsh, ed., *The Irish,* 228–43.

254. Ward, 141–213; Carroll, 89, 98, 106–7, 113–14, 126–28, and passim; Cuddy, "Irish-American Propagandists," 271; R. Jeffreys-Jones, "Massachusetts Labour and League of Nations Controversy in 1919," *IHS*, 19 (Sept. 1975), 396–416.

255. Ward, 214–35; Carroll, 149–76; McGurrin, 238–41; P. McCartan, *With De Valera in America* (NY, 1932), passim; Tarpey, 95–126; M. Sullivan, "Fighting for Irish Freedom: Irish-American Nationalism in St. Louis," in J. P. Walsh, ed., *The Irish*, 184–206; A. Kelly, 14 Mar. 1966 (Martin J. Kelly).

256. T. N. Brown, *Irish-American Nationalism*, passim; idem, "Origins," passim; Funcheon, *Chicago's Irish Nationalists*, esp. 32–38; Birmingham, *Irishmen All*, 157–58; Rossa, *Rossa's Prison Life*, 430–32; O'Brien and Ryan, II, 94–99, 250–51; Rodechko, 184; Reeve and Reeve, 158, 172–73, 188.

257. O'Brien and Ryan, I, 156, 281; Ibsen, 63–64; C. O'Conor, 29 Oct. 1883 (#9.4:139, O'CD); Bagenal, 232–39; Cuddy, "Irish-Americans and Election," 232–34; idem, "Irish Question and Revival of Anti-Catholicism in 1920s," passim; T. J. Sarbaugh, "Irish Republicanism vs. 'Pure Americanism': California's Reaction to Eamon de Valera's Visits," *CAH*, 69 (Summer 1981), passim.

258. Light, "Social Bases," and unpublished research generously shared with author; V. A. Walsh, "'Fanatic Heart,'" 196–97; M. Sullivan, "Fighting," 184–206; D. Brundage, "Denver's New Departure: Irish Nationalism and Labor Movement in Gilded Age," *SWES*, 5, no. 3 (Winter 1981), 12; Clark, *Irish Relations*, 115–19; Carroll, 197–98; Bagenal, 126; Plunkett, 13–15; Buenker, *Urban Liberalism*, 185; J. A. O'Leary, *My Political Trial and Experiences* (NY, 1919), 1–2 and passim; Flynn, 23, 29–33.

259. Rodechko, 56; Moody, *Davitt*, 415; Burke, *Lectures*, 235; Brundage, 13–15.

260. Rossa, *Rossa's Recollections*, 262; Ibsen, 106–20; J. Shields, 16 May 1875 (mf n5225, NLI); J. O'Connor, 14 Sept. 1932 (Doncha Ó Conchúir); Doyle, *Irish Americans*, 199–204, 295–303.

261. J. F. Connolly, *Philadelphia Archdiocese*, 332; Foner, 17; D. Clark, "*Éireannach Éigin:* William J. Bradley (1892–1981), Sinn Féin Advocate," *É-I*, 18, no. 2 (Summer 1983), 116–26; Reeve and Reeve, 264–65.

262. Cuddy, "Irish-Americans and 1916 Election," 236–41; idem, "Irish-American Propagandists," 256–57, 271–75; idem, "Irish Question," passim; Sarbaugh, passim; Tarpey, 95–126; McCartan, passim. For the conservative role generally played by middle-class Irish-American nationalists, see already cited works by T. N. Brown, Funcheon, Foner, V. A. Walsh, Brundage, M. Sullivan, Ward, Carroll, and Rodechko, esp. 243–73. Also, see McGurrin, 219–41; Reid, 185–86, 232–33; and British reports on Irish-American opinion in 1916–22 (FO 115/2073–751).

263. Gordon, "Labor Boycott," 204–5; J. Fitzgerald, 16 Feb. 1887 (Hayes Mss., MG24 D2, v.9, PAC); Foner, 21–30; V. A. Walsh, "'Fanatic,'" 191–96; Gordon, "Studies," passim; J. Rodechko, "Irish-American Society in Pennsylvania Anthracite Region, 1870–80," in Bodnar, *Ethnic Experience*, 19–35; Meagher, chaps. 9–10, unpublished research, courtesy of Profs. Dale Light, East Carolina Univ., and Timothy J. Meagher, Worcester Polytechnic Institute; F. P. Leahy, 2 May 1916 (FO 115/2073, PRO). The account book of the Gaelic-American Defense Fund (1918), a Clan na Gael "front," shows most individual contributions of $5.00 or less (sometimes four persons combined to send $2.00), indicating the relative poverty of Clan supporters (Ms. 9208, ULI); contributions to the Clan-dominated Gaelic League of the U.S. in 1911–13 show the same pattern (Ms. 3279, NLI); T. N. Brown, *Irish-American Nationalism*, 70; Gibson, 338–67; O'Brien and Ryan, I, 189–91, 256–57, 375–76, and II, 41–43, 178–89, 189–91; H. O'Daly, Life History (Rev. Patrick Daly); D. Clark, *Irish Relations*, 122–24.

264. Foner, 26–27 and passim; Gordon, "Boycott," passim; Brown, *Irish-American Nationalism*, 108; Flynn, 35; Montgomery, "Irish," 215–16; Higham, 80–87; Brusher, 70–83, 156–209; Carroll, 106–7; Sarbaugh, passim.

265. Foner, 20; Montgomery, "Irish," 216; V. A. Walsh, "'Fanatic,'" 191–96; unpublished research, courtesy of Prof. Dale Light; O'Brien and Ryan, I, 256–57, and II, 19–20; Morrison and Zabusky, 41; Hackett, 45; Brusher, 195.

266. See above, pp. 310–12; M. Flanagan, 14 Apr. 1877 (Peter & Mary Flanagan); P. O'Callaghan, 17 Aug. 1883 (Eugene O'Callaghan); O'Brien and Ryan, I, 147–49, 536–38, and II, 147–49.

267. F. P. Leahy, 11 Dec. 1916 (FO 115/2244, PRO); Anon., Account of Fenianism . . . (Ms. 5963, NLI); Devoy, 26–35; Ms. 1407, p. 209, Ms. 1408, pp. 127–29, and Ms. 1409,

p. 64 (DIF/UCD); W. Dermady, n.d. (Ms. 15,784, NLI); Pomfret, 257; Hackett, 15–16, 28; P. Ryan, Journal (WJSML).

268. Fallows, 83; Namias, 14–20; Derham, "Oral History,"; Hackett, 15–16, 28; M. Carroll (tc, San Francisco, 1977); J. F. Costello, 11 Jan. 1883 (AS); Morrison and Zabusky, 41; T. Cashman, Memories (Patrick Clancy); idem, "Irish Language: A Reading . . . 1913" (Patrick Clancy).

269. Unpublished research, courtesy of Profs. Dale Light and T. J. Meagher; see Appendix, this work, Table 4; see above, pp. 441–53; Tarpey, 23–32; T. Cashman, Memories (Patrick Clancy).

270. T. Cashman, "Irish Language" (Patrick Clancy); see above, pp. 469–81; Rossa, *Rossa's Prison Life*, 431; Brusher, 9, 165.

271. V. A. Walsh, " 'Fanatic,' " 190–96; B. O'Connor, 14; Ó Dúbhda, 127–33 (trans. BDB).

272. Ó Dúbhda, 127–33 (trans. BDB).

273. Ibid.; J. P. Walsh, *San Francisco Irish*, 7–8; E. Ua Cathail as cited in n. 197.

274. P. Kane, "Reflections," Chicago *New World*, 19 Nov. 1898 (courtesy of Dr. D. N. Doyle, UCD); P. Cunningham, 9 Jan. 1869 (Conlin S. Mulvihill, Arnprior, Ontario); T. Higgins, 16 May 1916 (J. S. Higgins, Longford).

275. For Irish-American reactions to the Anglo-Irish treaty and the Irish civil war, see Ward, 237–55, and Carroll, 177–87; or more intimately in Reid, 527–28; P. J. Dowling, 4 Sept. 1922 (Mrs. Catherine Cullen, Blanchardstown, Dublin); T. O'Brien, n.d. [1922–23] (Mrs. M. Cregan, Belfast); and J. D. Fitzgerald, 12 Dec. 1923 (Ann Delea, Douglas, Co. Cork). On post-1921 Catholic emigrants from Northern Ireland, see D. Clark, *Irish Blood: Northern Ireland and American Conscience* (Port Washington, NY, 1977).

Conclusion

1. Unless otherwise cited, the information on the "American wakes" in this and the following paragraphs is derived from A. Schrier, *Ireland and the American Emigration, 1850–1900* (NY, 1970 ed.), 84–91. A. Nicholson, *Ireland's Welcome to the Stranger* (London, 1847), 76–77; W. McElroy, Diary (AIAH); M. T. Mellon, ed., *Selections from Thomas Mellon and His Times . . .* (Belfast, 1968 ed.), 3–4; M. Carbery, *Farm by Lough Gur* (Cork, 1973 ed.), 232–43; S. Gwynn, *Holiday in Connemara* (London, 1909), 293; P. O'Farrell, "Emigrant Attitudes and Behavior as Source for Irish History," *HS*, 10 (1976), 111.

2. See Chapter 2, pp. 72–73; S. Ó Súilleabháin, *Irish Wake Amusements* (Cork, 1967), passim; A. and B. Rees, *Celtic Heritage . . .* (London, 1961), 314–25; E. Estyn Evans, *Irish Folkways* (London, 1957), 44–45; R. L. Praeger, *The Way That I Went: Irishman in Ireland* (Dublin, 1939 ed.), 158; information from BDB; T. Ó Crohan, *The Islandman* (London, 1934), 249; M. O'Sullivan, *Twenty Years A-Growing* (NY, 1933), 240; H. Brody, *Inishkillane: Change and Decline in West of Ireland* (NY, 1973), 84; Ms. 1411, pp. 90–91 (DIF/UCD).

3. See general descriptions of American wakes in Schrier, 84–91, and in Ms. 1410 (DIF/UCD). Ó Súilleabháin, 19–23, 146–57, for clerical condemnations of wakes; Rev. J. Guinan, *Scenes and Sketches in an Irish Parish . . .* (Dublin, 1906), 35–37; M. Kilcran, Journal (John & James Kilcran, Carrick-on-Shannon, Co. Leitrim).

4. On wake keens and their reproachful tone, see T. C. Croker, *Researches in South of Ireland* (London, 1824), 166–82; and idem, *Keen of the South of Ireland* (London, 1844), passim. D. B. Quinn, *Elizabethans and the Irish* (Ithaca, 1966), 82–83; A. Plumptre, *Narrative of a Residence in Ireland during . . . 1814 and 1815* (London, 1817), 354–55; Nicholson, 76–77; E. Costello, ed., *Traditional Irish Folk Songs from Galway and Mayo* (London, 1919), 44–45; P. Ua Duinnín, *Muinntear Chiarraidhe Roimh an Drochsaoghal* (Dublin, 1905), 55–56 (trans. BDB); Schrier, 87.

5. O'Sullivan, 221–22; Schrier, 88.

6. G.-D. Zimmermann, *Songs of Irish Rebellion . . .* (Dublin, 1967), 12, 22–23, and passim; S. F. and A. L. Milligan, *Glimpses of Erin* (London, 1888), 195–96; D. G. Boyce, *Nationalism in Ireland* (Baltimore, 1982), 246–48; C. D. Greaves, *Life and Times of James Connolly* (NY, 1971 ed.), 26; see Chapter 3, pp. 106–7.

7. Schrier, 95, 99; R. L. Wright, ed., *Irish Emigrant Ballads and Songs* (Bowling Green, Ohio, 1975), 12–13, 170, 201, 208, 415, 491; M. A. Gordon, "Studies in Irish and Irish-American Thought and Behavior . . ." (Ph.D. diss., Univ. of Rochester, 1977), 388; J. N.

Healy, ed., *Mercier Book of Old Irish Street Ballads*, vol. 4, *No Place Like Home* (Cork, 1969), 92–94.

8. See Chapter 6, pp. 223–24; Ms. 1408, p. 314 and passim, and Ms. 1407, pp. 23–26 (DIF/UCD); C. Mac Mathuna, "Song of the Exile," *Irish Times*, 16 Dec. 1976; Wright, 170; Ms. 1411, pp. 91, 217 (DIF/UCD).

9. Ms. 1410, p. 271 (DIF/UCD); Schrier, 95; Nicholson, 76; Wright, 59; "Three Leaved Shamrock" and testimony of Mrs. B. Douglass, in Ms. 1411 (DIF/UCD).

10. Ms. 1411, pp. 24–25 (DIF/UCD); Healy, 62–64; Wright, 79, 177; Ms. 1408, pp. 96–97, and Ms. 1409, pp. 248–49 (DIF/UCD); Zimmermann, 22–34, 60; Milligan, 195–96; "My Native Irish Home: New National Ballad" (James Bredin, Birmingham); see above, pp. 103–7; Croker, *Keen*, xx, xxviii–xxx, 97, 103.

11. Wright, 138, 192, 242–47, 503–25; Healy, 84–85.

12. Anon., *The Emerald: or, Book of Irish Melodies* (NY, 1863), 22–23; Wright, 153, 352, 506; Healy, 97; Gordon, xxxv.

13. Ms. 1411, pp. 90–91 (DIF/UCD).

14. E. C. Guillet, *Great Migration . . .* (Toronto, 1963), 44–45; S. Ó Súlleabháin, *Irish Folk Custom and Belief* (Dublin, n.d.), 29; Guinan, 41; Schrier, 89; O'Sullivan, 89; J. Greene, ? Aug. 1902 (Greene Mss., AD/UCD); M. J. H. Anderson, Memoir (MNHS); J. J. Mitchell, Journal (N-YHS).

15. Schrier, 89–90; P. Sayers, *Peig: Autobiography of Peig Sayers . . .* (Syracuse, 1974), 129–30; G. R. C. Keep, "Irish Migration to North America in Second Half of 19th Century" (Ph.D. diss., TCD, 1951), 242; Brody, 132.

16. Ms. 1410, p. 303 (DIF/UCD); M. McG. Elliott, Memoir (Alice L. McGuinness, Hampton Bays, NY); A. L. O'Brien, *Journal of Andrew Leary O'Brien* (Athens, Ga., 1946), 49; Rev. J. Guinan, *Soggarth Aroon* (NY, 1906), 54–55, 207, represented an especially blatant attempt to revive Irish-Americans' memories of parting scenes and of their promises to return—the nonfulfillment of which engendered guilt among emigrants such as A. L. O'Brien and Mary McGuinness Elliott. F.D., 12 Aug. 1835 (Box 45, RJP/CUA); Hibernicus, *Address to Irish and Their Descendants in the United States . . .* (Columbia, S.C., 1848), 12.

Bibliography of Manuscript Sources

I. IN PUBLIC COLLECTIONS

Canada

PUBLIC ARCHIVES OF CANADA (Ottawa, Ontario)
Beattie, Martin. Diary (MG29 C59).
Coulter, James. Voyage journal (MG24 H11).
Farmer, Hugh Hovell. Letters (MG23 H11/7).
Graves, William. Voyage journal (MC24 H7).
Hayes family papers (MG24 D2, vols. 2, 9).
Horton, Sir Robert Wilmot. Misc. correspondence relating to assisted emigration from Ireland, 1823–25, including Peter Robinson correspondence (mf 7–2167).
Nowlan family letters (MC24 I122).
O'Donohoe, John. Papers (MG27 IE12).

PUBLIC RECORD OFFICE OF CANADA (Ottawa, Ontario)
Bell, William. Letters (mf; originals in the Lennox and Addington Historical Society, Napanee, Ontario).

METROPOLITAN TORONTO CENTRAL LIBRARY (Toronto, Ontario)
McConnell and Johnson family letters.
Willcocks, Joseph. Letters.

Great Britain

DR. WILLIAM'S LIBRARY (London)
Griffith, Mattie. Letter (27 July 1863) in Mary Estlin papers (Ms. 24.120–7).

LIBRARY OF THE SOCIETY OF FRIENDS (Friends' House, London)
Bennis, Ernest H. Letters and reminiscences of Irish Quakers, late 19th and early 20th centuries (Ms. Box 1/12 and Portfolio C, letter 104).
Grubb, J. E. Letters (Portfolio C, letters 111–15).
Hodgkins, H. Letters to, from the west of Ireland, on distress and emigration, 1880–86 (Tuke Relief and Emigration, Ms. vol. S254).
Webb, R. D. Narrative of a Tour Through Erris . . . in . . . 1848.

PUBLIC RECORD OFFICE (London)
Petitions for assisted emigration to—and/or land grants in—British North America, primarily from Ireland; addressed to the Colonial Office, London, 1817–50 (Colonial Office papers, CO 384/1–88).
Reports and papers of the British ambassador and the British consuls in the United States, 1916–22 (Foreign Office papers, FO 115/2073–2751).

Northern Ireland

PUBLIC RECORD OFFICE OF NORTHERN IRELAND (Belfast)
Adams family letters (MIC 26).
Agnew, Jane. Letter (D.2013).
Aitken, Alexander. Letter (D.627).
Allen, Henry. Letter (T.3084).
Anderson family letters (T.1664).
Anderson family letters (D.1859).
Anon. "Letter from a United Irishman" (T. 2655).
Anon. Letter (D.2967).
Anon. Journal (D.280).
Anon. Letter (T.439).
Anon. Letters (T.2338).
Anon. Letters (T.1873).
Anon. Letters (T.2722).
Anon. Voyage journal (T.2620).
Anon. Letter (T.1866).
Ard-Dornan family letters (T.1597).
Armstrong family letters (D.682).
Armstrong family letters (T.1835).
Bacon-Kerr family letters (T.1639).
Baily, David. Letter (T.2332).
Barr, John. Letter (T.2229).
Beck, James. Letter (T.1468).
Best family letters (D.1846).
Black, Paul. Letters (D.2587).
Black, James. Diary (D.1725).
Blakely, Thomas. Letter (T.3055).
Broadman, Elizabeth. Letter (T.2460).
Boyd-Weir family letters (T.1873).
Breathwait, Richard. Letter (T.1362).
Breeze family letters (T.1381).
Brennan family letters (T.2140).
Brobston, William. Letter (T.1269).
Brooks, Mathew. Letters (T.2700).
Brown family letters (T.2675).
Bruce, Samuel. Letters (T.2919).
Bryson family letters and journal (T.1373).
Buchanan family letters (D.1473).
Byron, Robert. Letter (T.2227).
Campbell family letters (D.1781).
Campbell, William and Mina. Letters (D.693).
Campbell-Allen papers (D.1558).
Carlisle, James. Letters (MIC.143).
Carson family letters (T.2077).
Carson, James and Margaret. Letter (D.1520).
Charley ?. Letter (T.2085).
Chesney, Captain Alexander. Diary (D.2260 and T.1095).
Clark, Thomas. Letters (D.3127).
Clarke-Gordon family letters (D.1096).
Cleland family letters (MIC. 33/1).
Colhoun family letters (T.1466).
Collins family letters (T.2889).
Coulter, Henry. Voyage journal (T.3032).
Crawford family letters (T.2338).
Cumming, Mary. Letters (T.1475).
Cunningham, John. Voyage journal (D.394).
Cunningham, John. Letter (MIC. 32).
Cupples family letters (T.1476).

Daly, Patrick M. Notebook (MIC.179).
Dalzell, James. Letter (T.2298).
Dalzell, William and Sons, Ltd. Passenger and Emigration Account Books (MIC.203).
Dawson, Robert Peel. Letters and journals (T.850).
Denison, John. Letter (T.2294).
Doak family letters (D.682).
Dobbs, Arthur. Papers (D.162).
Doherty family letters (T.2606).
Donegall Estate letterbook (T.1893).
Donnan family letters (D.2795).
Donnelly, Dr. James. Diary (DIO[RC]1/11A/2).
Donnelly, Dr. James. Diary (DIO[RC]1/1013).
Doody, William. Letters (D.1384).
Dornan, E. Letter (T.1597).
Duff, John. Letter (T.2252).
Duffin family letters (T.1252 and T.710).
Duggan, Mary. Letter (T.2946).
Dunlop, John. Letters (T.1336).
Early, James. Letter (T.2541).
Edwards family letters (D.2547).
Egan, G. W. Journal (T.3056).
Elder, John J. Diary (T.1264).
Emmet, Thomas Addis. Letters (T.1815 and D.1759).
Ferris, James. Letter (T.1458).
Fleming, Elizabeth. Letters (T.1850).
Fleming, James. Letters (MIC.162).
Fleming, Jane. Letter (D.1047).
Forman, Samuel. Letter (D.354).
Fullerton, Robert. Letter (D.1951).
Gamble, Alexander. Letter (D.682).
Gass family letters (T.1396).
Given family letters (D.1141).
Girls' Friendly Society, Lists of Emigrants (D.648).
Glover, James. Letter (T.1347).
Graham, Hugh A. Letter (T.2186).
Graham, Thomas. Letter (D.1497).
Greenlees family letters (T.2046).
Greer family letters (D.1044).
Gribbin, John. Letter (D.2700).
Grimshaw family letters (T.1116).
Hagan family letters (MIC.181/1).
Hall family letters (D.2041).
Hamilton, John. Letter (T.2201).
Hamilton, J. B. Diary (D.1518).
Hanlon [O'Hanlon] family letters (D.885).
Hanna family letters (T.2193).
Harshaw, N. K. Letters (T.1505).
Heather, William and James. Letters (D.592–93).
Heazelton, William. Letters (D.592).
Henry, John. Letters (T.1480).
Hill, William. Letters (T.1830).
Hilton, John. Letters (D.1226).
Hobson, C. Letter (T.1795).
Holmes, William. Letter (D.1782).
Horner, A. A. Letters (D.2003).
Horner, James. Letters (T.1592).
Houston family letters (T.2581).
Hunter family letters (D.1441).
Hutton, William. Letters (D.2298).
Irvine, Abraham. Letter (T.2135).
Jennings family letters (D.1930).

Johnson family letters (T.2319).
Johnston-Fleming family letters (D.1047).
Journal of a voyage on board the *Glasgow* (D.280).
Journal of the *Christiana* (T.2581).
Kaine, Edmond. Letter (T.2529).
Kane family letters (D.1791).
Kennedy family letters (T.3152).
Kerr family letters (MIC.144/1/3–23).
Kirkpatrick family letters (D.1424).
Knox, James. Letter (T.1483).
Lawless, ?. Letter (T.2345).
Lewis family letters (T.1776).
Lindsey, David. Letter (T.2539).
Locke, Mrs. James. Letter (D.2709).
Lough family letters (MIC.138).
Love family letters (T.2393).
Lowrie family letters (T.2018).
Lynn-Lawther-Houston family letters [extracts] (T.439).
McBride, John. Letters (T.2613).
McCann family letters (T.1456).
McCarter, William. Letter (D.2298).
McClellan, John. Letters (D.1005).
McClelland, James. Letter (D.1712).
McClorg family letters (T.1227).
McCloskey, Hugh. Letter (T.1767).
McCloy, David. Diary (T.2515).
McConnell family letters (T.3081).
McCormick, William. Letters (D.2082).
McCoy family letters (D.1444).
McDowell family letters (T.2305).
McElderry family letters (T.2414 and MIC.26).
McFarland family letters (D.1665).
McFarland, W. Letter (D.732).
McGregor, Margaret. Letters (D.1522).
McKay, John. Letter (D.2007).
McKelvey, Robert. Letter (D.893).
McKenny, Edward. Letter (T.2838).
McKeown, Annie. Letter (T.1777).
McLees, John and Catherine. Letters (D.904).
McNally, Edward. Letter (T.1448).
McNally, Mrs. P. Letter (D.2721).
McSparron, William. Letters (T.2743).
Martin, Andrew. Letter (T.1752).
Martin family letters (D.2722).
Mayne family letters (T.2284).
Mayne family letters (T.2932).
Miller, John. Letter (D.2630).
Milliken-Gillespie family letters (D.985).
Misc. letters (T. 2125).
Misc. letters collected by Prof. E. R. R. Green (T.2345).
Mitchell, John. Letters (D.249, D.1078, and T.4134).
Montgomery family letters (D.2794).
Moody family papers (T.2901).
Moore family letters and journal (D.3165).
Moore family letters (D.877).
Mulligan family letters (D.1757).
Murphy, Jane. Letters (D.1789).
Murray, James. Letter (D.1809).
Neill, Henry. Letter (T.1796).
Northern Ireland Ministry of Finance Report on Emigration (FIN.18/4/94).
Nolan, John. Letters (D.2782).

Nolan, M. Letter (T.2340).
Nolan, Mrs. Letter (T.2054).
Notes on emigration, 1736–7 (T.342).
Notes on emigration, 1748 (T.1791).
Notes on emigration, 1836–7 (T.342).
Orr family letters (D.2908 and T.1336).
Patterson, John. Letter (D.556).
Patton family letters (D.3127).
Paul, Moses. Letters (T.1568 and T.2850).
Pennington, Sue. Letter (D.2630).
Phillips, John B. Letters (T.1449).
Porter family letters (D.682 and D.1152).
Potts family letters (D.2488).
Printed letters on emigration (T.2511).
Quin, Hugh, Jr. Journal and letters (T.2874).
Quin-Park family letters (D.1819).
Redford family letters (T.3028).
Redmond family letters (D.1364).
Robb family letters (T.1454 and T.1639).
Robinson, David. Letter (D.2013).
Sample-McIntyre-Galbraith letters (T.2722).
Scott family letters (T.2609).
Shaw, Robert. Diary and letter (T.1913).
Shaw-Shanks-Martin family letters (D.2709).
Shepard, Matilda, Letter (D.2594).
Shipboy family letters (D.530).
Simms, Robert. Letters from exiled United Irishmen in America (D.1759/3B/6).
Sinclair family letters (D.1497).
Sloan, James. Letters (T.2304).
Smiley family letters (D.2723).
Smith family letters (D.1828).
Smyth family letters (T.2212).
Spotten, Bert. Letter (D.693).
State Papers of Ireland. Transcripts of reports on emigration, 1756 (T.1060).
State Papers of Ireland. Transcripts of reports on emigration, 1729 (T.659).
Stavely family letters (D.1835).
Stewart, Alexander T. Papers (T.2753).
Stewart, Ezekiel. Letter (D.2092).
Tallon, Robert. Letter (T.3067).
Taylor family letters (T.1435 and T.2296).
Thompson, John. Letters (T.1585).
Thompson family letters (D.2035).
Thompson, ?. Letters (D.898).
Thompson-Mullen letters (T.1866).
Toal, James and Mary. Letter (T.1543).
Topley family letters (T.2149).
Treanor, Ellen. Letter (D.2981).
Tyrrell, A. Letter (D.2068).
Ulster emigrant's passport, 1760s (T.2779).
Vogan, Thomas. Letters (D.268).
Wallace family letters (D.1195).
Weir family letters (D.1140 and D.1948/3).
Whaley, William. Letter (D.2630).
White, Jane. Letters (D.1195).
Whitelaw, Mrs. Letter (D.1270).
Wightman family letters (D.1725).
Wightman, Nancy. Letter (D.1771).
Wightman-Cumming family letters (T.1475).
Willes, Edward. Journals (T.2368 and MIC.148).
Williamson family letters (T.2680).
Wilson family letters (D.1921).

Wilson-Easton, A. Letters (T.1370).
Wray family letters (T.1727).
Wyly, Annie. Letter (T.2393).
Wylly-Habersham-Lawrence letters (D.955).
Young, William. Letter (T.1823).

Republic of Ireland

CLOGHER HISTORICAL SOCIETY (Monaghan, Co. Monaghan)
McCusker, James. Letter.
McDonald, Alice. Letter.

CLONALIS HOUSE (Castlerea, Co. Roscommon)
O'Conor Don papers (courtesy of Josephine O'Conor and Gareth and Janet Dunleavy).

CORK ARCHIVES COUNCIL (Cork, Co. Cork)
Buckley family letters.
Hurley family letters.
Huston-Eady-Anstis family letters.
Quinlan, Dan. Letter.
Quinlan, John. Letters.
Richard, R. D. Letters.

FRANCISCAN LIBRARY (Dunn Mhuire, Killiney, Co. Dublin)
Reville, Fr. Clement. Letters (courtesy of Fr. Bartholomew Egan, archivist).

KINSALE REGIONAL MUSEUM (Kinsale, Co. Cork)
Dorman family papers.
Murphy family letters.
Sheehan-Hayes letters (in M. Hayes papers).
Williams, R. F. Letter (in Orr family papers).

LAOIS COUNTY LIBRARY (Portlaoise, Co. Laois)
Burke, Rev. Edmund. Papers.

LONGFORD-WESTMEATH COUNTY LIBRARY (Mullingar, Co. Westmeath)
Burdan, P. Letter.

MEATH COUNTY LIBRARY (Navan, Co. Meath)
O'Reilly, John Boyle. Notes and poems.

MEATH DIOCESAN ARCHIVES (Mullingar, Co. Westmeath)
Mulvaney, John James. Autobiog. letter.
O'Brien, Thomas S. Letters.

NATIONAL LIBRARY OF IRELAND (Dublin)
All Hallows College, Overseas Missionary Correspondence (mf p.2782 and p.3849–51).
"An Account of Fenianism . . . , 1866" (Ms.5963).
Anon. Letter (Ms.15,647).
Bourke, F. S. Collection (Ms.9870).
Buchanan, Samuel. Letters (Box PC431).
Campbell, Neal, Bernard M'Kenna, and Edward Toner. Letters (Ms.2300).
Clancy [Mac Fhlannchaidhe], John M. Voyage diary (ms.21,666; also see Mss.1330–1 for
        other Mac Fhlannchaidhe documents brought to America, in Irish).
Clarke, Wad. Letters (Ms.8746).
Cleburne family letters (Ms. 15,588).
Coolattin emigration record, 1840s (Ms.4974).
Cremen, Cornelius J. Papers (Ms.17,805; incl. Mary Anne Murphy letter).
Crosby, George. Letter (Ms.3549).
Devoy, John. Diaries (Mss.9819–20).
Dimond family papers (Ms.18,236; incl. W. Austin letter).
Edwards, Thomas. Journal (Ms.16,136).
Gaelic American Defence Fund. Account book (in John Devoy papers, Ms.9828).
Gaelic League of the United States. Ledger (in John Devoy papers, Ms.3278).
Gallagher, Frank. Papers (Ms.18,335 and 18,342).
Gaynor, Mathew. Letters (Ms. 13,554).

Green, Alice Stopford. Rough-draft essay on Irish in America (Ms.10,445).
Grimshaw, C., Shipping Agent. Emigrants' letters to . . . (Ms.15,784).
Hamilton, W. E. Letters (Ms.10,360).
Henry, Patrick. Letters (Ms.21,570).
Hickey collection. Includes letters from Young Ireland exiles in Australia and the United States (Ms.3225–6).
Holt family letters (mf n.6322).
Humphreys, Robert. Letters (Ms.8907).
Irish National League. Papers (incl. letters of Rev. Charles O'Reilly; Ms. 8582/2).
Kearney, Frederick. Memoir of Thomas Francis Meagher (Ms. 9728).
Kelly, Thomas J. Letter (Ms.18,437).
Keogh family letters (Ms.3885).
Lalor family letters (Ms.8567).
Larcom, Sir Thomas A. Papers (incl. reports on Irish-American nationalism, Ms. 7517–25).
Locke family letters (uncataloged collection).
Luby, Thomas Clarke. Brief synopsis of early Fenian events in Ireland and America (Ms.331).
McCall, John. Papers (incl. John Hughes letter; Mss.13,849–13,852).
Mansfield, Owen. Letters (Mansfield papers, in storage).
Meagher, Thomas Francis. Letters (Ms.15,776).
Meagher, Thomas Francis. Poems (Ms.16,209).
Misc. emigrants' letters, collected by Prof. Arnold Schrier (Ms.8347).
Misc. emigrants' letters, collected by Prof. E. R. R. Green (Ms.11,428).
North-Pilkington family letters (Ms.10,093).
O'Brien, William Smith. Papers, including letters from Young Ireland exiles in Australia and the United States (Mss.426–62).
O'Donovan Rossa, Jeremiah. Papers (Ms.10,974).
O'Hara, Major Charles. Papers, including letters of Thomas Gunning, Joseph Hunter, and William Simpson (Mss.20,328–29 and 20,340).
O'Neill family papers (Mss. 18,327, 18,327C, and 20,970).
Osborne, Richard Boyce. Diary (Mss. 7888–95).
Papers relating to emigration, 1851 (mf p.1395).
Passenger lists of vessels arriving at New York City, 1820–60 (mf).
Pillson, Robert. Letters (Ms.10,360).
Reilly, Thomas. Letters (Ms.10,511).
Shea family letters (Ms.17,799).
Shields, James. Letters (mf n.5225).
Smith, Philip. Autobiography (mf p.3235).
Stephens, James. Diary of a trip to the United States (Ms.4146).
Studdert family papers (Mss.20,628–9).
Sudbury, Ketchtichia. Diary (mf p.1560).
Ua Cathail, Eoin. Autobiographical description of life in the United States, poems, essays, etc., in Irish (Ms.G510).
Wilson-Slator family letters (Ms.10,193).
Wolfe, Maurice. Letters (mf p.3887).

OFFALY COUNTY LIBRARY (Tullamore, Co. Offaly)
Kelly, Mrs. Alo. Papers.

PUBLIC RECORD OFFICE OF IRELAND (Dublin)
Kells family letters (Ms. M7075).
McDonnell, James Joseph. Letters (Ms.999/49).
Stanley, H. and W. Papers (Ms.1061).

RELIGIOUS SOCIETY OF FRIENDS LIBRARY (Dublin)
Birbeck, Morris. Letter.
Chandlee, Benjamin. Letter.
Jordan, Richard. Letters.
Pim, Frederick W. Letters (Pim Mss., bundle f).
Wright family letters.

ROYAL IRISH ACADEMY (Dublin)
Lee, C. Letter (in Charlemont papers).

O'Brien, William Smith. Misc. letters, papers, and clippings concerning his travels in
America.

SAINT PAUL OF THE CROSS RETREAT (Mount Argus, Dublin)
Devine, Fr. Pius, C.P. Journal of a Voyage to America, 1870; and Adventures and Misadventures of a Jolly Beggar, 1872–75 (courtesy of Fr. Declan O'Sullivan, C.P.,
archivist).

STATE PAPER OFFICE (Dublin)
Doyle, Subinspector Thomas. Spy reports from the United States, 1859–61 (in carton 62,
Fenian Movement, Records).
Papers relating to illegal recruitment of Irishmen for the American army, 1861–65 (Ms.
16,765).
Russell, Thomas. Papers (in Rebellion papers).
"United Irishman." Letter of 1 Aug. 1797 (in Rebellion papers).

TRINITY COLLEGE (Dublin)
Corbett, William. Letters.
Crampton, Sir John. Correspondence.
De Vere, Stephen. Diary and letterbook.
Dillon, John. Papers, including correspondence from Irish emigrants and Irish-American
nationalists.
Harvey, Jacob. Letters.
Madden, R. R. Papers, including letters from United Irish exiles and their relatives in the
United States.
O'Reilly, George Beresford. Letters.
Purdon-Fetherston family letters.
Russell, Thomas. Papers, including letters of Wolfe Tone from exile in the United States.

UNIVERSITY COLLEGE DUBLIN
ARCHIVES DEPARTMENT (courtesy of Prof. Robert Dudley Edwards)
        Greene family letters.
        McCullough family letters.
        McDonnell-Mahony-Slattery family letters.

DEPARTMENT OF IRISH FOLKLORE
        Brown, Mary. Letters (Ms.1408).
        Notebooks on emigration (Mss.1407–11).

WEXFORD COUNTY LIBRARY (Wexford, Co. Wexford)
Devereux family letters.
Doyle, T. Letter.

WILLIAM J. SWEENEY MEMORIAL LIBRARY (Kilkee, Co. Clare)
Ryan, Patrick. Diary (courtesy of Ms. Mary Teresa Hynes, librarian).
Scanlan family letters and photographs.

United States of America

California

BANCROFT LIBRARY, UNIVERSITY OF CALIFORNIA (Berkeley)
        Bray, Edmund. Letter.
        Crowley, Thomas. Recollections.
        Murphy family papers.
        Nunan, Matthew. Autobiography.
        Phelan, James D. Papers, including letters from Maggie Quinn and Michael Delany.
        Riordan, James. Letters.
        Scanlon family letters.
        Sinclair, Samuel Fleming. Life and Travels (memoirs, 1895).

CALIFORNIA HISTORICAL SOCIETY (San Francisco)
        Lawlor, Teresa. Letters.
        McBride, William. Letters (in Josephine R. Ober papers).
        McCardle, James. Letters.

O'Farrell, Jasper. Papers.
O'Neal, James. Letters and documents.

UNITED IRISH CULTURAL CENTER LIBRARY (San Francisco)
Kelly family letters.
Transcripts of interviews with Michael Carroll, John Riordan, and other Irish immigrants.

District of Columbia

CATHOLIC UNIVERSITY OF AMERICA
Hughes, Archbishop John, and the Diocese of New York. Correspondence relating to . . . (microfilm).
Irish College of Rome. American correspondence to . . . , 1832–49 (microfilm).
O'Donovan Rossa, Jeremiah. Papers (microfilm).
Purcell, Dr. Richard J. Papers on Irish-American history, including some transcribed copies of emigrants' letters.

LIBRARY OF CONGRESS
McDermott, Michael. Recollections (Ms. 2–15–1000).
Sampson, William. Letters (mf #13,611).

NATIONAL ARCHIVES
U.S. Consular Despatches from Cork (mf T–196), Dublin (mf T–199), Londonderry (mf T–216), Belfast (mf T–368), and Galway (mf T–570), 1790–1906.

Georgia

EMORY UNIVERSITY LIBRARY (Atlanta)
Wesleyan Collections (boxes 1–3 contain letters to and from Ireland, 1800–50).

GEORGIA STATE ARCHIVES, MANUSCRIPT SECTION (Atlanta)
Griffin family letters (in Lewis Neale Whittle papers).

Illinois

CHICAGO HISTORICAL SOCIETY (Chicago)
Casey, Peter. Letters.
Conlan, Frank [Peter Murphy]. Reminiscences (in letter form).
Mulligan, Col. James A. Papers.

ILLINOIS STATE HISTORICAL SOCIETY (Springfield)
Cronin, Dr. Patrick. Material concerning the murder of. . . .
King family letters.
McConnell family letters.
Mahon, Dr. James. Letters.

Indiana

INDIANA HISTORICAL SOCIETY (Indianapolis)
Dowling, John. Papers.
Dwyer, Anne Faussett. Letters.
Erskine, Andrew. Letters.
Gallagher, Hugh D. Letters.
Hewitt, Joseph. Letters.

INDIANA STATE LIBRARY, MANUSCRIPT DIVISION (Indianapolis)
Ballard, Mrs. Charles W. Personal papers.
Hamilton, Allen. Personal papers.

UNIVERSITY OF NOTRE DAME, ARCHIVES (South Bend)
All Hallows College, Overseas Missionary Correspondence (microfilm).
Brownson, Orestes. Papers (Mss. I-3-d and I-5-d).
Diocese of Cincinnati papers. Including letters of Fr. John Brummer (Ms. II-4-m),

Bishop John England (Ms. II-4-e), Fr. P. D. O'Regan (ms. II-4-k), and Fr. William Purcell (Mss. II-4-j and II-4-k).
Diocese of Hartford papers. Including letter of Joseph Lynch (Ms. I-1-b).
Diocese of New Orleans papers. Including letters of Henry Brenan (Ms. V-5-i), Daniel L. Brodie (Ms. V-5-g), Mary Teresa Collis (Ms. V-5-h), Julian Guillou (Ms. VI-1-e), Martin Hart (Ms. V-5-i), Ann McRorty (Ms. VI-1-c), Thomas Maher (Ms. VI-1-c), and Lawrence O'Sullivan (Ms. V-5-g).

Kansas

UNIVERSITY OF KANSAS, KENNETH SPENCER RESEARCH LIBRARY (Lawrence)
    Costello, Augustine E. Letter (in O'Hegarty papers).

Kentucky

KENTUCKY HISTORICAL SOCIETY (Frankfort)
    Masterson family letters.

Maryland

MARYLAND HISTORICAL SOCIETY (Baltimore)
    Crawford, John. Letters (Ms.1246).
    McHenry family papers (Ms.647).
    Mayer family papers (Ms. 1574).
    Warden, David Bailey. Papers (Ms.871).
    Williams, O. H. Papers (Ms.908).

Michigan

UNIVERSITY OF MICHIGAN (Ann Arbor)
    Immigration Sources Project, Bentley Historical Library (courtesy of Profs. Francis X. Blouin and Jo-Ellen Vinyard)
    Flynn, Bernard. Letters.
    Hewitt, Ellen E. and Catherine Edgar. Letters.
    Landy, Mary Ann. Letters.
    Mackey, Molly [Sr. Agnes Frances]. Letters.
    Michigan Historical Collections
    Lyster, Rev. William N. Letters.
    McMahon, Joseph. Papers.

Minnesota

MINNESOTA HISTORICAL SOCIETY (St. Paul)
    Anderson, Mary Jane Hill. Autobiography.
    Callahan, Michael, and family. Papers.
    Christie family letters.
    McBeath, James, and family. Papers.
    Unthank, G., Jr. Letter.

Missouri

MISSOURI HISTORICAL SOCIETY (St. Louis)
    Doyle, Anthony. Letter.

MISSOURI STATE ARCHIVES (Jefferson City)
    Pardon and petition papers, on behalf of Michael Whelan, Peter Devlin, James McGuire, et al. (courtesy of Frank Whelan, assistant archivist).

New York

ALBANY INSTITUTE OF ART AND HISTORY (Albany)
    McElroy, William. Reminiscences.

COLUMBIA UNIVERSITY, BUTLER LIBRARY (New York)
Mitchel, John. Letters (in Maloney-Mitchel collection).

CORNELL UNIVERSITY LIBRARY (Ithaca)
Humphreys, Robert. Letters.
Kernan family papers.
McGraw family papers.
McNish family papers.
Stevenson family papers.

LONG ISLAND HISTORICAL SOCIETY (Brooklyn)
Kiernan, James. Letter.

NEW-YORK HISTORICAL SOCIETY (New York)
Burke, John. Reminiscences.
Chambers, John and Jane. Letter.
Donovan, Minerva Padden. Letters (in Beekman family papers).
Harvey, Jacob. Letter (in Luther Bradish papers).
Marshall, Charles H., Jr. Papers.
Matteson family papers.
Mitchell, James J. Journal.
Nagle, David M. Letters (in Luther Bradish papers).
Sypher, J. R. Letter (in J. Hale Sypher papers).
Wildes, Mary. Letter (in Beekman papers).

NEW YORK PUBLIC LIBRARY (New York)
Cúndún, Padraig. Songs, poems, etc., in Irish.
Fleming, Sampson. Letterbook.
Meagher, Thomas Francis. Letters.
Mitchel, Jane Vernor [Mrs. John]. Letters.

North Carolina

DUKE UNIVERSITY LIBRARY, MANUSCRIPT DIVISION (Durham)
Aglionby, Francis Yates. Papers.
Harty, William. Circular letter on Irish fever epidemic, 1818 (in the Sir John Newport papers).
Lawless, Valentine Browne, 2d Baron Cloncurry. Letter (in the Henry William Paget papers).
McCullough-Hutchinson family papers.
McMullen family papers.
Malet family papers.
Moore family papers.
Potts family papers.
Ramage, W. Report on the state of Ireland (in the Robert Saunders Dundas papers).
Staunton, Sir George L. and George T. Papers.
Wright, I. J. Letter (in the N. N. Renwick papers).

NORTH CAROLINA DEPARTMENT OF ARCHIVES AND HISTORY (Raleigh)
Dickson, William. Letters.
Dobbs, Arthur. Papers.
Donaldson, Robert. Letters.

UNIVERSITY OF NORTH CAROLINA (Chapel Hill)
Southern Historical Collection
Griffin family letters (in the Lewis Neale Whittle papers).
McGavock, Hugh. Papers.
Sproule family letters (in Andrew J. Sproule papers).
Steele, Ephraim. Papers.
Wilson Library
Burke, Thomas. Papers (mf 1-653).

Ohio

CINCINNATI HISTORICAL SOCIETY (Cincinnati)
    Kemper family letters.

OHIO HISTORICAL SOCIETY (Columbus)
    Harker, Mary. Letter.
    Martin, Sarah and Edward. Letter.

Pennsylvania

BALCH INSTITUTE (Philadelphia)
    Costello family letters.
    Curtis-Lynch-Dunne letters.
    Doyle, Michael. Reminiscences.
    Polin, Daniel. Letter.

HAVERFORD COLLEGE LIBRARY (Haverford)
    Burke, Aedanus. Letter (in the Members of Congress papers).
    Chandlee, Benjamin. Letter.
    Shackleton family letters (Ms. 859).
    Sheppard family letters (Ms.858).

UNIVERSITY OF PENNSYLVANIA LIBRARY, RARE BOOK DIVISION (Philadelphia)
    Carey, Mathew. Diary (photocopy).

UNIVERSITY OF PITTSBURGH, ARCHIVES OF INDUSTRIAL SOCIETY (Pittsburgh)
    Donohoe family letters.

WYOMING HISTORICAL AND GENEALOGICAL SOCIETY (Wilkes-Barre)
    Byrne, P. Letter (in Hendrick B. Wright papers).

South Carolina

UNIVERSITY OF SOUTH CAROLINA, SOUTH CAROLINIANA LIBRARY (Columbia)
    "Address to the Irishmen of Charleston," 1861.
    Bannon, Rev. John. Letters.
    Fullerton, Robert. Letter.
    Hill, William. Letters.
    Humphrey, William. Letter.
    McCormick, John and Ann. Letter.
    McDonald, Edgar E., ed. "The American Edgeworths: a Biographical Sketch of
        Richard Edgeworth, with Letters and Documents. . . ."
    McDowell, Davison. Letters.

Tennessee

TENNESSEE STATE LIBRARY AND ARCHIVES (Nashville)

    Bell family papers (mf).
    Orr family diaries (mf).

Virginia

UNIVERSITY OF VIRGINIA, ALDERMAN LIBRARY (Charlottesville)
    Sinton, William. Letters.

VIRGINIA HISTORICAL SOCIETY (Richmond)
    Joyce, John. Letter (in Dickson family letters).

Washington

WASHINGTON STATE HISTORICAL SOCIETY (Tacoma)
    Dalzell, Thomas. Letters (in Thomas N. Chambers letters).

West Virginia

WEST VIRGINIA UNIVERSITY LIBRARY (Morgantown)
  Harold, James. Letters.
  Neeson, Daniel. Letters.

Wisconsin

STATE HISTORICAL SOCIETY OF WISCONSIN (Madison)
  Griffith, S. Letter.
  Rankin, Francis. Letter.
  Solon, John. Reminiscences.

II. MANUSCRIPTS PRIVATELY HELD

(The manuscripts listed below were lent or shown to the author between 1972 and 1983. Most have since been photocopied and the copies deposited in the National Library of Ireland and the Public Record Office of Northern Ireland.)

Canada

Cunningham, Peter. Letter (Conlin S. Mulvihill, Arnprior, Ontario).
Mulholland, Henry. Letter (Eleanor Reesor, Markham, Ontario).
Skerry, John. Letter and related information (Dr. Terrence Punch, Halifax, Nova Scotia).

Great Britain

Bredin family letters and emigration ballads (James Bredin, Erdington, Birmingham).

Northern Ireland

A ?, Mary. Letter (Patrick Kelly, Draperstown, Co. Derry).
Alexander, Sarah. Information pertaining to . . . (Miss J. McAlister, Warrenpoint, Co. Down).
Anderson, family letters and memoirs (General Sir John Anderson, Ballyhossett, Downpatrick, Co. Down).
Bell, William. Voyage letters (Miss A. Hodgson, Derriaghy, Dunmurry, Co. Antrim).
Burns, Mary A. Letter (Alexander McCloy, Armoy, Ballymoney, Co. Antrim).
Caldwell, Robert. Letter (Mr. A. S. Caldwell, Tullynure, Donaghmore, Co. Tyrone).
Cameron, Adam Scott. Letters (Jean C. Young, Kircubbin, Newtownards, Co. Down).
Campbell, Patrick F. Journal (Paul Maguire, Cahore, Ederney, Co. Fermanagh).
Carswell, Joseph. Letters (James F. Alexander, Belfast).
Cooper, J. F. Autobiographical letters (James Gracey, Downpatrick, Co. Down).
Craig family diary and other information (Elizabeth Craig, Ballybeen, Dundonald, Belfast).
Devlin family letters (Mrs. Anna Clifford, Talteevagh, Lisnaskea, Co. Fermanagh).
Fleming, Fred. Letters and other information (Mrs. May Barclay, Durnascallon, Desertmartin, Co. Derry).
Gamble family letters (John Magaughey, Newtownards, Co. Down).
Gracey, William. Letter (Miss Maire Gribbon, Belfast).
Gracey-Maloney-Russell family letters (Maire Gribbon, Belfast, and James Gracey, Downpatrick, Co. Down).
Harvey, Samuel, and B. Craigy. Voyage journal (Mrs. Maureen McVea, Newtownards, Co. Down).
Heazelton-Heather-O'Brien letters (Lt. Col. J. R. A. Greeves, Belfast).
Hutcheson, Henry. Letter (Mrs. Alison Hutcheson, Mountnorris, Armagh, Co. Armagh).
John ?. Letter (Paul Maguire, Cahore, Ederney, Co. Fermanagh).
Kane, Patrick. Letter (Mr. T. F. McCarthy-Maguire, Belfast).
King, William. Letter (Miss L. Little, Magheraneely, Enniskillen, Co. Fermanagh).
Knilans, William. Diaries (Hubert C. Knilans, Omagh, Co. Tyrone).

Lawlor, Michael. Letter (Kathleen McAvinchey, Woodford, Armagh, Co. Armagh).
McCullough family letters (Mrs. Margaret MacArthur, Londonderry city).
McCurdy family information (Lyle McCurdy, Finaghy, Belfast).
McKenna-Bradley letters (Mrs. L. Bradley, Maghera, Co. Derry).
McKinley, Mary E. Letters (George Adamson, Banbridge, Co. Down).
Misc. emigrants' letters (a collection of 100 or more, made by the late Prof. E. R. R. Green, Queen's Univ., Belfast).
Montgomery, Samuel Stuart. Letter (Mrs. U. M. Lavery, Dromore, Co. Down).
Moon, John. Letters (Mrs. Fionnuala Williams, Belfast).
Mullen, Muriel A. Letter to author describing visit to America and Irish-American relatives (Portadown, Co. Armagh).
Nicholl, Samuel. Letter and family history (Mrs. Evelyn C. Crawford, Newtonabbey, Co. Down).
Quinn, James. Letters (Mrs. M. Cregan, Belfast).
Reese-Seawright family letters (W. James Quail, Banbridge, Co. Down).
Richey family letters (Prof. E. R. R. Green, Queen's Univ., Belfast).
Roycroft, Anne. Letters (Anne Roycroft, Bangor, Co. Down).
Whinnery, Attie. Letter (Isaac E. Bell, Holywood, Co. Down).
Wills, Capt. Patrick J. Autobiographical letter (Miss Mona Wills, Larne, Co. Antrim).

Republic of Ireland

Author unknown. Letter (William Connell, Ballydevlin, Goleen, Co. Cork).
Brick, Tom. Memoirs (Doncha Ó Conchúir, Ballyferriter, Co. Kerry).
Brien, Peter. Letter and life history (William McAuliffe, University College, Cork).
Brogan, Fr. James. Letter (Patricia Dillon, Scariff, Co. Clare).
Brosnan family letters (Mrs. Mary Gourley, Kilflyn, Tralee, Co. Kerry).
Burke, Sr. Mary R. Letter (John Heffernan, Clonmel, Co. Tipperary).
Burke-O'Boyce family letters (Bridget O'Callaghan, Kindrum, Letterkenny, Co. Donegal).
Burns family letters (Michael F. Cahill, Ballinamona, Ring, Co. Waterford).
Butler family letters (Martin J. Kelly, Celbridge, Co. Kildare).
Byrnes, S. M. Letter (Mary Nolan, Crumlin, Dublin).
Callaghan, John. Letter (Miss B. Dowd, Murrigrane, Brandon, Co. Kerry).
Carrigan, Andrew N. Letter (Kevin Fennessey, Lisronagh, Clonmel, Co. Tipperary).
Carroll-McMahon letters (Mrs. Kathleen McMahon, Martinstown, Co. Lough).
Cashman, Timothy and Daniel. Memoirs, letters, essays, and poems (Patrick Clancy, Youghal, Co. Cork; and Timothy D. Cashman, San Francisco, Calif.).
Comyn, Thomas, et al. Letters (Most Rev. Michael A. Harty, Bishop of Killaloe, Ennis, Co. Clare; and Rev. Ignatius Murphy, Carrigoran, Newmarket-on-Fergus, Co. Clare).
Connolly, Peter, and John J. Dwyer. Letters (Lassarine Morris, Raheny, Dublin).
Creedon family letters (Humphrey Twomey, Mayfield, Cork).
Dalton family letters (Mrs. A. Cheasty, Dunkitt, Kilmacow, Co. Kilkenny).
Dever and Nugent family letters (Mrs. Alice Timoney, Clontarf, Dublin).
Dowd, Fr. Patrick. Letter (Sr. Anne Matthews, St. Patrick's College, Maynooth, Co. Kildare).
Dowling, Peter J. Letter (Mrs. Catherine Cullen, Blanchardstown, Co. Dublin).
Downes, William H. Letters (William O'Shaughnessy, Pallaskenry, Co. Limerick).
Fields, Julia, and Anne Flood. Letters (Pádraig Ó Droighneain, Raistín, Navan, Co. Meath).
Fitzgerald, J. Letters (Alan Kennedy, Castletroy, Co. Limerick).
Fitzgerald, James D. Letters (Ann Delea, Douglas, Co. Cork).
Flanagan family letters (Peter and Mary Flanagan, Tubbertoby, Clogherhead, Co. Louth).
Flynn, Bernard. Letters (Dermot Sweeney, Loughrea, Co. Galway; courtesy of Prof. JoEllen Vinyard and Francix X. Blouin, Immigration Sources Project, Univ. of Michigan).
Gleeson, Sr. Rose. Letters (Sr. Oliver Gleeson, Dominican Convent, Wicklow, Co. Wicklow).
Grimes family letters (Christopher Fox, Old Skerries Society, Skerries, Co. Dublin).
Handy, Joe. Letter (Patrick O'Reilly, Ballycumber, Co. Offaly).
Harte-Connolly family letters (Nuala Simon, Knockvicar, Boyle, Co. Roscommon).
Healy family letters (Christopher Healy, Kilkenny, Co. Kilkenny).
Hewitt-Edgar family letters (Mary E. Edgar, Aghadoey, Ballintra, Co. Donegal; courtesy of Vinyard and Blouin).

Higgins, Thomas. Letter (Mr. J. S. Higgins, Longford, Co. Longford).
Kearsey, John. Letters (John Kiersey, Ballyhussa, Kilmacthomas, Co. Waterford).
Kelleher, John. Letters and memorabilia (George D. Kelleher, Inniscarra, Co. Cork).
Kelly family letters (Martin J. Kelly, Celbridge, Co. Kildare).
Kerns, John. Letter (Rev. Gerard Kennedy, Mellifont Abbey, Collon, Co. Louth).
Kiely, Richard. Letter (Mrs. Philomena Coffey, Carrick-on-Suir, Co. Tipperary).
Kilcran, Michael. Journal (John and James Joseph Kilcran, Corlaskagh, Kilnagross, Carrick-on-Shannon, Co. Leitrim).
La Fuente, Augustine. Letter (William T. Matthews, Killiney, Co. Dublin).
Landy, Mary Ann. Letters (Mrs. Eileen McKenna, Balbriggan, Co. Dublin; courtesy of Vinyard and Blouin).
Langan family letters (Gerald Perry, Rathfeigh, Tara, Co. Meath).
Lough family letters (Mrs. Eilish O'Mahony, Dundalk, Co. Louth).
Luttrell, William. Letter (Miss C. Greenham, Dublin).
McArthur family letters (Mrs. C. W. P. MacArthur, Port-na-Blagh, Co. Donegal).
McCue, John. Poem on voyage (Mrs. M. Bayers, High Glen, Glen, Co. Donegal).
Mackey, Molly [Sr. Agnes Frances]. Letters (Elizabeth O'Toole, Bray, Co. Wicklow; courtesy of Vinyard and Blouin).
Misc. letters and postcards from America (Mrs. M. Bayers, High Glen, Glen, Co. Donegal).
[Moran], Sr. Mary Alicia. Letters (Ann Moran, Clare Island, Co. Mayo).
Murphy, Daniel and Michael. Letters (Sheila A. Murphy, Cork).
Murphy, Julia A. Letter (Peter Levy, Tralee, Co. Kerry).
Neilan, Thomas. Letter (N. W. English, Old Athlone Society, Athlone, Co. Westmeath).
Nolan, ? . Letter (Mary Nolan, Crumlin, Dublin).
O'Callaghan family letters (Eugene O'Callaghan and Mary Flynn, Fallagh, Kilmacthomas, Co. Waterford).
[O'Connor?], Jerry. Letter (Doncha Ó Conchúir, Ballyferriter, Co. Kerry).
O'Daly, Hugh. Life History (Rev. Patrick Daly, St. Macartan's College, Monaghan, Co. Monaghan).
O'Gorman, Frederick J. Letter (Mrs. Kathleen O'Dwyer, Iyone, Nenagh, Co. Tipperary).
O'Sullivan, Michael L. Letter (Br. W. P. Allen, Dublin).
Parker, Patrick. Letters (Michael Parker, Enniscorthy, Co. Wexford).
Rowe, Mary Ann. Letter (Mrs. B. Galway, Barrowsland, Thomastown, Co. Kilkenny).
Ryan, Rev. P. J. Letter (Mrs. Katherine Crowe, Ballyvoneen, Thurles, Co. Tipperary, and Sgt. Robert Maher, Holycross, Co. Tipperary).
Sisters of Mercy in the United States. Information about . . . (Sr. M. Veronica, Convent of Mercy, Ballindeasig, Belgooly, Co. Cork).
Slattery, T. Patrick. Letter (Nell Martin, Donnybrook, Dublin).
Smith, Fr. Gregory. Letter (Mrs. M. Coby, Clondalkin, Co. Dublin).
Teresa, Sr. Mary. Letter (Mrs. Elizabeth Enright, Ballybunion, Co. Kerry).
"Tipperaryman, A Distinguished." Newspaper biography (clipping from Kathleen Hughes, Stillorgan, Co. Dublin).
? , Tom. Letter in verse (Paul McArdle, Louth Village, Co. Louth).
Twomey, D. Ryan. Letters (Catherine M. Twomey, Midleton, Co. Cork).
Tunney, Bridget. Letter (Elizabeth Binchy, Charleville, Co. Cork).
Waldron, Thomas. Letters (Patrick Waldron, Rathmines, Dublin).
Williams, Rose. Letters (Rose Olive McDonnell, Dublin).

United States

Acheson family letters (Russell Schrode, Charleston, W.Va.; courtesy of Prof. William Rorabaugh, Univ. of Washington, Seattle).
Arbuthnot family letters (Mrs. Earle G. Ridall, Elmira, N.Y.)
Armstrong-de Butts family letters (Mrs. Scott Lytle, Seattle; courtesy of Rorabaugh).
Brady, Michael. Papers (William Brady, Beverly Hills, Calif.).
Burns family letters (Prof. James F. Burns, Univ. of Florida, Gainesville).
Cashman, Timothy. Journal (Timothy D. Cashman, Los Angeles).
Connolly, James J. Diary (Mrs. Lenora Dolan, Bronx, N.Y.).
Farrell, Charles. U.S. citizenship petition (William Henhoeffer, Arlington, Va.).
Fouhey, David. Poems (John M. Tivnan, Woodbridge, Va.).
Fulton, Hugh. Letter (Mrs. Frederick A. Keyes, Edina, Minn.).

Garland, John. Material written by or to . . . , concerning Protestant Ulster-American public relations efforts in U.S.A. (John Garland, Rochester, N.Y.)

Horan family letters (Robert J. Horan, North Hollywood, Calif.).

Kelly family letters (Mrs. Patricia Shaw, San Francisco).

Keppel, Rev. John H. Letters (Roxanne Mankin, Berkeley, Calif.).

Lawless family letters (Charles A. O'Neill, Milwaukee, Wis.).

McBride, Arthur and Ellen. Letter (Martha Parker, San Carlos, Calif.).

McIlwaine family materials (Richard McIlwaine Dunn, Jr., Richmond, Va.).

McGuinness family letters, memoir, and memorabilia (Alice L. McGuinness, Hampton Bays, N.Y.).

McManus, Terrence Bellew. Diary (Ann Chamberlain, San Francisco).

Mangan, Owen Peter. Memoir (Gerald A. Fitzgerald, New York City).

Misc. emigrants' letters (over 200 Irish emigrants' letters, 1780s–1910s, collected by and in possession of Prof. Arnold Schrier, Univ. of Cincinnati, Ohio).

O'Mahoney, Henry. Autobiographical reminiscences (Bridget Lynch, Berkeley, Calif.).

O'Neill, O'Brien, Gleeson, Keogh, Tormey, Cooke, O'Conor, and Molony family letters (Vincent O'Brien, Berkeley, Calif.).

Seaghan ar Fan. Letter (Kenneth Nilsen, Cambridge, Mass.)

Shanley, Bohan, Dooner, and Bradley families. Misc. information (James W. Dooner, Brooklyn, N.Y.).

"Story of Melrose [New Brunswick]." Pamphlet describing early Irish settlement in Maritime provinces (John J. Morrissey, Palo Alto, Calif.).

Tyrrell family letters (Joseph A. King, Lafayette, Calif.).

Wilkinson family letters (Mrs. Gladys Wilkinson, Los Angeles).

Index

665

DESERT : HI

P9-AG

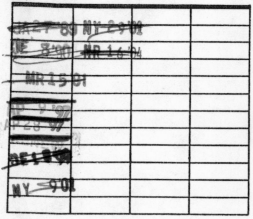
RIVERSIDE CITY COLLEGE

LIBRARY

Riverside, California

 NOV 1980

Dante, Poet of
the Desert

DANTE, POET OF THE DESERT

History and Allegory
in the *Divine Comedy*

Giuseppe Mazzotta

Princeton University Press
Princeton, N.J.

Published by Princeton University Press, Princeton, New Jersey
In the United Kingdom: Princeton University Press,
Guildford, Surrey

ALL RIGHTS RESERVED

Library of Congress Cataloging in Publication Data will be
found on the last printed page of this book

Publication of this book has been aided by a grant from
The Andrew W. Mellon Foundation.

This book has been composed in VIP Bembo

Clothbound editions of Princeton University Press books
are printed on acid-free paper, and binding materials are
chosen for strength and durability.

Printed in the United States of America by Princeton
University Press, Princeton, New Jersey

A mia madre
e in memoria
di mio padre

TABLE OF CONTENTS

PREFACE

It is well known that the quantity of scholarly publications on the *Divine Comedy* has reached such staggering proportions that Dante criticism, as practiced through the centuries, has itself become by necessity the object of a legitimate historical investigation. This brief prefatory note is certainly not, however, the place even to begin to assess the achievements of contemporary Dante scholarship. I shall only indicate the general critical context within which the present work has come into being.

There is no doubt that in recent times Dante scholarship, at its best, has shown a high degree of critical awareness and a truly compelling skill for unearthing factual sources and historical material. It is perhaps inevitable that philological research should produce results of more genuine value. The *Divine Comedy* contains such doctrinal complexities, its vocabulary, which resonates with prodigious pulsations, is so precise and highly specialized that scholars have realized the need to first identify Dante's wide array of extratextual traditions before engaging in interpretation. The work of scholars such as Contini, Pagliaro, Nardi, Petrocchi, W.H.V. Reade, Gilson, Kantorowicz, Auerbach, Singleton, Freccero, Sarolli and others, whatever the exegetic value of each contribution, is central to any critical investigation, for, taken cumulatively, it has attempted to map out the articulations of Dante's culture.

The disagreements among scholars have stemmed partly from the difficulty in establishing which tradition plays a canonical role in the *Divine Comedy*, partly, of course, from the natural bias of each perspective, partly from the rigidity of some critical procedures. There is still a strong interpretive tendency, possibly humanistic in origin, to translate literature into politics, to believe in the importance of the "literal" sense of the *Divine Comedy*, which is construed to be the concrete experience of the poet in his time and place. From the point of view of these "literalists," the method of allegorization, when it is not skillfully practiced, is reductive, for it imposes over-simplified schemes and generalized structures of meaning which impoverish the density of the text.

There may be some temerity in my suggesting that I have tried to explore both the distance and the alliance between "history" and "allegory"—the space of tradition—and, indi-rectly, between these two critical perspectives. Each chapter, whether it tests the possibilities of the "lectura dantis" or the importance of typological patterns, addresses itself to differ-ent strands of Dante's text: theology, political thought, bibli-cal exegesis, apocalyptic imagination, rhetoric, classical tradi-tions and what might be called the native strain of Dante's poetic language—all are shown to be vital parts of the *Divine Comedy*. They are tools by which Dante constructs his vision of the exile and the kingdom.

Finally two unrelated points have to be raised. The first is that I use the Letter to Cangrande as if it were Dante's. The second point concerns the use of quotations in the book. I have left the quotations in the original in the body of the text whenever I felt that the original might shed directly more light on the discussion than its translation would.

ACKNOWLEDGMENTS

I HAVE tried to acknowledge at every single point of this book my indebtedness to the previous scholarship on Dante. It is no easy task for me, however, to acknowledge the less palpable, but certainly no less real, debts I have contracted with my friends and associates over a long span of time. My foremost obligation is to my teacher and friend, John Freccero, who many years ago directed my doctoral dissertation at Cornell, "Dante's Theology of History." I welcome the opportunity to say that this book, which perhaps departs in some ways from the aims of the thesis, has grown out of steady meditation on Professor Freccero's work and teaching and is a tribute to their generosity. I am also most grateful to another teacher and friend, R. E. Kaske, who has unfailingly made available to me his vast knowledge and library and has given a most valuable reading of the manuscript. My other friends and colleagues in the Medieval Program at Cornell, James Cross, Thomas Hill, Winthrop Wetherbee, and especially Dan Ransom, have all helped and encouraged me in the writing of this book. It is with pleasure that I record my gratitude to them as well as to all the other friends who have stimulated me with their conversation and advice, among whom are James Hutton, Eugenio Donato, Roberto González Echevarría, Josué Harari and Piero Pucci.

Helen Calhoun has typed the manuscript.

Chapter 2 has appeared in a slightly different form as "Poetics of History: *Inferno* XXVI," in *Diacritics*, 5 (1975), pp. 37-44. Chapter 5, now greatly revised, appeared as "Dante's Literary Typology," in *Modern Language Notes*, 87 (1972), pp. 1-19. I want to express my thanks to these journals for granting permission to reprint.

I have greatly benefited from an ACLS grant-in-aid in the summer of 1975 which has enabled me to put the finishing touches to my research.

June 1978

NOTES ON DANTE'S TEXTS

Unless otherwise stated, all quotations from Dante's texts
are drawn from the following critical editions:

La Divina Commedia secondo l'antica vulgata, ed. Giorgio Petrocchi, 4 vols., Società Dantesca Italiana (Milan: Mondadori,
1966-67).

Convivio, ed. G. Busnelli e G. Vandelli, 2nd ed., ed. A. E.
Quaglio, 2 vols. (Florence: Le Monnier, 1964).

De Vulgari Eloquentia, ed. Aristide Marigo (Florence: Le
Monnier, 1968).

Monarchia, ed. Pier Giorgio Ricci (Milan: A. Mondadori,
1965).

The English renderings from the *Divine Comedy* are mine, but
I have depended heavily on these translations:

Dante Alighieri, *The Divine Comedy*, translated, with a commentary by Charles S. Singleton, Bollingen Series LXXX
(Princeton: Princeton University Press, 1970-76).

The Divine Comedy of Dante Alighieri, trans., John D. Sinclair
(New York: Oxford University Press, 1961).

ABBREVIATIONS

Biagi, ed., La Divina Commedia *nella figurazione artistica e nel secolare commento*, ed. Guido Biagi, 3 vols. (Inferno, Purgatorio, Paradiso) (Turin: Unione Tipografico-Editrice Torinese, 1924-29).

CCSL *Corpus Christianorum, Series Latina*

CSEL *Corpus Scriptorum Ecclesiasticorum Latinorum*

Etym. Isidore of Seville, *Etymologiarum sive Originum Libri XX*, ed. W. M. Lindsay (Oxford: Clarendon Press, 1966).

PG *Patrologiae Cursus Completus: Series Graeca*, ed. J. P. Migne (Paris: 1857-94).

PL *Patrologiae Cursus Completus: Series Latina*, ed. J. P. Migne (Paris: 1844-64), with later printings.

PMLA *Publications of the Modern Language Association of America*.

Summa Theologiae Thomas Aquinas, *Opera Omnia*, ed. S. E. Fretté and P. Maré, vols. i-v (Paris: L. Vivès, 1874-89).

Citations from other texts by Aquinas are drawn from this same series.

Dante, Poet of
the Desert

INTRODUCTION

THE general aim of this book is to probe Dante's sense of history in the *Divine Comedy* and to show that history is the question that lies at the very heart of the text. By examining some myths and metaphors of history (utopia, progress, millennium, tradition, memory, time, work, etc.), which are recurrently evoked in the movement of the poem, this study focuses essentially on three interrelated issues: (1) it plots the structure and language of history; (2) it explores the relationship between history and literary language; (3) it confronts the question of allegory and investigates the ambiguities or what might be called the historicity of interpretation.

It should be clear at the outset that one cannot expect this critical reading of the *Divine Comedy* to yield a systematic philosophy of history or the historical consciousness that classical historiographers are said to possess. For Thucydides and Livy, for instance, and even Dino Compagni and Villani, whether they write narratives of *res gestae*, annals or chronicles, *historia* is a special discipline and a form of inquiry, as the Greek etymology of the term suggests. They are the *logographoi*, record makers who are engaged in the investigation of particular events befalling the *polis*, and who seek the intellectual principles and causes for those events.

These inquiries, to be sure, are not always objective accounts resulting from a meticulous observance of the conventional laws of evidence. Livy himself frankly abandons the standards of impartiality in his avowed purpose to celebrate the apotheosis of Augustan Rome. But from Dante's perspective, Livy's own moral values, factual distortions and commitment to the ideology of Roman power are not to be construed as flaws that could account for Dante's own distance from the practices of classical historiography. Dante's own sense of history encompasses, after all, literary texts that we tend to classify as fictions, such as the *Aeneid* and the *Thebaid*. It is not surprising, then, that Livy, for all the personal prejudices that are contained in his *Histories*, should remain for Dante an infallible authority (*Inferno* xxviii, l. 12), and be referred to as "gestorum Romanorum scriba egregius" (*Monarchia* ii, iii).

In spite of the frequent and favorable acknowledgments of the works of *historiographi* such as Livy and, to some extent, of the political opinions of Cicero, Dante steers clear of the tacit assumptions that underlie their conception of history. It is well known that a contrast is generally posited between classical and biblical historiographies. Whereas the classical or "Hellenic" historiography produces abstract, formal inventories of events, whose only aim is to discover the principle that would make them intelligible, the Bible and Christianity feature a genuine sense of history—a history, that is, which cannot be surveyed simply with the intellectual detachment of an observer.

Though the Bible, with the possibly sole exception of Acts, does not even contain the word *historia*, it nonetheless discloses, more than any other text of historical scholarship, the historicity of human life. It dramatizes the precarious and temporal nature of existence and shows man dwelling in the concrete world of experience; it presents the view that the natural order is decisively shattered by the entrance of God in history, and that history is significant because it is the horizon within which God's mighty acts and purposes are unfolded. It is in history that the creation of man, the fall from the Garden, the Incarnation and Apocalypse take place.

If this contrast is more than simply a convenient fiction, Dante's sense of history is grounded in the biblical experience. The crucial and explicit structure which sustains the *Divine Comedy* is, as Singleton has shown, the story of Exodus, the account of the Jews who leave the house of bondage in Egypt, journey through the desert, and finally reach the promised land. This structure is the paradigm of the theological interpretation of history in that it typologically prefigures both the Incarnation, the hinge of salvation history, and the event of the New Jerusalem at the end of time. These are the two nodal centers that give the contingent and precarious elements of historical reality an irreducible sense and finality. The presence of this finality, it might be added, the conviction that there is nothing fortuitous and aimless in historical experience, annihilates the possibility of writing a philosophy of history. A philosophy of history always reduces history to a myth because, not possessing any metahistorical principle of order, it makes of any single principle or partial pattern of reality (the destiny of Rome, fortune, economics, ethnocentric myths or any other disembodied *logos* of philosophy) an absolute by which the knowledge of history may be possible.

A theology of history, on the other hand, denounces as arbitrary the variable and barren ideologies or abstract extrapolations which attempt to explain history. It emphasizes, in a forceful way, the problematical character of every individual with his irreducible fund of experience and values. From this point of view, one can hardly blame those Romantic critics who gave us still memorable pages on the "characters" of the *Divine Comedy*, say, Beatrice, Farinata or Ugolino. But history cannot be for Dante only a study of personalities: in the tradition of biblical exegesis and through an extensive use of *figura* and typology, he shows how individual lives and history vitally reenact and partake in the paradigmatic story of Exodus. Even the specifically political dimension of history, which plays such a prominent role in Dante's vision, appears to be part of the work of redemption.

Dante's scheme of secular order, consistently dramatized in texts as different as *De Vulgari Eloquentia*, *Monarchia* and the *Divine Comedy*, has frequently been summarized by critics. Actually, the value of political life, the particularity and concreteness of Dante's esthetic vision, and the moral temper of his language have appeared so pronounced that Auerbach's formula "Dante, poet of the secular world" and the phrase "prophet of the Empire" have gained wide currency in the scholarly circles.

On the strength of various passages from *Monarchia* (II,

i–xii), *Convivio* (IV, v) and scattered places in the *Divine Comedy*, the general outlines of his vision of political-moral history have been sharply drawn. The Roman Empire is the permanent structure of order and was appointed by God to carry out his providential design of universal history. And just as at the time of the Incarnation the Empire under Augustus established a *pax terrena*, so now, Dante's ideology is construed to be, a renewed empire, governed by the moral will of the emperor, can restore justice in the world and secure conditions favorable to man's spiritual ends.

This view of the providentiality of the temporal order does not completely exhaust the complexity of Dante's sense of history. One of the themes that run through this study is the definition of Dante's systematic correlation of the secular and sacred strands of history; an effort to show, that is, how terms such as nature and grace, temporality and eschatology, traditionally viewed as static and disjointed antitheses, are inextricably interdependent in his imagination. Dante captures, I argue in chapters 1 and 3, the movement whereby theology is historicized: the typology of Eden, for instance, or the doctrine of the mystical body are shown in chapter 3 to encompass respectively the city and the order of the body politic. At the same time, however, the world of contingency is drawn within the redemptive pattern of history: Cato, to give another instance from chapter 1, a pagan old man, inaugurates the new beginning of history. Outside of this economy of redemption, there is the failure of man-made history: chapter 2 focuses precisely on the failure of pagan political rhetoric in the earthly city, and on the tragedy of the utopian quest as part of Dante's strategy to expose the hollowness at the core of humanistic history.

The theological harmonization of the earthly and heavenly cities is achieved in the *Divine Comedy*, as I show in chapter 4, by a partial revision of St. Augustine's view of the Roman Empire. The fall of Rome entails for Augustine the bankruptcy of the very myth of the stability of the earthly city. Secular history is part of the ephemeral "cycle of the times," and enacts a pattern of repetition akin to the cycles of nature; and if justice is taken away, Augustine writes, kingdoms are but great robberies. The way out of the treachery of political life is, for Augustine, to retreat into the self and to find there, in the fragmentation of his inner life, the flicker of God's stability. But Dante's perception of the chaos of history is, in a real sense, more tragic than Augustine's. The harsh reality of history has become for him an intolerable nightmare, and he knows that nothing can shelter man's very self from history's sinister violence. In an open polemic with Augustine, Dante turns to Vergil and retrieves the ideology of the Empire, which, however ambiguously, the *Aeneid* contains and which alone, he believes, can put an end to the brutality of civil wars.

It must be clear, however, that the secular city, though it is a necessary myth against anarchy in Dante's moral world, is not given an absolute value in the *Divine Comedy*. Dante constantly vindicates the importance of earthly life, but he also warns us not to mistake the shadowy and insubstantial domain of temporal existence for the true things to come. There is, in brief, an antihistory at the heart of his historical imagination, a radical perspective from which the ultimately illusory values and idols of this world are relentlessly questioned. This profoundly Christian dimension of history is enacted by the Church, which, as I show in chapter 7, desecrates the myths of this world, even as it shares in the world's degradation.

This view of the Church goes counter to the Joachistic expectation of a new *status Ecclesiae*, a utopian age of the Spirit which would supersede the age of the Son. For Dante the Incarnation remains the pivot of history, the event that inaugurates the *eschata* which the Church embodies. It is actually the peculiarity of the Church to be a *casta meretrix*, in time and out of time, that make a theology of history a veritable paradox in which history has come to a closure, but we still wait for the end; the sense of history has been revealed, but we still see through a glass darkly. In this suspended time of history the Church is to speak the word of God and preach the message

of the kingdom. The task attendant on the Christian wayfarer, by the same token, is to scrutinize the signs of the times
and decipher the figures that God has stamped on the face of
the earth.

The structure of the poem, I argue in chapter 6, reflects
Dante's sense of the paradox of history simultaneously closed
and open-ended. The poem dramatizes a theological interpretation of history as a totality of unambiguous signs and in so
doing it mimes the commonplace that the world is a
storehouse of symbols to be interpreted, or as Alan of Lille
puts it, every creature "quasi liber et pictura / nobis est et
speculum." At the same time, however, I show that the poem
is open-ended, and that it is a mimetic representation of the
totality of the world as well as a gloss on the book of creation.
The poem dramatizes, in a fundamental way, the activity of
interpretation and recounts the effort of the poet-exegete to
restore the thread that binds signs and their meanings.

The question of interpretation, it can be shown, is an
explicit theme in most of Dante's writings. A glaring instance
occurs in the philosophical-poetic text such as *Convivio*,
where a theory of allegory is the preamble both to an extended self-exegesis and to a philosophical scrutiny of the
problematics of authority, language and glosses. The *Vita
nuova*, which like *Convivio* is also a story of self-reading, tells
a more oblique tale of a poet-lover, who, impelled by love,
wants to pierce the luminous mist that envelopes Beatrice's
appearance, grasp the signs she emits, and discover the sense
of her appearance. One could even go further and show that
Dante suggests—along with the more conventional
metaphoric bond between love and poetry—the profound
links which connect love and interpretation. The connection
was established by St. Augustine, who in *De Doctrina Christiana* makes *caritas*, the love of God, the exegetical principle by
which the ambiguities of the figurative language of the Bible
can be virtuously interpreted. St. Augustine's abstract formulation becomes the crucial concern of the *Vita nuova*, which is
built on the alternation of glosses and poems. In this "libello"

the lover, one could infer, bent on snatching the elusive secret of the beloved, suspiciously reading the signs of love and fearful of betrayals, is the very figure of the interpreter.

There is a way in which *Monarchia* dramatizes, among other things, what might be called the politics of interpretation. A famous instance occurs in the passage of this treatise (III, iv) in which Dante argues for the equality of the spiritual and temporal orders and refutes the principles by which the hierocrats justify their belief that the Empire ought to be subordinated to the authority of the Church. Their claim, Dante maintains, is based on an erroneous exegesis of Genesis 1:16, where it is said that God made "duo magna luminaria," the greater light to rule the day, and the lesser light to rule the night. In *Purgatorio* XVI the Latin phrase, by a deliberate mistranslation, is rendered as "due soli" (l. 108), to suggest the equality of pope and emperor in the guidance of human affairs. As Dante objects to the hierocrats' identification of the sun with the spiritual power, and the moon, which receives its light from the sun, with the temporal power, he discloses the political interests inherent in allegorical interpretations. He shows, to put it at its simplest, that conflicts of interpretation are not merely innocent academic debates but generate structures of meaning which legitimize power and establish ideological values.

The question of interpretation, with all its ideological and literary complications, is a central concern in this critical exploration of the *Divine Comedy*, and, I submit, even governs its poetics. There has been in recent years a heated debate aimed at deciding whether allegory is a mode of expression or whether it describes a theory of interpretation. The distinction is somewhat specious, for in the poem the mode of poetic expression coincides with the poet's exegesis of his own past experience. To show how paramount is the problem of interpretation in the *Divine Comedy*, I devote a substantial portion of this study to discussing the strategies of reading which Dante deploys in the text. There is a deliberate shift in focus away from abstract hermeneutics, the techniques and modes of interpretation, which scholars unearth, to the concrete textual situations where the poet and his characters are involved in imaginative interpretations, distortions and appropriations of the past. Chapter 5, for instance, focuses on literary history from the point of view of the poets.

In a primary way, such interpretative practices dramatize the essence of history as interpretation, the process by which tradition is handed down and, literally, manipulated. I do not view tradition, in my exegetical endeavor, simply as a likely background of patristic and mythographic *topoi*. I try, rather, to give a reasonably accurate picture of Dante engaged in a steady debate with the thought and language of figures such as Augustine, Vergil, Brunetto, Boethius, Ovid, Cavalcanti and others. This is not, to be sure, some belated exercise in positivistic history of stark facts and firmly rooted events. Such an indulgence in archeological research is certainly valid but is, ultimately, an illusory enterprise which runs counter to Dante's sense of tradition. For him tradition cannot be construed as an archive where one traces roots and records of the past. Tradition is the movement of history, the process by which the past is retrieved and is opened to the future. At the same time, the recalling of figures with whom Dante is engaged in a dialogue does not exhaust or circumscribe the horizon of Dante's intellectual preoccupations. They are the contours of the imaginative space in which Dante inscribes his text and which releases his text into a complex network of other texts.

The underlying problem in these textual strategies, which I explore in chapter 6, is to determine the historicity of the *Divine Comedy* and the question of how the reader is to interpret it. The fact that the Letter to Cangrande refers to the literal sense of the poem as *historialis* (a technical term used in biblical exegesis to qualify the historical nature of its literal sense), has led critics to argue that the poem tells a story the literal sense of which is to be taken as true. The poem is to be interpreted, their argument follows, according to the canons of theological allegory, a scheme which is rejected by those other scholars who believe that the poem is pure fiction, a text which mimes reality, but has no claims to be an "appendix to the Bible." It can be shown, however, that the question—as it stands—is ill posed. Several times in the course of the poem Dante alludes to the purely verbal construct of his poem. We should not see in these statements some banal version of poetics of failure in which referentiality is lost and the self-reflexive, autotelic nature of the text is disclosed. If in *De Vulgari Eloquentia* the whole of history appears as the history of language (the Edenic idiom of Adam, the loss of unity, the building of the Tower of Babel, the Incarnation of the Word, the necessity of grammar and poetry, etc.), in the *Divine Comedy* this concern is less systematic but no less explicit. Suffice it to say that in *Paradiso* xxvi, the canto where the fall of Adam is recounted in terms of the fall of language, God is also referred to as "Alfa e O" (l. 17), the boundaries of the letters of the alphabet which can be combined in and produce all possible words. As Dante views creation as a book and at the same time, dramatizes his perception of a gap that separates the words from the reality they try to represent (*Inferno* iv, ll. 145-7; xxxii, ll. 1-12; *Paradiso* i, ll. 70-2; xxxiii, ll.121-3), he implies that, as readers, we lodge in a world of language and to interpret means that we must travel the distance that separates signs and meanings. In a gesture that makes reading the imaginary extension of exile, he also implies that, as readers, we are dislocated in a space of radical ambiguity where the metaphors we encounter can be taken to be the glittering signs of God's presence or fictions emptied of any reality.

In this condition of ambiguity, interpretation cannot be a naive gesture of believing that we can demystify the poet or deconstruct his text. Nor should we see in this constitutive ambiguity of literary language the ironic predicament of the modern reader caught in the aporia of contrasting options which the text simultaneously issues. The plight of modern readers, it could be said, resembles the dilemma pictured in *Paradiso* iv, ll. 1-4. The problems of allegory and violence, which are debated in this canto, are introduced by a reference to the story—popular with the Scholastics—of what has come to be known as the Ass of Buridan who, suspended between two equally attractive foods, cannot choose. Dante, actually, has a way of anticipating and indeed dramatizing our interpretive choices or even our impasse. For Dante the ambiguities of language are crucial for our quest: they force us to interpret, to undertake itineraries that inevitably lead us to a self-disclosure. Understood in this sense, the text is a figure of the desert, in itself the metaphoric space of the quest, and a place to which Dante's imagination insistently returns.

In the dramatics of the poem the desert is the locus of encounters and radical decisions. It is in the desert of Exodus that the Jews enter a covenant with God; in that same desert, however, they yield to temptations by manufacturing idols and lapsing into nostalgia, in the etymological sense of entertaining a brooding wish to return home to Egypt. In *Inferno* I, the pilgrim is lost and it is in the "gran diserto" (l. 64) that he meets Vergil who guides him to the Garden of Eden. More important, the desert is also the radical emblem of history in the *Divine Comedy*. I argue, accordingly, that Dante removes man's utopian visions and pastoral dreams away from the boundaries of romances, where man's longing and disillusion have consigned them, to the world of the possibilities of history. This is not to believe that the world is a pastoral enclosure: Dante constantly warns us against acquiescing in the illusory stability of this world and tells us that history is the place where exiles work and wait.

As a metaphor for both history and text, the desert marks our estrangement from the world and is the perspective from which we can question the very language we use, the falsifications and ambiguities that language harbors. In both cases, from start to finish, the quest described in the *Divine Comedy* tells this effort to unsettle all complacencies, to leave behind familiar shores and shoals, to shed esthetic gardens of self-absorption, to expose ourselves to the possibilities and dangers of error.

Thus envisioned, the poet of the *Divine Comedy* is not some version of Socrates, the lover of wisdom and supreme ironist whose relentless questions checkmate facile intellectual certainties. In the measure in which Socrates' questions are an ironic intellectual exercise or an abstract love of wisdom, they are bound to appear simply useless to Dante, who more deeply than any other poet has pondered the links between intellect and love. Philosophy by itself, without faith, is useless for it is not enough, its knowledge is illusory, and Socrates is among the spirits wrapped in the half light of limbo, one of those who live in desire but without hope.

To the despair of the philosopher, Dante responds with an extraordinarily *untimely* sense of hope. This is neither the ambiguous blessing and/or evil of the Greek myth of Pandora's box, nor is it a cheat, as we moderns complacently may tend to believe. For Dante hope is a scandalous dimension of history, a virtue that tells us that despair is illusory, that nothing is ever final, and that the past has seeds for the future. Against the irony of the philosopher, Dante pits allegory, the figure which in Isidore's list of tropes is closest to irony, and the world of history, both figured in the desert. *There* is where we are like nomads and where we turn what is alien into the familiar; but *there* we also come to know that what is familiar is never a tamed truth, and that behind it steadily lurk signs that have to be interpreted and not simply understood. And to interpret, as the pilgrim's quest for Beatrice shows, is to be impelled by love.

CHAPTER 1

Opus Restaurationis

In *Inferno* xiv (ll. 94 ff.) the narrative action of the poem is briefly interrupted and Vergil explains to the pilgrim that the rivers of Hell have their origin in the cracks in the weeping statue of the Old Man of Crete. The interpretations that Dante scholarship has produced on the statue are well known: some critics have viewed it as an allegory of the corruption of the empires, as if Dante had assimilated into his fiction and basically preserved the substance of the biblical source, Nebuchadnezzar's dream of a statue glossed by Daniel as a prophecy of the ephemeral nature of earthly empires. An alternate critical opinion, reached largely by reinterpreting the existing evidence, suggests that the Old Man of Crete is an allegory of the crisis of both Church and Empire or the allegory of man redeemed but still subject to sin.[1] This raw

---

[1] The statue in the early commentaries of l'Ottimo and Benvenuto da Imola is taken to mean the course of history from Adam to the corruption of the Church. See Biagi, ed., *Inferno*, pp. 303-4. It was roughly within the last century that this general reading has been considerably sharpened. Giovanni Pascoli, *Sotto il velame* (Messina: Maglia, 1900), pp. 237 ff., advanced a theological rationale for the corruption of the statue. Francesco Flamini, *Avviamento allo studio della* Divina Commedia (Livorno: Giusti, 1906), pp. 57 ff., suggested that the four wounds are *vulnera naturae*. Giovanni Busnelli, *L'etica nicomachea e l'ordinamento morale dell'*Inferno *con in appendice la concezione dantesca del veglio di Creta* (Bologna: Zanichelli, 1907), pp. 159-91, understands the figure of the "veglio" as St. Paul's *vetus homo* but in psychological terms only; R. M. Dawkins, "The 'Gran Veglio' of *Inferno* xiv," *Medium Aevum*, 2 (1933), pp. 95-107, connects the legend to Hellenic sources. What is missing in these accounts is the integration of nature, history and psychology

summary of practically several centuries of scholarly research
on the statue clearly does not even begin to do justice to the
complex and subtle exegetical labors of past critics, and I shall
draw from them in the course of my own reinterpretation of
the episode. What has generally been neglected in the past,
and what I hope to account for, is the figurative pattern surrounding the Old Man, the dramatic significance of the island
of Crete, the rationale for allusions to Ovid's and Vergil's
texts, and, more important, the cracks in the statue.

The presence of Cato in the first two cantos of *Purgatorio*
has also been the object of considerable critical attention.[2] A
remarkable attempt at interpreting his specific role and his

achieved in *Inferno* xiv and their relationship in Dante's vision of the economy of salvation. The more recent scholarship has read the canto as an isolated textual unit. Salvatore Santangelo, "Il veglio di Creta," in *Studi letterari:
Miscellanea in onore di Emilio Santini* (Palermo: Manfredi, 1955), pp. 113-23,
reproposes the notion that the statue is the allegory of the Roman Empire in
its state of dissolution. Ettore Paratore, "Il canto xiv dell'*Inferno*," *Lectura
Dantis romana* (Turin: Società editrice internazionale, 1959), tempers somewhat Santangelo's interpretation. Claudio Varese, "Canto xiv," in *Letture
dantesche*. Inferno, ed. Giovanni Getto (Florence: Sansoni, 1955), pp. 251-66,
believes that the Old Man of Crete stands for "l'umanità dell'Inferno," and
that it is "l'umanità immobile, prima del veltro che dovrà rinnovarla" (p.
264). For the four rivers, see Theodore Silverstein, "The Allegorized Vergil
in the *Divina Commedia*," *Harvard Studies in Philology and Literature*, 14 (1932),
particularly pp. 54-9.

[2] The most important bibliographical item on Cato is still by E. Proto,
"Nuove richerche sul Catone dantesco," *Giornale storico della letteratura italiana*, 59 (1912), pp. 193-248; see also the earlier Nunzio Vaccaluzzo, "Le fonti
del Catone dantesco," *Giornale storico della letteratura italiana*, 40 (1902), pp.
140-50; Francesco D'Ovidio, *Nuovi studi danteschi. Il Purgatorio e il suo pre-
ludio* (Milan: Hoepli, 1906); André Pézard, "Le Chant premier du *Purgatoire*,"
Annales du Centre universitaire méditerranéen, 8 (1954-55), pp. 175-90; Emilio
Bigi, "Il canto i del *Purgatorio*," in *Letture dantesche. Purgatorio*, ed. Giovanni
Getto (Florence: Sansoni, 1958), pp. 5-16; various remarks of great interest
can be found in Paul Renucci, *Dante disciple et juge du monde greco-latin*
(Clermond-Ferrand: G. de Bussac, 1954); see also the suggestive reading of
Purgatorio i by Ezio Raimondi, "Rito e storia nel canto i del *Purgatorio*," *Let-
tere italiane*, 14 (1962), pp. 129-50. A typological reading of Cato as Moses is
proposed by Robert Hollander, *Allegory in Dante's* Commedia (Princeton:
Princeton University Press, 1969), pp. 123-9.

larger significance in the structure of the *Divine Comedy* was made by Erich Auerbach, who rigorously applied the figural principle and explained Cato as a *figura* of the providential redemption of the pagans.[3] Yet Auerbach, in my view, did not deal adequately at the time with the most crucial aspects of the question: why should it be precisely Cato who introduces *Purgatorio*? Why should this eminently Christian and resurrectional *cantica* start—and the paradoxes are flagrant—with a pagan and a well-known suicide? And, finally, what is the relationship between, on the one hand, the two enemies of Caesar, Brutus and Cassius, at the end of *Inferno*, and on the other hand, this other enemy of Caesar right at the beginning of *Purgatorio*? Or, more generally, does the historicity of Cato add any doctrinal element to Dante's conception of *Purgatorio*?

The general purpose of this chapter is to exemplify, by focusing on the Old Man of Crete and on Cato, the theological structure of Dante's language of history and to reflect on the myth of the origin of history both as a theological problem and a rhetorical strategy. Largely at stake are the question and techniques of historical knowledge, the process by which the unfolding of history appears as an intelligible and significant plot. Within this context it is my aim to explain the dramatic import of the two scenes by treating them as conceptually unified moments dramatizing two distinct phases of the pilgrim's progress from the chaos of fallen nature to the condition of *gratia sanans*. This is the middle ground where grace intervenes both to rescue and rectify fallen nature, and to ratify the importance of the natural virtues in the Christian scheme. These two stages, insofar as they are emblems of the pilgrim's spiritual growth, will be fullfilled at the top of Purgatory where their theological coordination comes into clearer perspective because it is there that healing grace is transformed into sanctifying grace. The dramatic movement

[3] Erich Auerbach, "Figura," in *Scenes from the Drama of European Literature: Six Essays*, trans. Ralph Manheim (New York: Meridian Books, 1959), pp. 11-76.

will appear in its essential triadic structure: from the instability of fallen nature, to redeemed nature, to the order of grace.[4] In specifically rhetorical terms, however, this linear theological pattern is complicated by the recurrence of metaphors and pervasive verbal recalls in the two scenes, so much so that, in many ways, the pilgrim's encounter with Cato is a rewriting of the allegory of the Old Man of Crete. Ostensibly, Dante is engaged in a palinode, a revisionary poetics which would be formally adequate both to the redemptive process of history which he envisions and to the spiritual conversion which the pilgrim experiences. More fundamentally, the palinode constitutes the temporal ground which sustains the possibility of dramatizing history's renewal. The theology of man's renewal is explicitly given in *Paradiso* VII where Dante draws the history of the Empire, treated in the preceding canto, within the totality of creation. Because of Adam's fall from Paradise, the Word of God descended in humility to restore man ("riparar l'omo a sua intera vita," l. 104) to the primal image forfeited by pride. In *Purgatorio* XVI, Dante describes, in the microcosmic terms of the journey of the soul away from God and back to God, what is in effect the substance of the whole poem—the "conversion" of the pilgrim to God—and what is also the dynamics of the historical process wherein fallen secular history is redeemed and rejoined with God. The structure of this historical process is traditionally explained in terms of *opus conditionis* and *opus restaurationis*.

These technical terms are never explicitly used by Dante; yet, regenerative concepts such as Resurrection, Re-creation,

---

[4] For a treatment of these two phases of grace the obvious point of reference is St. Thomas Aquinas, *Summa Theologiae,* Ia IIae, q. 110, a. 2, ad. 2, where he defines grace as an accidental form of the soul; see also Ia IIae, q. 111, a. 5, resp., where the sanctification process of man is defined. For an overall view, see René-Charles Dhont, *Le Problème de la préparation à la grâce: Etudes de science religieuse*, V (Paris: Editions franciscaines, 1946); Charles S. Singleton, *Dante Studies 2: Journey to Beatrice* (Cambridge, Mass.: Harvard University Press, 1967), pp. 39-56, has mapped the pilgrim's three conversions in the poem.

Reformation, Renovation, etc., stand at the center of his vision.[5] His ideology of renewal expressed through this unstable range of synonyms essentially hinges on the Incarnation, the radical event that transforms the sense of the past and imparts a definite direction to the future of history. In the two scenes I am about to consider, however, the conventional scheme of conversion, the Pauline typology of the Old Adam and New Adam, is only alluded to. What is singular in Dante's vision of salvation history is that the "renewed" man is not Christ but an old man drawn from the secular order, who in his historical existence lived outside the Revelation. It is in the fourth book of the *Convivio* that Dante provides a sustained framework of man's *restauratio* as a continuous historical process extending from the Fall and including the secular city.[6]

But why do I use this twelfth-century theological description of redemption as the structuring principle of history? In a sense, a thematic strand of this essay is the interplay of labor

---

[5] For some instances of these occurrences, see *Purgatorio* XXII, l. 70, "quando dicesti: 'secol si rinova' "; in *Purgatorio* I, l. 135 the humble plant that has been plucked "si rinacque"; there is an obvious symmetrical relationship between this rebirth of the plant and the "rinovellate di novella fronda" at the end of *Purgatorio* XXXIII, l. 144, to mark the pilgrim's emersion from the Eunoe River. *Paradiso* VII contains some versions of the motif; God's redemption of man is alluded to as the act of "riparar l'omo a sua intera vita," (l. 104). See also *Purgatorio* VI, ll. 145-7. The motif of reform—and its semantic refractions—in the patristic tradition up to St. Augustine is studied with great care by Gerhart B. Ladner, *The Idea of Reform: Its Impact on Christian Thought and Action in the Age of the Fathers*, rev. ed. (New York: Harper Torchbooks, 1967), particularly pp. 9-26.

[6] In *Convivio* IV, v, 3, Dante writes: "Volendo la 'nmensurabile bontà divina l'umana creatura a sé *riconformare*, che per lo peccato de la prevaricazione del primo uomo da Dio era partita e *disformata*, eletto fu in quello altissimo e congiuntissimo consistorio de la Trinitate, che'l Figliuolo di Dio in terra discendesse a fare questa concordia. . . . E tutto questo fu in uno temporale, che David nacque e nacque Roma, cioè che Enea venne di Troia in Italia, che fu origine de la cittade romana." See also *Convivio* II, v, 12, in which Dante, elaborating on the fallen angels explains that human nature was created to make up for that fall: "a la quale *restaurare fu l'umana natura poi creata*" (italics mine).

and grace. The statue is the obvious image of the artifact shaped by the hand of God and violated by sin. The recovery of Eden is primarily a restoring of the image by grace and human toil and effort, both directed to transform the desert of the Fall into a garden. Secondly, the patristic glosses on Nebuchadnezzar's statue—which give the ideological ground of this chapter—systematically connect *conditio* and *restauratio* as a dialectical totality of history. Thirdly, the tag I chose gives an exact presence to Alanus de Insulis and, to some extent, suggests a structural repetition of his myth of the fall from the golden age in *De Planctu Naturae* and the process of renewal in the *Anticlaudianus*.[7]

It is within this doctrinal field of reference that I believe an explanation of the postulated coordination of the Old Man of Crete and Cato can be made persuasive. There is an obvious discontinuity between these two scenes: the Old Man of Crete is represented in the context of the theology of the sin of pride; Cato is presented in a context of pride's opposite, ascetic humility.[8] This antithesis is precisely the antithesis of

[7] Textual parallels between Alanus and Dante have been pointed out by E. R. Curtius, *European Literature and the Latin Middle Ages*, trans. W. R. Trask (New York: Harper and Row, 1953), pp. 353–62. Some precise links have also been established by E. C. Witke, "The River of Light in the *Anticlaudianus* and the *Divina Commedia*," *Comparative Literature*, 2 (1959), pp. 144–56; see also Andrea Ciotti, "Alano e Dante," *Convivium*, 28 (1960), pp. 257–88; and the more recent item by Peter Dronke, "Boethius, Alanus and Dante," *Romanische Forschungen*, 78 (1968), pp. 119–25. I have found useful, for the rationale I propose in the *Divine Comedy*, a number of studies on Alanus de Insulis: Richard H. Green, "Alan of Lille's *Anticlaudianus: Ascensus Mentis ad Deum*," *Annuale Medioevale*, 8 (1967), pp. 3–16; also by R. H. Green, "Alan of Lille's *De Planctu Naturae*," *Speculum*, 31 (1965), pp. 649–74; Vincenzo Cilento, *Medioevo monastico e scolastico* (Milan-Naples: Ricciardi, 1961), pp. 234–80; Cesare Vasoli, "Le idee filosofiche di Alano di Lilla nel *De Planctu* e nell'*Anticlaudianus*," *Giornale critico della filosofia italiana*, 40 (1961), pp. 462–98; Winthrop Wetherbee, "The Function of Poetry in the *De Planctu Naturae* of Alain de Lille," *Traditio*, 25 (1969), pp. 81–125, and now partly incorporated in his *Platonism and Poetry in the Twelfth Century* (Princeton: Princeton University Press, 1972), pp. 188 ff.

[8] "O Capaneo, in ciò che non s'ammorza / la tua superbia, se' tu più punito"; *Inferno* XIV, ll. 63–4. The virtue of humility in *Purgatorio* I is rendered

the *opus conditionis* (which is articulated within the theology of original sin, wherein the Old Adam is wounded and stripped of grace) and the *opus restaurationis* wherein man, through the Incarnation or sacramental grace, is restored *in pristinum*, to the spiritual state of a prelapsarian innocence, and subsequently, *in melius*, to a condition of sanctifying grace surpassing the original beatitude of Adam before the Fall.[9]

The process of redemption here schematized, and it will reemerge in detail in the ensuing discussion, does not imply, however, that the movement is cyclic. Dante obviously cannot accept the myth of the circular, eternal return, because this would mean, as St. Augustine eloquently points out in *De Civitate Dei*, a negation of the linear movement of history and would represent a lapse into the historiography of the pagans.[10] The *circuitus temporum*, where events repeat themselves and fall upon themselves, flatly contradicts the view of time having a beginning and an end, and also contradicts implicitly the Incarnation, the radically new event which breaks open the pagans' circle. Dante dramatizes his conception of the linearity of history by dissociating the phase of corruption of the statue from the phase of redemption enacted in Cato. This point needs to be clarified. In the patristic glosses on Nebuchadnezzar's dream, as we shall see, the corruption of the statue is immediately followed by a renewal caused by a stone (*lapis*) unanimously interpreted in biblical exegesis as Christ. Dante alters this tradition. The statue—a microcosm of the sinful world—is eternal: it is symbolic of whatever is eternally damned and no redemption will ever be brought to

---

by the epithet in ll. 135-6; "l'umile pianta, cotal si rinacque / subitamente là onde l'avelse." For this moral antithesis between the *opus conditionis* and the *opus restaurationis*, see M.-D. Chenù, *La Théologie au douzième siècle* (Paris: J. Vrin, 1957), pp. 289-308.

[9] Hugh of St. Victor, *De Sacramentis* i, prol. 2, *PL* 176, col. 183 and cols. 203-4; see also *De Arca Noe morali*, *PL* 176, col. 667; *Expositio in Hierarchiam Coelestem*, *PL* 175, cols. 926-7. Alanus alludes to the *opus restaurationis* in his *De Planctu Naturae*, *PL* 210, cols. 444-6.

[10] St. Augustine, *De Civitate Dei*, xii, 10-20; *CCSL* xlviii; see also Hugh of St. Victor, *PL* 175, col. 144.

it. Redemption, or return to God, takes place in another order of experience, Purgatory. To be sure, by his separation of the intrinsic unity of processes of corruption and redemption of the statue as it had appeared in the Bible, Dante marks a transition from the abstract allegory of the artifact to the particularity and concreteness of history in Cato.

At first glance, what is at stake is the figural relationship between allegory and historical contingency. The complexity of this relationship is made apparent by a brief look at the specific rhetorical technique deployed by Dante: he grafts onto the prophetic statue dreamed by Daniel an extensive pattern of Ovidian and Vergilian allusions. The *contaminatio*, or conflation of disparate traditions, is a deliberate secularization of prophecy. On the other hand, Cato, a pagan, is the emblem that unfolds the process of the new creation of man: secular history is theologized. The chiasmus shows that terms such as secular and prophetic are reversible and elusive, but it also points to their radical identity. History and prophecy coexist and are not linked to temporal directions, history to the past, prophecy to the future. For Dante, as for St. Augustine, history and prophecy are synonymous in the total pattern of redemption.[11]

The ensuing discussion will return to and reexamine these lengthy opening remarks; in the meantime, without theorizing any further in a vacuum, let us handle more specifically these observable poetic patterns. I will first of all discuss the Old Man of Crete; I will, then, relate this myth to Cato, considering both figures as a paradigm of the process from the *opus conditionis* to *opus restaurationis* or as correlatives of the pilgrim as an "old man" and a "new man" in the Pauline sense of conversion. Finally, I will try to formulate some answers to the problems concerning the figure of Cato which Auerbach's interpretation leaves open to debate.

The digression on the Old Man of Crete in canto xiv of

---

[11] "Huius religionis sectandae caput est historia et prophetia dispensationis temporalis divinae providentiae, pro salute generis humani, in aeternam vitam reformandi et reparandi" (*De Vera Religione*, vii, 13, *CCSL* xxxii).

Inferno takes place in the context of the perversion of the moral order of nature, between the circle of the suicides and that of the sodomites.[12] But the most immediate dramatic backdrop of the statue is Capaneo's defiance of Jupiter (ll. 51-60), an ironic dramatic anticipation of Jupiter's own defiance of Saturn. Capaneo's sin repeats Adam's archetypal sin of pride (ll. 63-4), and it is also to be related to Lucifer's primal sin; their common blasphemy against the deity is also associated by Dante in the very adoption of the focal verb "maturi" (l. 48) or in the other cases the epithet "acerbo" (unripe) in order to describe their fall and distance from grace.[13] This association of sins transcends the mere interest of their moral and typological unity. These sins are the essential events upon which the dynamics and continuity of history find their fulcrum. Lucifer's pride generates a cosmic disruption which demands a *restauratio* by the creation of Adam, as Hugh of St. Victor explains; Adam's own sin of disruption of the Edenic order in turn demands the Incarnation in order to restore universal harmony.[14]

Capaneo's pride is delineated in this canto in the political context of the disintegration of the city of Thebes: whether or

[12] It might be pointed out that Alanus' own vision of the fall of man is framed in terms of sexual perversion as the sin that violates the order of nature; *PL* 210, cols. 449-50. Dante's dramatization of sodomy as a metaphor involving linguistic and sexual perversion is probed by André Pézard, *Dante sous la pluie de feu* (Paris: Vrin, 1950); Pézard links throughout the sin of Brunetto to Alanus' *De Planctu*.

[13] I follow here Charles S. Singleton's reading "maturi" against "marturi" which Petrocchi suggests; I also incorporate Singleton's rationale for following Vandelli's text. See Charles S. Singleton, *The Divine Comedy; Inferno 2: Commentary*, Bollingen Series LXXX (Princeton: Princeton University Press, 1970), p. 234. In *Inferno* xxv, l. 18, the proud Vanni Fucci is referred to as "acerbo." In *Paradiso* xxvi, l. 91, Adam is addressed as "O pomo che maturo / solo prodotto fosti, . . ."; Dante refers to Lucifer as ". . . 'l primo superbo, / che fu la somma d'ogne creatura, / per non aspettar lume, cadde acerbo"; (*Paradiso* xix, ll. 46-8).

[14] *De Sacramentis*, *PL* 176, col. 310. *Paradiso* vii is an extensive dramatization of the necessity of the Incarnation to redeem history and nature. Cf. appendix on this problem.

not Capaneo's sin calls for a political *restauratio*, Dante does not say. In *Purgatorio* VI (ll. 145-7) the possibility of historical renewal is by violent sarcasm evoked as a mere alternating of laws and images on coins. In *Purgatorio* VII (ll. 94-6), when the pilgrim meets the Emperor Rudolph, his speech implies the possibility of political re-creation that *Rex Medicus* will belatedly administer to the sick body politic of Italy. But Thebes, in the secular typology of the *Divine Comedy*, functions as the archetype of the irredeemable *civitas terrena*, the city of Oedipus where brothers are enemies. The passage on Thebes and Capaneo's sin is immediately followed by the description of the island of Crete and of the statue of the Old Man standing within a mountain:

"In mezzo mar siede un paese guasto,"
   diss' elli allora, "che s'appella Creta,
   sotto 'l cui rege fu già 'l mondo casto.
Una montagna v'è che già fu lieta
   d'acqua e di fronde, che si chiamò Ida;
   or è diserta come cosa vieta.
Rëa la scelse già per cuna fida
   del suo figliuolo, e per celarlo meglio,
   quando piangea, vi facea far le grida.
Dentro dal monte sta dritto un gran veglio,
   che tien volte le spalle inver' Dammiata
   e Roma guarda come süo speglio.
La sua testa è di fin oro formata,
   e puro argento son le braccia e 'l petto,
   poi è di rame infino a la forcata;
da indi in giuso è tutto ferro eletto,
   salvo che 'l destro piede è terra cotta;
   e sta 'n su quel, più che 'n su l'altro, eretto.
Ciascuna parte, fuor che l'oro, è rotta
   d'una fessura che lagrime goccia,
   le quali, accolte, fóran quella grotta.
Lor corso in questa valle si diroccia;

fanno Acheronte, Stige e Flegetonta;
poi sen van giù per questa stretta doccia,
infin, là dove più non si dismonta,
fanno Cocito; e qual sia quello stagno
tu lo vedrai, però qui non si conta."
Inferno xiv, ll. 94–120

("In the middle of the sea lies a wasted country," he then
said, "which is called Crete, under whose king the world
was once chaste. A mountain is there, called Ida, which
once was lush with waters and with leaves; now it is deserted like a thing outworn. Rhea chose it once as the secure cradle of her child and, the better to conceal him
when he cried, she made them raise shouts. Within the
mountain stands erect a great old man, who holds his
back turned against Damietta and gazes on Rome as on
his mirror. His head is fashioned of fine gold, and his
arms and breast are pure silver, then down to the fork he
is of brass and from there down he is all of choice iron,
except that the right foot is baked clay and he rests more
on this than on the other. Every part but the gold is
cracked by a fissure that drips with tears which, collected, come out through that cavern. They take their
course from rock to rock into this valley; they form
Acheron, Styx and Phlegeton; then their way is down by
this narrow channel, till, there where there is no more
descending, they form Cocytus; and what that pool is,
you shall see; therefore, I do not explain it here.")

This composite picture of a sterile landscape and the
wounded statue of the Old Man dramatizes the fallen world
of creation, at the center of which stands man, the flawed
image and literal artifact not of nature, as Bernardus Silvestris
had envisioned it, but of God.[15] Actually, man's disruption of

[15] Bernardus Silvestris, *De Mundi Universitate Libri Duo sive Megacosmos et
Microcosmos*, ed. C. S. Barach and J. Wrobel (Frankfurt: Minerva, 1964), ii,
xiv, 1-2; cf. Brian Stock, *Myth and Science in the Twelfth Century: A Study of
Bernard Silvester* (Princeton: Princeton University Press, 1972), esp. pp.

creation, is not the allegorical abstraction of either Bernardus
or Alanus, but is brought with sharp precision into the world
of history. Capaneus' proud defiance of Jupiter at the civil
war of Thebes marks the convergence of history and theology. Further, at line 105, Dante defines Rome as the reflected
image of the Old Man by employing the conventional neoplatonic analogy between the state and the human microcosm in order to emphasize the intimate bonds between man's
spiritual fall and the decrepit moral condition of the historical
city.[16] This analogy is reinforced by the personification of the
statue: what might seem to be a rhetorical motif, in effect, introduces the medieval commonplace of the corporate political
order based on the metaphor of the human body as the principle which subtends and sustains the rationale of the body
politic.

The fall, rooted in the sin of pride, is imaginatively turned
to invest space and time. The statue, in itself an emblem of
pride by the oblique recall of the commonplace of the *homo
erectus* (l. 111) and by its ironic juxtaposition to the proud sinners lying supine (l. 22), is situated in a spatial condition of
remarkable ambiguity. Properly speaking it is not even in
Hell but in this world, in Crete, both a mythic space of fallen
nature and a historical place, a station in an open-ended process which, as it will be shown, one can leave behind on the
way to salvation. The statue appears also as an extended allegory of time, enacting a temporal process (it is the figure of
an old man) and the totality of time. Its head, golden and in-

63-87; see also Winthrop Wetherbee's introductory remarks to his translation
of Bernard's *Cosmographia* (New York: Columbia University Press, 1973),
esp. pp. 34-45; for a general background, see George D. Economou, *The
Goddess Natura in Medieval Literature* (Cambridge, Mass.: Harvard University
Press, 1972); of great interest is Tullio Gregory, "L'idea di natura nella
filosofia medievale prima dell'ingresso della Fisica di Aristotele. Il secolo
XII," in *La filosofia della natura nel Medioevo. Atti del terzo congresso internazionale di filosofia medievale* (Milan: Vita e Pensiero, 1966), pp. 27-65.

[16] Benvenuto da Imola defines the statue as man called by the philosophers
"minor mundus." Cf. Biagi, ed., *Inferno*, p. 394; the analogy is also at the
heart of Bernard Silvester's *Cosmographia*, trans. W. Wetherbee, pp. 91-127.

tact, is explicitly related to the harmony of the golden age when Saturn was king of Crete. In mythographic traditions, Saturn is already represented as an old man to symbolize the plenitude of time and the origin of the gods. In the image of Saturn devouring his children, Isidore of Seville, for instance, sees the myth of temporal duration consuming whatever it engenders. Cronos, the name used for Father Time, is identified with Saturn, called thus because of his old age, "quasi saturetur annis."[17] Paradoxically, then, the world was already old when it was new, and this paradox will be more fully explored later on in the discussion of Cato's old age.

The intact head of the statue, symbolic of the golden age, is juxtaposed to the process of progressive deterioration of the quality of the metals and to the wasteland of Crete, two images designed to render the loss of the Garden of Eden. Benvenuto da Imola views Crete as the figuration of this world:[18] it is possible to extend his gloss and suggest that Dante's focus is to dramatize it as an anti-Eden. His emphasis on the fabled golden age once flourishing in Crete and on the fact that it is an island lying in mid-sea with a mountain rising from it, projects it as a garden where the original fecundity has turned into waste. The contrast with the original state of chastity, expressed through a series of temporal antitheses ("fu già," "già fu," "or," "già"), dramatizes this fall. Ironically, however, the sterility of the place and the fall into temporal corruption begin in a moment of sexual fecundity, the gener-

[17] "Saturnus origo deorum et totius posteritatis a paganis designatur. Hunc Latini a satu appellatum ferunt . . . a tempore longitudine, quasi saturetur annis. Unde et eum Graeci Cronos nomen habuere dicunt, id est tempus, quod filios suos fertur devorasse" (Isidore of Seville, *Etym.* VIII, xi, 30). See also Jean Pépin, *Mythe et allégorie* (Paris: Aubier, 1958), pp. 329-33; for a more general view, see E. Panofsky *et al.*, *Saturn and Melancholy: Studies in the History of Natural Philosophy, Religion and Art* (London: Nelson, 1964).

[18] "Est autem hic bene notandum, quod autor per istam insulam figurat nobis mundum istum, sive terram habitabilem, quia ista insula est circumcincta mari sicut terra tota oceano; . . . et est quasi in medio mundi, . . ." (Benvenuto da Imola, *Comentum super Dantis Aldigheris Comoediam*, ed. W. W. Vernon and I. F. Lacaita [Florence: Barberi, 1887], I, 489).

ation and survival of Jupiter and the periodic renovation of time: the substitution of the old Cronos by the child god. But this pattern of history is marked by ongoing violence: the giant Capaneus' defiance to Jupiter repeats Jupiter's rebellion against Saturn. In a sense, Dante echoes the broad outlines of Ovid's myth of the fall. In the *Metamorphoses*, after God had imparted order to the shapelessness of nature and man was fashioned in God's image, Ovid describes the succession of the four ages of gold, silver, brass, and iron during which "sons hustle fathers to death" and the giants attack the very throne of Heaven. Jupiter punishes the giants by hurling thunderbolts to destroy them.[19] The new race of men which springs from the blood of the giants is equally contemptuous of the gods much as for Dante is Capaneus, who is mindless of Jupiter's thunderbolts (ll. 52-60).

This primal violence against Saturn scores the beginning of history, for Saturn is traditionally correlated to the genesis of Rome. It was in Latium, according to the story Evander tells Aeneas, that Saturn after his fall reestablished his golden rule by teaching the art of agriculture. Vergil's myth suggests that Saturn's displacement from Crete results in the historicizing of the golden age and a localizing of it in Italy.[20] In *Purgatorio* XVI (ll. 94 ff.) the Roman emperor ideally should lead man at least to "discern the tower of the true city"; but here in *Inferno* XIV Rome is mirrored in the emblem of the fall from Eden, the statue of the Old Man of Crete. This ambiguity of Rome, the image of Eden and anti-Eden, reflects the contradictions which inhere in the world of history.

To be sure, the implications of this reflection do not come without warning. There are a number of details in the canto which function as dramatic and deliberate hints to adumbrate the iniquity of the historical Rome and signal that the city,

---

[19] *Metamorphoses* I, ll. 151-62.

[20] The myth is alluded to in *Aeneid* VII, ll. 45-9 where King Latinus' lineage is traced to Saturn; cf. also *Aeneid* VII, l. 203. Evander's account is found in *Aeneid* VIII, ll. 314-36. Saturn, in his hiding place, Latium, is said to have gathered together the unruly natives and given them laws.

bound to the earth and founded in the pride of fallen man, will be destroyed: the allusion to the rain of fire (ll. 28-30) recalling the rain that destroys Sodom in Genesis 19:24; the reference to Cato's journey through the Libyan desert at the time of the civil war between Caesar and Pompey (ll. 13-5); and finally the image of the city of Thebes destroyed by Jupiter— all are elements that reveal the chaos of history. Further, the position of the statue, situated to point toward Rome, draws attention to the implied doctrine of the *translatio imperii*, a view of history, that is, modeled on the east-west movement of the sun.[21] The *translatio* is the metaphor of history which maps the movement of tradition, the process by which the past is translated into another beginning. The island of Crete is associated with this doctrine in two crucial instances.

Crete was the island where Aeneas, journeying from Troy, stopped in order to found the city of Pergamea in the belief that this was the place willed by the gods for a renewed Troy.[22] In the Vergilian account, this is a false new start be-

---

[21] All the early commentators emphasize this symbolic detail in the statue. Boccaccio eloquently writes: "Appresso dice che tiene volte le spalle verso Dammiata, la quale sta a Creti per lo levante, volendo per questo mostrare il natural processo e corso delle cose mondane, le quali come create sono, incontanente volgono le spalle al principio loro e cominciano ad andare e a riguardare verso il fine loro: e per questo riguarda verso Roma, la quale sta a Creti per occidente; e dice la guata come suo specchio" (*Esposizioni sopra la Commedia di Dante*, ed. Giorgio Padoan [Milan: Mondadori, 1965], p. 659). Both Benvenuto and the Anonimo gloss the detail in the same way. See Biagi, ed., *Inferno*, pp. 392-4. The concept of *translatio imperii* is defined by Hugh of St. Victor as the coordination of time and space arranged by Divine Providence, "ut quae in principio temporum gerebantur in Oriente, quasi in principio mundi geruntur, ac deinde ad finem profluente tempore usque ad Occidentem rerum summa descenderet, ut ex ipso agnoscamus appropinquare finem saeculi, quia rerum cursus iam attigit finem mundi" (*De Arca Noe morali*, PL 176, col. 667). See also Otto of Freising, *The Two Cities: A Chronicle of Universal History of the Year 1146 A.D.*, ed. A. Evans and C. Knapp, trans. C. C. Mierow (New York: Columbia University Press, 1928), p. 94. For a general treatment of the doctrine, see P. Van den Baar, *Die Kirchliche Lehre der Translatio Imperii Romani* (Rome: Analecta Gregoriana LXXVIII, 1956); W. Goez, *Translatio Imperii* (Tübingen: J.C.B. Mohr, 1958); E. R. Curtius, *European Literature and the Latin Middle Ages*, pp. 29 and 384 ff.

[22] *Aeneid* III, ll. 225 ff.

cause Aeneas reduces the renewal to something past and now merely to be faithfully duplicated. The Trojan exiles, lured by the mirage that their quest for a new land may soon be over, decide to settle in Crete "gentis cunabula nostrae."[23] Prey to nostalgia, they call the city Pergamum, but in a vision Aeneas is told to leave Crete and resume the journey in search of Italy, their true promised land. Analogously in the Acts of the Apostles, St. Paul was lost in Crete and in a dream he was told that his mission to Rome would be fulfilled.[24] The journeys of both Aeneas and St. Paul prepare the advent of the last things, the consummation of history, by moving the world, as it were, to Rome. Bernardus Silvestris, in his neoplatonic allegorization of the *Aeneid* significantly contrasts Crete and Italy, one as the world of carnality and the other as the land of promise:

> Two ancient mothers, two regions, Crete and Italy, are the two beginnings of Aeneas, that is to say the nature of the body and the nature of the soul. By Crete, in fact, we understand bodily nature which is the beginning of the temporal life of Aeneas. And Crete is called by antiphrasis *crasis theos*, that is, divine judgment. For badly does carnal nature judge divine things when it puts them after temporal things. By Italy which is interpreted increase, we understand the nature of the soul, which is rationality and immortality, virtue and knowledge. These are the things which (Aeneas) is ordered by Apollo, that is to say, wisdom to seek. For wisdom warns that he love the divinity it possesses. But Aeneas mistakes the oracle when having been told to go to Italy, he seeks Crete.[25]

---

[23] *Aeneid* III, l. 105, which is clearly echoed in "cuna fida" of *Inferno* XIV, l. 100.

[24] Acts 27:13.

[25] Bernardus Silvestris, *Commentum super sex libros Eneidos Virgilii*, ed. Wilhelm Riedel (Greifswald: J. Abel, 1924), pp. 20-1. Cf. Giorgio Padoan, "Tradizione e fortuna del commento all'*Eneide* di Bernardo Silvestre," *Italia medioevale e umanistica*, 3 (1960), pp. 227-40. See also for further bibliography, *The Commentary on the First Six Books of the Aeneid of Vergil Commonly attributed to Bernardus Silvestris. A new critical edition by Julian W. Jones and*

Since the commentary on the third book of the *Aeneid* focuses explicitly on the parallels between the experiences of Ulysses and Aeneas, we ought to point out that the "scientiae et virtutes," which led Aeneas to flee Crete, resemble "virtute e canoscenza," the ostensible goal of Ulysses' quest (*Inferno* XXVI, 1. 120). But this world of carnality and error (Aeneas—and we shall see the significance of this later on—misinterprets Apollo's oracle) is only a stage in his quest and he will transcend it as mere illusion. In Dante's perspective, nonetheless, Crete is a recurrent possibility of history, and the historical Rome, in a real sense, looks back at and resembles its very antitype. Like Aeneas and Paul, who stand for the political and spiritual mission of Rome, Dante, too, seeks that Rome "onde Cristo è romano" (*Purgatorio* XXXII, 1. 102) and his journey parallels their journeys into the beyond. The pilgrim's disavowals when he resists Vergil's call to undertake his providentially willed voyage, "Io non Enea, io non Paulo sono" (*Inferno* II, 1. 32), ironically stresses the fact that both Aeneas and Paul are models for his own mission. The city of Rome, in other words, can be like Crete or Eden, and history appears as the precarious construct without any absolute order or value. Whereas for Bernardus Italy is the *telos* of Aeneas' quest, Dante breaks with this closed rational system and makes history the space of contingent and variable values, the reality and fulfillment of which lie in the spiritual man or the lapsed old man. In *Inferno* XIV, the wounded Old Man of Crete represents precisely the spiritual corruption that subtends the disorder of the city.

Dante's elaboration of the statue already appears in the Book of Daniel and is explained by the prophet himself as a historical political allegory of the ephemeral succession of earthly kingdoms till the advent of Christ. In the patristic exegeses on the biblical statue we can find more pertinent elements for our discussion. Richard of St. Victor allegorizes it as signifying the degenerate "human effigy" and the *conditio*

Elizabeth F. Jones (Lincoln and London: University of Nebraska Press, 1977), pp. xxv-xxxi.

of human life. "What is," he asks, "the statue if not the human effigy?" In it the condition of human life ("humanae siquidem vitae conditio") is figured.[26] It is further explained as the degeneration of man in time, from the Fall to the Redemption, till a stone, signifying Christ, will shatter the statue to pieces, and from the pieces a new man will be formed and the original effigy is restored as *imago Dei*. At the same time, Richard rigorously applies Hugh of St. Victor's notion of the historical process as a Christocentric movement from *conditio* to *restauratio*. The two terms are explained by Hugh as follows:

> Materia divinarum Scripturarum omnium, sunt opera restaurationis humanae. Duo enim sunt opera in quibus universa continentur quae facta sunt. Primum est opus conditionis. Secundum est opus restaurationis. . . . Ergo opus conditionis est creatio mundi cum omnibus elementis suis. Opus restaurationis est incarnatio Verbi cum omnibus sacramentis suis. . . . Nam opera restaurationis multo digniora sunt operibus conditionis; quia illa ad servitutem facta sunt, ut stanti homini subessent; haec ad salutem ut lapsum erigerent.[27]

More specifically for our present purpose, Philip of Harvengt glosses Nebuchadnezzar's dream as an allegory of the totality of salvation history from Adam to the sixth age of the world:

> Therefore the rock that was dislodged from the mountainside without hands is Christ, who without carnal

[26] *De Eruditione Hominis Interioris*, PL 196, cols. 1266-7.

[27] *De Sacramentis*, PL 176, cols. 183-4. The text reads as follows: "The works of human restoration are the subject of all the divine Scriptures. Two, in fact, are the works in which all the things which were made are contained. The first is the work of creation. The second is the work of restoration. . . . Accordingly, the work of creation is the creation of the world with all its elements. The work of restoration is the incarnation of the Word with all its sacraments . . . For the works of restoration are much worthier than the works of creation; because those were made for service, so that they would be subject to the upright man; these for salvation, so that they would raise up fallen man."

union was born from the sinning mass of mankind. . . .
But now let us see what is the meaning of that statue
which the rock shattered and reduced to ruins, for so
wonderful a dream . . . (is not) without the weight of a
great significance. Its head, he said, was of gold, its chest
and arms of silver, its feet partly of iron, partly of clay.
. . . If we then accept the statue as a symbol for this
world, and if by the seven parts of the statue and by the
five materials of which the statue is composed we understand five or seven ages of the world, we shall have its
probable sense and rational meaning. For those men who
were in the first age of the world from Adam to Noah
were as if they constituted the golden head of the statue,
because just as the head is the first part of the body, so
they were the beginning of the age to follow and of the
human race. . . . But by silver . . . is meant the second
age of the world which extends from Noah to Abraham.
. . . By bronze, which we are accustomed sometimes to
use as a symbol of patience and fortitude, we rightly understand the third age of the world from Abraham to
Moses. . . . The fifth age, however, which lasted from
the time of David to the advent of Christ, is properly understood to be symbolized by mud and clay, which, although it is conjoined with iron, yet also could not be
united with it. . . . Therefore in the sixth age the stone
was dislodged from the mountain . . . that is, Christ was
born. . . .[28]

Philip of Harvengt gives, then, a definite eschatological interpretation of Daniel's allegorization up to the end of time,
when in the sixth age of the world Redemption occurs.
Clearly, for Daniel and his commentators, the vision of the
degeneration of the world is tempered by a doctrine of partial
regeneration. This messianic motif of renewal finds a secular
counterpart in Ovid's *Metamorphosis*, where the account of the
four ages of man—conventionally taken to be the basis of
Dante's allegorical compound of the Old Man of Crete—ends

[28] *De Somnio regis Nabuchodonosor*, PL 203, col. 586.

with the renewal of man because of the residual innocence of Deucalion.[29]

But Dante radically suppresses in this scene the redemptive element from the scene of the statue: he leaves out the subsequent event, in Daniel, of the stone dislodged from the mountain without the help of human hands. Rather, the symbolic overtone of the clay foot implies that the statue in the end will be totally annihilated. The clay foot, with its suggestion of man's return to dust, provides the Christian perspective and Dante's indictment of pagan theories of continuous self-regenerative circularity. The eternal return, in a Christian context, means that the earthbound man will inevitably return to the clay out of which the divine artisan fashioned him.

By the suspension of Daniel's narrative sequence at the crucial juncture of the Incarnation, Dante means to represent a finalized destiny of the unregenerate part of human history. He also seems to imply that what can rescue human history from the tyranny of death is not the belief in the regenerative wonders within the natural order, for the instability of that order is such that every birth is swallowed by death. The renewal and the escape from death can only take place by a spiritual resurrection, and a detail in *Inferno* xiv subtly insinuates this hope. After hearing Vergil's exposition of the rivers of Hell, the pilgrim asks where Phlegethon and Lethe are to be found (ll. 130-2). The allusion to Lethe, the river of oblivion where the souls purify themselves when "la colpa pentuta è rimossa" (l. 138), points to the Garden of Eden and the new life available there and dramatizes the fact that the tragic reality of the Old Man is not the totality of history. But before we pursue the threads that stretch on to the resurrection and the *opus restaurationis*, there are other questions that have to be answered, namely, the significance of the old age and the four cracks in the statue.

In a passage in his commentary on the Epistle to the Romans, Thomas Aquinas establishes an eloquent parallel between moral "old age" and the sin of pride:

[29] *Metamorphoses* i, ll. 348-415.

Vetus homo noster, idest vetustas hominis per peccatum inducta, simul scilicet cum Christo crucifixus est, idest per crucem Christi est mortificatus. Sicut enim supra dictum est, vetustas hominis per peccatum inducta est in quanto per peccatum bonum naturae corrumpitur. Quae quidem vetustas in homine principatur quandiu homo peccato subjacet. . . . Vetustas autem peccati potest intellegi vel ipse reatus seu macula actualium peccatorum vel etiam consuetudo peccandi vel etiam ipse fomes peccati proveniens ex peccato primi parentis. . . .[30]

I have already shown how the typological sin of pride introduces the statue of the old man; in the wake of Aquinas it is possible to translate into moral terms the successive appearances of wounds in the statue. For him, virtually all sins preexist in the original sin and progressively manifest themselves; thus the decay of the metals from the noble gold to the base mixture of iron and clay is a mimetic dramatization of the progressive corruption of man as he recedes from his rational aim, God. The metaphor of time, so central to Dante's figuration, is also the governing principle for Aquinas to explain generation and corruption from the original prelapsarian purity of man till he reaches old age:

Nam unumquodque corrumpitur cum recedit ab origine naturae suae. Natura autem hominis est ut desiderium eius tendat ad id quod est secundum rationes. . . . Quando ergo ratio tendit ad errorem et desiderium ex hoc errore corrumpitur; tunc vetus homo dicitur. . . .[31]

[30] "Our old man, that is to say the old age of man introduced through sin, was crucified at the same time with Christ. That is, through the cross of Christ he was mortified. For as was said above, the old age of man was introduced through sin, in that through sin the goodness of nature is corrupted. Indeed, this old age is begun in man as long as man is subject to sin. . . . The old age of sin can also be understood either as the very sin or the stain of actual sins or also as the habit of sinning . . . or futhermore the very stimulus of sin deriving from the sin of the first father" (*In Epistolam ad Romanos*, VI, lect. 2, *Opera Omnia* xx).

[31] This passage is a gloss on Ephesians 4:22-3: "To put off, according to

It is at this state of moral disorder that man becomes the "old man" or "veglio" according to Pauline theology; or, to use the terms of St. Augustine, whenever a man lives according to the flesh, he is identified with the Old Adam. The different metals of which Dante's Old Man of Crete is made have been variously interpreted both *in bono* and *in malo*. Busnelli reports, for instance, how the gold of the head has been antithetically interpreted as signifying *caritas* for Bernard or *malitia* for Richard of St. Victor.[32] I suggest that in order to understand the moral qualities involved we must look at the four wounds. It has been widely acknowledged that they are the traditional *vulnera naturae*, the effect of Adam's sin on the totality of mankind.[33] Dante in *Paradiso* VII stresses the collective presence of the totality of human nature in the first sin:

> Vostra natura, quando peccò *tota*
> nel seme suo, da queste dignitadi,
> come di paradiso, fu remota;
>
> ll. 85-7

(Your nature, when it sinned totally in its seed, was removed from these dignities, even as from Paradise.)

---

former conversations, the old man who is corrupted according to the desire of error. And be renewed in the spirit of your mind." The gloss reads: "For something is corrupted when it recedes from the origin of its own nature. On the contrary, the nature of man is that his desire tends to that which is according to reason. . . . Consequently, when reason tends to error, even desire is corrupted by this error; then man is said to be old" (*In Epistolam ad Ephesios*, IV, lect. 7, *Opera Omnia* XXI).

[32] G. Busnelli, *L'etica nicomachea e l'ordinamento morale dell'*Inferno, pp. 174-80.

[33] See F. Flamini, *Avviamento allo studio della* Divina Commedia, pp. 57 ff. The link between Adam and the life of the whole human race (*Paradiso* VII, ll. 85-7) is given a precise theological rationale by St. Thomas, who writes that "omnes homines qui nascuntur ex Adam, possunt considerari ut unus homo, in quantum conveniunt in natura quam a primo parente accipiunt secundum quod in civilibus omnes homines qui sunt unius communitatis, reputantur quasi unum corpus et tota communitas quasi unus homo" (*Summa Theologiae*, Ia IIae, q. 81, c. 1).

The Venerable Bede was the first to enumerate and describe the *vulnera naturae* as *ignorantia*, *malitia*, *infirmitas*, and *concupiscentia*. Bede argues, moreover, that the wounds stripped man of the four cardinal virtues and wounded him *in naturalibus*.[34] Both the Pseudo-Alexander of Hales and Aquinas show that grace was needed in order that the wounds of the *status naturae lapsae* might be healed.[35]

More importantly for the dramatic coordination of the Old Man of Crete and Cato, in order for man to be restored to his prelapsarian condition, he has to be healed by recovering the four cardinal virtues, prudence, justice, fortitude, and temperance.[36] In the redemptive order, such a recovery is for Aquinas only the first stage toward complete justification. Such a stage, *gratia sanans*, justifies the soul insofar as it can make it acceptable to God. The second stage, *gratia sanctificans*, occurs when the soul in the Earthly Paradise is in possession of all the seven virtues.[37]

Keeping in mind this spiritual interpretation of the wounds of the human body, it seems appropriate to explain morally the static immobility of Dante's weeping statue. According to St. Bernard of Clairvaux, for instance, to keep both feet on the ground is to think of *quae mundi sunt*.[38] The feet, indicating the twin powers of the soul—*intellectus and affectus*[39]—are *infirm* precisely when they are, so to speak, most solidly *firm* on the ground. The pilgrim's limping in the prologue scene is an imperfection only in terms of movement of the soul to-

---

[34] *In Lucam, PL* 92, col. 460.

[35] See Pseudo Alexander, *Summa Theologica,* iv, tract. iii, quaest. iii, 1, 510 (Quaracchi: Coll. S. Bonaventure, 1928), ii, 746.

[36] *Summa Theologiae,* ia iiae, q. 85, a. 3. Cf. M. J. Gardar, *Les Vertus naturelles* (Paris: Lethielleux, 1901).

[37] A. Pézard, "Nymphes platoniciennes au paradis terrestre," in *Medioevo e Rinascimento: studi in onore di Bruno Nardi* (Florence: Sansoni, 1955), ii, 543 ff. See also C. S. Singleton, "Rivers, Nymphs and Stars," in *Dante Studies 2: Journey to Beatrice*, pp. 159-83.

[38] Guerricus, *PL* 185, col. 23.

[39] See John Freccero, "Dante's Firm Foot and the Journey Without a Guide," *Harvard Theological Review*, 52 (1959), pp. 245 ff.

ward God. To stand, moreover, and not to move, was exactly the condition of Adam between Creation and the infusion of grace; such a condition was described by the Church Fathers: "Adam could stand but could not move his feet."[40] If the process of *restauratio* of man after the Fall can start by the "healing grace" and the recovery of the four cardinal virtues, it is only proper that we should look at canto I of *Purgatorio* where Cato, another old man, becomes, by virtue of the recovered four stars shining on his face, the image of the regenerated man. There are many connections between the Old Man of Crete and the old man of *Purgatorio*. Apart from the notable fact that the word "veglio" is used only for the symbolic, decrepit statue and for Cato—a kind of conceptual unification of the two figures—it is also important to stress that both figures live in a desert. Speaking of the degraded *locus amoenus* of Crete where the statue stands, Dante writes that "ora è diserta come cosa vieta" (l. 99), which demands to be associated with the other desert of *Purgatorio* I: "venimmo poi in sul lito diserto" (l. 130). Singleton's analysis of the technical force of the desert has shown how Dante's journey is structured on the stages of the Jewish *transitus* from Egypt to the Promised Land, through the desert.[41] But the desert is not purely a stage toward glory; Dante uses the metaphor in the tradition of spiritual and mystical itineraries to describe Cato's and his own exilic condition in terms of the archetypal Exodus.[42] Yet the desert contains a conceptual ambiva-

---

[40] Henri de Lubac, *Le Mystère du surnaturel* (Paris: Aubier, 1965), pp. 105 ff. gives many instances of the formula and explores the centrality of Peter Lombard, *Sententiae* II, xxix, 1, to this formulation.

[41] Charles S. Singleton, "In Exitu Israel de Aegypto," in *Dante: A Collection of Critical Essays*, ed. John Freccero (Englewood Cliffs, N.J.: Prentice-Hall, Inc., 1965), pp. 102-21.

[42] The typological link between the historical Exodus and its sacramental reenactment in baptism is suggested by St. Paul in I Corinthians 10:1-4. Cf. also Jean Daniélou, *From Shadows to Reality: Studies in the Biblical Typology of the Fathers*, trans. W. Hibberd (London: Burns and Oates, 1960), pp. 153-226. For the liturgical aspects of Exodus, see J. W. Tyrer, *Historical Survey of Holy Week: Its Services and Ceremonial* (London: Oxford University Press, 1932).

lence.[43] In a sense, the desert is where you are, where you fall into idolatry, or where you discover God's presence, or better, man's presence to God. To stay in the desert is sin, but the desert, as the stage toward Jerusalem, signifies grace.[44]

I shall examine later the relevance of the desert in the context of Cato's conversion, specifically anticipated in this very canto XIV of *Inferno*; for present purposes, it is enough to stress the synthesis which Ambrose makes of the semantic ambiguity of "desert." Just as Adam was driven into the desert by his fall, so also the second Adam has to begin his work of redemption in the desert, overcoming there the various temptations of the devil.[45] Cato's desert, then, is the same condition of nature as the desert in Crete, but it is visited by grace which regenerates and literally recreates the land and the old man on it.

See particularly Jean Daniélou, *The Bible and the Liturgy*, trans. from French (Notre Dame: University of Notre Dame Press, 1956), pp. 70-113. A fairly conventional medieval paraphrase of Exodus is by Avitus, "De transitu Maris Rubri," *PL* 59, cols. 355-68; see also Cyprianus Gallus, "Exodus," *CSEL* XXIII, pp. 57-103.

[43] Richard of St. Victor, *PL* 196, col. 302, notes that "est namque desertum aliud bonum aliud malum." The ambiguity of the desert is anticipated by Guido da Pisa's gloss on "landa" (*Inferno* XIV, 1. 8): "Landa vero est proprie planities aliquando arenosa, omnino sicca et arida, in qua nulla planta oritur sive herba, ut hic; aliquando vero landa est locus amoenus herbis et floribus atque arboribus adornatus, ut infra in secunda cantica ibi: Giovane e bella in sogna mi parea / donna veder andar per una landa" (*Commentary on Dante's* Inferno, ed. V. Cioffari [Albany: State University of New York Press, 1974], p. 265).

[44] Gregory of Nyssa interprets the desert as sin: "Carry the gospel like Joshua the Ark. Leave the desert, that is to say, sin, cross the Jordan." Gregory the Great understands the desert as the path to be followed in order to reach Jerusalem: "The true husbandman is he who at the beginning in Paradise cultivated human nature which the Heavenly Father planted. But the wild boar (Psalm 80:13) has ravaged our garden and spoiled the planting of God. That is why he (the true husbandman) has descended a second time to transform the desert into a garden, ornamenting it by planting virtues and making it flourish with the pure and divine stream of solicitous instruction by means of the word." The two passages are quoted by George H. Williams, *Wilderness and Paradise in Christian Thought* (New York: Harper and Brothers, 1962), p. 40.

[45] St. Ambrose, *Epistola LXXI ad Horontianum, PL* 16, col. 1295.

Similar ambivalences are not limited to marginal linguistic aspects alone: if Cato, according to the present hypothesis, is the emblem of the secular "new man" in the economy of salvation, it may even seem paradoxical that he should be depicted as an old man, when it is widely known that the theological "new man" is traditionally represented in several popular medieval works as a young man. Rabanus Maurus, for instance, employs the direct symbolic analogy between youth and new life: "Iuventus, reversio ad bonum et in Psalmis: Renovabitur ut aquila vita tua" (Psalm 102:5).[46]

Dante's own *Vita nuova* is ambiguously articulated on the dramatic principle that the new life is both a biological quality and a metaphor for the experience of spiritual conversion.[47] In the hexaemeron literature, as in the quotation from Philip of Harvengt, the concept of the world growing older, based as it is on the analogy between the life of the world and individual man, one finds the motif of rejuvenation occurring *after* old age sets in. St. Augustine exploits this motif in a way which seems to have partial bearing on Dante's own imaginative resolution. In *De Genesi contra Manicheos*, while elaborating a parallelism between the seven days of the week, the seven ages of man, and the seven ages of the cosmos, St. Augustine speaks of the sixth age, the time of senescence, as the point at which the new man is born, the spiritual man fit to receive the teachings of Christ:

> The sixth (day) began in which old age appears. For it is in this age that carnal rule was violently attacked and the temple was destroyed and the sacrifices themselves ceased; and now that people attained the limits of its forces, as if it came to the end of life. Yet in that age, as in the old age of man, a new man is born who now lives spiritually . . . (*in ista tamen aetate tamquam in senectute veteris hominis, homo novus nascitur qui iam spiritualiter vivat . . .*). Then man was made in the image and likeness

---

[46] *Allegoriae in universam sacram scripturam, PL* 112, col. 975.

[47] J. E. Shaw, *Essays on the* Vita Nuova, Elliott Monographs 25 (Princeton: Princeton University Press, 1929), pp. 53–75, sheds some light on this ambiguity.

of God, as our Lord was in the sixth age born in the flesh.[48]

Augustine does not use this scheme of the ages as a model of universal history in his *City of God* where he interprets the events from secular and salvation history in terms of the great theme of the two antithetical loves, love of self and love of God. Yet, St. Augustine's view of the historical ages enjoyed great popularity throughout the Middle Ages, and his formulation reappears practically unchanged in Isidore, Bede, and others.[49] Dante in the *Convivio*, while reading the *Aeneid* in the tradition of Fulgentius and John of Salisbury, explains the vicissitudes of Aeneas as a neoplatonic allegoresis of the phases of growth of human life.[50] He refers to "senio" as the age when Marcia, symbolic figuration of the human soul, returns to her first husband Cato, the figure of the Creator. In terms of the *Convivio*, such a return is a veritable conversion, a shedding of the old self to put on the new man.

More fundamentally, in the *Anticlaudianus* the new man shaped by the virtues appears precisely as an old man:

> Munera leticie largitur grata Iuventus,
> Et quamvis huius soleat lascivia semper
> Esse comes, deponit eam moresque severos
> Induit atque senis imitatur moribus evum:
> In senium transit morum gravitate Iuventus.
> Sic etate viret iuvenis, quod mente senescit,
> Etatem superat sensus, primordia floris
> Anticipat fructus et rivum prevenit amnis.[51]

[48] *PL* 34, cols. 190 ff. On the symbolism of the week, see also Jean Daniélou, "La Typologie millénariste de la semaine dans le Christianisme primitive," *Vigiliae Christianae*, 2 (1948), pp. 1-16.

[49] Isidore of Seville, *Etym.* v, xxxviii, 5; Bede, *De Temporibus*, *PL* 90, col. 288; Rabanus Maurus, *Liber de computo*, *PL* 107, col. 726; Honorius of Autun, *De Imagine mundi libri tres*, *PL* 172, col. 156. A general survey of the motif of renewal can be found in George Boas, *Essays in Primitivism and Related Ideas in the Middle Ages* (Baltimore: Johns Hopkins University Press, 1948).

[50] *Convivio* IV, xxviii, 13-19.

[51] *Anticlaudianus*, ed. R. Bossuat (Paris: J. Vrin, 1955), VII, ll. 92-9. See also

If for Alanus the young man shares in the virtues of old age, Dante shifts the process around and shows how an old man is spiritually rejuvenated. They both tell us, by recalling what actually is the commonplace of the *puer senex*,[52] that in a world of grace where the fixing of physical categories is relentlessly questioned, the new age cannot be purely a literal biological phenomenon. More pointedly, by having an old man to inaugurate the spiritual renewal of man, Dante stresses how the new history is the interpretative retrieval of the old and no radical break is possible between them.

In the first canto of *Purgatorio*, as the pilgrim emerges to the light and the four stars, the linguistic structure of the text accentuates the resurrectional motifs.

> Per correr miglior acque alza le vele
> omai la navicella del mio ingegno,
> che lascia dietro a sé mar sì crudele;
> e canterò di quel secondo regno
> dove l'umano spirito si purga
> e di salire al ciel diventa degno.
> Ma qui la morta poesì resurga,
> o sante Muse, poi che vostro sono;
> e qui Calïopè alquanto surga,
> seguitando il mio canto con quel suono
> di cui le Piche misere sentiro
> lo colpo tal, che disperar perdono.
> Dolce color d'orïental zaffiro,

PL 210, col. 551. The text reads as follows: "Youth bestows the welcome gifts of joy. Though wantonness is her customary attendant, she discards it, adopts grave ways and patterns herself on the characteristics of an aged man. With grave character Youth makes the transition to Old Age. Thus the youth is in the robust years of bloom; but because he is mature in mind, sense prevails over years: the fruit comes before the first flowers, the river before the brook" (*Anticlaudianus or the Good and Perfect Man*, trans. James J. Sheridan [Toronto: Pontifical Institute of Mediaeval Studies, 1973], p. 176). The translation blurs the metaphor of the garb ("induit"), which is present also in *Purgatorio* I, l. 75 ("la vesta"), used to indicate the resurrected body.

[52] Some instances of this *topos* are given by E. R. Curtius, *European Literature and the Latin Middle Ages*, pp. 98-101.

che s'accoglieva nel sereno aspetto
del mezzo, puro infino al primo giro,
a li occhi miei ricominciò diletto,
     tosto ch'io usci' fuor de l'aura morta
     che m'avea contristati li occhi e 'l petto.
Lo bel pianeto che d'amar conforta
     faceva tutto rider l'orïente,
     velando i Pesci ch'erano in sua scorta.
I' mi volsi a man destra, e puosi mente
     a l'altro polo, e vidi quattro stelle
     non viste mai fuor ch'a la prima gente.
Goder pareva 'l ciel di lor fiammelle:
     oh settentrïonal vedovo sito,
     poi che privato se' di mirar quelle!

Purgatorio I, ll. 1-27

(To course over better waters the little bark of my genius
now lifts her sails, leaving behind her so cruel a sea; and I
will sing of that second realm where the human spirit is
purged and becomes worthy of ascending to heaven. But
here let dead poetry rise again, o holy Muses, since I am
yours; and here let Calliope rise up a little, accompanying
my song with that strain which smote the ears of the
wretched Pies so that they despaired of pardon. The
sweet hue of the oriental sapphire which was gathering in
the serene face of the sky, pure till the first circle, restored delight to my eyes as soon as I came out of the
dead air which had afflicted my eyes and breast. The fair
planet that prompts to love made the whole east laugh,
veiling the Fishes that were in her train. I turned to the
right and set my mind on the other pole and I saw four
stars never seen before but by the first people. The sky
seemed to rejoice in their flames. O widowed region of
the north since you are deprived of beholding them!)

It is Easter Sunday morning and for the pilgrim the night is
far spent and the time has come to put on the armor of light.
The canto is, in a real sense, an *aubade*. If in the secular lyrics

the aube is the hour when lovers sadly part, for the pilgrim this is the time of delight when he puts off the works of darkness.[53] The allusion to the "alba" (l. 115), actually, places the notion of time within a special theological perspective. Purgatory is conventionally seen as the world of time, and time here begins as it comes to an end, and, paradoxically, opens to futurity. Despite the *plenitudo temporis* that the Resurrection enacts, Dante introduces an *incrementum temporis* through the ensuing drama of purification and the direct reference to the *telos* of history:[54] the expectation of the final resurrection of the bodies as the cloth that on the great day will shine luminously (l. 75). This eschatological hope shows that, although the end has come, redeemed history is still intermediary time, the time of the veiled messianic kingdom during which we await the second coming and rediscover renewal both as a presence and as a promise of the future. The temporal references, futhermore, are an exact revision of the temporal plenitude figured in the myth of Saturn. In the statue Dante presented a waning fullness and the purely linear time of degeneracy ending in nothing. Here in *Purgatorio* i, plenitude is recovered and time is the measure of Creation's return to God.

The allusion to Venus as the fair planet that prompts to love (l. 19) brings to focus the possibilities of this return. Venus

[53] The detail prepares the encounter between the pilgrim and Beatrice in *Purgatorio* xxx, l. 10. For a general treatment of the *alba*, see Jonathan Saville, *The Medieval Erotic Alba: Structure and Meaning* (New York: Columbia University Press, 1972); see also the proceedings of the symposium *EOS: An Enquiry into the Theme of Lovers' Meetings and Partings at Dawn in Poetry*, ed. Arthur T. Hatto (The Hague: Mouton, 1965).

[54] For the doctrine of fulness of the time, cf. St. Paul, Galatians 4:4-5: "But when the fulness of the time was come, God sent forth his Son, made of a woman, made under the law, to redeem them that were under the law, that we might receive the adoption of sons." See also *Monarchia* i, xvi where Dante refers to the Pauline doctrine to justify the perfection of the Roman Empire under Augustus. For a patristic commentary on St. Paul's passage, see St. Bernard of Clairvaux, *PL* 185, cols. 38 ff. The idea of *incrementum temporis* is treated by St. Thomas Aquinas, *In Epistolam ad Hebraeos* i, lect. 1, *Opera Omnia* xiii, 668.

here no longer stands for the perverse passion that Dante celebrates in the *Rime Petrose*,[55] nor for the irrational love that Alanus de Insulis posits in his dramatization of man's corruption.[56] She is, rather, the emblem of natural justice and functions as a palinode of the mythographic pattern of *Inferno* xiv. For the myth of the origin of Venus is linked with the beginning of time subsequent to the fall of Saturn and the loss of the original golden age. Macrobius in his *Saturnalia* recounts the fable of Saturn, who cut off his father Cronos' genitalia and threw them into the sea. From them Venus emerged and received, because of the foam, her name Aphrodite.[57] Saturn's own fall, traditionally confused with Cronos' emasculation, contains the seeds for man's temporal process of recovery of the garden. Further, like Saturn, Venus, the mother of Aeneas, marks the beginning of the Roman order founded on an exercise of will and effort. These deeper sedimentations of the myths of Saturn and Venus do not imply that renewal is a pure reiteration of the past; rather, the genetic pattern allows us to view the possibility of new history as a revision, a palinode of the old.

The poet's strategy throughout the canto, actually, is both to mark a separation between the old and the new and at the same time to show how blurred is the boundary line between the two. At the very exordium, poetical activity, recalled through the *topos* of the bark of poetry, must itself experience a new departure;[58] the pilgrim's rebirth is signaled by his

[55] The line "lo bel pianeto che d'amar conforta" (*Purgatorio* i, 1. 19) recalls "la stella d'amor" and "quel pianeta che conforta il gelo" from Dante's famous poem "Io son venuto al punto de la rota" in *Rime*, ed. Gianfranco Contini (Turin: Einaudi, 1965), p. 152. A brief discussion of the poetic and doctrinal implications of the "rime petrose" will be found below in chapter 4, notes 28 and 29.

[56] *De Planctu Naturae*, *PL* 210, col. 431.

[57] The myth is extensively treated in Macrobius' *Saturnalia*, ed. James Willis (Leipzig: B. G. Teubner, 1970), i, viii, 5-12.

[58] For "ingegno" as the poetic faculty, see Philippe Delhaye, *Le Microcosmus de Godefroy de Saint Victor* (Lille: Editions J. Duculot, 1951), pp. 111 ff. See also the remarks by Winthrop Wetherbee, *Platonism and Poetry*, pp. 94-8

ritual turning to the right (l. 22) and to the east after the leftward descent in the topsy-turvy world of *Inferno*;[59] the humble plant with which the pilgrim girds himself (l.
134) is
miraculously resurrected, and the pilgrim's girding mimes
the traditional action of the *homo viator* as he sets out for a new
journey; finally, the cosmological emblem of the rising sun
(l. 122)[60]—all are details that announce and stress the new beginning. These elements, however, are given a dramatic twist
by the elegiac awareness that the first man and woman, who
saw the light of the four stars, are no longer there (l. 24). Even
the allusion to Calliope (l. 9), the mother of Orpheus and the
muse whose own name signifies "optima vox,"[61] reinforces
the elegiac strain. As Dante invokes the power of her song
with which she overcame the challenge of the daughters of
Pierus, he is obliquely conjuring up the myth of the fall.[62] For
the argument of Calliope's song at the contest is the story of
Ceres, who gave men the gifts of corn and harvest. Ostensibly the myth of Ceres is opposed to the metamorphosis of
Pierus' daughters into magpies: Ceres' seasonal cycles and agriculture prefigure the productive changes that will take place
in Purgatory while the magpies in their pride score, as it
were, changes *in malo*. But the myth of Ceres, as Calliope tells
it, is also the story of her sorrow for the loss of Proserpina,
the emblem of the world of nature brutally ravished by
death.[63] The memory of the fall, in a real sense, stands at the

---

and 116-8; Jane Chance Nitzsche, *The Genius Figure in Antiquity and the Middle Ages* (New York and London: Columbia University Press, 1975).

[59] For the symbolic motif of turning to the left and right, see E. Panofsky,
Hercules am Scheidewege (Leipzig: B. G. Teubner, 1930). See also below chapter 2, note 63.

[60] The history of the emblem is studied by Hugo Rahner, *Greek Myths and
Christian Mystery*, trans. B. Battershaw (London: Burns and Oates, 1963),
pp. 89 ff.

[61] See John Block Friedman, *Orpheus in the Middle Ages* (Cambridge,
Mass.: Harvard University Press, 1970), esp. pp. 6-8.

[62] *Metamorphoses* v, ll. 390 ff.

[63] Claudian, *De Raptu Proserpinae* I, ll. 248 ff., focuses on Pluto's rape of
Proserpina.

very heart of the representation of the new beginning of history, and the whole of *Purgatorio* enacts a steady oscillation between the memory of the fallen world and the longing for the new.

This strategy dramatizes Dante's sense that there is never a final and once-for-all conversion and that the beginning, to put it in the terms of the rhetoric of this chapter, is always begun again in insecurity and hope. The pilgrim's own spiritual renewal is initiated by the washing of his face with dew (ll. 121-9). Critics have spoken generically of this detail as Dante's "first baptism," with Vergil the sponsor.[64] By contrast a gloss by Alanus de Insulis from a sermon on the advent of the Lord will possibly explain more cogently the dramatic implications of the ritual portrayed by Dante. The sermon is, in effect, an extensive commentary on a line of Isaiah "rorate coeli de super" (45) and turns into a reflection on man's redemption. By this line, Alanus writes, is to be understood "primitiva gratia . . . quae post vitiorum tenebras in matutino fidei ad nos venerat, de quo dicitur sicut ros Hermon qui descendit in montem sion" (Psalm 132).[65] Alanus goes on to say that it "morbum purgat" and leads "ad sanitatem." His references to the transition from the dark night of Hell to the morning of faith, the typological nexus with the Exodus story and Sion which is the metaphoric framework of Dante's *Purgatorio*,[66] and the purgatorial and

---

[64] Ernest H. Kantorowicz, *The King's Two Bodies: A Study in Mediaeval Political Theology* (Princeton: Princeton University Press, 1957), pp. 492-4.

[65] *PL* 210, cols. 214-8. Cf. also St. Bernard's *Sermones*, *PL* 183, col. 886, where history is seen as divided into the time of creation and the time of "reconciliatio et reparatio." The time of reconciliation is marked by the dew that that drops from the heavens (Isaiah 45:8), the time, that is, when the land ". . . germinavit Salvatorem per quem facta est coeli terraeque reconciliatio."

[66] Carol V. Kaske, "Mount Sinai and Dante's Mount Purgatory," *Dante Studies*, 89 (1971), pp. 1-18. See also John G. Demaray, *The Invention of Dante's* Commedia (New Haven and London: Yale University Press, 1974), particularly pp. 168-77. The experience of Exodus as the informing principle of the *Divine Comedy* has been studied by Charles S. Singleton, *Dante Studies I:* Commedia: *Elements of Structure* (Cambridge, Mass.: Harvard University

remedial function of the dew constitute an extensive pattern of convergence of dramatic detail and theological structure with Dante's purgatorial scene. Apart from the way Alanus' gloss may explain the symbolic dew, the analogue ultimately shows that Dante's theology of history and nature is an affirmation of their reconstituted sacramental unity, unlike, however, the fallacy in *Inferno* XIV, where history was viewed as if it were like the process of nature.[67] Yet this unity is provisional: the precariousness of the dew fighting with the sun (l. 122) deftly prepares *Purgatorio* as the metaphoric area of spiritual warfare where reconciliation is presented as a continuous and difficult process.

It is within this Easter context that the pilgrim meets Cato. The surprise Cato expresses at seeing the two poets—for to him, their coming seems a violation of the eternal order of God (*Purgatorio* I, ll. 40-8)—is precisely the reader's own reaction to the unexpected presence of the "veglio solo" who appears—

> degno di tanta reverenza in vista,
> che più non dee a padre alcun figliuolo.
> Lunga la barba e di pel bianco mista
> portava, a' suoi capelli simigliante,
> de' quai cadeva al petto doppia lista.
> Li raggi de le quattro luci sante
> fregiavan sì la sua faccia di lume,
> ch'i' 'l vedea come 'l sol fosse davante.

Press, 1954), pp. 1-17. By the same author, "In Exitu Israel de Aegypto," in *Dante: A Collection of Critical Essays*, pp. 102-21. See also John Freccero, "The River of Death: *Inferno II*, 108," in *The World of Dante: Six Studies in Language and Thought*, ed. S. Bernard Chandler and J. A. Molinaro (Toronto: University of Toronto Press, 1966), pp. 24-61. The Easter Liturgy has been examined by Dunstan J. Tucker, " 'In Exitu Israel de Aegypto,' The *Divine Comedy* in the Light of the Easter Liturgy," *The American Benedictine Review*, 11 (1960), pp. 43-61.

[67] The sacramentality of the historical process is fully explored by M.-D. Chenù, *Nature, Man and Society in the Twelfth Century*, trans. J. Taylor and L. K. Little (Chicago: University of Chicago Press, 1968), pp. 162-201.

"Chi siete voi che contro al cieco fiume
fuggita avete la pregione etterna?"
diss' el, movendo quelle oneste piume.
"Chi v'ha guidati, o che vi fu lucerna,
uscendo fuor de la profonda notte
che sempre nera fa la valle inferna?
Son le leggi d'abisso così rotte?"

                                                    ll. 32-46

(Worthy in his looks of so great reverence that no son
owes more to his father. His beard was long and streaked
with white, like his hair, a double tress of which fell on
his breast. The rays of the four holy stars so adorned his
face with light that I saw him as if the sun were before
him. "Who are you that against the blind stream have
fled the eternal prison?" he said moving those venerable
locks. "Who has guided you or what was a lamp to you
in coming out of the deep night that ever makes the
infernal valley black? Are the laws of the abyss thus
broken?")

If the metaphor of the eternal prison of Hell prepares primarily the motif of "libertà" (l. 71) that the pilgrim seeks, it also
introduces the question of law and justice with which Cato is
traditionally associated. In book VIII of the *Aeneid*, Cato is described as "iura dantem";[68] in Lucan's *Pharsalia*, more cogently, Cato embodies the staunch opposition to the civil
war, the wicked crime that reverses "legesque et foedera rerum," and is shown as he fights what Lucan calls a "losing
battle for despised law and justice."[69] In *Purgatorio* I he appears fittingly as the custodian of the place and the keeper of
the law, in a landscape where natural justice is being reestablished and the law is being superseded by grace. This detail,
however, cannot begin to unravel the series of startling
paradoxes that Cato's presence elicits. We are told that he presides over the crucial middle between the captivity and dark

---

[68] *Aeneid* VIII, l. 670.   [69] *Pharsalia* II, ll. 2 ff.

night of Hell (1. 40) and the liberty of Jerusalem that the pilgrim seeks as Cato did (1. 78). But how can a suicide, a pagan,
and an enemy of Caesar play such a central role in the drama
of Exodus?

In the *effictio* of the old man Dante describes his face
adorned with light. The description (ll. 34-9) faintly recalls
the appearance of the exalted Christ in the Book of Revelation
(1:12-6): "his head and his hair were white as white wool
. . . and his face was like the sun shining in full strength." The
light on the old man's face, actually, is a *topos* of patristic reflections (which combine Revelation 1:12 and Psalm 4:7)[70]
and is explained by medieval commentators as a *gratia renova-
tionis* which operates through the Holy Spirit and the sacraments. This light, for Clement of Alexandria, removes both
ignorance from our eyes and the darkness that shuts us in like
a thick fog but it hardly becomes more than an individual sacramental act.[71]

Hugh of St. Cher, commenting on the famous line, "Sig-
natum est super nos lumen vultus tui Domine" (Psalm 4:7),
writes as follows:

> Lumen vultus tui . . . idest ratio. . . . Vultus Dei dicitur
> ratio, quia sicut per vultum homo homini assimilatur et
> homo cognoscit hominem, ita per rationem similes
> sumus Deo et Deum cognoscimus. . . . *Lumen huius vul-
> tus, est gratia*, quia sicut moneta est informis, donec
> Imago Regis ei per cuneum imprimatur, ita ratio nostra
> *deformis est donec* per Gratian Dei illustretur. *Ratio enim est
> imago creationis*: sed *gratia Dei est imago Recreationis*.[72]
>
> (Italics added.)

---

[70] "The Light of your countenance, O Lord, is signed upon us: you have
given gladness in my heart."

[71] For Clement of Alexandria, see Hugo Rahner, *Greek Myths and Christian
Mystery*, particularly "The Christian Mystery of Sun and Moon," pp. 89-
176.

[72] "The light of your countenance, that is reason. . . . The countenance of
God is said to be reason, for just as through the countenance man is made
similar to man and man recognized man, so through reason we are made in

More specifically, Peter Lombard relates such a renewing grace to the deformation of man by the original sin:

> Lumen vultus tui, scilicet lumen gratiae tuae, quo refor-matur imago tua in nobis, qua tibi similes sumus. . . . Vultus ergo Dei, ratio nostra accipitur. . . . Haec autem ratio per peccatum primi hominis deformata est . . . sed per gratiam Christi reformata est, vel recuperata.[73]

But Peter Lombard reads this line from Psalm 4 as a metaphor of the great acts of Creation, Fall, and Re-creation of the world (as Honorius of Autun also does),[74] but he also establishes an identity between "restoration" and "reformation" which is to some extent also Dante's. I have already, though in a general way, discussed the function of the four cardinal virtues to heal fallen man of the *vulnera naturae*. Before establishing the type of virtues Dante means in this context of renovation, I should mention how in medieval hexaemera the week of Creation is often correlated to the cardinal and theological virtues. It was common for Peter of Blois to draw parallels between the seven days of creation and the group of seven virtues (*fides, spes, caritas, prudentia, justitia, temperantia,* and *fortitudio*): the virtue of charity contains them all.[75] It is

---

the likeness of God and come to know God. . . . The light of this countenance is grace, for just as the coin is unformed till the Image of the king is impressed on it with a wedge, so our reason is disfigured till it is cleared through God's grace. . . . For reason is the image of creation: but the grace of God is the image of Re-creation." Hugh of St. Cher, *Opera omnia in universum Vetus et Novum Testamentum* (Lugduni: J. A. Hugvetom and G. Barbier, 1669), II, 9v.

[73] "The light of your countenance, that is to say the light of your grace, by which your image in us is reformed, so that we are like you. . . . Therefore the countenance of God is taken to be our reason. . . . Now this reason was deformed through the sin of the first man . . . but was reformed or recovered through the grace of Christ." *Commentarium in Psalmos, PL* 191, col. 88. See also St. Thomas Aquinas, *Summa Theologiae*, Ia, q. 93, a. 4.

[74] "De Inventione Sanctae Crucis," in *Speculum Ecclesiae, PL* 172, col. 941. In the homily Honorius puts the emphasis on the loss of the earthly paradise and the recovery of man's likeness to God through the sacrificial lamb.

[75] *De Charitate Dei et Proximi, PL* 207, col. 915.

precisely in terms of the doctrine of charity that Dante dramatizes the figure of Cato in this process of redemption. As the pilgrim and his guide emerge from Hell to the new world inaccessible to other travelers, Vergil appeals to Cato's affective memory, a solicitation which Cato rejects:

> "ma son del cerchio ove son li occhi casti
> di Marzia tua, che 'n vista ancor ti priega,
> o santo petto, che per tua la tegni:
> per lo suo amore adunque a noi ti piega.
> Lasciane andar per li tuoi sette regni;
> grazie riporterò di te a lei,
> se d'esser mentovato là giù degni."
> "Marzïa piacque tanto a li occhi miei
> mentre ch'i' fu'di là," diss' elli allora,
> "che quante grazie volse da me, fei.
> Or che di là dal mal fiume dimora,
> più muover non mi può, per quella legge
> che fatta fu quando me n'usci' fora.
> Ma se donna del ciel ti move e regge,
> come tu di', non c'è mestier lusinghe:
> bastisi ben che per lei mi richegge."
> *Purgatorio* I, ll. 78-93.

("But I am of the circle where are the chaste eyes of your Marcia, who in her look still prays you, o holy breast, that you hold her for your own. For her love, then, incline to us. Allow us to go on through your seven realms. I will report to her your kindness, if you deign to be mentioned there below." "Marcia so pleased my eyes while I was yonder," he said then, "that I did every favor she wished of me. Now that she dwells beyond the evil stream, no more can she move me, by the law which was made when I came forth from there. But if a lady from Heaven moves and directs you, as you say, there is no need of flattery: it is enough that you ask me for her sake.")

The evocation of Marcia, who is in Limbo, as a vehicle to assuage Cato's wrath gives a hint, fully explored in successive
cantos, that Purgatory is the world of reciprocity, the place
where we are keepers of one another. But no reciprocity is
possible between the lost and the elect: Cato, who now lives
under the new law, refuses Vergil's flattery, the *captatio benevolentiae* formulated in the language of earthly love. It is the
Lady of Heaven who is the intermediary for the pilgrim's ascent. The rhetoric of the eyes, so central in secular love lyrics,
is recalled only to be quickly dismissed. Marcia is mentioned
to Cato, metonymically, through her chaste eyes, and Cato
remembers how delightful she was to his eyes; but there is
no yielding in Cato to nostalgia and the insidious temptation
of the past. The palinode of earthly love marks his spiritual
regeneration.

The allusion to Marcia, actually, is also for the poet a
palinode of the *Convivio*. It might be pointed out that all three
canticas of the poem get started by the same gesture of breaking with the philosophical and moral assumptions of *Convivio*.[76] In *Inferno* I, the pilgrim's encounter with the shadow
of Vergil, who appears, as will be shown in a following chapter, as the poet of history, marks a radical departure from the
neoplatonic interpretation of the *Aeneid* contained in the
fourth book of the *Convivio*.[77] In *Paradiso* II, the poet's address
to those readers who have eaten the "pan de li angeli" recalls
the bread of the angels in *Convivio* I, where the metaphor refers to the bread eaten at philosophy's table;[78] in *Paradiso*, it is

[76] Critics have variously examined Dante's own critique of *Convivio*. See
Joseph A. Mazzeo, *Medieval Cultural Tradition in Dante's* Comedy (Ithaca:
Cornell University Press, 1960), pp. 174-204; Etienne Gilson, *Dante and Philosophy,* trans. David Moore (New York: Harper Torchbooks, 1963), pp.
83-161; Bruno Nardi, *Saggi di filosofia dantesca* (Florence: La Nuova Italia,
1967), pp. 3-39 particularly.

[77] Ulrich Leo, "The Unfinished *Convivio* and Dante's Rereading of the
Aeneid," *Medieval Studies*, 13 (1951), pp. 41-64.

[78] "Voi altri pochi che drizzaste il collo / per tempo al pan le li angeli, del
quale / vivesi qui ma non sen vien satollo" (*Paradiso* II, ll. 10-12). "Pan de li
angeli" echoes Psalm 77:25 and Wisdom 16:30. It appears also at the very be-

the metaphor for a journey to Heaven. By translating freely
from *Pharsalia* II (ll. 326 ff.), where Marcia after the death of
Hortensius returns to Cato, Dante in *Convivio* allegorizes the
episode as the story of the soul's return to God.[79] The same
scene of the *Pharsalia* is echoed in *Purgatorio* I: Lucan recounts,
for instance, how Cato at the wedding ceremony suffers the
grey hair to grow long over his stern brow in sign of mourning for the wanton civil war afflicting Rome.[80] But against the
neoplatonic allegory of the *Convivio*, *Purgatorio* I shows the
final separation between Marcia and Cato. Dante, in other
words, abandons poetic allegory and turns Cato into a figure
of history, partly the way Lucan, known to the Middle Ages
as the poet of history, represents him;[81] partly by superimpos-
ing, as we shall soon see, the pattern of universal history,
Exodus, on Lucan's own account.

If the poet is engaged in such complex revisionary practices
as the character Cato is, the pilgrim's own experience is remarkably at odds with those practices. *Purgatorio* II, after a description of dawn, tells of the arrival on the shores of the island of a vessel filled with souls all singing "in exitu Israel de
Aegypto" (l. 46), the psalm of Israel's deliverance from Egypt
through the desert to the promised land. After the celestial
steersman disappears, the crowd of new spirits, like the pilgrim and his guide, seem strange to the place (ll. 49-54), pil-

ginning of *Convivio*: "Manifestamente adunque può vedere chi bene consi-
dera, che pochi rimangono quelli che a l'abito da tutti desiderato possano
pervenire, . . . Oh beati quelli pochi che seggiono a quella mensa dove lo pane
de li angeli si manuca" (I, i, 5-7). See on this Daniel J. Ransom, *"Panis
Angelorum*: A Palinode in the *Paradiso*," *Dante Studies*, 95 (1977), pp. 81-94.

[79] "E che queste due cose convegnano a questa etade, ne figura quello
grande poeta Lucano nel secondo de la sua Farsalia, quando dice che Marzia
tornò a Catone e richiese lui e pregollo che la dovesse riprendere guasta: per la
quale Marzia s'intende la nobile anima" (*Convivio* IV, xxviii, 13-4).

[80] "Intonsos rigidam in frontem descendere canos / passus erat maestam-
que genis increscere barbam" (*Pharsalia* II, ll. 375-6).

[81] Under the rubric "De poetis," Isidore of Seville excludes Lucan from
the craftsman of fiction and lists him as a writer of histories: "Lucanus ideo in
numero poetarum non ponitur, quia videtur historias conposuisse, non
poema" (*Etym.* VIII, vii, 10).

grims unacquainted with the way up the mountain. In this unfamiliar landscape the pilgrim meets his friend Casella and to relieve the care and weariness of the journey asks him to sing. The pilgrim imaginatively visits his own native ground and his own past as Casella sings "Amor che nella mente mi ragiona" (l. 112), Dante's poem of the third book of *Convivio*. The song functions as a fictive space of gathering as the pilgrim and the souls listen ensnared and forgetful of their ascent, "come a nessum toccasse altro la mente" (l. 117). Unlike Cato, who refuses, mindful of the new law, to yield to the memory of Marcia, the pilgrim forgets the new law and lapses into the memory and practice of the songs of love (ll. 106-9).[82] Cato comes to scatter the gathering and remind them of their journey:

> . . . "Che è ciò spiriti lenti?
> qual negligenza, quale stare è questo?
> Correte al monte a spogliarvi lo scoglio
> ch'esser non lascia a voi Dio manifesto."
>   ll. 120-3

("What is this, you laggard spirits? What negligence, what stay is this? Haste to the mountain to strip off the slough that lets not God be manifest to you.")

From the perspective of the scattering even this scene represents a palinode in the pilgrim's process of conversion. But the poet insinuates that the sweetness of the song *"ancor dentro mi suona"* (l. 114), still lingers within him. The weight of the past, as it were, can never be completely effaced and disrupts the very possibility of a radical break with it. Against the explicit structure of conversion, *Purgatorio* appears as the domain where distinctions between the past and the new are blurred and, more precisely, as the realm of

---

[82] "E io: 'Se nuova legge non ti toglie / memoria o uso a l'amoroso canto / che mi solea quetar tutte mie voglie, / di ciò ti piaccia consolare alquanto / l'anima mia, che, con la sua persona / venendo qui, / è affannato tanto!' "(*Purgatorio* II, ll. 106-11).

choice. The reference to "negligenza" (l. 121) is a poignant illustration of this feature. Negligence is a version of the medieval *topos* of *acedia* and as such it aptly qualifies the sluggishness of the souls.[83] In Isidore's etymology, the word "neglegens" is taken to mean "nec legere," not to choose.[84] The souls, provisionally bound to the esthetic temptation, have neglected the ascent. Obliquely, *Purgatorio* is cast as the world of choice, either esthetic drifting into erotic poetry as an end in itself or the moral choice of the road to salvation. Nor does the choice end here: it is a steady exercise reoccurring throughout *Purgatorio* and repeated till the end comes.

This, in a fundamental way, is the historicity of *Purgatorio*, a world which combines the rigorous theological structure of renewal with the tentativeness of an open process. The ambivalence is evident in the symbolic value of the four stars—the four cardinal virtues—the pilgrim sees upon arriving at the southern hemisphere and which are reflected on Cato's face. A passage from Macrobius' commentary on the *Dream of Scipio* provides an important gloss for this interpretation. As Macrobius describes the view that Scipio Africanus the Younger has of some stars, he writes that "we never see (these stars) from the place where we are now."[85] The line bears a remarkable resemblance to Dante's reference to the northern hemisphere which we inhabit as "oh settentrïonal vedovo sito, / poi che privato se' di mirar quelle" (*Purgatorio*

---

[83] The moral tradition of the *topos* has been examined by Siegfried Wenzel, *The Sin of Sloth: Acedia in Medieval Thought and Literature* (Chapel Hill: University of North Carolina Press, 1967). See also Morton W. Bloomfield, *The Seven Deadly Sins: An Introduction to the History of a Religious Concept With Special Reference to Medieval English Literature* (East Lansing: Michigan State College Press, 1952).

[84] "Neglegens, quasi nec legens" (*Etym.* x, 193). *Purgatorio* as the area of drama is the object of Francis Fergusson, *Dante's Drama of the Mind: A Modern Reading of Purgatorio* (Princeton: Princeton University Press, 1953).

[85] Macrobius, *Commentarium in Somnium Scipionis*, ed. J. Willis (Leipzig: B. G. Teubner, 1970), I, xvi, 3. See also *Commentary on the Dream of Scipio*, trans. William Stahl (New York: Columbia University Press, 1952), pp. 152-3.

1, ll. 26-7). The virtues are then described by Macrobius as follows:

> Virtues alone make one blessed and in no other way can one obtain this name. Hence those who believe that the virtues are found in none but those who philosophize, affirm that none are blessed but the philosophers. They say that if wisdom is to be properly taken to be knowledge of divine things only those men who seek heavenly truths are wise. . . . In their opinion it is here alone that the virtues are exercised and they assign four functions to the virtues: prudence, that is, to hold in contempt this world and all that is in the world in contemplation of divine things, and to direct all the attention of the soul only to divine things; temperance, to abandon, in so far as nature allows, all that the habits of the body demand; fortitude, for the soul not to be in fear when it leaves the body, in a sense, under the guidance of philosophy and not to be in dread of the height of perfect ascension to the celestial world; justice to consent to the only way to this mode of life, that is to say, observance of each virtue. . . . But Plotinus . . . arranges . . . each of the above virtues in four types: the first, political virtues; the second, purgatorial virtues; the third, virtues of the soul already purged; and the fourth, the exemplary virtues. Man has political virtues because he is a social animal. By these virtues good men devote themselves to their commonwealths, protect cities, *revere parents*, *love their children*, are fond of their relatives. By these they govern the well being of the citizens. . . . Cicero is right in claiming for the rulers of the commonwealths a place where they may enjoy a blessed existence for ever.[86]

---

[86] *Commentarium* I, viii, 3-13. Cf. also Stahl, pp. 120-3. Brunetto Latini makes a remarkably similar distinction among the cardinal virtues: "Vertus sont en II manieres, une contemplative et une autre morale. Et se comme Aristotles dist, toutes choses desirant aucun bien, Ke est lor fin. Je di que vertus contemplative establist l'ame a la soveraine fin, c'est au bien des biens;

Even the line I have italicized in the passage ("parentes venerantur, liberos amant") seems to be faintly echoed in the pilgrim's first perception of Cato as "degno di tanta reverenza in vista, / che più non dee a padre alcun figliuolo" (*Purgatorio* I, ll. 32-3).[87] More to the point, according to Macrobius the cardinal virtues are operative in the political order of history; they coexist with purgatorial virtues and eventually become virtues of man cleansed of worldly passions. As such, the stars seen in *Purgatorio* are there for both the pilgrim and Cato and announce the Edenic condition where cardinal and theological virtues will shine together. In the opening canto of *Purgatorio*, however, they are, as Macrobius understands them, virtues of *praxis*, of work and effort through which the foundations of the city are laid and strengthened and man is purified.

Macrobius' gradual but continuous perfection in the exercise of these virtues is not altogether Dante's. Dante recognizes the presence and import of a synchronic pattern to the processes of secular history and salvation history, but, like St. Augustine, he senses the ultimately tragic disharmony between the secular order and the Christian dispensation.[88] The

---

mais la morale vertus establist le corage a la vertu contemplative. Et por ce volt li mestres deviser tot avant de la vertu moral que de la vertu contemplative, por ce k'ele est autresi comme matire par que on parvient a la contemplative" (*Li Livres dou Tresor*, ed. Francis J. Carmody [Berkeley and Los Angeles: University of California Press, 1948], p. 55).

[87] It may be pointed out that this metaphor of reverence for Cato, as that which a son owes to his father, faintly reverses the metaphor of strife between father and son (Saturn and Jupiter) in *Inferno* XIV. A further oblique link between *Inferno* XIV and *Purgatorio* I is suggested by the presence of the same rhyme scheme in the two cantos. In *Inferno* XIV, the fissures in the various parts of the statue are described: "Ciascuna parte, fuor che l'oro, è rotta / d'una fessura che lagrime goccia, / le quali, accolte, foran quella grotta" (ll. 112-4). In *Purgatorio* I, in an entirely different thematic context, Cato wonders whether the pilgrim's arrival to the island means that the laws of Hell are broken: "Son le leggi d'abisso così rotte? / O è mutato in ciel novo consiglio, / che, dannati, venite alle mie grotte?" (ll. 46-8; italics mine).

[88] St. Augustine's view of secular history is brilliantly treated by Charles Norris Cochrane, *Christianity and Classical Culture: A Study of Thought and Ac-*

unity of a spiritual and political renewal is, in part, the giving of a Christian hope to the open and uncertain adventure of man's history. But far from representing a total indentification of the two, Dante points to their separation when the pilgrim crosses the river of grace. The theology of the relationship between nature and grace will be treated in the fourth chapter of this essay. For the time being, let us examine how Dante imposes a redemptive rationale on Cato's own history, and how he exploits the resonances of his myth to exemplify the historical features of *Purgatorio*. Cato's salvation has been scrupulously analyzed by Proto in terms of the wider question of the salvation of the pagans present in the *Divine Comedy*.[89] To Proto's impressive research, one could add the *Disticha Catonis*, which in the Christian commentary of Hugo of Trimberg appears to be a book on the four cardinal virtues, and in the eleventh century was converted into a sapiential book, analogous to the wisdom literature of the Old Testament.[90] Or, one may point out the fact that Cato is used by Alanus de Insulis as one of the examples of virtue for the new man in the *Anticlaudianus*.[91]

More fundamentally, it could be remarked that Cato is represented on the shield of Aeneas—in the extended *ecphrasis* of book VIII of the *Aeneid*—as an opposer of the decay of the Roman republic. He is dramatically contrasted to Catiline in an antithesis which prefigures, in the economy of Vergil's

---

tion from Augustus to Augustine (Oxford: Oxford University Press, 1968), esp. pp. 359-516. Cf. also Giuseppe Amari, *Il concetto di storia in sant'Agostino* (Rome: Edizioni Paoline, 1950). For a traditional view on Dante's sense of history and the importance of the Roman Empire, see W.H.V. Reade, "Dante's Vision of History," in *Proceedings of the British Academy*, 25 (1939), pp. 187-215.

[89] E. Proto, "Nuove ricerche sul Catone dantesco." For the theology of the salvation of pagans, cf. Jean Daniélou, *Holy Pagans of the Old Testament*, trans. Felix Faber (London: Longmans, 1957), pp. 19 ff.

[90] Richard Hazelton, "The Christianization of Cato: The *Disticha Catonis* in the Light of Late Medieval Commentaries," *Medieval Studies*, 19 (1959), pp. 157-73.

[91] *Anticlaudianus*, PL 210, col. 544; Bossuat, ed., VI, l. 230, p. 147.

text, the Octavian-Antony conflict.[92] This aspect of Cato's history is important for an understanding of the spiritual distance Dante emphasizes between on the one hand, Cato, and on the other hand, Brutus and Cassius. The regicides and opposers of the providentiality of the empire are significantly associated with Judas in what is a representation of fallen history in its totality from Lucifer to the time of Christ's descent. By the overt juxtaposition to the traitors, Cato's presence in *Purgatorio* (and here Dante radically departs from St. Augustine) shows that there is a secular reality that can be integrated within a providential scheme of creation and history. More cogently, by the strategy of contrasting Cato to the regicides, Dante suggests that there is a latent duality within the very fabric of secular history, that there is a redeemed secular history that provides the moral middleness and area of choice between the antithetical cities of the end.

Because of this, it should be clear that the salvation of Cato does not figure simply the future salvation of good pagans, as Auerbach views it, but is private; yet it discloses the characteristic of *Purgatorio* as the locus of redemption in history; at the same time, Cato's role is to dramatize the historicizing of the typology of Eden (a problem more fully probed in the third chapter), to remove the myth of the quest for Eden from the realm of otherworldly utopia and give it an irreducibly historical sense.

Cato's own salvation can possibly be explained by the reference to him, in language that recalls once again Lucan's *Pharsalia*, in the very canto XIV of *Inferno*:

[92] *Aeneid* VIII, l. 670. Servius in his commentary expresses his incredulity that this should be Cato Uticensis, the opposer of Caesar, and explains it as a reference to Cato Maior; Servius, *Virgilii Aeneidos Commentarium*, ed. Georgius Thilo (Leipzig: B. G. Teubner, 1878), II, 297. A modern scholar, on the authority of Sallust, correctly interprets the Cato-Catiline antitheses as prefiguring, in Vergil's vision, the political conflict between Octavian and Antony. See Viktor Pöschl, *The Art of Vergil: Image and Symbol in the Aeneid*, trans. Gerda Seligson (Ann Arbor: University of Michigan Press, 1962), pp. 21 ff. The Vergilian opposition between Cato and Catiline, accordingly, places Cato on the side of the providential survival of Rome.

Lo spazzo era una rena arida e spessa,
non d'altra foggia fatta che colei
che fu da' piè di Caton già soppressa.

ll. 13-5

(The ground was a dry and thick sand not made differently from the one that was already trod by Cato's feet.)

The wayfarer has just come out of the circle of the suicides,
the sinners who have violated God's eternal plan, and is approaching Capaneus, the blasphemous challenger of Jupiter.
As he moves across the waste plain between the two sins, he
recalls Cato's own experience across the Libyan desert. Naming Cato, a suicide who is saved, right after the encounter
with the suicides and before the blasphemy against the deity,
is a deliberate strategy of juxtaposing them. Suicide is condemned because it is an act by which man denies both divine
ownership of his life and membership in the social body. For
Dante it is a sin of false transcendence, the narcissistic reifica-
tion of the self to himself.[93] Pier delle Vigne expresses this
self-doubling and estrangement in the general iterations
which punctuate his language, or, more precisely, in the
climactic line of his speech: "ingiusto fece me contra me
giusto" (*Inferno* XIII, l. 72).[94] By the contrast he establishes,
Dante asks us to view Cato's suicide as the enactment of a veritable voluntary death of the self by which he is reborn as a
new man.

In medieval historiography, from Henry of Ghent to Geoffrey of Monmouth and Dante, death in defense of the fatherland, "pro patria mori" (a phrase which is also to be found in

[93] This view of suicide as false transcendence is suggested by St. Augustine
in the *City of God* where he views Lucretia's suicide as a case of self-doubling,
"that Lucretia so celebrated and lauded slew the innocent, chaste, outraged
Lucretia" (I, 19; *The City of God*, trans. Marcus Dods [New York: The Modern Library, 1950], p. 24).

[94] The best analysis of the style of *Inferno* XIII is by Leo Spitzer, "Speech
and Language in *Inferno* XIII," *Italica*, 19 (1942), pp. 81-104, and now re-
printed in John Freccero, ed., *Dante: A Collection of Critical Essays*, pp. 78-
101.

the *Disticha Catonis*), appears as a work of *caritas*. They compare the self-sacrifice of a citizen for his community to the supreme self-sacrifice of Christ for the salvation of mankind.[95] Dante—to whom those giving their lives for the salvation of "patria," like the Roman Decii, appeared as "sacratissimae victimae Deciorum,"[96]—in *Convivio* links Cato to the Decii.[97] Such a link already existed in Lucan's *Pharsalia*, where Cato speaks and acts in ways that the Middle Ages found suggestive of Christ.[98] In the second book, where Brutus laments the onset of the civil war as a cosmic disaster banishing virtue from every land and calls on Cato not to keep aloof in the midst of a tottering world, Cato replies that he would willingly be a scapegoat for the nation in order to avert the madness of civil war.[99] As the world seems to fall down and is shaken with the weight "coeuntis mundi" (*Pharsalia* ii, l. 291), Cato wishes that his own blood might redeem the nations and his own death expiate the sacrilege of war: "Hic redimat sanguis populos, hac caede luatur" (l. 312). As has been pointed out, Pope Gelasius gives a Christological exegesis to this line and uses it to describe Christ's sacrifice for the re-

[95] E. H. Kantorowicz, *The King's Two Bodies: A Study in Medieval Political Theology*, pp. 240 ff. See also Hélène Pétré, *Caritas* (Louvain: Spicilegium Sacrum Lovaniense, 1948), pp. 35 ff.

[96] *Monarchia* ii, v, 15.

[97] *Convivio* iv, v, 14–6. Here there is to be found, further, the following phrase: "Onde si legge di Catone che non a se, ma a la patria e a tutto il mondo nato esser credea," which echoes Lucan's *Pharsalia*, filtered through the *Policraticus*. See on this, A. Pézard, "Du *Policraticus* à la *Divine Comédie*," *Romania*, 70 (1938–9), p. 28.

[98] The importance of Lucan for Dante has been stressed in traditional textual terms by Ettore Paratore, "Lucano e Dante," in *Antico e nuovo* (Caltanissetta: Sciascia, 1965), pp. 165-210. The tradition of Lucan in the Middle Ages, and the Christological elements of his epic, have been highlighted by Enrica Malcovati, *M. Anneo Lucano* (Milan: Hoepli, 1940), pp. 117-35 particularly.

[99] *Pharsalia* ii, ll. 286-325. A cogent study on Lucan is by Donato Gagliardi, *Lucano poeta della libertà* (Naples: Loffredo, 1958). See also C. Wirszubski, *Libertas as a Political Idea of Rome During the Late Republic and the Early Empire* (Cambridge: Cambridge University Press, 1950).

demption of mankind.[100] Above and beyond these extratextual bits of evidence, it can be shown that Dante imposes on
Cato's death the structure of Exodus.

The Libyan desert that he crosses is linked by Lucan, and
also by a widespread mythographic tradition, with Jupiter's
oracle. Labienus urges Cato, once they reach the temple of the
horned Jupiter, to consult the oracle and search into the mysterious designs of the gods.[101] The notion that in this hallowed ground Jupiter grants prayers to the travelers is held by
the second Vatican mythographer and by Servius in his
comments on the fourth book of the *Aeneid*, where Vergil
speaks of Jupiter Ammon granting the gift of water to
Dionysios.[102] But Cato, unlike Capaneus' blasphemy against
Jupiter in *Inferno* XIV, refuses to indulge in divination. He departs from the altar leaving Ammon "non exploratum" (*Pharsalia* IX, l. 586) and believing that "Juppiter est quodcumque
vides, quodcumque moveris" (l. 580), a line which is quoted
by Dante in the Epistle to Cangrande as the only pagan
auctoritas on the universality of the *lumen divinum* beside the
revelations that the Holy Ghost has proffered through

---

[100] A. Bourgery, ed., *La Guerre civile* (Paris: Les Belles Lettres, 1926), I, 45.
Bourgery quotes Pope Gelasius, *CSEL* XXXV, 458, 3. See also *Monarchia* II, v,
17 where, quoting Cicero's *De Officiis* I, 31, Dante writes of Cato's liberty:
"Catoni vero cum incredibilem natura tribuisset gravitatem, eamque perpetua constantia roborasset, semperque in proposito susceptoque consilio
permansisset, moriendum ei potius quam tyrampni vultus aspiciendus fuit."

[101] *Pharsalia* IX, ll. 545-65. It ought to be stressed that the Jews in the wilderness yielded to idolatry by making for themselves a molten calf and wor-
shiping and sacrificing to it (Exodus 32:6-9).

[102] The Second Vatican mythographer writes: "Mox ex arena aries ap-
paruit, qui pede elevato monstravit locum, ubi fodiens aquam posset inve-
nire. Tunc aperta terra, egressa est aqua largissima . . . in eo autem loco, ubi
aqua fluxit, templum constituit, quodo Jovis Ammonis dicitur" (G. H.
Bode, ed., *Scriptores Rerum Mythicarum Latini Tres* [Celle: 1934; rept. Hil-
desheim: G. Olms, 1968], II, pp. 102-3). Servius gives an analogous explanation: "Liber cum Indos peteret et per Xerolibyam exercitum duceret,
fatigatus siti Jovis sui patris imploravit auxilium et statim viso ariete fons
secutus est, unde factum est Jovi Ammoni ab arenis dicto simulacrum cum
capite arietino" (Thilo, ed., I, 498).

Jeremiah and the Psalms.[103] To Cato, actually, Jupiter in the shape of an animal "tortis cornibus" is a pure simulacrum, an idolatrous form of God; and Lucan remarks that "nulla sub illa cura jovis terra est" (*Pharsalia* ix, ll. 435-6), a statement which a twelfth-century anonymous commentator takes to be a pagan witnessing to the existence of the Holy Spirit.[104]

It is within this moral context that we can grasp the sense of Cato's quest for "libertà" (*Purgatorio* i, l. 71). In Lucan's epic, the civil war appears after Pompey's death as the never-ending contest between liberty and tyranny, and Cato's party is the party of liberty (*Pharsalia* ix, ll. 29-30), a virtue that can best be understood as the foundation of moral life against the sacrilege of tyranny. Cato's choice of liberty is glossed by John of Salisbury in his *Policraticus* as an act that brings together both the political and the spiritual aspects of that virtue. Although John follows St. Augustine in condemning Cato's suicide, he praises him, in a long chapter in which he denounces divination, for not lapsing into idolatrous practices, and postulates the moral identity between idolatrous worship and acquiescence to political tyranny:

> Cato in Libya extremae difficultatis angustia coarctatus Hammonem Jovem dedignatus est consultare ratus sibi rationem sufficere ut persuaderet servandam libertatem et non modo dominationis Caesareae iugum sed omnem notam turpitudinem licet in eo erraverit quod auctoritate propria vitae munus abiecit. . . .[105]

[103] *The Letters of Dante*, ed. Paget Toynbee, 2nd ed. (Oxford: Clarendon Press, 1966), Epistole x, paragraph 22, p. 185.

[104] Tullio Gregory, *Platonismo medioevale: studi e ricerche* (Rome: Istituto storico italiano per il Medio Evo, 1958), p. 129.

[105] John of Salisbury, *Policraticus*, ed. Clemens C. I. Webb (Frankfurt A.-M.: Minerva G.M.B.H., 1965), i, ii, 27. The passage reads: "When Cato, in Africa, found himself hemmed in by difficulties on all sides he did not deign to consult Jupiter Hammon, for he thought that reason sufficed to advise that liberty must be preserved and that not merely the yoke of Caesar's domination but even the slightest suspicion of baseness were to be shunned, though he did indeed err in casting away the gift of life by his own act." The translation is taken from *Frivolities of Courtiers and Footprints of Philosophers*,

Going beyond John of Salisbury, Dante views Cato's journey through the desert of temptation, his shunning the tyranny of the idols, his self-sacrifice for mankind, and his quest for freedom as elements that make Cato's redemption the secular reenactment of Exodus. This paradigm of history uncovers the meaning of history as a movement from the slavery of Egypt to the liberty of Jerusalem. Thus Cato's suicide, for Dante, far from being a sign of weakness in the face of adversity as Augustine had interpreted it, is a veritable martyrdom.[106] The body that he left in Utica, the "veste," he will wear more luminously on the day of the final Resurrection (ll. 73-5) at the end of time, when the perishable nature will be clothed with the imperishable (I Corinthians 15:53). In *Convivio*, Dante states that he has found no other man more worthy of signifying God than the Roman Cato.[107] It is only appropriate that in *Purgatorio* the new creation of history should start with this old man.

Let me summarize thus far by saying that Dante views history as the ground of God's providential purpose: the *opus conditionis*, dramatized in the corrupt human statue, belongs to the reality of a lost Eden, a state of perfection which man would have enjoyed on earth; the *opus restaurationis* is also of the temporal order, and, precisely because of the historical concreteness of Cato, Dante shows how Roman history is constitutive of the redemptive process. Through Cato, to whom Dante applies the typology of Exodus, the order of reality from time to nature and history is radically renewed or in the process of being renewed. The two figures, situated in two antithetical orders of spiritual experience, mark the pilgrim's own askesis from the condition of old man to his redemption in a new man. By the adoption of Cato to begin the new history, Dante figures the necessary unity between historical process and prophecy: the end of the historical process

---

trans. Joseph B. Pike (Minneapolis: The University of Minnesota Press, 1938), p. 142.

[106] *De Civitate Dei* xix, 4.

[107] *Convivio* iv, xxviii, 15.

can be none other than the imposition of redemption upon history.

A final remark must be made about the suggested analogue between the redemptive schemes of Dante and Alanus. The analogy is not simply a texture of verbal echoes and recalls; rather, it exemplifies in a fundamental way the strategy of repetition, in the etymological sense of the term as *re-petere*, to search again into the possibilities of conversion. History, as the allegory of renewal, makes a fresh start by going back to the past, and, through a theology of hope, opens up to the belief that the new will arrive. Like the figural pattern of history it describes, repetition is indeed a "recollection forward."[108]

In this back and forth movement of metaphors and concepts, the passage of *Purgatorio* seems to question the very figuration of renewal that ostensibly it celebrates. The episode of Cato is, in effect, a rewriting, a revision of the same metaphors of nature and history in *Inferno* xiv. Literary revision, for Dante, attempts to give a mimetic representation of the redemption of history, and by what might be called the figural openness of Dante's poetic language attempts to disclose history's quest for an *eschaton*, the silence of the end where history's meaning comes into being. But ironically, at the very moment of the palinode the text fleetingly alludes to its own possible poetic snares. I shall explore later the extension and centrality of this implied poetics in the *Divine Comedy*.

[108] For this sense of repetition, see S. Kierkegaard, *Repetition*, trans. Walter Lowrie (Princeton: Princeton University Press, 1941).

CHAPTER 2

Rhetoric and History

THE question of the relation between literary myth and history, the object of serious critical reflection throughout the Middle Ages, much as it is now, has elicited radically contrasting views. Isidore of Seville's canonical definitions distinguish between *historia*, *argumentum*, and *fabula*. *Historia*, to him, is the discipline in which events have a firm truth, "res vera"; *argumentum* is the mode in which the probability of events is envisioned; while *fabula* designates a fictional narrative without any basis in fact.[1] Isidore's sharp distinctions were followed but somewhat mitigated by Hugh of St. Victor, who acknowledges, as Chenù has shown,[2] the ambiguities inherent to the term *historia*. As a secular literary form, *historia*—what we now call historiography—belongs to grammar, the

---

[1] After discussing some types of historiography, such as annals, ephemerides and calendars, Isidore gives the following definitions: "Historiae sunt res verae quae facta sunt; argumenta sunt quae etsi facta non sunt, fieri tamen possunt; fabulae vero sunt quae non factae sunt nec fieri possunt" (*Etym.* I, xliv, 5).

[2] M.-D. Chenù, *Nature, Man and Society in the Twelfth Century*, trans. J. Taylor and L. K. Little (Chicago: University of Chicago Press, 1968), pp. 165–77. For a survey of the notion of history in the early Church Fathers, see Antonio Quacquarelli, *La concezione della storia nella società dei primi secoli dopo Cristo* (Bari: Adriatica Editrice, 1968). A convenient delineation of the patristic views on history can be found in L. G. Patterson, *God and History in Early Christian Thought: A Study of Themes from Justin Martyr to Gregory the Great* (London: Adam and Charles Black, 1967). A comprehensive view of *historia* in ancient and modern times is R. G. Collingwood, *The Idea of History* (Oxford: Clarendon Press, 1946).

science of letters in Isidore's etymology,[3] and is enumerated by Hugh along with fables and tropes. But *historia* also indicates for him the sequence of events in the Christian dispensation, the actual content of the religious experience, which, not at all a detemporalized and abstract doctrine, takes place in a world of history and is the basis of allegorical investigation.[4] Dante's theological structure of history, as has been delineated in the preceding chapter, falls partly within this category of salvation history.

Yet, there is a way in which Dante is far removed from the theoretical positions of Isidore and explores the very ambiguity of history posited by Hugh of St. Victor. In the fourth treatise of *Convivio* he refers to both the *Thebaid* and the *Aeneid* as "istoria,"[5] ostensibly to elide the line of demarcation between those literary myths and history. His procedure,

[3] "Grammatica est scientia recteque loquendi, et origo et fundamentum liberalium litterarum. Haec in disciplinis post litteras communes inventa est. . . . Grammatica autem a litteris nomen accepit: enim Graeci litteras vocant. . . . Divisiones autem Grammaticae artis a quibusdam triginta dinumerantur . . . prosae, fabulae, historiae" (*Etym.* I, v, 1-4). Cf. also Hugh of St. Victor, *Didascalicon*, trans. J. Taylor (New York and London: Columbia University Press, 1968), p. 88.

[4] In the prologue to *De Sacramentis Christianae Fidei*, *PL* 176, col. 185, Hugh writes that "historia est rerum gestarum narratio, quae in prima significatione litterae continetur." Cf. Chenù, p. 167. See also *Didascalicon* VI, 3-4: "But if we take the meaning of the word more broadly, it is not unfitting that we call by the name 'history' not only the recounting of actual deeds but also the first meaning of any narrative which uses words according to their proper nature. And in this sense of the word, I think that all the books of either testament, in the order in which they were listed earlier, belong to this study in their literal meaning. . . . You have in history the means through which to admire God's deeds, in allegory the means through which to believe his mysteries. . . . After the reading of history, it remains for you to investigate the mysteries of allegories" (Taylor's translation, pp. 137-9).

[5] Dante, *Convivio*. The passages read: "E però dice Stazio, lo dolce poeta, nel primo de la Tebana Istoria, che quando Adrasto, rege de li Argi, vide Polinice coverto d'un cuoio di leone, . . . esso divenne stupido" (IV, xxv, 6); "Quanto spronare fu quello, quando esso Enea sostenette solo con Sibilla a intrare ne lo Inferno a cercare de l'anima di suo padre Anchise, contra tanti pericoli, come nel sesto de la detta istoria si dimostra" (IV, xxvi, 9).

in effect, resembles St. Augustine's formulation. While in *De Musica* St. Augustine acknowledges that grammar is the custodian of history ("custos ille videlicit historiae"),[6] he gives in *De Ordine* a more complex and nuanced view of the problem. History is still considered a part of grammar, and the word grammar, he says, means literature, "unum nomen sed res infinita, multiplex," a body of knowledge which contains events worthy of being remembered and encompasses mythological events such as the flight of Daedalus.[7] Augustine, who, like Dante, compresses secular history and fables within the economy of the *ordo salutis*, will preserve especially in the *City Of God* the unique authority of salvation history but he also insists that there is a common moral exemplariness binding the domains of fiction and history.[8] In this sense he seems

[6] Augustine, *De Musica* II, i, 1: "Atque scias velim totam illam scientiam, quae grammatica graece, latine autem litteratura nominatur, historia custodiam profiteri, vel solam, ut subtilior docet ratio; vel maxime, ut etiam pinguia corda concedunt . . . reprehendet grammaticus, custos ille videlicit historia . . . " (*PL* 32, col. 1099).

[7] Augustine, *De Ordine* II, xii, 37: "Poterat iam perfecta essa grammatica sed, quia ipso nomine profiteri se litteras clamat—unde etiam Latine litteratura dicitur—factum est, ut, quicquid dignum memoria litteris mandaretur, ad eam necessario pertineret. Itaque unum quidem nomen, sed res infinita multiplex curarum plenior quam iocunditatis aut veritatis huic disciplinae accessit, historia non tam ipsis historicis quam grammaticis laboriosa. Quis enim ferat imperitum uideri hominem, qui volasse Daedalum non audierit, mendacem illum, qui finxerit, stultum, qui crediderit, impudentem, qui interrogauerit, non uideri, aut in quo nostros familiares grauiter miserari soleo, qui si non responderint, quid uocata sit mater Euryali, accusantur inscitiae, cum ipsi eos, a quibus ea rogantur, uanos et ineptos nec curiosos audeant appellare?" (*CCSL* XXIX).

[8] The notion of the exemplary value of history is practically a cliché in the Middle Ages. Isidore of Seville writes: "historia est narratio rei gestae quae in praeterito facta sunt dignoscuntur" (*Etym.* I, xli). Cf. St. Augustine, *De Doctrina Christiana* II, xxviii, in *CCSL* XXXII. Cf. also *De Vera Religione* XXVI, 49, in *CCSL* XXXII: "Primam (aetatem) in uberibus utilis historiae, quae nutrit exemplis." For a detailed study, see Giuseppe Amari, *Il concetto di storia in S. Agostino* (Rome: Edizioni Paoline, 1951), pp. 74-103. More generally, see Eva Matthews Sanford, "The Study of Ancient History in the Middle Ages," *Journal of the History of Ideas*, 5 (1944), pp. 21-43; D. T. Starnes, "Purpose in the Writing of History," *Modern Philology*, 20 (1922-3), pp. 281-300 for bibliography.

essentially to move in the fold of classical rhetoric[9] and particularly in the wake of Cicero, who systematically links rhetoric and history. In a remarkable passage on the importance of oratory, Cicero views history as "magistra vitae" and commends the orator as the best witness to the passing of the ages, with skills to distribute and arrange the subject matter and give guidance to human existence.[10] It is precisely against Cicero's sense of history as the world of man's own construction that Dante directs his critique in *Inferno* xxvi. By a close-up on the canto, I plan to show that these humanistic values by themselves issue into a tragic history but that at the same time for Dante there is a constant interplay and even reversals between history and rhetorical fictions: the distance between them is not as clear-cut as Isidore would want it.

The pivotal value of this canto in relation to the rest of the poem has frequently been remarked by critics even when they have not always agreed on its sense.[11] Their views range from

[9] Amari, pp. 27 ff. See also H. I. Marrou, *The Meaning of History*, trans. R. J. Olsen (Baltimore: Helicon, 1966). For St. Augustine's indebtedness to the classical tradition, see C. N. Cochrane, *Christianity and Classical Culture: A Study of Thought and Action from Augustus to Augustine* (Oxford: Oxford University Press, 1968); Harald Hagendahl, *Augustine and the Latin Classics*, 2 vols. (Stockholm: Almqvist and Wiksell, 1967).

[10] "Historia vero testis temporum, lux veritatis, vita memoriae, magistra vitae, nuntia vetustatis, quae voce alia nisi oratoris, immortalitati commendatur?" (*De Oratore* ii, ix, 36, in *Libri Rhetorici*, ed. J. A. Ernst [London: A. J. Valpy, 1830], ii, 961). For the relation between rhetoric and history in Cicero, see M. Rambaud, *Cicéron et l'histoire romaine* (Paris: Les Belles Lettres, 1953); B. L. Ullmann, "History and Tragedy," *Transactions of the American Philological Association*, 73 (1942), pp. 25-53. For a more general survey and bibliography, see Nancy S. Struever, *The Language of History in the Renaissance: Rhetoric and Historical Consciousness in Florentine Humanism* (Princeton: Princeton University Press, 1970), pp. 28-39.

[11] The bibliography on *Inferno* xxvi from 1950 up to 1964 is handily available in E. Esposito, *Gli studi danteschi dal 1950 al 1964* (Rome: Centro editoriale internazionale, 1965), pp. 269-75. Among the commentators, Hermann Gmelin conveniently gathers classical references to Ulysses; see his *Die Göttliche Komödie Kommentar I: Die Hölle* (Stuttgart: E. Klettverlag, 1954), pp. 380-402. I shall list here some of the items which directly or indirectly bear on my argument. Benedetto Croce, *La poesia di Dante*, 2nd ed. (Bari: Laterza, 1948), views Ulysses as "parte di Dante stesso, cioè

attempted definitions of Ulysses' sin as *mala curiositas*, evil counseling etc., to a reading of the canto as the dramatic focus for a series of moral oppositions (Ulysses-Aeneas, Ulysses-Cato, Ulysses-Adam, Ulysses-Dante). The specific nature of these oppositions is condensed admirably by Scott in a con-

dell'anelito al grande, che la reverenza e l'umiltà cristiana potevano in lui infrenare ma non distruggere" (p. 92). Bruno Nardi, *Dante e la cultura medioevale* (Bari: Laterza, 1949), pp. 153-64, insisting on the importance of Cicero's *De Finibus* v, xvii-xix, on Dante's conception, interprets Ulysses as the personification of reason "insofferente dei limiti" (p. 161), and in this sense, he is the antithesis of Vergil and the equivalent of Adam's pride. Rocco Montano, "I modi della narrazione di Dante," *Convivium*, 26 (1958), pp. 561-3, sees the sin of Ulysses as *mala curiositas*; so does Joseph A. Mazzeo, *Medieval Cultural Tradition in Dante's* Comedy (Ithaca, N.Y.: Cornell University Press, 1960), pp. 205-12, and Mario Fubini, "Il canto XXVI dell' *Inferno*," in *Letture dantesche*, ed. Giovanni Getto (Florence: Sansoni, 1962), pp. 491-513. John Freccero reads the story of Ulysses as the allegory of the flight of the soul analogous to Dante's attempt in *Convivio*, which the pilgrim transcends, in his "Dante's Prologue Scene: II. The Wings of Ulysses," *Dante Studies*, 84 (1966), pp. 12-25. David Thompson has examined the tradition of Ulysses both as the paradigm of *via philosophica* and in contrast to Aeneas, in "Dante's Ulysses and the Allegorical Journey," *Dante Studies*, 85 (1967), pp. 33-58; now in *Dante's Epic Journeys* (Baltimore: The Johns Hopkins University Press, 1974). More recently, John Freccero has given a more extended reading of the canto in his "Dante's Ulysses: From Epic to Novel," in *Concepts of the Hero in the Middle Ages and the Renaissance* . . . , ed. Norman T. Burns and Christopher J. Reagan (Albany: State University of New York Press, 1975), pp. 101-19. Giorgio Padoan, "Ulisse *fandi fictor* e le vie della sapienza, *Studi danteschi*, 37 (1960), pp. 21-61, argues for the view of Ulysses as a contriver of deceptions, "scelerum inventor" (p. 24). Antonino Pagliaro attempts to refute Padoan's argument by emphasizing that "l'Ulisse dantesco è l'immagine, a livello epico, dell'amore per il sapere" (*Ulisse: ricerche semantiche sulla* Divina Commedia [Messina and Florence: D'Anna, 1967], I, 403). The contrast between Ulysses and Cato has been highlighted by P. W. Damon, "Dante's Ulysses and the Mythic Tradition," in *Medieval Secular Literature*, ed. W. Matthews (Berkeley and Los Angeles: University of California Press, 1965), pp. 25-45. The contrast between Ulysses and Elijah in *Inferno* XXVI is treated by Richard H. Lansing, "Two Similes in Dante's *Commedia*: The Shipwrecked Swimmer and Elijah's Ascent," *Romance Philology*, 28 (1974), pp. 161-77. Most of these ideas are discussed by John A. Scott, *"Inferno* XXVI: Dante's Ulysses," *Lettere italiane*, 23 (1971), pp. 145-86. For a general view of Ulysses, see W. B. Stanford, *The Ulysses Theme*, 2nd ed. (Oxford: Blackwell, 1963).

clusive statement where the strands of his argument are brought together: "The Greek hero is guilty of transgressing the laws of nature and society. As a man, he should not have ventured into the uninhabitable world; as an old man, he should have returned to the haven of Ithaca and prepared himself for death; as a king, it was his duty to acquire the supreme virtues of justice and prudence."[12]

Most of these critical contributions have valuably probed the massive stratified allusions of the canto but they have tended to bypass, with few exceptions, a crucial aspect of *Inferno* XXVI, namely its rhetorical articulations. The neglect is not surprising: it has been a commonplace in Dante scholarship, ever since Auerbach,[13] to bracket the question of rhetoric on the implicit assumption that in Dante's text literary language gives a happy and unproblematical representation of the poet's moral vision. Accordingly, the critic's practice has been to acknowledge the correspondences and harmony that the text voices and to translate its rhetorical complexities into explicit thematic and ideological equivalents. The neglect, however, is remarkable since it is precisely Dante's own sense of the power of language which is thrown into doubt in the canto of Ulysses. The prophetic faith that often is assumed to sustain the poem is systematically questioned, not simply in terms of a deliberate secularism but, more fundamentally, by a reflection on the nature of language, its possibilities to produce knowledge and its constitutive error.

It can be easily shown that the primary concern of this canto is rhetoric: the tongues of fire that *conceal* the sinners; the oblique allusion to Elijah's prophecy (l. 35); the formal decor in the exchange between the poet and the hero of the epic world, Vergil and Ulysses; the frequent allusions to the

[12] Scott, pp. 185-6.

[13] A reading in essentially rhetorical-stylistic terms of *Inferno* is by Edoardo Sanguineti, *Interpretazione di Malebolge* (Florence: Olschki, 1961). The sense of the importance of genres can be obtained in Renato Poggioli, "Tragedy or Romance? A reading of the Paolo and Francesca Episode in Dante's *Inferno*," *PMLA*, 72 (1957), pp. 313-58.

epics, *Aeneid* (l. 93), *Thebaid* (l. 54) and *Achilleid* (l. 62); the more obvious fact that the canto tells the story of the mind-bewitching orator—the *fandi fictor* in G. Padoan's formula[14]—who moves men by rhetorical blandishments and incantatory language to the pursuit of "virtute e canoscenza" (l. 120) are explicit elements of the rhetorical substance of the canto.

Yet, although this aspect of language is given a thematic status, and in some measure affords a key to the interpretations of Ulysses, rhetoric does not exhaust itself purely in the deployment of the deceits and seductions of language. For the canto enacts, at the same time, a protracted reflection on the secular city and the pattern of secular history: Florence, Prato, Thebes, Troy, Rome and the quest for a "nova terra" (l. 137) constitute the geography, the space of history within which rhetoric acts out its pretension to be a creative discipline that fashions history, a veritable tool to manipulate and order historical consciousness.[15]

More explicitly, *Inferno* XXVI is articulated within a significant contrast: in the opening lines (ll. 1-12), there is Dante's own intimation that the city of Florence will soon reach its apocalyptic end; in the closing lines (ll. 136-42), Ulysses' vision of the new land climaxes in a catastrophe. Rhetoric shuttles between these poles and involves both the poet's own voice and Ulysses' task. To speak of rhetoric, on the one hand, in terms of its supposed perspectives on the historical

---

[14] Giorgio Padoan, "Ulisse *fandi fictor* e le vie della sapienza," pp. 21-61.

[15] The political values of rhetoric have been frequently the object of analysis. See Concetto Marchesi, "Il compendio volgare dell'etica aristotelica a le fonti del VI libro del *Tresor*," *Giornale storico della letteratura italiana*, 42 (1903), pp. 1-74; and by the same author, L'Etica Nicomachea *nella tradizione latina medievale* (Messina: Trimarchi, 1904). For the general idea of the importance of rhetoric on historiography, see Claudio Varese, *Storia e politica nella prosa del Quattrocento* (Turin: Einaudi, 1961); cf. also A. Galletti, *L'eloquenza* (*dalle origini al XVI secolo*), Storia dei generi letterari italiani (Milan: Vallardi, 1938); H. Wieruszowsky, "*Ars Dictaminis* in the Time of Dante," *Medievalia et Humanistica*, I (1943), pp. 95-108; Nancy S. Struever, *The Language of History*, pp. 101-15.

order, as if it were nothing less than a philosophy of history, an authoritative manner of choosing the possibilities of history, and, on the other hand, as a property of language forces us to clarify our exegetical procedure.

Dante's point of departure is precisely political rhetoric as a process of education by which the making of the city is attempted. But there is a drastic turn in his thought and we shall follow this logical shift from the political view of rhetoric to the awareness that language is an inherently unstable and murky instrument. If this is the case, what is the meaning of history governed by a language which is inevitably trapped in its own instability? What is the status of Dante's text? It is within this broad configuration of problems and questions here summarily sketched that this chapter inscribes itself.

In general, the symbolic interaction of city and language is a persistent motif in Dante's imagination, so much so that they are often interchangeable terms: Babel, the literal city of language and the radical emblem of chaos is, in Dante's typology, the antitype of the Incarnation. If the Incarnation is the account of the descent into humility of the Word as it bridges the gap between Heaven and Earth, Babel is the allegory of the confusion of tongues, the narrative of the failure of language to bridge that gap. But in *Inferno* XXVI, it is not through these conventional medieval archetypes that the relationship between history and language is worked out. Dante starts with a specific text and a ready-made manual as his polemical target: his own teacher Brunetto Latini's humanistic myth of rhetoric as man's medium to act upon the formlessness of the world and make the world the place of life.

In the *Tresor*, for instance, the book that Brunetto recommends to his student at the close of *Inferno* XV (after the evocation of the tragic history of Florence and the prophecy of Dante's exile from it),[16] the creative link between rhetoric and

---

[16] "Gente vien con la quale esser non deggio. / Sieti raccomandato il mio Tesoro, / nel qual io vivo ancora, e più non cheggio" (*Inferno* XV, ll. 118-20). For the prophecy of Dante's exile, see *Inferno* XV, ll. 61-6 and my chapter 3.

the possibilities of order in the city are the explicit center of reflection:

> Cicero says that rhetoric, that is to say the science of language, is the highest science for governing the city; for if there were no language, there would be no cities, nor would we establish justice and human company. And while speech is given to all men, Cato says that wisdom is given to a few.[17]

Rhetoric, for him, is a theory of education and even the foundation of history because it opens up the options of history, the continuous ethical choices man must make between violence and rational order.

It is precisely in terms of the myth of education that the conceptual substance of the canto is unfolded. We ought to remark, perhaps, on the aptness of the choice of Ulysses to illustrate this motif. For the Odyssey, in the tradition of neoplatonic philosophical allegoresis, is the allegory of education.[18] The story of Ulysses leaving Ithaca and returning,

[17] Brunetto Latini, *Li Livres dou Tresor*, ed. Francis J. Carmody (Berkeley and Los Angeles: University of California Press, 1948), p. 317: "Tulles dit que la plus haute science de cité governner si est rectorique, ce est a dire science dou parler; car se parleure ne fust, cités ne seroit, ne nus establissemens de justise ne de humaine compaignie; e sa soit ce que parleure soit donée a touz homes, Catons dit que sapience est donée a poi. . . . " For the importance of Brunetto's *Tresor* in Dante's works, see Luigi Mario Capelli, "Ancora del *Tresor* nelle opere di Dante," *Giornale dantesco*, 5 (1898), pp. 548-56. For the more general problem of Brunetto's political activity and Dante, see Walter Goetz, "Dante und Brunetto Latini," *Deutsches Dante Jahrbuch*, 20 (1938), pp. 78-99; cf. also more recent contributions by Charles T. Davis, *Dante and the Idea of Rome* (Oxford: Clarendon Press, 1957), pp. 86-94; and his "Brunetto Latini and Dante," *Studi medievali*, ser. 3, 8 (1967), pp. 421-50. For the "linguistic" perversion of Brunetto, as supposedly seen by Dante in *Inferno* xv, see André Pézard, *Dante sous la pluie de feu* (Paris: Vrin, 1950), pp. 113-30. Cf. also chapter 3, notes 49-50.

[18] The motif is studied by Hugo Rahner, "Odysseus at the Mast," in *Greek Myths and Christian Mystery*, trans. Brian Battershaw (London: Burns and Oates, 1963), pp. 328-86. Cf. Felix Buffière, *Les Mythes d'Homère et la pensée grecque* (Paris: Belles Lettres, 1956), particularly p. 376 where he quotes Seneca's *De Constantia Sapientis* ii, ii, 1. The passage is quoted by Padoan, "Ulisse

after twenty years of war and labors, back to Ithaca is the paradigm of the journey and education of the soul as it successfully returns, after its purification from the dross of materiality, to the place of origin. But to what extent is Dante's view of Ulysses' education specifically rooted in rhetoric and affected by it? Also, why should Dante draw Ulysses' philosophical experience into a distinctly rhetorical context?

The moral burden of Ulysses' "orazion picciola" in point of fact, shares the imaginative values of Ciceronian rhetoric:

> "Considerate la vostra semenza:
> Fatti non foste a viver come bruti,
> Ma per seguir virtute e canoscenza."
>
> ll. 118-20

("Consider the seed from which you spring: you were not made to live as brutes, but to follow virtue and knowledge.")

The tercet is, to begin with, a literal adaptation of the general intent of eloquence and echoes Cicero's definition that "in each part of the oration it must be considered what is fitting to life."[19] In the economy of the canto, the immediate function of the exhortation "fatti non foste a viver come bruti, / ma per seguir virtute e canoscenza," is to reverse Circe's metamorphosis of Ulysses' companions into beasts vaguely alluded to by the evocation of the goddess' lures (l. 90-2) and, in a larger sense, it connects this canto with the metamorphosis sequence of *Inferno* xxiv and xxv which will be discussed later on. More to our present concern, the lines explicitly focus on the process of *paideia*, the redemptive act of fashioning man's

---

fandi fictor," p. 34, and by Thompson, "Dante's Ulysses and the Allegorical Journey," p. 41. For a more general treatment of education, see Werner Jaeger, *Paideia: The Ideals of Greek Culture*, trans. G. Highet, 3 vols. (Oxford: Clarendon Press, 1938–45); see also H. I. Marrou, *A History of Education in Antiquity*, trans. G. Lamb (New York: New American Library, 1956).

[19] "Semperque in omni parte orationis ut vitae quid deceat est considerandum" (*Orator*, trans. H. M. Hubbell [Cambridge, Mass.: Harvard University Press, 1939], xxi, 71, p. 358).

moral life.[20] Further, the metaphor of "semenza" reinforces the motif of education: it announces a potential fruitfulness and—along with the verb "considerate"—implies man's imperative and choice to grow and shape his world; it also places the possibilities of self making—since the growth recalls the *topos* of the *homo faber* ("*fatti* non foste")—both within the will and reach of man and in the perspective of the natural order.

More important, in the elaboration of the tercet, Dante draws from Cicero's *De Inventione*[21] and, more lavishly, from a text written by his teacher Brunetto Latini. *La rettorica*, a partial translation and commentary of *De Inventione* is essentially a handbook of political education.[22] Composed while Brunetto was in exile from Florence,[23] it describes the origin of the city of life in terms of a rhetorical process, the language of which Dante weaves into the texture of *Inferno* XXVI.

In questa quarta parte del prologo vogliendo Tullio dimostrare che eloquenzia nasce e muove per cagione e per ragione ottima e onestissima, sì dice come in *alcuno*

[20] Cf. note 18. The motif of the *paideia* of Ulysses is alluded to by Bernardus Silvestris, *Commentum Super Sex Libros Eneidos Virgillii*, ed. G. Riedel (Greifswald: J. Abel, 1924), p. 21. For further bibliography, see Thompson, "Dante's Ulysses," pp. 56-7. The question of education in the *Divine Comedy* has been treated by John Freccero, "Infernal Inversion and Christian Conversion (*Inferno* XXXIV)," *Italica*, 42 (1965), pp. 35-41; see also Freccero's "The Sign of Satan," *Modern Language Notes*, 80 (1965), pp. 11-26.

[21] *De Inventione*, The Loeb Classical Library (Cambridge, Mass.: Harvard University Press, 1949). For the power of eloquence, see the initial remarks "multas urbes constitutas, plurima bella restincta, firmissimas societates, sanctissimas amicitias intelligo cum animi ratione, tum facilius eloquentia comparatas" (I, i). On the origin of the city: "Nam fuit quoddam tempus, cum in agris homines passim bestiarum modo vagabantur et sibi victu fero vitam propagabant; . . . Quo tempore quidam magnus videlicit vir et sapiens cognovit, quae materia esset, . . . deinde propter rationem atque orationem studiosius audientes ex feris et immanibus mites reddidit et mansuetos" (I, ii).

[22] Brunetto Latini, *La rettorica*, ed. Francesco Maggini (Florence: Le Monnier, 1968).

[23] On the importance of exile in Brunetto's text, cf. below chapter 3, note 51.

tempo erano gli uomini rozzi e nessci come bestie; . . . onde misusavano le forze del corpo uccidendo l'un l'atro, tolliendo le cose *per forza e per furto, luxuriando malamente* . . . Ma tuttavolta la natura, cioè la divina disposizione, non avea sparta quella bestialitade in tutti gli uomini igualmente; *ma fue alcuno savio e molto bello dicitore* il quale, vedendo che gli uomini erano acconci a ragionare *usò di parlare a lloro per recarli a divina connoscenza*, cioè ad amare Idio e 'l proximo . . . E là *dove dice dell'umano ufficio* intendo che non sapeano vivere a buoni costumi *e non conosceano prudenzia nè giustizia ne l'altre virtudi* . . . Et là dove dice "folle ardita" intendo che *folli arditi sono uomini matti e ratti* a ffare cose che non sono da ffare. . . .[24]

The series of verbal echoes in the tercet from this passage is truly impressive. Equally cogent, however, is Dante's assimilation of the conceptual structure of Brunetto's handbook to the point of turning Brunetto against himself. In the final pages of *La rettorica*, for instance, Brunetto alludes to Ulysses, much loved for his wisdom, and contrasts to him Ajax's rhetorical manipulations of the audience.[25] Dante, on the contrary, casts Ulysses as the very embodiment of persuasive eloquence. As we shall see presently, it is as if Dante views

---

[24] "In this fourth part of the prologue, Cicero wishing to show that eloquence moves and is born by a most excellent and honest cause and reason, it is said that at one time men were uncouth and unknowing like beasts; . . . thereby they misused the forces of the body, killing one another, taking things away by force and by thievery, inordinately lascivious. . . . But, nevertheless, Nature, that is to say divine disposition, had not assigned bestiality equally to all men; rather, there were some wise and very attractive speakers who, seeing that the men were wont to reason, used to speak to them in order to lead them to divine knowledge, that is, to love God and one's neighbor. . . . And there where it speaks of human duties, I understand that they did not know how to live with good customs, and they did not know prudence, nor justice, nor any other virtue. . . . And there where it says "mad and daring," I understand that mad and daring men are those mad and quick to do things which are not to be done (*La rettorica*, pp. 18-21).

[25] *La rettorica*, pp. 197-8. The story of Ulysses and Ajax is a thread running through the treatise; cf. pp. 93-4, 139.

Brunetto's statements as political idealism which he proceeds to deconstruct.

Brunetto roots the emergence of the political order in the gift of language as the fundamental tool of man's presence to himself and to the world. The orator is the civilizing agent, the Orpheus who assuages the beast within and teaches mankind the virtues of moral life.[26] This progress from the darkness of the natural condition to the stability of collective life is, to be sure, reversible. Man can always lapse into the original brutishness. Because of this, Cicero's authoritative text is always timely. By translating it Brunetto asserts the persistent historical validity of Cicero's scheme and suggests the exemplary repetition of historic patterns. Translation becomes, accordingly, the strategy by which the movement of history is enacted as an exemplary process and by which the assumption of a paradigm of a changeless history, in existence from the beginning, is disclosed. In *Inferno* xxvi Dante also dramatizes the reversibility of the process of education: Ulysses' companions are metamorphosed into beasts by "luxuriando malamente,"[27] as it were, with Circe, and Ulysses' attempt is to reshape them into their full humanity. Yet, in open contrast to Brunetto's myth of repetition, Dante shows Ulysses leading his men to final disaster.

We must stress, however, that there is no facile complacency in Brunetto's belief that order is not alien to history. Like Cicero who at the outset of *De Inventione* acknowledges the damages that eloquent men can cause to the state,[28] Bru-

[26] For the tradition of Orpheus as the poet taming beasts, see John B. Friedman, *Orpheus in the Middle Ages* (Cambridge, Mass.: Harvard University Press, 1970).

[27] Circe's metamorphosis of Ulysses' companions is strengthened by the allusion to Circe's enchantments in *Purgatorio* xiv, ll. 40-2. The inhabitants of the Arno Valley appear deprived of virtue, "ond' hanno sì mutate lor natura / li abitator della misera valle, / che par che Circe li avesse inpastura."

[28] "Saepe et multum hoc mecum cogitavi, bonine an mali plus attulerit hominibus et civitatibus copia dicendi ac summum eloquentiae studium. Nam cum et nostrae rei publicae detrimento considero et maximarum civitatum animo calamitates colligo, non minimam video per disertissimos homines invectam partem incommodorum" (*De Inventione* i, 1).

netto faces squarely the dangers of rhetoric; it can be a cohesive force and the means by which men share the same
world only if it is used wisely. But wisdom can be rhetorically simulated. Among orators, he writes, there were some
"calidi e vezzati . . . cioè per la frode e per la malizia che in
loro regnava parea che avessero in loro sapienza."[29] Ultimately, Brunetto must admit that rhetoric deals with the
world of opinion and the probable, that potentially it generates a distortion of the real because both truth and falsehood
are pleaded through this art. Because of this, he attempts to
give it philosophical dignity by making ethics its origin and
its object and by the conviction that the orator's primary obligation is the determination of moral questions.

Ostensibly Dante assimilates the conceptual framework of
Brunetto's text. Ulysses is "callido,"[30] inhabits the moral area
of fraud and claims to have wisdom. Yet he is shown at Troy
as he steals the Palladium (1. 63), the simulacrum of wisdom.
His extended claim (ll. 98-9) that he has experience of the
world as well as the vices and worth of men is undermined by
the theft of the *appearance* of wisdom. Dante even seems to
place Ulysses' experience within an ethical context. As Ulysses recounts his quest, he says:

> "Quando
> mi diparti' da Circe, che sottrasse
> me più d'un anno là presso a Gaeta,
> prima che sì Enëa la nomasse,
> né dolcezza di figlio, né la pieta
> del vecchio padre, né 'l debito amore
> lo qual dovea Penelopè far lieta,
> vincer poetero dentro a me l'ardore
> ch'i' ebbi a divenir del mondo esperto
> e de li vizi umani e del valore."
>
> ll. 90-9

[29] *La rettorica*, p. 32.

[30] For the importance of Ulysses *calliditas*, as a term indicating both heat
and astuteness, see A. Pagliaro, *Ulisse: ricerche semantiche sulla* Divina Commedia, ɪ, 380-2.

("When I parted from Circe, who held me more than a year near Gaeta before so Aeneas named it, neither fondness for my son, nor duty to an aged father, nor the love I owed Penelope and which should have made her glad, could conquer within me the burning desire I had to gain experience of the world and the vices and the worth of men.")

It has been remarked by Edward Moore that these lines bespeak Ulysses' self-dramatization as *alter Aeneas* since they are faintly modeled on Aeneas' speech to Dido.[31] The lines are also patterned on Cicero's *De Officiis*, a text of speculative philosophy largely dealing with the possibility of spiritual regeneration of Rome. In the context of moral duties, Cicero selects Ulysses as the hero who, as it is told by tragedians, feigns madness in order to remain in Ithaca and avoid the daily toil of war, a version of Achilles' own disguise for not going to Troy:

(. . . apud Homerum, optimum auctorem, talis de Ulixe nulla suspicio est), sed insimulant eum tragoediae simulatione insaniae militiam subterfugere voluisse. Non honestum consilium at utile, ut aliquis fortasse dixerit, regnare et Ithacae vivere otiose cum parentibus, cum uxore, cum filio.[32]

[31] *Aeneid* I, ll. 198-203; see also Horace, *Odes* I, vii, ll. 25-6; Edward Moore, *Studies in Dante* (Oxford: Clarendon Press, 1896), I, 180 ff. Cf. Hermann Gmelin, *Kommentar I: Die Hölle*, p. 392. The idea of duty expressed in *Inferno* XXVI, ll. 94-9 has been studied by Umberto Bosco, *Dante vicino* (Rome: Sciascia, 1966), pp. 173-96. See also the emphasis given to "debito" and "dovea" by J. M. Ferrante, "The Relation of Speech to Sin in the *Inferno*," *Dante Studies*, 87 (1969), p. 41. For an entirely different view, see Lanfranco Caretti, "Etica e retorica dantesche," in *Dante, Manzoni e altri studi* (Milan-Naples: Ricciardi, 1964), pp. 31-56.

[32] "Ulysses thought his ruse expedient, as the tragic poets have recounted it (for in Homer, a most reliable authority, no such suspicion is cast on Ulysses). But the tragedies charge him with trying to escape a soldier's service by simulating madness. The trick was not morally right; and someone might perhaps say that it was expedient for him to keep his throne and live at ease in

Cicero praises Ulysses for not persisting in that pretended madness and not acquiescing to the temptations of domestic tranquility. But Ulysses' new journey—in Dante's text—is not to Troy but on the open road of the quest: thus, the Ciceronian "source," where there is an indication of public duty, is ironic both because it is taken out of its original context and appropriated, and because Ulysses' speech resonates with its own surrogate language of domestic duty ("*debito amor*" "*dovea* far lieta"). As Ulysses quotes Cicero to justify the higher moral imperative of the journey, he contrives ethical fictions. Far from being an ethical quest, or the case of rhetoric supported by ethics, rhetoric appears without foundation and is itself the "ground" of choices given as ethics.

But there is a further reason for the philosophical allusion, one which has to do with the coupling of Ulysses—the paradigm of the philosophical journey—with Brunetto's rhetoric. In a sense, Dante's strategy is to reverse the neoplatonic commentators who extrapolate a truth and a model of certitude from the world of fiction. Dante, by contrast, historicizes philosophy, dissolves the abstract *exemplum* into the world of rhetoric and history, the ground where opinions are debated, where one continuously copes with the temptation of truth and falsehood. As Dante abandons the philosophical allegorizations of Ulysses and draws the Greek hero into a rhetorical context, he is engaged in a remarkable subversion of the very possibilities of philosophical discourse. The shift from the abstract rationality of philosophy to a recovery of the world of history is operative, it should be remarked, in the movement from the *Convivio* to the *Divine Comedy*: the *Convivio* ends with a neoplatonic interpretation of the *Aeneid*;

Ithaca with his parents, wife and son" (*De Officiis*, trans. W. Miller [New York: Putnam's Sons, 1928], III, xxvi, 97, pp. 372-3). Part of the irony of the passage is, of course, that the "folle volo" (*Inferno* XXVI, l. 125) is neither simulation nor a trick. It might be also mentioned that Brunetto Latini, in the context of faith, as opposed to deception which undermines the cities, mentions Cicero's "delli offici" (*La rettorica*, p. 26).

the *Divine Comedy* begins with the resumption of a neo-platonic attempt at self-transcendence which fails[33] and with the subsequent rediscovery of the *Aeneid* as the poem of history. By challenging the value of Ulysses as philosophy's *exemplum*, Dante is telling us that abstract models of philosophy, and its truth—by themselves—are useless insofar as they lack the mark of irreducible historicity, that truth is an involuntary event, part and parcel of the world of the probable and the contingent. At the same time, the irony of turning to one's teacher in order to dismantle the myth of education is transparent. For Dante the failure of political rhetoric does not depend simply on its inability to make crucial moral distinctions, but on something prior: the fundamental rupture between truth and a language which is caught up in the world of contingency. In this sense, fraud is not simply the sin of Ulysses, but the very condition of discourse.

An intimation of this problem occurs when Ulysses defines the object of his quest as "virtute e canoscenza" which bears a close verbal resemblance to Brunetto's formulation "non conosceano né prudenza né giustizia né l'altre virtudi." In Brunetto's text the recall to prudence and justice tells us that these are the cardinal virtues. More clearly, Cicero in *De Inventione* makes virtue the *telos* of rhetoric and describes how it subsumes the four moral virtues:

> Est igitur in eo genere omnes res una vi atque uno nomine amplexa virtus. Nam virtus est animi habitus naturae modo atque rationi consentaneus—Habet igitur partes quattuor: prudentiam, iustitiam, fortitudinem, temperantiam.[34]

---

[33] Ulrich Leo, "The Unfinished *Convivio* and Dante's Rereading of the *Aeneid*," *Medieval Studies*, 13 (1951), pp. 41-64. John Freccero, "Dante's Prologue Scene," pp. 4-7.

[34] "Everything in this class is embraced in one meaning and under one name, virtue. Virtue may be defined as a habit of mind in harmony with reason and the order of nature. . . . It has four parts: wisdom, justice, courage, temperance" (*De Inventione* II, 159, trans. H. M. Hubbell).

This definition of virtue suggests a further conceptual nexus connecting Ulysses' journey with the first canto of *Purgatorio*, where the four cardinal virtues are recovered by the pilgrim. Other links, to be sure, exist between the two scenes:[35] from our point of view, Dante does not seem so much to force upon us the moral ambiguity of virtue, pagan virtue versus Christian virtues, since *Purgatorio* I is the abode of Cato. The virtues are the same, part of the ongoing moral exercise. By making virtue the purpose of rhetoric Dante lays open the intrinsic error of rhetorical language: virtue is contained within the rhetorical statement but its fulfillment lies outside of that statement, is always at a distance. Ulysses attempts to travel the distance that separates words from facts and to fill those words with the reality of experience. In contrast to Cicero's notion of Ulysses' simulated madness, Dante shows the real madness of the Greek hero: his madness lies in his belief that the distance can be bridged by an act of knowledge.[36] Ulysses literally crosses the frontiers to reach an imaginary and truly "utopian" space where his language may have literal truth. For Dante this transgression is a tragic violation and actually exposes the madness of that philosophical discourse which pretends that there is an equivalence between virtue and knowledge and that it can reach the heart of knowledge where the differences of the world collapse into an absolute unity. The text gives a remarkable exemplification of the inadequacy of knowledge and rhetoric to reach truth. As Ulysses is about to trespass the world's boundaries, the address to his companions is Dante's pretext to reflect on the confusions inherent in language.

[35] P. W. Damon, "Dante's Ulysses and the Mythic Tradition," in *Medieval Secular Literature*, pp. 41-5.

[36] For a conventional gloss on "folle volo," see Rocco Montano, "Il 'folle volo' di Ulisse," *Delta*, N.S., 2 (1952), pp. 10-32. For the theme of madness in the *Divine Comedy*, cf. Umberto Bosco, "La 'follia' di Dante," *Lettere italiane*, 10 (1958), pp. 417-30. They both undervalue the imaginative and threatening power of madness which is probed in an entirely different context by Michel Foucault, *Folie et déraison: histoire de la folie à l'âge classique* (Paris: Plon, 1961). Cf. also my remarks on madness in chapter 7 of this study.

"L'un lito e l'altro vidi infin la Spagna,
  fin nel Morrocco, e l'isola d'i Sardi,
  e l'altre che quel mare intorno bagna.
Io e' compagni eravam vecchi e tardi
  quando venimmo a quella foce stretta
  dov' Ercule segnò li suoi riguardi
acciò che l'uom più oltre non si metta;
  da la man destra mi lasciai Sibilia,
  da l'altra già m'avea lasciata Setta.
'O frati,' dissi, 'che per cento milia
  perigli siete giunti a l'occidente,
  a questa tanto picciola vigilia
d'i nostri sensi ch'è del rimanente
  non vogliate negar l'esperïenza,
  di retro al sol, del mondo sanza gente.
Considerate la vostra semenza:
  fatti non foste a viver come bruti,
  ma per seguir virute e canoscenza.'
Li miei compagni fec' io sì aguti,
  con questa orazion picciola, al cammino,
  che a pena poscia li avrei ritenuti;
e volta nostra poppa nel mattino,
  de' remi facemmo ali al folle volo,
  sempre acquistando dal lato mancino.
Tutte le stelle già de l'altro polo
  vedea la notte, e 'l nostro tanto basso,
  che non surgëa fuor del marin suolo.
Cinque volte racceso e tante casso
  lo lume era di sotto da la luna,
  poi che 'ntrati eravam ne l'alto passo,
quando n'apparve una montagna, bruna
  per la distanza, e parvemi alta tanto
  quanto veduta non avëa alcuna.
Noi ci allegrammo, e tosto tornò in pianto;
  ché de la nova terra un turbo nacque
  e percosse del legno il primo canto."

Inferno XXVI, ll. 103–38

("The one shore and the other I saw as far as Spain, as far as Sardinia and the other islands which that sea bathes around. I and my companions were old and slow when we came to that narrow outlet where Hercules marked his limits so that man should not pass beyond. On my right hand I left Seville, on the other had already left Ceuta. 'O brothers,' I said, 'who through a hundred thousand perils have reached the west, to this so brief vigil of the senses that remain to us, choose not to deny experience, in the sun's track, of the unpeopled world. Consider the seed from which you spring: you were not made to live as brutes, but to follow virtue and knowledge.' With this little speech I made my companions so eager for the road that then I could hardly have held them back; and with our stern turned to the morning, we made of the oars wings for the mad flight, always gaining on the left. The night then saw all the stars of the other pole, and ours so low that it did not rise from the ocean floor. Five times had the light beneath the moon been rekindled and as often quenched since we had entered that deep passage, when there appeared to us a mountain, dim by distance, and it seemed to me of such a height as I had never seen before. We became glad and soon the joy turned to grief, for from the new land a whirlwind rose and struck the forepart of the ship.")

The speech is divided into two parts, the first half to his companions, the second to Vergil. The "orazion" is set within the fictional context of romance, in the imaginative area beyond the known world but not quite the Edenic place toward which the hero unwittingly ventures. It is in this open and unbounded region that the utopia of rhetoric is dramatized both because it is placed literally somewhere else than in the city, nowhere, and because it appears in its vital impulse to contain within itself the evocation of the past and the quest for knowledge. This strategy of isolating language in a spatial vacuum discloses its peculiar feature. There is no adequation of *res* and *signa*, nor is the sign the receptacle of a reality, its specular image. The logical and necessary continuity between words and things—exemplified throughout the poem by Dante's use of etymology—is subverted. Language seems to originate in the void, in a condition of total separation from the world of "reality," where it makes seductive promises to produce experience and is doomed to failure. Tragedy creeps into this epic quest from the ordinary world to the enchanted land the voyager approaches but never reaches. The vision of the mountain dark in the distance recoils into a tragic dénouement and is couched in a stylized rhetorical definition of tragedy: "Noi ci allegrammo, e tosto tornò in pianto; / Chè de la nova terra un turbo nacque . . ." (ll. 136-7). The line which translates almost verbatim the tragic formula "tragicum carmen quod incipit a gaudio et terminat in luctu" (tragic song begins in joy and ends in grief) describes the reversal of the hero's fortune. Yet, it is no longer a mere incident in life, part of the larger view of life as a cycle in which all things happen again and again. On the contrary, this tragic reversal gets the hero off the wheel of fortune and decisively shatters the illusion of the possible pattern of recurrence in life. The tragic finale marks the conclusion of the elaborate tour de force of the passage to which we now turn.

By the "orazion picciola," a *topos* of affected modesty, Ulysses draws his companions into a state of complicity ("o frati," "nostri sensi"), which in the exchange with Vergil is disclosed as being the circle of his authority "Li miei compagni fec' io sì aguti. . . ." The authority of the speaking voice, however, is undermined by the discrepancy between what his speech promises and the tragedy he himself confronts. His promises are unfulfilled: ironically, the golden world he dimly perceives seems to lie beyond his volition, and the language by which Ulysses manipulates and seduces his companions possesses both the companions, who can no longer be controlled (l. 123), and, as we shall see later on, the hero himself.

The address moves from the opening apostrophe to the

hyperbolic *captatio benevolentiae* celebrating the past common achievements, but it hinges on *amplificatio* and *antithesis*. The frequent and conspicuous enjambements (ll. 112-3; 114-5, etc.), the cosmic directions ("l'occidente," "nel mattino," "di retro al sol, del mondo sanza gente"), the antithetical sequence of hyperboles and litotes ("grande-piccolo") give appropriate relief to the grandeur of the quest. After the *peroratio*, there is a shift from the pathos of the appeal to a logical statement as the speech closes on the well-known aphorism "fatti non foste a viver come bruti, ma per seguir virtute e canoscenza." Recurrent sounds and alliterative modulations create the harmony of the speech: the repetitions compel the rhythm to return on itself and create an incantatory, suspended effect.

Though aware of the fallacy of a logical continuity between sound and sense, this melic aura must be stressed since Dante exposes precisely the techniques of rhetorical deception. The hypnotic, "poietic" quality of the speech makes it into a self-contained totality luring the audience within its deceptive circuit of hollow promises and hides its character as an exercise of persuasion, an instrument of manipulation of the audience's response.

But why remark on the *lexis*, the presence of figures of speech which, in effect, pervade *any* literary text whatsoever? They are, at one level, devices for structuring thought, through which the articulation of language naturally takes place. But there is more to it. The display of rhetorical virtuosity is not a gratuitous act: it confirms a hierarchy of knowledge between the orator and the audience at the very moment in which language challenges the presence of an authority and devalorizes knowledge. Paradoxically, the figures of speech are the place of encounter between orator and listeners, where a "recognition" or a complicity seems to occur. More fundamentally, they disclose the institution of dissimulation inherent in the structure of rhetorical discourse. In *De Doctrina Christiana*, Augustine reflects on the treachery of rhetorical figures, acknowledges them as weapons of power, and warns Christians not to leave them in the sole possession of the "salesmen of words."[37] Dante is equally aware of the mystifications of rhetorical figures. In the first canto of *Purgatorio* as the ascent of the pilgrim begins, Vergil speaks to Cato by a *captatio benevolentiae*—Cato rejects the insidious charm of pagan rhetoric, identified with man's bondage to sin.[38] Beatrice's own words, as referred to by Vergil are necessarily in the smooth and plain style.[39] Benvenuto da Imola's commentary on this line focuses on the opposition between the language of Beatrice and that of Vergil: "et bene dicit, quia sermo divinus est suavis et planus, non altus et superbus sicut sermo Virgili et poetarum."[40] Benvenuto's reflection reinforces the notion that rhetoric is not a pure art "bene loquendi": it has, on the contrary, pretensions to exceed itself, to transcend itself into the making of reality and to give an adequate representation of reality.

It is within this general claim of language to represent and order the world that we understand why it is Vergil who conducts the dialogue with Ulysses, while by an overt and significant contrast, Dante will speak to Guido in the following canto. Vergil provides the clue when approaching Ulysses and Diomed through the *captatio benevolentiae* "s'io meritai di voi assai o poco, / quando nel mondo li alti versi scrissi" ("if I deserved of you so much or little, when in the world I wrote the lofty verse") (ll. 81-2)—he refers to the "alti versi" (l. 82), the epic he wrote. The implication is clear: formal propriety is observed; an epic poet is the proper interlocutor of the epic

---

[37] Erich Auerbach, "Sermo humilis," in *Literary Language and Its Public in Late Latin Antiquity and the Middle Ages*, trans. Ralph Manheim (New York: Pantheon Books, 1965), pp. 27-66.

[38] Vergil's request to be allowed to climb the mountain is effected by a reference to Marcia, "per lo suo amore adunque a noi ti piega" (*Purgatorio* i, l. 81). Cato replies: "Ma se donna del ciel ti move e regge, / come tu di', non c'è mestier lusinghe: / bastisi ben che per lei mi richegge" (ll. 91-3).

[39] "Lucevan li occhi suoi più che la stella; / e cominciommi a dir soave e piana, / con angelica voce, in sua favella" (*Inferno* ii, ll. 55-7). On the *sermo planus*, see Auerbach, "Sermo Humilis," p. 66.

[40] Biagi, ed., *Inferno*, p. 63.

hero. Yet not only is this notion of the "proper" undercut, but in the canto that follows, Guido's apostrophe "O tu a cu' io drizzo / la voce e che parlavi pur mo lombardo" ("O you to whom I direct my voice and who just now spoke Lombard") (Inferno XXVII, ll. 19-20), retrospectively undercuts the possibility of rigidly formalized levels of representation. From one point of view, the presence of Ulysses, the only epic hero among so many contemporary Italians, marks the distance between his epic grandeur and the provincial and petty world of Guido. At the same time, there is the radical affirmation of the tragic spiritual sameness of these sinners in this eschatological area. Dante thus exemplifies and simultaneously abrogates the juxtaposition of the epic and the quotidian. Fictional separations of style—the doctrine that to each subject matter corresponds a fixed level of style—are misrepresentations in a Christian context.[41]

Furthermore, as Ulysses recounts his departure from Circe at Gaeta he explicitly mentions Aeneas "prima che sì Enëa la nomasse" (l. 93). The interpretative twist given to Aeneas' journey is remarkable. The hero's special fate to be the carrier of tradition from Troy to Italy emerges as an activity of naming, his history-making a "poietic" mission as he names the place in memory of his nurse. Apparently, naming is the process by which man memorializes the world, marks his losses and the world comes to be history, the place of man's nostalgic recollections. For Ulysses, however, to mention Aeneas naming places discloses a further irony: he seems to

---

[41] The stylistic aspects of *Inferno* XXVI have been studied by H. D. Goldstein, "Enea e Paolo: A reading of the 26th Canto of Dante's *Inferno*," *Symposium*, 19 (1965), pp. 316-27, mainly in the wake of the work by Erich Auerbach, "Sermo Humilis." The question of style, as is generally acknowledged, is pervasive in *De Vulgari Eloquentia*, II, iv, 4-8. See also Dante's own treatment in the tenth paragraph of his Epistle to Cangrande in *The Letters of Dante*, emended text and introduction by Paget Toynbee, 2nd ed. (Oxford: Clarendon Press, 1966), pp. 175-7, where he quotes Horace's *Ars Poetica*, ll. 93-5. More generally, see Richard McKeon, "Poetry and Philosophy in the Twelfth Century," *Critics and Criticism*, ed. R. S. Crane (Chicago: University of Chicago Press, 1952), p. 3.

disguise himself as Aeneas and identify with his *pietas*; yet, the priority he claims over the Trojan hero both reveals the illusoriness of the identification and denounces Ulysses' own failure to name. The canto, in general, exemplifies Ulysses' excessive naming of geographic points (ll. 103, 104, 110, 111), but as he comes closer to the unknown world, the world stands unknown and his language collapses into temporal specifications.

The irony does not envelop Ulysses alone. His shipwreck, expressed through the canonical formula of tragedy, defines the tragic history of utopia, of the hero barred from his object. But in this canto where Ulysses disguises himself as another Aeneas and Vergil speaks of his "alti versi," it is inevitable that we recall Vergil's own definition of the *Aeneid* as "alta mia tragedia" (*Inferno* xx, l. 113). This is the canto of the soothsayers, the sin of perversion of prophecy and it is in this context that the origin of the name of Mantua is debated. In the *Aeneid*, it was Ocnus who built and named Mantua. In this canto, instead, Dante has Vergil tell of the false prophetess Manto, daughter of the Theban Tiresias, who founded the city. The authority of Vergil is directly questioned: not only is the *Aeneid*, the privileged epic of Rome, the locus of error, but naming itself is part of the ambiguities of the divinitory claim of language.

In *Inferno* xxvi this ambiguity is exemplified by the tongues of fire that envelop and conceal the sinners but through which Ulysses tells his story (ll. 42, 48, 87 ff.). To be sure, Ulysses claims that he had an inward fire, "l'ardore" (l. 97), from which his desire to know the world originates. Ironically, he is now inside the flame, trapped by it. The implied correspondence of the inward fire that has become the outside flame might be construed as an instance of *contrappasso*, the law of retributive justice that governs Dante's *Inferno*. In rhetorical terms, however (and the flame is, as will be seen shortly, an emblem of rhetoric), the flame is outside because rhetoric is that which appears or, as Dante says of Venus (the planet of Love and of Rhetoric) in the *Convivio*,[42] is visible from everywhere, covers the inner substance.

Commentators have agreed that the flames are a pointed parody of the descent of the Pentecostal tongues of fire, because Ulysses' sin of evil counseling is primarily a sin against the good counsels of the Holy Spirit.[43] It might be added in this context that the production of sound through the metaphor of the wind (l. 88) ironically recalls Acts 2:2 in which the descent of the Spirit is described in tongues of flames and the sound of a mighty wind: "and they were all filled with the Holy Ghost and began to speak with other tongues as the Spirit gave them utterance." The allusion to the inspirational afflatus prepares a sustained reflection on the prophetic word and Ulysses' language: in both cases, the implication is that the speaker, far from being the master of language, is possessed by language in the moment of giving utterance to it. More important still, the Pentecostal resonance enacts the thematic antithesis between Elijah and Ulysses. As the pilgrim approaches the sinners, he recalls Elisha watching Elijah, the prophet who was taken up by a whirlwind in a chariot of fire. Elijah is the explicit antitype of Ulysses, and like Ulysses in canto XXVI, is conventionally described "et surrexit Elias propheta, *quasi ignis et verbum eius quasi facula ardebat.*"[44] This thematic contrast is, in effect, concerned with the division between spurious and genuine prophecy. This distinction is made more cogent by the fact that the tongue of

---

[42] "E lo cielo di Venere si può comparare a la Rettorica per due proprietadi: l'una sì è la chiarezza del suo aspetto, che è soavissima a vedere più che altra stella; l'altra sì è la sua apparenza, or da mane or da sera. E queste due proprietadi sono ne la Rettorica" (*Convivio* II, xiii, 13-14). Busnelli and Vandelli in their footnotes point out the similarities between this formulation and Cicero's and Brunetto's (I, 198-9).

[43] Acts 2:1-11. For the motif of the prophetic tongue and the flame, see Isaiah 5:27; Psalm 119:10; A. Pézard, *Dante sous la pluie de feu*, p. 293. Cf. also the recent article by James G. Truscott, "Ulysses and Guido: *Inferno* XXVI-XXVII," *Dante Studies*, 91 (1973), pp. 47-72.

[44] Ecclesiasticus 48:1.

fire is the characteristic property of Rhetoric. In the *Anticlaudianus*, Alanus de Insulis describes the seductive adornments of Rhetoric, through an extended *effictio*, the apt rhetorical figure of description of outside appearance:

> Exemplans auri speciem miraque polytus
> Arte iacet crinis, investit colla capillus
> In vultuque natat color igneus, *ignis in ore*
> Purpureus roseo vultum splendore colorat.[45]

Alanus' "ignis in ore," it must be stressed, comes from Statius' *Achilleid*, the epic fragment specifically alluded to in *Inferno* XXVI.[46] In the *Achilleid*, the phrase is part of the description of Achilles' travesty as a maiden till Ulysses and Diomed come and literally seduce him to the Trojan War.

The double exegesis of the flame in terms of rhetorical and prophetic allusions dramatizes the proximity of prophecy and rhetoric. At one level, it would seem that Ulysses' rhetoric is the degradation of prophecy or, vice versa, that prophecy establishes the normative canon for the lies of rhetoric, its ironic demystification. But the flow of irony is not closed and finite, a simple movement that leads directly to the assertion of the truth of prophecy over the shiftiness of rhetoric. Dante seems more interested, at this juncture of the journey, to map the threatening contiguity between them, to question precisely the possibility of distinguishing between them. Significantly,

---

[45] *Anticlaudianus*, ed. R. Bossuat (Paris: J. Vrin, 1955), III, ll. 151-4. James Sheridan's translation reads: "Her locks reflecting the gloss of gold lie adorned with wondrous artistry: her hair falls down to cover her neck. Her countenance is steeped in radiant colour: a brilliant red glow tints her face with roseate lustre" (Alan of Lille, *Anticlaudianus or the Good and Perfect Man* [Toronto: Pontifical Institute of Mediaeval Studies, 1973], p. 97). While the translation correctly gives the metaphoric sense of the original, it inevitably bypasses the literal force of "ignis in ore" as the "fire in the mouth," i.e., lips and tongue. Dante, my point is, literalizes Alanus' metaphor (which he derives from Statius, see note 46).

[46] "Niveo natat ignis in ore / purpureus" (*Achilleid* I, ll. 161-2). For the reference to Deidamia in *Inferno* XXVI, ll. 61-2, see *Achilleid* I, l. 884. For the recognition of Achilles by Ulysses and Diomede, cf. see *Achilleid* I, ll. 538 ff.

the canto opens with Dante's own prophetic wrath against the city of Florence:

> Godi, Fiorenza, poi che se' sì grande
> che per mare e per terra batti l'ali,
> e per lo 'nferno tuo nome si spande!
> Tra li ladron trovai cinque cotali
> tuoi cittadini onde mi ven vergogna,
> e tu in grande orranza non ne sali.
> Ma se presso al mattin del ver si sogna,
> tu sentirai, di qua da picciol tempo,
> di quel che Prato, non ch'altri, t'agogna.
>
> *Inferno* xxvi, ll. 1-9

(Rejoice, Florence, since you are so great that you beat your wings over land and sea and your name is spread through Hell. Among the thieves I found five of your citizens, such that shames come to me and you rise by them in no great honor. But if near morning our dreams are true, you shall feel before long what Prato, not to say others, craves for you.)

What follows the outburst (ll. 23 ff.) is a brief meditation of the poet who, threatened by the danger of his own poetic imagination, recoils into the self and bridles his creative powers. The curbing of "ingegno"—the poet's faculty[47]—is primarily Dante's suspicion that his own poetic venture may simply be a version of Ulysses' madness, that Dante, too, like Ulysses is actually reenacting by the virtue of poetic language, which for Plato is inspired madness, the quest of Ulysses. In the more immediate context of the outburst, however, the poet's self-reflexive posture is the ambiguous consequence of the authoritarian, prophetic voice he assumes and of the hybristic challenge to the ancient poets in *Inferno* xxv where he claims to have surpassed the poets of the past. Dante's own authority, in other words, is continuously caught between the elusive claim of speaking with prophetic self-assurance and

---

[47] Cf. chapter 1, note 58.

the awareness that this can be a supreme transgression. The authenticity of this threat emerges from the definition of poetry in terms of rhetoric in the De Vulgari Eloquentia "si poesis recte consideramus que nichil aliud est quam fictio rhetorica musicaque poita."[48] His self-doubt is, to be sure, a common feature of the prophet: St. Paul in the First Epistle to the Corinthians expresses this anguish in the peculiar tone of certainty: "My speech and my preaching were not in the persuasive words of human wisdom, but in the showing of the spirit and the power."[49] For Dante, the complicity of rhetoric and prophecy is continuous: it is rooted in the claim that the speaker is possessed by language and in their shared symbol of the flame. More conspicuously, Ulysses is damned but still exerts a singular fascination on the pilgrim-poet.

In the light of this, it should be clear why language is a fraud. Its inevitable condition is to provide the region, the "topics" of dissimulation and error: it always achieves something more and something else than it envisages. If for Brunetto political rhetoric aims at acquiring knowledge of the good life of the city, for Dante it would seem that it cannot be an instrument of knowledge because it is intrinsically ambiguous and shifty. The shiftiness does not depend merely on moral ambiguities, on the radical confusion of prophecy and rhetoric; it is, rather, the very specificity of language. We must look more closely at the tongues of fire—and their compressed textual references—because it is through them that Dante articulates the distinctiveness of poetic language.

The "ignis in ore" is no longer, in Dante's text, the seductive lure of Alanus' Rhetoric, a part of the Venus-like splendor that colors his personification; nor is it Achilles' own dis-

---

[48] De Vulgari Eloquentia II, iv, 2-3. See also A. Schiaffini, " 'Poesis' e 'poeta' in Dante," in Studia Philologica et Litteraria in Honorem L. Spitzer (Bern: Francke, 1958), pp. 379-89; August Buck, "Gli studi sulla poetica e sulla retorica di Dante e del suo tempo," in Atti del congresso internazionale di studi danteschi (Florence: Sansoni, 1965), pp. 349-78. On the notion of fictio, see G. Paparelli, "Fictio: La definizione dantesca della poesia," in Ideologia e poesia di Dante (Florence: Olschki, 1975), pp. 51-138.

[49] I Corinthians 2:4.

guise as a woman. The flame is a veritable metaphor, a figure of substitution that makes literal and visible the "ardore" within, but hides what was "outside." In a real sense, the flame is the locus where distinctions between the inside and the outside are confused. We note that the flame hides Ulysses, who speaks through this cover: in so doing, it acts out rhetoric's own ambiguous agon between concealment and appearance. The point has to be clarified. When Thomas Aquinas draws the theological distinction between *violentia* and *fraus*, he focuses on *rapina* and *furtum*, as an illustration of this difference: "si occulte unus rem alterius accipiat vocatur furtum, si autem manifeste, vocatur rapina."[50] Aquinas' connection between fraud and theft as acts of concealment may account for the metaphorics of hiding and thievery of *Inferno* XXVI. The fall of Troy is evoked through the contrivance of the wooden horse (Ulysses' stratagem) which hides the Greek soldiers; Achilles is ensnared away from the refuge where his mother had hidden him; the Palladium, the simulacrum of wisdom, is stolen. But how does this pattern of hiding and thievery illumine or amplify the conditions of language that we have described?

Dante, in effect, seems to establish a symbolic reciprocity between the two moments: the tongues of fire in which the sinners are hidden, literally "steal" them. The word Dante uses is "invola":

> Tal si move ciascuna per la gola
>   del fosso, ché nessuna mostra 'l furto,
>   e ogne fiamma un peccatore invola.
>
>   ll. 40-2

(So each flame moves along the gullet of the ditch for none shows the theft and every one steals away a sinner.)

"Invola" is etymologically related to *involucrum*, the technical term of medieval allegoresis, that which covers the substance

---

[50] *Summa Theologiae,* IIa IIae, q. 61, a. 3: "If the offense against property is carried out secretly it is a theft, if openly it is a robbery."

within.[51] But, as the allusion to the theft (l. 41) shows, it means also "steals." Like thievery, language is a secret and furtive activity: just as Ulysses defiles the holy by stealing what is inviolable in the temple, his language defiled the Word because it violated prophecy. More fundamentally, like thievery which is a transgression of property, language forever eludes the possibility of univocal, *proper* meaning. To say this is to talk of language as desire, originating in a condition of lack, in the Augustinian sense,[52] and failing to achieve a stable self-identity. The desire that subtends language (the "ardore" exposed by the tongue of fire) accounts for the inseparable link that exists between the promises of education and the seduction which actually takes place in Ulysses' speech. We must not confuse this question with, for instance, Jason's deliberate exploitation of the erotic force of rhetoric, his "parole ornate," by means of which he accomplishes what he had set out to accomplish, namely the seduction and deception of Hypsipyle.[53] Ulysses, on the contrary, moves toward the inaccessible goal and dies. Seduction is what is left over from the failure of the journey of education: his false promises depend on a language that is forever askew with its intents and which can never wrest truth from its concealment.

[51] For a discussion of *involucrum* as a veil of allegory, see M.-D. Chenù, "*Involucrum*: le mythe selon les théologiens médievaux," *Archives d'histoire doctrinale et littéraire du moyen-âge*, 22 (1955), pp. 75-9. See also Édouard Jeanneau, "La Notion d'integumentum," *AHDL*, 24 (1957), pp. 35-100.

[52] Throughout book one of the *Confessions*, St. Augustine dramatizes most explicitly his sense that the origin of language lies in want. In early "infancy" gestures are signs of desire (i, 6); in the transition to boyhood, "I learned to speak myself by the use of that mind which you, God, gave me. By making all sorts of cries and noises, all sorts of movements of my limbs, I desired to express my inner feelings, so that people would do what I wanted; . . . Then, having broken in my mouth to the pronunciation of these signs, I was at last able to use them to say what I wanted to say" (*The Confessions of St. Augustine*, trans. Rex Warner [New York and Toronto: The New American Library, 1963], i, 8, pp. 25-6).

[53] "Ello passò per l'isola di Lenno / poi che l'ardite femine spietate / tutti li maschi loro a morte dienno. / Ivi con segni e con parole ornate / Isifile ingannò, la giovinetta / che prima avea tutte l'altre ingannate" (*Inferno* xviii, ll. 88-93).

The pattern of appearance and concealment that the tongues of fire crystallize sustains, dimly visible, the poetic movement of the canto. We have already remarked on the presence of metaphors of wished-for renewal, of linearity from an "end" to a "new beginning," from the prophecy of the imminent destruction of Florence which opens the canto to the vision of the new land which closes it. These metaphors find a dramatic counterpart in the emblems of the continuous, repetitive cycles of the sun and the moon. Ulysses' voyage in the beyond follows the path of the sun (l. 117) and is recounted, as the journey approaches its tragic conclusion, in terms of the moon (l. 131). The quest for historic regeneration and the constant circularity of the natural order depend concomitantly on the metaphor of the sun.

The canto, in reality, has a hidden heliocentric structure and all the characters evoked seem to emanate from the sun or go toward it. The first allusion to the sun is oblique:

nel tempo che colui che 'l mondo schiara
la faccia sua a noi tien meno ascosa.
ll. 26-7

(. . . in the season when he that lights the world least hides his face from us.)

The sun is hidden in a periphrasis to describe the night. The veiled allusion introduces Elijah whose ascent, according to Sedulius' *Carmen Paschale*, for instance, is represented in terms of Helios in his chariot.[54] Hercules, who draws the boundaries of the world, is like the sun. Macrobius in his *Saturnalia* refers to him "nec Hercules a substantia solis alienus est, quippe Hercules ea est solis potestas quam humano generi virtutem et similitudinem praestat deorum," or even as "lustrator orbis, purgator ferarum, gentium

---

[54] *Carmen Paschale* I, 168, in *CSEL* x. Damon, p. 32, also mentions for this etymology Firmicus Maternus, *De Errore Profanarum Religionum*, and Paulinus of Nola. For a general synopsis of the sun symbolism, see H. Flanders Dunbar, *Symbolism in Medieval Thought and its Consummation in the Divine Comedy* (New York: Russell and Russell, 1961), pp. 106-239.

domitor."[55] Parenthetically, we might note that this view of
Hercules—adumbrated in *Inferno* xxv where he is shown killing Cacus[56]—reinforces the similarities with Ulysses who
also appears as educator of brutes. Circe, to continue our discussion, is conventionally "filia solis dicta";[57] finally, the oblique allusion to Daedalus (l. 125)[58] is again the story of flight
from the labyrinth into the sun and a timely return to earth
where he offers his wings to the Sun God, Apollo.

This double movement away from the sun and toward the
sun is essentially described in terms of the linearity of generation and attempted regeneration, a quest for eternity patterned on the cycle of death and resurrection of the sun. The
exordium of the canto with its ironic apostrophe to Florence's
wings (an anticipation of Ulysses' flight) is an allusion to
Fama, the classical myth of secular eternity and the other
name of Clio. The city's claim to sempiternity gives way to
the prediction of its imminent end and introduces the two
other cities of Thebes and Troy.

Thebes is the metaphoric archetype of the *civitas terrena*. It
originates, like all earthly empires, in violence and it provides
the dramatic storehouse of moral *exempla* for the horror of the
historical chaos. It constitutes also a persistent model of recurrence and periodical renewal. Thus Pisa is a "novella Tebe"
(*Inferno* xxxiii, l. 89) and, like Thebes, doomed to destruction. Troy, on the other hand, is part of a genetic and linear

---

[55] Macrobius, *Saturnalia*, ed. J. Willis (Leipzig: B. G. Teubner, 1970), i,
xx, 6. For a general view an extensive bibliography on the myth of Hercules,
see Marcel Simon, *Hercule et le Christianisme* (Paris: Les Belles Lettres, 1955).
See also Henri de Lubac, *Exégèse mediévale* (Paris: Aubier, 1964), ii,
pp. 222 ff.

[56] "Questi è Caco, / . . . Non va co' suoi fratei per un cammino, / per lo
furto che frodolente fece / del grande armento ch'elli ebbe a vicino; / onde
cessar le sue opere biece / sotto la mazza d'Ercule, che forse / gliene diè cento,
e non sentì le diece" (*Inferno* xxv, ll. 25-33).

[57] In Ovid's *Metamorphoses*, for instance, she is "filia solis" (xiv, l. 346).
See also *Aeneid* vii, l. 11; *De Consolatione Philosophiae* iv, meter iii, l. 5. Dante
obliquely alludes to Circe as the beautiful daughter "di quel ch'apporta mane
e lascia sera" (*Paradiso* xxvii, ll. 136-8).

[58] John Freccero, "Dante's Prologue Scene," pp. 13-4.

pattern: from its destruction Rome will emerge. If Dante imposes on Thebes' history the structure of a palimpsest because it, phoenixlike, dies and comes back to life in a perpetual self-circulation, he sees Troy as part of salvation history: its fall is the pivotal myth of history, the *felix culpa* of historic origination. Just as the fall of man is a happy sin because it made possible the supreme experience of the Incarnation, the fall of Troy is a happy fall because it makes possible the providential establishment of the Roman Empire. The reference to the Troy-Rome filiation (*Inferno* xxvi, 1. 60) enacts the fundamental metaphor of history: the *translatio imperii* and the idea of the linearity of the westward historic process.

Modeled on the movement of the sun from east to west, this doctrine is conventionally based on the analogy between the duration of the day and the totality of history. The movement of the sun gives a spatialized view of time and the end of the day, when the sun sets, is the end of both space and time. The doctrine of *translatio*, however, literally accounts for the view of history as a self-acknowledged metaphor, the world of translation, always foreign to itself, unrepeatable and pointing to its own end.[59] The rhetorical view of the historic process is by no means unusual and it depends on the assumption of the figurative nature of history. This is not to deny that history is not part of grammar: it is, indeed, the

[59] For the notion of *translatio* as a controlling metaphor of history, see Hugh of St. Victor, *De Arca Noe morali* iv, 9, in *PL* 176, col. 667: ". . . ut quae in principio temporum gerebantur in Oriente, quasi in principio mundi gerentur, ac deinde ad finem profluente tempore usque ad occidentem rerum summa descenderet, ut ex ipso agnoscamus appropinquare finem saeculi." Cf. also *PL* 176, col. 720. For a general view, see W. Goez, *Translatio Imperii* (Tübingen: J. C. B. Mohr, 1958). For *translatio* as the term for metaphor, see the definition given by Isidore of Seville: "metaphora est verbi alicuius usurpata translatio" (*Etym*. i, xxxvii, 2). It may be added that after listing the conventional four types of metaphor, Isidore gives as an instance of metaphor "nam et alae navium et alarum remigia dicuntur." Cf. *Inferno* xxvi, 1. 125: "de' remi facemmo ali al folle volo." For the same definition of metaphor, see also Matthieu de Vendôme, *Ars Versificatoria* iii, 19-24 in *Les Arts poétiques du XIIᵉ et du XIIIᵉ siècle*, ed. Edmond Faral (Paris: E. Champion, 1924), pp. 172-3.

"letter" which calls for interpretation, the "fundamentum allegoriae,"[60] a veritable metaphor. This view of history appears to be consecrated by St. Augustine, who illustrates the tragic duality of history in terms of an explicit rhetorical figure. The wickedness of the devil and of man coexist with the goodness of the Kingdom of God: together they embellish the process of history and make "the course of the ages, as it were an exquisite poem set off with antitheses."[61]

In the case of Aeneas, as I have argued in the first chapter, the *translatio* enacts the notion that history is the process of tradition, an attempt to recover anew what has been lost, by moving away from the origin or its identical replica (Pergamea). The empire moves with Aeneas and, in a real sense, his translation is the absolute paradigm of history because it is bound—and binds him—to a historic event, namely the new city. Italy is for Aeneas the promised land, the secular new land but it is not the last horizon in the space of history: it announces a new messianic earth, the *eschaton* of fulfillment and establishes itself as pure figure. To stop at Rome is thus a meditation on hope, a belief in God's promise and the recognition by Aeneas that he is subject to the contingent order of history, that he is between the "no longer" of Troy and the "not yet" of the fulfillment: he follows the sun but stops and awaits.

Ulysses' tragedy, on the contrary, consists in not *awaiting*; he follows the westward movement of the sun back to the east, "nel mattino" (l. 124), literally to its point of origin. His is a quest for regeneration—to be like the sun—dying and resurrecting like the sun: significantly, he begins his journey by placing himself outside the pattern of generation as he leaves behind his father and son. But, ironically, as Ulysses

[60] The *topos* is traced by Henri de Lubac, "Le Fondement de l'histoire," in *Exégèse mediévale* (Paris: Aubier, 1959), I, esp. pp. 425-39; the formula that in allegorical interpretation of Scripture "historia fundamentum est" can be found in Petrus Comestor, *PL* 198, col. 1054; cf. also *PL* 210, col. 209c.

[61] "Sicut ergo ista contraria contraris opposita sermonis pulchritudinem reddunt: ita quadam non verborum, sed rerum eloquentia contrariarum oppositione pulchritudo conponitur" (*De Civitate Dei* XI, 18, *CCSL* XLVIII).

literally follows the sun, the sun disappears and the night sets in (l. 130), and the quest takes on the form of a vigil through the dark underworld on the way to redemption. Although in narrative terms what is happening is a *peripetia*, a journey toward death, it is the quest for a new beginning that is emphasized. Ulysses' old age (l. 106) is more than an emblem of physical decrepitude. Old age, for Cicero, signifies wisdom because it is the time when man returns to philosophical studies;[62] in a Christian context, it is the time for spiritual regeneration, when the new man is born. The other detail of Ulysses' turning to the left, after passing beyond Hercules' pillars, reinforces the motif of rebirth. Left and right are standard symbolic terms of spiritual direction. In the philosopher's accounts of the process of education, human life is represented through the letter Y, the emblem of the crossroads which a person reaches in his youth and where he must make a moral choice.[63] But Ulysses' symbolic turn takes place in his old age and in the otherworldly context. He reverses Aeneas' moral drama in the otherworld when the Sybil points to him the *right* way.[64] His model is the sun: to go left is to return to the point of origin, to move in a circle or

[62] *De Senectute*, v, 13-14; vii, 22 ff.

[63] This symbolic motif has been studied by Erwin Panofsky, *Hercules am Scheidewege* (Leipzig: B. G. Teubner, 1930). See particularly Cicero, *De Officiis* I, xxxii, 118: "Nam quod Herculem Prodicus dicit, ut est apud Xenophontem, cum primum pubesceret, quod tempus a natura ad deligendum, quam quisque viam vivendi sit ingressurus, datum est, exisse in solitudinem atque ibi sedentem diu secum multumque dubitasse, cum duas cerneret vias, unam Voluptatis, alteram Virtutis, utram ingredi melius esset, . . ." See also F. Cumont, *Lux Perpetua* (Paris: P. Geuthner, 1949), p. 287; T. E. Mommsen, "Petrarch and the Story of the Choice of Hercules," *Journal of the Warburg and Courtauld Institutes*, 16 (1953), pp. 178 ff.

[64] "Nox ruit, Aenea; nos flendo ducimus hores. / Hic locus est, partes ubi se via findit in ambas: / dextera quae Ditis magni sub moenia tendit, / hac iter Elysium nobis; at laeva malorum / exercet poenas et ad inpia Tartara mittit" (*Aeneid* vi, ll. 540-3). For a patristic gloss, see Lactantius, *Divinae Institutiones* vi, 3, in *PL* 6, cols. 641-4. Cf. Servius' Commentary on *Aeneid* vi, l. 136, ed. G. Thilo (Leipzig: B. G. Teubner, 1888), pp. 30-1. For the importance of Servius, see Erich von Richthofen, "Traces of Servius in Dante," *Dante Studies*, 92 (1974), pp. 117-28.

reach the Blest Isles "sitae . . . in Oceano contra laevam Mauretaniae, occiduo proximae."[65] As he goes leftward, Ulysses follows the motion by which the universe returns to its point of origin[66] and begins all over again. But in place of the harmonious circularity of the myth of the eternal return, Dante asserts the discovery of the linear, open-ended translation of history. From this point of view, *Inferno* xxvi denounces the fact that man is not at one with the natural order, and more broadly, is Christianity's farewell to the pagan belief of a literal history of repetition and recurrence. Augustine attacks precisely the *philosophi mundi huius* who believe that the same revolutions of times and temporal schemes are repeated and are to be repeated through countless ages of the future. This repetitive circular pattern is sheer nonsense to him for Christ died once and for all. The perfect return to the point of origin—exemplified by Ulysses' experience as he begins from Ithaca, returns to Ithaca and starts his journey all over again—is an illusory "nostalgia."

I have spoken of the sun as a genetic and referential center, the hidden principle of authority, above and beyond, as it were, the challenge of authority that Dante enacts at the specific level of rhetoric. The sun is the foundation of history, its radical metaphor, yet it is, as the antithetical stories of Aeneas and Ulysses have shown, a deceptive sign. Later in *Paradiso* x its pure metaphoricity is acknowledged by the distinction between the "sole sensibile" and the true "Sol degli

---

[65] This imaginative geography is by Isidore of Seville, *Etym*. xiv, vi, 8-9. The definition might account for Ulysses' leftward turn after crossing Hercules' pillars. There is a utopian text, I would like to suggest, that gives weight to the notion that Ulysses is questing also for a utopian new land: in the political *Epode* xvi, Horace gives a picture of Rome torn by civil war (ll. 1-14) and calls on "the better part" of the Romans to seek the fabled Isles of the Blest (ll. 42 ff.) where the land unploughed yields corn, honey flows from oaks, etc. This mythic land has not been reached by the oarsmen of Argo, nor has the "laboriosa . . . cohors Ulixei" (l. 60), Horace goes on to say, set foot on it.

[66] *De Caelo* ii, ii, 285-6. Cf. John Freccero, "Dante's Pilgrim in a Gyre," *PMLA*, 76 (June 1961), pp. 168-71.

angeli";[67] in *Inferno* xxvi, however, it continuously appears by hiding and when Ulysses follows it, it is invisible. In this sense, because of its persistent self-dislocation, appearance and disappearance, it is the metaphor that sustains the extended figurative pattern of appearance and concealment (the flame which hides and reveals the sinner, the "orazion" which means something other than what it says, history which is grammar but must be seen rhetorically, the renewal which turns out to be death, the complex ambiguities of knowledge, etc.) that we have examined. We must briefly look at the canto of the thieves (*Inferno* xxiv) to understand this problem more clearly. The canto is articulated through a sequence of metamorphoses: the idyllic reference to the book of nature, its fields covered by snow and changing their appearance as the sun rises, is the pretext to introduce the motif of work and hope as the ironic counterpart of the world of thievery and despair of the sinners.[68] The canto ends with the assimilation of fallen history into the process of metamorphosis: the whiteness of the snow and the darkness of the night are translated into the struggle of Whites and Blacks of Pistoia.[69] In between, the endless movement of forms is described in terms of two magic fictional referents. The first is the

---

[67] "E Bëatrice cominciò: 'Ringrazia, / ringrazia il Sol de li angeli, ch'a questo / sensibil t'ha levato per sua grazia" (*Paradiso* x, ll. 52-4). For the sun as the metaphor of God, see *Convivio* iii, xii, 7: "Nullo sensibile in tutto lo mondo è più degno di farsi essemplo di Dio ch 'l sole."

[68] "In quella parte del giovanetto anno / che 'l sole i crin sotto l'Aquario tempra / e già le notti al mezzo dì sen vanno, / quando la brina in su la terra assempra / l'imagine di sua sorella bianca, / ma poco dura a la sua penna tempra, / lo villanello a cui la roba manca, / si leva, e guarda, e vede la campagna / biancheggiar tutta; ond' ei si batte l'anca, / ritorna in casa, e qua e là si lagna, / come 'l tapin che non sa che si faccia; / poi riede, e la speranza ringavagna, / veggendo 'l mondo aver cangiata faccia / in poco d'ora, e prende suo vincastro / e fuor le pecorelle a pascer caccia (*Inferno* xxiv, ll. 1-15).

[69] "Pistoia in pria d'i Neri si dimagra; / poi Fiorenza rinova gente e modi. / Tragge Marte vapor di Val di Magra / ch'è di torbidi nuvoli involuto; / e con tempesta impetüosa e agra / sovra Campo Picen fia combattuto; / ond'ei repente spezzerà la nebbia, / sì ch'ogne Bianco ne sarà feruto. / E detto l'ho perché doler ti debbia!" (*Inferno* xxiv, ll. 143-51).

Phoenix, the fabulous bird that after its cycle of five hundred years perishes in the flames and arises from its own glowing ashes.[70] Like the sun, to which it is related, it symbolizes the perpetuity, the rhythm of death and renewal of the fallen world of change. The second and more crucial referent is the heliotrope. The vision of horror in the canto is such that the pilgrim sees the sinners running naked "sanza sperar perturgio o elitropia" (l. 93), "without hope of hiding place or heliotrope." Singleton confesses his bafflement and laconically asks: "No heliotrope here (why should there be?)"[71] The unmistakable historical information commentators generally give is a reference to the fabulous precious stone that cures the bites of snakes and makes its bearers invisible.[72] It is literally a fictional trope, a figure of the sun that would conceal their visibility, their nakedness, and shelter their appearance. In the literalness of Hell, Dante alludes to the impossible "utopian" metaphor that could spare their pain of sheer appearance and rescue their literalness, for it is the letter, as St. Paul writes, that kills.[73] Rhetoric is not, then, simply a mystification: it is the cover necessary to hide and save us from an equally intol-

[70] For the myth of the Phoenix, focusing on Lactantius' *De Ave Phoenice* and its biblical and nonbiblical sources, see J. Hubaux and M. Leroy, *Le Mythe du Phénix dans les littératures grecque et latin* (Liège: Bibliothèque du philosophie et lettres de l'Université de Liège LXXXII, 1939). For the importance of the symbol of the phoenix in political theology, see Ernst H. Kantorowicz, *The King's Two Bodies: A Study in Mediaeval Political Theology* (Princeton: Princeton University Press, 1957), pp. 388-95. Cf. also P. Renucci, "Dante et les mythes du millénnium," *Dante et les mythes: tradition et rénovation*, special issue of *Revue des études italiens*, 11 (1965), pp. 393-421.

[71] Singleton's remark is to be found in his *The* Divine Comedy. Inferno 2: *Commentary*, Bollingen Series, LXXX (Princeton: Princeton University Press, 1969), p. 416.

[72] These virtues of the heliotrope are described by Marbodus, *Liber de Gemmis*, in *PL* 171, col. 1757; Pliny, *Natural History*, x, xxxvii, 165. The heliotrope, as the metaphor of metaphors, is the focus of an essay by Jacques Derrida, "La Mythologie blanche: la metaphore dans le texte philosophique," in *Marges de la philosophie* (Paris: Les Editions de Minuit, 1972), pp. 247-324.

[73] II Corinthians 3:6.

erable visibility. Ulysses dies when he *sees* the "montagna" in the distance. The duplicity and lying in Ulysses' speech seem to go deeper even than the complexities of his moral temptations. The language of political duplicity will be the explicit theme of *Inferno* XXVII where Guido da Montefeltro's advice to the pope is the advice to destroy the city.[74] For all his rhetorical mastery, Ulysses' deception is primarily a self-deception, a way of succumbing to the literalness of his language, of being trapped by his own tongue. Ironically, the craftsman of persuasion is spellbound by his own song, the way he is caught within the tongue of fire and spellbound by the song of the sirens (*Purgatorio* XIX, 1. 22).

For Dante, in the movement of the narrative, Ulysses is left behind but his tragedy produces no irrevocable catharsis. He will reappear again, even in *Paradiso*,[75] as a constant reminder to the poet of the possible treachery of his own language and the madness of his own journey. The sense of Dante's text—in *Inferno* XXVI—is to disrupt the complicity with Ulysses and to place his own voice in a condition of interpretative distance from both prophetic claims and rhetorical self-deception. He explicitly intimates this much (ll. 34 ff.) when he compares himself watching the tongues of fire to Elisha watching Elijah's ascent. The look, in both cases, implies both a threatening fascination and distance. More important still, Dante resorts to another form of rhetorical discourse, the allegory of writing. Over against the myth of plenitude and self-presence of the uttered voice of the orator, he retrenches into writing—where the presence of the author is still to be constituted and deferred—and into allegory. Founded on the displacement of sense, on the distance between signs and the sense, allegory acknowledges itself, as we shall see in chapter 6, as error.

[74] Cf. *Inferno* XXVII, ll. 94-111.

[75] "Da l'ora ch'ïo avea guardato prima / i' vidi mosso me per tutto l'arco / che fa dal mezzo al fine il primo clima; / sì ch'io vedea di là da Gade il varco / folle d'Ulisse" (*Paradiso* XXVII, ll. 79-83).

The radical sense of rhetoric in the canto of Ulysses is concealment and disclosure. The tongues of fire conceal and reveal the sinners; the sun is the metaphor of hiddenness and disclosure; the speech of Ulysses is the insidious trap of the literal; history as the ground of a providential order is a translation; language possesses and is stolen. It is Hermes, the thief and wing-footed traveler, who, if we may speculate, seems ironically evoked in *Inferno* xxvi. Horace associates oratory with Hermes,[76] the nightly god who bears and lays open the message. Boethius tells the fable of Circe who converts men into swine and it is because of the mediation of Hermes that Odysseus is not left helpless against her magic secrets.[77] The ironic and dark evocation of Hermes suggests the necessary activity of interpreting, of learning to "read" through the metaphoric ambiguities of the letter.

The process of education and the disclosure-hiddenness of rhetoric are essentially related in the canto of Ulysses. *Paideia*, as the journey to truth, appears as disclosure, as the process of being led out of brutishness. But what comes to life in *Inferno* xxvi is Ulysses' error or the quest. If it is true that for Dante there is a Revelation—beyond any deceptions and simulacra—which can come only from God, he remains in this context bound to rhetoric's "revelation," in the sense of *revelatio*, that which simultaneously unveils as it inevitably puts the veil on once again.

---

[76] Horace, *Odes*, i, 10; ii, 17. For the myth of Hermes, see also Norman O. Brown, *Hermes the Thief* (New York: Vintage Books, 1969), esp. pp. 145 ff.

[77] "And though the winged son of Jove from these bewitched cups' delightful taste to keep the famous captain strove, yet them the greedy mariners embraced with much desire, till turned to swine instead of bread they fed on oaken mast" (*The Consolation of Philosophy*, trans. H. F. Stewart, rev. for Loeb Classical Library [Cambridge, Mass.: Harvard University Press, 1968], iv, meter 3, ll. 18-24, pp. 321-3). It might be pointed out that Ulysses' companions, who in Boethius' poem "glande pabula verterant," faintly resemble Dante's sense of those who acquire vulgar knowledge and who "in bestiale pastura" eat "erba e ghiande" (*Convivio* i, i, 8-9).

CHAPTER 3

Communitas and its Typological Structure

THE shadow that the story of Ulysses casts on the possibilities for humanistic rhetoric to be the cohesive medium for the making of the city cannot be immediately construed as Dante's own paramount skeptical reflection on the relationship between literature and history. Quite to the contrary, Dante continuously dramatizes at various crucial junctures of the poem both a vision of order available to the historical city and his belief that he, as a poet, occupies a singular and creative role in the shaping of that order. The relationship between the poet and the world of history remains, however, a difficult one. We are reminded constantly that the earthly cities are fallen, torn by civil wars and that the two lights of Rome, Empire and Church, have eclipsed each other. At the same time, notwithstanding the passion and the moral urgency with which the poet calls for a reordering of the world, his voice arises in a condition of exile from the city of life. What is the nature of this exile, and how does it affect Dante's myth of order in history? Also, is there ever any homecoming for the poet? The chapter that follows will attempt to answer these questions by a close analysis of some of the images that occur at the exordium of *Paradiso* xxv. After a brief clarification of the terminology used in this discussion, I shall analyze the metaphoric pattern by which Dante envisions the possibility of order in the city. I shall argue that, by reinterpreting the pastoral tradition, Dante represents the city as a *locus amoenus*.[1] Secondly, drawing from other parts of the poem, I should like to suggest some ideological extensions that the configuration of the city as a garden has in Dante's imagination. Finally, I shall circle back to *Paradiso* xxv in order to examine Dante's sense of exile and the dramatic conditions that make possible the poet's public posture.

It must be said at the outset that there has not been any major effort to investigate the metaphorics of the city in the *Divine Comedy* and their interaction with the typological structure of Dante's vision of history.[2] When scholars have had to deal with Dante's myth of political order, their attention conventionally has focused on *Monarchia* either to ascertain and debate the philosophical assumptions that sustain its

---

[1] The phrase is never used in the *Divine Comedy*. It is used, however, to describe the city of Florence in *De Vulgari Eloquentia*: "Nos autem, cui mundus est patria velut piscibus equor, quanquam Sarnum biberimus ante dentes et Florentiam adeo diligamus ut, quia dileximus, exilium patiamur iniuste, rationi magis quam sensui spatulas nostri iudicii podiamus. Et quamvis ad voluptatem nostram sive nostre sensualitatis quietem *in terris amenior locus quam Florentia* non existat . . . multas esse perpendimus firmiterque censemus et magis nobiles et magis delitiosas et regiones et urbes quam tusciam et Florentiam" (I, vi, 3). In the *Divine Comedy* the metaphor of the garden is deployed, as we shall see further on in the chapter, to describe Italy as " 'l giardin dello 'mperio" (*Purgatorio* vi, l. 105); in *Purgatorio* xiv, Florence is referred to as "trista selva" (l. 64). For the motif of the *locus amoenus* as a description of nature, see E. R. Curtius, *European Literature and the Latin Middle Ages*, trans. W. R. Trask (New York: Harper and Row, 1953), pp. 192 ff.

[2] Most of the critical studies focus on Dante's view of political Rome; see G. De Leonardis, "La Roma di Dante," *Giornale dantesco*, 3 (1896), pp. 188–96; Charles T. Davis, *Dante and the Idea of Rome* (Oxford: Clarendon Press, 1957). A. Passerin d'Entrèves, *Dante as a Political Thinker* (Oxford: Clarendon Press, 1965), examines the importance of the "city-state" in Dante's thought and dismisses the poet's interest in political life as nostalgia (pp. 1-25). In an entirely different vein, Thomas Goddard Bergin, *A Diversity of Dante* (New Brunswick, N.J.: Rutgers University Press, 1969), sensitively suggests that the evocation of Florence by Cacciaguida is a "lost paradise of history" (p. 152). The typology of Jerusalem in the Old and New Testament, in liturgical traditions and Dante, without its extension into the political city, is carefully treated by Johan Chydenius, *The Typological Problem in Dante* (Helsingfors: Societas Scientiarum Fennica, 1958), pp. 51-91.

political theory or to establish the possible discrepancies, or coherence, between that tract and the political theology which, in the oblique forms of poetic language, figures prominently in the *Divine Comedy*. One can hardly account for the reluctance of critics to handle this question in more than literal and purely ideological terms since the study of the overt thematic strains of the poem inevitably leaves out of the picture the importance of the interdependence of the metaphors of order and exile. The coordinating principle of these two problems is the myth of *communitas*[3] which I now shall attempt to define by turning briefly to the hagiographic representation of St. Francis in *Paradiso* XI.[4]

The legend (ll. 43-117) in its broad outline tells the story of St. Francis leaving the "world" and its social structures to found his fraternal order (ll. 83 ff.). Yet, it is in the process of transition between the two events that the dramatic focus of the scene lies. Francis divests himself of the *insignia* of the world, gives up family bonds and wealth and becomes a scandal to the accepted values of the social fabric. By the public performance of self-dispossession, Francis moves to the fringes of society, to a symbolic area where the forms of the world lose whatever fixed and stable sense convention has imposed on them. In the liminal space where he withdraws, in fact, he is represented as he marries Lady Poverty:

'ché per tal donna, giovinetto, in guerra
del padre corse, a cui, come a la morte,
la porta del piacer nessun diserra;

[3] I am using the concept of *communitas* in the sense given to it by Victor Turner in his *The Forest of Symbols* (Ithaca: Cornell University Press, 1970), pp. 93 ff.; see also his *The Ritual Process* (Chicago: Aloline Publishing Co., 1969).

[4] For a detailed reading of *Paradiso* XI, see Erich Auerbach, *Scenes from the Drama of European Literature*, trans. Ralph Manheim (New York: Meridian Books, 1959), pp. 79-98; Umberto Cosmo, "Le mistiche nozze di Frate Francesco con Madonna Povertà," *Giornale dantesco*, 6 (1898), pp. 49-82; pp. 97-117; also his "Il canto di San Francesco," *Giornale dantesco*, 21 (1913), pp. 137-51; A. Chiari, *Tre canti danteschi* (Varese: Editrice Magenta, 1954), pp. 55-78.

> e dinanzi a la sua spirital corte
> *et coram patre* le si fece unito;
> poscia di dì in dì l'amò più forte.
> . . . .
> Ma perch' io non proceda troppo chiuso,
> Francesco e Povertà per questi amanti
> prendi oramai nel mio parlar diffuso.
> La lor concordia e i lor lieti sembianti,
> amore e maraviglia e dolce sguardo
> faceno esser cagion di pensier santi.
>
> ll. 58-63, and ll. 73-8

(. . . for while still a youth, he rushed into strife against his father for such a lady, to whom, as to death, none willingly unlocks the door; and before his spiritual court *et coram patre* he was joined to her, and thereafter from day to day he loved her ever more ardently. . . . But lest I proceed too darkly, take now Francis and Poverty for these lovers in all that I have said. Their harmony and joyous semblance made love and wonder and tender looks the cause of holy thoughts.)

The passage pivots on a process of compression of the concrete and the abstract, and I shall explore in chapter 7 the specific strategy by which its allegorical structure is literalized. Other details enact the reversal of opposite elements: the eminently spiritual love is portrayed in terms of a physical relationship between lovers; the poverty Francis embraces engenders spiritual riches (ll. 82-4); the spiritual ceremony is cast in legal language (*coram patre*). The representation shows Francis, in other words, moving to the edges of social structures and involved in a ritual where the boundaries between the physical and the spiritual are deliberately blurred and confused. The self-humiliation he chooses to experience gives him a paradoxically privileged perspective from which he is enabled to reverse and challenge the secular myths of the world. Possibly on the strength of the conventional view of Francis and the Franciscans as *ioculatores Domini*, Dante shows

Francis as he parodies the legal and institutional fictions of society. The ceremony makes a mockery of wealth, marriage, sex, the legal language of the contract, and even family. Pointedly, Francis leaves his real family to be with "la sua donna e con quella famiglia / che già legava l'umile capestro" (*Paradiso* xi, ll. 86-7). It might be remarked that *Paradiso* is largely, though not exclusively, inhabited by souls who in their earthly lives left behind the "world": to give a few instances, one can mention Piccarda who originally entered the convent from which her brother later will remove her; Romeo of Villeneuve, who abandoned the comforts of the court to live as a pilgrim; Folquet, who rejected his amatory poetry and joined the Cistercian Order; and finally, St. Bernard, who exemplifies the epitome of monastic life.

The liminality that characterizes the earthly existence of the blessed souls, the quality, that is, of their living in the world and yet outside of it, of being, in Turner's language, "betwixt and between" the structures of society and God's eternal order, is crucial to our understanding of St. Francis. The phase of liminality that he sets out to institutionalize by the foundation of the mendicant order (ll. 92-6) is the area of mediation between the world of contingency and history, and the absolute model of Paradise and a Christ-like existence. One of the conventional themes in monastic literature is that the cloister and convent are earthly prefigurations of heavenly Paradise, truly places of spiritual delights.[5] At the same time, the Christological patterns of the canto hardly need emphasizing: the legend is the apt rhetorical form to portray the saint's life. His birth in "Oriente" (l. 54), his marriage to Poverty, and the stigmata that Christ imprinted on his hands, feet and side (ll. 106-8) depict a veritable *imitatio Christi*. The model that is re-

[5] Jean Leclerq, *La Vie parfaite* (Turnhout and Paris: Brepols, 1948), pp. 164-9, has collected a number of references to this motif. Other references can be found in R. E. Kaske, "Langland and the *Paradisus Claustralis*," *Modern Language Notes*, 72 (1957), pp. 481-3. See also Morton W. Bloomfield, *Piers Plowman as Fourteenth Century Apocalypse* (New Brunswick, N.J.: Rutgers University Press, 1962), p. 197.

called and enacted in the liminal area is what we call *communitas*. *Communitas*, thus, is more than a condition of concrete existential communion, fleeting encounters and recognitions of which *Purgatorio* gives plenty of examples. It is a speculative myth of history, a scandalous utopia which is disengaged from history and yet has a radical historicity both because it is predicated as the *telos* of history and because it provides the perspective which makes possible a fresh and renewed apprehension of the structures of the world. It is within this context of problems that the poet's exile, far from being a mystical escape into some sort of visionary privacy, is the stance affording the detached vantage point from which he can speak to the world and impose his sense of order on it. It is not at all surprising that the fundamental model Dante has in mind is the City of God. In *Paradiso* xxx, he describes the circular shape of the mystical rose where the marriage banquet is celebrated (l. 135) and depicts it as existing in a condition of perennial spring:

> Nel giallo de la rosa sempiterna,
> che si digrada e dilata e redole
> odor di lode al sol che sempre verna,
> qual è colui che tace e dicer vole,
> mi trasse Bëatrice, e disse: "Mira
> quanto è 'l convento de le bianche stole!
> Vedi nostra città quant' ella gira;
> vedi li nostri scanni sì ripieni,
> che poca gente più ci si disira."
>
> ll. 124-32

(In the yellow of the eternal rose, which rises in ranks and expands and breathes odor of praise unto the sun which makes perennial spring, Beatrice drew me as one who is silent and wishes to speak, and she said, "Behold how great is the assembly of the white robes. See our city, how widely it goes around. See our seats so filled that few souls are now wanted here.")

In this eschatological area, aptly enough, the city is the Heavenly Jerusalem, and the phrase "bianche stole" is an unmistakable recall of Apocalypse 7:9. Like Jerusalem, the traditional bride and *hortus conclusus*, this city is also the perfected version of the Garden of Eden.[6] The convergence between city and garden is dramatized by other allusions. The alliterative description "si digrada e dilata e redole / odor di lode . . ." echoes both an image drawn from Vergil's *Georgics*[7] and, a suggestion made plausible by the word "convento," some stylized accounts of the cloister. Peter Damian, for instance, views the cloister as Heaven on earth, a "paradisus deliciarum, ubi tamquam *redolentium* species pigmentorum, . . . sic *fragrantia spirant odoramenta* virtutum. Ibi siquidem *rosae charitatis* ignes rubore flammescunt . . . et *perpetuae viriditatis* gratia incomparabiliter *vernant.*"[8] In a sense, it is as if Dante brings back to Heaven what the monks had imaginatively transposed down to earth.

Throughout his journey the pilgrim experiences what might be described as a pattern of synecdoches, a series of rehearsals of the event of the Heavenly Jerusalem, the symbolic center of his imaginative world. From Dis, the *civitas diaboli*, through Purgatory where the souls practice living in common, to the Earthly Paradise, Dante reviews corrupt but increasingly less imperfect images of the model. Of these images, the Garden of Eden stands as the ordering principle of

---

[6] A. Bartlett Giamatti, *The Earthly Paradise and the Renaissance Epic* (Princeton: Princeton University Press, 1969) has eloquently shown that in *Paradiso* xxx "where will and desire are one, where perfect stillness creates perfect motion, the twin images of Garden and City are married in the final, luminous vision" (p. 118). Johan Chydenius, *The Typological Problem in Dante*, has briefly probed the "affinity of Jerusalem and Paradise in medieval tradition" and Dante (pp. 103-5).

[7] *Georgics*, "redolentque thymo fragrantia mella" (iv, l. 169). For the problems surrounding the *Georgics* in the Middle Ages, see V. Zabughin, *Vergilio nel Rinascimento italiano da Dante a Torquato Tasso*, 2 vols. (Bologna: Zanichelli, 1921-3).

[8] *Laus Eremetical Vitae*, PL 148, col. 231-2.

history. This means both that the historical city is part of the typology of Eden and that Eden, like St. Francis' liminal area, is the perspective from which Dante puts forth his vision of secular order.

In an essay of a few years ago, Renato Poggioli deftly interpreted the pilgrim's experience of the terrestrial paradise as the "pastoral of happiness" that can be achieved only in personal justice exemplified by his encounter with Matelda-Astraea.[9] The barest summary of the dramatic content of the garden sequence at the top of Purgatory might show that the experience of Eden is more than the oasis of tranquility provisionally enjoyed by the pilgrim's weary mind. Dante seems intent on representing it as a place of radical ambiguity. Though removed from the world and outside of man's history, the garden is part of the geography of the world; it is a serene pastoral locale, and yet it is here, by an ironic counterpart that shatters the seemingly idyllic quality of the place, that the pilgrim experiences a painful confrontation with his own past (*Purgatorio* xxx, l. 73, to xxxi, l. 90); in the garden the pilgrim's journey under Vergil's guidance ends and the new journey led by Beatrice starts; moreover, this is the place where the Pauline *rite de passage* from the condition of the old man to the redeemed new man occurs and, at the same time, it appears as a veritable garden of love where the fall of man took place.

[9] Renato Poggioli, "Dante poco tempo silvano: or a 'Pastoral Oasis' in the *Commedia*," *Eightieth Annual Report of the Dante Society* (Cambridge, Mass., 1967), pp. 1-20. See also Charles S. Singleton, *Dante Studies 2: Journey to Beatrice* (Cambridge, Mass.: Harvard University Press, 1967), particularly pp. 141 ff. For a general treatment, see J. Daniélou, "Terre et Paradis chez les Pères de l'Eglise," *Eranus-Jahrbuch*, 23 (1954), pp. 433-72; A. Graf, *Miti, leggende e superstizioni del Medio Evo* (Turin: E. Loescher, 1892), I, chaps. I-IV; Bruno Nardi, "Intorno al sito del *Purgatorio* e al mito dantesco dell'Eden," *Giornale dantesco*, 25 (1922), pp. 290-300, and now expanded in *Saggi di filosofia dantesca* (Florence: La Nuova Italia, 1967), pp. 311-40; P. Gamberà, "La topografia del viaggio di Dante nel paradiso terrestre," *Giornale dantesco*, 9 (1902), pp. 126-7; Levi O. Kuhns, "Dante's Treatment of Nature in the *Divina Commedia*," *Modern Language Notes*, II (1896), pp. 1-17; finally, cf. A. Bartlett Giamatti, *The Earthly Paradise and the Renaissance Epic*, pp. 94-122.

Matelda in *Purgatorio* xxviii is perceived, as is well known, in terms of Cavalcanti's *pastorella* "In un boschetto" which celebrates the poet's erotic adventure with a shepherdess culminating with a joy that makes the poet believe that he has seen the very God of Love. To be sure, Dante recalls the genre and Cavalcanti's poem to alter its substance.[10] There is no erotic consummation for the pilgrim, and yet, there is a whole pattern of sexual imagery that Dante deploys to dramatize his encounter with the "bella donna." The memory of Proserpina that Matelda evokes in the pilgrim (*Purgatorio* xxviii, ll. 49-51) alludes to Proserpina's loss of Eden by the rape perpetrated by Pluto. As Matelda raises her eyes, the pilgrim is reminded of the light that shone from beneath Venus' eyelids when she was wounded by the arrows of Cupid (ll. 63-6). Finally, the text contains a reference to Leander's hatred of the Hellespont because it separates him from his beloved (ll. 71-5). In a sense, these erotic allusions are meant to suggest that the pilgrim is not in the position of Adam before the Fall, in total harmony with himself, nature and God.[11] More importantly, by the sequence of ambiguities Dante makes the garden the point of convergence between nature and grace; here, memory of the Fall and quest for redemption mingle; it is a place stripped of contingencies but where man, caught in the instability of the natural condition, may have access; it is the area where the language of secular history ("qui sarai tu poco tempo silvano; / e sarai meco sanza fine cive / di quella Roma onde Cristo è Romano," *Purgatorio* xxxii, ll. 100-2) is used to prefigure the City of God at the end of time; finally, this is the place where the fictions of the golden age coincide with the reality that the Garden has within the Christian dispensation.

Much like St. Francis in the blurred margin simultaneously outside of the world and in the world, Dante uses the Edenic

[10] See *La Divina Commedia*, ed. Natalino Sapegno (Milan and Naples: Ricciardi, 1967), p. 712.

[11] Emerson Brown, Jr., "Proserpina, Matelda, and the Pilgrim," *Dante Studies*, 89 (1971), pp. 33-48.

stance for a critique of the history and chaos of the world. As the heavenly procession in *Purgatorio* xxxii encircles the tree stripped of its flowers, the pilgrim hears the name "Adam" murmured by all. Adam means precisely the fallen world, the dissemination of men throughout the earth after the Fall, or as St. Augustine glosses it,

> Now Adam's name, as I have said more than once means in Greek the whole world. For there are four letters A,D,A,M, and with the Greeks the four corners of the world have these initial letters . . . Adam is thus scattered throughout the globe.[12]

Although Augustine goes on to say that the Divine Mercy gathered up the fragments from all sides and welded into the Church what had been broken, for Dante the reference to Adam is the pretext to introduce the allegory of the great drama of the Church, the traditional *hortus conclusus* violated by endless vicissitudes.[13] The allegory of the fortunes of the Church Militant climaxes with the prophecy of the advent of the "messo di Dio" who will come to restore the world to its idyllic order.

   Such a rudimentary summary of a most compact grid of images and allusions intends to show that Dante exploits the pastoral structure to bring together nature and history the way, for instance, Vergil does in the fourth eclogue. For Vergil, the bucolic landscape is bent to announce, through the symbolic birth of a child, the return of justice from its exile and the rejuvenation of the world. For Dante, Eden is the perspective from which he reflects on the garden's earthly projections, the Church and, as it will be presently shown, the city.

   Paradiso xxv, the canto where the pilgrim is examined on the theological virtue of hope, opens with a famous exordium:

---

[12] *PL* 37, col. 1236; cf. also *PL* 71, col. 786. St. Cyprian, *PL* 4, col. 248, makes the same point.

[13] R. E. Kaske, "Dante's *Purgatorio* xxxii and xxxiii: A Survey of Christian History," *University of Toronto Quarterly*, 43 (1974), pp. 193-214.

Se mai continga che 'l poema sacro
al quale ha posto mano e cielo e terra,
sì che m'ha fatto per molti anni macro,
vinca la crudeltà che fuor mi serra
del bello ovile ov' io dormi' agnello,
nimico ai lupi che li danno guerra;
con altra voce omai, con altro vello
ritornerò poeta, e in sul fonte
del mio battesmo prenderò 'l cappello.

ll. 1-9

(If it ever come to pass that the sacred poem to which
heaven and earth have so set hand, that it has made me
lean for many years should overcome the cruelty which
bars me from the fair sheepfold where I slept as a lamb,
an enemy to the wolves which war on it, with changed
voice now and with changed fleece a poet I will return,
and at the font of by baptism will I take the hat.)

Critics have chosen to read the passage either most literally as
the aging poet's concomitant expression of doubt and of hope
to return to his native city to take the poetic hat, or as the
statement of the theological certainty that the poet will return
to the city in order to fulfill the providential mediation of reconciling Church and Empire.[14] The lines, in effect, waver between concrete allusions to the city of Florence torn by the
tragic civil discord, and the typology of Eden.

Terms such as "ovile," "agnello," "lupi," and "vello"
adumbrate a decidedly pastoral configuration of the city. The
line "agnello, / nimico ai lupi che li danno guerra" actually

---

[14] Sapegno reads the passage in literal terms (pp. 1084-5) and quotes Boccaccio's *Vita di Dante*, ed. D. Guerri (Bari: Laterza, 1918), "sperando per la
poesì allo inusitato e pomposo onore della coronazione dell'alloro poter
pervenire, tutto a lei si diede e istitudiando e componendo" (p. 35). Niccolò
Rodolico, "Il canto xxv del *Paradiso*," in *Letture dantesche*, ed. Giovanni Getto
(Florence: Sansoni, 1961), III, 499-524, agrees with Sapegno. Dante's prophetic mission is put forward by Gian Roberto Sarolli, who has subjected the
lines to a detailed analysis, "Dante's Katabasis and Mission," in *Prolegomena
alla Divina Commedia* (Florence: Olschki, 1971), pp. 381-419.

brings together two different pastoral traditions. Isaiah in his prediction of the messianic kingdom when the disorder of the natural world will be restored into a new paradise, envisions that reign to come as the age when "the wolf shall dwell with the lamb and the leopard shall lie down with the kid" (Isaiah 11:6-7). The possibility that this biblical verse stands behind Dante's line is strengthened by the fact that later on in the canto the pilgrim defines the promise of Christian hope by referring to Isaiah. The new and old Scriptures promise the resurrection, "Dice Isaia che ciascuna vestita / ne la sua terra fia di doppia vesta" (*Paradiso* xxv, ll. 91-2). But the enmity between lamb and the wolves bears a remarkable resemblance to a description of the fall of the city of Mantua as the collapse of an Arcadian place. In an anonymous poem of the ninth century the city in ruins is figured as follows:

> Urbs quae tantum alias inter caput extulit urbes
> quantum lenta solent inter viburna cupressi
> Mantua ....
> ....
> Tytirus admonuit quam saepe cavere
> ne lupus in stabulis ovium misceret acervos.[15]

The metaphoric link between Mantua and the pastoral theme was perhaps made inevitable by the fact that Mantua is the city of Vergil, the poet of the bucolic world. One readily grants that the last line of the fragment is by no means to be construed as a "source" for Dante's own metaphor; it is, at best, a faint analogue of some cogency because of its identification of the fall of the city as a loss of the *locus amoenus*.

[15] "The city which held its head high among the other cities just as cypresses are accustomed to do among the bending osiers, Mantua . . . Tityrus often admonished to take care lest the wolf bring confusion to the heaps in the sheepfold." The poem is quoted by Jean Hubaux, *Les Thèmes bucoliques dans la poésie latine* (Brussels: M. Lamertin, 1930), p. 252. The first two lines are clearly a direct echo of Vergil's First Eclogue, ll. 24-5. It might be pointed out that the image of loftiness of the city is ironically undercut by the funereal implications of the cypresses. For the image of "acervos" as store or deposit, see *Georgics* I, ll. 158 and 185. For the *topos* of the wolf and lamb, see also *Georgics* IV, l. 435: "auditisque lupos acuunt balatibus agni."

Nonetheless, it is worth recalling that in *Purgatorio* VI what triggers the invective against the political chaos of the Italian cities is precisely the embrace between Vergil and Sordello when Mantua, their native city, is mentioned (*Purgatorio* VI, l. 72). These two traditions, Edenic and pastoral, seem to imply that Dante views the present discord of Florence as a tragic interlude between the loss of a *locus amoenus* and the expectation of a paradise to be regained. The motif of friendship, indirectly evoked through the enmity existing between the lamb and the wolves (l. 6), constitutes another major Edenic allusion.[16] Friendship, to be sure, is an essentially earthbound value, but Ambrose, in a deliberate attempt to Christianize this most pagan human bond, speaks of friendship as a foretaste of the harmony of Heaven and a veritable experience of the Garden of Eden on earth.[17] Paulinus of Nola is even more explicit in stating that friendship is the means of raising oneself to God.[18] Within this perspective one can understand, for instance, why it should be the act of friendship which brings the pilgrim out of his spiritual entanglement in *Inferno* I. In her plea to Vergil, Beatrice refers to Dante as "l'amico mio, e non de la ventura" (*Inferno* II, l. 61) which prepares and prefigures their reunion in the Garden of Eden.[19]

Yet, Ambrose and Paulinus define *amicitia* in a purely private form. To them, as in Dante's friendship with Beatrice, the friend is another self and a "pars animae." But by refer-

[16] The occurrence of the motif in patristic reflections is studied by A. Fiske, "Paradisus Homo Amicus," *Speculum*, 40 (1965), pp. 436-59. See also M. C. D'Arcy, *The Mind and the Heart of Love* (London: Faber and Faber, 1942), pp. 112-31. For *amicitia* as *concordia* in a Platonic context, see Leo Spitzer, *Classical and Christian Ideas of World Harmony: Prolegomena to the Word Stimmung* (Baltimore: The Johns Hopkins University Press, 1964), pp. 21 ff.

[17] St. Ambrose, *PL* 16, cols. 73-4; and cols. 179-84; see also A. Fiske, pp. 442-52 for further bibliography.

[18] Paulinus of Nola, *Epistola* xi, 6, *CSEL* XXIX, 64; see also *Epistola* xxiv, 9, *CSEL* XXIX, 209. The motif appears also in Aelred of Rievaulx, *De spiritali amicitia*, ed. Jean Dubois (Paris: Bayaert, 1948), II, 671D-673A. More generally, see Pierre Fabre, *Saint Paulin de Nole et l'amitié chrétienne* (Paris: Bibliothèque des Ecoles françaises d'Athènes et de Rome, 1949).

[19] *Purgatorio* xxx, ll. 11-19.

ring to the enmity within the city, Dante also historicizes the concept of friendship and makes it the metaphor of unity and the means by which the pristine harmony of the city can be restored. Enmity is precisely what destroys the garden: the *locus amoenus* of *Purgatorio* VII, the valley where the great rulers of the world are gathered, shelters the pilgrims from the imminent dark and its dangers. The "Salve, regina" (l. 82) which the penitents sing stresses the fact that they provisionally abide in a pleasant spot where the souls are exiles in what literally is a "lachrymarum valle," that the Garden is drawn within the exigencies of the world of history. As the temptations of the night creep upon the souls, they sing "Te lucis ante" (*Purgatorio* VIII, l. 13) and, as the remaining part of the hymn reveals, they pray that the dreams and phantoms of the night may be dispelled and "*hostemque* nostrum comprime." The enemy is the snake which comes but is exorcised by the arrival of two angels sent by Mary. The implication is that the Arcadian place is a precarious shelter threatened by enmity, in which the fall from Eden is typologically reenacted.

This typology of Eden is also suggested in the exordium to *Paradiso* XXV by the reference to the poet's longing to return home and take his hat "sul fonte del mio battesmo." In a way, the naming of the baptismal font reverses the literal burden of the passage and grounds the hope of the return into the typological frame of the whole poem. The poem, as is well known, is patterned on the story of Exodus, and in this very canto Beatrice glosses the pilgrim's journey in terms of the Jewish Exodus from Egypt to Jerusalem.

> "La Chiesa militante alcun figliuolo
>   non ha con più speranza, com' è scritto
>   nel Sol che raggia tutto nostro stuolo:
> però li è conceduto che d'Egitto
>   vegna in Ierusalemme per vedere,
>   anzi che 'l militar li sia prescritto."
>
>   ll. 52-7

("The Church Militant has not any child possessed of
more hope, as is written in the Sun which irradiates all
our host; therefore it is granted to him to come from
Egypt to Jerusalem, that he may see before his term of
warfare is completed.")

Exodus, as Daniélou has shown, is a type of baptism, the sacrament by which man is renewed by grace.[20] But baptism has
a double spiritual sense. It is primarily, in St. Paul's exegesis,
the typological reenactment of Exodus.

I would not have you ignorant brethren, that our fathers
(the Israelites) were all under the cloud and passed
through the sea. And all in Moses were baptized in the
cloud and the sea. . . . Now all these things were done in
figure for us.[21]

Along with this authoritative Pauline formulation, there is a
steady tendency to interpret the font of baptism as the very
figure of Eden. Origen glosses the soul's movement from sin
to the promised land exactly in terms of reaching the baptismal font:

And you who have just abandoned the darkness of
idolatry . . . then it is that you first begin to leave Egypt.
When you have been included in the number of
catechumens . . . you have passed over the Red Sea. And
if you come to the sacred font of baptism you shall enter
into the land of promise.[22]

The Church Fathers attempted to explain this seeming contradiction by distinguishing the two types of baptism administered to Christians: the first, a baptism of preparation to

[20] Jean Daniélou, *From Shadows to Reality; Studies in the Biblical Typology of
the Fathers*, trans. W. Hibberd (London: Burns and Oates, 1960), pp. 153-226,
for the general typology of Exodus.

[21] I Corinthians 10:1-6.

[22] *Commentary on St. John* I, 3, quoted by Daniélou, *From Shadows to Reality*, p. 269. For the importance of Origen in the Middle Ages, see Henri de
Lubac, *Exégèse médiévale* (Paris: Aubier, 1959), I, 198-304.

grace, the second the descent of grace itself.[23] In the moral structure of the *Divine Comedy*, this ambiguity is dramatized by the pilgrim's movement through Purgatory as an ascetic preparation for grace until, later in the Garden, Beatrice finally comes as sanctifying grace. More cogently to our passage, the double symbolic value of the baptismal font gives the poet's sense of the city an extraordinary coherence. It shows how in Dante's rigorously contrived universe, Exodus informs practically every aspect of the poem; it exemplifies the paradox that the city is the garden and, at the same time, far from being a contracted, seductive space of rest, is the area of history enacting the metaphorics of the desert. It bears the message, to put it in Pauline terms, that "civitatem manentem non habemus"[24] and that we are at home, like the penitents in the pleasant valley of *Purgatorio* VII or the pilgrim in Eden, by being in a continuous exile.

Dante's alteration of the limits of the pastoral tradition could not have been more radical. If the prominent thrust of the pastoral world is to figure the voluntary estrangement from the *negotium* of the city life to an imaginative bucolic *otium*, Dante collapses the conventional opposition between city and garden. To be sure, this static antithetical structure had been put into question by Vergil. In the fourth eclogue, as previously suggested, the pastoral is the landscape where the prophecy of renewal of history occurs.[25] In book VIII of the

[23] This distinction is based on the authority of Matthew 3:11: "I indeed baptize you with water unto repentance; but he that comes after me is mightier than I, whose shoes I am not worthy to bear: he shall baptize you with the Holy Ghost and with fire." Cf. the theological formulation by Thomas Aquinas, *Summa Theologiae*, III, q. 38, art. 2, resp. See the discussion by John Freccero, "The River of Death: *Inferno* II, 108," in *The World of Dante: Six Studies in Language and Thought*, ed. S. B. Chandler and J. A. Molinaro (Toronto: University of Toronto Press, 1966), especially pp. 37-9.

[24] "Let us go forth therefore unto him without the camp, bearing his reproach. For here we have no lasting city, but we seek one that is to come" (Hebrews 13:13-5).

[25] For the pastoral ideal as a retreat from the city to a world of esthetic repose (made of love, friendship, music and poetry), see R. Poggioli, "The

Aeneid, history also intrudes into the pastoral. In this idyllic interlude, marked by the symbolic reconciliation between two old enemies, Aeneas and Evander, Vergil represents this Arcadian world as the setting where the future city of Rome will be founded.[26] But for Vergil the setting has ambiguous implications: on the one hand, it is openly stated that Arcadia is the ground in which the justice of the empire is rooted; on the other hand, the implied continuity between history and the pastoral is subverted by the awareness of a temporal gap between the golden world of Arcadia and the imperial history. Arcadia itself, after all, is an illusory place encroached upon and shattered by the mythic violence of Hercules strangling Cacus who had stolen some of his cattle and the "furor impius" of the war between Aeneas and Turnus.[27] Ironically, the pastoral is for Vergil the perspective from which to expose the hollowness of the claims that the empire has restored the golden age on earth. He blurs the lines between history and the pastoral only to draw both within the same dark world of violence.

Oaten Flute," *Harvard Library Bulletin*, 11 (1957), pp. 148–84. See also William Empson, *Some Versions of Pastoral* (London: Chatto and Windus, 1935). On the Fourth Eclogue, see Jérôme Carcopino, *Virgile et le mystère de la IVième éclogue* (Paris: L'Artisan du Livre, 1943). For recent statements on Vergil's Eclogues, see Michael C. J. Putnam, *Virgil's Pastoral Art: Studies in the Eclogues* (Princeton: Princeton University Press, 1970), pp. 136–65.

[26] After recalling the fauns and nymphs that once lived in that landscape, and the civilizing action of Saturn, Evander points out the Capitol, golden now but once a tangle of wild woodland, the Forum, etc.; see *Aeneid* VIII, ll. 336–69.

[27] *Aeneid* VIII, ll. 193–267. H. Schnepf, "Das Herculesabenteur in Virgil's *Aeneid* (VIII, 184 ff.)," *Gymnasium*, 66 (1959), pp. 250–68, reads the victory of Hercules as the counterpart of Augustus' triumph. The sense of the "grievous burden of history" in the *Aeneid* has been highlighted by Viktor Pöschl, *The Art of Vergil: Image and Symbol in the Aeneid*, trans. Gerda Seligson (Ann Arbor: University of Michigan Press, 1962), p. 39. See also Adam Parry, "The Two Voices of Virgil's *Aeneid*," *Arion*, 2 (Winter 1963), p. 79. On the tragic elements in the *Aeneid*, see Lilian Feder, "Virgil's Tragic Theme," *Classical Journal*, 49 (1954), pp. 197–208. See also Kenneth J. Reckford, "Latent Tragedy in Aeneid VII," *American Journal of Philology*, 82 (July 1961), pp. 252–69.

The rhetorical model Dante uses for his own version of the identification of garden and city is not Vergil's, but a tradition established by Christian thinkers.[28] Taking Jerusalem, the city and the enclosed garden, as their point of departure, Endelechius, Paulinus and a host of other apologists in the wake of St. Jerome transpose the *locus amoenus* from the countryside (the region literally identified with paganism) to the city because of the presence of the Church, the new *hortus conclusus*, within its boundaries.[29] For Dante, as for the medieval exegetes, the *topos* of the *locus amoenus* to represent the city does not embody, plainly, a fictional ensemble of shadowy grove, birds singing and streams flowing. Nor is it an amiable, sentimental cipher of real and somewhat droll autobiographical elements that the poet uses in his correspondence with Giovanni del Virgilio.[30] Its main function, rather, is to show the city as a humble place marked by frugality and innocence.

The most elaborate description of the city as a spiritualized pastoral community occurs in the cantos of Cacciaguida. The encounter between the pilgrim and his ancestor in *Paradiso* xv focuses on the memory and praise of Florence of old. The rhetorical technique of the *encomium urbis* provides an obvious symmetrical antithesis to the city's present degeneracy chronicled in the successive canto. A brief close-up on his description of the city will show that Cacciaguida's words are a *laudatio temporis acti*, an elegiac reminiscence of Florence as a humble village:

"Fiorenza dentro da la cerchia antica,
        ond' ella toglie ancora e terza e nona,
        si stava in pace, sobria e pudica.
Non avea catenella, non corona,
        non gonne contigiate, non cintura
        che fosse a veder più che la persona."
                                        ll. 97-102

[28] The imaginative displacement in the early Church fathers was studied by Wolfgang Schmid, "Tityrus Christianus," *Rheinisches Museum für Philologie*, N.F., 96 (1953), pp. 101-65.

[29] Schmid, pp. 105-28.

[30] For the pastoral fiction that Dante uses in the exchange of epistles with

("Florence, within her ancient circle from which she still takes tierce and nones, abode in peace, sober and chaste. There was no necklace, no coronel, no embroidered gowns, no girdle that was more to be looked at than the person.")

The series of negatives, with their deliberate anaphoric redundance, ironically calls attention to the opulence and excesses of the present-day Florence and suggests the process of corruption of the city, what the city has become. At the same time, it acts as a way of stripping the city—the epithets "sobria" and "pudica" imply that the city is a woman—of all its superfluities, the decorative artifices that disfigure its natural chastity and continence.

In Cacciaguida's evocation, further, the city appears as a closed and self-sufficient universe, "dentro da la cerchia," a detail which is repeated in *Paradiso* XVI "nel picciol cerchio s'entrava" (l. 125). Its circular structure is emblematic of spatial perfection, analogous to the circularity of the mystical rose, we could say, if the application of this circular figure to mundane reality were not a fact surprising in itself. The primary form of the circle is God,[31] and the circle is adopted here as a symbolic sign of plenitude in poverty and as a way of discarding temptations of trespasses. The circular form draws attention to the centripetal nature of the city, to the necessity of abiding within a confined social microcosm. This notion is part of an extensive moral pattern in the poem, whereby the sins of Adam and Ulysses consist in their having trespassed beyond the limits respectively of the Garden and the world. At the same time, the walls that surround Florence are meant

Giovanni del Virgilio, see P. H. Wicksteed and E. G. Gardner, *Dante and Giovanni del Virgilio* (Westminster: A. Constable, 1902). In the first eclogue, for instance, Dante refers to the ten cantos of *Paradiso* he is sending to Giovanni del Virgilio as ten pails of milk he sends to Mopsus (p. 156). Dante, my point is, is in the tradition that holds Paradise to be the place of spiritual virtues. Cf. Jean Daniélou, *From Shadows to Reality*, pp. 57-65.

[31] The history of the emblem has been examined by Georges Poulet, *Les métamorphoses du cercle* (Paris: Plon, 1961). See also Bruno Nardi, *Nel mondo di Dante* (Rome: Edizioni di Storia e Letteratura, 1944), pp. 337-50.

to insulate the city from outside danger, the wilderness that is outside.

More importantly, Cacciaguida obliquely designates the city as a type of Jerusalem: along with the implication that it is a woman, the phrase "si stava in pace" recalls the standard biblical and patristic etymology of Jerusalem as *visio pacis*. The identification is borne out by the overt reference to the Heavenly City, the new abode of Cacciaguida, as "pace," "e venni dal martiro a questa pace" (l. 148). A correlation as well as a significant contrast is established: the Heavenly Jerusalem is reflected in the peace of Florence of old, but the permanence of one shows the earthly city to be a threatened and fragile construct.

Cacciaguida's nostalgia for the peaceful community is heightened by the fact that the scene takes place in the heaven of Mars, and Cacciaguida was a warrior in the Crusade for the liberation of Jerusalem. His nostalgia also sharply contrasts with the account of the fallen city in *Paradiso* XVI.[32]

> "Ma la cittadinanza, ch'è or mista
>   di Campi, di Certaldo e di Fegghine,
>   pura vediesi ne l' ultimo artista.
> Oh quanto fora meglio esser vicine
>   quelle genti ch' io dico, e al Galluzzo
>   e a Trespiano aver vostro confine,
> che averle dentro e sostener lo puzzo
>   del villan d'Aguglion, di quel da Signa,
>   che già per barattare ha l'occhio aguzzo!
> . . . .
> Sempre la confusion de le persone
>   principio fu del mal de la cittade,
>   come del vostro il cibo che s'appone."
>   ll. 49-57; 67-9

[32] See also the remarks by G. B. Salinari, "Il canto XVI del *Paradiso*," *Lectura Dantis Romana*, N.S. (Turin: Società Editrice Internazionale, 1965), pp. 1-27; see also Thomas G. Bergin, "Light from Mars," in *A Diversity of Dante*, pp. 143-66.

("But the citizenship which now is mixed with Campi, with Certaldo, and with Figline, saw itself pure down to the humblest artisan. Oh, how much better it would be that those folk of whom I speak were neighbors, and to have your boundary at Galluzzo and at Trespiano, than to have them within and endure the stench of the churl of Aguglione and of him of Signa who already has his eyes sharp for barter. . . . The confusion of people was always the beginning of harm to the city, as to you the food which is loaded onto the body.")

We might remark, to begin with, that Dante uses the term "città" in the sense that Isidore gives to it. In his *Etymologies*, Isidore distinguishes between "urbs" and "civitas" as follows: "civitas est hominum multitudo societatis vincula adunata . . . nam urbs ipsa moenia sunt, civitas autem non saxa sed habitatores vocantur."[33] Whereas the *urbs* can be threatened from without, the *civitas* is destroyed by internal discord. The decay, actually, is attributed to the mingling of people and "confusion de le persone." If the diagnosis resembles Plato's, who in the *Republic* attributes the corruption of the state to the confusion and meddling of people,[34] for Dante the analogy between the meddling harming the city and the excessive food harming the body prepares the motif of the body politic. Even the allusion to the "villan" threatening the stability of the city goes in that direction. In *De Planctu Naturae* the human body is metaphorically equated to the body politic, and the loins, which subvert the order of rationality, are compared to the *suburbia* inhibited by *villani*.[35] Order, the point is, can be achieved by binding desire, by knowing that for the city to exist in peace desire must be circumscribed and, in one word, controlled. More importantly, however, *confusio* is the etymological meaning of Babylon, the inverted counterpoint of the ordered city, where all bonds of family

---

[33] *Etym.* xv, 2.
[34] *Republic* iv, 434.
[35] *De Plantu Naturae*, in *PL* 210, col. 444.

and society are ignored.[36] Babylon itself, before its disintegration, was referred to by commentators as a *locus amoenus*. Bede, for instance, citing Orosius' *History*, writes that "haec campi planitia undique conspicua, natura loci laetissima."[37] Understandably, from Cacciaguida's eternal, synchronic perspective (where the sequence of contingent events is grasped in its totality, *Paradiso* xvii, ll. 37-9), the earthly city is viewed through the Augustinian paradigm of the eschatological cities of Jerusalem and Babylon. From this absolute standpoint, in fact, the earthly city is part of the world of finitude:

> "Le vostre cose tutte hanno lor morte,
> sì come voi; ma celasi in alcuna
> che dura molto, e le vite son corte.
> E come 'l volger del cielo de la luna
> cuopre e discuopre i liti sanza posa,
> così fa di Fiorenza la Fortuna."
>
> *Paradiso* xvi, ll. 79-84

("All your affairs have their death even as you do; but it is concealed in some things that last long, whereas lives are short. And as the revolution of the heaven of the

---

[36] For the commonplace, "quia Babylon confusio interpretatur," see *PL* 75, col. 742D; *PL* 40, col. 337. Mixture, confusion and *discordia* (*Inferno* vi, l. 63), I should like to add, as metaphors of disharmony, have musical-political overtones. See Leo Spitzer, *Classical and Christian Ideas of World Harmony*, pp. 17 ff., for the neoplatonic tradition of justice as concordance and harmony. In this context, it might be pointed out that the notion of peace has also musical resonances. In *The City of God*, trans. Marcus Dods (New York: Random House Inc., 1950), St. Augustine defines peace both by an analogy between body and the state, and by a music metaphor: "The peace of the body then consists in the duly proportioned arrangement of its parts. The peace of the irrational soul is the harmonious repose of the appetites. . . . Domestic peace is the well-ordered concord between those of the family who rule and those who obey. Civil peace is a similar concord among the citizens" (xix, 13, p. 690).

[37] *Hexaemeron*, in *PL* 91, col. 127; Bede quotes Orosius' *Historiarum Adversum Paganos Libri Septem* i, chap. 6. See also John T. Golden, "Societal Bonds in Old English Heroic Poetry: A Legal and Typological Study," Dissertation, Cornell University 1970, p. 27.

moon covers and uncovers the shores without pause, so Fortune does with Florence.")

The awareness of the ephemeral nature of all earthly things introduces Cacciaguida's chronicle of the fall of the great Florentine families and is linked to a general sense of mutability of the world of time governed by fortune. The brief span of individual lives discloses what the larger duration of the families seems to conceal, that the cycles of generations are like the phases of the moon and they perpetually ascend and descend around the revolving wheel of fortune till they finally die.

This fundamentally Boethian view of fortune presiding over the sublunary world of generation and corruption is associated with man's fall from the Garden into the shiftiness of time.[38] Cacciaguida's speech on the inevitable finitude of all temporal things is certainly valid from his perspective *sub specie aeternitatis*, but for Dante time is not the principle of the city's decay. Cacciaguida's reflections are actually modeled on a passage from Macrobius' *Commentary on the Dream of Scipio* where he describes the seasons of history and the pattern of the origin and collapse of civilizations.

People wander over the earth and gradually put aside the roughness of a nomadic existence and by natural inclination submit to communities and associations. Their mode of living is at first simple, knowing no guile and strange to cunning, called in its early stage the golden age. The more these populations progress in civilization and progress of the arts, the more easily does the spirit of rivalry creep in, at first commendable but imperceptibly changing to envy: this then is responsible for all the tribulations that the race suffers in subsequent ages. So much for the trouble that civilizations experience, of perishing and arising again as the world goes on unchanged.[39]

[38] For the motif of fortune, see Appendix.

[39] Macrobius, *Commentarium in somnium Scipionis*, ed. J. Willis (Leipzig: B. G. Teubner, 1970), II, x, 15, p. 127. The translation is by William H.

The passage is a cogent gloss on *Paradiso* XVI for a number of reasons. It is spoken by a grandfather (and Cacciaguida is the pilgrim's grandfather), its main thrust is the proposition that "glory is not to be sought after," and Dante introduces the canto with a tercet on the nature of nobility of blood and the pilgrim's glory in it in Heaven: "O poca nostra nobiltà di sangue, / se gloriar di te la gente fai / qua giù dove l'affetto nostro langue, / . . . nel cielo, io me ne gloriai" (ll. 1-6). For Macrobius the golden age is the period of simplicity and absence of envy. For Dante envy is repeatedly called the spark that perverts the order of Florence. For both, human history is not the story of a steady progress in time. Time, as an Aristotelean accident, is supplanted by the sense that it is a category existing in a moral dimension.[40] The notion of moral time is Dante's attempt to escape out of time, not through some conviction that time is unreal, since it is the framework of God's plan from Creation to Apocalypse, but because it has no ontological stability. When man clings to wealth, has his eye sharp for jobbery and trades and changes in imitation of the very operations of Fortune, then the city is fallen.

The hurlings and shifts of Fortune can be overcome by the exercise of continence and poverty, and by joining the acts of will to those of reason, as Dante implies in his discussion of Fortune in *Inferno* VII, the stability and permanence of the city can be regained. In this sense, the pastoral myth in which the political order is rooted is by no means the romantic fantasy and longing, however ironic and consciously hollow a fiction this may be with the Romantics, for a return to a pure state of nature where history can have a fresh start. The *locus amoenus*

Stahl, *Commentary on the Dream of Scipio* (New York: Columbia University Press, 1952), p. 219.

[40] The Aristotelian definition of time, drawn from his *Physics* (IV, xi), is given in *Convivio* IV, ii, 6. For what is here called moral time, see the extended reflections in St. Augustine, *Confessions* XI, viii and ff. See also the summary by Hans Urs Von Balthasar, "The Fragmentary Nature of Time," in *A Theological Anthropology*, trans. from German (New York: Sheed and Ward, 1967), pp. 1-42.

is not the enchanted ground for the making of history nor is it
its precondition; it is, on the contrary, made in history, contrived by man's will and effort. Using the strictly esthetic language of the pastoral convention, nature is not in contrast to
art but is perfected by art. Thus envisaged, the order that the
city may realize is "natural" but certainly not in the sense of a
spontaneous growth like the things of nature.

The pastoral metaphor transposed into the context of the
possibilities of history is the imaginative focus for Dante's
corporate ideology. We must look at the vituperative attack
on Italy in *Purgatorio* VI, a veritable *excursus* of the poet speaking *in propria persona*, to grasp its structure.

> Ahi serva Italia, di dolore ostello,
>> nave sanza nocchiere in gran tempesta,
>> non donna di provincie, ma bordello!
> Quell' anima gentil fu così presta,
>> sol per lo dolce suon de la sua terra,
>> di fare al cittadin suo quivi festa;
> e ora in te non stanno sanza querra
>> li vivi tuoi, e l'un l'altro si rode
>> di quei ch'un muro e una fossa serra.
> Cerca, misera, intorno da le prode
>> le tue marine, e poi ti guarda in seno,
>> s'alcuna parte in te di pace gode.
> Che val perché ti racconciasse il freno
>> Iustinïano, se la sella è vòta?
>> Sanz' esso fora la vergogna meno.
> . . . .
> O Alberto tedesco ch'abbandoni
>> costei ch'è fatta indomita e selvaggia,
>> e dovresti inforcar li suoi arcioni,
> giusto giudicio da le stelle caggia
>> sovra 'l tuo sangue, e sia novo e aperto,
>> tal che 'l tuo successor temenza n'aggia!
> Ch'avete tu e 'l tuo padre sofferto,
>> per cupidigia di costà distretti,
>> che 'l giardin de lo 'imperio sia diserto.

Vieni a veder Montecchi e Cappelletti

. . . .

Vieni a veder la tua Roma che piagne
vedova e sola, e dì e notte chiama:
"Cesare mio, perché non m'accompagne?"
Vieni a veder la gente quanto s'ama!

ll. 76-90, 97-106, 112-5

(Ah, servile Italy, hostel of grief, ship without pilot in
great tempest, no mistress of provinces but brothel. So
eager was that noble soul, just at the sweet name of his
land, to give glad welcome there to his fellow citizen;
and now in you your living are not without war and of
those whom one wall and one moat shut in, one gnaws at
the other! Search, wretched one, round the shores of
your seas and then look within your bosom, if any part
of you enjoy peace. What avails it that Justinian should
refit the bridle, if the saddle is empty? Without it the
shame would be less. . . . O German Albert, who do
abandon her that is become wanton and wild and who
should bestride her saddle bows, may just judgment fall
from the stars upon your blood, and be it so strange and
manifest that your successor may have fear thereof! For
you and your father, held back yonder by greed, have
suffered the garden of the empire to be laid waste. Come
to see Montecchi and Cappelletti, . . . Come to see your
Rome that weeps, widowed and alone, crying day and
night, "My Caesar, why do you abandon me?" Come
and see how the people love one another.)

The canto is symmetrically related to the other political cantos, *Inferno* VI and *Paradiso* VI, and, in effect, it looks forward
to the apotheosis of the Empire by the allusion to Justinian
and backward to the chaos of Florence (ll. 127-9) as if to
imply that each unit reflects and shares in the disorder of the
other. In the initial apostrophe, if the phrase "di dolore ostello" is the ironic reversal of Cacciaguida's sense of Florence
as "dolce ostello" (*Paradiso* XV, l. 132), the epithet "serva"

places Italy within the typology of the Exodus story. It exploits the ambiguity of moral and political captivity the way Cato's "libertà" was seen to encompass both spiritual and political liberty. More important, there are two crucial metaphors used to describe Italy. In the first she is explicitly referred to as "giardino" untended by the emperor and degraded into a desert. It might be pointed out that the motif of the desert is turned upside down in the following canto where the good princes are gathered to abide in a pleasant valley. In the second metaphor, the biblical lamentation for Jerusalem, she is cast as an adulterous woman, and further on, the city of Rome appears as a "vedova" crying night and day for her Caesar.

The tradition of characterizing the emperor in the guise of a bridegroom and the city as the bride was well known to Dante. In the *Pharsalia*, Cato is called "urbi pater urbique maritus" (ii, l. 388). More prominently, in the epistle to the King of Italy, Dante greets Henry VII in emphatic scriptural terms as "sponsus Italiae."[41] By the implied metaphor of marriage, Dante extends on to the secular order the mystical marriage between the Church and the pope. In *Inferno* xix, for instance, Pope Boniface VIII's abuses of the spiritual gifts of the Church are unmistakably presented as an adultery degrading the Church into the apocalyptic *magna meretrix* predicted by St. John.[42] The symbolic cluster of marriage and garden makes the earthly city the typological extension of the Church in another crucial sense. Medieval exegetes from Honorius Augustodunensis to Hugh of St. Victor and St.

[41] *The Letters of Dante*, emended text by Paget Toynbee (Oxford: Clarendon Press, 1966). The letter is written in the typological mode: the exiles who hope to return to Florence are referred to as the Jews in the captivity of Babylon (par. 8, particularly); cf. also Epistle vi, par. 6. In Epistle viii, par. 8, the emperor is alluded to as a new David. The "sponsus" derives from the biblical tradition of viewing Jerusalem as the woman and wife of the Lord. See Song of Songs 4:12-3.

[42] The unfaithful bride and harlot as a motif is in Jeremiah 3:6-10, and Isaiah 1:21. See also Dante's Epistle viii, par. 7, where Florence is spoken of as an unnatural Myrrha and Amata.

Bernard generally agree in allegorizing the love story in the garden of the Song of Songs as the epithalamium with the Church as the bride, and Christ as the bridegroom.[43] St. Paul himself in Ephesians 5:21-3 explains marriage as the act which typologically repeats the unity of Christ and the Church and as the sacrament by which the prelapsarian unity of Adam in the world of Eden is once again available to man.

Actually, St. Paul's formulation "for no man ever hates his own flesh, but nourishes and cherishes it, as Christ does the Church, because we are members of his body," along with other passages from the Epistles to the Corinthians and Colossians, is the metaphor for the *corpus mysticum* of the Universal Church, the economy embracing all the members from the beginning in Adam to the end of the world and whose head is Christ.[44] It is ironic, we might add, that in historical terms, this corporate doctrine should be advanced as a tenet of faith in the bull *Unam Sanctam* by Boniface VIII who, for Dante, is its foremost violator.[45] It is this idea of *communitas*, visible in the structure of the Church and the eucharistic sacrament which the Church administers, that Dante translates

---

[43] For the bride as the Church, see St. Ambrose, *De Isaac et Anima* 3, 8, in *CSEL* xxxii, i, 647. Cf. St. Jerome, *PL* 33, col. 547, and *De Civitate Dei* xvii, 20, in *CCSL* xlviii, for the marriage between Christ and Church.

[44] The quote is from Ephesians 5:29-30. The doctrine of the *Corpus Ecclesiae Mysticum* is derived from organic metaphors which St. Paul uses in other letters. See I Corinthians 12:12 and 6:15. Cf. Colossians 2:19. An excellent history of the controversies surrounding the doctrine is in Henri de Lubac, *Corpus Mysticum*, 2nd ed. (Paris: Aubier, 1949). See also Emile Mersch, *Le Corps mystique du Christ; Etudes de théologie historique*, 3rd ed. (Brussels: Desclee de Brouwer, 1951). More recently, a summary has been provided by Ernst H. Kantorowicz, *The King's Two Bodies: A Study in Mediaeval Political Theology* (Princeton: Princeton University Press, 1957), pp. 194-232.

[45] Gerhart B. Ladner, "The Concepts: *Ecclesia*, *Christianitas*, *Plenitudo Potestatis*," in *Sacerdozio e Regno da Gregorio VII a Bonifacio VIII*, Miscellanea Historiae Pontificiae, xviii (1954), pp. 49-77. For Dante's view of Boniface VIII, see *Inferno* xix: " 'Se' tu già costì ritto, / se' tu già costì ritto, Bonifazio? / Di parecchi anni mi mentì lo scritto. / Se' tu sì tosto di quell' aver sazio / per lo qual non temesti tòrre a 'nganno / la bella donna, e poi di farne strazio?' " (ll. 52-7).

into the metaphor of the body politic organically unified by the symbolic marriage between emperor and state in the garden. This doctrine had been displaced in Dante's time, as E. H. Kantorowicz has shown, into a concrete legal structure within which the articulation of political society could be envisioned.[46] But for Dante it seems that the model he evokes had become an empty and deluded abstraction which he arrays over and against the harshness and anarchy of political life. If in the Heavenly Jerusalem the members eat at the nuptial banquet of the Lord (*Paradiso* xxx, l. 135), here on earth "l'un l'altro si rode," a phrase which simultaneously implies the reciprocity of violence, and by the "si," the self-reflexiveness of violence: being members of the same body, cannibalism is inevitably reversed into self-cannibalism. And if the mystical body is governed by a bond of love, here on earth we are asked to see "la gente come s'ama," another phrase which is also doubly ironic because it can be read to mean both that no bond of love actually exists among the people and that everyone is caught in a love of self. The causes of such a radical mockery of the myth of order for Dante lie in the neglect of the laws (ll. 139 ff.), which, far from being rational norms for the rational ends of man, have been reduced to subtle provisions spun in October, to paraphrase the text, and never lasting till mid-November; the general unbridled greed; the strife within the leading families; and finally the lack of an emperor who would lead men in their journey to a point from which they catch a glimpse of at least the tower of the true city (*Purgatorio* xvi, l. 96).

By placing the invective within the scene of the recognition and embrace of the two Mantuan poets and through the sys-

[46] Ernst H. Kantorowicz, *The King's Two Bodies*, pp. 207 ff. The metaphor of the human body for the organic structure of the state has also a classical tradition, as shown by Wilhelm Nestle, "Die Fabel des Meninius Agrippa," *Klio*, 21 (1926-7), pp. 358 ff. Cf. John of Salisbury, *Policraticus*, ed. C. C. J. Webb (Frankfurt a. M.: Minerva G.M.A.H., 1965), II, 282 ff. See also Alan of Lille, in *PL* 210, col. 444. For a general view, see Leonard Barkan, *Nature's Work of Art: The Human Body as Image of the World* (New Haven and London: Yale University Press, 1975).

tematic pattern of allusions to the myth of order that families, cities, country and empire have betrayed, Dante emphasizes the corruption existing in the world of history. But his strategy goes beyond the mere suggestion of a contrast between an ideal vision and the reality of experience. For in this invective the poet is involved in a literal "digression" (l. 128); he literally steps outside of the narrative and insinuates that a rupture exists between history and the text. His public voice arises in a condition of marginality to both the historical nightmare and the idyllic communion between Vergil and Sordello.

Throughout the poem, actually, the poet subverts any temptation of pastoral complacency and retreats from the comfortable quarters that the poetic imagination seemingly affords. In the *locus amoenus* of limbo, the pilgrim encounters the community of poets living in the half-light of desire and hopelessness. Dante stops and speaks with them of beautiful things (*Inferno* IV, ll. 103-5), of literature, one surmises, beautiful in itself but like that *locus amoenus* a painfully incomplete act because it is pagan literature and, like that garden, is enclosed within itself. The poets are graphically relegated to the threshold of Hell in an absolute space where temporal differences are crushed and the contemporaneity of poets of different ages is a simulacrum of the eternity they grope for but will never achieve. Even Vergil, who because of the *Aeneid*, which for Dante is the book of history, leaves this *locus amoenus* to guide the pilgrim up to the Garden of Eden, will finally return to it. It is as if Dante constantly senses that poetry is always so threatened by the possibility of being a fictional self-enclosure that he emphatically breaks away from and insists that his own poetic voice has no place in the Garden.

All the prophecies about his own future that Dante registers are phophecies of exile; what is more, they are uttered by men in Hell who themselves were alienated from the city, and all predict the fall of the city. Ciacco's prophecy in *Inferno* VI of the civil war of Florence, which is the *leitmotif* of all other prophetic statements, comes from a man who refers to his own city as *"la tua città"* (l. 49), indicating his detachment from it. The prophecy of exile comes also from Farinata, portrayed in proud loneliness in the circle of the heretics, those who have torn the seamless tunic of Christ. Brunetto Latini's prediction is uttered by a man who is "del 'umana natura posto in bando" (*Inferno* xv, l. 81). Finally, the pilgrim's encounter with Cacciaguida climaxes with the painful prophecy of Dante's future exile from the city: "tu lascerai ogne cosa diletta / più caramente; e questo è quello strale / che l'arco de lo essilio pria saetta" and concludes ". ... sì ch'a te fia bello / averti fatta parte per te stesso" (*Paradiso* xvii, ll. 55-69).

Alienation for Dante is an ambiguous concept[47] and a passage from Gregory's *Moralia in Job* may help to illustrate this ambiguity. Gregory describes the fallen angels as "alieni" because of their estrangement from the divine order and to this angelic alienation juxtaposes the ascetic idea of the *homo viator* who consciously alienates himself from the world in the journey to the heavenly homeland:

> At contra justi . . . sic . . . refoventur subsidio, sicut viator in stabulo utitur lecto: pausat et recedere festinat; *quiescit corpore sed ad aliud tendit mente.* Nonnumquam vero et adversa perpeti appetunt, in transitoriis prosperare refugiunt, ne delectatione itineris a patriae perventione tardentur. . . .[48]

[47] A general statement on the medieval idea of alienation, particularly in Gregory, is by Gerhart B. Ladner, *"Homo Viator*: Mediaeval Ideas on Alienation and Order,"* Speculum*, 42 (1967), pp. 233-59. The motif of the Christian as a stranger on this earth can be found in Hebrews 11:13 ("They are pilgrims and strangers on the earth"); cf. also the First Epistle of St. Peter 2:11. Ladner (p. 236) lists examples of the Christian residing as a *peregrinus* in a foreign country from various places. A primary occurrence is in *De Civitate Dei* i, the preface, and xviii, 51; see also *PL* 38, col. 619; *PL* 44, col. 253; etc. Cf. G. N. Knauer, *"Peregrinatio Animae,"* Hermes*, 85 (1957), pp. 216 ff. In *Purgatorio* the metaphor of the pilgrimage is extensive: see "ma noi siam peregrin come voi siete" (*Purgatorio* ii, l. 63); " 'O frate mio, ciascuna è cittadina / d'una vera città; ma tu vuo' dire / chi vivesse in Italia peregrina' " (*Purgatorio* xiii, ll. 94-6).

[48] "But on the other hand, the just ones are so comforted by temporal pro-

Such a metaphor of man as a pilgrim on earth and a citizen of Heaven is extensively dramatized in *Purgatorio*: more poignantly, in canto II, as the pilgrim starts his ascent up the mountain, Dante writes: "Noi eravam lunghesso mare ancora, / come gente che pensa a suo cammino, / che va col cuore e col corpo dimora" (ll. 10-2), the last line of which translates *verbatim* "quiescit corpore sed ad aliud tendit mente," with the difference that for Dante, following Augustine, the heart, not the mind, is the locus of spiritual restlessness.

Dante, like Gregory, assigns a double moral value to alienation. It designates sin in the case of Ciacco, Farinata and Brunetto. But in the case of Dante's own alienation from the city predicted by Cacciaguida it is viewed positively as "a te fia bello / averti fatta parte per te stesso." This statement of isolation seems to contradict the stance the pilgrim takes in *Paradiso* VIII, where to Charles Martel's query whether it would be worse for man on earth if he were not a citizen, Dante replies "si, . . . e qui ragion non cheggio" (l. 117). The contradiction is only apparent: Dante's exile from the city is linked with the poetic act and is described as the transmission of truth to the people (*Paradiso* XVII, ll. 124 ff.). It is an act central to the idea of community because through the poetic discourse Dante acts upon the world by being outside of it.

Dante is aware, however, that this poetic exile may simply hide a darker version of self-enclosure, as a brief look at *Inferno* XV where Brunetto Latini is punished exemplifies. Brunetto's own sin is admittedly a sin of sodomy, either sexual or linguistic, but nonetheless a metaphor for the unnatural act of indulging in sterile and unfructifying actions.[49] The

---

visions as the wayfarer uses a bed in an inn: he stops and hastens to go away; he rests with the body, but with the mind he reaches out to another place. Sometimes they long to suffer misfortunes, avoid being happy in transitory things, lest they be delayed by the delight of the journey from reaching the country" (*Moralia in Job*, in *PL* 75, cols. 857c-858a). Also in the *Moralia in Job*, *PL* 75, col. 1005c; *PL* 76, col. 720d, Gregory makes the fallen angels those who are by definition *alieni*.

[49] E. G. Parodi, *Poesia e storia nella* Divina Commedia, 2nd ed. (Venice: Pozza, 1965), pp. 165-200. Umberto Bosco, "Il canto XV dell'*Inferno*," *Lec-*

focus of the canto falls on Brunetto's blindness to his own condition. Sodom, to be sure, is conventionally etymologized as *caecitas*,[50] and Dante's metaphor as he approaches the sinners subtly implies this much: ". . . e ciascuna / ci riguardava come suol da sera / guardare uno altro sotto nuova luna; / e sì ver' noi aguzza van le ciglia / come 'l vecchio sartor fa ne la cruna" (ll. 17-21). Brunetto's own blindness is ironically deployed throughout the exchange with his former disciple, and Dante capitalizes on this irony. As if blind to his own blindness, Brunetto speaks of the Florentines as "orbi" and "gente avara e invidiosa"[51] (ll. 67-8). Twice does Brunetto refer to

tura Dantis scaligera (Florence: Le Monnier, 1961). Of interest are also M. Casella, "Il canto di Brunetto Latini," in *Studi critici in onore di Emilio Santini* (Palermo: Manfredi, 1956), pp. 125-8. For the view of linguistic perversion, see André Pézard, *Dante sous le pluie de feu* (Paris: Vrin, 1950); more recently, M. Pastore Stocchi, "Delusione e giustizia nel canto XV dell'*Inferno*," *Lettere italiane*, 20 (1968), pp. 433-55.

[50] "Sodoma interpretatur caecitas," in *PL* 113, col. 131B. See also Isidore, *Quaestiones in Vetus Testamentum*, in *PL* 83, col. 246A-B; Gregory, *Moralia in Job*, in *PL* 75, col. 750B. The symbolic-spiritual relation between blindness and sodomy has been pointed out by the early Dante commentaries; see Biagi, ed. *Inferno*, particularly the "Chiose anonime edite dal Vernon," p. 408, and more generically, by Benvenuto, p. 408. The commentators also gloss "e ciascuna / ci reguardava come suol da sera / guardare uno altro sotto nuova luna" (*Inferno* XV, ll. 17 ff.) as the blindness of sodomy. Cf. Biagi, p. 402.

[51] These passions which pervert the order of the city echo almost verbatim the triad of sins listed by Ciacco in *Inferno* VI, l. 74. I would also suggest that this motif of blindness of love, which metaphorically links political chaos and Brunetto's own spiritual disorder, recalls Brunetto's *Tesoretto*, a poem of exile from Florence and an imaginative quest for a possible new order under the guidance of Nature. At the heart of the quest, Brunetto enters the Garden of Love pointedly represented as blind Cupid: "ch'avea l'arco e li strali / e avea penn' ed ali, ma neente vedea" (ll. 2263-5). It would seem, I believe, that it is this view of love that Dante indicts in *Inferno* XV. To be sure, the *Tesoretto* does not end there: Ovid leads the quester out of the Garden of Love, where things both are and are not what they seem to be (ll. 2204 ff.), and the penance begins eventually to climax with Brunetto's encountering Ptolomy, at which point the story is interrupted. It is difficult to resist the temptation to inscribe, at the metaphoric encounter with Ptolomy, Brunetto's crossing into the domain of science, the *Tresor*. The quotations from *Tesoretto* are taken from *Poeti del Duecento*, II, ed. Gianfranco Contini (Milan and Naples: Ricciardi, 1960).

Dante as "figliuol" (ll. 31 and 37), a claim to paternity which
is ironically undercut by his sodomy. Poignantly enough,
Dante stresses the illusoriness of the claim by referring to
Brunetto as "imagine paterna" (l. 83). Further, he mistakes
Dante's own quest as being parallel to his own. When Dante
recounts his own journey:

> "Là sù di sopra, in la vita serena,"
> rispuos' io lui, "mi smarri' in una valle,
> avanti che l'età mia fosse piena.
> Pur ier mattina le volsi le spalle:
> questi m'apparve, tornand' ïo in quella,
> e reducemi a ca per questo calle."
>
> ll. 49-54

("Up above there in the bright life," I answered him,
"before my age was at full, I lost my way in a valley.
Only yesterday morning I turned my back on it. He appeared to me when I was returning to it and by this road
he leads me home.")

The account recapitulates the very exordium of *Inferno* but is
faintly patterned, as has been widely acknowledged,[52] on the
opening lines of Brunetto's *Tesoretto*, the story of his exile
from the city. Brunetto here in *Inferno*, on account of the textual recalls of his poem, ironically believes that Dante's quest
reenacts his own. Thus, to his disciple's statement that he is
headed for home, he predicts that he will reach a "glorioso
porto" (l. 56), mindless of the discrepancy between his
earthly view of glory—rejected by Dante in the canto of
Cacciaguida—and the glory and the true home the pilgrim
seeks. More important, this man who is alienated from
human nature believes that he lives within his own *Tresor*, a
text written in exile, which he recommends to the pilgrim (ll.

---

[52] The echoes from the *Tesoretto* in Dante's text have been duly noted by
Nicolaus Delius, "Dante's *Commedia* und Brunetto Latini's *Tesoretto*,"
Jahrbücher der deutschen Dantesgesellschaft, 4 (1887), pp. 12-3; see also E. von
Richthofen, *Veltro und Diana* (Tübingen: M. Niemeyer 1956), pp. 33 ff.

119-20). The irony consists in the duplicity of the representation: on the one hand, the reality of Brunetto's factual life distorted and cramped, the disorder that the human flesh is prone to; on the other hand, the claims of a transfigured life provided by literature. This claim is another sign of Brunetto's sodomy because it implies his confusion between his own reality and the images of the text ·and makes the confines of the text the narcissistic, illusory house of his eternal death.

As Dante exposes Brunetto's self-deceptions, he seems to dismiss his notion that life and literature can even be together or that literature can reflect the author's life. Against the fiction that the self is contained in the text, he calls for a radical sense of exile, emptied of illusions of self-presence, as an ongoing quest which to him can only end in God. If this is the case, what is the meaning of his hope for a return to Florence in *Paradiso* xxv?

The medium for his homecoming is the "poema sacro" by which the poet would take the poetic hat at the baptismal font. The passage is colored by a language ("sacro," a spare reference to spiritual askesis in line 3, self-dramatization as a lamb, the baptismal font where the investiture should take place) that seems to give a quality of holiness to the bond that will link the poet to the reconciled city. This hoped-for return to the baptismal font, actually, is a pointed recall of the poet's breaking of the baptismal font recounted in *Inferno* xix (ll. 16-21). The correspondences between the two scenes are striking: both deal with autobiographical reflections; both are centered on the metaphor of the font; in *Inferno* xix, Dante speaks of "mio *bel* San Giovanni" (l. 17) and in *Paradiso*·xxv, of "*bell'* ovile" (l. 5). In the infernal scene the poem is used to assert the necessity for the poet's breaking the vessel ("e questo sia suggel ch' ogn' omo sganni," *Inferno* xix, l. 21), while in *Paradiso* the poem is an instrument of reconciliation. By recalling the previous violation, Dante stresses his hope that the past divisions within the city may be healed and the order of the city may be renewed.

This motif of renewal is obliquely hinted through the allusion to Jason's quest and his return with the Golden Fleece.[53] The myth of the Argonauts is recalled both at the beginning of *Paradiso* II (ll. 16 ff.) and at the very end, *Paradiso* XXXIII (ll. 94 ff.), as a metaphoric counter to the pilgrim's own journey in the unexplored domain of the blessed. But there is no identification with Jason who is damned for his seduction of Hypsipyle with "parole ornate" (*Inferno* XVII, l. 91). On the contrary, Dante is interested in marking the alterity (the emphasis falls on "*altra* voce," "*altro* vello"), the radical difference from Jason's signs and ornate words and his Golden Fleece. Jason's story of the return with the Golden Fleece is, in fact, subtly alluded to in Vergil's fourth eclogue precisely as an instance of residual fraud prior to the advent of the renewed golden age of history, and as such it seems to act as a hint of disruption of the eclogue's overt thematic design.[54] Unlike the mythic Jason, then, Dante figured as an old man, the time when one puts on the new man, would return to announce the renewed pastoral order in the city. As a poignant correlation to this, we might remember that in Dante's own second eclogue the ram's fleece that Jason brought back is periphrastically employed to describe the constellation of Aries, the emblem of spring and the new beginning of the year.[55]

This hope of a return is, however, reversed into an emblem for a new departure. The baptismal font, as I have shown, is

[53] The presence of the allusion is suggested by Gian Roberto Sarolli, pp. 401-3; and, extending Sarolli's insight, by Robert Hollander, *Allegory in Dante's* Commedia (Princeton: Princeton University Press, 1969), pp. 223-4.

[54] The first lines of the eclogue proclaim the future age of justice, while later (ll. 30-6) there is a compressed account of man's sins as follows: "Pauca tamen suberunt priscae vestigia fraudis / quae temptare Thetim ratibus, quae cingere muris / oppida, . . . alter erit tum Tiphys, et altera quae vehat Argo delectos heroas."

[55] "Velleribus Colchis praepes ditectus Eous / alipedesque alii pulcrum Titana ferebant" (ll. 1-2, *Dante and Giovanni del Virgilio*, p. 166). As the commentators of the eclogue suggest, the passage means that Eous (one of the horses of the sun) had "thrown off the golden clouds of the sunrise" (pp. 238-9). It is of interest to point out that in the eclogue Dante casts himself as a Ulysses unwilling to put himself into the powers of "Polyphemus" (ll. 44-62, p. 170).

the figure of Eden as well as the figure of Exodus. Furthermore, the phrase "poema sacro" contains an ambiguous resonance. The epithet "sacro" can be taken in the double sense, suggested by its Latin etymology, of profane and holy, and would thus describe the thematic substance of the poem, its infernal and heavenly content. The phrase, more cogently, translates Macrobius' definition of the *Aeneid*. In his *Saturnalia*, he rejects vulgar interpretations of the *Aeneid* in favor of the allegorical investigations of its deeper and arcane senses:

> . . . ultra quae siquis egredi audeat, introspexisse in aedem deae a qua mares absterrentur existimandus sit. Sed nos, quos crassa Minerva dedecet, non patiamur abstrusa esse adyta *sacri poematis*, sed arcanorum sensuum investigato aditu doctorum cultu celebranda praebeamus reclusa penetralia (emphasis mine).[56]

The passage in Macrobius is preeminently a vindication of an intellectual élite sensitive to the esoteric doctrines of the *Aeneid* and an attempt to mobilize the philosophical resources of an endangered pagan culture.[57] The force of the phrase in Dante's text can be gauged by looking at its slight variant, "sacrato poema," in *Paradiso* XXIII. After the pilgrim is unable to remember the vision of the triumph of Christ and Mary surrounded by the communion of saints, the poet acknowl-

---

[56] Macrobius, *Saturnalia*, ed. J. Willis (Leipzig: B. G. Teubner, 1970), I, xxiv, 13-14, p. 130. The text reads: ". . . and if anyone were to dare to overstep these prescribed limits, he would have to be deemed guilty of as heinous an offense as if he had peered into the temple from which all males are banned. But we, who claim to have a finer taste, shall not suffer the secret places of this sacred poem to remain concealed, but we shall examine the approaches to its hidden meanings and throw open its inmost shrine for the worship of the learned" (Macrobius, *The Saturnalia*, trans. Percival Vaughan Davies [New York and London: Columbia University Press, 1969], p. 156).

[57] The debate between the proponents of the Hellenic tradition and the Christians has been highlighted by F. Cumont, "La Polémique de l' Ambrosiaster contre les païens," *Revue d'histoire et de littérature religieuses*, 8 (1903), pp. 417-40; Pierre Courcelle, "Pagan Hellenism: Macrobius," in *Late Latin Writers and their Greek Sources*, trans. Harry E. Wedeck (Cambridge, Mass.: Harvard University Press, 1969), pp. 13-47.

edges that, even if Polyhymnia and her sisters sounded to aid him, he would be unable to recount the splendor of Beatrice's smile:

> e così, figurando il paradiso,
> convien saltar lo sacrato poema,
> come chi trova suo cammin riciso.
> Ma chi pensasse il ponderoso tema
> e l'omero mortal che se ne carca,
> nol biasmerebbe se sott' esso trema:
> non è pareggio da picciola barca
> quel che fendendo va l'ardita prora,
> né da nocchier ch'a sé medesmo parca.
>
> ll. 61-9

(. . . and so, picturing Paradise, the sacred poem must make a leap, like one who finds his way cut off. But he that considers the ponderous theme and the mortal shoulder that is laden with it, will not blame it if it tremble beneath the load. It is no voyage for a little bark, this which the daring prow cleaves as it goes, nor for a pilot who would spare himself.)

If for Macrobius "sacred poem" designates an allegorical edifice for the interpreters to enter and explore, for Dante it describes the poem as a journey marked by broken paths, short cuts and detours. In view of this, in *Paradiso* xxv the poet hopes to return to the baptismal font by the poem, and by it he seems to call upon the community to undertake the experience of exile that the poem tells. This call is exemplified by the frequent addresses to the readers by which they are asked to interpret and to share the poet's own journey. More prominently, the readers are asked to venture into unstable seas in the wake of the poet's own bark, through metaphors that echo Ulysses' journey. In *Purgatorio* I the poet sets the sails of poetry; in *Paradiso* II the readers are envisioned in a little bark following the path marked by the poet's ship, whereby some may go astray and few others may manage to hold to the furrow before the trace is effaced and the water turns smooth again (ll. 1-15). The navigational metaphor for the act of writing and interpretation recalls a long classical and patristic tradition.[58] It obliquely recalls also Psalm 76, the song of the restlessness of the exiled soul questing for God and of the knowledge that the paths that lead to God are not like the paths of the earth but are comparable, rather, to the sea itineraries which never leave any trace: "In mari viae tuae et semitae tuae in aquis multis, et vestigia tua non cognoscunt." For the psalmist, the only hope is God who in Exodus led his people "like a flock by the hand of Moses and Aaron" (Psalms 76:19-20). This psalm, we might add, is used by Joachim of Flora to introduce his own interpretive adventure into the depths of Scripture.[59]

Exile for the poet, then, is not merely a perspective from which he acknowledges the storms brooding over history and nostalgically relives the pastoral order of the city. It is also the very condition of the text, its most profound metaphor. Nor is the vision of the pastoral myth simply an elegy for dead hopes, a way of elaborating a city of the mind against the horrors of history; a city, that is, drawn upward into a more general metaphysical drama or, more precisely, into the eschatological expectation of the resurrection and the Heavenly Jerusalem. The elegy is also a hope that the order of Eden is typologically possible here on earth.

This possibility rests on the theological virtue of hope that governs *Paradiso* xxv. Hope, a metaphor of time opened to the future (l. 67), is the promise of the final times, but it also tells us that the past can never be regarded as a closed and dead

[58] The classical tradition of nautical metaphors is briefly sketched by Ernest Robert Curtius, *European Literature and the Latin Middle Ages*, trans. W. R. Trask (New York: Harper and Row, 1953), pp. 128-30. Besides the *Georgics* II, l. 41, and IV, l. 117, and Horace's *Carmen* IV, 15, 1, and others, Curtius lists Prudentius and Jerome's "Sails of interpretation" in *PL* 25, col. 903D. The motif of writing as a journey in Dante has been suggested by Philippe Sollers, "Dante et la traversée de l'écriture," *Tel Quel*, 23 (1965), pp. 12-33.

[59] *Liber Introductorius in Apocalypsin* (Venice, 1527), fols. 24-5. Quoted by Henri de Lubac, *Exégèse médiévale* (Paris: Aubier, 1964), II, 438.

archeology and that the past itself has seeds for the future.[60] This hope, to be sure, cannot be domesticated entirely within the bounds of history nor exhausted in messianic expectations. Dante's text in *Paradiso* xxv deliberately wavers between the vision of order in the empirical, concrete city of Florence and the "attender certo" of the glory of Jerusalem. This hope places us in history and against history, in a garden which is a desert where nomads are always on the way.

[60] In *Paradiso* xxv, ll. 67 ff. hope is defined as "attender certo / de la gloria futura." This sense of hope as promise of the future is studied by Jürgen Moltmann, *Theology of Hope*, trans. James W. Leitch (New York: Harper and Row, 1967). It might be pointed out that among contemporary writers Robert Penn Warren, has voiced a similar understanding, I think, of hope. His classic *All the King's Men*, which bears as epigraph Dante's line "Mentre che la speranza ha fior del verde," ends as follows: "We shall come back, no doubt, to walk down the Row. . . . But that will be a long time from now, and soon now we shall go out of the house and go into the convulsion of the world, out of history into history and the awful responsibility of Time." The quotation is taken from *All the King's Men* (New York: Bantam Books, 1959), p. 438.

CHAPTER 4

Vergil and Augustine

IN the previous chapter, I suggested that the Augustinian rationale of two cities governs Dante's sense of history *sub specie aeternitatis* and that, to a degree which is unknown to Augustine, Dante explicitly extends the concept of the eschatological cities to include the historical order. The divergence between Dante and Augustine over the status of the contingencies of history is particularly exemplified by their respective interpretations of Vergil's *Aeneid*, the contradictory views that each of them holds about the meaning of the Vergilian poem. Dante's journey, for instance, is significantly contained between two books, Vergil's volume and the volume of the universe:[1] the *Aeneid* is the privileged text by an author who guides the pilgrim from the chaos of materiality, the inverted Edenic landscape of the prologue scene, to the Earthly Paradise. This special role played by the *Aeneid* and Vergil in the *Divine Comedy* is a direct reversal of their function in Augustine's experience of conversion. For in the *Confessions*, he dramatizes his spiritual itinerary from the *Aeneid*, through complex intellectual temptations, to God's book.[2]

[1] *Inferno* I, l. 84; *Paradiso* XXXIII, l. 87.

[2] *Confessions*, I, xiii; the story ends (XIII, xxxviii) with Augustine "opening" God's book; *CSEL* XXXIII. On the dramatic significance of the word "aperietur" on which the *Confessions* comes to an end, see below chapter 5, note 38. For the intellectual quest recorded in the *Confessions*, see Pierre Courcelle, *Recherches sur les "Confessions" de Saint Augustin* (Paris: E. De Boccard, 1950), esp. pp. 49-138.

The *Aeneid*, however, is rejected as a blasphemous utterance (the reasons for which will be apparent later on) and Augustine ends with the affirmation of God's book: "and in your Book we read this as a presage that when our own work in this life is done, we too shall rest in You in the sabbath of eternal life."[3]

This divergence is not merely a matter of historical, extratextual interest. On the contrary, its significance lies in the fact that Dante is well aware of Augustine's critical reading of the *Aeneid*; indeed he both depends on it for his own interpretation and systematically weaves it into the texture of his poetry. In brief, from Dante's perspective, Augustine rescues the *Aeneid* from the conventional neoplatonic moralizations[4]

---

[3] *Confessions*, XIII, xxxvi. For the English translation, I have generally followed closely *The Confessions of Saint Augustine*, trans. Rex Warner (New York and Toronto: The New American Library, 1963) and Edward B. Pusey, *The Confessions of Saint Augustine* (New York: Collier Books, 1961).

[4] For the neoplatonic readings of Vergil in the Middle Ages, see Domenico Comparetti, *Virgilio nel Medioevo*, new ed., ed. Giorgio Pasquali (Florence: La Nuova Italia, 1937), I, esp. 61 ff.; Henri de Lubac, "Virgil philosophe et prophète," in *Exégèse médiévale* (Paris: Aubier, 1964), II, 233–62; Salvatore Battaglia, *Esemplarità e antagonismo nel pensiero di Dante* (Naples: Liguori, 1967), I, 271–301; H. T. Silverstein, "Dante and Vergil the Mystic," *Harvard Studies and Notes in Philology and Literature*, 14 (1932), pp. 51–82; Ulrich Leo, "The Unfinished *Convivio* and Dante's Rereading of the *Aeneid*," *Mediaeval Studies*, 13 (1951), pp. 41–64; Giorgio Padoan, "Tradizione e fortuna del commento all'*Eneide* di Bernardo Silvestre," *Italia medioevale e umanistica*, 3 (1960), pp. 227–40, which stresses the importance of Bernardus' commentary on the *Aeneid* in Pietro di Dante's glosses on the *Divine Comedy*; for the doubtful authorship of the commentary, see the remarks by Brian Stock, *Myth and Science in the Twelfth Century: A Study of Bernard Silvester* (Princeton: Princeton University Press, 1972), pp. 36–7. Recently, John Freccero, "Dante's Prologue Scene," *Dante Studies*, 84 (1966), pp. 1–25, has rightly probed the critical stance of both St. Augustine and Dante toward neoplatonic traditions. Dante's possible polemic with the neoplatonists is played down by David Thompson, who asserts that Bernardus' commentary is central to the structure of the *Divine Comedy* in his *Dante's Epic Journeys* (Baltimore: The Johns Hopkins University Press, 1976), pp. 25 ff.; for a more general account of medieval platonism, see E. Garin, *Studi sul Platonismo Medioevale* (Florence: Le Monnier, 1954); cf. also Joseph Mazzeo, *Structure and Thought in the Paradiso* (Ithaca: Cornell University Press, 1958), pp. 1–24.

and discerns in it a definite ideology of history, a tale of two secular cities which he reinterprets, in his theological frame of reference, as the city of God and the earthly city. This chapter, by focusing on some scenes of the poem where Augustinian and Vergilian elements are strategically deployed, will attempt to map Dante's effort to preserve Vergil's sense of history, perceived by Augustine but discarded by him, and to bring Vergil and Augustine together within the focus of his own vision. Yet, there is an ironic counterpart to this process of harmonization: from the vantage point of Augustine's critique of the *Aeneid*, Dante engages in an occasional undercutting of the privileged status that, on the face of it, he assigns to Vergil's text; at the same time, he challenges Augustine's critical reading of the *Aeneid* by pitting against him the views held by its neoplatonic commentators.

It should be clear at the very outset that the arguments which will be here advanced are not intended to minimize the importance of those respects in which I differ from the existing scholarly opinions on the role and meaning of Vergil in the *Divine Comedy*:[5] Vergil, in fact, often appears as a shorthand designation for "reason," or—in more recent and per-

---

[5] I list here some items on the *Aeneid* and the character Vergil in the *Divine Comedy* which I have found particularly useful for this chapter: Edward Moore, *Studies in Dante*, 1st series (Oxford: Clarendon Press, 1896); C. H. Moore, "Prophecy in the Ancient Epic," *Harvard Studies in Classical Philology*, 32 (1921), pp. 99-175; F. D'Ovidio, "Non soltanto lo bello stile tolse da lui," *Atene e Roma*, 1 (1898), pp. 15-25; Augustin Renaudet, *Dante Humaniste* (Paris: Les Belles Lettres, 1952), esp. pp. 71-100 and 147-61, in which Vergil appears as a symbol of human reason; cf. p. 95 and p. 537; Paul Renucci, *Dante disciple et juge du monde greco-latin* (Clermont-Ferrand: G. De Bussac, 1954), pp. 282-91; Charles T. Davis, *Dante and the Idea of Rome* (Oxford: Clarendon Press, 1957), pp. 100-38, in which Davis reviews existing scholarship and plays down the importance of neoplatonic mediations of the *Aeneid*. So does Robert Hollander, *Allegory in Dante's* Commedia (Princeton: Princeton University Press, 1969), esp. pp. 96 ff.; Bruno Nardi, "Tre momenti dell'incontro di Dante con Virgilio," in *Saggi e note di critica dantesca* (Milan and Naples: Ricciardi, 1966), pp. 220-37; see also Nardi's *Saggi di filosofia dantesca* (Florence: La Nuova Italia, 1967), pp. 215-75; Domenico Consoli, *Significato del Virgilio dantesco* (Florence: Le Monnier, 1967).

ceptive critical contributions—he is seen as the message bearer of the empire, the prophet of the secular world Dante tenaciously envisions. Eminent historians such as Bruno Nardi, A. Renaudet and Charles T. Davis have agreed on the special mission of Rome and the Roman Empire in Dante's plot of salvation history. Davis, in effect, goes further than this and in a dense chapter he delineates the increasing importance the Roman poet has for Dante at the time he wrote the *Commedia*. Vergil, Davis argues quite correctly, is now more than the poet of wisdom as he appeared in *Convivio* and more than the prophet of the empire as he appeared in the *Monarchia*: in the *Commedia*, in addition to this, Vergil takes on a new role, that of being, in Davis' own language, "a bridge between the two Romes."[6]

But what is the specific poetic mechanism that makes possible the simultaneous presence of these roles in the poem? Above and beyond the strategy of "reading" the *Aeneid* here summarily sketched, what is the dramatic substance of the *Aeneid* in the *Divine Comedy*, and how does it affect the role of Vergil in it? It is the contention of this chapter that Dante reads the *Aeneid* as a poem of love, the generalized desire that shapes the world of history and is the root of history. Dante, I wish to argue, is deeply interested like Vergil in the outward myth of the mission of Rome but, like Vergil, he wants to penetrate into it, to grasp the core of the ethical values of *Romanitas*, the voluntarism which supports these values. I might add, to anticipate, that Augustine discerns in the *Aeneid* precisely the erotics of history, the *amor sui* of the "world" and that Bernardus Silvestris, among the neoplatonists, has also read the Roman epic as the story of *libido* transcended by rationality.

Reading the *Aeneid* as a text with a philosophy of desire inevitably raises the problem of the act of reading (a question that will be extensively treated through the next chapters) in the *Divine Comedy*, the meaning of the activity of reading

---

[6] Davis, *Dante and the Idea of Rome*, p. 137.

books. This activity is given a conspicuous prominence in the poem: if one of the more ancient metaphors in literature is that of the universe as a book written by the hand of God and bound by his love,[7] in Dante the metaphor is subsumed and redeemed from its cliché status by a correlated series of statements on books (their promises and deceptions), so much so that, from one point of view, the *Divine Comedy* is a book about books. The *Aeneid* is the first explicit book of the series. In his exchange with Vergil, Dante professes ". . . lungo studio e 'l grande amore / che m'ha fatto cercar lo tuo volume" (*Inferno* I, ll. 83-4). This is more than merely rhetorical *captatio benevolentiae* of a man who is in dire need of help. For the *captatio* literally reflects the links between the quest and desire and places the act of reading within the context of desire. Neither an innocuous nor inconsequential experience, reading has a profound resonance in that it is an act of disclosure of the historicity of the self and one by which the self is engaged in an imaginary confrontation with the semblances of oneself and history.

The *Aeneid* appears at the outset as the literary *lieu de passage* to history. The dramatics of the first encounter between the pilgrim and Vergil are well known: the pilgrim has been driven by the she-wolf back to the dark night and its terrors when at last he catches a glimpse of, and appeals to, what is confusedly perceived as a shadow or a man. The pilgrim's doubt is part of the radical ambiguity that sustains the first canto.[8] This is the desert (l. 64), the symbolic space of the fall

---

[7] For the metaphor of the book, see E. R. Curtius, *European Literature and the Latin Middle Ages*, trans. W. R. Trask (New York: Harper and Row, 1953), pp. 302-47.

[8] I am referring to what John Freccero has rightly called *regio dissimilitudinis* in his "Dante's Prologue Scene," p. 12. For the history of the motif, see Pierre Courcelle, *Les "Confessions" de Saint Augustin dans la tradition littéraire: Antécédents et postérité* (Paris: Etudes Augustiniennes, 1963), pp. 623-40. See also F. Chatillon, "Regio Dissimilitudinis," in *Mélanges E. Podechard* (Lyon: Facultés Catholiques, 1903), pp. 85-102; Robert Javelet, *Image et ressemblance au douzième siècle* (Paris: Letouzey et Avé, 1967), I, pp. 266-85 for bibliography.

where all directions and contours are uncertain and blurred. We learn from his oblique response that Vergil gratuitously shows himself forth to rescue the wayfarer from his despair. His speech tells us that he lived in pagan Rome and is the poet of the *Aeneid*:

> Rispuosemi: "Non omo, omo già fui,
>   e li parenti miei furon lombardi,
>   mantoani per patria ambedui.
> Nacqui sub Iulio, ancor che fosse tardi,
>   e vissi a Roma sotto 'l buono Augusto
>   nel tempo de li dèi falsi e bugiardi.
> Poeta fui, e cantai di quel giusto
>   figliuol d'Anchise che venne di Troia,
>   poi che 'l superbo Ilion fu combusto."
>
>   ll. 67-75

("No, not a living man, though once I was," he answered me, "and my parents were Lombards, both Mantuans by birth. I was born *sub Julio*, although late, and I lived at Rome under the good Augustus, in the time of the false and lying gods. I was a poet and I sang of that just son of Anchises who came from Troy after proud Ilium was burned.")

The compressed view of the content of the *Aeneid*, Aeneas' journey from fallen Troy to Italy, deserves some comment. It is a poignant gloss on the pilgrim's fallen state and his own typological journey to that "Roma onde Cristo è romano" (*Purgatorio* xxxii, l. 102); it acts as the pivotal point from the massive and threatening materiality of the forest where the pilgrim is once again situated to the journey proper; and it marks the shift from a landscape of undefined sense to Vergil's sharp definitions of himself and his text. This point of transition is the emergence of the sense of history, the world of Rome disclosed by the *Aeneid* and its author. There seems to be, in effect, a typological nexus between the account of Vergil's life under Augustus and the events narrated

by his epic in the sense that the Augustan Rome is a fulfillment of Aeneas' quest for Italy. But it is the allusion to the fall
of Troy as "superbo Ilión" that places the *Aeneid* in the very
economy of salvation history: pride, the conventional *initium
omnis peccati* is man's primal sin which marks the fall from the
garden. Unsurprisingly in *Purgatorio* xii, where the examples
of punished pride are illustrated, the description of the fall of
Troy contains the acrostic VOM (ll. 61-3).

The claim that the *Aeneid* typologically adumbrates the history of the fall is also made for the *Divine Comedy*: the allusion
to the vernal equinox (*Inferno* i, ll. 37-40), which is a conventional *topos* of exordium,[9] hints at the symbolic date for the
beginning of the world, the fall of man and his redemption.
This detail of an *ab origine* commencement of the literary text
is picked up at the point where the pilgrim enters the gates of
Purgatory: among the examples of humility, there is, in fact,
the Annunciation (*Purgatorio* x, ll. 37-45); the Annunciation,
occurring as it does at the vernal equinox is the emblem for
the new beginning of the world and the apt correlative for the
pilgrim's spiritual rebirth. Like the *Commedia*, the *Aeneid* is
placed within a biblical perspective of salvation history, for to
Dante there is always an inner history that gives meaning to
the entire historical process. The anchorage to this process is
Christ whose advent took place when the world was united
under the hegemony of Rome.

The awareness of history represents for the pilgrim lost in
the forest a crucial detour from the vain attempts to reach salvation through philosophy: the philosophical quest is vain because its abstract, forever valid paradigms do not give access
to the irreducible historicity of the self, the depth of one's in-
teriority and confusion. The detour into history, dramatized
by the poem's movement from the neoplatonic language of

---

[9] For the motif, see Macrobius, *Commentarium in Somnium Scipionis*, ed.
J. Willis (Leipzig: B. G. Teubner, 1970), i, xxi-xxiv, pp. 88-9. Cf. commentary on the line by Benvenuto da Imola, *Comentum super Dantis Aldigheris
Comoediam*, ed. W. W. Vernon and I. F. Lacaita (Florence: Barberi, 1887), i,
37.

the first abortive ascent in the prologue scene to the encounter with Vergil, is condensed in Dante's very interpretation of the *Aeneid*.[10] His view of the *Aeneid* as history within the framework of the total redemptive activity of God is, as I shall try to show, a radical departure from the neoplatonic exegetes, whom he had echoed in the *Convivio* and echoes again in the *Commedia*. A glimpse of this tradition is discernible in the pilgrim's response to Vergil's speech:

> "O de li altri poeti onore e lume,
> vagliami.'l lungo studio e 'l grande amore
> che m'ha fatto cercar lo tuo volume.
> Tu se' lo mio maestro e 'l mio autore,
> tu se' solo colui da cu' io tolsi
> lo bello stilo che m'ha fatto onore."
>
> *Inferno* I, ll. 82-7

("Oh glory and light of other poets, may the long study and the great love that have made me search your volume avail me. You are my master and my author. You alone are the one from whom I took the beautiful style that has done me honor.")

The language of this appeal is strongly reminiscent of Vergil's neoplatonic commentators. The reference to him as "maestro e autore" recalls the Chartrian debate over *authentica* and *magistralia*:[11] the conventional opposition between incontrovertible *auctoritates* and the learned, but not binding, opinions of the *magistri* seems to collapse in Dante's line as the two terms are applied to Vergil but, in effect, they are symptomatic of the ambiguous reading that Dante will have of Vergil. Even more suggestive is the term "volume." Its symbolic value is provided by the fact that "volume" is also used to describe God's book, as we have hinted, in *Paradiso* XXXIII.

[10] Ulrich Leo, "The Unfinished *Convivio* and Dante's Rereading of the *Aeneid*," pp. 57 ff. John Freccero, "Dante's Prologue Scene," pp. 8-12.

[11] The background on the debate is treated by M.-D. Chenù, *La Théologie au douzième siècle* (Paris: Vrin, 1957), pp. 351-65.

In *Paradiso*, it designates the roll of parchment folding within it "substances and accidents" which, like a transparent allegory, are "explicated" through the universe. The definition of Vergil's *opus* as "volume" implies that it contains under the cover an inner substance; under the *cortex*—to use Isidore's term for the material out of which volumes are manufactured[12]—there hides a philosophical *medulla*. Significantly, Bernardus Silvestris repeatedly adopts the word "volumen" to describe the allegorical nature of the books of the *Aeneid*:

> Notandum est hoc in loco quemadmodum in aliis misticis voluminibus, ita et in hoc aequivocationes et multivocationes et integumenta ad diversa respicere. . . .[13]

The assumption that there was a philosophical substance under the poetic integument led Bernardus and the other Chartrians to consider Vergil (and Plato, for that matter) an *auctor*, in the sense that his symbolic vision is an oblique revelation of the nature of the universe and worthy—as Dante will etymologize in the *Convivio*—of being believed.[14] Further, when Dante refers to Vergil's "bello stilo"—and Vergil's rhetorical mastery had been cited in the *De Vulgari Elo-*

---

[12] Isidore of Seville, *Etym.* VI, xiii, 2-3: "Volumen liber est a volvendo dictus, sicut apud Hebraeos volumina Legis, volumina Prophetarum. Liber est interior tunica corticis, quod ligno cohaeret." In Book XVII, vi, 16, Isidore defines liber as "corticis pars interior, dictus a liberato cortice." Cf. Hollander, *Allegory in Dante's Commedia*, p. 79. See also chapter 6 below, note 59.

[13] "It must be noted that in this place just as in other mystical volumes, so also in this equivocations, multivocations and integuments refer to different things" (B. Silvestris, *Commentum super sex libros Eneidos Virgilii*, ed. W. Riedel [Greifswald: J. Abel, 1924], p. 9).

[14] *Convivio*, IV, vi, 5: "L'altro principio, onde 'autore' discende, sì come testimonia Uguiccione nel principio de le sue Derivazioni, è uno vocabulo greco che dice 'autentin', che tanto vole in latino quanto 'degno di fede e d'obedienza'." See also Chenù, *La Théologie au douzième siècle*, pp. 353 ff., for a historical sketch of the links between "auctoritas" and "authenticus." For some statements on the authority of the philosophers, see Abelard, *PL* 178, col. 1035; Alanus de Insulis, *PL* 210, col. 332.

quentia[15]—he again seems to move within the tradition of Bernardus' double view of the *Aeneid*:

> Geminae doctrinae observationem perpendimus in sola Eneide Maronem habuisse, teste namque Macrobius: "qui et veritatem philosophiae docuit et figmentum poeticum non praetermisit". . . . Sub integumento describit quid agat vel quid patiatur humanus spiritus in humano corpore temporaliter positus. Atque in hoc scribendo . . . utrumque narrationis ordinem observat, artificialem poeta, naturalem philosophus.[16]

Bernardus, recalling Macrobius' premise, acknowledges the presence of a double layer in the *Aeneid*, philosophical truth and poetic figment. But his commentary on the first six books of the *Aeneid* centers on the doctrine of what he takes to be the allegory of Aeneas' journey, the intellect's authentic experience of philosophical truth, and practically neglects the fictional surface. In Dante's vision, Aeneas' intellectual quest, as we shall see, owes a great deal to the neoplatonists' interpretations.[17] But Dante departs from Bernardus' exegesis at the very outset in a fundamental way. Vergil appears primarily as a poet. His own self-definition is "poeta fui, e cantai . . . ," which Dante picks up in his response: "o degli altri poeti onore e lume . . ." and "tu se' solo colui da cu' io tolsi / lo bello stilo che m'ha fatto onore."

The emphasis on Vergil as a poet serves for Dante as a way of focusing precisely on the tension—partly bypassed by Bernardus—between literature and philosophy and as a way

---

[15] *De Vulgari Eloquentia*, II, vi, 7; and II, viii, 4, where "arma virumque cano" is quoted as an instance of the "Cantio."

[16] "We consider that in the *Aeneid* alone Vergil observed a double doctrine, as Macrobius witnesses: 'he both taught the truth of philosophy and did not neglect the poetic figments'. . . . Under the integument he describes what the human soul, placed provisionally in a human body, does or suffers. And in writing this . . . he observes both orders of narrative: as a poet, the artificial; as a philosopher, the natural" (*Commentum super sex libros Eneidos*, pp. 1-3).

[17] A convenient summary of neoplatonic readings of the *Aeneid* is in D. Comparetti, *Virgilio nel Medioevo*, I, 61 ff.

of questioning the notion that poetic language can directly lead to an extrapolation of philosophical "truth." The ambiguities of poetic language are more valuable to Dante than explicit *sententiae*, and philosophy itself seems to be important in the measure in which it uses myths as fabulous disguises for its arcane secrets (*Paradiso* IV, ll. 22-57). Ambiguities are significant because they force us to *interpret*, place us in history, in the land of exile where things both are and are not what they appear to be.[18] It is in this ambiguous space that Vergil shows himself forth "ombra od omo certo" (*Inferno* I, l. 66), and the reflection on language in *Inferno* II subtly extends this point.

There Beatrice's address to Vergil centers, to a large extent, on the nature of speech: she speaks "soave e piana" (l. 55), "con angelica voce" (l. 56) and her language originates in desire: "amor mi mosse, che mi fa parlare" (ll. 71-2). By contrast, as she exhorts Vergil to help her friend she refers to his "parola ornata" (l. 67). The phrase translates the *ornatu verborum*—a rhetorical commonplace in the esthetic treatises of the twelfth century—and it describes the order and design of the poetic text much the way, in the neoplatonic tradition, *exornatio mundi* describes the design of the cosmos. Bernardus Silvestris refers to the *Aeneid*'s "ornatu verborum" to suggest the "quaedam delectatio" which the text generates.[19]

The allusion to Vergil's "parola ornata" in the second canto of *Inferno* is particularly ironic: it marks the distance, as Ben-

---

[18] I am echoing here the words of Benedetto Croce, *La poesia di Dante*, 2nd ed. (Bari: Laterza, 1948), p. 67. For a theological definition of these ambiguities, see Freccero, "Dante's Prologue Scene," p. 1. For the importance of the *narrationes fabulosae* leading to truth, see Macrobius, *Commentarium in Somnium Scipionis*, I, ii, 9, p. 5 and I, ix, 8, p. 41. Cf. also John of Salisbury, *Metalogicon*, II, 1, *PL* 199, col. 858A; Alanus de Insulis, *PL* 210, col. 541C. More generally, see D. W. Robertson, Jr., "Some Mediaeval Literary Terminology, with Special Reference to Chrétien de Troyes," *Studies in Philology*, 48 (1951), pp. 669-92. For the question of reading as exile, see below chapter 6, note 78.

[19] *Commentum super sex libros Eneidos*, p. 2: "Ex hoc opere ex ornatu verborum et figura orationis . . . quaedam habetur delectatio."

venuto da Imola perceived, between the language of the blessed and the pagan poet.[20] But the irony reaches further. Dante uses the same phrase to characterize Jason's deceptive love promises to Hypsipyle, when "con segni e con parole ornate / Isifile ingannò" (*Inferno* xviii, ll. 91-2). In a sense, the use of the same phrase establishes the dramatic contrast between Vergil and Jason and shows how rhetorical blandishments can be directed to good ends, as in the case of Vergil, and to evil purposes, as in the case of Jason. To reinforce this distinction, we might add that Beatrice's own *sermo planus*— directed as it is to good ends—also exhibits rhetorical lures through the extended *captatio benevolentiae* "O anima cortese mantoana / di cui la fama ancor nel mondo dura, / e durerà quanto 'l mondo lontana" (*Inferno* ii, ll. 58-60) to Vergil. But the contrast which is possibly intended cannot hide the sense of the inevitable duplicity of poetic language, its own inherent wavering between good and evil. By drawing attention to the ambiguities of Vergil's language, Dante makes it the vehicle of history; the world where events are caught in their symbolic process and the assumptions of a univocal sense generated by *a priori* fixed categories are jolted.

The thrust of the foregoing remarks is that Dante reads the *Aeneid* as a poem of history which, though immersed in a condition of temporality and finitude, strains toward the enduring atemporality of Heaven and enacts a view of history as a sequence of events significant in God's providential plan. But I am also suggesting that there is an ironic counterstatement to this fixed structure of order. The point is—and this will emerge in detail in the ensuing discussion—that if Vergil is the poet of history, history cannot be taken literally. It is a conventional motif to see the language of history literally: "Historia est rerum gestarum narratio, quae in prima significatione litterae continetur," as Hugh of St. Victor

[20] "Et dicit: et ista Domina *Soave e piana*, et bene dicit, quia sermo divinus est suavis et planus, non altus et superbus, sicut sermo Virg. et poetarum, *cominciommi a dire con angelica voce*" (Benvenuto da Imola, Biagi, ed., *Inferno*, p. 63; for "parola ornata" as "florida eloquentia," see p. 66).

writes.[21] Even in the *Didascalicon*, while he exploits the link
between language and history, he speaks of events themselves
as words, the "voice of God speaking to men."[22] But Dante
knew well that there is a gap between the language of God
and the language of men for the language of men is prone to
duplicity. To paraphrase Augustine's *De Ordine*, history is
grammar but also a word that includes an infinity of things
fuller of cares than of enjoyment or truth. This ambiguity of
the letter does not mean that the letter is useless or superfluous. On the contrary, it means that the letter is the necessary
envelope, the metaphor that must be continuously questioned
and interpreted. Does this ambiguity, this view of history as
an immanent, uncertain process disrupt the theological pattern of history, and how are the two related? It is this interplay between the open-ended ambiguous process of history
and its transcendent order that must be explored.

The teleological design that Dante attributes to the *Aeneid* is
a far cry from Augustine's reading of the Roman epic. When
Augustine glosses the Vergilian line describing the ideology
of Rome "imperium sine fine dedi" (*Aeneid* i, l. 279), he
transposes the *imperium* from the dimension of the intended
eternity of the earthly city to the heavenly city.[23] Rome can
be acceptable only as a prefiguration of the Church because to
him the history of the earthly Rome is another tragic and lamentable instance of the eternal corruption of secular life.
Dante, on the contrary, will use the same line from the *Aeneid*
to account for the providentiality of the Roman Empire. In
the *Convivio*, in fact he writes:

And because there never was and never will be (as may
be seen by experience) a nature more gentle in governing, more powerful in maintaining, and more subtle in
acquitting than that of the Latin people—therefore God

[21] Cf. note 4 to chapter 2.
[22] *PL* 176, col. 790; *Didascalion*, trans. Jerome Taylor (New York and London: Columbia University Press, 1968), v, 3, p. 121.
[23] *De Civitate Dei*, ii, 29, *CCSL* xlvii.

elected them for this office. . . . It was not by force that it was assumed in the beginning by the Roman people, but by Divine Providence, which is above all law. Vergil agrees with this in the first book of the *Aeneid*, where he says, speaking in the person of God, "To them, that is to the Romans, I have set neither limit of things nor of time; 'to them have I given an empire without end.' "[24]

Even in the *Divine Comedy*, the conviction that the historical Rome is the legitimate structure of history makes Dante part company with Augustine and turn to the neoplatonic commentaries. Such an attempt at harmonizing Augustine and the neoplatonists is made possible by the fact that they all agree, though they sharply differ in their evaluations, that the *Aeneid* is a story of desire. By focusing on canto v of *Inferno* it can be shown to what extent Augustine's reading of the *Aeneid* as a poem of love is drawn into Dante's cosmos.

This canto, where *luxuria* is punished, has been subjected by scholars to intensive and often remarkably lucid analyses. They have documented, for instance, among other prominent textual echoes (stilnovistic poetry, love formulas from *De arte Honeste Amandi*, etc.),[25] the overriding presence of the *Aeneid*

---

[24] *Convivio*, IV, iv, 11-12. The translation of the passage is from Katharine Hillard, *The Banquet* (London: Kegan Paul, 1889), pp. 241-2.

[25] A summary of the bibliographical items on *Inferno* v can be found in G. Baldo Curato, *II canto di Francesca e i suoi interpreti* (Cremona: Editrice Padus, 1963). I have found of interest the following contributions: Paget Toynbee, "Dante and the Lancelot Romance," in *Dante Studies and Researches* (London: Methuen and Co., 1902), pp. 1-37; Gianfranco Contini, "Dante come personaggio-poeta della *Commedia*," in *Varianti e altra linguistica* (Turin: Einaudi, 1970), pp. 343-8, where echoes from Andreas Capellanus' *De Arte Honeste Amandi* are noted; Bruno Nardi, "Filosofia dell'amore nei rimatori italiani," in *Dante e la cultura medioevale*, 2nd ed. (Bari: Laterza, 1949), pp. 1 ff. For the stilnovistic echoes of the canto, see also the comments by Natalino Sapegno in *La Divina Commedia*, ed. Natalino Sapegno (Milan and Naples: Ricciardi, 1967), pp. 64-5; Antonino Pagliaro, "Il canto di Francesca," in *Ulisse: ricerche semantiche sulla* Divina Commedia (Messina and Florence: D'Anna, 1967), I, 115-59. A. C. Charity, *Events and Their Afterlife: Dialectics of Christian Typology in the Bible and Dante* (Cambridge: Cambridge University Press, 1966), gives a reading of the episode in "esthetic" terms, pp. 214-7. Roger Dragonetti, *Aux Frontières du langage poétique*, Romanica Gan-

but have neglected the peculiar Augustinian mediation of this "source." In a real sense, *Inferno* v tells also the story of Dido who is mentioned twice in the canto; the first time is by a periphrasis in the general catalogue of love heroines that crowd this area of sin:

> L'altra è colei che s'ancise amorosa,
> e ruppe fede al cener di Sicheo.
>
> ll. 61-2

(The other is she who slew herself for love and broke faith to the ashes of Sicheus.)

The second time, she is named directly to describe the movement of Paolo and Francesca toward the poets:

> cotali uscir de la schiera ov'è Dido,
> a noi venendo per l'aere maligno,
> sì forte fu l'affettuoso grido.
>
> ll. 85-7

(So did they come out of the troop where Dido is, coming to us through the malignant air, so forceful was my compassionate cry.)

Dido would seem to be given, in reality, the status of the paradigm, the point of reference of all these adulterous sinners, among whom are Cleopatra and Semiramis. In *Paradiso* viii (ll. 1-9), in the heaven of Venus, while the poet's ostensible purpose is to correct the belief that mad love descends from the goddess, Dante associates Dido's "folle amor" with the myth of Venus.[26] More to the point, the rhyme scheme of the tercet we just quoted (Dido . . . grido), along with the

---

densia, 9 (Ghent: Rijksuniversiteit te Gent, 1961), pp. 98 ff., has suggested the pilgrim is himself charmed by Francesca's story.

[26] On the tradition of the "two Venuses," heavenly and earthly, see Bernardus, *Commentum*, pp. 9-10; cf. Alanus, *De Planctu Naturae*, PL 210, col. 571. See also Johannes Scotus, *Annotationes in Marcianum*, ed. Cora E. Lutz (Cambridge, Mass.: Harvard University Press, 1939), lxii, 12, p. 67. For further bibliography, see Arthur Groos, " 'Amor and his Brother Cupid': The 'Two Loves' in Heinrich Von Veldekes's *Eneit*," *Traditio*, 32 (1976), pp. 239-55.

language of the previous two lines, is an exact recall of the story of Dido as it appears in "Cosi' nel mio parlar voglio esser aspro."[27] This is a poem in which Dante describes his love for the so-called Donna Petra as an experience of spiritual degradation that threatens to transform the lover into a stone:

> E m'ha percosso in terra, e stammi sopra
> con quella spada ond'elli ancise Dido,
> Amore, a cui io grido . . .
>
> ll. 35-7

(Love has struck me to the ground and now stands over me with that same sword with which he slew Dido, Love to whom I cry out . . .)

What purpose does this recall serve in the economy of *Inferno* v? The question is worth pursuing because the myth of the Vergilian Dido in "Cosi' nel mio parlar. . . ." is grafted on an unequivocally Augustinian doctrine of love which is dramatized in the second stanza of the poem:

> Non trovo scudo ch'ella non mi spezzi
> nè loco che dal suo viso m'asconda:
> che come fior di fronda,
> Cotanto del mio mal par che si prezzi
> quanto legno di mar che non lieve onda;
> e il peso che m'affonda
> è tal che non potrebbe adequar rima.
>
> ll. 14-20

(I find no shield she does not shatter, nor a place to hide me from her look; because, like a flower on the stalk, she occupies the summit of my mind. She seems to take such a care of my suffering as does a ship of a sea that lifts no wave; and the weight that founders me is such that no poetry could be equal to it.)

This love occupies "de la mia mente la cima": the phrase actually translates the technical *apex mentis* or, as it is also

---

[27] *Rime*, ed. Gianfranco Contini (Turin: Einaudi, 1965), pp. 167-8.

known in medieval psychological treatises, *acies mentis*.[28] Among other things, the term designates the point of conjunction of intellect and will and describes the principle of moral choice, the infallible innate *habit* of the mind to make practical judgments. By the theological resonance, Dante clearly implies the absolute corruption of the intellect or, since *mens* is the faculty of intellectual vision,[29] the darkening of reason by the fleshly sight of the Medusa.

The first two lines of the stanza enact precisely an allusion to the myth of the Medusa threatening the unshielded lover who, in turn, is cast as an unsuccessful Perseus. Medusa, it might be pointed out, is a type of Dido: Perseus' victory is mentioned by Bernardus Silvestris in his commentary on the *Aeneid* as the illustration of Aeneas' triumph over the flesh and his achievement of philosophical wisdom.[30] More importantly, the dramatic process of the stanza hinges on the coherently related allusion to the Medusa and the definition of the poet's misdirected love as a weight that pulls the lover downward (ll. 20-1).

In St. Augustine's erotic typology, love is defined as the inner weight that urges the soul to seek its own place. In book XIII of the *Confessions* he discusses this doctrine of love, conventionally known as *pondus amoris*, through the metaphor of the law of physical gravity. In particular he employs the natural movement of stone and fire to provide the metaphoric illustration for a spiritual gravity or weight: the fire for the upward spiritual ascent, the stone for the erotic fall.

Requies nostra locus noster. Amor illuc attollit nos et spiritus tuus bonus exaltat humilitatem nostram de portis mortis. In bona voluntate pax nostra est. Corpore pondere suo nititur ad locum suum. Pondus non ad ima tan-

[28] Isaac de l'Etoile, *De Anima*, PL 181, col. 1881CD; for further bibliography, see Robert Javelet, *Image et ressemblance*, II, especially note 304 to chapter I, p. 37, and note 52 to chapter IV, p. 109.

[29] For "mens" as "oculus," here blinded by the sight of Medusa, see Isidore of Seville, *Etym*. XI, i, 12. Cf. also the discussion on Medusa in chapter VII, especially notes 16-29.

[30] *Commentum super sex libros Eneidos*, p. 73.

tum est, sed ad locum suum. Ignis sursum tendit, deor-
sum lapis. Ponderibus suis aguntur, loca sua petunt. . . .
Minus ordinata inquieta sunt: ordinantur et quiescunt.
Pondus meum amor meus; eo feror, quocumque feror.
Dono tuo accendimur et sursum ferimur; . . . Igne tuo,
igne tuo bono inardescimus et imus, quoniam sursum
imus ad pacem Hierusalem. . . .[31]

This citation is an overt gloss on Dante's stanza: the "peso che
m'affonda" is the downward *pondus* of the stone, the Donna
Petra—Medusa which reduces the lover to a stone. There is
further persuasive evidence of Dante's familiarity with this
specific Augustinian passage: the line "in bona voluntate pax
nostra est" is translated *verbatim* in *Paradiso* III: "in la sua vol-
untade è nostra pace" (l. 85).

This Augustinian doctrine of *pondus amoris* seems to shape,
partially at least, the general moral structure of *Inferno*.
Ciacco, for instance, enunciates the principle that the hierarchy of evil is represented in terms of gradations of symbolic
materiality (cf. particularly the line "diverse colpe giù li grava
al fondo," *Inferno* VI, ll. 85-7). More generally, the various
degrees of culpability in Hell are defined as degrees of progressively increasing weight, so much so that twice does
Dante refer to the center of Hell through images of weight
that gathers there: "lo mezzo / al qual ogne gravezza si rauna"
(*Inferno* XXXII, ll. 73-4), and "'l punto / al qual si traggon
d'ogne parte i pesi" (*Inferno* XXXIV, ll. 110-1).

This excursus, in a real sense, is a heuristic exercise to

---

[31] *Confessions*, XIII, viii. "Our rest is our place. Love lifts us up to it, and
your good spirit raises our lowness from the gates of death. In your good will
is our peace. A body tends to go of its own weight to its own place, not
necessarily downward toward the bottom, but to its own place. Fire tends to
rise upward; a stone falls downward. Things are moved by their own
weights and they go toward their proper places. . . . Put them back in order
and they will be at rest. My weight is my love; wherever I am carried, it is
my love that carries me there. By your gift we are set on fire and are carried
upward; . . . We are red hot with your fire, your good fire and we go; for we
are going upward toward the peace of Jerusalem" (trans. Warner, p. 322).

suggest primarily how Dante connects Dido's suicidal love with Augustine's doctrine of erotic weight. But the excursus will possibly help to illuminate some conceptual and dramatic features of *Inferno* v. The loss of rationality, for instance, in "Cosi' nel mio parlar" is rendered in *Inferno* v in explicit terms of the sinners' inversion of the order of reason over the will: "i peccator carnali, / che la ragion sommettono al talento" (ll. 38-9). From a dramatic standpoint, as Paolo and Francesca are shown endlessly whirling around, they seem to enact their existence of pure desire (l. 82), or, in Augustinian language, the restlessness of the heart forever out of place. In this sense, the setting for their expiation, "la bufera infernal, che mai non resta" (l. 31), is certainly a poignant detail of poetic justice as is the irony of the "pace" (ll. 92 and 99) that Francesca twice wistfully evokes. For Augustine, the fire of love, inspired by God, tends to the peace of Jerusalem: in *Inferno* v, the fire that kindled their love makes them wistful for "pace." The sinners' random motion (l. 43) is an apt counterpoint to the erratic impulses of the flesh, the aimlessness of their love, and a mockery of the perfect circle of God's love. At the same time, their floating weightlessly in the air (l. 75) ironically alludes to the fire of their passion (l. 100). In Augustine's metaphorics of love, the fire tends upward (and Dante has Vergil explain this law of spiritual gravity in his exposition on love in *Purgatorio* xviii, l. 28); yet, there is no ascent for Paolo and Francesca: trapped by their blind passion, they are enclosed in circuitous, aimless flights.

Augustine's presence in this episode, however, goes deeper than the excursus may indicate and calls directly into question the meaning of the *Aeneid*. The canto, as Poggioli has lucidly shown,[32] revolves around the question of desire mediated by literature: Francesca's love formulas (ll. 100-5) while they flat-

[32] Renato Poggioli, "Paolo and Francesca" in *Dante: A Collection of Critical Essays*, ed. John Freccero (Englewood Cliffs, N. J.: Prentice-Hall Inc., 1965), pp. 61-77. For the general problem, see René Girard, *Deceit, Desire, and the Novel*, trans. Yvonne Freccero (Baltimore: The Johns Hopkins University Press, 1965).

ter her sense of spontaneity,[33] ironically show that she is possessed by literature, that her desire is an imitation of the love
story of Lancelot and Guinevere she is reading. Thus, the
mystifications of love literature, the insidiousness of reading
"per diletto" (l. 127)—as she does—for pure esthetic enjoyment, are unveiled and indicted. It might be pointed out that
Francesca's reading "per diletto" faintly echoes Augustine's
categories of *uti* and *frui*. In *De Doctrina Christiana*, he distinguishes between things which are to be used, things which are
to be enjoyed and things which are to be used and enjoyed.[34]
The things which are to be enjoyed are the Father, the Son
and the Holy Spirit: to enjoy other things, to cling, that is to
say, to them with love for their own sake, is sinful. For
Francesca to read "per diletto" is nothing less than to be fet-
tered by the esthetic dimension of the book. Thus envisaged,
Dante's own text functions as an extended critique of the
seductions of the romance Francesca reads and implicitly
would seem to claim for itself an ironic authentic stance from
which to unmask the deceits of the "galeotto." This elaborate
scheme, however, is complicated by the presence in the canto
of another love book, the *Aeneid*, and we must pursue the
metaphor of reading further.

It had been pointed out, quite correctly, that the last line in
Francesca's speech "quel giorno più non vi leggemmo
avante" (l. 138), which symmetrically circles back to "noi
leggiavamo un giorno . . ." (l. 127), is an echo of St. Augustine's "nec ultra legere volui."[35] This is the moment when
Augustine breaks off the reading of St. Paul's Epistle in which
the apostle urges the reader to give up reveling and drunkenness, lust and wantonness, and reaches his conversion. Augustine's own reading of St. Paul's Epistle to the Romans
parallels and subsumes a previous scene in the *Confessions*,

[33] Sapegno, p. 64.   [34] *De Doctrina Christiana*, I, iii-v.

[35] T. K. Swing, *The Fragile Leaves of the Sybil* (Westminster, Md.: The
Newman Press, 1962), p. 299. See also R. Hollander, *Allegory in Dante's
Commedia*, pp. 112-4, for the literary implications of the echo. Of considerable interest is Giovanni Busnelli, "S. Agostino, Dante e il Medio Evo," *Vita
e Pensiero*, 21 (1930), pp. 502-8.

Augustine's account of his reading of the *Aeneid*. It is this scene that Francesca's reading experience directly recalls:

Nam utique meliores, quia certiores, erant primae illae litterae, quibus fiebat in me et factum est et habeo illud, ut et legam, si quid scriptum invenio, et scribam ipse, si quid volo, quam illae, quibus tenere cogebar Aeneae nescio cuius errores oblitus errorem meorum, et plorare Didonem mortuam, quia se occidit ab amore, cum interea me ipsum in his a te morientem, Deus, vita mea, siccis oculis ferrem miserrimus.

Quid enim miserius misero non miserante se ipsum et flente Didonis mortem, quae fiebat amando Aenean, non flente autem mortem suam, quae fiebat non amando te, Deus, lumen cordis mei et panis oris intus animae meae et virtus maritans mentem meam et sinum cogitationis meae? Non te amabam et fornicabar abs te et fornicanti sonabat undique "euge, euge," dicitur, ut pudeat, si non ita homo sit. Et haec non flebam et flebam Didonem "extinctam ferroque extrema secutam," sequens ipse extrema condita tua, relicto te, et iens in terram . . . Nam ecce paratior sum oblivisci errores Aeneae atque omnia eius modi, quam scribere et legere. . . . Peccabam ergo puer, cum illa inania istis utilioribus amorem praeponebam vel potius ista oderam, illa amabam. Iam vero unum et unum duo, duo et duo quattuor, odiosa cantio mihi erat, et dulcissimum spectaculum vanitatis equus ligneus plenus armatis et Troiae incendium "atque ipsius umbra Creusae."[36]

36 *Confessions*, I, xiii. "For by means of these rudiments I acquired and still retain the power to read what I find written and to write what I want to write myself; they are undoubtedly better, because more reliable, than those other studies in which I was forced to learn all about the wanderings of a man called Aeneas, while quite oblivious of my own wanderings, and to weep for the death of Dido, because she killed herself for love, while all the time I could bear with dry eyes, O God my life, the fact that I myself, poor wretch, was, among these things, dying far away from you.

"What indeed can be more pitiful than a wretch with no pity for himself, weeping at the death of Dido, which was caused by love for Aeneas, and not

The links between this long passage and the foregoing discussion are several. Dante, to begin with, seems to take over *verbatim* Augustine's description of Dido's suicide: "che s'ancise amorosa" translates "(quia) se occidit ab amore." The line in which Francesca recalls her fornication "se fosse amico il re de l'universo" (l. 91) seems to follow Augustine's "amicitia enim huius mundi, fornicatio est abs te." Even the "spada ond'elli ancise Dido" from the *Rime Petrose* echoes the Vergilian line which is quoted by Augustine "seeking by the sword her doom." But there are other remarkable analogies: Augustine's tears for Dido find a correlate in Dante's grief: "Francesca, i tuoi martiri / a lagrimar mi fanno tristo e pio . . ." (ll. 116-7). In passing, we should note that the word "martiri" subtly casts Francesca as a character in an ironic hagiography, the conventional legend of good women in the religion of the god of love. Further, in both scenes the act of reading is disclosed as an erotic experience: Augustine's pity for Dido is judged as a fornication against God; Francesca's reading results in a literal fornication. The *Aeneid* is for Augustine a potential "galeotto," threatening him with self-forgetfulness (in a book whose narrative paradigm is memory); Francesca, by surrendering to the erotic temptations of

weeping at his own death, caused by lack of love for you, God, light of my heart, bread of the inner mouth of my soul, strength of my mind, and quickness of my thoughts? You I did not love. Against you I committed fornication and in my fornication I heard all around me the words: 'Well done! Well done!' they have the effect of making one ashamed not to be that sort of person. But this was not what I wept for; I wept for dead Dido 'who by the sword pursued a way extreme' meanwhile myself following a more extreme way, that of the most extremely low of your creatures, having forsaken you, and being earth going back to earth. . . . For obviously I would rather forget about the wanderings of Aeneas and everything of that sort than how to write and read. . . . I sinned, therefore, in my boyhood when I showed greater affection for these empty studies than for the others that were most useful; or it would be truer to say, I loved the former and I hated the latter. At that time 'One and one make two; two and two make four' was a horrible kind of singsong to me. What really delighted me were spectacles of vanity—the wooden horse full of armed men, the burning of Troy and 'there the very shade of dead Creüsa' " (trans. Warner, pp. 30-2).

the "galeotto" forgets herself, and now that she is damned she belatedly remembers her "tempo felice" (l. 122). Moreover, in both scenes the submerged and unifying motif is literary retraction. Augustine reads Vergil and attempts to turn his own literary statement into an instrument for the exposure of the fallacy of the Vergilian text. The *Aeneid* is to him an empty deceitful fiction, a "choice spectacle of vanity," and he resists going astray in the footsteps of Aeneas' errors.[37] Augustine's dismissal of the love story he reads breaks into two distinct parts in *Inferno* v: Francesca goes into an illusory self-identification with the heroine of the romance; it might be said, exploiting the Augustinian resonance of her reading "per diletto," that she reads literally, according to the flesh, as it were, and mistakes the insubstantial shadows of the text for her own self. At the same time, the canto features Dante's own drama as he resists the temptation of succumbing to the pathos of Francesca's story. The words "pietade" (l. 140) and "pietà" (l. 93), which for Aeneas are virtues that prompt him to leave Dido, are turned around by Dante to indicate his compassion for the sinner and his moving toward her. He faints in the intense awareness, furthermore, that he, as an author, might trap the readers into the illusory self-enclosure of the romance, just as the stilnovistic poetry, which Francesca quotes in her speech, trapped her. Dante's own text, then, does not simply claim the privileged position of demystifying "romantic" lies; it acknowledges itself as part of the unavoidable ambiguities of the language of desire. The erotic force of literature, in other words, appears to involve in the spirals of desire all the principals of the canto in various degrees: Francesca is seduced by her "galeotto"; the pilgrim, like Augustine with the *Aeneid*, is fascinated by the love story he hears which, in turn, is the text we read. Dante, the poet of love, witnesses the potential dangers generated by the reading of love poetry, as if the *reprobatio amoris* is flanked by the possibility of it becoming a pretext for other perverse passions.

[37] *Confessions*, i, xiii ff., Warner, pp. 30 ff.

Finally, what connects *Inferno* v and the Augustinian experience of reading is the *Aeneid*: in the *Confessions*, the *Aeneid* is the object of overt critical confrontation. In *Inferno* v, Francesca's speech evokes the same scene of the *Aeneid* that Augustine reads. The lines ". . .'Nessun maggior dolore / che ricordarsi del tempo felice / ne la miseria; . . ." (ll. 121-3) echo, as has been often remarked, the beginning of Aeneas' speech to Dido "infandum, regina iubes renovare dolorem" (*Aeneid* II, l. 3).[38] In Vergil's context, Aeneas' account of the fall of Troy sets in motion at the same time the erotic seduction of Dido. Vergil's implication seems to be that Carthage will fall like Troy because of the lust on which it is founded. More to our concern, the *Aeneid* is for both Augustine and Dante a book of love; yet, it is the different value that each of them assigns to this love that ultimately separates them. In a real sense, Dante recalls Augustine's reading of the *Aeneid* in order to register his disagreement with it. This is more than an innocuous exegetical debate and—as we shall now see—the stakes involved are indeed high.

Augustine's distrust of the *Aeneid*—which of course cannot obscure his fascination and continuous absorption of it—betrays more than his revulsion at the formal seductions of the work of art. His attack is directed at what might be called the ideology of the text, the thinly disguised justification of the Roman state. Just as for Dante, who links the lust of the queens with their cities, respectively Babylon, Carthage, Egypt and Troy (ll. 52-66), so for Augustine, the tragedy of Dido is a metaphor for his vision of secular history grounded in *amor sui*, a sinister world of carnality and perversion. Her love is perceived as "friendship of the world," which varies in degree but not in kind from the "libido dominandi" of Rome. The *City of God*, from this perspective, contains the conceptual sequel to Dido's lust: in the treatise, "amor sui" is the explicit vital focus by which the twisted strands of secular history are identified and unraveled:

[38] Enzo Esposito, "Dante traduttore di Virgilio," *L'Italia che scrive*, 48 (1965), esp. pp. 335-6.

Accordingly, two cities have been formed by two loves: the earthly by the love of self, even to the contempt of God; the heavenly by the love of God even to the contempt of self. The former, in a word, glories in itself, the latter in the Lord. . . . In the one, the princes and the nations it subdues are ruled by the love of ruling (Illi in principibus eius vel in eis quas subiugat nationibus dominandi libido dominatur); in the other, the princes and subjects serve one another in love. . . .[39]

The ideology of power is thus disclosed as it is caught in the dynamics of desire and the city of Rome is no exception. Rather, in the measure in which it lays false claims to eternity, Rome is the very counterfeit of the heavenly community. In the *City of God*, as he introduces his theological pattern of history, Augustine writes:

The glorious city of God is my theme in this work. . . . I have undertaken its defence against those who prefer their own gods to the Founder of this city, a city surpassingly glorious, whether we view it as it still lives by faith in this fleeting course of time, and sojourns as a stranger in the midst of the ungodly, or as it shall dwell in the fixed stability of its eternal seat, which it now with patience waits for . . . the King and Founder of this city of which we speak, has in Scripture uttered to His people a dictum of the divine law in these words, "God resists the proud, but gives grace unto the humble." But this, which is God's prerogative, the inflated ambition of a proud spirit also affects, and loves to have this said in its praise, "show pity to those who are humbled and crush the proud ones." And therefore . . . we must speak also of the earthly city which . . . is itself ruled by its lust of rule.[40]

---

[39] *De Civitate Dei*, xiv, 28. The English text is from *The City of God*, trans. Marcus Dods (New York: The Modern Library, 1950), p. 477. It might be pointed out that book i of the *City of God* starts with a pointed recall of the Vergilian story of the fall of Troy recounted by Aeneas to Dido, *CCSL*, i, ii.

[40] *The City of God* i, 1, Dods, p. 3.

It is no impeccable logic to see the manifest Vergilian allusion (*Aeneid* vi, 1. 854) as a way of releasing the history of Rome into the general domain of sin and of seeing the city as the true inversion of the authenticity of God's kingdom. Hence, in a perfectly transparent polemic with Vergil, Augustine negates any providential mission to Rome which is consistently vindicated by its poet.[41] He goes so far as to dissociate the Vergilian text from any truth it may express: to the degree that Vergil may have had premonitions of the future, Augustine indicates the real source in the prophetic pronouncements of the Sybil.[42] If for Vergil Rome is the eternal city, willed by the gods and in radical antithesis to all other empires, for Augustine it is the epitome of the earthly city; like the city of Cain, it has its inception in a fratricide and no difference can be discerned "between the foundation of this city (Rome) and the earthly city, a product of spiritual lust."[43]

Yet, although Rome is inextricably part of the earthly city for Augustine, he preserves the Vergilian structure in his own theology of history: both see history as a process, for the one the *eschaton* is Christian freedom, for the other the finality is secular and Roman. Both postulate a dualistic substance in history. For Vergil, it is either Rome or Carthage; for Augustine, whose historical perspective is the chaos of the fallen city sacked by Alaric, and who writes, ironically, from Africa, the choice is between Babylon and Jerusalem. This parallel, to be sure, is not simply structural: for Augustine, the two cities belong to an eschatological dimension and have tem-

---

[41] *The City of God* iii, 2, Dods, 75.

[42] "It is of Him, too, that the most famous poet speaks, poetically indeed, since he applies it to the person of another, yet truly if you refer it to Christ, saying, 'Under thine auspices, if any traces of our crimes remain, they shall be obliterated, and each freed from its perpetual fear. . . .' For that he did not say this at the prompting of his own fancy, Virgil tells us in almost the last verse of that 4th eclogue, when he says, 'The last age predicted by the Cumaean sibyl has now arrived'; whence it plainly appears that this has been dictated by the Cumaean sibyl" (x, 27, Dods, p. 333).

[43] *The City of God* xv, 5, Dods, p. 482; cf. also xviii, 22, Dods, p. 628.

poral extensions; for Vergil, the two cities belong to a political order and are immutable models for history. [44]

In the light of this, Dante's agreement with, and departure from, Augustine's view of the *Aeneid* would seem to be inevitable. Dante shares, as we shall see later on, Augustine's sense of history as radical desire, but for him *amor sui* is redeemed by a belief in the providential structure of history. To give an instance for now, greed and avarice are the vices that threaten the order of the world, but they can be corrected by the exercise of rationality. This motif is highlighted by the famous invective against the "antica lupa" (*Purgatorio* xx, ll. 10 ff.) and the hopeful prayer that she may be banished and justice restored to the world.

In terms of the *Aeneid*, Dante's interpretative resolution gives an eloquent measure of his distance from Augustine. Unlike Augustine, who condemns both Aeneas and Dido, Dante deliberately discriminates between Dido's passion and Aeneas' transcendence of it; he even delineates his own experience in a way which admittedly parallels Aeneas' quest because he has a double awareness of Vergil's poem. Dante's polemic with Augustine over the meaning of the *Aeneid* is effected by turning, as we have hinted, to the interpretations which had been virtually institutionalized by the neoplatonic exegetes. In a sense, Fulgentius, Bernardus Silvestris and John of Salisbury dehistoricized the *Aeneid* and in their mythographic schematizations they interpret the experiences of Aeneas in purely ontological terms. [45] To them, Aeneas represents the myth of the platonic abstraction of the journey of life in its process of *paideia*. This general reading of the poem, with its emphasis on Aeneas' philosophical askesis and his redemptive hardships, allowed Dante to make a fruitful distinction between Dido and Aeneas.

---

[44] For Augustine's indebtedness to Vergil, see Brooks Otis, "Virgil and Clio," *Phoenix* 20 (1966), pp. 59-75. See also C. N. Cochrane, *Christianity and Classical Culture: A Study of Thought and Action From Augustus to Augustine* (Oxford: Oxford University Press, 1968), pp. 359 ff.

[45] Cf. R. Hollander, *Allegory in Dante's* Commedia, pp. 11-2.

Bernardus' commentary on the first six books of the *Aeneid* seems to be obliquely recalled precisely in canto v of *Inferno*, as Vergil points out to the pilgrim Semiramis and Dido:

> "La prima di color di cui novelle
> tu vuo' saper," mi disse quelli allotta,
> "fu imperadrice di molte favelle.
> A vizio di lussuria fu sì rotta,
> che libito fé licito in sua legge,
> per tòrre il biasmo in che era condotta.
> . . . .
> L'altra è colei che s'ancise amorosa."
>
> ll. 52-7, 61

("The first of these of whom you wish to hear news," he said to me then, "was empress of many tongues. She was so given to lechery that she made lust licit in her law, to take away the blame she had incurred. . . . The other is she who slew herself for love.")

Both Babylon, the city of confusion ("molte favelle") and Carthage, the city of Dido, are clearly alluded to in this brief enumerative sequence, and the sin of "libito" connects the two queens. The distance from Augustine, who had associated Babylon and Rome also in terms of *libido*, is self-evident. What is of interest is the fact that the linkage between Carthage and Babylon, because of the *libido* which characterizes both cities, was explicitly made by Bernardus in his moralized account of Aeneas' journey. Speaking of Carthage he says:

> . . . novam civitatem mundi . . . in hac civitate regnum habet Dido i.e., libido . . . in hac civitate [Aeneas] invenit regnantem mulierem i.e. Poenos servientes, quia in mundo isto talis est confusio quod imperat libido et opprimuntur virtutes, quas per Poenos, fortes et rigidos viros, intelligimus, atque ita servit virtus atque imperat libido. Ideo in divinis libris dicitur mundus Babylonis civitas i.e., confusionis.[46]

[46] "(Aeneas came to Carthage, that is) to the new city of the world. Dido,

The connection is made more strikingly by Dante in *De Vulgari Eloquentia*, where he describes the erection of the tower, a myth which he drew from Augustine's *City of God*, in terms which textually recall the building of Carthage in the first book of the *Aeneid*: "pars imperabant, pars architectabantur, pars muros moliebantur, pars amussibus regulabant, pars trullis lienbant, pars scindere rupes, pars mari, pars terra vehere intendebant, partesque diverse diversis aliis operibus indulgebant. . . ."[47] But Aeneas transcends "libido." Both Fulgentius and Bernardus contrast Aeneas' love for Dido to his love for Lavinia as polar opposites in his spiritual *paideia*. This is how Fulgentius interprets the moral function of Lavinia:

> Denique tunc et uxorem petit Laviniam, id est laborum viam; ab hac enim aetate unusquis suis utilitatum emolumentis laborum asciscit suffragia; unde et filia Latini dicta est, nepus Cauni; Latinus enim quasi a latitando dictus, quod omnis labor diversis in locis latitet, . . . Caunus vere id est quasi comnonus, est laborans sensus.[48]

that is, lust, has a kingdom in this city . . . Aeneas finds in this city a woman ruling, that is, Carthaginians in servitude, since in that world such is the confusion that lust rules and virtues are held in check, which we understand through the Carthaginians, brave and stalwart men, and thus virtue serves and lust rules. Therefore in divine books the world is said to be the city of Babylon, that is, of confusion" (*Commentum super sex libros Eneidos*, p. 12).

[47] "Some gave orders, others drew designs, some built walls, others made them straight by levels, some plastered them with trowels; some were busy in splitting rocks, and others were intent on transporting them by sea and land, and different groups devoted themselves to different other works" (*De Vulgari Eloquentia*, i, vii, 6). For the building of Carthage, see *Aeneid*, i, ll. 423 ff. For the building of the tower, see *De Civitate Dei*, xvi, 4.

[48] *Expositio Virgilianae Continentiae* in *Opera*, ed. R. Helm (Leipzig: B. G. Teubner, 1898), p. 105. "Then he seeks to marry Lavinia, that is, the road of toil (*laborum viam*), for at this stage Everyman (*unusquis*) learns the value of toil in worldly possession. She is also called the daughter of Latinus and the descendant of Caunus. Now Latinus is from *latitando*, being concealed, because toil is always concealed in various places, . . . And Caunus is for *camnonus*, that is toiling mind" (trans. Leslie G. Whitbread, *Fulgentius the Mythog-*

The same emphasis on "labor" as the rational activity by which man can attain spiritual wholeness is given by Bernardus for whom Aeneas, freeing himself from Dido and reaching Italy, shows "potentia animi" in "regna laborum."[49] Such a radical distinction in Aeneas' experience is articulated by Dante himself in the *Convivio*, where following the neoplatonic exegesis of Fulgentius, he reads the *Aeneid* as the allegory of human life in its various stages of "Adolescenzia, Gioventude, Senettute, and Senio."[50] While discussing the necessity that reason bridle desire, Dante refers to Aeneas as the emblem of a man who in his "gioventute" had the virtue of temperance and after leaving "dilettazione," chose "laudabile via e fruttuosa."

> E cosi' infrenato mostra Vergilio, lo maggiore nostro poeta, che fosse Enea, ne la parte de lo Eneida dove questa etade si figura; . . . E quanto raffrenare fu quello, quando, avendo ricevuto da Dido tanto di piacere quanto di sotto nel settimo trattato si dicerà, e usando con essa tanto di dilettazione, elli si partio per seguire onesta e laudabile via e fruttuosa come nel quarto de l'Eneida scritto è!

Later on in the same chapter, Dante elaborates on the necessity of having love for one's elders, and Aeneas' journey to Italy is explicitly stated in terms of "fatiche," the Italian equivalent of *labor*:

> . . . conviensi amare li suoi maggiori . . . e questo amore mostra che avesse Enea lo nomato poeta nel quinto libro

rapher [Columbus, Ohio: Ohio State University Press, 1971], p. 133). I would render the sentence starting "for at this stage" as follows: "for from this age everyone accepts the advantages of his labors as his own rewards for services."

[49] *Commentum*, p. 50.

[50] The pattern of the four phases of human life is treated in *Convivio* IV, xxiv, 1-10. The reference to the "figurato che questo processo de l'etadi tiene Virgilio ne lo Eneida" is in vol. II, pp. 312-3, and Busnelli and Vandelli rightly point out the allusion to *De Continentia Vergiliana*. Cf. also Domenico Comparetti, *Virgilio nel Medioevo*, I, 130-9.

sopra detto, quando lascio' li vecchi Troiani in Cicilia
raccomandati ad Aceste, e partilli da le fatiche. . . .[51]

These interpretations of the ascetic process of the *Aeneid* negate the undifferentiated, homogeneous view of Augustine
and contain for Dante *in embryo* the structure of the two secular cities: the self-destructive lust upon which the city of
Babylon or Carthage is founded is juxtaposed to love as a
moral virtue or labor as the basis of the city of Rome.

For Dante historicizes the purely intellectual, disembodied
pattern of Aeneas' askesis that Bernardus, Fulgentius and he
himself in the *Convivio* had articulated. Aeneas' labors in the
Commedia are not simply tests for the hero's philosophical
maturity or for his abstract rational control over circumstances that besiege his will. Labor is indeed desire restrained
by discipline, or more precisely, the activity which conveys a
real coherence and rationality upon history and by which man
shapes and shares the world.

The historicizing of the neoplatonists' view was partly
stressed in the discussion on the symbolic implications of the
island of Crete (chapter 1). It will be remembered that in the
allegorization of Bernardus, Crete is the world of carnality
antithetical to Rome, the promised land of Aeneas. Dante
transformed this interpretation by making the historical
Rome the mirrored image of the old man of Crete. He represented Crete as the crystallization of an anti-Eden, a mythic
prototype of degradation outside the direct experience of the
pilgrim. Rome, in turn, had a sort of moral neutrality: it can
be a historical projection either of Crete, an emblem of pure

---

[51] *Convivio* IV, xxvi, 8-9: "And Virgil, our greatest poet, tells us how
Aeneas was thus restrained in that part of the *Aeneid* which represents this
age. . . . And how he felt the curb, when, having received from Dido so
much pleasure (as will be told afterwards in the seventh treatise), and taking
such delight with her, he departed from her, that he might follow the virtuous, praiseworthy, and fruitful way, as is written in the fourth of the
Aeneid!" Later, xxvi, 10-11: "The youth should love his elders. . . . And this
love Aeneas felt, as the same poet shows us in the aforesaid fifth book, when
he left the aged Trojans in Sicily, recommended to Acestes, and freed them
from further toil" (trans. Katharine Hillard, pp. 364-6).

negativity, or of the Earthly Paradise, an emblem of work and love as Matelda's symbolic presence there pointedly suggests.

The dramatic nexus between work and desire is probed in the two cantos where Vergil, the character, acts as the philospher of love. In *Purgatorio* xvii he sets forth the theory of love which sustains the moral system of this second *cantica*. In his exposition, let us briefly recall, he distinguishes between unerring instinctive love and elective love which, subject to man's free will, can choose unworthy objects or be directed to the good. In the course of the "scholastic" *demonstratio*, the "alto dottore" (and the term ought to be taken in its strictest medieval acceptation) even alludes to Augustine's doctrine of desire as spiritual restlessness:

> Ciascun confusamente un bene apprende
> nel qual si queti l'animo, e disira;
> per che di giugner lui ciascun contende.
>
> ll. 127-9

(Each one apprehends confusedly a good wherein the mind may find rest, and this it desires; because of this each one strives to attain it.)

This recalls the opening of the *Confessions*: "fecisti nos ad te et inquietum est cor nostrum donec requiescat in te." This view of the apprehension of the good in which the self's restlessness is quenched is pursued in the following canto, *Purgatorio* xviii, where Vergil expatiates on love in its relation to acts of choice. His elaborate discourse, of which we have only given the salient point, is framed between a series of *exempla*, two of which are drawn from the *Aeneid*. The first, occurring in the ridge where wrath is punished, features Amata who hanged herself in a fit of rage and fear that her daughter, Lavinia, would marry Aeneas (*Purgatorio* xvii, ll. 34-9). Aeneas and Lavinia belong, in the fiction of the *Commedia*, together (significantly, they are both in Limbo, *Inferno* iv, ll. 122 ff.), and Amata's anger is the symbol of an irrational and unnatural opposition to God's plan. The other *exemplum* occurs in the following canto where the sin of *acedia* is expiated.[52] The term designates a spiritual weariness, the inactivity induced by the noonday devil; Dante figures the punishment of sloth by showing the children of Israel who chose to remain in the desert and lost their promised land, and by showing also the companions of Aeneas who remained behind in Sicily and never reached their promised land, Italy (*Purgatorio* xviii, ll. 133-8).

The correlation of episodes from biblical history and secular history in this instance reflects, once again, Dante's sense of the *Aeneid* as a text which belongs to salvation history. More pertinently to our concern, sloth is a form of insufficient love or, which amounts to the same thing, love is the impulse of every act. Obliquely, Aeneas' quest for Italy is qualified as "affanno" (l. 136), a term which—as in the case of Francesca (*Inferno* v, l. 80)—implies both craving and effort, and which explains work to be the medium for Aeneas' progressive purification from the misdirected love for Dido. Work is not simply the punishment of man who has fallen from the Garden; it is an ascetic exercise, the conscious praxis by which the recovery of the promised land or, as the dramatization of the four cardinal virtues in Cato has shown, the making of political life is possible. Accordingly the foundations of the Roman Empire, as we shall see shortly, have been laid in the marriage of Aeneas to Lavinia.

I have thus far argued that Vergil has provided Dante with a new and useful dichotomy between the love of Dido and the love of Lavinia. The Vergilian world of historical immanence, however, does not claim a love of God that might transcend the conditions of an earth-bound destiny. This specifically Vergilian conception of history, which on the face of it would seem to entail a contraction, a narrowing of focus in Dante's theology of history, is actually grafted on St. Au-

[52] Siegfried Wenzel, *The Sin of Sloth: Acedia in Medieval Thought and Literature* (Chapel Hill: University of North Carolina Press, 1967).

gustine's view of the two cities. This process of harmonization is quite appropriately dramatized in *Paradiso* VI, the heaven of Mercury, the lawgiver,[53] where God's justice and the underlying order of history are celebrated.

In rhetorical terms, Dante ostensibly writes a *laudatio* of the empire, and as such it is the reversal of the *vituperatio* of both city and Italy in *Inferno* VI and *Purgatorio* VI. More substantively, this is the canto of Justinian and the symbolic transparency of the name hardly needs belaboring: his name suggests that he is bound to the laws of justice, and quite in keeping with this tenet he is the lawgiver of the empire (*Paradiso* VI, ll. 11-3) who, finally stripped of the earthly attributes of Caesar (l. 10), describes God's great design in history in a chronological succession from the fall of Troy and the marriage of Lavinia and Aeneas to the days of the struggle between Guelfs and Ghibellines. The continuous narrative of the fragmented events of the empire is organized around the vicissitudes of the Roman eagle, the conventional emblem of justice, that followed Aeneas from Troy and was moved east by Constantine (ll. 1-3). But the eagle has other symbolic implications for the structure of the canto. The line from Psalm 102, "renovabitur ut aquila vita tua," is interpreted by Augustine, among others, to mean life's spiritual new beginnings.[54] By focusing on the eagle as the emblem of history, Dante shows the typological unity of history, its continuous renewal even as it appears to be defeated by its enemies. Further, by telling the story of the empire through its emblem, Dante implies that history is a representation and a purely symbolic construct; by this implication, he manages to preserve a crucial distinction between the providential, immutable structure of

[53] In *De Natura Deorum* III, 56, Cicero gives various types of Mercury. The fifth in the list is the one worshiped by the people of Pheneus and is said to have fled in exile to Egypt where he gave the Egyptians "leges et litteras."

[54] *Enarrationes in Psalmos CII*, CCSL XL, p. 1459. For the eagle as the emblem of the empire, see *Paradiso* XIX: "Poi si quetaro quei lucenti incendi / de lo Spirito Santo ancor nel segno / che fé i Romani al mondo reverendi" (ll. 100-2); see also *Paradiso* XVIII, ll. 94-108.

history and the changing process of events. This distinction is fundamental to explaining Dante's awareness that history enacts a providential plan—it is indeed the *ordo salutis*—but it appears on the stage of the world as a succession of violence. In effect, the canto is articulated ambiguously as the story of the chaos of secular history and the apotheosis of the "virtues" of the empire. The narrative opens *ex abrupto* with a quick reference to Constantine's violation of the doctrine of the *translatio imperii*, his turning the eagle from the westward course begun by the fortunate fall of Troy. Aeneas' journey to Italy and his marriage to Lavinia are actually alluded to as the focal point of the history of the empire, by and large patterned on the *Aeneid*. The death of Pallas at the hands of Turnus, the founding of Alba Longa and the rape of the Sabine women (ll. 35 ff.) are clear echoes, as commentators have noted, of the *Aeneid*.[55] But the rape of the Sabine women and that of Lucretia which culminates in suicide subtly insinuate the motif of lust in the fabric of Roman history. Moreover, this is the dramatic point where the Vergilian burden of the canto is given an Augustinian bent. The phrase "mal de le Sabine" (l. 40) echoes, more than the *Aeneid*, St. Augustine's account of the event. In the *City of God* he comments on the Romans' mischief of ravishing the women as follows: *"nec finis esset tanti mali*, nisi raptae illae laceratis crinibus emicanent et provolutae parentibus iram eorum iustissiman non armis victricibus, sed supplie pietate sedarent."*[56] Further, the refer-

---

[55] The canto is generally read as a poetic exemplification of and contrast to the view of Roman history that Dante puts forth in *Monarchia* II, iii-xi. Dante's echoes of Orosius in the canto have been pointed out by Paget Toynbee, *Dante Studies and Researches*, pp. 121-36. Francesco Torraca rightly remarks on the importance of *Aeneid* III to the whole canto. See his commentary on *La Divina Commedia* (Milan: Albrighi-Segati, 1921), pp. 679 ff.

[56] The passage in *The City of God* III, 13 reads: "But not even thus would the mischief have been finished, had not the ravished women themselves flashed out with dishevelled hair, and cast themselves before their parents, and thus disarmed their just rage, not with the arms of victory, but with the supplications of filial affection" (Dods, p. 84). The passage also echoes *Aeneid* VIII, l. 635. I am grateful to Silvia Rizzo of the University of Rome for bring-

ence to the war between Alba Longa and Rome "infino al fine / che i *tre* a' *tre* pugnar per lui ancora" (ll. 38-9) bears a pale resemblance to Augustine's description "a Romanis *tres* Horatii, ab Albanis autem *tres* Curiatii processerunt."[57] Finally, the eagle's triumph over neighboring people "vincendo intorno le genti vicine" (l. 42) recalls Augustine's account of the Romans' victory over the Sabines "At enim *vicerunt* in hac conflictione *Romani suos vicinos*."[58] These crimes, along with the violence perpetrated on Lucretia's body, are occasions for Augustine's indictment of Rome as a city founded on lust and impiety and whose legitimacy is continuously questioned. But Dante redeems this sinfulness even as he acknowledges Augustine's evaluations.

I am not trying, it should be made clear, to belittle the presence of the *Aeneid* in the canto: I simply wish to point out that there is a system of cross references at work to Vergil and Augustine. This technique was also deployed in *Inferno* v, and it is too frequent and extensive not to be part of a deliberate pattern. The line, for instance, which describes the eagle's triumph over the Arabs "esso atterrò l'orgoglio de li Aràbi / che di retro ad Anibale passaro" (ll. 49-50) echoes the Vergilian dictum "parcere subiectis, debellare superbos" which, however, Augustine had used to exemplify Rome's mockery of the city of God. If the pattern is deliberate, we must draw its inferences.

It would seem that from Justinian's eschatological standpoint, Dante shares Augustine's view of Vergilian history as a staging of lust and violence. But Dante twists Augustine's vigorous attack on Rome around; he implies that history enacts typologically the pattern of Exodus. When

---

ing to my attention the piece by Scevola Mariotti, "Il Canto vi del *Paradiso*," *Nuove letture dantesche*, v (Florence: Le Monnier, 1972), pp. 375-404, which also mentions the allusions to Augustine. For the importance of *The City of God* for Dante's conception of Roman history in both *Convivio* and *Monarchia*, see E. Moore, *Studies in Dante*, 1st series, pp. 188 ff.

[57] *The City of God* iii, 14; Dods, p. 85.
[58] *The City of God* iii, 13; Dods, p. 83.

Augustus was the "keeper" of the eagle, the defeat of
Cleopatra and the subsequent Augustinian peace are described
as follows:

> Piangene ancor la trista Cleopatra,
>   che, fuggendoli innanzi, dal colubro
>   la morte prese subitana e atra.
> Con costui corse infino al lito rubro;
> con costui puose il mondo in tanta pace, . . .
>
> ll. 76-80

(Because of it sad Cleopatra is still weeping, she who,
fleeing before it took from the viper sudden and black
death. With him it ran as far as the shore of the Red Sea;
with him it set the world in such peace. . . .)

The typological resonances of the passage are unmistakable:
the eagle's exploits and the peace later established are obliquely dramatized in terms of the underlying structure of history, Exodus, as a movement, that is, from Egypt (Cleopatra), a recall of love of self in *Inferno* v, through the Red Sea,
the "lito rubro" (l. 79), to Jerusalem, the conventional *visio
pacis*. But in addition to this suggested structure, there is
another submerged redemptive event that Dante places at the
very center of the tragic economy of history, namely the sacrifice of Christ.[59] His sacrifice, cryptically alluded to as "la
vendetta del peccato antico" (l. 93), is the act by which the
constitutive violence of history is redeemed: he is the
pharmakos—as we are told at some length in *Paradiso* vii (ll.
28-51)—the voluntary victim by whom the binding of man to
God takes place. To be sure, the provisional experience of the
harmony of the world willed by God at the time of Caesar (ll.
55-8) is elevated to the goal of history, but it cannot obscure
the deep sense of the reality of violence and Christ's violent
death which in turn demands a "revenge." Titus' destruction
of the temple of Jerusalem is interpreted precisely as the
"vendetta . . . de la vendetta." In spite of Christ's redemptive

[59] René Girard, *La Violence et le sacré* (Paris: Grasset, 1972).

act, the pervasive violence of history does not come to an end but, on the contrary, seems to proliferate. The violence of the empire, however, appears "justified" as it takes on the role of God's punitive instrument: Titus' revenge, Charlemagne's defense of the Church against the Longobards (ll. 94-6), and, more explicitly, the claim that the universal empire is directed by God (ll. 109-11) are unequivocal signs of its providential function in God's design. Thus envisaged, the empire enacts the Augustinian paradox: it originates in sin and is *remedium peccati*.[60]

This harmonization is carried out at the considerable expense of both Vergil and Augustine. Dante criticizes Augustine for his playing down the importance of the natural order celebrated, even if ambiguously, by Vergil. At the same time, by the weighty recall of Augustine's version of the history of Rome, he seems to imply that indeed the world of immanence, the world of Vergilian history, if left entirely to itself as Augustine sees it, would really be only a pageant of lust and violence. The point is borne out, in more general terms, in *Paradiso* VII where man's redemption by the grace of God is discussed: "non potea l'uomo ne' termini suoi / mai sodisfar, per non potere ir giuso . . ." (ll. 97-8). Dante's interpretive strategy between Augustine and Vergil is not a pure rhetorical exercise, the indulgence of a poet who is profoundly engaged in literary polemics. The strategy dramatizes, on the contrary, Dante's view of the relationship between the orders of nature and grace.

The problem between these two orders is not that of a failure to choose between them, but rather to establish the sense of their middle ground. Grace does not entail the abrogation of nature ("gratia non tollit naturam"), on the contrary it perfects nature.[61] Dante accepts this thomistic theological com-

---

[60] In *Monarchia*, Dante asserts that the foundation of the empire is human right (III, x, 7) and he also states that "regimina remedia contra infirmitatem peccati" (III, iv, 14).

[61] *Summa Theologiae*, Ia, q. I, art. 8, ad sec.; see also *De veritate*, XXVII, art. 6, ad primum.

monplace: he takes the world of immanence seriously (and it is here that for him Augustine possibly failed) and believes in the existence of a middle ground, a redeemed nature between fallen nature and the order of grace. This middle area is not given, to be sure, a metaphysical substantiality: in an *ab aeterno* condition, middleness is a theological impossibility and there are, in fact, no middle forms of beatitude.[62] The middle area is the region, on the contrary, of a *moral* middleness, the temporal and open-ended world where choices are made and the opportunity of transcending the order of nature is offered. Dante identifies the moral middle ground with the Garden of Eden and the precarious condition of *liberum arbitrium*.

Free will implies the possibility of doing good or evil, of choosing a disordered and idolatrous love of self or the love of God. The Garden of Eden is precisely the locus where reason holds sway over the will and where the pilgrim roams with Vergil until Beatrice comes. At the same time, the empire functions as a way of making possible this moral region within history: its aim is to establish peace and, by the exercise of justice, bring men to discern at least the tower of the true city.[63]

In the Garden of Eden, the transition from Vergil to Beatrice is effected by a radical revision of some lines from the *Aeneid*. Beatrice, who comes as Christ or sanctifying grace,[64] and Vergil actually represent two orders of being, grace and nature respectively, two spiritual states whose complete eventual separation is certain but in no sense drastic. As Beatrice

---

[62] The question has been treated, by focusing on angelology, by John Freccero, "Dante's 'per se' Angels: the Middle Ground in Nature and Grace," *Studi danteschi*, 39 (1962), pp. 5-38; see also his "Dante and the Neutral Angels," *The Romanic Review*, 51 (1960), pp. 3-14. Cf. Bruno Nardi, *Saggi di filosofia dantesca*, pp. 215-44.

[63] *Purgatorio* xvi, ll. 94-6. For the problem of justice in the *Divine Comedy*, see Allan H. Gilbert, *Dante's Conception of Justice* (New York: AMS Press, 1965).

[64] Charles Singleton, *Dante Studies 2: Journey to Beatrice* (Cambridge, Mass.: Harvard University Press, 1958), pp. 74 ff.

gets nearer to the pilgrim, he turns to Vergil (*Purgatorio* xxx, l. 43) to communicate to him his apprehension of Beatrice by the Vergilian line "conosco i segni dell'antica fiamma" (l. 48), a literal translation of Dido's protestation of love for Aeneas. Within this dramatic context, the ambiguity of the line is striking for it seals the separation between Vergil and Dante and, at the same time, it marks the encounter between Dante and Beatrice. In its original context, the line describes a self-annihilating and suicidal type of love and, in a real sense, when Dante recognizes Beatrice in this Vergilian language, he is turning away, like Augustine, from the Vergilian poetry of perverted love. Augustine reads the same Vergilian scene, as we have seen, and must leave it behind so that, like a Christian Aeneas, he may go on seeking his own real home, the Christian city of Rome. Dante, by the translation of the line, introduces an explicit *amor Beatricis*, expressed through a rectification of Dido's love for Aeneas. Translation is a veritable metaphor that dramatizes the ambiguous process of assimilating the line and betraying its original sense.[65] In doctrinal terms, the inversion of the object of love (from Dido to Beatrice) serves to postulate the ultimate discontinuity and inevitable caesura between fallen nature and the order of grace.

But apart from the doctrinal problems involved in the transition from Vergil to Beatrice, there are some specific literary questions worth considering. Perhaps no other single passage in the poem features a rhetoric more charged with Vergilian echoes, as if Dante wished to mitigate the pathos and abruptness of Vergil's dismissal. The triple invocation to Vergil (ll. 49-51), as Moore points out, is an echo of Orpheus' invocation to the lost Eurydice. In the *Georgics* Orpheus' descent to the underworld fails because of his mad love.[66] Orpheus can-

[65] It might be pointed out, in this context of Dante's betrayal of the original sense of Dido's words, that Dido in the *Aeneid* is herself a figure who "ruppe fede al cener di Sicheo" (*Inferno* v, l. 62); cf. "non servata fides cineri promissa Sychaeo," *Aeneid* iv, l. 552.

[66] Edward Moore, *Studies in Dante*, 1st series, p. 21, refers to *Georgics* iv, ll. 525-7. For the importance of Orpheus in Vergil, see Marie Desport, *L'Incantation Virgilienne: Virgile et Orphée* (Bordeaux: Imprimeries Delmas, 1952).

not conquer death but, unlike him, Dante enters the garden of a new life. Further, another line from the *Aeneid*, "manibus o date lilia plenis," is transposed untranslated into Dante's text (1. 21). The line in the *Aeneid* is an elegiac anticipation of Marcellus' premature death, an event by which Vergil obliquely undercuts the triumphant spectacle of Roman history staged for Aeneas and draws the fabric of history into the universe of death. That event is turned against Vergil into a greeting for Beatrice's own premature death and present resurrection and, implicitly, into an anticipation of the pilgrim's own renewed life.

As Vergil disappears, the poem actually seems to take on what might be called an Augustinian literary form. The poet, for the first and only time in the poem, registers his own name (1. 55). A gloss in *Convivio* explains that a man may speak of himself when "grandissima utilitate ne segue per via di dottrina," and, to substantiate the claim, Dante explicitly recalls both Boethius and Augustine's autobiographical focus in the *Confessions*.[67] Cantos XXX and XXXI enact precisely a confessional experience. The pilgrim voices his contrition and goes into a brief recapitulation of his past from the "vita nuova" (*Purgatorio* XXX, 1. 115) to the new encounter with Beatrice. Like Augustine in the *Confessions*, Dante's conversion is marked by a dismissal of Dido's love. But neither manages to break away completely from Dido's imaginative spell. Augustine rejects the *Aeneid* and finds himself drawn back by the vision of the burning city of Troy and "ipsius umbra Creusae."[68] Dante's own confession to the "cose fallaci" (*Purgatorio* XXXI, 1. 56) features a similar ambiguity. As he experiences a painful humiliation at Beatrice's rebuke, he alludes to the "terra di Iarba" (1. 72), he imaginatively returns,

---

[67] Cf. the gloss by John Freccero, "Dante's Prologue Scene," p. 2.

[68] The constant fascination that Augustine, the retraction in the *Confessions* notwithstanding, has for Vergil is documented by Karl Hermann Schelkle, *Virgil in der Deutung Augustinus* (Stuttgart and Berlin: Kohlhammer, 1939); see also Nancy Lankeith, *Dante and the Legend of Rome* (London: The Warburg Institute, 1952), pp. 33-4.

that is, to the very story of Dido's love for Aeneas that he must forsake, lapses into the past he wishes to transcend.

Beyond the suggestion of the formal shift from what might summarily be called the "epic" to Augustinian autobiography and the disruption of the conversion, we must face the question of Dante's reading of the *Aeneid*. This is the poem of history, the narrative of true and providential events, and yet it appears to be systematically subjected to interpretive violence: indeed, the letter of the text is turned against its author. Is this interpretive violence necessary, and how is it related to the ideology of history which, in purely human terms, also appears as desire and violence?

In order to give further probative evidence of the violations of the *Aeneid*, let us briefly look at *Inferno* xiii where Aeneas' encounter with Polydorus (*Aeneid* iii, ll. 39 ff.) is recast to dramatize the suicide of Pier delle Vigne.[69] But Dante's account is not a twice-told tale. On the contrary, there is a deliberate revision of the "source." A thematic thread, from our narrowly defined point of view, is the act of breaking. Pier delle Vigne denies that he has broken faith with the Emperor Frederick (l. 74) and Dante breaks the twig in which Pier delle Vigne is held (ll. 33 ff.). Further, the punishment on the sinners is meted out by unleashed dogs tearing apart the spendthrifts (l. 110). The act of breaking, clearly, is the counterpart of the sinners' transgression of the wholeness of the person and property. But Vergil, at the hideous scene of blood and words dripping from the bush, draws attention to his own text:

> "S'elli avesse potuto creder prima,"
> rispuose 'l savio mio, "anima lesa,
> ciò c'ha veduto pur con la mia rima,
> non averebbe in te la man distesa;

[69] For a general reading of the canto, see Ettore Paratore, "Analisi 'Retorica' del canto di Pier delle Vigne," in *Tradizione e struttura in Dante* (Florence: Sansoni, 1968), pp. 178-220. For the problem of faith in terms of its allegorical significance, see Gian Roberto Sarolli, *Prolegomena alla* Divina Commedia (Florence: Olschki, 1971), pp. 138-43.

ma la cosa incredibile mi fece
indurlo ad ovra ch'a me stesso pesa."
                                        ll. 46-51

("If he had been able to believe before," replied my sage,
"O wounded spirit, what he had seen in my verses, he
would not have stretched forth his hand against you; but
the incredible thing made me prompt him to a deed that
grieves me.")

The apologetic speech of Vergil is directed at luring the
branch to disclose its identity (ll. 52 ff.) and renew, thus, the
sinner's fame. There is an obvious ironic discrepancy between
the claim that Pier delle Vigne's fame will be "refreshed" and
the lifeless landscape (ll. 1-6), or, more importantly, the state
of the damned to whom no renewal is ever possible except for
the branches in which they dwell (l. 73). The motif of renewal
is, in effect, ironically turned around in this canto where the
doctrinal focus is on the sense of metamorphosis.[70] Far from
implying a renewal, the metamorphosis is a parody of conversion, a tragic and irretrievable fall into matter. Yet,
paradoxically, Dante renews the corresponding scene from
the *Aeneid* by imposing on it a Christian perspective: unlike
the story of Polydorus who will be reconciled by Aeneas'
pious ritual with the order of nature, the pain of Pier delle
Vigne's experience will never be relieved. There is more to
this revisionary poetic practice than simply the case of a subversive Christian interpretation of a pagan myth. Vergil, who
had described the scene in the *Aeneid* and now asserts his authorship ("ciò c'ha veduto pur con la *mia* rima"), is himself
perplexed by the experience he confronts (ll. 50-1), as if the
reality they witness exceeds his language. More important
still, Dante by not believing Vergil's original account ("s'egli

[70] Francesco D'Ovidio, *Nuovi studi danteschi*, I (Naples: A. Guida, 1932),
pp. 117-276, points out that Dante conflates the Vergilian source in *Aeneid* III,
ll. 39 ff. with Ovid's account of Acteon in *Metamorphoses* III, ll. 138 ff., pp.
126-31. See also Leo Spitzer, "Speech and Language in *Inferno* XIII," in Freccero, ed., *Dante: A Collection of Critical Essays*, pp. 78-101.

avesse potuto *creder* prima . . .") is, in effect, questioning Vergil's *auctoritas*, which means, as we have seen, that which is worthy of faith. The story of Polydorus, finally, will be recalled in *Purgatorio* XXII where Statius' conversion is dramatized and, as we shall explain in some detail in the next chapter, the literal sense of the *Aeneid* is deliberately reversed and appropriated by Statius as a gloss to his own life.

The movement of tradition that this pattern of reading describes, the process of interpretation by which the past is handed over, seems to imply that violence is the genuine and fruitful mode of preserving the past and that revision is inevitably an act of betrayal, a metaphor of appropriation. Significantly, in the canto of suicides—sinners who have arrogated to themselves *ownership* of their lives, and spendthrifts—those who have violated property, Dante raises the question of the proper sense, the *sensus proprius*, of literary language.[71] The revisionary poetics that sustains Dante's text questions the possibility of an inherent proper value of language and shows the act of reading as the movement of appropriation, the interpretive process by which the fiction of the proper sense is constituted.

[71] The relation between the "proper sense," and the "metaphoric sense" is possibly made clear by the famous reflection of Thomas Aquinas. In the wake of Aristotle, Aquinas writes that the phrase "homo ridet" has an inherent, proper sense, for laughter is man's distinctive faculty. When, on the contrary, one says "pratum ridet," the phrase has the metaphoric meaning of describing springtime. See *In Epistolam ad Galatas*, IV, lectio 7, in *Opera Omnia*, XXI, p. 230. For Aristotle, see his *Parts of Animals*, XXI, trans. A. L. Peck (Cambridge, Mass.: Harvard University Press, 1961), III, 10, p. 281. See also Dante's statement on the figure of Love (and generally on metaphoric representation) in his *Vita nuova*: "Dico anche di lui che ridea, e anche che parlava; le quali cose paiono essere proprie de l'uomo, e spezialmente essere risibile; . . . *La vita nuova*, ed. Tommaso Casini (Florence: Sansoni, 1962), XXV, p. 137. For "proper sense" as a term designating appropriation by the heretics of the original meaning of the Bible, see Henri de Lubac, "Où est le 'sens propre'?" in *Exégèse médiévale*, III, pp. 99-113. What is remarkable in de Lubac's survey of this patristic tradition is the fact that the exegetes, particularly Gregory the Great, view the perverse reading of the heretics as acts of violence. For further bibliography, see below chapter 5, note 15.

I have argued, on the one hand, that Dante reads the *Aeneid* through Augustine and the neoplatonic commentaries and that by his elaborate interpretive effort the *Aeneid* emerges as the authoritative text of history, the text of the desire that lies under the signs of history. On the other hand, I have examined instances where the authority of the *Aeneid* is challenged and disrupted and its sense is radically altered. In either case, the act of reading emerges as the fundamental metaphor upon which Dante's view of history depends. It is an act that can lead Francesca to fall into the trap of narcissistic literal identification with Guinevere and lust and violence: to take the metaphors of the text literally, as I have shown in the discussion of Ulysses, is to die. At the same time, reading is also the experience by which the reader resists the seductive authority of the text by doing violence to and interpreting the letter. More generally, it implies that history is a book that has to be interpreted: to read the book of history, like reading the *Aeneid*, is to enter an imaginary domain where its sense is asserted and, at the same time, suspended. In *Paradiso* VI, history appears precisely as the locus of articulation of lust and violence which Dante interprets as a theological construct, the enactment of God's purpose. This theological interpretation of history seems to resolve for Dante the confusions and ambiguities of the world of immanence and time. Yet, it will be shown in the next two chapters, his own text deliberately wavers between a vision of theological order and a view of allegory that continuously doubts the possibility of that order.

CHAPTER 5

Literary History

LONG a problem for interpretation, the dialogue between Dante and Bonagiunta (*Purgatorio* XXIV, ll. 40-63) nevertheless constitutes the dramatic center of an uninterrupted sequence of poetic encounters ranging from canto XXI to canto XXVI of *Purgatorio*. Its centrality lies mainly in the fact that at this stage of his spiritual ascent, the pilgrim experiences a moment of esthetic self-consciousness culminating in the explicit and puzzling formulation of his own principles of poetic composition:

> E io a lui: "I' mi son un che, quando
> Amor mi spira, noto, e a quel modo
> ch'e' ditta dentro vo significando."
> ll. 52-4

(And I to him: "I am one who, when Love inspires me, takes note and goes setting it forth in the manner in which he dictates within me.")

While there has been a consensus among critics that Dante is here propounding his own poetics, the specific sense of the enunciation is still open to debate.[1] On the one hand, it has

[1] A bibliographical inventory on the tercet is conveniently gathered in the volume by Emilio Pasquini and Antonio Enzo Quaglio, *Lo stilnovo e la poesia religiosa* (Bari: Laterza, 1971), pp. 141-8. The following items are, however, of particular interest: Francesco De Sanctis, *Storia della letteratura italiana*, chap. 2 in *Opere*, ed. N. Gallo (Milan and Naples: Ricciardi, 1961), pp. 20-57; Giorgio Petrocchi, "Il dolce stil novo," in *Storia della letteratura italiana*, eds. E. Cecchi and N. Sapegno, I (Milan: Garzanti, 1965), pp. 729-94; Mario

been suggested that this poetic self-definition has a proximate parallel in a dictum of Richard of St. Victor: "He alone speaks of that subject worthily who composes his words according to the dictates of the heart."[2] On the basis of this potentially cogent parallel, the tercet has been interpreted with near unanimity as a rhetorical formula by which Dante paradoxically rejects the very rhetoric of formalization of experience and claims spontaneity for his fiction. On the other hand, other critics have been interested in this passage as a focus for extrinsic problems of historical classification.[3] For them, the tercet contains the genesis of the stilnovistic school of poetry, the *Dolce stil nuovo*, and they proceed, consequently, to discuss the reasons for the legitimacy, or its limits, of this historiographic concept. The spectrum of critical interpretations would not be complete without reference to other critics who view the scene as a dramatization of a Platonic duality:[4]

Marti, *Storia dello stil nuovo*, 2 vols. (Lecce: Milella, 1973). More specifically: G. Bertoni, "Il dolce stil novo," *Studi medievali*, 2 (1907), pp. 352-408; G. A. Cesareo, "Amor mi spira," in *Studi e ricerche sulla letteratura italiana* (Palermo: R. Sandron, 1930), pp. 143-73; N. Sapegno, "Dolce stil novo," *La cultura*, 1 (1930), pp. 331-41, and 2 (1931), pp. 272-309; Domenico De Robertis, "Definizione dello stil novo," *L'approdo*, 3 (1954), pp. 59-64; S. Pellegrini, "Quando amor mi spira," *Studi mediolatini e volgari*, 11-12 (1954), pp. 157-67; more recently A. Jacomuzzi, *L'imago al cerchio: Invenzione e visione della Divina Commedia* (Milan: Silva, 1968) understands this love as "uno dei nomi di Dio," p. 65.

[2] The citation, first pointed out by Mario Casella, *Studi danteschi*, 18 (1934), pp. 105-26, is from Richard of St. Victor, *Tractatus de gradibus charitatis, PL* 196, col. 1195. The formula is also quoted by Maurice Valency, *In Praise of Love* (New York: Macmillan, 1969). Valency inaccurately attributes it to Hugh of St. Victor; see p. 305.

[3] E. Bigi, "Genesi di un concetto storiografico: 'Dolce stil novo,' " *Giornale storico della letteratura italiana*, 132 (1955), pp. 337-71; Umberto Bosco, "Il nuovo stile della poesia dugentesca secondo Dante," in *Medioevo e Rinascimento; studi in onore di B. Nardi* (Florence: Sansoni, 1955), I, pp. 77-101; Aurelio Roncaglia, "Precedenti e significato dello 'stil novo' dantesco" in *Dante e Bologna nei tempi di Dante* (Bologna: Commissione per i testi di lingua, 1967), pp. 13-34; Salvatore Santangelo, " 'Sole nuovo' e 'sole usato': Dante e Guittone," in *Saggi danteschi* (Padua: C.E.D.A.M., 1959), pp. 93-132.

[4] J. E. Shaw, "Dante e Bonagiunta," 52nd-54th *Annual Report of the Dante Society* (Cambridge, 1936), pp. 1-18. He summarizes his argument affirming

Bonagiunta's poetry is inspired by an essentially earthbound theory of love, whereas Dante claims that his own poetry represents a highly spiritualized philosophical cosmos governed by a view of love as an ennobling redemptive virtue.

The primary aim of this chapter is to propose a possibly more specific interpretation of Dante's own esthetic self-confrontation. He describes, I believe, his poetic practice as an instance of theological poetry and couches his definition in the language of the theology of the Word made flesh. Using this interpretation as a plastic center, the chapter will analyze the terms which unify into a significant pattern the sequence of cantos to which I have alluded. The element which gives an actively thematic unity to these cantos is literature itself: Dante is engaged, I would argue, in a sustained reflection on literary history and the powers of literature to engender a moral conversion, and in probing the inevitable limits of poetic fictions. That the extrapolation of this continuous literary nexus is possible will be shown here by a quick synopsis.

In both canto xxi and canto xxii, Dante dramatizes Statius' poetic apprenticeship and his conversion to Christianity through the mediation of Vergil's fourth eclogue. In what is actually an account of his life and works, Statius identifies himself as having lived in Rome in the time of Titus' reign where he won acclaim and wrote his *Thebaid* and the fragments of the *Achilleid* (*Purgatorio* xxi, ll. 82-93). Yet, while the *Aeneid* is acknowledged as the text which "mamma / fummi, et fummi nutrice, poetando: / sanz' essa non fermai peso di dramma" (ll. 97-9) and Vergil is singled out for pointing to Statius the way to Parnassus, the poetic dream of Eden, Statius' literary apprenticeship is not constrained by mere estheticism. He moves decisively beyond the fictions of a pastoral esthetic wonderland and becomes a Christian by

---

that in Dante's *terzina* he sees "no elaborate doctrine of the poetic arts . . . but it does contain the assertion of the superiority of poetry inspired by spiritual love over other kinds." A duality, in terms of "passione e virtù," is also seen by Maria Simonelli, "Bonagiunta Orbicciani e la problematica dello stil nuovo (*Purgatorio* xxiv)," *Dante Studies*, 86 (1968), pp. 65-83.

heeding Vergil's prophetic fourth eclogue and its shadowy announcement of the return of the golden age to the world (ll. 64-73). In canto XXIII, the focus shifts to another poet, Dante's contemporary and friend, Forese Donati, with whom Dante exchanged in his youth a sequence of vituperative sonnets. In their present encounter, however, there is an explicit revision of their previous exchange. For the pilgrim himself, the recall of his past life of dissipation marks his new moral vision; at the same time, the gluttonous Forese appears now disfigured and famished; his wife Nella, who in the dispute is the object of obscene insinuations, is recalled by Forese as a stilnovistic woman through whose prayers he has been brought so soon "a ber lo dolce assenzo d'i martìri" (l. 86) and who "Tanto è a Dio più cara e più diletta / la vedovella mia, che molto amai, / quanto in bene operare è più soletta" (ll. 91-3). Canto XXV is an excursus on the process of the creation of the human soul. What apparently is just a philosophical-scientific digression on the ontological quality of the shades will be shown to be vitally integrated into this singular inner structure: in effect, its function is to provide the theological coherence for the multiple spiritual problems dramatized over the six cantos. Finally, canto XXVI is again populated with poets. In the presence of Vergil and Statius, Dante recognizes his own literary progenitor, Guido Guinizzelli, who points out to Dante the "miglior fabbro del parlar materno" (l. 117), Arnaut Daniel.

Although there has been no attempt in the past to connect these cantos or to discern a rationale for this proposed inner structure, in no way do I wish to argue that this organic literary segment exhausts the particularized complexities of each of the cantos, or that, in their concatenation, they constitute an isolated poetic interlude. We are confronted, I take it, with a complex literary tour de force on the sense of literary tradition from the viewpoint of poets and on how the poet's world of experience constructs and tests his tradition. It should be clear that terms such as "literary tradition," "revisions" and "misreading of the authors of the past" which will be de-

ployed later on in the discussion, do not merely imply a
rhetorical mode. The underlying argument seeks to show
how Dante in the *Divine Comedy* adopts and transposes the
historiographic concept of figuralism from the more traditional domain of the historic process to the less usual region of
literary history. *Figura*, as Auerbach has shown, is the
prophetic structure of history which Dante identifies with the
biblical pattern of Exodus and, typologically, with Christ.[5]
Dante's formulation to Bonagiunta of the poetic process as an
act analogous to the Incarnation will be seen to be relevant to
this "figural" interpretation of the literary discourse, for
Dante applies to the esthetic dimension the very techniques of
figural interpretation adopted by the patristic exegetes of biblical history.

At the same time, however, Dante figures the breakdown
of the analogy between the biblical paradigm of history and
the literary structure: the revelatory, prophetic power of literature is put into question by the awareness that literature,
though striving to provide a focus on one's world, is confined
to its own boundaries and always ends up by folding back
upon itself. This doubleness of literature, simultaneously a
vehicle to moral truth and a self-enclosed entity, prevents the
viewing of literary history simply as a story of a moral progress. If in *Purgatorio* XXIV Dante announces his new poetics
of love, in canto XXVI he recognizes in Guinizzelli the
originator of the modern trend, but love—far from being a
virtue—is here lust and sodomy. More importantly, Guinizzelli's sin recalls the moral condition of Francesca, the sinner
who lapsed into lust by reading love books, and who in her
speech deploys the language of love which resembles both
Guinizzelli's and Dante's stilnovistic formulas.[6] From a moral
standpoint, the "new" poetry can be as "courtly" and

[5] Erich Auerbach, "Figura," in *Scenes from the Drama of European Literature:
Six Essays*, trans. Ralph Manheim (New York: Meridian Books, 1959), pp.
11-76.
[6] Gianfranco Contini, "Dante come personaggio–poeta della *Commedia*,"
in *Varianti e altra linguistica* (Turin: Einaudi, 1970), esp. pp. 343-61.

worldly as the old poetry that Dante is intent on seeing super-seded.

This is the general texture of problems and interpretative intents within which Dante's pivotal encounter with Bonagiunta takes place. The episode is, structurally, a narrative center for two reasons. First, it completes a process, giving a structure of linear progression to the first four cantos under discussion. It summarizes the movement from the literary exchange between Vergil and Statius, through the encounter with Forese, to be resolved in the explicit esthetic self-confrontation of *Purgatorio* xxiv. Secondly, like the Incarnation on which Dante's idea of the new poetry is modeled, the exchange with Bonagiunta has a proleptic function. In it, Dante obliquely claims a radical poetic novelty and dissociates himself from the literary tradition of Bonagiunta, Guittone and Iacopo da Lentini. The two questions of originality and tradition will be resolved later in canto xxvi of *Purgatorio*.

In *Purgatorio* xxiv, actually, Dante gives the doctrinal configuration for the sharp opposition between Bonagiunta's and his own poetry. Bonagiunta's initial query pointedly evokes the *Vita nuova*.

> "Ma dì s'i' veggio qui colui che fore
> trasse le nove rime, cominciando
> 'Donne ch'avete intelletto d'amore.' "
>
> ll. 49-51

("But tell me if I see here him who brought forth the new rhymes, beginning: 'Ladies that have understanding of love.' ")

In the *Vita nuova*, the poem here alluded to marks the shift to a "matera nuova," the artistic project to write poetry which would be "loda di questa gentilissima."[7] After a period of

---

[7] *La vita nuova*, ed. Tommaso Casini (Florence: Sansoni, 1962), xvii-xx, pp. 77-104. For a map of the poetic history of the *Vita Nuova*, see Domenico de Robertis, *Il libro della* vita nuova (Florence: Sansoni, 1961).

hesitancy during which the poet is suspended between the desire to write and the fear of beginning, he registers his newly found inspiration. He is seized by a "volontade di dire" till his tongue spontaneously speaks, "quasi per se stessa mossa," a song of praise for the wondrous powers that issue from Beatrice's soul and Heaven's own desire to have her among the elect. It falls outside of the present scope to establish whether in the movement of the *Vita nuova*, a text systematically punctuated by oscillations and imaginative and moral crises, this poem indeed constitutes a final conversion to a new style of moral consciousness. It does, nonetheless, place Beatrice between Heaven and earth, and maps, as it were, the path for the journey of love which the poet wishes to undertake. And, to stress the import of the "matera nuova," in chapter 20, Dante explicitly recalls the *auctoritas* of Guinizzelli, "Amore e 'l cor gentil sono una cosa, / si come il saggio in suo dittare pone" and the conjunction between the gentle heart and love is equated with the identity between the rational soul and reason.

But Bonagiunta has fiercely parodied the poetic novelties introduced by Guinizzelli and his effort to remake the poetic conventions.[8] The famous sonnet, "Voi che avete mutata la mainera / de li piacenti ditti dell'amore," attacks Guinizzelli primarily for employing scholastic language ("de la forma, dell'essere, là dov'era"); his poetry is, then, likened to a candle that gives a little brightness in the dark but is nothing when compared with the poetry of Guittone which surpasses

[8] "Voi, ch'avete mutata la mainera / de li plagenti ditti de l'amore / de la forma dell'esser là dov'ere, / per avansare ogn'altro trovatore, / avete fatto come la lumera, / ch'a le scure partite dà sprendore, / ma non quine ove luce l'alta spera, / la quale avansa e passa di chiarore. / Così passate voi di sottigliansa, / e non si può trovar chi ben ispogna, / cotant' è iscura vostra parlatura. / Ed è tenuta gran dissimigliansa, / ancor che 'l senno vegna da Bologna, / traier canson per forsa di scrittura" (*Poeti del Duecento*, ed. Gianfranco Contini [Milan and Naples: Ricciardi, 1960], II, 481). Cf. Mario Marti, "Sperimentalismo guinizzelliano," in *Storia dello stil nuovo*, II, pp. 351-76; see also F. Montanari, "La poesia di Guinizzelli come esperimento di cultura," *Giornale storico della letteratura italiana*, 104 (1934), pp. 241-54.

all in splendor; finally, he attacks Guinizzelli's poetry for its darkness and reliance on sources of intellectual speculation which, to Bonagiunta, falsify the essence of poetry. In his answer Guinizzelli defends his position by deploying a theological argument. "The greatest good in things created," Aquinas writes, "is the perfection of the universe consisting in the order of distinct things."[9] In much the same terms, Guinizzelli stresses the value of orderly diversity in a universe God has organized by degrees ("Deo natura e 'l mondo in grado mise, / e fe' despari senni e intendimenti: / perzò ciò ch'omo pensa non dé dire"). To believe, the intimation is, in uniformity, as Bonagiunta does, is a sheer madness which violates the rational order of God's creation. Bonagiunta's peculiar blindness and opposition to the new poetry, from Guinizzelli's perspective, is not directed merely to rhetorical techniques; he resists, rather, the doctrinal and theological substance to which Guinizzelli's poetry is yoked.

In a real sense, *Purgatorio* xxiv reenacts the terms of this literary debate with the difference that Bonagiunta now sees what in his poetic practice on earth he could not grasp. For there is a fundamental and emphatic admission of a temporal discontinuity between Bonagiunta's present mode of perception and his mode of perception in the earthly life. As soon as Dante has formulated the mechanism of his poetic process, Bonagiunta replies:

> "O frate, issa vegg'io," diss'elli, "il nodo
> che 'l Notaro e Guittone e me ritenne
> di qua dal dolce stil novo ch'i' odo!
> Io veggio ben come le vostre penne
> di retro al dittator sen vanno strette,
> che de le nostre certo non avvenne;

---

[9] *Summa contra Gentiles*, ed. English Dominican Friars (London: Burns and Oates, 1923), ii, 44, p. 101. For the broader implications of the question of inequalities in creation, see Etienne Gilson, *The Christian Philosophy of St. Thomas Aquinas*, trans. L. K. Shook (London: Gollancz, 1957), pp. 153 ff. See also Arthur O. Lovejoy, *The Great Chain of Being* (New York: Harper Torchbook, 1960), pp. 73 ff.

e qual più a gradire oltre si mette,
non vede più da l'uno a l'altro stilo";
e, quasi contentato, si tacette.

ll. 55-63

("O brother," he said, "now I see the knot which kept
the Notary, and Guittone and me short of the sweet new
style that I hear. Clearly I see how your pens follow close
after him who dictates, which certainly did not happen to
ours; and he who sets himself to seek farther can see no
other difference between the one style and the other."
And, as if satisfied, he fell silent.)

It is the perspective of Purgatory, the "issa" of a unidirectional, irreversible process of redemption or, in terms of time,
the present moment of redeemed temporality, which provides Bonagiunta the vantage point for detached self-
interpretation. Because ostensibly no such hiatus exists in the
case of Dante's own poetry, Bonagiunta's present revision accords with Dante's self-exegesis. Bonagiunta's distance from
his own poetic practice, while it implies a spiritual and moral
gap, is the exact parallel of the sharp distinction between
Dante's poetry and Bonagiunta's poetry. This epistemological discrepancy makes it necessary to reject the generic interpretation that Dante is formulating here a Crocean esthetics
avant la lettre, the doctrine of the inseparable synthesis of
the lyrical intuition of reality and its expression. It impels us,
on the contrary, to seek Dante's poetic self-definition in a profound interior dimension.

From Bonagiunta's perspective, the style is "dolce." This is
the formal *lenitas*, the quality of style which in *De Vulgari
Eloquentia* Dante attributes to Cino and himself as those who
"dulcius subtiliusque poetati vulgariter sunt" and which de-
materializes the corruption and facticiousness of everyday
language into the radiant nobility of art.[10] For Dante, no

---

[10] *De Vulgari Eloquentia*, I, x, 4. In this sense, "dolce stilo" is opposed to
rithimorum asperitas, allowed only when it is *lenitati permixta*, of *De Vulgari
Eloquentia*, II, xiii, 12.

doubt, this property is constitutive of authentic love poetry, and it is the sign of its harmonious resonances which Guittone's practice, as he implies in *De Vulgari Eloquentia*, lacks. But there is no connotation of moral virtue to the epithet "dolce." In effect, the word is used at various junctures of the *Divine Comedy* to imply the bewitching impressions and musical enchantments of love poetry. Thus, Casella sings "Amor che ne la mente mi ragiona" (*Purgatorio* II, l. 112), "dolcemente"; the siren who beguiles the sailors in mid-sea and turns Ulysses to her song is "dolce" (*Purgatorio* XIX, l. 19); Francesa's lapsing into lust is the time of "dolci sospiri" (*Inferno* V, l. 118). As a musical metaphor, much the way the word "modo" is, "dolce" defines the new poetry as rhetorical accomplishment and implies that style is exterior to moral truth, a cover for the inner feelings.[11] More precisely, this sweetness draws Dante's own poetry into the ambiguous area where the claim to moral rectitude is mixed with esthetic snares.

The first vague allusion to the nature of the difference between the two poetic modes occurs at line 55 where Bonagiunta defines his distance from the Sweet New Style as "nodo." There has been no specific critical explication of this knot except for an impressionistic gloss that it refers to sensuality or difficulty, probably technical, that hampered Bonagiunta's writings. While my interpretation of the whole passage in no way depends on this term, I tentatively offer a reading which will make sense both in terms of the narrative coherence that I have postulated in the six cantos and in terms of the solution to the tercet which I shall shortly present. In a searing poetic exchange with Forese Donati, Dante uses the image of the knot to indicate the sin of gluttony, "Ben ti faranno il nodo Salamone, / Bicci novello, e' petti de le starne."[12] Although only the word "nodo" appears both in

---

[11] *Convivio*, IV, ii, 11-2.

[12] *Rime*, ed. Gianfranco Contini (Turin: Einaudi, 1965), p. 87. For a traditional interpretation of the "knot" as the sin of gluttony in this poem, see Fredi Chiappelli, "Per l'interpretazione della tenzone di Dante con F.

the sonnet and in *Purgatorio* xxiv where the focus is also gluttony, it is of interest to point out that Dante was aware that
the metaphoric extension of the familiar figure of the knot of
Solomon, to which he gives a comical twist in the poem to
Forese, is conventionally synonymous with the endless pen-
tangle and symbolizes natural perfection, the condition of
human existence sundered from the perception of God.[13]
This gloss is admittedly marginal and approximate; yet, it
reinforces the concept of a moral gap in Bonagiunta's poetic
exercise. It further exemplifies the notion that his love poetry
(significantly, he appears as the poet of Love for Gentucca, l.
37) is rooted in the natural order, unable to transcend it and
come to a knowledge of God. That this is basically the focus
of the juxtaposition of the two esthetic modes is manifest
from an analysis of Dante's description of his poetic activity
to which we must now turn.

If the primary intent of Dante's self-definition is to qualify
his poetics of love, the mechanism of the poetic process is
characterized in terms of Love's "inspiration" and inner dictation which the poet notes down and translates into signs ("vo
significando," l. 54). The link between the inner dictation and
the poet's signification is provided by "a quel modo." In a
way, Dante alludes to the *modus significandi*, a notion which is

---

Donati," *Giornale storico della letteratura italiana*, 142 (1965), pp. 321-50; cf.
Michele Barbi, "La tenzone di Dante con Forese," in *Problemi di critica dantesca*, 2nd series (Florence: Sansoni, 1964), pp. 87-214.

[13] This sense of the knot of Solomon can be found in the anonymous Middle English poem *Sir Gawain and the Green Knight*, eds. J.R.R. Tolkien and E.
V. Gordon (Oxford: Clarendon Press, 1925), ll. 625 ff. For the relevance of
the knot of Solomon in this romance, see the remarks by Richard Hamilton
Green, "Gawain's Shield and the Quest for Perfection," *ELH: Journal of English Literary History*, 29 (1962), pp. 121-39. Dante uses the figure of the *penta-
gon* as an emblem of natural perfection: "Chè, sì come dice lo Filosofo nel
secondo de l'Anima, le potenze de l'anima stanno sopra sè come la figura de
lo quadrangulo sta sopra lo triangulo, e lo pentangulo, cioè la figura che ha
cinque canti, sta sopra lo quadrangulo: e così la sensitiva sta sopra la ve-
getativa, e la intellettiva sta sopra la sensitiva. Dunque, come levando l'ultima
canto del pentangulo rimane quadrangulo e non più pentangulo, così levando
l'ultima potenza de l'anima, cioè la ragione, non rimane più uomo, ma cosa
con anima sensitiva solamente, cioè animale bruto" (*Convivio*, iv, vii, 14-5).

central to a theory of metaphor in Aquinas' theology. Of more immediate interest, however, is the fact that by this adverbial phrase, Dante establishes the faithful analogy between the inner voice and its outer manifestation. The movement by which the inner idea is translated into speech is used by St. Augustine in his *De Doctrina Christiana* to develop his conception that human language is the immanent analogue of the Incarnation:

> How did he come except that "the Word was made flesh and dwelt among us"? (I Corinthians 1:21). It is as when we speak. In order that what we are thinking may reach the mind of the listener through the fleshy ears, that which we have in mind is expressed in words and is called speech. But our thought is not transformed into sounds; it remains entirely in itself and assumes the form of words by means of which it may reach the ears without suffering any deterioration in itself. In the same way the Word of God was made flesh without change that he might dwell among us.[14]

This Augustinian passage in reality discerns only a generic analogy between the physical utterance of the word and the manifestations of the Logos, yet it provides the context

[14] *De Doctrina Christiana*, I, xiii. The translation is by D. W. Robertson, Jr., *On Christian Doctrine* (New York: Liberal Arts Press, 1958), p. 14. A remarkably similar passage can be found in St. Augustine's *De Trinitate*, xv, ii, in *CCSL*, La. Here is the English translation: "Hence the word which sounds without is a sign of the word that shines within, to which the name of word properly belongs. For that which is produced by the mouth of the flesh is the sound of the word, and is itself also called the word, because that inner word assumed it in order that it might appear outwardly. For just as our word in some way becomes a bodily sound by assuming that in which it may be manifested to the senses of men, so the Word of God was made flesh by assuming that in which He might also be manifested to the senses of man. And just as our word becomes a sound and is not changed into a sound, so the Word of God indeed becomes flesh, but far be it from us that it should be changed into flesh" (*The Trinity*, trans. Stephen McKenna [Washington: The Catholic University of American Press, 1963], pp. 476–77). The passage is quoted unaltered by Vincent of Beauvais, *Speculum Naturale* (Douai: Belleri, 1624), xxvii, col. 1921.

within which to grasp Dante's claim that his poetry is the analogue of the Incarnation. A closer analysis of the terms he uses will reveal the existence of a coherent trinitarian pattern within which his poetic voice is couched.

The two verbs "spira" and "ditta" by which Dante formulates the activity of Love, have definite trinitarian resonances. In *Paradiso* x, for instance, Dante describes the circularity of the Persons of the Trinity joined together by the unifying inspiration of love:

> Guardando nel suo Figlio con l'Amore
> che l'uno e l'altro etternalmente spira,
> lo primo e ineffabile Valore. . . .
>
> ll. 1-3

(Looking upon his Son with the love which the One and the Other eternally breathe forth, the primal and ineffable Power. . . .)

The divine activity is the spiration of love, but in this context of *Paradiso* Dante formulates the transcendent unity of the Trinity which imparted its order on everything that revolves through the mind or through space (ll. 4-5). It is Thomas Aquinas, instead, who glosses this activity in a manner that provides the essential connection between inspiration and the Word.

In one of his articles on the Trinity, Thomas states that there are processions in God. The first is the procession of the word:

> . . . it must be known that in the divinity, as it was shown above, there are two processions, one by the way of the intellect, and this is the procession of the word, the other by way of the will, and this is the procession of love.

The second procession, the procession of love, is called spiration:

> While there are two processions in God, one of these, the procession of love has no proper name of its own, as

stated above. Hence, the relations also which follow from this procession are also without a name: for which reason the Person proceeding in that manner has not a proper name. But as some names are accommodated by the usual mode of speaking to signify the aforesaid relations, as when we use the names of procession and spiration which in their strictest meaning indicate characteristic acts rather than relations; in like manner the usage of holy Scripture has set apart this name "Holy Spirit" to signify a divine person. An explanation for the aptness of this usage can be drawn from two considerations. The first is that the one called "Holy Spirit" belongs to Father and Son together. As Augustine teaches, because the Holy Spirit is common to both, he has a proper name that they have in common; for the Father is spirit, the Son is spirit; the Father is holy, the Son is holy. A second point is the literal meaning of the name. For among corporeal beings the term "spirit" would seem to denote a surge and a movement; we give the name *spiritus* to breath and to wind. Now it is distinctive of love that it move and urge the will of the lover towards the beloved.[15]

[15] *Summa Theologiae*, Ia, q. 36, ar. 1, general edition T. C. O'Brien (New York: McGraw-Hill, 1976), p. 53. The preceding passage is from *Summa Theologiae,* Ia, q. 37, ar. 1, p. 80 in O'Brien's edition. The articles on the Processions and Relations of the Divine Persons referred to are S.T., Ia, 27-28. For an extended view of the theological structures of the questions, see Bernard J. Lonergan, S.J., *Verbum: Word and Idea in Aquinas* (Notre Dame: University of Notre Dame Press, 1967). It ought to be stressed at this point that Aquinas' reflections on the *modus significandi* are a way by which he explores the question of metaphor and analogy in theological language. Throughout the *Summa Theologiae,* Ia, 13, Aquinas turns his attention to "the names of God," and distinguishes between the "modus significandi," the *imperfect* vehicle by which man attempts to express the perfection of God, and the "res significata." St. Thomas concludes this section (*Summa Theologiae,* Ia, q. 13, ar. 5) by stating the impossibility of predicating anything univocally of God, and views theological language as one of analogy. Analogical language lies somewhere between "Puram aequivocationem et simplicem univocationem." For further bibliography, on this issue see Ralph McInerny, *Studies in Analogy* (The Hague: Martinus Nijhoff, 1968). These complications

The burden of Aquinas' reflection is to show the consubstantiality of the Father, the Word and the Spirit. But he is also putting forth a most complex theory of signification, a veritable inquiry into the nature of theological language. For him, the names "sonship," "procession," "inspiration" are not simply metaphors applied to divinity by human art and invention; they have a proper sense as handed down by Scripture and designate the inner life of the Trinity. To be sure, there ought to be no need to stress how for Aquinas the mystery of the godhead surpasses understanding; yet, he accepts the notion that biblical language is invested with a substantial, proper sense which truly, albeit inadequately, expresses the reality of the divine itself. Dante transposes this theory of signification into the context of his own poetic inspiration in the attempt to charge his own language with a theological sense and to imply that the poetic signs are commensurate and proper to the desire which generates them.

The theological framework of the doctrine of inspiration and its relationship to the production of the word is further elucidated by the resonances of the verbs "ditta" and "noto." "Noto" qualifies the role of the poet as a glossator of an inner book of memory (and in this sense it hints at the distance between himself and the "Notaro," l. 56);[16] "ditta," a term widely used in the rhetoric of poetic composition, casts Love as the poet. But dictation is the activity of God the Father, and a symmetrical correspondence of the inspired poet as a scribe and God as the inditer can be found obliquely expressed in Psalm 44, "My heart has uttered a good word: I speak my words to the king: my tongue is the pen of a scrivener that writes swiftly." It is in this context, it should be pointed out,

---

inherent in theological language, my point is, are the horns of Dante's dilemma.

[16] Frances A. Yates, *The Art of Memory* (Chicago: The University of Chicago Press, 1966), pp. 42-52, points out that *notae* are the marks placed at the crucial points one wishes to retain in the reading of a book. This act of noting is juxtaposed to what is possibly the legal sense of "notae," suggested by Dante's reference to the "Notaro" (*Purgatorio* XXIV, l. 56); see Isidore of Seville, *Etym.* I, xxii.

that Bonagiunta's lines, "Io veggio ben come le vostre penne /
di retro al dittator sen vanno strette" (ll. 58-9), can be taken to
mean his present understanding of the nature of the inspiration of the new poetry. More to the point, in the third book
of *Monarchia* Dante himself posits an incisive dialectical process between the Holy Spirit, God the Dictator and the
prophets-scribes:

Non enim peccatur in Moysen, non in David . . . sed in
Spiritum Sanctum qui loquitur in illis. Nam quanquam
scribe divini eloquii multi sint, unicus tamen dictator est
Deus, qui bene placitum suum nobis per multorum
calamos explicare dignatus est.[17]

The awareness that his own poetry has a theological foundation allows Dante to claim the singularity for his own poetic activity. This is the special force of the phrase "'I' mi son
un, che quando" (l. 52) by which he introduces his own definition to Bonagiunta. Its tone, as has often been remarked, is
one of humility and even self-deprecation, but one can hardly
imagine that a theological claim can be voiced in anything but
the language of humility. From Bonagiunta's standpoint, this
theological poetry is not Dante's own exclusive prerogative
and it is seen to invest the whole new poetic mode: "Io veggio
ben come le vostre penne / di retro al dittator sen vanno
strette, / che de' le nostre certo non avvenne" (ll. 58-60). For

[17] "One does not sin against Moses, against David . . . but against the
Holy Ghost who spoke in them. For although the scribes of the divine word
are many, the only dictator, however, is God, who deigned to explain to us
through many writers what pleases him" (*Monarchia*, III, iv, 11). Guillaume
de St. Thierry, *Liber de Natura et Dignitate Amoris*, PL 184, col. 394, writes:
"Affectus ergo charitatis indissolubiter inhaerens, et de vultu eius omnia
judicia sua colligenda, ut agat vel disponat exterius, sic voluntas Dei bona, et
beneplacens, et perfecta *dictat ei interius*" (italics mine). On the "ars dictandi,"
see the remarks by A. Schiaffini, *Tradizione e poesia* (Rome: Edizioni di storia
e letteratura, 1943), pp. 27-36; Marigo lists Dante's use of the words "dicta-
men," "dictator," "dicto," and "dictum" in *De Vulgari Eloquentia* to mean
poetic composition, p. 323. The word "dittare" is used in this sense also in
the *Vita nuova*, "si come il saggio in suo dittare pone" (xx,
p. 101).

Dante, who throughout the exchange says nothing about the novelty of the style, Bonagiunta's words seem to be a strategy by which he undercuts the very privilege and singularity he has just advanced. This wavering is a steady motif throughout the *Divine Comedy*, featuring the radical predicament of a Christian poet who seeks more than an esthetic humanistic redemption and less than to perform the supreme transgression of writing an appendix to the Bible. At the very outset of the poem, for instance, the poet conveys the notion that his journey embodies a special mission, and his text occupies a special role in the economy of salvation; but, at the same time, the metaphoric movement of the text subverts this claim and insinuates the poet's doubting his prophetic call. Before examining, however, the textual evidence for this wavering, I would like to deal with the problem of analogy within which the poetic process is rooted.

There is a way in which analogy is the crucial problem with the most eminent poets of what is known as the *Dolce stil novo*. Guinizzelli's "Al cor gentile rempaira sempre amore" or "Io voglio del ver la mia donna laudare / ed asembrarli la rosa e lo giglio"—among others—are built on a sequence of analogies.[18] Analogy, however, is not purely a technical expedient by which to establish and "find" the metaphoric elements that bind together the fragments of the natural order through the experience of love. From one point of view, analogy as the very specificity of literary language is *the* problem that Guinizzelli dramatizes in his poems. In "Al cor gentil," to mention the most flagrant occurrence, love is defined through a series of disparate comparisons: its fire takes hold in the gentle heart like the virtue in a precious stone ("come vertute in petra preziosa"); it dwells in the noble heart in the same way fire stays on the top of a torch, while a vile nature stops love as water does the burning fire. The lady herself looks like an angel from God's kingdom: yet, the underlying question of the poem is the potential deceitfulness and delud-

---

[18] Contini, ed., *Poeti del Duecento*, II, 460–64 and 472 respectively.

ing knowledge engendered by the image. In the final stanza the poet presents a picture both of God chiding him for lapsing in vain love and comparing God to this vain image, and of how he will justify himself, "Dir li porò: tenne d'angel sembianza / che fosse del tuo regno: / non me fu fallo, s'in lei posi amanza." The lines may well be taken as a mildly hyperbolic convention to praise the beauty of the woman; at the same time the world of analogy is exposed in its unavoidable illusory and insidious equivocations. In those lines the poet covertly intimates the suspicion that what seems to bear the likeness of an angel and be the instrument of the lover's ascent to God may in fact turn out to be the cause of his fall. Guinizzelli's own preoccupations with the errors of poetic language, it can be shown, also invests the poetics of the *Vita nuova* where the poet wistfully attempts to distinguish between idolatrous simulacra, empty images of love, and the figure of Beatrice who is portrayed in Christological language.

In *Purgatorio* xxiv the question of analogy is placed at the very heart of Dante's poetry-making and is unaccompanied by demurring doubts on its value: the poet transcribes in the same way as the voice of Love dictates. On the face of it, this concept of analogy does not entail the humanistic doctrine of the artistic creation as an *alter mundus*, a reified and self-contained heterocosm analogous to the real world and yet discontinuous from it. This view of an autonomous poetic universe, without a vital nexus with the Creator and contracted in the order of nature, is precisely the view of Bonagiunta, but it is ostensibly extraneous to Dante's poetics. For Dante the mode of analogy depends on and dramatizes a trinitarian pattern internalized in the mind. The creative process, because its inner life has a structural analogy to the Trinity, is a central cognitive act insofar as it reveals the immanence of the Trinity in the human mind.

Although Dante gives the philosophical basis for the immanence and participation of the Trinity in man in *Purgatorio* xxv, the analogy in canto xxiv reverses and complements the perspective because it shows the opposite movement of the word of man participating by analogy in the creative activity of God.[19] This esthetic theory in no way implies that the absolute self-sufficiency of God is less real: it bespeaks, rather, the vital function of the human word as the link with the divine. It is within this context that we have to see the poetic act as fundamentally analogous to the Incarnation. Like the Incarnate Word, which is its model, this human word is the vehicle to God. Dante, in effect, characteristically expands the metaphor of his journey as Exodus into a verbal cosmos. Critics in the past have agreed that Exodus is the declared figural structure of the *Divine Comedy*; while this is certainly true, it is not the whole truth because it is a definition that fails to see that Dante's principle of poetic construction is the dramatization of the typological equation postulated by St. Paul in I Corinthians: "Christ our Exodus."[20] The *Divine Gomedy* is, consequently, patterned on the figural experience of Exodus, but at the same time, it is a dramatic reenactment, as its precise liturgical time, of the descent of Christ to Hell on Good Friday and his resurrection on Easter Sunday. Since the poem is the record of the journey toward salvation, it has a structure analogous both to Exodus and to Christ. This thematic relationship of the poetic voice to both Exodus and the Logos is extended throughout the poem, and I will return to it later.

To summarize the discussion so far: I have analyzed the elements which point to Dante's esthetic self-awareness as a dramatic extension of the Exodus-Christ typology, the con-

[19] For the problem of analogy, implying at the same time identity and difference, see G. B. Phelan, *St. Thomas and Analogy* (Milwaukee: Marquette University Press, 1941); Marcia Colish, *The Mirror of Language: A Study in the Medieval Theory of Knowledge* (New Haven: Yale University Press, 1968); Cornelio Fabro, *Partecipazione e causalità secondo S. Tommaso d'Aquino* (Turin: Società editrice internazionale, 1960). More generally, see Enzo Melandri, *La linea e il circolo: studio logico-filosofico sull' analogia* (Bologna: Mulino, 1968).

[20] I Corinthians 5:7; "Etenim Pascha nostra immolatus est Christus." The typological nexus between *Pascha* and *transitus* has been documented by Christine Mohrmann, *Etudes sur le latin des chrétiens* (Rome: Edizioni di storia e letteratura, 1958), pp. 205-22.

trolling metaphor of the poem. The focus of discussion will now shift to canto XXV of *Purgatorio* where we shall find both a corroboration for our reading of the passage in *Purgatorio* XXIV and the distinctively philosophical structure underlying the problems exemplified by Dante's poetic self-exegesis and Bonagiunta's admission of a mode of vision, partial and bound within time.

Canto XXV of *Purgatorio*, structurally, exerts a centripetal pull on the two adjacent cantos. Its philosophical and abstract quality has led literary critics to dismiss it as a scholastic exercise,[21] a ratiocinative interpolation, so much so that only historians of medieval philosophy such as Bruno Nardi[22] and Etienne Gilson[23] have attempted to unravel its complex technical fabric. From our point of view, the canto subsumes the intellectural problems from the preceding canto and telescopes them toward *Purgatorio* XXVI.

A rudimentary summary of *Purgatorio* XXV, focusing on the thematic links with *Purgatorio* XXIV, is in order here. Dante's first concern is to reject the Averroistic doctrine of the possible intellect as a separate spiritual substance. He dismisses the idea of a metaphysical discontinuity between the vegetative-sensitive potencies of the soul and the intellective faculty, and expresses his belief in the unity and continuity of the soul. He gives prominence to this theory by describing the simultaneous three-fold activity within the soul, the coexistence of unity and trinity:

> lo motor primo a lui si volge lieto
> sovra tant' arte di natura, e spira
> spirito novo, di vertù repleto,
> che coì che trova attivo quivi, tira

---

[21] Benedetto Croce, *La poesia di Dante*, 2nd ed. (Bari: Laterza, 1948) introduces his analysis by stating that ". . . anche in questa parte cominciano a farsi frequenti ed estese le intramesse didascaliche," p. 114.

[22] Bruno Nardi, *Studi di filosofia medioevale* (Rome: Edizioni di storia e letteratura, 1960), pp. 9-68.

[23] Etienne Gilson, "Dante's Notion of a Shade," *Mediaeval Studies*, 29 (1967), pp. 124-42.

in sua sustanzia, e fassi un'alma sola,
che vive e sente e sé e sé rigira.

                                    ll. 70-5

(The First Mover turns to it with joy over such art of nature, and breathes into it a new spirit replete with virtue,
which absorbs that which is active there into its own substance, and makes one single soul which lives and feels
and circles on itself.)

While the activity of the Prime Mover textually recalls the
spiration of Love in the process of poetic creation of the
previous canto, the last line of the quotation is, in effect, a
graphic representation of the unity and continuity of the veg-
etative, sensitive and intellective faculties of the soul. The "sé
in sé rigira" is the formulaic description of the rational activity indicated by the traditional platonic emblem of the circular
movement of the intellectual act.[24]

A second concern of Dante, which definitely reinforces the
view that his poetry is couched in trinitarian rhetoric, is the
explicit consciousness of a literal immanence of the Trinity in
the human soul:

Quando Làchesis non ha più del lino,
    solvesi da la carne, e in virtute
    ne porta seco e l'umano e' 'l divino:
l'altre potenze tutte quante mute;
    memoria, intelligenza e volontade
    in atto molto più che prima agute.

                                    ll. 79-84

(When Lachesis has no more thread, the soul is loosed
from the flesh and carries with it, in potency, both the
human and the divine: all the other faculties mute, but
memory, intellect and will much more acute in action
than before.)

---

[24] A history of the symbolic value of the circle from antiquity on is found
in Georges Poulet, *Les Métamorphoses du cercle* (Paris: Plon, 1961); see also
Bruno Nardi, *Nel mondo di Dante* (Rome: Edizioni di storia e letteratura,
1944), pp. 337-50.

To be sure, these lines refer to the structure of the soul in its condition after death, yet they are of particular interest to the present discussion for several reasons. First, Dante is illustrating the continuity between the temporal, contingent existence, represented by the life of the body, and the eternal life of the resurrection. Second, Dante is giving a literal translation of a line in St. Augustine's *De Trinitate*,[25] whose quest for analogies and vestiges of the divine Trinity in the human soul is assimilated by Dante precisely to dramatize the reality of the participation of the Divine in the human.

It should be clear at this point how this philosophical canto illuminates retrospectively the problems debated in *Purgatorio* XXIV. Canto XXV provides the philosophical profundities for a critique of Bonagiunta's poetics confined to a vision of this-worldliness and contingency, unable to attain what to Dante is intellectual truth.[26] But an objection might be raised at this point: why would a problem of literary practice, judged autonomous from the order of grace as Bonagiunta's is, be connected with a doctrine of discontinuity in the soul? Dante, it seems to me, anticipates this question when in *Purgatorio* XXV he describes the transition from the sensitive to the rational faculty of the soul in terms of language.

> Ma come d'animal divenga fante,
>   non vedi tu ancor: quest'è tal punto,
>   che più savio di te fé già errante,
> sì che per sua dottrina fé disgiunto
>   da l'anima il possible intelletto,
>   perché da lui non vide organo assunto.
>
> ll. 61-6

(But how from animal it becomes a human being you do not see yet: this is such a point that once it made one

---

[25] "Haec igitur tria, memoria, intelligentia, voluntas, quoniam non sunt tres vitae sed una vita, nec tres mentes sed una mens, consequenter utique nec tres substantiae sunt sed una substantia" (*De Trinitate*, XI, xi, 18, in *CCSL* L).

[26] Cf. Dante's queries whether the soul inclines to the objects of love by natural impulses and whether free will is lost in this process, and Vergil's exposition, *Purgatorio* XVIII, ll. 46-75.

wiser than you to err, so that in his teaching he separated
the possible intellect from the soul because he saw no
organ assumed by it.)

The word "fante," human being, etymologically means "he
who speaks" and connects language indissolubly with the
creation of the soul. In *De Vulgari Eloquentia*, which is Dante's
essay on the origin of language, he extensively views language and the soul as part of a primordial unity. Language
was first created by God along with the soul ("dicimus certam
formam locutionis a Dei cum anima prima concreatam
fuisse");[27] Adam spoke in this tongue and so did all men until
the building of the Tower of Babel; since that confusion, he
states, the incorrupt primal language was inherited and used
only by the Hebrews so that the Redeemer "non lingua con-
fusionis, sed gratia frueretur." But in the *Divine Comedy* this
view that the prelapsarian language had been preserved in an
ordered state of grace in order that Christ would not speak the
fallen, sinful language of man, was radically altered. In
Paradiso xxvi, Adam's fall from Eden entails the loss of the
perfect language:

> La lingua ch'io parlai fu tutta spenta
>   innanzi che a l'ovra inconsummabile
>   fosse la gente di Nembròt attenta:
> ché nullo effetto mai razionabile,
>   per lo piacere uman che rinovella
>   seguendo il cielo, sempre fu durabile.
> Opera naturale è ch'uom favella;
>   ma così o così, natura lascia
>   poi fare a voi secondo che v'abbella.
>   ll. 124-32

(The tongue which I spoke was all extinct before the
people of Nimrod attempted their unaccomplishable

---

[27] *De Vulgari Eloquentia*, I, vi, 4 ff.; *De Civitate Dei*, xvi, 11, *CCSL* xlviii,
is the possible source for Dante's view of the continuity of the Hebrew
tongue up to the building of the Tower of Babel. See Francesco D'Ovidio,

work; for never was any product of reason forever dura-
ble, because of human liking which alters following the
heavens. It is nature's doing that man should speak, but
whether thus or thus, nature then leaves you to follow
your own pleasure.)

It might be remarked that this focus on language symmetrically connects *Paradiso* xxvi with both *Inferno* and *Purgatorio*
xxvi which deal respectively with the "humanistic" rhetoric
of Ulysses and the poetic language of Guinizzelli and Arnaut
Daniel. More explicitly in *Paradiso* xxvi than in the two other
corresponding cantos, language is viewed as caught in the spirals of a temporal instability, as a work of nature which can be
used to build the Tower of Babel or, the implication is, for
opposite ends.

This twofold possibility in the uses of language is the basis
for Dante's rejection of the literary tradition represented by
Bonagiunta, Guittone and Iacopo da Lentini. If their poetry
centers upon earthly objects of love, the woman at whose
service, as the Provençal tradition had codified the rules of
love, the lover places himself, Dante's poetry fixes itself on
the love of the rational soul and seeks the permanent order of
God. Also, the allusion to the error of Averroes (*Purgatorio*
xxv, l. 63), who separated the soul from the possible intellect,
hints at another, in a sense more painful, literary practice, that
of his friend Cavalcanti, to whom the *Vita nuova* is largely
directed.[28] Cavalcanti's poem "Donna me prega," which I
shall discuss in chapter 7, is a deliberate Averroistic exploration of love as a dark experience, a sensual urge which inexorably crushes the order of rationality. Every poetic text implies

---

"Sul trattato *De Vulgari Eloquentia* di Dante Alighieri," *Versificazione romanza*
(Naples: Guida, 1932), II, 217-332.

[28] On Cavalcanti, see Mario Casella, "La canzone d'amore di Guido
Cavalcanti," *Studi di filologia italiana*, 7 (1944), pp. 97-160; Bruno Nardi,
"Dante e Guido Cavalcanti," and "L'amore e i medici medioevali," in *Saggi e
note di critica dantesca* (Milan and Naples: Ricciardi, 1966), pp. 190-219, 238-
67; see also Bruno Nardi, "L'averroismo del primo amico di Dante," in
Dante e la cultura medievale, 2nd ed. (Bari: Laterza, 1949), pp. 93-129.

a metaphysical position, and for Dante, Guinizzelli and Cavalcanti, for all their specific differences, philosophy and theology are the constant, explicit interlocutors of poetry. They are dimensions of poetic knowledge to which Bonagiunta was blind, and which Dante exposes. In *Purgatorio* XXVI, however, Dante comes to a recognition of a literary tradition with which he identifies. Canto XXVI is, therefore, in a sharp thematic contrast to canto XXIV. Between these two cantos, as I have said, canto XXV acts as a theological center of convergence for this dramatic antinomy. Its function is to show that the discussion in canto XXIV and canto XXVI is not concerned with purely formal principles.

In canto XXV, from the point of view of its relevant links with canto XXVI, Dante accounts for the origin of the soul: its genetic process is extensively described, from the sperm of the father to its incarnation; its life is later viewed in the eschatological context of the Resurrection.[29] In *Purgatorio* XXVI, Dante transposes the doctrine of continuity in the structure of the soul from the dimension of metaphysics to the symbolic region of literary continuities. Furthermore, just as in canto XXV Dante illustrates the process of the creation of the soul from its point of origin, the father's blood, so he will also use this genetic perspective to describe the question of literary generation in *Purgatorio* XXVI. In contrast with the dramatization of literary and spiritual discontinuities of *Purgatorio* XXIV and XXV, Dante describes the notion of continuities in a spiritual and historical sense in *Purgatorio* XXV and XXVI.

In *Purgatorio* XXVI, the literary continuity is aptly expressed through organic metaphors of father-son relationship. When Dante encounters Guido Guinizzelli, he speaks to him in terms of poetic filiation:

> quand'io odo nomar sé stesso il padre
> mio e de li altri miei miglior che mai
> rime d'amore usar dolci e leggiadre;
>
> ll. 97-9

---

[29] *Purgatorio* XXV, ll. 37-108.

(when I hear name himself the father of me and of others my betters who ever used sweet and gracious rhymes of love).

I shall deal with the problem of Dante's expression of the literary activity in genetic terms further on. For the time being, I would like to point out another thematic nexus between cantos XXIV and XXVI of *Purgatorio* which makes clear that the two cantos must be seen as intimately related. In canto XXIV, Bonagiunta speaks of the stilnovistic poetry from which he, Guittone and Iacopo de Lentini are excluded.[30] In canto XXVI, instead, Guinizzelli refers again to Guittone's poetry, and sanctions, in a sense, his inferiority.[31] Canto XXVI is, thus, a dramatic account of a new poetry, a consciously different perspective on a literary tradition which both father and son have repudiated.

The question of tradition gives an internal unity to the six cantos and is systematically pursued by Dante through its metaphoric refractions. Poets beget poets: the *Aeneid* is literally a generous text, a "mamma" and "nutrice" to Statius' own *paideia* (*Purgatorio* XXI, ll. 94-100); Guinizzelli is "padre" to Dante and Arnaut is the "miglior fabbro del parlar materno" (*Purgatorio* XXVI, l. 117), their common point of origin. The creative process itself in Dante's own definition is cast in terms which resemble the natural production of the body when the soul is breathed into it. This rhetoric of natural fecundity is clearly deployed to render the idea of the sem-

---

[30] " 'O frate, issa vegg'io,' diss' elli, 'il nodo / che 'l Notaro e Guittone e me ritenne / di qua dal dolce stil novo ch'i' odo!' " (*Purgatorio* XXIV, ll. 55-7). The novelty is conventionally seen to be an echo of "Cantate Domino canticum novum" and "canticum novum hominis novi est" respectively from Psalm 32:3 and 39:4; cf. also Apocalypse 5:9 and 14:3. It ought to be pointed out that any claim of poetic novelty is a worn-out literary *topos*. See, as an instance, the title in Geoffrey of Vinsauf, *Poetria Nova*; also the lines by Guillaume IX, "Farai chansoneta nueva / ans que vent ni gel ni plueva."

[31] "Così fer molti antichi di Guittone, / di grido in grido pur lui dando pregio, / fin che l'ha vinto il ver con più persone" (*Purgatorio* XXVI, ll. 124-6). Cf. also *De Vulgari Eloquentia* II, vi, 8. On Guittone see also A. Schiaffini, *Tradizione e poesia*, pp. 39-81.

inality of literature, its power to proliferate itself and engender its own future. But the organic process of literary generation is not analogous to the generative process of the natural model: in the literary universe there is a marked reversal of the paternal order, for it is the son who chooses the father; each poet, that is to say, shapes his past and fathers his own tradition. More importantly, the acknowledgment of a literary tradition from which the "new" poetry derives, undercuts Dante's own notion that poetry springs spontaneously in the heart in the immediacy of inspiration. The modernity of Guinizzelli upon which Dante—echoing the sweetness that Bonagiunta recognizes in the "Stil novo"—insists, "Li dolci detti vostri, / che, quanto durerà l'uso moderno, / faranno cari ancora i loro incostri" (*Purgatorio* XXVI, ll. 112-4), is an equally ambiguous notion. Just as in *Paradiso* XXVI, Adam, the archetypal poet who first named the world and alone spoke the Edenic language, view the usage that mortals make of language as a metaphor for its impermanence (it is like a leaf on a branch, we are told, which goes away and another comes) (ll. 136-7), in *Purgatorio* XXVI, "uso moderno" displaces the "new" poetry into the mutability of time, where it always renews itself and the renewal has always already taken place.

From Guinizzelli's own perspective, actually, the tradition of literary history is not an original break with the past but simply a case of literary interpretation. The value of literary texts, he laments, is settled by opinions based on rumors: on account of this, Girault de Bornelh is thought to surpass in excellence the verses of love of Arnaut, and Guittone alone received the prize "fin che l'ha vinto il ver con più persone" (who know how to listen to art and reason, ll. 118-26). The "arte o ragione" clearly implies that for Guinizzelli the criterion of judgment lies in the empirical test of the concrete elements of the artifice. But, unlike him, Dante dramatizes his desire to make literary history into a history of faith-producing messages in which each text is translated into life, becomes the prophecy of an event which in turn may lead to that history that is at one with the Revelation of the Word.

This prophetic mechanism of the literary tradition, and its ambiguities, are fully probed in cantos XXI and XXII of *Purgatorio* where Statius, who has crossed a metaphoric river of grace, is shown as he decisively interprets and assimilates Vergil's poetry. Dante's attention to what might be called the "modernity" of Vergil's texts, their power to enter and affect their readers' present time, is primary in the two cantos just as it was primary to his own journey in the beyond.[32] In a sense, the encounter between Statius and Vergil is a more extended and elaborate version of the encounter between Dante and Vergil in the prologue scene with the difference that Vergil appears personally to guide the pilgrim, while in *Purgatorio* he is the author who meets his reader and confronts the destiny and transformation of his own texts.

Their encounter is introduced by a reference to the apparition on the road to Emmaus, the place where the risen Christ revealed himself on the afternoon of the day of his resurrection to two of his disciples who did not recognize him (*Purgatorio* XXI, ll. 7-10). The image aptly describes the state of Statius, who, newly risen and hence Christ-like, appears to Vergil and the pilgrim. It also prepares, by a reversal of terms, Statius' acknowledgment of his discipleship to Vergil. From one point of view, the two cantos turn into a veritable tribute to him and, more generally, into a celebration of the redemptive power of his literature. Large claims are actually made for it: in canto XXI, Statius presents his life as a poetic autobiography and stresses the pivotal importance of the *Aeneid* for his own poetic growth; in canto XXII, prompted by Vergil's questions, Statius views literature as part of his lived experience: in both cases, the dramatic thrust is to show that the world of poetic fiction is not an isolated, self-enclosed entity and that a symbolic coherence exists between literature and life.

---

[32] See *Inferno* I, ll. 79-87: Dante's acknowledgment of the importance of Vergil's poetry is echoed in *Purgatorio* XXI, ll. 94-9 where Statius refers to the *Aeneid:* "Al mio ardor fuor seme le faville, / che mi scaldar, de la divina fiamma / onde sono allumati più di mille; / de l' Eneïde dico, la qual mamma / fummi, e fummi nutrice, poetando: / sanz'essa non fermai peso di dramma."

This coherence is not, however, self-evident: Vergil points out to Statius that the *Thebaid*, a poem viewed as history and inspired by Clio (*Purgatorio* XXII, l. 58), does not appear to be touched by faith and asks what "sun or candles" dispelled his spiritual darkness. Statius replies:

> . . . "Tu prima m'inviasti
> verso Parnaso a ber ne le sue grotte,
> e prima appresso Dio m'alluminasti.
> Facesti come quei che va di notte,
> che porta il lume dietro e sé non giova,
> ma dopo sé fa le persone dotte,
> quando dicesti: 'Secol si rinova;
> torna giustizia e primo tempo umano,
> e progenie scende da ciel nova.'
> Per te poeta fui, per te cristiano."
>
> ll. 64-73

("It was you who first sent me toward Parnassus to drink in its caves, and first did light me on to God. You were like one who goes by night and carries the light behind him and avails not himself but makes those who follow him wise, when you said, 'The ages are renewed; Justice returns and the first age of man, and a new progeny descends from heaven.' Through you was I a poet, through you was I a Christian.")

From Statius' account, there is a real continuity between poetry and conversion and the iteration "per te" (l. 73) ostensibly establishes the link between the two experiences. Vergil's fourth eclogue, which in the Middle Ages is conventionally understood as a prophetic announcement of Christ's renewal of the world, is the vehicle for Statius' conversion. Moreover, Dante applies to Vergil's role a Pauline image which St. Augustine uses to describe the Jews' mission to the world. In the Letter to the Romans, St. Paul speaks of the Jew as "a guide to the blind, a light of them who are in blindness" (2:19); St. Augustine addresses the Jews as those who "carried in your hands the lamp of the law in order to show the way to others while you remained in darkness."[33]

Dante brings literary history within the focus of salvation history and transposes the methods of patristic hermeneutics from the Bible into secular literature. From the perspective of the Revelation, the Fathers of the Church could subvert whatever literal affirmation the Old Testament made: the ultimate irrelevance of anything literal found its authoritative maxim in St. Paul's formula, "the letter kills, but the spirit gives life" (II Corinthians 3:6). This common practice of moralizing pagan texts is dramatized by Dante in showing Statius subverting the literal thrust of the eclogue, which occasioned as a *genethliacon*, envisions the return of the golden age.[34] Statius changes the sense of the poem, reads it as poetry of spiritual inwardness, by deploying what in biblical exegesis is known as the technique of parallel texts.[35] He points out

[33] St. Augustine, *De Symbolo ad Catechumenos*, iv, 4, *PL* 40, col. 664. E. Moore, *Studies in Dante*, 1st series (Oxford: Clarendon Press, 1896), p. 260, recalls the following passage by Ennius (also used by Cicero in *De Officiis*, i, xvi, 51), "Homo, qui erranti comiter, monstrat viam, / quasi lumen de suo lumine accendat, facit / nihilo minus ipsi lucet, cum illi accenderit." See also *La Divina Commedia*, ed. Natalino Sapegno (Milan and Naples: Ricciardi, 1957), p. 647 for further bibliography. For the tradition of Vergil as a prophet, see Henri de Lubac, "Virgile philosophe et prophète," in *Exégèse médiévale* (Paris: Aubier, 1964), ii, 233–62.

[34] Jerome Carcopino, *Virgile et le mystère de la IVième éclogue* (Paris: L'Artisan du livre, 1943), esp. pp. 17–20 and 195 ff. For the moralized readings of Vergil, see Domenico Comparetti, *Virgilio nel Medioevo*, new ed., ed. Giorgio Pasquali (Florence: La nuova Italia, 1937), i, 61 ff. See also de Lubac, *Exégèse médiévale*, ii, 233–62. More generally on the patristic tradition of subversive interpretation of literal statements in the Bible, see Beryl Smalley, *The Study of the Bible in the Middle Ages* (Oxford: Clarendon Press, 1941), pp. 1–23, *et passim*.

[35] "Già era 'l mondo tutto quanto pregno / de la vera credenza, seminata / per li messaggi de l'etterno regno; / e la parola tua sopra toccata / si consonava a' nuovi predicanti;" (*Purgatorio* xxii, ll. 76–80). "Consonava," a metaphor for the harmony between the Word of Revelation and its pagan foreshadowing, is a technical term in biblical exegesis, and it designates the *concordance* between the Old and the New Testaments. Cf. St. Augustine, *Contra Faustum*, "ipsa tanta consonantia rerum praefiguratarum et nunc impletarum"

that Vergil's prediction, "si consonava a' nuovi predicanti" (l. 80), establishes a *concordance* between the messengers of the eternal kingdom, the *viva vox evengelii* disseminated through the world, and his veiled pronouncements.

It is by this elaborate interpretative process that the eclogue, which significantly deals with the renewal of the world, is made truly new. Vergil, in a real sense, is foreign to the meaning of his own text, and Statius literally remakes an entirely different poem from the perspective of his own life. This subversion of the author is even more evident in Statius' earlier reading of the *Aeneid*. The first impulse to repent from the sin of prodigality, he says, came to him when he understood the lines in which Vergil, as if enraged at the perversions of human nature, cries, "Per chè non reggi tu, o sacra fame / de l' oro, l'appetito dé mortali?" (*Purgatorio* XXII, ll. 40-1). The lines, drawn from a passage in which Vergil describes the death of Polydorus, state in the original precisely the opposite, "quid non mortalia pectora cogis, auri sacra fames?" Critics have spoken of a mistake that Dante inadvertently makes: in effect this is a mistake, but not in a banal philological sense. As Statius translates the text, he reads it against the author, deliberately alters the meaning of the words to accord with his own inner world. We might also note that this is the very passage that Dante, as has been shown in the previous chapter, rewrites in *Inferno* XIII. Translation provides an apt metaphor for literary history: it implies that texts have no preestablished fixed sense, and that to interpret is to undertake an "itinerary of error"[36] in a language which is foreign and through which moral truth can be extrapolated.

(*PL* 42, col. 275); cf. also *De Trinitate*, "Haec enim congruentia, sive convenientia, vel consonantia, . . . quod unum est ad duo" (IV, ii, in *CCSL*, L). For further bibliography, see de Lubac, "Concorde de deux testaments," in *Exégèse médiévale*, I, 328-55.

[36] For the implied sense of error, see Maurice Blanchot, *Le Livre à venir* (Paris: Gallimard, 1959), pp. 98 ff. See also chapter 6 below, particularly notes 77-81.

Dante, undoubtedly, rejects that literature which is an intransitive esthetic experience independent of the thought of God and believes, as the exchange with Bonagiunta exemplifies, that a literary text ought to be a vehicle to God, joining together the worlds of God and man. In *Purgatorio* II he explicitly suggests this much. Casella sings Dante's own poem "Amor che ne la mente mi ragiona" (l. 112) and the souls interrupt their purification, enthralled by the song, till Cato inexorably reminds them that they are in the desert of exile and their journey to God cannot be held back by nostalgia for the earth. Furthermore, what is more important is the fact that Dante juxtaposes to Casella's erotic, earthbound song its precise opposite, the Psalm of Exodus, "In exitu Israel de Aegypto" (l. 46), the controlling metaphor of his journey to God. Ostensibly, the literary act is not an esthetic enclosure but a veritable reenactment of Exodus. This view that a literary text darkly figures the story of the paradigm of salvation history is also implied by Statius in the account of his conversion:

E pria ch'io conducessi i Greci a' fiumi
di Tebe poetando, ebb' io battesmo;
ma per paura chiuso cristian fu'mi,
lungamente mostrando paganesmo.
Purgatorio XXII, ll. 88-91

(And before I brought the Greeks to the river of Thebes in my verse, I received baptism; but for fear I was a hidden Christian long making show of paganism.)

There is, actually, an oblique typological nexus between the scene of the *Thebaid* and the episode of conversion in Statius' autobiography: in the fiction the Greeks reach the rivers of Thebes, in his life the poet receives his baptism, crosses, that is to say, his Jordan; the poem conceals the newly found faith because Statius is a "chiuso cristian."

But for all this symbolic coherence that Statius posits between fiction and life, the morality of literature and personal redemption, his own revision of Vergil's writings against Vergil's authorial "intentions" shows that a rupture exists between literature and life. Statius' attempt to embrace Vergil when he recognizes him (*Purgatorio* xxi, ll. 130 ff.) creates a strong sense of ambiguity: here, just as in the case of the futile embrace of Casella, there is an illusion of real presence which is contradicted by the awareness that both lack any physical substance. What is more, as Vergil and Statius are engaged in a friendly conversation on their way up the mountain, the scene reenacts the shadowy world of Limbo: Homer, Euripides and all the other Greeks, "che già di lauro ornar la fronte" (l. 108), are recalled and Dante finds himself listening to their talk "ch' a poetar mi davano intelletto" (l. 129).

As if to emphasize that poetry is always threatened with turning into a pastoral self-enclosure, Dante ends the canto by dramatizing a mysterious voice crying from among the boughs of a tree:[37]

> Poi disse: "Più pensava Maria onde
>   fosser le nozze orrevoli e intere,
>   ch'a la sua bocca, ch'or per voi risponde.
> E le Romane antiche, per lor bere,
>   contente furon d'acqua; e Danïello
>   dispregiò cibo e acquistò savere.
> Lo secol primo, quant' oro fu bello,
>   fé savorose con fame le ghiande,
>   e nettare con sete ogne ruscello.
> Mele e locuste furon le vivande
>   che nodriro il Batista nel diserto;
>   per ch'elli è glorïoso e tanto grande
> quanto per lo Vangelio v'è aperto."
>   *Purgatorio* xxii, ll. 142-54

(Then it said, "Mary had more thought that the marriage feast should be honorable and complete than for her own

---

[37] For the identity of the tree, see Thomas D. Hill, "Dante's Palm: *Purgatorio* xxii: 130-35," *Modern Language Notes*, 82 (1967), pp. 103-5.

mouth which now answers for you. And the Roman
women of old were content with water for their drink,
and Daniel despised food and gained wisdom. The first
age was beautiful as gold; it made acorns savoury with
hunger and with thirst it made nectar of every brook.
Honey and locusts were the viands that nourished the
Baptist in the desert, for which he is glorious and as great
as by the Gospel it is made manifest for you.")

The voice introduces the moral area of gluttony where Forese
and Bonagiunta are situated; it juxtaposes gluttony to the
prophetic vision of Daniel and John the Baptist, and in this
sense casts Bonagiunta's poetic "nodo" as a truly spiritual
impediment. But the passage, defining the golden age as the
age of need in the desert and the Gospel as open, makes the
Gospel the privilegd text that fulfills and transcends what secular literature foreshadows: retrospectively, it also redefines
Vergil's own prophecy of the golden age (ll. 70-2). More to
the point, the passage makes the Gospel the only *open* book,
with a self-evident message. As Dante focuses on the openness of the Gospel (l. 154), his strategy resembles St. Augustine's, who, after a series of reflections on the books of
Vergil, the platonists and the Bible, ends the *Confessions* by a
scriptural citation, "pulsate et aperietur vobis."[38] For Au-

---

[38] The closing lines of the *Confessions* are, actually, "a te petatur, in te
quaeratur, ad te pulsetur: sic, sic accipitur, sic invenietur, sic aperietur" (XIII,
xxxviii, CSEL xxxiii). St. Augustine obviously alludes to Matthew 7:8.
Kenneth Burke, *The Rhetoric of Religion* (Berkeley and Los Angeles: University of California Press, 1970), in his analysis of the "Verbal Action in St.
Augustine's *Confessions*," pp. 43 ff., points out the "stylistic aspects of the
final sentence." More importantly, the metaphor of "opening" (and *clavis*,
which is its natural metaphoric extension) is applied by Dante and Augustine
to describe the act of glossing the biblical text. In *De Doctrina Christiana*, III,
xxx, CCSL xxxII, Augustine writes: "Tichonius . . . facit librum quem Re-
gularum vocavit, quia in eo quasdam septem regulas exsecutus est, quibus
quasi clavibus divinarum scripturarum aperientur occulta." In the *Vita
nuova*, the verb "aprire," in the sense of interpretation, occurs with high frequency; see Charles S. Singleton, *An Essay on the* Vita Nuova (Cambridge,
Mass.: Harvard University Press, 1958), p. 47. See also Francesco Tateo,
Questioni di poetica dantesca (Bari: Adriatica Editrice, 1972), pp. 53-75.

gustine, through the citation, his *Confessions* is literally an open-ended book; as it ends with the word "open," it explicitly defers the reader to the Word of God, makes the text a vehicle, an Exodus to the Book of God. Dante, too, attempts to make literature a prolongation of the concept of figural history, and assigns to the literary act a vital historicity exemplified by the fact that a Christian universe is, ultimately, a verbal universe of which the Logos made flesh is the divine center. But at the same time, he intimates that literature is not intrinsically part of the redeemed order and salvation history. The sense of the texts lies, paradoxically, outside of them. In this perspective, literary history is not the simplified myth of a unified culture as Bonagiunta believes, nor is it only some sort of positivistic history of formal techniques as Guinizzelli suggests. As Dante formulates his poetics of love he dramatizes both his desire to be a *poeta-theologus*[39] and his awareness that his poetry, like Guinizzelli's, falls short of this desire. Literary history is interpretation, a process of tradition whereby texts are betrayed, and in that act, renewed.

[39] Salvatore Battaglia, "Teoria del poeta teologo," in *Esemplarità e antagonismo nel pensiero di Dante*, Part I (Naples: Liguori, 1967), pp. 271-301. On the limits of the famous formula "Theologus Dantes nullius dogmatis expers," see Etienne Gilson, "Poésie et théologie dans la *Divine Comédie*," in *Dante et Béatrice; études dantesques* (Paris: Vrin, 1974), pp. 79-102.

CHAPTER 6

Allegory: Poetics of the Desert

No single issue in the *Divine Comedy* has been more divisive and more persistently debated by Dante scholarship than that of allegory. This is hardly surprising, one might add, for allegory is not merely a distinct, isolated theme which can be exhaustively treated by following its incidental textual movement. What is largely at stake in the recurrent critical debate is nothing less than the fundamental decision of how to read the poem, how to identify, that is to say, the interpretative laws which govern the poem and come to grips with the poet's authorial claims, his sense of the nature of figurative language, its relation to a moral truth and even the place, if any, that truth occupies in the economy of poetic fiction.

The truly problematic and elusive nature of these questions cannot be overemphasized: they reach into the very heart of Dante's literary enterprise and, it may be said without exaggeration, they determine the status, the epistemological value of the explicit thematic patterns of the text. Aware of the stakes, critics have recently probed anew medieval allegorical conventions, techniques of biblical exegesis and general theories of reading, the so-called *accessus ad auctores*, in the belief that a secure foothold in the massive and often contradictory documentary evidence of tradition can possibly help them to decipher these questions.[1]

---

[1] The renewed interest in the techniques of biblical interpretation and their

The critics' historical research came primarily as a genuine reaction to the impasse reached by Romantic principles and practices of literary interpretation. Croce, for instance, in the wake of German idealism, views allegory as an act of the will, a doctrinaire and discursive structure superimposed on and

extension to medieval poetry is exemplified by Henri de Lubac, *Histoire et esprit: l'intelligence de l'Ecriture d'après Origène* (Paris: Aubier, 1950), and more importantly, by his *Exégèse médiévale*, II (Paris: Aubier, 1959-64); see also Ceslaus Spicq, *Esquisse d'une histoire de l'exégèse latine au moyen âge* (Paris: Vrin, 1944); Beryl Smalley, *The Study of the Bible in the Middle Ages* (Oxford: Clarendon Press, 1941); Jean Pépin, *Mythe et allégorie* (Paris: Aubier, 1958); Jean Daniélou, G. Devoto, *et al.*, in *La Bibbia nell'Alto Medioevo* (Spoleto: Centro italiano di studi sull'Alto Medioevo, 1963); Robert E. McNally, *The Bible in the Early Middle Ages* (Westminster, Md.: Newman Press, 1959). The debate has affected the study of medieval literature: see E. Talbot Donaldson, "Patristic Exegesis in the Criticism of Medieval Literature," and R. E. Kaske, "The Defense," in *Critical Approaches to Medieval Literature*, ed. Dorothy Bethurum (New York: Columbia University Press, 1960); Judson Allen, *The Friar as Critic: Literary Attitudes in the Late Middle Ages* (Nashville: Vanderbilt University Press, 1971); Peter Dronke, *Fabula: Explorations into the Uses of Myth in Medieval Platonism* (Leiden: E. J. Brill, 1974); Andrea Ciotti, "Il concetto della 'figura' e la poetica della 'visione' nei commentatori trecenteschi della *Commedia*," *Convivium*, 30 (1962), pp. 264-92, 399-415; D. W. Robertson, Jr., "Some Medieval Literary Terminology, with Special Reference to Chrétien de Troyes," *Studies in Philology*, 48 (1951), pp. 669-92. As far as Dante goes, the debate has focused around his Epistle to Cangrande, mainly to establish or dispute its authenticity. See G. Boffito, "L'Epistola di Dante Alighieri a Cangrande della Scala: saggio d'edizione critica e di commento," *Memorie della Reale Accademia di Scienze di Torino*, 2nd series, 58 (1907), pp. 1-39; Francesco d'Ovidio, "L'Epistola a Cangrande," in *Studii sulla Divina Commedia* (Caserta: Moderna, 1931), II, 229-89; Francesco Mazzoni, "L'Epistola a Cangrande," *Rendiconti dell'Accademia Nazionale dei Lincei*, X, fasc. 3-4 (1955), pp. 157-98; and "Per l'Epistola a Cangrande," *Studi in onore di Angelo Monteverdi*, II (Modena: Società tip. editrice modenese, 1959), pp. 498-516; Bruno Nardi, "Osservazioni sul medievale *accessus ad auctores* in rapporto all'Epistola a Cangrande," in *Saggi e note di critica dantesca* (Milan and Naples: Ricciardi, 1966), pp. 268-305; see also L. Jenaro-MacLennan, *The Trecento Commentaries on the Divina Commedia and the Epistle to Cangrande* (Oxford: Clarendon Press, 1974). The specific aspect of the "reader" in the *Divine Comedy* has been treated by Erich Auerbach, "Dante's Addresses to the Reader," *Romance Philology*, 3 (1949), pp. 1-26, in which he points out the authority and prophetic urgency of Dante's voice; Leo Spitzer, "The Ad-

extraneous to the poetic immediacy of symbolic representation. [2] The lyrical substance, he argues, resides in fragments
where images and their meaning are bound together in a pure
and spontaneous intimacy, while allegory, because of the
heterogeneity which characterizes it, shatters the esthetic
unity of the symbolic discourse. Croce's sense of the intrinsic
superiority of symbol over allegory is certainly debatable just
as is his notion that sharp and stable distinctions can be drawn
between what is "poetry" and what is "non-poetry." Yet, his
insight into the disjunctions present in all allegorical writings
has been dismissed by medievalists, with quick and occasionally questionable condescension, as idealistic prejudice. They
have appealed to the canons of medieval esthetics as the background against which Dante's allegory can be legitimately assessed and through which the laws governing the imaginative
unity of "poetry" and "structure" in the text can be found.

It has been increasingly acknowledged that the allegory of
the *Divine Comedy*, far from being simply a device to induce
mechanically from the outside a moral sense into the poetic
texture or a rhetorical modality only sporadically present in
the poem, is indeed its very principle of structure. [3] It is the

---

dresses to the Reader in the *Commedia*," in *Romanische Literaturstudien 1936-
1956* (Tübingen: Niemeyer, 1959), pp. 574-95, insists on the human bond of
solidarity that by addresses Dante intends to establish between the reader and
himself. Among recent theories of reading, cf. Paul De Man, *Blindness and
Insight* (New York: Oxford University Press, 1971), especially pp. 102-41,
and "The Rhetoric of Temporality," in *Interpretation: Theory and Practice*, ed.
Charles S. Singleton (Baltimore: The Johns Hopkins University Press, 1969),
pp. 173-209; for a more traditional treatment, see E. D. Hirsch Jr., *Validity in
Interpretation* (New Haven: Yale University Press, 1967).

[2] Benedetto Croce, *La poesia di Dante*, 2nd ed. (Bari: Laterza, 1948), pp.
7-8, 14-18; see also his "Sulla natura dell'allegoria," in *Nuovi saggi di estetica*,
3rd ed. (Bari: Laterza, 1948), pp. 329-38. For a critical view of Croce's posi-
tion, see Salvatore Battaglia, "Linguaggio reale e linguaggio figurato nella
Divina Commedia," in *Esemplarità e antagonismo nel pensiero di Dante* (Naples:
Liguori ed., 1967), I, 51-82. See also Michele Barbi, "Poesia e struttura nella
Divina Commedia," in *Problemi fondamentali per un nuovo commento della* Divina
Commedia (Florence: Sansoni, 1956), pp. 7-19.

[3] For a sense of the episodic nature of allegory, see Antonino Pagliaro,

active framework within which the symbolic layers are invested with moral determinations and which sustains Dante's narrative strategy, the double perspective on which the movement of the poem is ostensibly articulated. John Freccero, for instance, has recently argued that Dante's allegory coincides with the structure of autobiography in that it affords precisely the temporal horizon within which the poet maps his spiritual conversion, the self-interpretative process of his prior experience as a pilgrim.[4]

Opinions are still divided, however, between those who believe that the *Divine Comedy* is an allegory of poets and those for whom the mode belongs to the tradition of the allegory of theologians.[5] The proponents of the allegory of poets see the *Divine Comedy* essentially as a *fabula*, a poetic

---

"Simbolo e allegoria," in *Ulisse: ricerche semantiche sulla* Divina Commedia (Messina and Florence: D'Anna, 1967), II, 467-527. For a nuanced version, see Michele Barbi, "Allegoria e lettera nella *Divina Commedia*," in *Problemi per un nuovo commento sulla* Divina Commedia, pp. 115-40.

[4] John Freccero, "Medusa: The Letter and the Spirit," *Yearbook of Italian Studies*, 2 (1972), pp. 1-18; for this idea that "Christian allegory . . . is identical with the phenomenology of confession," see also his introduction to *Dante: A Collection of Critical Essays*, ed. J. Freccero (Englewood Cliffs, N. J.: Prentice-Hall Inc., 1965), pp. 1-7; Gianfranco Contini, "Dante come personaggio-poeta della *Commedia*," in *Varianti e altra linguistica* (Turin: Einaudi, 1970), esp. pp. 335-9.

[5] Charles S. Singleton, *Dante Studies 1*: Commedia: *Elements of Structure* (Cambridge, Mass.: Harvard University Press, 1954), pp. 1-17, 84-98; R. H. Greene, "Dante's 'Allegory of the Poets' and the Medieval Theory of Poetic Fiction," *Comparative Literature*, 9 (1957), pp. 118-28, objects to Singleton's view; see Singleton's reply in "The Irreducible Dove," *Comparative Literature*, 9 (1957), pp. 129-35, in which he reaches the conclusion that the "fiction is not a fiction." The fictionality of the *Divine Comedy* had been asserted by Bruno Nardi, "I sensi delle Scritture," in *Nel mondo di Dante* (Rome: Edizioni di Storia e Letteratura, 1944), pp. 55-61; for a more general view of *fictio*, see Alfredo Schiaffini, " 'Poesis' e 'poeta' in Dante," in *Studia Philologica et Litteraria in Honorem L. Spitzer* (Berne: Francke, 1958), pp. 379-89; see also G. Paparelli, "*Fictio*: la definizione dantesca della poesia," in *Ideologia e poesia di Dante* (Florence: Olschki, 1975), pp. 53-138. For a general overview see Jean Pépin, *Dante et la tradition de l'allégorie* (Montréal: Institut d'études médiévales, 1970); see my review of this essay in *Italica*, 50 (1973), pp. 590-4.

construct in which theology, figuralism and Dante's prophetic vocation, which manifestly are the props of the poem,
are part and parcel of the fictional strategy, the literal sense of
which is a pure fiction. For those critics, such as Singleton,
who argue in favor of the allegory of theologians, the poem is
written in imitation of God's way of writing and, like Scripture, it exceeds metaphor and comes forth with the "irreduci-
bility of reality itself."[6] If for Singleton the historicity of the
literal sense is what might be called a formal quality of the
text, if it depends, that is to say, on a conniving reader manipulated by the author to believe that the "fiction is not a fiction," for Auerbach this historicity is the prominent feature of
biblical figuralism which Dante rigorously deploys in his
poem.[7] *Figura* is both a theory of interpretation of history and
a mode of writing in which signs and their significations are
historically true, and which—just as in the Bible, where the
reader is never pampered into the safety of esthetic illusions—demands the reader's radical commitment.

But Dante, Auerbach suggests in the last paragraph of his
chapter on "Farinata and Cavalcante" in *Mimesis*, no longer
believes in the figural grid which organizes his poem and, ultimately, subverts the order and stability of the world he represents. "By virtue of this immediate and admiring sympathy
with man," says Auerbach, "the principle, rooted in the divine order, of the indestructibility of the whole historical and
individual man turns *against* that order, makes it subservient
to its own purposes, and obscures it. The image of man
eclipses the image of God. Dante's work made man's
Christian-figural being a reality, and destroyed it in the very
process of realizing it."[8] This ironic disruption, which mark-

[6] Charles S. Singleton, *Dante Studies 1*, pp. 12-13.

[7] Erich Auerbach, "Figura," in *Scenes from the Drama of European Literature:
Six Essays*, trans. Ralph Manheim (New York: Meridian Books, 1959),
pp. 11-76.

[8] Erich Auerbach, "Farinata and Cavalcante," in *Mimesis: The Representation of Reality in Western Literature*, trans. Willard Trask (Princeton: Princeton
University Press, 1953), p. 202; this particular view echoes the following

edly resembles Croce's sense of the split between poetry and doctrine, has generally been neglected by critics, probably because Auerbach, with some hesitancy, places this view of Dante as a Romantic rebel *avant la lettre*, a Prometheus who steals the fire from the gods, outside of the text, and because the disruption for him is more the work of a Hegelian "cunning of history" than a conscious strategy of the text.

Most of the later critical strains flow either from the achievements of Singleton or the more orthodox insights of Auerbach, and frequently attempt to harmonize the two. G. R. Sarolli sees the *Divine Comedy* as a secularized prophecy, a visionary allegory which irrupts into a concrete historical crisis with the confessed intent to reshape the moral order of the world and reconcile its two providential structures, Empire and Church.[9] For A. C. Charity the poem is sustained by typology and carries out an interiorized, existential call for the reader's private redemption.[10] Mineo, in a systematic study, places Dante's voice in the line of biblical prophets;[11] Hollander and P. Giannantonio, on the other hand, accept Singleton's view of the poem as a fiction which predominantly employs the techniques of theological allegory.[12] It was left to Hollander, however, to exemplify, in a

conclusion by Francesco De Sanctis: "Dante è stato illogico; ha distrutto senza saperlo la sua poetica, ha fatto contro la sua intenzione. . . . La realtà distrae lui e distrae il lettore," in *Lezioni e saggi su Dante*, a cura di Sergio Romagnoli (Turin: Einaudi, 1955), p. 627.

[9] Gian Roberto Sarolli, *Prolegomena alla* Divina Commedia (Florence: Olschki, 1971), especially pp. 1-119. See also Bruno Nardi, "Dante profeta," in *Dante e la cultura medioevale*, 2nd ed. (Bari: Laterza, 1949), pp. 336-416.

[10] A. C. Charity, *Events and Their Afterlife: The Dialectics of Christian Typology in the Bible and Dante* (Cambridge: Cambridge University Press, 1966). See also Johan Chydenius, *The Typological Problem in Dante* (Helsingfors: Societas Scientiarum Fennica, 1958).

[11] Nicolò Mineo, *Profetismo e apocalittica in Dante* (Catania: Università di Catania, 1968); see also Giorgio Padoan, " 'La mirabile visione' di Dante e l'Epistola a Cangrande," in *Dante e Roma* (Florence: Le Monnier, 1965), pp. 283-314.

[12] Robert Hollander, *Allegory in Dante's* Commedia (Princeton: Princeton University Press, 1969); Pompeo Giannantonio, *Dante e l'allegorismo* (Florence: Olschki, 1969).

critical move aimed at capturing the text's internal correspondences, the controlled presence of the fourfold senses of
biblical exegesis. Paradoxically, while the historical research
has given the critics' own make-believe the strength of fact,
the critics have ended up disclosing, as is perhaps inevitable,
their own sense of esthetic values.

That such a self-disclosure should take place may not go entirely against the grain of Dante's poetry and its purposes, and
one concern of this chapter is to show that critics read the *Divine Comedy* in ways that Dante precisely anticipates. This
statement is not meant to justify or preempt likely interpretative errors: it is meant to suggest, rather, that the *Divine
Comedy* is the allegory of its possible readings, or to put it in
different terms, that the act of reading, essentially a critical-
philological operation, is at the same time for Dante a veritable allegory of the quest, the outcome of which is as tentative
and possibly aberrant as the significance we extract from that
reading. It has been my contention in the preceding chapters
that Statius' philological "mistake" in the reading of the
Aeneid turns out to be a spiritual insight into Vergil's text, and
that Francesca and Statius, much like Augustine reading the
Aeneid and St. Paul's Epistle to the Romans in the *Confessions*,
are paradigms of opposed experiences in which books come
forth as avenues of the readers' "fate," in the full meaning of
the word, as that which is spoken to them.

In this context, the question of whether Dante's allegory
belongs to a theological or fictional mode cannot be simply
solved, as critics would have it, by some *a priori* decision
about the fictiveness or reality of the literal sense. Dante's
reader is constantly reminded, in effect, that the practice of
reading deals precisely with how that decision can be made,
that reading is an imaginary operation in which truth and fiction, far from being mutually exclusive categories, are simultaneously engendered by the ambiguous structure of
metaphoric language. The *locus classicus* where the ambivalence of the literal sense is formulated is the passage in *Convivio* (II, i) in which Dante distinguishes between the allegory
of poets and the allegory of theologians.

I say that, as has been stated in the first chapter, this explanation should be both literal and allegorical. And to understand this, we should know that books can be understood, and ought to be explained, in four principal senses. One is called *literal*, and this it is which goes no further than the letter, such as the simple narration of the thing of which you treat: [of which a perfect and appropriate example is to be found in the third canzone, treating of nobility]. The second is called *allegorical*, and this is the meaning hidden under the cloak of fables, and is a truth concealed beneath a fair fiction; as when Ovid says that Orpheus with his lute tamed wild beasts, and moved trees and rocks; which means that the wise man, with the instrument of his voice, softens and humbles cruel hearts, and moves at his will those who live neither for science nor for art, and those who, having no rational life whatever, are almost like stones. And how this hidden thing [the allegorical meaning] may be found by the wise, will be explained in the last book but one. The theologians, however, take this meaning differently from the poets; but because I intend to follow here the method of the poets, I shall take the allegorical meaning according to their usage.[13]

[13] This is the text in the reconstruction by Busnelli and Vandelli: "Dico che, si come nel primo capitolo è narrato, questa sposizione conviene essere litterale e allegorica. E a ciò dare a intendere, si vuol sapere che le scritture si possono intendere e deonsi esponere massimamente per quattro sensi. L'uno si chiama litterale, [e questo è quello che non si stende più oltre che la lettera de le parole fittizie, sì come sono le favole de li poeti. L'altro si chiama allegorico,] e questo è quello che si nasconde sotto 'l manto di queste favole, ed è una veritade ascosa sotto bella menzogna: sì come sono quando dice Ovidio che Orfeo facea con la cetera mansuete le fiere, e li arbori e le pietre a sè muovere, che vuol dire che lo savio uomo con lo strumento de la sua voce fa[r]ia mansuescere e umiliare li crudeli cuori, e fa[r]ia muovere a la sua volontade coloro che non hanno vita di scienza e d'arte: e coloro che non hanno vita ragionevole alcuna sono quasi come pietre. E perchè questo nascondimento fosse trovato per li savi, nel penultimo trattato si mostrerà. Veramente li teologi questo senso prendono altrimenti che li poeti; ma però che mia intenzione è qui lo modo de li poeti seguitare, prendo lo senso allegorico secondo

In the subsequent paragraphs Dante describes the third sense, which is called moral, by referring to the account of Christ's transfiguration: the fact that Christ took with him only three of his twelve apostles exemplifies the moral that in the most secret things we should have but few companions. The fourth sense, the anagogical or "sovrasenso," occurs when even in the literal sense, by the very things it signifies ("la quale ancora sia vera eziandio nel senso litterale, per le cose significate"), it signifies the supernatural things of the eternal glory. The illustration for this "sovrasenso" is provided by the psalm, "In exitu Israel de Aegypto," which is historically true according to both the letter and its spiritual intentions.

The distinction between poetic allegory and theological allegory depends not on an intrinsic separation of truth and lies in the literal sense, but on an act of interpretation: "the theologians take the literal sense otherwise than the poets do"; the truth of the literal sense, then, lies not in the actual enunciation, but in what the literal sense signifies.[14] The same argument, as some critics have remarked, recurs in the Letter to Cangrande, which, in spite of its doubtful authenticity, is conventionally granted a privileged place in the debate over the *accessus* to the *Divine Comedy*. Here Dante claims that the underlying structural model for his allegory is Scripture and illustrates the four senses by expounding the verse from the psalm, "When Israel went out of Egypt, the house of Jacob from a people of strange speech, Judea became his sanctification, Israel his power." By virtue of this allusion, which indeed provides the pattern for the poem, scholars have recently

che per li poeti usato" (*Convivio*, II, i, 2-4). The English text is from Dante Alighieri, *The Banquet*, trans. Katharine Hillard (London: Kegan Paul, 1889), pp. 51-2.

[14] "Vera mente li teologi *questo senso prendono altrimenti che li poeti*" (emphasis mine). Cf. Francesco Tateo, "Sulla genesisi teorica dell'allegoria," in *Questioni di poetica dantesca* (Bari: Adriatica, 1972), especially pp. 110-13. Thomas Aquinas asserts the metaphorical nature of the literal sense as follows: "sensus parabolicus sub literali continetur; nam per voces significatur aliquid proprie et aliquid figurative. Nec est literalis sensus ipsa figura sed id quod est figuratum" (*Summa Theologiae* Ia, q. 1 art. 10, ad tertium).

argued for the historicity of the literal sense. Yet, in no less explicit terms the Letter asserts that the poem's *forma tractandi* is "poetic, fictive, descriptive, digressive, metaphorical, and, in addition, definitive, analytical, probative, censorious, and exemplificative." The metaphoricity of the text is stressed with equal overtness in parapraph 29 of the Letter where the line "which he has no knowledge or power to tell again" (*Paradiso* I, l. 6) is glossed as follows: "For there are many things which we see by the intellect for which verbal signs are lacking, which Plato suggests in his books by means of metaphors, for he saw many things by the light of his intellect that he could not express in suitable words."[15]

But critics, for all their specific differences, generally bypass the importance and complications of metaphor in the *Divine Comedy*.[16] They argue that Dante's language, like its biblical model, goes beyond metaphor and comes forth with the immediacy of reality itself; or, when Dante's representation is drawn within a Platonic theory of poetic expression, as in Mazzeo's essay, it is still believed that it manages to give an untroubled and direct access to reality. The common assumption is that literary language conveys a univocal sense and the critical efforts are directed at establishing whether the overall meaning of the poem is prophecy or political theology or spiritual intellectual conversion. Textual ambiguities are repressed in favor of univocal truth and the acknowledged

[15] *The Letters of Dante*, ed. Paget Toynbee, 2nd ed. (Oxford: Clarendon Press, 1966), p. 193. The reference to Psalm 113 and to the polysemous nature of the text is in paragraph 7, p. 173. The allusion to the twofold form of the text, the "forma tractatus" and the "forma tractandi," is in paragraph 9, p. 174. On the *modus tractandi*, see H. Pflaum, "Il 'modus tractandi' della *Divina Commedia*," *Giornale dantesco*, 39 (1936), pp. 163-4. For the relationship between *Convivio* and Epistola x, see Maria Simonelli, "Allegoria e simbolo," in *Dante e Bologna nei tempi di Dante* (Bologna: Commissione per i testi di lingua, 1967), pp. 207-26; see also Phillip W. Damon, "The Two Modes of Allegory in Dante's *Convivio*," *Philological Quarterly*, 40 (1961), pp. 144-9.

[16] There have been, however, some exceptions in recent years: Joseph A. Mazzeo, *Structure and Thought in* Paradiso (Ithaca: Cornell University Press, 1958), pp. 25-49; G. R. Sarolli, *Prolegomena*, pp. 5-39.

polysemy of Dante's poem is viewed to describe the steps in a hierarchy of fixed and stable meanings. Thus, allegory appears as the wrapping in which experience is packed, but the disguises can be penetrated by the application of the right exegetical tools.

While these critical perspectives cannot be dismissed as wrong, they are nonetheless partial, and the burden of this chapter is to show that Dante's allegory intends to provide a theological scheme by which the world of reality, history and the self can be intelligible in God's providential plan. But I also want to show that the metaphoric movement of the poem denounces the illusoriness of the project and draws the theological structure of sense into the possibility of error, that Dante writes in the mode of theological allegory and also recoils from it. This wavering, partially elaborated in the preceding chapters, is not simply a way of describing occasional moments of the poet's troubled doubt meant ultimately to heighten the poet's authority. It describes, rather, the bind within which the voice of the poet is forever caught and disrupts the sense of a stable continuity between reality and its representation. The poem, it must be stressed, is neither the imitation of God's way of writing nor a prodigious crystal, an idolatrous self-referential construct; it occupies the ambiguous space between these two possibilities; and allegory, as I see it, dramatizes the choice with which the reader is confronted. Is this ambiguous pattern at all necessary? What are the reasons for it? I shall try to answer these questions by focusing mainly on *Purgatorio* x and *Paradiso* xxxiii.

In *Purgatorio* x, the first ledge where pride is expiated, the pilgrim confronts the exemplary allegorical representations of humility carved on the marble sides of the cliff.[17] If pride is

---

[17] The canto has been mainly treated from the point of view of Dante's sense of the plastic arts. See H. Gmelin, "Canto x," in *Letture dantesche*, ed. G. Getto (Florence: Sansoni, 1958), ii, 205-14; Francesco Tateo, "Teologia e 'arte' nel canto x del *Purgatorio*," in *Questioni di poetica dantesca*, pp. 139-71. Maria Simonelli, "Il canto x del *Purgatorio*," *Studi danteschi*, 23 (1956), pp. 12-45, emphasizes the exaltation of humility as the poetic focus of the canto.

the root of all evils, humility is literally the "ground" from which the spiritual ascent of both penitents and pilgrim is to start. This is no mere abstract virtue statically opposed to pride in what is a purgatorial version of a *psychomachia*; humility also appears as the meaning that underlies the providential order of history. The icons, in effect, unfold the allegory of history and enact a compressed synopsis of salvation history. Gabriel's descent and the humility of the Virgin at the Annunciation (ll. 34-45), the Old Testament account of David dancing in front of the ark of the covenant (ll. 55-72), and finally Trajan's surrender to the widow's plea for justice (ll. 73-93) are images of prophetic and secular history drawn together into a coherent unity pivoted on the Incarnation. Christ's descent, the paradigm of humility, is tellingly adumbrated by the allusion to David. In patristic exegesis, the ark is the conventional prophetic sign of the Church[18] and David is both the type of the just emperor (he appears as more and less than King, l. 66) and a veritable *figura Christi*.[19] It is more openly hinted in the reference to Gabriel's salutation to the Virgin.

> Giurato si saria ch'el dicesse "Ave";
> perchè iv'era imaginata quella
> ch'ad aprir l'alto amor volse la chiave;
> e avea in atto impressa esta favella
> "Ecce ancilla Dei," propriamente
> come figura in cera si suggella.
>
> ll. 40-5

(One would have sworn that he was saying, "Ave," for there she was imaged who turned the key to open the supreme love, and these words were imprinted in her attitude: "Ecce ancilla Dei," as clearly as a figure is impressed on wax.)

"Ave" is commonly glossed as the typological reversal of Eve, the first woman who figures the pride of the Fall, and

---

18 Tertullian, *PL* 1, col. 1209; *PL* 50, col. 1084.
19 Cf. for instance, *PL* 79, col. 461; *PL* 109, col. 49; *PL* 191, col. 1253; etc.

the image of Mary as she who "volse la chiave" stresses the
reversal.[20] The birth of Christ, the new Adam, appears as the
unique event which transforms and redeems the Fall into the
new beginning of history. Its uniqueness is dramatized by a
significant detail in Dante's narrative: the Annunciation is the
only instance of the new life granted to the world whereas, in
contrast to it, Michal, as we gather from the biblical context,
is "sterilitati damnata,"[21] and the widow weeps for her dead
son.

Dante actually exploits for this synoptic theology of history
the force of the technical term "storia" and its variant
"storiato." The pilgrim turns his eyes beyond the representation of Mary to "un'altra storia ne la roccia imposta" (l. 52);
he moves his feet beyond the picture of Michal, "per avvisar
da presso un'altra istoria" (l. 71) in which "era storiata l'alta
gloria / del roman principato, il cui valore / mosse Gregorio a
la sua gran vittoria" (ll. 73-5). In the measure in which the
three representations are allegorical examples of humility,
Dante suggests, following upon rhetorical traditions, that history is an imaginative reservoir of *exempla* and moralized
myths.[22] At the same time, these are images seen and the emphasis on vision, which occupies a conspicuous place in the
canto, carries a more specialized overtone of the word
"storia." Hugh of St. Victor, among others, gives the
etymology of history precisely in terms of vision: "History is
derived from the Greek word 'istoreo' which means 'I see and
recount.' For this reason, among the ancients it was allowed
to no one to write about events unless he had seen them him-

---

[20] The reversal is a commonplace in the Middle Ages: see for instance,
"Ave non Evae meritum," "Ave maris stella, . . . mutans nomen Evae," etc.,
in *Analecta Hymnica Medii Aevi*, ed. Guido Maria Dreves (Leipzig: Fues's Verlag, 1886), I, 50; III, 40. See also the etymological jumble that Isidore of
Seville makes of "Eva": "vita sive calamitas sive vae" (*Etym.* VII, v, 5-6).

[21] II Kings 6:23.

[22] The word "storia" is actually used in the sense of *exemplum* in *Paradiso*
XIX, ll. 16-8: " 'e in terra lasciai la mia memoria / sì fatta, che le genti lì mal-
vage / commendan lei, ma non seguon la storia.' " On the didactic function
of history, see chapter 2, note 8 above.

self so that falsehood would not get mixed with truth. . . .
Thus is history properly and strictly defined."[23] But Dante's
historical sequence in *Purgatorio* x is unambiguous: it is a
theological allegory both because of the historicity of the
events and because the images are constructed by God himself, the *Deus Artifex*,[24]

> Colui che mai non vide cosa nova
> produsse esto visibile parlare,
> novello a noi perchè qui non si trova.
>
> ll. 94-96

(He who never beheld any new thing wrought this visible speech, new to us because it is not found here.)

The detail that this is God's work exemplifies, from one point
of view, the doctrinal counterpoint of pride and humility on
which the canto is explicitly articulated and is tailored to
suggest that this art surpasses and humbles both the imita-
tions of nature and the artifice of man (ll. 31-3).[25] It also
exemplifies what has come to be known as God's way of writing. Much as in Holy Scripture, God signifies his meaning by
both words and things, or as Aquinas puts it,

> Sicut enim dicit Apostolus ad hebr. "Lex vetus figura est
> novae legis," et ipsa nova lex, ut Dionysius dicit, "est
> figura futurae gloriae." In nova etiam lege et quae in ca-
> pite sunt gesta sunt signa eorum quae nos agere debe-
> mus.

---

[23] *PL* 175, col. 12; cf. also Isidore of Seville, *Etym.* I, xli, 1.

[24] For this motif, see "God as Maker," in E. R. Curtius, *European Literature and the Latin Middle Ages*, trans. W. R. Trask (New York: Harper and Row, 1953), pp. 544-6; see also Antonio Santi, "La questione della creazione nelle dottrine di Dante e del suo tempo," *Giornale dantesco*, 23 (1915), pp. 197-207.

[25] The motif of the vainglory of human art is raised in *Purgatorio* xi, ll. 90-102. It might also be pointed out that wax, the malleable material on which the images are impressed, is in direct contrast to Dante's sense of the intracta-ble matter in *Paradiso* I, ll. 127-9: "Vero è che, come forma non s'accorda / molte fïate a l'intenzion de l'arte, / perch' a risponder la materia è sorda"; see on this *Summa Theologiae*, Ia IIae, q. 4, art. 4.

Secundum ergo quod ea quae sunt veteris legis significant ea quae sunt novae legis est sensus allegoricus;
secundum vero quod ea quae in Christo sunt facta vel in
his quae Christum significant sunt signa eorum quae nos
agere debemus est sensus moralis; prout vero significant
ea quae sunt in aeterna gloria est sensus anagogicus.[26]

Aquinas' definition of the fourfold sense of biblical exegesis is
clearly applicable to the *ecphrasis* of *Purgatorio* x, a Christocentric vision of history which fulfills the Old Testament
figure, points out how the moral edification of the sinners can
be obtained, and foreshadows the glory to come.

The primary sense of the word "storia," however, is representation and Dante insistently focuses on the mimetic power
of the fiction, on the subtlety of God's craft by which the illusion of reality is achieved.[27] Thus, the angel "pareva sì verace" (l. 37), the fragrance of the incense seems real (ll. 61-3),
Trajan's banners "in vista" flutter in the wind (ll. 80-1), and
the little widow "pareva dir: 'Segnor, fammi vendetta' " (ll.
82-4). The central expedient in this fiction of reality is the

[26] *Summa Theologiae*, 1a, q. 1, art. 10, resp. The English text, in the
Blackfriars edition (New York: McGraw-Hill, 1964), reads:

For, as St. Paul says, "The Old Law is the figure of the New," and the
New Law itself, as Dionysius says, "is the figure of the glory to come."
Then again, under the New Law the deeds wrought by our Head are
signs of what we ourselves ought to do.

Well then, the allegorical sense is brought into play when the things of
the Old Law signify the things of the New Law; the moral sense when
the things done in Christ and in those who prefigured him are signs of
what we should carry out; and the anagogical sense when the things that
lie ahead in eternal glory are signified.

See Epistola x, par. 7 (Toynbee, p. 173) on the fourfold sense of the verse "In
exitu Israel de Aegypto, domus Iacob de populo barbaro, facta est Iudaea
sanctificatio eius, Israel potestas eius."

[27] The word is used to mean representation by Ristoro d'Arezzo, *La com-
posizione del mondo* (Milan: G. Daelli, 1864): "E pare che le figure del cielo
fossero disegnate e composte di stelle, a modo delli savi artefici che fanno la
nobilissima operazione mossaica ad adornare od a storiare le pareti e
pavimenti de' palazzi . . . e de' grandi templi" (I, 7, p. 13); cf. also *PL* 210,
col. 438.

"visibile parlare," the synesthesia which simulates the symbolic bond of words and vision and which organizes the triptych into a formal and sensorial totality. The phrase, to be sure, recalls the classical chiastic formula, here applied to sculpture, "poema loquens pictura pictura loquens poema."[28] But it recalls, more closely, St. Augustine's *verba visibilia*, an expression which he uses in at least two different but related contexts. In *De Doctrina Christiana*, a treatise which lays down the criteria for a Christian hermeneutics, Augustine devotes the third chapter of the second book to a description of conventional signs as distinguished from natural signs. The phrase "quasi quaedam verba visibilia" occurs to describe conventional signs such as silent gesticulations of mimes or military insignia which convey a full and unmistakable sense.[29] In *De Vera Religione*, in a section on the rules for interpreting Scripture, Augustine envisions fallen man delighting in "figmentis ludicris" and to them he opposes the semblances and parables, "quasi quaedam verba visibilia," given by God's mercy to cure "interiores oculos nostros."[30]

Much as for St. Augustine, for Dante the "visibile parlare" ostensibly designates God's art which, unlike man's figments, is removed from duplicity and deception and which cures pride's spiritual blindness, the condition of sinners whom the poet later in the canto refers to as being "de la vista de la mente infermi" (l. 122). The presence of the language of fiction in what is the allegory of God's way of writing in no way challenges the moral knowledge that Dante's passage conveys nor does it undermine the reality of its historical referents. It simply states, in Aquinas' words, that *fictio* can be a "figura veritatis"[31] and asserts the power of metaphors to duplicate

---

[28] The motif has been recently studied in general terms by F. Ulivi, *Poesia come pittura* (Bari: Adriatica, 1969), esp. chaps. 2 and 3, pp. 31-89.

[29] *De Doctrina Christiana*, II, iii, 4, in *CCSL* XXXII.

[30] *De Vera Religione*, I, 98, in *CCSL* XXXII.

[31] *Summa Theologiae*, IIIa, q. 55, a. 4, 1: "Non omne quod fingimus mendacium est . . . cum autem fictio nostra refertur in aliquam significationem, non est mendacium, sed aliqua figura veritatis."

the world of reality in all its sensuous multiplicity and to recover signs and meaning into a symbolic plenitude. Even the
Bible, according to St. Thomas, fittingly employs metaphorical language to deliver its spiritual realities. "For God provides for all things according to the kind of things they are.
Now we are of the kind to reach the world of intelligence
through the world of sense, since all our knowledge takes its
rise from sensation. Congenially, then, Holy Scripture delivers spiritual things to us beneath metaphors taken from bodily
things. Dionysius agrees, 'The divine rays cannot enlighten
us except wrapped up in many sacred veils.' "[32]

Aquinas, to be sure, proceeds to distinguish between secular poetry which employs metaphors for the sake of representation, for "repraesentatio naturaliter homini delectabilis est,"
and Scripture which adopts metaphors "propter necessitatem
et utilitatem."[33] In what seems to be a deliberate tempering of
St. Thomas' rigid dichotomy, Dante insists on the feeling of
delight engendered by God's art, "mentr'io mi *dilettava* di
guardare / l'imagini di tante umilitadi" (ll. 97-8). But this is no
illicita delectatio of the mind trapped by esthetic lures and
forgetful of its askesis:[34] rather it leads the pilgrim back to its
Creator, "per lo fabbro loro a veder care" (l. 99).

In this sense, Dante stresses the absolute morality of God's
art: unlike human art which in *Purgatorio* xi is symbolically

---

[32] *Summa Theologiae*, ia, q. 1, art. 9, resp. Blackfriars' translation, pp. 33-4.

[33] The whole passage reads: "Poetry employs metaphors for the sake of
representation, in which we are born to take delight. Holy teaching, on the
other hand, adopts them for their indispensable usefulness, as just explained"
(*Summa Theologiae*, ia, q. 1, art. 9, resp. p. 35).

[34] The classical text where the lure of beauty is probed, and indicted, is
Augustine's *De Doctrina Christiana*, i, iii-iv; see also his *De Vera Religione*,
xxxix, 52: "in quorum consideratione non vana et peritura curiositas exer-
cenda est, sed gradus ad immortalia et semper manentia faciendus." This
same opinion is followed by, among others, Jóhn the Scot, *De Divisione
Naturae*, PL 122, cols. 825-9. More generally, see Edgar De Bruyne, *Etudes
d'esthétique médiévale*; *III. Le XIIIe siècle* (Bruges: "De Tempel," 1946); cf.
also D. W. Robertson, Jr., *A Preface to Chaucer* (Princeton: Princeton University Press, 1962), pp. 52-137.

envisioned as the impermanent work of pride the fame of which lasts briefly (ll. 91-102), God's exemplary art does not stand isolated from moral practice and actually contains within itself its own interpretative paradigms and, in turn, inspires man to moral action. Although in *Purgatorio* XI Dante releases his own work within a temporal succession whereby the earthly fame procured by art is but a breath of wind (ll. 97-9), he also claims that his own poetics is subsumed under the general category of ethics. The claim is common in medieval critical theories and as the Letter to Cangrande has it, "the branch of philosophy which regulates this work in its whole and its parts is morals or ethics, because the whole was undertaken not for speculation but for practical results."[35]

This ethical finality is concretely borne out in *Purgatorio* X by the allusion to the legend of Trajan's salvation. The legend, which was very popular throughout the Middle Ages, tells how Pope Gregory was moved to prayer after hearing the accounts of Trajan's humility and seeing his statue in the Roman forum.[36] It is borne out, more dramatically, by the pilgrim's own process of education which is consistently played out in the canto. The pilgrim is absorbed by the imaginative wonders of God's art and Vergil interrupts him, first, prompting him not to fix "ad un loco la mente" (l. 46), second, announcing the arrival of the proud penitents (ll. 100-3). The pilgrim doubts his perception: in sharp contrast to the clarity of the divine artifice, these shapes are disfigured, veritable images of dissemblances, "maestro, quel ch'io veggio / muover a noi, non mi sembian persone, / e non so che, sì nel veder vaneggio" (ll. 112-4). In effect, we are confronted here by what Dante in the Letter to Cangrande calls the literal

---

[35] Epistola X, par. 16; Toynbee, pp. 178-9.

[36] "Dum igitur quadam vice diu iam defuncto Trajano Gregorius per forum Trajani transiret et huius mansuetudinem judicis recordatus fuisset" (Jacobus a Voragine, *Legenda Aurea*, ed. Th. Graesse [Leipzig: Libreriae Arnoldianae, 1850], p. 196). For the diffusion of the legend in the Middle Ages, see Gaston Paris, *La Légende de Trajan* (Paris: Imprimerie Nationale, 1878), pp. 261-98.

sense of the poem, "the subject of the whole work, understood only literally, is simply the state of the souls after death. For the course of the whole work turns from and around this."[37] The literal sense, however, does not speak its univocal meaning: the shapes are literally figures which, as Buti glosses the line, deceive the sight, "parendo ora una cosa et ora un'altra."[38] To remove the confusion, Vergil provides the doctrinal rationale for the sinners' cramped forms, "la grave condizione / di lor tormento a terra li rannicchia" (ll. 115-6). The phrase "a terra" renders graphically and even extends the etymological overtone of humility; the epithet "grave" alludes to *gravitas*, the burden of sinful love that pulled the sinners downward, under the stones, from which finally they can begin their ascent.[39]

Dante, in a gesture that mimes Vergil's repeated moral guidance of the pilgrim, addresses his readers urging them to look beyond the corrupt forms:

> Non vo' però, lettor, che tu ti smaghi
> di buon proponimento per udire
> come Dio vuol che 'l debito si paghi.
> Non attender la forma del martìre:
> pensa la succession; pensa ch'al peggio
> oltre la gran sentenza non può ire,
>
> ll. 106-11

(But, reader, I would not have you turned from good resolution for hearing how God wills the debt shall be paid. Heed not the form of the pain: think what follows, think that at the worst it cannot go beyond the great Judgment.)

---

[37] "Est ergo subiectum totius operis, literaliter tantum accepti, status animarum post mortem simpliciter sumptus. Nam de illo et circa illum totius operis versatur processus" (Epistola x, par. 8; Toynbee, p. 174).

[38] Francesco da Buti, *Commento sopra la* Divina Commedia *di Dante Allighieri*, ed. Crescentino Giannini (Pisa: Fratelli Nistri, 1860), ii, 239.

[39] See above, chapter 4, note 31.

In a real sense, the address is a miniature compression of the dialectical movement of the poem, the effort of the poet, that is to say, to make his text an act of knowledge, an "essemplo," and give the reader the same cognitive standpoint as the poet. Just as Cato and Vergil have alerted the pilgrim to the dangers of the esthetic snares, Dante now moves to dispel the possible enchantments and to remind the reader of the wedge that separates the form from its truth. This *caveat* hinges on the word "smaghi"; this word, used elsewhere to describe the guiles of the sirens, the false honey of their songs and promises,[40] or Rachel enthralled by self-reflection in the mirror,[41] provides an esthetic context for the temptation that might otherwise lead the reader away from good resolve. Obliquely, Dante raises the possibility that the moral meaning of the image may be forfeited by the appearance and that a temporal split exists between appearance and meaning.

To be sure, critics have always noted the ambiguities in what is often referred to as the poet's drama, the tension between "esthetic" compassion and "ethical" distance in the representation of characters punished in Hell.[42] In *Paradiso*, the appearance of the souls is overtly given as a pure metaphor drained of any substantial reality.[43] In *Paradiso* IV, we are told at some length, the spirits showed themselves forth in the heaven of the Moon, not because that sphere is allotted to them, but "per far segno" (l. 38) of the degree of beatitude they enjoy. In poetic terms this is a metaphoric ac-

[40] " 'Io son,' cantava, 'io son dolce serena, / che 'marinari in mezzo mar dismago; / tanto son di piacere a sentir piena! / Io volsi Ulisse del suo cammin vago / al canto mio' " (*Purgatorio* XIX, ll. 19-23).

[41] " 'Per piacermi a lo specchio, qui m'addorno; / ma mia suora Rachel mai non si smaga / dal suo miraglio, e siede tutto giorno' " (*Purgatorio* XXVII, ll. 103-5).

[42] This antinomy, which is stressed in the work of Nardi, Fubini, etc., is at the center of the Romantic assumptions of Francesco De Sanctis, *Lezioni e saggi su Dante*, ed. Sergio Romagnoli (Turin: Einaudi, 1955).

[43] For the metaphoric nature of *Paradiso*, see Mazzeo, pp. 46-7; see also John Freccero, "*Paradiso* x: The Dance of the Stars," *Dante Studies*, 86 (1968), pp. 85-111; Marguerite Mills Chiarenza, "The Imageless Vision and Dante's *Paradiso*," *Dante Studies*, 90 (1972), pp. 77-91.

commodation of spiritual realities to sense perception, a condescension to the human faculty which can only apprehend
through visible representations. This same principle, Beatrice
says, alluding to Aquinas' account of biblical metaphor, sustains Scripture which metaphorically "piedi e mano / at-
tribuisce a Dio e altro intende" (ll. 44-5).[44] Even the opinion
of the *Timaeus* to the effect that the souls return to the stars
cannot be taken literally, "e forse sua sentenza è d'altra guisa /
che la voce non suona" (ll. 55-6). The two phrases, "altro intende," and "altra guisa che la voce non suona," it might be
pointed out, echo the conventional terminology of allegory.
Isidore of Seville defines allegory as "alieniloquium. Aliud
enim sonat, et aliud intelligitur."[45]

Though without the moral implications that characterize
the representations of *Inferno*, metaphor in *Paradiso* dramatizes
the internal distance between signs and their reality in both
biblical and secular texts and in the pictorial representation of
the angels in Church (ll. 46-8). This distance is the thread that
also runs through the various modes of representation that
Dante deploys in his poem. The sense of a deeply divided perception has thematic weight in *Purgatorio*: on the one hand,
experience is arranged according to degrees and quality of sin
which convey the poet's firm and unremitting moral judgment; on the other hand, we are confronted with the figments
of both penitents and pilgrim variously seeking esthetic relief,
tempted by nostalgia and the chimeras of the night which
threaten that moral pattern with disruption.[46] All of these un-

[44] "Non enim cum scriptura nominat Dei brachium, est literalis sensus
quod in Deo sit membrum huiusmodi corporale: sed id quod per hoc membrum significatur, scilicet virtus operativa" (*Summa Theologiae*, Ia, q. 1, art.
10, ad tertium).

[45] *Etym.*, I, xxxvii, 22; cf. also Epistola x, par. 7 (Toynbee, p. 174): "Nam
allegoria dicitur ab *alleon* graece, quod in latinum dicitur alienum, sive
diversum."

[46] *Purgatorio* II, ll. 106-23; VIII, ll. 1-6 where the motif of nostalgia for the
homeland is alluded to (on this question see notes 77-80 of this chapter); XIX,
ll. 10-33. See, more generally, Francis Fergusson, *Dante's Drama of the Mind*
(Princeton: Princeton University Press, 1953).

certainties have always been treated as local oscillations,
momentary illusory lapses which the poet always transcends
in the compass of his moral vision.

And more forcefully now than ever before, the poet interrupts the narrative to correct the faulty vision of fallen man
and give the "superbi cristian" an insight beyond the blindness of self-deception.

> O superbi cristian, miseri lassi,
>   che, de la vista de la mente infermi,
>   fidanza avete ne' retrosi passi,
> non v'accorgete voi che noi siam vermi
>   nati a formar l'angelica farfalla,
>   che vola a la giustizia sanza schermi?
> Di che l'animo vostro in alto galla,
>   poi siete quasi antomata in difetto,
> sì come vermo in cui formazion falla?
>
> *Purgatorio* x, ll. 121-9

(O proud Christians, weary wretches who, sick in the
mind's vision, put trust in backward steps, are you not
aware that we are worms born to form the angelic butterfly that flies to judgment without defences? Why does
your mind soar up so high, since you are as it were imperfect insects, like the worm in which full form is wanting?)

The rapid shift of pronoun, "voi," "noi" overtly collapses the
distance between the poet, who generally occupies an omnis-
cient perspective, and fallen man by the suggestion that either
is caught in the bane and sorrow of original sin. The image of
"vermi," employed in *Inferno* for Lucifer and in patristic
exegesis for the fallen children of Adam, stresses precisely the
reality of the Fall and the sense of shared degradation. But this
identification with the sinners is also a strategy to give weight
to the poet's moral wisdom, root it in the awareness of a
common plight and, thus, sanction the authority of his
stance. This is, in reality, the tone of Dante's voice that

readers are most familiar with: a voice which combines affective identification with ethical detachment and which, for all the alliterative resonances of the apostrophe (the fricatives "v" and "f" abound), does not cajole the reader into fatuous complacencies but forces him to stare into the depths of man's misery and glimpse, beyond that, beneath the cocoon the redemption available to him.

The soul's redemption, described through the metamorphosis of the worm into a butterfly, is primarily a specimen of Dante's revision of the neoplatonic allegoresis of the flight of the soul. Though in Plato the myth is generally represented in the guise of a bird in flight, the symbolic equation between soul and butterfly depends on the ambivalence of the term *psyché*, an equivocal homonym which designates both the soul and the butterfly. Undoubtedly, the ambivalence of the Greek word was not directly available to Dante. Yet, the association persisted in a Latin tradition which is highly significant to Dante's present context of plastic representations. It can be found in an epitaph on a Florentine gravestone;[47] in addition, among the symbolic bas-reliefs and decorations hewn on murals, monuments and cinerary urns, a steady emblem is precisely the allegory of Psyche in the form of a butterfly to mark death as the point where the perilous journey into the beyond begins.[48] There is good reason to believe

[47] "Papilio volitans texto religatus aranist: illi praeda ripens, huic data mors subitast." This is inscription 1063 in *Carmina Latina Epigraphica*, ed. Franciscus Buecheler, II (Amsterdam: Adolf M. Hakkert, 1972), p. 489. For the butterfly as the symbol of the soul, and extensive bibliography, see *Dictionnaire d'archéologie chrétienne et liturgie*, ed. F. Cabrol (Paris: Letouzey and Ane, 1907), under "Ame," I, 1543-54; cf. also Maxime Colligon, *Essai sur les monuments grecs et romains relatifs au mythe de Psyché* (Paris: Thorin, 1877), pp. 13 ff. and esp. p. 41, where another funereal inscription is recorded in which the word *papilio* is employed for *anima*.

[48] Colligon, *Essai sur les monuments*, gives a detailed catalogue of the representation of Psyche on monuments, murals at Pompei, Florence, Rome, etc., pp. 85-159. For further bibliography, see *Ausführliches Lexikon der griechischen und römischen Mythologie*, ed. W. H. Roscher (Leipzig: B. G. Teubner, 1902-1909), 3.2, cols. 3240-58; for a general view of the question, see Franz Cumont, *After Life in Roman Paganism* (New Haven: Yale University Press, 1922).

that this figurative tradition stands behind Dante's own dramatic embodiment of the flight of the soul: in a canto filled with allegorical sculptures, it is apt that Dante should employ an allegorical motif which in all likelihood could only be found as a sculpture.

In the pagan representations, largely inspired by Apuleius' *Metamorphosis*, the fabulous allegory of the ascent of Psyche is consigned to the natural order: the soul is a butterfly when at death the tortures of Eros cease and the garments of the body are finally shed. Dante displaces this allegory into the order of grace, moors the myth to a theological structure. The key word for this conceptual transvaluation is the epithet "superbi." *Superbia*, etymologically an upward flight of the natural man, turns out for Dante to be inevitably a fall. The word "lassi," on which line 121 comes to an end, carries with it the overtone of the Latin "lapsi" and seals this fall. The soul returns to its pristine purity not when it is a disembodied spirit: in Dante's context, it is beyond death, through the pain of purification, that the worm is metamorphosed into a butterfly.

If the doctrinal strain of the apostrophe is to invert both the substance and the direction of the soul's *paideia*, its main burden is to refocus on the notion of form. In the address to the reader, "forma" as a mere esthetic category darkening the reader's moral judgment had to be eschewed by him. In the apostrophe to the "superbi cristian," Dante redefines form in rigorously ethical terms: "formar" and "formazion" imply that form cannot designate a fixed and self-enclosed totality; it epitomizes, on the contrary, an ongoing process of spiritual unfolding, an emblem of a constant and gradual movement to be perfected when the soul reaches the "giustizia senza schermi." It is, in effect, only after this detour on the ethical value of form that Dante returns to the narrative and clearly discerns the distorted shapes of the penitents which he likens to the classical caryatids, the figures that lend support to ceilings.

Come per sostentar solaio o tetto,
per mensola talvolta una figura
si vede giugner le ginocchia al petto,
la qual fa del non ver vera rancura
nascere 'n chi la vede; così fatti
vid' io color, quando puosi ben cura.

ll. 130-5

(As for corbel to support a ceiling or a roof, sometimes a
figure is seen to join the knees to the breast which,
though unreal, begets real distress in him that sees it, so
fashioned did I see these when I gave good heed.)

The force of the simile is extraordinary: in literal terms, it
resumes and extends the iconographic metaphorics which
sustain the vault of the canto; it hints at the same time, by
comparing the low-lying souls with the figures set on high, at
those souls' askesis; it implies that, like corbels supporting a
roof, the sinners' suffering is no gratuitous esthetic decora-
tion, but is functional to their redemption; it renders exactly
the patient appearance of the penitents. From Buti to
Sapegno, critics have remarked on the realism of the simile,[49]
but have neglected the complications of the term "figura":[50]
for the caryatid is literally a *fictura*, a mere fictional surface devoid of depth and, for all its materiality, is an empty stone, an
image of "non ver." In the address to the reader, the appearance was a potentially misleading illusion, a contingent condi-

[49] N. Sapegno in his commentary, *La Divina Commedia* (Milan and Naples:
Ricciardi, 1957), p. 511, writes: "Le cariatidi erano un elemento importante
nell'architettura romanica e gotica ed erano ritratte con spirito fortemente
realistico." He then goes on to quote Buti's view that "si scolpiscono alcuna
volta omini co le ginocchia al petto che paiono sostenere tutto quel carico,
sicché chi li vede n'hae rancura."

[50] H. Gmelin, *op. cit.*, p. 209: "figura significa anche 'detto,' 'parola,'
'frase.' " A much more thorough view of *figura* as *fictura* can be found in
Gioacchino Paparelli, "*Fictio*," in *Ideologia e poesia di Dante*, pp. 99-103; Erich
Auerbach, "Figura," in *Scenes from the Drama of European Literature*, pp.
11-76.

tion distracting the mind from the inner truth of the appearance, the *forma perfectior* which awaits the sinners; now, the simile, which ostensibly denotes the ultimate unreality of the "forma del martire," reverses the terms: it gives substantiality to the fictional appearance and is not itself directed toward a meaning to be eventually disclosed. More important, however hollow the outside surface may be, it cannot be bypassed and, actually, it begets a real pathos which resists and is possibly foreign to facile transpositions to a definite moral sense.

By so doing, Dante insinuates the oblique and shadowy path of metaphoric language in which truth and fiction have a simultaneous existence and the presumed unity of sign and meaning is shattered. He decidedly obliterates, in other words, the distinction between allegory of poets and allegory of theologians conventionally based on the fictive or nonfictive status of the literal sense, and in effect, he absorbs what is radically new in Aquinas' hermeneutics. Aquinas knew well that because of figurative language, the road of understanding is not *a priori* certain and that the very foundation of scriptural meaning could be sapped by the presence of metaphors. He short-circuits the impasse by claiming that we should interpret the semantic doubleness of metaphors and bring to a closure the displacements of meaning from the perspective of the Divine Author.[51] It is from this same awareness that Dante's sense of the necessity of interpretation derives. Because literary language is engulfed in duplicity, whereby things are not what they appear and images are seductive traps, Dante interprets the neoplatonic allegory from a definite theological standpoint; at the same time, the reader is overtly urged to transcend the contingent and deceptive forms and see the pen-

[51] "That God is the author of Holy Scripture should be acknowledged. . . . Now because the literal sense is what the author intends, and the author of Holy Scripture is God who comprehends everything all at once in his understanding, it comes not amiss as St. Augustine observes, if many meanings are present even in the literal sense of one passage of Scripture. Hence: I. These various readings do not set up ambiguity or any other kind of mixture of meanings." *Summa Theologiae*, Ia, q. 1, art. 10; Blackfriars' translation pp. 37-8.

itents from the endpoint of the temporal sequence. The lines, "pensa la succession; pensa ch'al peggio / oltre la gran sentenza non può ire," refer precisely to the Day of Judgment, the apocalyptic time when the drama of history reaches its denouement and no rupture will exist between appearance and reality.

The emphasis on the "end" is possibly the most Augustinian trait in Dante's poetics. In St. Augustine's epistemology, signs and their meanings never coincide and it is in the silent space of the end, when the articulation of the syllables of a text, a life, and history is over, that meaning surfaces. The present has no space and, as he writes in the famous passage in book XI of the *Confessions*, understanding has necessarily a retrospective structure:

> Suppose I am about to recite a psalm which I know. Before I begin, my expectation [or "looking forward"] is extended over the whole psalm. But once I have begun, whatever I pluck off from it and let fall into the past enters the province of my memory [or "looking back at"]. So the life of this action of mine is extended in two directions—toward my memory, as regards what I have recited, and toward my expectation, as regards what I am about to recite. . . . And as I proceed further and further with my recitation, so the expectation grows shorter and the memory grows longer, until all the expectation is finished at the point when the whole of this action is over and has passed into the memory. And what is true of the whole psalm is also true of every part of the psalm and of every syllable in it. The same holds good for any longer action, of which the psalm may be a part. It is true also of the whole of a man's life, of which all of his actions are parts. And it is true of the whole history of humanity, of which the lives of men are parts.[52]

[52] St. Augustine, *Confessions*, XI, xxviii; *CSEL* XXXII. The English text is from *The Confessions of St. Augustine*, trans. Rex Warner (New York and Toronto: The New American Library, 1963), p. 282.

Critics have variously spoken of the "typology of death" in
the *Divine Comedy*, and have given a special importance to the
end as the point where the temporal dislocation of meaning
ceases and in retrospect the sense of one's life emerges in its
immutable essence.[53]

This notion of the end, it has been maintained, structures
the very movement of the poem. The poet writes from the
point of view of a self that has reached self-understanding in
God and looks back in memory to recount the stages of the
pilgrim's painful itinerary to God. In this sense, the vision of
God's book in *Paradiso* XXXIII is the solid ground, the substance on which the poet's authority rests; and it is the point
where the linear quest of the pilgrim ends, bends into a circle
and its metaphoric narrative starts.[54] This dramatic strategy
accounts for the double focus of the poem as it is conventionally understood: as a story of a conversion that the poem
tells, the poet knows more than the pilgrim does and the text
is seen to enact an extended series of palinodes, a systematic
discharging of convictions and beliefs the pilgrim once held

[53] This view was reemphasized by Erich Auerbach's notion that death dis-
closes and fulfills the historical existence of each soul. See both his essay,
"Figura" in *Scenes from the Drama of European Literature*, pp. 60-76; and
Mimesis, pp. 166-77. See also the more recent probings by A. C. Charity,
Events and Their Afterlife, pp. 184-207.

[54] See, for instance, John Freccero, "Dante's Prologue Scene," *Dante
Studies*, 84 (1966), esp. p. 20, where he writes that "for Dante, the distance
between protagonist and poet is at its maximum distance at the beginning of
the story and is gradually closed by the dialectic of poetic process until pilgrim and poet coincide at the ending of the poem, which gives unity and
coherence to all that went before. . . . It is at the last moment that the
metamorphosis of the pilgrim's view of the world is completed, when he
himself has become metamorphosed into the poet, capable at last of writing
the story we have read." See also Singleton's remarks that at the end "the
poem comes full circle. . . . [The poet's] voice speaks, of course, in the present tense, for the poet's struggle is *now*. This *now* alternates from here on
with the *then* of the narrative, and when the *then* and the *now*, as the two lines
of this final action, merge, the poem ends, in a focus of eternity" (*Paradiso 2*.
Commentary, Bollingen Series LXXX [Princeton: Princeton University Press,
1975], pp. 571-2).

while the text is an experience which in itself is outside of error. The critical fruitfulness of this notion of the end and its concomitant view of conversion has been such that one hesitates to reexamine and probe its limits. Yet, it can be shown that this image of reassuring coherence that the text overtly displays is unsettled at its very core. For in the *Divine Comedy* writing is not a pure act of recollection of the pilgrim's past experience or a metaphoric version of that past. It is, rather, an interpretative quest which throws into question the poet's voice of authority and the stability of his standpoint. To illustrate briefly this point let us look at *Inferno* xxv where the poet *qua* poet starts the gruesome description of the thieves metamorphosed into snakes and breaks out into a poetic challenge to the poets of the pagan past.

> Taccia Lucano omai là dov' e' tocca
> del misero Sabello e di Nasidio,
> e attenda a udir quel ch'or si scocca.
> Taccia di Cadmo e d'Aretusa Ovidio,
> ché se quello in serpente e quella in fonte
> converte poetando, io non l'invidio
>   ll. 94-9

(Let Lucan from this moment on be silent, where he tells of wretched Sabellus and of Nasidius, and wait to hear that which now is uttered. Let Ovid be silent concerning Cadmus and Arethusa, for if, poetizing, he converts one into a snake and the other into a fountain, I envy him not.)

By this hybristic apostrophe (an extension of the *taceat* or *cedat nunc* rhetorical motif)[55] Dante crushes any lingering impression that the limbo of poets, among whom he met both Ovid and Lucan, is an imaginative oasis where poets are engaged in

---

[55] For the *topos*, see E. R. Curtius, *European Literature and the Latin Middle Ages*, pp. 162-5.

serene conversation. More to the point, the apostrophe marks a dramatic and hidden discrepancy between the pilgrim's descent into humility and the poet's voice of pride. As the poet lapses into pride, he insinuates that he is caught in a precariousness which both undermines any claim of the poet, who has reached a synoptic view of reality, to a privileged position, and negates the notion that the poem is simply an "essemplo," a moral and ironic fable in which time is the ironic principle of knowledge.

One cannot dismiss the scene simply as an imaginative experience bound to Hell: on the contrary, much like the paradigmatic canto of Ulysses, which follows this act of hybris and which to a large extent is occasioned by it, the scene is a warning that the poem, in spite of its doctrine and its subtle moral distinctions, has no quick moral substance that the reader can extract. Writing is an act fraught with threats and temptations in the same way that the journey of the pilgrim was, and the text describes more than a temporal movement from the partial, fragmented knowledge of the pilgrim to the poet's total view at the end. The poem is actually open-ended, with the poet away from his promised land and still in exile.

If the journey of writing has not an end where all its promises are fulfilled, how does the poem come to an end? What is the exile with which poetry seems to be synonymous? We must provisionally single out as having a special, revelatory function the ending of the poem, the point which is conventionally given special importance, because it is there that the sense of the poem lies. Quite explicitly, in *Paradiso* XXXIII, the focus of attention is the mighty effort to bring the poem to a closure and sanction it as a totality.[56] The canto is articulated

[56] The prayer to the Virgin has been studied by Erich Auerbach, "Dante's Prayer to the Virgin (*Paradiso* XXXIII) and Earlier Eulogies," *Romance Philology*, 3 (1949), pp. 1-26. A number of important historical suggestions has been advanced by Aldo Vallone, *Studi su Dante medioevale* (Florence: Olschki, 1965), pp. 83-109; for an esthetic reading of the canto, see Benedetto Croce, "L'ultimo canto della *Divina Commedia*," in *Poesia antica e moderna* (Bari: Laterza, 1950), pp. 151-61; see also Mario Fubini, "L'ultimo canto del *Paradiso*," in *Il peccato di Ulisse e altri scritti danteschi* (Milan: Ricciardi, 1966),

along a metaphoric pattern of gathering and closing, which, though it has gone unnoticed by critics, is of paramount importance to Dante's poetic strategy. The canto opens with St. Bernard's prayer to the Virgin, who is still point in the chain of mediations to God. Through her, the hierarchical order of the universe reverses into paradoxes, and her womb appears, in the tradition of St. Bernard's own commentary on the Song of Songs, as the sacred space, the *hortus conclusus* in which Christ, the flower, has spontaneously blossomed.[57] More fundamentally, the anaphoric sequence on which the prayer is articulated insists on the Virgin as the fixed point to which all things return, the enclosure of salvation history, "In te misericordia, in te pietate, / in te magnificenza, in te *s'aduna* / quantunque in creatura è di bontate" (ll. 19-21).

The metaphorics of ingathering and closure are explicitly recalled both at the point where the poet defines the supreme light as that in which the good "tutto s'accoglie in lei" (l. 104) and where the pilgrim looks into the universal form of the knot, the holy center that sustains and binds the scattered multiplicity of the world.

> Nel suo profondo vidi che s'interna,
>   legato con amore in un volume,
>   ciò che per l'universo si squaderna:
> sustanze e accidenti e lor costume
>   quasi conflati insieme, per tal modo
>   che ciò ch'i' dico è un semplice lume.
> La forma universal di questo nodo
>   credo ch'i' vidi, perchè più di largo,
>   dicendo questo, mi sento ch'i' godo.
>   ll. 85-93

---

pp. 101-36; see also M. Rossi, "L'ultimo canto del poema," in *Gusto filologico e gusto poetico* (Bari: Laterza, 1942), pp. 129-48.

[57] " 'Nel ventre tuo si raccese l'amore, / per lo cui caldo ne l'etterna pace / così è germinato questo fiore' " (*Paradiso* xxxiii, ll. 7-9); cf. "Non est locus voluptatis nisi uterus Virginis" (*In nativitate Domini*, PL 184, col. 837); cf. also "Hortus deliciarum nobis est . . . tuus uterus, o Maria; electus est" (*PL* 184, cols. 1011-2); for other references, see Vallone, p. 96.

(In its depth I saw ingathered, bound by love in one
single volume, that which is dispersed in leaves throughout the universe: substances and accidents and their relations, as though fused together in such a way that what I
tell is but a simple light. The universal form of this knot I
believe that I saw, because, in telling this, I feel my joy
increase.)[58]

The metaphor faintly recalls Ezekiel's vision of the book,
"and behold, a hand was sent to me, wherein was a book
rolled up, and he spread it before me, and it was written
within and without," which Aquinas glosses as "liber involutus ornatu verborum . . . Est etiam involutus profundi-
tate mysteriorum."[59] The pilgrim stands and gains access to
the love that binds the book together, the Author, who, according to the definition Dante gives in *Convivio*, chains
words together. In book IV, chapter vi, Dante defines "authority" as follows:

We must know, then, that authority is nothing else than
an act of an author. This word [that is *autore* and without
its third letter c] may have two origins: one from a verb
quite fallen into disuse in grammar which means to link
words together, namely AUIEO ("che significa tanto
quanto 'legare parole,' cioè auieo"). And anyone who
considers it in its first voice will plainly see that it demonstrates itself, that it is made entirely of the links of
words, that is of the five vowels alone which are the soul
and connecting links of every word; and is composed of
them in a way that may be varied to represent the image

[58] It might be pointed out that in the *Vita nuova* (ed. Tommaso Casini
[Florence: Sansoni, 1962], xxv), Dante describes the process of poetic
myth-making as a movement from accidents to substances: "Dunque se noi
vedemo, che li poeti hanno parlato a le cose inanimate sì come se avessero
senso o ragione, e fattale parlare insieme; e non solamente cose vere, ma cose
non vere (ciò è che detto hanno . . . che molti accidenti parlano, sì come fossero sustanzie ed uomini)" (p. 140). Dante, I would suggest, views God in
Paradiso XXXIII as the maker of the perfect metaphor.

[59] Thomas Aquinas, *In Threnos Jeremiae Expositio*, *Opera Omnia* XIX, 199.

of a link ("che solo di legame di parole è fatto, cioè di sole cinque vocali, che sono anima e legame d'ogni parole, e composto d'esse per modo volubile, a figurare imagine di legame"). Because beginning with A we then turn back into U and come directly by I into E, whence we turn again to the O; so that this figure of a link really represents the vowels aeiou. And how far "author" comes from this verb we learn only from the poets, who have linked their words together with musical art.[60]

In the context of *Convivio*, this is the significance that Dante leaves behind in favor of philosophical authority in the sense of "autentin," that which is worthy of faith.[61] Here in *Paradiso*, the notion of God the Poet and Author, "Alfa" and "O" (*Paradiso* XXVI, l. 17) is retrieved to seal, as it were, by the authority and power of the Logos the poet's words.

St. Bernard's prayer culminates with a reference to the saints, who, interceding that the final vision may be granted to the pilgrim, emblematically "chiudon le mani" (l. 39). The prayer also requests that the fog of the flesh may be dispelled from the pilgrim, ". . . tutti miei prieghi / ti porgo, e priego che non sieno scarsi, / perchè tu ogne nube li disleghi / di sua mortalità co' prieghi tuoi" (ll. 29-30). The phrase, "ogne nube li disleghi di sua mortalità" partially translates "dissice terrenae nebulas et pondera molis" from the famous ninth hymn of the third book of *De Consolatione Philosophiae*. The context that surrounds the line is immediately relevant, I would like to propose, to the thematics of *Paradiso* XXXIII. In strictly neoplatonic language, Boethius addresses the Creator as "Tu numeris elementa ligas" and celebrates the order of

---

[60] *Convivio*, IV, vi, 3-5. The English version is by Katharine Hillard, pp. 252-3.

[61] "The other origin of 'author,' as Uguccione witnesses in the beginning of his Derivations, is a Greek word, *autenta*, which is equivalent in Latin to 'worthy of faith and obedience.' . . . That Aristotle is most worthy of faith and obedience, and that his words are of supreme and highest authority, can be proved thus" (*Convivio*, IV, vi, 5-6; Hillard, p. 253). See also above, chapter 4, note 14.

creation held together by "sure knots which nothing can un-
tie";[62] in this context, the prayer that the earthly weight may
be cast off is for him, as well as for Dante, the condition
which allows man to be part of the harmonious whole of the
universe. But Dante, unlike the neoplatonists, also insists that
man cannot measure the design of creation: by an oblique recall of the metaphors of enclosure, he describes the vision of
the Trinity as three circles of three colors and one magnitude,
each circle reflecting the other (ll. 116-9). The pilgrim seems
to see the circling depicted "de la nostra effige" (l. 131), but
he, like the geometer who cannot square the circle, cannot
find the principle and the point at which the image is conformed to the circle (ll. 133-8). The allusion to the geometer,
etymologically the earth measurer who tries to establish
boundaries and the shape of space, implies that the mathe-
matical representation of nature does not give an exact
knowledge and is thwarted by an elusive surd. The final vision is granted to the pilgrim by a special grace whereby the
mind is smitten by a flash and joins the whirling spheres revolving concentrically around the Prime Mover.

These images of binding, gathering, and untying are the
thematic scaffolds which dramatize the perfection of the cosmos and within which the poet attempts to recollect and en-
close all he has seen within the intelligibility of his language.
Memory is the crucial metaphor for this process of gathering.
For Augustine, who ponders the problem of memory in order
to find God's traces in it, memory is the "belly of the mind,"
"a large and boundless chamber" which contains "reasons
and laws innumerable of numbers," the affections of the mind
and the "treasures of innumerable images." Experiences glide
into its deeper recesses and to think means to collect the images out of their dispersion ("ex quadam dispersione colligenda") and rearrange them in the memory.[63] More

---

[62] Boethius, *The Consolation of Philosophy*, with the English translation rev.
by H. F. Stewart (Cambridge, Mass.: Harvard University Press, 1968), III,
meter II, p. 233. For a general view of the relationship of Dante to Boethius,
see Rocco Murari, *Dante e Boezio* (Bologna: Zanichelli, 1905).

[63] *Confessions*, x, viii.

explicitly, as Hugh of St. Victor explores the didactic function of memory, he defines it as an act of gathering.

I do not think one should fail to say here that just as ap-
titude investigates and discovers through analysis, so
memory retains by gathering. The things which we have
analysed in the course of learning and we must commit
to memory we ought, therefore, to gather. Now
"gathering" is reducing to a brief and compendious outline which has been written or discussed at some length
[. . . Memoria colligendo custodit. Oportet ergo ut quae
discendo divisimus commendando memoriae ea col-
ligamus. Colligere est ea de quibus prolixius vel scriptum
vel disputatum est ad brevem quamdam et compen-
diosam summam redigere]. The ancients called such an
outline an "epilogue," that is, a short restatement, by
headings, of things already said. . . . The fountainhead is
one, but its derivative streams are many: why follow the
windings of the latter? Lay hold upon the source and you
have the whole thing. I say this because the memory of
man is dull and likes brevity, and, if it is dissipated in
many things, it has less to bestow upon each of them. We
ought, therefore, in all that we learn gather brief and de-
pendable abstracts to be stored in the little chest of memory, so that later on, when need arises, we can derive everything else from them. . . .[64]

The importance of mnemonic devices and techniques for
Hugh's theory of learning is the very principle of structure in
Dante's literary works. The *Vita nuova* is openly acknowledged as a book of memory. Its exordium states that in that
part of the "libro de la mia memoria dinanzi a la quale poco si

[64] *The Didascalicon of Hugh of St. Victor*, trans. Jerome Taylor (New York
and London: Columbia University Press, 1968), III, 11, pp. 93-4. The Latin
paragraph is from *PL* 176, cols. 772-3 (where it is given as chapter 12). For
the problem of memory in Hugh, see Grover A. Zinn, Jr., "Hugh of Saint
Victor and the Art of Memory," *Viator*, 5 (1974), pp. 211-34. For the more
general problem of memory, see Frances Yates, *The Art of Memory* (Chicago:
The University of Chicago Press, 1966), esp. pp. 50-81.

potrebbe leggere, si trova una rubrica la quale dice: Incipit
Vita Nova," and that the poet's intention is to "assemplare,"
to copy and edit into a little book the essential meaning (the
"sentenzia") of the larger book of memory. In this autobiographical account, memory gives itself as the paradigm which
grounds the representation not in a fine fabling ("parlare
fabuloso"), but in the poet's personal history.[65]
The *Divine Comedy* is also a book of memory. In the pro-
tasis of *Inferno*, the invocation of the Muses "O muse, o alto
ingegno, or m' aiutate; / o mente che scrivesti ciò ch'io vidi, /
qui si parrà la tua nobilitate" (*Inferno* II, ll. 7-9), casts memory
as the custodian of the pilgrim's vision and the metaphor
which scans the unfolding of the poem. In *Paradiso* XXIII,
while the poet has no remembrance of the spectacle of
Christ's triumph, he cannot efface from the book that records
the past ("non si stingue / del libro che 'l preterito rassegna,"
ll. 53-4) Beatrice's proffer that he open his eyes and look on
her.

We cannot minimize, in effect, the poet's intense effort to
remember in *Paradiso* XXXIII: repeatedly the poet asks the
"somma luce" to relend to his mind "un poco di quel che
parevi" (l. 69) for "per tornare alquanto a mia memoria / e per
sonare un poco in questi versi, / più si conceperà di tua vittoria" (ll. 73-5). And he registers both the memory of his
boldness in sustaining with his gaze the keenness of the living
ray (ll. 76-81) and the faint recollection of the light in which
all the good is gathered (ll. 99-108). We cannot minimize the
importance of the memorative effort because it implies more
than simply a nostalgia for the original epiphany. It brings
into focus, rather, the poet's desire to give his language a referential stability, to found the traces and signs of memory in
the substance of God's vision. It is from the standpoint of this
remembered final vision that the author can be led to a retrospective unification of his experience and the reader to a
critical decipherment of the work.

[65] On this aspect of the *Vita nuova*, cf. Charles S. Singleton, *An Essay on
the* Vita Nuova (Cambridge, Mass.: Harvard University Press, 1949), pp.
26-9.

But memory, conventionally the mother of the Muses and a priviledged metaphor because through it the images of the past survive and are given a renewed presence, fails the poet. It fails primarily because it cannot duplicate the world of reality. Dante, actually, entertains no naive illusion about the power of memory to recover the past in its immediacy. As the *oculus imaginationis*, which is its standard definition, memory preserves only images and phantasms and always lags behind the experience it attempts to represent.[66] In *Paradiso* I, while the poet states his theme to be what memory has treasured up (ll. 10-11), he also acknowledges that memory cannot follow the movement of the intellect, "che dietro la memoria non può ire" (l. 9). Memory is a metaphor of time in the most profound sense of the term: it tries to recover the past and safeguard it from oblivion; by the same token, it marks the temporal distance between reality and its image and makes the text a pure representation, not in the sense of a mimesis, but in the sense of an interpretation, just as in the *Vita nuova*, of the experience it attempts to renew. This interpretation has no absolute validity because memory is endangered by forgetfulness.

Statements of forgetfulness abound in *Paradiso* XXXIII: "Da quinci innanzi il mio veder fu maggio / che 'l parlar mostra, ch'a tal vista cede, / e cede la memoria a tanto oltraggio" (ll. 55-7); the single moment of vision, we are told, is shrouded in more oblivion than "venticinque secoli a la 'mpresa / che fè Nettuno ammirar l'ombra d'Argo" (ll. 94-6);[67] the poet's speech falls shorter, "pur a quel ch'io ricordo," than that of an infant still bathing his tongue at the breast (ll. 106-8). In a sense, this oblivion is as important as the act of remembrance. For by forgetting the final vision Dante gives what is forgotten a unique and unrepeatable presence and preserves it intact and inviolate. Yet, the logical implications of forgetting are such that it releases the presence it supposedly guards into a

[66] Yates, pp. 32 ff.
[67] Peter Dronke, "Boethius, Alanus and Dante," *Romanische Forschungen*, 78 (1966), pp. 119-25.

fundamental paradox. To forget means that the past is kept hidden and concealed, it reveals what is hidden. At the same time, forgetting suggests the corruption and unreliability of memory, opens up a gap in the book of memory. Memory, the exercise by which the vision reappears from what has not been concealed and which gathers the fragments out of their dispersion, is laid open and scattered into the shapelessness of oblivion.

> e cede la memoria a tanto oltraggio.
>
> Qual è colui che sognando vede,
>   che dopo 'l sogno la passione impressa
>   rimane, e l'altro a la mente non riede,
> cotal son io, chè quasi tutta cessa
>   mia visione, e ancora mi distilla
>   nel core il dolce che nacque da essa.
> Così la neve al sol si disigilla;
>   così al vento ne le foglie levi
>   si perdea la sentenza di Sibilla.
>
>   ll. 57-66

(And at such excess memory fails. As is he who dreaming sees, and after the dream the passion remains imprinted and the rest returns not to the mind; such am I, for my vision almost wholly fades away, yet the sweetness that was born of it still drops within my heart. Thus is the snow unsealed by the sun; thus in the wind, on the light leaves, the Sybil's sentence was lost.)

In flagrant contrast to the metaphors of gathering and closure which pervade the doctrinal substance of the canto, we are confronted here with a double image of opening and dispersion, the unsealing of the snow in the sun and the scattering of the Sybil's leaves when the door of her cave is opened. Since the thematic burden of the passage is forgetfulness, it is possible to understand the two images as an explicit reversal of commonplace definitions of memory. From Aristotle on to medieval theorists, the impressions on memory are conven-

tionally described as analogous to the imprinting on waxed
tablets and to the permanent marks of a seal on wax;[68] at the
same time, the scattering of leaves in the Sybil's cave turns
around the view held by Augustine that memory is the dark
cave where images are stored to be gathered "ex quadam dispersione" by an act of thought. But beyond these reversals by
which Dante insinuates a breach in the book of memory, the
word "disigilla" has another important resonance. The *sigillum* marks the act of creation; the process of imposing a form
and sealing it with authority:[69] "disigilla," thus, traces the
distance between the book of the gathering Logos and the
dispersion and openness of the poet's book of memory; it
stresses Dante's technique of giving up the myth of the poet
as *Autore* who binds and is conspicuously in charge of his creation and who, like the Creator, shapes a self-sufficient closed
form.

His text, actually, originates from the confusion and fragmentation of a blotted memory, the only lingering trace of
which is the impression of sweetness in the heart. It ought to
be remarked that the phrase "ancora mi distilla nel core il
dolce che nacque da essa" gives the thematic movement of the
poem an unmistakable dramatic coherence. In *Inferno* I, the
poem starts by recording the sense of bitterness of the pilgrim
lost in the dark wood ("Tant'è amara che poco è più morte,"
l. 7), and the fear which "nel lago del cor m'era durata" (l.
20). In *Paradiso* XXXIII, the heart is the receptacle where
sweetness is distilled and gathered. Ostensibly, the poem

---

[68] Cicero, *De Oratore*, II, lxxxvi and lxxxviii; Quintilian, *Institutio oratoria*,
XI, ii; Martianus Capella, *De Nuptiis Philologiae et Mercurii*, ed. A. Dick (1925;
rpt. Stuttgart: B. G. Teubner, 1969), pp. 268-70; for Aristotle, see Yates, pp.
33-6.

[69] The word "sigillum" is used in this precise sense by Alanus de Insulis in
his description of the creation of the soul: "tunc ille sigillum / sumit, ad ipsius
formae vestigia formam / dans animae vultum qualem deposcit idea / im-
primit exemplo, totas usurpat imago / exemplares opes, loquiturque figura
sigillum" (*PL* 210, col. 548). See also Dante's use of the word for the authenticity of money: "Ivi è Romena, là dov'io falsai / la lega suggellata del Batista"
(*Inferno* XXX, ll. 73-4); cf. also *Inferno* XIX, l. 21.

maps a linear movement which consists in the purification of the affections, troubled by sin in the plight of Hell but now experiencing joy after the final vision. The phrase, in effect, is introduced to suggest that the text is what is left over from the vision—as if the text, unable to sustain the visionary burden in its totality, still shares in the original emotion: by what is possibly a pun on the etymology of "ricordo," the "core" preserves a faint memory of the vision.

But this memory is encased in oblivion. *Paradiso* XXXIII, from this point of view, gives a sustained interplay of memory and forgetfulness which symmetrically echoes the one in *Purgatorio* XXXIII. In *Purgatorio* we witness the pilgrim's immersion first into Lethe, which induces a cathartic oblivion of his sinful past, then into Eunoe which revives his weakened faculty. The cleansing ritually prepares the pilgrim to enter the domain of the blessed and, in this sense, it dramatizes the moral import of memory, its central role in the spiritual askesis of the pilgrim. Memory and forgetfulness are coextensive in his moral progress; they implicate and complement each other: the two rivers, we are explicitly told, issue from the same spring, "dinanzi ad esse Eufratès e Tigri / veder mi parve uscir d'una fontana, / e, quasi amici, dipartirsi pigri" (ll. 112-4). In *Paradiso* XXXIII Dante's language oscillates between efforts to remember and statements of oblivion which are simultaneously applied, not to the moral experience of the pilgrim, but to the constitution of the text.

This means that for Dante memory is not the only starting point by which his poetic account is determined and projected, but that the outer layers of memory are blurred by forgetfulness. To say that the matrix of the text is the interplay of memory and forgetfulness is also to imply that memory is always a forgetful memory, permeated by error and forever telling the story of a representation punctuated by absences and gaps which both reveal and hide its significance. There is a special aptness, it should be remarked, in the metaphoric bond that Dante suggests between memory and the revelatory power of dreams. In a sense, he restates the traditional link between memory and the imagination. Like memory, imagination is the world of phantoms deprived of substantiality and arises when its contacts with reality are precarious and uncertain. The famous apostrophe to, and exploration of, the "imaginativa," the image-receiving faculty, in the very center of the poem (*Purgatorio* xvii, ll. 13-45) is introduced by an appeal to the readers' memory which evokes a landscape of half light perceived as if through a thick mist dissipated by the feeble rays of the setting sun (ll. 1-11).[70] This half light mediates between the blinding cloud of smoke in the preceding circle of wrath and the revelation that the eye of the imagination produces. The "imaginativa" does not stem from the impressions of the senses; it descends directly from God who grants to the "alta fantasia" (l. 25) three images of punished wrath, which disappear "come si frange il sonno ove di butto / nova luce percuote il viso chiuso" (ll. 40-1).

In *Paradiso* xxxiii, the content of the vision remains an undeciphered enigma, and as the poet remembers that yet "mi distilla / nel core il dolce che nacque da essa," he casts himself as a writer of glosses. The phrase, I submit, closely echoes a stylized definition of the tropological intelligence of Scripture. In the mystical tradition of biblical exegesis, which owes a great deal to St. Bernard's homilies on the Song of Songs, the tropological level was referred to as a honeycomb, "favus distillat quia quanta dulcedo sapientiae in corde lateat."[71] This was a floating formula which had variations such as "qualia mella sacri favus distillat eloquii" and which is often crystallized in the expression "stillat dulcedo."[72] As the poet registers the sediment of memory, in itself an interpretative process, the sediment constitutes the poet as a reader of God's

[70] For an extended view of the function of the imagination, see Murray Wright Bundy, *The Theory of Imagination in Classical and Medieval Thought* (Urbana: The University of Illinois Press, 1927), pp. 225-56.

[71] Quoted by Henri de Lubac, "Doctor Mellifluus," in *Exégèse médiévale*, ii, 615.

[72] The list of formulas can also be found in Henri de Lubac, *Exégèse médiévale*, ii, 599-620.

book. The hint of the poet as interpreter is countered by the allusion to the loss of the "sentenza di Sibilla." The term "sentenza," which Dante employs in the *Vita nuova* to indicate the allegorical substance extrapolated from the book of memory and in *Paradiso* IV to describe the allegorical sense of Plato's myth of the return of the souls to the stars, calls attention to the poet's interpretative operation.[73] But the "sentenza" is lost and the metaphor of the scattering of the Sybil's leaves, actually, discloses the impossibility of reading and interpreting. In the third book of the *Aeneid*, widely acknowledged as the source of the image, Helenus describes to Aeneas the leaves with signs and dark symbols which flutter in the rocky cave of the Sybil when its door opens, and which cannot be read: the oracle remains undeciphered and the questers who consult the prophetess depart uncounseled, "inconsulti abeunt sedemque odere Sybillae" (l. 452). Even in the *Aeneid* Aeneas' vision of the future of his own life and Roman history, under the guidance of the Sybil, ends on a note that ironically undercuts the substantiality of his vision. The House of Sleep, we are told, has two gates: one is of ivory and it gives exit to delusions and false dreams; the other is of horn and through it pass true shades. After leading Aeneas over every scene of his future, Anchises dismisses the Sybil and his son through the gate of polished ivory (*Aeneid* VI, ll. 893-901). Just as in the *Aeneid*, there is no univocal truth in the vision at the end of the *Divine Comedy*. There is only an interpretation countered by the presence of a concealed and impenetrable message and both together dramatize what might be called the marginality of the text to the Logos.

It is possible to view this marginality of the poet's language, the speechlessness that threatens its articulation (ll. 106-8), as the consequence of a moral choice: the choice, that is, to stop on the threshold of profanation, the poet's humble withdrawal into silent listening before the ineffable presence

---

[73] " 'Quel che Timeo de l'anime argomenta / non è simile a ciò che qui si vede, . . . e forse sua sentenza è d'altra guisa / che la voce non suona, ed esser puote / con intenzion da non esser derisa' " (*Paradiso* IV, ll. 49-57).

of God. More to the point, this marginality discloses the errors of metaphoric language, its attempt and inability to achieve an absolute self-identity and recover full sense. No poet, it must be added, attributes more import to error than Dante. As I have shown in the discussion of Ulysses, the paradigm of the erratic voyager, Dante gives error an epic status and makes it the other name of the quest. In the case of Ulysses, error is madness, a radical mistaking of words for things; in *Paradiso* xxxiii, it designates the poet's suspension in a world of forgetful memory and shifty impressions, of a truth found and another one lost, of metaphors that bear simultaneously a likeness and unlikeness to the reality they represent.

These ambiguities of metaphor account for and engender the possibility of a double reading of the poem. The *Divine Comedy* overtly tells the story of the pilgrim's progress from the sinful state of the "selva oscura" to the beatific vision of *Paradiso* xxxiii. From this point of view, Dante dramatizes the spiritual conversion of the self and envisions the providential order of history and the cosmos as a significant totality. Critics have correctly pointed out that this is a theological allegory, for the poem presents itself as reflecting and sharing in man's pilgrimage to God. It is a text, that is, which belongs to a redeemed order and which shifts its modes of representation, the *visio corporalis, spiritualis* and *intellectualis*, according to the order of reality it renders.[74] But the poem undercuts, and recoils from, this prominent pattern of clear and distinct order. It also tells the story of the persistent ambiguity of metaphoric language in which everything is perpetually fragmented and irreducible to any unification. Alongside the presence of a representation adequate to its spiritual reality, the poem repeatedly dramatizes a world of dissemblance, empty forms and illusory appearances which the poet repeatedly demystifies but to which the poem is irrevocably

[74] Bundy, pp. 169-72 and 233-4. Entirely within the scheme of Bundy is the article by Francis X. Newman, "St. Augustine's Three Visions and the Structure of the *Commedia*," *Modern Language Notes*, 82 (1967), pp. 56-78.

bound. In this sense, the poem always places us in the land of unlikeness of *Inferno* I; it reverses the conventional hierarchy of the pilgrim's distorted vision transcended by the poet's synoptic view and, more generally, it shows that poetry is at odds with its own explicit statement.

There is an important understanding, after all, in Croce's notion of the rupture at the heart of the text and in Auerbach's hesitant conclusion that Dante disrupts the order he creates. These insights are valid, to be sure, only if they are read against the possible intentions of their conceivers—the assumptions, respectively, that the rupture depends on the shortcomings of allegory or on the belief that the ironic movement of history consumes and empties of its sense every literary text. This disruption cannot be accounted for by extrinsic categories of a critic's taste or philosophical bias. It is the very sinew of the text and a consistent and controlled strategy by which Dante turns every statement into an interrogative sentence, reopens questions that seem settled once and for all, asserts the authority of his voice and also knows how fragile the claim to authority can be. It is a banality to say that a reader is a poet's invention; yet, in the case of Dante, one truly feels inescapably caught in the web of his design. The reader is confronted in the *Divine Comedy* with the possibility of two opposed readings which do not deconstruct and cancel each other out, but are simultaneously present and always involve each other.

Allegory describes the process by which the reader (and this, it might be added, is the empirical reality of existing criticism) decides whether the metaphor of the pilgrim's ascent to God is an illusory fiction or has the weight of a truth guaranteed by God; whether the sweetness that distills in the heart is the spiritual joy released by Scripture or simply a variant of that other sweetness which "ancor dentro mi suona" (*Purgatorio* II, l. 114), the esthetic snare of Casella's song. That decision, like Augustine's view of meaning which lies at the end of the temporal articulation of language, places us outside of the text and to decide means that something is always left out, that the poem, bound to a world of representation made of absence and presence, has no simple truth to give; it tells us that the truth of representation is allied to the possibility of error, and the two are undecidable, that the language of man always prevaricates, follows a crooked path and cannot snatch the secrets that lie deep in a dark cave. In this sense, the *Divine Comedy* is a text that transgresses the very possibility of "being read." But Dante has a way of turning this limit and error of language into a value: the veiled signs of the quest force us to interpret and decipher; to seek the truth for a truth which is given becomes valuable only when it is found and, in one word, produced.

For Dante production and work are the true essence of art. In *Purgatorio* x, God is the "fabbro" (l. 99), who "produsse esto visibile parlare" (l. 95); in *Purgatorio* xxi the *Aeneid* is the embodiment of fecundity, "mamma . . . c . . . nutrice" (ll. 97-8). In *Inferno* xi, while Vergil explains to the pilgrim the sin of usury, he goes into an elaborate and essentially scholastic definition of art as production.[75] Usury is a mockery of *poiesis*, a parasitic gain obtained in violation of the productive processes of nature and human industry ("e perchè l'usuriere altra via tene, / per sè natura, e per la sua seguace / dispregia, poi ch' in altro pon la spene," ll. 109-11). Art, a virtue of the practical intellect, belongs in the order of making: it is God's grandchild, for it follows nature which in turn follows the supreme Artifex. If the language of filiation (l. 105) clearly implies that art imitates the productivity of nature, the allusion to Genesis (ll. 106-8), where man is told to tend the Garden and to eat bread by the sweat of his face, makes work of art. This metaphor of work, the principal metaphor of history as I have shown in chapter 4, discloses the time of need and places

[75] Jacques Maritain, *Art and Scholasticism and the Frontiers of Poetry*, trans. Joseph W. Evans (New York: Scribner's Sons, 1962), pp. 10-37. This sense of production brings to focus the concept of author as "he who augments"; see Honorius of Autun: "Sic et *auctor* est aequivocum. . . . Est auctor civitatis. . . . Est quoque auctor libri. . . . Est etiam auctor commune nomen, ab augendo dictum" (*PL* 172, col. 348). See also, M.-D. Chenù, "Auctoritas," in *La Théologie au douzième siècle* (Paris: Vrin, 1957), pp. 353-7.

us in the desert where art is needed to transform the desert into a garden.

To be a reader is to be in the desert of exile or, as the Fathers of the Church understood it, to undertake a journey in a foreign land. The Bible is commonly seen to be like the world, a deep forest and a labyrinth, an "infinita sensuum silva."[76] These patristic commonplaces, to be sure, are caused by Scripture's wondrous depth; yet, exegetes like Honorius of Autun and Hugh of St. Victor go into a literal identification of reading as exile.[77] In the *Didascalicon*, which is a treatise on the art of reading, Hugh devotes a paragraph to *De Exsilio* and writes:

> Finally, a foreign soil is proposed, since it, too, gives a man practice. All the world is a foreign soil to those who philosophize. However, as a certain poet says: "I know not by what sweetness native soil attracts a man / and suffers not that he should ever forget." It is, therefore, a great source of virtue for the practiced mind to learn, bit by bit, first to change about in visible and transitory things, so that afterwards it may be able to leave them behind altogether. The man who finds his homeland sweet is still a tender beginner; he to whom every soil is as his native one is already strong; but he is perfect to whom the entire world is as a foreign land. The tender soul has fixed his love on one spot in the world; the strong man has extended his love to all places; the perfect man has extinguished his. From boyhood I have dwelt on foreign soil, and I know with what grief sometimes

---

[76] The phrase is by St. Jerome, Epistola 64, and is quoted with a number of other formulas— "scripturarum . . . oceanum et mysteriorum Dei, ut si loquar, labyrinthum" (*PL* 25, col. 448D)—by Henri de Lubac, *Exégèse médiévale*, I, 119-21.

[77] For the motif of exile, see Honorius of Autun, *De Animae Exsilio et Patria*, *PL* 172, cols. 1241-6. For Honorius exile is the state of "hominis ignorantia" and typologically Babylon; the "patria" is "sapientia" and typologically Jerusalem and Scripture; in between, Honorius figures the journey of knowledge through the citadels of the liberal arts, "physica," "mechanica," and "oeconomica."

the mind takes leave of the narrow hearth of a peasant's hut, and I know, too, how frankly it afterwards disdains marble firesides and panelled halls.[78]

The allusions to the poetry of Ovid, where exile is turned into a nostalgia for a homecoming, sharpens Hugh's view of the exile of reading as a turning away from the traps of literature and its precious metaphors. To him, as he says elsewhere, "all the world is a foreign soil to those whose native land should be heaven. . . . Therefore comes a 'time for scattering stones' (Ecclesiastes 3:5), so that man may see he has no stable dwelling here and may get used to withdrawing his mind and freeing it from the chains of earthly pleasures."[79] This motif of the exile's longing for the homeland is explicitly thematized in *Purgatorio*,[80] but Dante, unlike Hugh or Aquinas for that matter, does not think of poetry as a mere *appendix artium*:[81] it is the ground of exile where questions that seem settled once and for all are rethought in their original problematical char-

[78] *The Didascalicon*, III, 19; Taylor, p. 101; *PL* 176, col. 778 (given as chap. 20). As Taylor points out, the allusion to Ovid is from *Epistolae ex Ponto*, I, iii, 35-6. See Taylor, p. 216.

[79] Hugh of St. Victor, *In Ecclesiasten Homiliae*, *PL* 175, col. 221C; Taylor, p. 216.

[80] Constant exile is, of course, the feature of *Inferno*: see Vergil's remark, " 'che me rilega ne l'etterno essilio' " (*Purgatorio* XXI, l. 18); see also, however, *Paradiso* X, l. 129: " 'e da essilio venne a questa pace.' " In *Purgatorio*, the theme of exile is explicitly expressed by the souls: " 'O frate mio, ciascuna è cittadina / d'una vera città; ma tu vuo' dire / che vivesse in Italia peregrina' " (XIII, ll. 94-6); in this sense, see the definition of Romeo of Villeneuve as " 'Romeo, persona umìle e peregrina' " (*Paradiso* VI, l. 135); cf. *Purgatorio* VII, l. 40: " 'Loco certo non c'è posto;' " see also above chapter 3, notes 47, 48 and 58.

[81] "The appendages of the arts, however, are only tangential to philosophy. . . . Of this sort are all the songs of the poets—tragedies, comedies, satires, heroic verse and lyric, iambics, certain didactic poems, fables and histories, and also the writings of these fellows whom today we commonly call philosophers and who are always taking some small matter and dragging it out through long verbal detours" (*The Didascalicon* III, 4; Taylor, p. 88). See also Aquinas' statement: "Fictiones poeticae non sunt ad aliud ordinatae nisi ad significandum; unde talis significatio non supergreditur modum litteralis sensus" (*Questiones Quodlibetales* VII, vi, art. 16).

acter; it is the imaginative area where faith is exposed to the possibility of faithlessness and error; it figures a radical displacement where memory is shifty and any univocal meaning is elusive and itself exiled. In this condition, one must be willing to take hints, follow leads, surrender to encounters, as the pilgrim does in *Inferno* I, where he confusedly perceives "ombra od omo certo" (l. 66), and always be alert to the possibility that every garden may hide a snake, every definitive answer may be a mirage. One must be a restless nomad, like the poet, till the end comes. In this sense, it makes little difference whether we speak of Dante's poetry as fiction or truth, a secular or theological endeavor. Dante abolishes the boundaries between theology and poetry and carves a metaphoric space of dispersion where exiles seek and work.

Later on in the history of poetic forms a counter tendency develops. We reach with Petrarch the historical moment when Humanism forges its own simulacra and erects its own monuments. Petrarch gathers his three hundred and sixty-six fragments into a *florilegium*, the ephemeral leaves into a flower. But this unity is fictive and illusory and, as I shall show in the following chapter, from Dante's viewpoint this faith in the self is a work of madness. The flower's name is Narcissus.

CHAPTER 7

The Language of Faith: Messengers and Idols

THE practice of reading, as has been seen in the previous chapters, leads the reader into the center of an imaginative maze, to the awareness of an impasse where the primary plot of the pilgrim's ascetic experience harbors within itself a counterplot, the sense that the explicit moral weight of the text is drawn within the possibility of error. The question must now be asked whether this view of the poet, and the reader, cast in a condition of exile, where everything appears uncertain, open-ended and tentative, is simply the reflection of too modern a critical temper suspicious of firm answers, an interpretative heresy of sorts in projecting on to the text strictly subjective preoccupations. The question is not a gratuitous exercise of the mind doubting, as it were, its own doubts. It must be raised because the dramatic action of the *Divine Comedy* depends, to a large extent, on the persistent presence of guides and the occasional intervention of messengers who point the way to the pilgrim, remove obstacles from his journey, and whose primary role is to dramatize the fact that this is not the journey of a man entirely left to himself. The pilgrim is ostensibly unlike Ulysses whose mad flight is the emblematic story of a voyager who relies exclusively on his own intellectual powers and leads himself and his companions to a tragic end.

What is true for the pilgrim is equally true for the poet's own sense of history, shaped, as it is, by the steady acknowledgments of guides, prophets and mediators who bear and interpret God's Word to man. The readers are reminded that they have the Old and New Testament and " 'l pastor de la Chiesa che vi guida; / questo vi basti a vostro salvamento" (*Paradiso* v, ll. 76–8); in spite of the contingent crisis of authority, pope and emperor ideally ought to be guides to the world (*Purgatorio* xvi, ll. 91 ff.); and if these two "suns" have eclipsed each other and have left the world in a state of blindness, St. Francis and St. Dominic are the two "princes" of the Church, "che quinci e quindi le fosser per guida" (*Paradiso* xi, l. 36), veritable angels who herald and preach God's love and wisdom. Dante himself frequently takes a prophetic posture and calls for the reform of the Church: at the top of Purgatory, Beatrice, for instance, promises the imminent advent of a "messo di Dio," the "cinquecento, diece a cinque" (*Purgatorio* xxxiii, ll. 43–4) who will come to kill the Whore dallying with the Giant.

To suggest, therefore, as I have done, that the reader is left alone in a space of contradictory and indeterminate choices, is, on the face of it, to lapse into what might be called a heresy of reading, the doctrinal error of extrapolating, unaided, one's own truth from the poem. In *Inferno* ix and x, where heresy is punished, Dante dramatizes precisely this error and juxtaposes to it the virtue of faith in God's Word as the perspective from which the spiritual interpretation of the poem can be attained. The question of interpretation, thus, must be reexamined from the point of view of the language of faith: by focusing on the messengers and interpreters of God's Word (without giving, however, a full inventory of their role and occurrence in the poem), this chapter will map out first the relation between heresy and faith, and secondly it will describe the prophetic content of Dante's own message. Prophecy is, in a real sense, the language of faith, the way faith speaks; but I shall also argue that, for Dante, prophecy itself is vulnerable to the possibility of turning into blasphemy. He systematically opposes heresy to faith, idolatry to prophecy, and yet he is also aware that the line which separates belief from unbelief is precarious, that metaphoric language is never impervious to those interpretive errors which he unequivocally condemns in his treatment of heresy. In *Inferno* IX, on the threshold of the city of Dis, the pilgrim is about to enter the circle of the heretics, but experiences what to him is a veritable impasse. The three Furies, handmaids of Hecate (ll. 43-4) and guardians of the gates, obstruct his passage by calling on Medusa to appear and, by the power of her gaze, transform him into a stone (ll. 52-4). Vergil, who in the preceding canto had failed to persuade the devils to allow them to enter Dis, now quickly instructs his disciple not to look, turns his head backward and shuts the pilgrim's eyes with his own hands (ll. 55-60). An angel, "da ciel messo" (l. 85), comes and, by a touch of his wand, opens the gates for the pilgrim and his guide. In the middle of this action, the poet interrupts the narrative and urges the readers to look under the veil of the "strange verses."

> O voi ch'avete li 'ntelletti sani,
>   mirate la dottrina che s'asconde
>   sotto 'l velame de li versi strani.
>   ll. 61-3

(O you who are of sound understanding, look at the doctrine that is hidden beneath the veil of the strange verses.)

Since the early commentators, the passage has been subjected to the allegorical reading the poet calls for. Iacopo della Lana, for instance, interprets Medusa as the emblem of heresy; Boccaccio sees her as the image of obstinacy that blinds man; by virtue of her etymology, "quod videre non possit," she has been taken to be the allegory of *invidia*; other critics gloss the Furies and the threatened apparition of Medusa as abstract figurations of remorseful terror and despair; some others explain Medusa as the sin of *malitia* and the angel as the allegory of imperial authority.[1] From this political perspective, since

---

[1] Iacopo della Lana writes: "In questo nono capitolo intende l'autore circa la fine toccare alcuna cosa delli eresiarchi. . . . Circa lo qual trattato, per al-

the immediate context of the scene is the civil war ravaging Florence, one might infer that Dante is dramatizing the crisis of what has come to be known as an Averroistic political vision. The scene, actually, is so complex that no single critical formula can account for its metaphoric and doctrinal density.

---

legoria mette tre furie infernali, le quali portano pene da serpenti e bestie venenose, che come l'eresia e li eretici è venenosa e corrompente cosa. . . . Poscia introduce una favola poetica d'una Medusa, la quale per un fallo che commise facea tramutare in pietra chi la vedea. . . . E questa per allegoria hae a significare che la eresia fa diventare l'uomo pietra, perchè lo eretico vuole più credere a la sensualitadi ch'enno indicii e prove corporee, che alla Sacra Scrittura che è per revelazione avuta da Spirito santo." The rest of Iacopo's introduction to the canto enumerates the various heretical opinions against the Christian faith; see *Commedia di Dante degli Allagherii col commento di Iacopo della Lana*, ed. Luciano Scarabelli (Bologna: Tipografia regia, 1866), I, 191. For Boccaccio, Medusa is specifically the emblem of "ostinazione, in quanto essa faceva chi la riguardava divenir sasso, cioè gelido e inflessibile." He goes on to say that we look at the Gorgon insofar as we are "ostinati cultivatori delle terrene cose." After explaining that the eyes stand for the affections of the irascible and concupiscent appetites, Boccaccio goes on to show why "possonsi . . . gli eretici simigliare alle sepolture." For Boccaccio's allegorization, see his *Esposizioni sopra la Commedia di Dante*, ed. Giorgio Padoan (Milan: Mondadori, 1965), pp. 505-9; among recent commentators, Raffaello Fornaciari explains the scene as the allegory of *invidia* in his "Il mito delle Furie in Dante," *Nuova antologia di scienze lettere ed arte*, 2nd series, 16 (1879), pp. 627-56; the episode is seen by Margaret N. Mansfield to dramatize a kind of conversion from despair in her "Dante and the Gorgon Within," *Italica*, 47 (1970), pp. 143-60. She also reemphasizes the etymology of Medusa, "quasi *mèidesan*, quod videre non possit." Cf. Fulgentius, *Mitologiarum libri tres*, in *Opera*, ed. R. Helm (Leipzig: B. G. Teubner, 1898), I, xxi, p. 33. For a political-religious account of heresy, there is a passage from Giovanni Villani's *Cronica*, ed. F. Gherardi Dragomanni, 4 vols. (Florence: S. Coen, 1844-45), which relates the problem to the moral reform brought about by Franciscans and Dominicans, as will be seen later in this chapter: "la città era malamente corrotta di resia, intra l'altre della setta degli epicurei, per vizio di lussuria e di gola, e era sì grande parte, che intra' cittadini si combatteve per la fede . . . e durò questa maledizione in Firenze molto tempo infine alla venuta delle sante religioni di santo Francesco e di santo Domenico, le quali religioni per gli loro santi frati, commesso loro l'officio della eretica pravità per lo papa, molto la stirparo in Firenze e in Milano." The passage is from vol. I, bk. IV, 30. For a modern political view, see the extensive comments in *La Divina Commedia*, ed. Daniele Mattalìa (Milan: Rizzoli, 1960), pp. 181-2.

Its primary concern, I would like to suggest, is heresy, a sin that for Dante involves the failure of understanding and imagination, and which he equates with the madness of those who produce poetic and philosophical discourses but have no faith in God.

The phrase "intelletti sani," I submit, calls immediate attention to what might be called the heresy of reading and translates a commonplace of biblical exegesis. The Church Fathers, denouncing the error of the heretics who expounded the doctrine of the Bible in any sense but that imparted by faith and the Holy Ghost, consistently use the formula "sanus intellectus" to qualify a faithful interpretation of Scripture.[2] The heretics apply their own "sensus proprius" or "bovinus intellectus," and fall into an illusory subjectivism which disrupts the prophetic integrity of the biblical text. Those with a "sanus intellectus," on the contrary, interpret the doctrine for what it is and do not hold false opinions in matters pertaining to Christian faith. The same phrase, "intelletto sano," is employed in this precise sense in *Convivio*.[3] In the fourth treatise, while giving a systematic critique of Frederick the Second's false opinion that nobility resides in fine manners and wealth, Dante appeals to those with "intelletti sani" who would discern the falseness of the emperor's doctrine. In the subsequent commentary on the line, the phrase is glossed as meaning that "tempo è d'aprire li occhi a la veritade," and "sano intelletto" means a mind which is not petrified and knows "quello che le cose sono."[4] This particular meaning, and the metaphor of

---

[2] A full documentation on the patristic formulas describing a heretical reading of the Bible is provided by Henri de Lubac, "Subjectivisme et intelligence spirituelle," in *Exégèse médiévale* (Paris: Aubier, 1961), II, esp. pp. 99-181.

[3] The phrase " 'ntelletti sani" occurs in the third song (l. 74) of *Convivio* and in the subsequent commentary, *Convivio* IV, xv, 10-16.

[4] The whole passage reads: "Then when it says, 'Because to the healthy mind 'Tis manifest these words of theirs are vain,' I conclude their error to be confuted; and I say that it is time to open their eyes to the truth. And this I mean when I say, 'And now I wish to say after my thought.' I say, then, that from what has been said, it is evident to the healthy intellect that the words of

opening the eyes, clearly carried over in *Inferno* IX, has an extraordinary dramatic aptness because heresy, as we shall now see, is a sin that forfeits and darkens the sanity of the intellect.

Indeed, even at first glance the circle of the heretics appears to be literally the graveyard of that philosophy that believes in the perishability of the soul along with the death of the body. The sinners, Epicurus and his followers, "che l'anima col corpo morta fanno" (*Inferno* x, 1. 15), Frederick the Second (and the irony of the name, Federico, is transparent), Cavalcanti and Farinata, by a stark *contrappasso* are buried in tombs to live out, as it were, the eternal death they upheld in life.[5] In a real sense, this is the exact reversal of the value that Dante assigned to the Epicureans in *Convivio*. In its fourth treatise, Dante describes, using Cicero as his source, the philosophical schools of active life (namely the Stoics, the Peripatetics and the Epicureans) as the three Marys who go to the tomb, the receptacle of corruptible things, where the Savior, that is to say, beatitude, is buried. But the "monimento" is empty, and an angel of God, who had rolled the stone away, tells them that Christ has risen and has gone before them into Galilee where those who seek can find him.[6] Quite overtly, this is the

these men are vain, that is, without any marrow of truth. And it is not without reason that I say *healthy*. For we must know that our intellect can be called healthy or diseased. And I mean by intellect the noble part of our soul which may be called by the common word *mind*. It may be said to be healthy, when it is not hindered in its operations by any evil disposition of soul or body; which is to know things as they are, as Aristotle has it, in the third *Of the Soul*" (Dante Alighieri, *The Banquet*, trans. Katharine Hillard [London: Kegan Paul, 1889], p. 304).

[5] See, for instance, Benvenuto da Imola's gloss: "sunt mortui quantum ad fidem, et viventes sepulti, quia eorum vitium occultant nec audent propalare" (Biagi, ed., *Inferno*, p. 284).

[6] The description of the three philosophical sects as the three Marys is in *Convivio* IV, xxii, 15. Cf. also *Convivio* IV, vi, 11-12; IV, xxii, 4. The allegorical interpretation that Dante gives of this imaginative philosophical quest may have been partly inspired, as Busnelli and Vandelli suggest (II, pp. 284-5), by Hugh of St. Cher. The source for Dante's information about the Epicureans is Cicero's *De finibus* I, 9, etc. See Busnelli and Vandelli's commentary, *Convivio*, vol. II, p. 64. Giorgio Padoan, "Il canto degli epicurei,"

story of understanding seeking faith, an explicit turning around of the formula *fides quaerens intellectum* which in the philosophical context of *Convivio* is viewed as a legitimate and positive undertaking. But in *Inferno* x, Epicurus, instead of seeking the risen Christ in Galilee, has remained at the tomb, the "monimenti," as Dante, echoing the passage of *Convivio*, calls it (*Inferno* ix, l. 131), and he literally dwells in it. We can, perhaps, account for this shift of views from *Convivio* to the *Divine Comedy*. If in *Convivio*, where philosophy is celebrated as the sovereign source of authority, Athens is the celestial city,[7] in the *Divine Comedy*, Dante juxtaposes Jerusalem to Athens. There is a great deal of irony in Vergil's words, "Tutti saran serrati / quando di Iosafàt qui torneranno / coi corpi che là sù hanno lasciati" (*Inferno* x, ll. 10-2). From this perspective of the valley in Jerusalem, where the Last Judgment and the resurrection of the flesh will take place, philosophy leads as far as the tomb and no further. In *Convivio* philosophy may even offer consolation to death;[8] in *Inferno* x, the tomb is the scandal against which philosophy stumbles.

Dante's way of experiencing the opposition between Athens and Jerusalem is by no means unusual. When St. Paul

Convivium, N.S., 27 (1959), pp. 12-39, argues that Dante, at the time of the *Convivio*, knew only partially Cicero's *De finibus*, and later on he came to see the materialistic basis of Epicurean thought. For Dante's view of Epicurus and heretics in general, see Felice Tocco, *Quel che non c'è nella* Divina Commedia *o Dante e l'eresia* (Bologna: Biblioteca storico-critica della letteratura dantesca, 1899); Alfonso De Salvio, *Dante and Heresy* (Boston: Dumas Bookshop, 1936), esp. pp. 2-11; Joseph A. Mazzeo, *Medieval Cultural Tradition in Dante's* Comedy (Ithaca, Cornell University Press, 1960), pp. 174-204; André Pézard, "Un Dante Epicurien?" in *Mélanges offerts à Etienne Gilson* (Paris: Vrin, 1959), pp. 499-536. Emerson Brown, Jr., of Vanderbilt University, is preparing a full-fledged study of the tradition of Epicurus in the Middle ages.

[7] "Per le quali tre virtudi si sale a filosofare a quelle Atene Celestiali, dove gli Stoici e Paripatetici e Epicurii, per la luce de la veritate etterna, in uno volere concordevolmente concorrono" (*Convivio* iii, xiv, 15).

[8] Quite explicitly Dante states in *Convivio* ii, xii, 2-4 that following the death of Beatrice, he attempted to find consolation in the reading of Boethius' *De consolatione philosophiae* and Cicero's *De amicitia*.

preaches in Athens that God is not like gold or stone, a representation by the art and imagination of man, and announces the resurrection of the dead, the Athenians laugh at him (Acts 17:22 ff.). Later on, his belief in life after death is dismissed as sheer madness: "Paul, you are mad; much learning is turning you mad" (Acts 26:24).[9] The distance that separates philosophical reason from the madness of faith is also the brunt of Tertullian's *De Praescriptione Haereticorum*. When Tertullian asks "quid ergo Athenis et Hierosolymis? quid academiae et ecclesiae? quid haereticis et Christianis?" he answers that the two have nothing to do with each other.[10] Tertullian's position, to be sure, depends largely on the assumption that faith believes what is rationally impossible;[11] for Dante, it is not that reason is insignificant or absolutely inept in matters of faith. Reason, left to itself, is found wanting because it can grasp neither the mystery which belongs to faith nor the wisdom of God who chooses foolish things, in the language of St. Paul, to confound the wise. Confronted with death conquered, the empty tomb of Christ, Epicurus remains entrenched in his own unbelief, and *Inferno* x bears witness to the wreckage of his philosophy: his philosophical quest of *Convivio* is exposed as madness, the doctrinal error that litters the path to God's wisdom.

It has not been clear to scholars, however, why heresy, a philosophical error, should be punished in the sixth circle of

[9] The belief in the Incarnation and resurrection from the dead is, for the Athenians, the madness of faith; for Dante unbelief in the proclamation of these events is the madness of philosophy. Cf. *Purgatorio* iii, ll. 34-6: "Matto è chi spera che nostra ragione / possa trascorrer la infinita via / che tiene una sustanza in tre persone." The lines that follow explicitly allude to the inadequate knowledge of Plato and Aristotle. More cogently, *Inferno* xi starts with an allusion to "Anastasio papa" (l. 8), who in Dante's view was led by Photinus into the heretical denial of the divinity of Christ and into accepting the "body" of Christ as naturally begotten.

[10] *PL* 2, col. 20b.

[11] "Falsa est igitur et fides nostra, et phantasma est totum quod speramus a Christo? . . . Natus est Dei Filius; non pudet, quia pudendum est: et mortuus est Dei Filius; prorsus credibile est, quia ineptum est; et sepultus resurrexit; certum est quia impossibile" (*De carne Christi*, *PL* 2, cols, 760-1).

Inferno, between the sins of incontinence and those of mad bestiality.[12] The critical confusion stems from the fact that in his exposition of the moral structure of Hell, Vergil says nothing about heresy, and also from the fact that in Aristotle's ethical system there is no rationale to view it even as a sin. In his pagan frame of reference, heresy is simply a perversion of the speculative intellect, which results neither from any infirmity of the will nor from the impulses of the flesh. On the other hand, for Dante it must be stressed that sin always involves the various functions of the will. Because of the apparent contradiction, W.H.V. Reade concludes his examination of the problem by stating that Dante "did not know what to say about the moral causes of heresy."[13] In effect, Dante develops his figuration of heresy along the broad lines of Thomas Aquinas' conception. In an elaborate passage of the *Summa*,[14] Aquinas views heresy as a sin of choice (the word comes, he says quoting Jerome and Isidore, from the Greek *hairesis* meaning choice); as a misinterpretation of Scripture, it is a denial of the truth on which faith is founded and, in this

[12] G. Fraccaroli, *Il cerchio degli eresiarchi* (Modena: Angelo Namias, 1894); Edward Moore, *Studies in Dante*, 2nd series (Oxford: Clarendon Press, 1899), esp. pp. 152-82; W.H.V. Reade, *The Moral System of Dante's* Inferno (Oxford: Clarendon Press, 1909), esp. pp. 367-81; see also Alfred A. Triolo, "Matta‑Bestialità in Dante's 'Inferno': Theory and Image," *Traditio*, 24 (1968), pp. 247-92. See also Dante's statement: "Dico che intra tutte le bestialitadi quella è stoltissima . . . chi crede dopo questa vita non essere altra vita" (*Convivio* II, viii, 8).

[13] Reade, p. 378.

[14] The question of heresy is treated at length in the *Summa Theologiae*, IIa IIae, q. 11. In article one, Aquinas quotes Jerome (*PL* 26, col. 445) and writes that "heresy, the word comes from the Greek for choice, whereby a man selects for himself the teaching he thinks the better." In article two, Aquinas states that "heresy is not just about things, but also about words and interpretations of Holy Scripture. Jerome says that whoever expounds Scripture in any sense but that of the Holy Ghost by whom it was written may be called a heretic even though he may not have left the Church." He concludes the article as follows: "We take heresy at present to mean a corruption of the Christian faith." The English version is from St. Thomas Aquinas, *Summa Theologiae*, IIa IIae, q. 11, ar. 2, ed. Thomas Gilby (New York: McGraw-Hill, 1975), p. 85.

sense, it designates an intellectual error. But it is also more than a sin of opinion: it is an act that involves the flesh and arises, as Aquinas puts it, "from pride or covetousness or even some illusion of the imagination which according to Aristotle is a source of error."[15] A more careful reading of the pattern of allusions and metaphors obliquely woven in the folds of *Inferno* ix and x will show that Dante gives an essentially Thomistic account of heresy, one in which the affections are engaged, much as the intellect was, and like the intellect, they are threatened by a veritable madness.

The Furies' call for Medusa to appear dramatizes in a primary way a case of madness: the epithet "sani" (*Inferno* ix, l. 61) signals that whatever we are witnessing verges on *insania*. Medusa's own story, as told by Ovid, is an experience of mad love. Among the early commentators on the passage, Boccaccio and Buti rightly recall the Ovidian account of the myth: once a beautiful maiden, Medusa was raped by Neptune in the temple of Minerva, the goddess of wisdom, who avenges the violation by turning Medusa's golden curls into snakes and, eventually, by giving Perseus the mirrored shield by which he can kill her.[16] In several mythographic glosses, the Gorgons (l. 56) are interpreted as women who disrupt the sanity of the mind. In Fulgentius' *Mythologicon*, the first of the three sisters stands for "mentis debilitas"; the second, "terrore mentem spargit"; the third, "mentis intentum, vero

[15] The whole passage reads: "Heresy takes its name from choosing and sect takes its name from cutting, as Isidore notes. A heresy and a sect are the same. Each is a work of the flesh, on account, not of the act itself of unbelief in respect to its proximate object, but of its cause, which is either the desire for an improper end, arising from pride or covetousness, as we have mentioned, or even some illusion of the imagination, which according to Aristotle is a source of error. The imagination somehow belongs to the flesh in that it acts with a bodily organ" (*Summa Theologiae*, IIa IIae, q. 11, art. 1, resp.; Gilby, p. 83).

[16] *Metamorphoses* IV, ll. 744-803. The story of the rape of the Medusa by Neptune and the violation of the temple of Minerva is recalled by Boccaccio, Buti, Ottimo and Lana; see Biagi, ed., *Inferno*, pp. 270-1.

etiam caliginem ingerit visus."[17] Further, both John of Garland and Arnulf of Orleans explain the metamorphosis into stone by Medusa as the allegory of the *stupor* that she engenders in the mind;[18] this gloss, it may be pointed out, is obliquely picked up by Benvenuto da Imola, who interprets the pilgrim's threatened petrification as meaning to be "stupidum."[19]

A number of other dramatic elements in *Inferno* IX suggests this motif of madness. The three Furies are conventionally etymologized as the three affections, namely, wrath, cupidity and lust, which "stimulis suis mentem feriant";[20] Tisiphone (l. 48), Juno's messenger, is also said to bring "insania."[21] But there is a more compelling allusion that gives madness a central place in the canto: the fearful summons to Medusa to appear. Medusa, to be sure, does not appear; nonetheless, her name is to the pilgrim a shock of recognition, literally a ghost issued from his own past, and her name reenacts the *amor insanus* that Dante celebrated in his *Rime Petrose*. In a powerful piece of literary criticism, John Freccero has recently shown that the *Rime Petrose* are textually recalled in the rhyme scheme, "alto . . . smalto . . . assalto" (ll. 50-4), to dramatize the memory of the pilgrim's erotic fascination with the

[17] *Mitologiarum libri tres*, pp. 32-3. The description in its entirety reads: "But let me explain what the Greeks, inclined as they are to embroider, would signify by this finely spun fabrication. They intended three Gorgons, that is, the three kinds of terror: the first terror is indeed that which weakens the mind; the second, that which fills the mind with terror; the third, that which not only enforces its purpose upon the mind but also its gloom upon the fact" (*Fulgentius the Mythographer*, trans. Leslie George Whitbread [Columbus: Ohio State University Press, 1971], I, 21, p. 62).

[18] Fausto Ghisalberti, ed., "Arnolfo d'Orléans, un cultore di Ovidio nel secolo XII," *Reale instituto lombardo di scienze e lettere*, 24, 3rd series, no. 15, fasc. 4 (Milan, 1932), p. 312.

[19] Biagi, ed., *Inferno*, p. 271.

[20] Isidore of Seville, *Etym.* VIII, xi, 95-6.

[21] *Metamorphoses* IV, ll. 481-511 tells of Tisiphone, who, at the request of Juno, drives Athamas mad. In her journey out of Avernus, Tisiphone is accompanied by Insania (l. 485).

stonelike woman of that poetic sequence.[22] The myth of Medusa, I would like to add, explicitly governs one of those poems.   In "Così nel mio parlar voglio esser aspro," the poet, installed in an eerie spiritual landscape, recounts the tortures of his obstinate passion for the *Donna Petra* and the condition of his mind which has been shattered by the madness of his vain pursuit.[23]

> Non trovo scudo ch'ella non mi spezzi
> nè loco che dal suo viso m'asconda:
> chè come fior di fronda,
> così de la mia mente tien la cima.
>
> ll. 14-7

(I cannot find a shield that she does not shatter, nor a place to hide from her look; like the flower on the stalk, she occupies the summit of my mind.)

As I have shown earlier in chapter 4, the lover is an unsuccessful Perseus, without a shield and unable to sustain the lady's glance. This myth of the woman as Medusa is countered by another myth that runs through Dante's imaginative contrivance. The poet obliquely casts himself as Pygmalion: like Pygmalion, who, by the intervention of Venus, breathes life into the statue, the idol he wrought with his own hands, the poet wishes to instill life into the loved lady, who is a "dura petra / che parla e sente come fosse donna."[24] The lady, however, will remain an unresponsive stone, and the poet's love is a hopeless obsession which borders on death.

This effort to give life to what is only a stone is placed in *Inferno* IX within a context of magic and witchcraft. It ought to be remarked that Pygmalion's transformation of the statue

[22] John Freccero, "Medusa: The Letter and the Spirit," *Yearbook of Italian Studies*, 2 (1972), pp. 1-18.

[23] Quotations are from Gianfranco Contini's edition of *Rime* (Turin: Einaudi, 1965), p. 167.

[24] "The hard stone that speaks and feels as if it were a woman." These are lines 5-6 of "Al poco giorno," *Rime*, p. 158. The Pygmalion motif is also alluded to in "Amor, tu vedi ben," *Rime*, p. 162, ll. 10-13.

into a human being is understood by the Ovidian mythographers as a magic mutation.[25] More importantly, *Inferno* IX opens with an allusion to Erichtho, the sorceress, who, as it is told by Lucan, conjures the shades from Hades to foretell the future events in the civil war at Pharsalia, and whose necromancy involves Vergil himself.[26] The Furies, the grim shapes howling in the night, are identified as the handmaids of Hecate (ll. 43-4), the goddess of the lower world, who presides over demons and phantoms, and who is said to have taught sorcery and witchcraft.[27] In Latin love lyrics, where the focus is the enchantment of love, it may be added, Hecate's magic spells are invoked to engender or cure the incantations and delusions of love.[28] Even the angel "da ciel messo" (l. 85), who opens the gates of Dis with his wand, bears overtones of magic. Ever since the early commentators, he has been identified as Mercury, Jupiter's faithful messenger from Statius' *Thebaid*.[29] In *Inferno* IX, to be sure, the angel is the emblem of

[25] The types of metamorphosis depend on the threefold distinction set by Boethius, *De consolatione philosophiae* IV, pros. iii, m. iii; they are called natural, spiritual and magic mutation by Giovanni del Virgilio; cf. F. Ghisalberti, ed., "Giovanni del Virgilio espositore delle *Metamorfosi*," *Giornale dantesco*, 29, N.S. 4 (1931), p. 17; the myth of Pygmalion as magic mutation is alluded to by Arnulf of Orléans, in F. Ghisalberti, ed., "Arnolfo d'Orléans," p. 181.

[26] *Pharsalia* VI, ll. 507-830. The importance of magic in Lucan has been stressed by L. Paoletti, "Lucano magico e Vergilio," *Atene e Roma*, 8 (1963), pp. 11-26; see also S. Eitrem, "La Magie comme motif littéraire chez les grecs et les romains," *Symbolae Osloenses*, 21 (1941), pp. 39-83. The legend of Vergil's association with magic is documented by Domenico Comparetti, *Virgilio nel Medioevo*, new ed., ed. Giorgio Pasquali (Florence: La Nuova Italia, 1943), II, 22-68.

[27] For the link of Hecate with magic, see *Thebaid* IV, ll. 514 ff.; *Metamorphoses* VII, ll. 74-5, 174, 194 (where the focus of the story is Medea, the famous *maga* of antiquity); see also *Metamorphoses* XIV, ll. 403-11, where Circe, the other practitioner of magic enchantments, is discussed.

[28] When Propertius and Tibullus, who allude to Cynthia and Trivia in their love poems, refer to magic, it is generally a metaphor deployed to dramatize the disorder of the lover's mind. See on this aspect Eugene Tavenner, *Studies in Magic from Latin Literature* (New York: Columbia University Press, 1916), esp. pp. 33-40; see also Archibald W. Allen, "Elegy and the Classical Attitude Toward Love: Propertius, I, 1," *Yale Classical Studies*, 11 (1950), pp. 253-77.

[29] "Inter gelidis Maia satur aliger umbris / iussa gerens magni remeat Iovis;

divine eloquence, the bearer of God's message, who defeats the devils and lets the pilgrim continue his journey.[30] Dante, in effect, alludes to and revises his source, the *Thebaid*, where the messenger's function is to summon back the dead soul of Laius to foment the civil war of Thebes.

These allusions in the canto to magic heighten the sense of the madness of the pilgrim's experience. Like madness, which violates the rigor of the intellect and mistakes one thing for another, magic creates deceptive semblances and false figments of the mind. This metaphoric link between magic and madness did not escape Isidore of Seville, who, quoting the same passage of Erichtho in Lucan's *Pharsalia* which Dante recalls in lines 22 to 27, views magic precisely as the practice in which "the mind, though polluted by no venom of poisoned draught, perishes by enchantment."[31] For Dante the links between the two are such that they invest the very substance of *Inferno* IX. As magic designates the tampering with the natural order, it discloses Dante's madness and unnatural passion for the *Donna Petra*; as the demonic art of conjuration of the dead, it further discloses as pure illusion the poet's idolatrous attempt in his past to give life to what is only a stone and an insubstantial form.

In the case of Epicurus, who is blind to the fact that Christ's

---

undique pigrae / ire vetant nubes et turbidus implicat aer" (*Thebaid* II, ll. 1-3). Isidore of Seville, *Etym*. VIII, ix, 7-8, quotes Prudentius in listing Mercury among the "magi" and conjurers of the dead. See also *Etym*. VIII, ix, 32-3, where Mercury is said to have first found the "praestigium," explained to mean "quod praestringat aciem oculorum." See also Waldemar Deonna, *Le Symbolisme de l'oeil* (Paris: Editions De Boccard, 1965).

[30] Benvenuto da Imola glosses the descent of the angel as follows: "Hic A. ostendit terrorem quem faciebat Mercurius per loca per que transibat. . . . Per hoc autem figurat A. quod rei fugiunt a facie oratoris et advocati eloquentis, et abscondunt" (Biagi, ed., *Inferno*, p. 278).

[31] *Etym*. VIII, ix, 10. Tertullian, *Liber de anima*, *PL* 2, cols. 748-9, also links magic and heresy in discussing Simon Magus. For a historical sketch of magic, heresy and madness, see Jeffrey Burton Russell, *Witchcraft in the Middle Ages* (Ithaca, Cornell University Press, 1972); see also the more general overview by E. M. Butler, *The Myth of the Magus* (Cambridge: Cambridge University Press, 1948), esp. pp. 66-111.

empty tomb is a sign of his resurrection from the dead, philosophy goes mad; in *Inferno* IX it is the poetry of the *Rime Petrose*, which attempts to give life to a stone, that retrospectively is seen to suffer the same fate. This is not the classical madness of poetry, the powerful frenzy that is traditionally said to possess and engender poetic divinations. It is the spiritual derangement of the imagination, as Aquinas understands it, that operates all sorts of "magic" changes: it believes it can transform death into immortality, and make of a stone the monument for one's own self. These errors of the imagination are given an ironic twist in the two cantos of the heretics: the monument is an illusory and hollow emblem of death; the poet's attempt to give life to the Donna Petra-Medusa is reversed into a threat to reduce the pilgrim to a veritable tomb, like the one inhabited by the heretics, to petrify his intellect and make him blind.

The metaphor of blindness is crucial, actually, to the question of heresy, and it sustains the unfolding of both cantos IX and X of *Inferno*. In canto IX, Medusa herself blinds those who gaze at her; Vergil shuts the pilgrim's eyes; the poet enjoins his readers to open their eyes. In canto X, Hell is referred to as "cieco carcere" (ll. 58-9), and the sinners, we are told, see the faraway future, but are blind to the present. The question of blindness figures so prominently in the exchange between Cavalcanti and the pilgrim that we must look at it closely in order to assess its exact significance for the problem of heresy.

The passionate partisan exchange between Farinata and Dante about the civil war ravaging Florence (*Inferno* X, ll. 22 ff.) is interrupted by Cavalcanti's anxious query about his son Guido:

> Dintorno mi guardò, come talento
>   avesse di veder s'altri era meco;
>   e poi che 'l sospecciar fu tutto spento,
> piangendo disse: "Se per questo cieco
>   carcere vai per altezza d'ingegno,
>   mio figlio ov' è? e perché non è teco?"

E io a lui: "Da me stesso non vegno:
colui ch'attende là, per qui mi mena,
forse cui Guido vostro ebbe a disdegno."
Le sue parole e 'l modo de la pena
m'avean di costui già letto il nome;
però fu la risposta così piena.
Di sùbito drizzato gridò: "Come?
dicesti "elli ebbe"? non viv' elli ancora?
non fiere li occhi suoi lo dolce lume"?
Quando s'accorse d'alcuna dimora
ch'io facëa dinanzi a la risposta,
supin ricadde e più non parve fora.

ll. 55-72

(He looked round about me as if he had a desire to see
whether someone was with me, but when his expectation was all quenched he said weeping: "If you go
through this blind prison by height of genius, where is
my son and why is he not with you?" And I answered
him: "I come not of myself; he that waits there is leading
me through here perhaps to that one whom your Guido
held in disdain." His words and the nature of his
punishment had already told me his name, so that I replied thus fully. Suddenly erect, he cried: "How did you
say, 'he held'? Does he no longer live? Does not the
sweet light strike his eyes?" When he perceived that I
made some delay before replying he fell back again and
was seen no more.)

The phrase "cieco carcere" translates, as is generally acknowledged, "Carcere caeco" from *Aeneid* vi, l. 734. But the
importance of the context which the phrase evokes has not, to
my knowledge, been stressed. It occurs, in effect, at the very
center of Anchises' exposition of the theory of the reincarnation of the souls. The souls destined to return to the light,
Anchises says, are held in a blind prison, but after their guilt is
washed away, they drink of the waters of the river Lethe and
return to the world. As the Vergilian context is evoked, it is

ironically turned around. For these heretics do not believe in the immortality of the soul, and Cavalcanti is no Anchises speaking to a son who has providentially descended to Hades and will return back to the light; at the same time, from Dante's Christian perspective the Vergilian notion of the eternal return of the souls is deflated and emptied of any validity.

This ironic twist of the passage of the *Aeneid* is not an isolated occurrence; actually, it is extended to cover the whole of Cavalcanti's speech. The very phrase "altezza d'ingegno," which is his humanistic perception of the pilgrim's descent, shows the old man's peculiar blindness to the vanity of the intellect, a blindness which Dante dispels by replying that he is not undertaking the journey on his own but is guided by Vergil to that one whom Guido held in disdain.[32] The use of the past absolute, as Pagliaro has shown,[33] is mistakenly construed by the sinner as an intimation that his son has died. The mistake is primarily Dante's strategy to sanction Guido's spiritual death, or at least suggest the uncertainty of his future. For, ironically, Cavalcanti's questions, which ostensibly ask whether Guido is alive, in reality allude to the philosophical reasons for his spiritual loss. Just as in *Inferno* IX Dante recalled the rhyme scheme of his own poetry, here he

[32] The "disdain" of Guido and its referent have been the object of a long controversy. A bibliographical review of the various critical opinions has been compiled by S. A. Chimenz, "Il 'disdegno' di Guido e i suoi interpreti," *Orientamenti culturali*, 1 (1945), pp. 179-88. More recently, Charles S. Singleton, "Guido's Disdain," *Modern Language Notes*, 77 (1962), pp. 49-65, argues that the one held in disdain refers to Vergil. Gianfranco Contini, "Dante come personaggio-poeta della *Commedia*," in *Varianti e altra linguistica* (Turin: Einaudi, 1970), p. 351, believes that the "cui" refers to Beatrice and concludes: "La renitenza di Guido non è solo quella, pur probabile, dell'ateo che rifiuta la grazia, ma quella del poeta contento alla letteratura con i suoi sistemi di metafore." See also Letterio Cassata, " 'Il disdegno di·Guido' (*Inferno* x, 63)," *Studi danteschi*, 46 (1969), pp. 5-49.

[33] Antonino Pagliaro, "Il disdegno di Guido," in *Ulisse: saggi di critica semantica* (Messina and Florence: D'Anna, 1953), pp. 357-79. See also the review article by M. Lucidi, "Ancora sul 'disdegno' di Guido," *Cultura neolatina*, 14 (1954), pp. 203-16.

echoes the same rhyme scheme, "nome," "come," and "lume," which Guido, with the important variation of "lome" for "lume," had deployed in *Donna me prega*, his philosophical meditation on the nature of love.[34] Love, in Guido's formulation, proceeds from the darkness of Mars, the sphere of the irascible, and dwells, stripped of any moral quality, in the sensitive faculty. If the *Divine Comedy* dramatizes the perfection of love stretching from the Intellectual Light through the layers of Creation, Cavalcanti's poem projects love as a tragic experience, which robs the human self of any rationality and makes intellect and love radically heterogeneous entities. Practically following Isidore's etymology, "A Marte mors nuncupatur,"[35] Cavalcanti sees love as war, the activity of Mars, which ends in death, "di sua potenza spesso segue morte."[36] This view of love as war and death is heightened by Dante in both cantos IX and X of *Inferno*: in canto IX, the recall of the *Petrose* is framed within two allusions to civil wars, the *Pharsalia* (ll. 21 ff.) and the *Thebaid* (ll. 88 ff.). In canto X, the explicit focus is the civil war of Florence. In a sense, Dante draws the internal strife of the cities within the moral category of heresy, for civil war perverts the bond of love that alone orders the city.[37] As such, the metaphors of civil war expose the tragic reality that lies under Cavalcanti's view that love shatters the intellect. The celebration of love as death is a veritable heresy, as the phrase "dolce lume" implies.

Editors of the *Divine Comedy* still debate whether "lume" or the variant "lome" is the proper *lectio* of the text.[38] I con-

---

[34] *Poeti del duecento*, ed. Gianfranco Contini (Milan and Naples: Ricciardi, 1960), II, 522-19. It should be noted that Contini gives "lume" instead of "lome" at l. 17 of Guido's poem. E. Monaci, "Canzone di Guido Cavalcanti," in *Crestomazia italiana dei primi secoli*, new ed., rev. Felice Arese (Rome: Società editrice Dante Alighieri, 1955), gives "lome," l. 17, p. 574.

[35] *Etym.* VIII, xi, 51.

[36] Contini, II, 526, l. 35. For bibliography on "Donna me prega," see above chapter 5, note 28.

[37] D. Mattalia, ed., *La Divina Commedia*, pp. 181-2.

[38] When Heinrich Kuen, "Dante in Reimnot?" *Germanisch-Romanische*

tend that Dante deliberately changes Guido's "lome" into "lume" in order to graft onto the allusions to *Donna me prega* an echo from Ecclesiastes, "*dulce lumen* et delectabile oculis videre solem" (11:7). Together these allusions afford the perspective from which he indicts Guido's intellectual errors. There are at least two medieval texts, I would like to suggest, which give cogency to this strategy. St. Jerome interprets the passage of Ecclesiastes as an invitation to man to rejoice in his youth, but warns not to think that the words of the preacher are meant "hominem ad luxuriam provocare, *et in Epicuri dogma corruere.*"[39] More importantly, Ecclesiastes 11:7 is used by Aquinas in an article which probes whether blindness of mind ("caecitas mentis") is or is not a sin.[40] His authorities are St. Augustine, who asserts that "all love to know the shining truth," and Ecclesiastes, which says that "light is sweet and it is delightful for the eyes to see the sun." On the other hand, Aquinas acknowledges that Gregory places "blindness of mind among the vices originating from lust." His conclusion is that blindness of mind is a privation of intellectual vision which can occur for three reasons. The most important one, for our purpose, is the first, which concerns the light of natural reason "of which a rational soul is never deprived, though its proper exercise may be hindered as in the insane and the mad."[41] Against what is possibly Cavalcanti's nostalgia for the delights of life, Dante obliquely insinuates, by the

Monatsschrift, 28 (1940), pp. 305-14, pointed out the allusion in Dante's text to Guido's poem and argued that Dante's word "lume" should be "lome." Mattalia, for instance, chooses "lome," p. 216; Petrocchi in his edition argues for the rhyme "come / lume" because of a "larghissima testimonianza dei codici" (*Inferno* x, l. 69, note).

[39] Jerome, *Commentarius in Ecclesiasten*, *PL* 23, col. 1106.

[40] *Summa Theologiae,* IIa IIae, q. 15, art. 1, 3.

[41] *Summa Theologiae*, ed., Thomas Gilby, pp. 135-7. The Latin text reads: "Et hoc lumen, cum pertineat ad speciem animae rationalis, nunquam privatur ab anima. Impeditur tamen quandoque a proprio actu per impedimenta virium inferiorum, quibus indiget intellectus humanus ad intelligendum, sicut patet in amentibus et furiosis, ut in *Primo* dictum est" (*Summa Theologiae,* IIa IIae, q. 15, art. 1, resp.)

allusion to "dulce lumen," that Guido and his poem are wrapped in the darkness of the Epicurean heresy and that the poem dramatizes a veritable madness of love which eclipses the mind.

In view of the foregoing, it is appropriate that heresy should be placed midway between the sins of incontinence and those of mad bestiality, for it is a sin that involves the passions and also implies a violence against the intellect. It is a sin that entails the bankruptcy both of that philosophical discourse which literally leads man to the tomb but cannot show him how to transcend it, and of that poetic imagination which erects illusory monuments to eternity. More important, heresy is an interpretive perversion: as Dante transposes the patristic commonplace "intelletti sani," to his own text, he claims that his own poem demands the same interpretive discipline accorded to the Bible; by that phrase, the poet directs the readers to look beyond the blinding appearances of deceitful and insubstantial forms, which mask death. He asks that we read not with a human eye, which as St. Augustine already knew is always bound to doubt and contemptuous disbelief,[42] but with a mind sustained by the light of faith. The messenger from Heaven, who in *Inferno* ix comes to open the gates of Dis, is precisely the faithful interpreter of God who removes the obstacles from the pilgrim's ascent and opens the way to God.

The centrality of faith to the allegorical interpretation of Scripture can hardly be exaggerated. Biblical exegetes state it succinctly by formulas such as "allegoria fidem aedificat"[43] and "littera gesta docet, quid credas allegoria."[44] Accordingly, Dante makes faith the prerequisite for understanding

---

[42] *De trinitate* xiii, i, 3, in *CCSL* la.

[43] The formula is used by Gregory the Great, *PL* 76, col. 1302A; Guibert of Nogent, *PL* 156, col. 26A; John of Salisbury, *PL* 199, col. 666B. More generally, see Henri de Lubac, "L'édification de la foi," in *Exégèse médiévale*, ii, 522-36.

[44] This is part of the famous distich, "Littera gesta docet, quid credas allegoria, / moralis quid agas, quo tendas anagogia." It is generally attributed to Nicholas of Lyra, *Ad Galathas*, iv, 85H in *Biblia sacra cum glossa interlineari ordinaria*, vi (Venice, 1588).

and the virtue which is radically opposed to heresy. While in the symbolic world of heresy there is only death and the madness of illusory changes, faith ostensibly affords the perspective from which language can have a precise signification, and the contingent and the eternal are fused together. In this sense, Dante's indictment of heresy is not an arbitrary theological choice: he is bent, actually, to show that faith has a necessary value over and against the errors of heresy. We must look at the story of St. Dominic in *Paradiso* xii to probe Dante's sense of faith further.[45]

St. Dominic marries faith (ll. 61-3), and he appears as the knight of faith who stands at the center of the Church Militant to uproot the heretics and nurture the vineyard of the Lord (ll. 100-3). He achieves this by his being a preacher, a reliable messenger who proclaims God's Word to the end of the earth so that the whole world may be gathered into the truth of the Logos. In *Paradiso* xi, actually, both Francis and Dominic are introduced as the two guides of the Church (ll. 31-6) and, by echoing Ubertino da Casale's definition, they are referred to as veritable angels, "L'un fu tutto *serafico* in ardore; / l'altro per sapienza in terra fue / di *cherubica* luce uno splendore." In the wake of St. Gregory, Aquinas defines the cherubim as fullness of knowledge and the seraphim as the zeal of charity.[46] The two hagiographies of Francis and Dominic, in effect, enact the interdependence of will and intellect and, from this point of view, retrospectively show and remedy the double *obduratio* of heart and mind which heresy embodies.

The interdependence of *Paradiso* xi and xii is reflected, as is

---

[45] Some *letture* of the canto of general interest are F. Crispolti, *Il canto XII del Paradiso* (Florence: Sansoni, 1923); L. Cicchitto, "Il canto di Dante a San Domenico," *Miscellanea francescana*, 48 (1948),. pp. 306-28; Gioacchino Paparelli, "Il canto xii del *Paradiso*," in *Ideologia e poesia di Dante* (Florence: Olschki, 1975), pp. 283-316.

[46] "Ad primum ergo dicendum quod Cherubim interpretatur plenitudo scientiae, Seraphim autem interpretatur 'ardentes,' sive incendentes" (*Summa Theologiae*, Ia, q. 63 art. 7 resp.). See also *PL* 76, col. 666. Cf. U. Cosmo, "Le mistiche nozze di Frate Francesco con Madonna Povertá," *Giornale dantesco*, 6 (1898), pp. 49-82, 97-117.

well known, in the rhetorical structure of the cantos.[47] Each hagiography is recounted in exactly forty-six lines; in canto XI, at line 51, St. Francis' birthplace is linked, by an etymological pun on Assisi, with the rising sun; in canto XII, line 52, Dominic's place at Calagora is associated with the setting sun, as if to suggest that the whole world is held within the compass of their light. In *Paradiso* XI, the Dominican St. Thomas delivers the eulogy of St. Francis, while in the successive canto the Franciscan Bonaventure celebrates the accomplishments of St. Dominic. Reversing the practice of the two fraternal orders on earth, each speaker praises the virtue of the opposite order and attacks the moral erosion of his own. By such strategies, Dante elicits the picture of the genuine fellowship of the Church bent on questioning itself and confronting its own need of spiritual reform in order to carry out the providential mission with which it is invested.

If by focusing on preachers Dante implies the necessity for the proclamation of faith so that the Word of God may be heard, he also gives a representation in *Paradiso* XII of how language sustained by faith achieves its full sense. The canto is deliberately organized to evoke a significant and providential design of history:

> Come si volgon per tenera nube
>   due archi paralleli e concolori,
>   quando Iunone a sua ancella iube,
> nascendo di quel d'entro quel di fori,
>   a guisa del parlar di quella vaga
>   ch'amor consunse come sol vapori,
> e fanno qui la gente esser presaga,
>   per lo patto che Dio con Noè puose,
>   del mondo che già mai più non s'allaga:

[47] A. Sorrentino, *L'unità concettuale dei canti XI e XII del* Paradiso *e una leggenda riferita dal Passavanti* (Florence: Olschki, 1927); Howard Needler, *Saint Francis and Saint Dominic in the* Divine Comedy (Cologne: Petrarca-Instituts, 1969). See my review of this monograph in *Italica*, 49 (1972), pp. 506-8.

così di quelle sempiterne rose
volgiensi circa noi le due ghirlande.
ll. 10-20

(As two bows, parallel and like in color, bend across a
thin cloud when Juno gives the order to her handmaid,
the one without born of the one within, like the voice of
that wandering nymph whom love consumed as the sun
does vapors, and makes the people here presage, by reason of the covenant that God made with Noah, that the
world shall never again be flooded; so the two garlands
of those sempiternal roses circled round us, and so did
the outer correspond to the inner.)

The overt dramatic purpose of the passage is to describe the
dance of the two garlands of saints in the shape of two con-
centric and equidistant semicircles of the rainbow. It also
functions as an expedient to set apart and, at the same time,
provide a smooth transition from one hagiography to the
other. Yet, the mythological and biblical allusions to the rainbow are thematically relevant to the central topics of the
canto. The rainbow appearing after the flood is the prophetic
sign of history as the alliance between man and God. As a sign
of the restored peace, it both contrasts with the motif of the
war that St. Dominic will wage on the heretics and prefigures
the final peace that will come at the end of that war. This
technique of prefiguration, of signs that foretell future events,
invests the whole structure of the canto.

Critics have pointed out that the allusion to Iris echoes the
first book of Ovid's *Metamorphoses* (ll. 271 ff.) where she
draws water from the teeming earth and feeds it into the
clouds to produce the flood which will punish the wickedness
of the world. In this sense, one might add, there is an important symmetry at work in the passage: Iris prepares the flood,
while Noah's rainbow appears when the flood is over to mark
the covenant between man and God. But there is another reference to Iris in Ovid's *Metamorphoses* which critics have
neglected and which is also recalled in *Paradiso* xii. In book xi

of *Metamorphoses*, Ovid recounts the death of Ceix and his wife Halcyon's prayer to Juno that the fate of her husband may be disclosed to her. Juno sends Iris to the House of Sleep:

> "Iri, meae" dixit "fidissima nuntia vocis
> Vise soporiferam somni velociter aulam
> extintique iube Ceycis imagine mittant
> somnia ad Alcyonem veros narrantia casus."[48]

Iris, "a rainbow through the skies," descends to Morpheus, the artificer of dreams, who counterfeits a dream to reveal to Halcyon her husband's shipwreck. The story sheds considerable light on canto XII of *Paradiso*. One could point out the presence of "iube" in the passages of both Ovid and Dante (l. 12); moreover, like Iris, the messenger of Juno and her "nuntia vocis," Dominic is *"messo* e famigliar di Cristo" (l. 73); like Iris, who is "fidissima," Dominic is consistently linked to faith. Further, the Ovidian passage focuses on the prophetic powers of dreams and establishes the difference between Morpheus, who sends true visions, and Phantasos, who takes on deceptive shapes. In *Paradiso* XII, there are two prominent prophetic dreams. The first concerns the saint's mother who dreamt she would bear a black and white hound (ll. 58-60); the second concerns his godmother who receives a prophetic dream disclosing Dominic's future mission in the service of the Church (ll. 64-6). But in contrast to Ovid's story, in which the dream reveals the widowhood of Halcyon, in Dante, the godmother, emblem of spiritual regeneration, dreams of the marriage between Dominic and Faith.[49]

This pattern of prophetic signs is extended to two other

---

[48] *Metamorphoses* XI, ll. 585-88: "She said: 'Iris, most faithful messenger of mine, go quickly to the drowsy house of Sleep, and bid him send to Alcyone a vision in dead Ceyx' form to tell her the truth about his faith' " (Ovid, *Metamorphoses*, trans. F. J. Miller [Cambridge, Mass.: Harvard University Press, 1946], p. 163).

[49] The episode is repeatedly found in all biographies of the saint. Cf. Vincent of Beauvais, *Speculum historiale* (Douay: Belleri, 1624), XXIX, 94.

characters in the canto. As St. Bonaventure points out from among the blessed "Natàn profeta" (l. 136) and Joachim "di spirito profetico dotato" (l. 141), Dante seems to imply that prophecy is the language of faith. Prophecy is not simply the prediction of events to come. The prophet, for Dante, is one who is engaged in *reading* the signs of the times and who, sustained by faith, bears witness to his own words with the reality of his life. This was exactly the conduct of the Hebrew *nabi*, who would, for instance, marry a prostitute in order to give credence to his denunciation that Israel was unfaithful to her God. Accordingly, faith is a condition whereby words are bound to things (l. 44) and, far from being obstacles obscuring their sense, they contain a univocal and proper meaning. The extensive presence of etymology in the canto explicitly dramatizes this fact of language. Dominic, for instance, is interpreted as the possessive of *Dominus* (ll. 67-70); his father is interpreted as "veramente Felice" (l. 79), and we are told that his mother Giovanna, correctly interpreted, was really what the word means (ll. 80-1). Words, as the metaphor of etymology and derivations suggests, are not equivocal designations prone to misunderstanding and entangling us in interpretative contradictions. There is the possibility of order and sense, and the presence in the canto of the grammarian Donatus reinforces this point. He is praised for deigning to set his hands on the "prim' arte" (l. 138), grammar, which is to be understood as the effort to rescue language out of the historical chaos into which it has plunged since the Fall, arrange it according to standards of order, and return it to the prelapsarian origin of history.[50] This effort, it must be remembered,

---

[50] Priscian, the grammarian (*Inferno* xv, l. 109), is traditionally seen as "Apostata"; cf. *PL* 210, col. 508. Peter Damian links grammar to the enemies of faith, *PL* 145, cols. 695-704; cf. the attack by Isidore against both Priscian and Donatus, *PL* 83, col. 907; see also Dante's definition of grammar in *De Vulgari Eloquentia* I, ix, 11; more generally, see from this point of view, André Pézard, *Dante sous la pluie de feu* (Paris: Vrin, 1950), pp. 151-72. See also Roger Dragonetti, *Aux Frontières du langage poètique*, Romanica Gandensia, 9 (Ghent: Rijksuniversiteit te Gent, 1961), pp. 36-45.

was Dante's own in his unfinished *De Vulgari Eloquentia*. In this sense, grammar is the first art, the ground in which the split between words and things, which characterizes the language of the fallen world, is healed and correct interpretation is envisioned.

This celebration of order in the language of faith is ostensibly refracted in Dante's own hagiographic representation in *Paradiso* XI and XII. The biographical mode which he deploys implies that the legends, for all the stylized features that conventionally characterize these narratives of sainthood,[51] are not just empty words but point to, and are charged with, the reality of life. The preaching of the Word, it would seem, is "faithful" in the measure in which one's own life is involved and Christ's life is reenacted. This motif is the overt dramatic substance of the hagiographies of both Dominic and, even more explicitly, of Francis.

I have pointed out earlier in chapter 3 that Francis' conversion (*Paradiso* XI, ll. 55 ff.) is marked by his moving away from the social structures to a liminal space, and that this metaphor of apartness is Francis' mocking counterpoise to the institutional values of this world. But the canto's central concern is to show Francis' life as a mimetic representation of Christ's own life. The impressions of the stigmata on his body (ll. 106–8) are literally the seal by which he shares in the suffering of the Crucifixion. On the other hand, the wooing of Lady Poverty, who had mounted the cross with Christ (ll. 64–72), completely realizes Francis' *imitatio Christi*.[52] This im-

---

[51] A paradigmatic study of the stylizations which punctuate the accounts of the saints' lives is Pierre Courcelle, *Recherches sur les 'Confessions' de Saint Augustin* (Paris: E. De Boccard, 1950), esp. "Le 'tolle, lege'; fiction littéraire et réalité," pp. 188–202; the figural elements in the hagiography of St. Francis are borne out by Erich Auerbach, "St. Francis of Assisi in Dante's *Commedia*," trans. Catherine Garvin, in *Scenes from the Drama of European Literature* (New York: Meridian Books, 1959), pp. 79–98.

[52] For the relevant bibliography on *Paradiso* XI, see above chapter 3, note 4; the importance of St. Francis in medieval eschatology and Dante has been probed by Silvio Pasquazi, "San Francesco in Dante," in *Studi in onore di Alberto Chiari*, II (Brescia: Paideia, 1973), pp. 939–70.

itation is not a purely symbolic gesture, nor is the allegory of his marriage to Lady Poverty simply a moral abstraction. The canto opens, significantly enough, with the poet's attack against the senseless care of men embroiled in the emptiness of syllogisms and aphorisms (ll. 1-9). To these, Dante contrasts Francis' experience in which the imitation of Christ and the representation of poverty, far from being mere fiction, are rooted in the reality of his lived life. From this point of view, it could be argued that the allegory of his marriage to Poverty is a theological allegory: if Christ is the Word made flesh, Francis, stripped of clothes and wounded in the flesh, makes his own body into a word, a text in which the signs, literally inscribed on the flesh, *are* their own unambiguous allegorical meaning and reenact Christ's life.

Obliquely, a contrast is established between the canto of Medusa and the cantos of Francis and Dominic. In *Inferno* IX, Dante evokes, and discards, a version of the allegory of poets as he represents the illusory efforts of his past life to move and give life, like Orpheus, to empty stones, which, from the perspective of the present, appear as the erection of a monument to the self.[53] In the theological allegory of *Paradiso* XI, Francis is the image of Christ and gives life to that image; by the same token, in the representation of Dominic's life, words are shown to be receptacles of reality and to contain within themselves their own referents.

This contrast is not accidental: it is part of Dante's systematic attempt to set up a pattern of oppositions between faith and heresy. Thus, if heresy engenders petrification, the pilgrim's examination on faith in *Paradiso* XXIV is conducted by Peter, whose own name is the stone on which faith is built.

[53] It will be remembered that in his discussion of the allegory of poets Dante refers to Orpheus as he who moves with his lute, trees and rocks, and he adds that "coloro che non hanno vita ragionevole alcuna sono quasi come pietre" (*Convivio* II, i, 3-4). In *Inferno* the allegory of poets fails because Orpheus, as it were, cannot move the tombstones. For the notion of monument, see Boccaccio's gloss: "Chiamasi 'monimento' per ciò che ammoniscono la mente de' riguardanti, recando loro a memoria la morte o il nome di colui che in esso è sepellito" (*Esposizioni sopra la* Comedia di Dante, p. 493).

Significantly, the line spoken by Farinata to Dante in *Inferno* x, "La tua loquela ti fa manifesto" (l. 25) echoes "loquela tua manifestum te facit" said of St. Peter in Matthew (26:73). If heresy is blindness of the mind, to have faith, the pilgrim says quoting St. Paul's Epistle to the Hebrews, is to assent to what is not visible, to what on earth is hidden and concealed truth: "fede è sustanza di cose sperate / e argomento de le non parventi" (ll. 65–6). These contrasts between heresy and faith are even more evident in *Paradiso* xii.

As I have shown earlier in the analysis of *Inferno* ix, heresy designates primarily the act of tenaciously adhering to interpretive errors; by an overt contrast, the canto of St. Dominic reverses this aspect of heresy by focusing on those biblical exegetes, such as Rabanus Maurus, Hugh of St. Victor and Petrus Comestor (ll. 133–40), who faithfully interpret the Word of God. In *Inferno* ix there are some references to insubstantial magic apparitions; in *Paradiso* xii, Dante alludes to prophetic dreams. Heresy is characterized by a rhetoric of love and war; there is also a decidedly martial strain in Dominic's activity: as the embodiment of the ideals of Christian chivalry, he is the "paladino" who leads the army of Christ (ll. 37 ff.) and the "amoroso drudo" (l. 55) of faith. Finally, in *Inferno* ix, the allusion to Proserpina (l. 54) dramatizes the loss of the Garden, and the Gorgons, conventionally etymologized as "cultivatrices terrae,"[54] are now emblems of the stoniness of the landscape without a hint of a possibly benign natural recurrence; in *Paradiso* xii, St. Dominic's faith is translated into work: he is the "agricola" (l. 71), chosen by Christ to tend his orchard and pluck its "sterpi eretici" (l. 100).

By these contrasts, Dante makes faith the doctrinal opposite of heresy; yet, by overhauling the same metaphors, Dante implies both that the moral oppositions are formally contiguous, and that, in purely rhetorical terms, the "madness" of faith bears a close and almost parodic affinity to the madness

[54] John of Garland, *Integumenta Ovidii. Poemetto inedito del secolo XIII*, ed. Fausto Ghisalberti (Messina and Milan, 1933), p. 55.

of heresy. That the line of division between the two is not
very sharp is dramatized by the presence of Siger of Brabant
in *Paradiso* x (l. 136), and Joachim of Flora in *Paradiso* xii.
Joachim is pointed out as "il calavrese abate Giovacchino / di
spirito profetico dotato" (ll. 140-1), a phrase which translates
the formula "spiritu prophetico dotato," used by Joachim's
followers in the antiphon sung to commemorate his death.[55]
The phrase is the more interesting in that Bonaventura, the
speaker in the canto, has dismissed Joachim's views on the
Trinity as heretical. Joachim's views on the three stages of history, it may be added, and the announcement that history is
about to enter the third stage, that of the Spirit, that would
supersede and fulfill the preceding age of the Father and the
Son, were, and still are, objects of heated controversy.[56] Yet,
while orthodox opinion holds that Joachim's vision of a chiliastic spiritual age soon to come diminishes the role of Christ
in the economy of history and subverts the simultaneity of the
three Persons of the Trinity, for Dante, Joachim is not a heretic. As the presence of other biblical exegetes and theologians
of history implies, he appears to Dante to be a reader of the
Bible and an interpreter of the prophetic structure of history.
Like Petrus Comestor (*Paradiso* xii, l. 134), and more radically
than his *Historia scholastica*, which maps the history of the
Church from the beginning to the time of the apostles,
Joachim reads history as the place of an ongoing theodicy. As
Dante reconciles the quarrels that divided the theologians on
earth, he also shows that faith, far from speaking an absolute
unequivocal language, has an inevitable proximity to heresy.

[55] The detail has been treated by Francesco Russo, *Gioacchino da Fiore e le
fondazioni florensi in Calabria* (Naples: F. Fiorentino, 1958), pp. 15 and ff.

[56] Henri de Lubac, "Joachim de Flore," in *Exégèse médiévale*, ii, 437-558,
concludes that in Joachim one finds only an "exégèse aberrante et chimère."
For a view of Joachim as a theorist of history, and excellent bibliography, see
Morton W. Bloomfield, "Joachim of Flora: A Critical Survey of His Canon,
Teachings, Sources, Biography and Influence," *Traditio*, 13 (1957), pp. 249-
311; a survey of the polemics over the work of Joachim is by Marjorie
Reeves, *The Influence of Prophecy in the Later Middle Ages: A Study in
Joachimism* (Oxford: Clarendon Press, 1969).

The possibility that the language of faith degrades into and engenders interpretive contradictions is more explicitly raised in the cantos of Dominic and Francis, the Wordbearers of the Lord. Francis' own preaching to the sultan does not produce his conversion (*Paradiso* XI, ll. 99-104), as if this "text," with the living and unambiguous signs of Christ carved on it, were illegible. Also, after Francis' death, a divisive struggle arises between Conventuals and Spirituals. The Spirituals, guided by Ubertino da Casale, interpret the Franciscan rule to the letter; the Conventuals, guided by Matteo d'Acquasparta, shun its observance (*Paradiso* XII, ll. 124-6). This interpretive crisis dramatizes, in a primary way, the moral degeneracy of both Franciscans and Dominicans: Dominic eats the "verace manna" (*Paradiso* XII, l. 84), in what is his own spiritual Exodus, but his followers are gluttonous of "nova vivanda" (*Paradiso* XI, l. 125); the followers of Francis have equally wandered off the path of their founder and have betrayed his message. Within the Joachistic speculations on the new age about to dawn on history, the friars occupy a central role, but for Dante the fraternal orders are themselves in need of reform. More generally, the split between literalists and spiritualists both shows that Francis' followers have converted his message into half-dead significations, and exemplifies the inevitable error inherent in the interpretation of texts. The life and words of St. Francis, emptied of the concreteness of his presence, have become an allegorical text generating contradictory modes of apprehension. In *Inferno* IX, the sin of heresy, which involves will and intellect, appears as an interpretive error; in *Paradiso* XI and XII, which dramatize the proper exercise of will and intellect, the hagiographies are only fictions of lives, the language of which, hollowed of its vital content, is prone to misunderstanding and is subject to interpretive quarrels. In *Inferno* IX, the faithful messenger comes to open the gate of Dis; in the two cantos of *Paradiso*, God's messengers of love and faith are misunderstood by their followers, and the two cantos ultimately enact the interpretive strife that Dominic intended to solve.

This sense of the contiguity between faith and heresy is extended by Dante to his own text, and in the remaining pages of this chapter I shall describe Dante's own prophetic message and the doubt which encases it. I shall argue, that is to say, that in strictly thematic terms Dante grants a special status to the language of faith as the virtue which gives coherence to the text and to life, but that he is aware that language, divorced from the reality of experience, is always open—as in the case of the account of Francis' life—to misunderstanding. It must be clear, however, that faith, for Dante, is not a mere formal strategy to produce sense in his own poetic account. Faith has a historical content in his poetic vision, and the Church, founded on faith in the Word of God, is the carrier of a central prophetic message to the world. It is a fact, however, that this aspect of the historical function of the Church in the *Divine Comedy* is somewhat neglected by critics. Conventionally, Dante scholarship has attempted to view the role of the Church only in relation to the Empire, usually simply to point out Dante's strong persuasion that Empire and Church must be kept as distinct and autonomous structures, the "due soli" to the pilgrimage of human history to God.[57] Often, actually, scholars stress their belief that the Empire is central to the redemptive pattern of history, and several lines of the poem are frequently extrapolated to suggest the notion that Dante hallows the secular world and judges it to be the instrument of God's designs in history.

Yet, Dante's sense of history cannot be limited simply to a process of canonizing the political world, of discovering and asserting the signs of God's presence in the secular order. There is in Dante's moral imagination another history which is not political, and which transcends the values of the political world. This other history might best be called an antihistory, which is embodied by the Church in its ideal function to negate and counter the myths and idols of the world. The

---

[57] " 'Soleva Roma, che 'l buon mondo feo, / due soli aver, che l'una e l'altra strade / facean vedere, e del mondo e di Deo. / L'un l'altro ha spento; ed è giunta la spada / col pasturale' " (*Purgatori* xvi, ll. 106–10).

tragic reality of the Church, however, is that it espouses the very worldliness that it ought to subvert and denounce. We must look at the salient features of *Inferno* xix where Dante exposes the worldliness and perversion of the Church.[58] This is the canto of the simonists, who, unlike St. Francis's *commercium cum paupertate* or St. Dominic's refusal of *"decimas, quae sunt pauperum Dei"* (*Paradiso* xii, 1. 93), sell spiritual gifts of prophecy upon which the Church is founded. The initial apostrophe, "O Simon mago, o miseri seguaci / che le cose di Dio, che di bontate / deon essere spose, e voi rapaci / per oro e per argento avolterate" (ll. 1-4), places the sin in the specific time of the origin of the Church, the Pentecostal season when the tongues descend on the apostles. Simon the sorcerer of Samaria, according to Acts (8:9-13), offers Peter money in exchange for his prophetic powers. It might be pointed out that Simon is the other name of Peter before he was elected to be the cornerstone of the Church: as in the case of heresy and faith, here, too, Dante seems interested in separating but also marking the threatening contiguity between prophecy and simony. Peter never asked for "oro e argento" (l. 94), yet these sinful popes are successors of Simon and have made "dio d'oro e d'argento; / e che altro è da voi a l'idolatre, / se non ch'elli uno, e voi ne orate cento?" (ll. 112-4). Like Tertullian, for whom the exercise of Simon's sorcery "inter idolatrias deputabatur,"[59] Dante views Simon as a *magus* and the practice of the simonists a magic, illusory change of the free flow of the Spirit into empty idols, a reduction of what is a spiritual gift into a market commodity.

As if to underscore the perversion of prophecy into idolatry, the canto is systematically organized around a series of inversions. In direct opposition to the abuses of the spiritual power by the popes, Constantine has alienated the property of the Empire to the Church (ll. 115 ff.). Boniface, in

[58] An extensive bibliography on the canto can be found in the article by Gianluigi Berardi, "Dante, *Inferno* xix," in *Letteratura e critica: Studi in onore di Natalino Sapegno* (Rome: Bulzoni editore, 1975), ii, 93-147.

[59] *PL* 2, col. 46; see also *PL* 1, col. 672; Isidore of Seville, *Etym.* viii, iv, 2; *PL* 157, col. 227.

spite of the etymology of the name, is an evil doer; the popes are turned upside down and in a grim inversion of Pentecost, the flames of fire are on their feet;[60] the pilgrim stands near the hole where Pope Nicholas is planted like a stake, as if he were a confessor and the pope a "perfido assessin" (l. 50). The epithet "perfido" alludes to the pope's *infidelitas* and prepares the motif of adultery, the canto's central notion that the mystical marriage of the popes to the Church has been profaned and the Church has become *ecclesia carnalis*. It is precisely this awareness that the simonists have deceived the "bella donna" (l. 57) that prompts Dante to attack the popes for corrupting the purity of faith and turning the Church, the house of holiness, into the *magna meretrix* of the Apocalypse:

> Di voi pastor s'accorse il Vangelista,
> quando colei che siede sopra l'acque
> puttaneggiar coi regi a lui fu vista;
> quella che con le sette teste nacque,
> e da le diece corna ebbe argomento,
> fin che virtute al suo marito piacque.
>
> ll. 106-11

(It was shepherds such as you that the Evangelist had in mind when she that sits upon the waters was seen by him committing fornication with the kings: she that was born with the seven heads, and from the ten horns had her strength, so long as virtue pleased her spouse.)

This view of the Church no longer faithful to the gifts of the Holy Ghost has become the focus of much laborious and controversial exegesis. It is argued, for instance, that Dante embraces the central theme of Joachistic eschatological speculation which expects the present *ecclesia carnalis* to be superseded by a renewed *ecclesia spiritualis* in a chiliastic age, Joachim's third *status mundi*, heralded by the preaching of the Franciscan and Dominican Orders.[61] In the measure in which such a

---

[60] Acts 2:1-11. Cf. also *Paradiso* xxiv, ll. 91-3.

[61] A. Ricolfi, "Influssi gioachimitici su Dante e i 'Fedeli d'Amore,' " *Giornale dantesco*, 33 (1930), pp. 169-87; Antonio Crocco, *Gioacchino da Fiore: La*

view entails both the dissolution of the Church as an institution, and the attendant expectation of a spiritual utopia to be realized in history, it is not Dante's. To him, the Church in history is always and simultaneously spiritual and carnal, a *casta meretrix*, a paradox that will be resolved only at the end of time. The myth of Rahab is crucial to this conception.[62]

In the heaven of Venus Dante encounters the troubador Folquet of Marseilles, the poet who gave up his mad love and amatory poetry and joined the Cistercian Order. After explaining to the pilgrim his previous life as surpassing the passions of Dido and Demophon (*Paradiso* IX, ll. 97-101), Folquet points out Rahab:

> Or sappi che là entro si tranquilla
> Raab; e a nostr' ordine congiunta,
> di lei nel sommo grado si sigilla.
> Da questo cielo, in cui l'ombra s'appunta
> che 'l vostro mondo face, pria ch'altr' alma
> del trïunfo di Cristo fu assunta.

più singolare ed affascinante figura del Medioevo cristiano (Naples: edizioni Empireo, 1960), esp. pp. 167-80; see also E. Buonaiuti, *Dante come profeta*, 2nd ed. (Modena: Collezione uomini e idee, 1936); Leone Tondelli, *Da Gioacchino a Dante: nuovi studi-consensi e contrasti* (Turin: Società Editrice Internazionale, 1944); for further bibliography on the Joachimites and Dante, see Bloomfield, pp. 310-11. G. Papini, *Dante vivo* (Florence: Libreria editrice fiorentina, 1933), pp. 367-90, believes that the prophecy of the "veltro" (*Inferno* I, l. 101) refers to the eternal Gospel of Joachim; Charles T. Davis, *Dante and the Idea of Rome* (Oxford: Clarendon Press, 1957), pp. 230-1, holds that the reforms the "veltro" should enact reflect the Franciscan ideals of reform; for a non-Joachistic, political view of the "veltro" see M. Barbi, "Il gioachimismo francescano e il Veltro," *Studi danteschi*, 18 (1934), pp. 209-11; see also the extended argument, with which I am in substantial agreement, by Gian Roberto Sarolli, "Dante e la teologia politica: simbolismo cristologico e cristomimetico," in *Prolegomena alla Divina Commedia* (Florence: Olschki, 1971), pp. 248-88.

[62] Paget Toynbee, *Dante Studies and Researches* (London: Methuen and Co., 1902), pp. 287-8, first pointed out the typology between Rahab and the Church in the light of a passage by Peter Comester, *Historia Scholastica*, PL 198, cols. 1263-4; in the same vein is Erich Auerbach, "Figurative Texts Illustrating Certain Passages of Dante's *Commedia*," *Speculum*, 21 (1946), pp. 482-4.

Ben si convenne lei lasciar per palma
in alcun cielo de l'alta vittoria
che s'acquistò con l'una e l'altra palma,
perch' ella favorò la prima gloria
di Iosüè in su la Terra Santa,
che poco tocca al papa la memoria.

ll. 115-26

(Know then that within it Rahab is at peace, and, since
she is joined by our order, it is sealed with her in its highest rank; by this heaven, where the shadow ends that is
cast by your world, she was taken up before any other
soul of Christ's triumph. It was indeed fitting to leave
her in some heaven as a trophy of the lofty victory that
was gained with the one and the other palm, because she
favored Joshua's first glory in the Holy Land, a place that
little touches the pope's memory.)

It might be stressed that this reference to Rahab's assumption
to Heaven symmetrically relates *Paradiso* ix to the ninth cantos of both *Inferno* and *Purgatorio*. In *Purgatorio*, the dramatic
focus falls on the pilgrim lifted, while he is asleep, to the gate
of Purgatory by Lucy; in *Inferno* ix, in the context of the mad
love Medusa represents, Vergil recalls being sent by the sorceress Erichtho to fetch a soul from the pit of Hell. More to
the point, the passage in *Paradiso* ix tells the story of Rahab,
the harlot, who, during the siege of Jericho gave shelter to the
two spies sent by Joshua into the city. The two spies promised to spare her and her relatives from death when Jericho
should fall and, as a sign, she was to bind a line of scarlet
thread at the window. As related in Joshua (6:17), "only
Rahab the harlot shall live, she and all that are with her in her
house, because she hid the messengers that we sent."

Biblical commentators consistently gloss the series of
events as prophetic signs of God's saving works in history. If
in *Purgatorio* xx (ll. 109-11), Joshua is the type of the perfect
king, here he is the *figura Christi*; Rahab is the Church and the
two messengers are the two Testaments sent to her; Jericho is
a figure of the world that at the end of time will be destroyed

by the service of the Church.[63] Hence, Rahab as the harlot who will be saved is the *casta meretrix*, a formula which in the Old Testament is applied to Jerusalem and in the New Testament to the Church.[64] From Isaiah to Jeremiah to Ezekiel, Jerusalem, the Holy City, is a harlot whose infidelity makes her the equal of Babylon.[65] In the New Testament, Rahab, who appears mentioned in the genealogy of Christ, is interpreted as both work and faith;[66] in patristic exegesis, she is the typological prefiguration of the Church, who fornicates with idols and is transformed into a virgin by Christ.[67] The

[63] These typological correspondences in tradition have been examined by Jean Daniélou, "The Mystery of the Name of Jesus," and "Rahab, a Type of the Church," in *From Shadows to Reality: Studies in the Biblical Typology of the Fathers*, trans. W. Hibberd (London: Burns and Oates, 1960), pp. 229-60.

[64] Hans Urs Von Balthasar, "Casta Meretrix," in *Sponsa Verbi*, Ital. trans. G. Colombi and G. Moretto (Brescia: Morcelliana, 1969), pp. 189-283.

[65] See, for instance, Isaiah 1:21; Jeremiah 4:29-31; Ezekiel 16:2-50.

[66] Matthew 1:5; St. Paul refers to Rahab as the harlot who "By faith . . . perished not with the unbelievers" (Hebrew 11:31); James refers to Rahab ". . . The harlot, was she not justified by works . . . ?" (James 2:25).

[67] In a number of patristic texts Rahab is *meretrix*, insofar as she represents the pagan temple given to idols, and *casta*, insofar as she becomes the Church of Christ. Cf. *PL* 65, cols. 543-5; *PL* 120, col. 61 Cd; *PL* 167, cols. 1008-9. But in other authoritative patristic commentaries the Church of Christ still appears to be, like Rahab, Thamar and Mary Magdalen, a *casta meretrix*. Augustine thinks of both Synagogue and Church as the two prostitutes arguing in front of Solomon, *PL* 38, cols. 92-5; see also *PL* 79, cols. 486-8; St. Bernard's gloss on *"nigredine et formositate sponsae"* echoes the same motif: "si diceret, quia nigredinem non haberet, se ipsam seduceret, et veritas in ea non esset" (*PL* 183, col. 900 b). An eloquent identification between Rahab and the Church up to the end of the world is made by Isidore of Seville: "donec in fine temporum mors novissima inimica destruatur, et ex impiorum perditione unica domus Raab, tanquam unica Ecclesia, liberetur, munda a turpitudine fornicationis per fenestram confessionis, in sanguine remissione: ista enim meretrix in Jericho, tanquam in hoc saeculo moratur" (*PL* 83, col. 374 c). For a theological idea of the Church always in a pilgrimage toward the "patria" to be reached only at the end of time, see *Summa Theologiae,* iiia, q. 8, art. 3 ad secundum. This sense of the Church vulnerable to corruption is inspired by the words of St. Paul: "For I have espoused you to one husband, that I may present you as a chaste virgin to Christ. But I fear lest, as the serpent seduced Eve by his subtlety, so your minds should be corrupted" (II Cor. 11:2-3).

purification will be achieved at the end of time: her own name, actually, is taken to mean *dilatatio* or *amplificatio*,[68] a description of the ongoing, fruitful process of transformation until the Church completely supplants Jericho, the fallen world; by her purification, those who were born strangers to the promise are called to share in it.

This typological pattern is suggested by Dante in our very canto IX of *Paradiso*. Folquet goes into an extended attack against the city of Florence, whose florin has waylaid "le pecore e li agni" (l. 131) and has changed the shepherd into a wolf. The canto ends by conjuring up a vision of pope and cardinals whose thoughts do not turn to Nazareth, "lá dove Gabriello aperse l'ali" (l. 138). A typological nexus is obliquely established between Rahab and the Virgin Mary by recalling the event of the Word made flesh, the announcement that the new time of the promise has dawned on history. Yet, the Church is again meretricious (l. 142), and Folquet looks ahead to an imminent time when the unholy union of corrupt papacy and Church will be over.

Undoubtedly, the passage echoes the prophecy of the advent of the "messo di Dio" (*Purgatorio* XXXIII, ll. 43-5), who will come to put an end to the wickedness of history. The critical debate in recent years has renewed its attempts to define the sense of this promised "cinquecento diece e cinque" (l. 43). In R. E. Kaske's reading, it refers to the final denouement of the temporal process with the second coming of Christ;[69] for G. R. Sarolli, on the contrary, it is to be seen as referring to a Christomimetic emperor who will come to restore justice to the world, on the assumption that Dante actually secularizes eschatology and changes a religious chiliastic myth into one of political messianism.[70] Both the sys-

---

[68] "Raab lata sive dilatata," Jerome, *Liber interpretationis Hebraicorum nominum*, *CCSL* LXXII, p. 138; Isidore, *Etym.* VII, vi, 51; for a traditional link between Rahab and the Virgin Mary, see *PL* 174, col. 1025.

[69] Robert E. Kaske, "Dante's 'DXV' and 'Veltro'," *Traditio*, 17 (1961), pp. 185-254.

[70] Gian Roberto Sarolli, *Prolegomena alla* Divina Commedia, pp. 259-73.

tematic correlation of sacred and secular events (the coexten-
siveness of a thematic thread of political reform and apocalyptic impulse in Dante's imagination), and the interchangeable
rhetoric in tradition to describe the advent of Christ and of a
perfect emperor invested with the attributes of Christ make
the meaning of this prophecy somewhat ambiguous.

The equivocation is made stronger by the fact that the political structure is drawn by Dante within the providential design of history and that it even partakes in the process of the
consummation of history. *Paradiso* VI, for instance, opens
with the famous allusion to Constantine's turning the imperial emblem of the eagle against the "corso del ciel" (l. 2).
This is, in a primary way, a violation of the natural direction
of the *translatio imperii*. But the violation possesses poignant
eschatological dimensions. The theory of *translatio imperii* implies the necessary simultaneity and coincidence of time and
space in the movement of history.[71] The *translatio* follows the
movement of the sun and is arranged by Divine Providence
so that, as Hugh of St. Victor puts it, "those things which
happened at the beginning of time should happen in the East,
as at the beginning of the world; and that then as time moved
on toward the end, the climax of events should pass to the
West, from which we might conclude that the end of time is
approaching, since the course of events has now reached the
end of the world."[72] The Roman Empire was placed at the
end of the line of succession of empires to prepare the advent
of Christ and, eventually, the end of the world.[73] In this
sense, Constantine's reversal of the unidirectional movement
of the eagle is a disruption of the cosmic order and a delay of
the eschatological events. Understandably, in the epistle to
Henry VII, Dante describes the procrastination of the em-

[71] See above chapter 1, note 21; chapter 2, note 59.

[72] Hugh of St. Victor, *De arca Noe morali*, *PL* 176, col. 667; see also *PL* 176,
col. 720.

[73] Hugh of St. Victor, *De vanitate mundi*, *PL* 176, cols. 732-33. See M.-D.
Chenù, *Nature, Man, and Society in the Twelfth Century*, trans. J. Taylor and
L. K. Little (Chicago: University of Chicago Press, 1968), pp. 185-7.

peror to come to Italy as a postponement of the end of the day, a typological repetition of Joshua arresting the sun in the skies.[74]

Jean Daniélou has fully documented the eschatological relevance of the biblical episode, and, as an instance, I transcribe Origen's gloss:

> Until the father's promise be accomplished and the Church is built up from all the nations and the fullness of the peoples come in so that Israel will then be saved, until then, the day is prolonged and the sinking of the sun delayed and it does not set; but it is ever risen while the sun of Justice sheds its light and truth in the hearts of believers. When the full measure of believers is completed and the corrupt and exhausted time of the final generation has come, when as wickedness increases and charity grows cold and the number of those who believe grows less and less, then the days will be shortened.[75]

But for Dante history has come to a complete standstill as the two "suns" of Rome, rather than guiding the world, have eclipsed each other and have left the world blind (*Purgatorio* XVI, ll. 64-114). The cause of the crisis of both religious and secular institutions is attributed to the cursed "old wolf" of avarice (*Purgatorio* XX, ll. 10 ff.), on account of which Boniface VIII was seized and humiliated by Philip the Fair. In this very context of radical disillusionment with both Church and State, the two vehicles in the redemptive process of the world, Dante voices his hope that the heavens send a savior to restore justice to the earth ("O ciel, nel cui girar par che si creda / le condizion di qua giù transmutarsi, / quando verrà per cui questa disceda?" ll. 13-5).

[74] "Verum quia sol noster (sive desiderii fervor hoc submoenat, sive facies veritatis) aut morari iam creditur, aut retrocedere supputatur, quasi Iosue denuo" (*The Letters of Dante*, ed. Paget Toynbee, 2nd ed. [Oxford: Clarendon Press, 1966], VII, 2, p. 90).

[75] Jean Daniélou, "The Fall of Jericho and the End of the World," in *From Shadows to Reality*, pp. 283-4.

The very rhyme scheme of this prophetic expectation recalls the rhyme scheme in the announcement of the "messo di
Dio" ("Non sarà tutto tempo sanza reda / l'aguglia che lasciò
le penne al carro, / per che divenne mostro e poscia preda,"
Purgatorio xxxiii, ll. 37-9). I side with Kaske's view that the
DXV is the prophecy of the messenger who will come at
the end of history, the announcement of the *eschaton*, which is
the irrevocable promise in the Christian vision of history.
This "sense of the ending" of history is the perspective from
which the process of history is given a "finality" and becomes
an intelligible totality.[76] But this view of a closed structure
should not imply, I hasten to add, a dehistorization, as it
were, of history swallowed up in an apocalyptic eschatology;
nor should it be construed as a reduction of the temporal-
eschatological dialectic of Dante's vision to a myth of a
monastic millennium. History, for Dante, is undoubtedly a
history of failures of both Church and State, but it preserves
for him an enduring hope and promise that both Church and
State can regain their vital function in the conduct of human
affairs.

The structural paradox of history as a closed totality and
process finds a correlative in the simultaneous closed and
open-ended form of the poem, which was described in chapter 6. Dante sees that the end of history has already appeared:
the Incarnation has anticipated it and has brought history to
a closure—"noi siamo già ne l'ultima etade del secolo, e
attendiamo veracemente la consumazione del celestiale movi-
mento."[77] But he would also agree that the time of the

[76] This is the principle that subtends St. Augustine's view of the importance of the "ending." In his famous reflection on the recitation of a psalm,
Augustine shows that from the point of view of the end, the temporal fragments of a song, a man's life and the whole age of the sons of men emerge as a
total and intelligible structure. See *Confessions* xi, xxviii, *CSEL* xxxiii. See
also my remarks above in chapter 6, and esp. notes 53 and 54. For a general
exploration of this question in modern literary structures, see John Frank
Kermode, *The Sense of an Ending: Studies in the Theory of Fiction* (New York:
Oxford University Press, 1967).

[77] *Convivio* ii, xiv, 13. The full text reads: "For from the beginning of the

end cannot be calculated (Luke 17:21-3 and ff.) and that the Father alone knows the hour when the plot of history will reach its denouement (Matthew 24:36). In *Paradiso* xx, the eagle warns men to restrain in judging, for "noi, che Dio vedemo, / non conosciamo ancor tutti li eletti" (ll. 134-5).

The promise of the end, I would suggest, provides the conditions which make it possible to envision a theological scheme of history, but it does not abolish the sense of historicity, of the ongoing temporal process of events. The tension of the poem, as has been argued throughout this study, lies precisely in the coextensive presence of what is partial and problematic in the order of contigency with the closedness and totality *sub specie aeternitatis*, and in the simultaneously retrospective and proleptic structure of the poem, which at the very end is oriented toward the future, the "futura gente" (*Paradiso* xxxiii, l. 72). This paradox of eschatology and history in the *Divine Comedy* is exemplified by the respective roles that Church and Empire play in the economy of history: the action of the Empire belongs to the world of time; the Church enacts the eschatological hope in time, and is envisioned as the structure that is both inside and outside the structures of the world, whose mission is to transform the "world" into God's sanctuary. Only when the change is completed, will the end come.

Above and beyond this description of the prophetic content of history, we must raise the problem of Dante's own poetic stance. In the foregoing pages I have argued that Dante juxtaposes the madness of heresy and idolatry to faith and prophecy, and that the juxtaposition hinges on metaphors (blindness, petrification, magic, etc.) which draw the explicit moral oppositions within an area of figurative contiguity. The language of faith, however, has a special value because it provides a world of sense, and actually, Dante's own language constantly strives to reach an unambiguous state where

---

world, little more than the sixth part hath been traversed; and we are already in the last age of the world and verily await the consummation of the celestial movement" (*The Banquet*, trans. K. Hillard, p. 118).

words and their reality coincide in a clear articulation. At the very opening of *Paradiso* XII, for instance, we are told that the song of the heavenly spirits exceeds the beauty of "nostre muse, / nostre serene in quelle dolci tube" (ll. 7-8). Critics have variously tried to determine the exact tenor of the comparison, whether the muses and sirens are to be understood as referring to mythic symbols of harmony, or, on the contrary, to the acutal practices of poets and singers.[78] It seems hardly to be a matter of choice: the repeated possessive "nostra" decisively implies that the myth of poetry and poetic practices fall short of the heavenly language. The motif is resumed in *Paradiso* XIII, where Dante contrasts the content of pagan songs to the theological hymn of the blessed: "Lì si cantó non Bacco, non Peana, / ma tre persone in divina natura, / e in una persona essa e l'umana" (ll. 25-7).

In effect, after all the ambiguities which punctuate his sense of the value and power of literature in both *Inferno* and *Purgatorio*, Dante reverses in *Paradiso* the conventional humanistic defense of fiction, whereby the fables and poetic myths are upheld as vehicles to truth.[79] There are no poets in *Paradiso*, with the exception of Folquet, who has given up the mad poetry and mad love of his past to join the Cistercians and fight the heretics. In *Paradiso*, both the heavenly language of the blessed and the truth of the faith become the single perspective from which secular poetry is found wanting and deceptive. From this standpoint, it is understandable why Dante should assume a prophetic posture, should speak in the language of faith which would produce, in turn, faith. Yet, this deliberate posture is never exempt from the awareness that it might be another mad gesture, a lapsing into the very madness which he systematically indicts.[80]

[78] Natalino Sapegno, ed., *La Divina Commedia* (Milan and Naples: Ricciardi, 1957), p. 932.

[79] See, for instance, Giovanni del Virgilio's statement: "Sed cui parti philosophiae supponatur dico quod supponitur ethyce i. morali philosophiae, nam omnes poete tendunt in mores" (Fausto Ghisalberti, ed., *Giornale dantesco*, p. 19).

[80] See the remarks on madness above in chapter 2, note 36, and chapter 7, note 9.

Madness, actually, constitutes the constant boundary of Dante's discourse, a threat which he steadily discards, but which steadily reappears in the movement of the text. Like Folquet in *Paradiso* IX, in *Inferno* IX the poet eschews the madness of heresy and idolatrous poetry. The threat, and the memory of petrification, however, are never completely effaced. In *Purgatorio* XIV, the canto of the sinners blinded by envy, Dante puts among the examples of punished envy the story of the petrification of Aglauros of Athens. Dante drew the account from Ovid's *Metamorphoses*, where we are told that Minerva, to punish Aglauros, descends to the house of Envy and orders her to instill her poison into the girl's breast. Aglauros becomes envious of her sister Herse's love for Mercury, and, as she tries to block the god's entrance to Herse's chamber, she is metamorphosed by Mercury into a lifeless statue of stone.[81] The Ovidian fable is allegorized both by Arnulf of Orléans and John of Garland to mean that divine eloquence, Mercury, rescues what is memorable from the threat of oblivion.[82] For Dante, the blindness and petrification of Aglauros are literally an enduring monument, a veritable metaphor of memory: as the story of Aglauros is recalled, he draws close to Vergil and remarks that "in destro feci, e non innanzi, il passo" (*Purgatorio* XIV, l. 141). In *Paradiso* XXXIII, memory was seen to be endangered by forgetfulness; now, the terms are reversed: the threat of petrification and blindness in *Inferno* IX has been transcended, but their memory lingers and, in effect, forever reenacts the previous impasse.

The possibility that Dante's own prophetic voice is encroached upon by madness is more directly dramatized in *Inferno* XIX. As his language quickens with prophetic urgency against the simonists, he obliquely acknowledges the madness

[81] *Metamorphoses* II, ll. 708-820.

[82] Arnulf of Orleans glosses the myth as follows: "Aglauros invida Mercurium volens expellere mutata est in lapidem quia ipsa est oblivio que Mercurium id est facundiam, vel res a facundis pertractatas, nititur estinguere id est oblivioni dare. . . . Prevalent enim res memorande nec omnino deleri possunt" (*Allegoriae super Ovidii Metamorphosin* II, 12, Ghisalberti, p. 206). See also John of Garland, *Integumenta Ovidii* II, ll. 149-50, Ghisalberti, p. 47.

of his posture: "Io non so s'l' mi fui qui troppe folle, / ch'i' pur rispuosi lui a questo metro: 'Deh, or mi dì: quanto tesoro volle . . .' " (*Inferno* xix, ll. 88-90). And, as if to stress the awareness that prophecy is vulnerable to error, *Inferno* xx features the false prophets and soothsayers. By the strategy, Dante ostensibly implies that he is not a fortuneteller, like Tiresias and Manto, nor an idolater like the simonists; but he also implies, as the allusion to his breaking of the baptismal font indicates (*Inferno* xix, ll. 19 ff.), that his gesture borders on blasphemy and must be freed from the suspicion to which it is liable.

Undoubtedly, the poet asks that we believe and that we interpret sustained by belief. He also tells us that only those words filled with reality are worthy of belief and that pure signs, voided of reality, and even the life of St. Francis, inevitably engender a crisis in allegorical interpretations. The poem is a metaphor that maps these constant oscillations between prophecy and idolatry and gropes to be taken for reality, urges the readers into a performance whereby words may be translated into life. Whether this metaphor is taken to be a symbolic transaction endorsed by God, or an illusory, magic act of poetic mythmaking; whether we believe that the poem is a stone that edifies our faith, or is an artifice that barely conceals the grave—is a question Dante poses, but it remains necessarily an open one.

A Pattern of Order:
Inferno VII
and *Paradiso* VII

IN his recent monograph, F. P. Pickering maintains that there are two distinctive and contradictory models for medieval historiography, respectively inspired by St. Augustine and Boethius.[1] Whereas the Augustinian model deals with the transcendent and linear order of universal history, from Creation through the Fall and Redemption to the Apocalypse, the Boethian model focuses on the contingent and concrete events of secular history-writing (lives of individuals, dynastic histories, shifting fortunes of people, etc.).

The difference between these two possible schemes of history would seem to depend on the opposed value that Augustine and Boethius assign to Fortune. St. Augustine's *heilsgeschichte* has no place for a goddess *Fortuna*, the voluble and blind deity of the pagans. Accordingly, the paradigm of history that he elaborates in his *De Civitate Dei*, for instance, is overtly regulated by a providential order.[2] Boethius, on the

---

[1] F. P. Pickering, *Augustinus oder Boethius? Geschichtsschreibung und epische Dichtung im Mittelalter-und in der Neuzeit*, Part I (Berlin: Erich Schmidt Verlag, 1967). See also F. P. Pickering, *Literature and Art in the Middle Ages* (Coral Gables: University of Miami Press, 1970), esp. pp. 168-96.

[2] St. Augustine's attack against Fortune is contained in *De Civitate Dei*, IV, 18 and 19, respectively dealing with the myth of the good and bad Fortune, and *Fortuna Muliebris*. Cf. also the remark, "Non enim eas causas, quae dicuntur fortuitae, unde etiam Fortuna nomen accepit, non esse dicimus nullas, sed

contrary, has a view of the role of Fortune which accounts for
the mutability and vicissitudes of real experiences, not *sub
specie aeternitatis* as St. Augustine would, but as *res gestae* in
time and place. In the Boethian hierarchy of the universe, to
be sure, Fortune mediates between God and his Providence
on the one hand, and man and his fate and free will on the
other. Yet Fortune is still a capricious and erratic entity
forever playing her game and delighting in it.[3]

One doubts that these Augustinian and Boethian models
can be envisioned, as they are by Pickering, as being rigidly
juxtaposed. At any rate, it can be shown that Dante cuts
through these categories in his *Divine Comedy*, and even combines the main lines of the insights of Boethius and Augustine
in his representation of Fortune in the famous digression of
Inferno VII.[4]

The canto opens with a reference to the unintelligible and
threatening language of Plutus, the "wealthy one," according
to a standard etymology of the name.[5] Plutus' two traits, un-

---

latentes: easque tribuimus . . . veri Dei . . . voluntati, . . ." (*De Civitate Dei*,
v, 9, in *CCSL* xlvii).

[3] Boethius links Providence, Fortune and Fate most explicitly in book iv,
pros. 6 of *De Consolatione Philosophiae*; at the same time, he writes earlier in
the text: "The pride of fickle fortune spareth none, / And, like the floods of
swift Euripus borne, / Oft casteth mighty princes from their throne, / . . . She
cares not for the wretch's tears and moan, / And the sad groans, which she
hath caused, doth scorn. / Thus doth she play, to make her power more
known, / Showing her slaves a marvel, when man's state / Is in one hour both
downcast and fortunate" (*The Consolation of Philosophy*, English trans. rev.
H. F. Stewart (Cambridge, Mass.: Harvard University Press, 1968), ii, m. 1,
pp. 177-9. See also *De Consolatione*, ii, pros. 2 and m. 2, 1-8. For a general
view, cf. Howard R. Patch, *The Goddess Fortuna in Mediaeval Literature*
(Cambridge, Mass.: Harvard University Press, 1927). See also the important
remarks by Vincenzo Cilento, *Medio evo monastico e scolastico* (Milan and
Naples: Ricciardi, 1961), pp. 41-73.

[4] A recent reading of the canto is by Gianluigi Toja, "Canto vii dell'*Inferno*," *Convivium*, 35 (1967), pp. 129-54. See also V. Cioffari, *The Conception
of Fortune and Fate in the Works of Dante* (Cambridge, Mass.: Dante Society,
1940). Cf. Howard R. Patch, *The Tradition of Boethius* (New York: Oxford
University Press, 1935).

[5] Cicero, *De Natura Deorum*, ii, xxvi, 66.

intelligibility and wealth, are the conceptual coordinates around which the doctrine of Fortune is largely plotted. If in *Convivio* Dante questions the justice in Fortune's distribution of wealth,[6] here in *Inferno* vii he alters that conception. We are told now that Fortune does not hold the things of this world in her clutches: she is an angelic intelligence, a "general ministra e duce" (l. 78), appointed by God to preside over the "splendor mondani" (l. 77), the wealth and power that lie in the sublunary world of change and corruption. From this point of view it is significant that Dante should link Fortune to wealth and represent her in the area where avaricious and prodigals are punished: their contrary sins—the hoarding or dissipation or riches—disrupt the economy of the world governed by Fortune, and violate the principle, implicit in the wheel of Fortune, of exchange and circulation of common goods. In what clearly is a deliberate counterpoint to the circular motion of the wheel, the sinners are shown to move in half-circles, doomed, ironically, to exchange insults (ll. 28-33).

This irony has a dramatic value in the unfolding of the canto, for it is a sign of the reversals which Fortune enacts and, at the same time, it is a detail by which Dante points to Fortune's mockery of human attempts at mastery and control over the things of the world. The perpetual shifts of Fortune, who blindfolded changes "vain wealth" from race to race, follow a providential but inscrutable design, which teases man's efforts and sanctions the limitations of his reason. Since Fortune transcends human understanding, Vergil's rational exposition on her workings only heightens the sense that reason is precariously poised between the unintelligible bestiality of Plutus and the hidden purposes of this "ministra," who, in openly Boethian phraseology, appears as the distant spectator laughing at her own games in the world.

---

[6] "Dico che la loro imperfezione delle ricchezze primamente si può notare ne la indiscrezione del loro avvenimento, nel quale nulla distributiva giustizia risplende, ma tutta iniquitade quasi sempre, la quale iniquitade è proprio effetto d'imperfezione" (*Convivio*, iv, xi, 6 ff.).

The distance between man and Fortune is suggested by her description as an entity contained in a self-enclosed circularity:

> ma ella s'è beata e ciò non ode:
> con l'altre prime creature lieta
> volve sua spera e beata si gode.
>
> ll. 94–6

(But she is blest and does not hear this: happy with the other primal creatures she turns her sphere and rejoices in her bliss.)

The tercet, by the emphasis on the steady rotation of the wheel; the self-reflexiveness in two verbs ("s'è beata". . ."si gode"), the stylistic stratagem of repeating (and reversing the order of) the same phrase ("s'è beata" turns into "e beata si gode"), mimes the movement of Fortune, from a human standpoint, as a circular and self-enclosed totality.

This Boethian view of the cyclical turns of man's fortunes seems, on the face of it, to be remarkably at odds with Dante's conception of history (derived from St. Augustine) with its beginning in the Creation of the angels and its consummation in the Apocalypse. However, the contradiction is only apparent, for Dante, in effect, harmonizes the conception of Boethius and Augustine. Fortune, the text states, came into being with the other primal angelic intelligences at the time of Creation (*Inferno* VII, ll. 73–6); in addition, Vergil quiets Plutus by referring to the war in Heaven, the epic battle between Michael and Satan, whose "superbo strupo" (l. 12) is the primal Fall which has rent the order of the cosmos. Finally, the canto also contains a direct allusion to the resurrection, when these sinners shall rise from their grave, "col pugno chiuso, e questi coi crin mozzi" (l. 57).

The Augustinian focus in Dante's representation of Fortune is further implied by the context of pride within which she is evoked in *Inferno* VII as well as in other glaring instances. *Paradiso* XVI, which in a way is the poetic counterpart of the

Florentine chronicles, such as Villani's, tells the decline of the great Florentine families.[7] While their "dynastic history" is viewed as part of the ceaseless turning of Fortune's wheel (ll. 79-141), the sin of pride introduces their decline to reinforce the suggestion that Fortune rules over the world of the Fall.[8] In the representation of Fortune, in other words, Dante shares the Augustinian view of the providentiality of events. Like Augustine, he rejects as illusory the classical belief in chance: ultimately, the faith in the arbitrariness of chance is untenable because it completely abolishes the possibility of moral choice and the making of history.

By coupling Boethius' language with the fundamental elements of Augustinian historiography, Dante preserves the ambiguity which is the distinctive feature of Fortune's deceptiveness. It is only a commonplace to remark that for Boethius, Fortune first allures man with enticements of simulated bliss, only to cast him later into grief; for Alanus, she embodies all possible oxymora: reliably unreliable, blind seer, constant in fickleness, etc. For Dante, however, Fortune is deceptive only for those who abide in the darkling world of the Fall: in the instability of the fallen world, the more one attempts to hold on to the goods of Fortune, the more one plunges down to the bottom of the wheel. Fortune can be conquered by the exercise of poverty: by giving up the very

[7] It is well known that the picture of serene life of the Florence of old that Cacciaguida evokes in *Paradiso* xv (ll. 97 ff.) bears a striking resemblance to the account in Giovanni Villani, *Cronica*, ed. F. Gherardi Dragomanni, 4 vols. (Florence: S. Coen, 1844-45), I, bk. VI, 69. In *Paradiso* xvi, for instance, the feud between the house of the Amidei and the Buondelmonti's (ll. 136-54) parallels the account by Villani's *Cronica*, I, v, 38. For further bibliography, see Giovanni Aquilecchia, "Dante and the Florentine Chroniclers," *Bulletin of the John Rylands Library*, 48 (1965), pp. 30-55, now rep. in *Schede di italianistica* (Turin: Einaudi, 1976), pp. 45-72.

[8] " 'Oh quali io vidi quei che son disfatti / per lor superbia! e le palle de l'oro / fiorian Fiorenza in tutt' i suoi gran fatti' " (*Paradiso* xvi, ll. 109-11). It might also be pointed out that Fortune is linked to the fall of Troy and its traditional pride: "E quando la fortuna volse in basso / l'altezza de' Troian che tutto ardiva, . . ." (*Inferno* xxx, ll. 13-14).

material elements that she controls, and acknowledging its inherent providentiality. In this sense, the wheel of Fortune is a basic metaphor in Dante's vision of history, for it discloses the order that lies under the confusions and impermanence of temporal life.

This view of order underlying the darkness of the world of Fortune finds a direct extension in *Paradiso* VII, where Dante probes the question of the fall and redemption of man within the economy of Creation. In *Paradiso* VI, Justinian refers to two "vengeances" occurring within the plan of salvation history: the crucifixion of Christ was a "vendetta" for Adam's sin, while Titus' destruction of Jerusalem was the just revenge for the crucifixion (ll. 88-93). From one point of view, these two events dramatize the centrality of the Roman Empire in the providential structure of history. At the same time, the pilgrim perceives them as a moral paradox, which Beatrice untangles in *Paradiso* VII in terms of the divine and human natures of Christ. Since Christ is the nodal center of both history and the cosmos, her explanation turns, in effect, into a complex rationale which discloses the justice and order in God's scheme of things.

The whole of creation, Beatrice states, is shaped by God's boundless love and goodness. There are some elements in creation which have been touched directly by the hand of our maker and which, therefore, will never perish. But God has also acted through the agency of vicarious Nature: this is the so-called secondary creation, which comprises the four elements, their mixtures and compounds, and which is subject to the penalty of corruptibility and death (*Paradiso* VII, ll. 124-8). The primary creation, on the other hand, which consists of brute matter, the heavens, the angels and the soul, includes also the human flesh, which shares in God's immortality and will be resurrected at the end of time (ll. 130-48). However, man can conquer death only because of Christ's atonement and sacrifice, the only way, actually, by which man's redemption could take place. Man was originally fashioned by God in his image and likeness, but the Fall disfigured him, banished him from Paradise and stripped him of his dignities (ll. 36-9 and 79-87). His inability to reach salvation "ne termini suoi" (l. 97) was such that the crucifixion was needed to "riparar l'omo a sua intera vita" (l. 104) and rescue him from the burden of sin.

This brief summary was necessary to show the several links, forged both in terms of conceptual frame and detail, which exist between *Inferno* VII and *Paradiso* VII. In *Inferno* VII Fortune is introduced by an allusion to the cosmic disruption caused by the pride of the fallen angels, and Fortune herself is an angelic intelligence which came into being at the time of creation. In *Paradiso* VII the burden of Beatrice's exposition is creation, the pride and disobedience of man and the restoring of harmony in the universe. If Fortune in *Inferno* VII is depicted as the governess of the world, in *Paradiso* VII Dante explores how God governs the world through Nature. The two cantos, actually, enact the interdependence that is conventionally posited between Fortune's outward goods and Nature's works and gifts.[9]

More cogently, in *Inferno* VII Fortune is cast in Boethian language; in *Paradiso* VII, the description of the universe created by God's goodness, "La divina bontà, che da sé sperne / ogne livore, ardendo in sé, sfavilla / sì che dispiega le bellezze etterne" (ll. 64-6), translates a passage from *De Consolatione Philosophiae*, in which Boethius addresses the Creator who made his work from chaotic matter, not impelled by external causes, but by virtue of the highest good existing within him without envy.[10]

[9] *De Consolatione Philosophiae*, bk. II, pros. 5, tells the distinction between Fortune and Nature. Cf. Alanus de Insulis, *Anticlaudianus*, ed. R. Bossuat (Paris: J. Vrin, 1955), VIII, ll. 45-146. Cf. also H. R. Patch, *The Goddess Fortuna in Mediaeval Literature*, pp. 65-75.

[10] "O qui perpetua mundum ratione gubernas / Terrarum caelique sator qui tempus ab aeuo / Ire iubes stabilisque manens das cuncta moueri, / Quem non externae pepulerunt fingere causae / Materiae fluitantis opus, uerum insita summi / Forma boni liuore carens, . . ." *De Consolatione Philosophiae*, III, m. 9. The hymn is also quoted in *Convivio*, III, ii, 17. It must be mentioned, however, that G. Fraccaroli, "Dante e il Timeo," an appendix to *Il Timeo*,

There are other minor correspondences between the two cantos,[11] but an important common feature is that just as in *Inferno* VII Dante placed Boethius' view of Fortune within the Augustinian focus of the Fall, in *Paradiso* VII the allusion to Boethius' text is placed within a rigorous theological perspective. The famous ninth hymn of the third book of *De Consolatione*, to be sure, recapitulates the great themes of Plato's *Timaeus* and, along with the *Timaeus*, was the object of persistent and controversial exegeses, especially at the School of Chartres.[12] That the language of *Paradiso* VII is punctuated with a number of textual recalls from Chalcidius' version of the *Timaeus* has been pointed out ever since the early commentators of the poem.[13] It has been suggested that Dante is aware of Guillaume de Conches' controversial speculations over the *Timaeus* and the hymn, "O qui perpetua mundum. . . ." I would suggest, however, that in *Paradiso* VII Dante argues against the naturalistic thrust of Guillaume's position from the standpoint of Anselm's theology of the Incarnation.[14]

---

trans. G. Fraccaroli (Turin: Bocca, 1906), pp. 391-424, believes that *Paradiso* VII, ll. 64-6, echoes Plato's *Timaeus* directly.

[11] Gian Roberto Sarolli, *Prolegomena alla* Divina Commedia (Florence: Olschki editore, 1971), p. 290 points out the "antithethical parallelism" between Plutus' "voce chioccia" in his "Pape Satàn, pape Satàn aleppe." (*Inferno* VII, ll. 1-2), and the "cantare" of "Osanna, sanctus Deus sabaòth," of *Paradiso* VII, ll. 1-5. Another link is possibly to be found in the fact that the two cantos follow two parallel political cantos, thus stressing the point that a providential order lies under the chaos of history.

[12] An account of the debate can be found in J. M. Parent, *La Doctrine de la création dans l'école de Chartres* (Paris: J. Vrin, 1938), pp. 29-112. See also Pierre Courcelle, "Étude critique sur les commentaires de la Consolation de Boèce," *Archives d'histoire doctrinale et littéraire du moyen âge*, 12 (1939), pp. 5-140; Tullio Gregory, *Platonismo medievale: studi e ricerche* (Rome: Istituto storico italiano per il Medio Evo, 1958); Winthrop Wetherbee, *Platonism and Poetry in the Twelfth Century* (Princeton: Princeton University Press, 1972), pp. 19-36.

[13] Pietro di Dante mentions Boethius' ninth hymn of the third book; Francesco da Buti suggests that both Boethius and Plato's myth of creation are echoed by Dante. See Biagi, ed., *Paradiso*, pp. 166-7.

[14] Tullio Gregory, *Anima Mundi: la filosofia di Guglielmo di Conches e la*

For if the impulse behind the work of Guillaume is a faith in the natural world, in the ability of reason to grasp the structure of the universe, Anselm gave Dante the perspective from which he can question the basic optimism and, in one word, the humanism of Guillaume. Anselm's *Cur Deus Homo* is the perception of the radical evil that perverts man's will to the extent that redemption itself is not a natural desire, but a desire that comes from God.[15] The goodness of the natural order, the "naturalis iustitia" of Guillaume's glosses on the *Timaeus*, for Anselm had been shattered by the original sin, and his own argument, condensed in the now classical formula "faith seeking understanding," bears witness to the limitations of reason. In *Inferno* VII Dante explicitly warns against the presumption of reason to grasp the mystery of Fortune; in *Paradiso* VII the universe follows a pattern of order and rationality which is given to man by the grace of God.

It is of some significance, finally, that this doctrine of order in the cosmos should take place in the seventh cantos of *Inferno* and *Paradiso*. Seven is the symbolic number of creation and its harmonious perfection,[16] which, as has been shown, is

scuola di Chartres (Florence: Sansoni, 1955), pp. 100 ff. suggests Dante's place in the ideological debate around Guillaume's doctrines. For the naturalistic elements in the doctrines, see R. W. Southern, *Medieval Humanism and Other Studies* (New York and Evanston: Harper and Row, Publishers, 1970), pp. 29-85. For a more tempered view, see M.-D. Chenù, *Nature, Man and Society in the Twelfth Century*, trans. Jèrome Taylor and Lester K. Little (Chicago and London: University of Chicago Press, 1968), pp. 1-48. See also Wetherbee, *Platonism and Poetry*, pp. 74-125. The presence of St. Anselm in *Paradiso* VII has been documented by A. Agresti, *Dante e S. Anselmo* (Naples: Tipografia Luigi De Bonis, 1887), pp. 25-32. Cf. also Hermann Gmelin, *Die Göttliche Komödie: Das Paradies* (Stuttgart: E. Klett Verlag, 1957), III, pp. 139-44.

[15] Dante's sense of the Incarnation is partly inspired by Thomas Aquinas, *Summa Theologiae*, IIIa, q. 31, a. 1, resp. For a more radical view of Redemption, see *Cur Deus Homo*, I, 5, and II, 6 and *passim*. I am quoting from *Sancti Anselmi Liber Cur Deus Homo*, ed. F. S. Schmitt (Bonn: P. Hanstein, 1929). See also Karl Barth, *Anselm: Fides Quaerens Intellectum*, trans, Ian W. Robertson (Richmond: John Knox Press, 1960).

[16] For the value of number seven, see *De Civitate Dei*, XI, 31-32, *CCSL* XLVIII. See also Macrobius, *Commentary on the Dream of Scipio*, trans. W. H. Stahl (New York: Columbia University Press, 1952), p. 71 and pp. 100-08.

central to the theme of the two cantos. The symmetrical correspondences between these two cantos, or the other numerous parallelisms of the poem for that matter, are not to be construed merely as an exercise which maps out the formal mechanisms of the text. For Dante they exemplify, rather, the design and order of history, in which the haphazard and chance are of necessity excluded. The poet's own symbolic construction mimes the plan of the Divine Architect who has fashioned creation, as the Book of Wisdom has it, "in measure, and number and weight" (11:21). This is the world of order which the poet constantly evokes for the benefit of man who dwells in the shadows of time, buffeted by shifting desires and banished from Paradise into the land of exile.[17]

More generally, see Vincent F. Hopper, *Medieval Number Symbolism* (New York: Columbia University Press, 1968).

[17] It ought to be pointed out that Adam's fall is described as a fall into exile: " 'Or, figliuol mio, non il gustar del legno / fu per sé la cagion di tanto essilio, / ma solamente il trapassar del segno.' " (*Paradiso* xxvi, ll. 115-17).

INDEX

Library of Congress Cataloging in Publication Data

Mazzotta, Giuseppe, 1942–
  Dante, poet of the desert.

  Includes index.
  1. Dante Alighieri, 1265–1321. Divina commedia.
  2. Dante Alighieri, 1265–1321—Allegory.   I. Title.
  PQ4390.M54   851′.1   78-27468
  ISBN 0-691-06399-0